WORLD ENCYCLOPEDIA OF CIVIL AIRCRAFT

FROM LEONARDO DA VINCI TO THE PRESENT

WORLD ENCYCLOPEDIA OF CIVIL AIRCRAFT

FROM LEONARDO DA VINCI TO THE PRESENT

Enzo Angelucci

English-language edition
supervised by John Stroud

Crown Publishers, Inc.
New York

conceived and edited by
ENZO ANGELUCCI

written by
PAOLO MATRICARDI

created by
ADRIANO ZANNINO

advisor on English-language edition
JOHN STROUD

Editor-in-chief
SERENELLA GENOESE ZERBI

color illustrations by Nicola Arolse, Vincenzo Cosentino, Amedeo Gigli, Valeria Matricardi, Studio Kromos

black and white illustrations by Roberto Clementi, Daniela Dazzi, Marcello Giuseppini, Paolo Riccioni, Benedetto Tari, Claudio Tatangelo

cutaway drawings on pages 96, 144, 198, 270 by kind permission of Pilot Press

The Publisher would like to extend his sincere thanks to the Museums of Aviation and to the Press Offices of aeronautical industries and airlines throughout the world for their help in supplying data and information which have contributed to the making of this book.

Translated from the Italian by S. M. Harris

Originally published in Italian in 1981 by Arnoldo Mondadori Editore S.p.A., Milano under the title *Atlante Enciclopedico degli Aerei Civili del Mondo da Leonardo a oggi*

Published in the U.S.A., 1982
by Crown Publishers, Inc.,
One Park Avenue, New York, New York 10016

Published simultaneously in Canada by General Publishing Company Limited

Library of Congress cataloging in publication data

Atlante Enciclopedico degli Aerei Civili del Mondo.
English.
World Encyclopedia of Civil Aircraft.

Translation of: Atlante Enciclopedico degli Aerei Civili del Mondo.
Bibliography: P
Includes Index.
1. Airplanes – History. 1. Angelucci, Enzo.
TL515. A8413 1982 629.133′09 82–4642
ISBN 0–517–54724–4

Printed and bound in Italy by Arnoldo Mondadori Editore
Officine Grafiche, Verona

Twelve months after the publication of this book's twin volume covering military aircraft, this companion volume completes the years of work and research by a group of sixteen contributors who, at the outset, might well have thought themselves over-ambitious in setting out to compile an encyclopedia of aviation from the days of Leonardo da Vinci to the present.

Now that the *World Encyclopedia of Military Aircraft* has been translated into five languages and has proved so popular, we are confident that this book will prove a useful work of reference since it is unique in covering all the aircraft of importance which have been designed and built since the earliest days of aviation anywhere in the world. Technical data is given for each aircraft, together with three-views, color-plates, scale views, photographs and historical background. We feel this will provide any would-be aviation expert—or enthusiast—with an indispensable basis and point of departure from which to pursue more in-depth study of the subject.

More than four hundred civil aircraft are covered in this book (early flying machines, airliners, freighters, research and experimental aircraft, competition and record-breaking airplanes and trainers) as well as certain military aircraft which have contributed more to the development of civil aviation than to their original role.

Obviously some readers will accuse us of certain omissions, but the sheer breadth of the subject means that we have had to be selective and therefore *some* aircraft which never progressed beyond the prototype stage or were only built in very small numbers have unfortunately had to be sacrificed. When faced with such a choice we have tried to be impartial and select the more interesting and important airplanes.

We should like to dedicate this book to the aircraft designers and constructors of both the past and the present; to the brave pioneers of early aviation, some of whom gave their lives to further the development of heavier-than-air flight. We also dedicate our work to the pilots of our day and age, who carry such responsibility for the lives and safety of so many millions of people every year, so that passengers feel they can travel safely all over the world—a world which has become so much smaller since the beginning of air travel. We like to think that this book will appeal to anyone who feels a thrill when he sees an aircraft flying high in the sky overhead, and who pauses to think that one of man's oldest dreams is now a part of everyday life which most of us accept unquestioningly—and yet it is only eighty years since the first airplane rose uncertainly a couple of feet into the air and was airborne for a few seconds, on 17 December 1903, and in terms of history only yesterday.

Enzo Angelucci

CONTENTS

The numbers in bold to the right of the main contents column indicate page numbers of color plates; the numbers in normal type refer to pages where the corresponding texts will be found.

The dates shown in the "Entry into Service" plates correspond to those shown in the specifications accompanying the color illustrations and the relevant text.

In the series of scale views of aircraft, two different scales have been used. For aircraft from 1903 to 1940 the scale is 2.16 cm = 3 m (Plates 16, 34, 58, 79); for aircraft after 1940 the scale is 2.16 cm = 4 m (Plate 117).

In the photographic appendices the captions are followed by a number in brackets indicating the plate in which the aircraft appears.

Country abbreviations in the scale views and the "Entry into Service" plates are as follows:
A—Austria; **AUS**—Australia; **B**—Belgium; **BR**—Brazil; **CDN**—Canada; **CH**—Switzerland; **CS**—Czechoslovakia; **D**—Federal Republic of Germany; **DK**—Denmark; **DZ**—Algeria; **E**—Spain; **ET**—Egypt; **F**—France; **GB**—Great Britain; **H**—Hungary; **I**—Italy; **IL**—Israel; **IND**—India; **IR**—Iran; **IRL**—Ireland; **IRQ**—Iraq; **J**—Japan; **KWT**—Kuwait; **N**—Norway; **N.G.**—New Guinea; **NL**—Netherlands; **NZ**—New Zealand; **P**—Portugal; **PI**—Philippines; **PL**—Poland; **R**—Romania; **RA**—Argentina; **RCH**—Chile; **RY**—Lithuania; **S**—Sweden; **SF**—Finland; **SYR**—Syria; **TJ**—China; **TR**—Turkey; **U**—Uruguay; **USA**—United States of America; **USSR**—Soviet Union; **VO**—Newfoundland; **YU**—Yugoslavia; **ZA**—South Africa.

Chapter 5

The glamorous years of civil aviation: 1928–1940

Chapter 6

The great age of expansion in civil aviation

Chapter 7

Supersonic and space flight

INTRODUCTION

At the beginning of the 1980s there were nearly 300,000 civil aircraft of all types registered in the 145 member countries of ICAO—the International Civil Aviation Organization. In 1979, of this immense number, 8,590 were transport aircraft, with a takeoff weight in excess of 198,450 lb (90,000 kg); 1,230, or 14 percent of these were still powered by piston engines. There is a correlation between the growth in the world fleet of commercial aircraft and that of the annual growth rate of airline traffic: new orders, which averaged between 400 and 500 aircraft per annum between 1971 and 1974, fell to 257 by the end of 1976 and then rose slowly to total 989 by the end of 1979.

Apart from the increase in traffic (over 100 million passengers were carried on scheduled flights in 1960; rising to 300 million ten years later, to over 600 million in 1977 and to 748 million by the end of the decade) and of the forecasts of future growth (some predict over 3,500 million airline passengers in the year 2000, a number which it is difficult for us to grasp today) the industry nowadays is characterized by these mind-boggling statistics. This volume of traffic is backed up by an extremely sophisticated industrial infrastructure which can call on the vast sums necessary to finance development and keep pace with the market's growth and also to enable vital research work to continue.

Civil and commercial aviation is, however, only one facet of the airplane. Its military role is just as important. These two functions may sometimes appear to be incompatible, but in reality they are complementary and both further the evolution of the airplane. The aeronautical industry of today could not apply the sophisticated technology which is necessary to produce a modern airliner (in areas such as aerodynamics, metallurgy, electronics and aero-engines) if most of the research and development had not already been undertaken for military aircraft. None of the leading international aircraft manufacturers—especially the giant U.S. companies—could build successful commercial aircraft without a simultaneous research and experimental production program for military aircraft. The vast sums of money needed to finance R & D aircraft must come to a large extent from governments wishing to maintain their strength and therefore willing to invest in armament and military aircraft development and construction.

Nearly forty years after World War II, the great powers continue to maintain the balance of power through an arms race. Ironically, after eighty years' existence, the aircraft would not have achieved anything like the high levels of sophistication and complexity of today were it not for military needs which had to be satisfied in two world wars and in hundreds of more localized conflicts.

This was the case from the very beginning of the airplane's evolution. Orville and Wilbur Wright were the first to seek to exploit this potential as far back as 1905. In their efforts to overcome official prejudice against their experiments in the United States, the two pioneers had no hesitation in offering their Flyer No. 3 to the War Department after it had successfully undergone a series of important proving trials, which had culminated in a record flight lasting 38 minutes 3 seconds on 5 October 1905. This first attempt proved futile and they failed to arouse any interest at all, but just over two years later a second attempt met with success: the military authorities ordered a Wright Model A for evaluation and finally, in 1909, the U.S. Army Signal Corps took delivery of its first "heavier-than-air" craft.

Europe soon followed the example of America, even though the prevailing attitude toward aviation was only just changing from incredulity to enthusiasm with the first flights and feats of the early aviators. On 12 July 1909, the French War Ministry officially recognized the airplane's military potential by buying a Wright biplane. In Great Britain, in 1910 three artillery officers started the first flying school; in Italy in spring 1909, Wilbur Wright himself trained the first Italian pilot, Engineer Sub-Lieutenant Mario Calderara and the following year the first military flying school was established at the Centocelle field. In November 1910 in the United States, the Curtiss pilot, Eugene Ely, made the first takeoff from a ship and in January 1911 he made the first landing on a ship. Progress from the experimental stage to practical deployment was rapid and in 1911 the Italians were the first to use the airplane on reconnaissance and bombing missions during the invasion of Libya.

The military contribution to the development of the airplane is apparent from the earliest years and was, of course, bound go increase steadily as its military scope was increasingly appreciated. Production reflected this tendency, especially in Europe, where aircraft were no longer built by small numbers of pioneer-craftsmen. When ordered in increasing numbers by the general staffs of the more advanced nations, aircraft had to be manufactured on an industrial scale which meant mass-production and a continual improvement in construction standards.

World War I was to provide clear proof of this direct link and of the impetus which military demands gave to the development of the airplane. Such skepticism as still persisted at the beginning of that long and somber conflict as to whether the aircraft could play an effective role in modern warfare, gave way in the face of a surge of enthusiasm. Manufacturers and designers were encouraged in every way; new manufacturing companies were established and production monitoring was introduced. This was the beginning of a boom which lasted five years due to the merciless demands of war, during which the world first fully realized what a weapon it had in the airplane. The fighter was the embodiment of the technical and technological effort which the main belligerents brought to bear on their aircraft production. The fighter became a really decisive force in the war and could to some extent shield countries from the menace of bombing raids, enemy reconnaissance flights and attacks on ground forces, in short, from danger which threatened from the sky. If a country's fighters were superior to those of its enemies then, of course, it had the key to air supremacy within its grasp. As a result, from 1915, when the first extremely effective German Fokker monoplanes had appeared, this aim was given top priority by each nation involved in the fighting and the almost incredible pace at which the fighter was developed affected aviation as a whole.

At the outbreak of war two basic tendencies were evident in French and German aero-engine production: France had concentrated on improving the rotary engine which had originally been developed in the pioneering years. Germany had mainly worked on stationary inline liquid-cooled engines. Both types had their advantages and drawbacks, but were consistently improved during the war years. The rotary engine proved to be the ideal engine for fighters, since its design bestowed high manoeuvrability, and within only four years these engines reached the peak of their performance, more than doubling their original power. The original inline engines, however, were gradually replaced by the more modern and efficient Vee engines which were mainly developed in France (the Hispano-Suiza V-8); Great Britain (the Rolls-Royce V-12); and the United States (the Liberty V-12). The V-12 engines were soon capable of developing 300–400 hp (three times the power of engines in 1914).

Naturally the demand for increasingly powerful engines and its achievement had a direct influence on design, on construction techniques and on materials used. Fabric-covered wooden airframes gave way to part-plywood coverings, to wooden monocoque structures and to fabric-covered tubular steel frames, and later aluminum was also used. Excellent monoplanes were built, reviving a formula which had been eclipsed by the biplane before the war, and the first all-metal airplanes were produced. The typical fighter in 1918 was a tractor-propeller biplane, usually powered by a 220 hp engine, which had combat speeds of 125–130 mph (200–210 km/h) at an altitude of about 20,000 feet (6,000 m), armed with two synchronized machine guns. World War I stimulated the growth of the newly formed aircraft industry enormously in numbers of aircraft built. In 1913 France produced 1,294 aircraft, during the war a total of 60,000 aircraft of all types was built; Great Britain produced 58,000 aircraft in the war years, reaching a production peak of 3,500 per month; Germany's aircraft production rose from 24 aircraft in 1911 to 1,348 in 1914, to 19,746 in 1917 and totaled 14,123 in 1918, reaching an overall wartime total of 48,537 aircraft of all types.

With the coming of peace, another important stage in the aircraft's development began. The formidable machine of wartime production, which appeared to have gathered irresistible momentum, ground to a halt within a few months. The airplane, however, continued to evolve. Other stimuli were at work, such as commercial aviation, competition flying and the enthusiasm aroused by long-distance flights, but the contribution they made was less spectacular than that afforded by the war. This is reflected by the fact that the airplane changed relatively little until the beginning of the thirties and that, in spite of many innovations and the progress made in performance, that yardstick of progress, the fighter stayed very much as it had been at the end of World War I.

This situation started to change as soon as the world realized that another war was imminent. Air power was once more uppermost in the calculations of politicians and military strategists. All the inter-war years' progress and achievements were quickly harnessed to military production.

Once more, as in the previous world conflict, aviation surged ahead in response to the demands of war. Between 1939 and 1945, terror and destruction brought with them far greater advances in aeronautics than had occurred in the preceding twenty years of peace. By the end of the war, the best piston-engine fighters flew at speeds of 465 mph (750 km/h), nearly twice that of the last biplanes. The most advanced bomber in service, the American Boeing B-29, flew at such high altitude and speed as to be practically immune to interception. Immense progress was made in the technology of construction materials and of engines, where the piston engine was followed by the jet engine, the power unit of the future.

During those six somber years, the main belligerents never underestimated the importance of air power and spared no efforts to increase their capability. So much hinged on this one particular arm; too much was at stake. Historians agree that air power was the vital element which determined the entire course of the war, deciding which way the battle would swing. Each stage in the conflict was swayed by the airplane: in Europe, beginning with the Battle of Britain, followed by the strategic bombing of Germany and later by the Allied landings in Normandy; in the Pacific, starting with the Japanese attack on Pearl Harbor and then in the Battle of Midway and the other great air-sea battles, the American raids on Japan and ending with the historic dates of 6 and 9 August 1945, when atomic bombs were dropped on Hiroshima and Nagasaki, forcing Japan to surrender.

In terms of numbers of aircraft, progress can be directly measured by the production figures of the principal combatants. In 1942 the U.S.A. built a total of 47,836 aircraft of all types (including 10,769 fighters and 12,627 bombers, of which 2,615 were four-engine and 7,247 twin-engine aircraft); in 1943 the total was 85,898 (including 23,988 fighters and 29,355 bombers, of which 9,615 were four-engine and 10,361 twin-engine); the peak was reached in 1944: 96,318 aircraft (including 38,873 fighters and 35,003 bombers, out of which 16,331 were four-engine types and 10,058 twin-engine); finally, in the last year of the war 47,714 airplanes left the assembly lines, of which 21,696 were fighters and 16,492 bombers (6,865 four-engine and 4,454 twin-engine). The total number of combat aircraft built from 1941 to 1945 was 297,199: 99,742 fighters and 97,592 bombers—35,743 of which were four-engine aircraft and 35,369 twin-engine.

Great Britain did just as well, considering the enormous difference between her manufacturing capacity and that of the U.S.A. In 1940 15,000 airplanes were built, rising to 20,100 in 1941, 23,671 in 1942 and 26,263 in 1943; in the following year production reached its peak, totaling 29,220; by the end of the war the overall total of aircraft built stood at 125,254. The third great Allied power, the U.S.S.R., only managed to get its manufacturing industry organized and have major production under way in 1942; in that year 8,000 aircraft were built; in 1943 18,000; in 1944 30,000 were constructed and 25,000 in the first months of 1945.

Among the Axis powers, the Germans were obviously the top producers of aircraft in Europe and the Japanese led the way in Asia. By 1939 Germany had the most powerful air force in the world and in that same year produced 10,800 aircraft, 11,800 in the next year, 15,600 in 1942, 25,500 in 1943, 39,800 in 1944 and 8,000 in the first five months of 1945. Japanese aircraft production also ran at very high levels. 1940's total of 4,768 was followed by 5,800 in 1941 (of which 1,080 were fighters and 1,461 bombers); 8,861 aircraft were manufactured in 1942 (2,935 fighters and 2,433 bombers); 16,639 aircraft were built in 1943 (7,147 fighters and 4,189 bombers) and in 1944 the total rose to 28,180 (13,811 fighters and 5,100 bombers); in the eight months of war before the Japanese surrender in 1945, 11,066 combat aircraft came off the assembly lines and of these 5,474 were fighters and 1,934 bombers.

The greatest technical advance made during the war years was, of course, the introduction of the jet engine, on which both Great Britain and Germany had been working, progressing through the experimental to the operational stage. The Germans introduced their first operational jet aircraft when they put the Messerschmitt Me 262 into operational service during October 1944, a few months after its British counterpart, the Gloster Meteor, which first entered squadron service in July 1944. This meant that the first effective jet engines were soon to open a new chapter in the history of aviation, albeit at a cost of so much destruction.

The upheaval caused by World War II in the lives of nations and peoples had brought with it an alteration in the balance of power which henceforth hinged on two opponents: the United States and the Soviet Union. This tendency was reflected in the world of aviation: the U.S.A. and the U.S.S.R. became the unchallenged leaders and other countries which had been extremely important and influential on the international aviation scene had to be content with secondary roles.

During the years since 1945 aviation has become a vital element in world development. On the one hand it is a service and a benefit, on the other the key to a complex mechanism which maintains the balance of military power, underlining the contradictions inherent in its dual role, a dichotomy which had started to appear as far back as the years following World War I. The ostensible aim of the superpowers, that of maintaining world peace, is based more than ever before on the balance of armaments, on each side's counterattack potential with increasingly deadly weapons and also relies on stressing the possibility of total annihilation. This is a finely tuned dynamic balance, a process which over the last forty years has led to a horrifying growth in the size of stockpiles of weapons and an almost incredible increase in their sophistication. The airplane has been no exception to this trend and the arms race has made it evolve at an unprecedented rate. As we have seen, World War II not only affirmed the aircraft's importance as a strategic weapon, it also led to the development of the jet engine. The amount of effort devoted to developing this totally new means of propulsion produced constant advances. To gauge the extent of this progress one has only to look at forty years of world records.

In October 1938 the Fédération Aéronautique Internationale (FAI) recognized the following world records: distance in a closed circuit: 7,235 miles (11,651 km), Japan–Koken monoplane, 15 May 1938; distance in a straight line: 6,300 miles (10,148 km), U.S.S.R.–Tupolev ANT-25, 15 July 1937; speed: 440.85 mph (709.902 km/h), Italy–Macchi-Castoldi MC.72 seaplane, 23 October 1934. The altitude record was at that time still held by a balloon, the American *Explorer II*, and stood at 72,375 feet (22,066 m) achieved on 11 November 1935 but, on 22 October 1938, the Italian pilot Mario Pezzi, flying a Caproni Ca 161bis, reached an altitude of 56,032 feet (17,083 m). By September 1978, the numbers involved had changed dramatically: the world distance record (closed circuit) was now 11,330 miles (18,245 km), held by the U.S.A.'s Boeing B-52H Stratofortress, set on 7 June 1962; while the distance record in a straight line achieved by the same aircraft on 11 January 1962, had risen to 12,525 miles (20,168.78 km); speed: 2,191.86 miles (3,529.56 km), U.S.A.–Lockheed SR-71A, 28 June 1976; altitude: 123,492 feet (37,650 m), U.S.S.R.—MiG-25, 31 August 1977. At the end of 1981 these records had yet to be broken.

At the same time as this spectacular vindication of the airplane's potential, its military capability was being developed in new directions. Defensive and offensive weaponry became ever more effective and sophisticated, and included nuclear warheads and successive generations of increasingly accurate and "intelligent" missiles, operated as part of integrated electronic systems which meant that the pilot's only decision need be the choice of whether or not to fire. This altered traditional concepts of the use of combat aircraft once again beyond all recognition compared with previous generations of military aircraft. The conventional bomber is now being superseded by strategic intercontinental ballistic missiles (ICBMs); increasingly effective tactical fighters have been put into service and the multi-role combat aircraft (MRCA) has emerged, one of its assets being economy in view of today's staggering costs per single aircraft. Instead of several specialized aircraft having to be developed and built, the MRCA can perform a wide range of operational duties, from ground attack to reconnaissance and interception. Meanwhile interceptors themselves have become even more sophisticated, since the manned fighter is still needed in spite of startling advances in the field of missiles.

During this period of accelerated progress, great strides were made in the understanding and use of technology in electronics, aerodynamics and metallurgy. The two branches of space travel and conventional flight were interdependent, co-existing in what could be described as a form of osmosis. This close linkage is illustrated very clearly by the Fédération Aéronautique Internationale's figures for world records in conventional flight when compared with space flight data. The seven space records, as at the end of September 1980, were as follows: duration of flight in orbit round the earth: U.S.S.R., Vladimir Lyakhov and Valery Ryumin in Soyuz 32–Salyut 6–Soyuz 34, from 25 February–19 August 1979, a total of 175 days, 35 minutes, 36 seconds; altitude: U.S.A., F. Borman, J. A. Lawell and W. Anders in Apollo 8, 21–27 December 1968, reaching 234,532 miles (377,668 km); maximum weight put into orbit was achieved by the same satellite and crew on the same dates as above and stands at 282,196 lb (127,980 kg); distance covered in orbit round the earth: U.S.S.R., Lyakhov and Ryumin in their 1979 flight, when the spacecraft travelled 72,291,578 miles (116,411,557 km); the record for time spent by a member of the crew outside the spacecraft is held by the U.S.A.: E. Cernan, from the lunar module Apollo 17, 12–14 December 1972, 21 hours 31 minutes and 44 seconds; the record number of astronauts outside the spacecraft at the same time was set up by the U.S.S.R. when two astronauts, A. Eliseiev and E. Khrounov stayed outside their spacecraft Soyuz 4 and 5 for 37 minutes during the 14–18 January 1969 flight; the record length of time spent in space flight is held by the U.S.S.R., when V. Ryumin made his flight on board Soyuz 25, 32 and 34 and Salyut 6, and totals 117 days 1 hour 20 minutes and 21 seconds.

But to what extent has civil and commercial aviation been influenced by all these achievements? The answer is, to a tremendous extent and more than is immediately apparent, in fields such as aerodynamic research and analysis, and work on structural components; in metallurgy, electronics and computerized control systems. As for engines, a high proportion of modern airliners is powered by engines which were originally developed for military aircraft.

It is easy to find illustrations to prove this. The irony is that most new inventions which have led to a step forward in civil aviation and have brought about changes in the commercial aviation scene, are derived, directly or indirectly, from military research and development. The majority of airliners was developed to satisfy military requirements or was derived from bombers. Even the Boeing 707, the embodiment of the modern commercial jet, was produced by Boeing, drawing on the experience they had gained during the construction of the B-47 bomber. The Boeing 747, the first of the wide-body jet transports, was designed following the introduction of successful giant military jet transports. Many aircraft besides these have a less obvious debt to the same source.

1.

FOUR CENTURIES OF DREAMS AND EXPERIMENTS

Twelve seconds. On 17 December 1903, Orville Wright's first powered flight lasted just this long. In those few seconds a dream which was as old as mankind came true. A dream which had been kept alive by centuries of myths, fantasy, legends and speculation, a kind of magic which had fascinated madmen and fanatics, and the enquiring minds of artists, scientists and philosophers.

Evidence of man's preoccupation with the mystery of flight goes back as far as recorded history and leaves such traces as winged figures in prehistoric cave paintings, while the winged gods of Egyptian mythology were echoed by the flying bulls of the ancient Assyrians and the winged horses in Greek myths. In those far-off times the concept of flight was always bound up with the supernatural and the divine, belonging to a world which remained beyond the reach of mankind.

But this taboo was to be shattered—man decided that he, too, wished to possess the power to fly, just as the gods he worshipped. The earliest story of human flight known to most people is the tale of Daedalus and Icarus and their escape from prison with wings made from birds' feathers held together with wax. Daedalus, the older and more prudent, got safely away, while his rash son, Icarus, being younger and bolder was foolish enough to fly so high that the sun melted the wax and he fell to his death—the first recorded example of a structural failure in flight. The traditions of many peoples, not just the folklore of the Mediterranean civilizations, tell us what happened when men had the temerity to imitate the gods. In 2200 B.C. the Chinese emperor Shin jumped off a high tower wearing two very large straw hats and, luckier than Icarus, landed safely. Around 1500 B.C. the Persian king Kai Kawus is said to have made a fantastic journey, flying across the sky in a chariot drawn by eagles. Alexander the Great is supposed to have made a similar journey when he wanted to explore the wide blue skies; he embarked in a wicker basket and was pulled along by griffins which he persuaded to fly by the simple expedient of suspending food either just above or just below their ravening mouths, depending on which direction he wished to take.

This legend of flight by Alexander the Great was very popular with painters and chroniclers of the Middle Ages and was so often depicted and recounted that it was accepted as historical fact, in spite of the inconsistencies and widely differing versions. As late as the fifteenth century Giovanni da Fontana wrote in his *Metrologum de pisce, cane et volucre*: "Alexander was determined to rule the skies as well as the earth, so he had the clever idea of sitting astride great flying griffins and held pieces of roasted meat on the tip of his sword just above their heads. the griffins smelt the meat and leapt upward attempting to seize it. Once Alexander had climbed high into the sky and wished to descend, he simply held the meat below the griffins' jaws and in their efforts to reach the food below them they took Alexander safely back to earth. Whether this story is true or false, the idea is one of genius, although it shows a certain presumption in a mere human."

English legend reverts to the idea of "birdmen" and in the *Historia regum Britannize* of Geoffrey of Monmouth we are told of a mythical king of Britain, Bladud, who is supposed to have founded the city of Bath and to have been the father of King Lear. He wished to test his own magical powers and tried to fly with a pair of wings strapped to his shoulders, but he fell "on the roof of the temple and broke every bone in his body."

Birdmen and flying machines were the first two methods of flying which occurred to man's imagination. These ideas persisted for many hundreds of years, moving from folklore into chronicles, but progress of a sort was made, although the flying ships and carriages only existed on paper, in drawings and far-fetched designs, since attempts by birdmen to fly were made ever more frequently.

The first historically recorded attempt dates from 852 in Spain, when a Muslim holy man, Armen Firman, tried to fly in Cordoba. Nearly two centuries later, in 1020, a Saxon Benedictine monk called Aelmer tried to fly by jumping from the roof of Malmesbury Abbey and broke both his legs in the attempt. This event is recorded in some detail by William of Malmesbury, who relates in his *Chronicle of the Kings of England* that in his youth Aelmer had conceived the daring idea of imitating Daedalus, his ambition being to turn an ancient myth into reality. The young man had tied wings in some fashion to his arms and legs and then jumped off the top of a high tower. The wind happened to be so strong that it hampered his movements and he was unable to fly, plummeting to earth, but fortunately escaping with his life, although he was lame from then onward. William tells us that Aelmer ascribed his failure to his lack of tail-feathers, which might have given him more stability in flight.

Another attempt, which was made at Constantinople (now Istanbul) in the same century by an unknown Saracen resulted in death. In 1496 an elderly chorister of Nuremberg risked a jump and only broke his arm, while in 1503 it was the turn of the mathematician Giovanni Battista Danti of Perugia to launch himself into the air in front of an incredulous crowd with a pair of wings attached to his shoulders. He fell on to the dome of a church and broke his leg. According to a contemporary historian, Danti (who was also known as the Daedalus of Perugia) would have managed to fly had not a joint in one of his wings given way. He had apparently successfully tested these wings previously on Lake Trasimene and they had worked perfectly well.

Four years later another Italian adventurer, who had come to Scotland and taken the name John Damian, repeated Giovanni Battista Danti's experiment and jumped off the walls of Stirling Castle and ended up just as Danti had done. Damian had been made Abbot of Tungland by James IV of Scotland, but was held in great scorn by contemporary chroniclers, who called him a charlatan and a buffoon. In 1536, yet another Italian, a clockmaker named Bolori, decided to show how man could fly, leapt from the top of Troyes Cathedral wearing a pair of wings, and was killed.

The list of attempts could be continued indefinitely: men

went on trying to fly in the centuries which followed, even when a more rational and scientific approach toward the problem was becoming apparent. In 1628 Paolo Guidotti, the artist, scientist and writer from Lucca found the challenge irresistible and hurt his leg badly. A detailed contemporary account of his attempt has survived which tells us that the wings were made from a whale-bone framework into which Guidotti had painstakingly inserted feathers and the wings were then strapped under his arms. The flight covered about a quarter of a mile and an observer comments that it was not so much a flight, more a controlled descent, "falling more slowly than he would have done without wings." He relates that Guidotti grew weary of flapping his arms and fell on to a roof. This gave way and the enthusiast landed in the room below, breaking his thigh, which left him crippled.

But there were other experiments made besides those which imitated birds and other schemes besides the far-fetched myths of chariots being drawn along in the air by strange creatures. Countless experiments were carried out which led to nothing, but are interesting for what they reveal about the approach to flight.

The method of propulsion for a flying machine, which was only invented in the nineteenth century, had taxed people's ingenuity hundreds of years earlier. The rockets and fireworks of Imperial China are probably the earliest example of power being used to make objects fly. The Italian, Giovanni da Fontana, explored this idea in 1420 in his rudimentary design for a mechanical bird powered by a rocket in its tail. There are also records of experiments carried out by Heron of Alexandria, who discovered steam power and constructed a rotating boiler, which had four lateral vents. Archytas of Tarentum (444 B.C.) is supposed to have made a wooden dove powered by a steam jet which was tested while attached to a rotating arm which gave it horizontal support.

Archimedes invented the screw, and this principle was to be applied to the aircraft's propeller (hence air screw). This idea had been applied—but in a different way—in ancient China, where the first recorded use was made of windmills, in which the blades were arranged horizontally.

This method was not altered until the fourteenth century when the propeller was used as an active rather than a passive force. The first European windmills had vertically arranged blades and appeared in the thirteenth century. Drawings of toys subsequently came to light in old documents which can be described as rudimentary helicopters: they had little propellers which were worked by the string-pulling method and some could rise into the air, others simply whirled round fanning the air.

One of the most interesting methods of flight—which was totally distinct from the flapping-wing concept—was by kite. Once more China was the setting for the earliest known account of this use, and kites were widely employed to chase away evil spirits and were flown above houses and fields for protection. We are also told by many sources that kites were used for more practical purposes, such as war, and man-lifting kites were flown so that the enemy's movements could be observed. Another type of kite was something like a modern wind-sock and was widely used in the Mediterranean civilisations and later throughout Medieval Europe: its principal use was as a military standard and in appearance it remained curiously faithful to its ancient oriental origins, representing a grotesque dragon or serpent. More ambitious ideas were dreamed up, however. In a manuscript by Walter de Milemete, called *De Nobilitatibus, Sapientiis et prudentiis regum*, which dates from 1326, a drawing shows what then must have been a science fiction scene, with a city surrounded by high walls and towers, over which a large and sinister kite is hovering menacingly, flown at the end of a long rope which is held by three soldiers, and a bomb with stabilizing fins is hurtling from it onto the city. This is the first known European illustration of aerial bombardment and is also probably the first example of a direct link being made between a flying machine and a practical although unpleasant application.

What principles and theories lay behind these partly-thought out and rudimentary uses for flying machines? The answer has to be, none at all. Aerodynamics would only become a science in modern times and for many centuries "aeronautics" remained the exclusive province of philosophy and religion, and became further and further divorced from the realms of reality and increasingly far-fetched.

The first person to show any signs of breaking away from the old tradition and of approaching the problem from a different angle was Roger Bacon who in about the year 1250 wrote a book entitled *De mirabili potestate artis et naturae* (Of the wonderful power of art and nature) in which he made mention of hollow copper spheres filled with some sort of ethereal air which could float up into the air. And Bacon also describes a flying machine: "Engines for flying, a man sitting in the midst thereof, by turning only about an Instrument, which moves artificial wings made to beat the Aire, much after the fashion of a Bird's flight."

This was a first tentative step, and four centuries later, in 1670, Bacon's vaguely-formulated ideas were to be echoed and elaborated by Francesco de Lana de Terzi. This tremendous time lapse is explained by the fact that Bacon's work was lost for hundreds of years and was only published for the first time in Paris in 1542. It is doubtful, however, that man would ever have achieved flight had it been left to the philosophers. The writings of John Wilkins, a seventeenth-century English bishop, show how entrenched the old misconceptions about flight were and how persistent, when he states that there were four ways in which man can fly: by using birds, by attaching wings to one's body. in a flying chariot and—most helpful of all—with the assistance of the spirits and the angels.

Cutaway drawing of William Samuel Henson's monoplane **Plate 1**

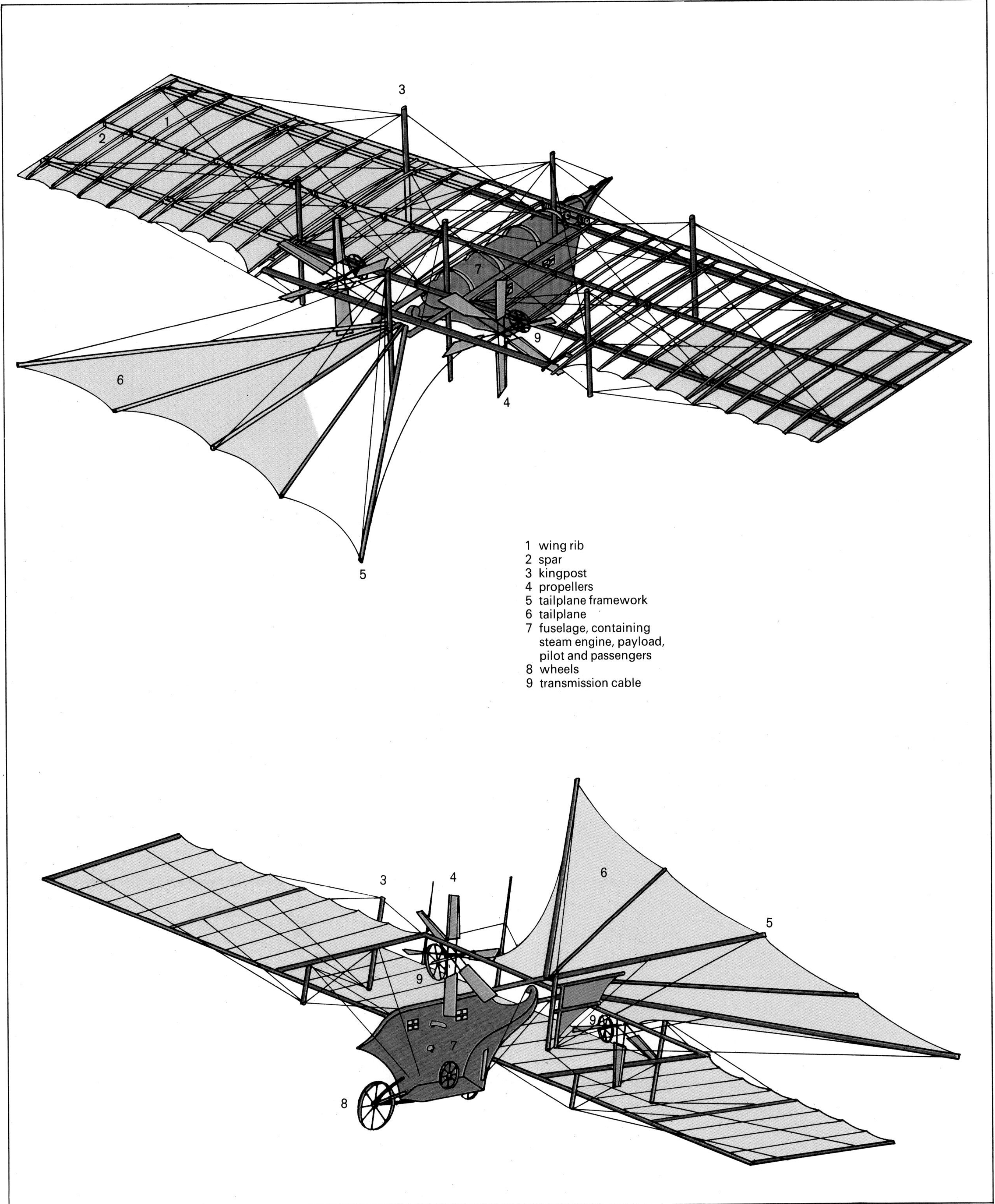

Plates 2–14
From Leonardo da Vinci to Langley

In his treatise *Sul Volo degli Uccelli* (*On the Flight of Birds*) of 1505, which was the product of nearly twenty years' study on the subject, Leonardo da Vinci (1452–1519) stated: "In order to fly a bird uses its wings in the same way as a swimmer moves his arms and legs." In fact da Vinci had misinterpreted his observations and this false premise meant that much of the immense amount of work he had done in his endeavor to achieve one of man's oldest and most exciting dreams was of little value. But the contribution which this man of genius from Tuscany made to the history of flight marks a turning point, a brief isolated flash of inspiration and insight into the problems which man faced in his efforts to fly. After centuries of dreams and myths, of impractical attempts at flight based on irrational principles and mistaken ideas, da Vinci's writings and drawings represent the first truly scientific treatment of the subject, covering five thousand manuscript pages (thirty-five thousand words and 150 diagrams) which have survived to this day.

Leonardo's mistaken interpretation is surprising when one remembers the uncompromisingly rigorous scientific method which the great inventor applied to other engineering and mechanical problems. He was hampered by his fixed idea that only by imitating birds could man learn to fly, and we have it from one of his biographers that this was the dream which persistently fascinated and obsessed him. Apparently he was so emotionally involved in this "quest" that his faculties of rational deduction were blunted. This becomes clear when we look at those of the line drawings which have survived and see that most of them concentrate on one particular mechanical device, the ornithopter, by means of which da Vinci set out to put his theories to practical application and achieve lift and flight by means of mobile—or flapping—wings, which were to function in much the same way as birds' wings when in flight—or, to be more accurate, their flight as da Vinci understood it. Only toward the end of his life did da Vinci realize that this was not a practical solution and hit upon the correct one: the use of the fixed wing—and by then time had almost run out. So keen was da Vinci to resolve this tantalizing problem that he underestimated another fundamental problem—that of the energy which was needed to power the machine. He was convinced that human muscle power could provide sufficient energy to lift a man's body and the machine as well, by means of working a complicated wing mechanism. It appears that da Vinci eventually realized that this line of research was futile; some of his drawings show an ornithopter and a rudimentary helicopter powered by a spring, which was obviously meant to supplement the muscle power of the "pilot." This idea had, however, come to da Vinci too late in life for him to have enough time to develop it further. Even had he never hit upon an alternative means of supplying power, da Vinci's research might well have led him to a second, correct solution: gliding flight.

Da Vinci began his study of the flight of birds in 1486, while he was in Milan in the service of the Sforzas, and he continued his studies until shortly before his death. Although the value of this vast amount of work was prejudiced by erroneous basic assumptions, it reveals his incredible ingenuity and the almost uncanny insight which typifies his scientific work. His drawings and diagrams include design sketches of several types of ornithopter (in which the pilot was either to lie flat or stand on a platform) and detailed drawings which anticipate certain structural concepts only rediscovered and used many hundreds of years later, such as the retractable "legs" of his ornithopter; a complicated system of controlling the elevons by means of straps attached to the pilot's head, so that he could steer up or down by nodding his head, altering the angle of the movable wing tips on the ornithopter. This system was adopted four centuries later by Otto Lilienthal with some modifications. Da Vinci's design sketches for a rudimentary helicopter have also survived (an "air screw" driven by a spring), as have his parachute designs (which look like a pyramid-shaped tent, with cables strapped to the parachutist's shoulders), but da Vinci's most outstanding invention in this field was probably the propeller. He designed a propeller as the driving force to turn a spit! The propeller blades were in turn to be driven round by the hot air from the fireplace. Many centuries were to pass before it was realized that a helicopter achieves vertical flight by means of aerodynamic lift from rotor blades which are rotated under power.

Leonardo da Vinci's ideas were to lie hidden for centuries and, by one of the quirks of history, were only brought to light three centuries later or, to be exact, 278 years later. Da Vinci died on 2 May 1519, at the Château de Cloux in France and in 1797 the first rediscovery was made of some of the notebooks. Thus a vast corpus of work was lost to those who were trying to progress towards manned flight, deprived as they were of the discoveries da Vinci had made through his research and the problems he had articulated concerning flight. Mistaken avenues of enquiry were therefore pursued, false hopes

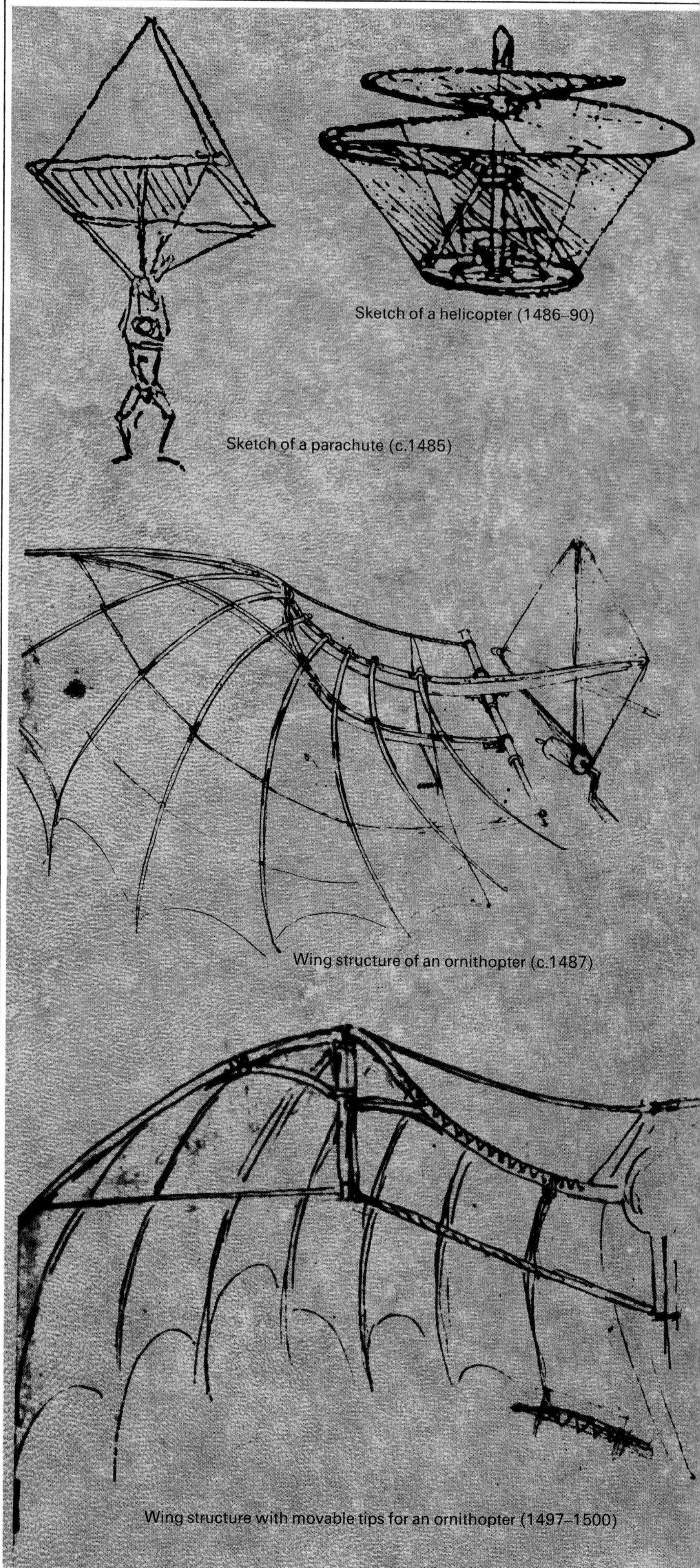
Sketch of a helicopter (1486–90)

Sketch of a parachute (c.1485)

Wing structure of an ornithopter (c.1487)

Wing structure with movable tips for an ornithopter (1497–1500)

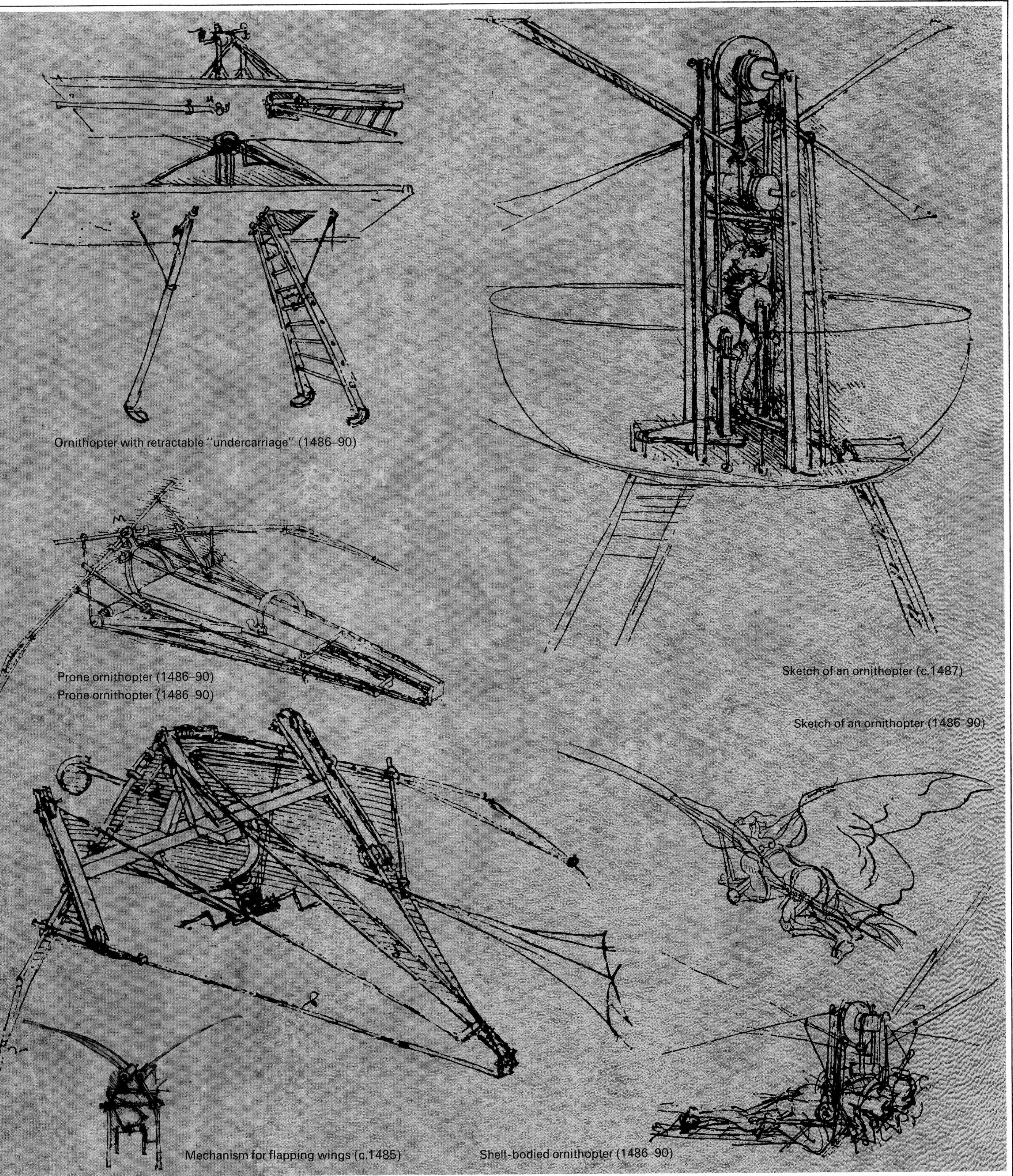

Ornithopter with retractable "undercarriage" (1486–90)

Sketch of an ornithopter (c.1487)

Prone ornithopter (1486–90)
Prone ornithopter (1486–90)

Sketch of an ornithopter (1486–90)

Mechanism for flapping wings (c.1485)

Shell-bodied ornithopter (1486–90)

raised and theories, which da Vinci had already disproved, explored anew. Da Vinci's genius, however, strikes us as even more phenomenal when we consider the "dark ages" which followed his death, insofar as the world of aeronautics was concerned.

In 1595, or thereabouts, a work by Fausto Veranzio was published in Venice entitled *Machinae novae* (New machines), containing an illustration which represented an original idea, since it could not have been inspired by the lost papers of da Vinci. A man is shown suspended from what could be described as a rudimentary type of parachute, which can be seen to derive from the structure of a sail, and one can discern a rigid framework which supports the four sides of the spread of fabric. This is the first known publication of a drawing of a parachute.

A very much more far-fetched inventor's description of a projected airship was given by Francesco de Lana de Terzi (1631–87) in a book entitled *Prodromo, overo saggio di alcune invenzioni nuove* (1670) (Prodrome, or an essay on some new inventions). De Lana was a Jesuit from Brescia who taught literature and science in a convent in Rome. Having made a study of the subject and carried out certain experiments, de Lana had succeeded in determining the pressure of the atmosphere at sea level with a fair degree of accuracy and he demonstrated that air is lighter—or as we would say, thinner—at higher altitudes. He attempted to put this knowledge to a practical use by designing a flying machine. He envisaged an airship and described it in the most minute detail—it was to have a hull like that of a ship and would be held aloft by four very large copper vacuum spheres, each measuring about six metres in diameter (19.5 ft); the airship was also to have a mast and a sail. The theory which determined the means of becoming airborne was based on the fact that a vacuum sphere weighs less than a similar sphere full of air; thus, on creating a vacuum in all four spheres, they would rise and float upward, taking the airship up into the air. Francesco de Lana also managed to devise a system of regulating climbing speed by the use of small sacks of sand for ballast, and descent was to be controled by means of special valves which would allow for the gradual introduction of air into the vacuum spheres, thus making them heavier. The sail was to be used to "steer" the airship or "gondola." The good Jesuit's imagination ran riot once he had disposed of the practical aspects of flight to his own satisfaction, and he went on to envisage and describe airborne invasions and bombardments using his flying machine.

The merit of De Lana's invention lay in its being one of the first examples of a completely new method of getting a craft airborne, which differed totally from all previous schemes which had been dreamt up by would-be inventors who had devoted all their energies to finding a way in which man could fly by imitating birds' flight and using wings. In much the same way, however, as da Vinci's theories had been postulated in isolation, so de Lana's ideas were not followed up and designs for ornithopters and men with wings were to come thick and fast. In 1678, at Sablé in France, a locksmith named Besnier tried to fly with two pairs of wings on rods driven by his arms and legs. Contemporary reports have it that Besnier carried out several trials with his invention which culminated in "a safe jump from a rooftop and a safe landing," but in all probability Besnier only escaped breaking his neck by luck rather than to the viability of his invention. In 1709, in Lisbon, the Brazilian Jesuit, Bartholomeu Lourenço de Gusmâo (1686–1724) tried to launch his bird-shaped glider which he called the *Passarola.* It is more than likely that Gusmâo constructed a life-size mock-up of the craft and that he only carried out his experiments with a small-scale model. In the year 1742 in Paris, Jean-François Boyvin de Bonnetot, Marquis de Bacqueville, tried out much the same experiment as Besnier had done and, fastening four wings to his arms and legs, jumped off the roof of a house overlooking the Seine. His brief moment of glory was somewhat marred when he broke both his legs on landing.

Among the more interesting ideas which were put forward in the eighteenth century was the fixed-wing flying machine designed by a German, Melchior Bauer, in 1764. The many detailed drawings which Bauer had made of his invention only came to light in 1921 in the Greiz town archives. These show that the wing had pronounced dihedral and was supported by sturdy struts; below was a single platform on four wheels for the pilot. The pilot himself had to power the machine by means of a complicated system of rotating blades fixed to a pole.

The designs of the French inventor Jean-Pierre Blanchard were somewhat similar, although on a much larger scale. This Parisian inventor had always been fascinated by the challenge of flight and in 1781 he designed an aircraft which consisted of a hull with a large mast, at the top of which was fixed a complicated system of six large revolving sails. This rigging could, according to its designer, not only keep the craft aloft, but also give it considerable climbing speed. Power was to be strictly muscular, supplied by the pilot and his crew.

In the same year, 1781, a German architect Karl Friedrich Meerwein

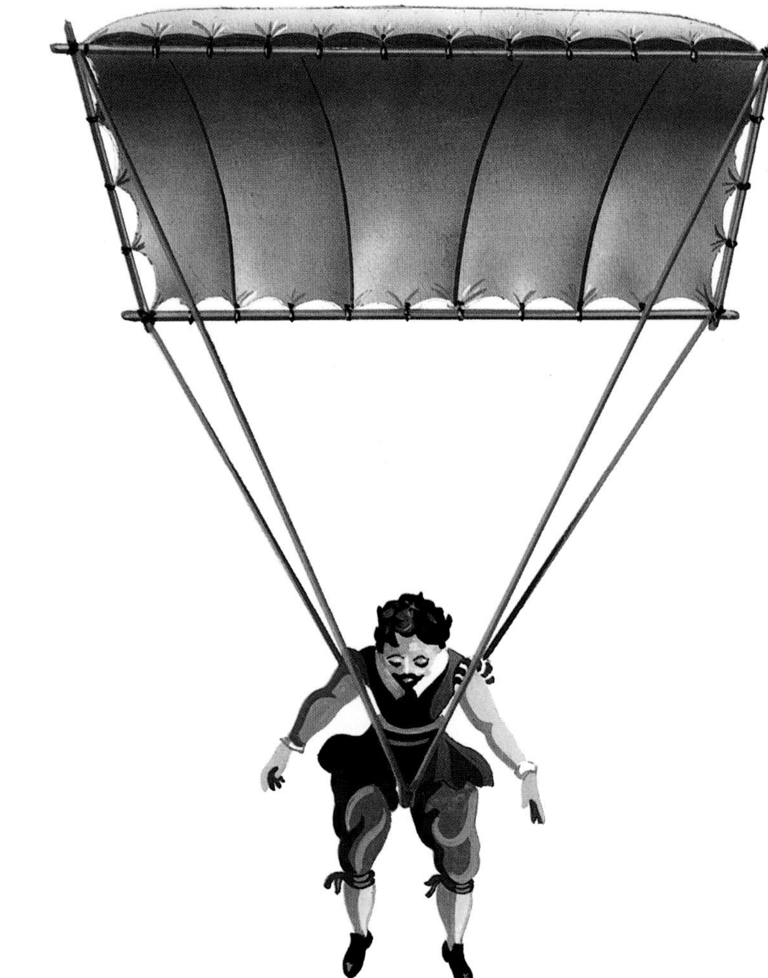

Veranzio's parachute (c.1595)

De Gusmâo's airship *Passarola* (1709)

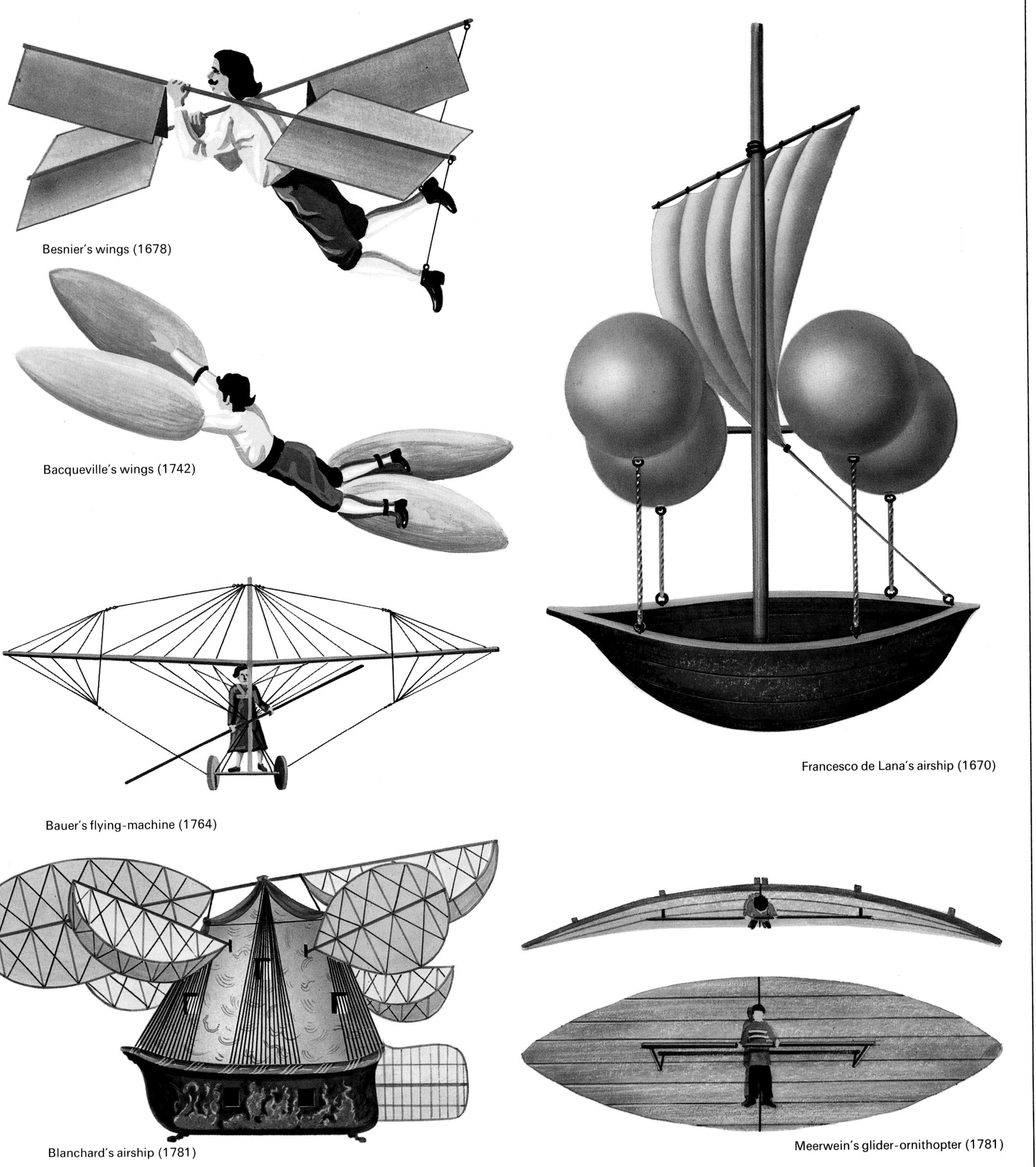

Besnier's wings (1678)

Bacqueville's wings (1742)

Bauer's flying-machine (1764)

Blanchard's airship (1781)

Francesco de Lana's airship (1670)

Meerwein's glider-ornithopter (1781)

returned to the idea of beating wings to power his glider, which was in fact a cross between a glider and an ornithopter. Meerwein had attempted to work out a surface-to-weight ratio and built a structure which he calculated would be able to bear his own weight. After a couple of experiments with the machine, however, he abandoned any further attempts but in 1784 described the machine and his working methods in his book *L'art de voler à la manière des oiseaux* (The art of flying like the birds). The wing was elliptical and strapped to the pilot's shoulders and was to be flapped by him in some way—Meerwein does not specify how. The surface area of the flapping wing was to be 11.68 square meters (108 sq ft). More than 100 years were to pass before winged flight became a practical proposition.

The laws governing flight, aerodynamics and the need to instal some form of power unit in flying machines so that they could be controled under all sorts of different conditions, had yet to be fully understood. Inventors, scholars and enthusiasts were all pursuing the same goal as Leonardo da Vinci had done so many years earlier: that of building a heavier-than-air machine which could fly. Meanwhile, a completely different approach met with some success, and 120 years before the Wright brothers' first flights, man's age-old dream of being airborne came true. At 1.53 p.m. on the afternoon of 21 November 1783, in Paris, François Pilâtre de Rozier (1756–85), a professor of chemistry, and François Laurent, Marquis d'Arlandes, made an ascent in an oval-shaped hot air balloon, approximately 49 feet (15 m) in diameter and 78 feet (22 m) high.

This achievement had been made possible by the brilliant inspiration of two Frenchmen, Joseph (1740–1810) and Etienne Montgolfier (1745–99), brothers who owned a paper mill in Annonay, near Lyons. They observed the ascending force of smoke and saw that paper bags placed over a fire also tended to rise, pushed upwards by the hot air. (Some historians describe the source of their inspiration somewhat quaintly, saying that the two brothers noticed how a shirt which had been hung to dry over the fire billowed upward, borne upward and inflated by the hot air and this led to their idea for a balloon.) From there it was but a short step. They concluded that if they managed to enclose what they thought was gas inside a fairly large and very light "envelope," this container, or bag would rise from the ground. Etienne Montgolfier carried out the first experiment at Avignon in September 1782, proving their theory to be sound. After further experiments with increasingly large models, they finally built a cloth and paper balloon 38 feet (11.5 m) in diameter and tested it on 4 June 1783, in the marketplace of Annonay, where a wool and straw fire had been prepared to fill the balloon with hot air. The balloon—which was called a Montgolfière from that day on—left the ground and rose into the air, reaching a height of about 6,560 feet (2,000 m).

Much encouraged by their success, the Montgolfier brothers went to Paris and built another larger balloon. On 19 September, in the same year, this aerostat made the first recorded air voyage of history—although the terrified "passengers" happened to be a sheep, a cock and a duck. The flight took place at Versailles, in the presence of Louis XVI, Marie Antionette and the whole court, as well as an enthusiastic crowd of some 130,000 people. The flight lasted eight minutes and the balloon covered nearly 2 miles (about 3 km) with no mishaps, bringing its occupants safely back to earth. Two months later, a third balloon, also built by the Montgolfier brothers, safely completed the first manned flight, with Pilâtre de Rozier and the Marquis d'Arlandes as the two-man crew.

The historic flight of 21 November had been preceded by a less ambitious trial ascent on 15 October, when the balloon was only allowed to rise a few feet with the two men on board and was anchored to the ground with ropes. A detailed record of this trial ascent has survived in Tiberio Cavallo's work *Storia e pratica dell' aerostatica* (History and practice of aerostation), published in 1785. His description of the balloon is particularly interesting: "It was elegantly decorated and painted on the outside with the signs of the zodiac, and the monogram of the king, fleur-de-lys, etc. The lower opening of the aerostat was encircled by a wickerwork gallery which was about three feet wide with a balustrade round the inner side and the outside edge about three feet high. The inside diameter of this gallery and of the opening of the balloon (the neck of which was surrounded by the gallery), was almost 16 feet. There was an iron grate or brazier in the middle of this opening secured by chains to the sides of the craft. This arrangement made it easy for a member of the crew who was positioned in the gallery to stoke a fire which had been lit on this grate with fuel, of which he had a store, thus keeping the hot air flowing into the opening of the balloon." Cavallo gives a very clear description of the ascent: "The balloon rose and floated safely over some trees, drifting slowly and majestically up into the sky. When they had reached a height of about 280 feet, the balloonists doffed their hats to the astonished crowd of spectators." The balloon was carried right across Paris by the wind and after about 25 minutes came down "in a field beyond the new Boulevard about 9,000 meters from the Château de la Muette." The only nasty moment for the passengers occurred immediately after the balloon had touched ground. The Marquis d'Arlandes jumped from the gallery as the balloon landed, but de Rozier was enveloped in the folds of the balloon's fabric as it suddenly deflated; he was, however, able to free himself very promptly from this somewhat precarious situation. From then on lighter-than-air flight was well and truly launched and a few days later Jacques Alexandre César Charles (1746–1823), a member of the French Academy of Sciences, successfully tested a new type of balloon, in which hot air had been replaced by hydrogen, the "inflammable air" which the English scientist, Henry Cavendish, had discovered 17 years before. Charles had already tested an unmanned hydrogen balloon on 27 August. After a long flight it came down near Paris, where it was destroyed by some terrified peasants. On 1 December 1783, the new balloon, called *La Charlière*, after its inventor's name, successfully took off from the gardens of the Tuileries in Paris, before a crowd of 400,000 people, carrying Charles and an assistant, M. N. Robert, as the passenger. *La Charlière* covered 27 miles (43 km) before touching down safely at Nesle.

On 25 February 1784, the first balloon ascent was made in Italy. It took place near Milan in a Montgolfier balloon with Paolo Andreani and the Gerli brothers. The Neapolitan diplomat, Vincenzo (Vincent) Lunardi, used a hydrogen balloon for the first ascent in England on 15 September 1784, although the first ascent in the British Isles had been made some three weeks earlier, on 25 August at Edinburgh, by James Tytler in a Montgolfier balloon. Lunardi took off from the Honourable Artillery Company's Ground near Moorfields in London, landing at Standon near Ware in Hertfordshire. On the way Lunardi unloaded his passenger, a cat, which, he said "had suffered dreadfully from the cold." In June 1785 the Italian diplomat had the honor of having the first woman air traveler on board his balloon: a certain Mrs Letitia Ann Sage, whom the journalists of the time gallantly described as being "of a Junoesque beauty, weighing about 15 stone 10 lb." The voyage was not entirely without incident since, on landing, Mrs Sage was confronted by an infuriated farmer whose field of peas she had trampled and ruined.

The new craze for lighter-than-air flight spread quickly. On 7 January 1785, the first real milestone was reached: the crossing of the Channel by the American, Dr John Jeffries, and Jean-Pierre Blanchard who had designed a rather fanciful airship but came up against insuperable problems. Unable to resolve the complexities of

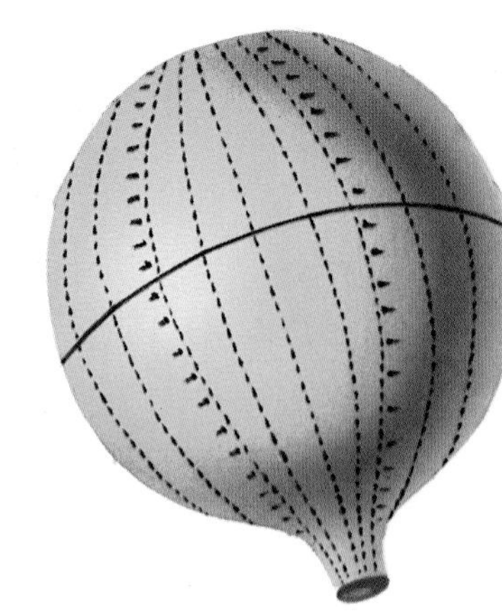

The Montgolfier brothers' first balloon (4 June 1783)

The balloon in which de Rozier and Romain met their deaths (15 June 1785)

Lunardi's hydrogen balloon (15 September 1784)

Montgolfier balloon (19 September 1783)

Pilâtre de Rozier and the Marquis d'Arlandes in the first manned balloon ascent (21 November 1783)

La Charlière (1 December 1783)

L'Entreprenant, the first balloon put to military use (1794)

▲ First balloon ascent in the United States and first airmail delivery: Blanchard (9 January 1793)

The balloon in which Blanchard and Jeffries crossed the Channel (7 January 1785) ▶

Nassau, the large balloon in which Charles Green flew from London to Weilburg in Germany (November 1836)

heavier-than-air and winged flight, Blanchard decided to opt for the aerostat. Their balloon measured 27 feet (8.3 m) in diameter and had a boat-shaped passenger car. An attempt to emulate this feat cost Pilâtre de Rozier his life. On 15 June 1785, the French professor of chemistry and a friend, Pierre Romain, took off from Boulogne for the crossing to Great Britain in a balloon containing both hot air and hydrogen, which de Rozier had built. At an altitude of about 2,950 feet (900 m) above the French coast, a spark from the brazier ignited the hydrogen and the two men plummeted to the ground. Thus manned flight had claimed its first two victims: de Rozier and Romain.

These accidents did not, however, dampen the prevailing enthusiasm. On 9 January 1793, Blanchard (who by now was totally committed to proving the aerostat's versatility) made the first ascent in the United States, at Philadelphia, and also made the first airmail delivery of a letter from George Washington. The widespread interest in this new means of air travel became evident the following year when it was first put to military use. The French used a captive hydrogen balloon, *L'Entreprenant*, at the battles of Maubeuge, Charleroi and Fleurus, in the spring and summer of 1794, for observation of artillery fire.

Further achievements in manned flight were to thrill those who followed the progress of this new method of exploration and travel. On 7–8 November 1836, one of the best-known aeronauts of the time, Charles Green, flew from London to Weilburg, Germany, covering a distance of 480 miles (772 km) in 18 hours; when the journey had been safely completed the balloon was named *Nassau*. A Frenchman, François Arban was the first man to fly over the Alps on 2–3 September 1849, starting from Marseilles and descending near Turin. On 2 July 1859, John Wise and John La Mountain flew from St Louis to Jefferson County, New York, in a balloon called *The Atlantic* covering about 810 miles (1,305 km) in 19 hours 50 minutes.

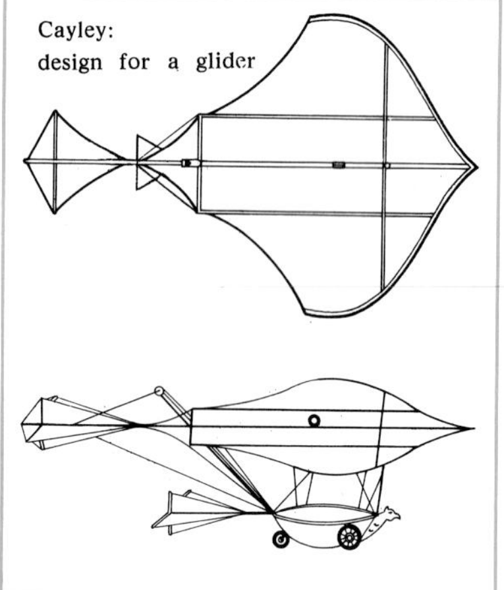

Cayley: design for a glider

Heavier-than-air flight was meanwhile not neglected. One of the most outstanding personalities of this field was a versatile English baronet, Sir George Cayley (1773–1857), whose contribution has in recent years been compared with that of Leonardo da Vinci. He has been described as "the true inventor of the airplane and one of the most powerful geniuses in the history of aviation."

Cayley discovered and defined the principles of mechanical flight: the relationship between weight, lift, drag and thrust. He was effectively the first person to think in modern aerodynamic terms and to reject da Vinci's idea of imitating birds. In Cayley's own words, the problem of mechanical flight could be solved by "making a surface support a given weight by the application of power to counteract the resistance of air." In 1799 he depicted his ideas on a small silver disc, one side of which showed a simple diagram of the forces which govern mechanical flight and on the other face an aircraft is engraved, designed as a logical application of these theories. It is shown as having a fixed wing, tailplanes with surfaces for vertical and horizontal control, a cockpit for the pilot and even a rudimentary means of propulsion using revolving vanes which foreshadow the use of the propeller. In the same year, Cayley made detailed technical drawings of his design.

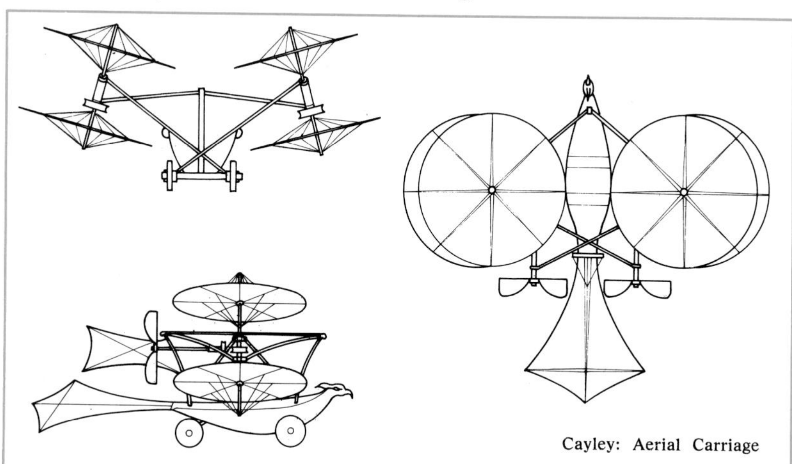

Cayley: Aerial Carriage

Three years earlier Cayley had carried out successful experiments to support his theories of aerodynamics. In 1792 or 1796 (Cayley gave both dates in different documents), he had built a small helicopter model. It was, in fact, very like the design drawn up in 1784, by two Frenchmen, Launoy and Bienvenu, but it is unlikely that he was aware of their work. Cayley's design went some way towards understanding how a propeller would work, as well as furthering his constant ambition of finding a means of powering a flying machine. Dissatisfied with his progress, Cayley reverted or rather regressed, somewhat surprisingly, to the da Vinci idea of flapping wings, and his design of 1843 for a convertiplane was the result.

Apart from this aberration, Cayley's research proved very fruitful. In 1804, after having carried out some experiments with model gliders to learn more about aerodynamics and wing structures using an ingenious rotating arm device, he put his theories to the test and constructed what is considered the first real airplane of history. This was a glider about 5 feet (1.5 m) long, with a fixed wing set at an angle of 6 degrees and cruciform tailplane which was attached to the fuselage by universal joints. Movable ballast was used to control the center of gravity. In 1809, Cayley built a larger glider (with a total wing area of approximately 172 square feet (18.5 sq m), which was successfully flown.

After having built several other models with an interruption for the design in 1843, of an ingenious convertiplane which was called the Aerial Carriage, Cayley concentrated on experiments with full-size gliders. The fundamental aim was, of course, to enable a man to fly and he went a long way towards it. His first glider was built in 1849, and trials were first carried out with ballast and then with the ten-year-old son of one of his servants. Although not fully satisfied with the results of these experiments, Cayley persevered. Four years later, in 1853, a second glider was built and he made his coachman, John Appleby, get into it. The glider, together with its terrified occupant, was launched from a hilltop, and after a fast swoop downward, crashed to the ground. We are told that the coachman quit Sir George's service after this ordeal, but Cayley had the satisfaction of achieving the first heavier-than-air flight. The 1853 glider used in these experiments had adjustable tailplanes and a rudimentary fuselage on wheels in which the occupant was positioned.

Apart from these practical experiments, Cayley's influence was widespread, due to the dissemination of his theories in the scientific journals of the period. What is considered his most important work *On Aerial Navigation*

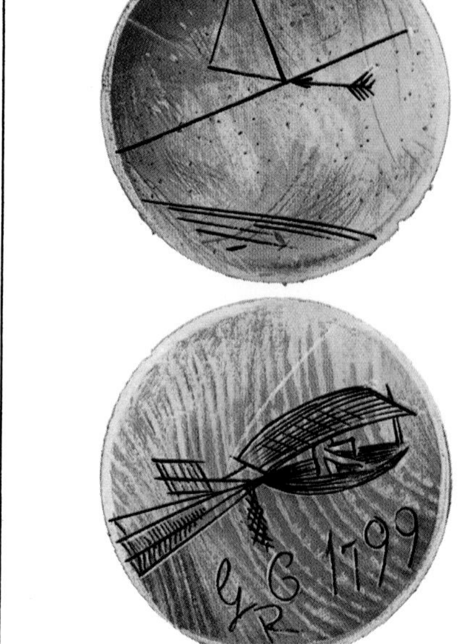

Two sides of a silver coin with Cayley's diagram of forces used in flight, and design of an airplane (1799)

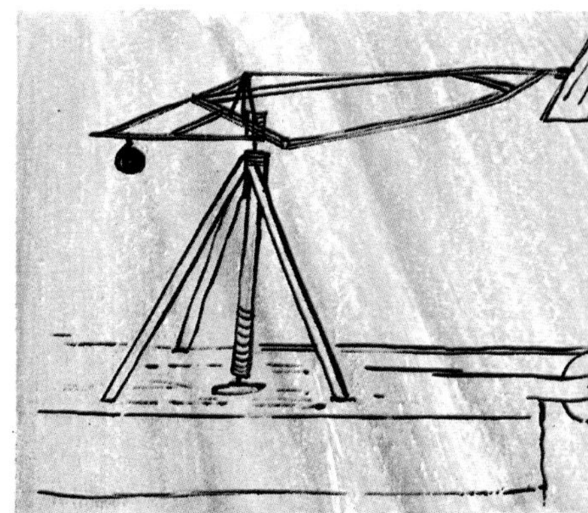

Drawing of a rotating arm for aerodynamic tests (1804)

Model of a helicopter (1796)

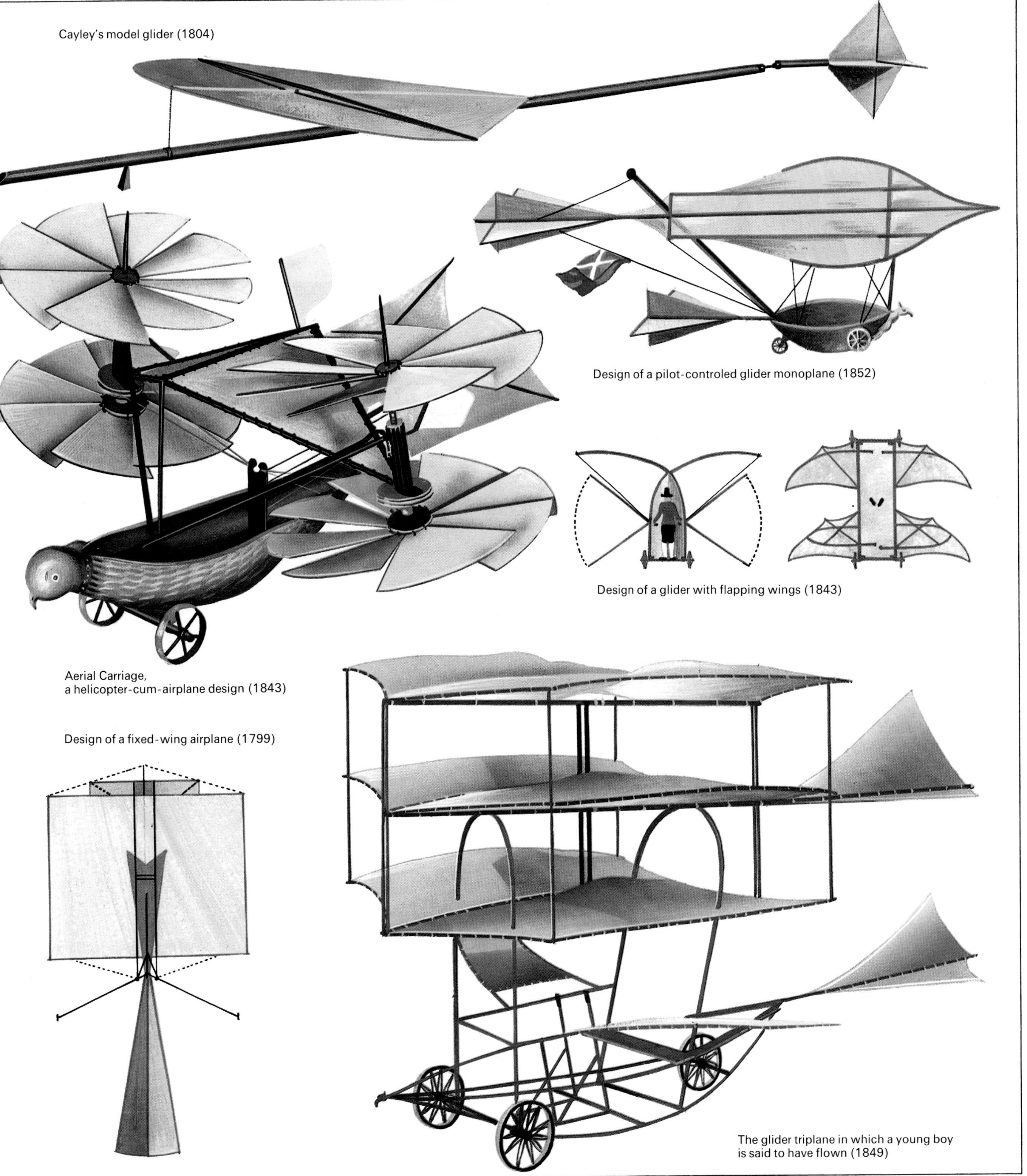

Cayley's model glider (1804)

Design of a pilot-controled glider monoplane (1852)

Design of a glider with flapping wings (1843)

Aerial Carriage,
a helicopter-cum-airplane design (1843)

Design of a fixed-wing airplane (1799)

The glider triplane in which a young boy is said to have flown (1849)

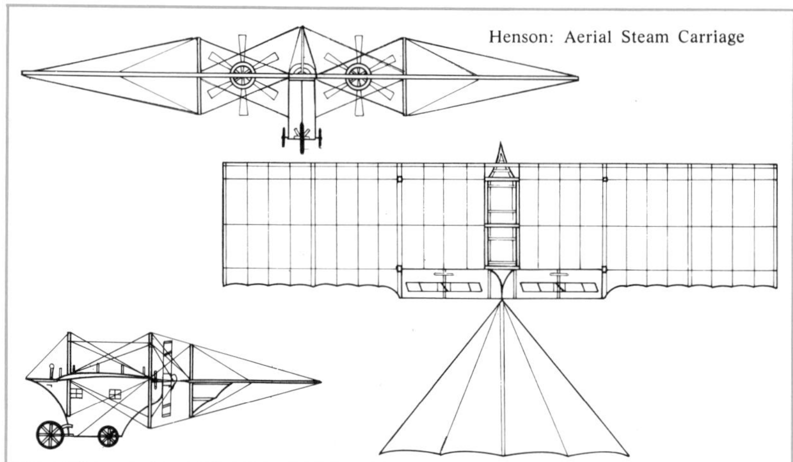
Henson: Aerial Steam Carriage

appeared in 1809–10 in *Nicholson's Journal of Natural Philosophy, Chemistry and the Arts*, in which the principles of aerodynamics were discussed as well as their practical application. It was some time, however, before Cayley's seminal work was widely known and acknowledged by the scientific establishment (his writings were only published more than twenty years after his death; in England in 1876 and in France in 1877). Nevertheless his research played its part in molding the ideas of aeronautical inventors. Even if we set aside the contribution made by Cayley's practical experiments, the theories he propounded form the scientific framework underlying mechanical flight, such as the concept of load-bearing, the study of stress, the analysis of the aerodynamics of heavier-than-air flight and the suggestion that an internal combustion engine should be used in the context of aviation. Cayley's written works show how fascinated he was by the last idea. In one passage, which was to prove prophetic, he states that he is "totally convinced that this noble art will soon be within man's competence and that we will eventually be able to travel with our families and baggage more safely than by sea, and at a speed of 20 to 100 miles an hour. All that is needed is an engine which can produce more power per minute than can the human muscular system."

The experiments which were carried out by Cayley's contemporaries throw his exceptional achievements into even sharper relief. The experiment of a Swiss clockmaker, Jacob Degen, (1756–1846) who lived in Vienna, was one of the best-known and also somewhat misleading. He must have got his ideas from the Frenchman, André-Jacques Garnerin, who had made the first parachute landing on 22 October 1797, managing to release himself and his parachute successfully from the hydrogen balloon which he had used to reach the necessary altitude. Degen designed and built a complicated ornithopter which he planned to use in conjunction with a balloon. In 1809 he carried out his first experiments, which resulted in "hops" rather than flights; Degen's own illustration left out any reference to the balloon thus deluding the public into thinking that he had achieved flight with his own muscle power. This rumor met with differing responses. On the one hand George Cayley made haste to publish his treatise *On Aerial Navigation* in order to debunk this claim; it also almost cost Degen his life when in October 1812 he was assaulted and roughed up by a disillusioned and infuriated crowd in Paris who had expected to see him fly.

The English artist, Thomas Walker, was also interested in ornithopters, and in 1810 he published a pamphlet on the subject (called *Treatise on the Art of Flying by Mechanical Means*), in which he put forward a design for a flying machine with flapping wings to be worked by the arms and legs of the occupant. Walker stated that he had carried out successful experiments with his ornithopter, which was not true. In a later edition of this work, published in 1831, he put forward another design, this time for a tandem wing monoplane, to be driven by flapping wings positioned in the center of the fuselage; at the end of the century the American inventor, Samuel Pierpont Langley, was to use the same configuration.

There were, however, some inventors who were receptive to Cayley's influence. In 1842 an Englishman, William Samuel Henson (1805–88), designed and patented a flying machine which was to have a tremendous influence on his contemporary would-be aviators. This was the Aerial Steam Carriage, which was, in fact, never built. This aircraft design, which drew its inspiration from the theories of Cayley, was to have a wingspan of 150 feet (45.72 m), a wing area of 4,500 square feet (418 sq m) and a 25–30hp steam engine installed in the fuselage to drive two pusher propellers. This was the first design ever for a propeller-driven fixed-wing airplane which approached the modern conception. Henson (who was an engineer in Somerset) had ambitious plans for developing and using his flying machine and publicized his invention extremely energetically, even before carrying out tests with a scale model:

Thomas Walker's design for an ornithopter (1810)

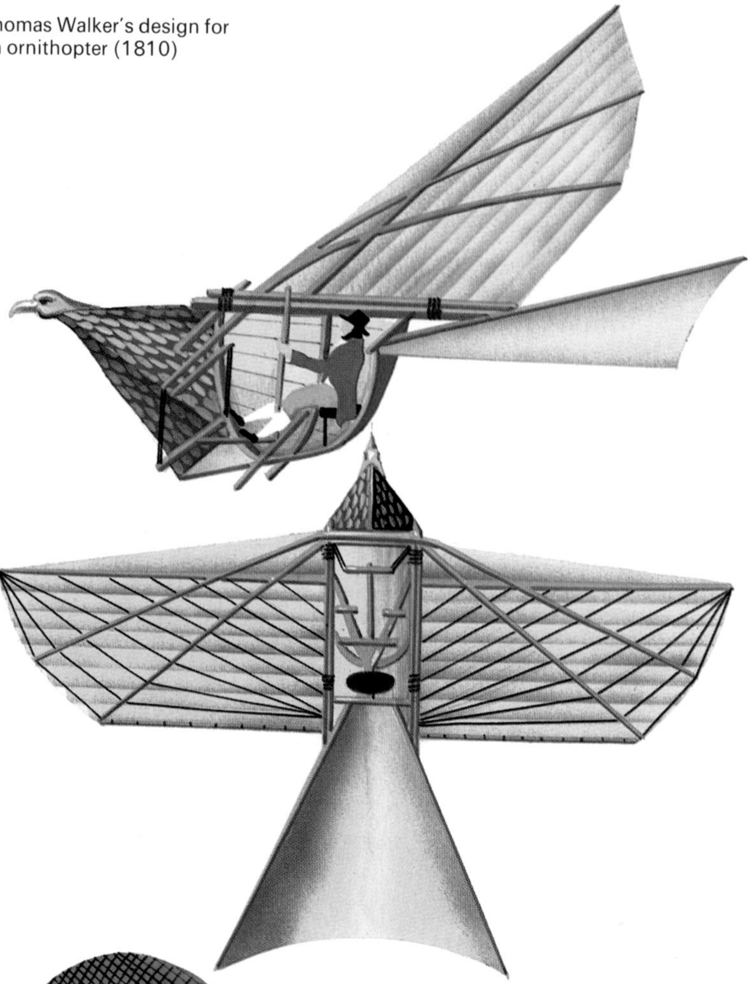

André-Jacques Garnerin's balloon-parachute (1797)

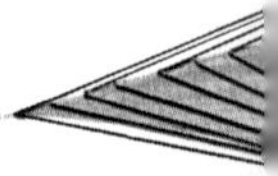

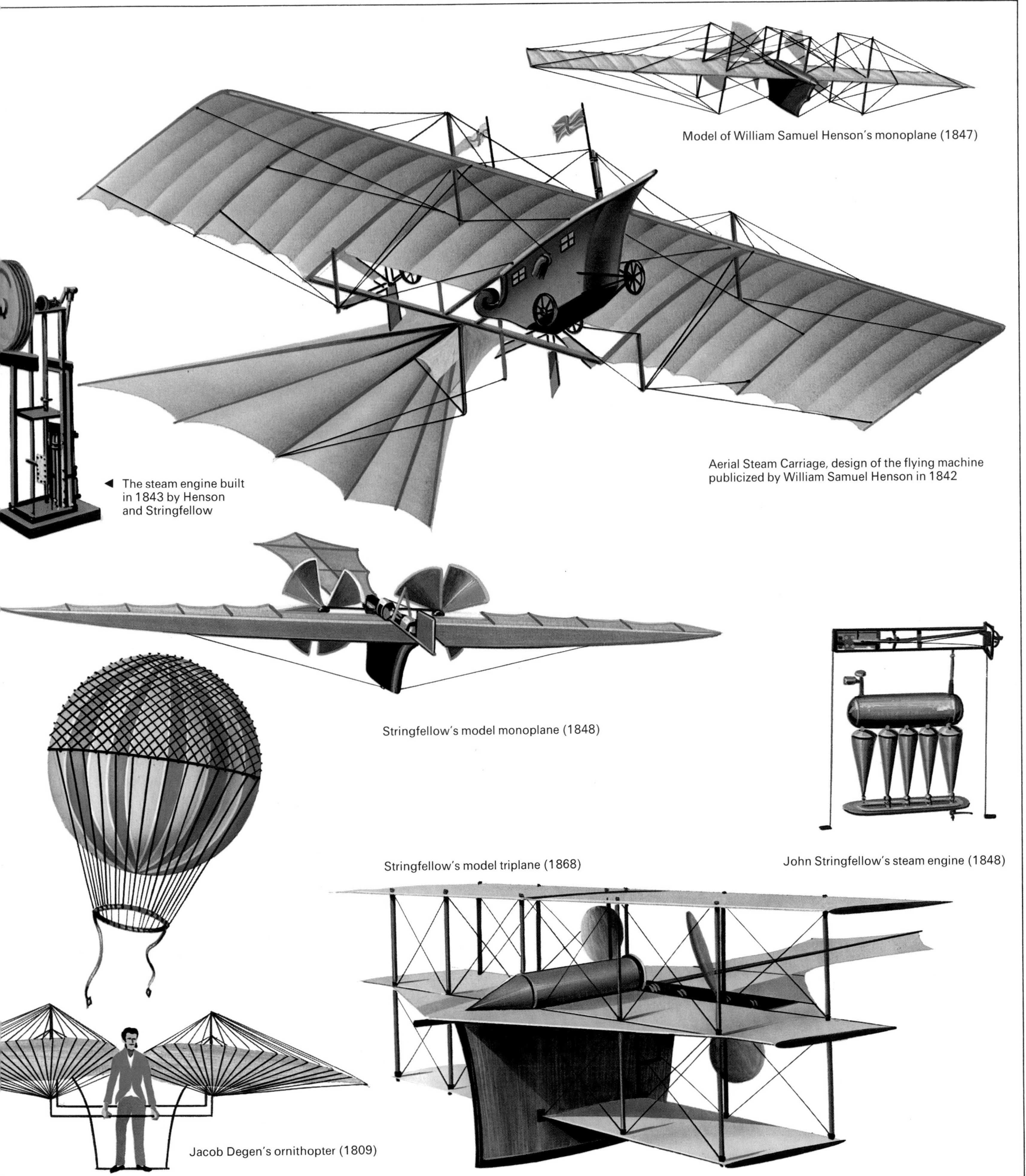

Model of William Samuel Henson's monoplane (1847)

Aerial Steam Carriage, design of the flying machine publicized by William Samuel Henson in 1842

◀ The steam engine built in 1843 by Henson and Stringfellow

Stringfellow's model monoplane (1848)

John Stringfellow's steam engine (1848)

Stringfellow's model triplane (1868)

Jacob Degen's ornithopter (1809)

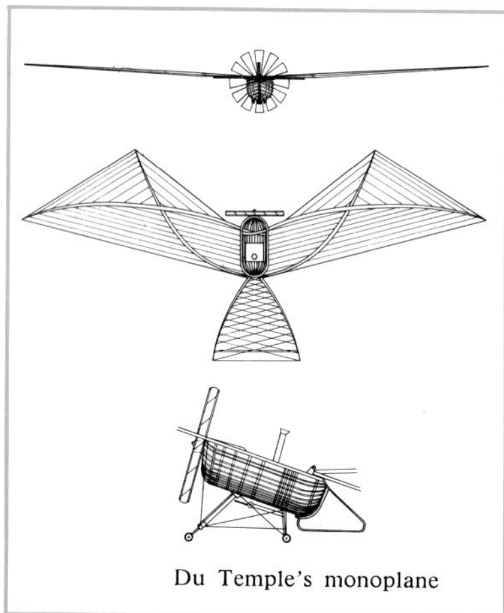
Du Temple's monoplane

he even tried to set up an air freight company, the Aerial Steam Transit Company, going into partnership with his friend John Stringfellow (1799–1883). It was Stringfellow who took pains to improve the little steam engine which Henson had built, and which was to power the small scale model of the Aerial Steam Carriage (wingspan approximately 20 feet (6 m) with which unsuccessful tests were carried out in 1847. Henson immediately lost all interest in the project; his disappointment was such that in 1848 he abandoned everything and emigrated to the United States.

Stringfellow, however, had much more tenacity of purpose and was much less easily discouraged and in the same year which saw his friend's departure for the United States he built a new monoplane model with about 10 feet (3 m) wingspan, powered by a little steam engine which was an improved version of the earlier power unit. Tests were carried out in 1848, but were disappointing. After a long interval Stringfellow made another attempt in 1868, with a triplane—the superimposed form of the wing surfaces excited great interest—but although it was a highly original aircraft it was not fully tested. Stringfellow exhibited this model at the first aeronautical exhibition ever, held at the Crystal Palace in that same year, where the merit of his design was recognized in the form of an Aeronautical Society prize of £100 for his steam engine which was found to have the best power-to-weight ratio of those tested.

Henson and Stringfellow were the first to tackle the problem of designing and building an efficient propulsion unit for a flying machine. As Cayley had maintained, the absence of an efficient power unit was the main stumbling block to mechanical flight, and this was to become increasingly obvious in the second half of the nineteenth century. Nowhere were aeronautical enthusiasts more acutely aware of it then in France where experiments proliferated.

In 1853, an engineer named Michel Loup designed a large-winged "bird" with a three-wheeled undercarriage and two enormous counter-rotating propellers which were to drive it. About ten or twelve years later another Frenchman, the engineer Charles de Louvrié was even further ahead of his time. In the early 1860s he designed a flying machine called the Aéronave or Aéroscaphe and outlined what could be considered a precursor of today's jet engines; thrust was to be supplied by the combustion of "hydrocarbons or preferably, vaporized petrol" and the gas given off was to escape through two nozzles in the rear. In 1867 this idea was taken up in England by Butler and Edwards who patented flying machines with a delta wing, no doubt inspired by the paper airplanes which the schoolboys of those days amused themselves with, as they still do today. These were to be powered by one of two forms of "jet propulsion." In the first design compressed air was to be used (or steam or the gas given off by combustion) which escaped through a rear vent; the second design was for a biplane, in which the propeller was to be turned by the action of small exhaust tubes positioned at the tips of the blades.

Meanwhile, in France, one of the most important pioneers of the period, Alphonse Pénaud (1850–80)—whose work is sometimes considered to be almost as significant as Cayley's—had developed theories about wing contours and aerodynamic principles, applying them successfully to model airplanes, helicopters and ornithopters. Pénaud's answer to the problem of propulsion was a brilliant development of a system which had already been tried out: that of twisted rubber strips. His best-known model was probably the *Planophore* of 1871, one of the forerunners of the modern airplane. This was a monoplane with an 18-inch (45 cm) wingspan, with wingtips which were bent to provide lateral stability and a two-blade pusher propeller, 8 inches (20 cm) in diameter, powered by a twisted elastic band. This model airplane was the first really stable aircraft ever constructed. It was tested in the Tuileries Gardens in Paris on 18 August 1871, and flew 131 feet (40 m) in 11 seconds.

The high point of Pénaud's career—which was short since he committed suicide at the age of 30—was his amphibious monoplane, which he designed with his mechanic, Paul Gauchot. The patent was applied for in 1876, although the actual aircraft remained at the drawing-board stage. This design for a two-seat airplane incorporated many brilliant ideas: two counter-rotating propellers, double elevators, a rudder connected to a fixed vertical fin, a glazed cockpit, retractable landing gear and a system of controls for the pilot. Pénaud had also worked out the weight and speed of the

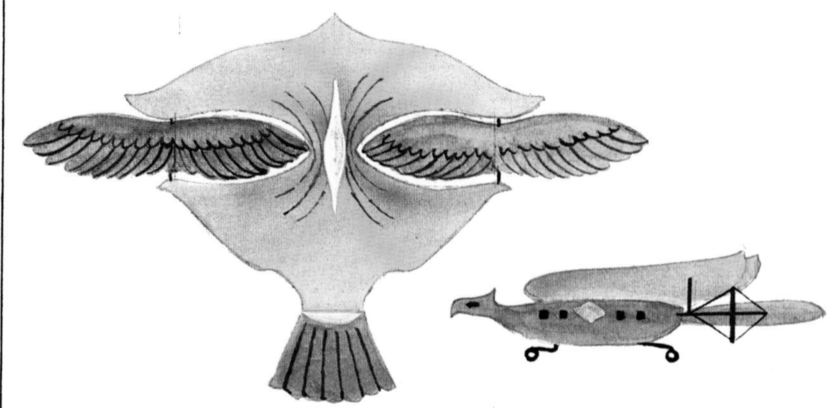
A design by Michel Loup (1853)

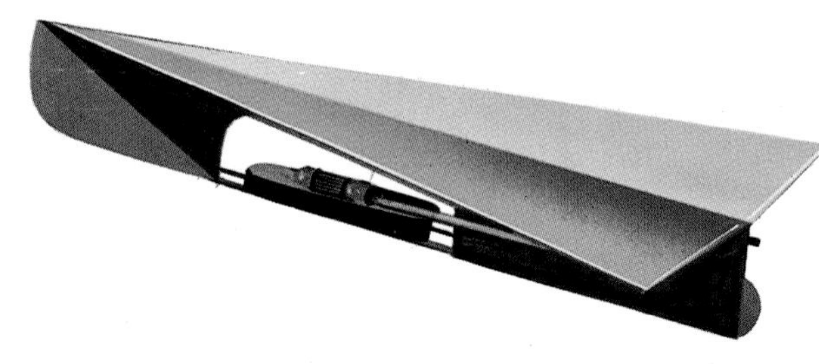

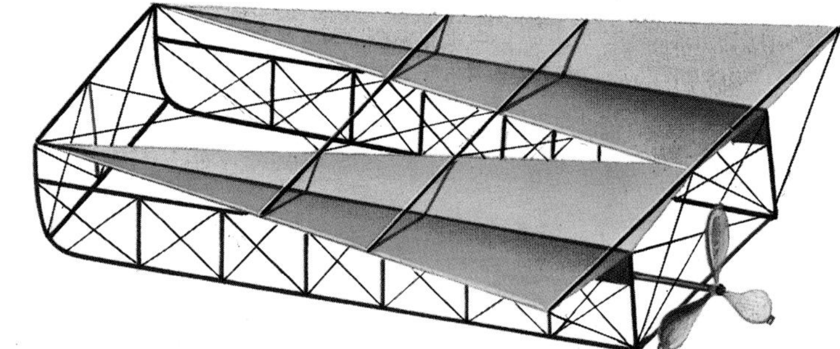
Designs by Butler and Edwards (1867)

Vincent de Groof's ornithopter (1874)

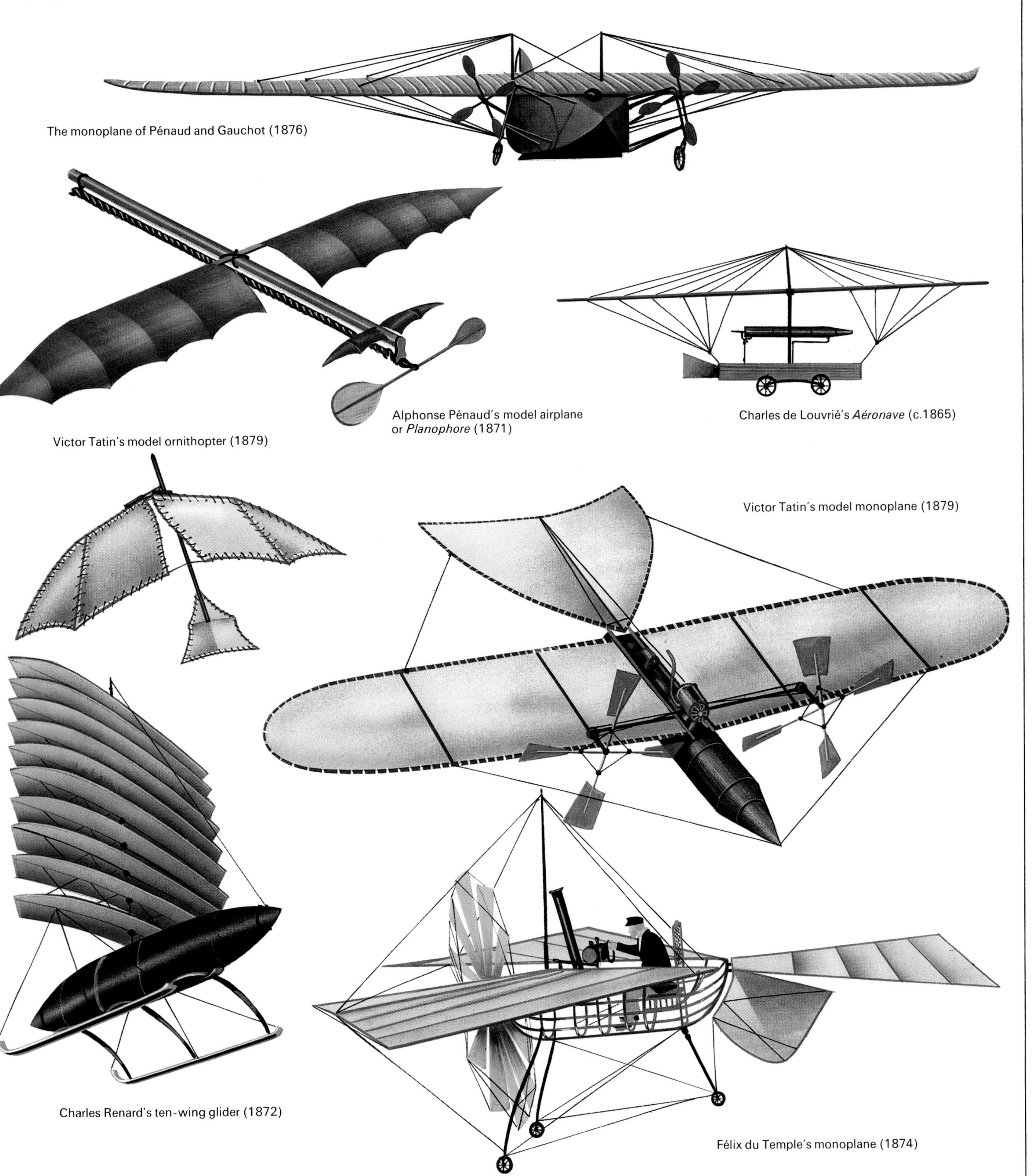

The monoplane of Pénaud and Gauchot (1876)

Victor Tatin's model ornithopter (1879)

Alphonse Pénaud's model airplane or *Planophore* (1871)

Charles de Louvrié's *Aéronave* (c.1865)

Victor Tatin's model monoplane (1879)

Charles Renard's ten-wing glider (1872)

Félix du Temple's monoplane (1874)

airplane: 2,635 lb (1,195 kg) with a speed of 60 mph (96.5 km/h).

Pénaud was, however, too far ahead of his time to be properly appreciated, as Cayley had been before him. The climate in which his ideas struggled for recognition was one which still produced far-fetched schemes for birdmen.

In 1872, Charles Renard designed a glider; this flying machine had as many as ten superimposed wings. Two years later a Belgian shoemaker, Vincent de Groof, died when he launched himself from a balloon in his ornithopter. Some attempts had happier outcomes. In 1874, a French naval officer, Félix du Temple (1823–90) tested his monoplane, which was driven by a tractor propeller and powered by a steam engine; the machine leapt into the air, having been launched from a downward-sloping ramp but it was more of an uncontroled "hop" than a real flight. Another noteworthy French pioneer was Victor Tatin (1843–1913) who was a friend of Pénaud and who became one of the most authoritative theorists in early aviation. He built a model of an ornithopter which actually managed to fly—the first of its kind to do so properly. His later design of 1879 was completely different: the fuselage acted as a tank for the compressed air which drove a small engine linked to two tractor propellers. This small-scale flying model had a wingspan of 6 feet 3 inches (190 cm) and the first model of this design flew in circles round a central pole to which it was attached managing to stay airborne for about 49 feet (15 m). It was not only for heavier-than-air flight that a power unit was so vital; the airplane's rival, the balloon, also needed an effective engine and here the inventors' efforts met with greater success and rapid progress was made. The main purpose of building a "powered balloon" or dirigible was to ensure that horizontal balloon flight could be controled. So far it had only been possible to control the ascent and descent of a balloon by using ballast and the balloon relied on the wind for movement which was far too unpredictable a force.

Jean-Baptiste Marie Meusnier (1754–93) designed the first dirigible in 1784; this was to be oval in shape and driven by three propellers but it remained at the design stage, not only because of construction difficulties but also for the obvious reason that there was no known power unit which could drive it. In 1804 the Swiss gunsmith Samuel John Pauly constructed a fish-shaped balloon and made some trials in France. In 1815 Pauly went to London and in collaboration with another Swiss gunsmith, Durs Egg, began construction of the fish-shaped *Dolphin* but this 90 feet (27.4 m) long balloon was never completed. Halfway through the nineteenth century the first workable dirigible was designed by a French engineer, Henri Giffard (1825–82) who fitted a balloon with a 3-hp steam engine which drove a propeller, and installed a rudimentary rudder. This aerostat's maiden flight took place on 24 September 1852, when it took off from the Hippodrome in Paris and then covered nearly 17 miles (27 km) at an average speed of 5.5 mph (9 km/h), landing at Trappes. This craft had considerable limitations both in speed and maneuvrability, mainly due to the engine's limited power but it represented a great step forward. Similar attempts were made in 1859 by Camille Vert with a two-propeller dirigible and in 1865 by E. Delamarne and Gabriel Yon with a more complicated but no more effective machine. Experiments carried out in the United States, where there was considerable enthusiasm for lighter-than-air flight, were also disappointing. In 1869 an engineer named Marriott constructed several model dirigibles in an attempt to achieve maneuvrability but met with little success. In France, government support encouraged Dupuy de Lôme, a well-known naval design engineer, to design a dirigible which was to be physically driven by eight of the fourteen people it could carry, who were to use muscle power to turn a four-blade propeller, 29 feet 6 inches (9 m) in diameter, but the machine made only one short flight, on 2 February 1872. In 1883 another solution to the power unit problem was tried out by two brothers, Albert and Gaston Tissandier, who chose an original type of engine for their airship: a 1.5-hp Siemens electric engine, powered by 24 batteries. This idea was imitated a year later by Charles Renard and A. C. Krebs, two French army officers who designed and built a large dirigible, 164 feet (50 m) long, named *La France*. The airship was powered by a 9-hp electric engine which had to have a set of fully-charged batteries to supply the necessary electricity. The problem of having to keep the batteries constantly charged led to all further development of this type of engine being abandoned after the early tests, although the dirigible was able to travel at about 12 mph (20 km/h); the airship was underpowered and thus too slow to achieve adequate control, and maneuvrability was hampered by the excessive weight of the batteries.

The internal combustion engine was to hold the key to success and a Brazilian, Alberto Santos-Dumont (1873–1932), who was later to pioneer the use of the airplane in Europe, successfully flew his dirigible No. 1, which was driven by a twin-cylinder tricycle engine, in Paris in 1898. A year before Santos-Dumont's test flight, David Schwarz experimented in Germany with an all-metal structure, a metal-clad rigid airship driven by a 12-

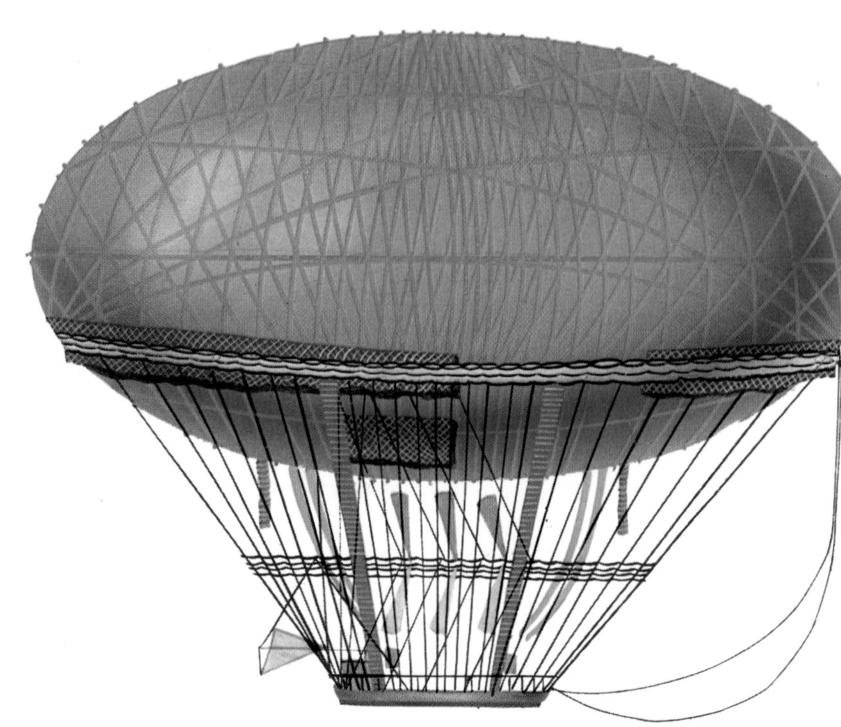
Jean-Baptiste Marie Meusnier's design of a dirigible (1784)

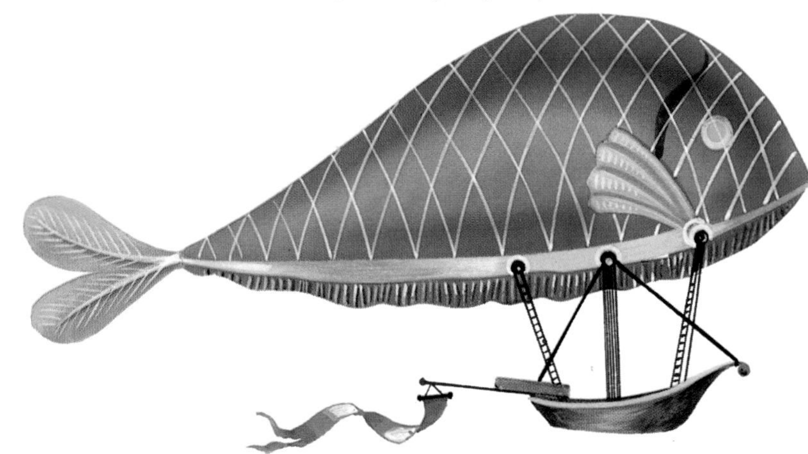
Design by Pauly (1804)

Delamarne's dirigible (1865)
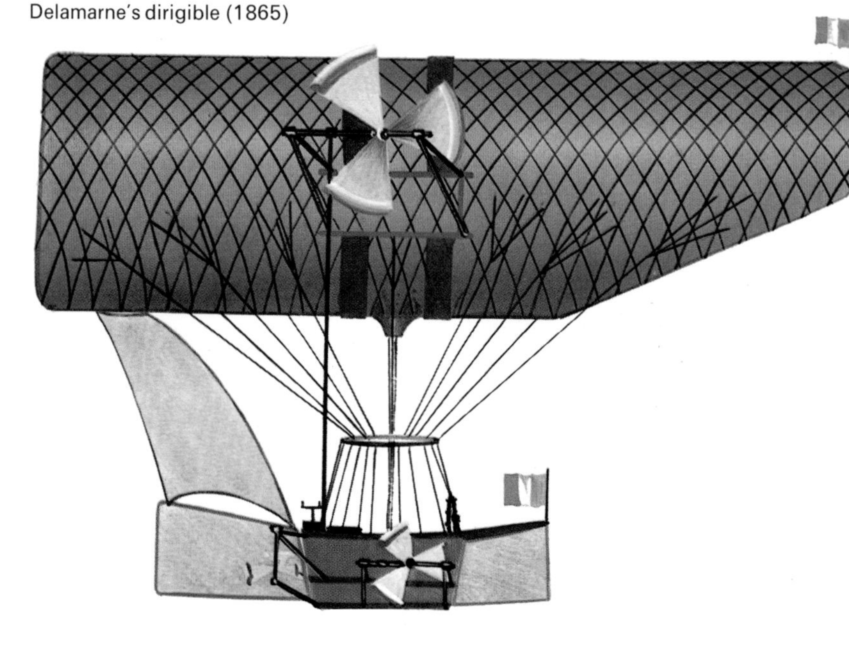

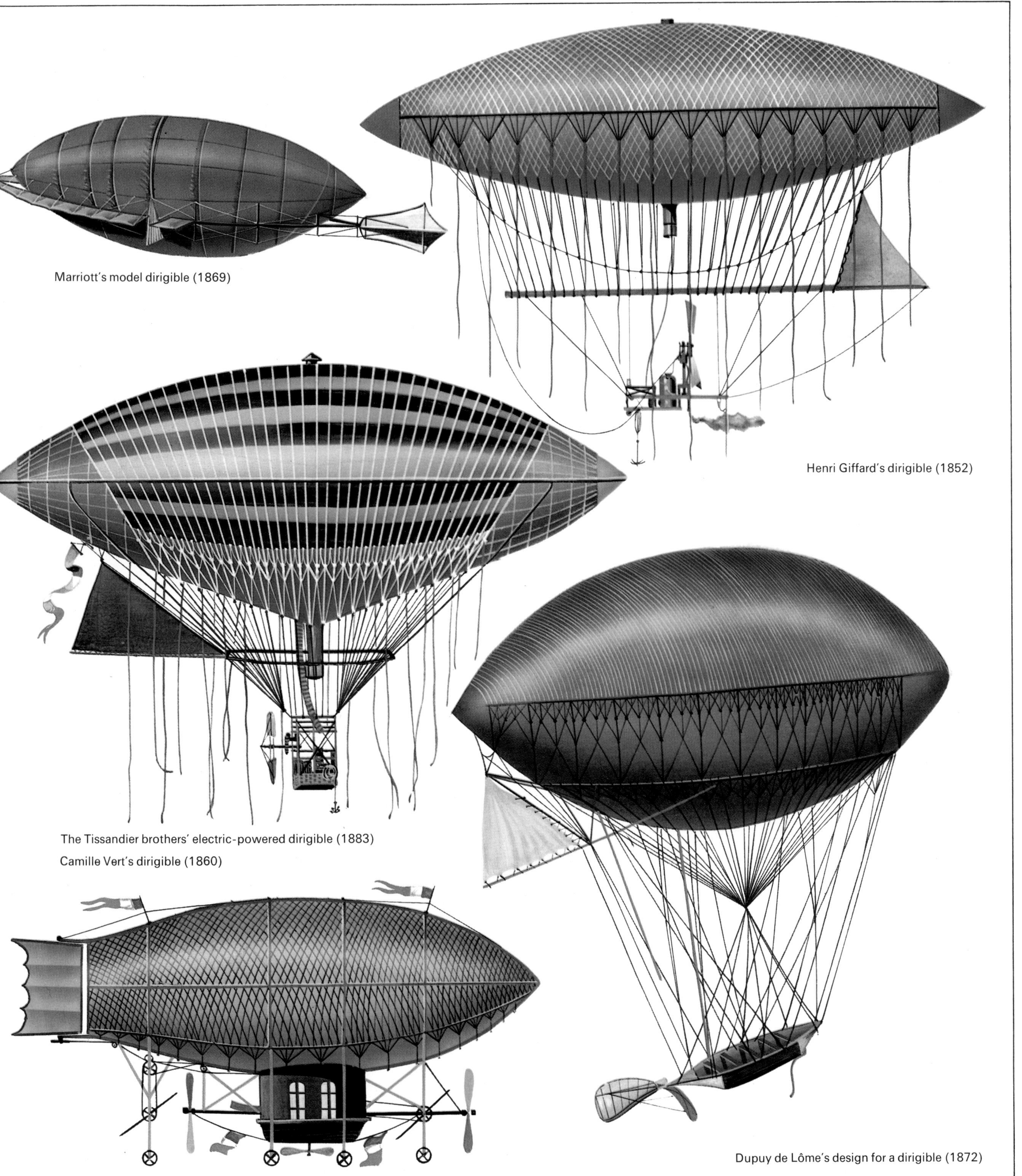

Marriott's model dirigible (1869)

Henri Giffard's dirigible (1852)

The Tissandier brothers' electric-powered dirigible (1883)

Camille Vert's dirigible (1860)

Dupuy de Lôme's design for a dirigible (1872)

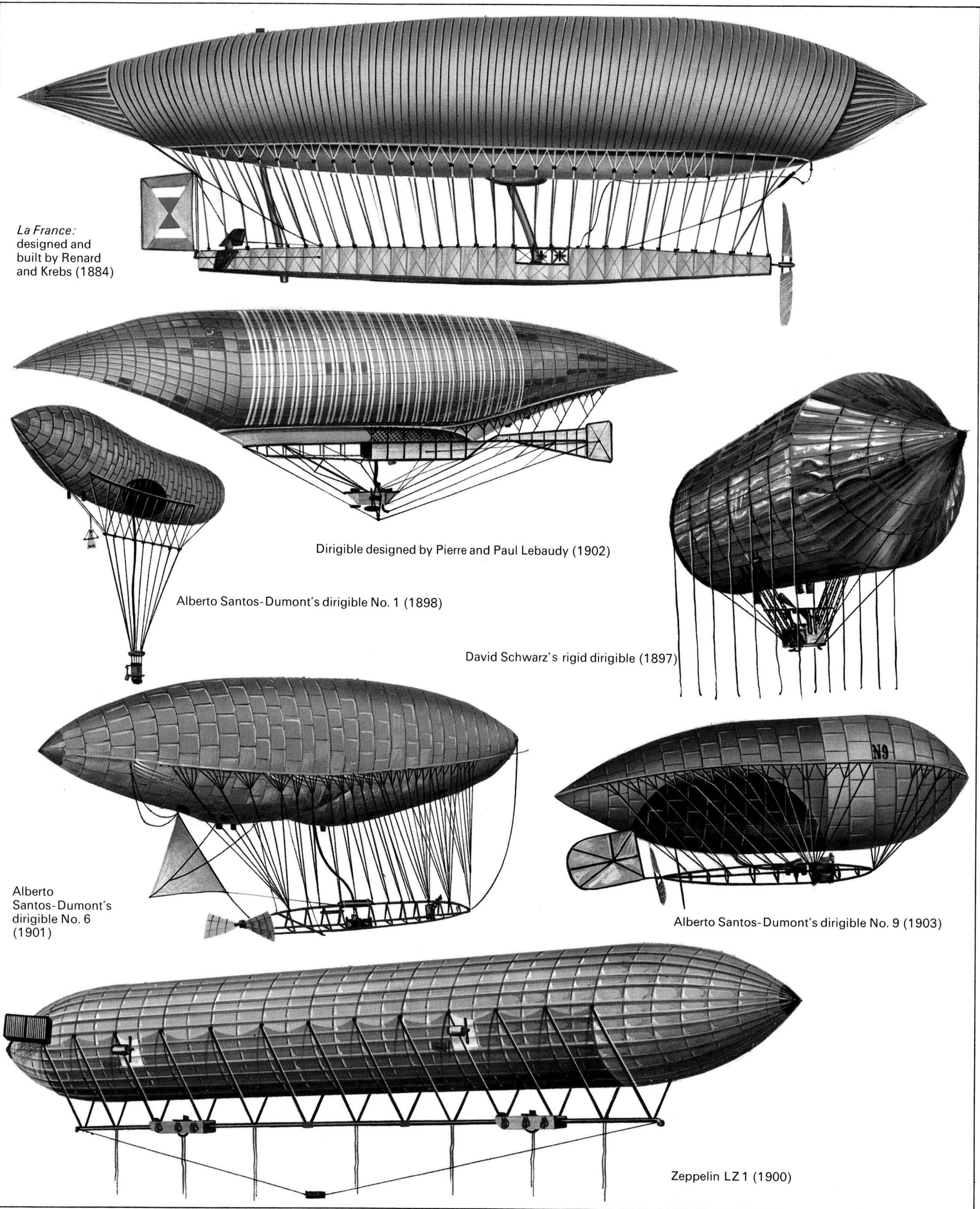

La France: designed and built by Renard and Krebs (1884)

Dirigible designed by Pierre and Paul Lebaudy (1902)

Alberto Santos-Dumont's dirigible No. 1 (1898)

David Schwarz's rigid dirigible (1897)

Alberto Santos-Dumont's dirigible No. 6 (1901)

Alberto Santos-Dumont's dirigible No. 9 (1903)

Zeppelin LZ 1 (1900)

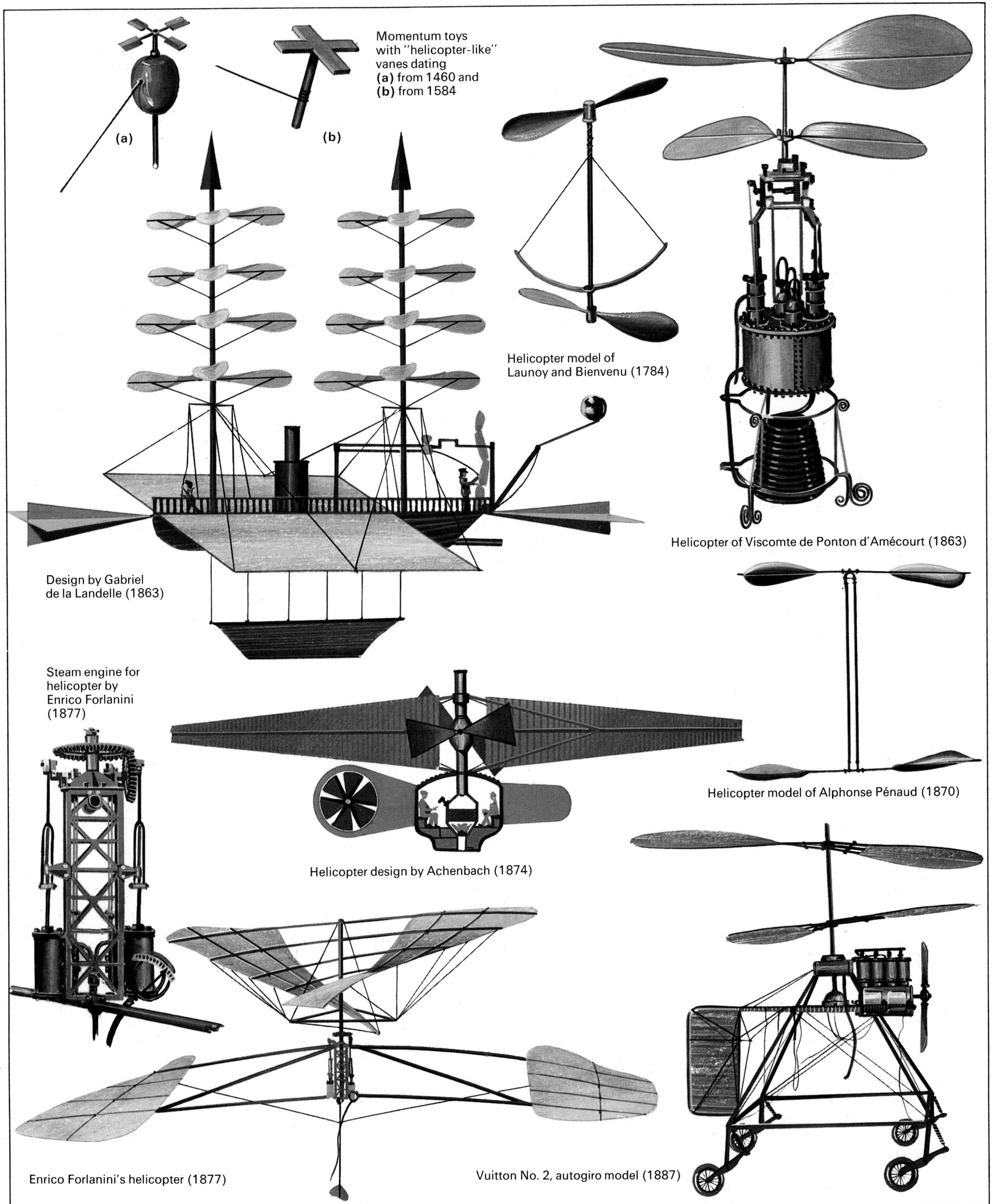

Momentum toys with "helicopter-like" vanes dating **(a)** from 1460 and **(b)** from 1584

Helicopter model of Launoy and Bienvenu (1784)

Helicopter of Viscomte de Ponton d'Amécourt (1863)

Design by Gabriel de la Landelle (1863)

Steam engine for helicopter by Enrico Forlanini (1877)

Helicopter model of Alphonse Pénaud (1870)

Helicopter design by Achenbach (1874)

Enrico Forlanini's helicopter (1877)

Vuitton No. 2, autogiro model (1887)

hp Daimler engine, but a trial flight from the Tempelhof field in Berlin was a failure and the airship was destroyed.

Alberto Santos-Dumont carried on building small dirigibles for several years before turning to heavier-than-air flight. In October 1901 he became famous when he made his spectacular flight round the Eiffel Tower in his airship No. 6 and won the Deutsch prize of 100,000 francs. He also became well-known for his frequent air trips just above the roofs of Paris, flying his dirigible No. 9, which was a smaller and more maneuvrable machine.

Santos-Dumont's airships were, however, too small to be used for anything but demonstration flights. The first very large dirigibles made their appearance at the beginning of the twentieth century. The forerunner of the new generation of French airships was that built in 1902 to the design of two brothers, Paul and Pierre Lebaudy. In Germany, the LZ 1 was to be the prototype of all the rigid dirigibles and was built by Count Ferdinand von Zeppelin (1838–1917) who became world-famous. This German aristocrat made a name for himself through the research, development and testing of this type of craft and was responsible for the revolution in lighter-than-air flight. His LZ 1 airship was built in a floating hangar at Manzell on Lake Constance. It took thirty workers a year to build the fabric-covered, cylindrical, light metal structure, inside which were 17 drum-shaped cells for hydrogen. The airship was driven by propellers powered by two 14-hp Daimler engines. The LZ 1's maiden flight took place on 2 July 1900, and was rather disappointing: the dirigible was slow, hard to control and structurally weak. It was dismantled a few months later, after two more flights. Zeppelin was not discouraged, however, and over the next 14 years he built many other dirigibles—the predecessors of the giant airships of World War I and the 1920s and 1930s.

In the second half of the nineteenth century there was no longer any doubt that the propeller was the only feasible and reliable means of achieving powered flight. It was at this time that the use of engines to power aerostats stimulated research into vertical flight. The results of this work were eventually to lead to the helicopter as we know it today and also formed an invaluable fund of technical knowledge which could be applied to horizontal flight—much of this progress stemmed from the experiments of Alphonse Pénaud and Enrico Forlanini.

The first practical experiment, carried out by two Frenchmen, Launoy and Bienvenu in 1784, was only a more sophisticated development of the momentum toys shown in fourteenth and fifteenth century paintings. Nearly a hundred years were to pass before any really original and worthwhile experiments were made. All that Gabriel de la Landelle (1863) and Achenbach (1874) were to contribute was a series of designs for weird and wonderful flying machines. Vicomte de Ponton d'Amécourt did, however, make considerable progress towards achieving vertical flight. In 1863 he built a steam-powered helicopter model driven by twin counterrotating screws which failed to lift although some of his simpler models flew. At about this time Alphonse Pénaud's observations and theories of aerodynamics and stability made a great contribution to the understanding of the principles of vertical flight. His theories stemmed from meticulous studies of the flight performance of small model helicopters during experiments carried out in 1870. The propellers of these models were driven by twisted elastic bands, a similar mechanism to that used in his famous *Planophore*.

Many experiments were carried out in France. In 1871 Pomès and de la Pauze designed a helicopter whose rotors were to be powered by gunpowder. In 1877 Emmanuel Dieuaide completed a design for a machine with counterrotating rotor blades; the boiler of the engine was to be on the ground and connected to the machine by a flexible tube. Mélikoff conceived the idea of a helicopter with a conical rotor which would double as a parachute to slow down the craft's descent. In 1878 Castel perfected this formula, when he designed and built a helicopter with eight rotors mounted on two counterrotating axles, driven by compressed air. This model failed to work, but some smaller ones built by Dandrieux in 1878 and 1879 and driven by elastic bands did manage to function quite well.

An Italian engineer, Enrico Forlanini, constructed models of helicopters which were technically sound and worked extremely well. Forlanini was later to become famous as a designer of dirigibles. In 1877 he built a very small model helicopter, weighing

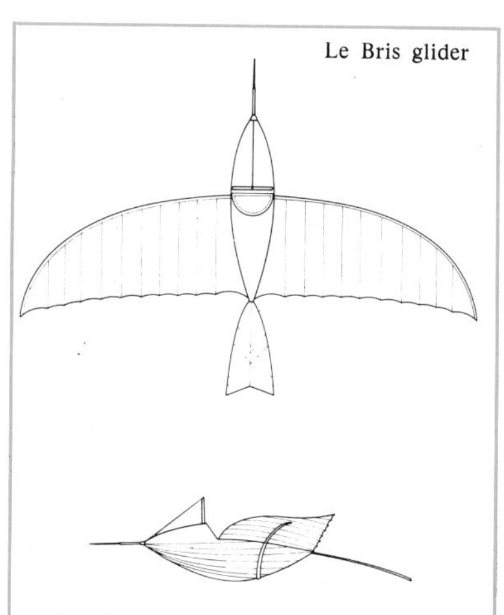
Le Bris glider

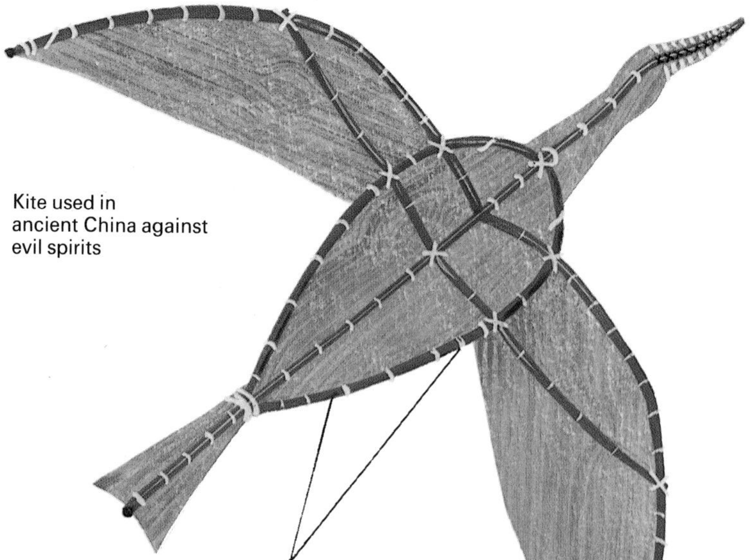

Kite used in ancient China against evil spirits

Drawing of a kite (1634)

Drawing of a kite (15th century)

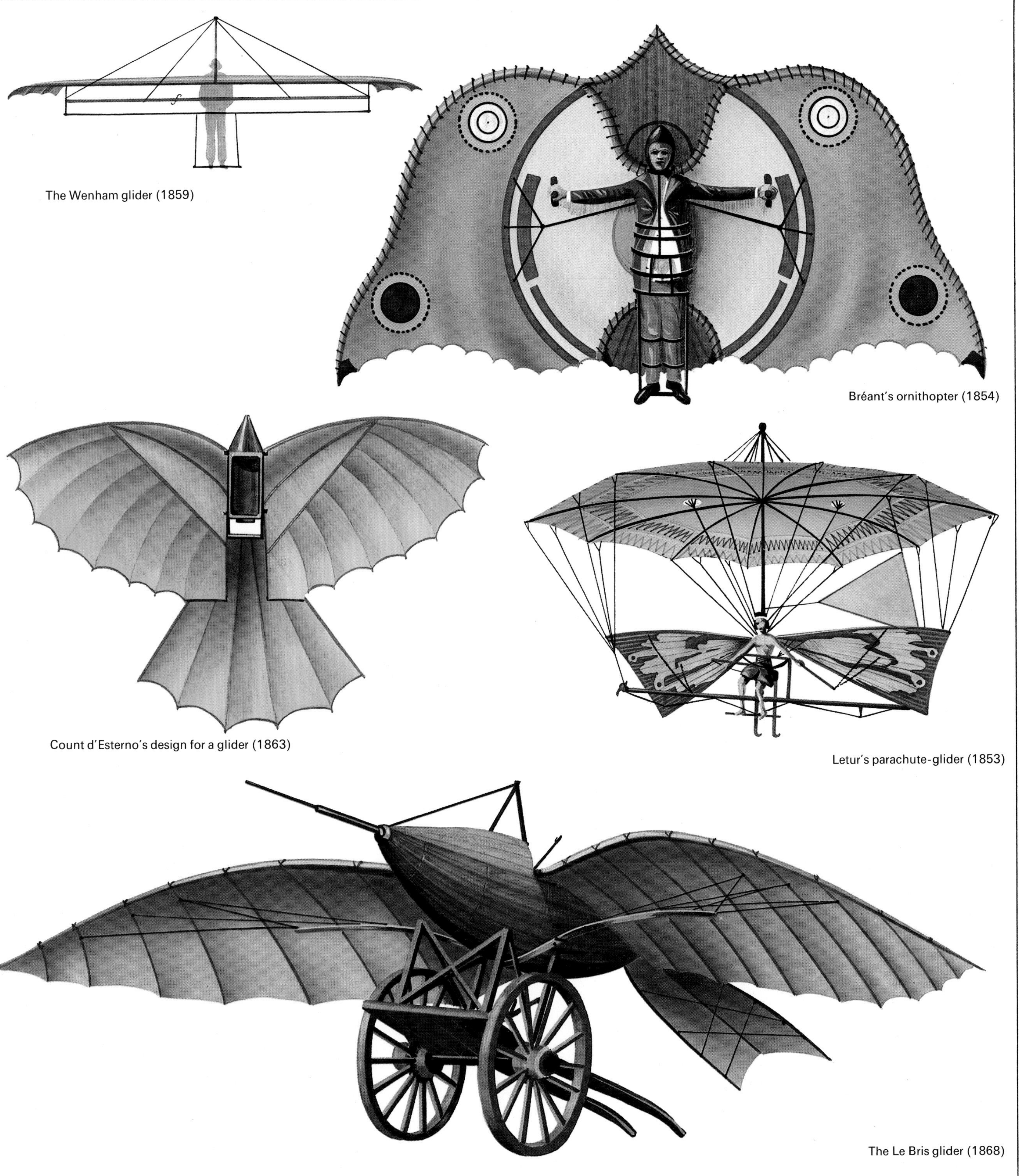

The Wenham glider (1859)

Bréant's ornithopter (1854)

Count d'Esterno's design for a glider (1863)

Letur's parachute-glider (1853)

The Le Bris glider (1868)

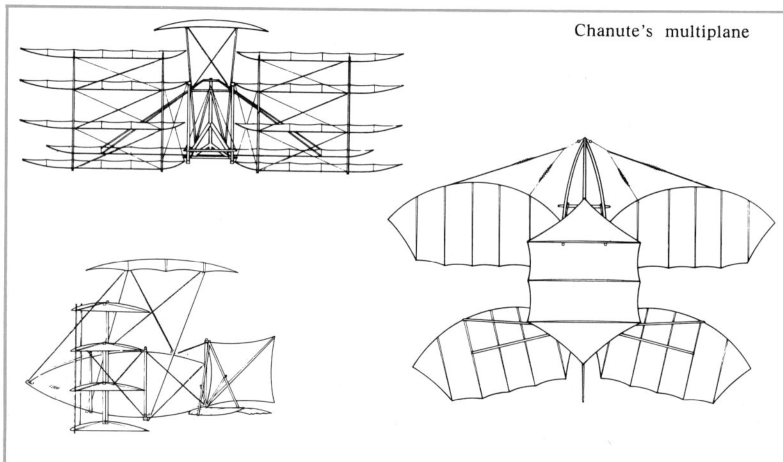
Chanute's multiplane

about 8.8 lb (4 kg), driven by a tiny, efficient steam engine. The two counterrotating blades had a large surface area and one was directly mounted on the driving shaft and the second on the structure proper. The machine was exhaustively tested, the last test taking place in Milan on 15 April 1877, when it managed to take off, reaching a height of some 40 feet (about 12 m) and remaining airborne for 20 seconds. Such very limited endurance was mainly due to the small size of the steam engine.

Among the more important investigations carried out in this field before the end of the century was that of the Frenchman, Vuitton, whose second design for an autogiro is preserved in the Musée des Arts et Métiers. But in spite of all these efforts and endeavors, the main problem, which was how to achieve piloted heavier-than-air flight, was still unsolved. Much more was understood about aerodynamics and science was making such progress that it was only a matter of time before an engine was invented which could drive the propeller and thus give the necessary thrust described by Cayley so many years before but which had proved so elusive. There was still a great deal to be learned about the design and function of the wing, as this was another vital element which alone could keep an airplane airborne, once the principle of lift and the wing's function in helping to control flight were grasped.

In ancient China much was understood about the function of the wing through flying kites, and kites shaped like birds were used to drive away evil spirits. Pictures of similar kites appear in European texts from the fifteenth century onward and are often in the form of dragons which betrays their oriental origins. Man, however, seemed intent on imitating birds in his attempts to fly and, as late as the nineteenth century, in spite of all Cayley had written on the subject, many ornithopters and gliders which were designed or actually constructed were in the shape of birds. Bréant's ornithopter of 1854 was one example of this tendency and was to be driven by both the muscular power of the pilot and by elastic cords. A similarly-shaped glider design by the French Count Ferdinand Charles Honoré Philippe d'Estienne (1806–83) was published in 1863. Another glider of this type was built by the naval officer Jean-Marie Le Bris, who built two flying machines inspired by the albatross which he had closely observed whilst at sea. These he tested between 1856 and 1868. Experiments with the first of the two gliders met with some success, although Le Bris broke both legs when he crash-landed. The second glider, which flew, unmanned, in 1868, was the first flying machine ever to be photographed.

Once inventors understood the principles of aerodynamics so much more clearly, they had the confidence to stop imitating birds and as early as 1853 the Frenchman, François Letur, built and tested a parachute-glider in which the only feature reminiscent of a bird was the shape and positioning of the two lifting surfaces which were on a level with the pilot's shoulders. Being dropped from balloons, Letur carried out a series of tests in France and England with this apparatus which might be considered the first piloted heavier-than-air craft to be tested in flight. After several successful descents, Letur had a serious accident near London on 27 June 1854 and died of his injuries. Five years later the Englishman, Francis Herbert Wenham, designed and built several models and a full-scale version of a multi-wing glider, but his most important contribution to flight was his study of the properties of the cambered wing.

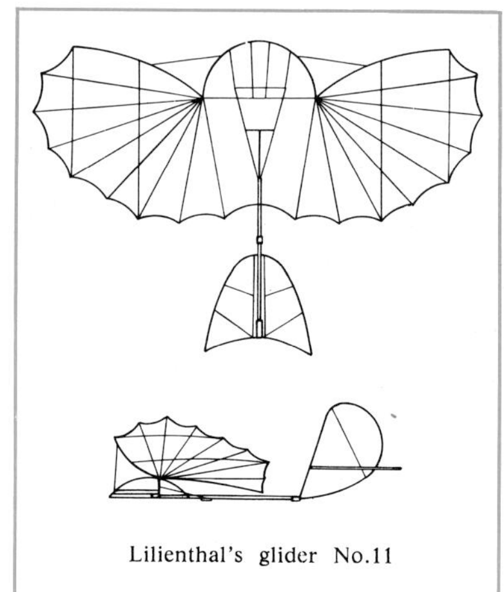
Lilienthal's glider No.11

The last lap of progress before heavier-than-air flight was to become a reality was covered in the final decade of the century. Decisive contributions were made by such men as Otto Lilienthal, Lawrence Hargrave, Percy Pilcher and Octave Chanute, who have gone down in history as the men who prepared the way for the final breakthrough. Otto Lilienthal (1848–96) was a German engineer and inventor and was the first man ever to take off and fly. It is interesting to speculate whether he might not have grasped the prize which was to be won by the Wright brothers had he not been killed during one of his gliding experiments, on 9 August 1896, near Stölln. Lilienthal had been caught up in the world of aviation when very young (he first experimented with two rudimentary wings when only fourteen) and in 1889 he published a book on the flight of birds in which he outlined his theories. Between 1891 and 1896 he built a succession of monoplane and biplane gliders, in which he applied and tested the ideas which his research had suggested. He met with almost immediate success: after the first tentative launchings Lilienthal was soon covering quite considerable distances. He made several hundred glider flights and in the last years of his life was working on the application of power to his gliders.

Lilienthal's designs had a great deal of influence on two of his contemporaries: the Australian, Lawrence Hargrave (1850–1915) and a Scottish engineer, Percy Sinclair Pilcher (1866–99). To Hargrave must go the credit for formulating the theory which enables the kite to stay airborne and he also managed to learn a great deal about the stability of the kite from the many experiments he carried out, demonstrating the direct relationship which existed between multiple wings and efficient lift. The basic model with which his research was carried out was called the "Cellular Kite" of 1893 and this was a biplane kite, the two wing surfaces meeting at their tips. Hargrave also managed to be lifted a few yards into the air by a system of kites which were kept aloft by a wind of approximately 18 mph (30 km/h). Pilcher chose to experiment with a hang-glider, as Lilienthal had done before him, and in 1895 he built his first aircraft which he called *The Bat*. *The Bat* had evolved after a visit to Germany when Pilcher bought one of Lilienthal's gliders. Pilcher built two more gliders, *The Beetle* (1895) and *The Gull* (1896) which were both unsuccessful, but in 1897 he set a distance record of 250

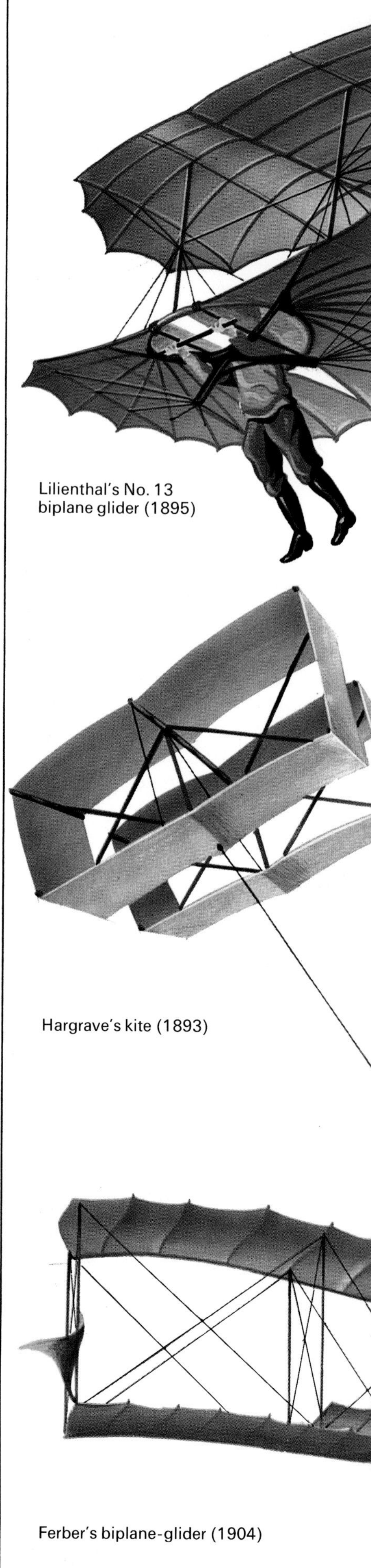
Lilienthal's No. 13 biplane glider (1895)

Hargrave's kite (1893)

Ferber's biplane-glider (1904)

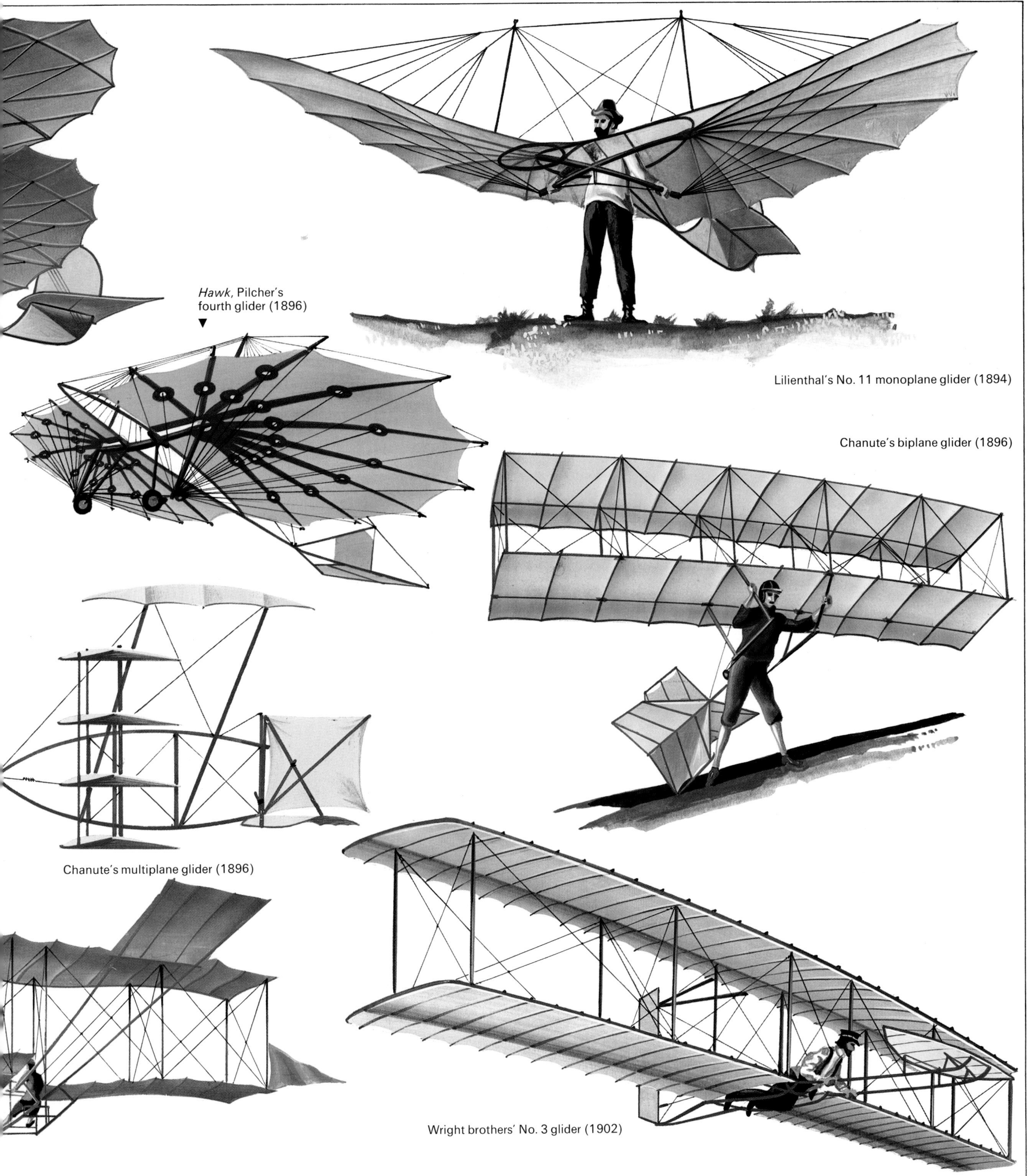

Hawk, Pilcher's fourth glider (1896)

Lilienthal's No. 11 monoplane glider (1894)

Chanute's biplane glider (1896)

Chanute's multiplane glider (1896)

Wright brothers' No. 3 glider (1902)

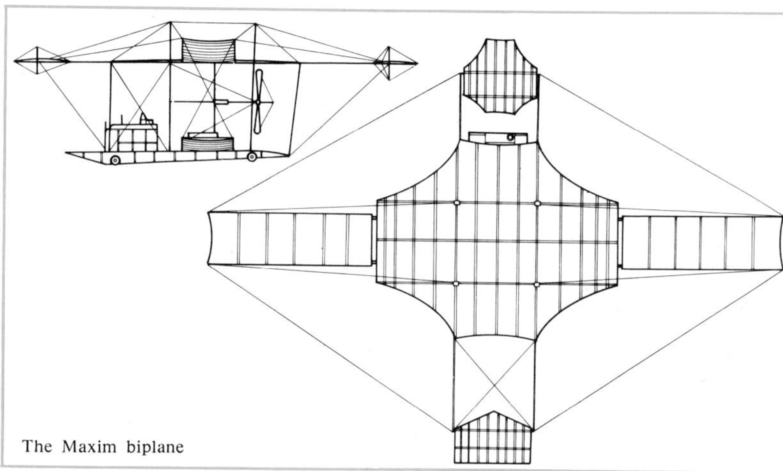
The Maxim biplane

yards (229 m) in his most famous aircraft, *The Hawk*. In 1899 Pilcher met his death in this same aircraft when he crashed while undertaking a towed flight. Pilcher was contemplating fitting an engine in a glider and at the time of his death a 4-hp engine was under construction for this purpose.

By 1899 Orville and Wilbur Wright had already become interested in flight. They were encouraged and influenced by Octave Chanute (1832–1910), an engineer of French origin who had taken U.S. citizenship. By this time Chanute was too old to fly himself, but in 1894 he published a lengthy work called *Progress in Flying Machines* which was a compilation and appraisal of all experiments in flight carried out up to that date—he can thus be called the first aviation historian. But this was not his only contribution: he designed a series of hang-gliders based on Lilienthal's ideas which worked well. His first two gliders were built in 1896, one being a multiplane which flew successfully and the other was a biplane. This latter inspired the Wright brothers when they came to build and test their first two gliders (in 1900 and 1901), subsequently achieving success with fully controled flights in their third glider, of 1902.

The general lines of the Wright brothers' flying machines in turn helped a Frenchman, Ferdinand Ferber, when he came to develop his first successful design for a glider in 1904. This glider, No. 6, was to set the standard for all European aircraft which followed, and in it Ferber achieved the first heavier-than-air flight with a passenger on board at Chalais-Meudon where he made a very brief flight with his mechanic, Burdin. No. 6 was fitted with a 12-hp engine in 1905.

By this time the scene was ostensibly set for powered flight. Designers had arrived at the correct wing configuration, and had effective propellers and power units: all that was needed was someone who could combine and sychronize these various elements and weld them into an efficient flying machine. Orville and Wilbur Wright's achievement was the product of an enormous number of experiments and tests, directed towards this end, some of which had proved successful and some futile.

In 1874 an English engineer, Thomas Moy, designed a large model tandem-wing monoplane driven by a steam engine which he called the Aerial Steamer. It was first tested in June 1875, at Crystal Palace, London. The model was connected to a central pole, round which it flew, reaching a height of 6 inches (15 cms). It was the first machine of its kind to fly successfully. Moy had succumbed to the fascination of aviation in 1865 after several balloon experiments, but he was not a really original thinker and his monoplane design had no lasting effect on later flying machines. The front wing of this model had an area of 50 square feet (4.6 sq m), the rear wing 64 square feet (5.9 sq m). It had two large fan-shaped propellers driven by a 3-hp steam engine; these propellers were 6 feet (1.82 m) in diameter and were positioned between the two wings and just managed to provide sufficient thrust to lift the 120-lb (55 kg) airplane a few inches off the ground. In 1879, the Secretary of the Aeronautical Society of Great Britain, F. W. Brearey, produced a totally anachronistic project which consisted of a model aircraft with an undulating wing, driven by elastic, which flew a distance of 60 feet (18 m). In 1886, John Stringfellow's son designed a steam-powered biplane model with twin propellers which was simply known by his initials, F.J., but this was also a failure.

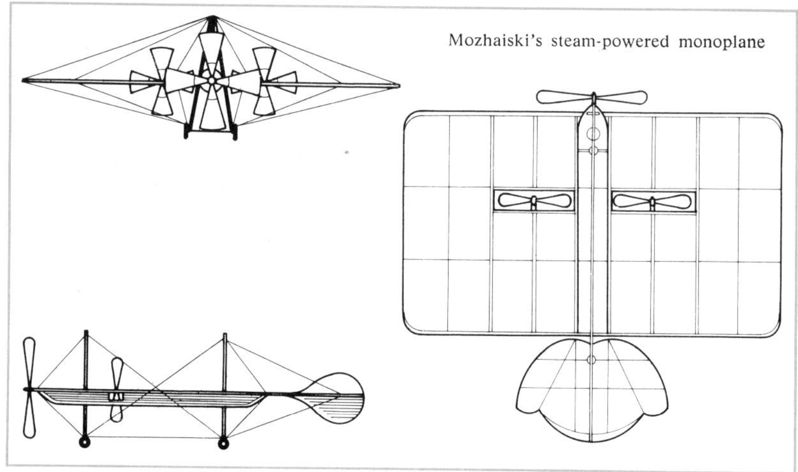
Mozhaiski's steam-powered monoplane

Other contemporary inventors, however, were not discouraged. Two years earlier, in 1884, the second powered takeoff in history had taken place (the first having been achieved with a model built by Félix du Temple in 1874); this was the work of a captain in the Russian Imperial Navy, Alexander F. Mozhaiski. In 1881 he had designed a steam-powered monoplane with three tractor propellers, two of which were positioned within the trailing edge of the wing. In 1884 it was successfully tested at Krasnoye Selo near St Petersburg, with a volunteer named Goluber at the controls; having been launched down a ramp it used the momentum to cover about 100 feet (about 30 m) in what amounted to an uncontroled leap.

At this time the steam engine was the common power unit adopted in designs which were elaborated; such as the multiplane built in 1893 by Horatio F. Phillips (1845–1906), a strange flying machine with 50 rows of superimposed small winglets, arranged like the slats of a Venetian blind, which was tested at Harrow in May 1893 attached to a central pole. This model aircraft ran round a circular track with a circumference of 628 feet (191.4 m) and managed to rise about 3 feet (91 cm) once it had reached a speed of 40 mph (64.37 km/h). But this was not the most important facet of the test, rather that it showed that Phillips' basic idea of having superimposed wings one above the other was given a practical trial after years of research. Phillips had patented his wing design as early as 1884 and he had carried out tests in a special experimental workshop which he had built himself. His analyses of wing performance were invaluable and, as he himself said, these tests had been carried out with the widest possible variety of wing profiles imaginable. His conclusions obviously had a lot of bearing on the relationship between lift and the wing section and this was the first time it had been demonstrated

Aerial Steamer: Thomas Moy's steam-driven monoplane (1874–75)

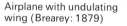

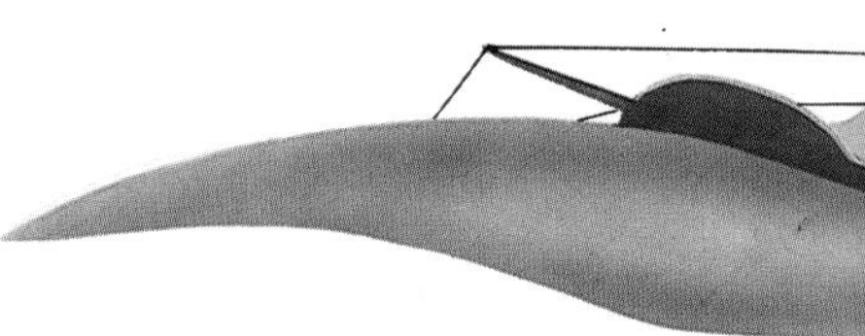
Airplane with undulating wing (Brearey: 1879)

Maxim's steam engine (1894)

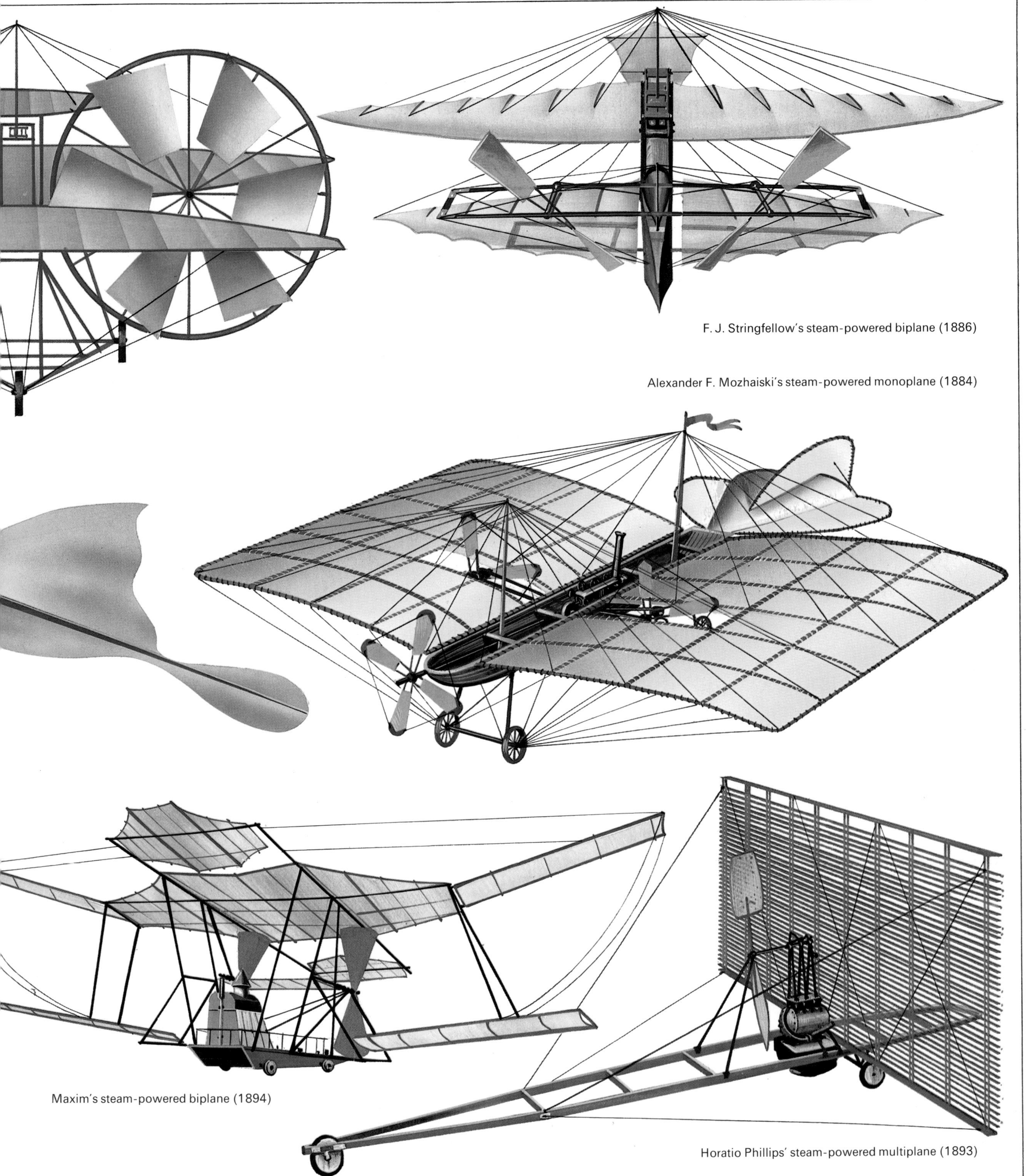

F. J. Stringfellow's steam-powered biplane (1886)

Alexander F. Mozhaiski's steam-powered monoplane (1884)

Maxim's steam-powered biplane (1894)

Horatio Phillips' steam-powered multiplane (1893)

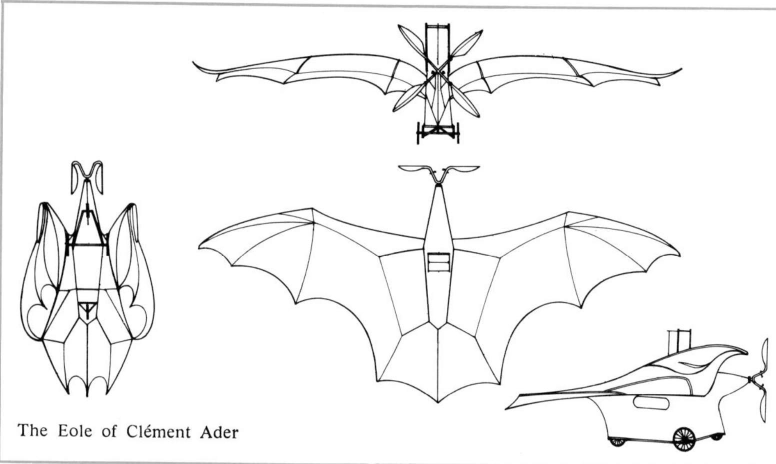
The Eole of Clément Ader

since the publications of Cayley's theories.

The famous American inventor, Sir Hiram J. Maxim (1840–1916) who took British nationality, used rails to launch his giant steam-powered biplane but to no avail. During the 1880s Maxim set out to "construct a flying machine which could become airborne," and he commenced a series of experiments whereby he could study the aerodynamic performance of wings and propellers and he also designed a very light steam engine. He started to build his flying machine in 1891, at Baldwyn's Park, Bexley, his country home. Maxim's aeronautical activities were to cost him a great deal of money—as much as £20,000, an enormous sum in those days—and work continued on the aircraft for more than a year. The product of all this effort was a large biplane of 104 feet (31.69 m) span with pronounced dihedral on its outer wing panels and with elevators at the nose and the tail. It had two 180-hp engines which drove two propellers, each 17 feet 9 inches (5.42 m) in diameter. The four wheels of the flying machine rested upon straight rails which were 1,800 feet (548.6 m) long and the total weight, including the three-man crew, was over 7,900 lb (3,600 kg). For safety during early tests there were restraining rails alongside the track to limit the height which could be attained by the aircraft. During the third experiment, in July 1894, the aircraft lifted clear of the rails but breakages occurred and the steam was shut off. Maxim lost interest in aviation for a while, only to make an equally unsuccessful venture in 1910.

By the end of the nineteenth century there were two more noteworthy attempts to fly before the Wright brothers' success. One was made by a Frenchman, Clément Ader (1841–1925) and another by an American, Samuel Pierpont Langley (1834–1906) and these were to prove the last of the countless far-fetched schemes before the Wrights heralded the age of modern aviation. Clément Ader was an engineer from Toulouse, and an enthusiast and dreamer. Had he paid more attention to contemporary experiments and used the information gained from them, he might well have achieved great things, as he was extremely gifted and capable. The aircraft which he built and tested (the *Eole* in 1890 and the *Avion III* in 1897) were still rather fantastic creations, weirdly-shaped with great bat-like wings. They belonged to the past and like their predecessors were to be forgotten.

In order to realize his flying ambitions, Ader made a study of bird flight and researched bat flight even more thoroughly, copying bats' wings when building his flying machines. He carried out experiments with small scale models and in 1873 tested a glider which was linked to the ground by ropes. In 1882 Ader started building his first full-scale aircraft, capable of carrying a man: this was the *Eole*. It was basically a monoplane with large concave wings with a span of approximately 46 feet (14 m), powered by a 20-hp steam engine which drove a four-blade bamboo propeller. The steam engine was a small masterpiece of ingenuity and had been designed and built by Ader himself; it had two cylinders, weighed 200 lb (91 kg) allowing for 66 lb (30 kg) of water and 22 lb (10 kg) of spirit fuel. It had a power/weight ratio of about 10 lb (4.5 kg) per hp which fell to 5.5 lb (2.5 kg) per hp dry weight.

The *Eole* was completed in 1890 and had its first test flight at 4 p.m. on 9 October in the grounds of the Château d'Armainvilliers, near Gretz. There was great excitement during the five-minute test: once the engine had been started up, Clément Ader positioned himself at the controls and got the aircraft under way, taxi-ing a short way and then rising a few inches into the air and covering about 50 yards, skimming along just above the ground. Thus for the first time an aircraft had managed to take off under its own power. Previous tests such as those of Du Temple and Mozhaiski had relied on launching the aircraft down a ramp in order to gather speed.

Ader's test with the *Eole* was certainly a significant step forward, although it could not strictly be described as a flight. There were many problems still to be solved, such as control and stability, which had not been tackled in the *Eole*. Ader was nonetheless encouraged by this success and went on with his research and experiments, aided by a subsidy from the French War Ministry which awarded him a generous grant in 1892, commissioning him to design and build another aircraft for military purposes. At this point Ader made the mistake of simply building a larger version of the *Eole* with two engines instead of one, when he should have tried out a new design. This new flying machine was named the *Avion III* and Ader spent five years on its design and construction. It had the same bat-wings, this time with a 52 feet 6 inches (16 m) wingspan and the most noticeable difference was that this aircraft had twin tractor propellers, each driven by the same type of steam-engine as had been used for the *Eole*.

The *Avion III* was not fitted with an elevator or any other means of flight control. Only two tests were carried out and these showed all too clearly that Ader had once more chosen to ignore what contemporary inventors were learning from their experiments. The *Avion III* was tested on 12 and 14 October 1897 at the Satory military base near Versailles. On the first occasion the machine simply rolled along the circular track laid out for it. When tested again two days later it rolled a short way, then shot off the track and ended up in a nearby field. Tests were then abandoned without the *Avion III* ever having left the ground. For some years the only official acknowledgement of the aircraft's failure was a meticulously detailed report drawn up by General Mensier, and this was filed away in the War Ministry's archives.

Nevertheless, it was widely believed at the time that Ader was the first European to fly and, in 1906, so irritated was Ader by all the publicity about Santos-Dumont's flights, that he gave it out as official that on 14 October 1897—the day of the *Avion III*'s final test—he had flown for about 1,000 feet (300 m) which was, of course, untrue. His claim was accepted without question until 1910 when the French War Ministry, seeing that their official refutation of Ader's claim had had no effect, decided to publish Mensier's report. Clément Ader's behaviour undoubtedly puts him in a very bad light, but can perhaps be understood when one remembers his obsessive enthusiasm for aviation which may have led to his tendency to live in a fantasy world, out of touch with what was going on in contemporary aeronautical circles.

Samuel Pierpont Langley (1834–1906) was a somewhat similar personality, and failed to achieve his ambition largely through paying too little attention to the discoveries of his fellow inventors.

Langley's aircraft, the *Aerodrome*, was a tandem-wing monoplane with a 48 feet (14.63 m) wingspan and a wing area of 1,040 square feet (96.6 sq m), weighing 730 lb (330 kg). The engine drove two propellers positioned between the two wings. Langley would probably have stood a better chance of success had he not persisted in using the same catapult launching system for his full-size aircraft as had been used previously for his model aircraft. He intended to take off from a specially constructed houseboat on the Potomac River. Tests took place on 7 October and 8 December 1903, and on both occasions the flying machine was damaged and fell into the water. These were to be the only tests. Like others before him, Samuel Pierpont Langley believed he had thoroughly thought out every aspect of powered flight and in his case it was the launching system which seems to have been the stumbling block. Only nine days after his *Aerodrome*'s brief career was brought to an end the Wright brothers made the first successful flights.

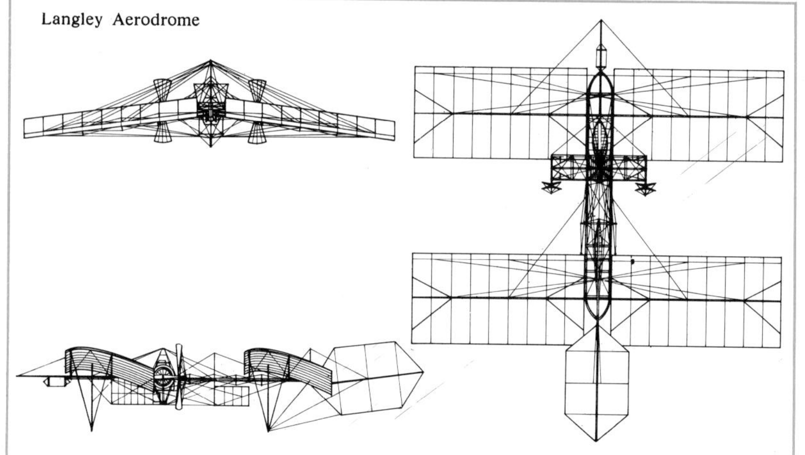
Langley Aerodrome

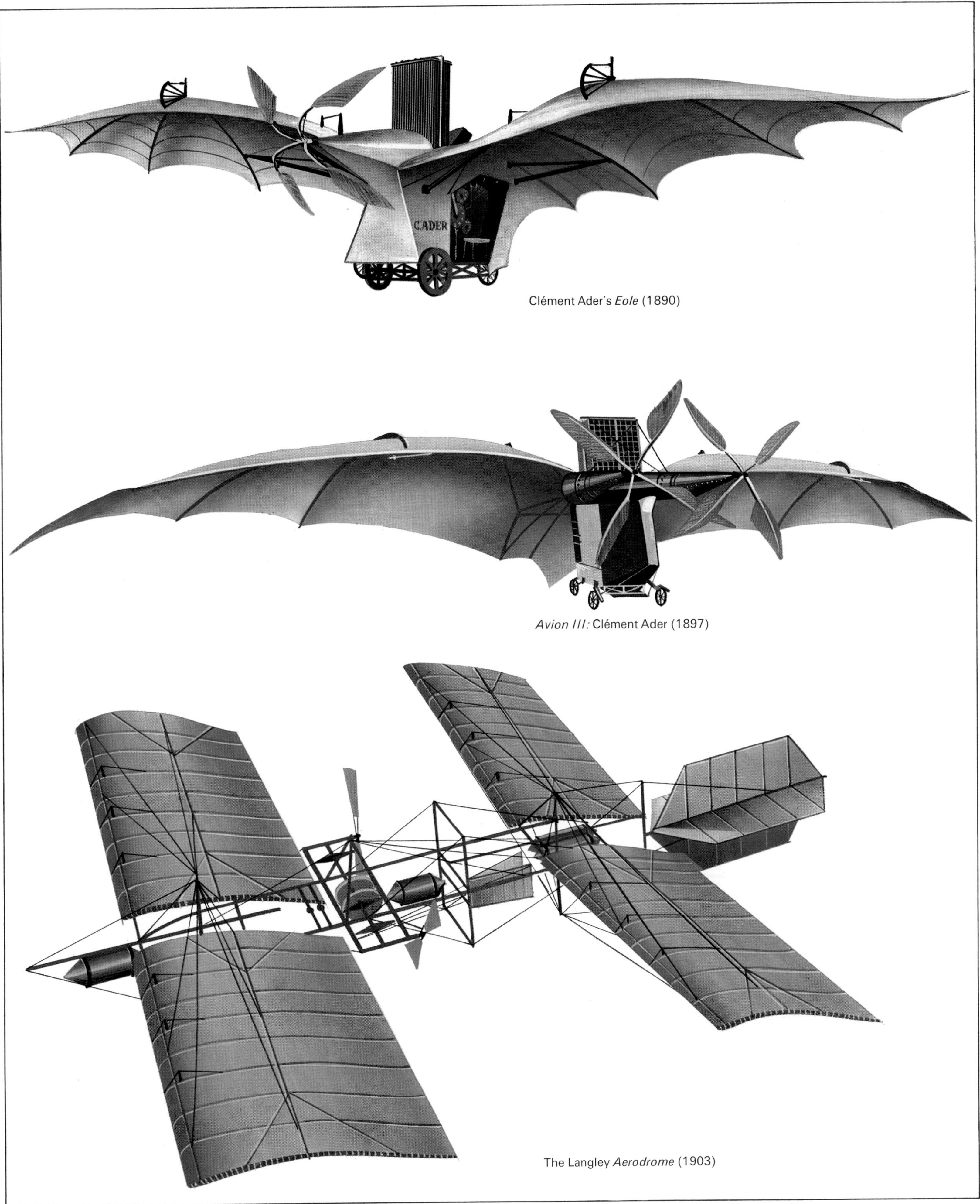

Clément Ader's *Eole* (1890)

Avion III: Clément Ader (1897)

The Langley *Aerodrome* (1903)

Photographic Appendix

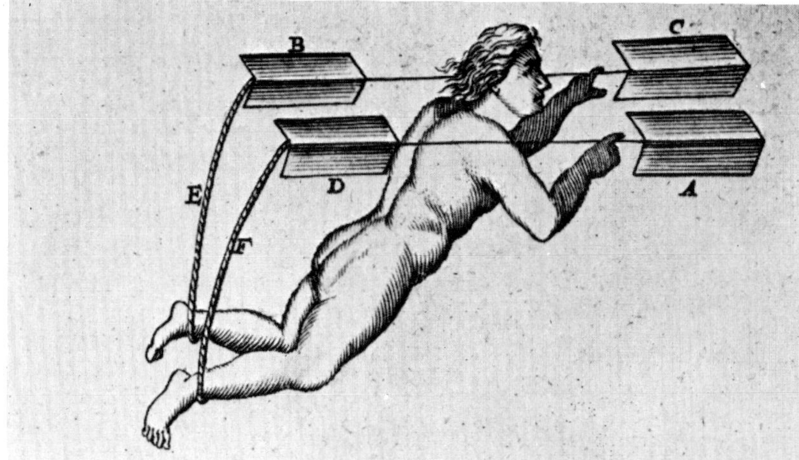

Besnier's wings, 1678 (3)

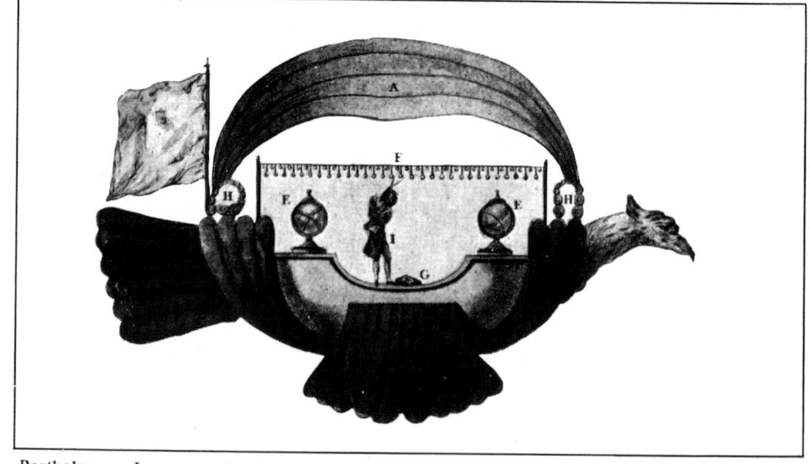
Bartholomeu Laurenço de Gusmâo's Passarola, 1709 (3)

Blanchard's aircraft, Paris 1781 (3)

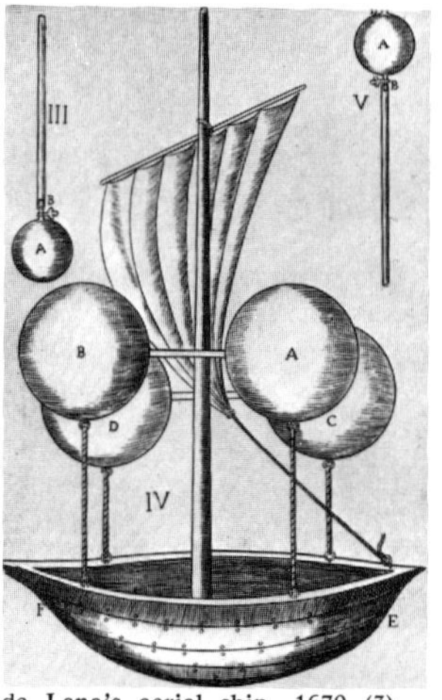

de Lana's aerial ship, 1670 (3)

De Rozier and d'Arlandes's free hot-air balloon, 1783 (4)

Montgolfier gas balloon, Versailles, 1783 (4)

Charles Green's balloon, Nassau, Paris, 1836 (4)

André-Jacques Garnerin's parachute, 1797 (6)

Victor Tatin's monoplane, 1879 (7)

Camille Vert's dirigible, 1859 (8)

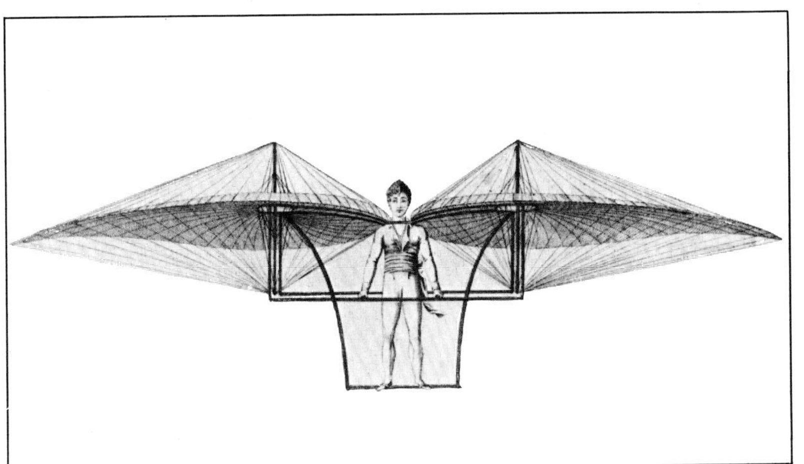

Jacob Degen's ornithopter, Paris, 1812 (6)

Pénaud's model airplane, Planophore, 1871 (7)

Victor Tatin's ornithopter, 1879 (7)

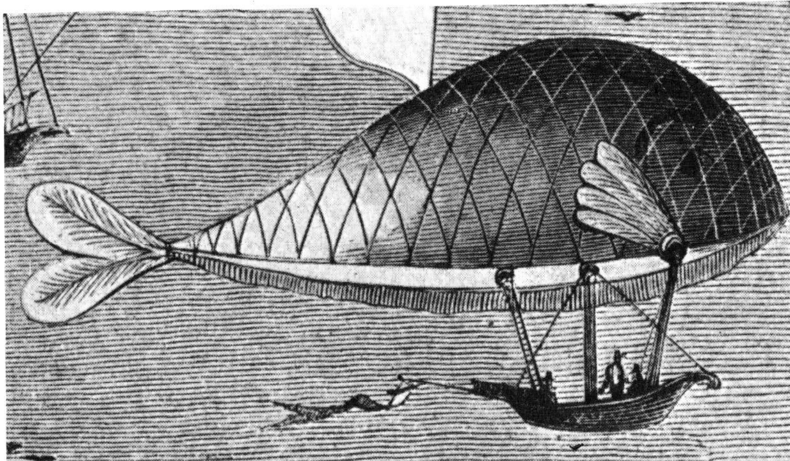

Pauly's design for a dirigible, 1804 (8)

The second Henri Giffard dirigible, 1855 (8)

Photographic Appendix

Dupuy de Lôme's dirigible; below, detail of a gondola, 1872 (8)

Marriott's dirigible, San Francisco, 1869 (8)

Jean-Baptiste-Marie Meusnier's dirigible in its tent hangar, 1784 (8)

The Lebaudy brother's dirigible, Champ de Mars, 1903 (9)

Renard and Krebs's dirigible La France, Chalais-Meudon, 1884 (9)

Ferdinand von Zeppelin's first dirigible in its floating hangar, 1900 (9)

Alberto Santos-Dumont's dirigible No.1, 1898 (9)

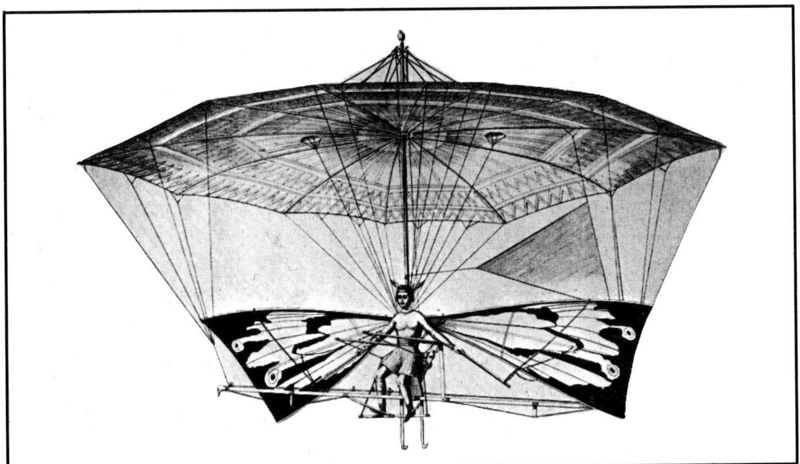
François Letur's parachute-glider, 1853 (11)

Le Bris glider, 1868 (11)

Lilienthal's monoplane glider No.11, 1894 (12)

The Wright brothers' No.3 glider, Kitty Hawk, 1902 (12)

Ferdinand Ferber's biplane glider No.5, Chalais-Meudon, 1904 (12)

Clément Ader's Avion III, 1897 (14)

Langley's Aerodrome on its houseboat catapult-launching platform, Potomac River, 1903 (14)

2. DREAMS COME TRUE - THE FIRST FLIGHTS IN THE USA AND EUROPE

Orville and Wilbur Wright's four successful flights made on 17 December 1903, the first controled and sustained flights by a power-driven heavier-than-air craft, were received with apathy and skepticism, and although their Flyer's achievement was to become a great historical event, American public opinion of the day refused to take it seriously and it was some time before it was generally believed. Although the Wright brothers had not wanted to publicize their experiments, the first reports of their achievement at Kitty Hawk, North Carolina, filtered through that same day and on the following days in the daily press. It was not particularly good publicity since the first report was largely vague and fabricated with few facts and failed to arouse the editors' interest and was treated as just one of the dozens of routine news items which came in each day. The long and meticulously detailed account which Orville and Wilbur Wright sent to the Associated Press news agency on 5 January 1904, should have scotched the mistaken impressions which had been given by the earlier inaccurate and embroidered reports published in the papers, but somehow it had little effect. Octave Chanute, the expert on the subject of aviation, and his associates were the only people in the United States to be fully convinced of the Wrights' success.

Bad luck was then to turn the prevailing climate of indifference into downright disbelief. By May 1904, the Wright brothers reckoned they were ready to give their first public demonstration, since they now thought they had perfected their machine and were experienced in piloting it. They had prepared Flyer No. 2, but the wind and then problems with the engine meant that the machine could not take off in front of the assembled journalists and photographers. People simply refused to believe their claims and official and public skepticism was to dissuade others from following the Wrights.

The United States refused to recognize the immense value of these experimental flights, and there followed three years of complete stagnation in aeronautical research during which time America lost her head start to Europe.

Ironically enough, it was the European pioneers' achievements and experiments which were to awaken and stimulate air-mindedness in the New World under the momentum of the surge of world-wide interest which these early aviators excited. But this was only to happen in 1908, the year in which Orville and Wilbur Wright decided to display their machine in public once more, having retired completely from the public eye in a self-imposed isolation which was devoted to perfecting their airplane.

Meanwhile Europe had made up for lost time amazingly quickly. After the death of Lilienthal in 1896 there was a lull in aeronautical activity and it was only in 1901 that a French army captain, Ferdinand Ferber, took up the German pioneer's ideas. Ferber spent about three years carrying out experiments, first with gliders very much like those flown by Lilienthal and then with gliders and powered flying machines which owed much to schemes outlined by the Wright brothers. In 1904, Ferber achieved his aim and produced an original glider design which was to serve as the basis for all subsequent European airplane design: this was a biplane glider with a fixed tail which was inherently stable.

Success appeared to be within reach. Enthusiasts were greatly encouraged by all this activity, particularly when confirmation of the Wright's powered flights came from the United States. In France, particularly, there was no holding the surge of projects and initiative largely due to the efforts of such well-known personalities as Louis Blériot, Gabriel Voisin, Ernest Archdeacon and Robert Esnault-Pelterie. In sharp contrast with the indifference in America, the Aéro Club de France offered various prizes to stimulate the growth of aviation in Europe. Among them was the Archdeacon Cup, to be won by the pilot of the first airplane to fly more than 25 meters, a prize of 1,500 francs for the first to fly more than 100 meters and the Grand Prix Deutsch-Archdeacon: 50,000 francs to the first pilot to complete a circuit of one kilometer.

Two years went by before the first two trophies were awarded. Alberto Santos-Dumont won them on 23 October and 12 November 1906, watched by a wildly excited crowd of spectators. The Brazilian pioneer's short flights could certainly not be compared with those made exactly one year earlier by the Wright brothers with their Flyer No. 3, but this seemed unimportant in the first flush of success.

1908 was a momentous year: the event which thrilled the aviation world was the Wright brother's decision to make demonstration flights with their own machines which they had by that time perfected. They could not have picked a better time, and Wilbur Wright chose shrewdly when he made France his destination for this vitally important European trip. Orville stayed behind in the United States to carry out evaluation flights which were to convince the U.S. Government and Army of the airplane's potential. Wilbur Wright gave demonstration flights from August to December at a racecourse near Le Mans and won the astonished admiration of European enthusiasts. Not only were they impressed by his flying machine (the Wright Model A) but even more by his obvious mastery of the machine and his exceptional flying technique, qualities almost unknown to the French pioneers.

The Wrights were unquestionably the best flyers, but they were no longer alone. Equally important milestones were soon to be set up by the record flights of Farman, Delagrange and Blériot. Great Britain, which had got off to a slow start, entered the field with such pioneers as Samuel Franklin Cody and Alliott Verdon Roe.

In the United States the efforts of the Aerial Experiment Association led to the construction of successful flying machines such as Glenn Curtiss's *June Bug* and J. A. D. McCurdy's *Silver Dart*. In Italy—where the first nationally built airplanes made their appearance the following year—Leon Delagrange's demonstration flights in Rome, Turin and Milan aroused great enthusiasm and stimulated further research and experiments.

The day was in sight when aviation would come of age, and 1909 can be considered the year when the airplane was no longer regarded as a curiosity but was generally accepted as a practical and reliable, albeit new, product of man's resourcefulness. Two important events helped to establish this new attitude, one was Louis Blériot's crossing of the English Channel and the other was the Reims Aviation Meeting. Blériot's flight was proof positive of the aircraft's capabilities and potential, while the Reims air show paved the way for the great sporting events and air displays which, besides making hundreds of thousands of people air-minded, were also to have a great influence on the future development of airplanes and engines. The Grande Semaine d'Aviation de la Champagne, organized by the Champagne Wine Growers Association under the patronage of the President of the Republic, offered a total of 200,000 francs prize money and led to an almost incredible number of records being set. These records included: distance, 112 miles (180 km) in 3 hours 4 minutes and 56 seconds set by a Henry Farman III, piloted by Farman himself; speed, 47.03 mph (75.7 km/h) by the Curtiss *Reims Racer*; altitude, 508 feet (155 m) by Hubert Latham in an Antoinette. Thirty-eight airplanes were entered, although only twenty-three managed to leave the ground, and 87 flights exceeding the 5 kilometers of the course were officially logged.

The contribution which the Reims meeting made to the development of aviation lay not only in the series of records it produced; it also made a very significant contribution in the purely technical sphere. Sharing the limelight with the pilots were two new component parts vital to the airplane's success: the propellers built by Lucien Chauvière—the first practical and efficient ones to be made in Europe—and the Gnome rotary engine designed by the Seguin brothers. Coming after Léon Levavasseur's engine, which had made possible the successes of the first French pioneers, the rotary engine designed by the Seguins had introduced a type of engine that typified a whole era of aviation history. Henry Farman was the first to show his confidence in the engine when at Reims on 27 August, only forty minutes before the distance contest was due to start, he replaced the eight-cylinder Vivinus engine in his biplane with a Gnome engine, and his decision was amply justified.

The momentum generated by the Reims air display was to lead to the almost uninterrupted series of sporting events which became increasingly popular. These included such races as the Circuit of Britain, the Circuit of Europe of 1911, the Gordon Bennett speed Trophy and the Michelin Trophy for endurance. There were a great many aviation meetings, including the famous Schneider Trophy seaplane speed races. Besides these organized air meetings, to which spectators flocked in their thousands and aviators in their hundreds, the significance of aviation was also brought home to the world by individual achievements, often accomplished alone. One was the ill-fated Alpine crossing by the Peruvian Jorge Chávez, whose Blériot monoplane crashed on landing on 23 September 1910, having successfully flown over the Alps. In 1911, the American, Calbraith Rodgers made a flight across the United States, covering 3,100 miles (5,000 km) in a special Wright EX, between 17 September and 10 December 1911.

The aviation craze gradually settled down into an acceptance that the age of the airplane had arrived, even in those countries which had been slow to take an interest in flying. In Italy, after the unsuccessful flight of the first Italian-built aircraft (Aristide Faccioli's triplane on 13 January 1909) the Club Aviatori was founded in Rome and was active from 9 February 1909 onwards. It was this body, to which all the successful pioneers and enthusiasts of the day flocked, which brought Wilbur Wright to Italy with one of his airplanes. Wright stayed in Rome for twenty-five days, from 1 to 26 April, and on 15 April he began a long series of demonstration flights at the Centocelle military base. During his epoch-making visit, Wilbur trained a naval officer, Engineer Sub Lieutenant Mario Calderara, who was to become the first Italian pilot. The following year the first military flying school was established at Centocelle. Inspired by the prevailing enthusiasm—and thanks to the technical expertise learned from Wilbur Wright—more frequent experiments were made. In the same year (1909), the first really efficient airplanes appeared in Italy, such as those built by the Turin engineer, Franz Miller, the Asteria company and Giovanni Caproni's aircraft. On top of all this, the first important aviation rally, the Circuito Internazionale di Brescia took place from 9 to 20 September 1909.

The year leading up to World War I saw a virtually unstoppable expansion of aviation. Only a few months before the outbreak of war in Europe, another extremely important phase of the aircraft's career commenced with the first regular passenger service. The little Benoist XIV flying-boat which took off from St Petersburg, Florida, to fly to Tampa on 1 January 1914, carrying only one passenger, was to be the precursor of the commercial fleets which were to fill the world's skies some years later.

By now the aircraft could be used for other purposes. The Italians were the first to convert the airplane from a peacetime, sporting machine into a weapon of war, which was to revolutionize military tactics. The first theoretical consideration of the use of the airplane for military purposes was formulated in 1909 by Major Giulio Douhet, who said: "We are already aware of the importance of sea power, in the near future it will be no less vital to achieve supremacy in the air."

These theories were first put to the test two years later in the Italian invasion of Libya. The first reconnaissance flight was made on 23 October 1911, by Captain Carlo Piazza, and the first aerial "bombardment" was carried out by Second Lieutenant Giulio Guidotti on 1 November. These were portentous events which other nations were quick to note. Meanwhile Europe drew closer to war, during which the competitive events and sporting achievements of the pre-war era faded as memories of happier times.

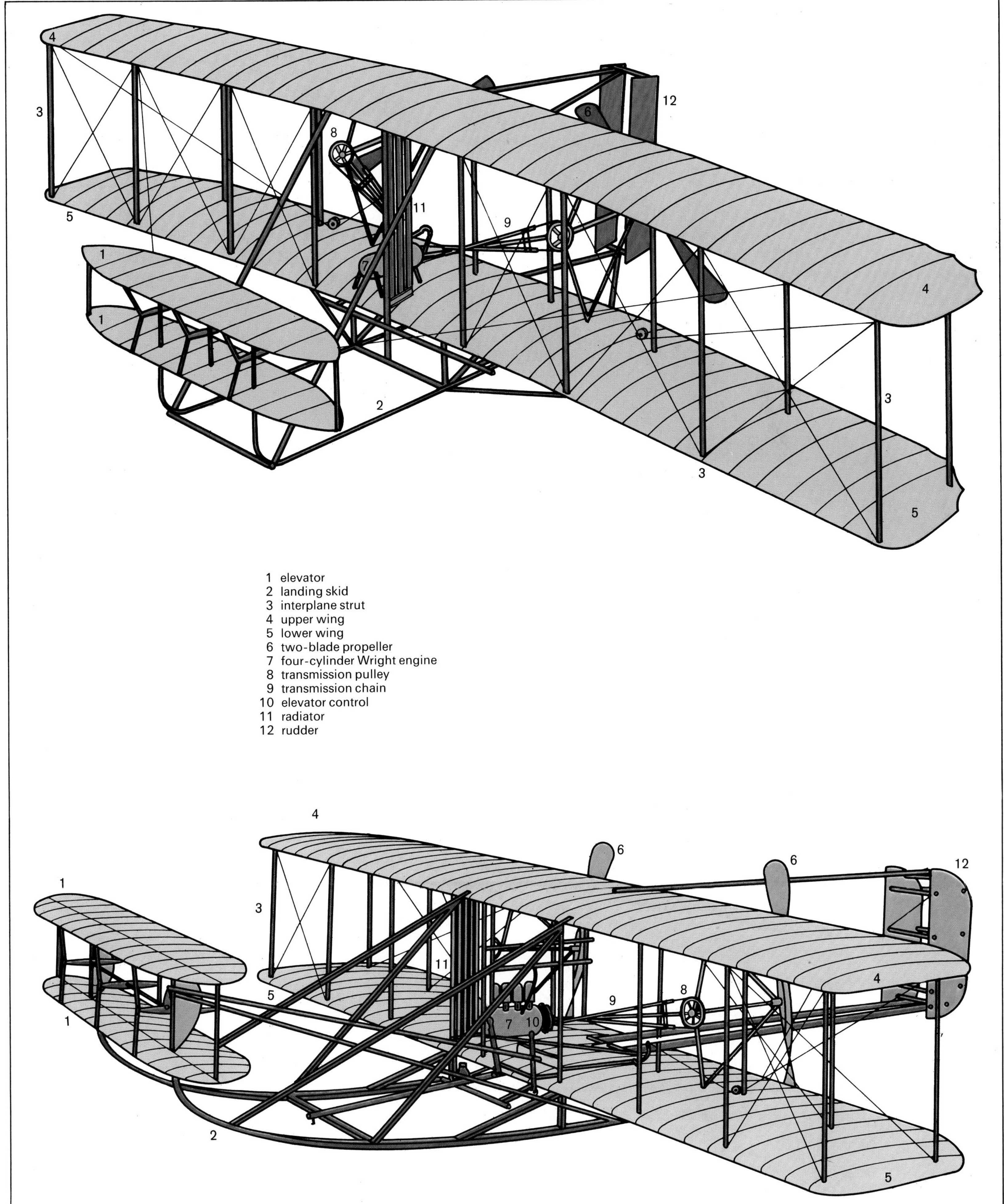
1
2
3
4
5
6
7
8
9
10
11
12
1 elevator
2 landing skid
3 interplane strut
4 upper wing
5 lower wing
6 two-blade propeller
7 four-cylinder Wright engine
8 transmission pulley
9 transmission chain
10 elevator control
11 radiator
12 rudder

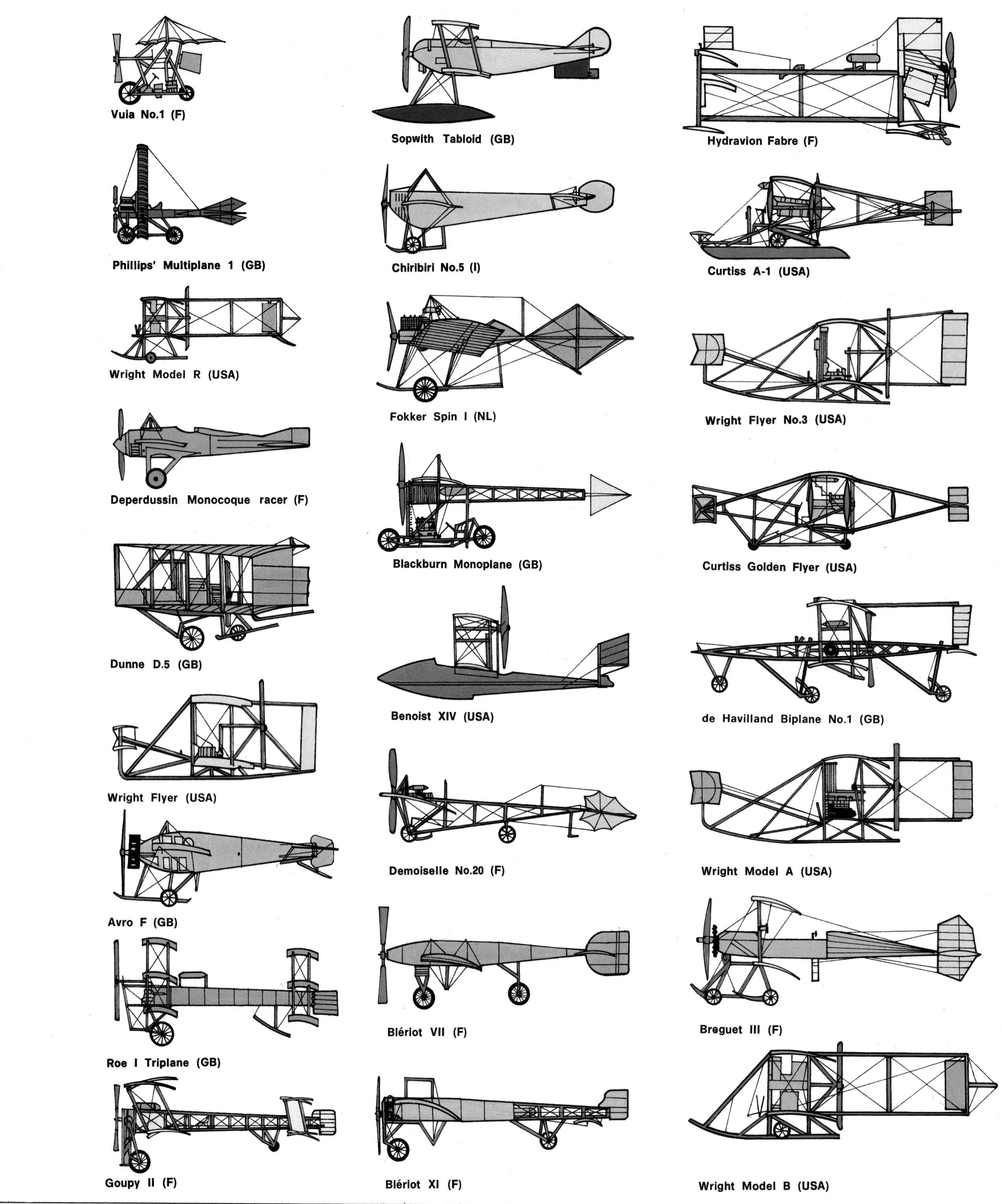
Vuia No.1 (F)
Sopwith Tabloid (GB)
Hydravion Fabre (F)
Phillips' Multiplane 1 (GB)
Chiribiri No.5 (I)
Curtiss A-1 (USA)
Wright Model R (USA)
Fokker Spin I (NL)
Wright Flyer No.3 (USA)
Deperdussin Monocoque racer (F)
Blackburn Monoplane (GB)
Curtiss Golden Flyer (USA)
Dunne D.5 (GB)
Benoist XIV (USA)
de Havilland Biplane No.1 (GB)
Wright Flyer (USA)
Demoiselle No.20 (F)
Wright Model A (USA)
Avro F (GB)
Blériot VII (F)
Breguet III (F)
Roe I Triplane (GB)
Goupy II (F)
Blériot XI (F)
Wright Model B (USA)

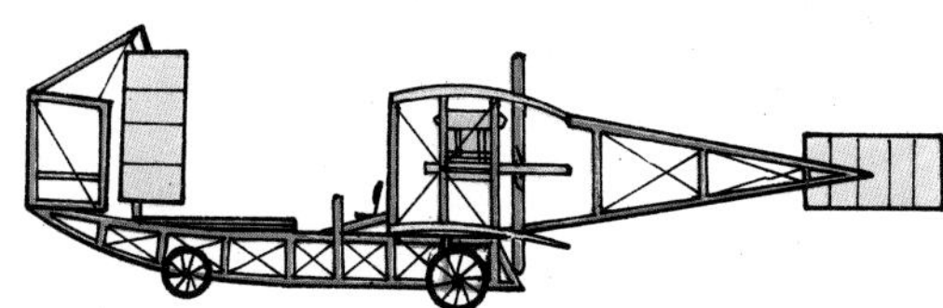

Short No.3 (GB)

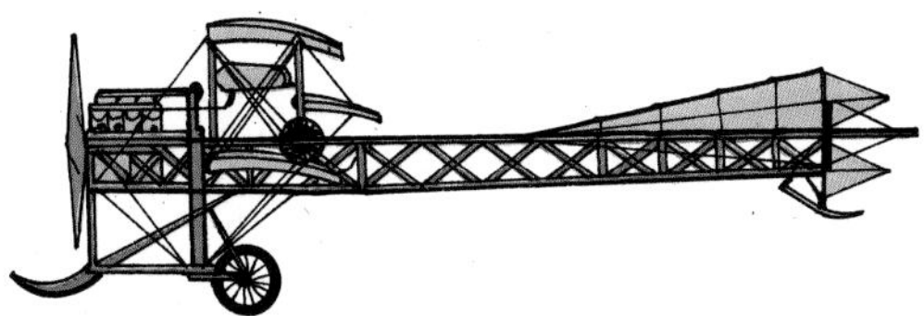

Dufaux 4 (CH)

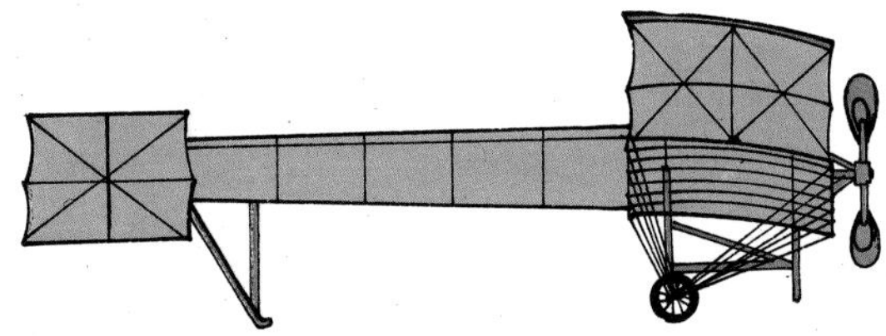

Santos-Dumont 14bis (F)

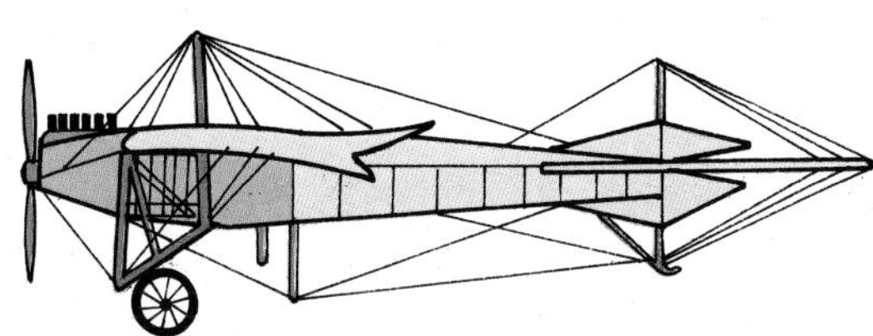

Etrich Taube (A)

Deperdussin Monocoque floatplane racer (F)

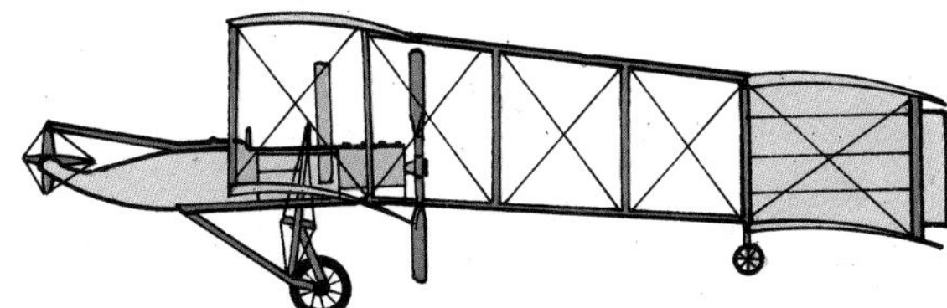

Voisin-Farman I (F)

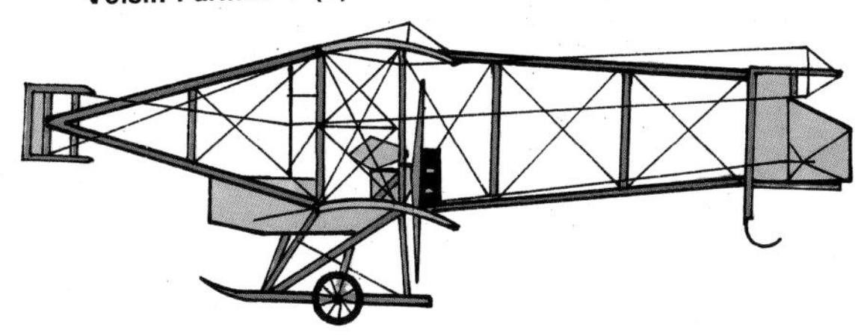

Asteria No.3 (I)

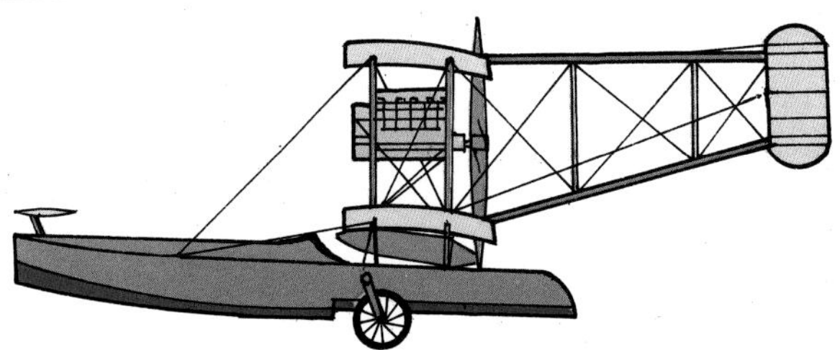

Sopwith Bat Boat II (GB)

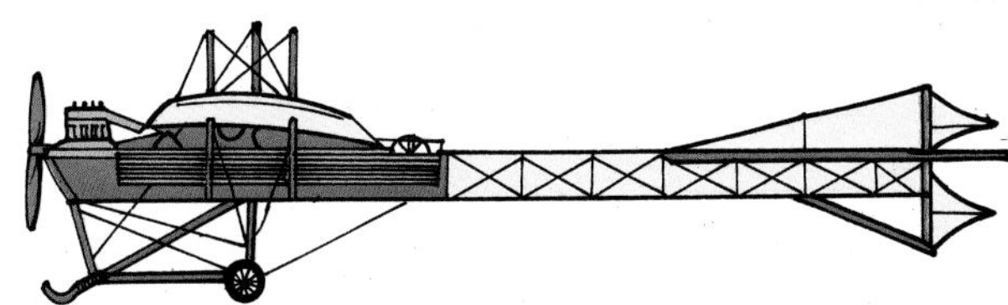

Antoinette IV (F)

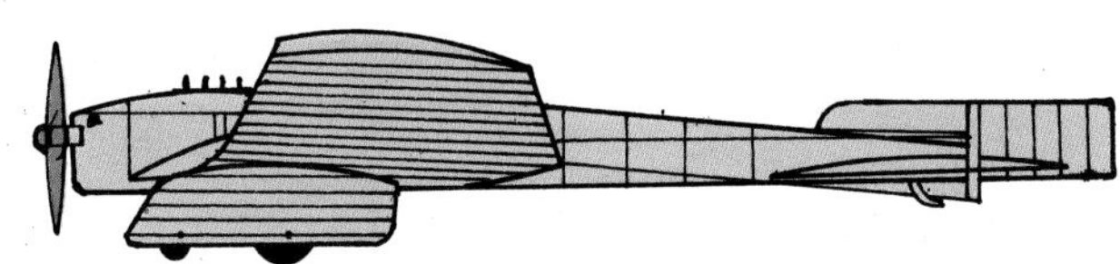

Antoinette Latham (Monobloc) (F)

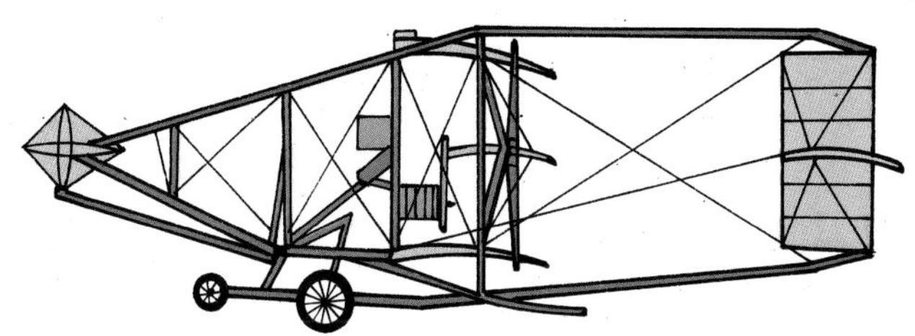

Cody Michelin Cup (GB)

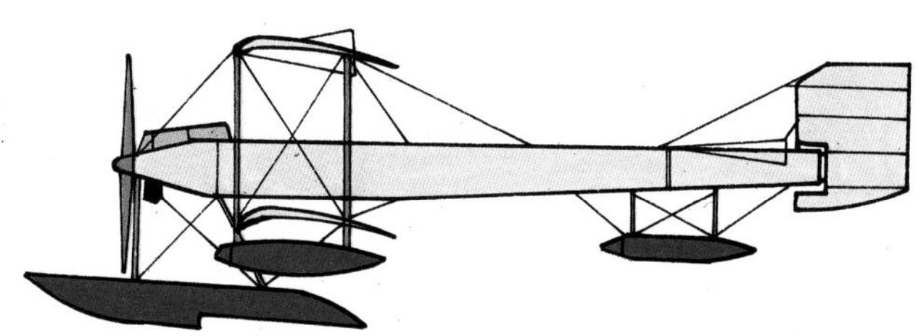

Short S.41 (GB)

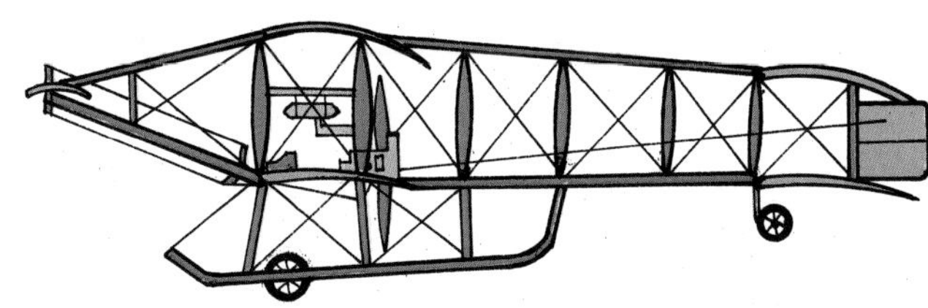

Henry Farman III (F)

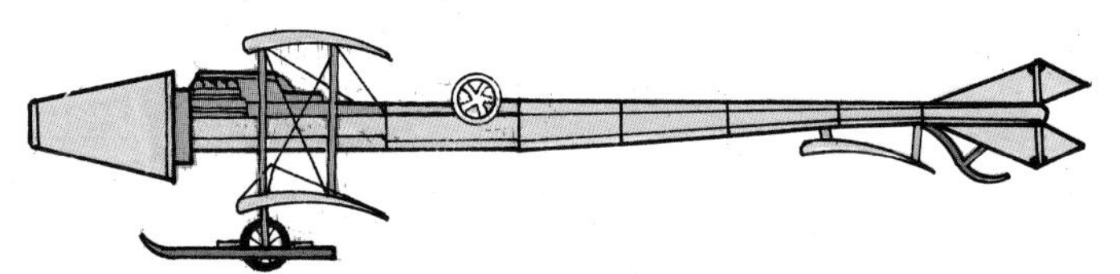

Coanda (F)

0 3 6 9m

3m = 2,16 cm

Some of the most important civil aircraft: 1903–1914

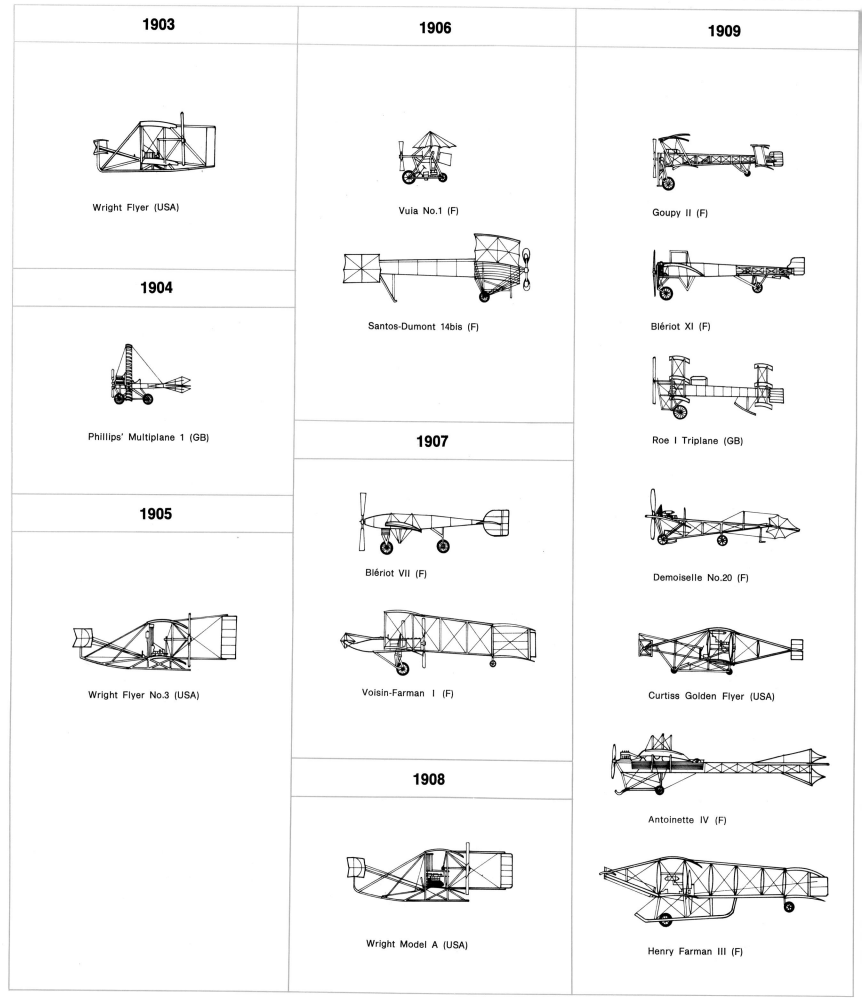

1903

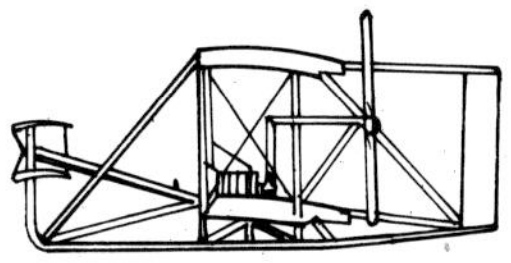

Wright Flyer (USA)

1904

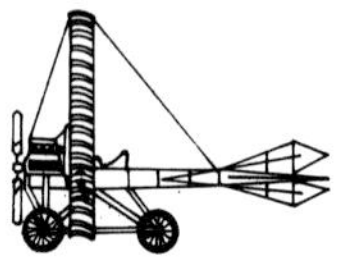

Phillips' Multiplane 1 (GB)

1905

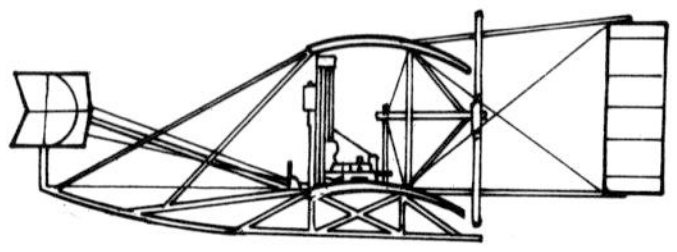

Wright Flyer No.3 (USA)

1906

Vuia No.1 (F)

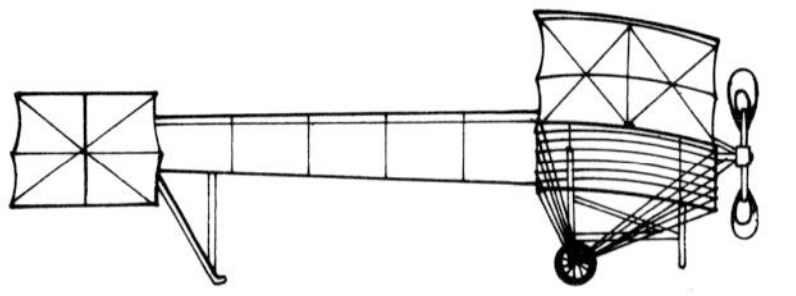

Santos-Dumont 14bis (F)

1907

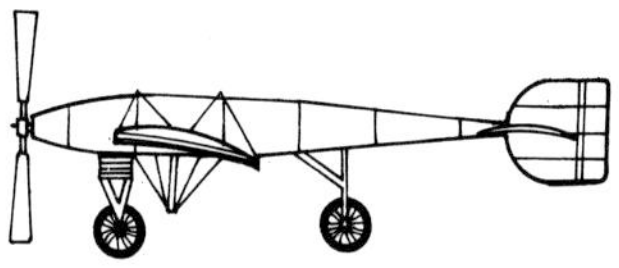

Blériot VII (F)

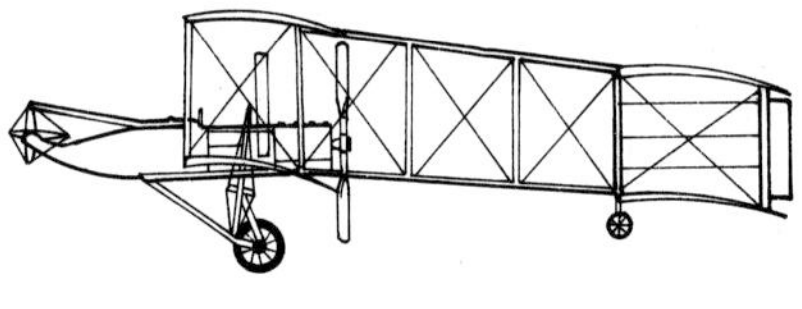

Voisin-Farman I (F)

1908

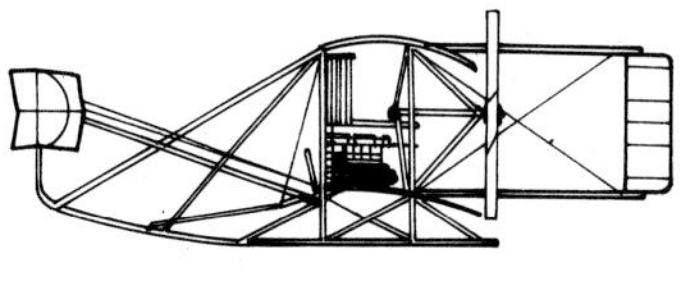

Wright Model A (USA)

1909

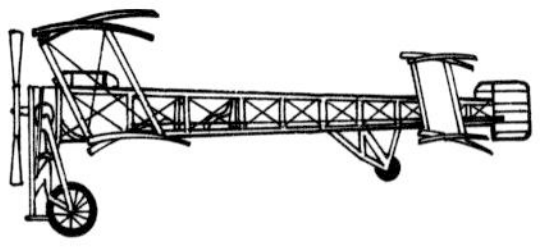

Goupy II (F)

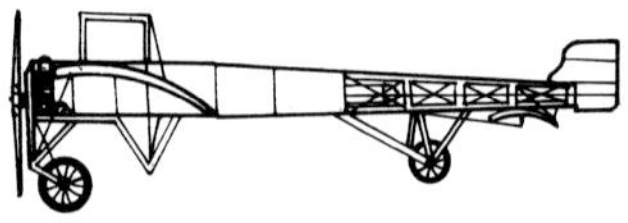

Blériot XI (F)

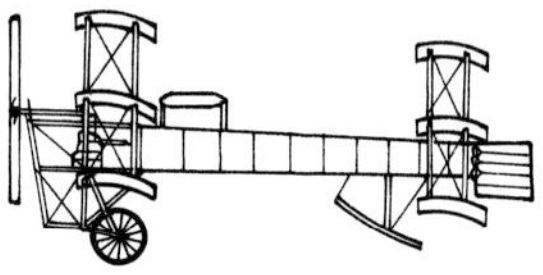

Roe I Triplane (GB)

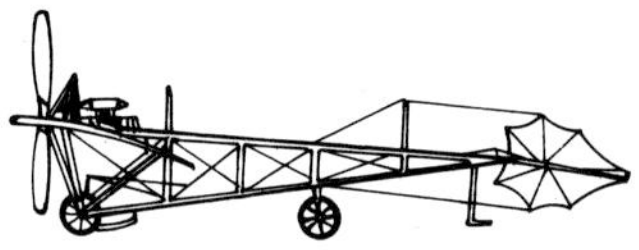

Demoiselle No.20 (F)

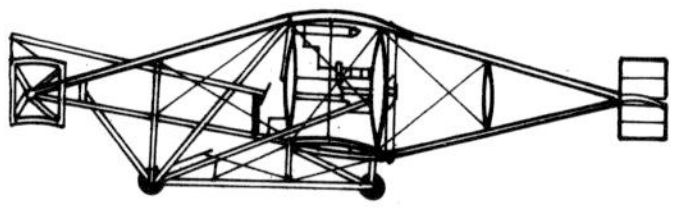

Curtiss Golden Flyer (USA)

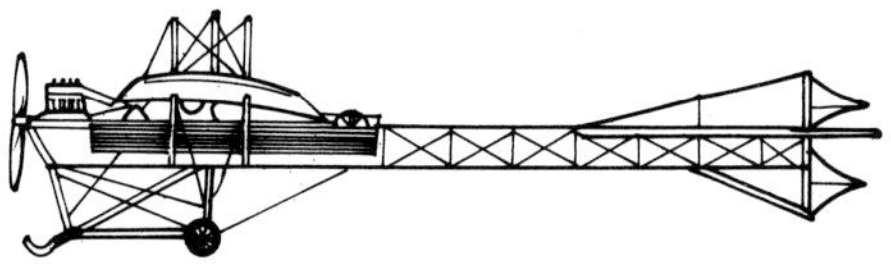

Antoinette IV (F)

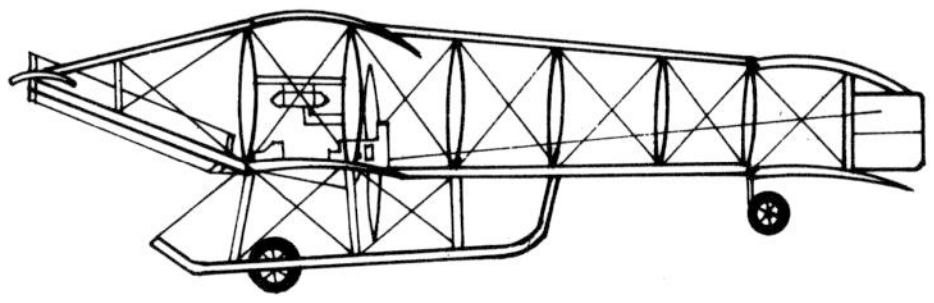

Henry Farman III (F)

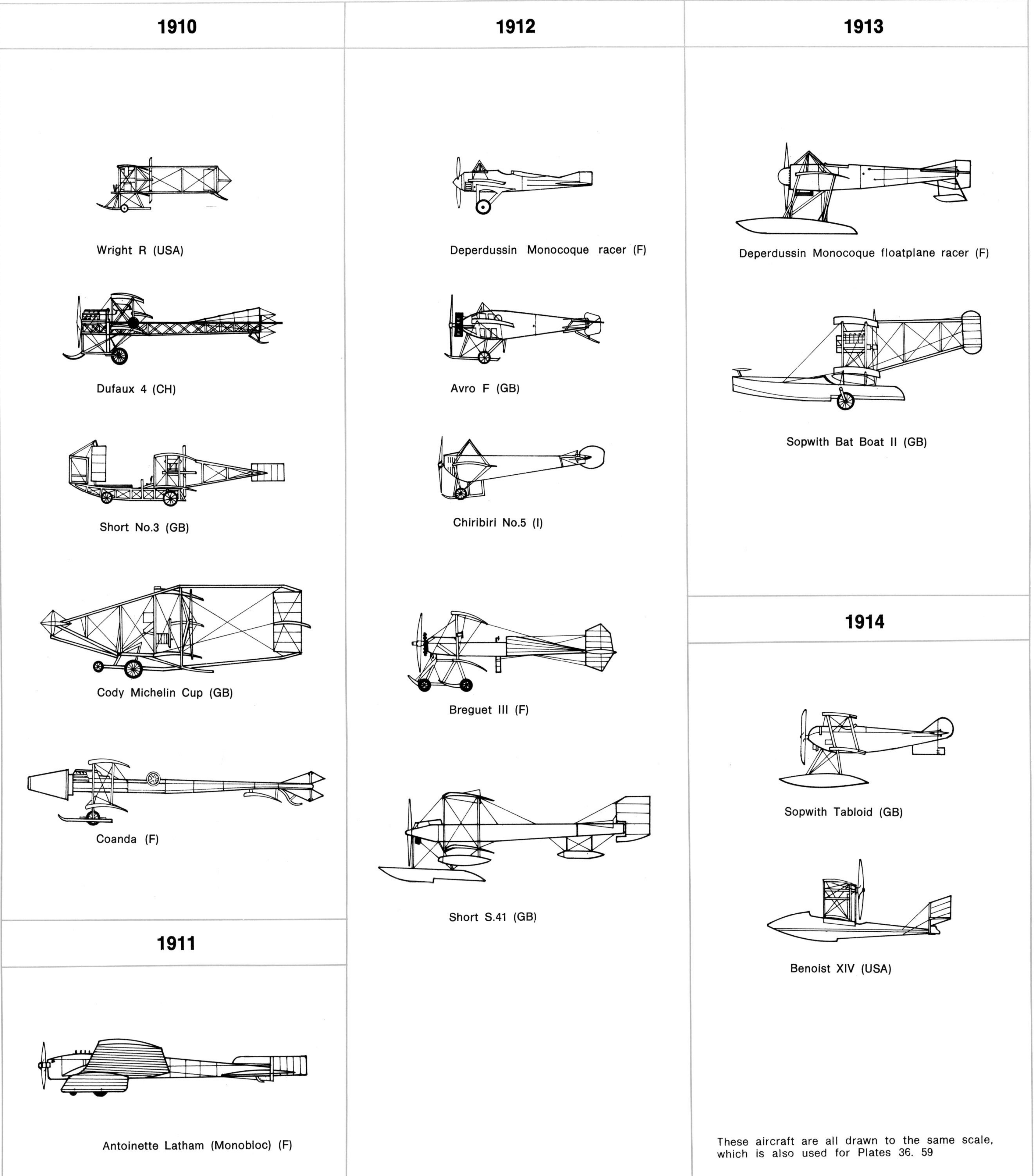

These aircraft are all drawn to the same scale, which is also used for Plates 36. 59

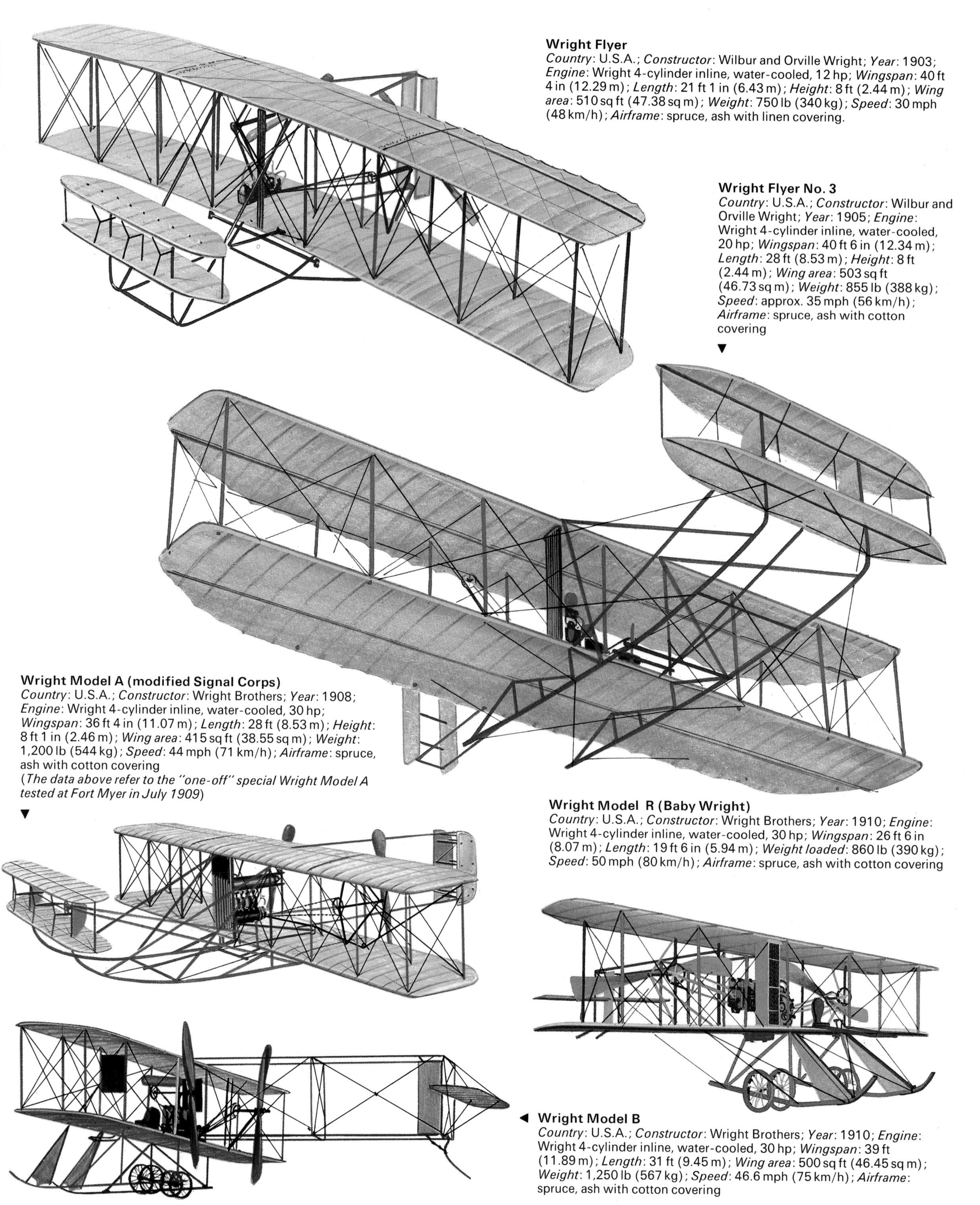

Wright Flyer
Country: U.S.A.; *Constructor*: Wilbur and Orville Wright; *Year*: 1903; *Engine*: Wright 4-cylinder inline, water-cooled, 12 hp; *Wingspan*: 40 ft 4 in (12.29 m); *Length*: 21 ft 1 in (6.43 m); *Height*: 8 ft (2.44 m); *Wing area*: 510 sq ft (47.38 sq m); *Weight*: 750 lb (340 kg); *Speed*: 30 mph (48 km/h); *Airframe*: spruce, ash with linen covering.

Wright Flyer No. 3
Country: U.S.A.; *Constructor*: Wilbur and Orville Wright; *Year*: 1905; *Engine*: Wright 4-cylinder inline, water-cooled, 20 hp; *Wingspan*: 40 ft 6 in (12.34 m); *Length*: 28 ft (8.53 m); *Height*: 8 ft (2.44 m); *Wing area*: 503 sq ft (46.73 sq m); *Weight*: 855 lb (388 kg); *Speed*: approx. 35 mph (56 km/h); *Airframe*: spruce, ash with cotton covering
▼

Wright Model A (modified Signal Corps)
Country: U.S.A.; *Constructor*: Wright Brothers; *Year*: 1908; *Engine*: Wright 4-cylinder inline, water-cooled, 30 hp; *Wingspan*: 36 ft 4 in (11.07 m); *Length*: 28 ft (8.53 m); *Height*: 8 ft 1 in (2.46 m); *Wing area*: 415 sq ft (38.55 sq m); *Weight*: 1,200 lb (544 kg); *Speed*: 44 mph (71 km/h); *Airframe*: spruce, ash with cotton covering
(*The data above refer to the "one-off" special Wright Model A tested at Fort Myer in July 1909*)
▼

Wright Model R (Baby Wright)
Country: U.S.A.; *Constructor*: Wright Brothers; *Year*: 1910; *Engine*: Wright 4-cylinder inline, water-cooled, 30 hp; *Wingspan*: 26 ft 6 in (8.07 m); *Length*: 19 ft 6 in (5.94 m); *Weight loaded*: 860 lb (390 kg); *Speed*: 50 mph (80 km/h); *Airframe*: spruce, ash with cotton covering

◀ **Wright Model B**
Country: U.S.A.; *Constructor*: Wright Brothers; *Year*: 1910; *Engine*: Wright 4-cylinder inline, water-cooled, 30 hp; *Wingspan*: 39 ft (11.89 m); *Length*: 31 ft (9.45 m); *Wing area*: 500 sq ft (46.45 sq m); *Weight*: 1,250 lb (567 kg); *Speed*: 46.6 mph (75 km/h); *Airframe*: spruce, ash with cotton covering

Santos-Dumont 14 bis
Country: France; *Constructor*: Alberto Santos-Dumont; *Year*: 1906; *Engine*: Antoinette 8-cylinder inline V, evaporative-cooled, 50 hp; *Wingspan*: 36 ft 9 in (11.2 m); *Length*: 31 ft 10 in (9.7 m); *Height*: 11 ft 2 in (3.4 m); *Wing area*: 560 sq ft (52 sq m); *Weight*: 661 lb (300 kg); *Speed*: 25 mph (40 km/h); *Airframe*: bamboo, pine with cotton covering

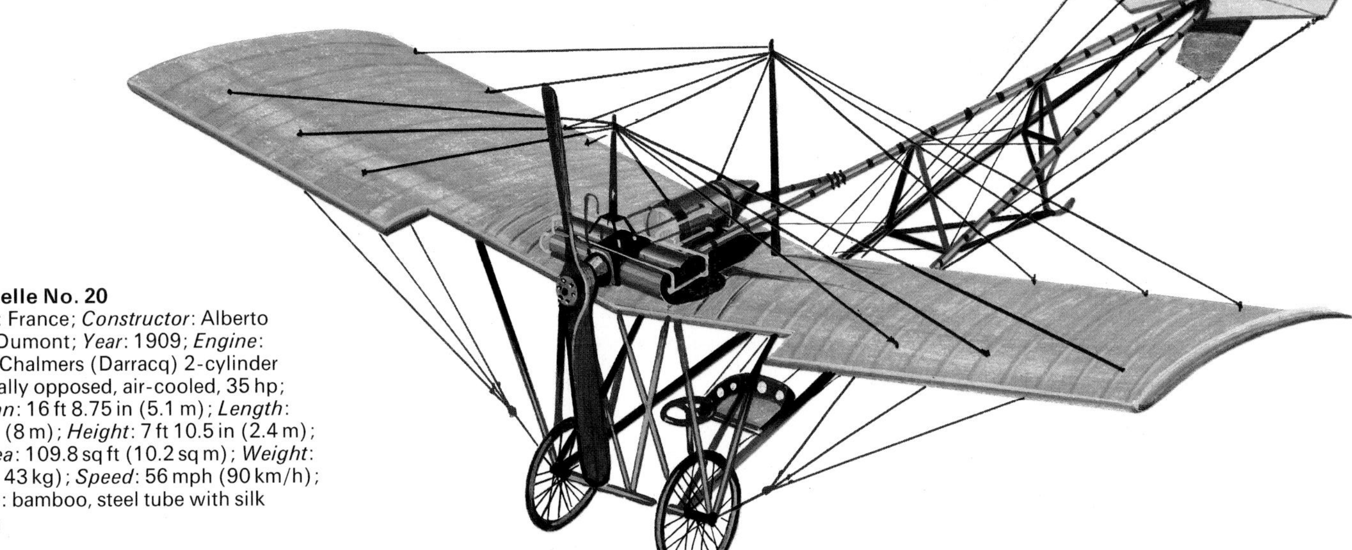

Demoiselle No. 20
Country: France; *Constructor*: Alberto Santos-Dumont; *Year*: 1909; *Engine*: Dutheil-Chalmers (Darracq) 2-cylinder horizontally opposed, air-cooled, 35 hp; *Wingspan*: 16 ft 8.75 in (5.1 m); *Length*: 26 ft 3 in (8 m); *Height*: 7 ft 10.5 in (2.4 m); *Wing area*: 109.8 sq ft (10.2 sq m); *Weight*: 315 lb (143 kg); *Speed*: 56 mph (90 km/h); *Airframe*: bamboo, steel tube with silk covering

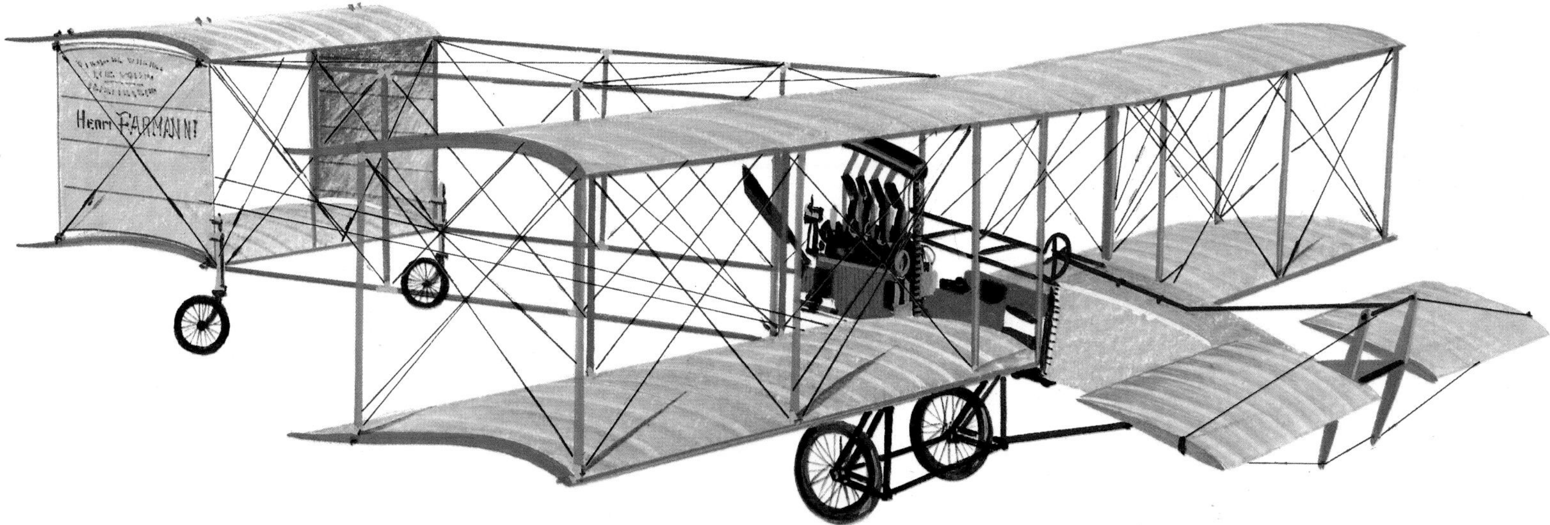

Voisin-Farman I
Country: France; *Constructor*: Voisin Frères; *Year*: 1907; *Engine*: Antoinette 8-cylinder inline V, evaporative-cooled, 50 hp; *Wingspan*: 33 ft 5.5 in (10.2 m); *Length*: 34 ft 5 in (10.5 m); *Height*: 11 ft (3.35 m); *Weight*: 1,150 lb (522 kg); *Speed*: 34 mph (55 km/h); *Airframe*: ash, steel tube with cotton covering

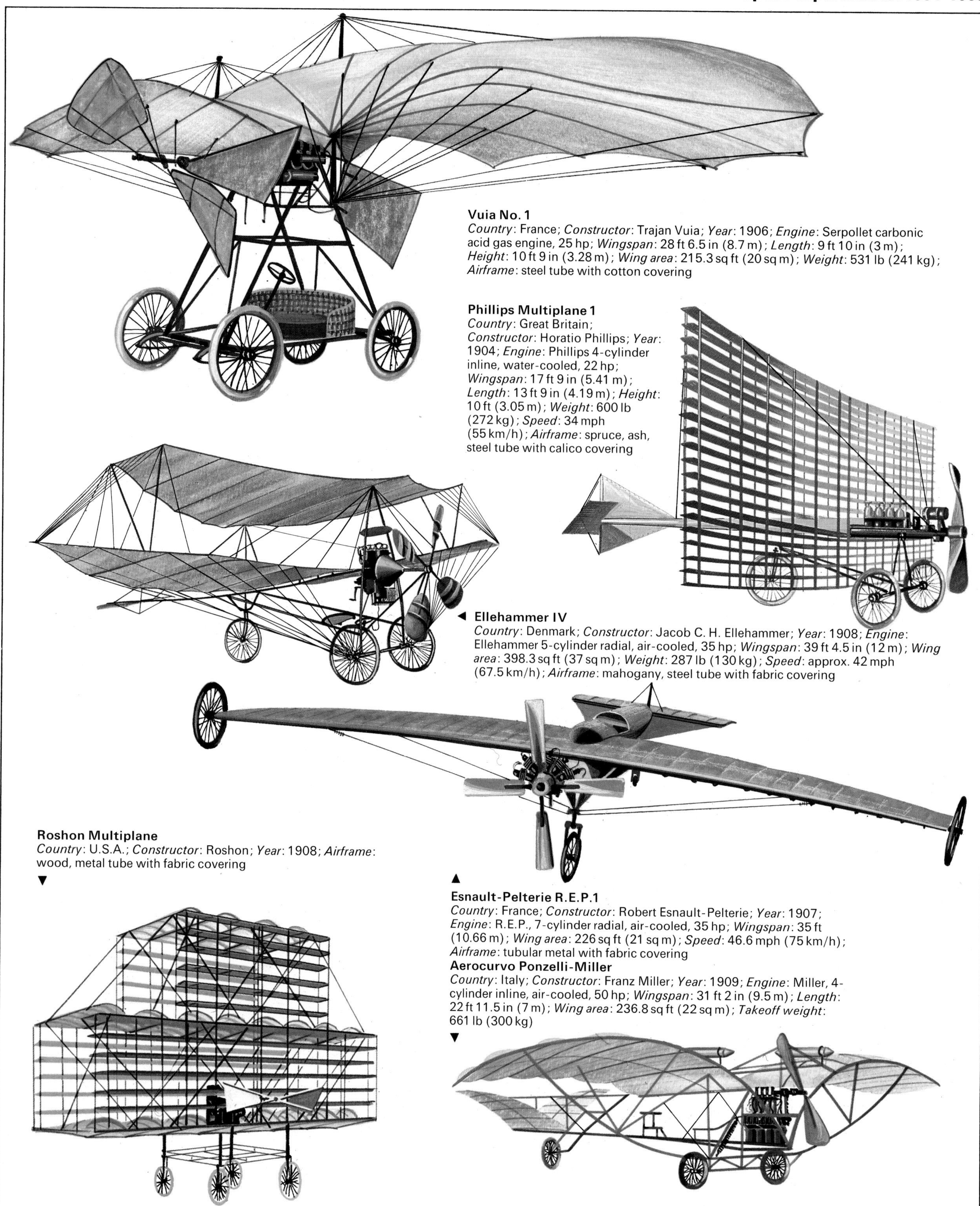

Vuia No. 1
Country: France; *Constructor*: Trajan Vuia; *Year*: 1906; *Engine*: Serpollet carbonic acid gas engine, 25 hp; *Wingspan*: 28 ft 6.5 in (8.7 m); *Length*: 9 ft 10 in (3 m); *Height*: 10 ft 9 in (3.28 m); *Wing area*: 215.3 sq ft (20 sq m); *Weight*: 531 lb (241 kg); *Airframe*: steel tube with cotton covering

Phillips Multiplane 1
Country: Great Britain; *Constructor*: Horatio Phillips; *Year*: 1904; *Engine*: Phillips 4-cylinder inline, water-cooled, 22 hp; *Wingspan*: 17 ft 9 in (5.41 m); *Length*: 13 ft 9 in (4.19 m); *Height*: 10 ft (3.05 m); *Weight*: 600 lb (272 kg); *Speed*: 34 mph (55 km/h); *Airframe*: spruce, ash, steel tube with calico covering

◀ **Ellehammer IV**
Country: Denmark; *Constructor*: Jacob C. H. Ellehammer; *Year*: 1908; *Engine*: Ellehammer 5-cylinder radial, air-cooled, 35 hp; *Wingspan*: 39 ft 4.5 in (12 m); *Wing area*: 398.3 sq ft (37 sq m); *Weight*: 287 lb (130 kg); *Speed*: approx. 42 mph (67.5 km/h); *Airframe*: mahogany, steel tube with fabric covering

Roshon Multiplane
Country: U.S.A.; *Constructor*: Roshon; *Year*: 1908; *Airframe*: wood, metal tube with fabric covering
▼

▲
Esnault-Pelterie R.E.P.1
Country: France; *Constructor*: Robert Esnault-Pelterie; *Year*: 1907; *Engine*: R.E.P., 7-cylinder radial, air-cooled, 35 hp; *Wingspan*: 35 ft (10.66 m); *Wing area*: 226 sq ft (21 sq m); *Speed*: 46.6 mph (75 km/h); *Airframe*: tubular metal with fabric covering

Aerocurvo Ponzelli-Miller
Country: Italy; *Constructor*: Franz Miller; *Year*: 1909; *Engine*: Miller, 4-cylinder inline, air-cooled, 50 hp; *Wingspan*: 31 ft 2 in (9.5 m); *Length*: 22 ft 11.5 in (7 m); *Wing area*: 236.8 sq ft (22 sq m); *Takeoff weight*: 661 lb (300 kg)
▼

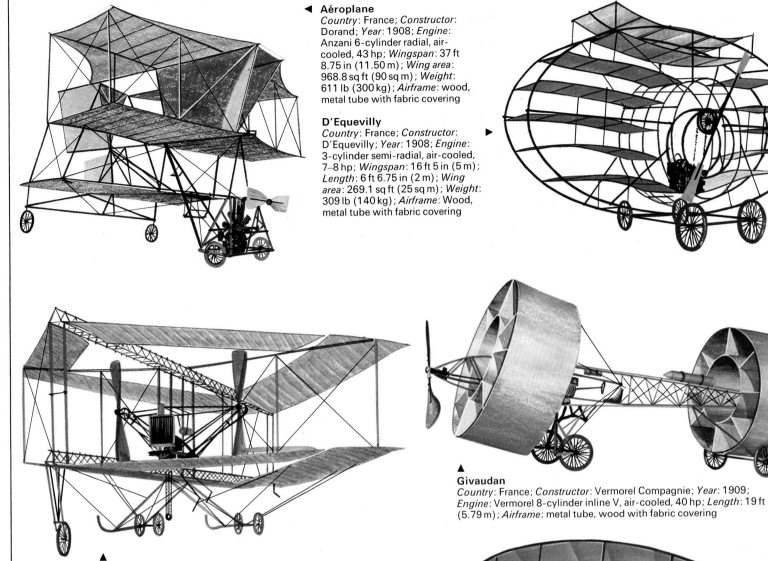

◀ **Aéroplane**
Country: France; *Constructor*: Dorand; *Year*: 1908; *Engine*: Anzani 6-cylinder radial, air-cooled, 43 hp; *Wingspan*: 37 ft 8.75 in (11.50 m); *Wing area*: 968.8 sq ft (90 sq m); *Weight*: 611 lb (300 kg); *Airframe*: wood, metal tube with fabric covering

D'Equevilly
Country: France; *Constructor*: D'Equevilly; *Year*: 1908; *Engine*: 3-cylinder semi-radial, air-cooled, 7–8 hp; *Wingspan*: 16 ft 5 in (5 m); *Length*: 6 ft 6.75 in (2 m); *Wing area*: 269.1 sq ft (25 sq m); *Weight*: 309 lb (140 kg); *Airframe*: Wood, metal tube with fabric covering ▶

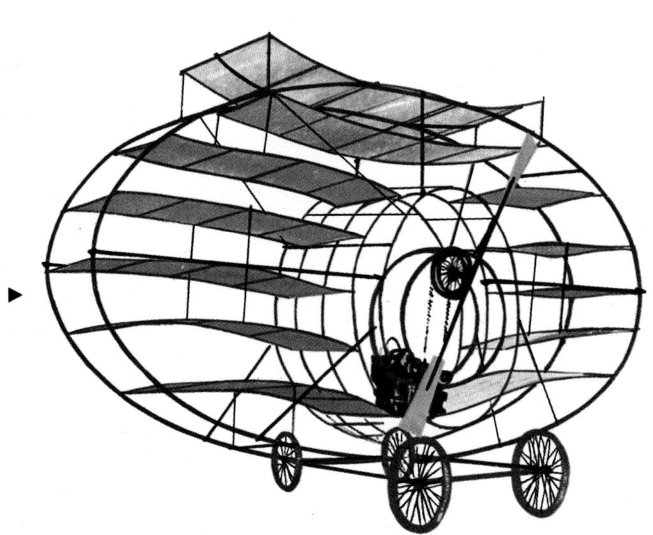

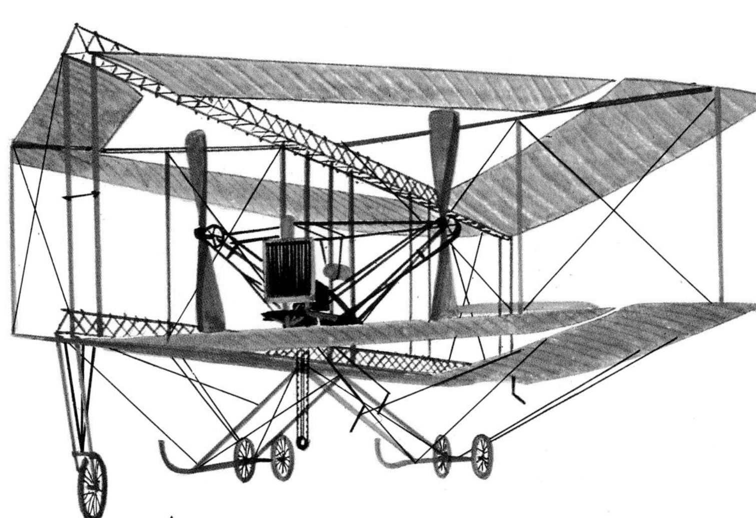

▲
Givaudan
Country: France; *Constructor*: Vermorel Compagnie; *Year*: 1909; *Engine*: Vermorel 8-cylinder inline V, air-cooled, 40 hp; *Length*: 19 ft (5.79 m); *Airframe*: metal tube, wood with fabric covering

▲
Edwards Rhomboidal
Country: Great Britain; *Constructor*: Edwards; *Year*: 1911; *Engine*: Humber 4-cylinder inline, water-cooled, 50 hp; *Wingspan*: 38 ft (11.58 m); *Length*: 48 ft (14.62 m); *Wing area*: approx. 1,200 sq ft (111.48 sq m); *Weight empty*: 1,600 lb (726 kg)

Mortimer and Vaughan Safety Biplane
Country: Great Britain; *Constructor*: Mortimer and Vaughan; *Year*: 1910; *Airframe*: wood, metal tube with fabric covering

Seddon Biplane
Country: Great Britain; *Constructor*: Accles and Pollock; *Year*: 1910; *Engines*: Two N.E.C. inline, water-cooled, 65 hp each; *Wing area*: 1,000 sq ft (93 sq m); *Weight empty*: 2,600 lb (1,178 kg); *Airframe*: steel tube with fabric covering

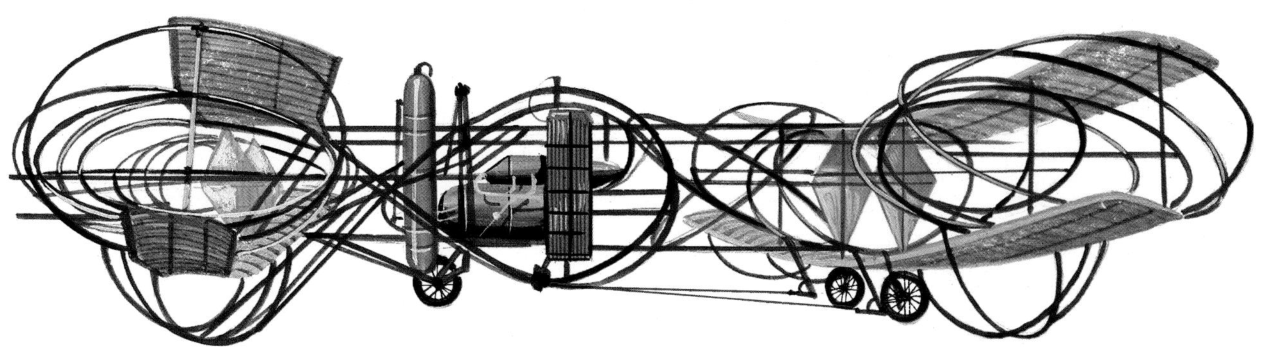

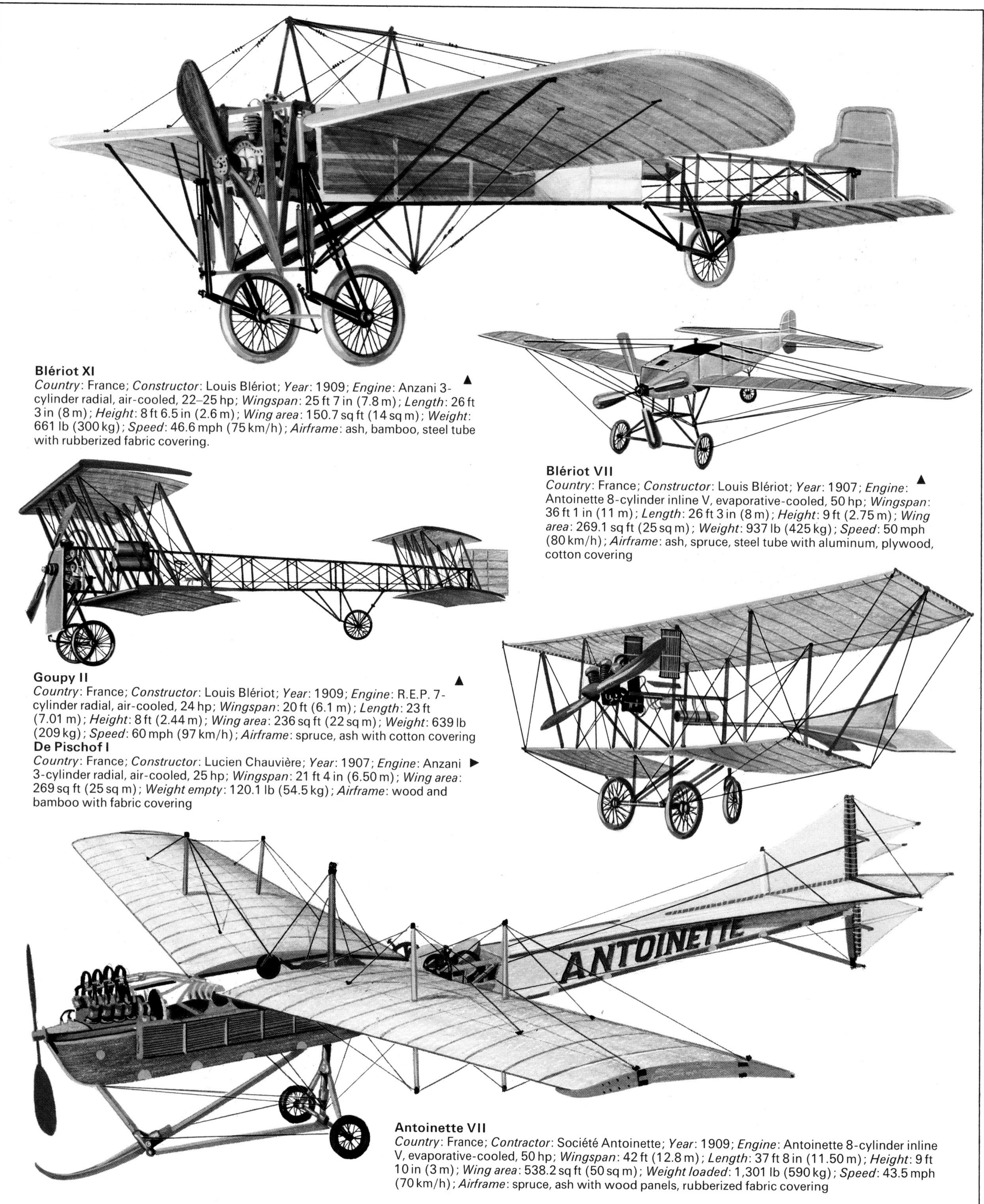

Blériot XI ▲
Country: France; *Constructor*: Louis Blériot; *Year*: 1909; *Engine*: Anzani 3-cylinder radial, air-cooled, 22–25 hp; *Wingspan*: 25 ft 7 in (7.8 m); *Length*: 26 ft 3 in (8 m); *Height*: 8 ft 6.5 in (2.6 m); *Wing area*: 150.7 sq ft (14 sq m); *Weight*: 661 lb (300 kg); *Speed*: 46.6 mph (75 km/h); *Airframe*: ash, bamboo, steel tube with rubberized fabric covering.

Blériot VII ▲
Country: France; *Constructor*: Louis Blériot; *Year*: 1907; *Engine*: Antoinette 8-cylinder inline V, evaporative-cooled, 50 hp; *Wingspan*: 36 ft 1 in (11 m); *Length*: 26 ft 3 in (8 m); *Height*: 9 ft (2.75 m); *Wing area*: 269.1 sq ft (25 sq m); *Weight*: 937 lb (425 kg); *Speed*: 50 mph (80 km/h); *Airframe*: ash, spruce, steel tube with aluminum, plywood, cotton covering

Goupy II ▲
Country: France; *Constructor*: Louis Blériot; *Year*: 1909; *Engine*: R.E.P. 7-cylinder radial, air-cooled, 24 hp; *Wingspan*: 20 ft (6.1 m); *Length*: 23 ft (7.01 m); *Height*: 8 ft (2.44 m); *Wing area*: 236 sq ft (22 sq m); *Weight*: 639 lb (209 kg); *Speed*: 60 mph (97 km/h); *Airframe*: spruce, ash with cotton covering

De Pischof I ►
Country: France; *Constructor*: Lucien Chauvière; *Year*: 1907; *Engine*: Anzani 3-cylinder radial, air-cooled, 25 hp; *Wingspan*: 21 ft 4 in (6.50 m); *Wing area*: 269 sq ft (25 sq m); *Weight empty*: 120.1 lb (54.5 kg); *Airframe*: wood and bamboo with fabric covering

Antoinette VII
Country: France; *Contractor*: Société Antoinette; *Year*: 1909; *Engine*: Antoinette 8-cylinder inline V, evaporative-cooled, 50 hp; *Wingspan*: 42 ft (12.8 m); *Length*: 37 ft 8 in (11.50 m); *Height*: 9 ft 10 in (3 m); *Wing area*: 538.2 sq ft (50 sq m); *Weight loaded*: 1,301 lb (590 kg); *Speed*: 43.5 mph (70 km/h); *Airframe*: spruce, ash with wood panels, rubberized fabric covering

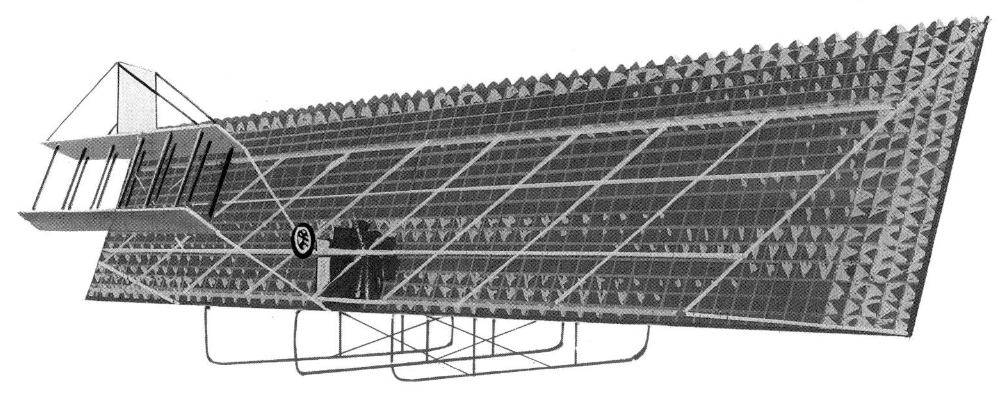

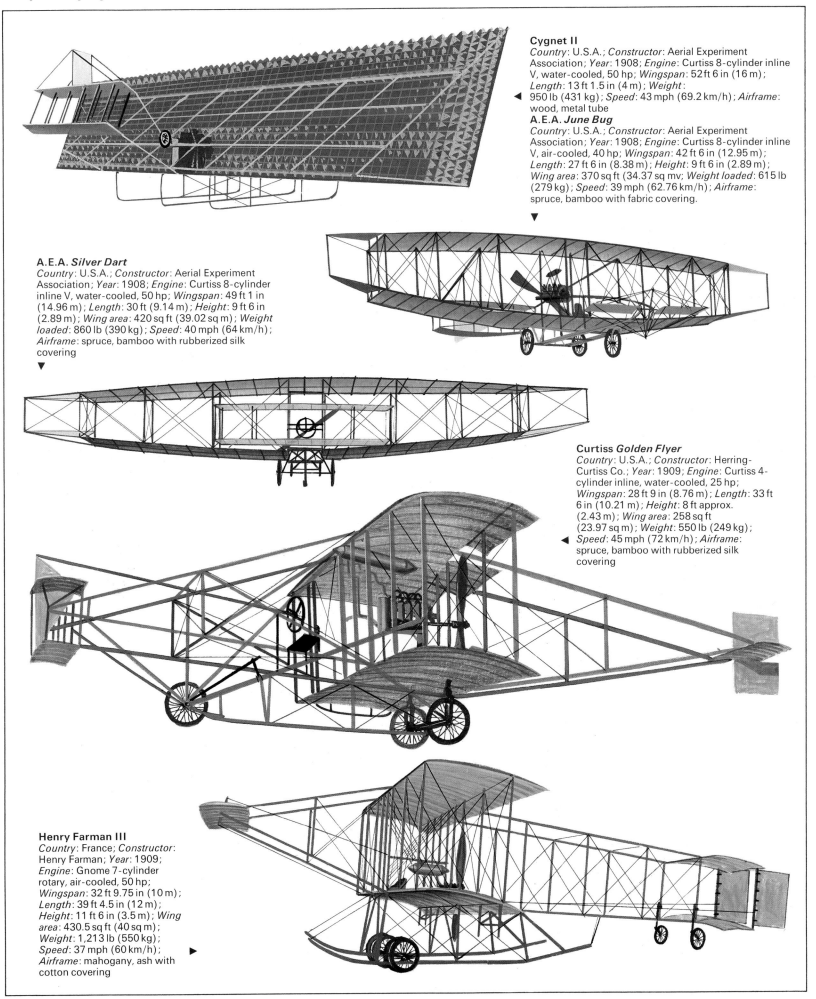

Cygnet II
Country: U.S.A.; *Constructor*: Aerial Experiment Association; *Year*: 1908; *Engine*: Curtiss 8-cylinder inline V, water-cooled, 50 hp; *Wingspan*: 52 ft 6 in (16 m); *Length*: 13 ft 1.5 in (4 m); *Weight*: ◄ 950 lb (431 kg); *Speed*: 43 mph (69.2 km/h); *Airframe*: wood, metal tube

A.E.A. *June Bug*
Country: U.S.A.; *Constructor*: Aerial Experiment Association; *Year*: 1908; *Engine*: Curtiss 8-cylinder inline V, air-cooled, 40 hp; *Wingspan*: 42 ft 6 in (12.95 m); *Length*: 27 ft 6 in (8.38 m); *Height*: 9 ft 6 in (2.89 m); *Wing area*: 370 sq ft (34.37 sq mv; *Weight loaded*: 615 lb (279 kg); *Speed*: 39 mph (62.76 km/h); *Airframe*: spruce, bamboo with fabric covering.
▼

A.E.A. *Silver Dart*
Country: U.S.A.; *Constructor*: Aerial Experiment Association; *Year*: 1908; *Engine*: Curtiss 8-cylinder inline V, water-cooled, 50 hp; *Wingspan*: 49 ft 1 in (14.96 m); *Length*: 30 ft (9.14 m); *Height*: 9 ft 6 in (2.89 m); *Wing area*: 420 sq ft (39.02 sq m); *Weight loaded*: 860 lb (390 kg); *Speed*: 40 mph (64 km/h); *Airframe*: spruce, bamboo with rubberized silk covering
▼

Curtiss *Golden Flyer*
Country: U.S.A.; *Constructor*: Herring-Curtiss Co.; *Year*: 1909; *Engine*: Curtiss 4-cylinder inline, water-cooled, 25 hp; *Wingspan*: 28 ft 9 in (8.76 m); *Length*: 33 ft 6 in (10.21 m); *Height*: 8 ft approx. (2.43 m); *Wing area*: 258 sq ft (23.97 sq m); *Weight*: 550 lb (249 kg); ◄ *Speed*: 45 mph (72 km/h); *Airframe*: spruce, bamboo with rubberized silk covering

Henry Farman III
Country: France; *Constructor*: Henry Farman; *Year*: 1909; *Engine*: Gnome 7-cylinder rotary, air-cooled, 50 hp; *Wingspan*: 32 ft 9.75 in (10 m); *Length*: 39 ft 4.5 in (12 m); *Height*: 11 ft 6 in (3.5 m); *Wing area*: 430.5 sq ft (40 sq m); *Weight*: 1,213 lb (550 kg); *Speed*: 37 mph (60 km/h); ► *Airframe*: mahogany, ash with cotton covering

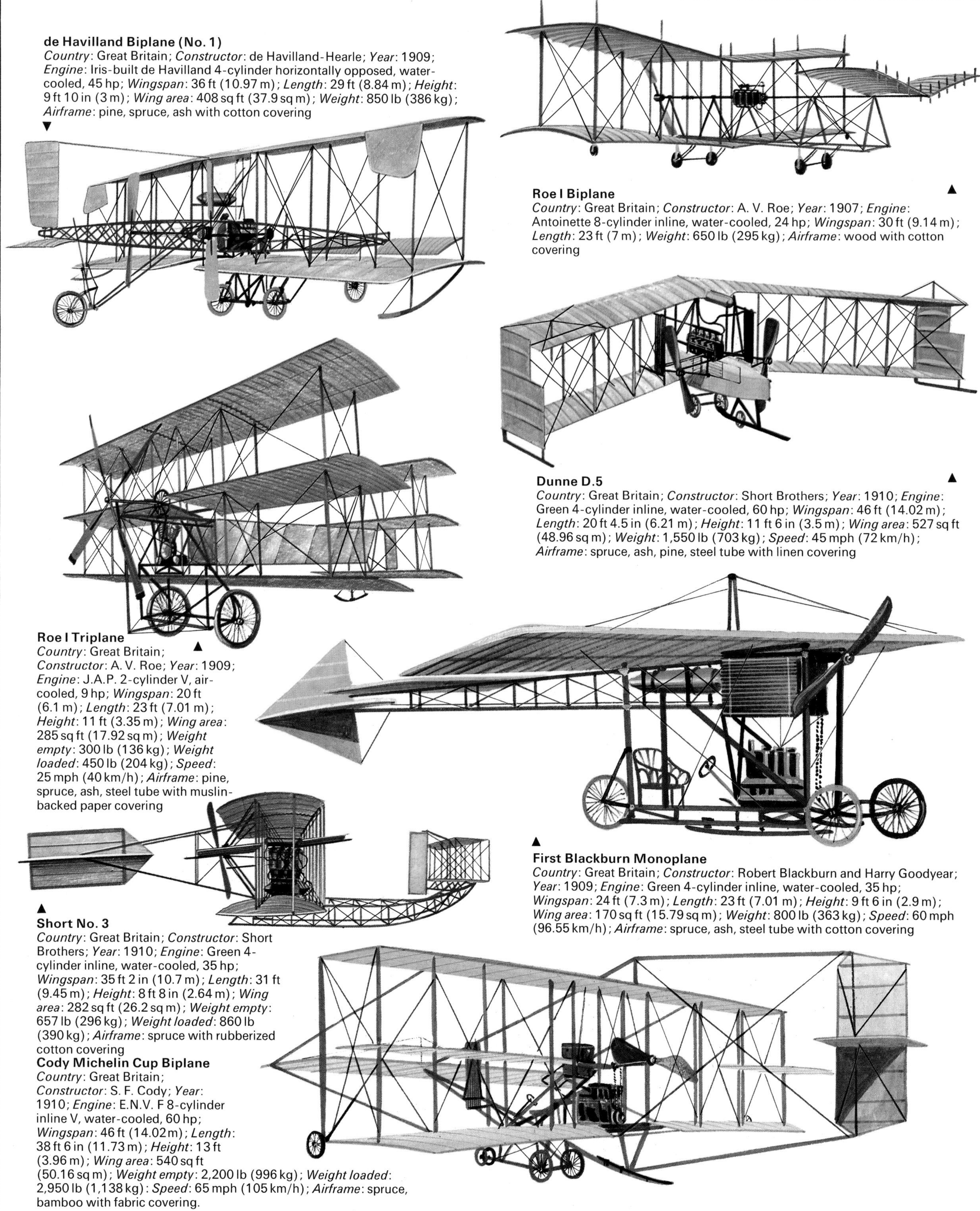

de Havilland Biplane (No. 1)
Country: Great Britain; *Constructor*: de Havilland-Hearle; *Year*: 1909; *Engine*: Iris-built de Havilland 4-cylinder horizontally opposed, water-cooled, 45 hp; *Wingspan*: 36 ft (10.97 m); *Length*: 29 ft (8.84 m); *Height*: 9 ft 10 in (3 m); *Wing area*: 408 sq ft (37.9 sq m); *Weight*: 850 lb (386 kg); *Airframe*: pine, spruce, ash with cotton covering

Roe I Biplane
Country: Great Britain; *Constructor*: A. V. Roe; *Year*: 1907; *Engine*: Antoinette 8-cylinder inline, water-cooled, 24 hp; *Wingspan*: 30 ft (9.14 m); *Length*: 23 ft (7 m); *Weight*: 650 lb (295 kg); *Airframe*: wood with cotton covering

Dunne D.5
Country: Great Britain; *Constructor*: Short Brothers; *Year*: 1910; *Engine*: Green 4-cylinder inline, water-cooled, 60 hp; *Wingspan*: 46 ft (14.02 m); *Length*: 20 ft 4.5 in (6.21 m); *Height*: 11 ft 6 in (3.5 m); *Wing area*: 527 sq ft (48.96 sq m); *Weight*: 1,550 lb (703 kg); *Speed*: 45 mph (72 km/h); *Airframe*: spruce, ash, pine, steel tube with linen covering

Roe I Triplane
Country: Great Britain; *Constructor*: A. V. Roe; *Year*: 1909; *Engine*: J.A.P. 2-cylinder V, air-cooled, 9 hp; *Wingspan*: 20 ft (6.1 m); *Length*: 23 ft (7.01 m); *Height*: 11 ft (3.35 m); *Wing area*: 285 sq ft (17.92 sq m); *Weight empty*: 300 lb (136 kg); *Weight loaded*: 450 lb (204 kg); *Speed*: 25 mph (40 km/h); *Airframe*: pine, spruce, ash, steel tube with muslin-backed paper covering

First Blackburn Monoplane
Country: Great Britain; *Constructor*: Robert Blackburn and Harry Goodyear; *Year*: 1909; *Engine*: Green 4-cylinder inline, water-cooled, 35 hp; *Wingspan*: 24 ft (7.3 m); *Length*: 23 ft (7.01 m); *Height*: 9 ft 6 in (2.9 m); *Wing area*: 170 sq ft (15.79 sq m); *Weight*: 800 lb (363 kg); *Speed*: 60 mph (96.55 km/h); *Airframe*: spruce, ash, steel tube with cotton covering

Short No. 3
Country: Great Britain; *Constructor*: Short Brothers; *Year*: 1910; *Engine*: Green 4-cylinder inline, water-cooled, 35 hp; *Wingspan*: 35 ft 2 in (10.7 m); *Length*: 31 ft (9.45 m); *Height*: 8 ft 8 in (2.64 m); *Wing area*: 282 sq ft (26.2 sq m); *Weight empty*: 657 lb (296 kg); *Weight loaded*: 860 lb (390 kg); *Airframe*: spruce with rubberized cotton covering

Cody Michelin Cup Biplane
Country: Great Britain; *Constructor*: S. F. Cody; *Year*: 1910; *Engine*: E.N.V. F 8-cylinder inline V, water-cooled, 60 hp; *Wingspan*: 46 ft (14.02 m); *Length*: 38 ft 6 in (11.73 m); *Height*: 13 ft (3.96 m); *Wing area*: 540 sq ft (50.16 sq m); *Weight empty*: 2,200 lb (996 kg); *Weight loaded*: 2,950 lb (1,138 kg): *Speed*: 65 mph (105 km/h); *Airframe*: spruce, bamboo with fabric covering.

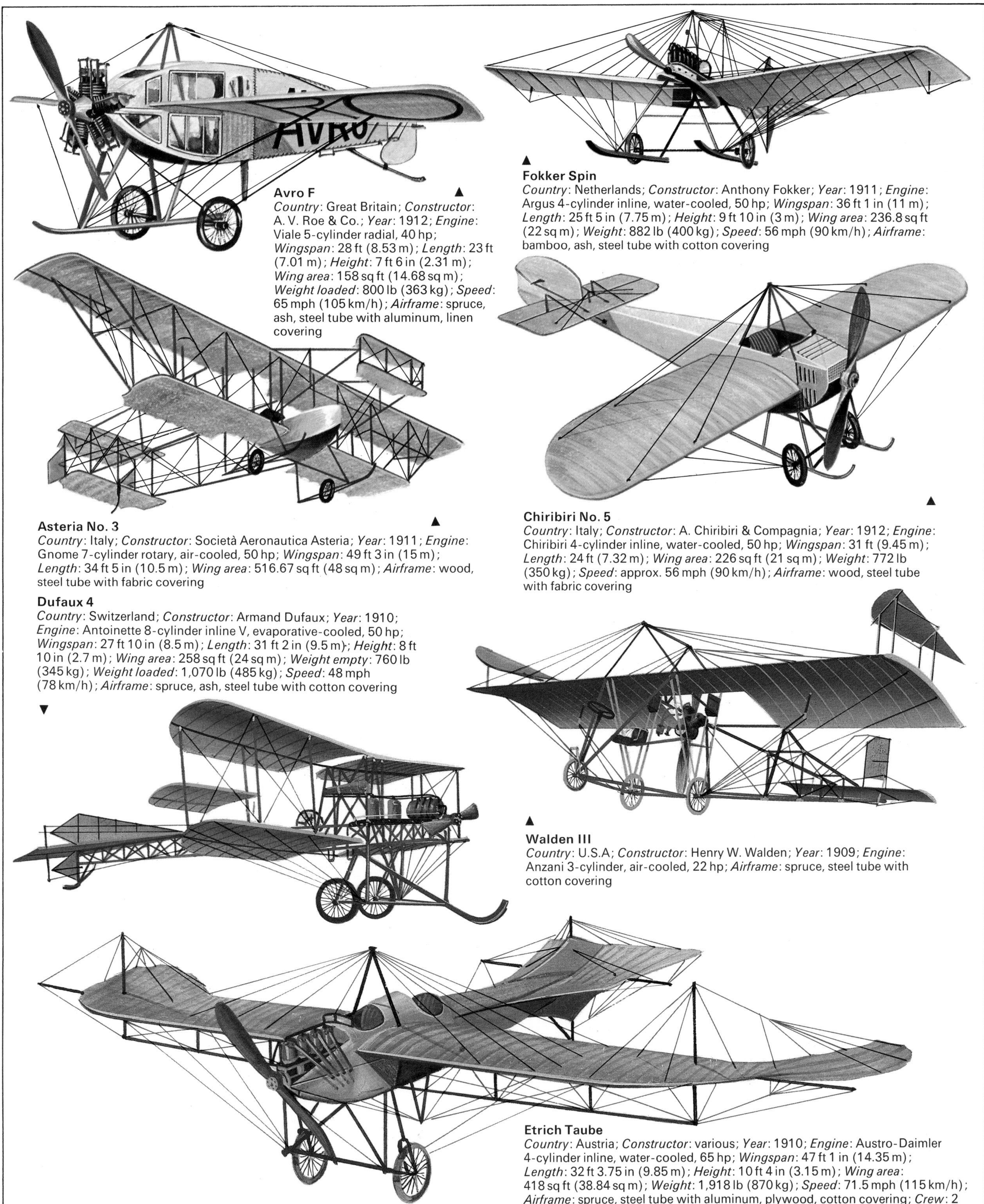

Avro F ▲
Country: Great Britain; *Constructor*: A. V. Roe & Co.; *Year*: 1912; *Engine*: Viale 5-cylinder radial, 40 hp; *Wingspan*: 28 ft (8.53 m); *Length*: 23 ft (7.01 m); *Height*: 7 ft 6 in (2.31 m); *Wing area*: 158 sq ft (14.68 sq m); *Weight loaded*: 800 lb (363 kg); *Speed*: 65 mph (105 km/h); *Airframe*: spruce, ash, steel tube with aluminum, linen covering

▲
Fokker Spin
Country: Netherlands; *Constructor*: Anthony Fokker; *Year*: 1911; *Engine*: Argus 4-cylinder inline, water-cooled, 50 hp; *Wingspan*: 36 ft 1 in (11 m); *Length*: 25 ft 5 in (7.75 m); *Height*: 9 ft 10 in (3 m); *Wing area*: 236.8 sq ft (22 sq m); *Weight*: 882 lb (400 kg); *Speed*: 56 mph (90 km/h); *Airframe*: bamboo, ash, steel tube with cotton covering

Asteria No. 3 ▲
Country: Italy; *Constructor*: Società Aeronautica Asteria; *Year*: 1911; *Engine*: Gnome 7-cylinder rotary, air-cooled, 50 hp; *Wingspan*: 49 ft 3 in (15 m); *Length*: 34 ft 5 in (10.5 m); *Wing area*: 516.67 sq ft (48 sq m); *Airframe*: wood, steel tube with fabric covering

▲
Chiribiri No. 5
Country: Italy; *Constructor*: A. Chiribiri & Compagnia; *Year*: 1912; *Engine*: Chiribiri 4-cylinder inline, water-cooled, 50 hp; *Wingspan*: 31 ft (9.45 m); *Length*: 24 ft (7.32 m); *Wing area*: 226 sq ft (21 sq m); *Weight*: 772 lb (350 kg); *Speed*: approx. 56 mph (90 km/h); *Airframe*: wood, steel tube with fabric covering

Dufaux 4
Country: Switzerland; *Constructor*: Armand Dufaux; *Year*: 1910; *Engine*: Antoinette 8-cylinder inline V, evaporative-cooled, 50 hp; *Wingspan*: 27 ft 10 in (8.5 m); *Length*: 31 ft 2 in (9.5 m); *Height*: 8 ft 10 in (2.7 m); *Wing area*: 258 sq ft (24 sq m); *Weight empty*: 760 lb (345 kg); *Weight loaded*: 1,070 lb (485 kg); *Speed*: 48 mph (78 km/h); *Airframe*: spruce, ash, steel tube with cotton covering
▼

▲
Walden III
Country: U.S.A; *Constructor*: Henry W. Walden; *Year*: 1909; *Engine*: Anzani 3-cylinder, air-cooled, 22 hp; *Airframe*: spruce, steel tube with cotton covering

Etrich Taube
Country: Austria; *Constructor*: various; *Year*: 1910; *Engine*: Austro-Daimler 4-cylinder inline, water-cooled, 65 hp; *Wingspan*: 47 ft 1 in (14.35 m); *Length*: 32 ft 3.75 in (9.85 m); *Height*: 10 ft 4 in (3.15 m); *Wing area*: 418 sq ft (38.84 sq m); *Weight*: 1,918 lb (870 kg); *Speed*: 71.5 mph (115 km/h); *Airframe*: spruce, steel tube with aluminum, plywood, cotton covering; *Crew*: 2

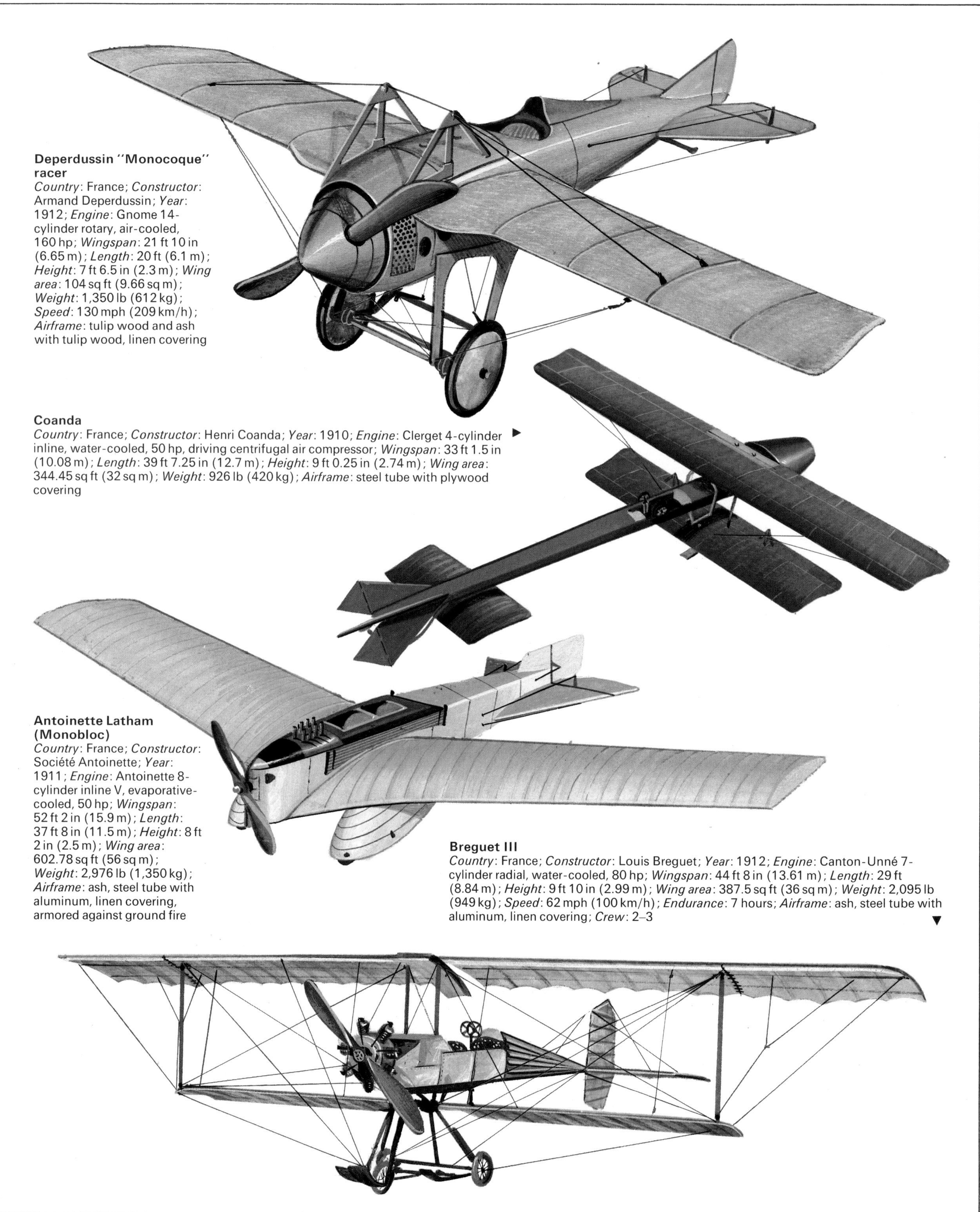

Deperdussin "Monocoque" racer
Country: France; *Constructor*: Armand Deperdussin; *Year*: 1912; *Engine*: Gnome 14-cylinder rotary, air-cooled, 160 hp; *Wingspan*: 21 ft 10 in (6.65 m); *Length*: 20 ft (6.1 m); *Height*: 7 ft 6.5 in (2.3 m); *Wing area*: 104 sq ft (9.66 sq m); *Weight*: 1,350 lb (612 kg); *Speed*: 130 mph (209 km/h); *Airframe*: tulip wood and ash with tulip wood, linen covering

Coanda
Country: France; *Constructor*: Henri Coanda; *Year*: 1910; *Engine*: Clerget 4-cylinder inline, water-cooled, 50 hp, driving centrifugal air compressor; *Wingspan*: 33 ft 1.5 in (10.08 m); *Length*: 39 ft 7.25 in (12.7 m); *Height*: 9 ft 0.25 in (2.74 m); *Wing area*: 344.45 sq ft (32 sq m); *Weight*: 926 lb (420 kg); *Airframe*: steel tube with plywood covering ▶

Antoinette Latham (Monobloc)
Country: France; *Constructor*: Société Antoinette; *Year*: 1911; *Engine*: Antoinette 8-cylinder inline V, evaporative-cooled, 50 hp; *Wingspan*: 52 ft 2 in (15.9 m); *Length*: 37 ft 8 in (11.5 m); *Height*: 8 ft 2 in (2.5 m); *Wing area*: 602.78 sq ft (56 sq m); *Weight*: 2,976 lb (1,350 kg); *Airframe*: ash, steel tube with aluminum, linen covering, armored against ground fire

Breguet III
Country: France; *Constructor*: Louis Breguet; *Year*: 1912; *Engine*: Canton-Unné 7-cylinder radial, water-cooled, 80 hp; *Wingspan*: 44 ft 8 in (13.61 m); *Length*: 29 ft (8.84 m); *Height*: 9 ft 10 in (2.99 m); *Wing area*: 387.5 sq ft (36 sq m); *Weight*: 2,095 lb (949 kg); *Speed*: 62 mph (100 km/h); *Endurance*: 7 hours; *Airframe*: ash, steel tube with aluminum, linen covering; *Crew*: 2–3 ▼

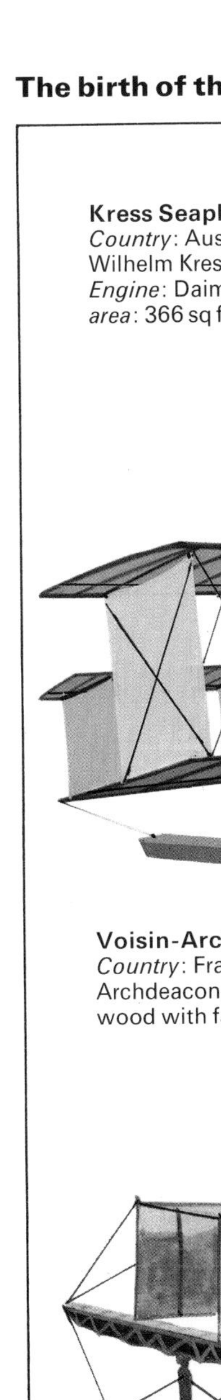

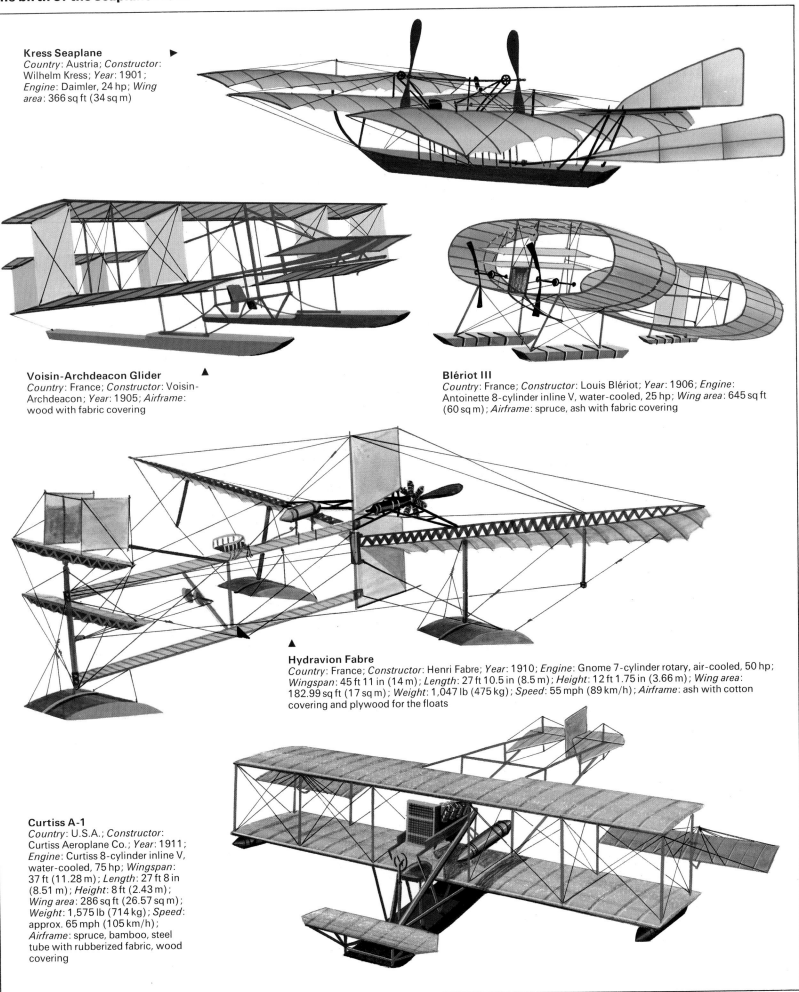

Kress Seaplane ▶
Country: Austria; *Constructor*: Wilhelm Kress; *Year*: 1901; *Engine*: Daimler, 24 hp; *Wing area*: 366 sq ft (34 sq m)

Voisin-Archdeacon Glider ▲
Country: France; *Constructor*: Voisin-Archdeacon; *Year*: 1905; *Airframe*: wood with fabric covering

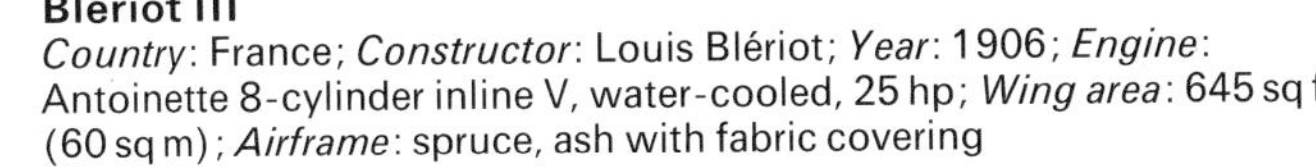

Blériot III
Country: France; *Constructor*: Louis Blériot; *Year*: 1906; *Engine*: Antoinette 8-cylinder inline V, water-cooled, 25 hp; *Wing area*: 645 sq ft (60 sq m); *Airframe*: spruce, ash with fabric covering

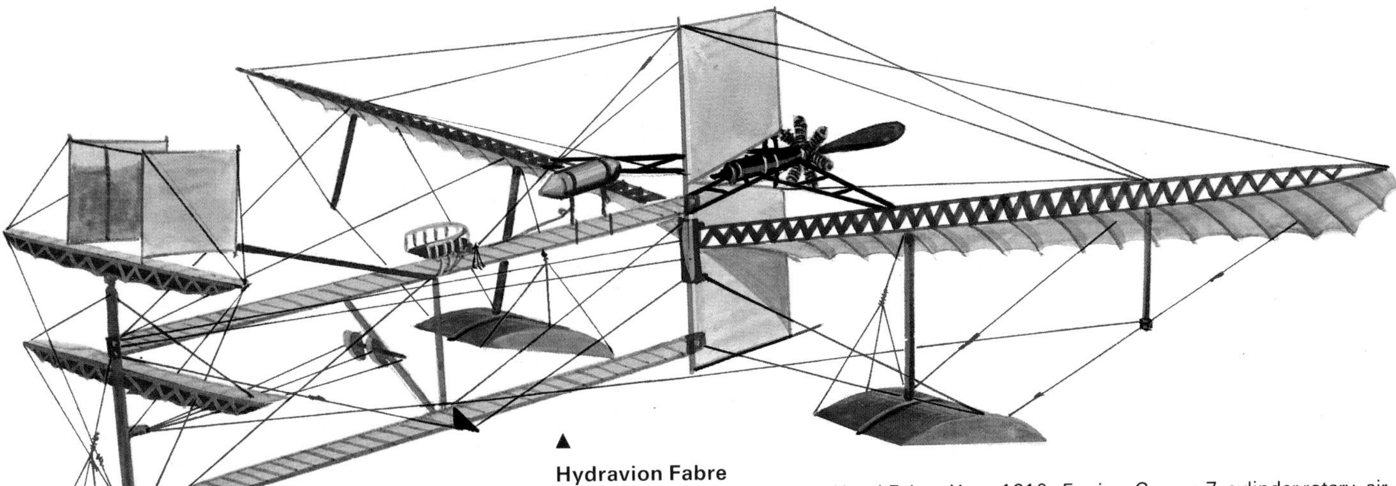

▲
Hydravion Fabre
Country: France; *Constructor*: Henri Fabre; *Year*: 1910; *Engine*: Gnome 7-cylinder rotary, air-cooled, 50 hp; *Wingspan*: 45 ft 11 in (14 m); *Length*: 27 ft 10.5 in (8.5 m); *Height*: 12 ft 1.75 in (3.66 m); *Wing area*: 182.99 sq ft (17 sq m); *Weight*: 1,047 lb (475 kg); *Speed*: 55 mph (89 km/h); *Airframe*: ash with cotton covering and plywood for the floats

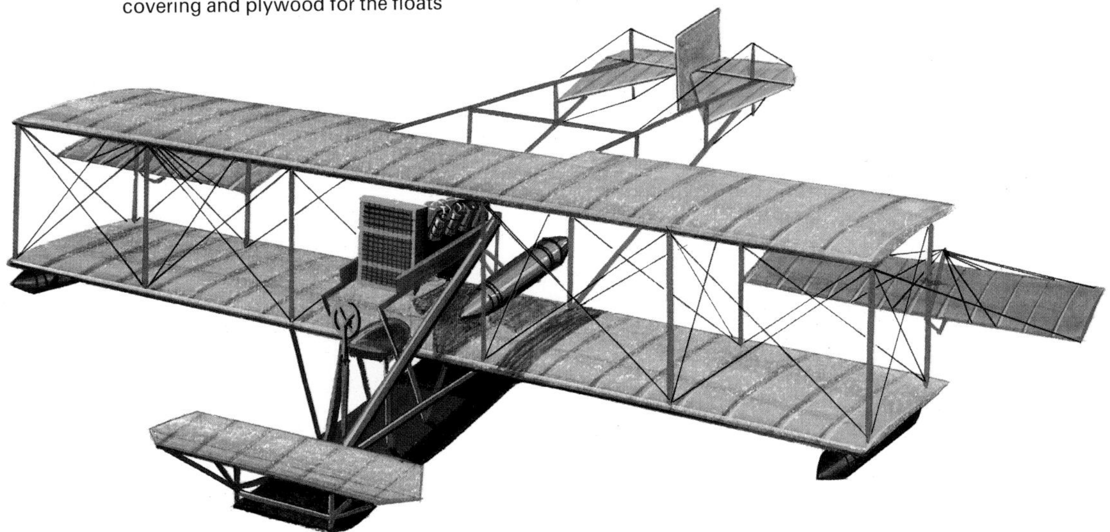

Curtiss A-1
Country: U.S.A.; *Constructor*: Curtiss Aeroplane Co.; *Year*: 1911; *Engine*: Curtiss 8-cylinder inline V, water-cooled, 75 hp; *Wingspan*: 37 ft (11.28 m); *Length*: 27 ft 8 in (8.51 m); *Height*: 8 ft (2.43 m); *Wing area*: 286 sq ft (26.57 sq m); *Weight*: 1,575 lb (714 kg); *Speed*: approx. 65 mph (105 km/h); *Airframe*: spruce, bamboo, steel tube with rubberized fabric, wood covering

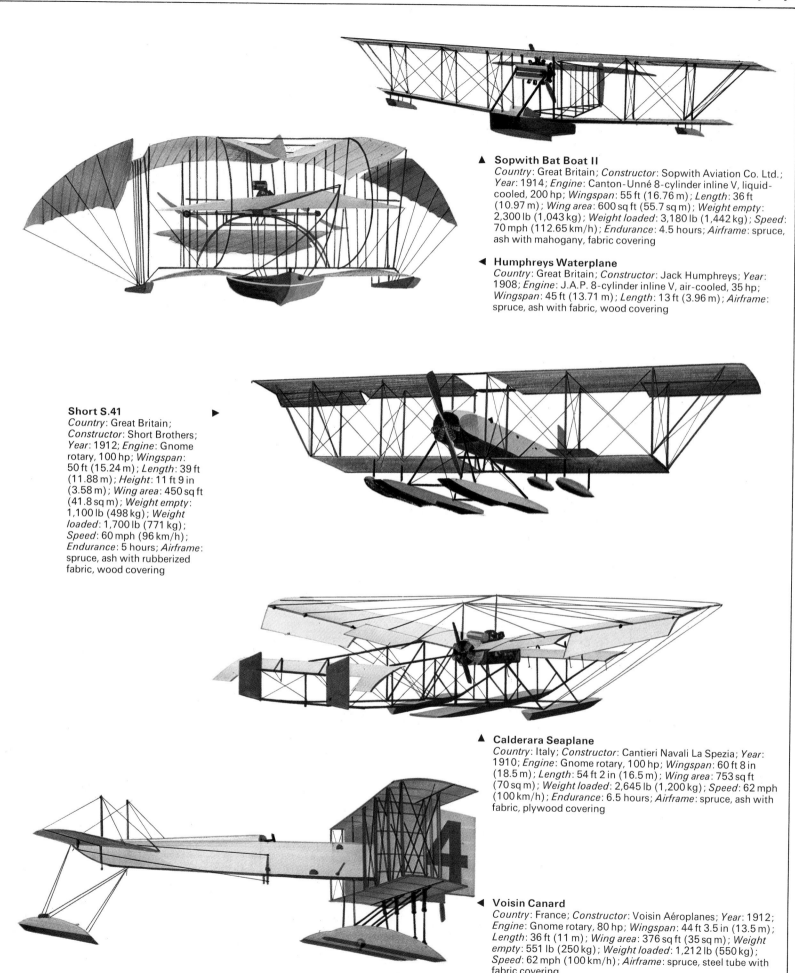

▲ **Sopwith Bat Boat II**
Country: Great Britain; *Constructor*: Sopwith Aviation Co. Ltd.; *Year*: 1914; *Engine*: Canton-Unné 8-cylinder inline V, liquid-cooled, 200 hp; *Wingspan*: 55 ft (16.76 m); *Length*: 36 ft (10.97 m); *Wing area*: 600 sq ft (55.7 sq m); *Weight empty*: 2,300 lb (1,043 kg); *Weight loaded*: 3,180 lb (1,442 kg); *Speed*: 70 mph (112.65 km/h); *Endurance*: 4.5 hours; *Airframe*: spruce, ash with mahogany, fabric covering

◀ **Humphreys Waterplane**
Country: Great Britain; *Constructor*: Jack Humphreys; *Year*: 1908; *Engine*: J.A.P. 8-cylinder inline V, air-cooled, 35 hp; *Wingspan*: 45 ft (13.71 m); *Length*: 13 ft (3.96 m); *Airframe*: spruce, ash with fabric, wood covering

Short S.41 ▶
Country: Great Britain; *Constructor*: Short Brothers; *Year*: 1912; *Engine*: Gnome rotary, 100 hp; *Wingspan*: 50 ft (15.24 m); *Length*: 39 ft (11.88 m); *Height*: 11 ft 9 in (3.58 m); *Wing area*: 450 sq ft (41.8 sq m); *Weight empty*: 1,100 lb (498 kg); *Weight loaded*: 1,700 lb (771 kg); *Speed*: 60 mph (96 km/h); *Endurance*: 5 hours; *Airframe*: spruce, ash with rubberized fabric, wood covering

▲ **Calderara Seaplane**
Country: Italy; *Constructor*: Cantieri Navali La Spezia; *Year*: 1910; *Engine*: Gnome rotary, 100 hp; *Wingspan*: 60 ft 8 in (18.5 m); *Length*: 54 ft 2 in (16.5 m); *Wing area*: 753 sq ft (70 sq m); *Weight loaded*: 2,645 lb (1,200 kg); *Speed*: 62 mph (100 km/h); *Endurance*: 6.5 hours; *Airframe*: spruce, ash with fabric, plywood covering

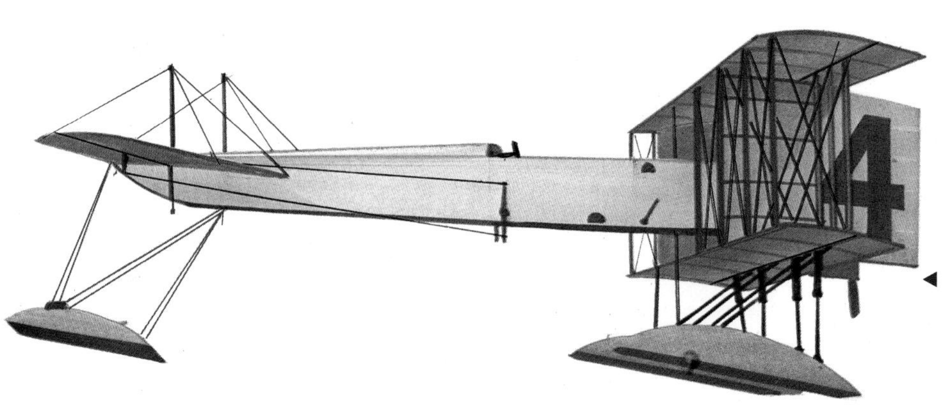

◀ **Voisin Canard**
Country: France; *Constructor*: Voisin Aéroplanes; *Year*: 1912; *Engine*: Gnome rotary, 80 hp; *Wingspan*: 44 ft 3.5 in (13.5 m); *Length*: 36 ft (11 m); *Wing area*: 376 sq ft (35 sq m); *Weight empty*: 551 lb (250 kg); *Weight loaded*: 1,212 lb (550 kg); *Speed*: 62 mph (100 km/h); *Airframe*: spruce, steel tube with fabric covering

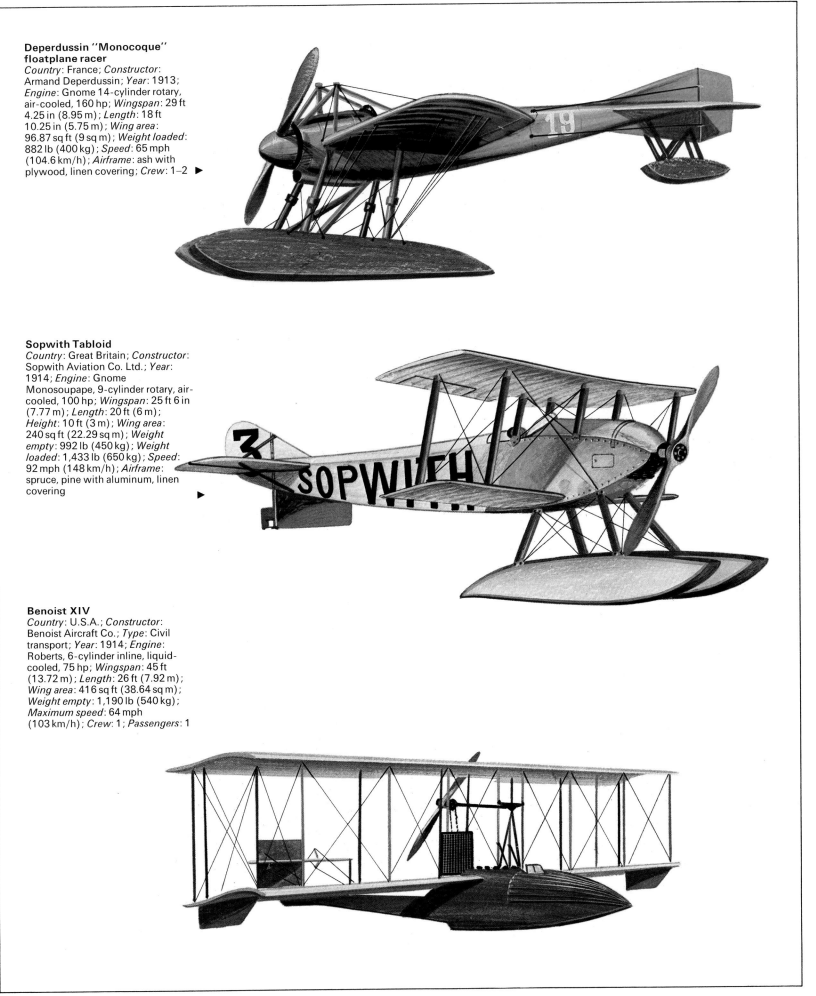

Deperdussin "Monocoque" floatplane racer
Country: France; *Constructor*: Armand Deperdussin; *Year*: 1913; *Engine*: Gnome 14-cylinder rotary, air-cooled, 160 hp; *Wingspan*: 29 ft 4.25 in (8.95 m); *Length*: 18 ft 10.25 in (5.75 m); *Wing area*: 96.87 sq ft (9 sq m); *Weight loaded*: 882 lb (400 kg); *Speed*: 65 mph (104.6 km/h); *Airframe*: ash with plywood, linen covering; *Crew*: 1–2 ▶

Sopwith Tabloid
Country: Great Britain; *Constructor*: Sopwith Aviation Co. Ltd.; *Year*: 1914; *Engine*: Gnome Monosoupape, 9-cylinder rotary, air-cooled, 100 hp; *Wingspan*: 25 ft 6 in (7.77 m); *Length*: 20 ft (6 m); *Height*: 10 ft (3 m); *Wing area*: 240 sq ft (22.29 sq m); *Weight empty*: 992 lb (450 kg); *Weight loaded*: 1,433 lb (650 kg); *Speed*: 92 mph (148 km/h); *Airframe*: spruce, pine with aluminum, linen covering ▶

Benoist XIV
Country: U.S.A.; *Constructor*: Benoist Aircraft Co.; *Type*: Civil transport; *Year*: 1914; *Engine*: Roberts, 6-cylinder inline, liquid-cooled, 75 hp; *Wingspan*: 45 ft (13.72 m); *Length*: 26 ft (7.92 m); *Wing area*: 416 sq ft (38.64 sq m); *Weight empty*: 1,190 lb (540 kg); *Maximum speed*: 64 mph (103 km/h); *Crew*: 1; *Passengers*: 1

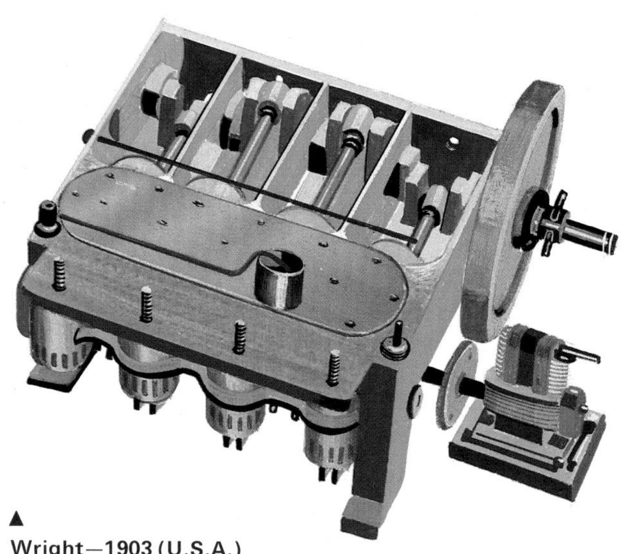

▲
Wright—1903 (U.S.A.)
The first engine to be installed successfully in an airplane: designed and built by the Wright brothers it was fitted to their 1903 Flyer. It was a 4-cylinder inline, water-cooled, 12-hp engine

Antoinette—1906 (F)
The most widely used engine in Europe up until 1909–10. Designed by Léon Levavasseur it was an 8-cylinder V, vapor-cooled, direct injection engine capable of producing 50 hp ▶

Anzani—1909 (F)
Louis Blériot used this engine in the first flight across the English Channel in 1909. It was a semi-radial, 3-cylinder, air-cooled engine producing 25 hp at 1,600 rpm

Gnome 50 HP—1909 (F)
This revolutionary engine marked a turning point in aviation history. Designed by the Seguin brothers it was an air-cooled rotary, 50-hp engine and was the first of a long series

Curtiss—1909 (U.S.A.)
Designed by Glenn Hammond Curtiss, this V-8 was first installed in the biplane the Reims Racer, one of the competitors in the 1909 Reims race. It was a water-cooled, 50-hp engine

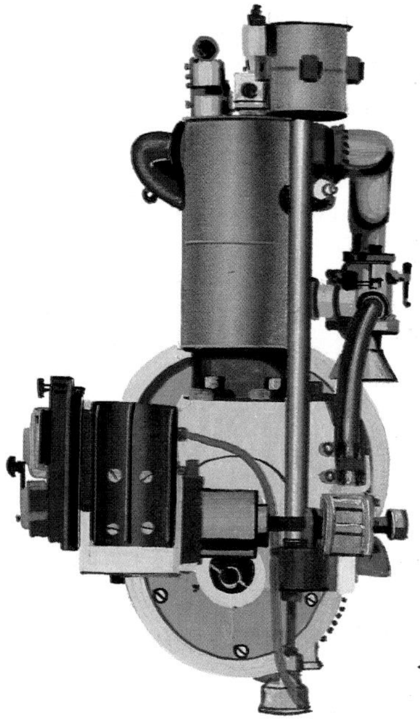

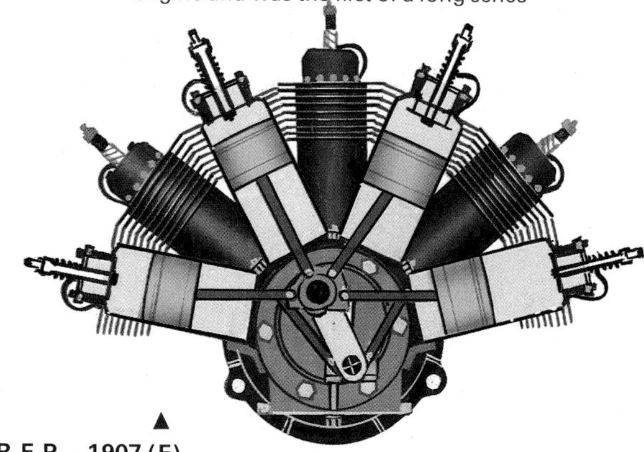

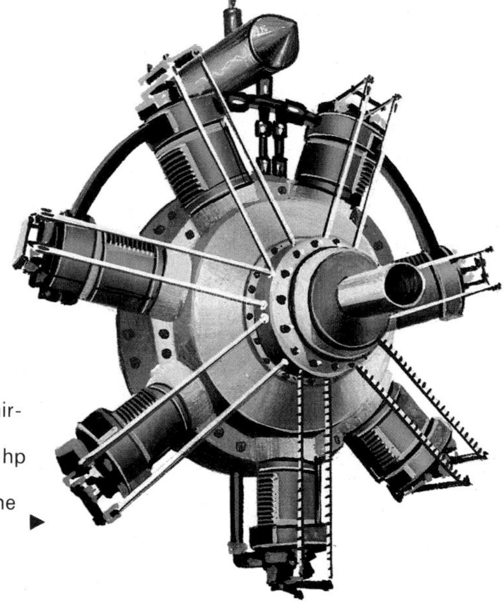

▲
R.E.P.—1907 (F)
Designed by Robert Esnault-Pelterie, this semi-radial, 7-cylinder, air-cooled engine was installed in all three of the aircraft this French pioneer built between 1907 and 1909. The basic version was of 30 hp

Canton-Unné—1910 (F)
At a time when rotary engines were predominant, this was one of the few stationary radials. This 7-cylinder engine was water-cooled, which was unusual. Initially it gave 60 hp ▶

◀ **Green—1909 (G.B.)**
One of the best-known British airplane engines in the pioneering days, it was a 4-cylinder inline, water-cooled engine, of 35 hp in the first version. Later the power was doubled

Plate 18
The Wright Brothers: 1903–1910

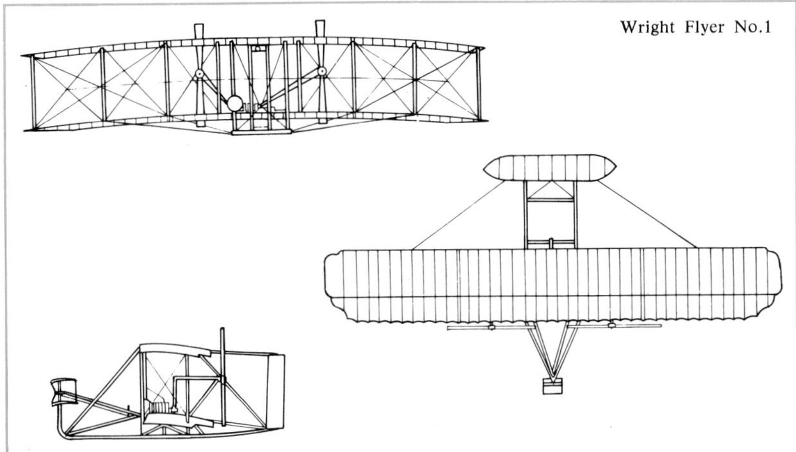

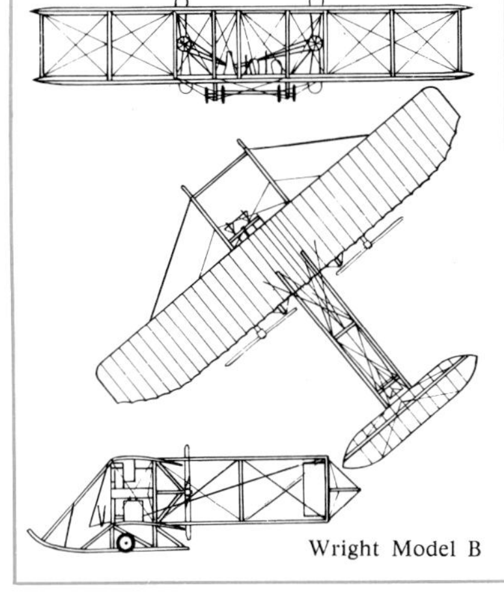

Nine days after the widely-reported failure of Samuel Pierpont Langley's attempt to fly his *Aerodrome*, Orville and Wilbur Wright ushered in the age of modern aviation, but the historic event which took place on the morning of 17 December 1903, at Kill Devil Hills, Kitty Hawk, North Carolina, passed almost unnoticed, due perhaps to the remoteness and obscurity of the site chosen for these experiments, or to the two brothers' wish to avoid all publicity at that stage. The most vivid description of the first successful flight made by the Flyer on the morning of 17 December is probably Orville Wright's diary entry for that day:

"After running the motor a few minutes to heat it up, I released the wire that held the machine to the track and the machine started forward into the wind. Wilbur ran at the side of the machine, holding the wing to balance it on the track. (Unlike the start on the fourteenth, made in a calm, the machine, facing a 27-mile wind, started very slowly.) One of the life-saving men snapped the camera for us, taking a picture just as the machine had reached the end of the track and had risen to a height of about two feet.

"The course of the flight up and down was exceedingly erratic, partly due to the irregularity of the air and partly to lack of experience in handling this machine. The control of the front rudder was difficult on account of its being balanced too near the center and thus had a tendency to turn itself when started so that the rudder was turned too far on one side and then too far on the other. As a result the machine would rise suddenly to about 10 feet and then as suddenly, on turning the rudder, dart for the ground. A sudden dart when about 100 feet from the end of the track ended the flight. (Time about 12 seconds.) As the velocity of the wind was over 35 feet per second and the speed of the machine over the ground against the wind ten feet per second, the speed of the machine relative to the air was over 45 feet per second and the length of the flight was equivalent to a flight of 540 feet made in calm air.

"This flight lasted only 12 seconds but it was nevertheless the first in the history of the world in which a machine carrying a man had raised itself by its own power into the air in full flight, had sailed forward without reduction of speed and had finally landed at a point as high as that from which it started."

Under prevailing wind conditions they did not feel it safe to rise far from the ground and this, Wilbur wrote, was why their flights were so brief—the fourth successful flight lasted 59 seconds.

Success came to the Wright brothers after years of research and observation and many attempts. They studied the flight of birds and were well aware of the German pioneer Otto Lilienthal's experiments with gliders. Comparing the two, they drew significant inferences: that it was impossible to maintain balance and lateral control of a flying machine by movements of the pilot's body to alter the aircraft's center of gravity. A completely different technique had to be adopted—that of adjusting the position of the wing-tips. This theory was put into practice in 1899 when they constructed a model glider-kite and the results of this test confirmed their theories. In September 1900, Orville and Wilbur Wright built a larger model and the following year they carried out piloted test flights at Kill Devil Hills with an even larger glider. It was necessary to build another glider, which flew in September and October 1902, before they were satisfied that all problems of control and balance had been solved. The fundamental modification which had been made was the substitution of a movable rudder for the double fixed fin of the first two gliders. Everything was now ready for the next step to be taken—that of powered flight. There was, however, no piston engine available which was both light and powerful enough and the propellers of the time were, aerodynamically speaking, not really efficient. The Wrights set to work and built a 12 hp 4-cylinder in-line engine and propellers. Once these two absolutely fundamental problems had been solved, the two brothers proceeded to build their flying machine.

The first Flyer—it later became known as the Flyer No. 1 since the Wrights called all their aircraft by this name—was constructed in the summer of 1903. It was a biplane with a skid undercarriage, the biplane elevator was installed forward of the wings with a double rudder to the rear. The engine drove two counterrotating pusher propellers by means of a double transmission chain. The pilot lay prone on the center section of the wing.

After success was achieved on 17 December 1903, the first Flyer was replaced by a second machine which was finished in May 1904, and which had some changes made (for instance the engine increased in power to 15–16 hp). Tests with the Flyer No. 2 took place between 23 May and 9 December. The aircraft, however, was not yet totally satisfactory and showed a tendency to stall when turning sharply. These faults were eliminated in the Flyer No. 3 of 1905, and this machine became the first real aircraft in history. Although it kept the same general lines of its predecessors, the Flyer No. 3 was considerably longer (in order to improve stability) and had new, more efficient propellers. Flights continued between 23 June and 16 October 1905, and the endurance record was set on 5 October at 38 minutes 3 seconds. During the course of these tests the Wrights successfully tried out a derrick and weight assisted takeoff system which meant that the airplane could become airborne irrespective of wind conditions. The Flyer No. 3 was offered to the U.S. War Department for evaluation, but was turned down.

Lack of official interest drove the Wright brothers to a drastic decision—they would have to improve their airplane still further and wait until the climate of opinion was more favorable.

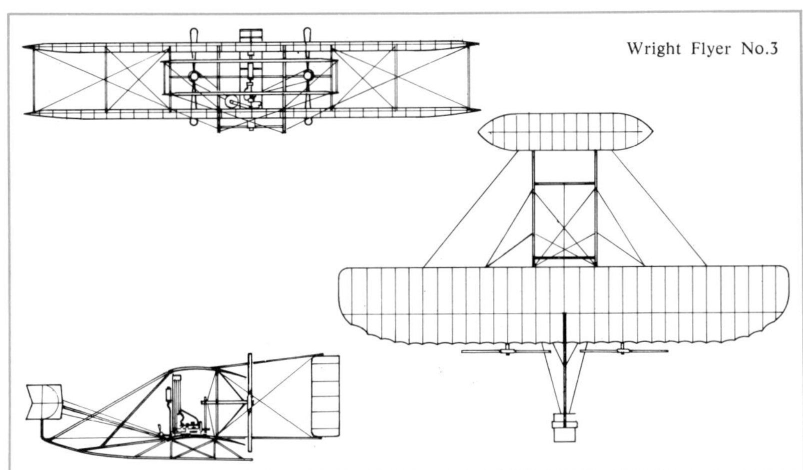

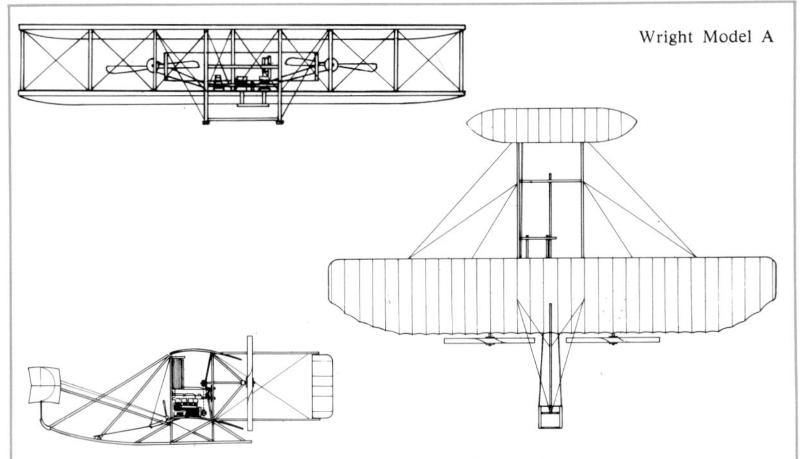

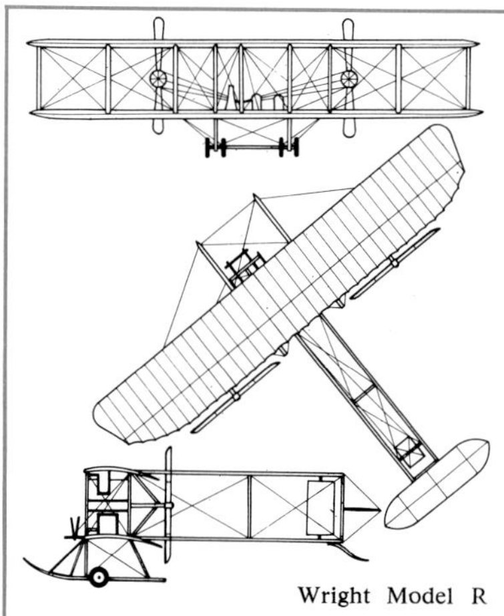
Wright Model R

After two and a half years had gone by, they were once more to be in the field, but with a far more efficient aircraft which could carry a passenger as well as the pilot, and which had a more powerful engine and a much improved control system. The Wright A first flew on 8 May 1908 and was the most commercially successful of their aircraft and the most widely known to the general public. It was to be instrumental in overcoming the hitherto unyielding skepticism in official circles (in 1909, after endless tests, the War Department finally accepted a Wright Model A for military use). It also swept the board in Europe. Commercial success was assured when construction licences were sold in Britain, France and Germany.

Feeling themselves vindicated, Orville and Wilbur Wright waited until 1910 before modifying their design, but when they were carried out these changes were radical. The configuration of the Wright Model B was more conventional, in terms of modern aircraft design; the elevators were positioned at the tail and a four-wheel landing gear was added to the skids of the earlier types. The aircraft won immediate acclaim and two were even ordered by the United States Army. A smaller single-seat version, the EX, was also developed. Other variants were the competition Model R, also known as the "Baby Wright," and a derivative of this model the Baby Grand, which had a 60 hp engine, and in which Orville Wright took part at the 1910 Belmont Park meeting, reaching speeds of between 71 and 75 mph (115 and 120 km/h).

Plate 19
Two great pioneers: Santos-Dumont and Henry Farman

Europe was three years behind America in achieving powered flight and it was, in fact, not a European, but a Brazilian, Alberto Santos-Dumont, who led the field. He settled in Paris in 1897, and became very well known through his many dirigibles, which he designed and constructed one after the other. When he heard of the Wright's success, Santos-Dumont decided to concentrate on designing and building a powered aircraft. Following his own numbering system, Santos-Dumont designated this plane 14bis. It was a canard type biplane—in effect a tail-first box kite. The box kite tail unit was connected to the fuselage in such a way that it could be moved up and down to act as an elevator and from side to side to act as a rudder. The engine was a 50 hp Antoinette which drove a metal pusher propeller 6 feet (1.82 m) in diameter. The main landing gear consisted of two wheels with rubber shock absorbers. A skid supported the front part of the aircraft. The pilot stood in a wicker basket just ahead of the engine; there was a control wheel linked by cables to the forward surfaces, and for later trials there were ailerons mounted in the outer wing bays. Because the pilot's hands were fully engaged with the other controls, the ailerons were linked to a metal T-piece attached to a special coat and the airplane's lateral control had to be attained by body movement.

The 14bis was constructed at Neuilly-St. James on the outskirts of Paris and was tested exhaustively. The first attempt at flight was made on 13 September 1906, at Bagatelle near Paris. The 14bis made what could be described as a "hop" of only 23 feet (7 m) rather than a flight, and was damaged on landing. Nearly six weeks later, on 23 October, things went far better: the plane flew 197 feet (60 m), winning Santos-Dumont the Archdeacon Prize of 3,000 francs for the first airplane in Europe to fly more than 25 meters (80 feet). On 12 November, the Brazilian won another prize, this time of 1,500 francs, awarded by the Aéro Club de France for the first plane to fly more than 100 meters; on this occasion his flight lasted just over 21 seconds and he landed 722 feet (220 m) from his takeoff point.

Santos-Dumont persevered with his interest in heavier-than-air machines and succeeded in flying a new model, the Santos-Dumont No. 20 Demoiselle which bore far more resemblance to the airplane as we know it than the 14bis. This little monoplane made its debut at St. Cyr in March 1909. The true prototype of the Demoiselle, however, had been built nearly two years previously. It had been designated project No. 19 and had made hops in 1907. It had a 20 hp engine, and a bamboo fuselage with cruciform tail surfaces and a framework beneath the wings which housed the pilot and the landing gear. The No. 19 was not an exceptional aircraft, and after two short hops on 17 November 1907, when it failed to fly any higher than 656 feet (200 m) and was damaged on landing, Santos-Dumont decided not to make any more tests with this model and redesigned the wing and fitted a more powerful engine to complete his No. 20 Demoiselle. The fuselage of the Demoiselle No. 20 was still of bamboo, but strengthened, the wing area was the same, but it was powered by a 35-hp engine. During tests in September 1909 it succeeded in flying for 16 minutes, covering about 11 miles (18 km). The much modified No. 19 was exhibited during that same month at the Grand Palais in Paris and was received with considerable enthusiasm. Santos-Dumont allowed anyone to copy his aircraft and it is believed that between ten and fifteen Demoiselles were built by other people.

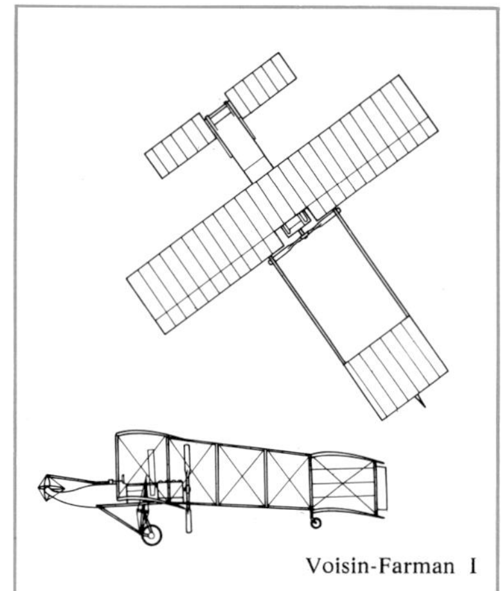
Voisin-Farman I

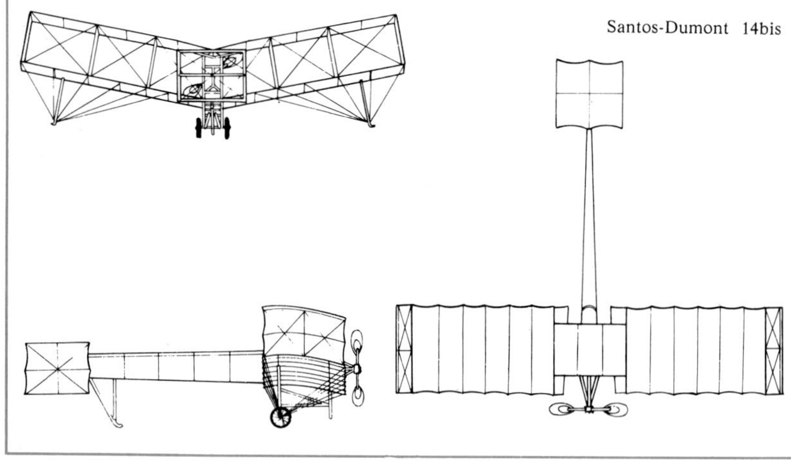
Santos-Dumont 14bis

Much work was also being done by other pioneers at this time, and France produced aircraft constructors who built more efficient machines—thus French aviators were in the forefront of aeronautical progress. Among them was Henry Farman who, on 9 November 1907, had flown for over a minute and completed a circuit of 3,380 feet (1,030 m) in 74 seconds at Issy. Henry Farman was of British origin but the spelling "Henri" appeared on some of his aircraft.

Henry Farman's early career was inextricably bound up with that of two other great French pioneers: two brothers, Gabriel and Charles Voisin who were the first men to build powered aircraft in Europe on a commercial scale. Their first success came with the aircraft they built for Farman. Work was started on the new Voisin-Farman biplane on 1 June 1907 and, after testing, Farman made extensive modifications to its general configuration, the structure of the wings and the elevator. The results were startling. When the aircraft was flown on 7 October at Issy it was a great success. On 26 October it flew 2,530 feet (771 m) in 52.6 seconds; on 5 November, it made its first turn in flight and the day after it broke the "one kilometer in one minute" barrier.

With the prize money of 50,000 francs awarded by Deutsch and

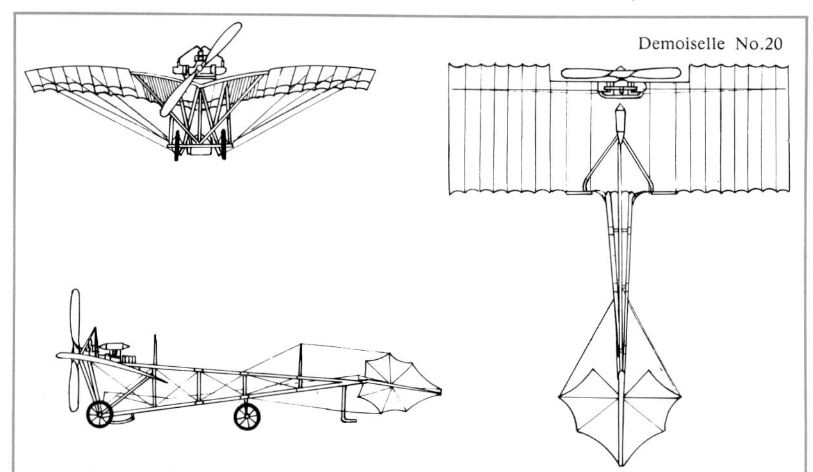
Demoiselle No.20

Archdeacon for the first officially logged flight of more than one kilometer (3,280 feet), which he had won on 13 January 1908 at Issy, Henry Farman completely re-covered the biplane. In May he added two side curtains between the wings to increase stability and, in October, he installed ailerons on all four wings. In this modified form the aircraft made the first proper cross-country flight in Europe, covering 17 miles (27 km) from Bouy to Reims on 30 October 1908.

Plate 20
European experiments: 1904–1909

These early achievements had a tremendous effect on aviation enthusiasts, kindling incredible excitement. Activity was intense: meetings of aeronautical associations and clubs attracted hundreds of fervent aviation enthusiasts. Inventors, designers and other pioneers fed the craze with a continual stream of proposals, theories and solutions. Inevitably, many of these ideas were useless; there were many impractical flying machines which appeared on airdromes together with the truly viable airplanes. Many never managed to take off, and complicated freakish machines abounded, which looked like contraptions dreamed up by a madman. Some of the seemingly improbable concepts were, however, to lead to workable designs in the future.

The theory of multiple lifting surfaces which had been put forward between 1884 and 1891 and tested with a steam-powered model in 1893, was first given practical application by an Englishman, Horatio F. Phillips, in 1904. His first Multiplane had 20 superimposed winglets, rather like a venetian blind. The aircraft had a cruciform tail unit and a three-wheel undercarriage. The engine, which had been built by Phillips himself, drove a two-blade puller propeller. This aircraft, however, was not a success. When it was tested at Streatham it proved unstable and impossible to control. Only three years later, in 1907, was Phillips able to fly for 490 feet (150 m), using another multiplane with some 200 narrow-chord wings.

The tractor monoplane formula, which was to have an illustrious future in the hands of men such as Blériot, had its first application in the Vuia of 1906, which proved a failure. It had been designed and built by a Romanian lawyer named Trajan Vuia, who had taken French citizenship. This monoplane had a bat-like wing structure mounted on top of a frame which carried the engine, the pilot, the directional rudder and the four-wheel pneumatic-tired landing gear, the front two wheels of which were steerable. The aircraft had no elevators but these were replaced by a device which was designed to change the wings' angle of incidence in flight. The Vuia was tested on 18 March 1906, and other proving flights were attempted in July and on 12 and 19 August at Montesson. The best the Vuia monoplane could do was to make a long leap of about 80 feet (24 m) and was destroyed when it crash-landed.

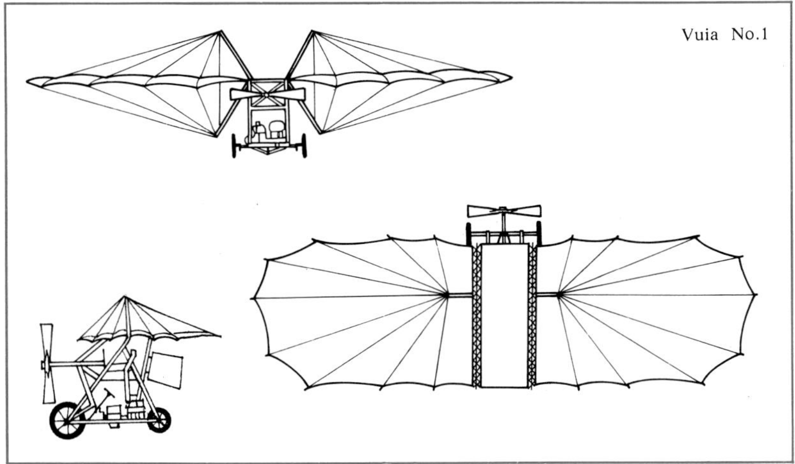
Vuia No.1

The following year the tractor propeller formula was used by another French enthusiast, Robert Esnault-Pelterie. His R.E.P. 1 was tested in November and December 1907 and was not a success, nor were the next two models which were built in 1908 and 1909, the R.E.P. 2 and the R.E.P. 2bis. The airplane lacked longitudinal and directional stability whilst the engine had not been properly tuned and developed overheating problems. The R.E.P. 1 managed to take off five times, making hops of varying length each time, the longest of which was about 1,970 feet (600 m) on 16 November 1907. This monoplane had wings with slight negative dihedral (anhedral), a very short fuselage, a tailplane and an elevator but no rudder. Control was achieved by warping the wings downwards only and by using the elevator, both being operated by a single control lever. The aircraft was powered by a 7-cylinder 30-hp radial engine, built by Esnault-Pelterie himself in 1907, which drove a four-blade metal propeller.

Esnault-Pelterie became famous for his technical solutions to a variety of subsidiary aviation problems, rather than through his flying machines themselves. He devised safety-belts, methods of load testing, material fatigue, hydraulic brakes for landing gears, engines, and aircraft controls.

A parallel could be drawn between the results of Robert Esnault-Pelterie's research and that of a Dane, Jacob Christian Hansen Ellehammer. Although his flying machines made a limited contribution to the development of the airplane, it is remarkable that he managed to achieve such interesting results working completely on his own, without any contact with contemporary pioneers in this field. His most promising design was the Ellehammer IV, built in 1908, which was a tractor biplane and was tested in Germany in June that same year, when its first short flight marked the beginning of the era of heavier-than-air flight in that country. Subsequent proving flights showed an improvement in the aircraft's performance: at Kiel on 28 June, it remained airborne for 11 seconds and won a prize of 5,000 marks for its designer. The machine's longest flight over a distance of 558 feet (170 m) was made on 14 January 1909, but this was more of a "hop" than a truly controlled flight.

Some time afterwards Ellehammer gave up aircraft construction, being unable to raise finance for further projects, and when one considers what he had achieved all on his own, this was a pity. He had built his first flying machine in 1905 which had a 9-hp engine, which he constructed himself; the aircraft was meant to fly in circles while attached to a central pole whilst semi-automatically controlled. This aircraft was for a while thought to have a better claim than Santos-Dumont's 14bis to have made the first flight in Europe: on 12 September 1906 (the day before the 14bis's unsuccessful attempt), Ellehammer's machine made a hop of 140 feet (42 m). Before completing the Ellehammer IV, several other designs had been built, including a "semi-biplane" and a triplane powered by up-rated versions of his own engines.

Heavier-than-air flight was introduced to Italy in the summer of 1908 by the French pioneer Léon Delagrange in his Voisin biplane. The Italian Aeronatical Society had been founded in the early years of the century, but only in 1909 were the first successful tests carried out with machines both designed and built in Italy. The first attempt on 13 January 1909 by a biplane which had been built in Turin by Aristide Faccioli was not a success, and the plane only managed to make a

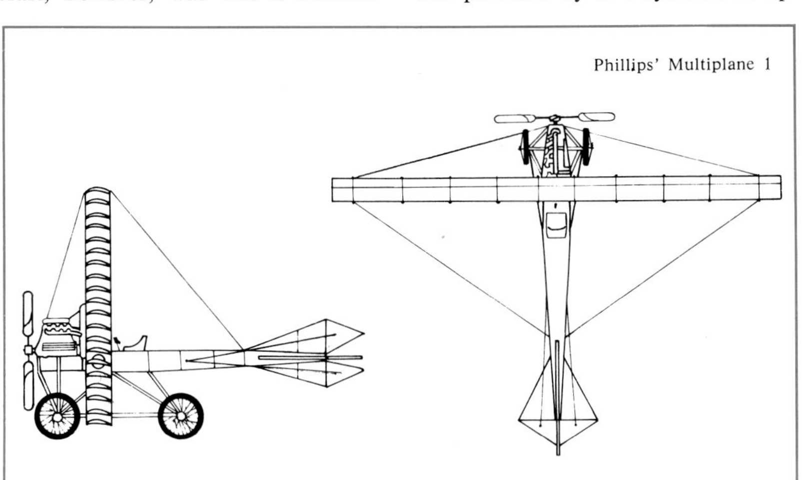
Phillips' Multiplane 1

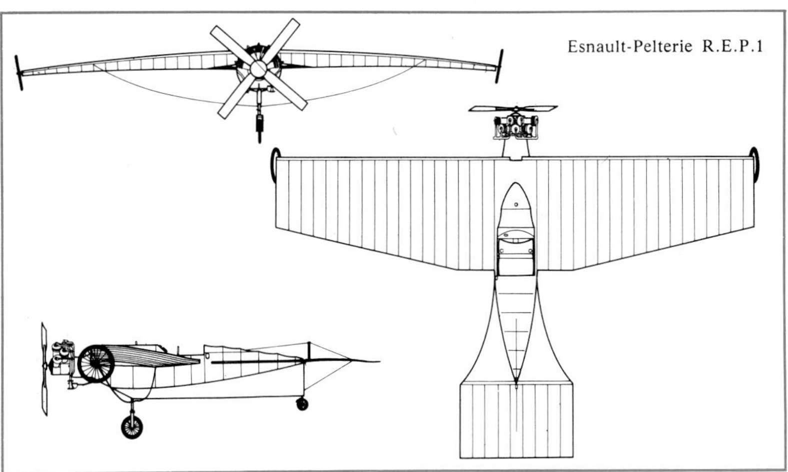
Esnault-Pelterie R.E.P.1

hop of a few yards before crashing to the ground. Also in Turin at the same time, Franz Miller, an engineer and an immensely active aviation enthusiast, established the first Italian aircraft factory and placed it at the disposal of anyone who wanted to build a flying machine. One of the very first airplanes to be produced in this factory was the Aerocurvo: an unusual looking monoplane with curved wings which, although unsuccessful, did help to stimulate public interest in aviation and make some contribution towards subsequent, more fruitful experiments.

The Aerocurvo was designed in collaboration with Riccardo Ponzelli and after a series of tests in Turin at the beginning of 1909, it was taken to Brescia to take part in the International Air Circuit, with Leonino Da Zara as pilot. The Aerocurvo failed to take off. Only after modifications and weight reduction did it manage to make a very short flight.

While the more successful flying machines which were the products of a methodical and sound scientific approach to the absorbing problem of flight, were being built and tested, there appeared a great many other machines which were freakish and unworkable. The Roshon Multiplane of 1908 is a particularly intriguing example of these machines since it was designed in the United States, home of the Wright brothers, and yet one can see that its structure seems to take no account of the basic principles of aerodynamics. Needless to say, Roshon's Multiplane never left the ground. Similar aircraft proliferated during the next few years at a time when the airplane as we know it was already developing and becoming more a part of everyday life, and many of them originated in Europe which by now had become the development center of heavier-than-air flight.

Plate 21
Freakish flying machines: 1908–1910

In France and England hundreds of machines appeared which were very strange indeed. In 1908 an obscure nobleman, the Marquis d'Equevilly, decided to try his hand at building a heavier-than-air flying machine and produced an odd elliptical structure, the idea for which had probably been suggested to d'Equevilly by Phillips' theories on multiple, superimposed wing surfaces. Photographs of the time show two oval frames mounted on four bicycle-type wheels; the lifting surfaces, the engine and the pilot were to be surrounded by this elliptical structure. The wing cellule was made up of 12 elements, five winglets on each side and two on top. The engine drove a twin-blade metal propeller by means of a transmission chain reduction gear, which reduced the engine's 1,500 rpm to the 500 rpm of the propeller.

In the same year another Frenchman, Captain Dorand, an army officer, hit upon the idea of constructing an aircraft expressly designed for military use. Dorand's chief concern was to provide the pilot with maximum visibility, and with this in mind he built an enormous structure in which the lifting surfaces were positioned aft of and above the "main fuselage" framework. The Aéroplane—as Dorand prosaically named his new flying machine—had a basic framework which housed the landing gear, the pilot and the engine which drove a two-blade propeller. This framework was more or less triangular; the two front wheels were attached to a structure on which the engine was mounted, and the two rear wheels were placed at the two extremities of the base of the rear structure to ensure stability on the ground. The wing cellule was a biplane-type arrangement, but with the two lifting surfaces attached to a triangular "box" in the center. A similar triangular structure to the rear was to function as the tailplane. The wing had a pronounced positive angle of attack in order to increase lift during takeoff—but this remained strictly theoretical since the aircraft never flew.

An extremely original design was built in the early summer of 1909 by an enthusiast named Givaudan and aroused great interest but proved to be totally impracticable. Although it never managed to get off the ground, the designer's remarkable structural and aerodynamic ideas made it intriguing. It was built in May 1909 at the Vermorel factory in Villefranche (Rhône) and had cylindrical, or annular, wings positioned at the front and rear ends of a metal tubular fuselage structure. The annular wings comprised two concentric sections with small wing sections inserted between the inner and outer sections. The control system was also extremely original and worked by moving the front wing which could be tilted in any direction since it was connected to the fuselage by a universal joint. The aircraft was powered by a 40-hp V-8 air-cooled Vermorel engine and was installed just aft of the front wing, driving a propeller 7 feet 10.5 inches (2.4 m) in diameter through a transmission shaft which protruded in front of the forward wing. The pilot was to sit behind the engine. The landing gear had four bicycle-type wheels, two of which were attached directly to the undersurfaces of the rear wing and the other two to the forward part of the fuselage.

In 1909 and 1910 British designers vied with their French counterparts and, caught up in the general excitement of the time, designed some extremely odd flying machines which blithely ignored all the recently discovered structural and technical principles, knowledge of which was already leading to the first triumphant steps towards the "classic" airplane and laying the foundations for its future development.

Among the many freakish and fantastic flying machines which appeared on the airdromes of the time was Edward's outdated Rhomboidal design, which took its name from the unusual structure of the two wings which were rhomboid-shaped and arranged in biplane configuration. The engine, pilot and the two propellers were in a central position between the two wings. The Rhomboidal was a failure when tested at Brooklands in 1911. The two rhomboidal lifting surfaces were linked by vertical struts and braced by wires. Tension cables were used as the "spars" of the wings which had a single expanse of canvas kept taut and curved by wooden battens inserted lengthwise like those used for sails. The 50-hp engine was mounted centrally in front of the pilot and drove the two propellers by means of transmission chains. A rudder was positioned above the upper wing where it was totally ineffective.

The Seddon flying machine, built in 1910 and designed by Lieutenant J. W. Seddon, R.N., and A. G. Hackett was a good advertisement for Accles and Pollock, the steel tube manufacturer, who built it, but worthless as an airplane. It was a positive maze of steel tubing—over 2,000 feet (600 m), weighing almost a ton (1,016 kg), a fantastic structure of hoops and geodetic shapes. This aircraft was a tandem biplane: the front wings also acted as elevators while the rear wings were only for lift. A pair of rudders was positioned between the two wings, and the whole contraption was held together by the intricate fuselage, in which two 65-hp N.E.C. engines were mounted and drove two Beedle-type tractor propellers. The fuselage also housed the landing gear and the passengers (five plus the pilot). The Seddon was unsuccessfully tried out at the Midland Aero Club flying ground before it was dismantled, but not before having acquired a transitory fame as "the world's largest aircraft."

Had the Safety of 1910 ever managed to fly, it would surely have gone down in history as the first flying saucer. This strange machine was designed by two enthusiasts, Mortimer and Vaughan, from Edgware, Middlesex, and had two pairs of semicircular superimposed wings which gave it its remarkable ring shape, in the center of which was the fuselage—rectangular in section, almost completely enclosed and tapering sharply at the forward end. The landing gear had four wheels and the flying machine was to have been driven by three propellers—one forward and the other two on either side of the fuselage within the circular wings. The Safety was once airborne—but only when suspended from heavy cables—for the indispensable photograph for posterity.

Plate 22
The tractor monoplane conquers the Channel: 1909

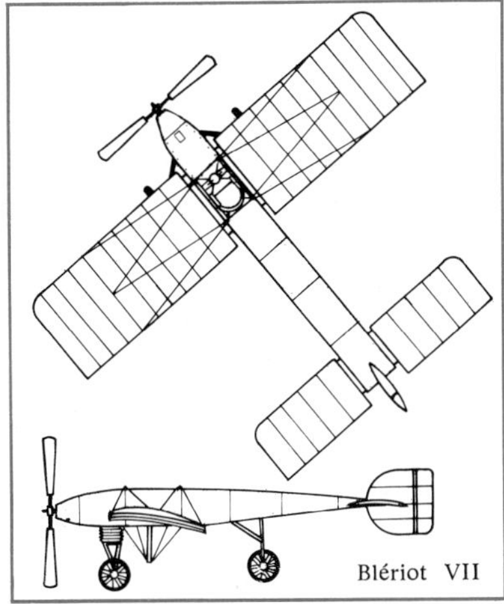
Blériot VII

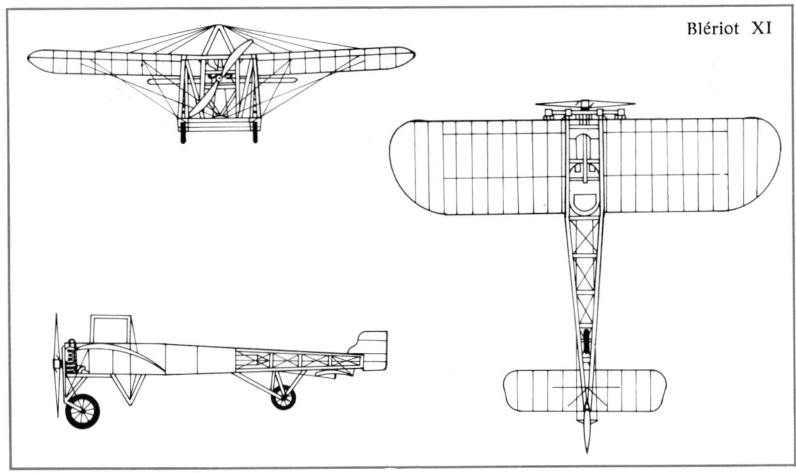
Blériot XI

Meanwhile "mainstream" aviation had made great progress towards its coming of age. On 25 July 1909, the French pioneer, Louis Blériot, achieved a feat which made the world gasp in admiration, when he completed the first powered flight across the English Channel. "England's isolation has ended once and for all," as an English daily paper put it the day after this historic flight of nearly 24 miles (38 km), almost entirely over the sea.

His aircraft was a specially modified Blériot XI, a small tractor monoplane, and he took off at 4.35 a.m. from Les Baraques, near Calais, and landed at 5.12 p.m. in Northfall Meadow, near Dover. This exploit meant that the French pioneer and his aircraft were both assured of fame and success.

Blériot had been involved in the world of aviation for some years. After designing some fairly unexciting flying machines he was inspired by the Romanian, Trajan Vuia's design to build a tractor monoplane and on 17 September 1907, at Issy, he covered a distance of 603 feet (184 m) in his tandem-wing *Libellule*. In 1908 he achieved a flight of 2,296 feet (700 m) with his tractor monoplane VIIIbis and on 31 October 1908, flew his Blériot VIII a distance of 8.7 miles (14 km) in 11 minutes.

At the Salon de l'Automobile et de l'Aéronautique in December 1908, in the aeronautical section, Blériot exhibited three flying machines: the Type IX (another tractor monoplane); the Type X (a pusher biplane) and the Type XI which was to prove the making of him as a designer and aviator. The Blériot IX only managed to make a few "hops" in January and February 1909 but the Blériot XI showed great promise from its very first flight at Issy on 23 January 1909.

The Type XI's first propulsion unit was a 30-hp R.E.P. engine which drove a four-blade metal propeller. As the tests proceeded, however, this was replaced by a 22/25-hp Anzani engine and a Chauvière two-blade propeller was installed. Changes were also made to the control system: the rudder was enlarged and the elevons at the outer ends of the tailplane were used as elevators only; lateral control was effected by warping the trailing edges of the wings. Thus modified, the Blériot XI assumed its definitive configuration and proved an outstanding aircraft.

It was to have a distinguished career. Apart from its sporting achievements, it was the first airplane sold to the French Army and the first to be used in war, when it was flown by Captain Carlo Piazza, who used it to carry out a reconnaissance mission over enemy lines in Libya on 23 October 1911, during the Italo-Turkish War.

In October 1908, the London *Daily Mail* offered a prize of £1,000 to the first aviator to cross the English Channel in either direction, and when Hubert Latham made his attempt on 19 July 1909, six days before Blériot, it proved a good test of the qualities of another tractor monoplane, the Antoinette IV of 1909. The attempt was unsuccessful, for, less than 8 miles (12.9 km) out, the engine failed and the Antoinette came down in the sea. Latham was, however, safely picked up by the French destroyer *Harpon*.

The Antoinette aircraft company owed much of its fame to the aircraft's designer, Léon Levavasseur. This engineer's contribution to the development of aviation in Europe did not stem from his aircraft design alone, but also from his excellent engines which were specially tailored for aircraft propulsion. The Antoinette IV made its first flight at Issy in 1908, but Levavasseur waited until January-February of the following year before making the final adjustments to the aircraft. The basic modification consisted of considerably increasing (in fact, nearly doubling) the monoplane's wing area, from the prototype's 322.9 square feet to the 538.2 square feet (30 sq m to 50 sq m) of the final model. From its very first appearance the Antoinette was considered an extremely elegant design, with its slim fuselage, trapezoidal wings with pronounced dihedral and cruciform tail surfaces. Only one aesthetic feature (a functional one as well) was changed in later models, starting with the Type VI: the ailerons at the wing-tips were replaced by a warping control system on the trailing edges of the wings.

In this definitive form the Antoinette immediately proved its worth, flying 3.1 miles (5 km) at Mourmelon, on 19 February 1909. A month later the Antoinette was turned over to Hubert Latham, who gradually brought it up to peak performance. Latham made his second attempt to cross the Channel on 27 July 1909, in a modified version of the monoplane, the Antoinette VII. This, however, also came down in the sea. It was retrieved, repaired, and taken to Reims, where it won the Prix de l'Altitude (508.5 feet or 155 m) and came second in the Prix de la Vitesse on 29 August.

Tractor propeller aircraft were by no means all monoplanes. Inspired by the idea that had led de Pischof to build a tractor biplane in 1907, Ambroise Goupy designed his Goupy II in 1909. Unlike de Pischof's biplane which was a complete failure, the Model II did manage to fly. Goupy had help when designing his aircraft from the Italian aviator, Lieutenant Mario Calderara. The Goupy II only made two flights before it was modified, during one of which it was piloted by Calderara himself.

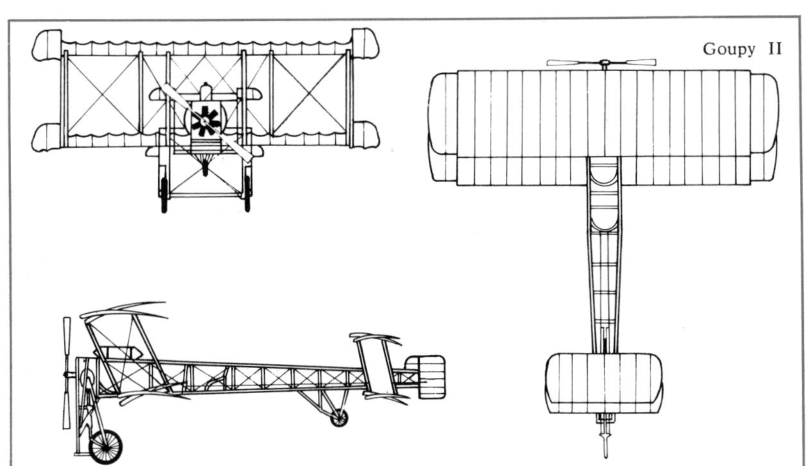
Goupy II

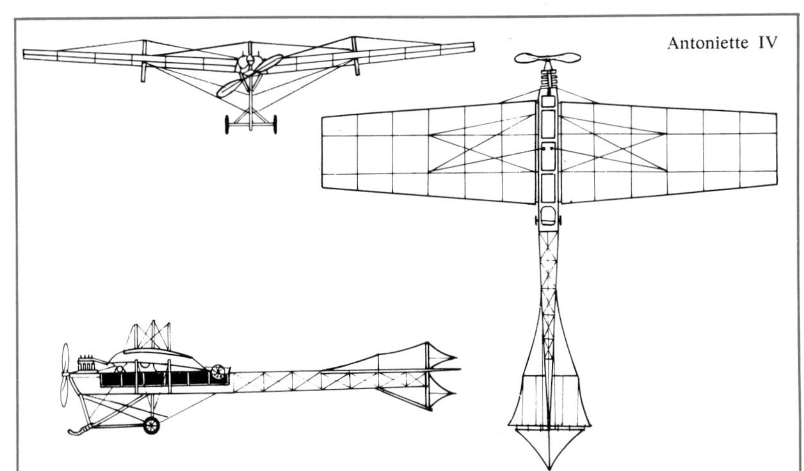
Antoinette IV

Plate 23
The pusher propeller wins at Reims: 1909

The tractor layout did not have a monopoly of success in 1909. The older formula of the pusher propeller, which had been launched by the Wright brothers, easily kept pace with the newer formula. An important contribution was made by an aeronautical society called the Aerial Experiment Association which had been founded in the United States on 1 October 1907 by Dr. Alexander Graham Bell.

Bell's main purpose in creating the Aerial Experiment Association (together with Glenn Curtiss, Lieutenant Thomas Selfridge, J. A. D. McCurdy and F. W. "Casey" Baldwin) had been to develop a competent working team to help him in his research with one particular facet of aerodynamics: multicellular-type supporting surfaces. The A.E.A undertook to fly Dr. Bell's Cygnet man-carrying tetrahedral kite, and with Lieutenant Selfridge it reached a height of 168 feet (51.2 m), but was destroyed after landing. The next project was the building of the powered tetrahedral kite, Cygnet II, which was completed on 19 February 1909. The aircraft structure consisted mainly of a massive bank of 2,152 cells which spanned 52 feet 6 inches (16 m) and which were to act as lifting surfaces. The aircraft was powered by a 50-hp Curtiss engine which drove a pusher propeller and was mounted on skids instead of the usual wheels. It was unsuccessfully tested on Lake Keuka near New York. The smaller Cygnet III did make some short flights early in 1912.

The structural formula of the Cygnets was not a practical proposition and when Bell realized this he dissolved the association. During its short life, however, the A.E.A. had built and tested other machines which were much more practical propositions than the Cygnet. The first of these was the *Red Wing* of 1908, designed by Selfridge, who never actually put it through its paces himself. It was tested twice on 12 March 1908 on Lake Keuka and before crashing on landing it managed to "hop" 319 feet (97 m). The pilot on this occasion was Frank Baldwin who designed the A.E.A.'s second airplane, the *White Wing* of 1908, which managed five takeoffs between 18 and 23 May. The best result was obtained on 21 May when it covered 1,017 feet (310 m).

The Association's next design was to launch one of the most famous aircraft constructors—Glenn Hammond Curtiss—on his career. He built an airplane, the *June Bug*, which made over thirty successful takeoffs during the last ten days of June 1908. The final accolade came on 4 July 1908, when the *June Bug* and its pilot were awarded the challenge prize offered by the journal *Scientific American* for the first official flight made in the United States to cover a distance of more than a kilometer: the *June Bug* covered 6,000 feet (1,829 m) in a flight lasting 1 minute 42.5 seconds.

The last aircraft to be designed and built by the Aerial Experiment Association was McCurdy's *Silver Dart*, which first flew in December 1908 before going to Canada where on 23 February 1909, flying from the frozen surface of Baddeck Bay in Nova Scotia, it covered about 2,400 feet (800 m). On 24 February the *Silver Dart* accomplished a flight of 4.5 miles (7.25 km) and a few weeks later, 12 miles (19 km)—a long-distance flight in those days!

Although the A.E.A. was wound up in March 1909, Glenn Curtiss continued to go from strength to strength. In the spring of that year this great American aviation pioneer built the first airplane of his own after leaving the A.E.A., which was called the *Gold Bug* or *Golden Flyer* and was produced in partnership with Augustus M. Herring for the New York Aeronautical Society who paid 5,000 dollars for it. The aircraft was lent to Curtiss who, on 17 July 1909, again won the *Scientific American* prize, this time for a nonstop flight of 25 miles (40 km).

From its first test flights the *Gold Bug* proved to be strong, fairly fast and easy to handle. This last quality mainly resulted from the installation of ailerons between the two wings. Curtiss had opted for these instead of the wing-warping system. A development of the *Golden Flyer*, the *Reims Racer*, with reduced wing area and powered by a 51.2-hp 8-cylinder in-line V engine was built to take part in the Grande Semaine d'Aviation de la Champagne held in Reims in August 1909, winning the Gordon Bennett Trophy on 28 August and the Prix de la Vitesse the day after.

Later Curtiss aircraft made the first takeoff ever from the deck of a warship and the first deck landing. These proving flights—which signalled the beginning of the era of the aircraft-carrier—were made on 14 November 1910, from the light cruiser U.S.S. *Birmingham* at Hampton Roads, Virginia, and on 18 January 1911, on the armored cruiser U.S.S. *Pennsylvania* anchored in San Francisco Bay. The aircraft were piloted by Eugene Ely on both occasions and were respectively the *Albany Flier* and the first Model D-IV. In 1911 the U.S. Navy purchased two Curtiss Model E biplanes which took the official designations A-1 and A-2.

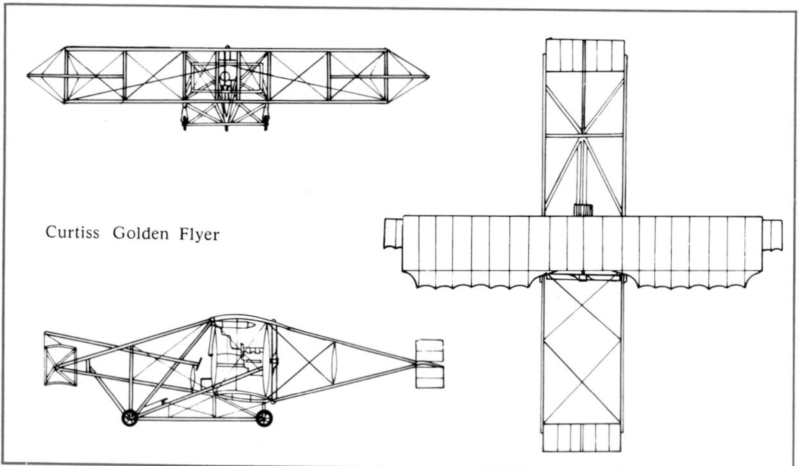
Curtiss Golden Flyer

Another immensely successful aviation pioneer was also to be seen at the Reims meeting—the Frenchman, Henry Farman. When the two Voisin brothers sold the aircraft he had ordered in 1908 to someone else, the infuriated Farman decided to set up a small factory in which to build a new airplane of his own design. The result of this snap decision was the Henry Farman III which was the world's most popular biplane between 1909 and 1911. At the Reims aviation rally in 1909 this aircraft won the Grand Prix, with a distance of 112 miles (180 km) flown in 3 hours 4 minutes 56 seconds; the Prix des Passagers, with two passengers on board besides the pilot; and second place in the Prix de l'Altitude (361 feet: 110 m) behind Hubert Latham's winning Antoinette VII.

The aircraft's maiden flight took place on 6 April 1909, at Châlons, powered by a 4-cylinder 50-hp Vivinus engine. This was followed by months of exhaustive tests and proving flights during which the aircraft was improved, changes being made to the ailerons and tailplanes. The last significant alteration was made at Reims, when the original Vivinus engine was replaced by a 50-hp Gnome rotary engine.

After its dazzling performance during the Grande Semaine de l'Aviation de la Champagne the Farman III was still further improved; it was enlarged, the wing area was increased and its performance generally up-rated. The modified version was an immediate success and became the most widely used aircraft in the years prior to World War I.

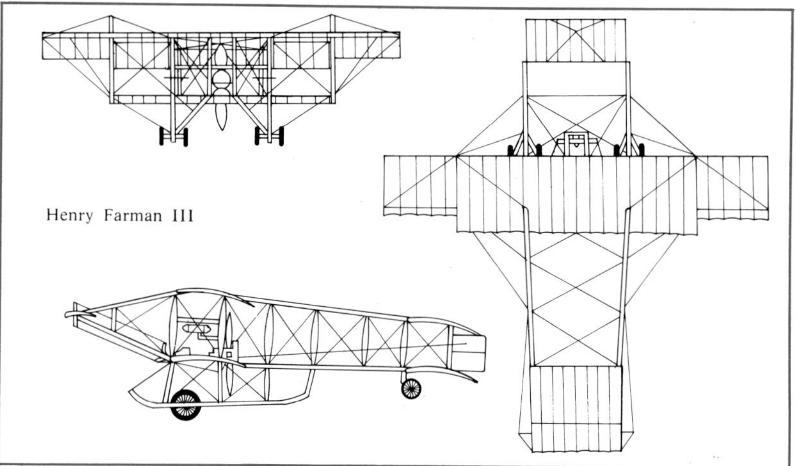
Henry Farman III

Plate 24
British aircraft: 1908–1910

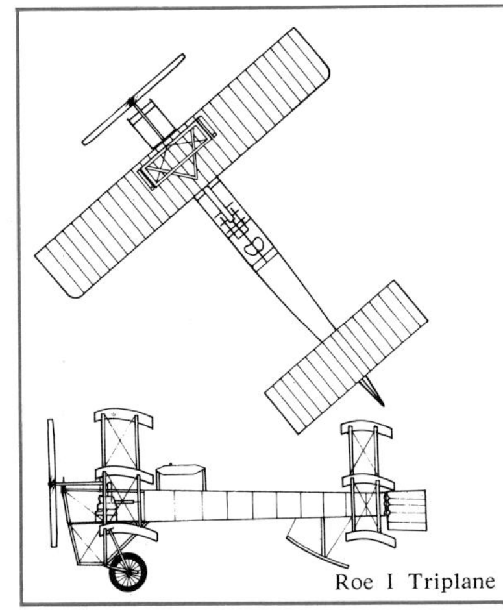
Roe I Triplane

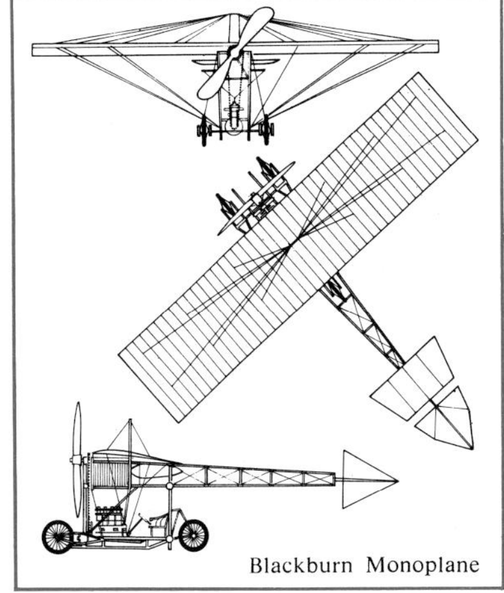
Blackburn Monoplane

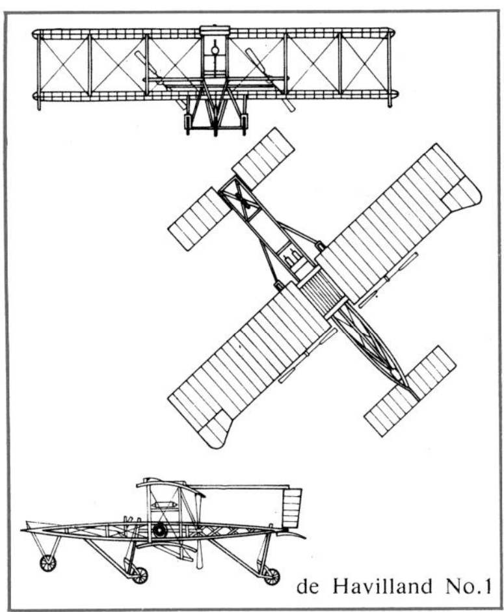
de Havilland No.1

Great Britain had at first been slightly left behind in the early days of international aviation but soon made up for lost time. The first true flight made in England by a British-designed airplane powered by a British engine took place on 23 July 1909, with Alliot Verdon Roe at the controls.

This aircraft was a triplane (the Roe I Triplane), the first of four that Roe built in 1909–10. The first triplane turned out to be underpowered: the best it could do on 23 July, powered by a 9-hp J.A.P. engine, was a hop of about 880 feet (270 m). In his second model, the Roe II Triplane, Roe used a 35-hp engine and the aircraft flew successfully at Brooklands.

Alliot Verdon Roe embarked on his career as an aircraft designer and constructor in the spring of 1907. The future founder of the famous A. V. Roe and Company Limited (Avro) made a start with a canard biplane with a pusher propeller, the Roe I Biplane, which he intended to enter for the prize of £2,500 for the first flight round Brooklands race track to be made before the end of that year. Roe made an unsuccessful attempt at the prize but was not discouraged. He replaced the 9-hp 4-cylinder J.A.P. motorcycle engine with a 24-hp Antoinette engine which he borrowed, changed the propeller and added small extra winglets between the main wings at the inner ends. On 8 June 1908 the machine just managed to rise 2 or 3 feet (60 or 90 cm) into the air under its own power. For some time this attempt was considered to be the first successful flight ever made in England by an Englishman, but in 1928 it was decided that this "hop" did not qualify as true flight and the credit was then given to J. T. C. Moore-Brabazon who had flown a Voisin biplane at Shellbeach on 2 May 1909.

Other men who were later to become famous in Great Britain as aircraft constructors also started their aviation careers in 1909 and 1910, such as Robert Blackburn, Geoffrey de Havilland and the Short brothers—Horace, Eustace and Oswald.

Robert Blackburn was a civil engineer who became a convert to heavier-than-air flight after seeing Wilbur Wright fly at Issy in 1908. Blackburn's first airplane was designed in Paris, but as soon as the plans were completed he returned to England and built the aircraft in a Leeds workshop with the help of Harry Goodyear. The result was the high-wing Blackburn Monoplane, so strongly built as to earn itself the nickname of "the Heavy Type Monoplane." It was tested at Marske on the Yorkshire coast in the spring of 1909, and it managed to take off after some taxiing tests but once in the air Blackburn lost control when he tried to make a turn and the "heavy monoplane" crashed into the sand dunes and was never repaired.

The same fate awaited Geoffrey de Havilland's first aircraft, the de Havilland Biplane No. 1, at the end of the year. It crashed during its only test at Seven Barrows, near Newbury, in December 1909, when one wing collapsed after a few seconds' flight. de Havilland had started work on the airplane in 1908, helped by a friend, F. T. Hearle. de Havilland also designed and built the engine, a 45-hp four-cylinder horizontally opposed unit which was salvaged from the Biplane No. 1 wreckage and installed in his next aircraft.

The Short brothers' early progress was more immediately successful, but also somewhat erratic. Horace, Eustace and Oswald Short's second design, the Short Biplane No. 2, was a good machine: a Wright-type biplane which J. T. C. Moore-Brabazon flew on 30 October 1909, to win the £1,000 *Daily Mail* prize for the first Briton to cover a mile (closed circuit) in a British airplane. The Short Biplane No. 3 represented an unusual example of technological regression. It was designed and built in the wake of the successful No. 2 and was exhibited at the Olympia Aero Show in 1910, but repeated takeoff attempts were all unsuccessful. This was also a financial blow to the Shorts since it led to the cancellation of five orders for the aircraft which had been placed before the exhibition opened.

The designer John William Dunne produced an extremely original aircraft. Working at the Farnborough Balloon Factory, Dunne produced designs for sweptback tailless gliders and powered machines. The first "flying wing" ever to fly was the Dunne D.5, built by Short Brothers in 1910; test flights started on 11 March at Eastchurch. In May the D.5 flew 2 miles (3.22 km) with such perfect stability that the pilot was able to maintain correct flying trim without touching the controls. Test flights continued throughout 1911 until the D.5 was destroyed in an accident, but it was rebuilt in 1912 as the D.8.

Samuel Franklin Cody, an American expatriate, made a great contribution to British aeronautical research, and it was he who made the first powered heavier-than-air flight in Great Britain at Farnborough on 16 October 1908, in a large biplane which he had built for the British Army at the Balloon Factory, the first officially designated army aircraft. After more than a year of test flights, Cody decided to build another biplane to compete for the first Michelin Cup. This aircraft, the Cody Michelin Cup Biplane, resembled his first machine but had improved controls and was equipped with ailerons. Before the competition, Cody replaced the original 60-hp Green engine with an E.N.V. of the same power and set British records for endurance and distance: 94.5 miles (152.08 km) in 2 hours 24 minutes. On 31 December 1910, he won the Michelin Cup and broke his own records, covering 185.46 miles (298.47 km) in 4 hours 47 minutes.

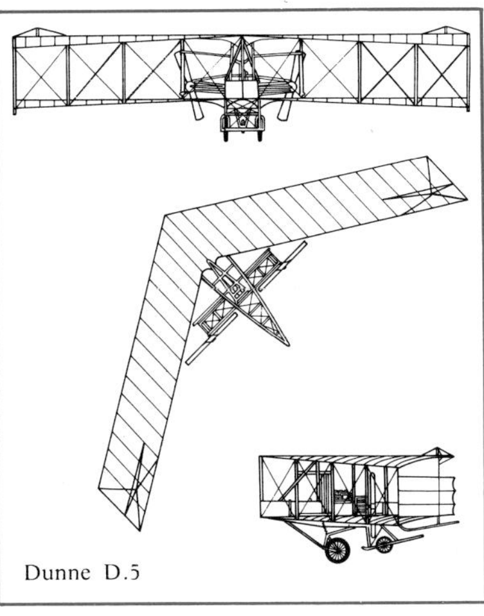
Dunne D.5

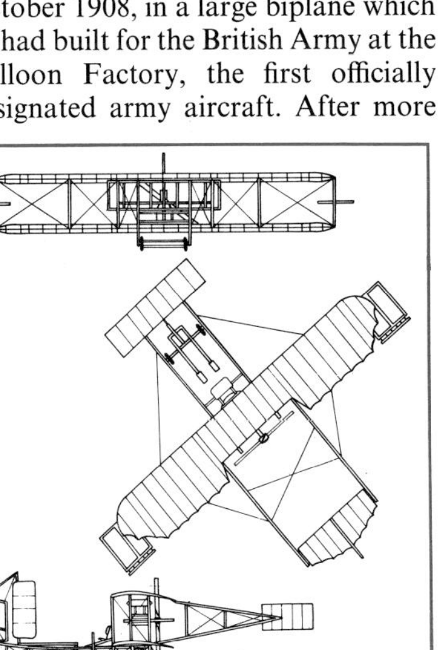
Short No.3

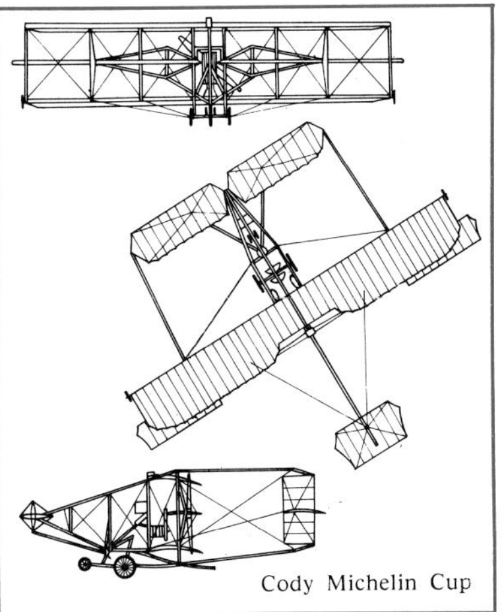
Cody Michelin Cup

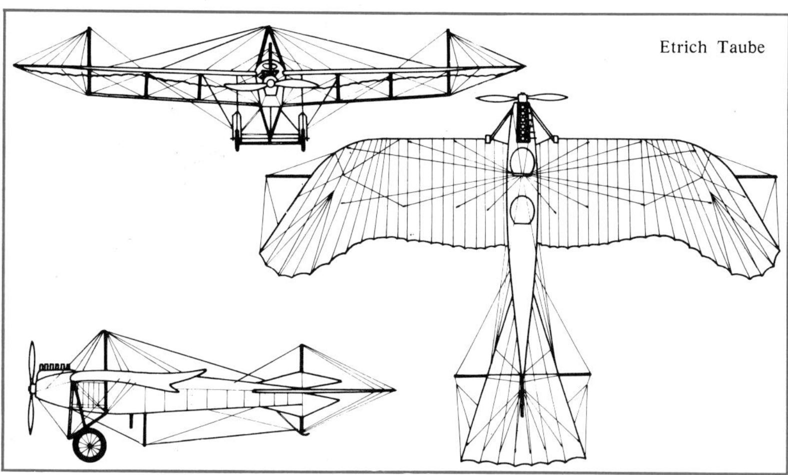

Etrich Taube

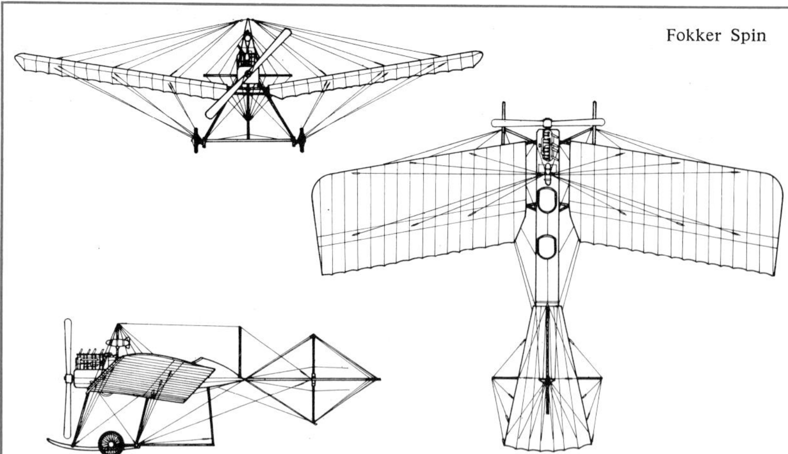

Fokker Spin

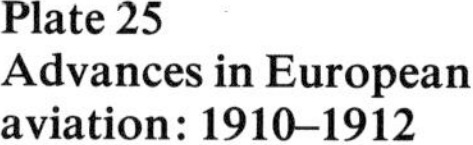

Plate 25
Advances in European aviation: 1910–1912

The years 1910–12 saw the rest of Europe busily engaged in developing new aircraft.

In Austria, the engineer, Igo Etrich designed a monoplane which proved enormously successful, especially in terms of numbers built: the *Taube* (Dove). The basic formula of the aircraft clearly derived from the designs of Vuia and Blériot but in appearance it looked very like a bird—especially the wings and tail. The *Taube* prototype was built in 1910 and was powered by an Austro-Daimler engine. After his first flights, Etrich granted construction rights to the Rumpler factory in Johannisthal near Berlin and subsequently the power unit used was a 100-hp Mercedes. Etrich later gave up his rights in the airplane altogether, after disagreements, and about ten different firms then began building *Taubes* in different variants and with different engines.

In 1910 it was Switzerland's turn to have her own nationally-produced aircraft. The Dufaux 4 had been built in 1909 by Armand Dufaux, Switzerland's first pilot, and was a biplane with tractor propeller reminiscent of de Pischof's 1907 tractor biplane. On 28 August 1910, Dufaux crossed Lake Geneva in his aircraft.

Another monoplane which was to enhance a formula which had already proved successful in the case of the *Taube* was the Fokker Spin, the first aircraft of the Dutch constructor Anthony Fokker. In 1910, in Wiesbaden, Germany, Fokker went into partnership with Franz von Daum and built his first airplane which is commonly called the Spin I. This monoplane was powered by a 50-hp Argus and the young enthusiast managed a few 100-yard (100 m) hops, in December 1910. Von Daum destroyed the aircraft when he crashed into a tree, but Fokker managed to salvage the engine and built another monoplane with the help of Jacob Goedecker, a boat-builder who was also a flying enthusiast. The Spin II was a great improvement on its predecessor. In August a third Spin was built after von Daum had managed to wreck the Spin II. The Spin III was even better than the Spin II and Fokker was so encouraged by its satisfactory performance that he decided to start building aircraft commercially. Early in 1912 he founded Fokker Aeroplanbau G.m.b.H., at Johannisthal, where he turned out new variations of the Spin with structural modifications and different engines. Two of the second 1913 variant were bought by the German military authorities, who designated the plane the M.I.

Pioneer constructors of this period were greatly excited and stimulated by the potential of the monoplane and devoted a great deal of energy and thought to its development. Even in the United States where the biplane appeared to reign supreme, great publicity was given to the first monoplane flight, on 9 December 1909. This was the Walden III, designed by Henry W. Walden, a New York dentist who found time to build and test twelve aircraft of this type between 1909 and 1913!

Monoplanes were also built in Italy where some of the earliest were designed by Antonio Chiribiri in Turin between 1911 and 1913. The Chiribiri No. 5 made its debut in July 1912, and can be considered the peak of this designer's output. After lengthy proving trials, the aircraft was submitted for the 1913 military competition. In spite of its good performance, it failed to secure orders and as a result Antonio Chiribiri gave up aircraft construction for want of finance.

A Farman-type biplane which had been designed and built by another designer from Turin, Francesco Darbesio, was more successful. This was the Asteria No. 2 which was bought by the Italian Government and sent to Benghazi for operations against the Turks. Encouraged by this, the Società Aeronautica Asteria produced a new, slightly larger model with a small nacelle for the pilot and passenger. The Asteria No. 3 did a great deal of flying and on 20 September 1911, it set an Italian endurance record. In far from perfect weather conditions, pilot and passenger managed to remain airborne for 2 hours 2 minutes 29 seconds.

The problem of protecting the occupants of an airplane from the elements was tackled by Alliott Verdon Roe who had founded the aviation company, A. V. Roe & Co., in 1910. He conceived an original idea which worked well. Two aircraft were built, a monoplane and a biplane both of which had completely enclosed fuselages with celluloid windows for the pilot. The monoplane, Avro Type F, was tested on 1 May 1912, at Brooklands with total success, confounding the critics who had predicted that the pilot's visibility would be totally obscured by oil and exhaust fumes from the engine. Flights continued smoothly until, on 13 September, the Avro F was damaged beyond repair. The biplane was the Avro Type G.

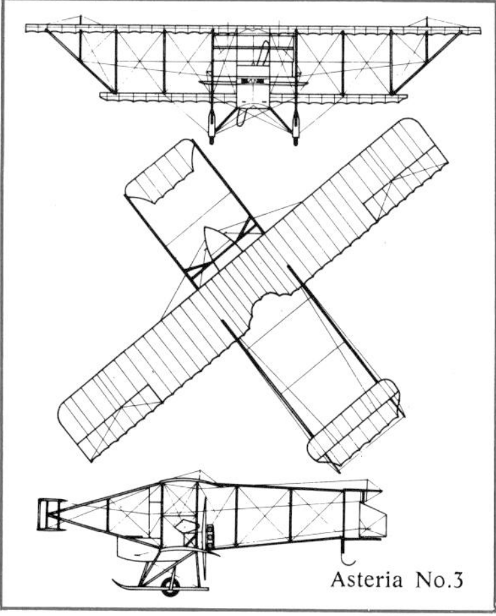

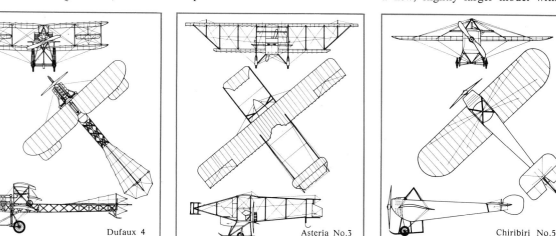

Dufaux 4

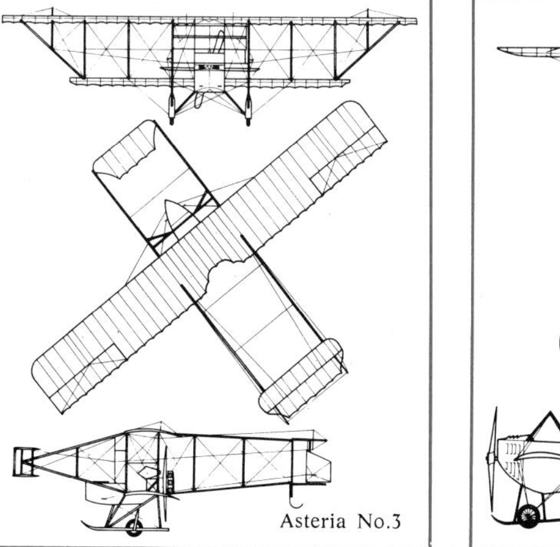

Asteria No.3

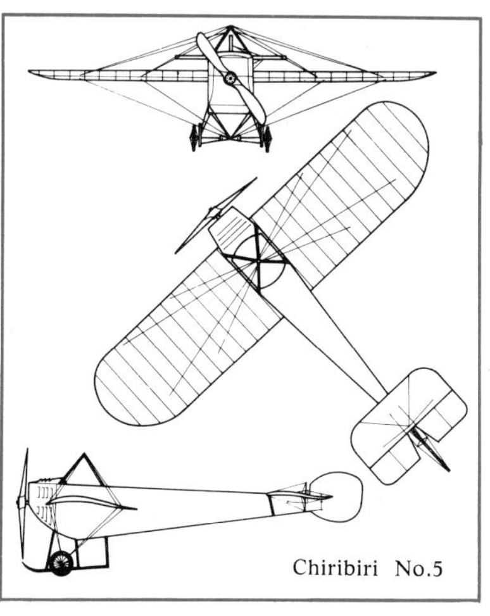

Chiribiri No.5

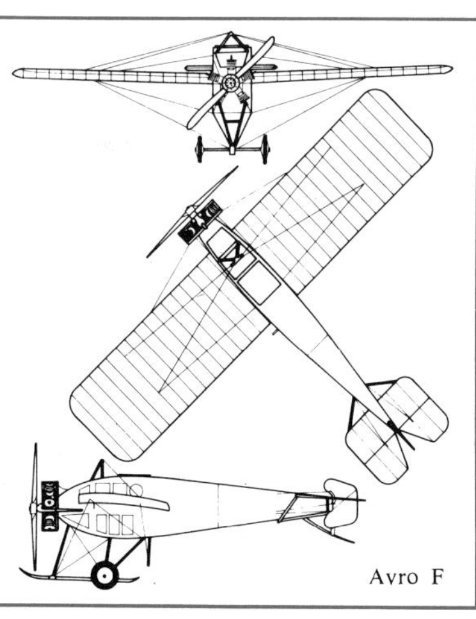

Avro F

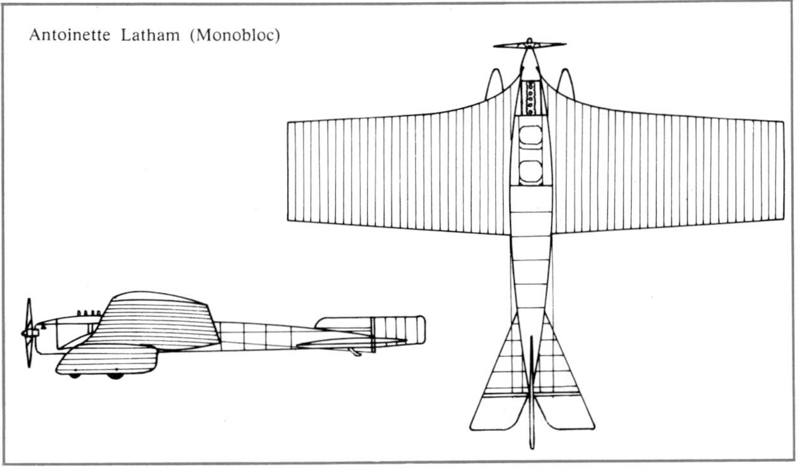
Antoinette Latham (Monobloc)

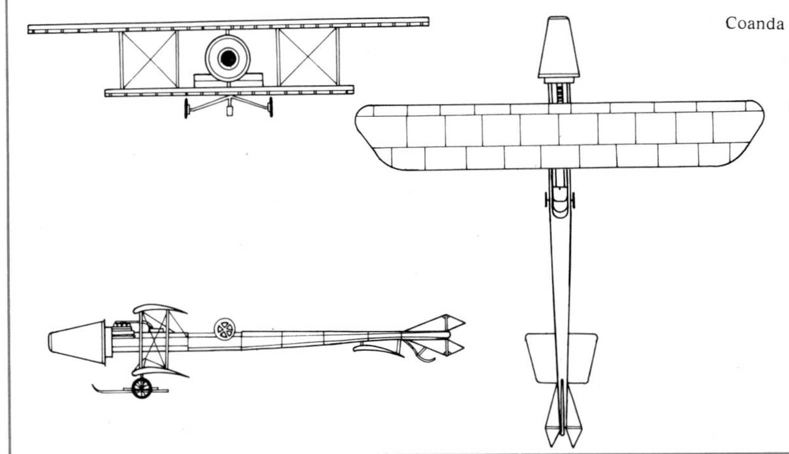
Coanda

Plate 26
Guesswork and genius: 1910–1912

During this time France kept up her role as the most innovative and enthusiastically air-minded nation. There was continuous activity, introducing new ideas into the aeronautical field, many of which had a lasting effect on the development of aviation.

One of the most revolutionary airplanes was designed and built by Henri Coanda; it was named after him and was certainly ahead of its time—it could, in fact, be considered the first "jet" aircraft in history. It never actually managed to fly, but was ample evidence of the talent of its young Romanian designer who built it when he was only twenty-four. It was presented at the Salon de l'Aéronautique in Paris in October 1910. Through a series of multiple gears, the airplane's piston engine drove a centrifugal compressor installed in the forward part of the fuselage. The main reason for its failure was the weak thrust supplied by the compressor (450 lb = 220 kg). Apart from this revolutionary form of propulsion, the Coanda biplane also impressed those who saw it with its elegance and structural ingenuity. For the first time struts and bracing wires had been reduced to a minimum and, also for the first time, the airplane was completely wooden skinned.

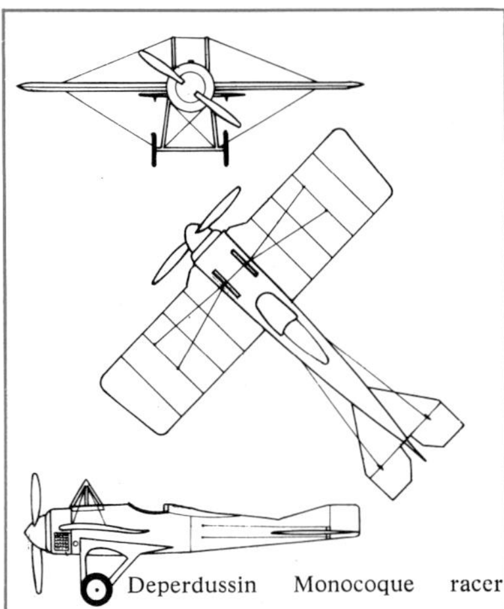
Deperdussin Monocoque racer

In 1911, Coanda built another interesting aircraft. Its structure was very similar to the previous aircraft and it was powered by two 70-hp Gnome rotary engines, positioned very unconventionally crosswise in the forward part of the fuselage, which drove a four-blade tractor propeller. The aircraft was not a success and after this new setback Coanda settled in England in 1912, where he was to have an outstanding career as a designer with the British and Colonial Aeroplane Co. (Bristol).

In the same year, 1911, another exciting airplane made its debut: the Antoinette Latham Monobloc. This was a three-seat low-wing monoplane with the crew accommodated in a completely enclosed fuselage. In order to obtain maximum performance, the Société Antoinette's designers had sought to improve the streamlining of the aircraft in every possible way: the wings were cantilevered with internal control cables and the landing gear was enclosed in streamlined fairings. Much of the skin was made up of sheets of aluminum. The overall design was, however, not fully thought out and the power-weight ratio of the machine had been underestimated. The Monobloc's takeoff weight was over 2,970 lb (1,350 kg) and it was powered by a 50-hp engine which only had enough power to lift it a few feet into the air. After some unsuccessful attempts to modify the aircraft its designer abandoned the project.

All the efforts which had been made to reduce drag and improve aerodynamic efficiency were to bear fruit in 1912, when for the first time an airplane was specifically designed for high-speed flying. The first to break the 200 km/h (124 mph) barrier and the first winner of the coveted Schneider Trophy was the Deperdussin monoplane which also won other competitions and became the speed king of the pre-war years. The aircraft was developed early in 1912 by Louis Béchereau, who was then the designer for the Société pour les Appareils Deperdussin. Béchereau took an idea of the Swedish engineer, Ruchonnet, as his starting point and built a very streamlined monocoque fuselage in plywood with a large spinner to fair in the nose. To achieve maximum power a two-row Gnome engine was fitted.

The first noteworthy achievement of this outstanding airplane was when it won the Gordon Bennett Cup in 1912 with a speed of 108.1 mph (174.01 km/h), piloted by Jules Védrines. The Deperdussin racer defended its title the following year when Maurice Prévost won the speed race, flying at an average of 124.6 mph (200.5 km/h). During this race the airplane performed spectacularly, beating the world speed record three times, and reaching a maximum speed of 126.7 mph (203.85 km/h).

Sporting and competition success did not, however, lead to commercial success for Armand Deperdussin's aircraft company. In spite of its victories and record-breaking performances, no orders were forthcoming for the aircraft and in 1913 mounting debts led to the French constructor's arrest and bankruptcy. The company survived in spite of this; it was rescued the following year by Louis Blériot who changed its name to the Société pour l'Aviation et ses Derivés. Louis Béchereau stayed on as chief designer and was to become famous, as was the acronym of the company, S.P.A.D., for the fighters they designed and built during World War I. Another exceptional designer who was to play a considerable part in the development of aviation also showed talent at this time: Louis Breguet. His ability is well illustrated by his Breguet III of 1912 and represents the tractor biplane in its definitive form. The aircraft attracted great interest, chiefly because of its military potential: in 1912 alone the French Army ordered 32 Breguet III's, the British Army ordered five, the Italian Army bought three and Sweden took one.

Louis Breguet had first taken an interest in aviation when he was at the École Supérieure de l'Électricité. In 1909 he built his first "gyroplane" with his brother Jacques and an engineer named Charles Richet. This was a kind of helicopter with four large vertical propellers driven by an Antoinette engine, which had managed to rise a few inches from the ground. After a series of gyroplane projects (the model 2-bis rose just over 13 feet (4 m) into the air on 22 July 1908), Breguet founded the Société des Ateliers d'Aviation Breguet-Richet and decided to switch to fixed-wing aircraft. He produced his first biplane in 1909 and this was successfully flown at Reims, although only over short distances. The Breguet I was an influential design since it had some highly original technical and structural features, such as the considerable use of metal components and

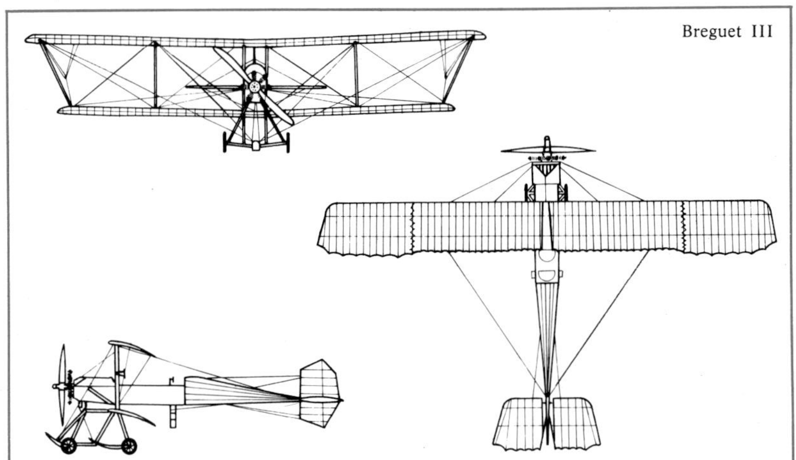
Breguet III

the ingenious controls for elevators and ailerons. Although the aircraft was seriously damaged when landing after its third flight at Reims, it had taught Breguet a great deal and he used this knowledge when designing his next model, from which the Breguet III was derived.

The designer made even greater use of metal components in his Model III biplane. Apart from the all-steel tube basic frame, Breguet used sheet aluminum to cover the forward part of the fuselage. This gave the aircraft such an unusual appearance that the Royal Navy pilots lost no time in giving it the nickname "The Tin Whistle"—no doubt prompted to do so in part by the fact that it made metallic whistling noises in flight. Different engines were installed in various models of this type, each of which gave rise to a variant with its own name. The engines most commonly used were the 60-hp V-8 Renault air-cooled, the 50-hp or 80-hp Gnome rotary and the Canton-Unné 80-hp or 110-hp 7-cylinder water-cooled radial. Some Breguets with Canton-Unné engines were still in squadron service in August 1914.

Plate 27
The birth of the seaplane: 1910

Another Frenchman, Henri Fabre, introduced a new member to the growing family of aircraft types and one which was to play a considerable role in the future. On 28 March 1910, the first ever powered takeoff from water was made from La Mède harbor, near Marseilles. Fabre's Hydravion looked like an extremely fragile and clumsy canard monoplane, bristling with spars and with three convex flat-bottomed floats. Henri Fabre had never piloted an airplane before, but on that historic morning, once he had flown just over two kilometers, skimming along about two meters above the surface of the water, and alighted safely, he became a celebrity in aviation history.

The first attempts to produce a flying machine which could take off from water went back to the beginning of the century. William Kress, an Austrian, was unsuccessful in his endeavors. He had devoted himself to the design and construction of "heavier-than-air" flying machines from 1877 onwards and had experimented with flying models powered by elastic bands until, in 1898, he came to the conclusion that takeoff would be much more easily achieved from a liquid surface than from *terra firma*. It took him three years of hard work to design and build the first floatplane in history: this was a complicated machine with three tandem wings, elevators and rudders on the tail and driven by two pusher propellers powered by a petrol engine. The designer, who was by then over 68 years of age, wanted to test the aircraft himself and, in October 1901, the one and only test was made on Lake Tullnerbach near Vienna. The seaplane floated for a little while, but failed to rise from the water and then, after a sudden turn, it capsized and sank. This experiment was not repeated.

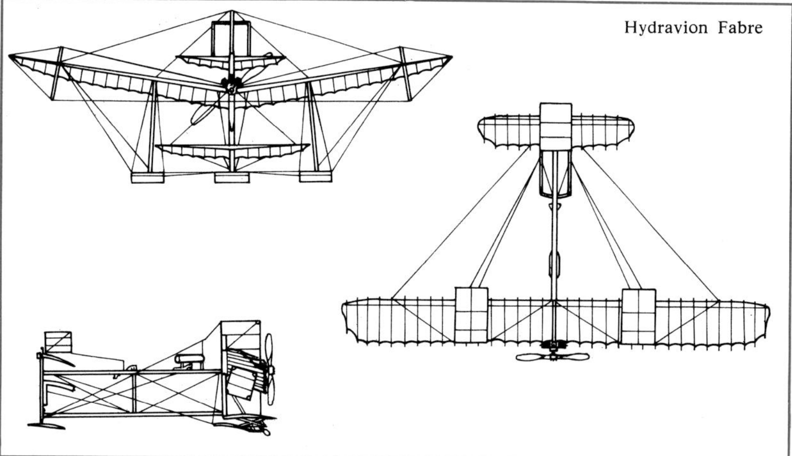
Hydravion Fabre

It was not until 1905 that another seaplane was tested, this time in France, being the result of a joint venture by two famous aviation pioneers, Gabriel Voisin and Ernest Archdeacon. They had carried out experiments with aircraft which resembled the Wright brothers' biplanes, and constructed a machine of that type which was mounted on floats. The Voisin-Archdeacon float-glider was tested twice, on 8 June and 18 July 1905, on the Seine on a stretch of the river between Sèvres and Billancourt. The machine was pulled by a steamer and on the first attempt it managed to rise above the water and fly for about 490 feet (150 m). Twice this distance was covered when the glider was tested again on 18 July.

Louis Blériot also started his aviation career with a seaplane in the same year. In 1905 Blériot had ordered a variant of the Voisin-Archdeacon float-glider (from Gabriel Voisin, which was subsequently known as the Blériot-Voisin). Blériot narrowly escaped drowning when he unsuccessfully tested it for the only time. After this Blériot designed an unusual aircraft with wings which were elliptical when seen from the front or rear, which was called the Blériot III and was tested for the first time in May 1906 on Lake Enghien. Neither this first model nor two subsequent variants (one a seaplane, one a landplane) ever managed to fly.

The next year Henri Fabre's seaplane success was emulated across the Atlantic, in the United States, by Glenn Hammond Curtiss who was already famous for his *Golden Flyer*.

In 1908 Curtiss began testing a seaplane version of his first plane, the *June Bug*, but it was only on 26 January 1911, at San Diego, California, that the first Curtiss seaplane took off from the water. The seaplane, the D Hydro, was equipped with a central float and two stabilizers under the wingtips. On 17 February 1911, the Curtiss D-III Tractor Hydro carried out a demonstration flight from North Island naval base at San Diego to the cruiser U.S.S. *Pennsylvania* anchored in San Diego harbor. Being convinced by the demonstration, the U.S. Navy purchased two E models and designated them A-1 and A-2. There followed a period of intense activity aimed at developing and broadening co-operation between ships and aircraft. The first U.S. Navy pilots were Lieutenants Theodore G. Ellyson and John H. Towers who made numerous test flights and experiments, the most important of which were concerned with perfecting launching techniques. Various systems were tried, including catapulting the aircraft with a compressed-air launcher developed for torpedoes. During these exhaustive tests Ellyson set up several new records, including a flight of 112 miles (180 km) from Annapolis, Maryland, to Milford Haven, Virginia, in 2 hours 2 minutes with a passenger on board.

The Curtiss A-1 and A-2 were followed by other models, which only differed in minor details. The A-2 underwent an interesting transformation, a superstructure being added to the central float originally fitted, forming a proper hull inside which the pilot was positioned, fully protected from the elements.

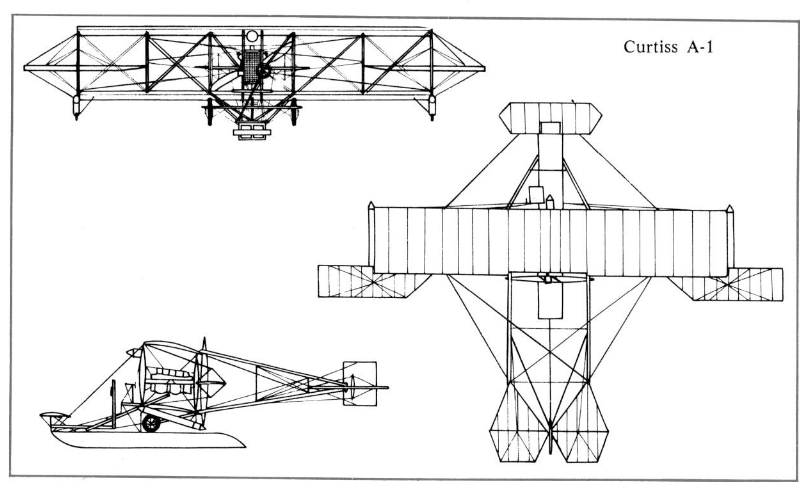
Curtiss A-1

Plate 28
The seaplane—early days

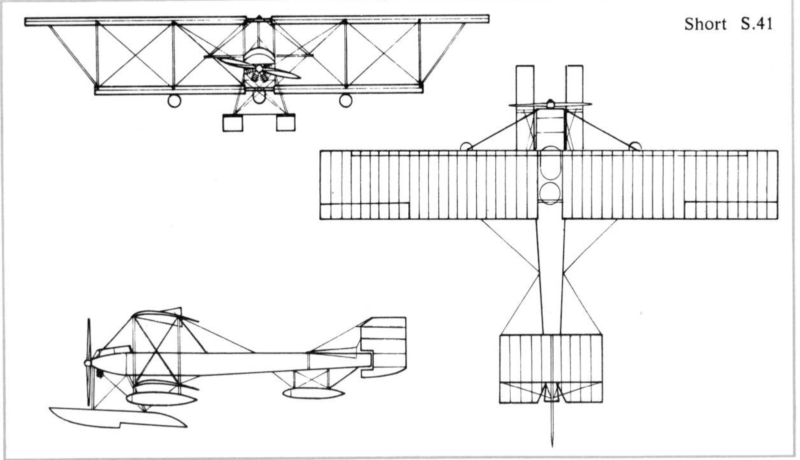
Short S.41

After Fabre's venture and Curtiss's resounding success, the seaplane became as much an accepted part of the aviation scene as the conventional landplane, and Great Britain was soon to set much store by the development and use of these aircraft, following the lead of France and the United States.

Some early experiments had been carried out in 1909 by Jack Humphreys with his Waterplane. This was in essence a sesquiplane with twin pusher-propellers driven by a 35-hp J.A.P. engine. The triangular tailplane was mounted on a universal joint which meant that it could be rotated in all directions and thus act as elevators and rudder. Two triangular ailerons were fitted on to the tips of the upper wing. The machine's buoyancy and stability on the water was to be ensured by its boat-shaped fuselage and two lateral stabilizers which were attached to the hull and braced to the upper wing by long struts. Humphreys had hoped to exhibit his Waterplane at the 1909 Olympia Aero Show but it was too large to get into the exhibition hall. In April 1909 the seaplane was tested on the River Colne at Wivenhoe in Essex, but here disaster struck. The hull filled with water and sank. The machine was salvaged and was refloated, but never managed to take off.

Short Brothers made a great name for themselves with their marine aircraft. They first made their reputation in this class with the S.41 of 1912 which went into series production for the Royal Navy. The prototype of the S.41 appeared at the beginning of 1912, but as a landplane. It was quickly converted by fitting floats and successfully tested.

The seaplane with its float undercarriage did not for long have the market all to itself. In 1913 Sopwith's Bat Boat I introduced the flying boat with a central hull to Europe. This aircraft was exhibited at the Olympia Aero Show in February 1913 and so impressed the Admiralty that they bought it.

In the Spring of 1913 the American tycoon Mortimer Singer offered a prize of £500 to the first all-British amphibian to complete a course of six return flights between two points 5 miles (8 km) apart, one of which was on land, one at sea. There was a time limit of five hours in which to complete the course. Sopwith decided to enter and, after changing the Bat Boat's engine from a 90-hp Austro-Daimler to a British 100-hp Green to meet the prize rules and fitting a pair of retractable wheels to turn it into an amphibian, chose the trial date for 8 July 1913. Carrying chief test pilot Harry Hawker and an observer from the Navy, the Bat Boat completed the competition course in 3 hours 25 minutes.

This victory encouraged Sopwith to start work on an even further improved version of the Bat Boat. Added incentive was given by the competition organized by the *Daily Mail* with a prize of £5,000. Sopwith built two models of the new and larger version, called, predictably, Bat Boat II, with the next year's (1914) *Daily Mail* Hydro-Aeroplane Trial in mind, and one of these flying boats was supplied to Germany. The bigger Bat Boats were fitted with 200-hp Salmson Canton-Unné engines.

Both Bat Boats were found to be very satisfactory when flown in 1914, proving to be sturdy, fast and particularly stable. The one bought by the German Navy was used over the Baltic and the other was eventually bought by the Royal Navy and was kept in service until 1915. The war meant that the *Daily Mail*'s 1914 competition was cancelled and so the Bat Boat II never got the opportunity to show how it could perform in competitive flying.

Italy was also very interested in the military potential of the seaplane and in 1910 one had been built in the naval yards at La Spezia. It was designed by Mario Calderara, the naval officer who had been taught to fly by Wilbur Wright in 1909. The following year Captain Alessandro Guidoni modified a Henry Farman biplane and turned it into a seaplane. In June 1912, Captains Crocco and Ricaldoni flew a seaplane at Vigna di Valle, which they had jointly designed and built. None of these seaplanes had any lasting effect on the aviation scene and the Pateras-Pescara seaplane which appeared two years later was also to prove unimpressive. This was certainly a very original design: a high-wing monoplane with twin floats, powered by two Gnome rotary engines installed on the fuselage center-line and driving a pusher and a tractor propeller.

While the military potential of the seaplane was being discovered, this type was also doing extremely well in competitive flying. The first international Hydro-Aeroplane Meeting was held in the Principality of Monaco in 1912 and attracted many French and foreign competitors. Trials had been specifically set up to see that competing aircraft had to cope with rough water as well as calm seas for takeoff and alighting, to test both pilots and aircraft to the full. Two Farman biplanes which had been converted into floatplanes carried off the laurels by winning first and second places. The two Canard-Voisins which took part were less successful. These had been built by the Voisin brothers the year before, and were of unusual design. They were given several proving flights in August 1911, to gauge the possibility of using them as seaplanes. (The Canard-Voisin had originally been built with landing undercarriage and was then fitted with four Fabre-type floats.) In this "hybrid" configuration the aircraft was successfully flown on 3 August, taking off from Issy airfield and coming down safely on the Seine near Billancourt. There had been some misgivings about the aircraft's ability to take off from water for the return journey but all went well.

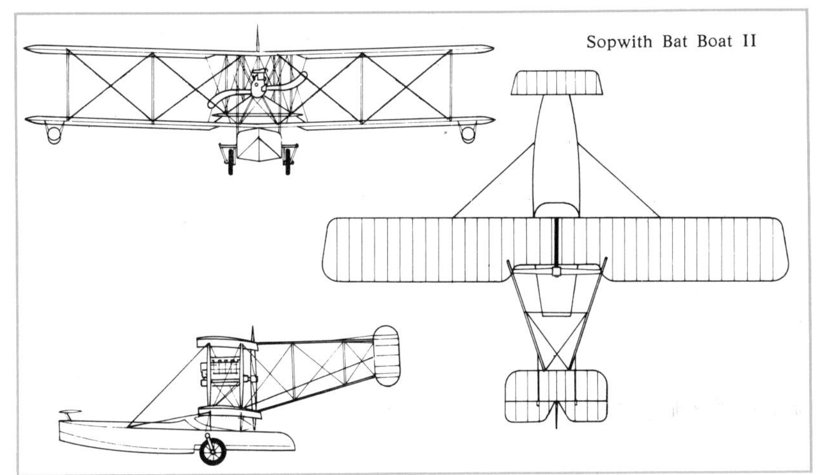
Sopwith Bat Boat II

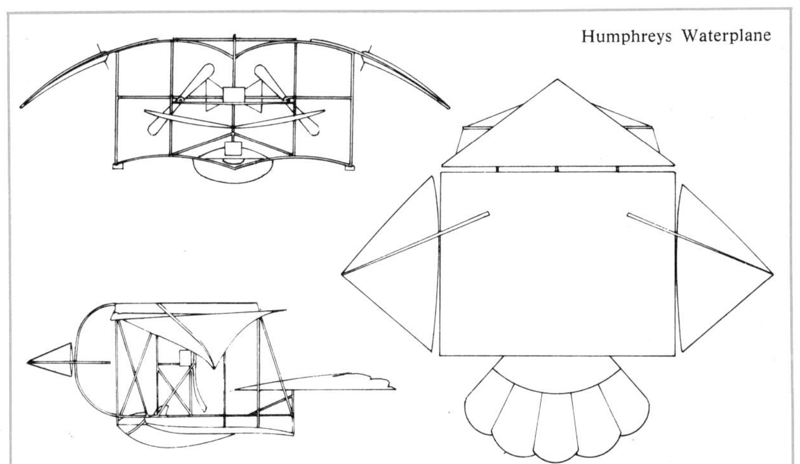
Humphreys Waterplane

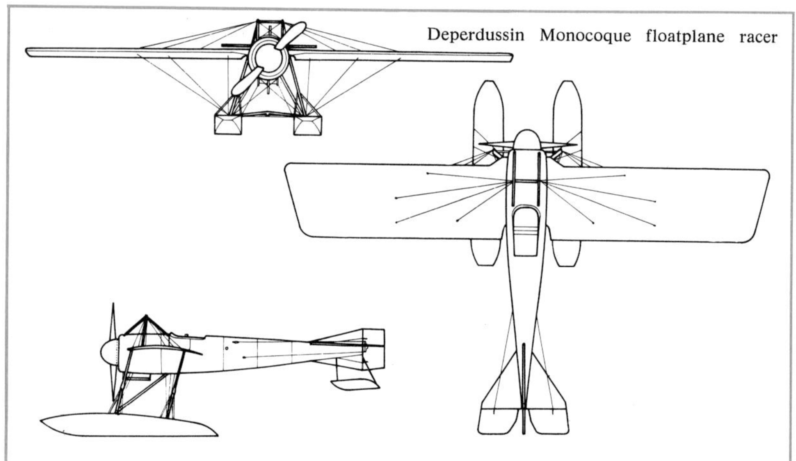
Deperdussin Monocoque floatplane racer

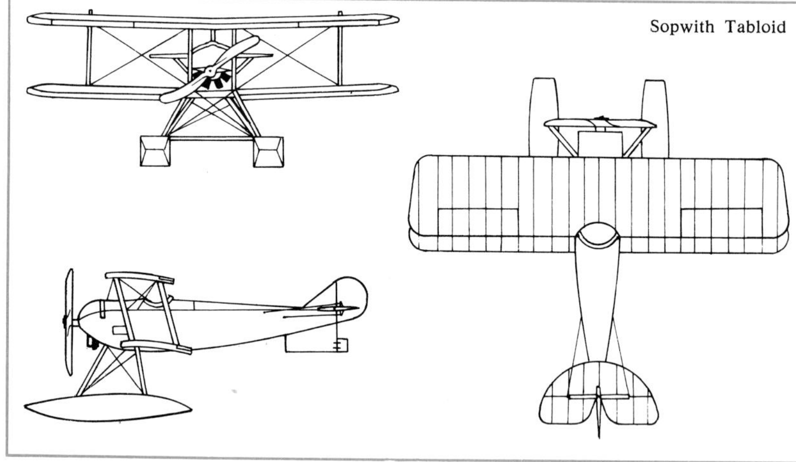
Sopwith Tabloid

Plate 29
The world's first passenger service is started with a flying boat

The first Schneider Trophy Contest was included as one item of the second international Hydro-Aeroplane Meeting held at Monaco in 1913 and the course consisted of twenty-eight 6-mile (10 km) laps.

A French industrialist, Jacques Schneider, had announced on 5 December 1912, that he was putting up the prize money in order to promote the development of the seaplane. The first year's prize went to an aircraft which was already famous: the Deperdussin "Monocoque" racer, the landplane version of which had left all its rivals far behind in the 1912 Gordon Bennett Cup. The Deperdussin "Monocoque" floatplane racer was a larger version of Louis Béchereau's original design, with three floats—two large floats forward and one small float under the tail. The Deperdussin made what was to be the first of two takeoffs in this race at 8.05 a.m. on the morning of 16 April piloted by Maurice Prévost. There were only three other competitors: Roland Garros in a Morane-Saulnier, Gabriel Espanet in a Nieuport and the American, Charles T. Weymann (the only foreign competitor) in another Nieuport. The Deperdussin monoplane was far and away the best: it won the race in spite of the fact that the judges made Prévost repeat his takeoff and fly an extra 6-mile (10 km) lap because of a supposed violation of the rules. Because of this Prévost's average speed appeared to be low: 45.75 mph (73.63 km/h).

This was to be the one and only French victory in the Schneider Trophy race, which for the rest of its history (1913–31) was to be dominated by the fierce rivalry of the Americans, the Italians and the British.

The British won the 1914 Schneider Trophy, which was to be the last race until after World War I, with a specially modified Sopwith Tabloid biplane, which had had two large floats fitted to enable it to compete, and was powered by an outstanding engine. On 20 April at Monaco, Howard Pixton flew at an average speed of 86.78 mph (139.66 km/h) and in two extra laps he reached 92 mph (148 km/h) establishing a new seaplane record and giving Great Britain its first major international success in aviation. The special version of the Sopwith Tabloid prepared for the Schneider Trophy race was not substantially different from the model which had appeared the previous autumn. The original landplane was designed by T. O. M. Sopwith and F. Sigrist whose aim was to produce a fast tractor biplane which could be used for military reconnaissance duties. The prototype was built in great secrecy and preliminary tests were carried out at Brooklands in November 1913. These were followed by the official evaluation tests in which the Tabloid immediately gave proof of its speed and maneuvrability. These tests were conducted at the Royal Aircraft Factory at Farnborough and, on 29 November, the Tabloid reached a top speed of 92 mph (148 km/h) in horizontal flight and showed a rate of climb of 1,200 feet (336 m) per minute. On the same day the test pilot, Harry Hawker, flew the Tabloid to Hendon where one of the popular Saturday air meetings was being held. More than 50,000 spectators saw the new Sopwith fly two low-altitude laps round the course at more than 90 mph (145 km/h). It made such an impression that it was ordered in large numbers by the Army and the Navy as a single-seat reconnaissance aircraft.

This success prompted Sopwith to get a Tabloid ready for the second Schneider Trophy race. Since the race was only open to seaplanes, the machine was modified by fitting a large central float in place of the landing gear. The 100-hp Gnome engine was also installed for the occasion. When the plane was first tested it suddenly capsized when still floating on the water. The design team decided to have two floats instead of one; time was, by now, very short and so it was decided to slice the original float in half to make two new ones which proved to be the ideal solution. The final modification before the race was the replacement of the original propeller with a better one and the little seaplane was all set to win the Trophy.

Once back in England after its victory, the floats were removed at Sopwith's factory at Kingston-on-Thames and a V-strut landing gear was fitted. The Tabloid was flown by R. H. Barnwell in the 1914 Aerial Derby, but owing to very poor visibility it did not complete the course.

The flying boat made an even more significant and lasting contribution to the history of aviation than these sporting achievements. On 1 January 1914, a Benoist XIV flying boat inaugurated the first scheduled passenger airline service, flying the 21 miles (34.5 km) between St. Petersburg and Tampa, both in Florida, on a regular basis. The little biplane could carry one passenger besides the pilot and had been designed and built by a St. Louis industrialist, Thomas Benoist, who had hit upon the idea of starting up a commercial airline towards the end of 1913. On 13 December that same year Benoist signed a contract with the municipal authorities of St. Petersburg, Florida, who agreed to his project provided he received official approval and could provide the initial investment.

The St. Petersburg–Tampa Airboat Line started operations on 1 January 1914, and continued to run two regular daily flights until the end of March. The fare was five dollars—although a certain A. C. Pheil paid four hundred dollars for the privilege of being the airline's first passenger.

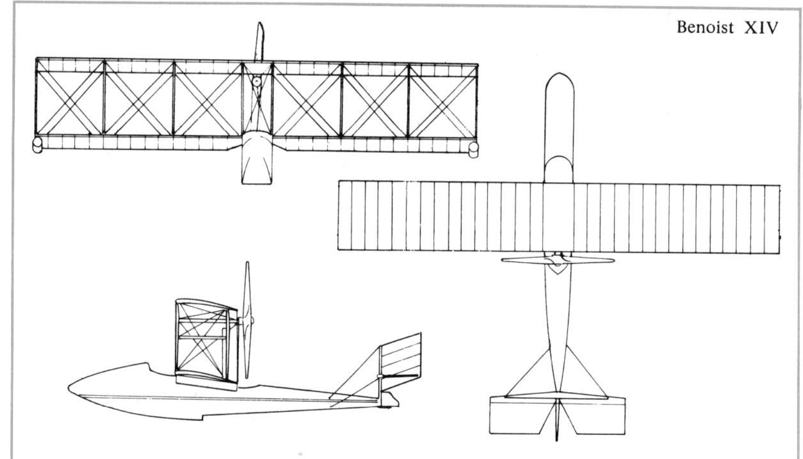
Benoist XIV

Speed and endurance records: 1906–1914

Plate 31

Date	Place	Pilot	Aircraft	Engine	(km/h)	(mph)
1908 21 IX	Auvours (F)	Wilbur Wright	Wright Model A	30 HP Wright	44	27.2
1909 31 V	Juvisy (F)	Léon Delagrange	Voisin	45 HP Antoinette	45	27.9
1909 3 IX	Juvisy (F)	Cap. Ferber	Voisin	45 HP Antoinette	48	29.7
1909 28 VIII	Reims (F)	Louis Blériot	Blériot	60 HP E.N.V.	76,9	47.8
1910 29 X	Belmont Park (USA)	Alfred Léblanc	Blériot	100 HP Gnome	109,7	68.2
1911 1 VII	Eastchurch (GB)	C. Weymann	Nieuport	100 HP Gnome	125	70.5
1912 9 IX	Chicago (USA)	Jules Védrines	Deperdussin	100 HP Gnome	174,1	108
1913 29 IX	Reims (F)	Marcel Prévost	Deperdussin	160 HP Le Rhône	204	124.5

km/h/mph 10/6 20/12 30/19 40/25 50/31 60/37 70/43 80/50 90/56 100/62 110/68 120/75 130/81 140/87 150/93 160/99 170/106 180/112 190/118 200/124

Date	Place	Pilot	Aircraft	Engine	Time (hrs	mins	secs)
1906 12 XI	Bagatelle (F)	Santos-Dumont	Santos-Dumont 14bis	50 HP Antoinette	0	0	21
1907 26 X	Issy (F)	Henry Farman	Voisin	40 HP Vivinus	0	0	52
1908 13 I	Issy (F)	Henry Farman	Voisin	50 HP Antoinette	0	1	28
1908 21 III	Issy (F)	Henry Farman	Voisin	50 HP Antoinette	0	3	39
1908 11 IV	Issy (F)	Léon Delagrange	Voisin	40 HP Vivinus	0	6	39
1908 30 V	Rome (I)	Léon Delagrange	Voisin	50 HP E.N.V.	0	15	26
1908 6 VII	Issy (F)	Henry Farman	Voisin	50 HP Antoinette	0	20	19
1908 6 IX	Issy (F)	Léon Delagrange	Voisin	40 HP Vivinus	0	29	53
1908 21 IX	Auvours (F)	Wilbur Wright	Wright Model A	30 HP Wright	1	31	25
1908 18 XII	Auvours (F)	Wilbur Wright	Wright Model A	30 HP Wright	1	54	53
1908 31 XII	Auvours (F)	Wilbur Wright	Wright Model A	30 HP Wright	2	20	23
1909 27 VIII	Béthény (F)	Louis Paulhan	Voisin	50 HP Gnome	2	43	24
1909 27 VIII	Béthény (F)	Henry Farman	H. Farman III	50 HP Gnome	3	4	56
1909 3 XII	Mourmelon (F)	Henry Farman	H. Farman III	50 HP Gnome	4	17	53
1910 9 VII	Reims (F)	Labouchère	Antoinette VII	50 HP Antoinette	4	19	0
1910 10 VII	Reims (F)	Jan Olieslaegers	Blériot	50 HP Gnome	5	3	5
1910 28 X	Étampes (F)	Maurice Tabuteau	M. Farman	70 HP Renault	6	0	0
1910 18 XII	Étampes (F)	Henry Farman	H. Farman III	50 HP Gnome	8	12	47.4
1911 11 IX	Buc (F)	Fourny	M. Farman	70 HP Renault	11	1	29.2
1911 11 IX	Buc (F)	Fourny	M. Farman	70 HP Renault	13	17	57.2
1914 4 II	Johannisthal (D)	Langer	L.F.G. Roland	100 HP Mercedes	14	7	0
1914 24 IV	Étampes (F)	Poulet	Caudron	50 HP Gnome	16	28	56
1914 24 VI	Johannisthal (D)	Basser	Rumpler	100 HP Mercedes	18	10	0
1914 26-27 VI	Johannisthal (D)	Landmann	Albatros	100 HP Mercedes	21	48	45
1914 10 VII	Johannisthal (D)	Boehm	Albatros	100 HP Mercedes	24	12	0

0 1 2 3 4 5 6 7 8 9 10 11 12 13 14 15 16 17 18 19 20 21 22 23 24 25 h

Plate 32

Distance records: 1906–1914

Date	Place	Pilot	Aircraft	Engine	Distance (km)	Distance (ml.)
1906 14 IX	Bagatelle (F)	Santos-Dumont	Santos-Dumont 14bis	50 HP Antoinette	7,8 m	8.6 yd
1906 12 XI	Bagatelle (F)	Santos-Dumont	Santos-Dumont 14bis	50 HP Antoinette	220 m	240.6 yd
1907 26 X	Issy (F)	Henry Farman	Voisin	40 HP Vivinus	770 m	855.5 yd
1908 13 I	Issy (F)	Henry Farman	Voisin	50 HP Antoinette	1	0.625
1908 21 III	Issy (F)	Henry Farman	Voisin	50 HP Antoinette	2	1.25
1908 11 IV	Issy (F)	Léon Delagrange	Voisin	40 HP Vivinus	3,925	2.439
1908 30 V	Roma (I)	Léon Delagrange	Voisin	50 HP E.N.V.	12,75	7.923
1908 6 IX	Issy (F)	Léon Delagrange	Voisin	40 HP Vivinus	24,125	14.991
1908 16 IX	Issy (F)	Léon Delagrange	Voisin	40 HP Vivinus	66,6	41.385
1908 21 IX	Auvours (F)	Wilbur Wright	Voisin	24 HP Wright	97	60.9
1908 18 XII	Auvours (F)	Wilbur Wright	Wright Model A	30 HP Wright	99,8	62.016
1908 31 XII	Auvours (F)	Wilbur Wright	Wright Model A	30 HP Wright	124,7	77.488
1909 27 VIII	Reims (F)	Henry Farman	H. Farman III	50 HP Gnome	180	112
1909 3 XI	Mourmelon (F)	Henry Farman	H. Farman III	50 HP Gnome	210	150
1910 10 VII	Reims (F)	Jan Olieslaegers	Blériot	50 HP Gnome	225	139.5
1910 20 VII	Reims (F)	Jan Olieslaegers	Blériot	50 HP Gnome	397,75	247.162
1910 28 X	Étampes (F)	Maurice Tabuteau	M. Farman	70 HP Renault	465.72	289.398
1910 30 XII	Buc (F)	Maurice Tabuteau	M. Farman	70 HP Renault	584,745	363.361
1911 16 VII	Kiewitt (D)	Jan Olieslaegers	Blériot	50 HP Gnome	625	388.375
1911 1 IX	Buc (F)	Fourny	M. Farman	70 HP Renault	722,935	449.232
1911 24 XII	Pau (F)	Gobé	Nieuport	70 HP Gnome	740,299	460.022
1912 11 IX	Étampes (F)	Fourny	M. Farman	70 HP Renault	1.010,9	628.173
1914 28 VI	Johannisthal (D)	Landmann	Albatros	100 HP Mercedes	1.900	1178

km/ml: 100/62, 200/124, 300/186, 400/248, 500/310, 600/372, 700/434, 800/496, 900/558, 1000/620, 1100/682, 1200/744, 1300/806, 1400/868, 1500/930, 1600/992, 1700/1054, 1800/1116, 1900/1178, 2000/1240, 2100/1302

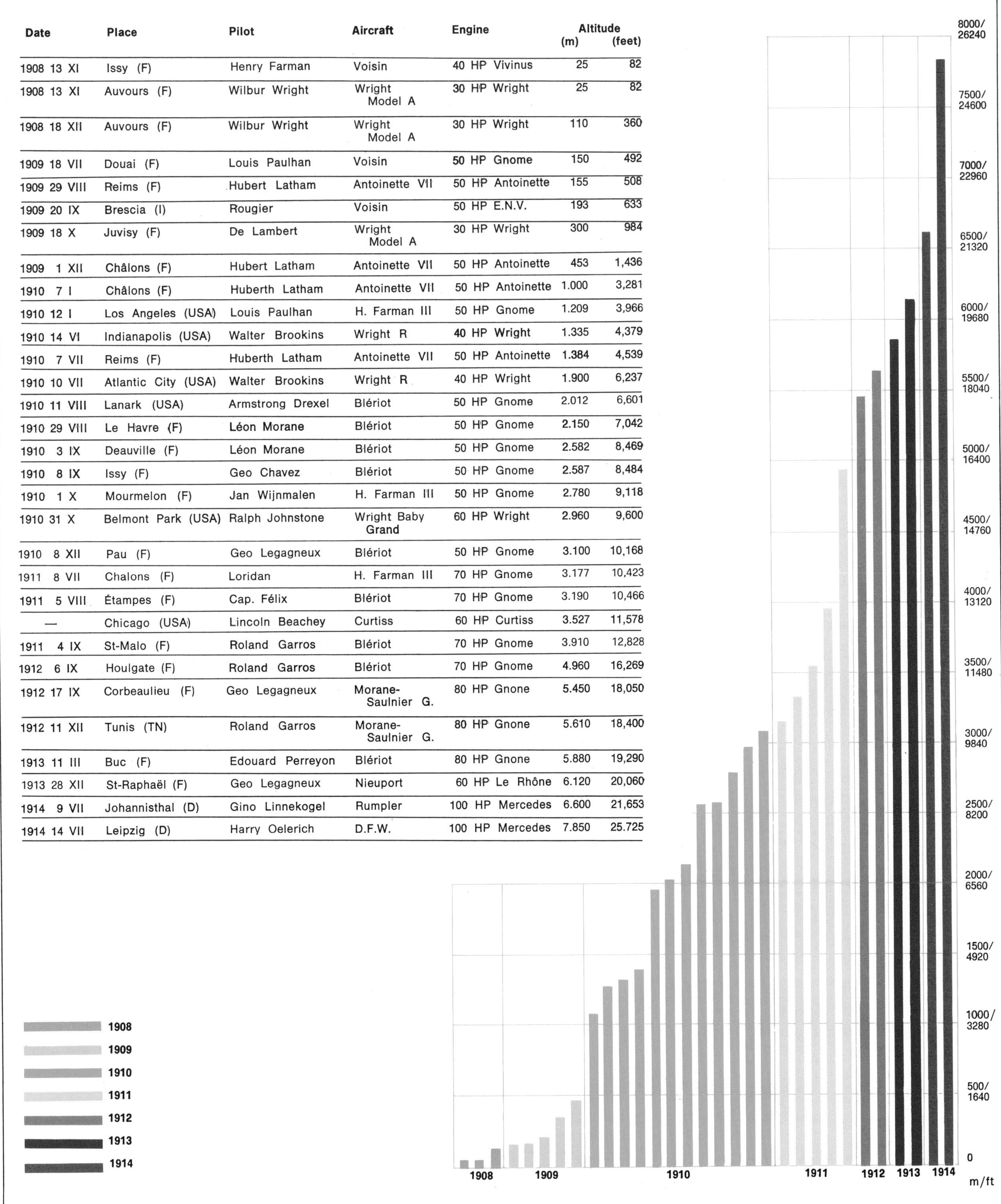

Date	Place	Pilot	Aircraft	Engine	Altitude (m)	(feet)
1908 13 XI	Issy (F)	Henry Farman	Voisin	40 HP Vivinus	25	82
1908 13 XI	Auvours (F)	Wilbur Wright	Wright Model A	30 HP Wright	25	82
1908 18 XII	Auvours (F)	Wilbur Wright	Wright Model A	30 HP Wright	110	360
1909 18 VII	Douai (F)	Louis Paulhan	Voisin	50 HP Gnome	150	492
1909 29 VIII	Reims (F)	Hubert Latham	Antoinette VII	50 HP Antoinette	155	508
1909 20 IX	Brescia (I)	Rougier	Voisin	50 HP E.N.V.	193	633
1909 18 X	Juvisy (F)	De Lambert	Wright Model A	30 HP Wright	300	984
1909 1 XII	Châlons (F)	Hubert Latham	Antoinette VII	50 HP Antoinette	453	1,436
1910 7 I	Châlons (F)	Huberth Latham	Antoinette VII	50 HP Antoinette	1.000	3,281
1910 12 I	Los Angeles (USA)	Louis Paulhan	H. Farman III	50 HP Gnome	1.209	3,966
1910 14 VI	Indianapolis (USA)	Walter Brookins	Wright R	40 HP Wright	1.335	4,379
1910 7 VII	Reims (F)	Huberth Latham	Antoinette VII	50 HP Antoinette	1.384	4,539
1910 10 VII	Atlantic City (USA)	Walter Brookins	Wright R	40 HP Wright	1.900	6,237
1910 11 VIII	Lanark (USA)	Armstrong Drexel	Blériot	50 HP Gnome	2.012	6,601
1910 29 VIII	Le Havre (F)	Léon Morane	Blériot	50 HP Gnome	2.150	7,042
1910 3 IX	Deauville (F)	Léon Morane	Blériot	50 HP Gnome	2.582	8,469
1910 8 IX	Issy (F)	Geo Chavez	Blériot	50 HP Gnome	2.587	8,484
1910 1 X	Mourmelon (F)	Jan Wijnmalen	H. Farman III	50 HP Gnome	2.780	9,118
1910 31 X	Belmont Park (USA)	Ralph Johnstone	Wright Baby Grand	60 HP Wright	2.960	9,600
1910 8 XII	Pau (F)	Geo Legagneux	Blériot	50 HP Gnome	3.100	10,168
1911 8 VII	Chalons (F)	Loridan	H. Farman III	70 HP Gnome	3.177	10,423
1911 5 VIII	Étampes (F)	Cap. Félix	Blériot	70 HP Gnome	3.190	10,466
—	Chicago (USA)	Lincoln Beachey	Curtiss	60 HP Curtiss	3.527	11,578
1911 4 IX	St-Malo (F)	Roland Garros	Blériot	70 HP Gnome	3.910	12,828
1912 6 IX	Houlgate (F)	Roland Garros	Blériot	70 HP Gnome	4.960	16,269
1912 17 IX	Corbeaulieu (F)	Geo Legagneux	Morane-Saulnier G.	80 HP Gnone	5.450	18,050
1912 11 XII	Tunis (TN)	Roland Garros	Morane-Saulnier G.	80 HP Gnone	5.610	18,400
1913 11 III	Buc (F)	Edouard Perreyon	Blériot	80 HP Gnone	5.880	19,290
1913 28 XII	St-Raphaël (F)	Geo Legagneux	Nieuport	60 HP Le Rhône	6.120	20,060
1914 9 VII	Johannisthal (D)	Gino Linnekogel	Rumpler	100 HP Mercedes	6.600	21,653
1914 14 VII	Leipzig (D)	Harry Oelerich	D.F.W.	100 HP Mercedes	7.850	25.725

Photographic Appendix

Orville Wright making the first controled and sustained powered flight, in The Flyer, at Kitty Hawk - 1903, USA (18)

The original Wright Flyer - 1903, USA (18)

Wright Flyer No.3 - 1905, USA (18)

Santos-Dumont 14bis - 1906, F (19)

Ellehammer IV - 1908, DK (20)

Vuia No.1 - 1906, F (20)

Esnault-Pelterie R.E.P.1 - 1907, F (20)

Blériot VII - 1907, F (22)

De Pischof-Koechlin - 1907, F (22)

Voisin-Farman on first 1 km flight - 1908, F (19)

Voisin-Farman - 1907, F (19)

Léon Delagrange and Henry Farman in the Voisin-Farman at Issy - 1908, (18)

Goupy II - 1909, F (22)

June Bug - 1908, USA (23)

Cygnet II - 1908, USA (23)

Photographic Appendix

Silver Dart - 1908, USA (23)

Cody Michelin Cup - 1910, GB (24)

Ponzelli-Miller - 1909 (20)

Etrich Taube - 1910, A (25)

Dunne D.5 - 1910, GB (24)

Dufaux 4 - 1910, CH (25)

Wright R (Baby Wright) - 1910, USA (18)

Antoinette IV - 1909, F (22)

Hydravion Fabre - 1919, F (27)

Walden III - 1909, USA (25)

Antoinette Latham Monobloc - 1911, F (26)

Curtiss A-1 - 1911, USA (27)

Chiribiri No.5 - 1912, I (25)

Deperdussin Monocoque racer - 1912, F (26)

Deperdussin Monocoque floatplane racer - 1913, F (29)

3.

THE BIRTH OF COMMERCIAL AVIATION

The coming of peace meant that the brakes were suddenly applied to the enormous expansion of the aeronautical industry, halting the momentum which had gathered pace during the four years of war. Production was reduced to the bare minimum and was just allowed to tick over. By now, however, the airplane had really come of age and was universally accepted almost without question as an indispensable part of the contemporary scene. The time had come for Europe to repair the devastation caused by the war and for both victors and vanquished to reorganize themselves, and the airplane was to play a fundamental role in postwar reconstruction, after having helped to shape the course and alter many aspects of the war. Aircraft development continued and in the ten years after the war, it was in Europe that the foundations were laid for what was to be the great commercial aviation industry of the years to come. This only evolved slowly, but continual progress was made. It is ironic that the first European civil airline was started by those who had lost the war, the defeated Germans; this was also the first sustained regular air passenger service in the world and predated the first airline in France, the most advanced aeronautical nation, by just over a month. The historic date was 5 February 1919, when Deutsche Luft-Reederei inaugurated its daily service from Berlin to Weimar—120 miles (193 km)—using A.E.G. biplanes—war surplus machines converted to carry two passengers.

This was not, however, the first time such a service had been launched. Apart from the experiment in the U.S.A. in the first three months of 1914 (the St. Petersburg—Tampa Airboat Line); five years earlier on 16 November 1909, Count Ferdinand von Zeppelin (the inventor of the rigid airship) had founded the first commercial air transport company, DELAG, but the company used dirigibles, not airplanes, and did not operate scheduled services. Up to the start of World War I DELAG's seven Zeppelins made 1,588 flights, carrying 33,722 passengers and crew and flying 107,205 miles (172,535 km). In 1910 and 1911 several experimental postal flights had been made in Great Britain, Italy and the United States. The first official postal flight took place in India on 18 February 1911.

France was not slow in reacting to the German initiative. On 22 March 1919, Lucien Bossoutrot flew a Farman F.60 Goliath to inaugurate the Paris–Brussels regular passenger route (the first international service in Europe). Farman had founded his own airline, and called it Lignes Aériennes Farman. The new airline had a lot of custom from the outset. Farman also made experimental flights to London, Northern Europe and to Africa to evaluate the possibility of opening routes to those destinations. A second French airline was founded at about the same time, Compagnie des Messageries Aériennes (CMA), by a group that included some of the most famous French aircraft manufacturers. The company began its activities on 1 May with a daily mail and goods flight between Paris and Lille, a service which was extended to Brussels in August. On 16 September their first passenger flight to London was made. The third French company to establish regular flights was the Compagnie des Transports Aéronautiques du Sud-Ouest which opened services in the Bay of Biscay in July 1919 and a route to Spain in September 1919.

Commercial aviation was consolidated and expanded in the 1920s in France. The French Government was well aware of the importance of this sector of the transport industry and gave large subsidies to the airlines and took the far-sighted step of appointing an Under Secretary of State for Aviation in January 1920. This ministry was subdivided into departments with responsibility for technical services, factories, air navigation and a national meteorological network. The airlines took full advantage of the government's recognition and official encouragement, to place their organizations on a firm footing and to widen their operations. During the course of 1920 new routes linking different parts of Europe were planned and some 2,400 commercial flights were made. Among the most dynamic companies were the Compagnie Franco-Roumaine de Navigation Aérienne (CFRNA), founded in April 1920, and Lignes Latécoère (this adopted the name of Compagnie Générale d'Entreprises Aéronautiques, CGEA, on 21 April 1921)which flew the first route proving flights from Toulouse to Barcelona, Alicante and Rabat in late 1918 and early 1919, using Breguet 14 and Salmson 2-A-2 biplanes. The end of 1922 saw the first mergers of companies in order to combine forces and improve services; the first important merger was effected by Compagnie des Grands Express Aériens and Compagnie des Messageries Aériennes, on 1 January 1923, to form Air Union. The new company concentrated its efforts on the Paris–London route with connections to Lyons, Marseilles and Geneva.

France's keenest rival, Germany, had an extremely competitive commercial aviation industry. The historic inauguration of Deutsche Luft-Reederei's service had been followed by others. By the spring of 1919 there were airlines which had services covering much of Germany. These included Lloyd-Luftverkehr Sablatnig, the Sächsische Luft Reederei, Bayerischer Luft Lloyd and Albatros. Rivalry between nations in the commercial sector was keen but Germany was to retain her lead for many years to come. The authorities took a very keen interest in the potential of the airplane as a means of transport. The development of a national aeronautical industry was considered so vital that the Germans used all their ingenuity to circumvent the restrictions imposed by the Treaty of Versailles, which prohibited them from designing and constructing other than low-powered airplanes. While appearing to observe the restrictive clauses of the treaty to the letter, the German aviation industry managed to carry out research and development and produced first-class aircraft which far outstripped those of other European nations.

In 1924 the German airlines were efficiently reorganized and several smaller airlines were consolidated into two major companies: Junkers-Luftverkehr (founded in 1921) and Deutscher Aero Lloyd. These two main companies served the whole of Germany and much of Europe, as a result of agreements with the leading companies in other countries. In 1921 an important breakthrough was achieved when Aero Union completed negotiations with the Soviet Government which resulted in the founding of the Deruluft company; this was not only a pioneer Russian airline but also one of the first attempts at international co-operation. 1926 was an even more significant year; on 6 January, Junkers-Luftverkehr and Deutscher Aero Lloyd were merged into a new, officially recognized company which was given very considerable government backing. This new company was called Deutsche Luft Hansa and was to make a name for itself as the busiest and most enterprising company in Europe. Luft Hansa's first commercial flight was made on 6 April and within a few months the company's routes extended well beyond Germany's borders, soon establishing a reputation for efficiency and dependability. In 1927 Luft Hansa had a fleet of about 120 airplanes, including some of the most advanced aircraft of the time.

In Great Britain civil aviation only received official recognition in April 1919, and A.V. Roe and Company, one of the oldest established aircraft companies in Britain, was the first to try to set up a regular air transport service. The first sustained service was inaugurated on 24 May, between Alexander Park (Manchester), Southport and Blackpool. Avro three-seat biplanes were used to cover a distance of about 50 miles (80 km). On 30 September, however, after only 194 flights had been made, the company decided to suspend the service. On 5 October 1916, another air transport company had been founded: Aircraft Transport and Travel Ltd. (AT&T). In February 1919 AT&T had begun a parcel service between Hawkinge and Ghent to carry food and urgent supplies to areas of Belgium suffering acute postwar shortages, and thereafter operated charter flights. This company was the first in the world to operate sustained regular civil daily international passenger flights. The company started its services with some war-surplus bombers, converted to de Havilland D.H.4A and D.H.16 cabin aircraft, commencing regular commercial flights between London and Paris on 25 August 1919. It was, however, to prove a conspicuous example of how an efficient company could go under in the face of subsidized competition. Due to the British Government's total lack of any interest in air transport, its operations ceased on 17 December 1920, because of serious financial difficulties.

The second British airline, Handley Page Transport, was founded on 14 June 1919. Adapting the O/400 heavy bombers for civil use, they inaugurated regular services between London and Paris on 2 September 1919, in direct competition with AT&T. Success encouraged Handley Page to introduce one of the first British aircraft to be expressly designed and built for civil aviation, the W.8. This aircraft gave the company a commanding lead in the commercial transport market. Even this clear proof of the potential of civil aviation did not induce the government to take a more active interest in civil aviation and it continued to turn a deaf ear to appeals for support and backing for the new industry. By 1921 the situation had become so serious that even the strongest companies, Handley Page Transport and Instone (the latter had begun public services on 18 February 1920, and became The Instone Air Line on 12 December 1921), found themselves in a very precarious situation. Due to financial difficulties, on 28 February 1921 these two companies suspended all services.

Cessation of all British cross-Channel services forced the government to appoint a commission of enquiry to examine the problems of the airlines. At length a decision was reached to allocate £25,000 to each company—a small sum but which represented the first official recognition of civil aviation in Great Britain and the first step towards formulating a new aviation policy. The results of this changed attitude soon became evident. First of all Handley Page and Instone resumed flights; then new ventures were undertaken and new companies formed, including The Daimler Airway, founded in 1922, and British Marine Air Navigation the following year. In order to rationalize operations, the four companies shared out their routes. Handley Page concentrated its efforts and put its best aircraft on the London–Paris route; Instone took over the Brussels route and Daimler had the Dutch route with the Amsterdam run. British Marine Navigation operated routes which linked Southampton with Guernsey.

1923 was a crucial year in the development of British commercial aviation. The government decided to implement a long-term plan and on 3 November an agreement was signed merging the four major companies into a single organization. The new company would take over all routes and all operational aircraft: it would use only British-built aircraft and engines; and, if it flew a stipulated minimum annual mileage, it would receive government subsidies amounting to £1 million over ten years. On 31 March 1924, the merger took effect and the new company, Imperial Airways Ltd., should have begun operations the next day but a pilot's strike prevented all flying until 26 April. From that time onward recovery was slow but steady. For a while Imperial Airways concentrated its efforts on consolidating its main European routes and on improving the quality of its service. It gradually extended its routes to Africa, the Far East and Australia.

Among the major aeronautical powers, Italy was the last to enter the field of European civil aviation. Although the first companies were founded in 1923—Aero Espresso Italiana (AEI) and Società Italiana Servizi Aerei (SISA)—followed in 1925 by S.A. Navigazione Aerea (SANA) and Transadriatica, regular commercial flights were not inaugurated until 1926. On 1 February the Transadriatica line launched its Rome–Venice route; on 1 April SISA inaugurated the Turin–Venice–Trieste line; this was followed on 7 April by SANA's commencement of services between Genoa, Rome and Naples and, on 1 August, Aero Espresso made its first flight from Brindisi to Constantinople (now Istanbul). During the next two years, two new companies were founded: Società Aerea Mediterranea (SAM), in March 1926, and Avio Linee Italiane (ALI) in November 1926. By the end of the 1920s these six companies were operating over a large area with flights to Rhodes, Tripoli, in Libya, and Berlin.

While the four major European aviation countries were forging ahead, other nations which had played a secondary role in the development of aviation exploited the potential of the airplane very enthusiastically. The Netherlands is a particularly interesting example, since the history of aviation in that country is to a large extent synonymous with the name of Anthony Fokker. Fokker managed to return home from Germany immediately the war was over and started designing and building aircraft again, switching to civil models. He sold many of them to a small company which was to become one of the world's major airlines, KLM (Koninklijke Luchtvaart Maatschappij—Royal Dutch Airlines). The airline had been founded on 7 October 1919, under the leadership of Albert Plesman, and had inaugurated its London–Amsterdam service on 17 May the following year, using a D.H.16 chartered from the British company, AT&T. On 1 September, KLM joined forces with the German company DLR and started a service to Copenhagen via Hamburg. A KLM demonstration flight using its own aircraft, a Fokker F.II, took place on 30 September 1920, from Amsterdam to Croydon. This was just the beginning of a long association between the great Dutch aircraft designer and KLM, which continued uninterruptedly until 1934.

Meanwhile, what was happening in the United States? Commercial aviation had a fairly checkered career in its early stages. The U.S. authorities had concentrated their efforts on the development of military aviation and the commercial sector was neglected for some years. The first progress was in airmail services, with the support of the United States Post Office. The first route, flown by the Army, was inaugurated on 15 May 1918, between New York and Washington, D.C., using obsolescent military trainers, Curtiss JN-4H Jennys. On 12 August, when the Post Office took over, these airplanes were replaced by new, specially built aircraft and at the beginning of 1919 the postal fleet was increased to 120 aircraft with the acquisition of some 100 D.H.4s left over from the war. The airmail network gradually expanded and by 8 September 1920, stretched from Washington and New York to Chicago and San Francisco. The East-West flight from New York to San Francisco took 34 hours 20 minutes, while the West-East flight lasted 29 hours 15 minutes. Aircraft were changed six times during the transcontinental journey: in Cleveland, Chicago, Omaha, Cheyenne, Salt Lake City and Reno. The service was a great success and in 1927 the postal authorities handed over the operation of airmail flights to private companies. Boeing Air Transport took over the San Francisco–Chicago route and National Air Transport handled the Chicago–New York run. By 31 August 1927, when the last Post Office-operated flight was made, almost 15 million miles (24 million km) had been flown with more than 300 million letters. In 1923 a record number of letters was carried: 67,875,840.

The airmail service had fostered the growth of airmindedness and changed attitudes toward air transport; as a result several small companies had sprung up to operate subsidiary routes. Among the more flourishing were Colonial Air Transport; the Robertson Aircraft Corporation; Western Air Express; Varney Air Lines; and the Ford Motor Company's airline. Western Air Express was the first company to commence operating regular passenger flights, albeit on a very limited trial basis, and the first large-scale undertakings were only begun in 1927, after Lindbergh's historic solo transatlantic flight which aroused enormous interest in passenger air travel and in flying generally throughout the United States. Transcontinental Air Transport (TAT) was the first major airline to be founded in this new climate of enthusiasm in the United States. The company was established on 16 May 1928, and its shareholders included such important companies as Wright, Curtiss and the Pennsylvania Railroad. The technical director was Charles Lindbergh, then at the height of his fame after his long-distance solo flight. From then onward the American civil aviation industry expanded steadily and assumed a position of prime importance in the world market.

Lindbergh's feat had brought home the importance of civil aviation to the American public, but it was really the culmination of what could be called the adventuring years, during which the airplane had been the means of achieving other thrilling "firsts" which were all to play their part in furthering the cause of commercial aviation. The first challenge to be met was the crossing of the Atlantic and in 1919 this was achieved on four separate occasions; in May, with a flight with refueling stops by the American Navy Curtiss NC-4 flying boat; in June, when Alcock and Brown flew eastward nonstop in a British Vickers Vimy from Newfoundland to Ireland, followed in July by nonstop out and back flights by the British airship R.34. The long-distance flights which followed were no less spectacular: in February 1920, the Italians Ferrarin and Masiero flew from Rome to Tokyo in an S.V.A.9; in May 1923 a U.S. Army Fokker T-2 made the first nonstop coast-to-coast crossing of the United States, from New York to San Diego; between 6 April and 28 September 1924, a round-the-world flight was made by Army Air Service Douglas DWC biplanes. A year later, two Italians, De Pinedo and Campanelli, completed the longest flight to date when they flew 34,155 miles (55,000 km) from Rome to Australia and Japan and back in a Savoia S.16 flying boat. In May 1926 Richard Byrd and Floyd Bennett made the first flight over the North Pole, in a three-engine Fokker. These achievements dispelled any doubts about the viability and safety of air travel and exploded the myth that the airplane was still at an experimental stage.

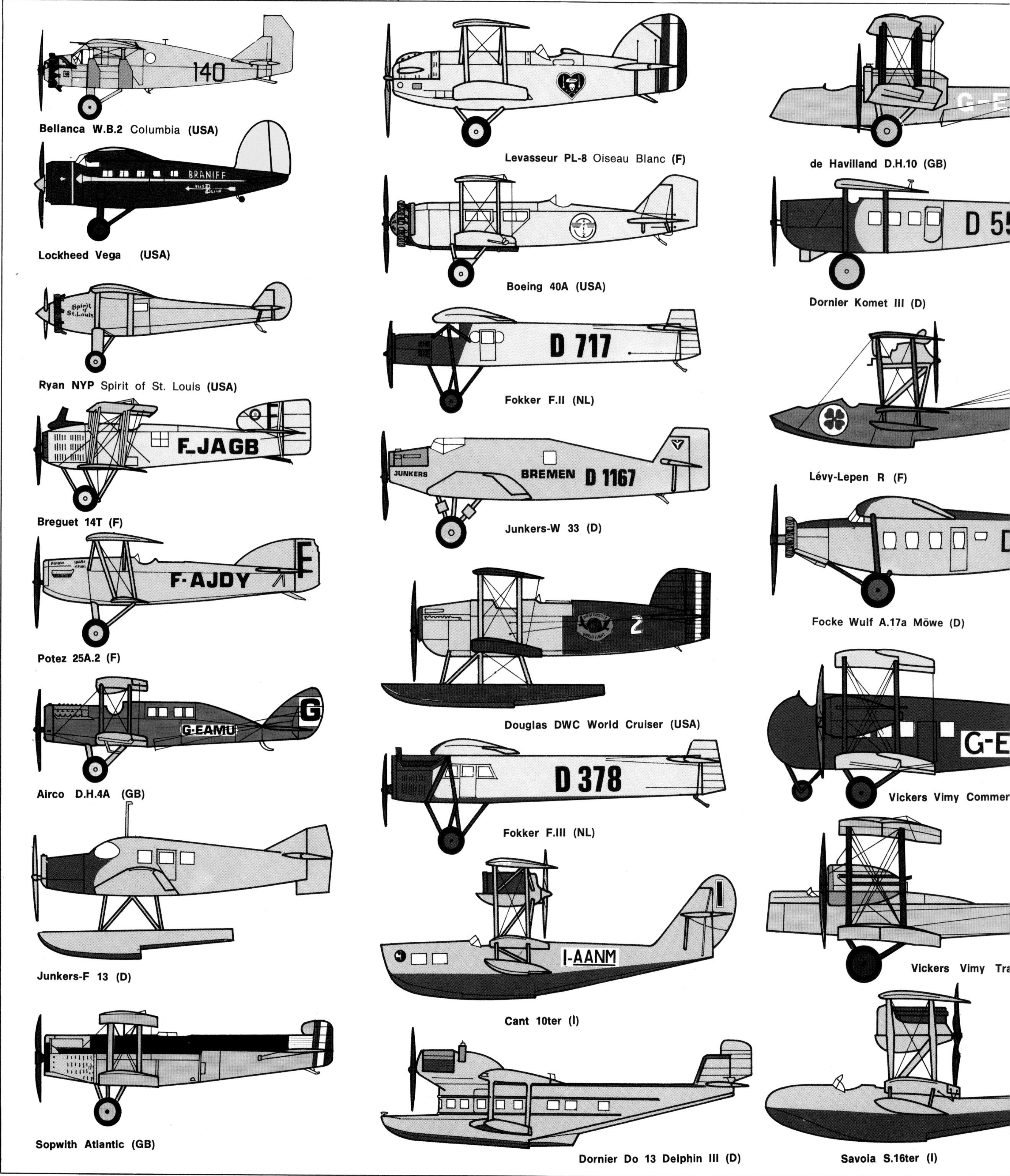
140
Bellanca W.B.2 Columbia (USA)
BRANIFF
Lockheed Vega (USA)
Spirit of St. Louis
Ryan NYP Spirit of St. Louis (USA)
F-JAGB
Breguet 14T (F)
F-AJDY
Potez 25A.2 (F)
G-EAMU
Airco D.H.4A (GB)
Junkers-F 13 (D)
Sopwith Atlantic (GB)
Levasseur PL-8 Oiseau Blanc (F)
Boeing 40A (USA)
D 717
Fokker F.II (NL)
JUNKERS
BREMEN D 1167
Junkers-W 33 (D)
2
Douglas DWC World Cruiser (USA)
D 378
Fokker F.III (NL)
I-AANM
Cant 10ter (I)
Dornier Do 13 Delphin III (D)
de Havilland D.H.10 (GB)
Dornier Komet III (D)
Lévy-Lepen R (F)
Focke Wulf A.17a Möwe (D)
G-E
Vickers Vimy Commer
Vickers Vimy Tra
Savoia S.16ter (I)

1909 On 16 November, in Germany, the first commercial air transport company, Die Deutsche Luftschiffahrts Aktien-Gesellschaft (DELAG), was formed by Count Ferdinand von Zeppelin, to operate Zeppelin airships. The company was very active; between June 1910 and August 1914 DELAG completed 1,588 flights, covered 107,205 miles (172,535 km) and carried 33,722 passengers and crew.

1910 On 10 August, the first, unofficial, airmail flight took off from Blackpool, England. Claude Grahame-White in a Blériot monoplane.

1911 In India a small quantity of letters and postcards was carried on 18 February, in a Humber biplane piloted by Henri Piquet, over a distance of 5 miles (8 km) from Allahabad to Naini Junction. It was an isolated experiment, but was the first government-sponsored airmail delivery, for which the stamps had been postmarked.
In England, from 9 to 26 September, the Grahame-White Aviation Company operated a regular mail flight from London (Hendon) to Windsor on the occasion of the Coronation of King George V. The pilot of the first flight was Gustav Hamel on a Blériot monoplane. A Farman was also used, and a total of 25,000 letters and 90,000 postcards was carried.
On 19 September the first mail flight in Italy took place between Bologna and Venice and Venice and Rimini.
In the United States, from 23 September to 2 October, Earle Ovington flew experimental airmail deliveries in a Blériot monoplane between Nassau Boulevard and Mineola, Long Island.

1914 The first regular passenger service in the world started on 1 January in Florida, between St. Petersburg and Tampa. The 21-mile (34.5-km) flight was made once, and later, twice a day in a small Benoist XIV flying boat belonging to the St. Petersburg-Tampa Airboat Line. After three months, the service came to an end, having carried 1,200 passengers.

1917 In May and June, military aircraft operated experimental mail flights from Turin to Rome; Brindisi to Valona in Albania; and Naples to Palermo.
In Germany, by the end of the year, there was a regular airmail service between Berlin and Cologne. Similar flights were made in France and Britain, also with military aircraft.

1918 Austria opened the first regular international airmail service on 20 March, between Vienna and Kiev.
On 15 May, in the United States, the first airmail route was opened between New York and Washington. Operated by the Army, it was taken over on 12 August by the U.S. Post Office; thus began the Unites States Air Mail, which up to 1927 made an enormous contribution to the development of U.S. air transport.
In Italy, on 25 November, the company Posta Aerea Transadriatica inaugurated a regular airmail service covering the northern Adriatic, between Venice and Trieste.

1919 The first sustained daily passenger service in the world was inaugurated on 5 February by Deutsche Luft-Reederei between Berlin and Weimar, a distance of 120 miles (193 km).
The first international commercial passenger route was opened on 22 March with a French Farman F.60 Goliath between Paris and Brussels. The once-weekly journey took 2 hours 50 minutes and cost 365 francs.
On 1 May, the French airline, CMA—Compagnie des Messageries Aériennes—commenced operations; it was soon to become one of the major European carriers.
The first regular domestic service in Great Britain began on 20 May. Three-seat Avro biplanes, operated by A.V. Roe and Company, linked Alexander Park, Manchester, with Southport and Blackpool.
On 14 July, Handley Page Transport was formed; it operated services between London and Paris from 2 September.
The first regular sustained scheduled daily passenger service between London and Paris was inaugurated on 25 August, by the British company—Aircraft Transport and Travel Ltd.
On 16 September, the French company, Compagnie des Messageries Aériennes, started a cross-Channel service between Paris and London.
Royal Dutch Airlines, KLM, which was to become one of Europe's leading airlines, was founded on 7 October. Its first regular service, however, only started on 17 May 1920, from Amsterdam to Croydon.
The first American international scheduled passenger service was inaugurated on 1 November by Aeromarine West Indies Airways from Key West in Florida to Havana. These services were only flown at certain times of the year.
South America's oldest established airline, SCADTA, was formed in Colombia on 5 December.

1920 In France, on 23 April, the Compagnie Franco-Roumaine de Navigation Aérienne was founded. It commenced flights between Paris and Strasbourg on 20 September and this was the first step in its gradual expansion of services to Eastern Europe. By October 1922, it had extended its routes to Constantinople (now Istanbul), via Strasbourg, Prague, Vienna, Budapest, Belgrade and Bucharest.
On 25 May the Belgian national airline, SNETA (which was to become SABENA on 23 May 1923), began operating services. On 1 July 1920, LARA (Ligne Aérienne du Roi Albert) began flying boat services in the Belgian Congo. The Kinshasha–N'Gombe route was extended to Stanleyville a year later.
The Danish airline, Det Danske Luftfartselskab (DDL), started its first services on 7 August and at about the same time the Norwegian airline, Det Norske Luftfartrederi, was founded.

1921 On 4–5 December, West Australian Airways started the first subsidized airmail service in Australia, between Geraldton and Derby.
On 15 October, the Compañía Española de Trafico Aereo (CETA) inaugurated an airmail service between Seville and Larache in Spanish Morocco.
At the end of the year, the joint German-Soviet airline, Deruluft, was formed. Its first route, Königsberg–Moscow, was inaugurated on 1 May 1922.

1922 Commercial aviation in Japan began on 4 June with the formation of Nihon Kokuyuso Kenkyujo (NKK), which began a mail service on 12 November from Osaka to Tokushima (Shikoku Island).
On 2–3 November QANTAS—Queensland and Northern Territory Aerial Services—commenced a scheduled service between Charleville and Cloncurry in Queensland.

1923 In order to pool resources and improve services, the French airlines, CGEA and CMA, merged to form Air Union on 1 January; this was to become one of Europe's most successful airlines.
ČSA Czechoslovak State Airlines began route proving flights in late October and scheduled flights at the beginning of 1924.
The first Finnish airline, Aero O/Y, was founded on 1 November and started regular services on 20 March 1924.

1924 Imperial Airways, which was to re-establish Britain's dominant position in civil aviation, was formed on 31 March as a result of the merger of Handley Page Transport, The Instone Air Line, Daimler Airway and British Marine Air Navigation Co.
The first Swedish airline ABA—AB Aerotransport, was formed, and services to Helsinki began on 2 June.
On 1 July, regular night flying began on the United States Post Office's coast-to-coast mail service between New York and San Francisco.

1925 Under the Kelly Act United States mail contracts began to be leased to private airlines. Twelve companies began service between February 1926 and April 1927 and these services were designed to act as feeders to the routes operated by the Post Office.

1926 Deutsche Luft Hansa, one of the giants of European air transport, was formed by the merger of Junkers-Luftverkehr and Deutscher Aero Lloyd on 6 January. The new company made its first commercial flight on 6 April.
In Italy, on 1 February, Transadriatica inaugurated its Rome–Venice service and, on 1 April, SISA launched its Turin–Venice–Trieste service. On 7 April SANA began to operate flights between Genoa, Rome and Naples. On 1 August, Aero Espresso opened its service between Brindisi and Constantinople.
The first sustained scheduled passenger service in the United States was started on 23 May by Western Air Express.

1927 Società Aerea Mediterranea, SAM, began operations on 4 February, with a service from Brindisi to Albania.
On 14 March the company which was to become the world's largest international airline in the 1930s, Pan American Airways, was founded, an event which passed almost unnoticed at the time. The first mail flight was between Key West and Havana on 19 October using a Fairchild seaplane which the new company had chartered. Regular flights began on 28 October with Fokker monoplanes.
The Yugoslav airline, Aeroput, was formed in May and scheduled flights from Belgrade to Zagreb began on 28 February 1928.
The U.S. Post Office made its last mail flight with its own aircraft on 31 August before handing its entire operation over to private companies.

1928 The first major airline to be formed in the United States in the wake of Lindbergh's transatlantic flight was Transcontinental Air Transport, established by a group of industrialists on 16 May.
Avio Linee Italiane (ALI), founded on 13 November 1926, inaugurated its Milan–Trento–Munich service and, on 9 October, started its Milan–Rome service.

Entry into service of the most important aircraft: 1919–1927

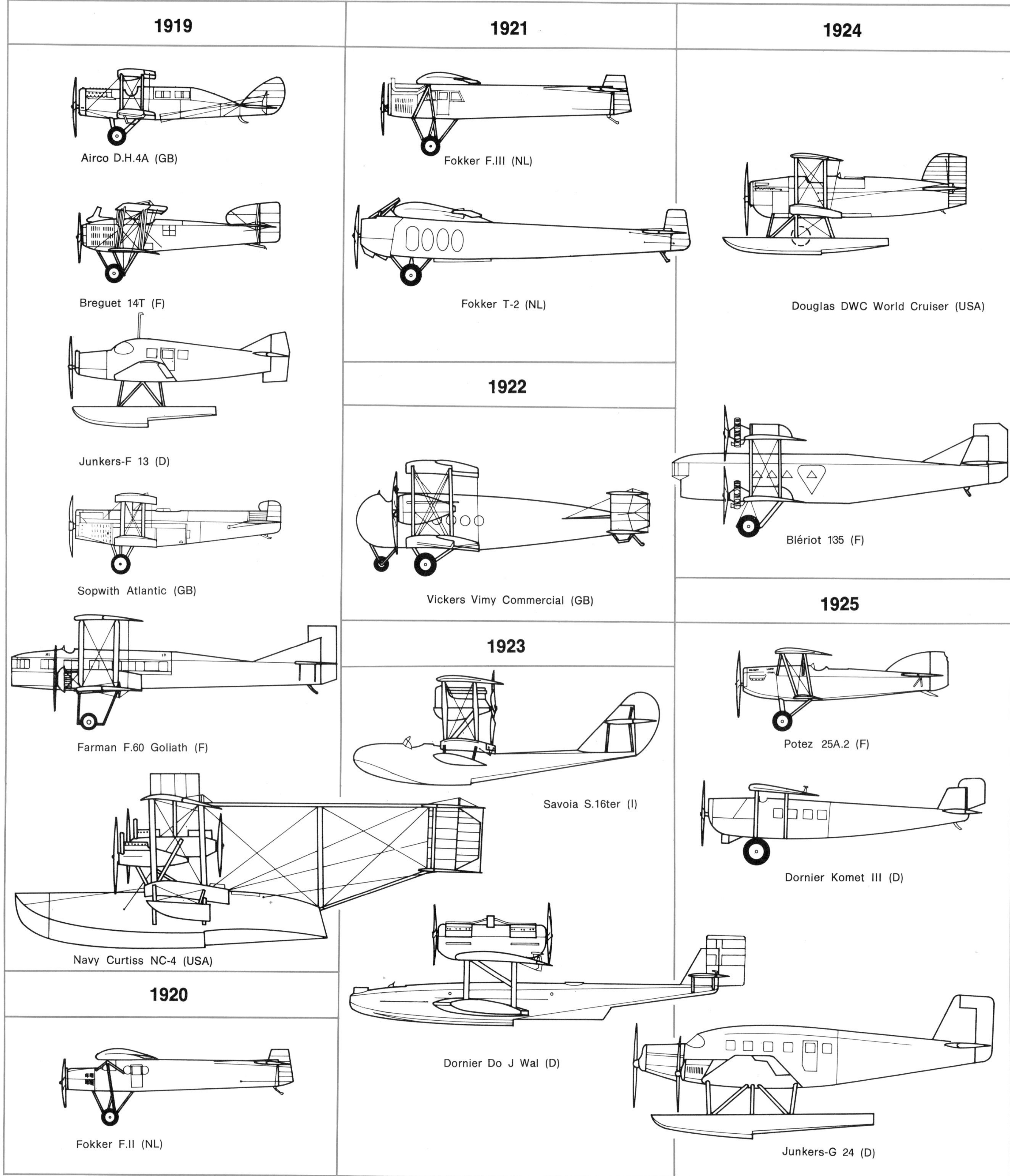

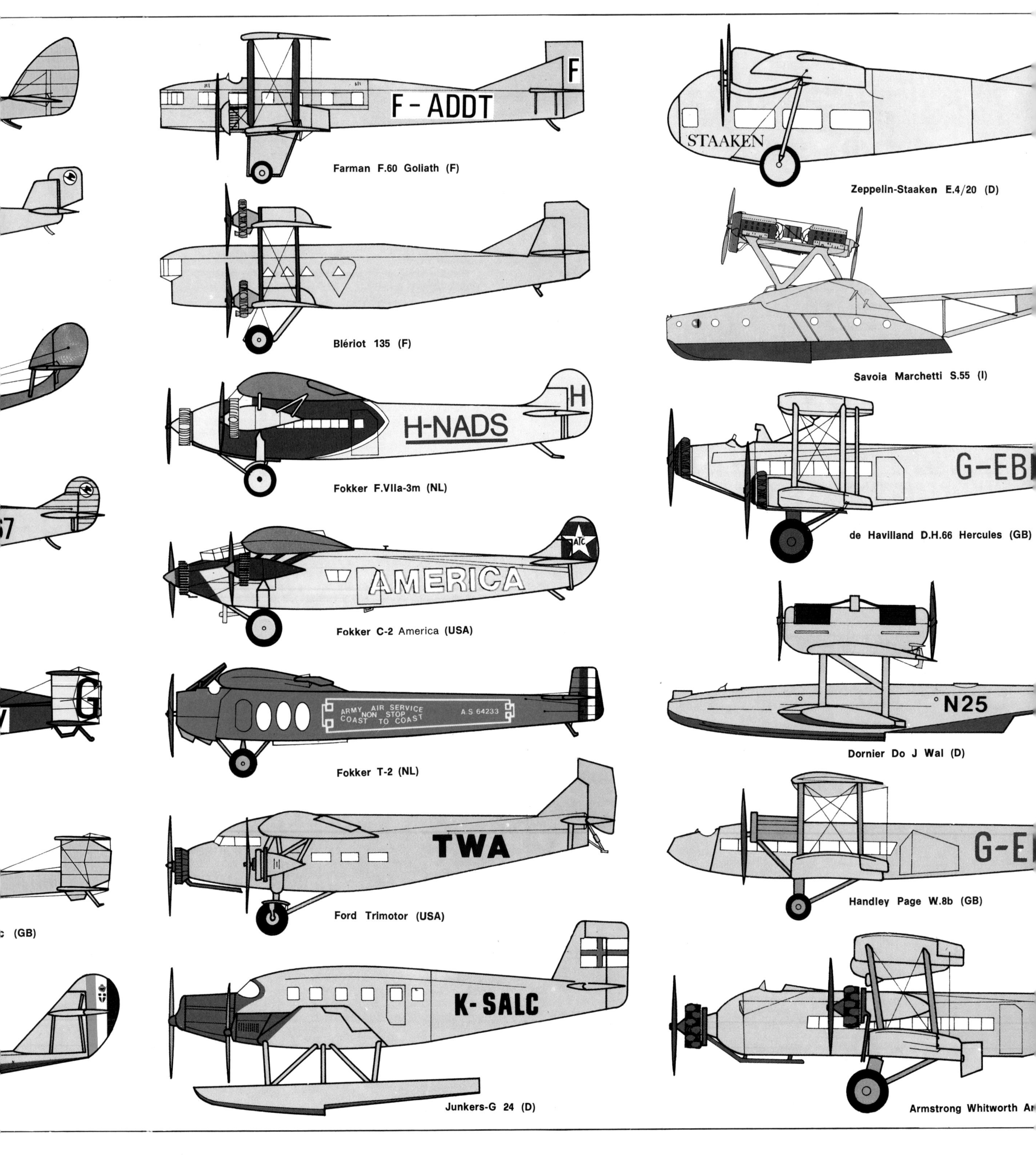

c (GB)

Farman F.60 Goliath (F)

Zeppelin-Staaken E.4/20 (D)

Blériot 135 (F)

Savoia Marchetti S.55 (I)

Fokker F.VIIa-3m (NL)

de Havilland D.H.66 Hercules (GB)

Fokker C-2 America (USA)

Fokker T-2 (NL)

Dornier Do J Wal (D)

Ford Trimotor (USA)

Handley Page W.8b (GB)

Junkers-G 24 (D)

Armstrong Whitworth Ar

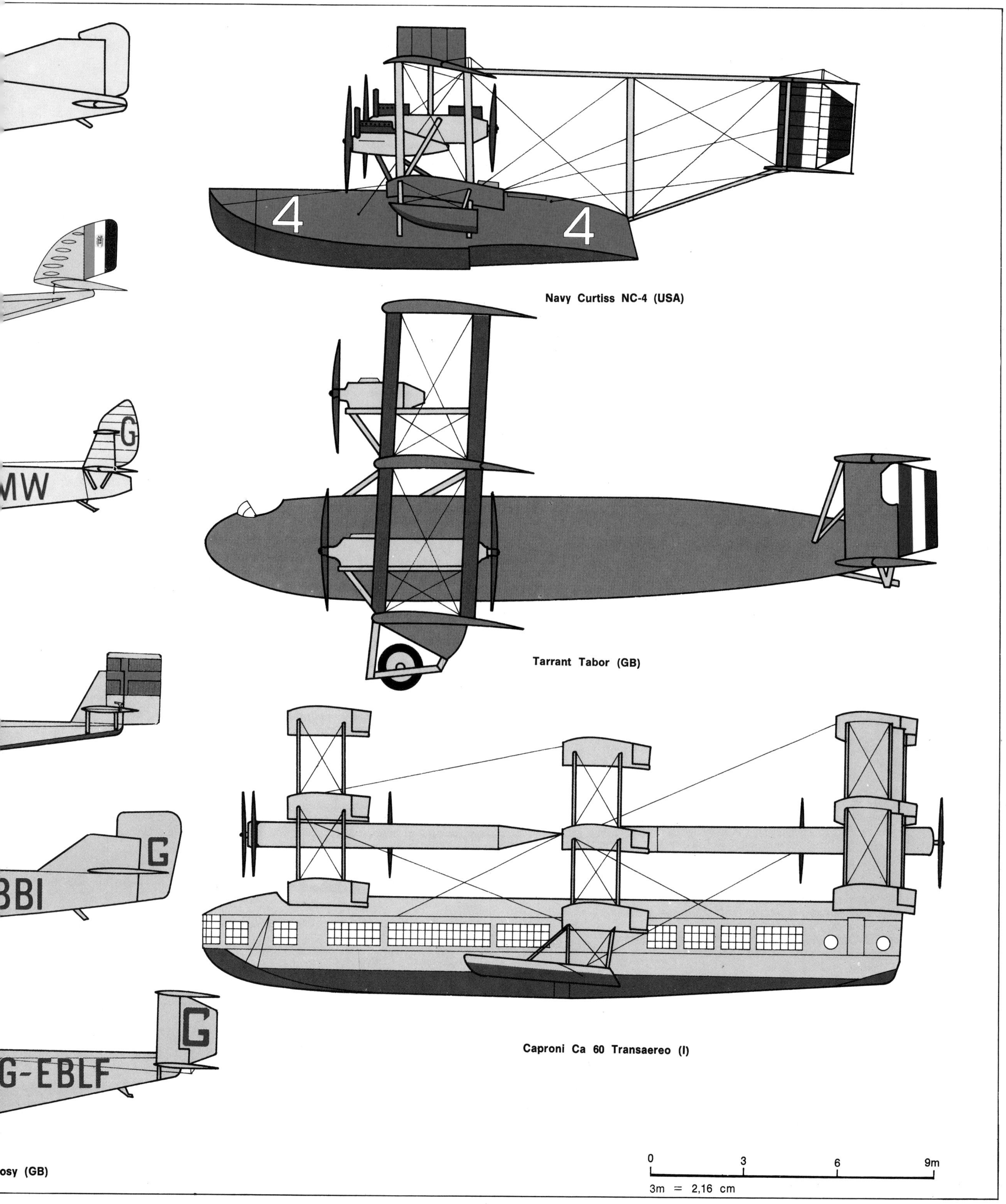

Navy Curtiss NC-4 (USA)

Tarrant Tabor (GB)

Caproni Ca 60 Transaereo (I)

osy (GB)

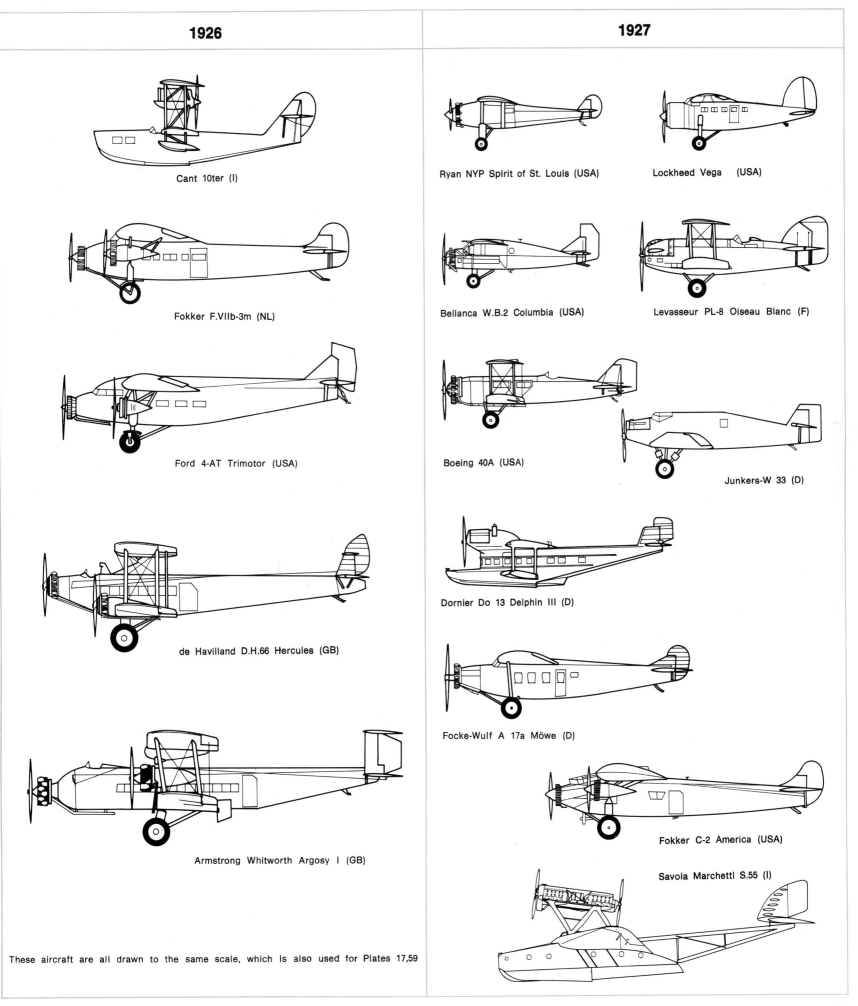

1926	1927

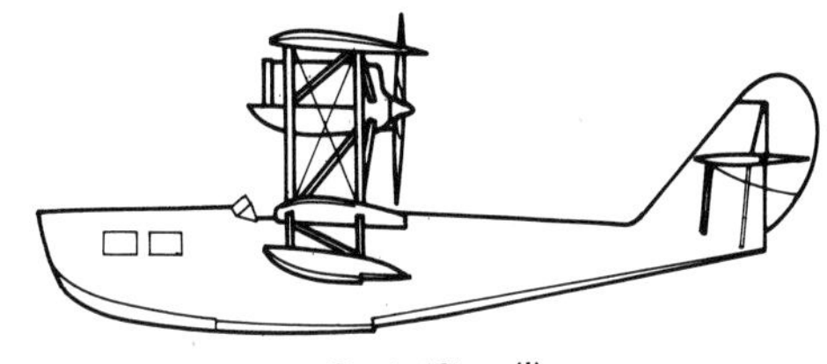
Cant 10ter (I)

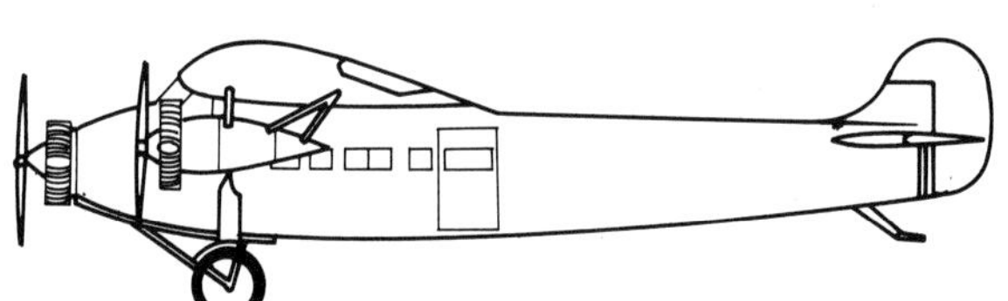
Fokker F.VIIb-3m (NL)

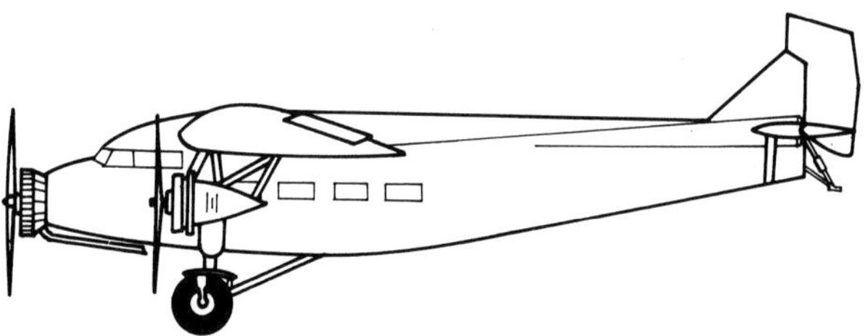
Ford 4-AT Trimotor (USA)

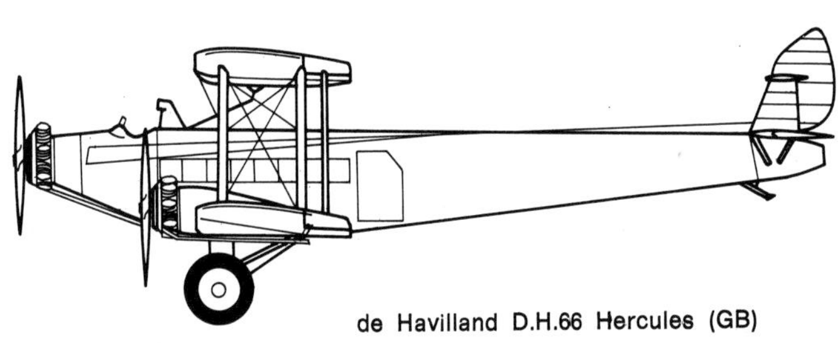
de Havilland D.H.66 Hercules (GB)

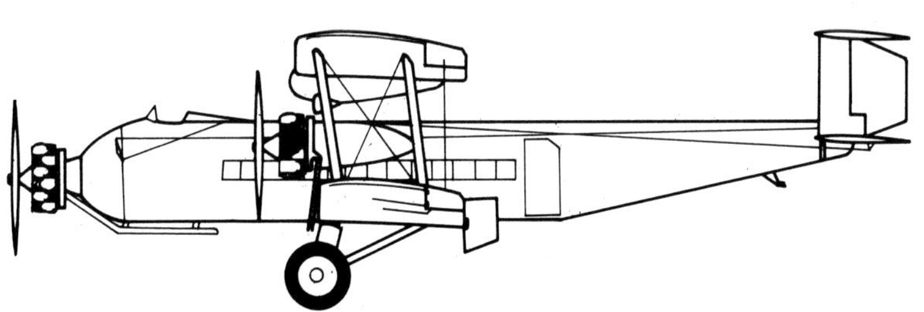
Armstrong Whitworth Argosy I (GB)

These aircraft are all drawn to the same scale, which is also used for Plates 17,59

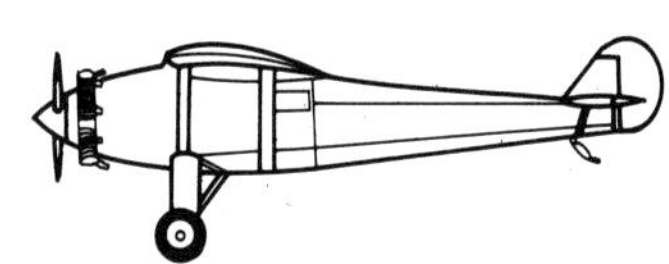
Ryan NYP Spirit of St. Louis (USA)

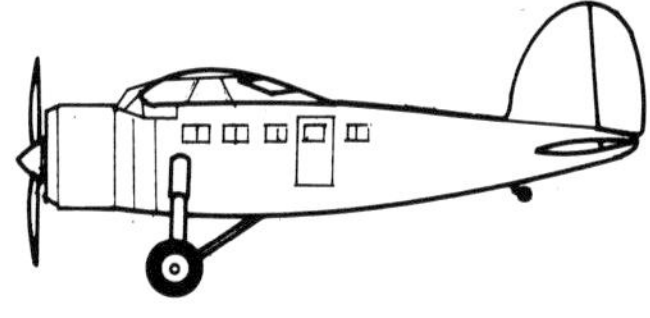
Lockheed Vega (USA)

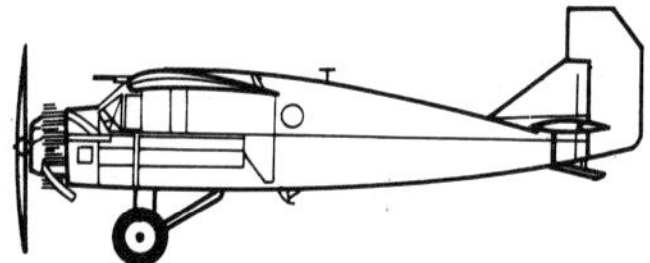
Bellanca W.B.2 Columbia (USA)

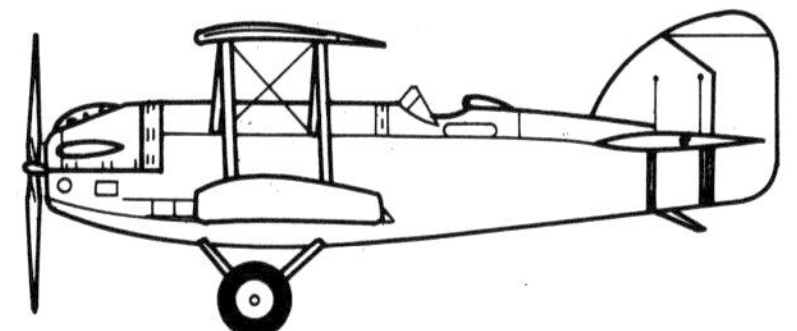
Levasseur PL-8 Oiseau Blanc (F)

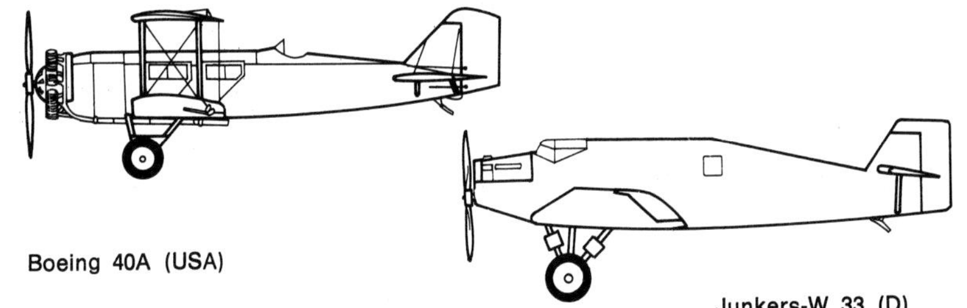
Boeing 40A (USA)

Junkers-W 33 (D)

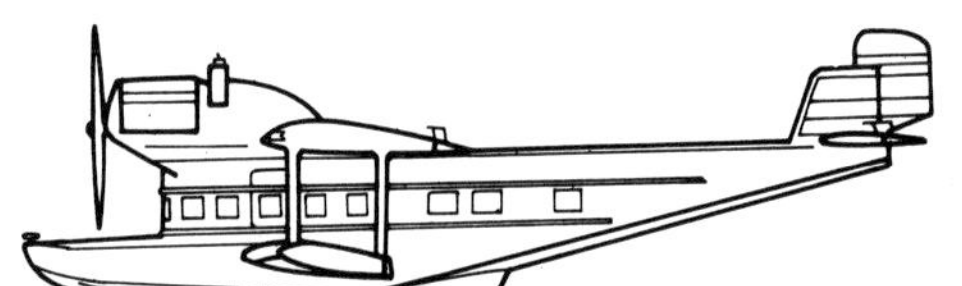
Dornier Do 13 Delphin III (D)

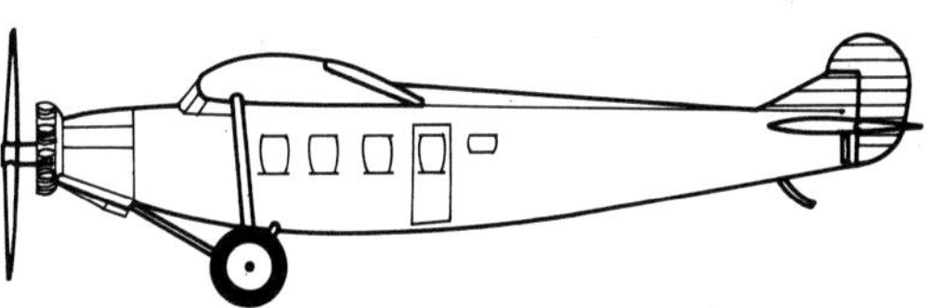
Focke-Wulf A 17a Möwe (D)

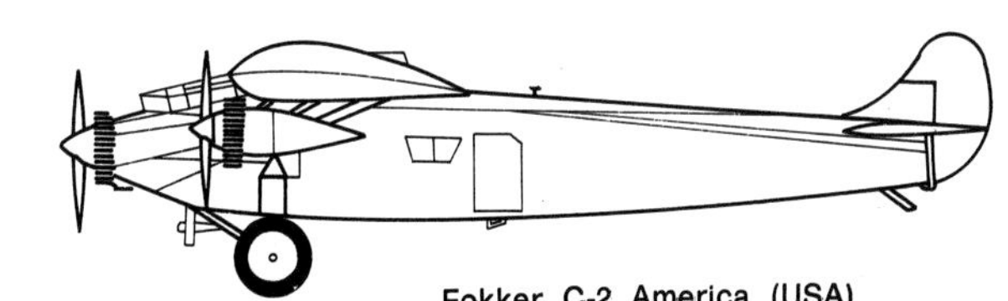
Fokker C-2 America (USA)

Savoia Marchetti S.55 (I)

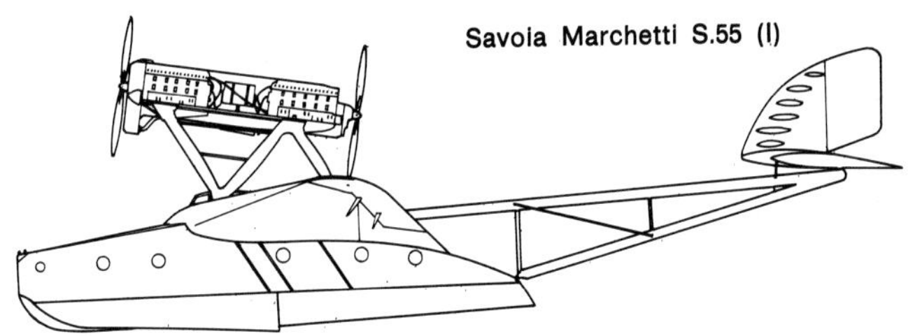

Plate 37

Cutaway drawing of the Fokker F. VIIb – 33m

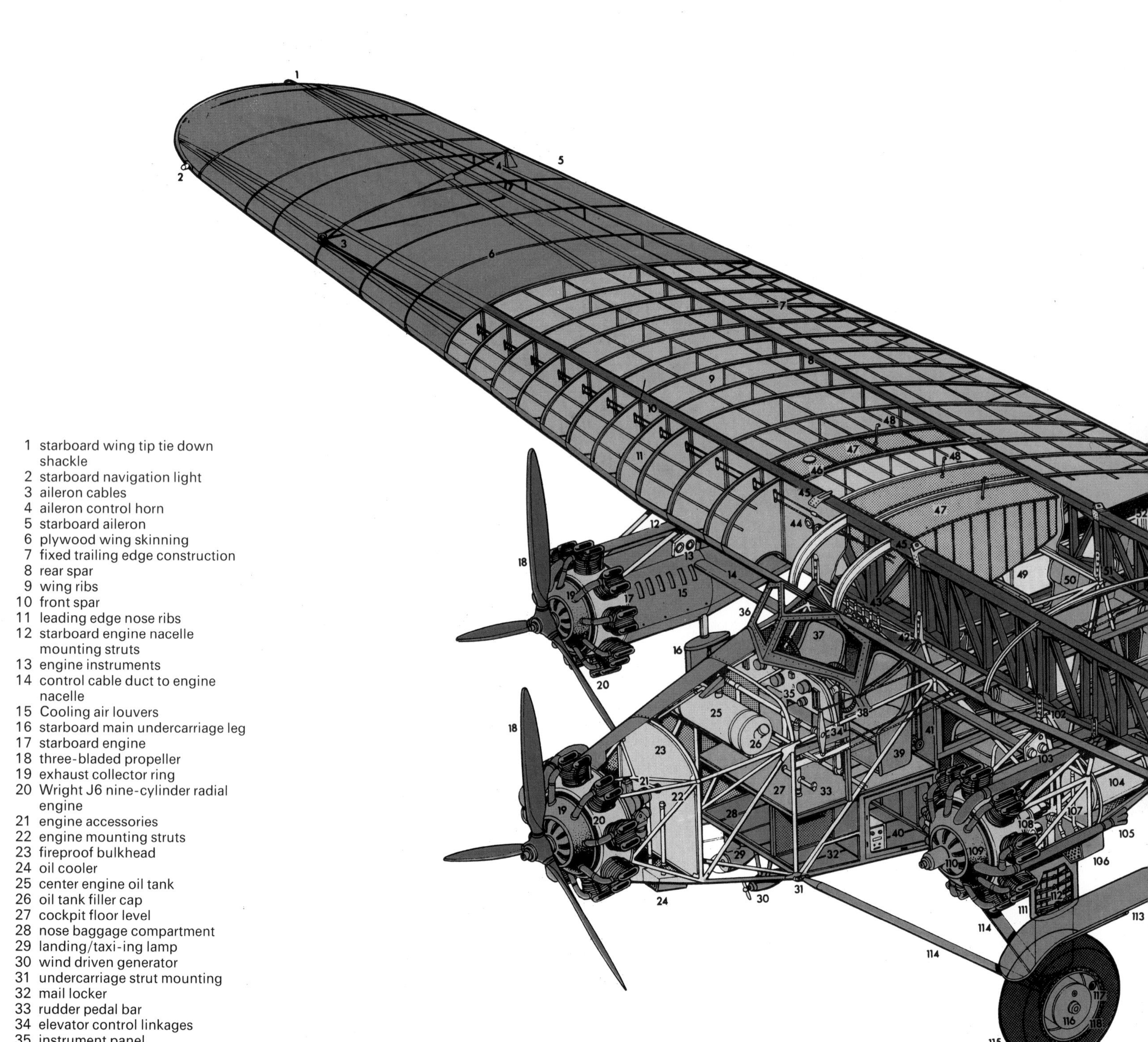

1 starboard wing tip tie down shackle
2 starboard navigation light
3 aileron cables
4 aileron control horn
5 starboard aileron
6 plywood wing skinning
7 fixed trailing edge construction
8 rear spar
9 wing ribs
10 front spar
11 leading edge nose ribs
12 starboard engine nacelle mounting struts
13 engine instruments
14 control cable duct to engine nacelle
15 Cooling air louvers
16 starboard main undercarriage leg
17 starboard engine
18 three-bladed propeller
19 exhaust collector ring
20 Wright J6 nine-cylinder radial engine
21 engine accessories
22 engine mounting struts
23 fireproof bulkhead
24 oil cooler
25 center engine oil tank
26 oil tank filler cap
27 cockpit floor level
28 nose baggage compartment
29 landing/taxi-ing lamp
30 wind driven generator
31 undercarriage strut mounting
32 mail locker
33 rudder pedal bar
34 elevator control linkages
35 instrument panel
36 windscreen panels
37 co-pilot's seat
38 control column handwheel
39 pilot's seat
40 radio
41 cockpit bulkhead
42 wing spar/fuselage attachment
43 fuel selector cocks
44 aileron cable runs
45 wing lifting lugs
46 fuel tank filler cap
47 fuel tanks
48 fuel vent pipes
49 starboard cabin window panel
50 passenger seats
51 rear spar/fuselage attachment
52 overhead luggage racks
53 cabin rear bulkhead
54 cabin doorway
55 toilet compartment
56 water tank
57 starboard baggage door
58 entry door
59 rear baggage compartment
60 steel tube upper longerons
61 fuselage stringers
62 control cable runs
63 horizontal spacers
64 starboard tailplane
65 elevator horn balance
66 starboard elevator
67 fin construction
68 rudder horn balance
69 sternpost
70 fabric covered rudder construction
71 tailplane bracing wire
72 elevator control horn
73 fabric covered port elevator construction
74 elevator horn balance
75 tailplane construction
76 rudder control horn
77 tailplane bracing strut
78 fuselage fabric covering
79 tailplane trim adjustment
80 tailskid
81 elastic cord shock absorber
82 vertical spacers
83 diagonal wire bracing
84 steel tube bottom longeron
85 welded fuselage construction

Fokker F.VIIb–3m

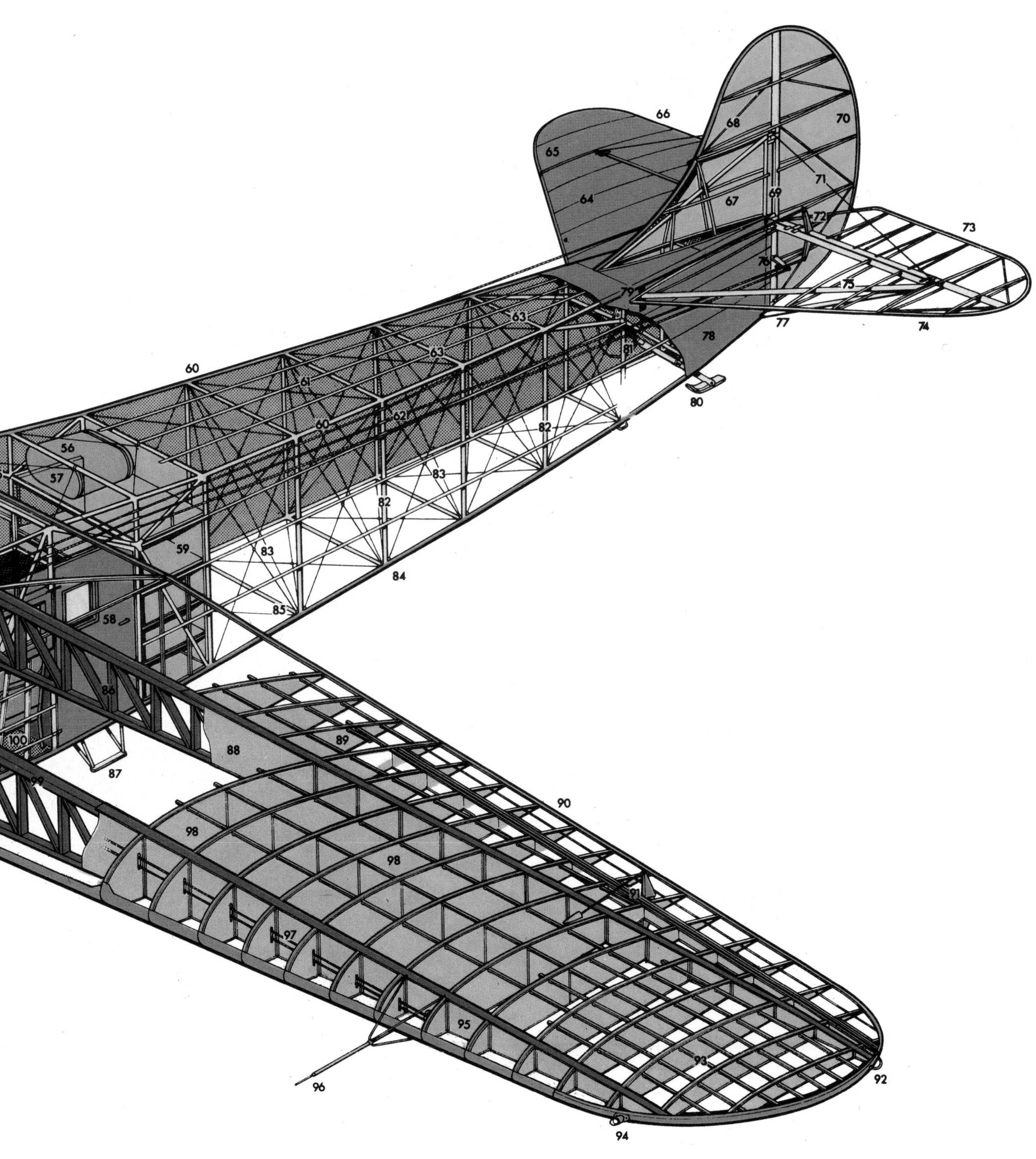

86 rear spar girder construction
87 step
88 spar plywood facing
89 trailing edge ribs
90 port aileron construction
91 aileron control horn
92 wing tip tie down shackle
93 wing tip stringer construction
94 port navigation light
95 leading edge construction
96 pitot tube
97 aileron cables
98 plywood ribs
99 front spar girder construction
100 passenger cabin floor level
101 engine nacelle rear struts
102 nacelle attachment joints
103 port engine instruments
104 oil tank
105 exhaust pipe
106 oil cooler
107 welded steel tube nacelle construction
108 port Wright J6 engine
109 exhaust collector ring
110 cooling air intake louvers
111 main undercarriage leg strut
112 elastic cord shock absorber
113 mudguard
114 undercarriage lower V-struts
115 port mainwheel
116 hydraulic brake
117 tire valve access
118 wheel disc cover/tire lacing

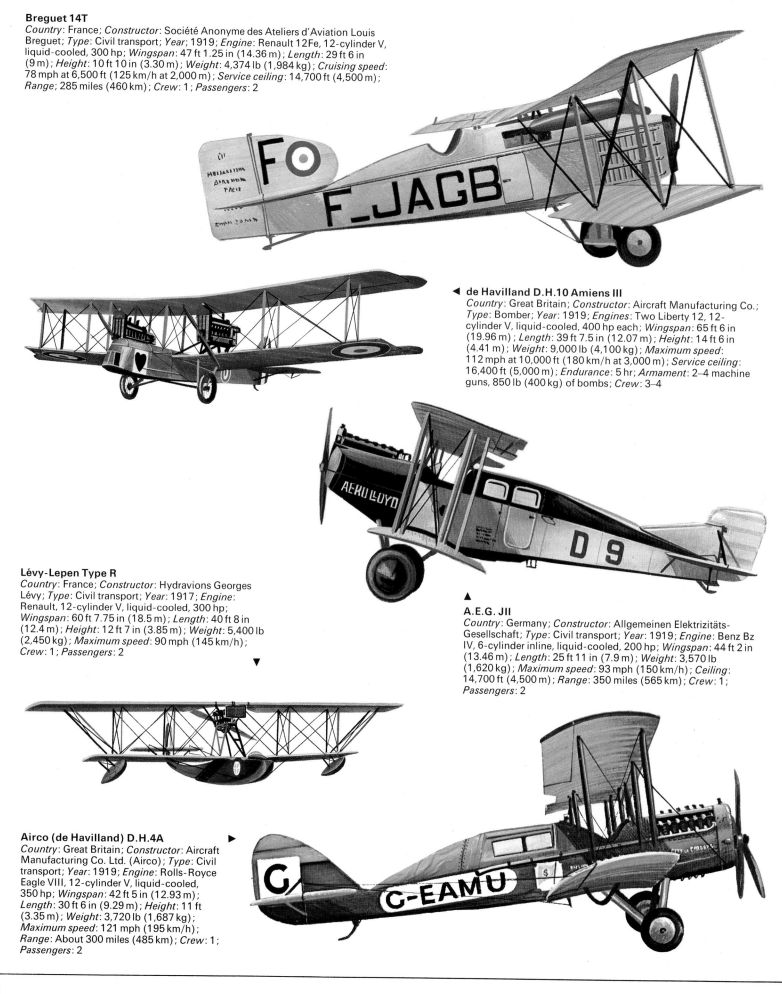

Breguet 14T
Country: France; *Constructor*: Société Anonyme des Ateliers d'Aviation Louis Breguet; *Type*: Civil transport; *Year*; 1919; *Engine*: Renault 12Fe, 12-cylinder V, liquid-cooled, 300 hp; *Wingspan*: 47 ft 1.25 in (14.36 m); *Length*: 29 ft 6 in (9 m); *Height*: 10 ft 10 in (3.30 m); *Weight*: 4,374 lb (1,984 kg); *Cruising speed*: 78 mph at 6,500 ft (125 km/h at 2,000 m); *Service ceiling*: 14,700 ft (4,500 m); *Range*; 285 miles (460 km); *Crew*: 1; *Passengers*: 2

◄ **de Havilland D.H.10 Amiens III**
Country: Great Britain; *Constructor*: Aircraft Manufacturing Co.; *Type*: Bomber; *Year*: 1919; *Engines*: Two Liberty 12, 12-cylinder V, liquid-cooled, 400 hp each; *Wingspan*: 65 ft 6 in (19.96 m); *Length*: 39 ft 7.5 in (12.07 m); *Height*: 14 ft 6 in (4.41 m); *Weight*: 9,000 lb (4,100 kg); *Maximum speed*: 112 mph at 10,000 ft (180 km/h at 3,000 m); *Service ceiling*: 16,400 ft (5,000 m); *Endurance*: 5 hr; *Armament*: 2–4 machine guns, 850 lb (400 kg) of bombs; *Crew*: 3–4

Lévy-Lepen Type R
Country: France; *Constructor*: Hydravions Georges Lévy; *Type*: Civil transport; *Year*: 1917; *Engine*: Renault, 12-cylinder V, liquid-cooled, 300 hp; *Wingspan*: 60 ft 7.75 in (18.5 m); *Length*: 40 ft 8 in (12.4 m); *Height*: 12 ft 7 in (3.85 m); *Weight*: 5,400 lb (2,450 kg); *Maximum speed*: 90 mph (145 km/h); *Crew*: 1; *Passengers*: 2 ▼

▲ **A.E.G. JII**
Country: Germany; *Constructor*: Allgemeinen Elektrizitäts-Gesellschaft; *Type*: Civil transport; *Year*: 1919; *Engine*: Benz Bz IV, 6-cylinder inline, liquid-cooled, 200 hp; *Wingspan*: 44 ft 2 in (13.46 m); *Length*: 25 ft 11 in (7.9 m); *Weight*: 3,570 lb (1,620 kg); *Maximum speed*: 93 mph (150 km/h); *Ceiling*: 14,700 ft (4,500 m); *Range*: 350 miles (565 km); *Crew*: 1; *Passengers*: 2

Airco (de Havilland) D.H.4A ►
Country: Great Britain; *Constructor*: Aircraft Manufacturing Co. Ltd. (Airco); *Type*: Civil transport; *Year*: 1919; *Engine*: Rolls-Royce Eagle VIII, 12-cylinder V, liquid-cooled, 350 hp; *Wingspan*: 42 ft 5 in (12.93 m); *Length*: 30 ft 6 in (9.29 m); *Height*: 11 ft (3.35 m); *Weight*: 3,720 lb (1,687 kg); *Maximum speed*: 121 mph (195 km/h); *Range*: About 300 miles (485 km); *Crew*: 1; *Passengers*: 2

Navy Curtiss NC–4
Country: U.S.A.; *Constructor*: Curtiss Aeroplane and Motor Co.; *Type*: Reconnaissance; *Year*: 1919; *Engines*: Four Liberty 12, 12-cylinder V, liquid-cooled, 400 hp each; *Wingspan*: 126 ft (38.4 m); *Length*: 68 ft 2 in (20.77 m); *Height*: 24 ft 5 in (7.44 m); *Maximum weight on takeoff*: 28,000 lb (12,700 kg); *Maximum Speed*: 91 mph (146 km/h); *Service ceiling*: 2,500 ft (762 m); *Range*: 1,470 miles (2,366 km); *Crew*: 6

Vickers Vimy Transatlantic
Country: Great Britain; *Constructor*: Vickers Ltd.; *Type*: converted bomber; *Year*: 1919; *Engines:* Two Rolls-Royce Eagle VIII, 12-cylinder V, liquid-cooled, 360 hp each; *Wingspan*: 67 ft 2 in (20.47 m); *Length*: 43 ft 6 in (13.26 m); *Height*: 15 ft 3 in (4.65 m); *Maximum weight on takeoff*: 13,285 lb (6,026 kg); *Maximum speed*: 100 mph (161 km/h); *Service ceiling*: 10,500 ft (3,200 m); *Range*: 2,440 miles (3,926 km); *Crew*: 2

Sopwith Atlantic
Country: Great Britain; *Constructor*: Sopwith Aviation Co.; *Type*: competition; *Year*: 1919; *Engine*: Rolls-Royce Eagle VIII, 12-cylinder V, liquid-cooled, 350 hp; *Wingspan*: 46 ft 6 in (14.18 m); *Length*: 32 ft (9.75 m); *Height*: 11 ft 1 in (3.38 m); *Maximum takeoff weight*: 6,130 lb (2,780 kg); *Maximum speed*: 118 mph (189.89 km/h); *Service ceiling*: 12,988 ft (3,960 m); *Range*: 1,860 miles (3,000 km); *Crew*: 2

R.34
Country: Great Britain; *Constructor*: William Beardmore and Co.; *Year*: 1919; *Engines*: Five Sunbeam Maori, 250 hp each; *Volume*: 1,950,000 cu.ft (55,217 cu.m); *Length*: 643 ft (196 m); *Diameter*: 78 ft 9 in (24 m); *Gross lift*: 59.2 tons; *Cruising speed*: 62 mph (100 km/h); *Range*: 4,812 miles (7,750 km); *Crew*: 22

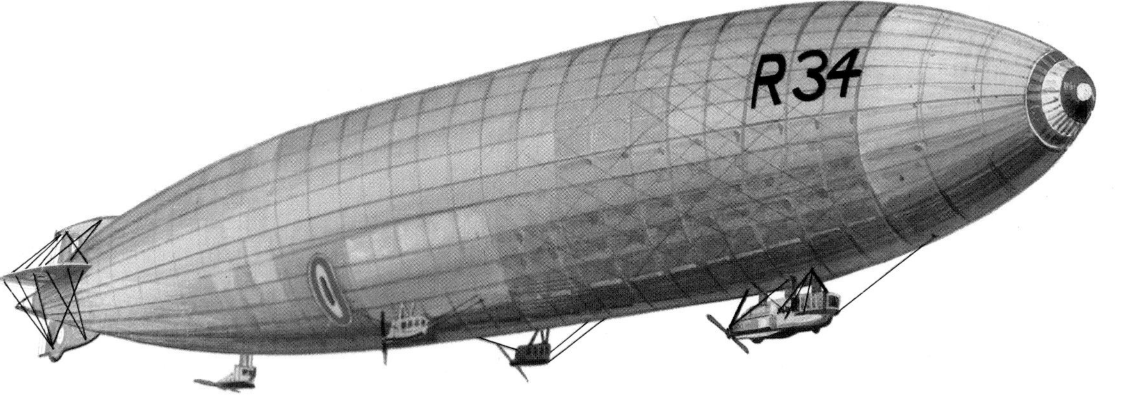

Tarrant Tabor
Country: Great Britain; *Constructor*: W. G. Tarrant Ltd.; *Type*: Heavy bomber; *Year*: 1919; *Engines*: Six Napier Lion, 12-cylinder broad-arrow, liquid-cooled, 450 hp each; *Wingspan*: 131 ft 3 in (40 m); *Length*: 73 ft 2 in (22.3 m); *Height*: 37 ft 3 in (11.35 m); *Weight*: 44,672 lb (20,262 kg); *Estimated maximum speed*: 108 mph (175 km/h); *Ceiling*: 13,000 ft (5,000 m); *Range*: 900–1,200 miles (1,500–1,900 km); *Armament*: 4,650 lb (2,109 kg) of bombs; *Crew*: 5

Zeppelin-Staaken E.4/20
Country: Germany; *Constructor*: Zeppelin-Werke GmbH; *Type*: Civil transport; *Year*: 1920; *Engines*: Four Maybach Mb.IVa, 6-cylinder in-line, liquid-cooled, 245 hp each; *Wingspan*: 101 ft 8.5 in (31 m); *Length*: 54 ft 1 in (16.49 m); *Weight*: 18,739 lb (8,500 kg); *Cruising speed*: 124 mph (200 km/h); *Range*: 740 miles (1,200 km); *Crew*: 3; *Passengers*: 12–18

Caproni Ca 60 Transaereo
Country: Italy; *Constructor*: Società Aviazione Ing. Caproni; *Type*: Civil transport; *Year*: 1921; *Engines*: Eight Liberty, 12-cylinder V, liquid-cooled, 400 hp each; *Wingspan*: 98 ft 5 in (30 m); *Length*: 77 ft (23.45 m); *Height*: 30 ft (9.15 m); *Weight*: 55,100 lb (26,000 kg); *Maximum speed*: 80 mph (130 km/h); *Range*: 410 miles (660 km); *Crew*: 8; *Cargo*: 12,000 lb (5,445 kg)—intended to accommodate 100 passengers

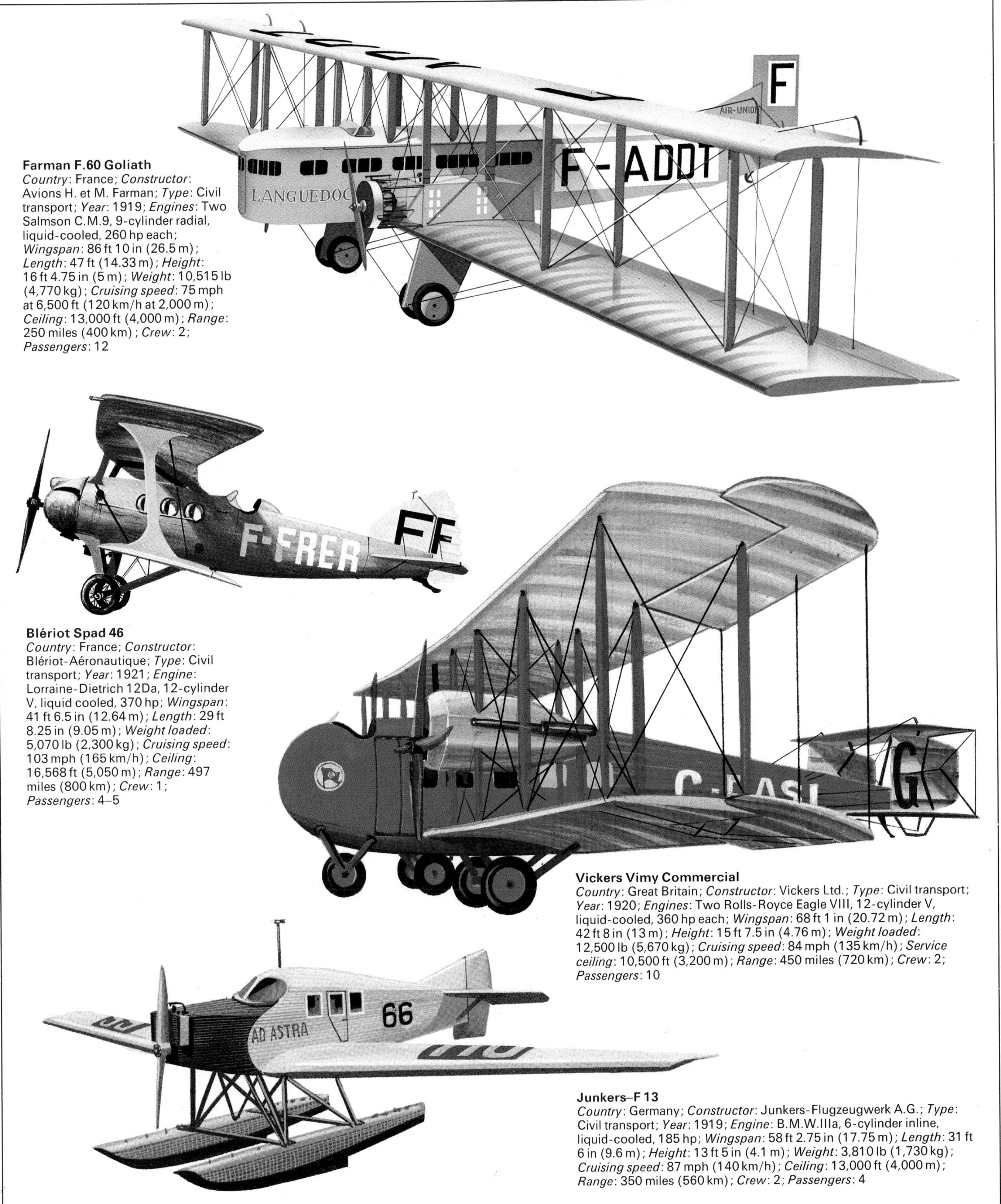

Farman F.60 Goliath
Country: France; *Constructor*: Avions H. et M. Farman; *Type*: Civil transport; *Year*: 1919; *Engines*: Two Salmson C.M.9, 9-cylinder radial, liquid-cooled, 260 hp each; *Wingspan*: 86 ft 10 in (26.5 m); *Length*: 47 ft (14.33 m); *Height*: 16 ft 4.75 in (5 m); *Weight*: 10,515 lb (4,770 kg); *Cruising speed*: 75 mph at 6,500 ft (120 km/h at 2,000 m); *Ceiling*: 13,000 ft (4,000 m); *Range*: 250 miles (400 km); *Crew*: 2; *Passengers*: 12

Blériot Spad 46
Country: France; *Constructor*: Blériot-Aéronautique; *Type*: Civil transport; *Year*: 1921; *Engine*: Lorraine-Dietrich 12Da, 12-cylinder V, liquid cooled, 370 hp; *Wingspan*: 41 ft 6.5 in (12.64 m); *Length*: 29 ft 8.25 in (9.05 m); *Weight loaded*: 5,070 lb (2,300 kg); *Cruising speed*: 103 mph (165 km/h); *Ceiling*: 16,568 ft (5,050 m); *Range*: 497 miles (800 km); *Crew*: 1; *Passengers*: 4–5

Vickers Vimy Commercial
Country: Great Britain; *Constructor*: Vickers Ltd.; *Type*: Civil transport; *Year*: 1920; *Engines*: Two Rolls-Royce Eagle VIII, 12-cylinder V, liquid-cooled, 360 hp each; *Wingspan*: 68 ft 1 in (20.72 m); *Length*: 42 ft 8 in (13 m); *Height*: 15 ft 7.5 in (4.76 m); *Weight loaded*: 12,500 lb (5,670 kg); *Cruising speed*: 84 mph (135 km/h); *Service ceiling*: 10,500 ft (3,200 m); *Range*: 450 miles (720 km); *Crew*: 2; *Passengers*: 10

Junkers–F 13
Country: Germany; *Constructor*: Junkers-Flugzeugwerk A.G.; *Type*: Civil transport; *Year*: 1919; *Engine*: B.M.W.IIIa, 6-cylinder inline, liquid-cooled, 185 hp; *Wingspan*: 58 ft 2.75 in (17.75 m); *Length*: 31 ft 6 in (9.6 m); *Height*: 13 ft 5 in (4.1 m); *Weight*: 3,810 lb (1,730 kg); *Cruising speed*: 87 mph (140 km/h); *Ceiling*: 13,000 ft (4,000 m); *Range*: 350 miles (560 km); *Crew*: 2; *Passengers*: 4

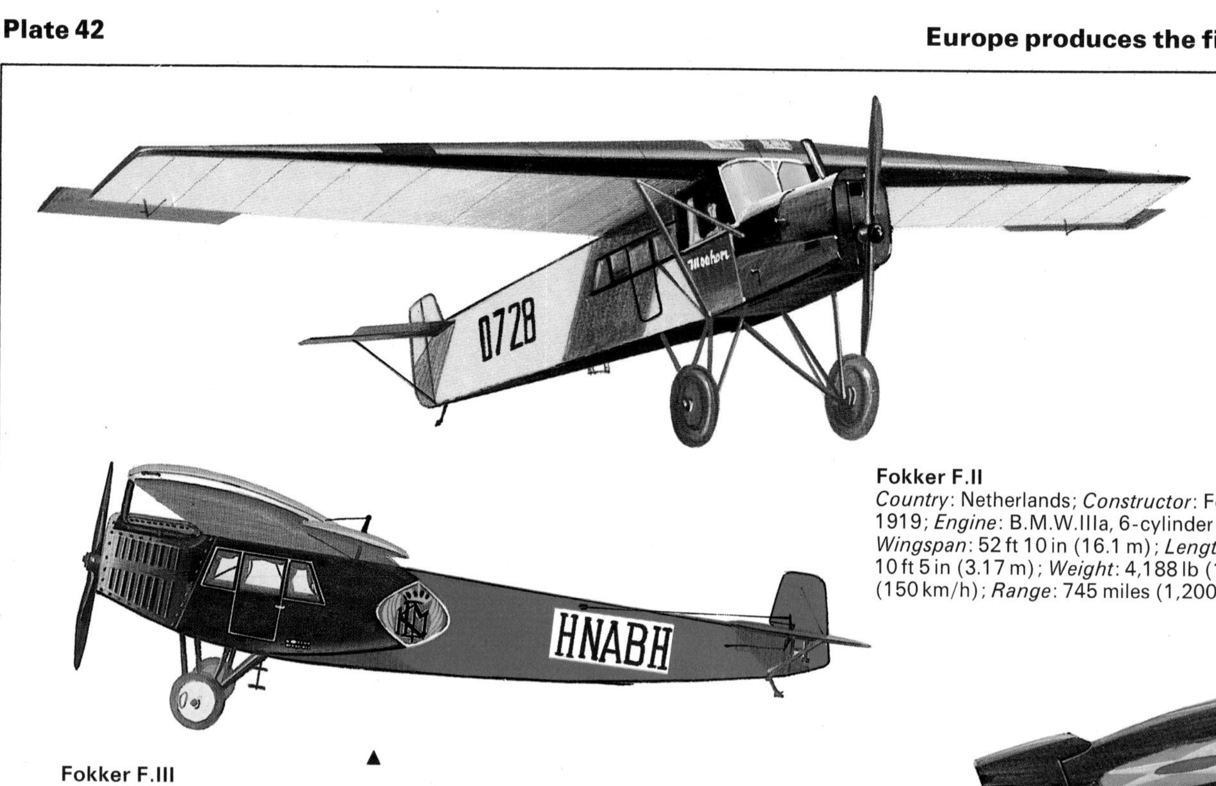

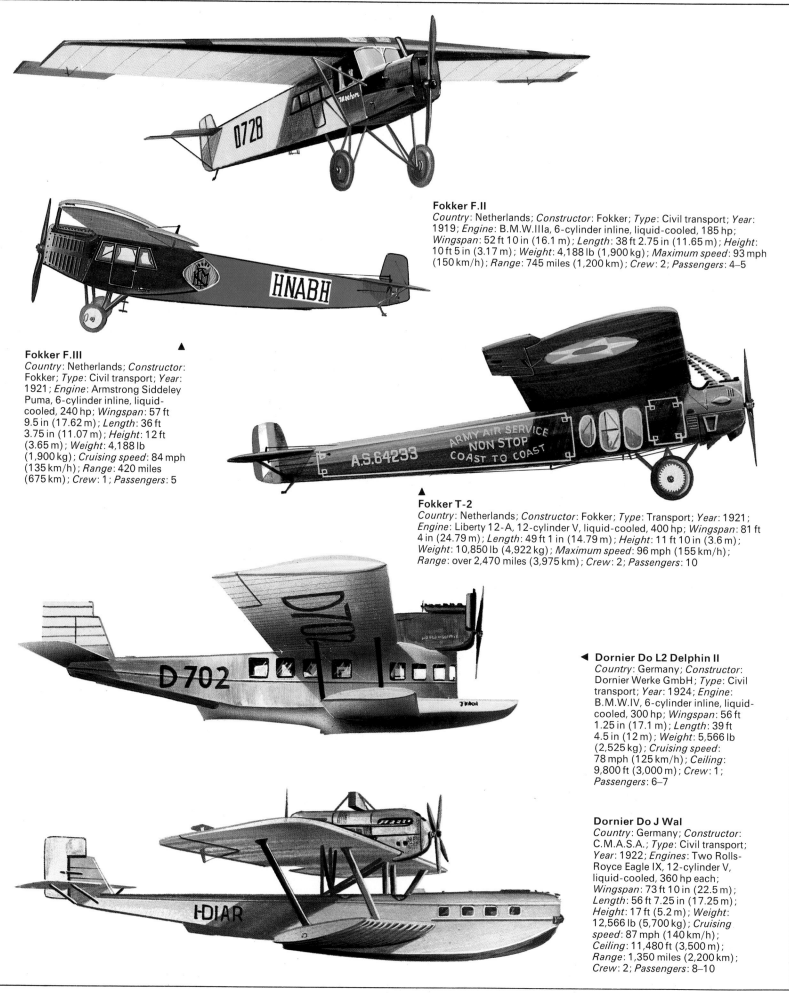

Fokker F.II
Country: Netherlands; *Constructor*: Fokker; *Type*: Civil transport; *Year*: 1919; *Engine*: B.M.W.IIIa, 6-cylinder inline, liquid-cooled, 185 hp; *Wingspan*: 52 ft 10 in (16.1 m); *Length*: 38 ft 2.75 in (11.65 m); *Height*: 10 ft 5 in (3.17 m); *Weight*: 4,188 lb (1,900 kg); *Maximum speed*: 93 mph (150 km/h); *Range*: 745 miles (1,200 km); *Crew*: 2; *Passengers*: 4–5

▲ **Fokker F.III**
Country: Netherlands; *Constructor*: Fokker; *Type*: Civil transport; *Year*: 1921; *Engine*: Armstrong Siddeley Puma, 6-cylinder inline, liquid-cooled, 240 hp; *Wingspan*: 57 ft 9.5 in (17.62 m); *Length*: 36 ft 3.75 in (11.07 m); *Height*: 12 ft (3.65 m); *Weight*: 4,188 lb (1,900 kg); *Cruising speed*: 84 mph (135 km/h); *Range*: 420 miles (675 km); *Crew*: 1; *Passengers*: 5

▲ **Fokker T-2**
Country: Netherlands; *Constructor*: Fokker; *Type*: Transport; *Year*: 1921; *Engine*: Liberty 12-A, 12-cylinder V, liquid-cooled, 400 hp; *Wingspan*: 81 ft 4 in (24.79 m); *Length*: 49 ft 1 in (14.79 m); *Height*: 11 ft 10 in (3.6 m); *Weight*: 10,850 lb (4,922 kg); *Maximum speed*: 96 mph (155 km/h); *Range*: over 2,470 miles (3,975 km); *Crew*: 2; *Passengers*: 10

◀ **Dornier Do L2 Delphin II**
Country: Germany; *Constructor*: Dornier Werke GmbH; *Type*: Civil transport; *Year*: 1924; *Engine*: B.M.W.IV, 6-cylinder inline, liquid-cooled, 300 hp; *Wingspan*: 56 ft 1.25 in (17.1 m); *Length*: 39 ft 4.5 in (12 m); *Weight*: 5,566 lb (2,525 kg); *Cruising speed*: 78 mph (125 km/h); *Ceiling*: 9,800 ft (3,000 m); *Crew*: 1; *Passengers*: 6–7

Dornier Do J Wal
Country: Germany; *Constructor*: C.M.A.S.A.; *Type*: Civil transport; *Year*: 1922; *Engines*: Two Rolls-Royce Eagle IX, 12-cylinder V, liquid-cooled, 360 hp each; *Wingspan*: 73 ft 10 in (22.5 m); *Length*: 56 ft 7.25 in (17.25 m); *Height*: 17 ft (5.2 m); *Weight*: 12,566 lb (5,700 kg); *Cruising speed*: 87 mph (140 km/h); *Ceiling*: 11,480 ft (3,500 m); *Range*: 1,350 miles (2,200 km); *Crew*: 2; *Passengers*: 8–10

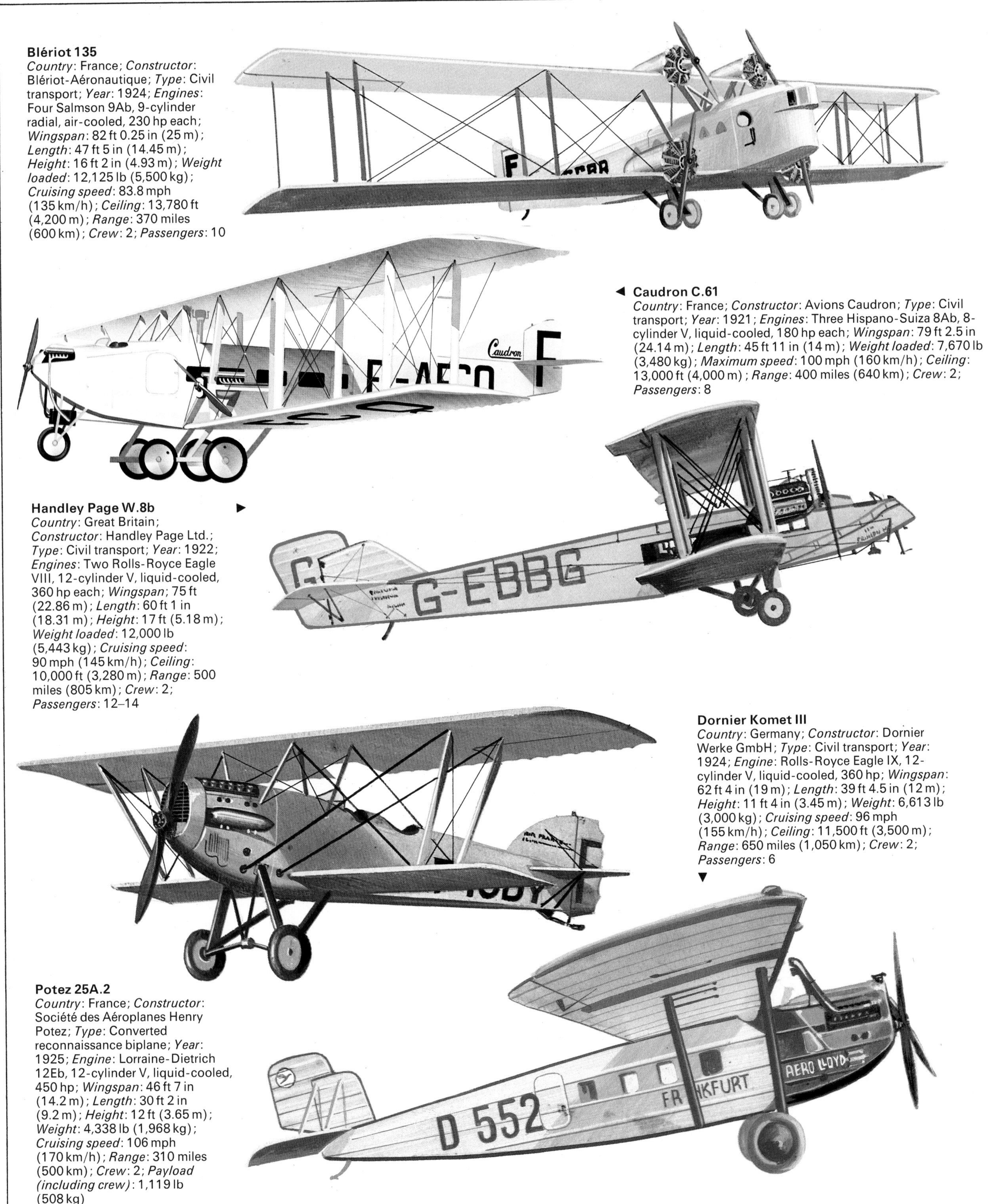

Blériot 135
Country: France; *Constructor*: Blériot-Aéronautique; *Type*: Civil transport; *Year*: 1924; *Engines*: Four Salmson 9Ab, 9-cylinder radial, air-cooled, 230 hp each; *Wingspan*: 82 ft 0.25 in (25 m); *Length*: 47 ft 5 in (14.45 m); *Height*: 16 ft 2 in (4.93 m); *Weight loaded*: 12,125 lb (5,500 kg); *Cruising speed*: 83.8 mph (135 km/h); *Ceiling*: 13,780 ft (4,200 m); *Range*: 370 miles (600 km); *Crew*: 2; *Passengers*: 10

◀ **Caudron C.61**
Country: France; *Constructor*: Avions Caudron; *Type*: Civil transport; *Year*: 1921; *Engines*: Three Hispano-Suiza 8Ab, 8-cylinder V, liquid-cooled, 180 hp each; *Wingspan*: 79 ft 2.5 in (24.14 m); *Length*: 45 ft 11 in (14 m); *Weight loaded*: 7,670 lb (3,480 kg); *Maximum speed*: 100 mph (160 km/h); *Ceiling*: 13,000 ft (4,000 m); *Range*: 400 miles (640 km); *Crew*: 2; *Passengers*: 8

Handley Page W.8b ▶
Country: Great Britain; *Constructor*: Handley Page Ltd.; *Type*: Civil transport; *Year*: 1922; *Engines*: Two Rolls-Royce Eagle VIII, 12-cylinder V, liquid-cooled, 360 hp each; *Wingspan*: 75 ft (22.86 m); *Length*: 60 ft 1 in (18.31 m); *Height*: 17 ft (5.18 m); *Weight loaded*: 12,000 lb (5,443 kg); *Cruising speed*: 90 mph (145 km/h); *Ceiling*: 10,000 ft (3,280 m); *Range*: 500 miles (805 km); *Crew*: 2; *Passengers*: 12–14

Dornier Komet III
Country: Germany; *Constructor*: Dornier Werke GmbH; *Type*: Civil transport; *Year*: 1924; *Engine*: Rolls-Royce Eagle IX, 12-cylinder V, liquid-cooled, 360 hp; *Wingspan*: 62 ft 4 in (19 m); *Length*: 39 ft 4.5 in (12 m); *Height*: 11 ft 4 in (3.45 m); *Weight*: 6,613 lb (3,000 kg); *Cruising speed*: 96 mph (155 km/h); *Ceiling*: 11,500 ft (3,500 m); *Range*: 650 miles (1,050 km); *Crew*: 2; *Passengers*: 6
▼

Potez 25A.2
Country: France; *Constructor*: Société des Aéroplanes Henry Potez; *Type*: Converted reconnaissance biplane; *Year*: 1925; *Engine*: Lorraine-Dietrich 12Eb, 12-cylinder V, liquid-cooled, 450 hp; *Wingspan*: 46 ft 7 in (14.2 m); *Length*: 30 ft 2 in (9.2 m); *Height*: 12 ft (3.65 m); *Weight*: 4,338 lb (1,968 kg); *Cruising speed*: 106 mph (170 km/h); *Range*: 310 miles (500 km); *Crew*: 2; *Payload (including crew)*: 1,119 lb (508 kg)

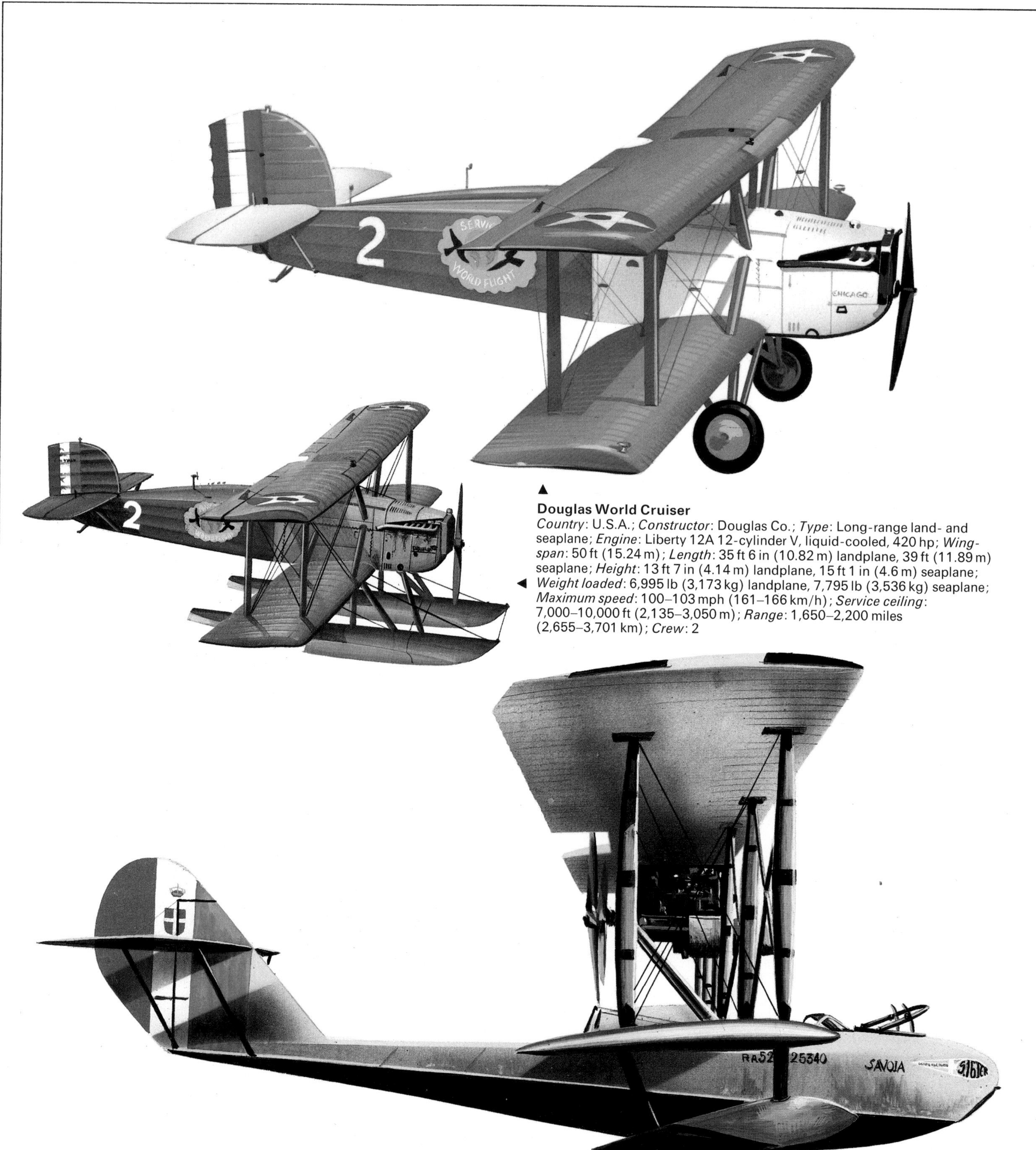

▲
Douglas World Cruiser
Country: U.S.A.; *Constructor*: Douglas Co.; *Type*: Long-range land- and seaplane; *Engine*: Liberty 12A 12-cylinder V, liquid-cooled, 420 hp; *Wing-span*: 50 ft (15.24 m); *Length*: 35 ft 6 in (10.82 m) landplane, 39 ft (11.89 m) seaplane; *Height*: 13 ft 7 in (4.14 m) landplane, 15 ft 1 in (4.6 m) seaplane; ◀ *Weight loaded*: 6,995 lb (3,173 kg) landplane, 7,795 lb (3,536 kg) seaplane; *Maximum speed*: 100–103 mph (161–166 km/h); *Service ceiling*: 7,000–10,000 ft (2,135–3,050 m); *Range*: 1,650–2,200 miles (2,655–3,701 km); *Crew*: 2

Savoia S.16ter
Country: Italy; *Constructor*: Società Idrovolanti Alta Italia; *Type*: Passenger transport; *Year*: 1923; *Engine*: Lorraine-Dietrich (Isotta-Fraschini), 12-cylinder V, liquid-cooled, 400 hp; *Wingspan*: 50 ft 10.25 in (15.5 m); *Length*: 32 ft 5.75 in (9.91 m); *Height*: 12 ft (3.66 m); *Weight*: 5,732 lb (2,600 kg); *Cruising speed*: 93 mph (150 km/h); *Ceiling*: 9,800 ft (3,000 m); *Range*: 620 miles (1,000 km); *Crew*: 1; *Passengers*: 4

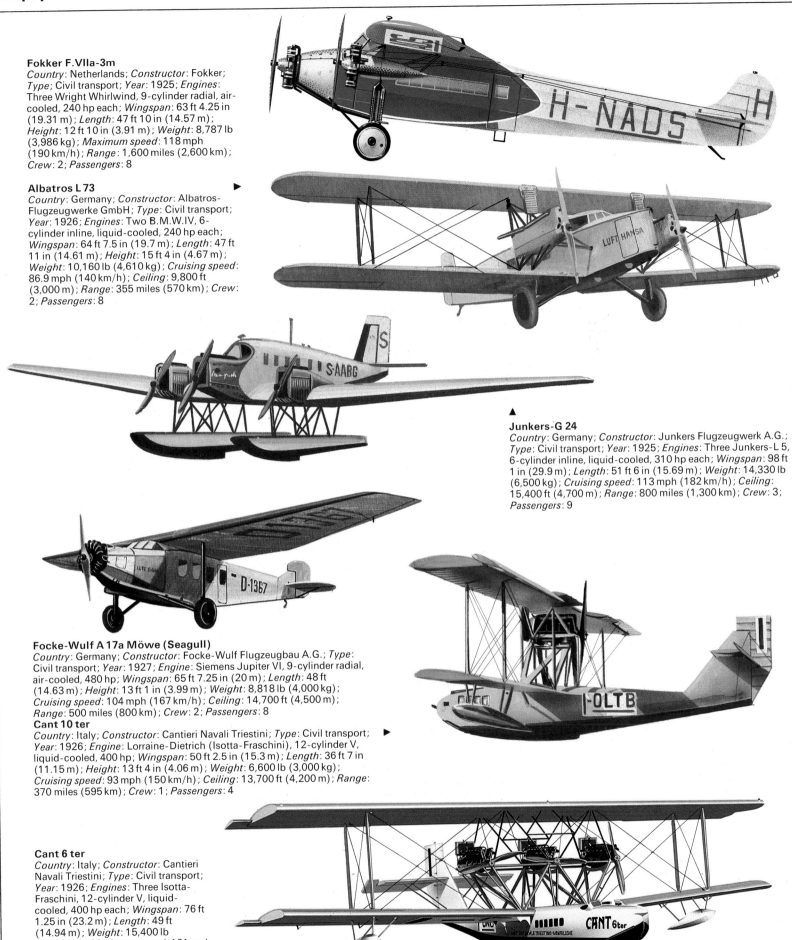

Fokker F.VIIa-3m
Country: Netherlands; *Constructor*: Fokker; *Type*: Civil transport; *Year*: 1925; *Engines*: Three Wright Whirlwind, 9-cylinder radial, air-cooled, 240 hp each; *Wingspan*: 63 ft 4.25 in (19.31 m); *Length*: 47 ft 10 in (14.57 m); *Height*: 12 ft 10 in (3.91 m); *Weight*: 8,787 lb (3,986 kg); *Maximum speed*: 118 mph (190 km/h); *Range*: 1,600 miles (2,600 km); *Crew*: 2; *Passengers*: 8

Albatros L 73 ▶
Country: Germany; *Constructor*: Albatros-Flugzeugwerke GmbH; *Type*: Civil transport; *Year*: 1926; *Engines*: Two B.M.W.IV, 6-cylinder inline, liquid-cooled, 240 hp each; *Wingspan*: 64 ft 7.5 in (19.7 m); *Length*: 47 ft 11 in (14.61 m); *Height*: 15 ft 4 in (4.67 m); *Weight*: 10,160 lb (4,610 kg); *Cruising speed*: 86.9 mph (140 km/h); *Ceiling*: 9,800 ft (3,000 m); *Range*: 355 miles (570 km); *Crew*: 2; *Passengers*: 8

▲
Junkers G 24
Country: Germany; *Constructor*: Junkers Flugzeugwerk A.G.; *Type*: Civil transport; *Year*: 1925; *Engines*: Three Junkers-L 5, 6-cylinder inline, liquid-cooled, 310 hp each; *Wingspan*: 98 ft 1 in (29.9 m); *Length*: 51 ft 6 in (15.69 m); *Weight*: 14,330 lb (6,500 kg); *Cruising speed*: 113 mph (182 km/h); *Ceiling*: 15,400 ft (4,700 m); *Range*: 800 miles (1,300 km); *Crew*: 3; *Passengers*: 9

Focke-Wulf A 17a Möwe (Seagull)
Country: Germany; *Constructor*: Focke-Wulf Flugzeugbau A.G.; *Type*: Civil transport; *Year*: 1927; *Engine*: Siemens Jupiter VI, 9-cylinder radial, air-cooled, 480 hp; *Wingspan*: 65 ft 7.25 in (20 m); *Length*: 48 ft (14.63 m); *Height*: 13 ft 1 in (3.99 m); *Weight*: 8,818 lb (4,000 kg); *Cruising speed*: 104 mph (167 km/h); *Ceiling*: 14,700 ft (4,500 m); *Range*: 500 miles (800 km); *Crew*: 2; *Passengers*: 8

Cant 10 ter
Country: Italy; *Constructor*: Cantieri Navali Triestini; *Type*: Civil transport; ▶
Year: 1926; *Engine*: Lorraine-Dietrich (Isotta-Fraschini), 12-cylinder V, liquid-cooled, 400 hp; *Wingspan*: 50 ft 2.5 in (15.3 m); *Length*: 36 ft 7 in (11.15 m); *Height*: 13 ft 4 in (4.06 m); *Weight*: 6,600 lb (3,000 kg); *Cruising speed*: 93 mph (150 km/h); *Ceiling*: 13,700 ft (4,200 m); *Range*: 370 miles (595 km); *Crew*: 1; *Passengers*: 4

Cant 6 ter
Country: Italy; *Constructor*: Cantieri Navali Triestini; *Type*: Civil transport; *Year*: 1926; *Engines*: Three Isotta-Fraschini, 12-cylinder V, liquid-cooled, 400 hp each; *Wingspan*: 76 ft 1.25 in (23.2 m); *Length*: 49 ft (14.94 m); *Weight*: 15,400 lb (7,000 kg); *Maximum speed*: 121 mph (195 km/h); *Crew*: 2; *Passengers*: 11

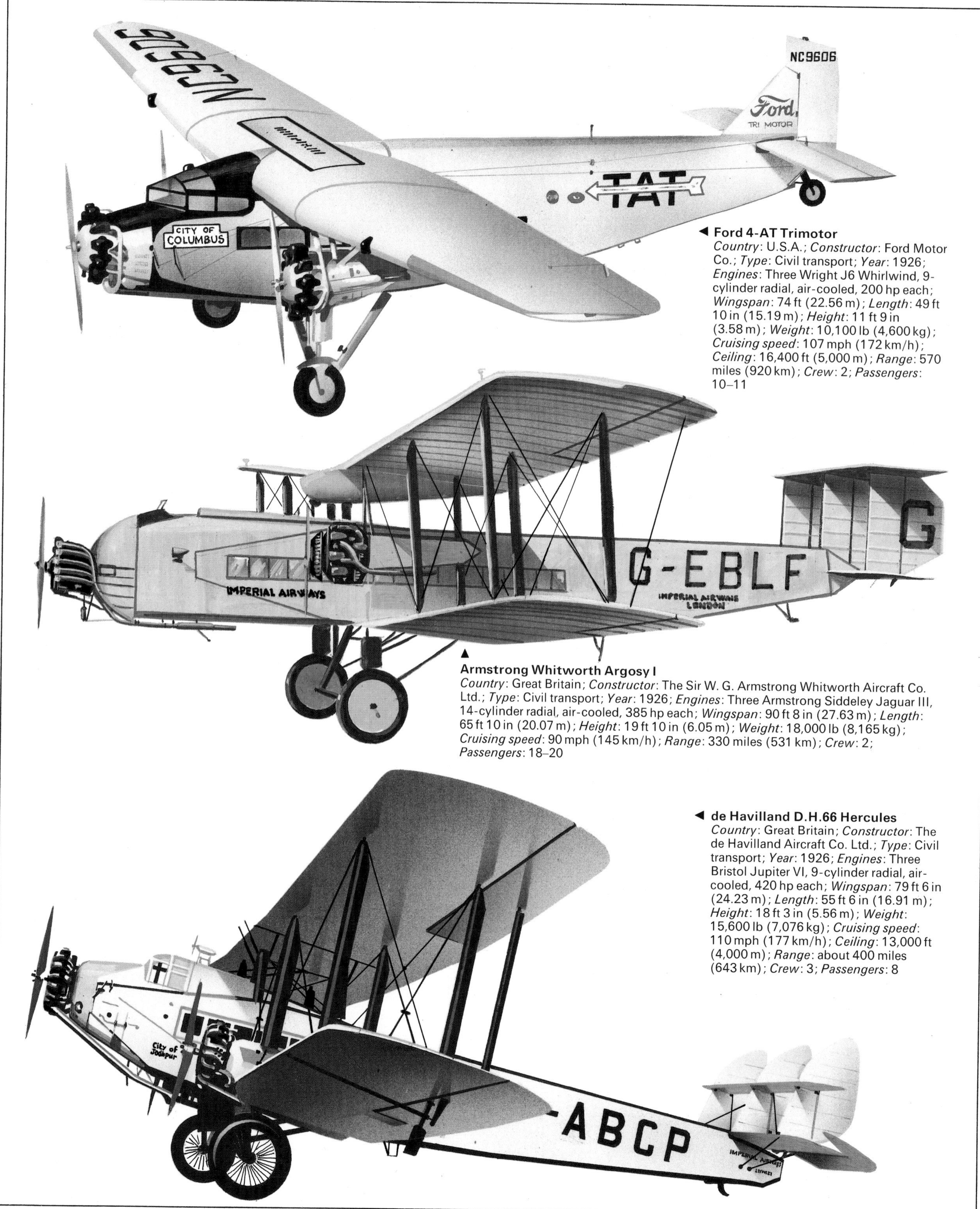

◄ **Ford 4-AT Trimotor**
Country: U.S.A.; *Constructor*: Ford Motor Co.; *Type*: Civil transport; *Year*: 1926; *Engines*: Three Wright J6 Whirlwind, 9-cylinder radial, air-cooled, 200 hp each; *Wingspan*: 74 ft (22.56 m); *Length*: 49 ft 10 in (15.19 m); *Height*: 11 ft 9 in (3.58 m); *Weight*: 10,100 lb (4,600 kg); *Cruising speed*: 107 mph (172 km/h); *Ceiling*: 16,400 ft (5,000 m); *Range*: 570 miles (920 km); *Crew*: 2; *Passengers*: 10–11

▲
Armstrong Whitworth Argosy I
Country: Great Britain; *Constructor*: The Sir W. G. Armstrong Whitworth Aircraft Co. Ltd.; *Type*: Civil transport; *Year*: 1926; *Engines*: Three Armstrong Siddeley Jaguar III, 14-cylinder radial, air-cooled, 385 hp each; *Wingspan*: 90 ft 8 in (27.63 m); *Length*: 65 ft 10 in (20.07 m); *Height*: 19 ft 10 in (6.05 m); *Weight*: 18,000 lb (8,165 kg); *Cruising speed*: 90 mph (145 km/h); *Range*: 330 miles (531 km); *Crew*: 2; *Passengers*: 18–20

◄ **de Havilland D.H.66 Hercules**
Country: Great Britain; *Constructor*: The de Havilland Aircraft Co. Ltd.; *Type*: Civil transport; *Year*: 1926; *Engines*: Three Bristol Jupiter VI, 9-cylinder radial, air-cooled, 420 hp each; *Wingspan*: 79 ft 6 in (24.23 m); *Length*: 55 ft 6 in (16.91 m); *Height*: 18 ft 3 in (5.56 m); *Weight*: 15,600 lb (7,076 kg); *Cruising speed*: 110 mph (177 km/h); *Ceiling*: 13,000 ft (4,000 m); *Range*: about 400 miles (643 km); *Crew*: 3; *Passengers*: 8

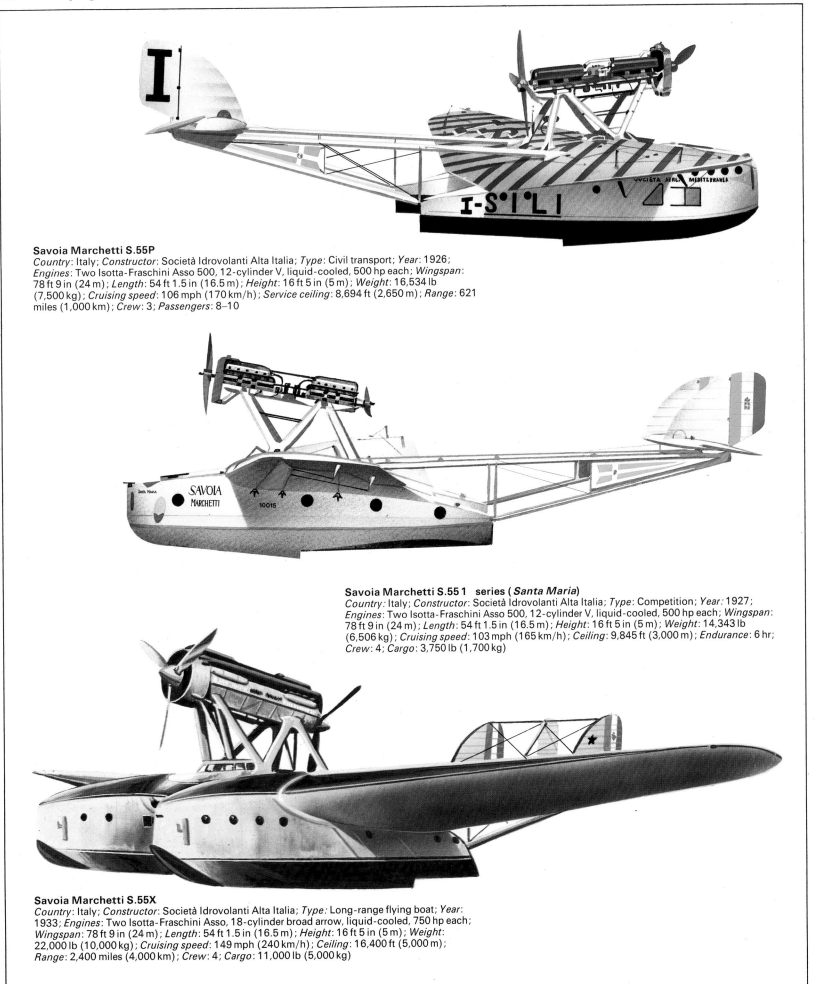

Savoia Marchetti S.55P
Country: Italy; *Constructor*: Società Idrovolanti Alta Italia; *Type*: Civil transport; *Year*: 1926; *Engines*: Two Isotta-Fraschini Asso 500, 12-cylinder V, liquid-cooled, 500 hp each; *Wingspan*: 78 ft 9 in (24 m); *Length*: 54 ft 1.5 in (16.5 m); *Height*: 16 ft 5 in (5 m); *Weight*: 16,534 lb (7,500 kg); *Cruising speed*: 106 mph (170 km/h); *Service ceiling*: 8,694 ft (2,650 m); *Range*: 621 miles (1,000 km); *Crew*: 3; *Passengers*: 8–10

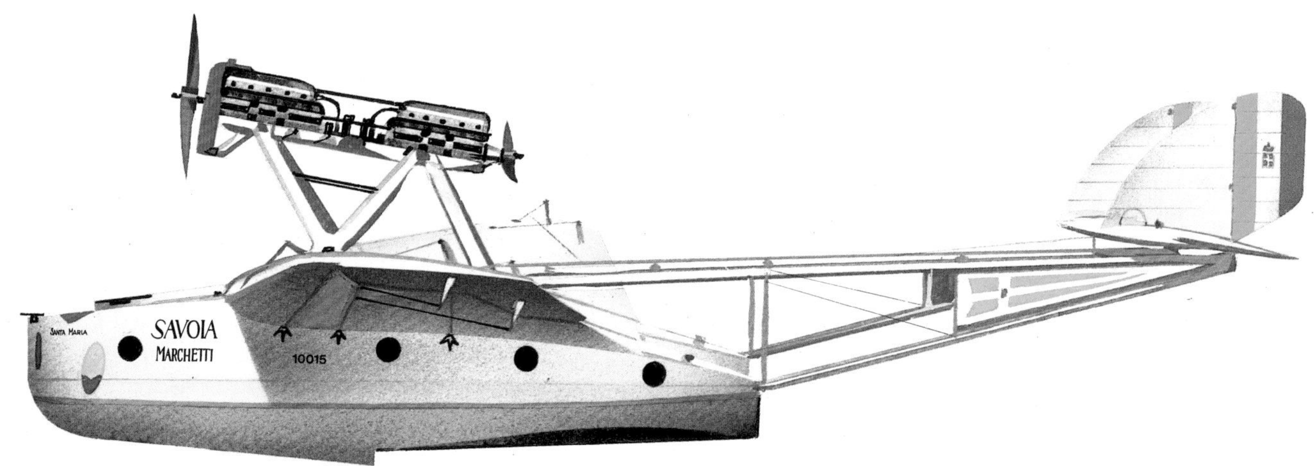

Savoia Marchetti S.55 1 series (*Santa Maria*)
Country: Italy; *Constructor*: Società Idrovolanti Alta Italia; *Type*: Competition; *Year*: 1927; *Engines*: Two Isotta-Fraschini Asso 500, 12-cylinder V, liquid-cooled, 500 hp each; *Wingspan*: 78 ft 9 in (24 m); *Length*: 54 ft 1.5 in (16.5 m); *Height*: 16 ft 5 in (5 m); *Weight*: 14,343 lb (6,506 kg); *Cruising speed*: 103 mph (165 km/h); *Ceiling*: 9,845 ft (3,000 m); *Endurance*: 6 hr; *Crew*: 4; *Cargo*: 3,750 lb (1,700 kg)

Savoia Marchetti S.55X
Country: Italy; *Constructor*: Società Idrovolanti Alta Italia; *Type*: Long-range flying boat; *Year*: 1933; *Engines*: Two Isotta-Fraschini Asso, 18-cylinder broad arrow, liquid-cooled, 750 hp each; *Wingspan*: 78 ft 9 in (24 m); *Length*: 54 ft 1.5 in (16.5 m); *Height*: 16 ft 5 in (5 m); *Weight*: 22,000 lb (10,000 kg); *Cruising speed*: 149 mph (240 km/h); *Ceiling*: 16,400 ft (5,000 m); *Range*: 2,400 miles (4,000 km); *Crew*: 4; *Cargo*: 11,000 lb (5,000 kg)

Four famous American single-engine aircraft: 1927

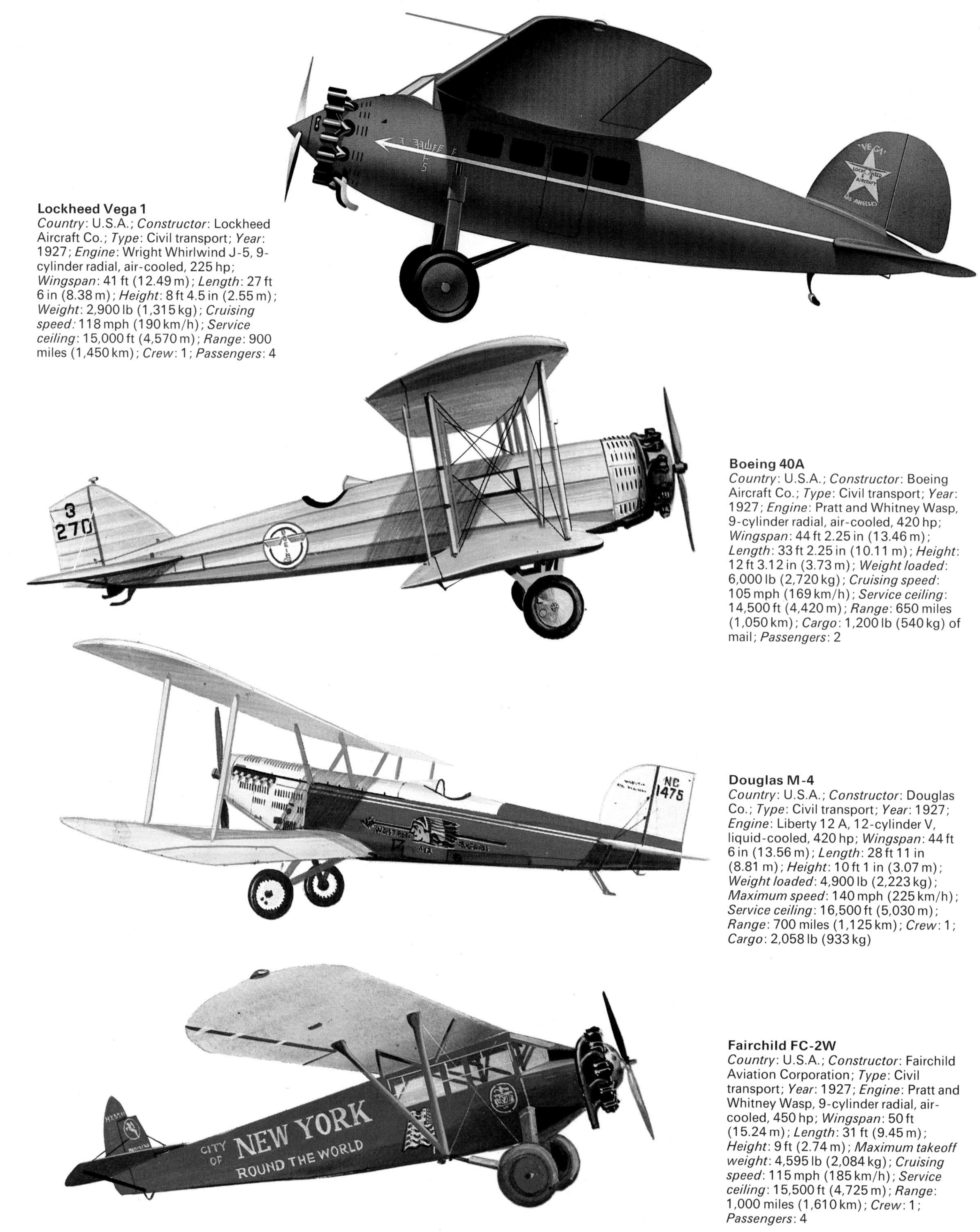

Lockheed Vega 1
Country: U.S.A.; *Constructor*: Lockheed Aircraft Co.; *Type*: Civil transport; *Year*: 1927; *Engine*: Wright Whirlwind J-5, 9-cylinder radial, air-cooled, 225 hp; *Wingspan*: 41 ft (12.49 m); *Length*: 27 ft 6 in (8.38 m); *Height*: 8 ft 4.5 in (2.55 m); *Weight*: 2,900 lb (1,315 kg); *Cruising speed*: 118 mph (190 km/h); *Service ceiling*: 15,000 ft (4,570 m); *Range*: 900 miles (1,450 km); *Crew*: 1; *Passengers*: 4

Boeing 40A
Country: U.S.A.; *Constructor*: Boeing Aircraft Co.; *Type*: Civil transport; *Year*: 1927; *Engine*: Pratt and Whitney Wasp, 9-cylinder radial, air-cooled, 420 hp; *Wingspan*: 44 ft 2.25 in (13.46 m); *Length*: 33 ft 2.25 in (10.11 m); *Height*: 12 ft 3.12 in (3.73 m); *Weight loaded*: 6,000 lb (2,720 kg); *Cruising speed*: 105 mph (169 km/h); *Service ceiling*: 14,500 ft (4,420 m); *Range*: 650 miles (1,050 km); *Cargo*: 1,200 lb (540 kg) of mail; *Passengers*: 2

Douglas M-4
Country: U.S.A.; *Constructor*: Douglas Co.; *Type*: Civil transport; *Year*: 1927; *Engine*: Liberty 12 A, 12-cylinder V, liquid-cooled, 420 hp; *Wingspan*: 44 ft 6 in (13.56 m); *Length*: 28 ft 11 in (8.81 m); *Height*: 10 ft 1 in (3.07 m); *Weight loaded*: 4,900 lb (2,223 kg); *Maximum speed*: 140 mph (225 km/h); *Service ceiling*: 16,500 ft (5,030 m); *Range*: 700 miles (1,125 km); *Crew*: 1; *Cargo*: 2,058 lb (933 kg)

Fairchild FC-2W
Country: U.S.A.; *Constructor*: Fairchild Aviation Corporation; *Type*: Civil transport; *Year*: 1927; *Engine*: Pratt and Whitney Wasp, 9-cylinder radial, air-cooled, 450 hp; *Wingspan*: 50 ft (15.24 m); *Length*: 31 ft (9.45 m); *Height*: 9 ft (2.74 m); *Maximum takeoff weight*: 4,595 lb (2,084 kg); *Cruising speed*: 115 mph (185 km/h); *Service ceiling*: 15,500 ft (4,725 m); *Range*: 1,000 miles (1,610 km); *Crew*: 1; *Passengers*: 4

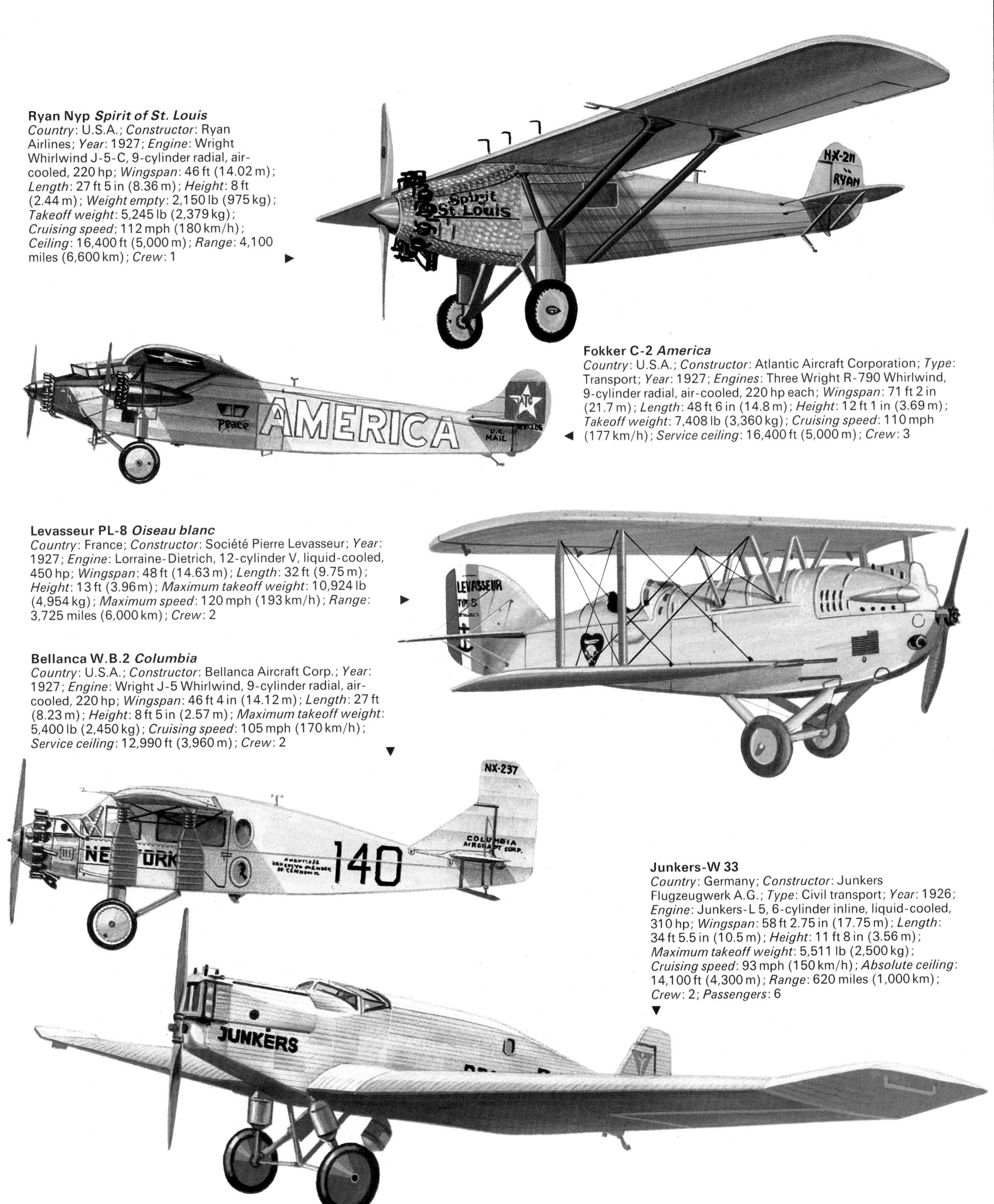

Ryan Nyp *Spirit of St. Louis*
Country: U.S.A.; *Constructor*: Ryan Airlines; *Year*: 1927; *Engine*: Wright Whirlwind J-5-C, 9-cylinder radial, air-cooled, 220 hp; *Wingspan*: 46 ft (14.02 m); *Length*: 27 ft 5 in (8.36 m); *Height*: 8 ft (2.44 m); *Weight empty*: 2,150 lb (975 kg); *Takeoff weight*: 5,245 lb (2,379 kg); *Cruising speed*: 112 mph (180 km/h); *Ceiling*: 16,400 ft (5,000 m); *Range*: 4,100 miles (6,600 km); *Crew*: 1 ▶

Fokker C-2 *America*
Country: U.S.A.; *Constructor*: Atlantic Aircraft Corporation; *Type*: Transport; *Year*: 1927; *Engines*: Three Wright R-790 Whirlwind, 9-cylinder radial, air-cooled, 220 hp each; *Wingspan*: 71 ft 2 in (21.7 m); *Length*: 48 ft 6 in (14.8 m); *Height*: 12 ft 1 in (3.69 m); *Takeoff weight*: 7,408 lb (3,360 kg); *Cruising speed*: 110 mph ◀ (177 km/h); *Service ceiling*: 16,400 ft (5,000 m); *Crew*: 3

Levasseur PL-8 *Oiseau blanc*
Country: France; *Constructor*: Société Pierre Levasseur; *Year*: 1927; *Engine*: Lorraine-Dietrich, 12-cylinder V, liquid-cooled, 450 hp; *Wingspan*: 48 ft (14.63 m); *Length*: 32 ft (9.75 m); *Height*: 13 ft (3.96 m); *Maximum takeoff weight*: 10,924 lb (4,954 kg); *Maximum speed*: 120 mph (193 km/h); *Range*: 3,725 miles (6,000 km); *Crew*: 2 ▶

Bellanca W.B.2 *Columbia*
Country: U.S.A.; *Constructor*: Bellanca Aircraft Corp.; *Year*: 1927; *Engine*: Wright J-5 Whirlwind, 9-cylinder radial, air-cooled, 220 hp; *Wingspan*: 46 ft 4 in (14.12 m); *Length*: 27 ft (8.23 m); *Height*: 8 ft 5 in (2.57 m); *Maximum takeoff weight*: 5,400 lb (2,450 kg); *Cruising speed*: 105 mph (170 km/h); *Service ceiling*: 12,990 ft (3,960 m); *Crew*: 2 ▼

Junkers-W 33
Country: Germany; *Constructor*: Junkers Flugzeugwerk A.G.; *Type*: Civil transport; *Year*: 1926; *Engine*: Junkers-L 5, 6-cylinder inline, liquid-cooled, 310 hp; *Wingspan*: 58 ft 2.75 in (17.75 m); *Length*: 34 ft 5.5 in (10.5 m); *Height*: 11 ft 8 in (3.56 m); *Maximum takeoff weight*: 5,511 lb (2,500 kg); *Cruising speed*: 93 mph (150 km/h); *Absolute ceiling*: 14,100 ft (4,300 m); *Range*: 620 miles (1,000 km); *Crew*: 2; *Passengers*: 6 ▼

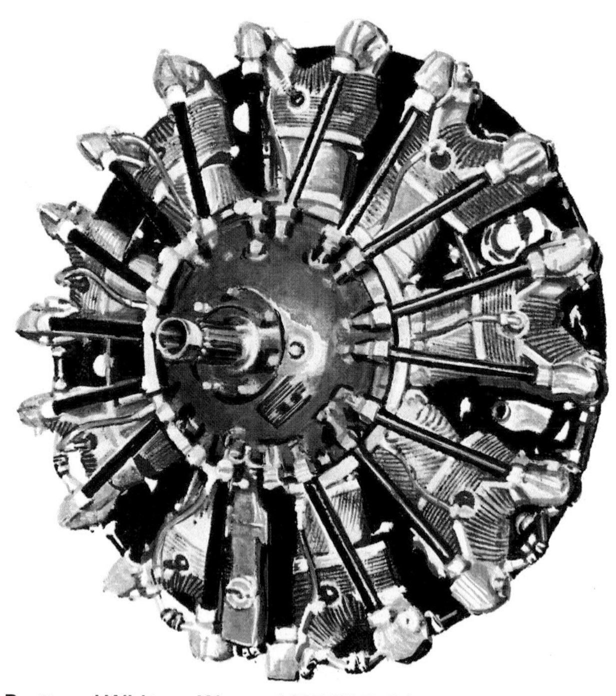

Pratt and Whitney Wasp—1925 (U.S.A.)
This was the first engine developed by Pratt and Whitney soon after the company was founded. It had the standard layout for radial air-cooled engines of the time (9 cylinders) and was fairly high powered (400 hp at first) and this together with its reliability made it very successful. After the Wasp came the Hornet and Wasp Junior series although these were in other power categories.

Wright Whirlwind—1925 (U.S.A.)
Like the Wasp, the Wright Whirlwind engine made a major contribution to the development of aviation in the United States, and was associated with some of the greatest feats in aviation such as the Lindbergh solo North Atlantic flight. It was a 9-cylinder radial engine, capable of producing 200 hp in its first version. The series was developed over many years, and with ever increased power. The Whirlwind was much used for light transport and private airplanes.

de Havilland Gipsy Major I—1932 (G.B.)
The first Gipsy 4-cylinder air-cooled inline engine was delivered in June 1928. It was a small upright engine and powered large numbers of light airplanes including the Moth. The Gipsy Major, illustrated, was an inverted development which appeared in 1932. The Gipsy Major I developed 130 hp and more than 14,000 were built. It was the power unit of the famous Tiger Moth. Final developments of the Gipsy Major gave 215 hp.

Wright Cyclone R-1820—1931 (U.S.A.)
The 9-cylinder Cyclone air-cooled radial engine first appeared in 1925 and produced 450 hp. The Cyclone was widely adopted for civil and military use and so developed that by the early 1930s the R-1820 version was producing more than 700 hp. This engine was later to produce more than 1,000 hp and developed into the 14-cylinder Double Cyclone and eventually the 3,500 hp Turbo-Cyclone.

Plate 38
Military aircraft adapted for use in peacetime: 1919

The first commercial routes were inaugurated and operated with aircraft which had been built as military aircraft and had been hastily converted for civil use. Although such a source of equipment had its drawbacks, these aircraft served their purpose well and played an important part in the expansion of commercial aviation. The Breguet 14 was just such a type and was as successful in the immediately post-war years as it had been during the war, when it had seen long and hard service. It was a very reliable, robust and safe aircraft and, most important of all, large numbers of Breguet 14s were immediately available. They were the obvious choice for some of the first passenger and mail services. Pierre Latécoère, an industrialist from Toulouse, was quick to realize this and he founded his airline, Lignes Aériennes Latécoère, with a fleet of some hundred converted military Breguet 14s. The first survey flight, between Toulouse and Barcelona, was flown on 24 December 1918, and by September 1919 services were being operated as far as Casablanca. In 1919 a group of French aircraft manufacturers, including Breguet, Caudron, Blériot, Farman and Morane, joined forces and founded the Compagnie des Messageries Aériennes (CMA), with the object of opening commercial routes to Great Britain and Belgium initially using Breguet 14Ts. CMA had a fleet of at least 25 Breguet 14s and operations were commenced on 18 April 1919, with flights between Paris and Lille. Services to Brussels and London started in August and September of the same year.

The first airline in Equatorial Africa was inaugurated with a French seaplane, the Lévy-Lepen R, which had been built in 1917 for the Navy. The first leg linking Kinshasha and N'Gombe was opened on 1 July 1920, by SNETA, the official Belgian airline. A second stretch, from N'Gombe to Lisala, was opened on 3 March 1921. This Congo river operation was known as Ligne Aérienne Roi Albert (LARA) and on 1 July 1921, the last leg of the route ending at Stanleyville was opened. It was operated until 7 June 1922. In the two years its aircraft had flown 77,671 miles (125,000 km) and carried 4,409 lb (2,000 kg) of mail and 95 passengers.

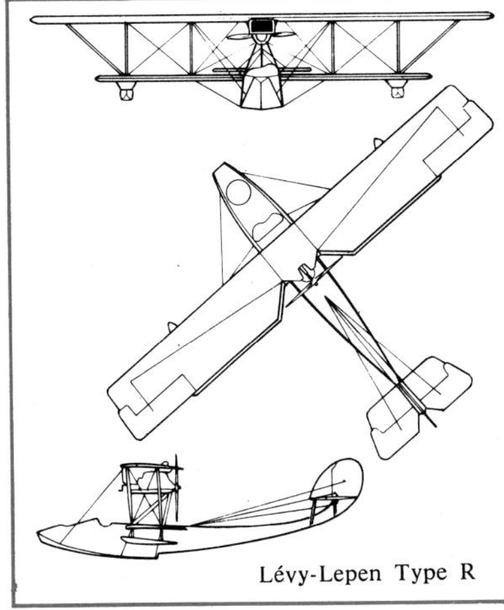
Lévy-Lepen Type R

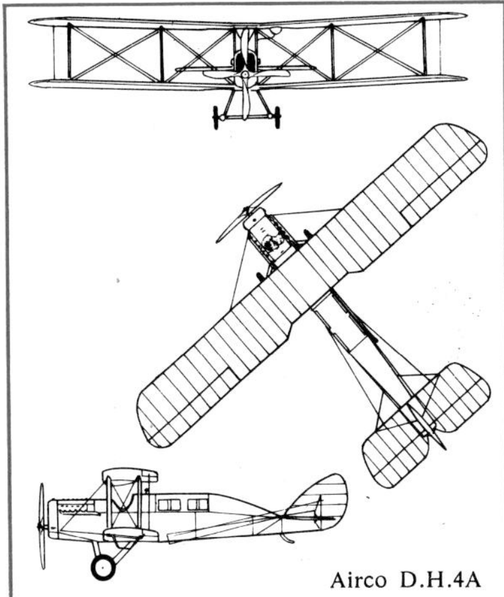
Airco D.H.4A

Great Britain also used converted military aircraft for the first commercial flights. The de Havilland D.H.4 (built by Airco) was one of the first to be adapted for airline use and was flown on regular services in 1919 by Aircraft Transport and Travel Ltd, the London–Paris service being opened on 25 August. A Handley Page Transport D.H.4A set a record on 4 December 1920, when it flew from London to Paris in one hour forty-eight minutes with two passengers on board. Another de Havilland type, the D.H.10, was used by the Royal Air Force for airmail services and saw very limited civil use.

The D.H.10 was a twin-engine bomber which had been completed too late to see action in the war. From 1919 onward the "Amiens," as the D.H.10 was called, equipped No. 120 Squadron R.A.F. and flew regular postal services, delivering mail to the British forces stationed on the Rhine in Germany. Two years later in 1921, the D.H.10s in service in Egypt assisted in inaugurating a far more adventurous mail service between Cairo and Baghdad, flying across the desert and having to rely on ploughed furrows in the sand when navigating over part of the route.

The German A.E.G. J II which was derived from a ground attack biplane was put to much the same civil uses as the French Breguets and the British D.H.4s. This type was stripped of all armament and some had a cabin installed in place of the rear open cockpit. From 1919 onward Deutsche Luft-Reederei ran regular commercial passenger and mail services using a variety of aircraft including J IIs. Four J IIs survived until 1926 when they were taken over by the newly-formed national company, Deutsche Luft Hansa.

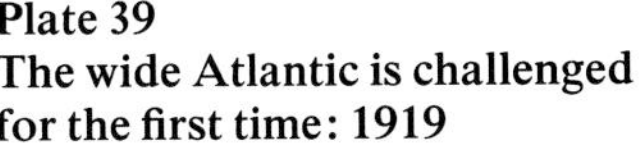

Plate 39
The wide Atlantic is challenged for the first time: 1919

The end of World War I signaled the beginning of an era which was to see immensely exciting events in the aviation world; the great long-distance flights and spectacular competition achievements were to thrill enthusiasts all over the world. The Atlantic presented one of the most tempting challenges and was to continue to inspire pilots and aircraft designers and constructors to use all their skill and ingenuity. It fell to the two Englishmen, John Alcock and Arthur Whitten Brown, to achieve the first nonstop flight across the Atlantic, earning themselves first place on the long list of pioneers who were to conquer that ocean. Their historic flight was made in a modified twin-engine bomber, a Vickers Vimy which had been especially prepared for the attempt. Alcock and Brown took off on 14 June 1919, at 16.12.5 GMT from Lester's Field near St. John's, Newfoundland, and set out across the 1,933 miles (3,110 km) of sea toward Clifden, in Ireland. Their transatlantic flight took 16 hours 27.5 minutes of which 15 hours 57 minutes was the coast-to-coast time and it was not without its hair-raising moments. The most persistent and the most dangerous problem was that of ice forming in the fuel tanks and on the control surfaces which nearly led to disaster. The aircraft which Alcock and Brown used was a normal Vickers Vimy bomber production model from which the military equipment had been removed to make room for supplementary fuel tanks, bringing the aircraft's total fuel capacity to 865 gallons (3,932 liters).

In the previous month an attempt had been made to cross the Atlantic by two other British pilots, Kenneth Mackenzie-Grieve and Harry Hawker, on 18 May 1919, flying a specially designed single-engine biplane, the Sopwith Atlantic. Spurred on by the hope of winning the £10,000 prize which had been offered by Lord Northcliffe, the proprietor of the *Daily Mail*, for the first successful nonstop transatlantic flight, these two enthusiasts were ready to make the attempt before their rivals, but they were unlucky. Nearly six hours out from Newfoundland on their way to Ireland, the engine developed cooling problems. Hawker and Mackenzie-Grieve flew on until early on the 19th, desperately trying to sight a ship. They finally spotted a Danish merchant vessel, SS *Mary*. They brought the Sopwith down in the sea near her and were rescued by her crew.

A successful American attempt to cross the Atlantic was made barely a month before Alcock and Brown's flight, but this was made in several stages, touching down at various points. Three large four-engine Navy Curtiss flying boats set out on the journey, but only one completed the flight. This spectacular, if less significant, feat was enough to make the Navy Curtiss NC-4 famous as the first airplane to fly the 1,400 miles (2,250 km) from Newfoundland to the Azores. The NC-4 was the fourth in a series of flying boats built in the last year of World War I to protect Allied convoys from German submarines in

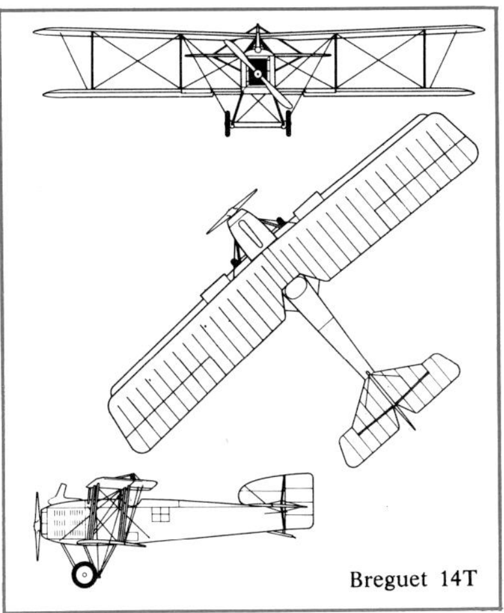
Breguet 14T

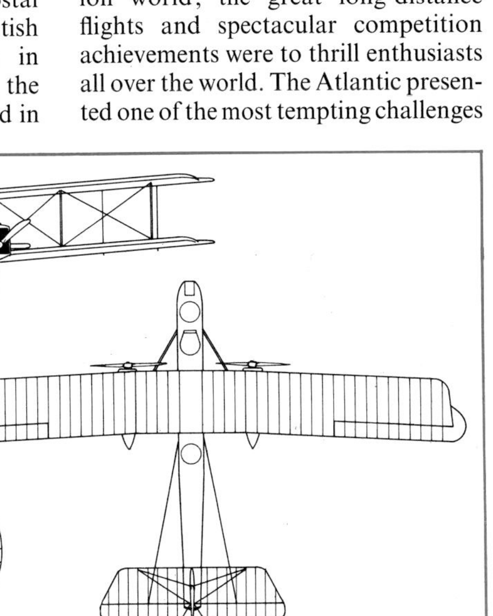
de Havilland D.H.10 Amiens III

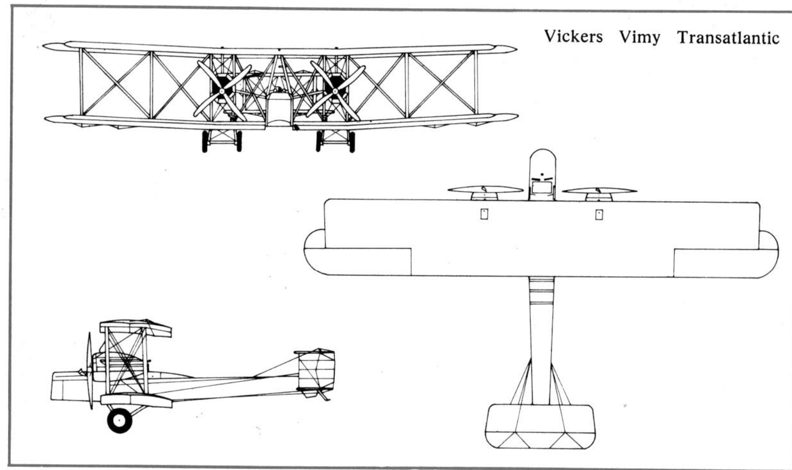
Vickers Vimy Transatlantic

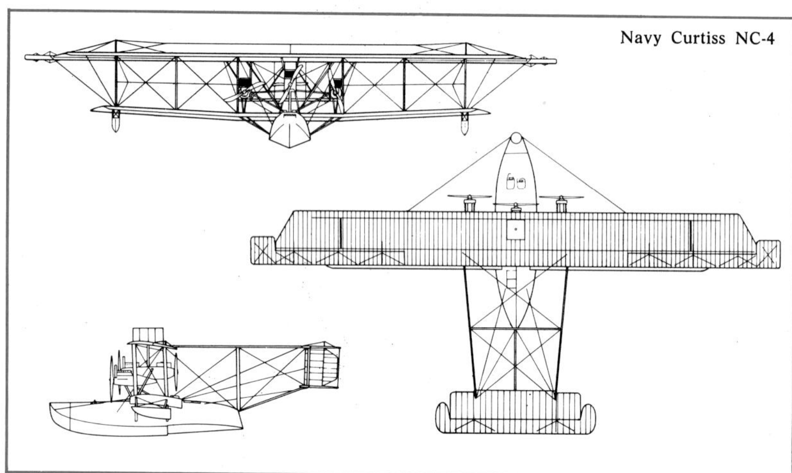
Navy Curtiss NC-4

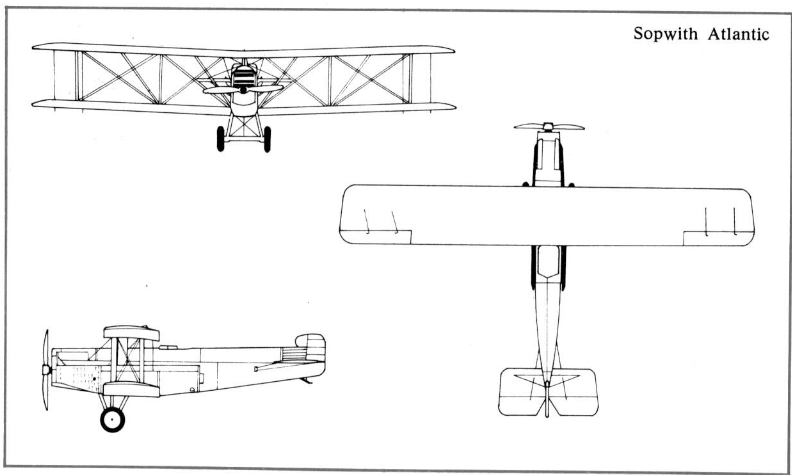
Sopwith Atlantic

the Atlantic. The first model, the NC-1, had made its maiden flight on 4 October 1918, and was powered by three 360 hp Liberty engines. It was followed by the three-engine NC-2 (12 April 1919) and the NC-3 (23 April 1919) which had four 400 hp Liberty engines. With the NC-3, the definitive design formula was reached—three tractor engines plus a fourth pusher engine housed in the center nacelle. With the coming of peace these aircraft were no longer needed for their original role and the decision was taken to test their capabilities in a transatlantic flight. On 16 May 1919, the NC-1, the NC-3 and the NC-4 took off from Trepassey Bay, Newfoundland, and headed for Horta in the Azores, 1,400 miles (2,250 km) away. The first two aircraft had to make forced alightings in the sea, thus abandoning the attempt, but the third, the NC-4, with Lieutenant Commander Albert C. Read at the controls, managed to reach the Azores and on 20 May it took off again for Portugal. On 31 May the NC-4 reached Plymouth where it was given a great welcome. Having been returned to the United States, the NC-4 then undertook a long publicity tour of the Eastern and Southern seaboard cities. The hull of the NC-4 was subsequently presented to the Smithsonian Institution in Washington. In 1969 the entire aircraft was rebuilt and the NC-4 put on view at the Naval Aviation Museum, Pensacola.

Yet another historic Atlantic crossing was made only eighteen days after Alcock and Brown's flight, this time by the R.34 rigid airship, the second of the Class 33 airships built in 1918 and 1919. The airship flew from East Fortune, Scotland, to Mineola, Long Island, in 108 hr 12 min. Four days later the R.34 made the return journey. This was the first Atlantic crossing in an airship, the first East-West crossing and the first return trip across the Atlantic between Europe and the United States. This successful flight started at 1.42 a.m. on 2 July 1919, when the R.34 ascended with thirty-one on board, including a stowaway, and left British shores behind her as she flew westward across the Atlantic. All went smoothly until the airship crossed the coast of Nova Scotia where she was caught in a violent squall and, for a while, it looked as though she might have to make a forced landing. The weather improved, however, and shortage of petrol became the main danger. The airship continued on its way, landing at Mineola at 1.54 p.m. on 6 July, with only enough fuel left for 40 minutes flying. The R.34 airship set off on the return journey on 10 July, shortly before midnight, local time, and reached England safely in only 75 hours 3 minutes.

Plate 40
The vulnerable giants of commercial aviation: 1919–1921

The first attempts to produce specially-designed commercial aircraft rather than adapting military types were made by several nations immediately after the war. The most ambitious designs put forward were for enormous airplanes which could carry dozens of passengers over long distances in comfort. Most of these projects came to nothing and their only significance was to show what tremendous enthusiasm and inventiveness were aroused in the early years of commercial aviation. In 1920 the Germans completed the Zeppelin-Staaken E.4/20, a large four-engine aircraft which was to be a casualty of the Treaty of Versailles. Had it been put into production it would probably have advanced the development of civil aviation by about ten years. It was an all-metal machine, of very advanced design and concept, which could carry 12–18 passengers in a roomy cabin over distances of up to 740 miles (1,200 km) at a cruising speed of 124 mph (200 km/h). Immediately after test flights had started and the potential of the airplane became obvious, the program was scrapped by the Allied Control Commission, ever watchful and determined that Germany should not rebuild any air power in the postwar years. Given the size of the airplane, it was feared that the Germans might develop this formidable aircraft into a highly efficient bomber and thus clandestinely regain air supremacy—and this was to be avoided at all costs. The E.4/20's designer, Adolf Rohrbach, protested, but in vain, and attempts by the management of the Zeppelin-Werke to persuade the members of the Commission to allow them to continue with the project proved equally fruitless. In November 1922 the E.4/20 was destroyed on Allied orders.

Another ambitious project which was launched at this time also came to nothing, but for completely different reasons. This was an Italian design for a gigantic nine-wing flying boat, the Caproni Ca 60 Transaereo. This giant was driven by eight engines and was designed to carry 100 passengers across the Atlantic. The Ca 60 only managed to fly once, however, when it rose about 60 feet into the air over Lake Maggiore on 4 March 1921, before nose-diving into the water and breaking up. Caproni had launched the project immediately after the war, confident that the experience gained during the war years building large-multi-engine

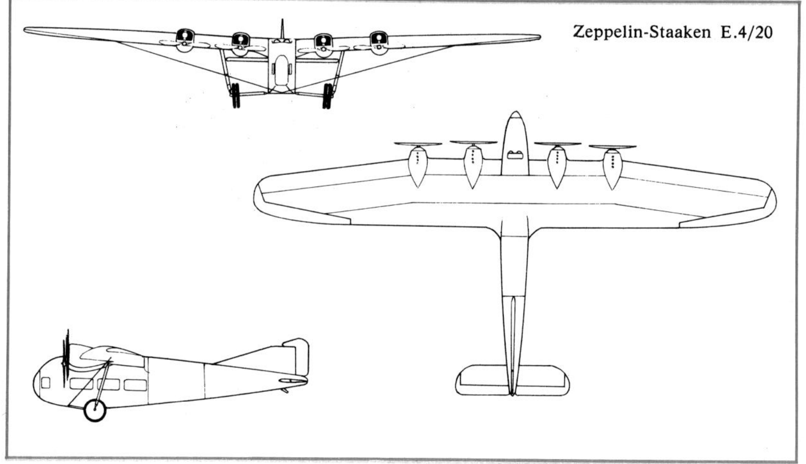
Zeppelin-Staaken E.4/20

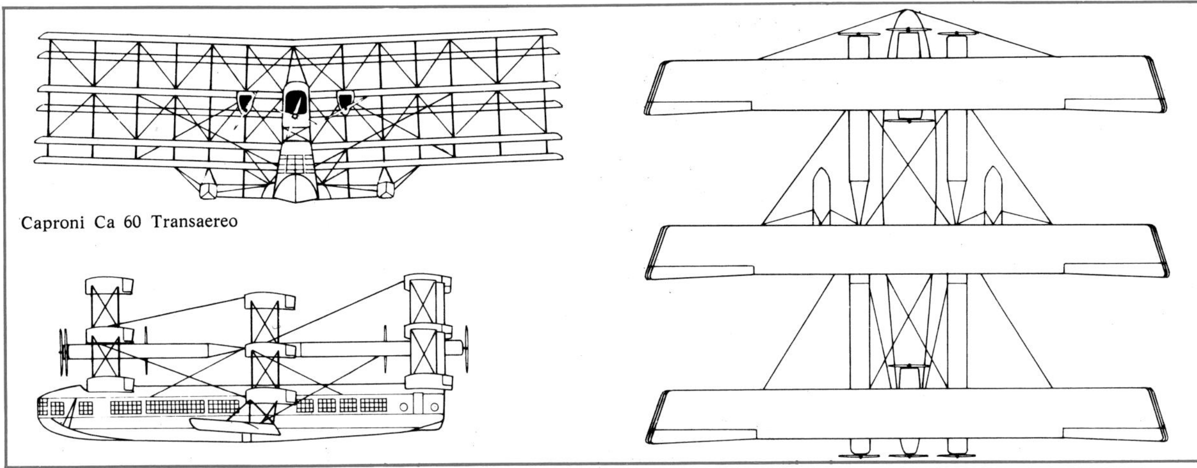
Caproni Ca 60 Transaereo

bombers which had proved so successful would enable them to produce an even larger civil transport with exceptional performance. The unusual structure of the Ca 60 made it an impressive sight: the fuselage was like a ship's hull, above which three triplane wings were positioned in tandem, supporting eight Liberty engines which were installed in a mixed tractor-pusher arrangement on the forward and aft center wings. The aircraft had two lateral pontoons to give stability on the water. In spite of its lack of success, the Transaereo did at least go down in history as the largest airplane of its day, as the first "triple triplane" ever and the first airplane designed to carry 100 passengers across the Atlantic.

Another enormous triplane, the Tarrant Tabor, built in Britain during the last year of the war, was equally unsuccessful. It was designed in response to the need for a very large strategic bomber capable of bombing Berlin and was of ingenious construction, with almost as much power as the Ca 60—2,700 hp, supplied by six Napier Lion engines installed in two tandem pairs on the lower wing and two further engines driving tractor propellers on the center wing. The only takeoff attempt was made on 26 May 1919 and led to the destruction of the prototype and the deaths of the two pilots.

Plate 41
The first aircraft for the first regular airline services: 1919–1921

While over-ambitious dreams were being shattered and far-fetched projects proving impracticable, the first regular airlines were starting operations. Among the more important aircraft of civil aviation's early years was the French twin-engine Farman F.60 Goliath. This large biplane was designed in 1918 as a bomber and was soon adapted for civil use. It was widely used for more than ten years and became one of the most famous civil transports immediately after the war. It was used by several leading European airlines and saw service in Belgium, Czechoslovakia, Poland and Romania. Before the Goliath was adopted by the Compagnie des Grands Express Aériens for regular use on the Paris–London route (29 March 1920) the Farman F.60 had already been in service for about a year, and some had set a number of world records. These can be considered as some of the more important milestones in early commercial aviation.

On 1 April 1919, a Farman F.60 with four passengers on board reached an altitude of 20,600 feet (6,300 m) in one hour and five minutes; two days later fourteen passengers were carried to an altitude of 20,300 feet (6,200 m) in the same time. On 5 May, with twenty-five passengers on board, the Goliath reached an altitude of 16,700 feet (5,100 m) in 1 hour and 15 minutes. In August the Farman flew the 1,270 miles (2,050 km) from Paris to Casablanca in 18 hours 23 minutes carrying an eight-man crew.

Soon after entering regular service in the livery of the Compagnie des Grands Express, the Farman Goliath was adopted by another company which also operated a Paris–London route, the Compagnie des Messageries Aériennes; and when the Paris–Brussels line was opened on 1 July 1920 by the Société Générale de Transports Aériens (also known as Lignes Farman—the Farman Line) which later extended their services to Amsterdam and Berlin, the Farman F.60 was their choice.

A total of about sixty Goliaths was used on regular services and a few survived until 1933. Considering that these were still formative years in civil aviation, the amount of use which was made of the Farman F.60 is all the more remarkable: by 1930 one of the Farmans had clocked up 2,962 hours 25 minutes flying time; another had flown 3,843 hours by 1933.

Another very popular and widely-used series of light transport biplanes, the Blériot Spads, was to reach the end of its development line in 1929 with the Spad 126. The first in the series was the Spad 33 which made its debut in December 1920 and was a small single-engine biplane which could accommodate four passengers in the cabin and a fifth sitting beside the pilot. The type proved successful and forty were built, to see service with French, Franco-Romanian and Belgian companies. In 1921 the next variant, the Spad 46, appeared which was powered by a different engine, had a greater wingspan and a higher operating ceiling. A total of at least 51 Spad 46s were produced and the Compagnie Franco-Roumaine de Navigation Aérienne took delivery of 38 of these, flying them on routes linking France with east European countries.

In Great Britain one of the first postwar commercial aircraft was derived from the Vickers Vimy heavy bomber. After Alcock and Brown's great achievement which proved that this large twin-engine type could be used in civil aviation to good account, some Vimys were converted: a completely new fuselage with enclosed cabin could accommodate ten passengers. The Vimy Commercial prototype made its maiden flight on 13 April 1919, and the best known example, *City of London*, was delivered to Instone on 30 April 1920. It operated Instone's first London–Cologne service on 1–2 October 1922, and in 1924 passed to Imperial Airways. Forty other Vimy Commercials were built for China in 1920–21, one was used by a French airline and the last one, with different engines and modified wings, was delivered to the U.S.S.R. in September 1922.

In spite of all the restrictions placed on her aircraft production by the Allied Control Commission, Germany managed to build and make good use of an excellent little single-engine civil transport, the Junkers-F 13 which was the first all-metal cantilever monoplane with an enclosed cabin. This aircraft's career shows what an outstanding contribution it made to the development of commercial aviation and the more than 320 F 13s built saw service

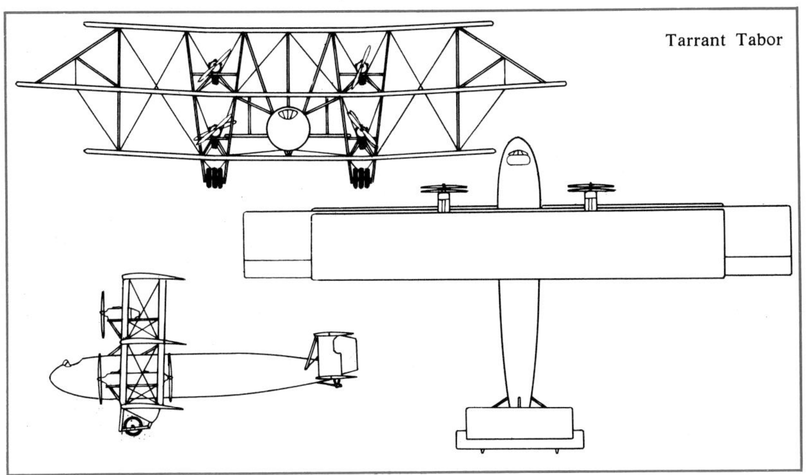
Tarrant Tabor

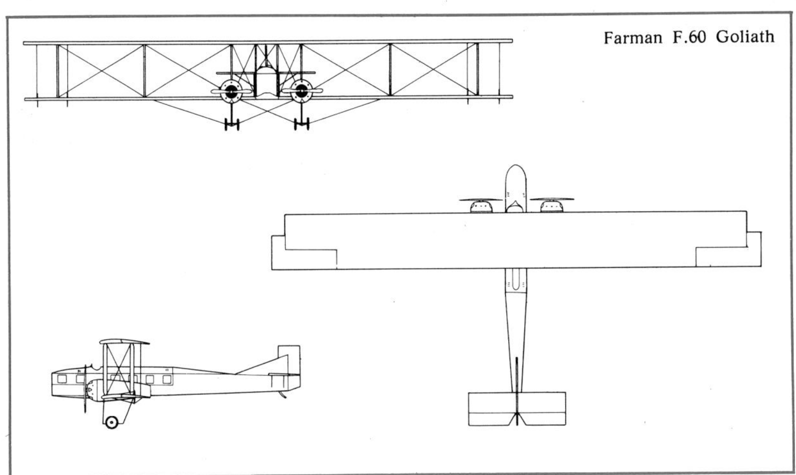
Farman F.60 Goliath

throughout the period between the two World Wars with airlines almost throughout the world. Much of this success was due to the F 13's sturdiness and reliability, but credit must also go to Junkers for their far-sighted company policy in encouraging the creation and development of airlines, offering easy terms for purchase as well as lending, renting and even giving away aircraft. The F 13 prototype made its first flight on 25 June 1919, and that same year established a record, reaching an altitude of 22,145 feet (6,750 m) with eight people on board. Despite this encouraging start, the F 13 only met with success in 1921 when Junkers formed its own airline, Junkers-Luftverkehr, and established routes between Germany and Hungary, Switzerland and Austria using no less than 60 F 13s. By 1926 these aircraft had flown 9.5 million miles (15 million km) and carried 281,748 passengers. When Deutsche Luft Hansa was formed, about 50 F 13s were absorbed into the new national airline's fleet and started a second, equally busy stage of their careers. In 1928 they were flying on forty-three German domestic passenger and two freight routes, and finally withdrawn in 1938.

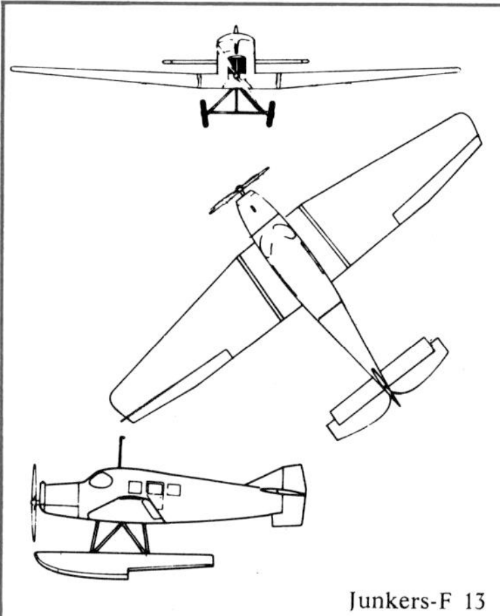
Junkers-F 13

Plate 42
Europe produces the first classic airliners: 1920–1924

It was during these first years of peace that the Dutch company KLM, later to become one of the major international airlines, really began to make an impact on the civil transport market. This phase of KLM's development coincided with the appearance of the first post-World War I civil aircraft of a famous designer, Anthony Fokker. Dutch by birth, he had hitherto been famous for the military aircraft he had built in Germany where he had gone to live in 1912. His first postwar civil transport, the F.II, originally built in Germany as the V.45, was launched on the market by Fokker after his return to Holland. (He had managed to get out of Germany in the closing stages of the war with the intention of starting up a new aircraft factory.) The F.II was KLM's first Fokker and it made a demonstration flight from Amsterdam to Croydon on 30 September 1920. The prototype first flew in October 1919 and was flown to the Netherlands in March 1920. This aircraft was the forerunner of all Fokker's transport aircraft. About thirty were built, most in Germany, and they were used by various German airlines and by Sabena.

Once he had launched his new enterprise, Fokker developed new civil variants of this family of light transports. In 1920 this talented designer started work on a new version of the F.II, which was larger, more powerful and had better performance and increased payload. This new aircraft, the Fokker F.III, lived up to expectations and was as successful as its predecessor. The F.III sold to KLM and other European airlines and more than thirty aircraft were manufactured in the Netherlands and Germany. The next model, however, did not enjoy the same market success as its two predecessors. As part of his policy of developing increasingly large and powerful variants as the series progressed, in 1921 Fokker built an aircraft which was still larger than the F.III and which could carry eleven passengers. The airlines, however, were simply not interested in such a large airplane and only two F.IVs were built. These were eventually sold to the United States Army, designated T-2 and used as military transports for some time. One of these T-2s became famous in May 1923, when it was flown by Macready and Kelly on the first nonstop coast-to-coast flight across the United States, thus breaking the world's long-distance record.

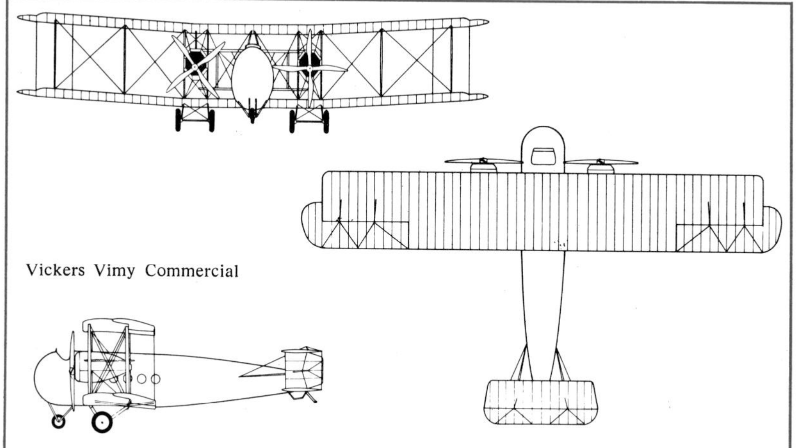
Vickers Vimy Commercial

Germany was among the first countries to use flying boats as commercial transports. The Delphin series built by Dornier between 1920 and 1928 were particularly interesting airplanes, more by virtue of the originality of construction formulae used rather than any great commercial success. Only a few models of the four series were built and they were chiefly employed on German domestic routes. They were all-metal single-engine monoplanes with short hulls and stabilizing sponsons. In the first versions the power unit was installed in the nose with the cockpit just behind. The cabin of the earlier versions could accommodate 5–6 passengers while the final variant, the much improved Delphin III of 1927, had space for 12–13 seats. The Do L.2 Delphin II was the third model of the four produced in the series and made its debut in 1924. It was of cleaner design and had an enclosed cockpit within the fuselage.

Another, much more successful series of flying boats was very widely used for some fifteen years: the Dornier Do J Wal. The prototype of this twin-engine aircraft was built in Germany in 1922, but in order to circumvent the restrictions imposed by the Peace Treaty, production was launched in Italy by a new, specially formed company, Construzioni Meccaniche Aeronautiche S.A. (CMASA) at Marina di Pisa. More than half the estimated three hundred Dornier Do J Wals, constructed in various models, were manufactured in Italy, which was to contribute towards the flying boat's success. In 1928 military versions of the Do J Wal were built in Spain by CASA and the Netherlands Aviolanda built about 40 between 1927 and 1931. In 1931 or 1932 the Dornier company itself began production of larger and more powerful models and continued to manufacture Wals until 1936. The first orders came from Spain, followed by Brazil, Colombia and Germany. Italy was one of the best customers for the passenger versions, but Germany herself really ensured that the aircraft's qualities were well publicized by using the improved 8-ton Wal from May 1933 for the demanding transatlantic mail runs to South America. The Wals used on these routes were catapulted from depot ships and made 328 South Atlantic crossings by the time they were taken out of service.

Plate 43
French, British and German passenger and mail aircraft: 1922–1925

During the first half of the 1920s several multi-engine landplanes were built in France and Great Britain specifically designed as civil transports. The Caudron C.61 made its appearance in 1921: a large three-engine biplane which could carry eight passengers and went into service with the Compagnie Franco-Roumaine de Navigation Aérienne in 1923. Great importance was attached to the im-

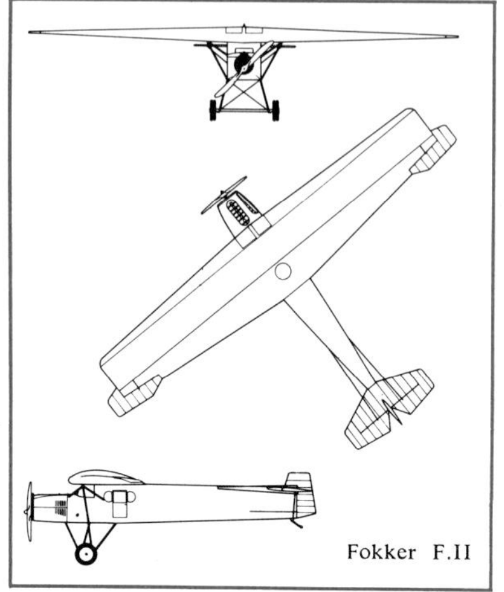
Fokker F.II

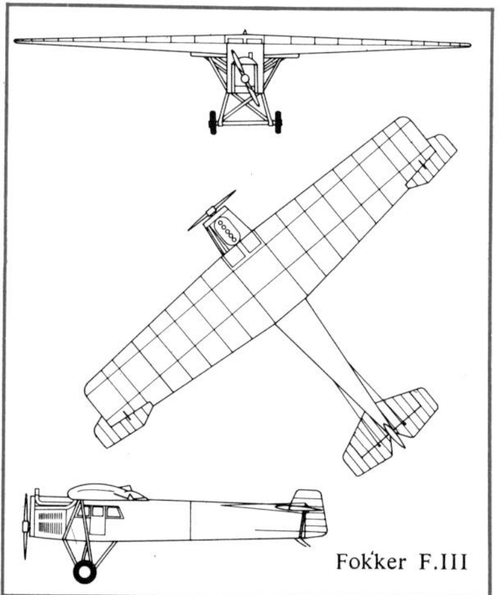
Fokker F.III

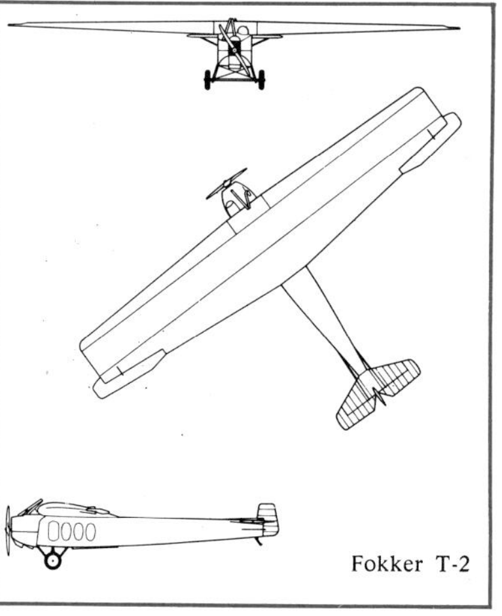
Fokker T-2

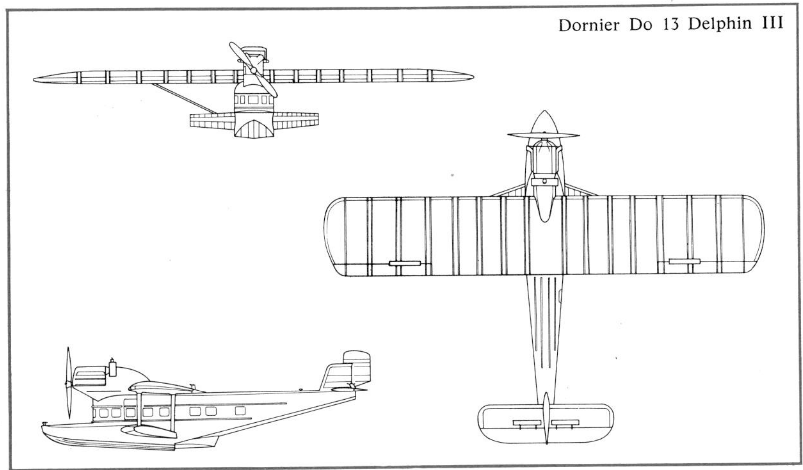
Dornier Do 13 Delphin III

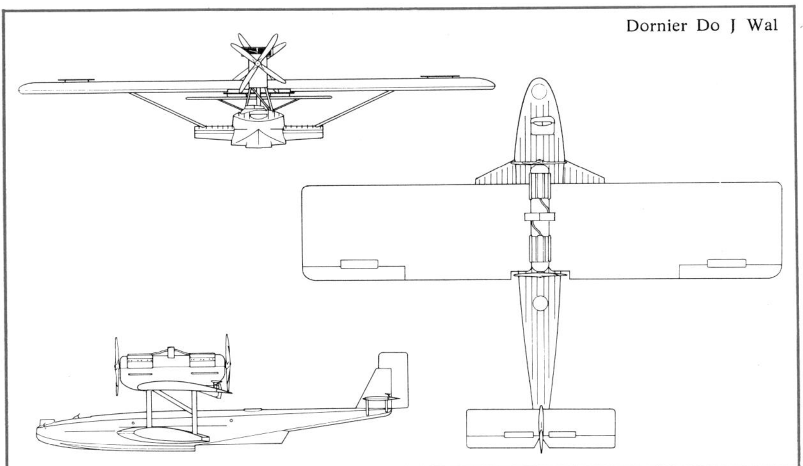
Dornier Do J Wal

provement of these somewhat primitive machines and at least seven C.61s underwent modifications in 1924 in order to improve their performance. The original outer engines (180 hp Hispano Suiza V-8s) were replaced by a pair of 260 hp Salmson C.M.9 liquid-cooled radials; the central engine remained a Hispano Suiza. This aircraft, known as the C.61bis, thus had its cargo capacity increased by some 440 lb (200 kg), but as a result its range and operational ceiling were significantly reduced. About twelve C.61s were built and they were mainly used on night flights between Belgrade and Bucharest.

An early attempt at designing a four-engine airliner was made in France and this rather ugly biplane, the Blériot 115, made its first flight on 9 May 1923. The prototype was then modified to become the Blériot 135 and two were used on the Paris–London route by Air Union from 8 August 1924. In 1925 a slightly bigger and heavier version, the Blériot 155, appeared and two of these were put on the London route by Air Union in 1926. These Blériot biplanes, which had accommodation for 10–17 passengers, were unusual in having two of the four engines mounted above the upper wing.

Handley Page, having founded Handley Page Transport on 14 June 1919, and begun regular services between London and Paris and London and Brussels that September, with converted O/400 bombers, designed and built a purely commercial transport aircraft, the W.8, which made its first flight on 4 December 1919. Although the W.8 attracted a lot of attention at that year's Exposition Internationale de Locomotion Aérienne in Paris, the aircraft did not go into service until October 1921. From the W.8, Handley Page developed the W.8b, of which three served Handley Page Transport from 1922 until passing to Imperial Airways in 1924. One, named *Prince Henry*, remained in service until 1932. A fourth W.8b was sold to Sabena and three more were built in Belgium. A small series of airliners based on the W.8bs—some with three engines—were built in Britain and Belgium, culminating in four W.10s delivered to Imperial Airways in 1926.

In Germany Dornier developed a series of all-metal high-wing monoplane transports, beginning in 1920 with the small Delphin flying boat and continuing in 1921 with the very similar Komet landplane. Bearing little resemblance to the earlier Komets, a larger Komet III made its first flight in December 1924. The Komet III had accommodation for six passengers and could be powered by a variety of engines. The type was used in Germany, Denmark, the U.S.S.R., Switzerland, and in Japan where the type was put into production. In 1925 Dornier began building the very similar Merkur and subsequently some Komet IIIs were modified to Merkur standard. Luft Hansa had a fleet of Merkurs and the type was also used in Brazil, Colombia, Japan, Switzerland and the U.S.S.R. One Merkur on floats flew from Zürich to Cape Town in 100 hours during the European winter of 1926–27.

The Potez 25 was one of the most popular French military aircraft in the 1920s and was subsequently used for postal flights. The aircraft first appeared in 1924 and nearly 4,000 of these small biplanes were manufactured. Three Potez 25A.2s were used for some years on the first commercial mail service across the Andes, between Buenos Aires and Santiago (Chile), inaugurated in 1929 by Aéropostale. These aircraft passed to Air France and were withdrawn in 1936. Potez 25s also became famous for several long-distance flights during their extensive careers.

Plate 44
The first transoceanic and transcontinental flights: 1923–1924

In 1923 the U.S. Army Air Service began to take an interest in making a round-the-world flight and sought a suitable aircraft. To meet this requirement, the Douglas Company proposed building a large single-engine biplane based on the U.S. Navy's Douglas DT-2 which could operate as a landplane or a seaplane. The new type, designated D-WC but soon changed to DWC (Douglas World Cruiser), was chosen, a prototype built and four production aircraft ordered, all delivered by 11 March 1924. Each with a crew of two, the four World Cruisers set off as seaplanes from Lake Washington at Seattle at the beginning of April 1924. Their route was across the Pacific via the Aleutians to Japan, on across Asia and Europe, across the North Atlantic via Iceland and Greenland, and finally across the continent to Seattle where the surviving aircraft arrived on 28 September having flown 26,345 miles (42,398 km) in an elapsed time of 176 days. The four World Cruisers had been named *Seattle*, *Chicago*, *Boston* and *New Orleans*. The *Seattle* crashed in Alaska, and *Boston* was lost in the North Atlantic. For the long overland sections of this flight the World Cruisers had their twin floats replaced

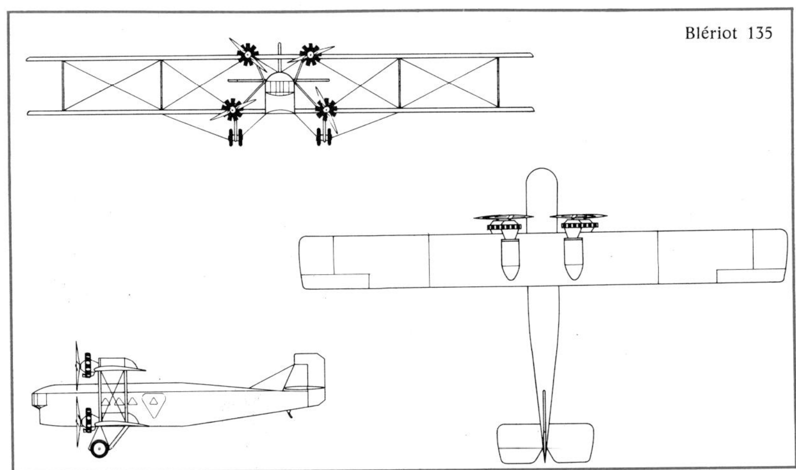
Blériot 135

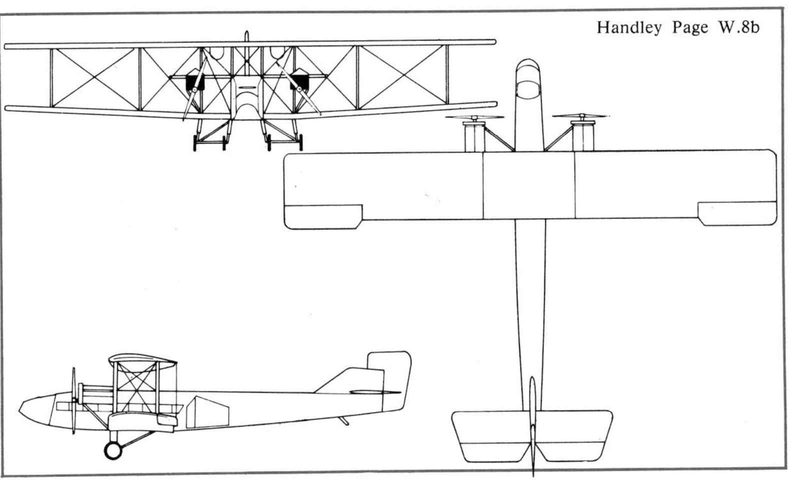
Handley Page W.8b

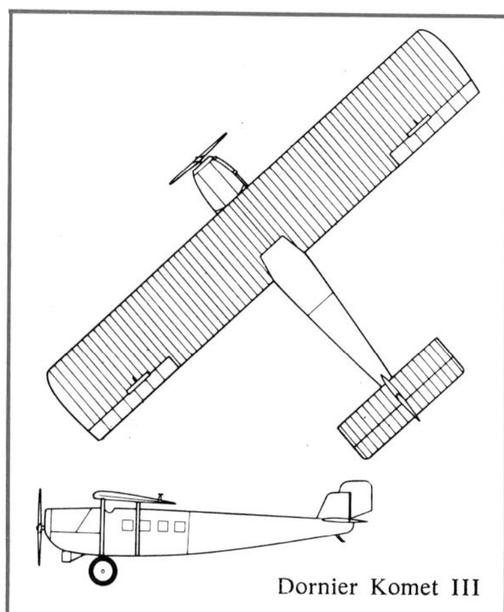

Dornier Komet III

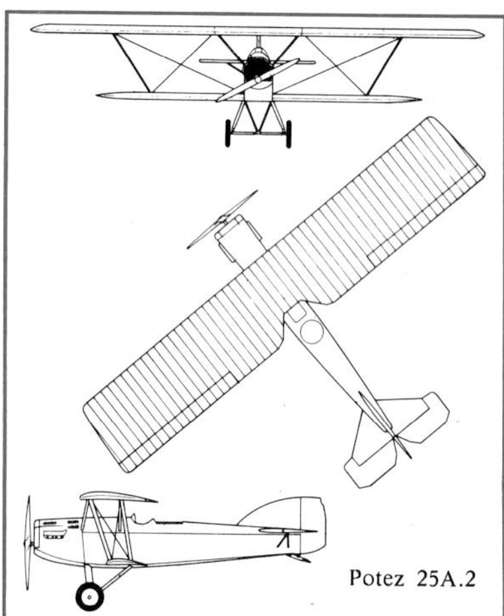

Potez 25A.2

by land undercarriages.

A year later, the distances flown by the World Cruisers was easily surpassed by an Italian aircraft: the Savoia S.16ter flying boat, called the *Gennariello*, piloted by Francesco De Pinedo with Ernesto Campanelli as flight engineer. The little flying boat took off from Sesto Calende on Lake Maggiore on 20 April 1925, on the longest flight yet to have been attempted: a total of 35,000 miles (55,000 km) in 360 flying hours, crossing three continents. The main stages on the flight were Rome, Melbourne, Tokyo and the return to Rome again, out of an overall total of 67 touchdowns in just over six and a half months. On 7 November 1925, Savoia finally moored on the Tiber. The S.16ter was derived from a civil transport—the S.16 of 1919 which had been a commercial failure. In 1921 a bomber version was built, the S.16bis, which was the first flying boat bomber to be used by the Aeronautica Militare after it became an independent service. In 1923 the final model, the S.16ter, made its appearance; this had a longer hull, a much more powerful engine than its two predecessors and was faster. After De Pinedo's feat, several airlines chose the aircraft for their fleets: in 1926 or 1927 two S.16ters were purchased by Aero Espresso and in 1929 SISA took delivery of four and SITA took six of three different versions, using them on its San Remo–Genoa route. The S.16ter achieved other sporting triumphs apart from the historic world flight, demonstrating its performance with such records as that set in September 1920, by one of the first production series aircraft, for the longest nonstop flying boat flight, of 2,095 miles (3,375 km) from Sesto Calende to Helsinki with Umberto Maddalena at the controls. In 1924 an S.16ter set a world altitude record for flying boats at 15,081 feet (4,597 m).

Plate 45
Europe produces the first classic trimotor: 1925–1927

Meanwhile, in spite of the restrictions imposed by the Peace Treaty, Germany also manged to produce effective transport aircraft, some of which were extremely innovative, such as those produced by Junkers in 1924 and 1925. The prototype of these aircraft—which were the first all-metal multi-engine monoplanes to go into commercial service—was the G 23. Because of Allied Control Commission curbs, several false starts were made before adequate engine power was achieved. The designers finally found the solution in 1925, when a larger version, the G 24, was built and about seventy were manufactured and sold to various airlines. Another type, the Albatros L 73, was especially designed for Deutsche Luft Hansa who used this large twin-engine biplane for night flights on the Berlin–Lübeck–Copenhagen–Malmö route. This airline took delivery of two L 73s, named *Preussen* and *Brandenburg* and put them into service in 1926. One of them, *Preussen*, was still flying in 1932. Deutsche Luft Hansa was also the biggest operator of a series of single-engine monoplanes built by Focke-Wulf between 1927 and 1931, all called Möwe (Seagull). Ten of the first model, the Focke-Wulf A 17, flew on a number of domestic and international routes carrying passengers to begin with and, from 1935, freight. Several of Luft Hansa's A 17s were re-engined and designated A 17a. The German airline also used four A 29s, a model which had been produced in 1929, and four A 38s (1931); these Möwe variants had larger fuselages and more powerful engines and the A 38 had increased seating capacity.

At about this time the Italian aviation industry was concentrating its efforts on manufacturing effective commercial flying boats. Cantieri Navali Triestini (CANT) were already well known for their military airplanes, and it was in the mid-1920s that this company entered the field of civil aviation. Among the more important types produced was the Cant 6ter of 1926, which was a large three-engine biplane flying boat accommodating eleven passengers. This design, however, was not a success and only one production model was built after the prototype. It was purchased by Società Italiana Servizi Aerei (SISA) for use as a trainer. The Cant 10ter, which appeared in the same year, was a smaller version of the Cant 6ter with only one engine and capacity for four passengers, and did rather better. SISA took delivery of at least seven and used them from April 1926, on the Trieste–Venice–Pavia–Turin services. In 1930 an improved and strengthened version of the Cant 10ter was produced, of which four were built with more powerful engines. These had metal hulls in place of the wooden structures of the earlier examples.

In 1925 the first of a long line of famous aircraft made its debut, leading to a succession of Fokker transport monoplanes which were to have great influence on commercial aircraft design for many years. The three-engine Fokker F.VIIa–3m was to win lasting fame when Richard E. Byrd and Floyd Bennett used the first of these (called the *Josephine Ford*) for their epoch-making flight over the North Pole on 9 May 1926. The first of the F.VII series was built in 1924 and was a single-engine, high-wing monoplane, typical of Fokker's construction formula of metal tube fuselage and wooden wing, and was designed as a long-distance transport. It vindicated Fokker's hopes for it when the prototype flew from Amsterdam to Batavia (now Djakarta), carrying mail. KLM took delivery of the production run of five aircraft, but meanwhile Fokker had been working on a much improved version, the F.VIIa, which first flew in 1925. This aircraft was an immediate success and it is thought that 41 were built, which were not only bought by KLM but also by Swiss, Danish, French, Polish, Hungarian and Czechoslovak airlines. The most significant change, the adoption of three engines, was made after Fokker visited the U.S.A. in May 1925, in order to assess the U.S. market and to check on what progress was being made by his U.S. subsidiary. Fokker found that a competition was being sponsored by the motor magnate, Henry Ford (this was the Ford Reliability Tour, a circuit of 1,860 miles (3,000 km) starting and finishing in Detroit) and decided to enter a specially adapted F.VIIa. The idea of installing two more engines in such a sturdy airplane seemed an excellent one and Fokker's chief designer, Reinhold Platz, made the conversion within the space of three

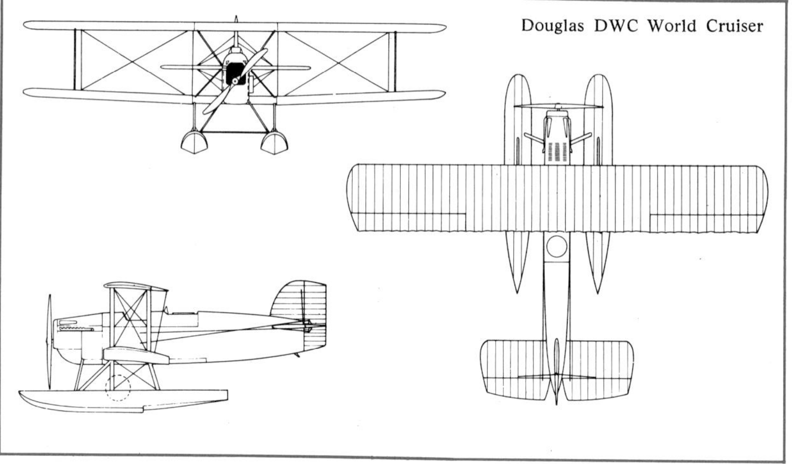

Douglas DWC World Cruiser

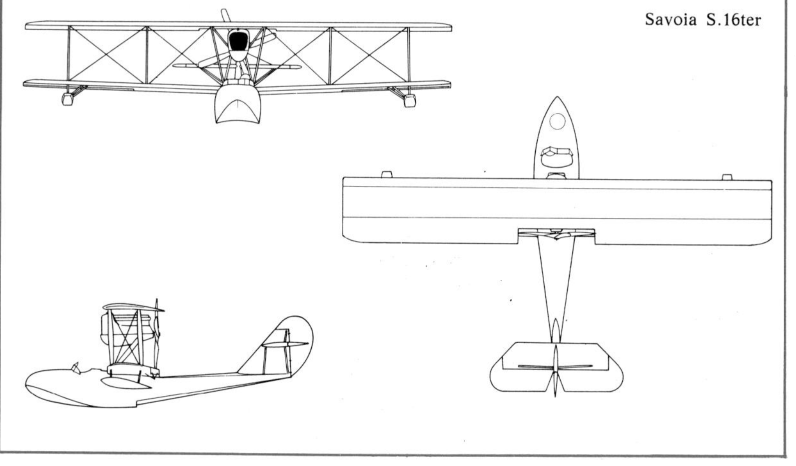

Savoia S.16ter

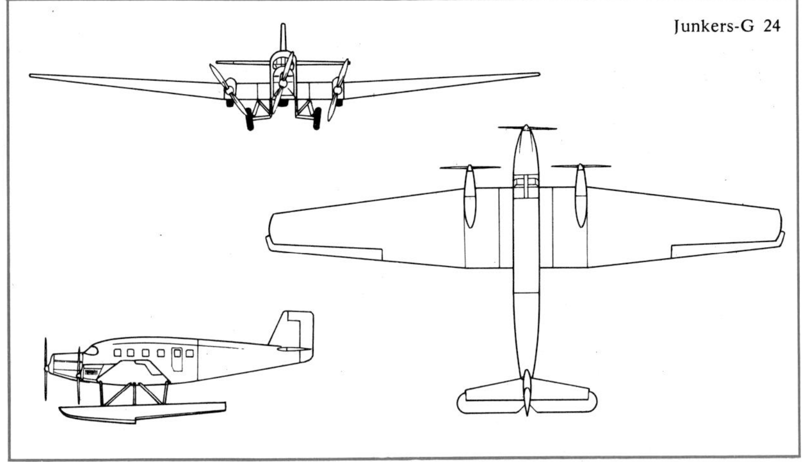
Junkers-G 24

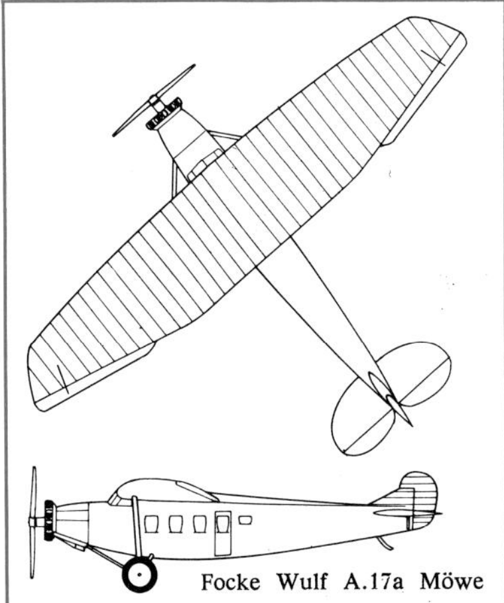
Focke Wulf A.17a Möwe

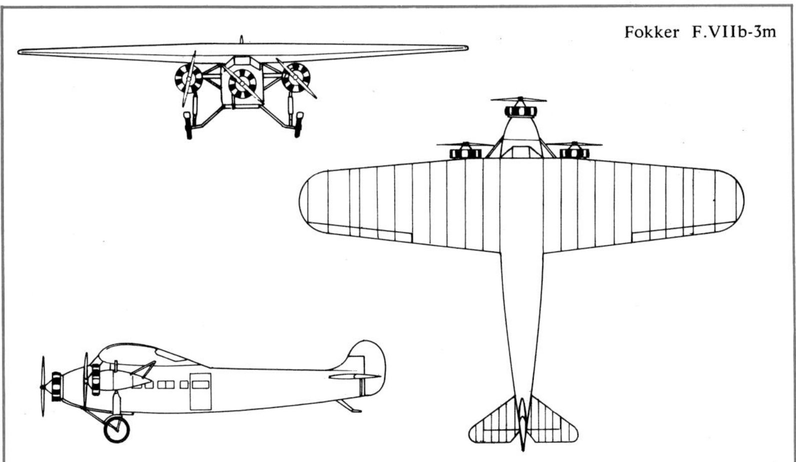
Fokker F.VIIb-3m

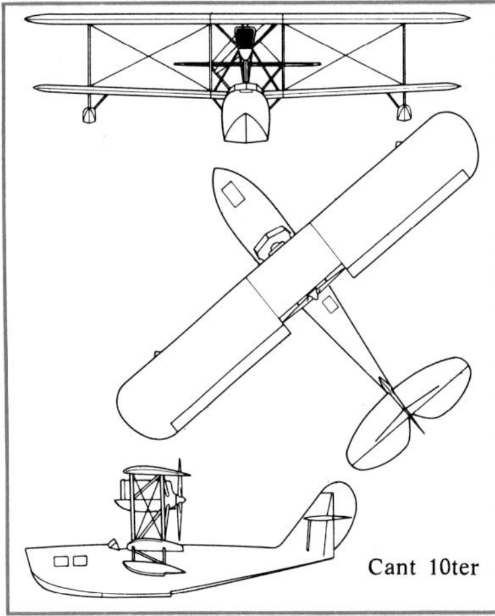
Cant 10ter

months. Henry Ford bought the first F.VIIa–3m and later lent it to Byrd for his historic Polar flight. As the other F.VIIa–3ms came off the assembly line, they were bought by a great many European airlines and were kept very busy for many years. They were subsequently joined by a new model, the F.VIIb–3m, similar in its general lines but with a larger wing. This model was to become one of the most famous and trusted transport aircraft.

Plate 46
Trimotors for European and American airlines: 1926

The Fokker F.VIIa–3m had an immediate effect on aircraft design and construction and Henry Ford was one of the first to draw inspiration from it. In 1925 he took over a small aircraft manufacturing company, the Stout Metal Airplane Company, with the intention of widening his business interests by extending his activities into the aeronautical industry. George H. Prudden, the company designer, was told to produce a three-engine transport and the result was the Ford 4–AT Trimotor, the prototype of what was to be an important aircraft in the history of aviation. Between 11 June 1926 (when the prototype made its maiden flight) and 7 June 1933, 194 Ford 4–AT and 5–AT Trimotors left the assembly lines, and these airplanes, nicknamed the Tin Goose, were used by nearly all the major U.S. airlines and played a considerable part in the development of the vast North American system of domestic routes until 1934, when they were replaced by the Boeing 247 and Douglas DC–2. Nor did their career end there; they were operated by individuals and small airlines in many countries (including Canada, Mexico, Central and South America, Europe, Australia and even China). Some Ford Trimotors survived World War II and one or two were still flying in the early 1980s. One of the Trimotor's more famous exploits was Richard Byrd's flight to the South Pole on 28–29 November 1929 in the fifteenth production 4–AT, called *Floyd Bennett*.

The British aviation industry was also attracted to the three-engine formula and in 1926 two transport aircraft types appeared which, in spite of being less up to date and original and having a shorter service life than the Ford 4–AT, were also instrumental in the expansion of commercial aviation networks. The Armstrong Whitworth Argosy and the de Havilland Hercules were specifically developed to meet Imperial Airways' need for comfortable and efficient passenger airliners and, equally vital, to provide postal and freight transport on European and Empire routes. The Argosy met the first requirement very satisfactorily indeed and three Argosies first flew the London–Paris and London–Brussels–Cologne routes in 1926. On 1 May 1927, the de luxe "Silver Wing" service was introduced on the London–Paris route, and from July was in direct competition with Air Union's LeO 212 "restaurant" flights. In 1929 Argosy Imperial's fleet was joined by four aircraft of the second Argosy production series, the Argosy Mk. II. The airline operated a few of these until 1934. Imperial Airways also took delivery of five de Havilland Hercules for the long-haul to India, the first sector of which, between Basra and Cairo, was opened in January 1927. West Australian Airways put four Hercules into mixed passenger-mail service linking Perth and Adelaide from 29 May 1929. These Australian Hercules could carry fourteen passengers.

Plate 47
The S.55 flying boat—a success story: 1926–1934

The Italian aeronautical industry's efforts to produce a worthwhile commercial flying boat bore fruit in the late 1920s when the extremely successful Savoia Marchetti S.55 appeared. The outstanding career of this very original twin-engine, twin-hull aircraft can be summed up by a few facts and figures. After the 1924 prototype had established fourteen world records, in 1927, Francesco De Pinedo and Carlo Del Prete flew the *Santa Maria*, one of the first production series aircraft, 27,230 miles (48,820 km) round the Atlantic. In 1928 two Brazilians, Braga and De Barros, flew across the South Atlantic and, in the same year, Umberto Maddalena and Stefano Cagna took part in the search for the wreck of Umberto Nobile's dirigible in the Arctic. On 17 December 1930, fourteen S.55As under the command of General Italo Balbo set off from Orbetello, north of Rome, and eleven reached Rio de Janeiro on 15 January 1931, having covered 6,462 miles (10,400 km). In 1933 a formation flight to commemorate the tenth anniversary of the formation of the Italian Air Force, again under the command of General Balbo, flew from Orbetello to Chicago and back to Rome, a return trip of 12,300 miles (19,800 km).

Besides all this, the S.55 was in commercial service for eleven years (1926 to 1937) on Mediterranean routes with such airlines as Aero Espresso, SAM and Ala Littoria. The prototype appeared in 1923, designed by Alessandro Marchetti who had

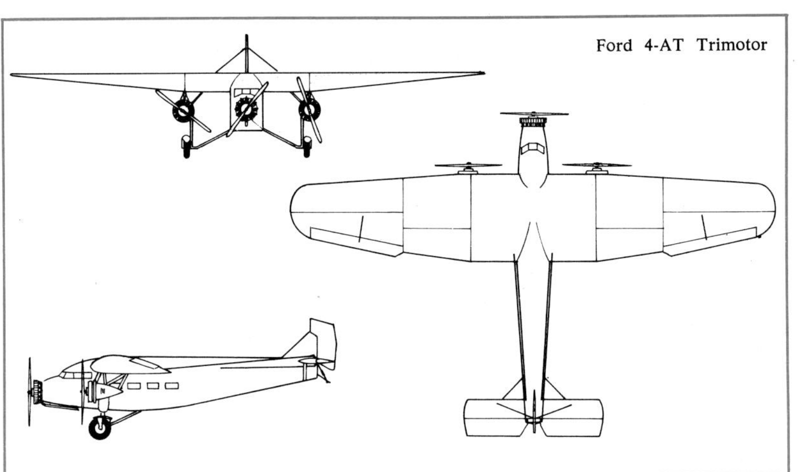
Ford 4-AT Trimotor

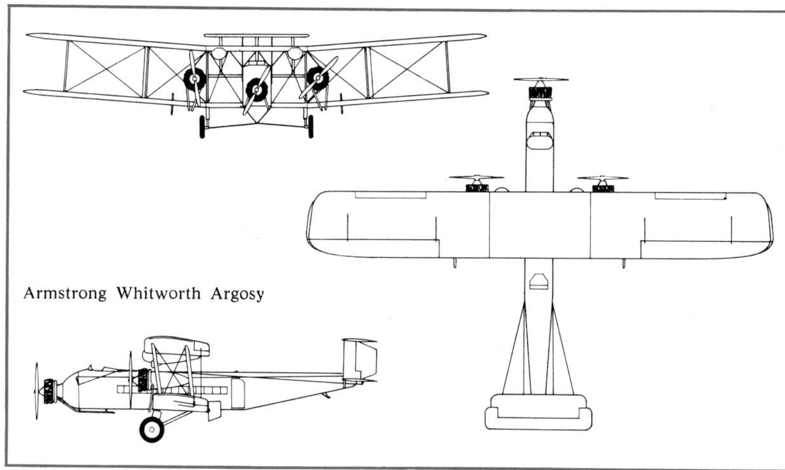
Armstrong Whitworth Argosy

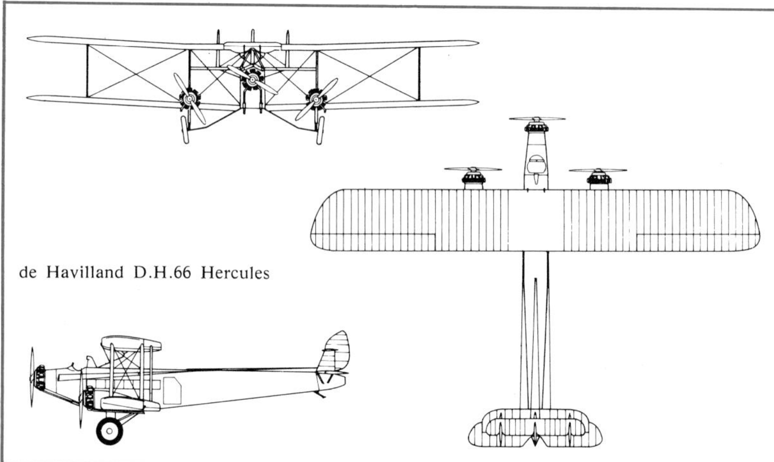
de Havilland D.H.66 Hercules

produced an extremely original design in response to a military specification for a torpedo bomber. The air force, however, found the flying boat too unorthodox for its taste and turned it down; two years went by before the aircraft's merits were fully appreciated. Only in 1925 did the Regia Aeronautica finally order the S.55 and was thoroughly satisfied with it. Production got under way without delay and over 170 S.55s were manufactured, deliveries commencing in 1926.

The S.55 was of very unorthodox design. There were two relatively short hulls above which was mounted a very thick wing in the center section of which the crew was housed. The tailplane, elevator, twin fins and three rudders were carried on booms running aft from the twin hulls. The two engines were mounted back-to-back on struts above the wing and drove a tractor and a pusher propeller. The hulls and the wing were constructed entirely of wood.

There were several variants of the S.55, with different structural details and varying performance, weight and size. There were three military versions, the A, M and X models, and two commercial models, the S.55C and the S.55P which had accommodation for eight to twelve passengers.

Plate 48
Four famous single-engine American aircraft: 1927

In the second half of the 1920s, the United States' comprehensive domestic network found a great deal of use for small transport aircraft to complete the nationwide communications coverage over the vast territory of the United States. One of the most famous single-engine types of this era was the Lockheed Vega; a high-wing monoplane with great purity of line and smoothly streamlined appearance unusual at that time. This was the first of Lockheed's transport monoplanes and the prototype made its maiden flight on 4 July 1927, showing very good general performance. It was designed by John K. Northrop and purpose-built to compete in the "Dole Race," a transpacific race from California to Hawaii. The prototype met with a tragic end in the Pacific during this race. A second Vega was built as a demonstrator and soon attracted orders. The production lines got to work, and eventually 128 Vegas were manufactured in several basic variants. Besides being used on regular commercial routes, Vegas also won races and set up new records including a new endurance record in May 1929, when one was airborne for just under 37 flying hours. But the most famous feats achieved by a Vega were undoubtedly the two round-the-world flights made by Wiley Post in 1931 and 1933.

On the first of these flights Post, with Harold Gatty as his navigator, set off from New York on 23 June 1931, in a Vega 5, the famous *Winnie Mae*, and flew 15,474 miles (24,902km) in 8 days 15 hours 51 minutes flying time. Two years later, on 15 July 1933, Post set out to break this record, flying solo this time, and completed his round-the-world flight in 7 days 18 hours and 43 minutes. His total time in the air was 115 hours 36.5 minutes and his achievement was not to be matched for another fourteen years.

The Douglas M–4 and the Boeing 40A biplanes were both designed for use on the U.S. airmail services and were used from 1927 onward. The first, the Douglas M–4, was the last of the M series of mail carriers that the Douglas Company began producing in 1925 for the U.S. Post Office airmail services. What makes these aircraft important is that they were trail-blazers, opening routes in near-primitive conditions, flying millions of miles across America, unobtrusively performing a vital service. They flew by day and night, over long distances and with few navigational aids. Yet many of the great names in aviation began their careers in the postal service. Charles Lindbergh is the most famous example; he used to fly the mail run from St. Louis to Chicago in war-surplus DH–4s for some years, before becoming world famous after his solo flight across the North Atlantic.

Unlike the Douglas M–4, the Boeing 40A biplane was built specifically for Boeing Air Transport, a large company which had been founded by the aircraft manufacturer to carry mail on the San Francisco–Chicago route. Besides carrying more than half a ton of mail, the Boeing 40A could carry two passengers who were accommodated in a cabin in the forward fuselage. The first Boeing 40A took to the air in May 1927, and a further twenty-three aircraft were delivered to the airline by 29 June.

One of the first all-purpose workhorses of American civil aviation appeared in the same year. The Fairchild FC–2W was a tough little monoplane which soon became widely known as a safe, reliable all-rounder which could transport virtually anything which would fit into its fuselage. Although this aircraft was mainly used as a freighter—both for mail and cargo—it also sprang into the limelight in June 1928, when John Henry Mears and Charles B.D. Collyer made their round-the-world flight, lasting 23 days 15 hours, in their FC–2W *City of New York*. Among its less glamorous duties, the Fairchild FC–2W was used by the Bell Telephone Laboratories in a series of important scientific experiments in radio communications.

Plate 49
Lindbergh makes the first solo flight across the Atlantic: 1927

The Atlantic challenge which had led to Alcock and Brown's historic flight in 1919 was answered by just as spectacular a feat of daring in 1927. Charles A. Lindbergh, a young American flying enthusiast and air mail pilot, attempted and succeeded in crossing the North Atlantic nonstop and solo. His story is very well known. On 20 May 1927, at 7.52 local time, the *Spirit of St. Louis* a small, high wing monoplane took off from Roosevelt Field, New York, with difficulty, since it was so laden with fuel. Lindbergh flew for 33 hours 30 minutes 28 seconds, at an average speed of 116 mph (188 km/h), over the Atlantic and landed at Le Bourget airport near Paris, having flown 3,520 miles (5,670 km). This was, of course, not the first crossing of the Atlantic, nor the first nonstop crossing, but Lindbergh's was the first solo flight. The airplane which made it all possible—the Ryan NYP *Spirit of St. Louis*—had been built in only two months (26 February–26 April) by a small, little known aircraft manufacturer in San Diego where, after many rebuffs, Lindbergh had finally found a like-minded designer who

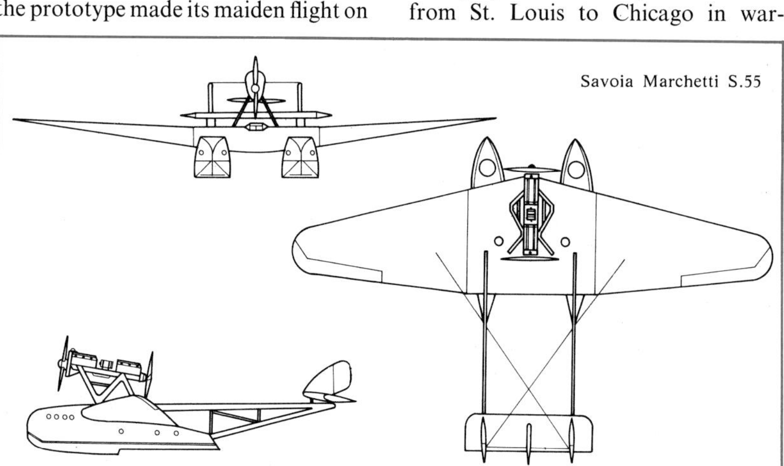
Savoia Marchetti S.55

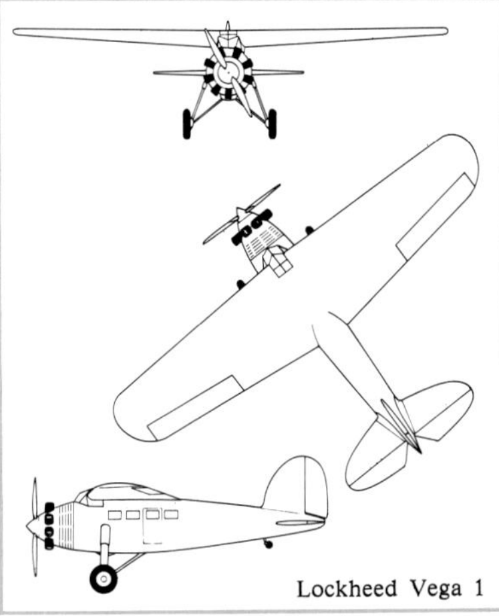
Lockheed Vega 1

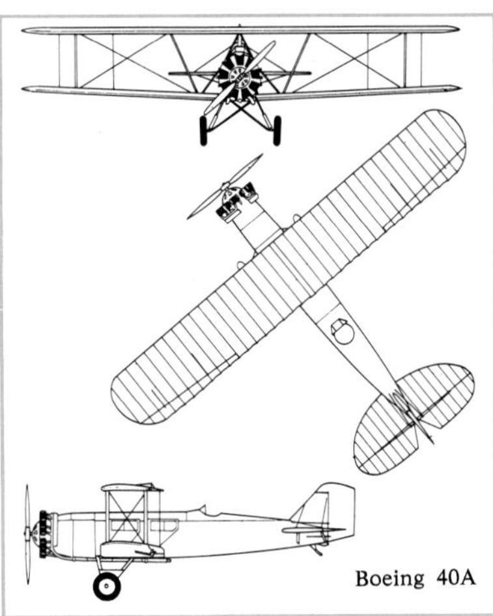
Boeing 40A

shared his enthusiasm for the enterprise.

The *Spirit of St. Louis*'s great adventure was preceded and followed closely by several other similar attempts which were not all successful. On 8 May (twelve days before Lindbergh's departure) an unwieldy biplane took off from Le Bourget and started flying westward. This was the Levasseur PL–8 *Oiseau Blanc* and on board were World War I ace, Charles Nungesser, and Captain François Coli: their aim was to be the first to reach North America flying nonstop in an east–west direction. Their aircraft, which was derived from a military reconnaissance type, had been specially adapted to give it 30 hours' endurance. All their enthusiasm and effort, however, came to nothing; Nungesser and Coli flew into a snow-storm over Newfoundland and no more was ever heard of them. A year later, however, on 12–13 April 1928, a second attempt was successful. A German monoplane, the Junkers–W 33 *Bremen* crewed by Hermann Köhl, Baron von Huenefeld and the Irishman James Fitzmaurice, took off at 5 a.m. from Baldonnel on the outskirts of Dublin and managed to reach the Straits of Belle Isle between Newfoundland and Labrador where they made a forced landing on Greenly Island. The flight lasted 37 hours, covering 2,173 miles (3,500 km). The W 33 was derived from the Junkers–F 13 and this achievement was a great boost to the aircraft's commercial success; 199 were built and were used for a long time as civil transports with companies in Europe, Canada, South America and New Guinea.

Only a matter of days after Lindbergh's flight other transatlantic crossings were achieved by two separate American crews. The first was made by Clarence D. Chamberlin and Charles A. Levine in a Bellanca W.B.2 monoplane called *Columbia*, with the object of flying nonstop from New York to Berlin. They were not strictly successful, since their aircraft, which had taken off on 4 June 1927, overshot the German capital and landed at Eisleben two days later. The second attempted transatlantic flight was unsuccessful: Richard Byrd, Bert Acosta, Bert Balchen and George O. Noville on board a three-engine Fokker C–2 called the *America* left New York on 29 June for Paris. But as they neared Le Bourget fog prevented them from landing and they had to come down in the sea off Ver-sur-Mer.

Plates 51–54
Long-distance and round-the-world flights

In the early days of civil aviation, one of the most challenging objectives was to extend the aircraft's potential by undertaking transcontinental and intercontinental flights to ever more distant destinations. One of the pioneers of this sort of endeavor was Louis Blériot. On 25 July 1909, this great French aviator achieved the first cross-Channel flight in his Type XI monoplane which had been specially modified for the attempt, flying from France to England in just under forty minutes. His Blériot XI monoplane was an extremely fragile flying machine and the distance which he had to cover before touching down in a field near Dover seems negligible today, but in those days of aviation's infancy his feat aroused tremendous enthusiasm and he was treated as a hero by the public of the time. Later aviation pioneers were to be accorded the same sort of adulation when they succeeded in making longer distance flights in the years to come.

The golden age of long-distance flying began in 1919, when the airplane had evolved considerably during World War I. The most exciting undertaking which many early aviation enthusiasts were determined to achieve was to fly across the North Atlantic which lay between the two continents which had given birth to the "heavier-than-air" flying machine. The first successful crossing, in an easterly direction, was made by John Alcock

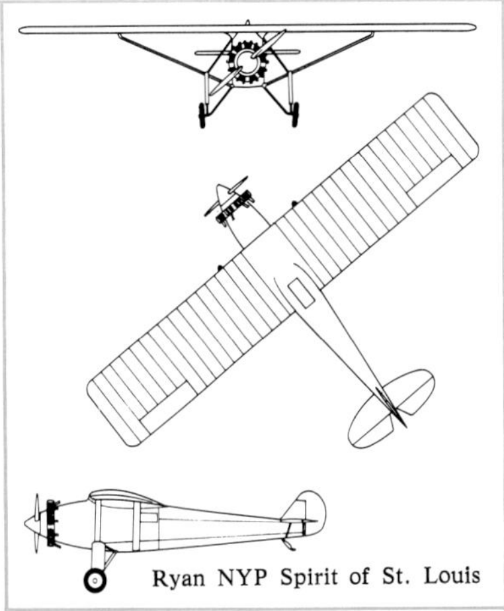
Ryan NYP Spirit of St. Louis

and Arthur Whitten-Brown, in a twin-engine Vickers Vimy bomber. The flight was made on 14–15 June, setting off from St. John's, Newfoundland, and lasted 15 hours 57 minutes before the aircraft landed at Clifden in Ireland. Only a month earlier, however, the first crossing of the Atlantic in stages had been carried out by three Navy Curtiss flying boats (the NC–1, the NC–3 and the NC–4). This flight had started from Trepassey Bay in Newfoundland bound for Horta in the Azores, over 1,400 miles (2,250 km) away. This long-distance flight had actually started off on 6 May from New York, but the first two aircraft had to make forced landings; only the NC–4, piloted by Albert C. Read, had managed to reach the Azores and set off from there for Portugal and then for Plymouth, where it arrived on 31 May. Another achievement was added to these successful Atlantic crossings; it was, however, made by a dirigible, the British R.34 airship which made a return trip between 2–13 July 1919, only eighteen days after Alcock and Brown's flight. The R.34 took off from East Fortune in Scotland at 1.42 a.m. with thirty-one people on board, and after considerable difficulties due to bad weather on the way over, managed to reach Mineola, Long Island, at 1.54 p.m. on 6 July. The airship set off on the return journey at 3.45 a.m. on 10 July and safely reached Pulham after 75 hours 3 minutes flying time.

Another tempting challenge was presented by the South Atlantic and the first attempt to cross it was made in 1922. On 30 March two Portuguese aviators, Sacadura Cabral and Gago Coutinho, set off from Lisbon in a Fairey III seaplane to make the flight to Brazil in stages, arriving on 5 June, in a third seaplane, the first having been damaged at St. Paul's Rocks and the second on the way to Fernando Noronha. This achievement was emulated in 1926 in the Dornier Wal *Plus Ultra* under the command of Major Franco with a crew of three, leaving Seville on 22 January and reaching Buenos Aires on 10 February

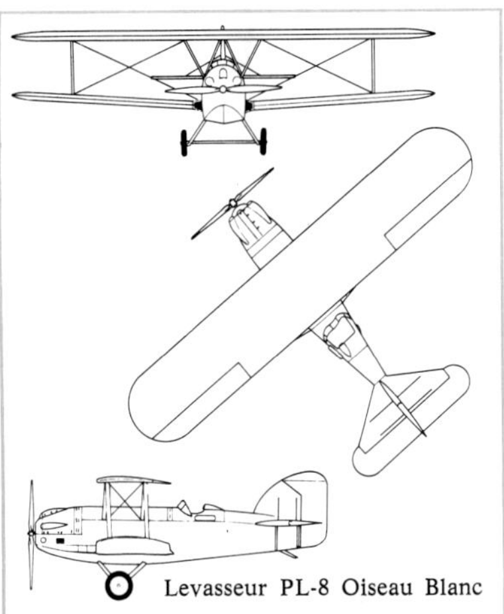
Levasseur PL-8 Oiseau Blanc

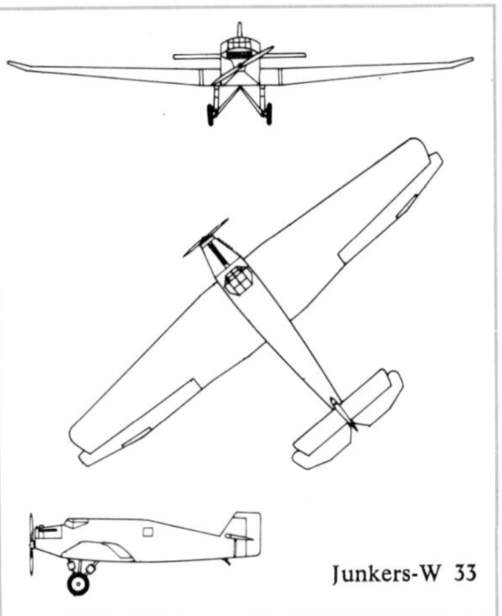
Junkers-W 33

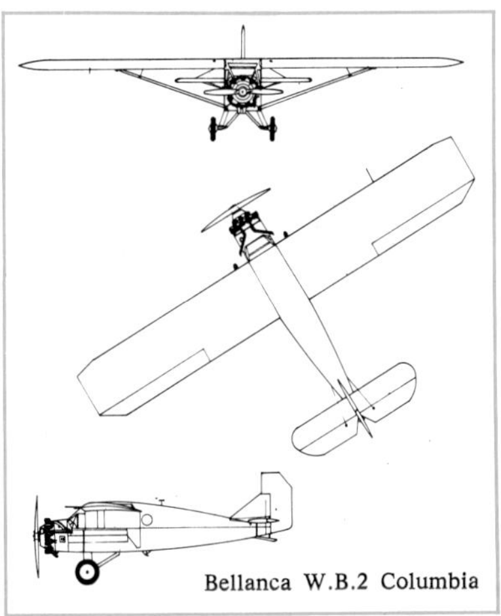
Bellanca W.B.2 Columbia

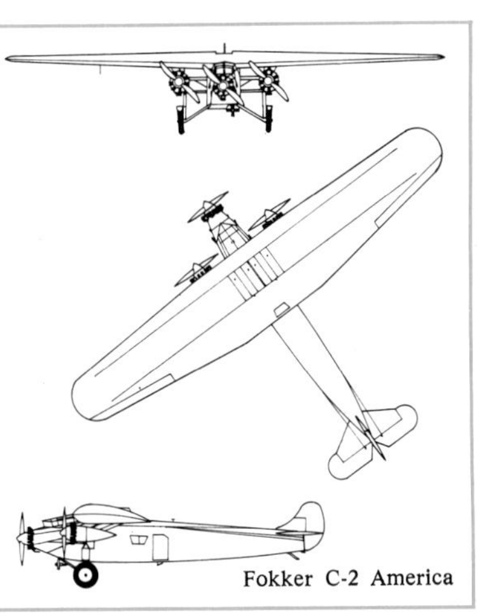
Fokker C-2 America

after a flight full of mishaps. The first nonstop South Atlantic flight was made in October 1927 by Dieudonné Costes and Joseph Le Brix in the Breguet XIX *Nungesser–Coli*. The Breguet left Paris on 10 October and flew nonstop to St. Louis in Sénégal in 26 hours 30 minutes. On the 14th the flight continued to Port Natal in Brazil with a 19 hours 50 minutes ocean crossing. In 1928 the famous Italian Savoia Marchetti S.64, with Arturo Ferrarin and Carlo Del Prete as crew, made a successful nonstop crossing of the South Atlantic, setting the world distance record by flying from Montecelo to Natal (Brazil), a distance of 4,464 miles (7,188 km) on 3–5 July. This was the first nonstop flight from Europe to South America. A year later an unsuccessful attempt was made to break this record over the same route by two Breguet XIX aircraft; the first with the Spanish crew, Jimenez and Iglesias, who had called their aircraft (a Breguet built in Spain under licence) *Jesús del Gran Poder*, and they took off from Seville on 24 March, flew 4,061 miles (6,540 km) over the South Atlantic and reached Bahia (Brazil) on 26 March. The second aircraft, flown by the Frenchman, Challe, and Borges from Uruguay, left Seville on 15 December and crashed on landing on 17 December, near Pernambuco.

The Atlantic, however, did not have a monopoly on the efforts of the adventurous. In 1919, five months after Alcock and Brown's historic flight, another Vickers Vimy linked Great Britain with Australia by air for the first time, covering 11,123 miles (17,912 km) between London (departing on 12 November) and Port Darwin (10 December) in just under 136 flying hours; a great achievement by two brothers, Ross and Keith Smith and their crew of two. In 1920 it was the Italians' turn to carry out an even more spectacular long-distance flight with two little single-engine S.V.A.9s, from Rome to Tokyo, a distance of 11,243 miles (18,105 km) which was flown by Ferrarin and Masiero from 11 February to 30 May. In the same year, on 4 February–20 March, two South Africans, Pierre von Ryneveld and Quintin Brand, made a successful flight from London to Cape Town, using two Vickers Vimys and finally a D.H.9. In 1925 the Italians repeated Ferrarin's earlier success and completed the longest flight undertaken up to that date, setting off from Sesto Calende on 20 April 1925, and flying to Tokyo; then from Tokyo to Rome via Australia, a total of 35,000 miles (55,000 km) in 360 flying hours and in sixty-seven stages. The aircraft used for this marathon flight was the small Savoia S.16ter biplane flying boat, piloted by Francesco De Pinedo.

Enthusiasm for long-distance flights soon spread to the United States. The first nonstop coast-to-coast flight across the United States was made by two military pilots, Macready and Kelly, in a single-engine Fokker T–2, on 2–3 May 1923, covering a distance of 2,470 miles (3,975 km) between New York and San Diego at an average speed of about 92 mph (148 km/h). A year later another trans-continental flight was made, this time between New York and San Francisco (2,698 miles–4,345 km), in a Curtiss PW–8 monoplane, piloted by Lt. Maughan on 23–24 June, in 18 hours 12 minutes actual flying time.

Europe and Africa had strong trading links and the French were the first to undertake long-distance flights in Africa. As early as 1919 they had used the airplane to map and explore the whole of East Africa. The first flight across the Sahara was achieved by Vuillemin and Chalus in a Breguet 16 Bn–2. This was a long-distance flight which had begun from Paris on 24 January 1920. Four airplanes had originally set out, but due to various vicissitudes only one aircraft managed to complete the flight, arriving in Dakar on 31 March. The London–Cape Town route was flown for the second time by the English pilot, Alan Cobham (16 November 1925–13 March 1926) in a de Havilland 50J. In the winter of 1926–27 the two French pilots, Dagnaux and Dufert, flew from France to Tananarive in a Breguet XIX, leaving Paris on 28 November 1926 and arriving in Madagascar on 10 February 1927. The first flight right round Africa was made by Sir Alan Cobham and his crew between 17 November 1927 and 31 May 1928. This was a survey made in the Short Singapore flying boat and covered a distance of about 20,000 miles (32,000 km) along the Nile and great lakes to Durban and Cape Town and back via the west coast.

During the twenties and thirties the North Atlantic route once more became the center of attention. The first solo nonstop crossing was achieved by Charles Lindbergh, on 20–21 May 1927 in the Ryan NYP *Spirit of St. Louis* monoplane, covering 3,520 miles (5,670 km) in 33 hours 30 minutes and 30 seconds at an average speed of 117 mph (188 km/h). On 4 June 1927, this feat was emulated by Clarence D. Chamberlin and Charles A. Levine in the single-engine Bellanca W.B.2 *Columbia*; this time the destination was Eisleben, near Berlin, which they reached on 6 June after covering 3,909 miles (6,294 km). At the end of the same month a Fokker C–2 trimotor named *America* set off from New York bound for Paris with Richard Byrd, Bert Acosta, Bert Balchen and George O. Noville on board but was forced to fall short of its destination, and came down near Vers-sur-Mer, after a flight of 3,478 miles (5,600 km). The first nonstop east–west crossing of the North Atlantic was by the *Bremen*, a Junkers W.33, on 12–13 April 1928. The crew was Hermann Köhl, Baron von Huenefeld and James Fitzmaurice, and they took off from Dublin for a flight lasting 37 hours covering 2,173 miles (3,500 km), landing at Greenly Island, Newfoundland.

The first flight from Paris to New York was made on 1–3 September 1930 by Dieudonné Costes and Maurice Bellonte in the French single-engine Breguet XIX Super TR *Point d'intérrogation* after which they flew on to Dallas; a total of 5,216 miles (8,400 km). In 1933 the first formation flight across the Atlantic was made by twenty-five S.M.55X flying boats commanded by Italo Balbo from Orbetello to New York. In 1930 a formation flight had been made with fourteen S.M.55A flying boats to Rio de Janeiro, a distance of 6,458 miles (10,400 km).

One of the truly great pioneering long-distance flights was the first crossing of the Pacific from the United States to Australia. On 31 May 1928, Charles Kingsford Smith, C. T. P. Ulm (pilots), Harry Lyon (navigator) and James Warner (radio operator) left Oakland, California, in the Fokker F.VIIb–3m *Southern Cross*, and with intermediate stops at Honolulu and Suva in Fiji, reached Brisbane on 9 June, with a flying time of 83 hr 11 min. On 10–11 September that year Kingsford Smith and Ulm, with a different crew, made the first flight across the Tasman Sea, the *Southern Cross* making the journey from Sydney to Christchurch in 14 hr 25 min. During 1931 Kingsford Smith flew the *Southern Cross* to Europe and after a while continued to the United States, thus the famous *Southern Cross* completed a circumnavigation of the world.

Another round-the-world flight was that made in August 1929 by the *Graf Zeppelin* which flew eastbound from Lakehurst, New Jersey, and completed the 21,000-mile (34,795-km) journey in 21 days 7 hours 34 minutes. As related earlier Wiley Post was to make high speed flights round the globe in a Lockheed Vega in 1931 and 1933.

Long-distance flights over Africa: 1920–1928

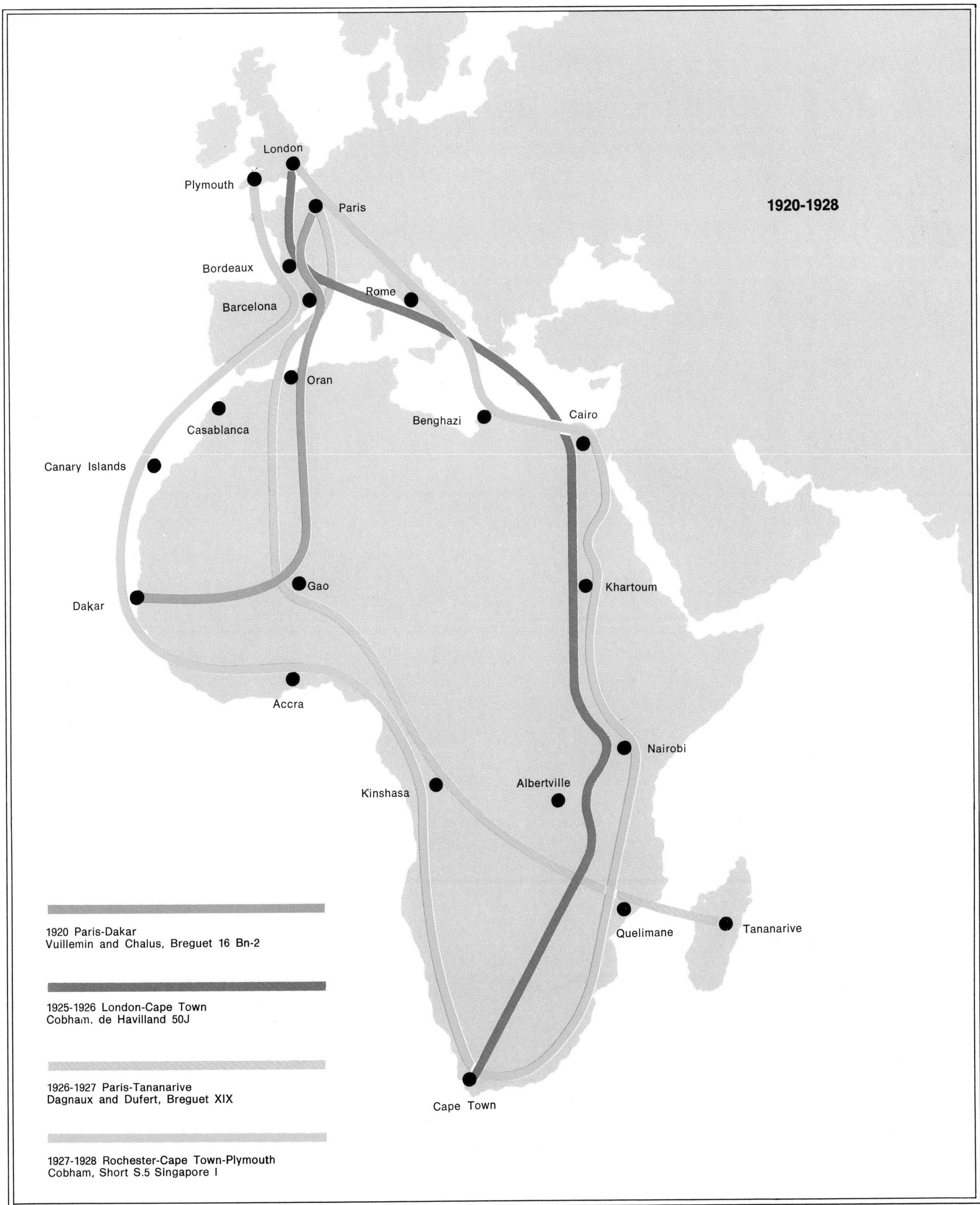
1920-1928
London
Plymouth
Paris
Bordeaux
Rome
Barcelona
Oran
Casablanca
Benghazi
Cairo
Canary Islands
Khartoum
Gao
Dakar
Accra
Nairobi
Kinshasa
Albertville
Quelimane
Tananarive
Cape Town
1920 Paris-Dakar
Vuillemin and Chalus, Breguet 16 Bn-2
1925-1926 London-Cape Town
Cobham, de Havilland 50J
1926-1927 Paris-Tananarive
Dagnaux and Dufert, Breguet XIX
1927-1928 Rochester-Cape Town-Plymouth
Cobham, Short S.5 Singapore I

Plate 52 Long-distance flights over the North Atlantic and the South Atlantic and the first round-the-world flight: 1919–1929

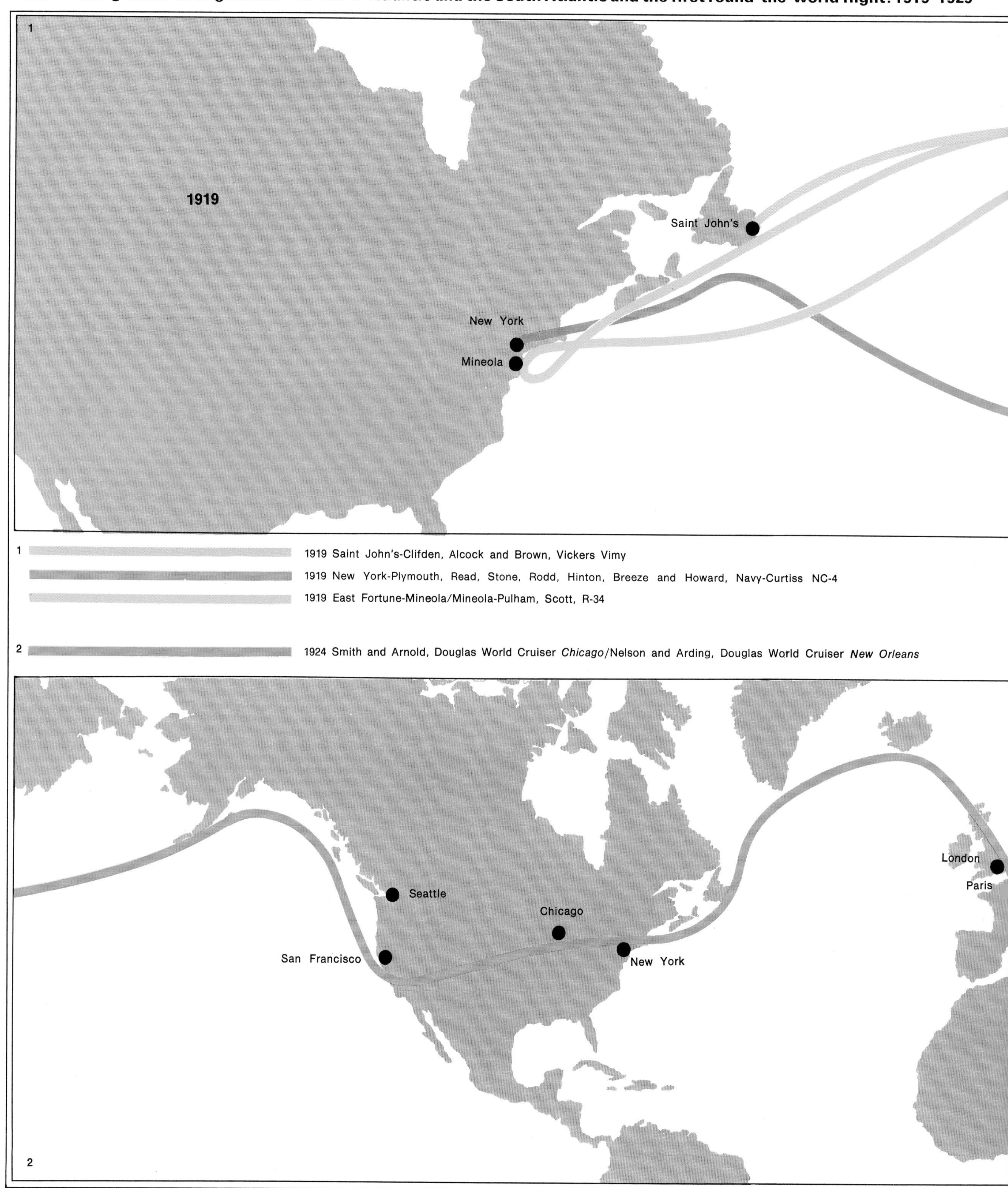

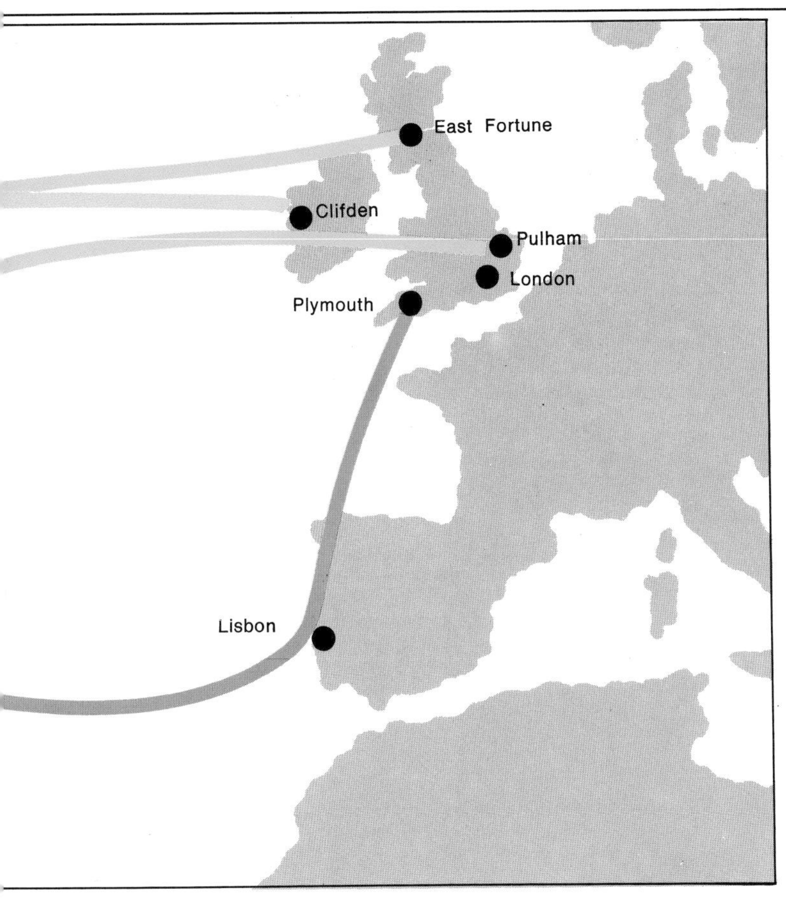

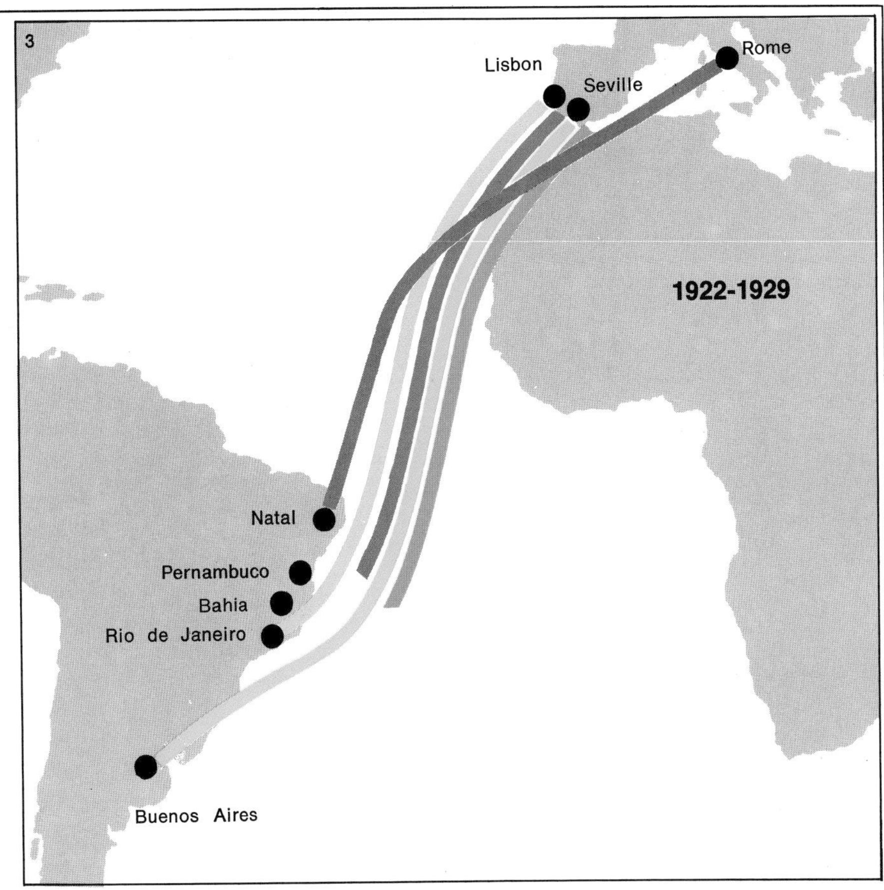

3

1922 Lisbon-Rio de Janeiro, Coutinho and Cabral, Fairey III
1926 Seville-Buenos Aires, Franco, De Alda, Duran and Rada, Dornier Do J Wal *Plus Ultra*
1928 Montecelio (Rome)-Natal, Ferrarin and Del Prete, Savoia Marchetti S.64
1929 Seville-Pernambuco, Challe and Borges, Breguet XIX
1929 Seville-Bahia, Jimenez-Iglesias, Breguet XIX *Jesús del Gran Poder*

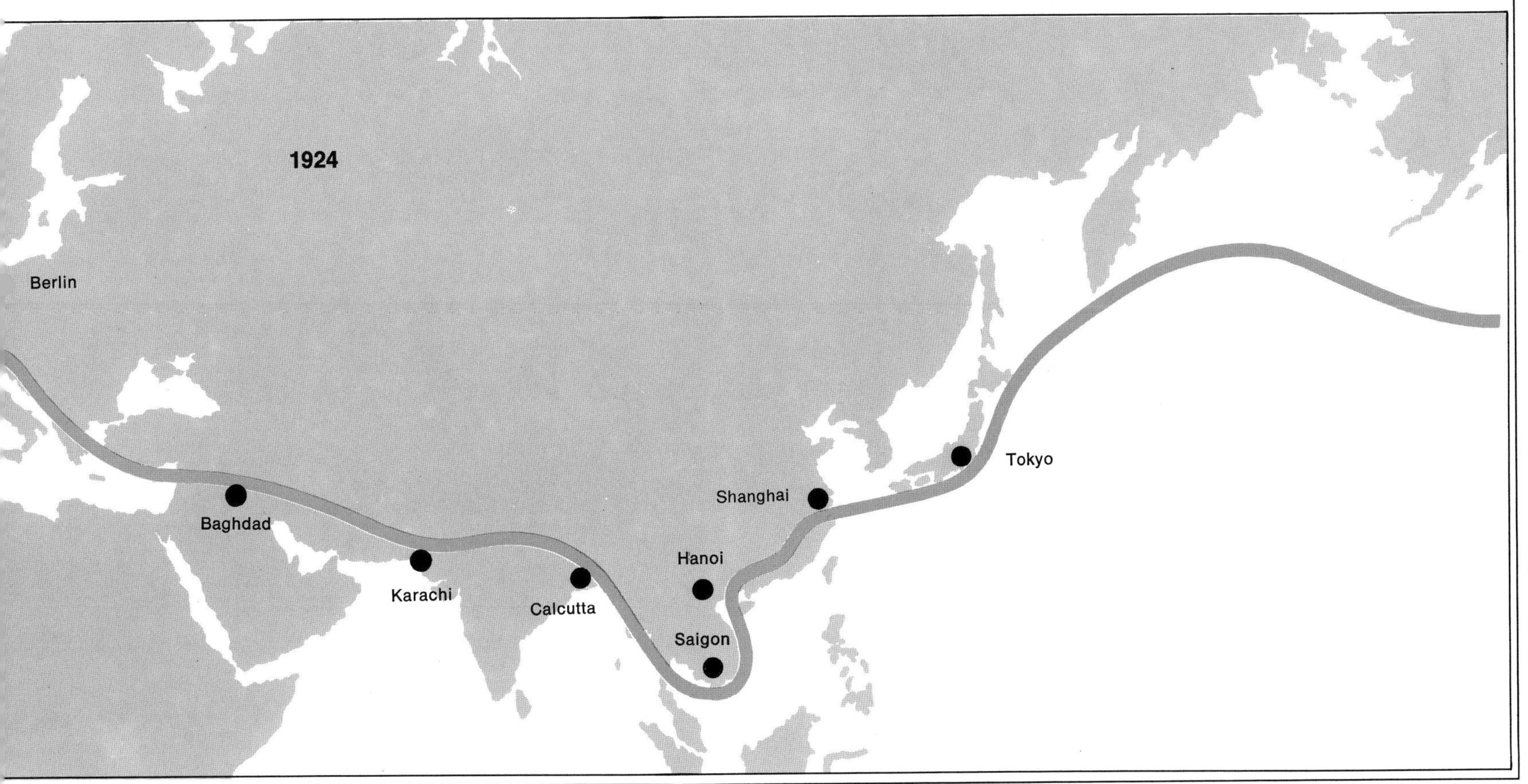

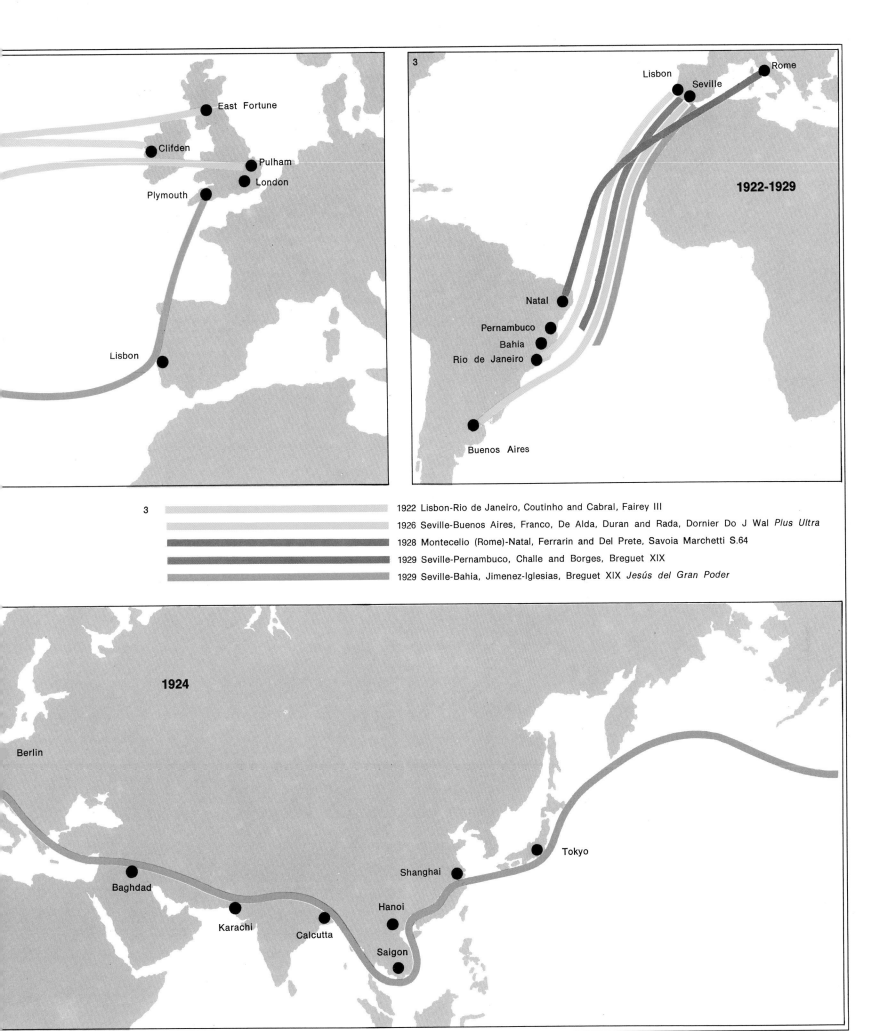

Transcontinental flights: 1919–1925

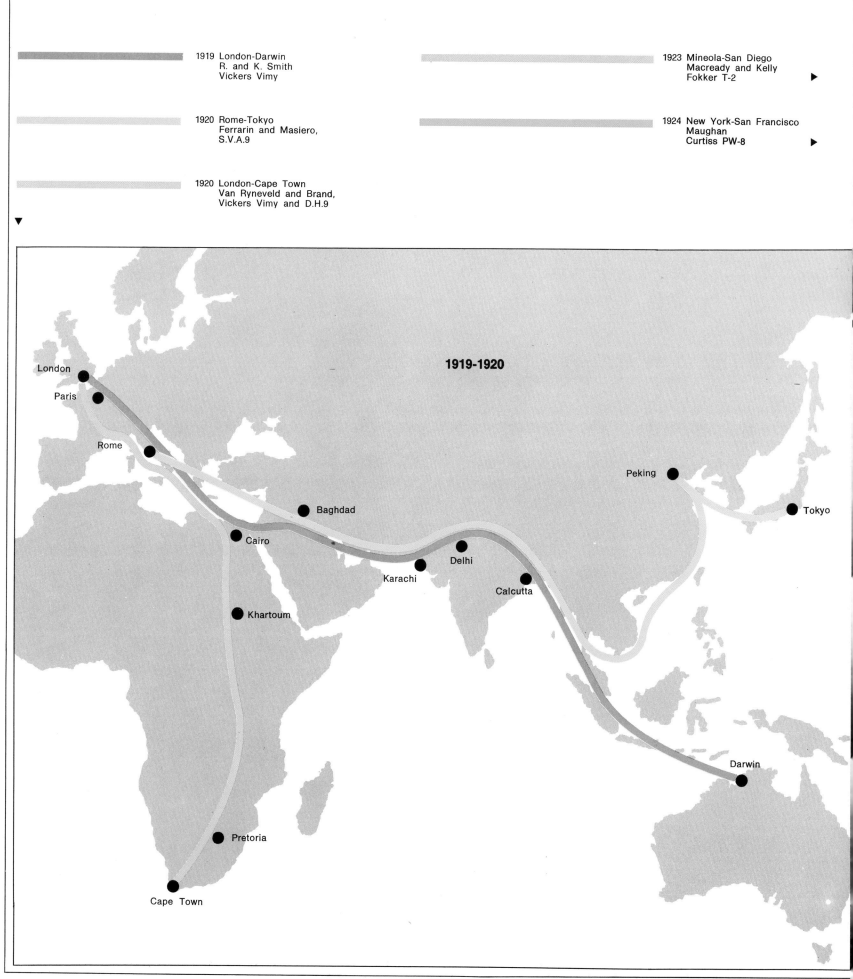

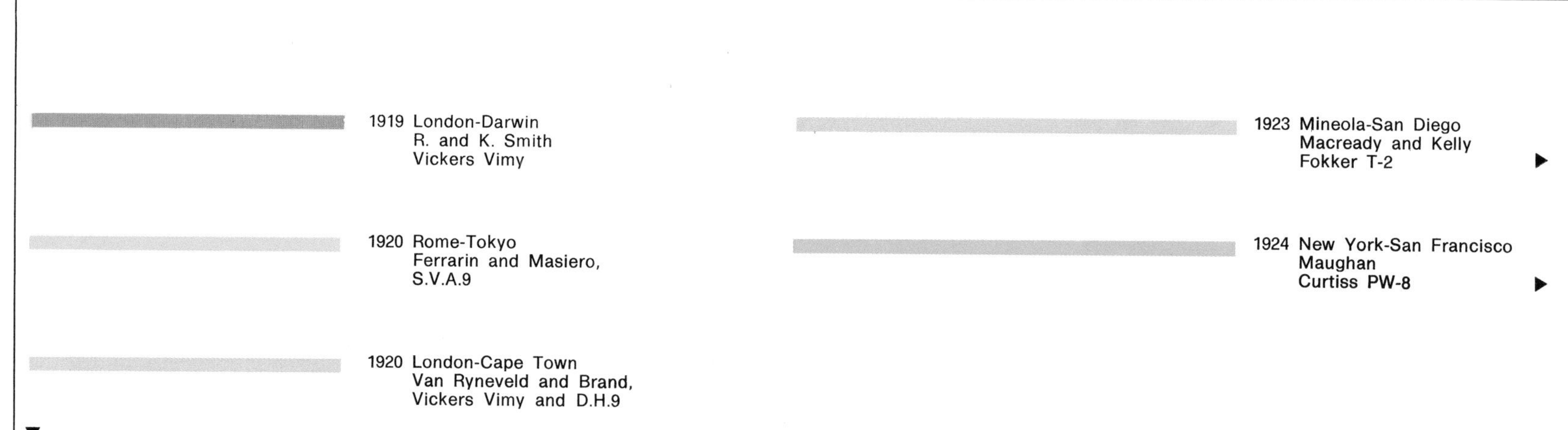

1919-1920

London
Paris
Rome
Baghdad
Cairo
Khartoum
Pretoria
Cape Town
Karachi
Delhi
Calcutta
Peking
Tokyo
Darwin

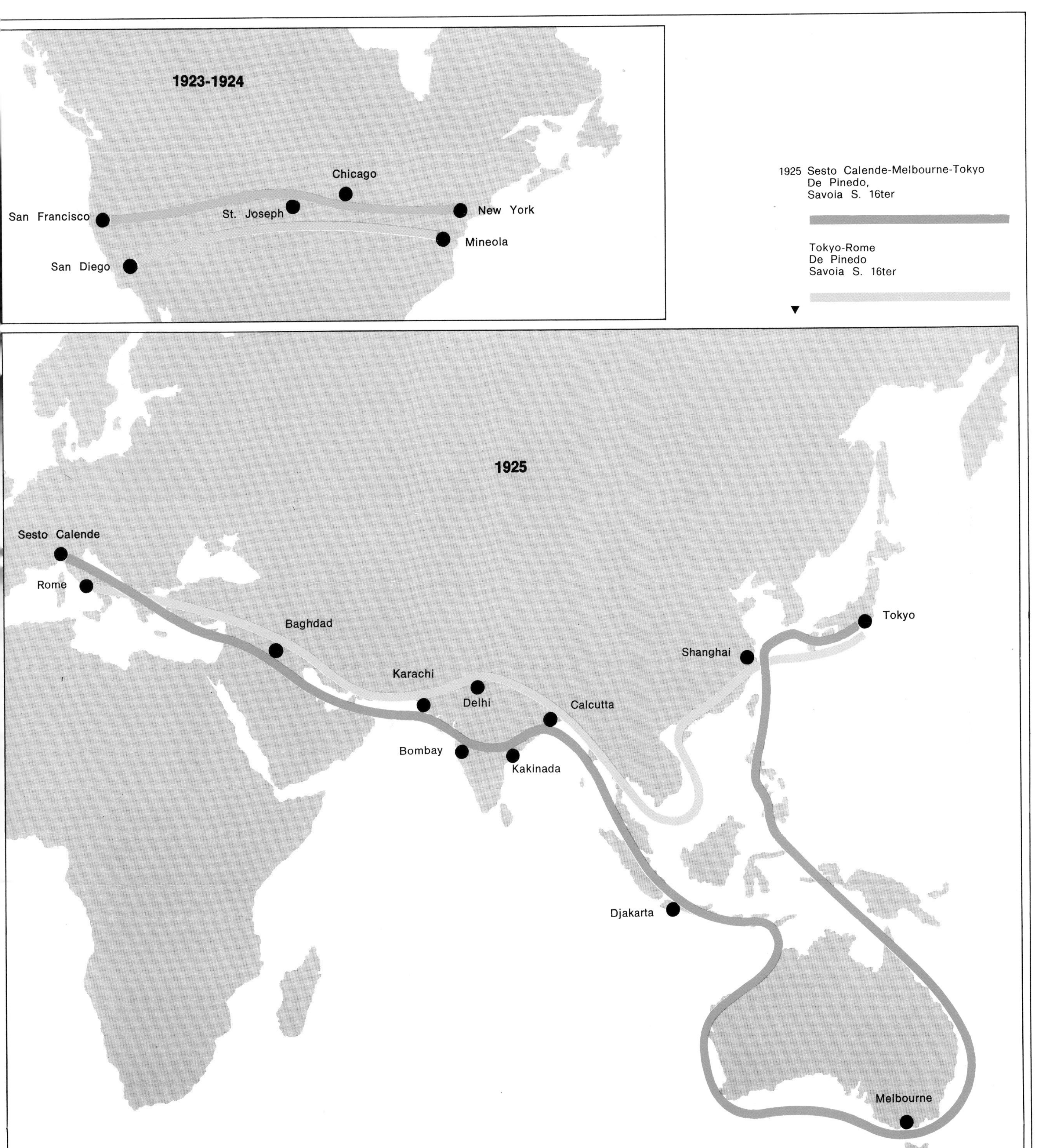

1925 Sesto Calende-Melbourne-Tokyo
De Pinedo,
Savoia S. 16ter

Tokyo-Rome
De Pinedo
Savoia S. 16ter

▼

Famous long-distance flights: 1927–1933

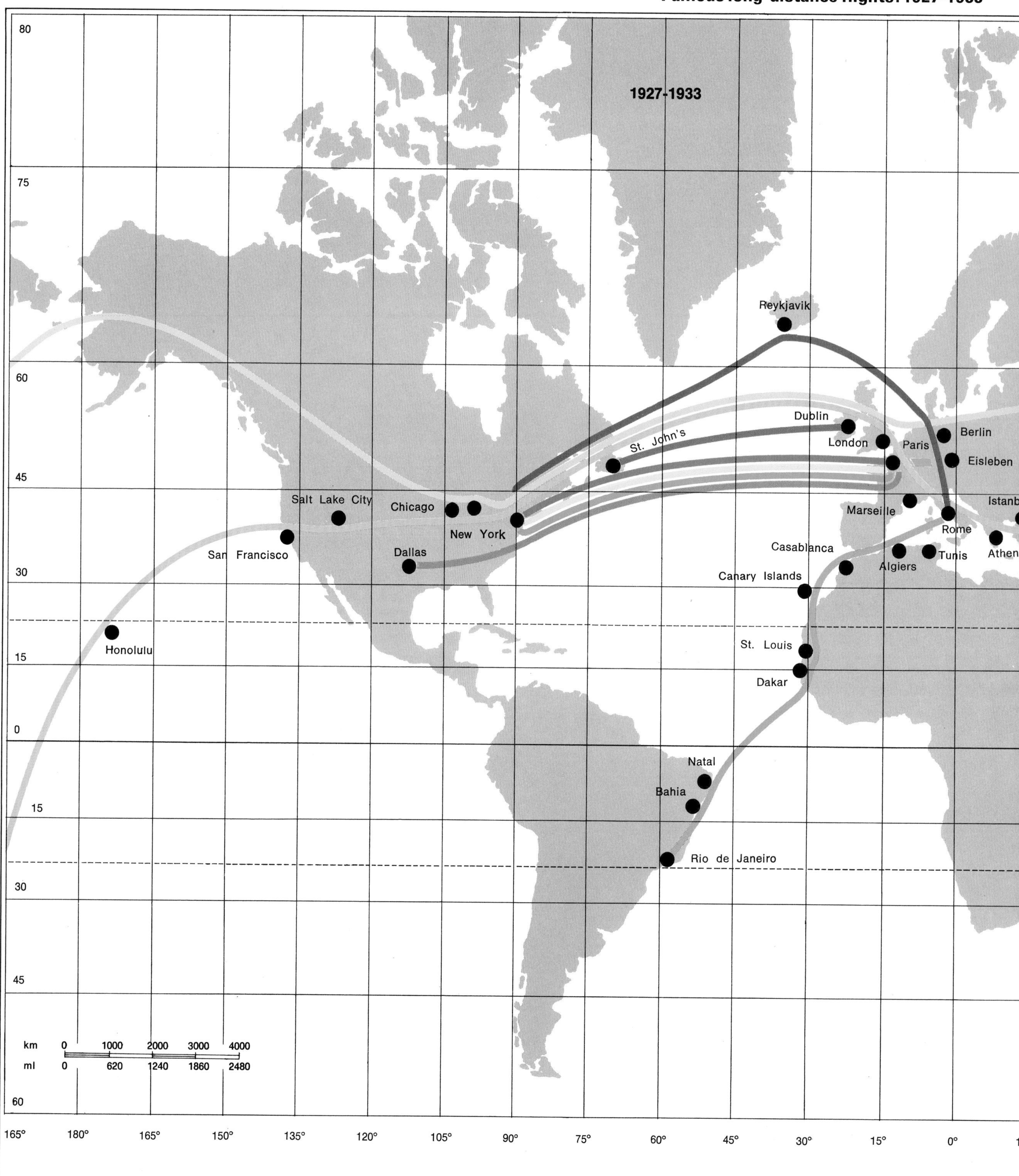

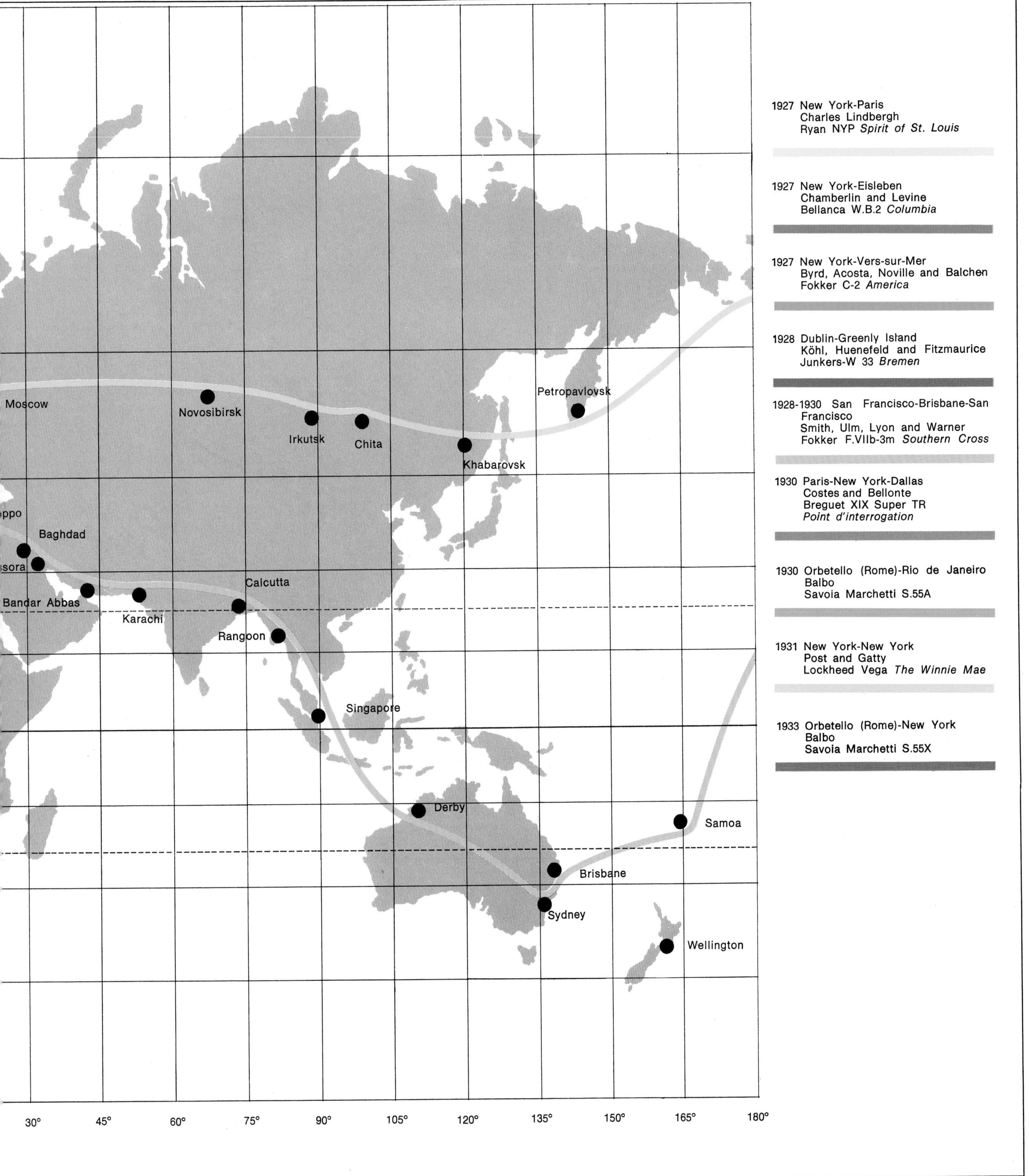
Moscow
Novosibirsk
Irkutsk
Chita
Khabarovsk
Petropavlovsk
ppo
Baghdad
sora
Bandar Abbas
Karachi
Calcutta
Rangoon
Singapore
Derby
Samoa
Brisbane
Sydney
Wellington
30°
45°
60°
75°
90°
105°
120°
135°
150°
165°
180°
1927 New York-Paris
Charles Lindbergh
Ryan NYP *Spirit of St. Louis*
1927 New York-Eisleben
Chamberlin and Levine
Bellanca W.B.2 *Columbia*
1927 New York-Vers-sur-Mer
Byrd, Acosta, Noville and Balchen
Fokker C-2 *America*
1928 Dublin-Greenly Island
Köhl, Huenefeld and Fitzmaurice
Junkers-W 33 *Bremen*
1928-1930 San Francisco-Brisbane-San Francisco
Smith, Ulm, Lyon and Warner
Fokker F.VIIb-3m *Southern Cross*
1930 Paris-New York-Dallas
Costes and Bellonte
Breguet XIX Super TR
Point d'interrogation
1930 Orbetello (Rome)-Rio de Janeiro
Balbo
Savoia Marchetti S.55A
1931 New York-New York
Post and Gatty
Lockheed Vega *The Winnie Mae*
1933 Orbetello (Rome)-New York
Balbo
Savoia Marchetti S.55X

1 S.V.A.9 (I)
1920 Rome–Tokyo (11,243 miles: 18,105 km)
Crew: Ferrarin and Masiero

2 Bellanca W.B.2 *Columbia* (U.S.A.)
1927 New York–Eisleben (3,909 miles: 6,294 km)
Crew: Chamberlin and Levine

3 Ryan NYP *Spirit of St. Louis* (U.S.A.)
1927 New York–Paris (3,520 miles: 5,670 km)
Pilot: Charles Lindbergh

4 Lockheed Vega *The Winnie Mae* (U.S.A.)
1931 Round the world: New York–New York (15,474 miles: 24,902 km)
Crew: Post and Gatty

5 Savoia Marchetti S.64 (I)
1928 Rome–Natal (Brazil) (4,464 miles: 7,188 km)
Crew: Ferrarin and Del Prete

6 de Havilland D.H.50J (G.B.)
1925–1926 London–Cape Town–London (15,990 miles: 25,750 km)
Crew: Cobham and Elliott

7 Junkers-W 33 *Bremen* (D)
1928 Dublin–Greenly Island (2,173 miles: 3,500 km)
Crew: Köhl, von Huenefeld and Fitzmaurice

8 Douglas DWC World Cruiser *Chicago* (U.S.A.)
1924 Round the world, Seattle–Seattle (26,345 miles: 42,398 km)
Crew: Smith and Arnold

9 Breguet XIX (F)
1929 Seville–Pernambuco
Crew: Challe and Borges

10 Breguet XIX *Jesús del Gran Poder* (F)
1929 Seville–Bahia (4,061 miles: 6,540 km)
Crew: Jimenez and Iglesias

11 Breguet XIX Super TR *Point d'intérrogation* (F)
1930 Paris–New York–Dallas (5,216 miles: 8,400 km)
Crew: Costes and Bellonte

12 Fairey III (G.B.)
1922 Lisbon–Rio de Janeiro
Crew: Cabral and Coutinho

13 Vickers Vimy (G.B.)
1919 St. John's–Clifden (1,933 miles: 3,110 km)
Crew: Alcock and Brown

14 Savoia S.16ter (I)
1925 Sesto Calende–Melbourne–Tokyo–Rome (35,000 miles: 55,000 km)
Crew: De Pinedo and Campanelli

15 Fokker F.VIIb-3m *Southern Cross* (NL)
1928 Oakland–Brisbane (7,316 miles: 11,774 km)
Crew: Kingsford Smith, Ulm, Lyon and Warner

16 Fokker T-2 (NL)
1923 Mineola–San Diego (2,470 miles: 3,975 km)
Crew: Macready and Kelly

17 Fokker C-2 *America* (U.S.A.)
1927 New York–Vers-sur-Mer (3,478 miles: 5,600 km)
Crew: Byrd, Acosta, Noville and Balchen

18 Savoia Marchetti S.55X (I)
1933 Orbetello–Chicago (6,065 miles: 9,760 km)
Twenty-five aircraft flown in formation commanded by Balbo

19 Savoia Marchetti S.55A (I)
1930 Orbetello–Rio de Janeiro (6,462 miles: 10,400 km)
Fourteen aircraft in formation commanded by Balbo.

20 Dornier Do J Wal *Plus Ultra* (D)
1926 Seville–Buenos Aires
Crew: Franco, De Alda, Duran and Rada

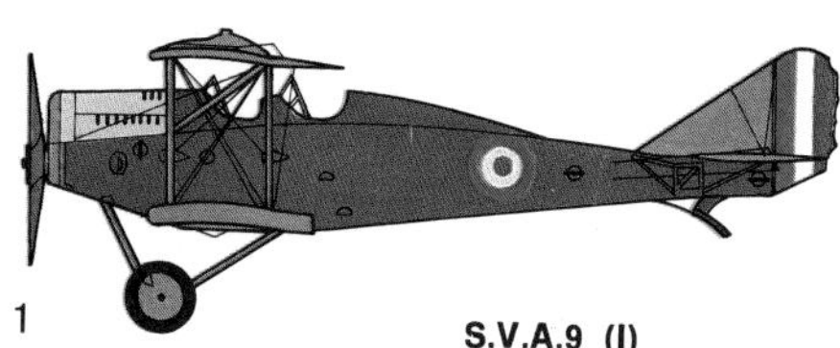
1 **S.V.A.9 (I)**

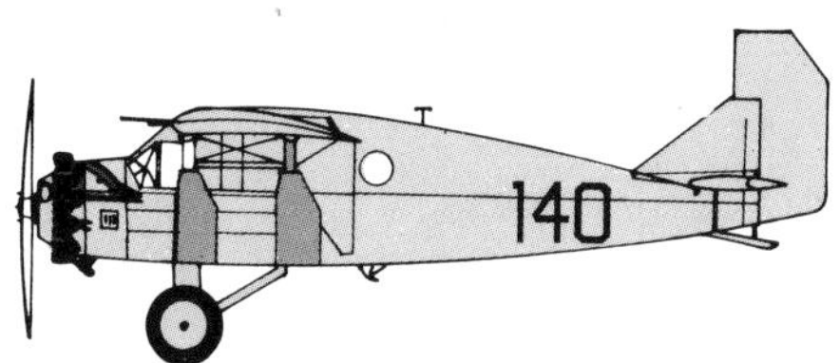

2 **Bellanca W.B.2** Columbia **(USA)**

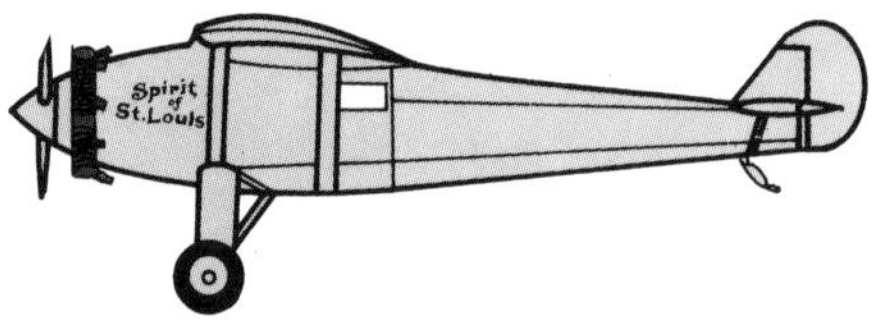

3 **Ryan NYP** Spirit of St. Louis **(USA)**

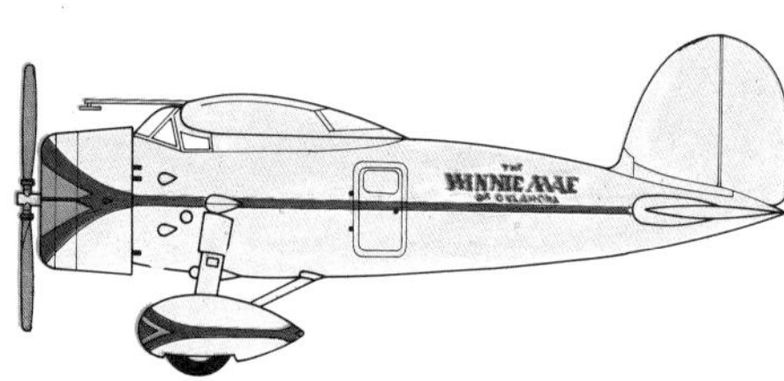
4 **Lockheed Vega** The Winnie Mae **(USA)**

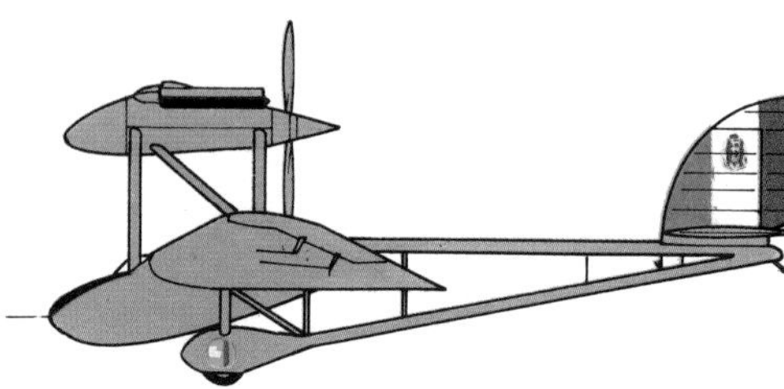
5 **Savoia Marchetti S.64 (I)**

6 **de Havilland D.H.50J (GB)**

21 Short S.5 Singapore I (G.B.)
1927–1928 Round Africa: Rochester–Cape Town–Plymouth (20,000 miles: 32,000 km)
Pilot: Cobham

22 Navy Curtiss NC-4 (U.S.A.)
1919 Newfoundland–Plymouth
Crew: Read, Stone, Rodd, Hinton, Breeze and Howard

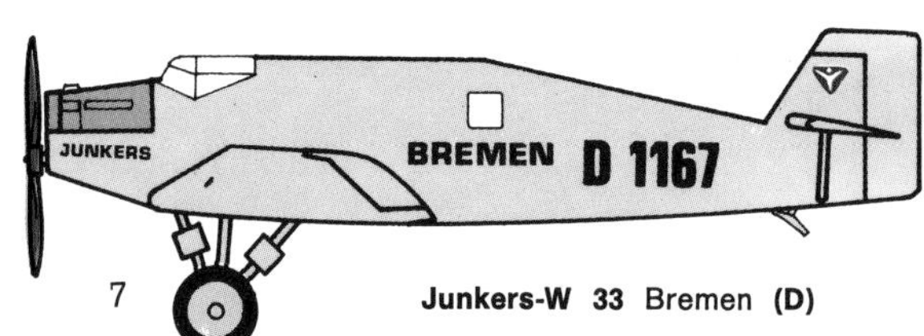

7 **Junkers-W 33** Bremen **(D)**

8 **Douglas DWC World Cruiser** Chicago **(USA)**

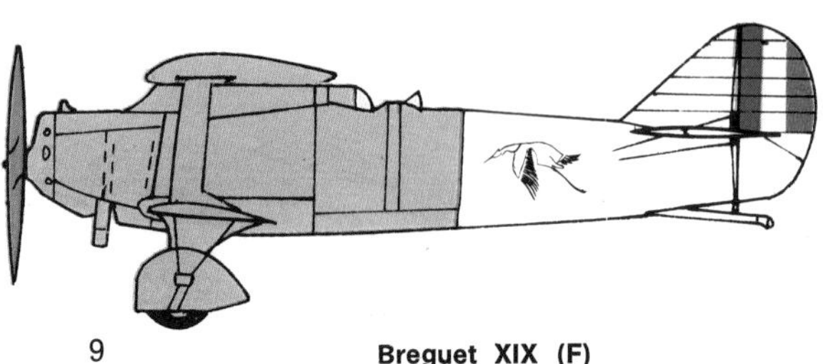
9 **Breguet XIX (F)**

10 **Breguet XIX** Jesús del Gran Poder **(F)**

11 **Breguet XIX Super TR** Point d'interrogation **(F)**

12 **Fairey III (GB)**

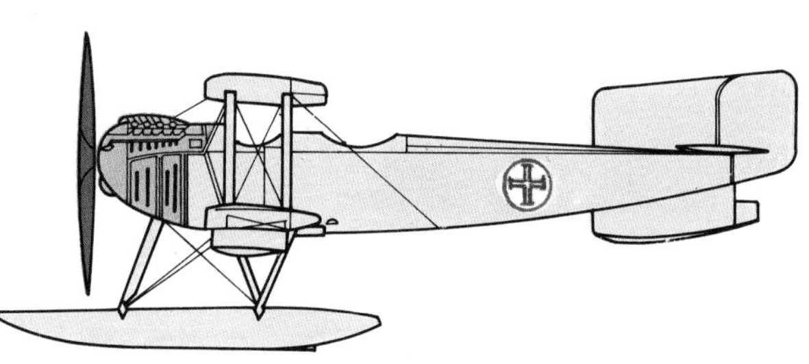

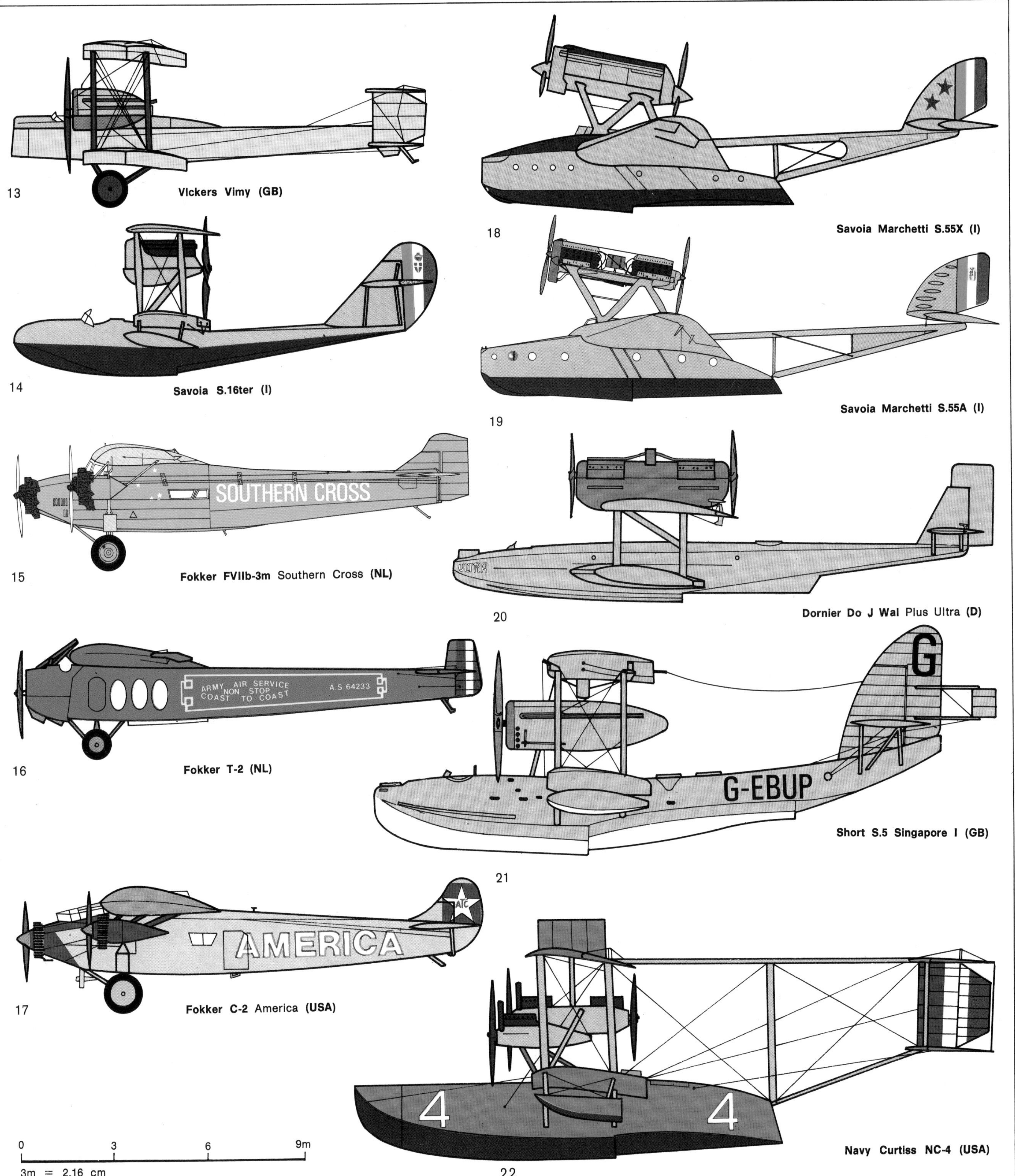

13 Vickers Vimy (GB)

14 Savoia S.16ter (I)

15 Fokker FVIIb-3m Southern Cross (NL)

16 Fokker T-2 (NL)

17 Fokker C-2 America (USA)

18 Savoia Marchetti S.55X (I)

19 Savoia Marchetti S.55A (I)

20 Dornier Do J Wal Plus Ultra (D)

21 Short S.5 Singapore I (GB)

22 Navy Curtiss NC-4 (USA)

Date	Route	Crew	Aircraft	Engine	km	miles
1919 16-23 May	New York (USA) - Plymouth (GB)	Read-Stone-Hinton-Rodd-Breeze-Howard (USA)	Navy-Curtiss NC-4 *Colossus*	Liberty 400 HP	3.920	2,436
1919 14-15 June	St. John's (VO) - Clifden (IRL)	Alcock-Brown (CDN)	Vickers Vimy	Rolls Royce Eagle 360 HP	3.032	1,884
1919 2-6 July (return 10-13 July)	East Fortune (GB) - Mineola (USA)	Scott (GB) and crew	R.34 *(Airship)*	Sunbeam Maori 250 HP	5.600	3,480
1922 30 March-17 June	Lisbon (P) -Rio de Janeiro (BR)	Coutinho-Cabral (P)	Fairey III	Rolls Royce Eagle 350 HP	6.034	3,750
1924 2 August- 1 September	London (GB)- New York (USA)	Smith-Arnold (USA)	Douglas DWC World Cruiser *Chicago*	Liberty 420 HP	3.500	2,175
1924 2 August - 1 September	London (GB) - New York (USA)	Nelson-Arding (USA)	Douglas DWC World Cruiser *New Orleans*	Liberty 420 HP	3.500	2,175
1924 12-15 October	Friedrichshafen (D) - Lakehurst (USA)	Eckener (D) and crew	LZ 126 *(Airship)*	Maybach	8.500	5,282
1926 22 January - 10 February	Seville (E) - Buenos Aires (RA)	Franco-De Alda-Duran-Prata (E)	Dornier Wal *Plus Ultra*	Napier Lion 450 HP	6.240	3,878
1927 13-24 February	Elmas (I) - Pernambuco (BR)	De Pinedo-Del Prete-Zacchetti (I)	Savoia Marchetti S.55 *Santa Maria I*	Isotta Fraschini Asso 500 HP	3.350	2,082
1927 12-20 March	Lisbon (P) - Rio de Janeiro (BR)	De Beires-Cabral-De Castillo-Gouveia (P)	Dornier Wal Marina *Argus*	Napier Lion 450 HP	3.000	1,864
1927 20-21 May	New York (USA) - Paris (F)	Lindbergh (USA)	Ryan NYP *Spirit of St.Louis*	Wright Whirlwind 220 HP	5.670	3.627
1927 23 May - 11 June	New York (USA) - Rome (I)	De Pinedo-Del Prete-Zacchetti (I)	Savoia Marchetti S.55 *Santa Maria II*	Isotta Fraschini Asso 500 HP	3.894	2,420
1927 4-6 June	New York (USA) - Eisleben (D)	Chamberlin-Levine (USA)	Bellanca W.B.2 *Columbia*	Wright Whirlwind 220 HP	6.294	3,904
1927 29 June - 1 July	New York (USA) - Vers-sur-Mer (F)	Byrd-Acosta-Noville (USA) Balchen (N)	Fokker C-2 *America*	Wright Whirlwind 220 HP	5.600	3,791
1927 10 October	St. Louis (SN) - Natal (BR)	Costes-Le Brix (F)	Breguet XIX *Nungesser-Coli*	Hispano-Suiza 600 HP	3.500	2,175
1928 12-13 April	Baldonnel (IRL) - Greenly Is. (VO)	Koehl-Huenefeld (D) - Fitzmaurice (IRL)	Junkers-W 33 *Bremen*	Junkers L.5 310 HP	3.500	2,175
1928 17-18 June	Trepassy Bay (VO) - Barry Port (GB)	Earhart-Stultz-Gordon (USA)	Fokker F.VIIb-3m/W *Friendship*	Wright Whirlwind 300 HP	3.940	2,448
1928 3-5 July	Montecelio (I) - Natal (BR)	Ferrarin-Del Prete (I)	Savoia Marchetti S.M.64	Fiat A.22 T 590 HP	7.188	4,467
1929 24-25 March	Seville (E) - Bahia (BR)	Jimenez-Iglesias (E)	Breguet XIX *Jesús del Gran Poder*	Hispano-Suiza 500 HP	6.540	4,064
1929 13-14 June	Old Orchard Beach, Maine (USA) - Santander (E)	Assolant-Lefèvre-Lotti (F)	Bernard 191 G.R. *Oiseau Canari*	Hispano-Suiza 600 HP	5.500	3,418
1929 8-9 July	New York (USA) - Rome (I)	Williams-Jancey (USA)	Bellanca *Pathfinder*	Wright J-6 300 HP	5.500	3,418
1929 15-17 December	Seville (E) - Pernambuco (U)	Challe (F) - Borges (U)	Breguet XIX	Lorraine-Dietrich 450 HP	5.670	3,523
1930 12-13 May	St. Louis (SN) - Natal (BR)	Mermoz-Dabry-Gimié (F)	Latécoère 28-3 *Conte de la Vaulx*	Hispano-Suiza 600 HP	3.180	1,976
1930 24-25 June	Dublin (IRL) - New York (USA)	Smith (AUS) - Soul (IRL) - Van Dyck (NL) - Stannage (USA)	Fokker F.VIIb-3m *Southern Cross*	Wright Whirlwind 300 HP	3.220	2,001
1930 29-30 June	New York (USA) - Bermuda	Williams (USA)	Bellanca	Wright J-6 310 HP	2.512	1,561
1930 29 July - 1 August (return 16-18 August)	Cardington (GB) - Montreal (CDN)	Booth and crew (GB)	R.100 *(Airship)*	Rolls Royce	6.000	3,729
1930 18-23 August	Warnemünde (D) - New York (USA)	Von Gronau-Zimmar-Albrecht-Hack (D)	Dornier Wal	BMW 600 HP	4.700	2,921
1930 1-4 September	Paris (F) - New York-Dallas (USA)	Costes-Bellonte (F)	Breguet XIX Super TR *Point d'interrogation*	Hispano Suiza 600 HP	6.400	3,977
1930 9-10 October	Harbour Grace (VO) - Tresco, Scilly Is. (GB)	Boyd-Connor (CDN)	Bellanca *Miss Columbia*	Wright Whirlwind 220 HP	3.637	2,260
1930 17 December (return 1931 - 15 January)	Orbetello (I) - Rio de Janeiro (BR)	Balbo (I)	Savoia Marchetti S.55A	Fiat A.22 R 550 HP	10.400	6,436
1931 29 April - 6 May (return end May)	Sweden - Greenland	Ahremberg-Floden-Junglund (S)	Junkers-W 33 *Sverige*	Junkers L.5 310 HP	2.100	1,305
1931 4-5 June	Lisbon (P) - Rio de Janeiro (BR)	Christiansen-Merz-Niemann-Schildauer (D)	Dornier Do.X	Curtiss Conquerors 600 HP	2.350	1,460
1931 24-25 June	Harbour Grace (VO) - Krefeld (D)	Hilling-Hoiriis (DK)	Bellanca K *Liberty*	Wright J-6 300 HP	4.600	2,858
1931 15-16 July	Harbour Grace (VO) - Bicske (H)	Endresz-Magyar (H)	Lockheed Sirius *Justice for Hungary*	P.&W. Wasp 425 HP	5.600	3,480
1931 28-30 July	New York (USA) - Istanbul (TR)	Boardman-Polando (USA)	Bellanca Peacemaker *Cape Cod*	Wright Cyclone 600 HP	8.070	5,015
1931 8-29 August	Warnemünde (D) - New York (USA)	Von Gronau-Zimmer-Albrecht-Hack (D)	Dornier Wal *Gronenlandwal*	BMW 600 HP	4.400	2,734
1931 26-27 November	Natal (BR) - Bathhurst (W. Africa)	Hinkler (AUS)	de Havilland Puss Moth	de Havilland Gipsy Major 120 HP	3.200	1,988
1932 21-22 May	Harbour Grace (VO) - Culmore (N. Ireland)	Earhart (USA)	Lockheed Vega	Wright Cyclone 665 HP	3.100	1,926
1932 21-22 May	New York (USA) - Berlin (D)	Christiansen-Niemann-Merz (D)	Dornier Do X	Curtiss Colossus 600 HP	4.000	2,486
1932 June	Italy-Reykjavik (IS)	Cagna (I)	Savoia Marchetti S.55	Isotta Fraschini A 750 HP	—	—

Date	Route	Crew	Aircraft	Engine	km	miles
1932 18-19 August	Portmarnock (IRL) - Pennfield Ridge, New Brunswick (CDN)	Mollison (GB)	de Havilland Puss Moth *The Heart's Content*	de Havilland Gipsy Major 130 HP	4.180	2,597
1933 9 February	Dakar (SN) - Natal (BR)	Mollison (GB)	de Havilland Puss Moth *The Heart's Content*	de Havilland Gipsy Major 130 HP	3.200	1,988
1933 7 May	Warsaw (PL) - Rio de Janeiro (BR)	Skarzynski (PL)	RWD 5	de Havilland Gipsy Major 130 HP	3.650	2,268
1933 9-10 June	Seville (E) - Camaguey (Cuba)	Collar Serra-Tros de Llarduya (E)	Breguet XIX Super TR *Cuatro Vientos*	Hispano-Suiza 600 HP	7.893	4,905
1933 2-12 July (return 8-9 August)	Orbetello (I) - Chicago (USA) - New York (USA)	Balbo (I)	Savoia Marchetti S.55X	Isotta Fraschini Asso 800 HP	19.800	12,305
1933 21 July - 26 September	New York (USA) - Copenaghen (DK)	Charles & Anne Lindbergh (USA)	Lockheed Sirius	Wright Cyclone 665 HP	5.500	3,418
1933 22-23 July	Pendine Sands, Wales (GB) Bridgeport, Conn. (USA)	Mr. & Mrs. Mollison (GB)	de Havilland Dragon *Seafarer*	de Havilland Gipsy Major 260 HP	5.000	3,107
1933 5-7 August	New York (USA) - Riyaq (SYR)	Codos-Rossi (F)	Blériot 110 *Joseph Le Brix*	Hispano-Suiza 600 HP	9.104	5,658
1933 6 December	Lisbon (P) - Atlantic round-trip	Charles & Anne Lindbergh (USA)	Lockheed Sirius	Wright Cyclone 665 HP	3.100	1,926
1934 3-4 January (return 30-31 January)	St. Louis (SN) - Natal (BR)	Bonnot-Jeanpierre-Gauthier (F)	Latécoère 300 *Croix du Sud*	Hispano-Suiza 650 HP	3.100	1,926
1934 14-15 May	New York (USA) - Lahinch (IRL)	Sabelli (I) - Pond (USA)	Bellanca K *Leonardo da Vinci*	Wright J-6 330 HP	5.000	3,107
1934 27-28 May	Paris (F) - New York (USA)	Codos-Rossi (F)	Blériot 110 *Joseph le Brix*	Hispano-Suiza 600 HP	5.950	3,719
1934 29-30 June	New York (USA) - St.André de Messel (F)	B. & G. Adamowitz (PL) and H. Hoirüs (DK)	Bellanca K *City of Warsaw*	Wright J-6 330 HP	4.600	2,858
1934 20 July - 10 September	Rochester (GB) - Ottawa (CDN) - New York (USA)	Grierson (GB)	de Havilland *Fox Moth*	de Havilland Gipsy Major 130 HP	5.000	3,107
1934 8-9 August	Wasaga Beach (CDN) - Heston (GB)	Reid (CDN) - Ayling (GB)	de Havilland Dragon *Trail of the Caribou*	de Havilland Gipsy Major 270 HP	5.800	3,604
1934 15 August-8 September	Cartwright, Labrador (CDN) - Edinburgh (GB)	Light-Wilson (USA)	Bellanca *Asulinak*	P.&W. Wasp 450 HP	5.000	3,107
1934 27 November (return 11 December)	Dakar (SN) - Natal (BR)	Bossoutrot-Givon (F)	Blériot 5190 *Santos Dumont*	Hispano-Suiza 650 HP	3.100	1,926
1934 19-20 December	Amsterdam (NL) - Paramaribo (Dutch Guyana)	Van der Molen-Stolk (NL)	Fokker F-7 *Snip*	P.&W. Wasp 250 HP	3.600	2,237
1935 21 May	Madrid (E) - Mexico	Pombo (E)	Klemm Eagle	de Havilland Gipsy Major 130 HP	3.100	1,926
1935 25 July-16 August	Cartwright, Labrador (CDN) - Bergen (N)	Solberg-Oscanyan (N)	Loening *Leiv Eriksson*	Wright Cyclone 750 HP	5.200	3,231
1935 21-22 September	New York (USA) - Ballinrobe (IRL)	Waitkins (RY)	Lockheed Vega *Lithuanica II*	P.&W. Hornet 750 HP	5.000	3,107
1935 13 November	London (GB) - Rio de Janeiro (BR)	Batten-Young (NZ)	Percival Gull	de Havilland Gipsy Six 200 HP	3.200	1,988
1935 14 December	Paris (F) - Martinique	Bonnot-De Jozan-Casselari (F)	Latécoère 521 *Lieutenant de Vaisseau Paris*	Hispano-Suiza 650 HP	3.100	1,926
1936 10-11 February	Cuba-Spain	Mendendez (C)	Lockheed Vega	P.&W. Wasp J 600 HP	3.100	1,926
1936 2-3 September (return 14 September)	Harbour Grace (VO) - Llandilo, Wales (GB)	Merrill-Rickman	Vultee V.1A *Lady of Peace*	Wright Cyclone 735 HP	5.300	3,293
1936 4-5 September	Abingdon (GB) - Cape Breton Is (CDN)	Beryl Markham (GB)	Percival Vega Gull *Messenger*	de Havilland Gipsy Six 200 HP	4.500	2,796
1936 28-29 October	Harbour Grace (VO) - Croydon (GB)	Mollison (GB)	Bellanca *Dorothy*	Wright Cyclone 750 HP	3.780	2,349
1936 31 December	Paris (F)-Buenos Aires (RA)	Marisa Bastié (F)	Caudron-Renault C-635	Renault 6 Pri Bengali 180 HP	3.100	1,926
1937 8-9 May (return 13-14 May)	New York (USA) - North Weald (GB)	Merrill-Lambie (USA)	Lockheed Electra	P.&W. Hornet 750 HP	5.600	3,480
1937 25-26 October (return 29 October)	Biscarrosse (F) - Maceio (BR)	Guillaumet-Leclaire (F)	Latécoère 521 *Lieutenant de Vaisseau Paris*	Hispano-Suiza 650 HP	5.771	3,586
1937 27-28 December	Trieste (I)-Buenos Aires (RA)	Stoppani-Comani Jaria-Pogliani (I)	Cant Z.506 B	Alfa Romeo 750 HP	7.013	4,358
1938 24-25 January	Rome (I) - Rio de Janeiro (BR)	Biseo-Paradisi (I)	Savoia Marchetti S.M.83	Alfa Romeo 750 HP	5.350	3,325
1938 20-26 March	Italy-Argentina	Klinger-Tonini (I)	Cant Z.506	Alfa Romeo 750 HP	4.000	2,486
1938 27-29 March	Plymouth (GB)-Brazil	Von Engel (D)	Dornier Do 18	Junkers Jumo 205 600 HP	8.500	5,282
1938 29 May	Los Angeles (USA)-Warsaw (PL)	Mokowsky (PL)	Lockheed 14	P.&W. Wasp J	3.100	1,926
1938 17-18 July	New York (USA) - Baldonnell (IRL)	Corrigan (USA)	Curtiss Robin *Sunshine*	Curtiss 300 HP	5.300	3,293
1938 20-21 July	Foynes (IRL)-Montreal (CDN) New York (USA)	Bennet-Coster (GB)	Short Composite *Mercury*	Napier Rapier 370 HP	4.600	2,858
1938 10-11 August (return 13-14 August)	Berlin (D)-New York (USA)	Henke-Von Moreau-Koder-Dierberg (D)	Focke Wulf Fw 200 Condor *Brandenburg*	BMW 720 HP	6.550	4,070
1939 4-12 February	Rome (I) - Buenos Aires (RA)	Biseo-Tonini (I)	Savoia Marchetti S.M.83	Alfa Romeo 750 HP	3.100	1,926
1939 28-29 April	Moscow (USSR)-New York (USA)	Kokkinaki-Gordienko (USSR)	Ilyushin *Moskva*	M85 1700	6.516	4,049
1939 29-30 June	Senegal-Antilles	Archbold (USA)	Consolidated PBY *Guba*	Wright Cyclone 800 HP	4.148	2,577

Chronology of transpacific and round-the-world flights: 1924–1939

Dates of transpacific flights: 1925-1938

Date	Route	Crew	Aircraft	Engine	km	miles
1925 31 August-1 September	San Pablo Bay (USA) - Honolulu (Hawaiian Is.)	Rodgers-Connell-Bowlin-Pope-Stanz (USA)	Curtiss	Packard 400 HP	2.963	1,841
1927 28-29 June	Oakland (USA) - Honolulu (Hawaiian Is.)	Maitland-Hegemberger (USA)	Fokker F.VII *Bird of Paradise*	Wright Whirlwind 220 HP	3.875	2,408
1927 14-15 July	Oakland (USA) - Molokai (Hawaiian Is.)	Smith-Bronte (USA)	Travel Air *City of Oakland*	Wright Whirlwind 220 HP	3.800	2,361
1927 17-18 August	Oakland (USA) - Honolulu (Hawaiian Is.)	Goebel-Davis (USA)	Stinson Detroiter *Woolaroh*	Wright Whirlwind 220 HP	3.875	2,408
1928 31 May-9 June	Oakland (USA) - Brisbane (AUS)	Smith-Ulm (AUS), Lyon-Warner (USA)	Fokker F.VIIb-3m *Southern Cross*	Wright Whirlwind 300 HP	11.823	7,348
1929 12-29 September	Moscow (USSR) - New York (USA)	Shestakov-Boltov-Sterlingov-Fufaev (USSR)	Tupolev	BMW 600	3.200	1,988
1931 14-23 August	New York (USA) - Shanghai (TJ)	Charles & Anne Lindbergh (USA)	Lockheed *Sirius*	P.&W. Wasp 425 HP	4.300	2,672
1931 3-5 October	Tokyo (J) - Wenatachee (USA)	Herndon-Pangborn (USA)	Bellanca Peacemaker *Miss Veedol*	P.&W. Wasp 425 HP	8.000	4,972
1934 11-12 January (return 8-9 March)	San Francisco (USA) - Honolulu (Hawaiian Is.)	Hellers (USA)	Consolidated	Wright Cyclone 750 HP	3.860	2,399
1934 21 October-4 November	Brisbane (AUS) - Oakland (USA)	Smith-Taylor (AUS)	Lockheed Altair *Miss Southern Cross*	P.&W. Wasp J 600 HP	11.634	7,230
1935 12 January	Honolulu (Hawaiian Is.) - Oakland (USA)	Earhart (USA)	Lockheed Vega	P.&W. Hornet 375 HP	3.870	2,405
1936 15-30 August	California (USA) - USSR	Levanewski-Levtchenko (USSR)	Vultee	Wright Cyclone 800 HP	4.200	2,610
1937 27-28 January	San Diego (USA) - Honolulu (Hawaiian Is.)	Mac'Dade (USA)	Consolidated XPBY	Wright Cyclone 800 HP	3.860	2,399
1937 13-17 April	San Diego (USA) - Manila (PI)	Pope (USA)	Consolidated XPBY	Wright Cyclone 800 HP	13.000	8,079
1938 2-25 June	San Diego (USA) - Darwin Lea (N.G.)	Archbold-Rogers-Yancey-Booth-Brown-Barrinka (USA)	Consolidated PBY *Guba*	Wright Cyclone 750 HP	12.000	7,458

Dates of round-the-world flights: 1924-1939

Date	Place	Crew	Aircraft	Engine
1924 6 April-28 September	Seattle (USA)	Smith-Arnold (USA)	Douglas DWC World Cruiser *Chicago*	Liberty 420 HP
1924 6 April-28 September	Seattle (USA)	Nelson-Arding (USA)	Douglas DWC World Cruiser *New Orleans*	Liberty 420 HP
1927 27-28 August	Detroit (USA)	Brock-Schlee (USA)	Stinson Detroiter *Pride of Detroit*	Wright Whirlwind 220 HP
1928 31 May-4 July 1930	San Francisco-Brisbane-San Francisco	Smith-Ulm (AUS), Lyon-Warner (USA)	Fokker F.VIIb-3m *Southern Cross*	Wright Whirlwind 300 HP
1929 31 July-4 September	Friedrichshafen (D)	Eckener (D)	*Graf Zeppelin*	Maybach
1931 23 June-1 July	New York (USA)	Post (USA)-Gatty (AUS)	Lockheed Vega *Winnie Mae*	P.&W. Wasp 420 HP
1931 28-29 July	New York (USA)	Herndon-Pangborn (USA)	Bellanca Peacemaker *Miss Veedol*	P.&W. Wasp 425 HP
1932 5-6 July	New York (USA)	Griffin-Mattern (USA)	Lockheed Vega *Century of Progress*	P.&W. Wasp 425 HP
1932 22-25 July	Sylt Isld. (D)	Von Gronau-Von Roth-Albrecht-Hack (D)	Dornier Do J Wal *Gronenlandwal*	BMW 600 HP
1932 24-30 August	Chicago (USA)	Von Gronau-Von Roth-Albrecht-Hack (D)	Dornier Do J Wal *Gronenlandwal*	BMW 600 HP
1933 3-4 June	New York (USA)	Mattern (USA)	Lockheed Vega *Century of Progress*	P.&W. Wasp 425 HP
1933 15-21 July	New York (USA)	Post (USA)	Lockheed Vega *Winnie Mae*	P.&W. Wasp J 750 HP
1937 18-20 March	Oakland (USA)	Earhart-Manz-Nooman-Manning (USA)	Lockheed Electra	P.&W. Wasp J 600 HP
1937 1 June	Miami (USA)	Earhart-Nooman (USA)	Lockheed Electra	P.&W. Wasp J 600 HP
1938 10-14 July	New York (USA)	Hughes-Thurlow-Connor-Stoddart-Lund (USA)	Lockheed Electra	P.&W. Hornet 750 HP
1939 26 August - 20 October	Tokyo (J)	Nakao - Yoshida - Shimokawa - Saeki - Sato-Yaokawa (J)	Mitsubishi G3M2 *Nippon*	Mitsubishi Kinsei 41 1075 HP

Vickers Vimy Transatlantic - 1919, GB (39)

Handley Page W.8 - 1919, GB (43)

de Havilland D.H.66 Hercules - 1926, GB (46)

Breguet 14 - 1916, F (38)

Levy-Lepen R - 1917, F (38)

Junkers-F 13 - 1919, D (41)

Albatros L 73 - 1926, D (45)

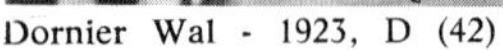

Dornier Wal - 1923, D (42)

Caproni Ca 60 Transaereo - 1921 I (40)

Savoia S.16ter - 1923, I (44)

Cant 6ter - 1926, I (45)

Cant 10ter - 1926, I (45)

Savoia Marchetti S.55A Santa Maria - 1927, I (45)

Fokker F.VIIb-3m - 1925, NL (45)

Fokker F.III - 1921, NL (42)

Lockheed Vega - 1927, USA (48)

4. THE PURSUIT OF SPEED:

TWENTY YEARS OF COMPETITIONS

Concurrently with ever longer flights being achieved, both in duration and distance covered, perhaps the most exciting element of flight, that of speed, was the foremost consideration between the two wars. During World War I it had been vital to provide combat machines which could outgun their adversaries, and the frantic efforts made to produce efficient fighters and bombers which were mass-produced and increasingly heavily armed meant that speed had been assigned a lower priority. This is illustrated by the fact that in spite of the enormous technical advances made in response to the demands of war, only in 1917–18 were fighters produced which could exceed the speed of the Deperdussin monoplane in which, on 29 September 1913, Maurice Prévost had set up the last world speed record at Reims, flying at 126.59 mph (203.85 km/h).

But in peacetime it was possible to strive for new speed records, with the advantage of new technology, new materials and the new aero-engines which had been developed during the war. Aviation enthusiasts were the principal driving force behind this phenomenon, but considerable impetus was also forthcoming from government and military circles, who realized that faster aircraft would lead to more effective military aircraft. Encouragement was also given by sponsors, for the most part industrialists and newspaper proprietors, who put up substantial sums in prize money, providing tempting incentives for pilots and designers.

The era which is now referred to by historians as the boom era of the competition aircraft was borne along on the same tide of enthusiasm in both Europe and the New World, although it evolved differently, reaching a peak in the second half of the 1920s and then gradually declining during the 1930s. Air rallies and displays with speed events were organized everywhere in Europe and the United States, but there were certain competitions which were to assume particular importance and prestige from very early on and these provided the most reliable measure of progress, attracting thousands of enthusiasts.

Some of these important competitions were revivals of events which had become internationally famous some years earlier, such as the Gordon Bennett Aviation Cup which had had a great influence during the pioneering years and had helped to popularize early aviation; others, such as the Pulitzer Aviation Trophy (which was first held in the United States in 1920), were competitions which, although only recently introduced, had a glamor about them that captured the imagination and fervent support of both participants and spectators. The results of these competitions speak for themselves: the first Gordon Bennett event in 1909 at Reims was won by Glenn Curtiss at an average speed of 46.908 mph (75.492 km/h), while the Frenchman, Sadi Lecointe, won the last, held in 1920, at an average speed of 168.731 mph (271.548 km/h). The first Pulitzer Trophy was won by Corliss C. Moseley, flying at an average speed of 156.539 mph (251.921 km/h); Cyrus Bettis won the last Pulitzer Trophy in 1925 with a speed of 248.975 mph (400.68 km/h). But the most influential competition of all was the Schneider Trophy which continued until 1931 and which stimulated such international rivalry that the governments of four nations gave their official backing to their entrants. On 5 December 1912, the French industrialist and patron of aviation, Jacques Schneider, announced that he was inaugurating La Coupe d'Aviation Maritime Jacques Schneider and offering an impressive trophy which was to be awarded outright to the first nation to win the competition three times within the space of five years. His aim was very straightforward—to promote the development of seaplanes and their commercial use. The original objective was soon completely forgotten, however, and the Schneider Trophy became a pure speed contest. In contrast with Jacques Schneider's laudable entrepreneurial spirit, which had as its object the promotion of investment in a commercially productive means of transport, the Trophy triggered off a series of increasingly expensive prestige machines and the scale of government subsidy and obsession with winning the Trophy for motives of national prestige reached such proportions that the United States decided to withdraw after the 1926 competition.

The expense which participation in the Schneider Trophy races involved was, indirectly, an investment. The very fact that the competition was exclusively for marine aircraft meant that designers had their skills taxed to the utmost and had to undertake a formidable amount of research and development, which has not been equaled in peacetime until the advent of today's space race. This competitive spirit furthered the development of aeronautical technology. The Italians and the British, in particular, gained an understanding of aerodynamics, airframes, materials and powerplants from the twelve Schneider races, which they could have acquired by no other means. The Italian aircraft industry finally produced the sophisticated and outstanding Macchi-Castoldi MC.72, holder of the officially unbeaten speed record for seaplanes, but its British counterpart's contribution was farther-reaching, since the immortal Spitfire fighter which was to play such a conspicuous part in World War II was derived from the Supermarine seaplanes which won the last three Schneider races.

Speed was, therefore, the yardstick of the progress which the Schneider Trophy stimulated. The first Schneider race attracted relatively little interest when it was included as part of the second international Hydro-Aeroplane Meeting at Monaco in 1913. Maurice Prévost gained France's only victory in the competition that year at an average speed of 45.7 mph (73.56 km/h) in his Deperdussin. This speed was almost doubled the following year when the Englishman, Howard Pixton, won in a Sopwith Tabloid, clocking up an average speed of 86.78 mph (139.656 km/h). The first post-war races saw speeds rise rapidly: in 1920 Luigi Bologna flew a Savoia S.12bis at a winning average speed of 105.971 mph (170.541 km/h) and in 1922 Henri C. Biard averaged 145.721 mph (234.516 km/h) in the Supermarine Sea Lion II. The Americans decided to enter the competition and won it with a Navy Curtiss CR–3 in 1923 and again in 1925 with a Curtiss R3C–2: Rittenhouse's average speed of 177.278 mph (285.303 km/h) in 1923 and James H. Doolittle's 1925 average speed of 232.573 mph (374.284 km/h) meant that the 300 km/h barrier had been broken and speeds were fast approaching a new target of 400 km/h. In 1927 S. N. Webster's Supermarine S.5 achieved this when he won the Trophy at an average speed of 281.655 mph (453.273 km/h) and in 1929 the 500 km/h milestone was passed when H. R. D. Waghorn flew at an average speed of 328.629 mph (528.869 km/h). The average speed in the last Schneider Trophy race to be held was not much higher: the outright winner, John H. Boothman, reached 340.08 mph (547.297 km/h) in 1931 in a Supermarine S.6B. In many ways the last Schneider Trophy race marked both the climax and the end of the great European flying competitions, and no comparable race was held in Europe after 1931.

This was not so in the United States, where the Army's decision to end the government-sponsored competitions met with fierce criticism and angry reaction, but did not signal the end of competitive flying. Although the most coveted prize in the U.S. aviation world, the Pulitzer Trophy, drew much of its excitement and interest from the fierce rivalry between the Army and Navy entrants, in the early thirties two other important competitions were introduced which were just as hotly contested until shortly before World War II: the Thompson Trophy and the Bendix Trophy.

But the American aeronautical world was very different from its European counterpart. In Europe flying was a sport which only relatively few people could afford and which attracted nothing like the vast crowds of wildly enthusiastic supporters who flocked to air displays in the United States. From 1920 onward, the airplane was the center of attention during the National Air Races, which were a large-scale, week-long, annual event. People came in their hundreds of thousands from all over the United States to watch these races, which took on the atmosphere of an aeronautical rodeo show. Events included formation flying; parachute drops; aerobatic displays and, of course, speed contests. It was on such occasions that aviator heroes and the legends surrounding them were created; hitherto unknown men and airplanes achieved overnight fame and adulation throughout the United States. This was just what was needed to promote the popularity of the airplane, leading to a craze which engulfed the United States in the immediately postwar years and stimulated the creation and expansion of a market with almost unlimited potential. This was the era of individual ventures, of countless small constructors who produced aircraft which were often superior to those produced by the large aircraft manufacturers. The latter were wary of running up excessive research and development costs and were still thinking in terms of large-scale wartime production, which meant that they were slow to think in terms of high-performance machines which were needed for competition flying. This was the golden age of American competitive flying and of the craftsman-produced airplanes such as the Gee Bee, Wedell-Williams and Laird which were unique and unrepeatable products of their time.

All this activity and enthusiasm was to have a profound effect on the course of aeronautical development. It is true to say that the twenty years of sporting events between the two wars in America and Europe did more to shape the modern airplane than anything else. The races, long-distance flights and continual setting of new records had far wider significance than mere fame for the pilots and aircraft manufacturers or national prestige. Their vital importance lay in overcoming technical problems and in advancing technology. With each innovation, one more step had been taken in the slow but sure evolution of airframes and engines.

The years between the two World Wars saw remarkable progress in engine technology. World War I had witnessed the decline of the first mass-produced power-unit, the rotary engine. The Seguin brothers' original rotary engine design gave way to the more conventional, stationary engines which were adapted for use as aero-engines having been originally developed for the automobile. Two basic layouts were adopted: the inline engine typical of German manufacture and the V-engine favored by the British and the French; both types were liquid-cooled. Among the best known were Mercedes, Rolls-Royce and Hispano-Suiza, excellent power-units which were continually up-dated.

The United States' dramatic entry into the aviation industry immediately after the end of World War I gave great impetus to the evolution of the airplane. During the war, the European aviation industry had forged ahead, leaving the Americans well behind, and it was only in 1917 that the United States caught up when they produced the 400 hp V-12 Liberty engine. This meant that America could henceforward produce military aircraft of equal, if not better, quality than those built in Europe. Enormous numbers of Liberty engines were manufactured (17,935 had been built by the end of 1918), but they arrived too late to fill the role for which they were intended, since the war ended before effective combat aircraft could be designed round them. These Liberty engines were a great step forward, though they were less sophisticated than their French and British counterparts. The next important American engine was built by one of the great pioneers of American aviation, Glenn Curtiss. Adopting the V–12 liquid-cooled formula, from 1917 onward Curtiss developed a series of engines which were to become world-famous, powering some of the greatest competition aircraft of the 1920s. Starting with the K–12 model and progressing to the C–12 of 1920, Glenn Curtiss's team of engineers (which included Charles B. Kirkham and Arthur Nutt) succeeded in perfecting the basic model, the D–12, which incorporated some completely new ideas, especially in the lay-out of the cylinders and cooling jackets; solutions to problems which had cropped up while building aircraft to compete in the most important races of the time. The Curtiss D–12 engine powered the winners of the Pulitzer Trophy in 1922, 1923 and

1924, and of the 1923 Schneider Trophy when this engine successfully challenged European domination. And as if that were not enough, a long line of engines was derived from the Curtiss D–12 which were used to power many American military aircraft of the 1920s.

Another development had far wider repercussions: the overwhelming success of a new powerplant—the radial engine. The names of Wright and of Pratt & Whitney are synonymous with the excellent engines which were to replace most others in the United States during the second half of the 1920s. The early types, the Cylcone and the Whirlwind, were launched on their long careers in 1926, when the U.S. Navy stipulated that radial engines should be used in all their future aircraft and the radial engine's qualities were confirmed when it powered competition aircraft to sporting triumphs in some of the most important American competitions. Radial engines dominated the U.S. aviation scene and were unchallenged until just before World War II, by which time they had become identified with the most popular aircraft and pilots participating in the National Air Races.

The U.S. aero-engine industry went over almost entirely to the manufacture of radial engines, a choice which meant that in the early stages of World War II, the United States would have to rely largely on the British aero-engine industry to provide the liquid-cooled V–12 engines which could develop enough power for fighters to compete with enemy aircraft. European designers, however, continued to develop the liquid-cooled inline engine as well as radial engines. One reason for this lay in the specific aerodynamic requirements of racing aircraft and in particular those designed for the all-important Schneider Trophy races. Some of the finest engines developed for racing were built by the two remaining participants in the Schneider Trophy when the United States had withdrawn: Great Britain and Italy.

The British built their Rolls-Royce R engine especially for the Schneider races and the Italians planned to have their Fiat A.S.6 ready in time for what proved to be the last Scheider Trophy Competition. Although the problems encountered with the Fiat engine could not be corrected in time, it powered Francesco Agello's seaplane when he set the world seaplane speed record. Both these engines were masterpieces of engineering and aero-engine design with outstanding performance. The Rolls-Royce R was a liquid-cooled 12-cylinder V-engine which could develop its full 2,350 hp at 3,200 rpm. The Fiat A.S.6 was a twenty-four cylinder V-engine which developed over 3,000 hp at 3,300 rpm, driving two counterrotating propellers. Whereas the Fiat engine was not developed further, the famous Merlin engines were directly derived from the Rolls-Royce R.

Other components of the aircraft were also becoming more sophisticated. Metal airscrews replaced wooden ones, and later on the variable-pitch propeller was introduced. The American, Sylvanus Albert Reed, built the first really efficient metal propellers in 1923. These contributed to the victories of the U.S. Navy's racing airplanes in the Pulitzer and Schneider Trophies of 1923 and this type of propeller was subsequently used throughout the world. Radiator design advanced to meet the demands for efficient cooling systems for the liquid-cooled engines used in competition aircraft, leading to the ingenious arrangement of radiators built into the wing surfaces in the most outstanding racing types. The first aircraft with an efficient, manually retractable undercarriage was a competition aircraft, the unfortunate Dayton-Wright RB monoplane which was specially built to compete in the 1920 Gordon Bennett Cup.

Significant progress was also made in airframe construction. One of the greatest benefits to accrue from competition flying was the vindication of the monoplane formula, which had been almost totally neglected after being used in World War I. The monoplane was only very gradually accepted over the next decade.

Although monoplanes had done well in speed competitions (the excellent performance of the French Deperdussin was a prime example) it was not until 1924, when the Verville-Sperry R–3 won that year's Pulitzer Trophy and the French Bernard V.2 set the world speed record at 278.48 mph (448.171 km/h), that the monoplane regained its former prestige. The main obstacle was fundamentally structural; the biplane had the advantage of providing a large wing area and was very robust due to the strut and wire bracing which linked the upper and lower wings. The large area of lifting surface made up for the lack of power in the engines available at that time. Very high construction standards had been achieved in aeronautical production by manufacturers during World War I and, as a result, designers tended simply to concentrate their efforts on improving the biplane still further. The innate conservatism of military thinking led to a mistrust of any proposals for change in the equipment which had become so familiar. In Britain this attitude was particularly deeply entrenched, to the extent that monoplanes had been officially banned from military use, following a number of accidents. The Netherlands and Germany were exceptions to this prevailing attitude, mainly because Fokker and Junkers had designed and built excellent combat monoplanes.

During the years following the end of World War I it was, once again, competition aircraft which revived the monoplane formula. The Dayton-Wright RB is considered by many to have been the forerunner of the modern monoplane, with its cantilever wing with variable camber achieved by the use of leading- and trailing-edge flaps. But this was an isolated experiment in spite of its great potential. In France progress was more gradual and several Nieuport-Delage sesquiplanes appeared before Adolphe Bernard's classic monoplanes were built. From 1925, however, the aerodynamic advantages of the monoplane formula had become so obvious that the monoplane had to be the airplane of the future if higher speeds were to be attained. The Macchi and Supermarine seaplanes were the standard-bearers, showing what the monoplane could achieve.

Scale view of selected competition aircraft: 1919–1940

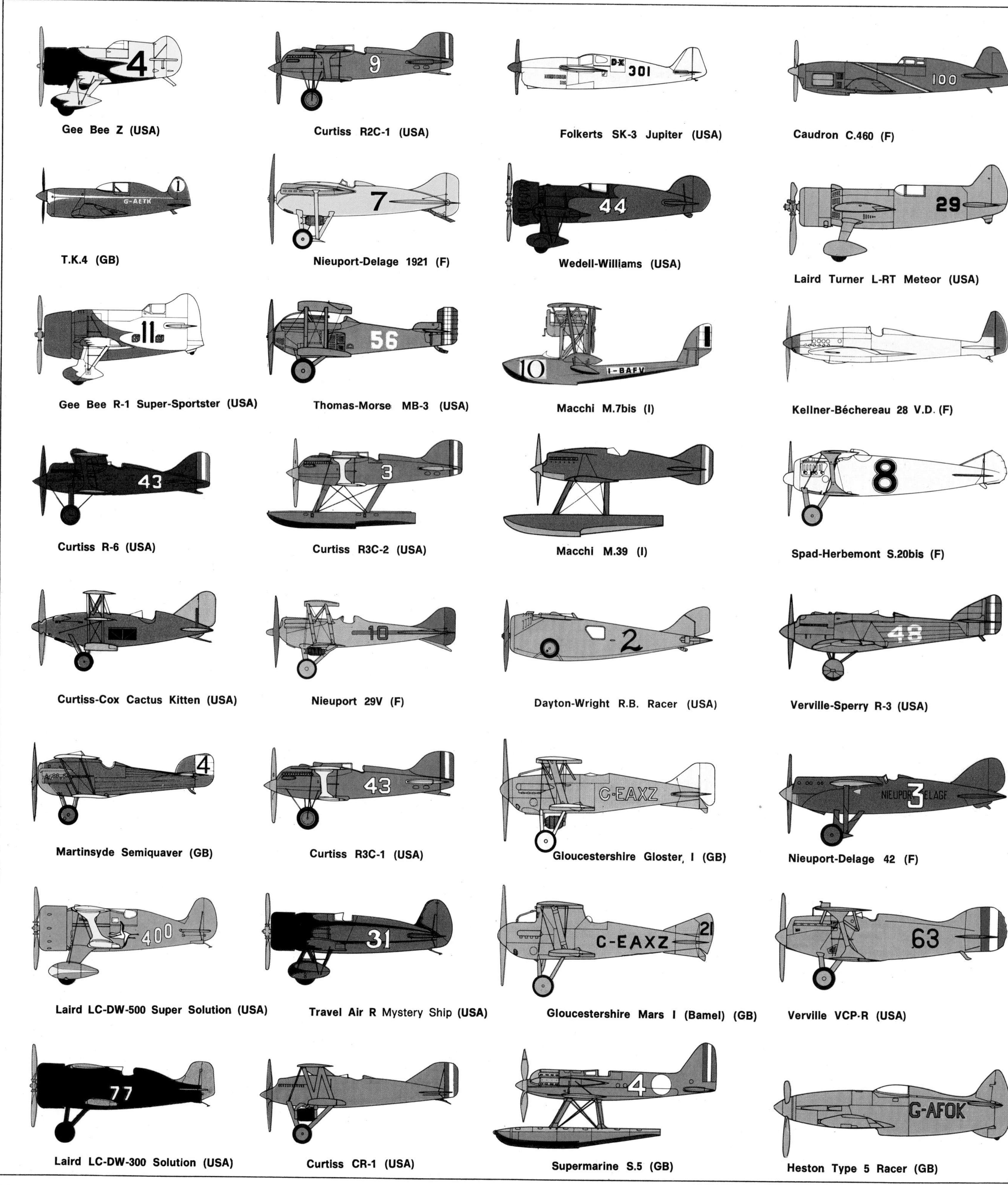

Gee Bee Z (USA)
Curtiss R2C-1 (USA)
Folkerts SK-3 Jupiter (USA)
Caudron C.460 (F)
T.K.4 (GB)
Nieuport-Delage 1921 (F)
Wedell-Williams (USA)
Laird Turner L-RT Meteor (USA)
Gee Bee R-1 Super-Sportster (USA)
Thomas-Morse MB-3 (USA)
Macchi M.7bis (I)
Kellner-Béchereau 28 V.D. (F)
Curtiss R-6 (USA)
Curtiss R3C-2 (USA)
Macchi M.39 (I)
Spad-Herbemont S.20bis (F)
Curtiss-Cox Cactus Kitten (USA)
Nieuport 29V (F)
Dayton-Wright R.B. Racer (USA)
Verville-Sperry R-3 (USA)
Martinsyde Semiquaver (GB)
Curtiss R3C-1 (USA)
Gloucestershire Gloster, I (GB)
Nieuport-Delage 42 (F)
Laird LC-DW-500 Super Solution (USA)
Travel Air R Mystery Ship (USA)
Gloucestershire Mars I (Bamel) (GB)
Verville VCP-R (USA)
Laird LC-DW-300 Solution (USA)
Curtiss CR-1 (USA)
Supermarine S.5 (GB)
Heston Type 5 Racer (GB)

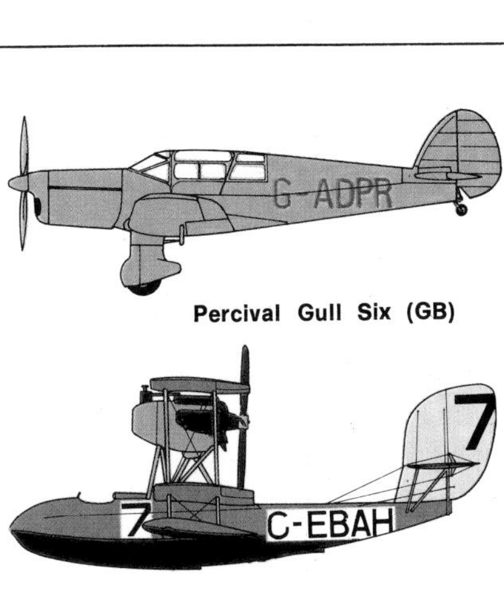

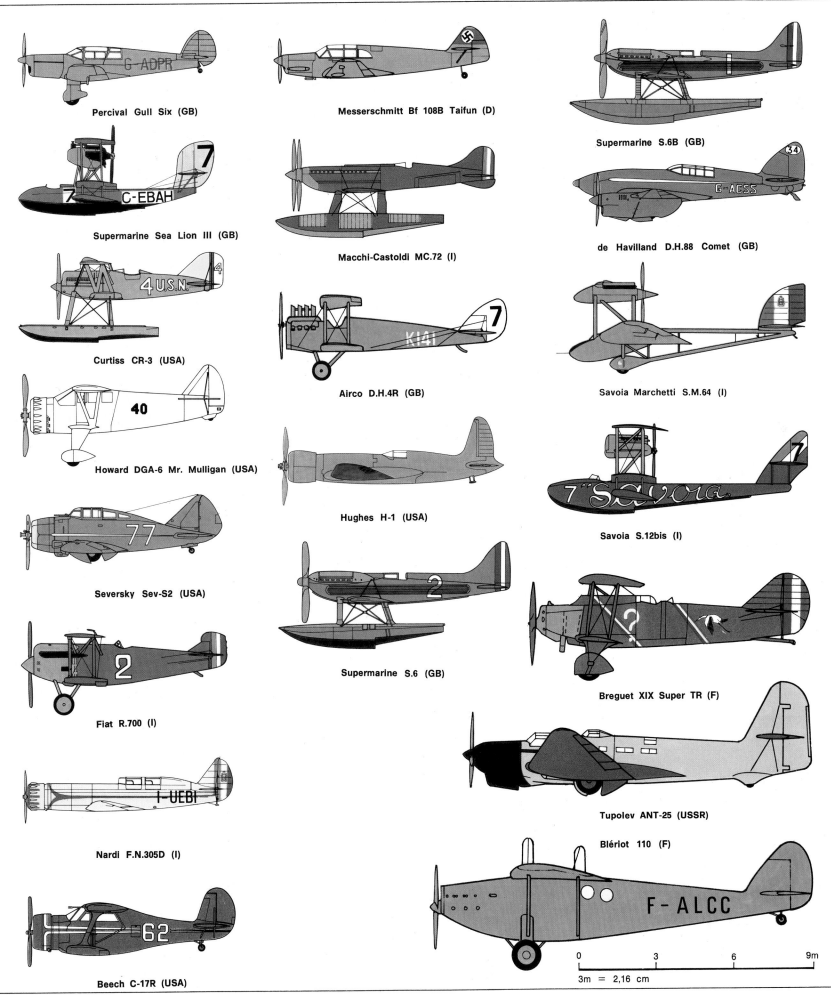

Percival Gull Six (GB)

Supermarine Sea Lion III (GB)

Curtiss CR-3 (USA)

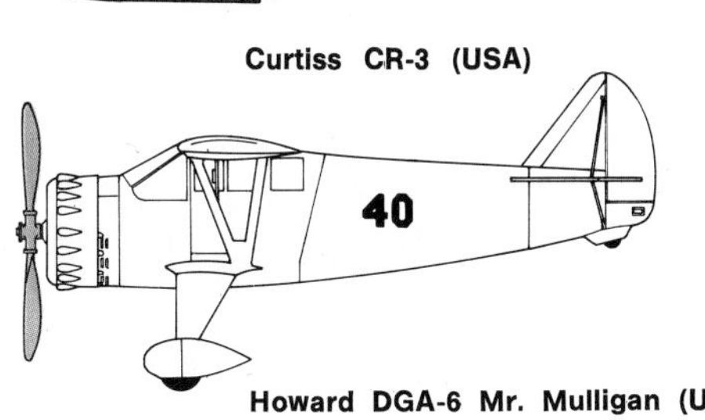

Howard DGA-6 Mr. Mulligan (USA)

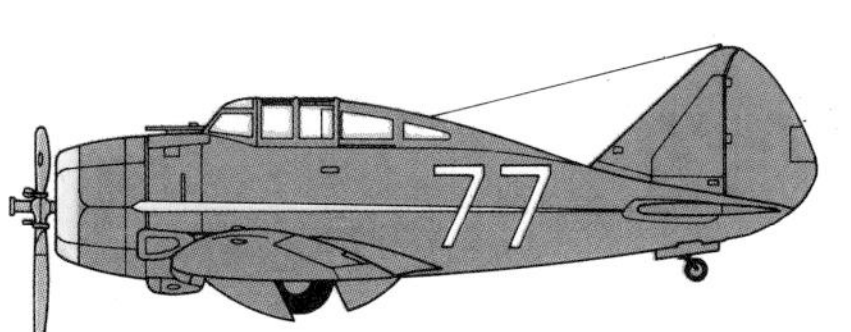

Seversky Sev-S2 (USA)

Fiat R.700 (I)

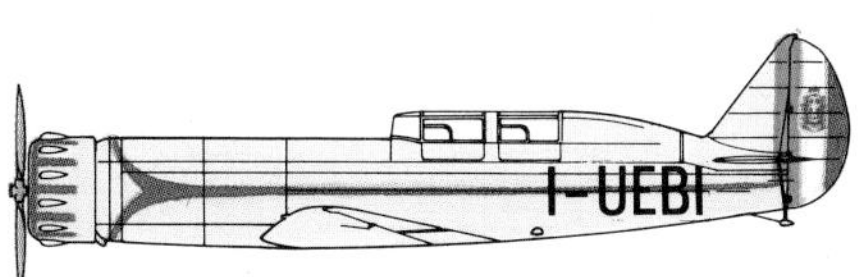

Nardi F.N.305D (I)

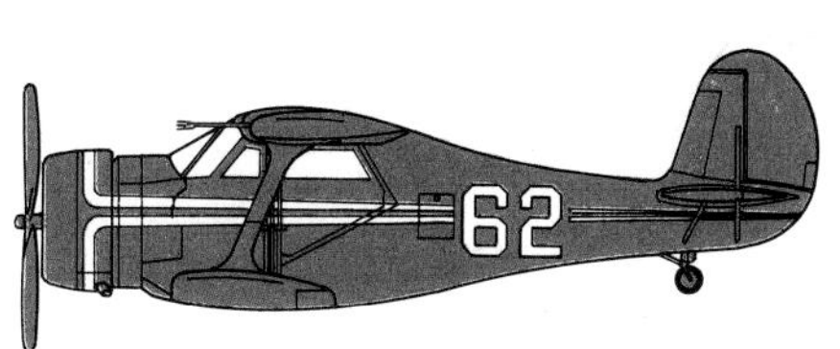

Beech C-17R (USA)

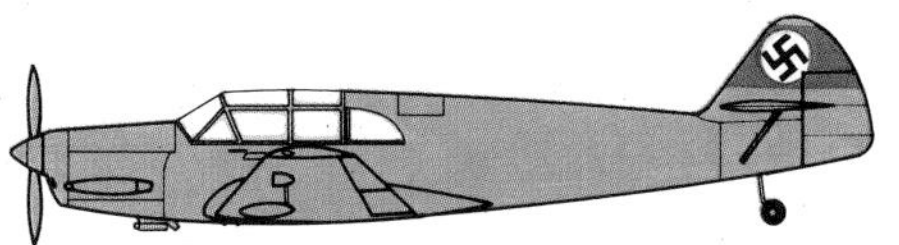

Messerschmitt Bf 108B Taifun (D)

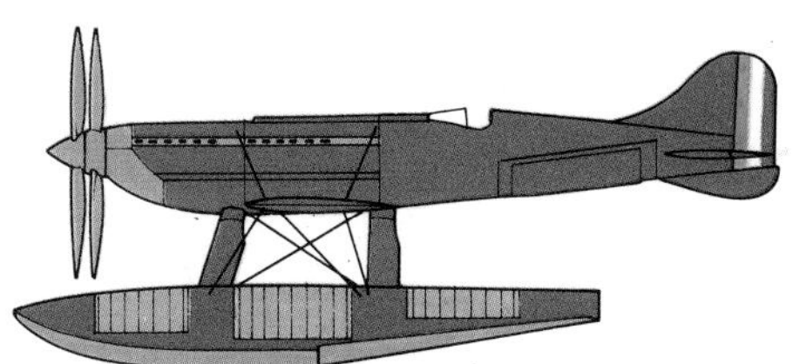

Macchi-Castoldi MC.72 (I)

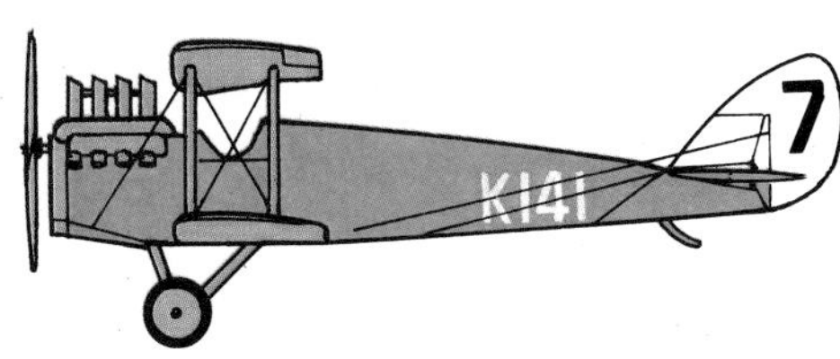

Airco D.H.4R (GB)

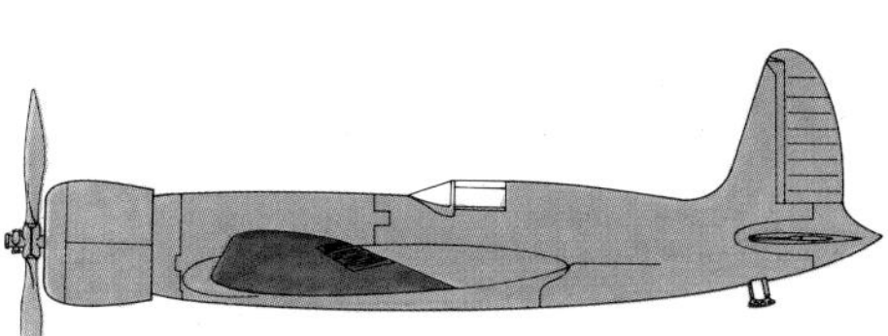

Hughes H-1 (USA)

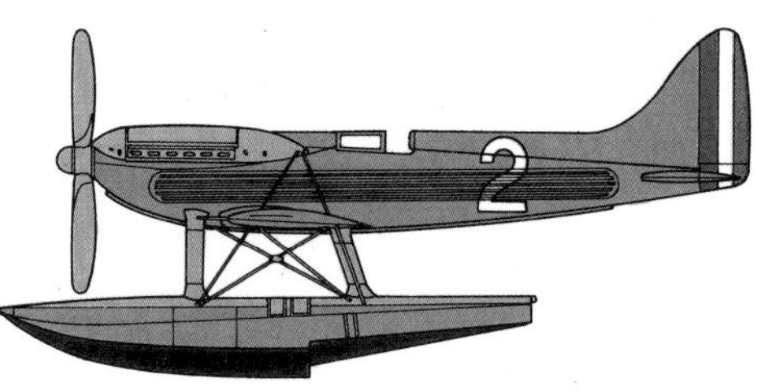

Supermarine S.6 (GB)

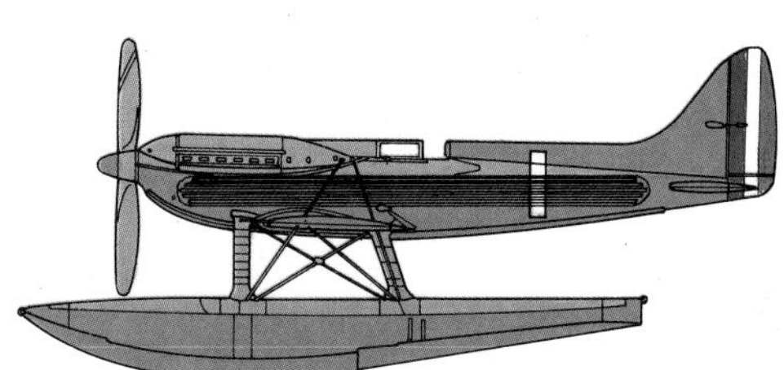

Supermarine S.6B (GB)

de Havilland D.H.88 Comet (GB)

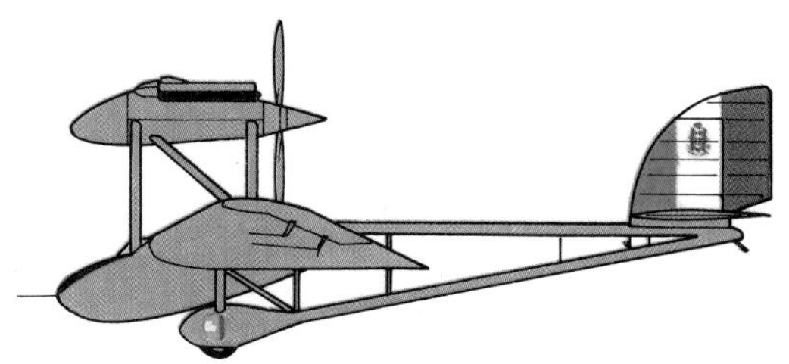

Savoia Marchetti S.M.64 (I)

Savoia S.12bis (I)

Breguet XIX Super TR (F)

Tupolev ANT-25 (USSR)

Blériot 110 (F)

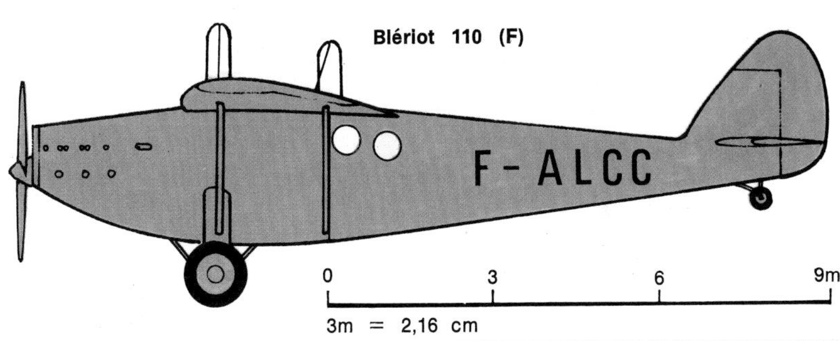

1919

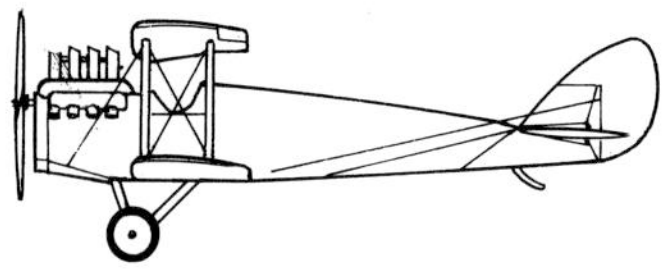

Airco D.H.4R (GB)

1920

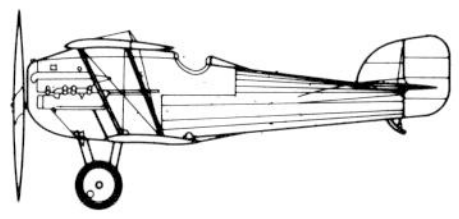

Martinsyde Semiquaver (GB)

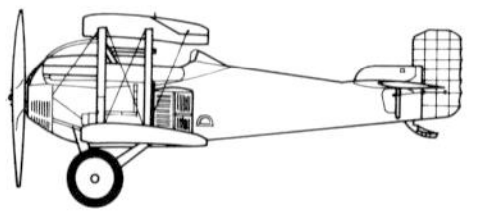

Thomas-Morse MB-3 (USA)

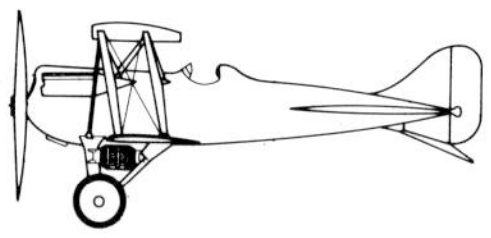

Nieuport 29V (F)

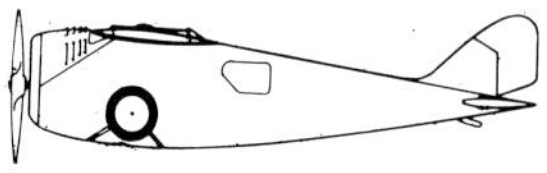

Dayton-Wright R.B. (USA)

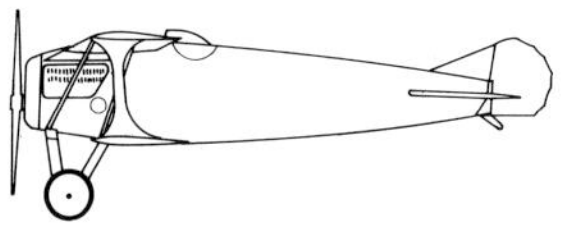

Spad-Herbemont S.20bis (F)

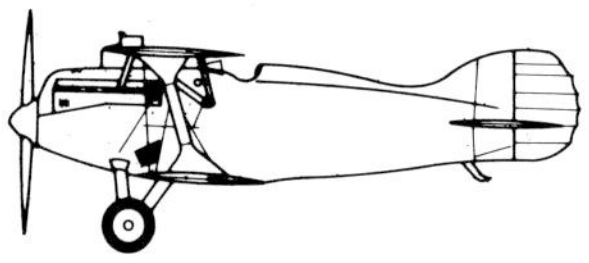

Verville VCP-R (USA)

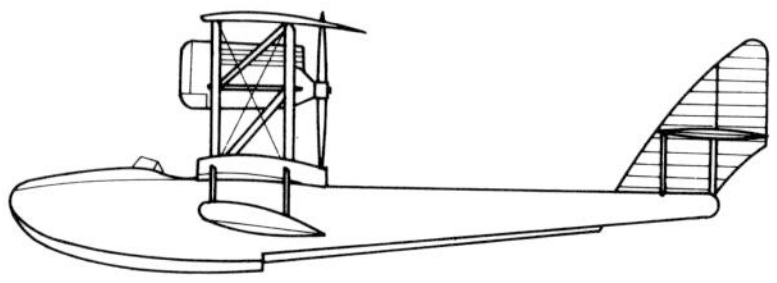

Savoia S.12bis (I)

1921

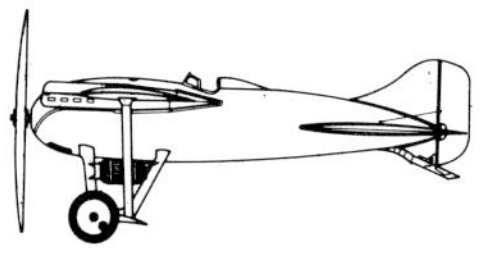

Nieuport-Delage 1921 (F)

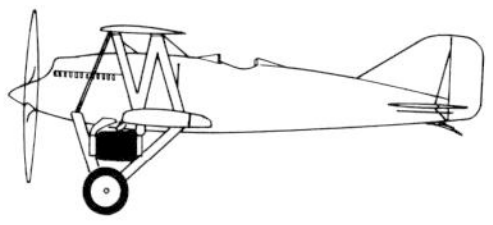

Curtiss CR-1 (USA)

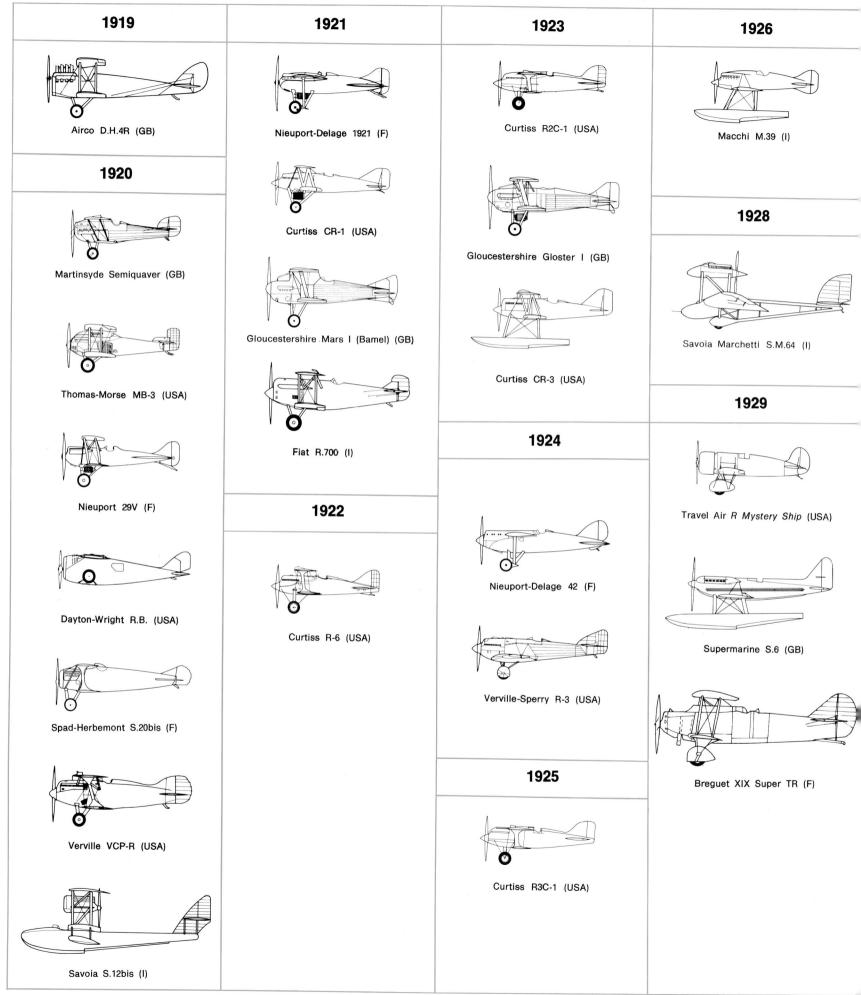

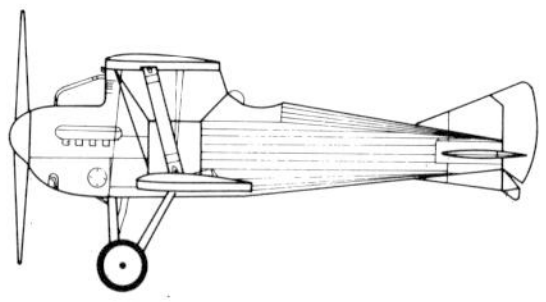

Gloucestershire Mars I (Bamel) (GB)

Fiat R.700 (I)

1922

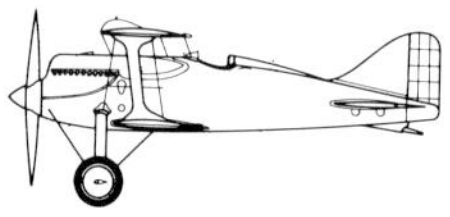

Curtiss R-6 (USA)

1923

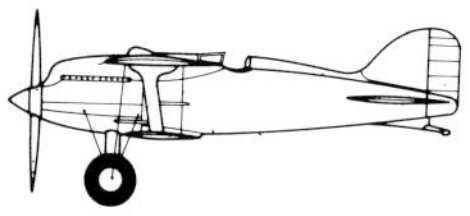

Curtiss R2C-1 (USA)

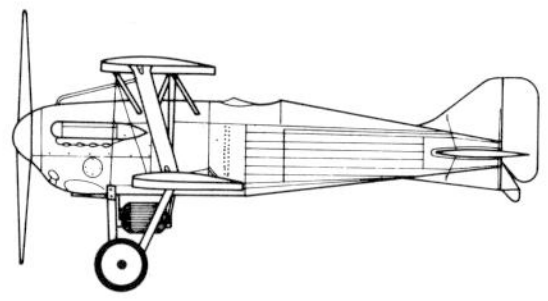

Gloucestershire Gloster I (GB)

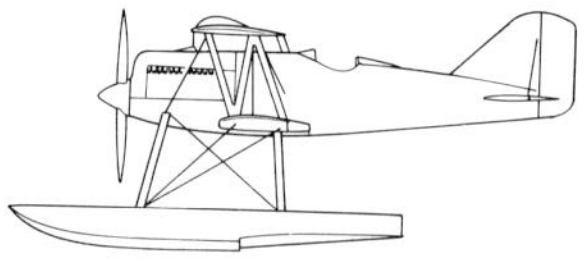

Curtiss CR-3 (USA)

1924

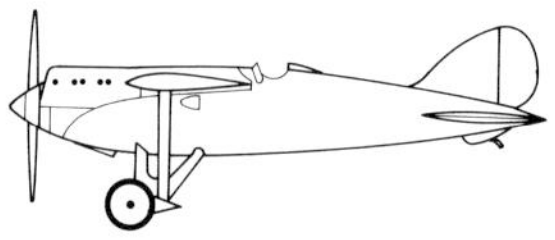

Nieuport-Delage 42 (F)

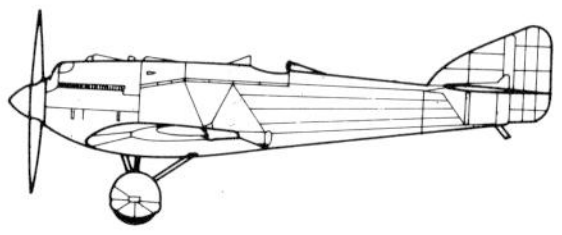

Verville-Sperry R-3 (USA)

1925

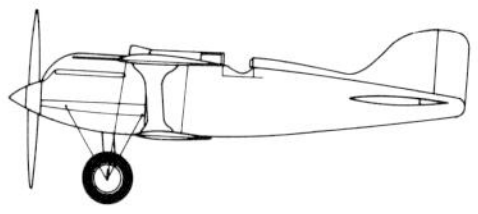

Curtiss R3C-1 (USA)

1926

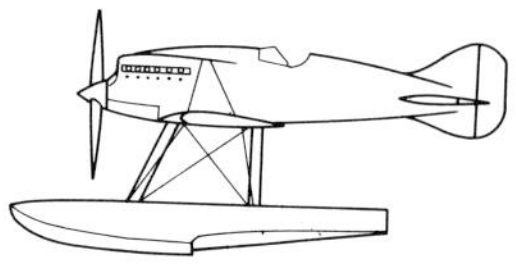

Macchi M.39 (I)

1928

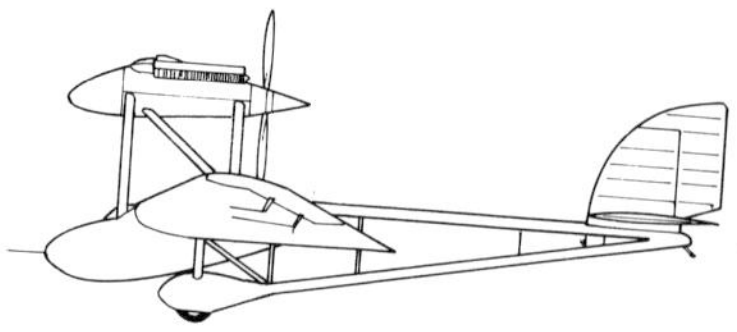

Savoia Marchetti S.M.64 (I)

1929

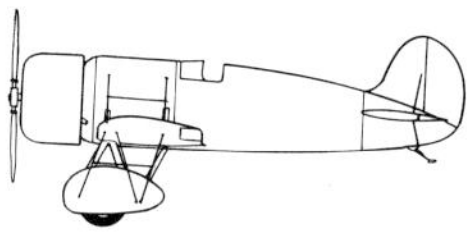

Travel Air R *Mystery Ship* (USA)

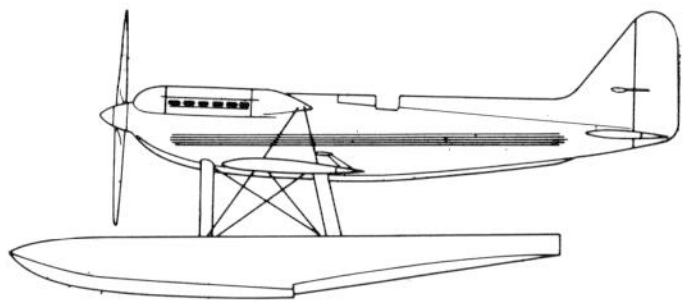

Supermarine S.6 (GB)

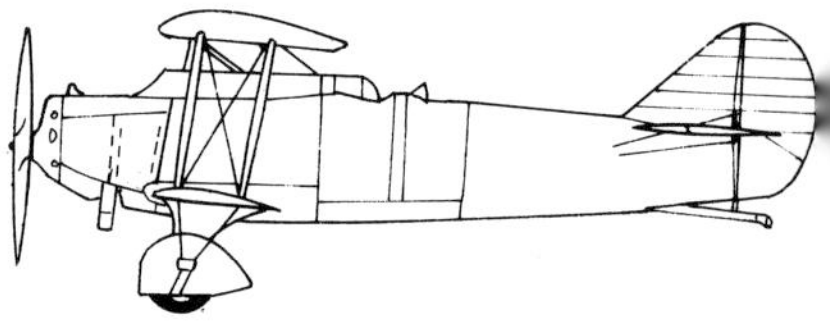

Breguet XIX Super TR (F)

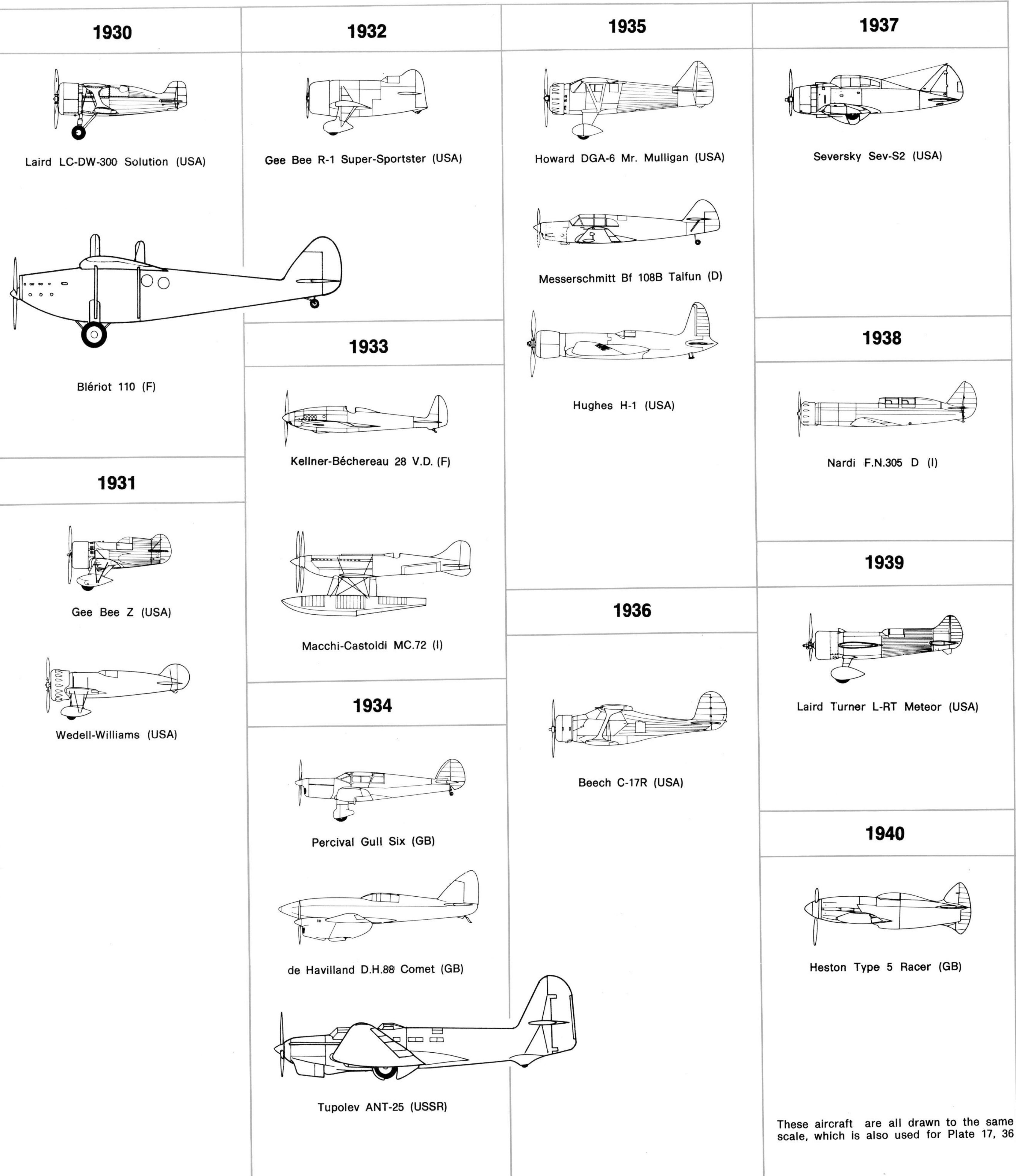
1930
Laird LC-DW-300 Solution (USA)
Blériot 110 (F)
1931
Gee Bee Z (USA)
Wedell-Williams (USA)
1932
Gee Bee R-1 Super-Sportster (USA)
1933
Kellner-Béchereau 28 V.D. (F)
Macchi-Castoldi MC.72 (I)
1934
Percival Gull Six (GB)
de Havilland D.H.88 Comet (GB)
Tupolev ANT-25 (USSR)
1935
Howard DGA-6 Mr. Mulligan (USA)
Messerschmitt Bf 108B Taifun (D)
Hughes H-1 (USA)
1936
Beech C-17R (USA)
1937
Seversky Sev-S2 (USA)
1938
Nardi F.N.305 D (I)
1939
Laird Turner L-RT Meteor (USA)
1940
Heston Type 5 Racer (GB)
These aircraft are all drawn to the same scale, which is also used for Plate 17, 36

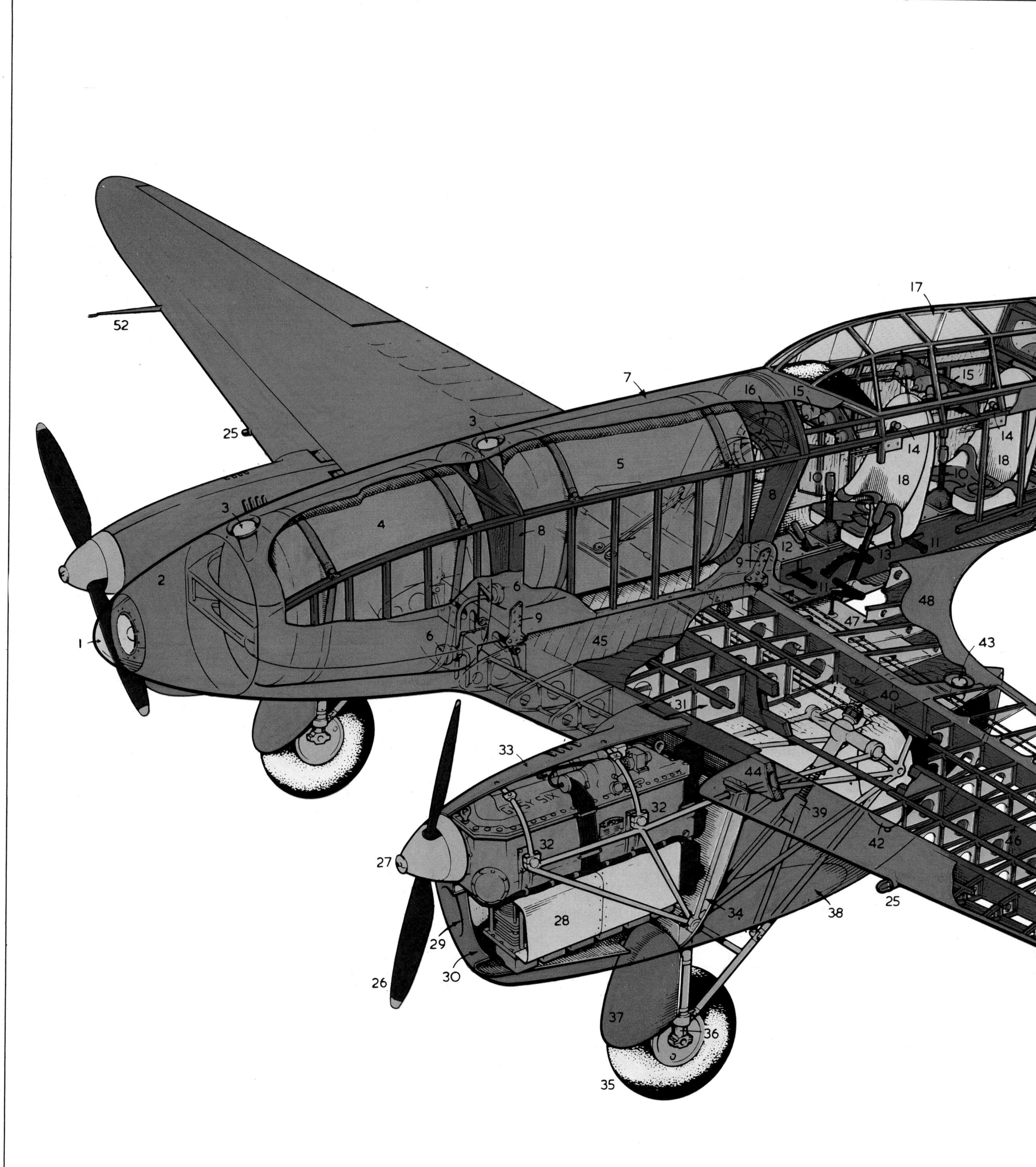
52
7
17
16
15
15
14
14
18
18
10
10
25
3
3
5
4
8
8
2
6
9
9
12
13
11
11
48
47
1
6
45
43
40
31
33
44
32
32
39
42
46
27
28
34
38
25
29
30
26
37
36
35

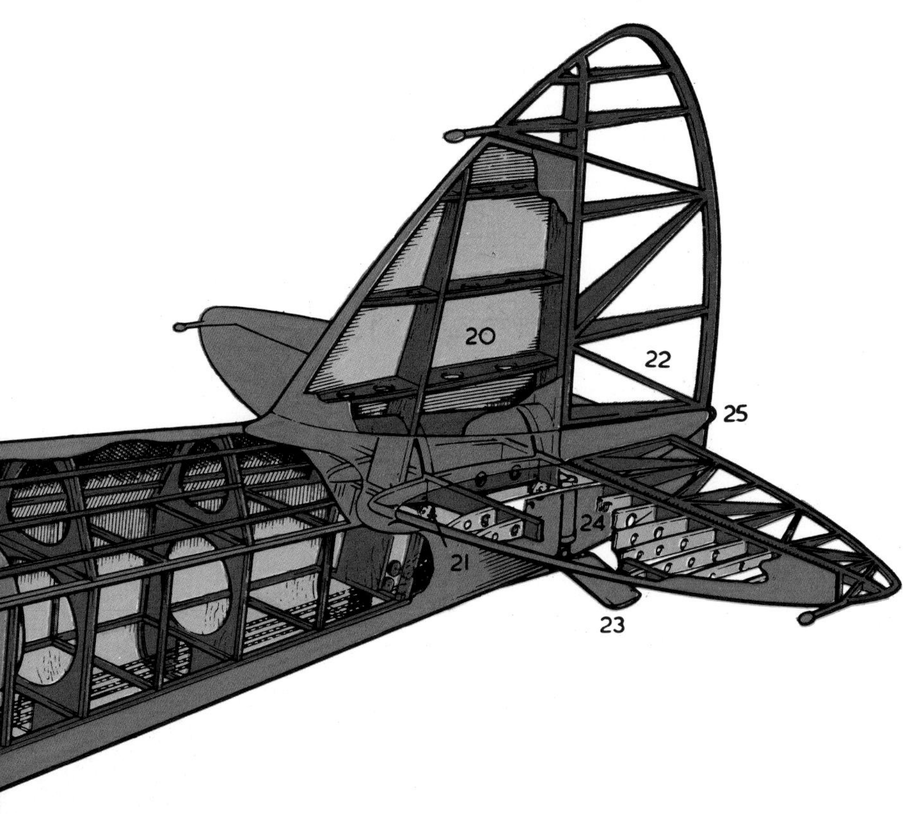

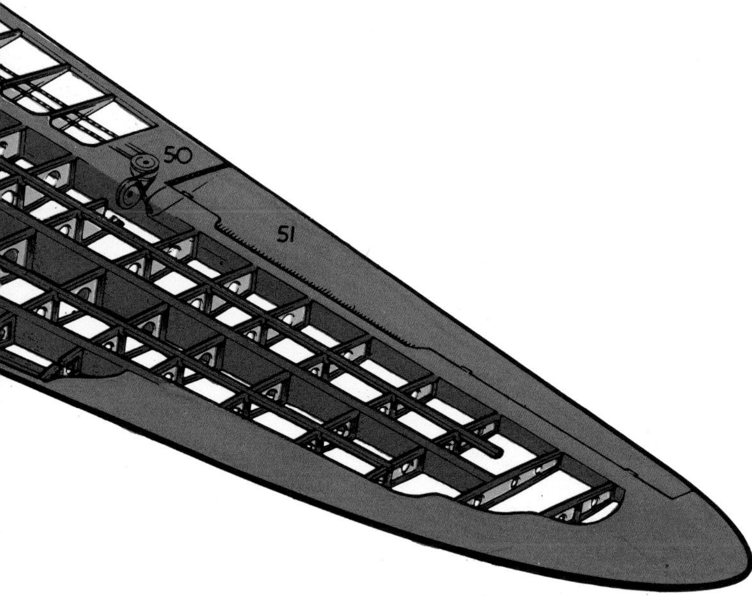

de Havilland D.H.88 Comet

1 landing light
2 detachable nose-cone
3 fuel tank fillers
4 front fuel tank, capacity 128 Imp gal (581 l)
5 midship fuel tank, capacity 110 Imp gal (500 l)
6 fuel jettison valves
7 fuselage skin, diagonally cross-laminated spruce
8 main bulkheads, plywood
9 fuselage/wing attachment points
10 control columns
11 rudder bars
12 wheel-brake lever
13 flap control lever
14 throttle controls
15 front and rear instrument panels
16 undercarriage retraction handwheel
17 one-piece canopy, hinged to starboard
18 fixed tandem seats, aluminum
19 rear fuel tank, capacity 20 Imp gal (91 l)
20 plywood-covered fin and tailplane
21 tailplane attachment points
22 rudder and elevators, plywood-covered
23 fully castoring tailskid
24 tailskid shock absorber
25 navigation lights
26 Ratier two-pitch propeller, 78.75-in (2-m) diameter
27 pitch control disc
28 230 hp de Havilland Gipsy Six R engine
29 carburetor air intake
30 cooling air intake
31 exhaust air outlet
32 four-point engine mounting
33 two-piece detachable aluminum engine cowling
34 aluminum and asbestos engine firewall
35 landing wheel, Dunlop 26.5 x 8.5
36 shock absorber, compressed rubber blocks
37 wheel fairing, retracts with wheel
38 one-piece rear aluminum fairing
39 retracting fork
40 screw-jack cable drum
41 screw-jack endless cable
42 oil tank, capacity 6.9 Imp gal (31 l)
43 oil tank filler
44 front, center and rear spars, plywood webs and spruce flanges
45 wing skins, diagonally cross-laminated spruce
46 wing ribs, birch plywood
47 split flaps
48 plywood-covered trailing edge
49 fabric-covered trailing edge
50 aileron control linkage
51 plywood-covered aileron, Frise type
52 pitot tube

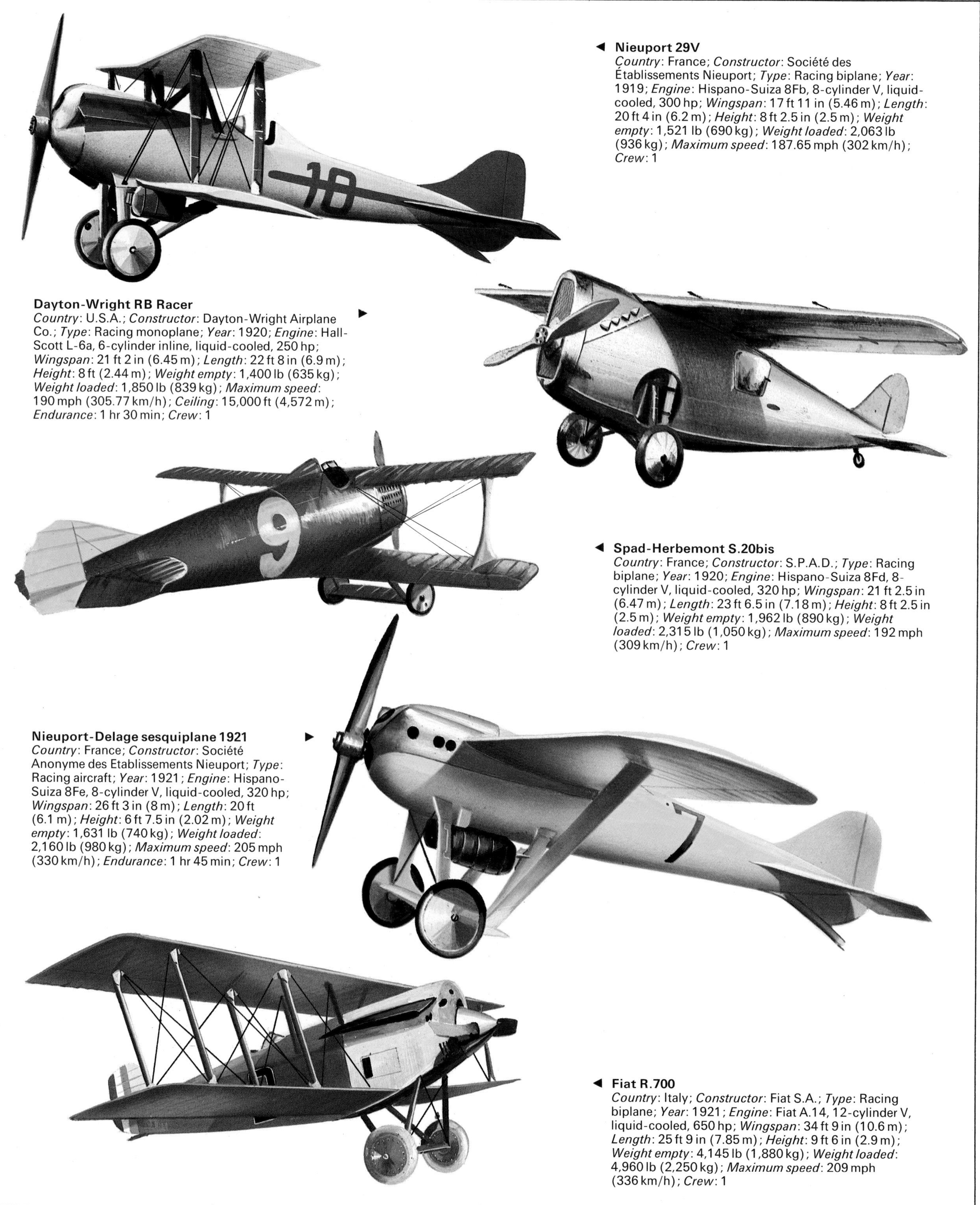

◄ **Nieuport 29V**
Country: France; *Constructor*: Société des Établissements Nieuport; *Type*: Racing biplane; *Year*: 1919; *Engine*: Hispano-Suiza 8Fb, 8-cylinder V, liquid-cooled, 300 hp; *Wingspan*: 17 ft 11 in (5.46 m); *Length*: 20 ft 4 in (6.2 m); *Height*: 8 ft 2.5 in (2.5 m); *Weight empty*: 1,521 lb (690 kg); *Weight loaded*: 2,063 lb (936 kg); *Maximum speed*: 187.65 mph (302 km/h); *Crew*: 1

Dayton-Wright RB Racer ►
Country: U.S.A.; *Constructor*: Dayton-Wright Airplane Co.; *Type*: Racing monoplane; *Year*: 1920; *Engine*: Hall-Scott L-6a, 6-cylinder inline, liquid-cooled, 250 hp; *Wingspan*: 21 ft 2 in (6.45 m); *Length*: 22 ft 8 in (6.9 m); *Height*: 8 ft (2.44 m); *Weight empty*: 1,400 lb (635 kg); *Weight loaded*: 1,850 lb (839 kg); *Maximum speed*: 190 mph (305.77 km/h); *Ceiling*: 15,000 ft (4,572 m); *Endurance*: 1 hr 30 min; *Crew*: 1

◄ **Spad-Herbemont S.20bis**
Country: France; *Constructor*: S.P.A.D.; *Type*: Racing biplane; *Year*: 1920; *Engine*: Hispano-Suiza 8Fd, 8-cylinder V, liquid-cooled, 320 hp; *Wingspan*: 21 ft 2.5 in (6.47 m); *Length*: 23 ft 6.5 in (7.18 m); *Height*: 8 ft 2.5 in (2.5 m); *Weight empty*: 1,962 lb (890 kg); *Weight loaded*: 2,315 lb (1,050 kg); *Maximum speed*: 192 mph (309 km/h); *Crew*: 1

Nieuport-Delage sesquiplane 1921 ►
Country: France; *Constructor*: Société Anonyme des Etablissements Nieuport; *Type*: Racing aircraft; *Year*: 1921; *Engine*: Hispano-Suiza 8Fe, 8-cylinder V, liquid-cooled, 320 hp; *Wingspan*: 26 ft 3 in (8 m); *Length*: 20 ft (6.1 m); *Height*: 6 ft 7.5 in (2.02 m); *Weight empty*: 1,631 lb (740 kg); *Weight loaded*: 2,160 lb (980 kg); *Maximum speed*: 205 mph (330 km/h); *Endurance*: 1 hr 45 min; *Crew*: 1

◄ **Fiat R.700**
Country: Italy; *Constructor*: Fiat S.A.; *Type*: Racing biplane; *Year*: 1921; *Engine*: Fiat A.14, 12-cylinder V, liquid-cooled, 650 hp; *Wingspan*: 34 ft 9 in (10.6 m); *Length*: 25 ft 9 in (7.85 m); *Height*: 9 ft 6 in (2.9 m); *Weight empty*: 4,145 lb (1,880 kg); *Weight loaded*: 4,960 lb (2,250 kg); *Maximum speed*: 209 mph (336 km/h); *Crew*: 1

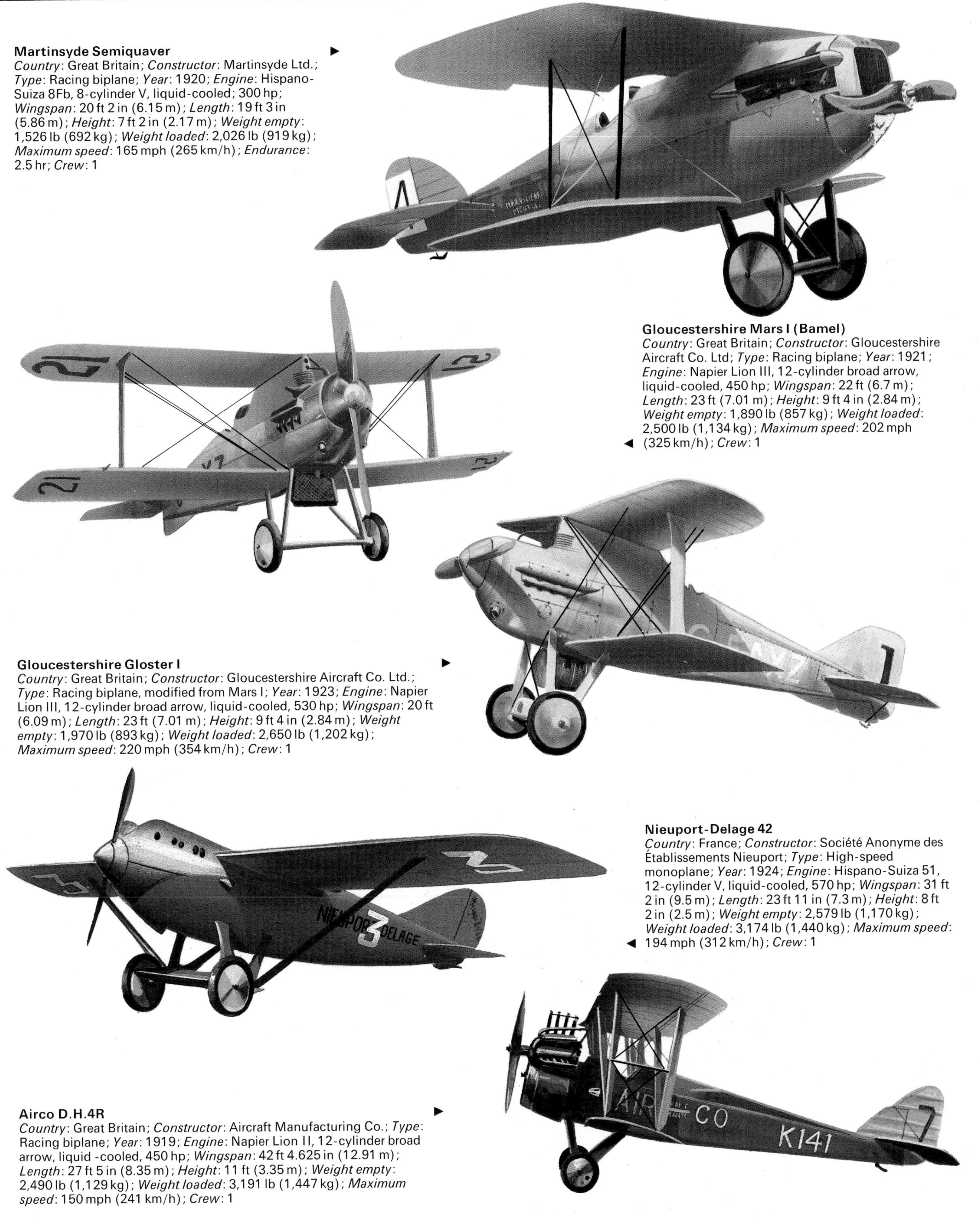

Martinsyde Semiquaver ►
Country: Great Britain; *Constructor*: Martinsyde Ltd.; *Type*: Racing biplane; *Year*: 1920; *Engine*: Hispano-Suiza 8Fb, 8-cylinder V, liquid-cooled; 300 hp; *Wingspan*: 20 ft 2 in (6.15 m); *Length*: 19 ft 3 in (5.86 m); *Height*: 7 ft 2 in (2.17 m); *Weight empty*: 1,526 lb (692 kg); *Weight loaded*: 2,026 lb (919 kg); *Maximum speed*: 165 mph (265 km/h); *Endurance*: 2.5 hr; *Crew*: 1

Gloucestershire Mars I (Bamel)
Country: Great Britain; *Constructor*: Gloucestershire Aircraft Co. Ltd; *Type*: Racing biplane; *Year*: 1921; *Engine*: Napier Lion III, 12-cylinder broad arrow, liquid-cooled, 450 hp; *Wingspan*: 22 ft (6.7 m); *Length*: 23 ft (7.01 m); *Height*: 9 ft 4 in (2.84 m); *Weight empty*: 1,890 lb (857 kg); *Weight loaded*: 2,500 lb (1,134 kg); *Maximum speed*: 202 mph ◄ (325 km/h); *Crew*: 1

Gloucestershire Gloster I ►
Country: Great Britain; *Constructor*: Gloucestershire Aircraft Co. Ltd.; *Type*: Racing biplane, modified from Mars I; *Year*: 1923; *Engine*: Napier Lion III, 12-cylinder broad arrow, liquid-cooled, 530 hp; *Wingspan*: 20 ft (6.09 m); *Length*: 23 ft (7.01 m); *Height*: 9 ft 4 in (2.84 m); *Weight empty*: 1,970 lb (893 kg); *Weight loaded*: 2,650 lb (1,202 kg); *Maximum speed*: 220 mph (354 km/h); *Crew*: 1

Nieuport-Delage 42
Country: France; *Constructor*: Société Anonyme des Établissements Nieuport; *Type*: High-speed monoplane; *Year*: 1924; *Engine*: Hispano-Suiza 51, 12-cylinder V, liquid-cooled, 570 hp; *Wingspan*: 31 ft 2 in (9.5 m); *Length*: 23 ft 11 in (7.3 m); *Height*: 8 ft 2 in (2.5 m); *Weight empty*: 2,579 lb (1,170 kg); *Weight loaded*: 3,174 lb (1,440 kg); *Maximum speed*: ◄ 194 mph (312 km/h); *Crew*: 1

Airco D.H.4R ►
Country: Great Britain; *Constructor*: Aircraft Manufacturing Co.; *Type*: Racing biplane; *Year*: 1919; *Engine*: Napier Lion II, 12-cylinder broad arrow, liquid-cooled, 450 hp; *Wingspan*: 42 ft 4.625 in (12.91 m); *Length*: 27 ft 5 in (8.35 m); *Height*: 11 ft (3.35 m); *Weight empty*: 2,490 lb (1,129 kg); *Weight loaded*: 3,191 lb (1,447 kg); *Maximum speed*: 150 mph (241 km/h); *Crew*: 1

Savoia S.13bis
Country: Italy; *Constructor*: Società Idrovolanti Alta Italia; *Type*: Racing flying boat; *Year*: 1919; *Engine*: Isotta-Fraschini V–6, liquid-cooled, 6-cylinder inline, 250 hp; *Wingspan*: 26 ft 7 in (8.1 m); *Length*: 27 ft 5 in (8.36 m); *Height*: 10 ft (3.05 m); *Weight empty*: 1,609 lb (730 kg); *Weight loaded*: 2,072 lb (940 kg); *Maximum speed*: 151 mph (243 km/h); *Crew*: 1

Savoia S.12bis
Country: Italy; *Constructor*: Società Idrovolanti Alta Italia; *Type*: Racing flying boat; *Year*: 1920; *Engine*: Ansaldo-San Giorgio 4E-29 V–12, liquid-cooled, 550 hp; *Wingspan*: 38 ft 5.5 in (11.72 m); *Length*: 32 ft 10 in (10 m); *Height*: 12 ft 5.5 in (3.8 m); *Weight empty*: 3,438 lb (1,560 kg); *Weight loaded*: 5,202 lb (2,360 kg); *Maximum speed*: 138 mph (222 km/h); *Crew*: 1

Macchi M.7bis
Country: Italy; *Constructor*: Società Anonima Macchi; *Type*: Racing flying boat; *Year*; 1921; *Engine*: Isotta-Fraschini Semi-Asso, 6-cylinder inline, liquid-cooled, 260 hp; *Wingspan*: 25 ft 5 in (7.75 m); *Length*: 22 ft 3 in (6.78 m); *Height*: 9 ft 9 in (2.97 m); *Weight empty*: 1,709 lb (775 kg); *Weight loaded*: 2,270 lb (1,030 kg); *Maximum speed*: 160 mph (257 km/h); *Crew*: 1

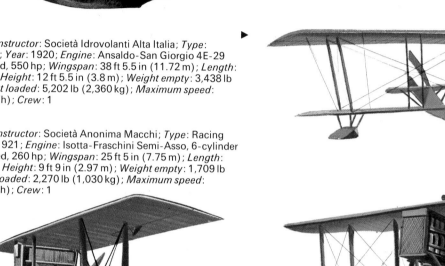

Supermarine Sea Lion II
Country: Great Britain; *Constructor*: The Supermarine Aviation Works Ltd.; *Type*: Racing flying boat; *Year*: 1922; *Engine*: Napier Lion II, 12-cylinder broad arrow, liquid-cooled, 450 hp; *Wingspan*: 32 ft (9.75 m); *Length*: 24 ft 9 in (7.54 m); *Height*: 12 ft (3.65 m); *Weight empty*: 2,115 lb (959 kg); *Weight loaded*: 2,850 lb (1,292 kg); *Maximum speed*: 160 mph (257 km/h); *Endurance*: 3 hr; *Crew*: 1; Converted from Sea King II.

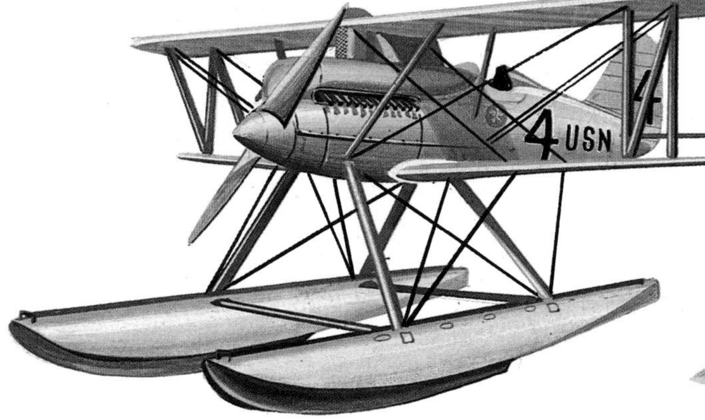

Curtiss CR-3
Country: U.S.A.; *Constructor*: Curtiss Aeroplane and Motor Co.; *Type*: Racing biplane; *Year*: 1923; *Engine*: Curtiss D–12, 12-cylinder V, liquid-cooled, 450 hp; *Wingspan*: 22 ft 8 in (6.9 m); *Length*: 25 ft (7.63 m); *Height*: 10 ft (3.05 m); *Weight empty*: 2,119 lb (961 kg); *Weight loaded*: 2,746 lb (1,246 kg); *Maximum speed*: 188 mph (302 km/h); *Range*: 520 miles (840 km); *Crew*: 1

Curtiss R3C–2
Country: U.S.A.; *Constructor*: Curtiss Aeroplane and Motor Co.; *Type*: Racing biplane; *Year*: 1925; *Engine*: Curtiss V–1400, 12-cylinder V, liquid-cooled, 565 hp; *Wingspan*: 22 ft (6.7 m); *Length*: 22 ft (6.7 m); *Height*: 10 ft 4 in (3.14 m); *Weight empty*: 2,135 lb (968 kg); *Weight loaded*: 2,738 lb (1,242 kg); *Maximum speed*: 245 mph (394 km/h); *Ceiling*: 21,200 ft (6,460 m); *Range*: 290 miles (467 km); *Crew*: 1

▲

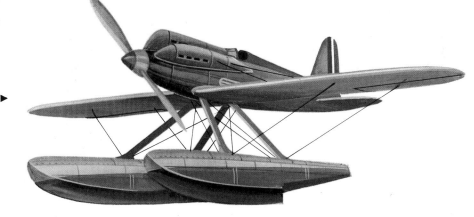

Macchi M.39
Country: Italy; *Constructor*: Aeronautica Macchi; *Type*: Racing seaplane; *Year*: 1926; *Engine*: Fiat A.S.2, 12-cylinder V, liquid-cooled, 800 hp; *Wingspan*: 30 ft 4.5 in (9.26 m); *Length*: 22 ft 1 in (6.73 m); *Height*: 9 ft 9 in (2.97 m); *Weight empty*: 2,772 lb (1,257 kg); *Weight loaded*: 3,465 lb (1,572 kg); *Maximum speed*: 272.13 mph (439.44 km/h); *Crew*: 1

Supermarine S.5 ►
Country: Great Britain; *Constructor*: The Supermarine Aviation Works Ltd.; *Type*: Racing seaplane; *Year*: 1927; *Engine*: Napier Lion VIIB, 12-cylinder broad arrow, liquid-cooled, 875 hp; *Wingspan*: 26 ft 9 in (8.15 m); *Length*: 24 ft 3.5 in (7.4 m); *Height*: 11 ft 1 in (3.38 m); *Weight empty*: 2,680 lb (1,215 kg); *Weight loaded*: 3,242 lb (1,470 kg); *Maximum speed*: 319.57 mph (514.29 km/h); *Crew*: 1

Supermarine S.6B
Country: Great Britain; *Constructor*: The Supermarine Aviation Works Ltd.; *Type*: Racing seaplane; *Year*: 1931; *Engine*: Rolls-Royce R, 12-cylinder V, liquid-cooled, 2,300 hp; *Wingspan*: 30 ft (9.14 m); *Length*: 28 ft 10 in (8.79 m); *Height*: 12 ft 3 in (3.73 m); *Weight empty*: 4,590 lb (2,082 kg); *Weight loaded*: 6,086 lb (2,760 kg); *Maximum speed*: 407.5 mph (655.79 km/h); *Crew*: 1

Verville VCP–R
Country: U.S.A.; *Constructor*: Verville; *Type*: Racing biplane; *Year*: 1920; *Engine*: Packard 1A–2025, 12-cylinder V, liquid-cooled, 638 hp; *Wingspan*: 27 ft 6 in (8.38 m); *Length*: 24 ft 2 in (7.36 m); *Height*: 8 ft 8 in (2.64 m); *Weight empty*: 2,450 lb (1,111 kg); *Weight loaded*: 3,200 lb (1,451 kg); *Maximum speed*: 186 mph (299 km/h); *Endurance*: 1 hr 15 min; *Crew*: 1

Thomas-Morse MB–3
Country: U.S.A.; *Constructor*: Thomas-Morse Aircraft Co.; *Type*: Fighter; *Year*: 1919; *Engine*: Wright H–2 Hunter, 8-cylinder V, liquid-cooled, 358 hp; *Wingspan*: 26 ft (7.92 m); *Length*: 20 ft (6.09 m); *Height*: 8 ft 5.5 in (2.56 m); *Weight empty*: 1,505 lb (683 kg); *Weight loaded*: 2,095 lb (950 kg); *Maximum speed*: 164 mph (264 km/h); *Ceiling*: 19,500 ft (5.945 m); *Endurance*: 3 hr; *Crew*: 1

Curtiss CR–1
Country: U.S.A.; *Constructor*: Curtiss Aeroplane and Motor Co.; *Type*: Racing biplane; *Year*: 1921; *Engine*: Curtiss CD–12, 12-cylinder V, liquid-cooled, 425 hp; *Wingspan*: 22 ft 8 in (6.3 m); *Length*: 21 ft (6.4 m); *Height*: 8 ft 4.5 in (2.55 m); *Weight empty*: 1,665 lb (755 kg); *Weight loaded*: 2,095 lb (950 kg); *Maximum speed*: 185 mph (297.72 km/h); *Service ceiling*: 24,000 ft (7,315 m); *Range*: 235 miles (378 km); *Crew*: 1

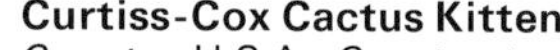

Curtiss-Cox Cactus Kitten
Country: U.S.A.; *Constructor*: Curtiss Aeroplane and Motor Co.; *Type*: Racing triplane; *Year*: 1921; *Engine*: Curtiss C–12, 12-cylinder V, liquid-cooled, 427 hp; *Wingspan*: 20 ft (6.09 m); *Length*: 19 ft 3 in (5.86 m); *Maximum speed*: 196 mph (315 km/h); *Ceiling*: 25,000 ft (7,600 m); *Endurance*: 1 hr 10 min; *Crew*: 1

Curtiss R–6
Country: U.S.A.; *Constructor*: Curtiss Aeroplane and Motor Co.; *Type*: Racing biplane; *Year*: 1922; *Engine*: Curtiss D–12, 12-cylinder V, liquid-cooled, 460 hp; *Wingspan*: 19 ft (5.79 m); *Length*: 18 ft 11 in (5.75 m); *Height*: 7 ft 11 in (2.41 m); *Weight empty*: 1,454 lb (659 kg); *Weight loaded*: 1,950 lb (884 kg); *Maximum speed*: 236 mph (380 km/h); *Range*: 283 miles (455 km); *Crew*: 1

Curtiss R2C–1
Country: U.S.A.; *Constructor*: Curtiss Aeroplane and Motor Co.; *Type*: Racing biplane; *Year*: 1923; *Engine*: Curtiss D–12A, 12-cylinder V, liquid-cooled, 507 hp; *Wingspan*: 22 ft (6.7 m); *Length*: 19 ft 8.5 in (6 m); *Height*: 6 ft 10 in (2.08 m); *Weight empty*: 1,677 lb (761 kg); *Weight loaded*: 2,071 lb (939 kg); *Maximum speed*: 266 mph (428 km/h); *Ceiling*: 31,800 ft (9,692 m) estimated; *Endurance*: 42 min; *Crew*: 1 ▼

Verville-Sperry R–3
Country: U.S.A.; *Constructor*: Verville; *Type*: Racing monoplane; *Year*: 1922; *Engine*: Curtiss D–12A, 12-cylinder V, liquid-cooled, 520 hp; *Wingspan*: 30 ft 7 in (9.32 m); *Length*: 23 ft 6 in (7.16 m); *Height*: 7 ft 1 in (2.16 m); *Weight empty*: 2,006 lb (910 kg); *Weight loaded*: 2,478 lb (1,124 kg); *Maximum speed*: 235 mph (378 km/h); *Crew*: 1 — ◄ (*Figures for modified aircraft 1923–24*)

Curtiss R3C–1 ►
Country: U.S.A.; *Constructor*: Curtiss Aeroplane and Motor Co.; *Type*: Racing biplane; *Year*: 1925; *Engine*: Curtiss V–1400, 12-cylinder V, liquid-cooled, 565 hp; *Wingspan*: 22 ft (6.71 m); *Length*: 20 ft (6.09 m); *Height*: 6 ft 9.5 in (2.07 m); *Weight empty*: 1,792 lb (813 kg); *Weight loaded*: 2,150 lb (975 kg); *Maximum speed*: 263 mph (423 km/h); *Ceiling*: 26,400 ft (8,046 m); *Range*: 216 miles (348 km); *Crew*: 1

◄ **Travel Air R *Mystery Ship***
Country: U.S.A.; *Constructor*: Travel Air Manufacturing Co.; *Type*: Racing monoplane; *Year*: 1929; *Engine*: Wright R–975 Whirlwind, 9-cylinder radial, air-cooled, 400 hp; *Wingspan*: 29 ft 2 in (8.89 m); *Length*: 20 ft 2 in (6.15 m); *Height*: 7 ft 9 in (2.36 m); *Weight empty*: 1,475 lb (670 kg); *Weight loaded*: 1,940 lb (880 kg); *Maximum speed*: 235 mph (378 km/h); *Ceiling*: 30,000 ft (9,145 m); *Range*: 525 miles (845 km); *Crew*: 1

◄ **Laird LC–DW–300 Solution**
Country: U.S.A.; *Constructor*: The E.M. Laird Airplane Co.; *Type*: High-speed biplane; *Year*: 1930; *Engine*: Pratt and Whitney Wasp Jr., 9-cylinder radial, air-cooled, 470 hp; *Wingspan*: 21 ft (6.4 m); *Length*: 19 ft 6 in (5.94 m); *Weight empty*: 1,380 lb (626 kg); *Weight loaded*: 1,895 lb (860 kg); *Maximum speed*: 202 mph (325 km/h); *Crew*: 1

Wedell-Williams
Country: U.S.A.; *Constructor*: Wedell Williams; *Type*: Racing monoplane; *Year*: 1931; *Engine*: Pratt and Whitney Wasp Jr, 9-cylinder radial, air-cooled, 550 hp; *Wingspan*: 26 ft 2 in (7.98 m); *Length*: 21 ft 3 in (6.48 m); *Height*: 8 ft (2.44 m); *Weight empty*: 1,500 lb (680 kg); *Weight loaded*: 2,200 lb (998 kg); *Maximum speed*: 305 mph (491 km/h); *Crew*: 1
▼

▲
Gee Bee Z
Country: U.S.A.; *Constructor*: Granville Brothers Aircraft; *Type*: Racing monoplane; *Year*: 1931; *Engine*: Pratt and Whitney Wasp Jr., 9-cylinder radial, air-cooled, 535 hp; *Wingspan*: 23 ft 6 in (7.16 m); *Length*: 15 ft 1 in (4.6 m); *Weight empty*: 1,400 lb (835 kg); *Weight loaded*: 2,280 lb (1,030 kg); *Maximum speed*: 286 mph (460 km/h); *Range*: 1,000 miles (1,600 km); *Crew*: 1

◄ **Gee Bee R–1 Super-Sportster**
Country: U.S.A.; *Constructor*: Granville Brothers Aircraft; *Type*: Racing monoplane; *Year*: 1932; *Engine*: Pratt and Whitney Hornet, 9-cylinder radial, air-cooled, 900 hp; *Wingspan*: 25 ft (7.62 m); *Length*: 17 ft 9 in (5.41 m); *Height*: 8 ft 1 in (2.47 m); *Weight empty*: 1,840 lb (835 kg); *Weight loaded*: 3,075 lb (1,395 kg); *Maximum speed*: 296.246 mph (476.741 km/h); *Crew*: 1

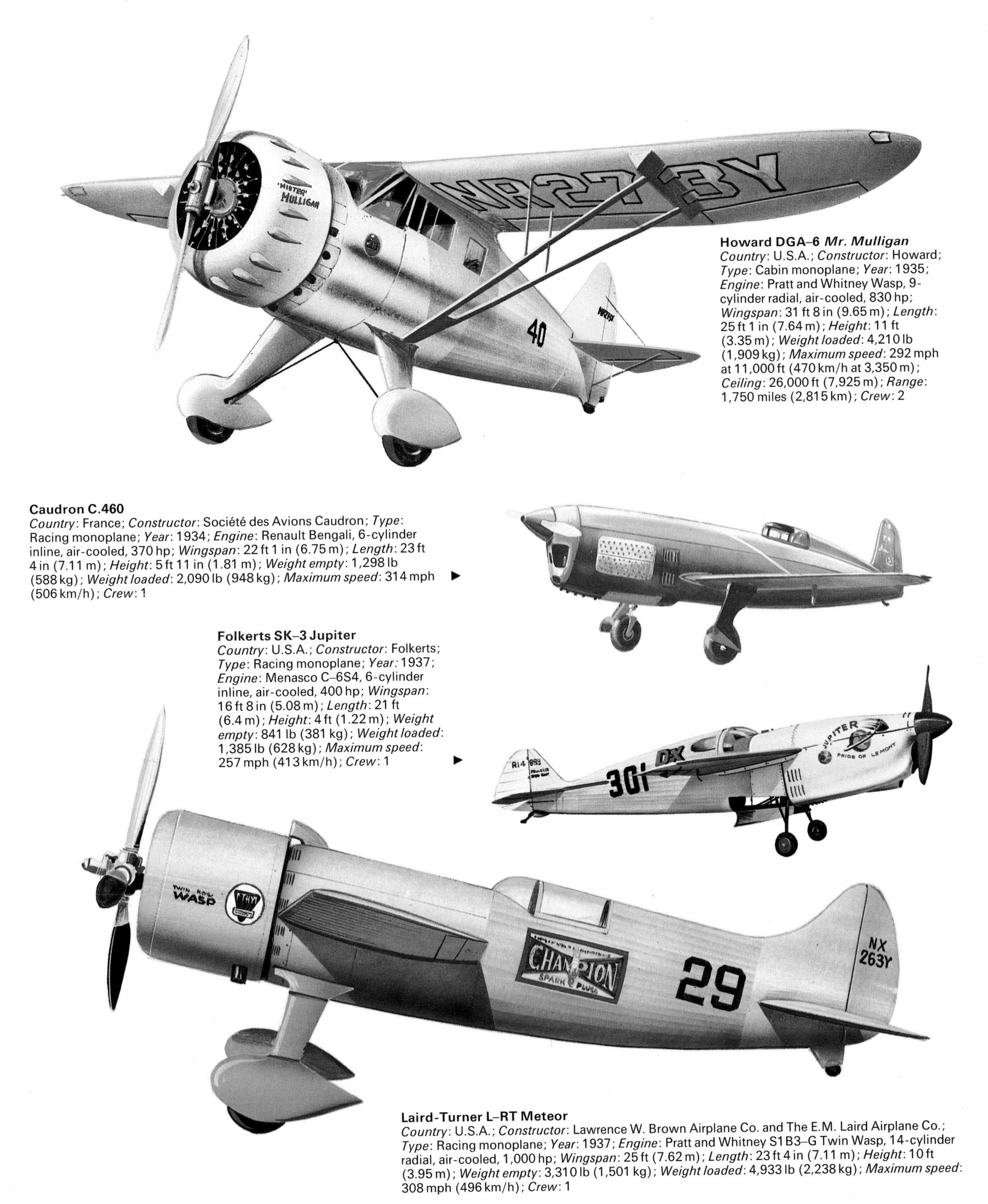

Howard DGA–6 *Mr. Mulligan*
Country: U.S.A.; *Constructor*: Howard; *Type*: Cabin monoplane; *Year*: 1935; *Engine*: Pratt and Whitney Wasp, 9-cylinder radial, air-cooled, 830 hp; *Wingspan*: 31 ft 8 in (9.65 m); *Length*: 25 ft 1 in (7.64 m); *Height*: 11 ft (3.35 m); *Weight loaded*: 4,210 lb (1,909 kg); *Maximum speed*: 292 mph at 11,000 ft (470 km/h at 3,350 m); *Ceiling*: 26,000 ft (7,925 m); *Range*: 1,750 miles (2,815 km); *Crew*: 2

Caudron C.460
Country: France; *Constructor*: Société des Avions Caudron; *Type*: Racing monoplane; *Year*: 1934; *Engine*: Renault Bengali, 6-cylinder inline, air-cooled, 370 hp; *Wingspan*: 22 ft 1 in (6.75 m); *Length*: 23 ft 4 in (7.11 m); *Height*: 5 ft 11 in (1.81 m); *Weight empty*: 1,298 lb (588 kg); *Weight loaded*: 2,090 lb (948 kg); *Maximum speed*: 314 mph (506 km/h); *Crew*: 1 ►

Folkerts SK–3 Jupiter
Country: U.S.A.; *Constructor*: Folkerts; *Type*: Racing monoplane; *Year*: 1937; *Engine*: Menasco C–6S4, 6-cylinder inline, air-cooled, 400 hp; *Wingspan*: 16 ft 8 in (5.08 m); *Length*: 21 ft (6.4 m); *Height*: 4 ft (1.22 m); *Weight empty*: 841 lb (381 kg); *Weight loaded*: 1,385 lb (628 kg); *Maximum speed*: 257 mph (413 km/h); *Crew*: 1 ►

Laird-Turner L–RT Meteor
Country: U.S.A.; *Constructor*: Lawrence W. Brown Airplane Co. and The E.M. Laird Airplane Co.; *Type*: Racing monoplane; *Year*: 1937; *Engine*: Pratt and Whitney S1B3–G Twin Wasp, 14-cylinder radial, air-cooled, 1,000 hp; *Wingspan*: 25 ft (7.62 m); *Length*: 23 ft 4 in (7.11 m); *Height*: 10 ft (3.95 m); *Weight empty*: 3,310 lb (1,501 kg); *Weight loaded*: 4,933 lb (2,238 kg); *Maximum speed*: 308 mph (496 km/h); *Crew*: 1

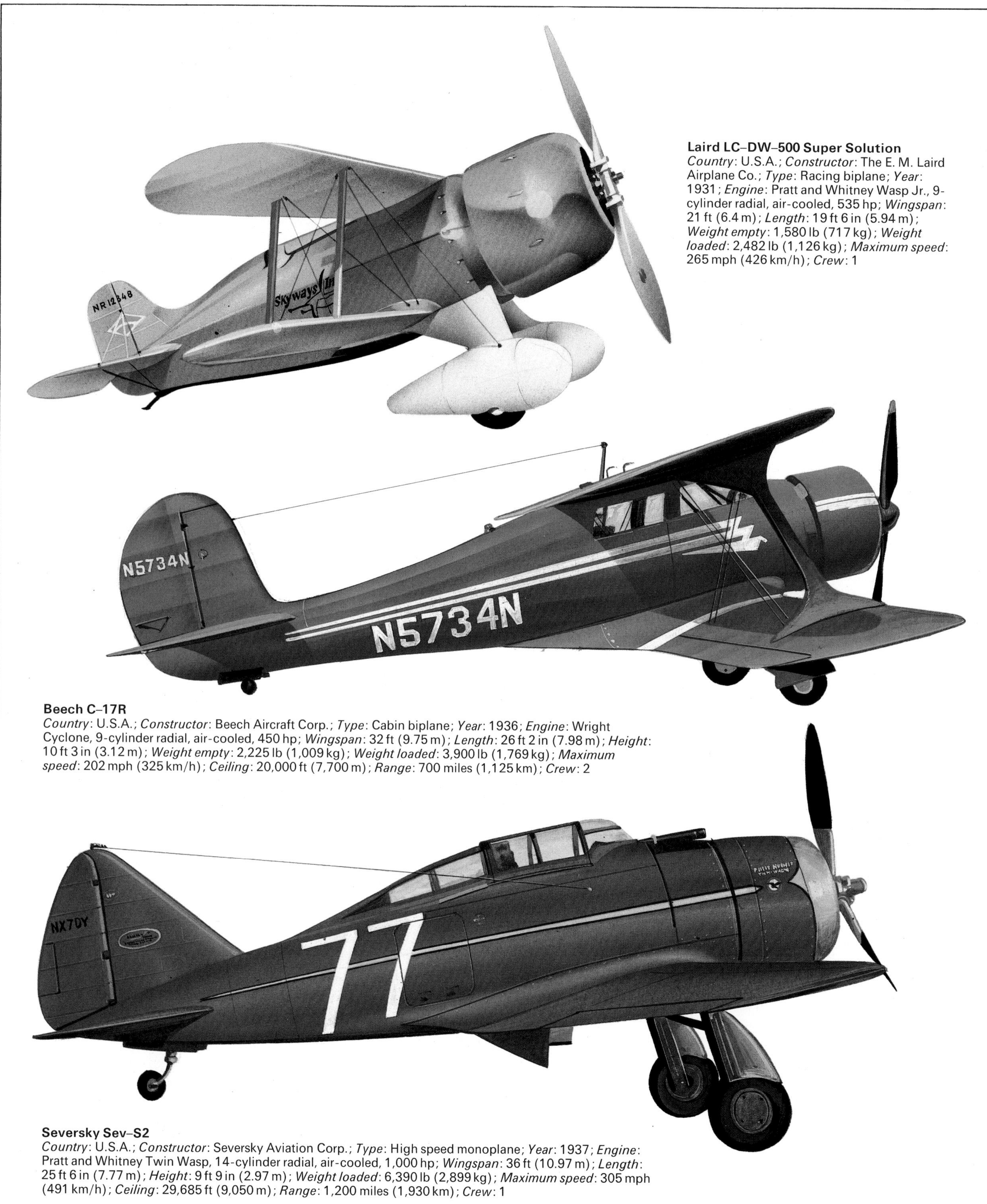

Laird LC–DW–500 Super Solution
Country: U.S.A.; *Constructor*: The E. M. Laird Airplane Co.; *Type*: Racing biplane; *Year*: 1931; *Engine*: Pratt and Whitney Wasp Jr., 9-cylinder radial, air-cooled, 535 hp; *Wingspan*: 21 ft (6.4 m); *Length*: 19 ft 6 in (5.94 m); *Weight empty*: 1,580 lb (717 kg); *Weight loaded*: 2,482 lb (1,126 kg); *Maximum speed*: 265 mph (426 km/h); *Crew*: 1

Beech C–17R
Country: U.S.A.; *Constructor*: Beech Aircraft Corp.; *Type*: Cabin biplane; *Year*: 1936; *Engine*: Wright Cyclone, 9-cylinder radial, air-cooled, 450 hp; *Wingspan*: 32 ft (9.75 m); *Length*: 26 ft 2 in (7.98 m); *Height*: 10 ft 3 in (3.12 m); *Weight empty*: 2,225 lb (1,009 kg); *Weight loaded*: 3,900 lb (1,769 kg); *Maximum speed*: 202 mph (325 km/h); *Ceiling*: 20,000 ft (7,700 m); *Range*: 700 miles (1,125 km); *Crew*: 2

Seversky Sev–S2
Country: U.S.A.; *Constructor*: Seversky Aviation Corp.; *Type*: High speed monoplane; *Year*: 1937; *Engine*: Pratt and Whitney Twin Wasp, 14-cylinder radial, air-cooled, 1,000 hp; *Wingspan*: 36 ft (10.97 m); *Length*: 25 ft 6 in (7.77 m); *Height*: 9 ft 9 in (2.97 m); *Weight loaded*: 6,390 lb (2,899 kg); *Maximum speed*: 305 mph (491 km/h); *Ceiling*: 29,685 ft (9,050 m); *Range*: 1,200 miles (1,930 km); *Crew*: 1

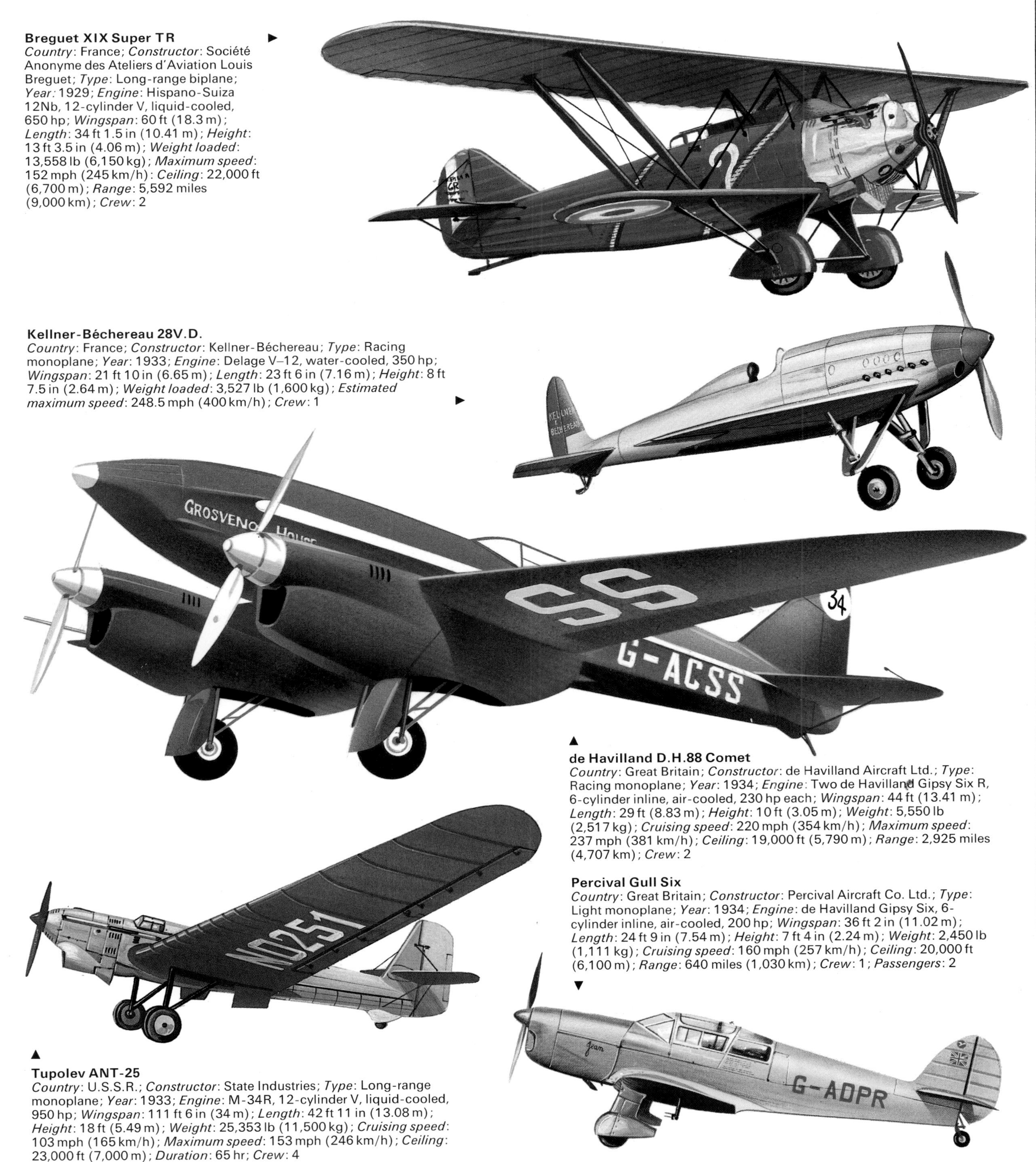

Breguet XIX Super TR ►
Country: France; *Constructor*: Société Anonyme des Ateliers d'Aviation Louis Breguet; *Type*: Long-range biplane; *Year*: 1929; *Engine*: Hispano-Suiza 12Nb, 12-cylinder V, liquid-cooled, 650 hp; *Wingspan*: 60 ft (18.3 m); *Length*: 34 ft 1.5 in (10.41 m); *Height*: 13 ft 3.5 in (4.06 m); *Weight loaded*: 13,558 lb (6,150 kg); *Maximum speed*: 152 mph (245 km/h): *Ceiling*: 22,000 ft (6,700 m); *Range*: 5,592 miles (9,000 km); *Crew*: 2

Kellner-Béchereau 28V.D.
Country: France; *Constructor*: Kellner-Béchereau; *Type*: Racing monoplane; *Year*: 1933; *Engine*: Delage V–12, water-cooled, 350 hp; *Wingspan*: 21 ft 10 in (6.65 m); *Length*: 23 ft 6 in (7.16 m); *Height*: 8 ft 7.5 in (2.64 m); *Weight loaded*: 3,527 lb (1,600 kg); *Estimated maximum speed*: 248.5 mph (400 km/h); *Crew*: 1 ►

▲
de Havilland D.H.88 Comet
Country: Great Britain; *Constructor*: de Havilland Aircraft Ltd.; *Type*: Racing monoplane; *Year*: 1934; *Engine*: Two de Havilland Gipsy Six R, 6-cylinder inline, air-cooled, 230 hp each; *Wingspan*: 44 ft (13.41 m); *Length*: 29 ft (8.83 m); *Height*: 10 ft (3.05 m); *Weight*: 5,550 lb (2,517 kg); *Cruising speed*: 220 mph (354 km/h); *Maximum speed*: 237 mph (381 km/h); *Ceiling*: 19,000 ft (5,790 m); *Range*: 2,925 miles (4,707 km); *Crew*: 2

Percival Gull Six
Country: Great Britain; *Constructor*: Percival Aircraft Co. Ltd.; *Type*: Light monoplane; *Year*: 1934; *Engine*: de Havilland Gipsy Six, 6-cylinder inline, air-cooled, 200 hp; *Wingspan*: 36 ft 2 in (11.02 m); *Length*: 24 ft 9 in (7.54 m); *Height*: 7 ft 4 in (2.24 m); *Weight*: 2,450 lb (1,111 kg); *Cruising speed*: 160 mph (257 km/h); *Ceiling*: 20,000 ft (6,100 m); *Range*: 640 miles (1,030 km); *Crew*: 1; *Passengers*: 2
▼

▲
Tupolev ANT-25
Country: U.S.S.R.; *Constructor*: State Industries; *Type*: Long-range monoplane; *Year*: 1933; *Engine*: M-34R, 12-cylinder V, liquid-cooled, 950 hp; *Wingspan*: 111 ft 6 in (34 m); *Length*: 42 ft 11 in (13.08 m); *Height*: 18 ft (5.49 m); *Weight*: 25,353 lb (11,500 kg); *Cruising speed*: 103 mph (165 km/h); *Maximum speed*: 153 mph (246 km/h); *Ceiling*: 23,000 ft (7,000 m); *Duration*: 65 hr; *Crew*: 4

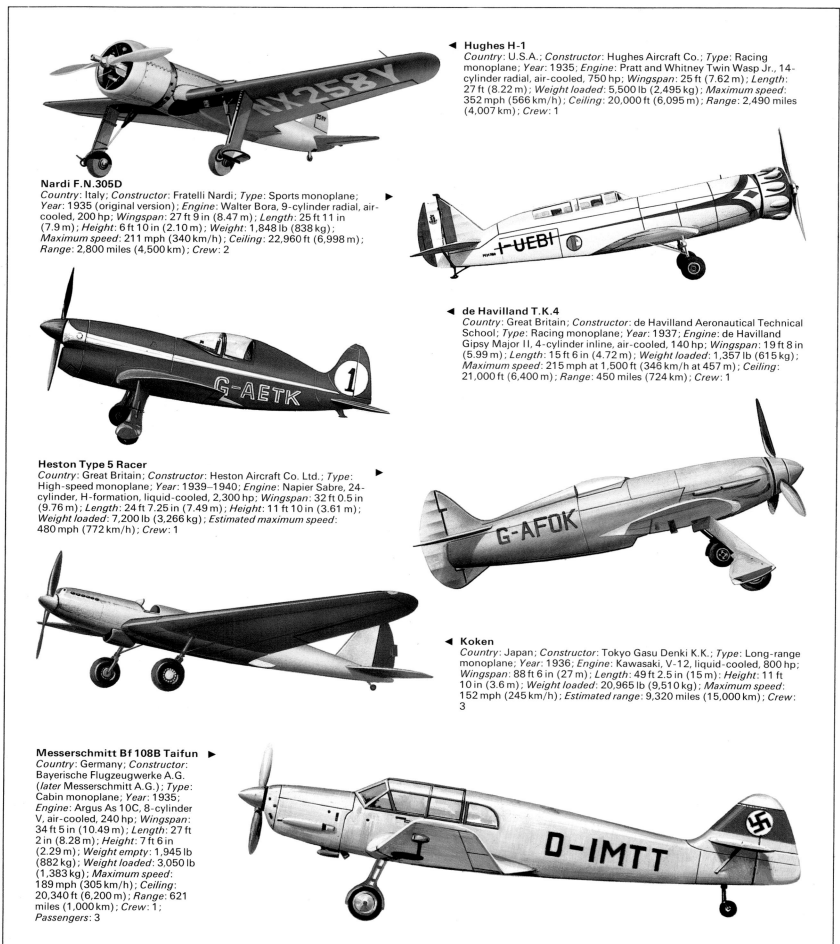

◄ **Hughes H-1**
Country: U.S.A.; *Constructor*: Hughes Aircraft Co.; *Type*: Racing monoplane; *Year*: 1935; *Engine*: Pratt and Whitney Twin Wasp Jr., 14-cylinder radial, air-cooled, 750 hp; *Wingspan*: 25 ft (7.62 m); *Length*: 27 ft (8.22 m); *Weight loaded*: 5,500 lb (2,495 kg); *Maximum speed*: 352 mph (566 km/h); *Ceiling*: 20,000 ft (6,095 m); *Range*: 2,490 miles (4,007 km); *Crew*: 1

Nardi F.N.305D ►
Country: Italy; *Constructor*: Fratelli Nardi; *Type*: Sports monoplane; *Year*: 1935 (original version); *Engine*: Walter Bora, 9-cylinder radial, air-cooled, 200 hp; *Wingspan*: 27 ft 9 in (8.47 m); *Length*: 25 ft 11 in (7.9 m); *Height*: 6 ft 10 in (2.10 m); *Weight*: 1,848 lb (838 kg); *Maximum speed*: 211 mph (340 km/h); *Ceiling*: 22,960 ft (6,998 m); *Range*: 2,800 miles (4,500 km); *Crew*: 2

◄ **de Havilland T.K.4**
Country: Great Britain; *Constructor*: de Havilland Aeronautical Technical School; *Type*: Racing monoplane; *Year*: 1937; *Engine*: de Havilland Gipsy Major II, 4-cylinder inline, air-cooled, 140 hp; *Wingspan*: 19 ft 8 in (5.99 m); *Length*: 15 ft 6 in (4.72 m); *Weight loaded*: 1,357 lb (615 kg); *Maximum speed*: 215 mph at 1,500 ft (346 km/h at 457 m); *Ceiling*: 21,000 ft (6,400 m); *Range*: 450 miles (724 km); *Crew*: 1

Heston Type 5 Racer ►
Country: Great Britain; *Constructor*: Heston Aircraft Co. Ltd.; *Type*: High-speed monoplane; *Year*: 1939–1940; *Engine*: Napier Sabre, 24-cylinder, H-formation, liquid-cooled, 2,300 hp; *Wingspan*: 32 ft 0.5 in (9.76 m); *Length*: 24 ft 7.25 in (7.49 m); *Height*: 11 ft 10 in (3.61 m); *Weight loaded*: 7,200 lb (3,266 kg); *Estimated maximum speed*: 480 mph (772 km/h); *Crew*: 1

◄ **Koken**
Country: Japan; *Constructor*: Tokyo Gasu Denki K.K.; *Type*: Long-range monoplane; *Year*: 1936; *Engine*: Kawasaki, V-12, liquid-cooled, 800 hp; *Wingspan*: 88 ft 6 in (27 m); *Length*: 49 ft 2.5 in (15 m): *Height*: 11 ft 10 in (3.6 m); *Weight loaded*: 20,965 lb (9,510 kg); *Maximum speed*: 152 mph (245 km/h); *Estimated range*: 9,320 miles (15,000 km); *Crew*: 3

Messerschmitt Bf 108B Taifun ►
Country: Germany; *Constructor*: Bayerische Flugzeugwerke A.G. (*later* Messerschmitt A.G.); *Type*: Cabin monoplane; *Year*: 1935; *Engine*: Argus As 10C, 8-cylinder V, air-cooled, 240 hp; *Wingspan*: 34 ft 5 in (10.49 m); *Length*: 27 ft 2 in (8.28 m); *Height*: 7 ft 6 in (2.29 m); *Weight empty*: 1,945 lb (882 kg); *Weight loaded*: 3,050 lb (1,383 kg); *Maximum speed*: 189 mph (305 km/h); *Ceiling*: 20,340 ft (6,200 m); *Range*: 621 miles (1,000 km); *Crew*: 1; *Passengers*: 3

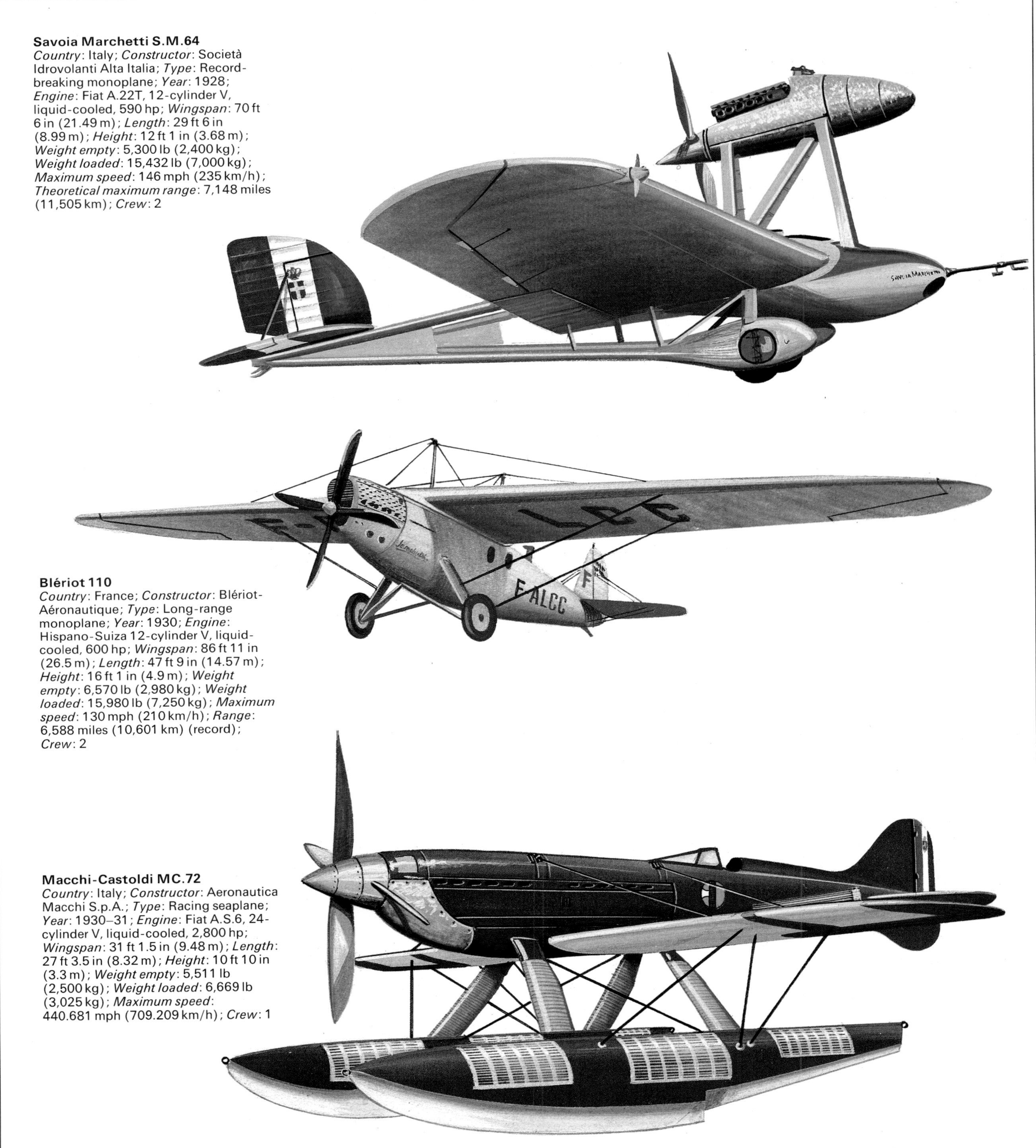

Savoia Marchetti S.M.64
Country: Italy; *Constructor*: Società Idrovolanti Alta Italia; *Type*: Record-breaking monoplane; *Year*: 1928; *Engine*: Fiat A.22T, 12-cylinder V, liquid-cooled, 590 hp; *Wingspan*: 70 ft 6 in (21.49 m); *Length*: 29 ft 6 in (8.99 m); *Height*: 12 ft 1 in (3.68 m); *Weight empty*: 5,300 lb (2,400 kg); *Weight loaded*: 15,432 lb (7,000 kg); *Maximum speed*: 146 mph (235 km/h); *Theoretical maximum range*: 7,148 miles (11,505 km); *Crew*: 2

Blériot 110
Country: France; *Constructor*: Blériot-Aéronautique; *Type*: Long-range monoplane; *Year*: 1930; *Engine*: Hispano-Suiza 12-cylinder V, liquid-cooled, 600 hp; *Wingspan*: 86 ft 11 in (26.5 m); *Length*: 47 ft 9 in (14.57 m); *Height*: 16 ft 1 in (4.9 m); *Weight empty*: 6,570 lb (2,980 kg); *Weight loaded*: 15,980 lb (7,250 kg); *Maximum speed*: 130 mph (210 km/h); *Range*: 6,588 miles (10,601 km) (record); *Crew*: 2

Macchi-Castoldi MC.72
Country: Italy; *Constructor*: Aeronautica Macchi S.p.A.; *Type*: Racing seaplane; *Year*: 1930–31; *Engine*: Fiat A.S.6, 24-cylinder V, liquid-cooled, 2,800 hp; *Wingspan*: 31 ft 1.5 in (9.48 m); *Length*: 27 ft 3.5 in (8.32 m); *Height*: 10 ft 10 in (3.3 m); *Weight empty*: 5,511 lb (2,500 kg); *Weight loaded*: 6,669 lb (3,025 kg); *Maximum speed*: 440.681 mph (709.209 km/h); *Crew*: 1

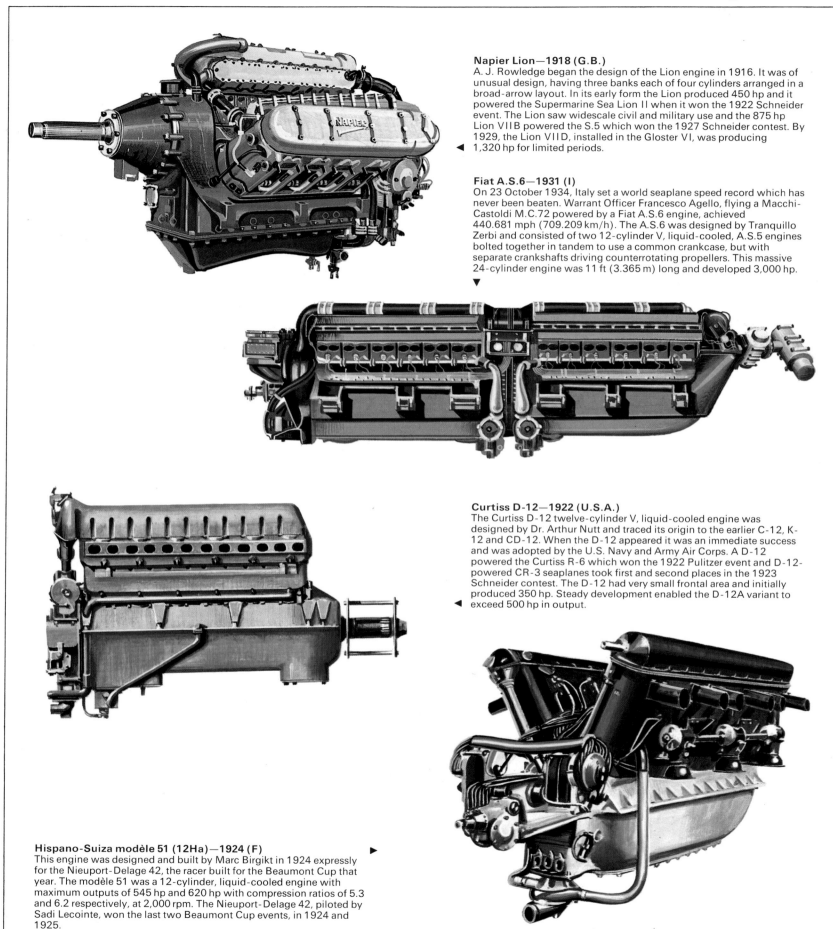

Napier Lion—1918 (G.B.)
A. J. Rowledge began the design of the Lion engine in 1916. It was of unusual design, having three banks each of four cylinders arranged in a broad-arrow layout. In its early form the Lion produced 450 hp and it powered the Supermarine Sea Lion II when it won the 1922 Schneider event. The Lion saw widescale civil and military use and the 875 hp Lion VIIB powered the S.5 which won the 1927 Schneider contest. By 1929, the Lion VIID, installed in the Gloster VI, was producing 1,320 hp for limited periods.

Fiat A.S.6—1931 (I)
On 23 October 1934, Italy set a world seaplane speed record which has never been beaten. Warrant Officer Francesco Agello, flying a Macchi-Castoldi M.C.72 powered by a Fiat A.S.6 engine, achieved 440.681 mph (709.209 km/h). The A.S.6 was designed by Tranquillo Zerbi and consisted of two 12-cylinder V, liquid-cooled, A.S.5 engines bolted together in tandem to use a common crankcase, but with separate crankshafts driving counterrotating propellers. This massive 24-cylinder engine was 11 ft (3.365 m) long and developed 3,000 hp.

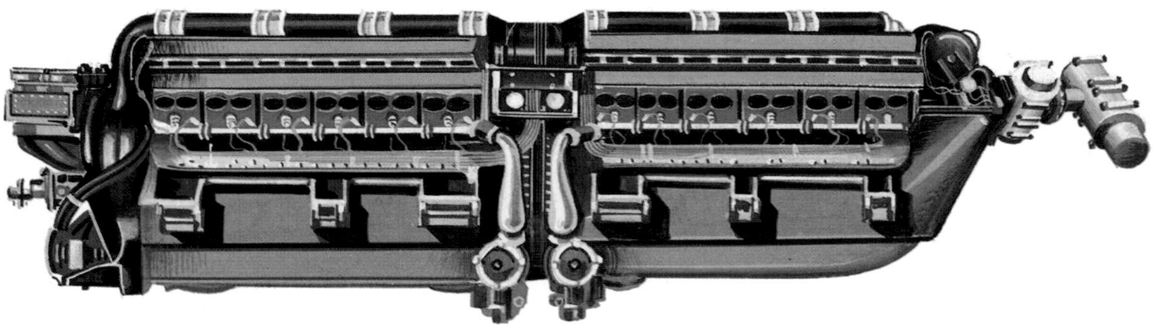

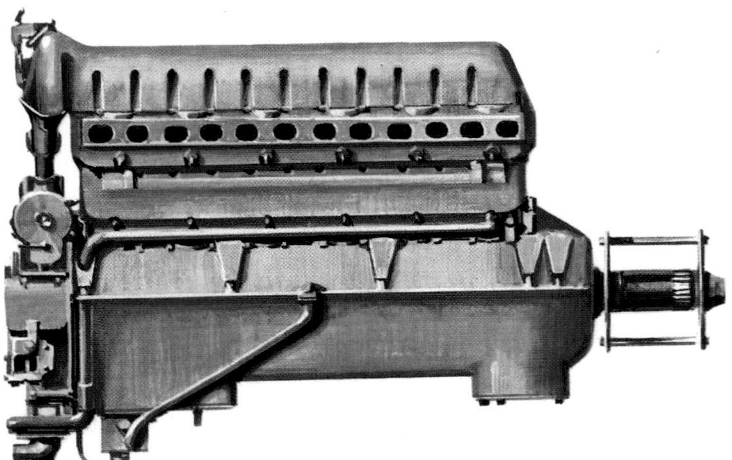

Curtiss D-12—1922 (U.S.A.)
The Curtiss D-12 twelve-cylinder V, liquid-cooled engine was designed by Dr. Arthur Nutt and traced its origin to the earlier C-12, K-12 and CD-12. When the D-12 appeared it was an immediate success and was adopted by the U.S. Navy and Army Air Corps. A D-12 powered the Curtiss R-6 which won the 1922 Pulitzer event and D-12-powered CR-3 seaplanes took first and second places in the 1923 Schneider contest. The D-12 had very small frontal area and initially produced 350 hp. Steady development enabled the D-12A variant to exceed 500 hp in output.

Hispano-Suiza modèle 51 (12Ha)—1924 (F)
This engine was designed and built by Marc Birgikt in 1924 expressly for the Nieuport-Delage 42, the racer built for the Beaumont Cup that year. The modèle 51 was a 12-cylinder, liquid-cooled engine with maximum outputs of 545 hp and 620 hp with compression ratios of 5.3 and 6.2 respectively, at 2,000 rpm. The Nieuport-Delage 42, piloted by Sadi Lecointe, won the last two Beaumont Cup events, in 1924 and 1925.

Plate 61
The Gordon Bennett Aviation Cup and the Deutsch de la Meurthe Trophy: 1920–1922

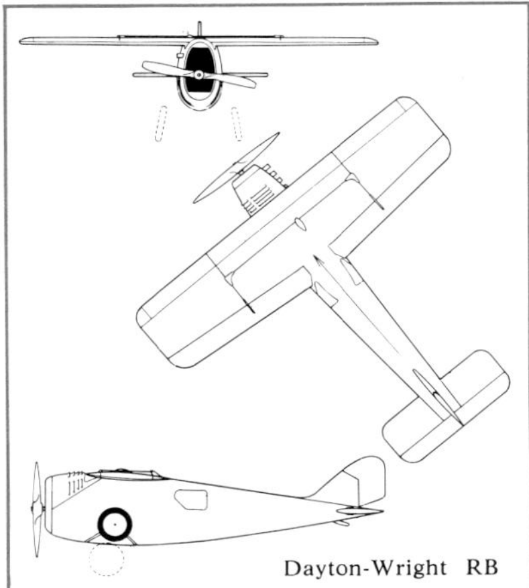

Dayton-Wright RB

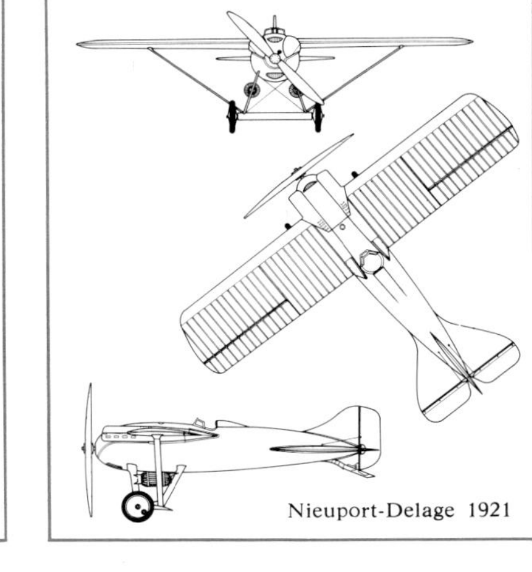

Nieuport-Delage 1921

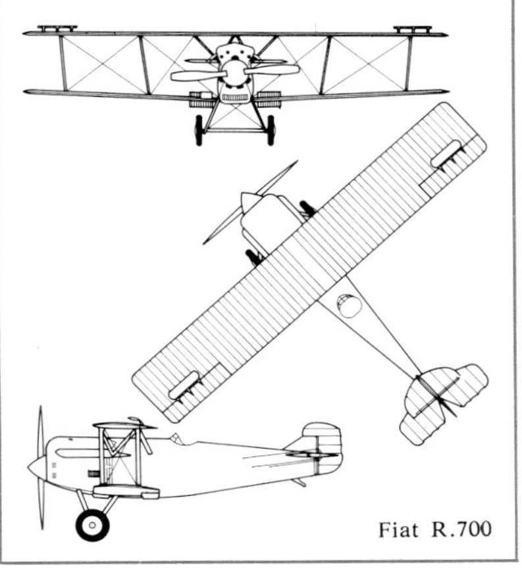

Fiat R.700

The oldest and most famous speed competition, the Gordon Bennett Aviation Cup, was held again in 1920 after an interval of seven years due to the war. The prospect of entering for this race aroused enormous excitement, particularly in France, since Deperdussins had won the last two contests in 1912 and 1913 when they were piloted by Jules Védrines and Maurice Prévost respectively. The revival of the competition gave France her chance to win the contest a third time and to keep the trophy. But other countries had also entered highly competitive machines and were there in force, including Great Britain and the U.S.A. The Americans made a particularly strong challenge in the shape of a small airplane, the Dayton-Wright RB, which was a real threat to all the contenders, so original and aerodynamic was its design. It was a fast, clean-lined monoplane which had been designed with the help of Orville Wright especially for the Gordon Bennett Cup. The aircraft's most noteworthy design features—apart from the fact that it was a monoplane, which was unusual at the time—were the construction materials used (plywood and balsa wood), its manually retractable undercarriage and closed cockpit, and the introduction of a variable-camber wing with leading- and trailing-edge flaps. The RB was, however, very unlucky on this occasion; it had to withdraw from the race after the first lap because of a jammed or failed control cable.

The competition was held at Étampes, about forty miles from Paris, on 28 September 1920. The race was flown over a 300-kilometer course consisting of three circuits from Villesauvage airdrome to a farm near Gidy and back. The competing aircraft were allowed to take off in handicap order at intervals between 07.00 hours and 19.00 hours. The first to go was the French pilot, Georges Kirsch, in his Nieuport 29V, at 13.37. He was followed at 13.42 by Bernard de Romanet in his Spad S.20bis. At 14.09 Sadi Lecointe took off in the other Nieuport 29V which had been entered and two minutes later Howard M. Rinehart took to the air in the Dayton-Wright. The other American who had entered the competition, Rudolph W. Schroeder, flying a Verville VCP-R which had the most powerful engine (638 hp) of any of the competing aircraft there, left at 14.37 and was followed at 16.36 by the only British contender left in the race, Frederick P. Raynham in the Martinsyde Semiquaver. Only two competitors completed the course and they were both French: Sadi Lecointe and Bernard de Romanet, only the former having had a smooth flight; Romanet had been forced to land and spend half an hour on the ground due to a lubrication fault. He then set off round the circuit again. Sadi Lecointe clocked up a time of 1 hour 6 minutes and 17 seconds; his fastest lap was flown at 172.522 mph (277.649 km/h); his fastest time had, however, been achieved during one of the practice flights: 173.674 mph (279.503 km/h). Besides winning the Gordon Bennett Cup outright for the Aéro-Club de France, these results broke the 100-kilometer and 200-kilometer closed-circuit speed records.

French aircraft also won the last three competitions of the Deutsch de la Meurthe Prize. These races had been named after the industrialist Henry Deutsch de la Meurthe. In 1912 this famous and immensely rich air enthusiast had offered prizes to be awarded to the winner of a race over 200 kilometers around Paris. The first year the prize was won by Emmanuel Helen in a 70-hp Nieuport at an average speed of 77.9 mph (125.37 km/h); in 1913 Eugène Gilbert won in a 180-hp Deperdussin at a speed of 101.563 mph (163.451 km/h). The third race was held between 12 September 1919 and 24 January 1920, over a distance of 118.3084 miles (190.3993 km). Sadi Lecointe won this time, in his Nieuport 29V, flying at a speed of 165.479 mph (266.314 km/h) on 3 January, winning the prize money of 20,000 francs. After the death, on 24 November 1919, of its founder, it was decided that the race should be discontinued in its old form, and in the two following years a Cup was offered named after Henry Deutsch de la Meurthe who had been such a great patron of aviation. The course was also changed, being increased to 186.4 miles (300 km). On 1 October 1921, Georges Kirsch beat four other competitors when he flew his new sporting airplane, a Nieuport-Delage Type 1921 at 172,994 mph (278.408 km/h). This airplane had been developed by Gustave Delage after his success with military aircraft. Fernand Lasne, flying the Nieuport 29V which had won the race in 1920, was second with a speed of 159.879 mph (257.302 km/h) and it was this Nieuport which won the following year's Deutsch de la Meurthe Cup on 30 September 1922, again piloted by Fernand Lasne with an average speed of 179.827 mph (289.405 km/h) and setting a new 200-kilometer closed-circuit speed record.

Among the numerous foreign participants in these two Deutsch de la Meurthe competitions, an Italian aircraft, the Fiat R.700 attracted a great deal of attention. It had been specially designed for this contest by Celestino Rosatelli who had installed one of the most powerful engines then available in it, the 650 hp Fiat A.14. This large biplane did not, however, do particularly well; in 1921 it had to withdraw at the end of the second lap owing to a fuel leak; in 1922 it developed a fault in the carburetor. On both occasions, however, it showed that it had potential. Before retiring from the race in 1921 it reached a speed of 185.575 mph (298.656 km/h), setting a new 100 kilometer closed-circuit world record: the following year its fastest lap speed was 179.875 mph (289.482 km/h) rivaling the winner's speed. On both occasions the pilot was Francesco Brak-Papa.

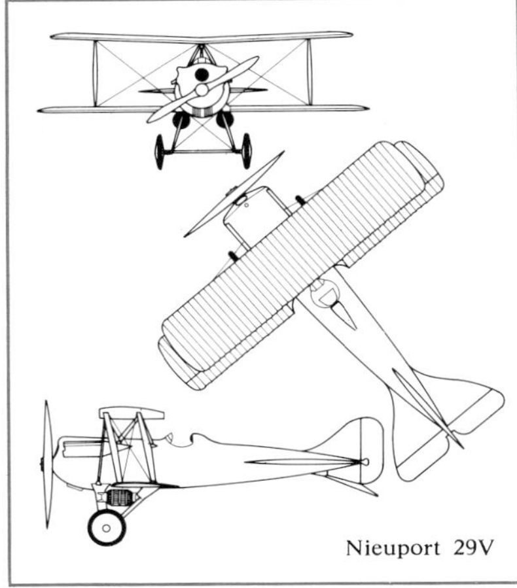

Nieuport 29V

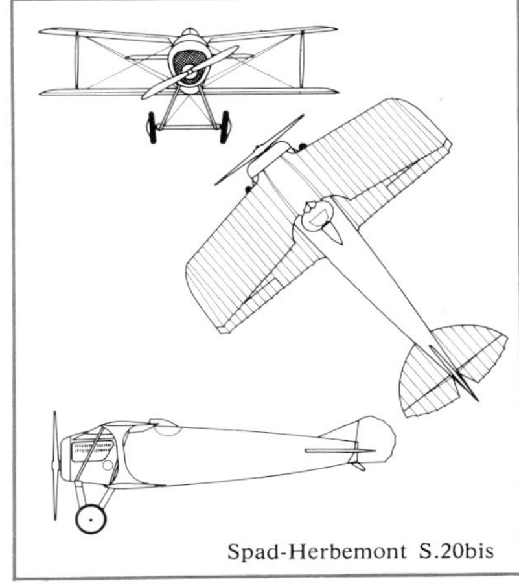

Spad-Herbemont S.20bis

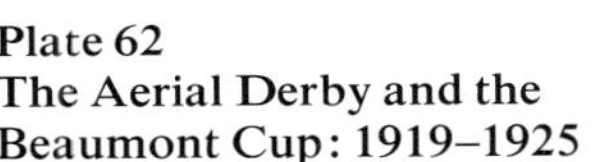

Plate 62
The Aerial Derby and the Beaumont Cup: 1919–1925

There was just as much enthusiasm for flying competitions in Britain as in France. After the enforced suspension of all activity in this field during the war, the first important peacetime speed competition was held at Hendon on 21 June 1919, on the longest day of the year. This was the fourth occasion on which the Aerial Derby had been flown. It was a race around London for prize money and the Daily Mail Trophy. The other three Derby races had been held in 1912, 1913 and 1914 and victory had gone each time to French aircraft; in 1912 to a Blériot XI piloted by T. O. M. Sopwith (58.46 mph–94.08 km/h) and in 1913 and 1914 Morane-Saulnier monoplanes had won, piloted by Gustav Hamel and William L. Brock respectively. The 1919 Aerial Derby attracted a very large field of British pilots and airplanes. The first place in the handicap race went to Captain H. A. Hamersley in the Avro 543 Baby (70.267 mph–113.082 km/h) and the speed event was won by Captain Gerald Gathergood, in the Airco

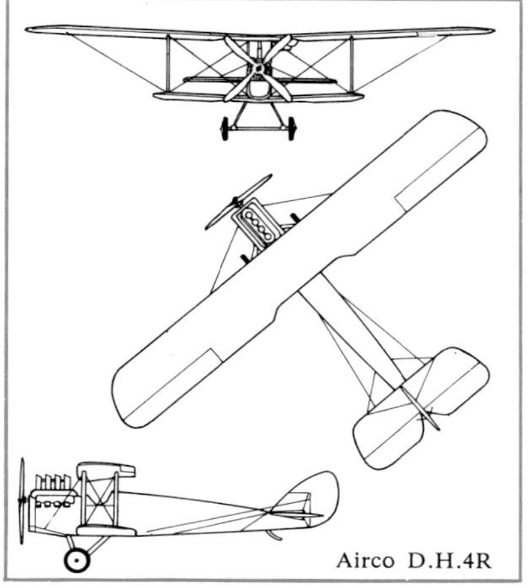

Airco D.H.4R

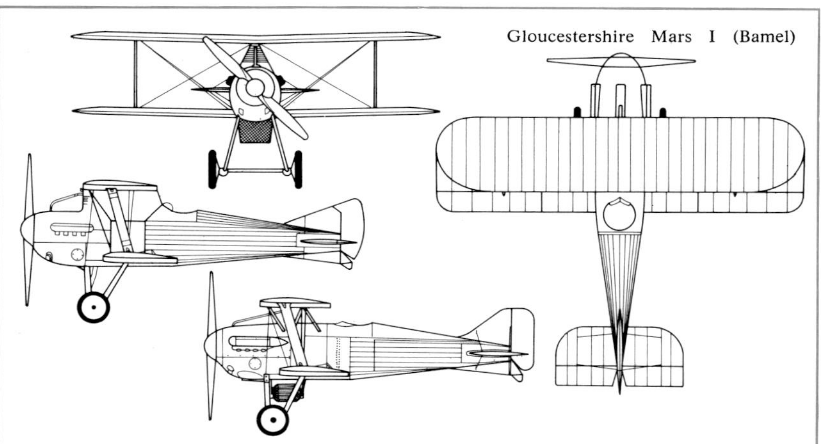

Gloucestershire Mars I (Bamel)

D.H.4R, at 129.304 mph (208.091 km/h). His aircraft was derived from the famous D.H.4 biplane bomber; the airplane had been given much improved performance by shortening the lower wing and by installing the more powerful 450 hp Napier Lion engine. After this exciting revival of the competition in peacetime, the Aerial Derby was held for another four years and became known as a classic race throughout the aviation world, stimulating designers and manufacturers who were now starting to recover from the difficulties of the immediate post-war period.

The four subsequent competitions were won by British aircraft, none of the overseas entries actually taking part. In 1920 the handicap race was again won by an Avro 543 Baby (again piloted by Hamersley with a speed of 78.895 mph–126.967 km/h), while the speed race was won by the Martinsyde Semiquaver which, with Francis T. Courtney at the controls, achieved 153.446 mph (246.943 km/h). The following year both events in this Derby were won by the same competitor (the only time this was to happen)—the Gloucestershire Mars I (nicknamed Bamel), flown by James H. James, whose fastest recorded speed was just over 163 mph (262 km/h). The Mars was an elegant biplane which had been developed from the Nieuport Nighthawk by Henry Folland to attain the highest possible speed and with which he hoped to attract the attention of the R.A.F. and arouse interest in the Gloucestershire Aircraft Company.

Mars I was designed and built in less than four weeks and completed its trials in time for the qualifying heats for the Aerial Derby. After its victory the Mars competed unsuccessfully for the Deutsch Cup and, in 1922, it was again entered for the Derby. The aircraft's performance (enhanced by improved streamlining) was enough to win the race again with a fastest lap speed of 178.7 mph (287.58 km/h). Yet again, in the next Derby, in 1923, it was to meet with success after considerable structural modifications had been carried out and a more powerful engine installed. Renamed Gloster I, it won the speed contest again with a best lap speed of 195.652 mph (314.866 km/h). In the 1922 Derby the handicap event was won by Larry L. Carter piloting a Bristol 77 monoplane (maximum speed 108.586 mph–174.749 km/h) and in 1923 H. A. Hamersley won in an Avro 522 (109.157 mph–175.668 km/h).

In 1924, the Aerial Derby having been discontinued, the Gloster I was entered for a new contest, the Beaumont Cup (Coupe Commodore Louis D. Beaumont) to be held in France. This competition had been sponsored by Louis D. Beaumont, an American industrialist who had taken French nationality, who had put up the prize money for a speed competition over a 300-kilometer course. The race was to be flown over six laps of a 50-kilometer circuit and the winner had to exceed 180 mph (290 km/h) to qualify for the lucrative prizes. In 1923, however, there was, to put it mildly, an extremely small field (only one pilot at the starting line) and the Cup was therefore not awarded. The next year there were five entrants, but the British aircraft, the only foreign aircraft to be entered, was not ready in time. Out of a wholly French field, Sadi Lecointe came first, flying a new Nieuport-Delage 42, derived from the famous series of competition aircraft built by this French manufacturer. The same Nieuport-Delage also carried off the Cup when the Beaumont contest was held for the second and last time in 1925, although on this occasion its only rivals had to retire. The top speeds logged were: 197.26 mph (317.46 km/h) in 1924 and 194.155 mph (312.464 km/h) in 1925.

Plates 63–64
The Schneider Trophy: 1919–1931

Once the war was over, another extremely famous contest was revived and enthralled the world of aviation for more than ten years. This was the Schneider Trophy, a seaplane speed competition. The two pre-war Schneider races had been won by the Frenchman Maurice Prévost (in 1913 flying a Deperdussin), and by the Englishman Howard Pixton (in 1914, in a Sopwith Tabloid). After the war Britain and France were joined by the Italians who, from the outset, proved to be very strong contenders. On 10 September 1919, at Bournemouth, Guido Jannello in his Savoia S.13bis was the only entrant who managed to complete the course in dense fog, averaging 125 mph (201 km/h). His splendid effort was not to win him the Trophy, however, since in the thick fog Jannello had mistakenly flown round a buoy which was not an official course marker and had repeated this error on each circuit. His victory was disallowed in spite of vehement protests.

In Venice, on 21 September 1920, the Italians had their revenge when Luigi Bologna's Savoia S.12bis won the race with an average speed of 105.971 mph (170.541 km/h). This time there was no quibbling with the result, even though no other country took part in the contest (the British and the French who constituted the main opposition had not been able to get their aircraft ready in time). When the competition was again held in Venice the following year, on 7 August 1921, the only non-Italian entry was the French pilot, Sadi Lecointe, with a Nieuport-Delage 29, which had, however, been damaged during practice flights. Another military flying boat, the Macchi M.7, which had been adapted for speed (as had been the case with the Savoias in 1919 and 1920) won with an average speed of 117.859 mph (189.677 km/h); this Macchi M.7 was piloted by Giovanni De Briganti. The Italians now had to win only one more race, that of 1922,

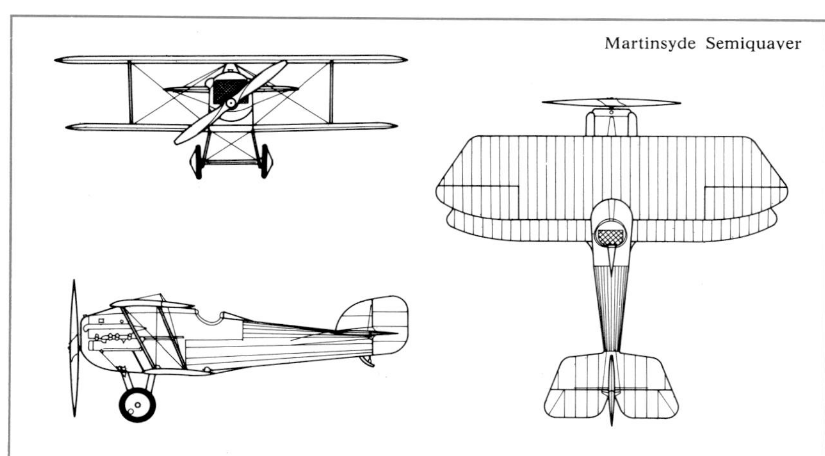

Martinsyde Semiquaver

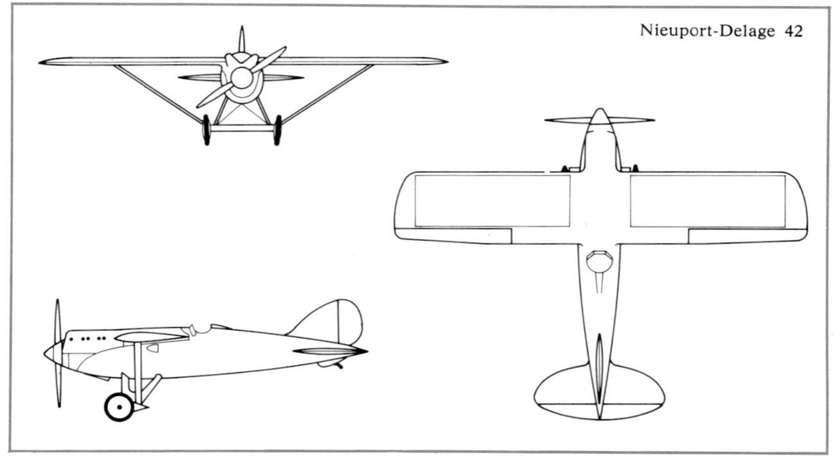

Nieuport-Delage 42

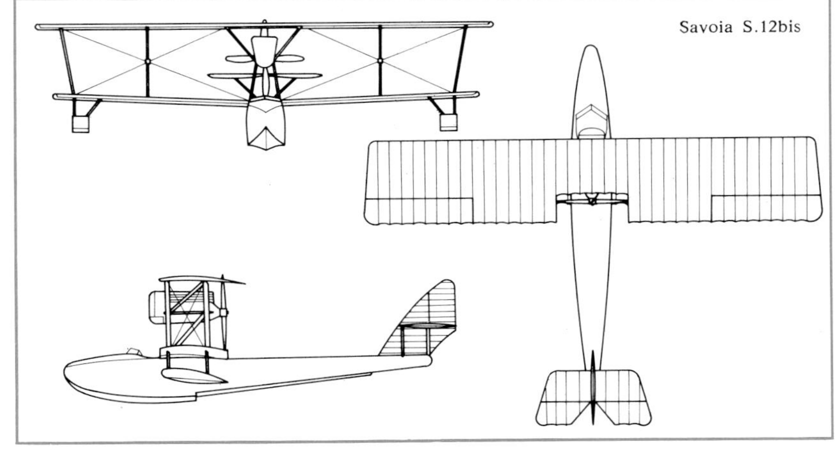
Savoia S.12bis

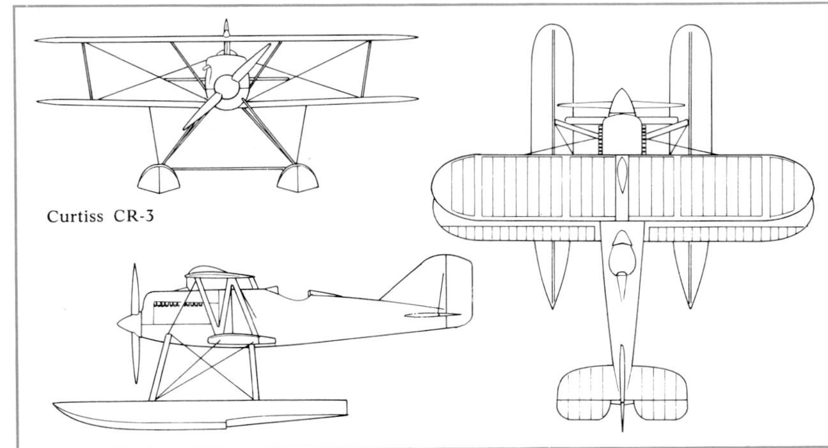
Curtiss CR-3

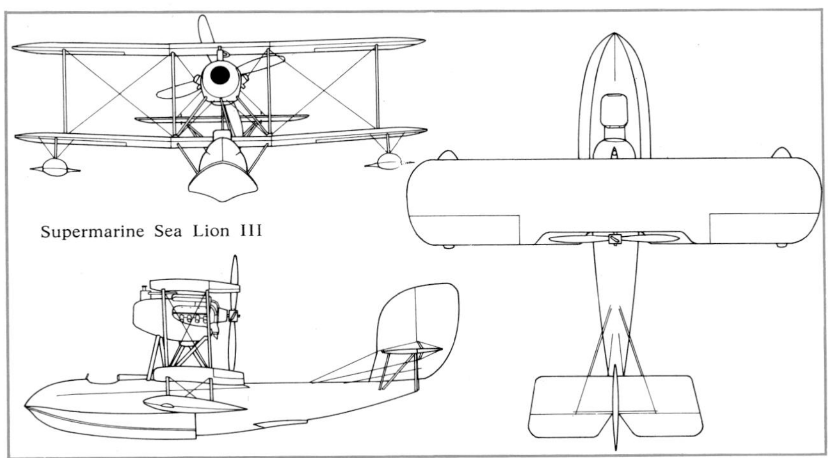
Supermarine Sea Lion III

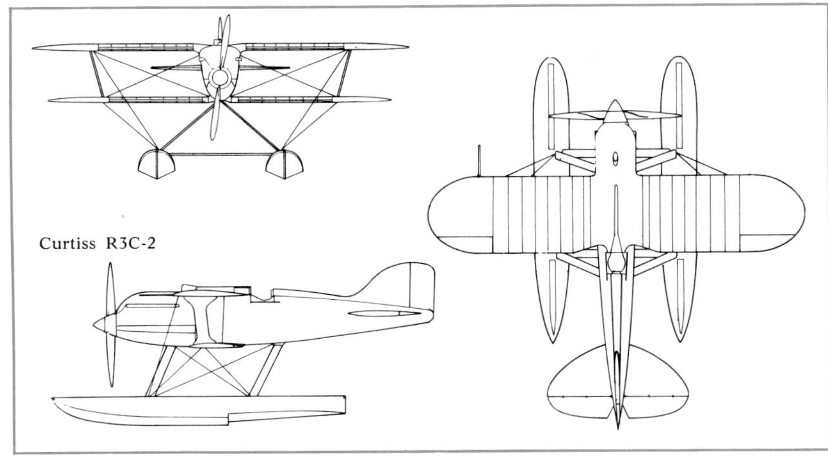
Curtiss R3C-2

to win the Trophy outright but, on 12 August at Naples, the only British contender managed to beat the three Italian entries and take the Schneider Trophy back to Britain. The winner was Henri C. Biard, flying the Supermarine Sea Lion II at an average speed of 145.721 mph (234.516 km/h). The preparation of this outstanding competition biplane showed that the British were not content to sit back and watch the Trophy slip from their grasp.

A new and very effective challenge was forthcoming, however, and British aircraft designers and constructors soon had to face the threat from the United States. During the postwar years enthusiasm in the U.S.A. for competition flying had known no bounds and American aircraft designers and builders had produced some formidable machines. Their quality was such that, in the 1923 Schneider races at Cowes, Isle of Wight, held on 27 and 28 September, the American Navy Curtiss CR-3 outflew the British competitor. This seaplane was a much modified landplane, the CR-1 biplane, built in 1921, which had been constructed to compete for the Pulitzer Trophy. Besides having had floats fitted, the CR-3 had a more powerful engine and was generally more streamlined.

Macchi M.7bis

CR-3s came first and second at Cowes; David Rittenhouse won with an average speed of 177.278 mph (285.303 km/h); and Rutledge Irvine averaged 173.35 mph (278.97 km/h). The British entry, the improved Sea Lion had to be content with third place. There were no Italian entrants on this occasion. The United States won the Schneider race again the next year when it was held on 26 October 1925, at Baltimore, Maryland. The date had originally been fixed for 24 and 25 October 1924, but since the British and the Italians had no hope of getting their new aircraft ready in time, the Americans very sportingly decided to put off the competition for a year. The winning seaplane, the Curtiss R3C-2 had again been derived from a landplane. Piloted by James H. Doolittle, its average speed was 232.573 mph (374.284 km/h). The British came second with the Gloster IIIA with an average speed of 199.17 mph (320.53 km/h) and the Italian Macchi M.33 was third (168.44 mph–271.08 km/h).

The Trophy went back to Italy the following year after an enthralling contest with the Americans, who had been determined to win the Trophy outright with a third successive victory. The ninth Schneider Trophy contest took place on 12 and 13 November 1926, at Hampton Roads (Norfolk, Virginia) and developed into a confrontation between the Italian and American seaplanes. Italy had entered three Macchi M.39s, piloted by Mario De Bernardi, Arturo Ferrarin and Adriano Bacula, two of whom completed the course: De Bernardi came first with a speed of 246.496 mph (396.698 km/h); Bacula was third (218 mph–350.845 km/h) and the American Curtiss R3C-2 was second (231.36 mph–372.34 km/h). The impressive performance of De Bernardi's M.39 led to the American decision not to have official entries in future Schneider Trophy races. The reason given when this decision was announced by the U.S. Government some time later was the prohibitive costs involved in developing competition aircraft for the races.

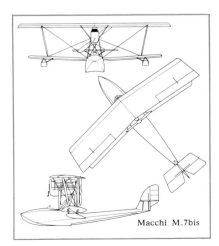

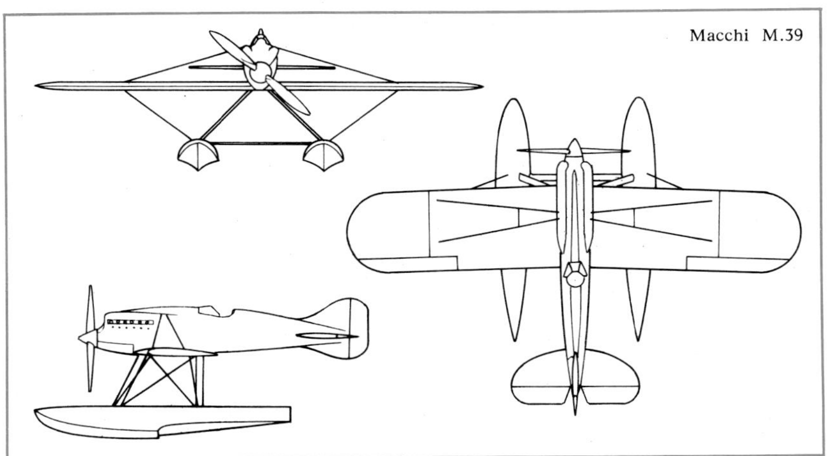
Macchi M.39

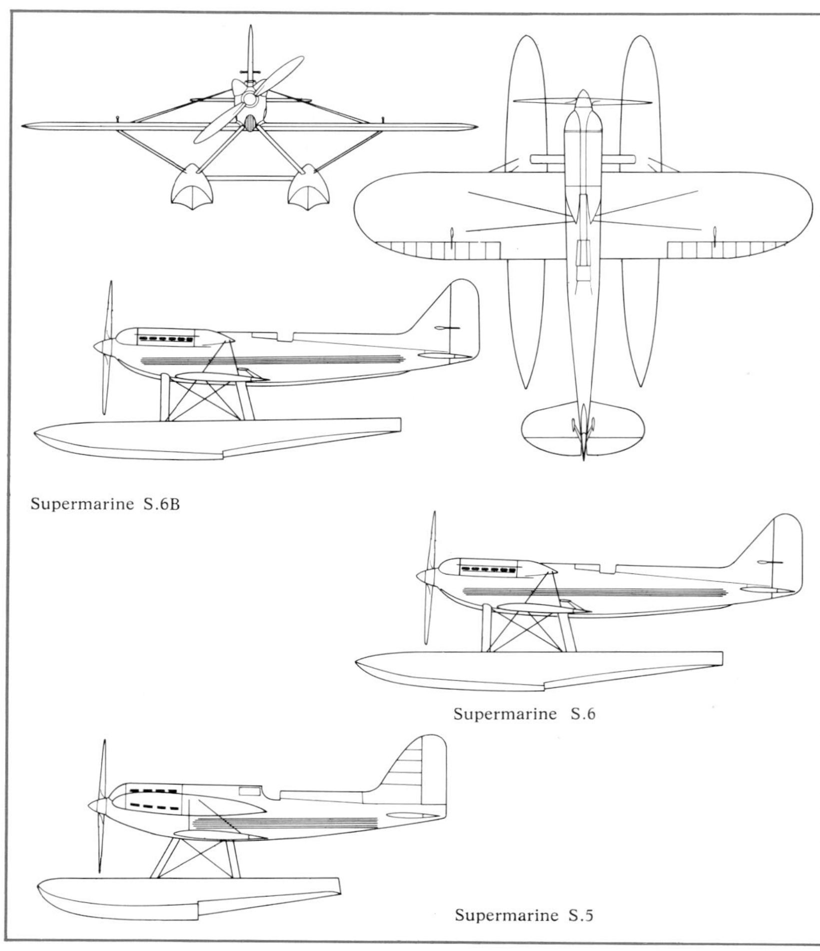

Supermarine S.6B

Supermarine S.6

Supermarine S.5

This left only the British and the Italians in the field. The next contest was fixed for 26 September 1927, in Venice, and both countries entered three aircraft. Italy fielded three Macchi M.52 seaplanes, which were improved and more powerful versions of the M.39; Great Britain was relying on two Supermarine S.5s and a Gloster IV biplane. The British S.5s took first and second places, piloted by S. N. Webster and O. E. Worsley; their respective average speeds were 281.655 mph (453.273 km/h) and 273.07 mph (439.45 km/h). This was the first of three victories which eventually led to Great Britain winning the Schneider Trophy outright. The Supermarine S.5 was the first of a series of highly sophisticated seaplanes designed especially for the competition by Reginald J. Mitchell and embodied the most advanced design techniques of the time.

The S.5's direct successor, the Supermarine S.6 won the 1929 Schneider Trophy (after 1927 it had been decided to hold the competition every two years to give the competing countries time to develop new and improved seaplanes). This took place at Cowes on 6 and 7 September. The winner, H. R. D. Waghorn, flew at an average speed of 328.629 mph (528.869 km/h) outflying the Italian Macchi M.52 piloted by Dal Molin who was second with an average speed of 284.2 mph (457.38 km/h). Two years later this most exciting series of competitions came to an end with the Supermarine S.6B (an S.6 with a 2,350 hp Rolls-Royce R engine) winning an uncontested race, flying only against time since the French and the Italian entries were not ready in time. At Calshot, John H. Boothman flew at 340.08 mph (547.297 km/h). After the contest an S.6B set a new world speed record of 407.5 mph (655.8 km/h).

Plates 65–66
The Pulitzer Trophy: 1920–1925

The Curtiss CR-3 and R3C-2 seaplanes which won the 1923 and 1925 Schneider Trophy races were outstanding examples of a generation of competition aircraft produced in America in the 1920s, where they enjoyed great popularity. The development of this type of aircraft was fostered and publicized by a succession of competitions, many of which aviators set as much store by winning as their equivalents in Europe. The Pulitzer Trophy was an enormously popular contest and stimulated both pilots and designers to produce exceptional aircraft. It was started in May 1919 as an endurance competition by the newspaper owners, the Pulitzer brothers Ralph, Joseph Jr. and Herbert. The following year, as part of the National Air Races, it became a closed-circuit speed competition and grew increasingly popular over the next five years.

In 1920 it was held on 25 November at Mitchel Field (Long Island, New York) and attracted as many as sixty-five entries. Only twenty-four finished and the winner was Corliss C. Moseley in the Verville VCP-R, averaging 156.539 mph (251.921 km/h), followed in second place by Harold E. Hartney flying a Thomas-Morse MB-3, with an average speed of 148.187 mph (238.438 km/h). Both these aircraft were derivatives of military models and were the U.S. Army's official entries. This marked the beginning of an increasingly keen participation by the armed forces in competition flying, which was to have a considerable effect on the choice of aircraft and was greatly to improve training standards. Many aircraft manufacturers started to feel confident enough to build aircraft specifically for these competitions, as a showcase to attract military orders. One such constructor was Glenn Curtiss who developed a formidable array of aircraft during these years. The precursor of this long line of airplanes was the Curtiss CR-1 which had been constructed to participate in the 1921 Pulitzer Trophy. This was held at Omaha, Nebraska, on 3 November and was won by Curtiss's elegant CR-1 biplane piloted by Bert Acosta, averaging 176.75 mph (284.44 km/h). Another Curtiss racer came second; a rather unusual triplane called the Curtiss-Cox Cactus Kitten, built for the oil magnate S. E. J. Cox. Its average speed was 170.336 mph (274.125 km/h).

Curtiss machines won three further Pulitzer races; in 1922, 1923 and, the last to be held, in 1925. The venue for the Trophy races on 14 October 1922, was Selfridge Field, Michigan, and Curtiss R-6s came first and second; first was Russell L. Maughan (205.856 mph–331.288 km/h) and Lester J. Maitland came second (198.85 mph–320.01 km/h). These racers were in effect scaled-down and more streamlined versions of the earlier CR-1 and Curtiss had been directly commissioned to build them by the Army. Curtiss's next design was for the Navy, the Curtiss R2C-1, which won the 1923 Pulitzer. This was held at Lambert Field, St. Louis, Missouri, on 6 October, and once again Glenn Curtiss's racers took the first two places, piloted by Alford J. "Al" Williams (243.673 mph–392.147 km/h) and Harold J. Brow (241.779 mph–389.099 km/h). The Navy decided to concentrate its efforts on a 1924 Schneider Trophy victory

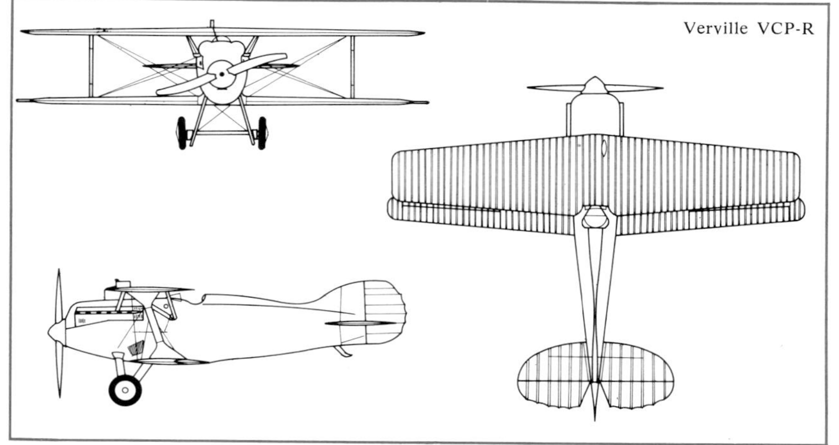

Verville VCP-R

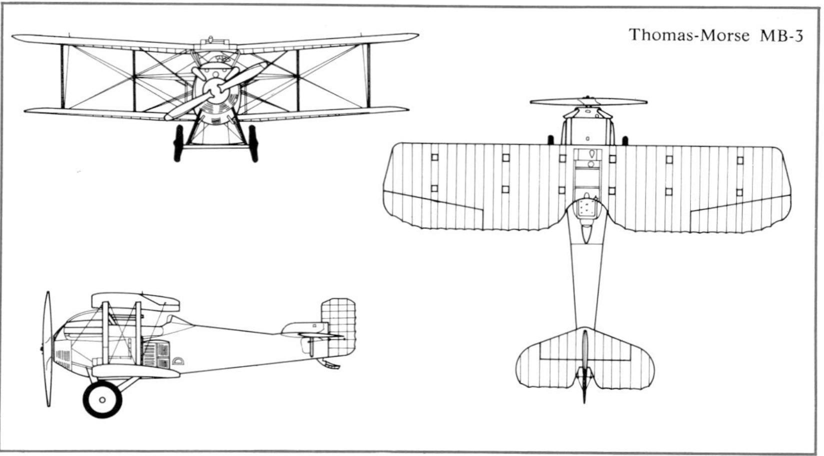

Thomas-Morse MB-3

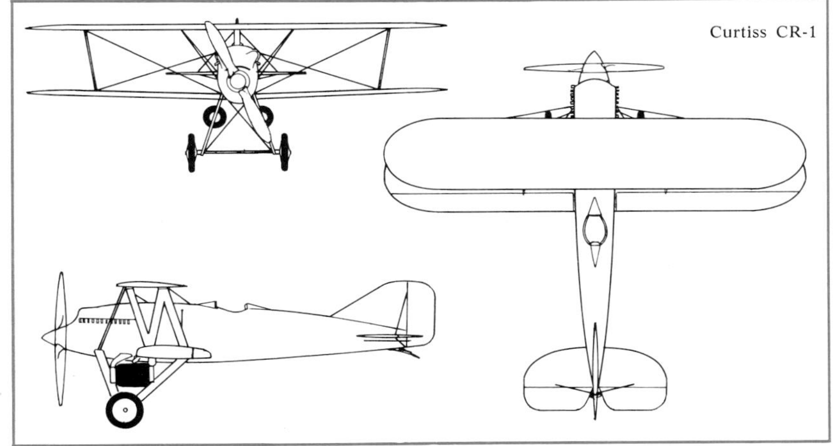

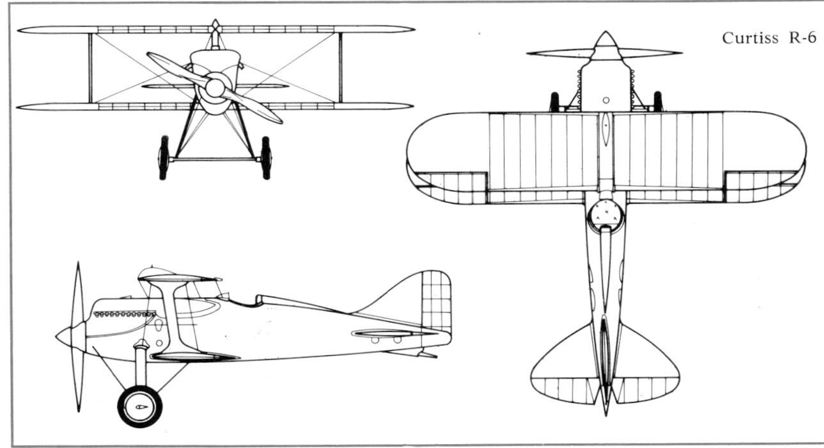

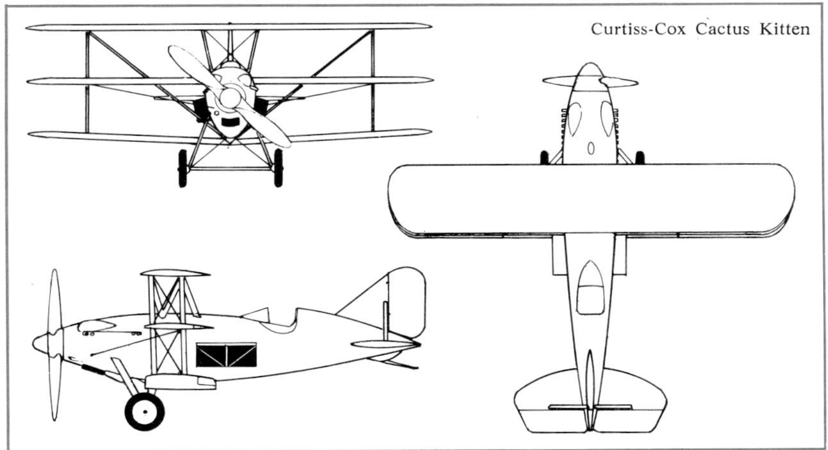

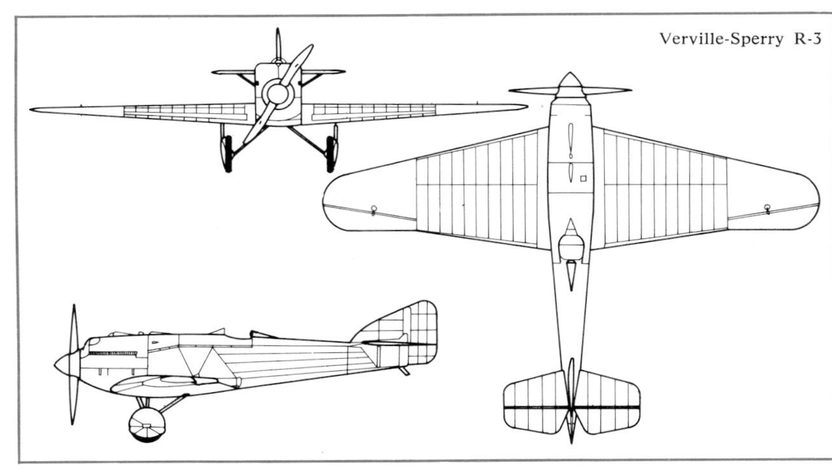

and did not participate in the next Pulitzer race, leaving the field to the Army.

On 4 October 1924, at Dayton, Ohio, the "old" Curtiss R-6 only achieved second place, just behind the Verville-Sperry R-3 monoplane piloted by Harry H. Mills, who won the competition with an average speed of 216.554 mph (348.504 km/h). This was well below the speeds reached by the R2C-1s in 1923, but the following year Curtiss designed a new version, building one for the Army and one for the Navy. In the 1925 Pulitzer Trophy races the Curtiss R3C-1 crushed all opposition. The contest was held at Mitchel Field, again, on 12 October, and the Army R3C-1, flown by Cyrus Bettis won with an average speed of 248.975 mph (400.68 km/h). Its naval "twin" came second, the pilot being Alford J. Williams, averaging 241.695 mph (388.964 km/h). After the competition, Williams's performance came in for a good deal of criticism in naval circles. Whether this was due to disappointment and pique at losing, or whether his airmanship really was somewhat at fault, remains unclear. Observers said they particularly noticed that the U.S. Navy's aircraft consistently fell behind its Army twin on each circuit, and this discrepancy in performance was put down to Williams having been too rough on the engine. Be that as it may, the Curtiss racer was an ideal competition aircraft. Just as the navalized version of the CR-1 had won the 1923 Schneider Trophy and also the Pulitzer a few days later, so the R3C-2 seaplane also triumphed at Baltimore. With James Doolittle at the controls it reached an average speed of 232,573 mph (374.284 km/h) and on the following day the world seaplane record of 245.713 mph (395.43 km/h).

Plate 67
The Thompson Trophy: 1930–1934

The U.S. Government's decision not to fund any more competition flying and not to sponsor experimental aircraft was attacked by the American press as being short-sighted and unwise. Public opinion was also extremely hostile and grew even more vociferous in 1929 when, during that year's National Air Races, which was by now a far less exciting event since the Pulitzer Trophy had been discontinued, a private aircraft commissioned and built by an enthusiast of limited means trounced the Army and Navy official entrants

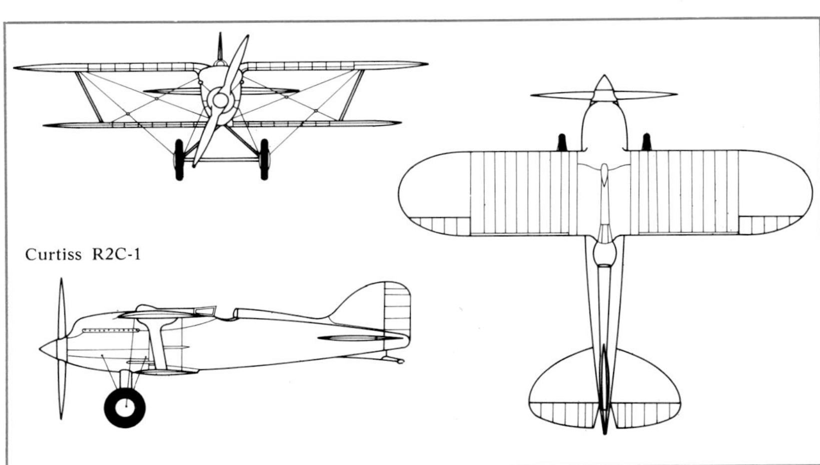

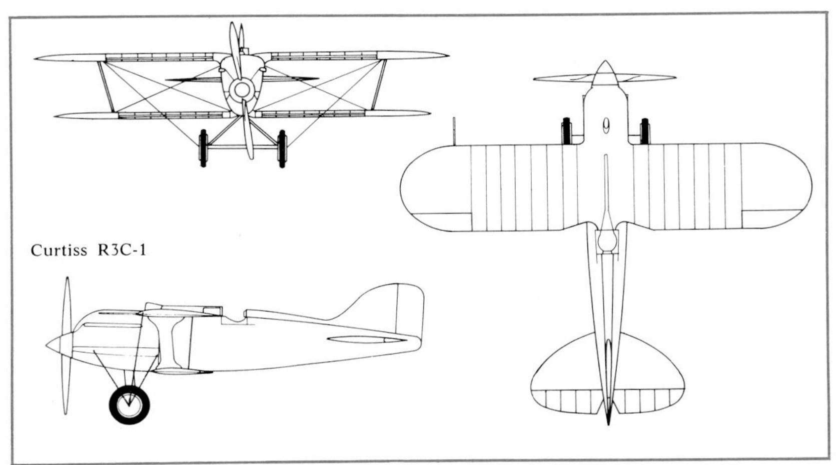

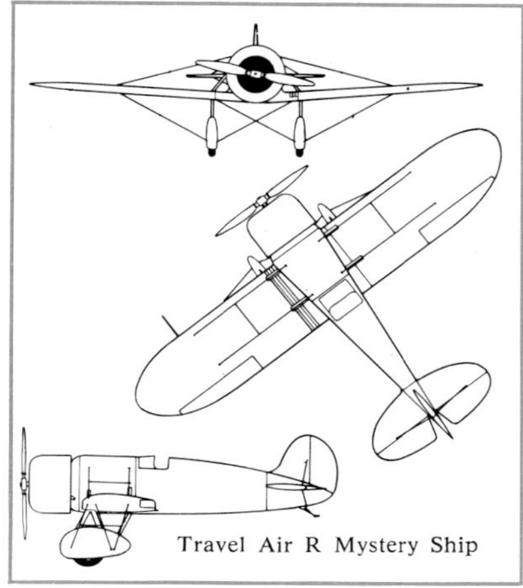
Travel Air R Mystery Ship

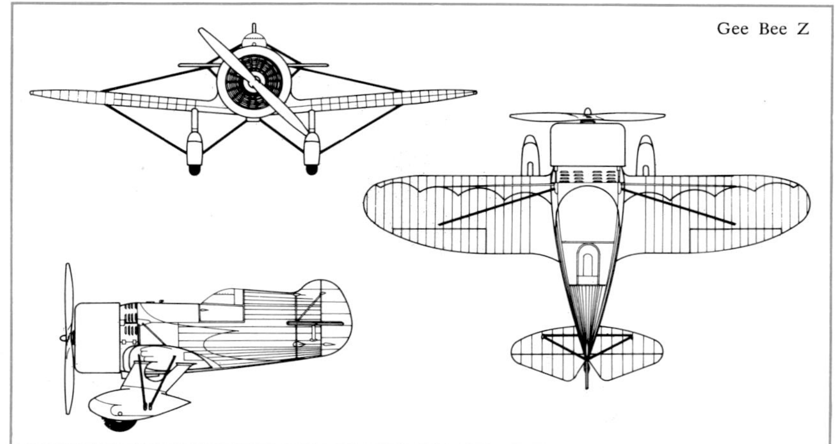
Gee Bee Z

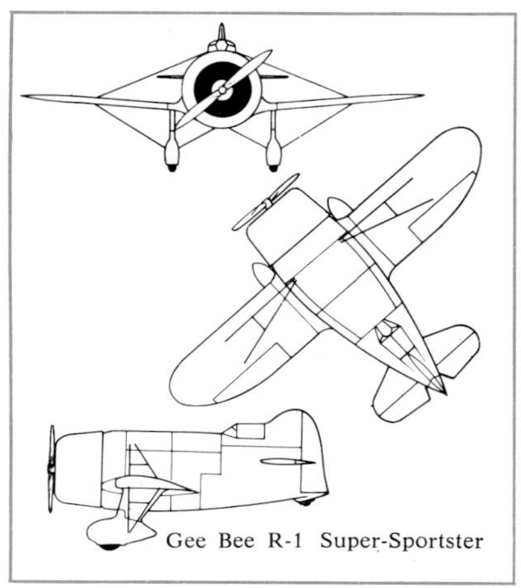
Gee Bee R-1 Super-Sportster

who were racing with their most up-to-date fighters. This was unheard of, and Douglas Davis's Travel Air *Mystery Ship* was so outstanding that it won this open competition with an average speed of 194.85 mph (313.59 km/h) and on its fastest lap reached 208.64 mph (335.79 km/h). The name by which this attractive monoplane came to be known among air enthusiasts arose from the mystery surrounding its arrival at the airfield and from the unusual reticence of its owner/pilot when questioned about his aircraft by the aviation press. The *Mystery Ship* had been designed by Herbert Rawdon and Walter Burhan in the summer of 1928 and great care had been taken in perfecting the engine, a 300 hp Wright Whirlwind radial, which had been so finely tuned that it could develop a third more power.

Davis's achievement sparked off renewed enthusiasm and the following year the decision was taken to hold a pure speed contest, a closed-circuit race which would recapture some of the glamor of the Pulitzer races. Another aviation patron, Charles E. Thompson, an industrialist from Cleveland, Ohio, put up the prize money and this competition was keenly contested every year until 1939, becoming one of the classic air races.

Some idea of the stimulus it gave to aviation may be gained from the first year's results and the field it attracted when it was held on 1 September 1930, at Chicago, when the excellent performance of the Travel Air entries was surpassed by a new, privately-built aircraft, the Laird LC-DW-300 Solution, a biplane which repeated the lines of Glenn Curtiss's racers but which differed in having a radial engine. This aircraft had been designed and built in exactly one month by Matty Laird. The Solution won the Trophy with a speed of 201.78 mph (324.93 km/h). The following year (7 September, Cleveland) a new airplane stole the show, winning the Trophy and showing how the challenge such a competition presented could inspire individual designers. This was the Gee Bee Z, a small, squat monoplane which was to become more famous than any other American competition aircraft. Its victory in the 1931 contest, reaching 236.239 mph (380.184 km/h), piloted by Lowell Bayles was repeated the next year, when the 1932 Thompson Trophy was again held in Cleveland and a more powerful Gee Bee, the R-1 model with James Doolittle at the controls, won with an average speed of 252.48 mph (406.57 km/h). This was the sum total of the little Gee Bee's Thompson victories, but it took the fancy of the hundreds of thousands of aviation fans who flocked to the flying competitions. The Gee Bees were the ideal competition airplanes for the American scene in the thirties, but they were tricky and demanding to fly and earned themselves the reputation of being "mean" airplanes which needed to have a skilled and daring pilot to coax the best performance out of them.

Just how tricky they were, is shown by the fact that on 5 December 1931, Lowell Bayles, the winner of the Thompson Trophy, crashed in his aircraft while trying for a new record; the Gee Bee R-1 which had won the 1932 Thompson Trophy, crashed a year later, killing the pilot Russell Boardman, and in the same year, 1933, another Gee Bee (Y model) disintegrated in flight while being flown by Florence Klingensmith. In 1935 the final model (Gee Bee R-1/R-2) broke up on takeoff at the start of the Bendix Trophy race, killing its owner/pilot, Cecil Allen.

The Gee Bee series had been specially built for speed. The designer, Robert Hall, had finished work on the model Z only a month before the 1931 Thompson Trophy race and its construction and participation in the race had been financed by the Springfield Air Racing Association, which had been set up to provide the backing for the Gee Bees. All the Gee Bees were similar in design and structure; they were initially built round the large 535 hp Pratt & Whitney Wasp Jr. radial engine while keeping the airframe as small as possible and the fuselage had to be faired into the very large engine cowling and yet still be as aerodynamically clean as possible. This gave the Gee Bees their distinctive "flying barrel" appearance and, to offset the weight of the engine, the cockpit was moved as far aft as possible, just forward of the tail. With each successive model the engine became more powerful.

The widely-publicized success of Robert Hall's racers was short-lived and the following year victory in the Thompson Trophy meant fame for an airplane which was to win the race two years running: the Wedell-Williams, designed and built by James Robert Wedell, who won the 1933 race in it at an average speed of 237.95 mph (382.93 km/h) on 4 July in Los Angeles. The aircraft had made its debut in the 1931 Trophy race, coming second to Lowell Bayles in his Gee Bee Z. In 1932 it had repeated this performance again coming second, but this time two more Wedell-Williams came third and fourth.

1934 saw another Wedell-Williams victory in the Thompson Trophy on 3 September at Cleveland, Ohio, with Roscoe Turner at the controls, averaging 248.13 mph (399.33 km/h). Yet more triumphs were in store for James Wedell's monoplane; it won the Bendix

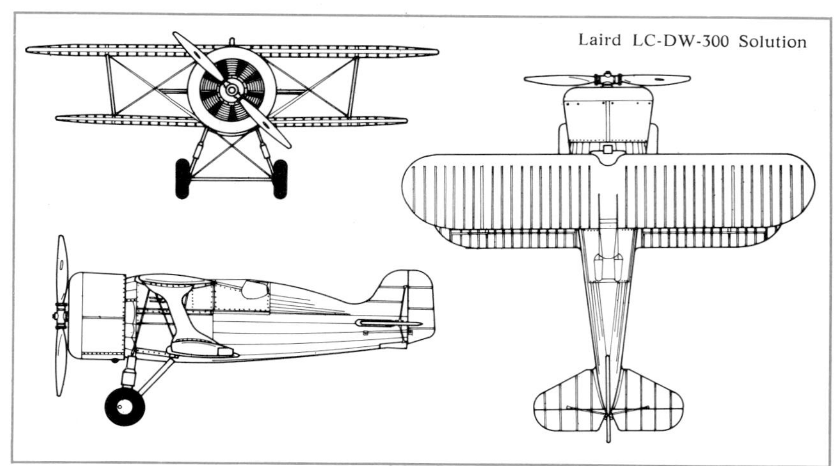
Laird LC-DW-300 Solution

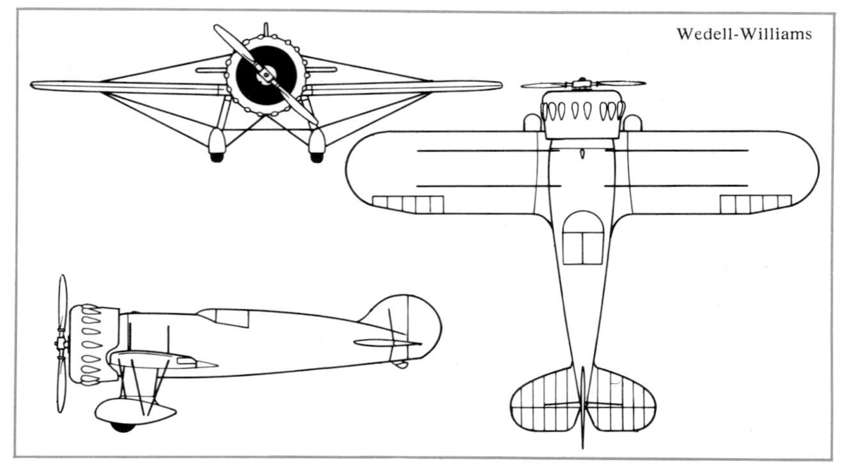
Wedell-Williams

Trophy three times in succession; in 1932 at an average speed of 245 mph (394.27 km/h); in 1933 averaging 214.78 mph (345.64 km/h), and in 1934 with 216.24 mph (347.99 km/h). On 4 September 1933, it shattered the world speed record for landplanes, reaching 305.24 mph (491.22 km/h); this record was set towards the end of a minor competition held in Chicago: the Frank Phillips Trophy.

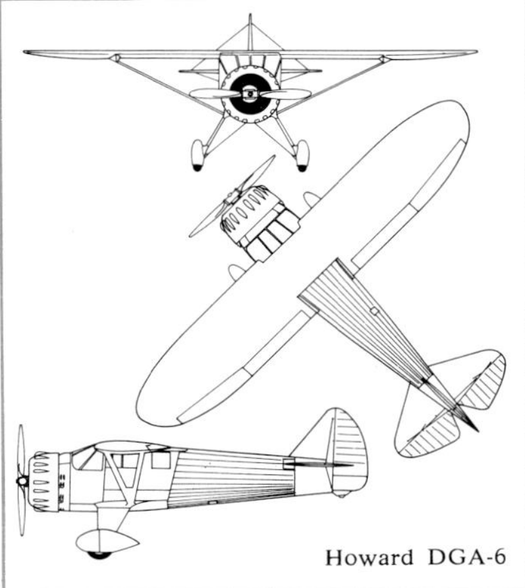
Howard DGA-6

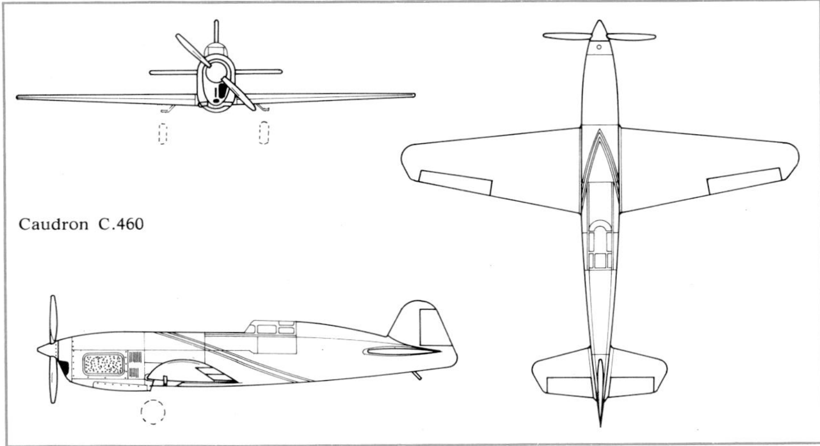
Caudron C.460

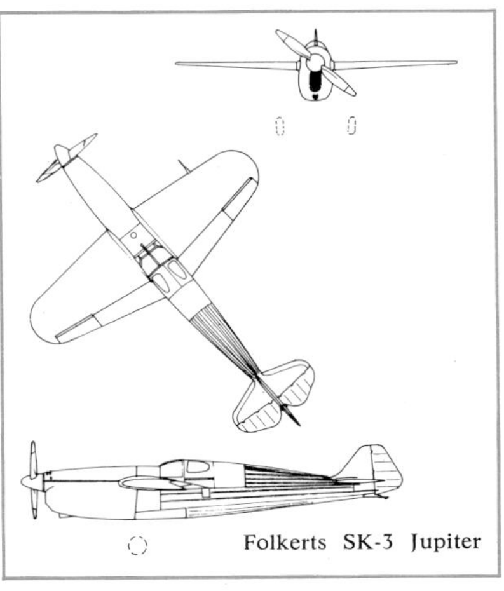
Folkerts SK-3 Jupiter

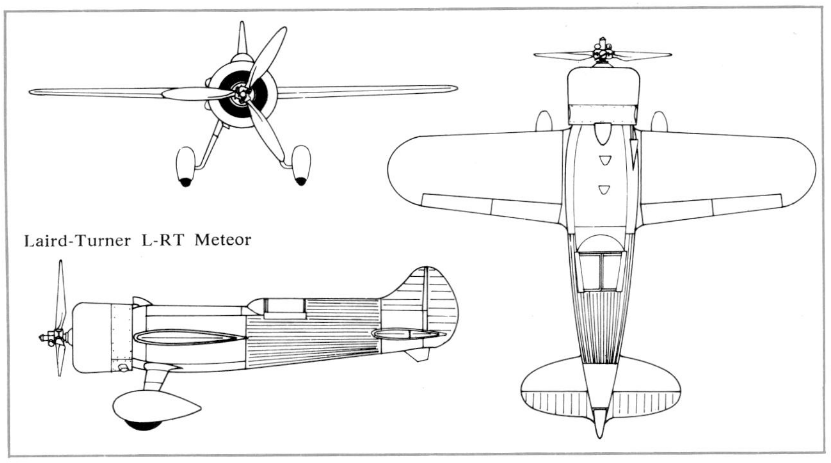
Laird-Turner L-RT Meteor

Plate 68
The Thompson Trophy: 1935–1939

The last four years of the Thompson Trophy races brought a number of excellent new aircraft to the fore. In 1935 the Trophy went to an airplane which looked more like a tourer than a racer: the Howard DGA-6 *Mr. Mulligan*, an elegant, high-wing monoplane which had been designed by one of the most famous personalities in the world of competition flying in the 1930s: Ben Howard. On 2 September at Cleveland, *Mr. Mulligan*, piloted by Harold Neumann, clocked up an average speed of 220 mph (354.29 km/h). Only two days before, flown by its designer, the aircraft had won the other coveted prize, the Bendix Trophy, at the National Air Races, when Ben Howard and Gordon Israel had reached average speeds of 236.69 mph (384.14 km/h) just beating their direct rival, Roscoe Turner in the Wedell-Williams, by 23 seconds. The next year great excitement was caused by the entry of the first European competitor in the National Air Races, challenging the Americans on their home ground.

The Caudron C.460 was a monoplane which already had a considerable reputation when it arrived in the U.S.A. It was one of the most famous French competition aircraft ever built and had been designed by Marcel Riffard to participate in the new series of the Deutsch de la Meurthe Cup. In 1934 it had set a new world speed record for landplanes, reaching 314 mph (505.335 km/h). This was the first time that the hitherto exclusively American field had had to face a European challenge, and the Caudron did, in fact, win The Thompson Trophy. The races were held from 4–7 September in Los Angeles, and the C.460 came first with an average speed of 264.04 mph (425.19 km/h) and also won the Greve Trophy averaging 247.1 mph (397.9 km/h); in both races it was flown by Michel Detroyat.

This European victory was, however, to be an isolated phenomenon. In 1937 (6 September, in Cleveland) the Thompson Trophy was won by a small American monoplane, the Folkerts SK-3 Jupiter, which was piloted by Rudy Kling, and which also won the Greve Trophy with an average speed of 232.08 mph (373.72 km/h). Kling had only just won the Thompson race by a last minute burst of speed.

In the last two years that the Thompson race was held, before the rumblings of another world war put paid to competition flying, one of the most celebrated flyers of the time, Roscoe Turner, rounded off his career in competitive flying with a thrilling achievement. Having won the race in 1934, he was again in the field, piloting an airplane which was as outstanding as the Wedell-Williams: the Laird-Turner L-RT Meteor. This was known as the *Turner Special* and was a small, powerful monoplane which was renamed several times, changing from *Pesco Special* in 1938 to *Miss Champion* in 1939. In both the 1938 and 1939 Thompson races it proved to be a splendid racer. The Meteor brought the golden years of the Thompson Trophy races to a fitting end when Turner won the last two contests: both took place in Cleveland and in 1938 (3–5 September) Turner averaged 283.419 mph (456.021 km/h) and won again in 1939 (2—5 September) with an average speed of 282.31 mph (454.6 km/h). Turner's performance in 1939 was astonishing; he was trailing at the beginning of the race, having missed a marker and having had to turn back again, but he gradually caught up, overtaking competitor after competitor over nine laps, streaking above the heads of a crowd of sixty thousand who rose to applaud his amazing airmanship. By the time he passed the finishing post, Turner had lapped all the other competitors.

Plate 69
The Bendix Trophy: 1931–1939

From 1931 onward another competition vied with the Thompson Trophy for popularity and prestige. This was the Bendix Trophy which was not a closed circuit race. It had been started by Vincent Bendix who was chairman of the Bendix Aeronautical Company and the prize was to be fought out right across the North American continent, from Burbank, California, to Cleveland, Ohio—a distance of nearly 2,050 miles (3,300 km), entailing some ten flying hours. This thrilling race was a regular event from 1931 to 1939 and the course only diverted twice from the original route, in 1933 and 1936, when it was flown from New York to Los Angeles.

During these nine years the average increase in speed of the aircraft taking part in the race was just as breathtaking as in the Thompson Trophy races, in spite of the much greater length of the Bendix flight. The first winner, on 4 September 1931, was James Doolittle, averaging 232.84 mph (374.95 km/h) in a Laird LC-DW-500 Super Solution, an improved, more powerful variant of the Solution which had won the first Thompson Trophy a year earlier. There was a great disparity in speeds between the Super Solution and the other three competitors, which were all commercial Lockheed Orion monoplanes, the fastest of which could not exceed an average speed of 198 mph (320 km/h). The next three Bendix races were won by another famous racer, the Wedell-Williams monoplane which for two years running captured both the Thompson and the Bendix Trophies. On 29 August 1932, James Haizlip reached an average speed of 244.8 mph (394.2 km/h); the following year, on 1 July, Roscoe Turner's Wedell-Williams won at an average speed of 214.78 mph (345.64 km/h) and on 31 August 1934, Douglas Davis piloted the Wedell-Williams to victory, reaching 216.24 mph (347.99 km/h). Exactly one year later, Roscoe

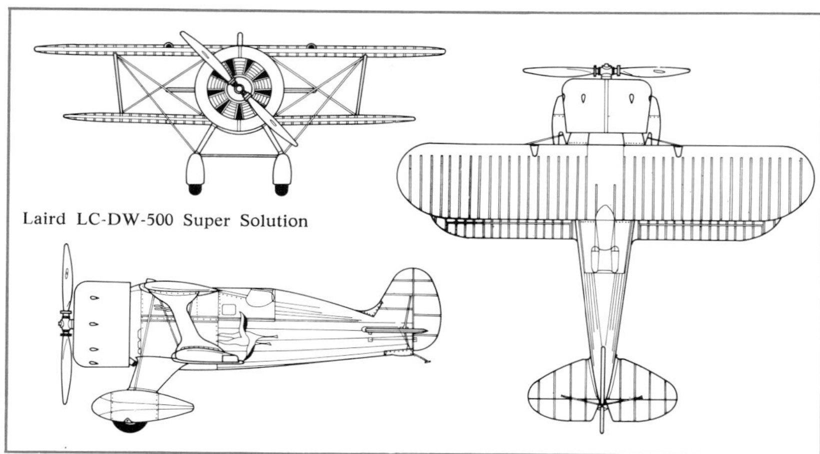
Laird LC-DW-500 Super Solution

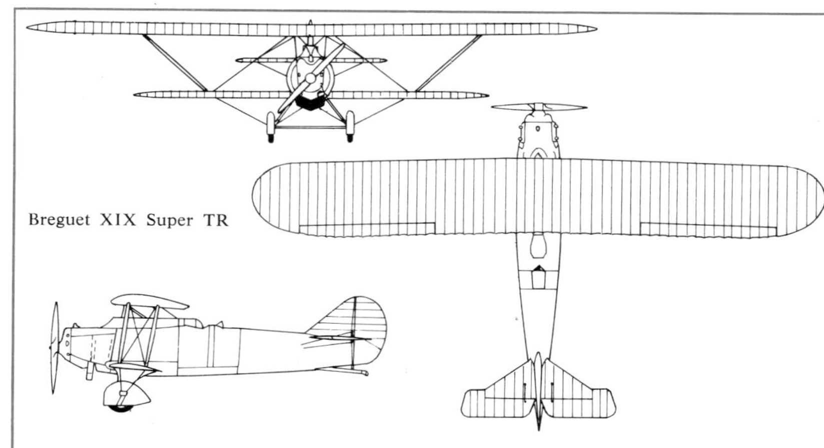
Breguet XIX Super TR

Turner's monoplane was just pipped at the post. At the end of a hard-fought battle he was beaten by Ben Howard in *Mr. Mulligan*, who averaged 238.51 mph (384.07 km/h) and who was also to win the Thompson Trophy two days later.

On 4 September 1936 there was another surprise result in the Bendix race when a standard commercial aircraft, a Beech C-17R flown by Louise Thaden and Blanche Noyes, came in first. These two pilots turned in a rather low average speed, 165.23 mph (266.08 km/h), but this set a new women's record for an East-West crossing of the United States. The most formidable contenders had dropped out of the race, among them *Mr. Mulligan*, again flown by Ben Howard who had to make a forced landing when his propeller failed.

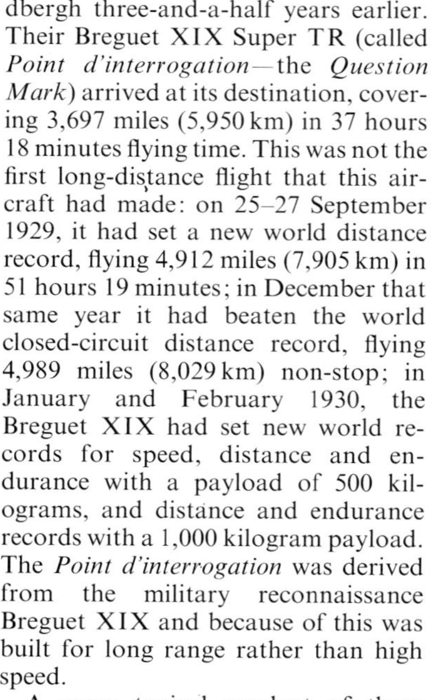
Beech C-17R

The last three years' Bendix Trophy races were dominated by a military aircraft, for the first time for several years. The Seversky Sev-S2 was almost identical to the U.S. Army Air Corps' P-35 which was at this time undergoing proving trials. The Sev-S2 was lent to some enthusiasts who were able to use it in competitions. This small, compact monoplane was entered for the 1937 Bendix Trophy without any advance preparation except for mirror-finishing of metal surfaces. On 3 September, with Frank Fuller at the controls, it won at an average speed of 258.2 mph (415.51 km/h), having flown for 7 hours 54 minutes 26 seconds. The same result recurred the following year, again on 3 September, when it was piloted by Jacqueline Cochran, winning at an average speed of 249.6 mph (401.83 km/h).

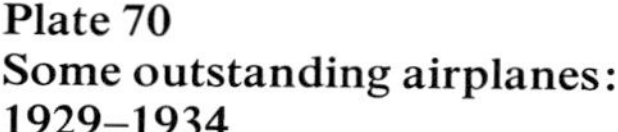
Plate 70
Some outstanding airplanes: 1929–1934

The entire aviation world tended to look to the United States as the leader in the development of racing aircraft, since the important competitions in America fascinated thousands of enthusiasts and drew hundreds of thousands of spectators. During the 1930s, however, European activity and enthusiasm also ran very high. In France, another attempt was made to cross the Atlantic on 1 September 1930. At 10.54 am a red biplane piloted by Dieudonné Costes and Maurice Bellonte took off from Le Bourget heading straight for New York with the objective of flying across the Atlantic in the opposite direction to Charles Lindbergh three-and-a-half years earlier. Their Breguet XIX Super TR (called *Point d'interrogation*—the *Question Mark*) arrived at its destination, covering 3,697 miles (5,950 km) in 37 hours 18 minutes flying time. This was not the first long-distance flight that this aircraft had made: on 25–27 September 1929, it had set a new world distance record, flying 4,912 miles (7,905 km) in 51 hours 19 minutes; in December that same year it had beaten the world closed-circuit distance record, flying 4,989 miles (8,029 km) non-stop; in January and February 1930, the Breguet XIX had set new world records for speed, distance and endurance with a payload of 500 kilograms, and distance and endurance records with a 1,000 kilogram payload. The *Point d'interrogation* was derived from the military reconnaissance Breguet XIX and because of this was built for long range rather than high speed.

A more typical product of these years, when the main emphasis was on racing, was the Kellner-Béchereau 28V.D., a racer built for the 1933 Deutsch de la Meurthe Cup, which was very streamlined, and of quite advanced design, capable of high performance with a relatively small engine. But this small monoplane, which was in some respects reminiscent of its transatlantic counterparts, was unlucky. During proving trials, on 14 May 1933, it developed serious faults and had to be withdrawn.

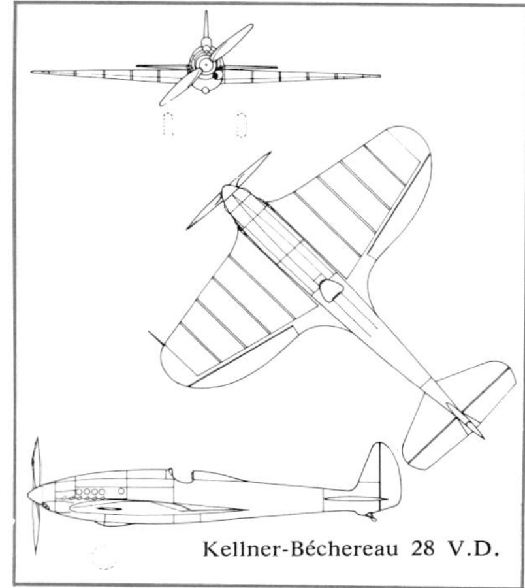
Kellner-Béchereau 28 V.D.

Contemporary British aircraft also made spectacular long-distance flights during these adventuring years. One of the most famous airplanes of this era was the de Havilland D.H.88 Comet, an elegant twin-engine aircraft specially built for the London–Melbourne race, sponsored by Sir MacPherson Robertson in 1934 to commemorate the centenary of the founding of the State of Victoria. The Comet not only won the race, leaving Mildenhall, England, on 20 October 1934, and

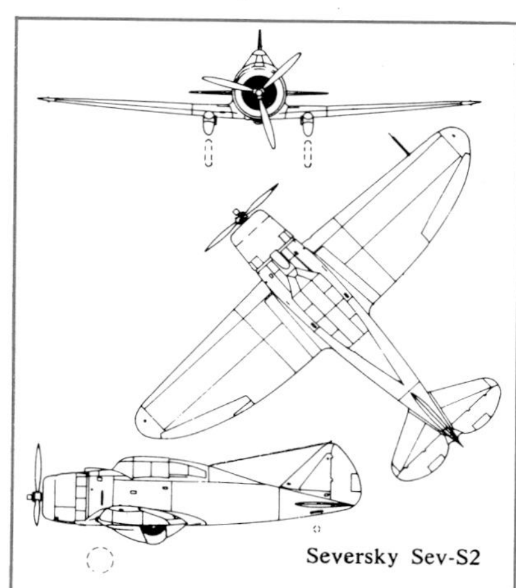
Seversky Sev-S2

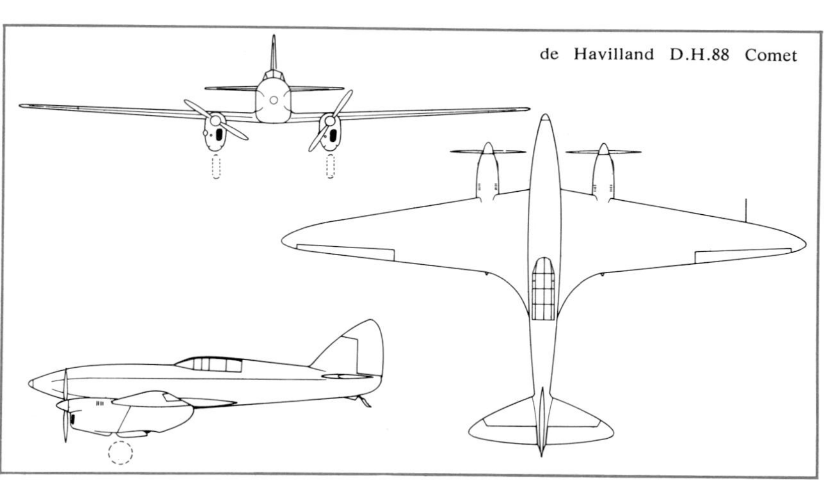
de Havilland D.H.88 Comet

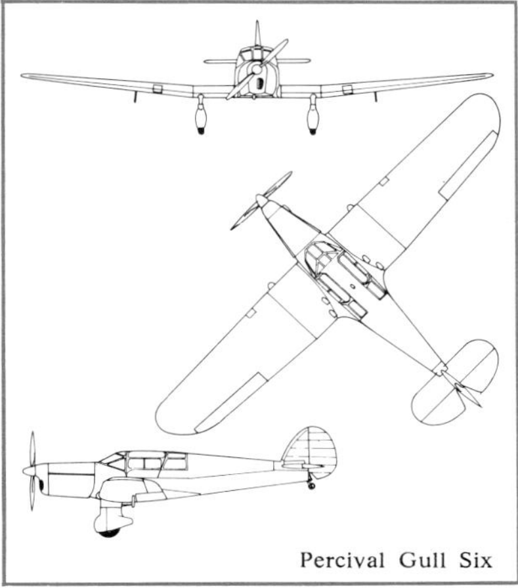
Percival Gull Six

completing the journey in 70 hours 54 minutes 18 seconds flying time but later flew 26,450 miles (42,566 km) from Gravesend (England) to Sydney and then on to Blenheim in New Zealand and back to England again, completing this epic journey in 10 days 21 hours 22 minutes. In 1936 a little single-engine tourer, the Percival Gull Six, piloted by Jean Batten, flew the same outward route (but starting from Lympne in Kent), arriving in New Zealand in 11 days 45 minutes. The year before, this intrepid woman aviator had broken the record for crossing the South Atlantic in the same aircraft, when she flew from England to Brazil, with an ocean crossing, taking 13 hours 15 minutes.

The Soviet Union was also attracted by the challenge of long-distance flights and in 1934, on 10–12 September, a Tupolev ANT-25 broke the world closed-circuit distance record, covering 7,712 miles (12,411 km) in 75 hours 2 minutes; on 18–20 June 1937, the first nonstop flight from Moscow to Portland, Oregon, was made, a distance of 5,284 miles (8,504 km) covered in 63 hours 25 minutes. A month later the ANT-25 set a new long-distance record, flying from Moscow to San Jacinto, California, a distance of 6,303 miles (10,148 km) in 62 hours 17 minutes.

Plate 71
The products of five nations: 1935–1940

In 1938 the Tupolev ANT-25's achievements were emulated by a Japanese aircraft, the Koken. This aircraft, named *Wind of the Century*, had been designed specifically for an attempt on the world closed-circuit record by the Institute for Aeronautical Research at Tokyo University. With a crew of three, the Koken flew 7,235.271 miles (11,643.86 km) on 13–15 May, staying airborne for 62 hours 23 minutes. A year later on 5–6 March 1939, another impressive long-distance flight by a small Italian aircraft, a Nardi F.N.305D, piloted by Giovanni Zappetta and Leonardo Bonzi clocked up 2,773.7 miles (4,463.77 km) in 18 hours 49 minutes from Rome to Addis Ababa, to set a record for light aircraft, an exceptional achievement since the F.N.305D was a trainer, although it had undergone major modifications. It had a stretched fuselage to accommodate extra fuel tanks and, most important change from the series aircraft, a Walter Bora radial engine installed in place of the usual Fiat or Alfa Romeo inline engine. Comparable long-distance flights were made in 1936 and 1938 by the German Messerschmitt Bf 108B, an aircraft which bore some resemblance to the Nardi. The first version of the Bf 108, the A model, had been built to compete in the 1934 "Europa-rundflug" (Circuit of Europe); the next model was an improved version which, apart from entering service with the Luftwaffe, chalked up many sporting triumphs. In 1936 Elly Beinhorn flew a Bf 108B from Berlin to Istanbul and back in a single day; in 1937 and 1938 the Bf 108 did extremely well in a number of aviation rallies in Great Britain, Germany and Belgium.

The late 1930s saw the last of the great racing aircraft. In America on 13 September 1935, the Hughes H-1 broke the world speed record, flying at 351.99 mph (566.49 km/h) at Santa Ana, California. In Great Britain two racers built to break landplane speed records, both failed to do so. The T.K.4 was built in 1937 and came ninth in that year's King's Cup Race with an average speed of 230.5 mph (370.94 km/h), but crashed on 1 October. The Heston Type 5, built in 1939–40 was damaged beyond repair on 12 June 1940, when it crashed during its one and only flight.

The Hughes H-1 was one of the "flying millionaire" Howard Hughes's pet projects and he had designed and built this aircraft merely for the pleasure of producing an exceptionally fast and impressive competition aircraft. The idea first came to him in 1935 and the H-1 was originally intended to enter and, needless to say, win the following year's Thompson and Bendix Trophies. Hughes's talents and unlimited wealth meant that he was a privileged contestant and after the H-1 had beaten the world speed record in 1935, vociferous complaints about his unfair advantage from the other regular American competitors grew so strident that Hughes withdrew his entry in some irritation. He was not, however, going to renounce an opportunity of showing off the potentail of his aircraft. On 19 January 1937, the

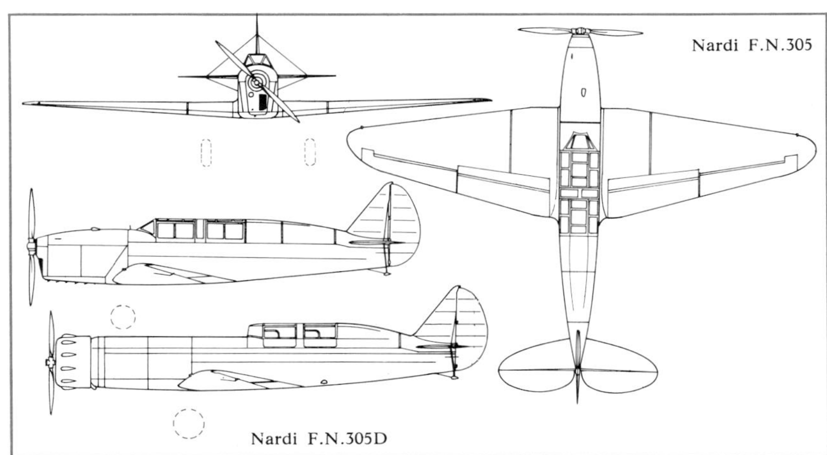
Nardi F.N.305
Nardi F.N.305D

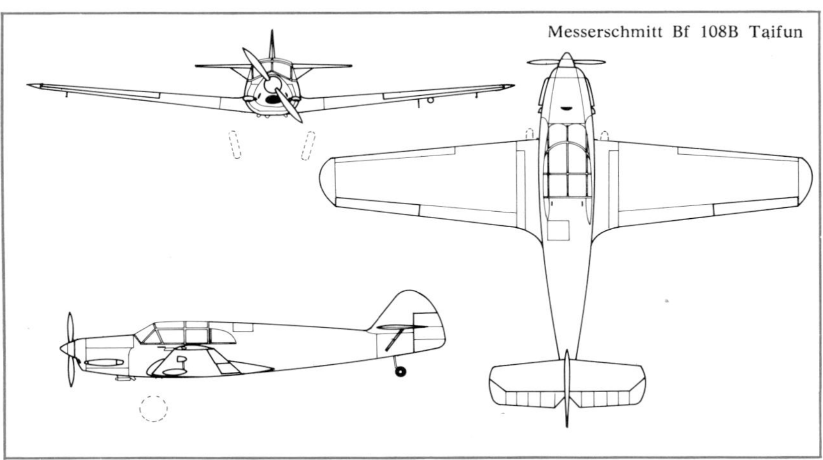
Messerschmitt Bf 108B Taifun

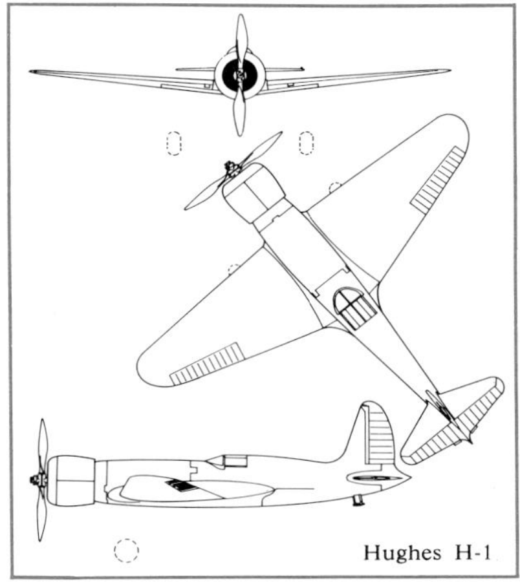
Hughes H-1

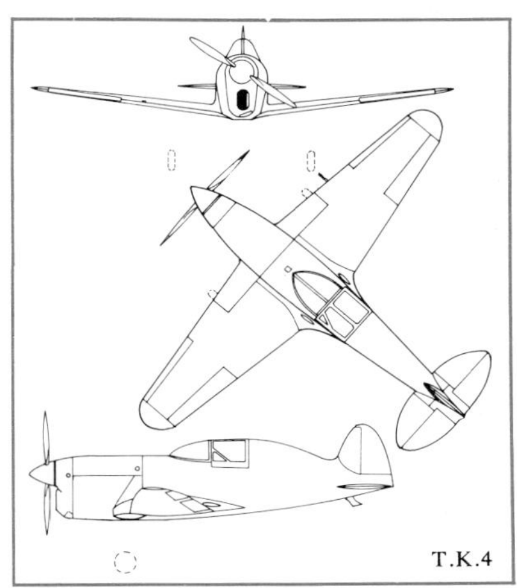
T.K.4

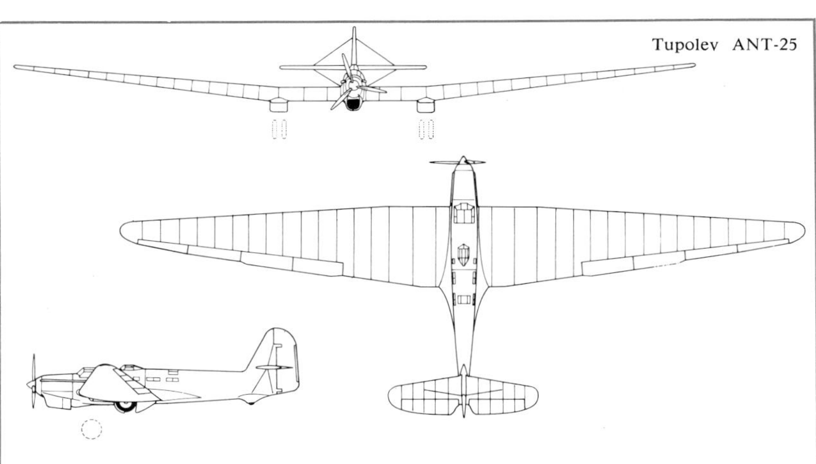
Tupolev ANT-25

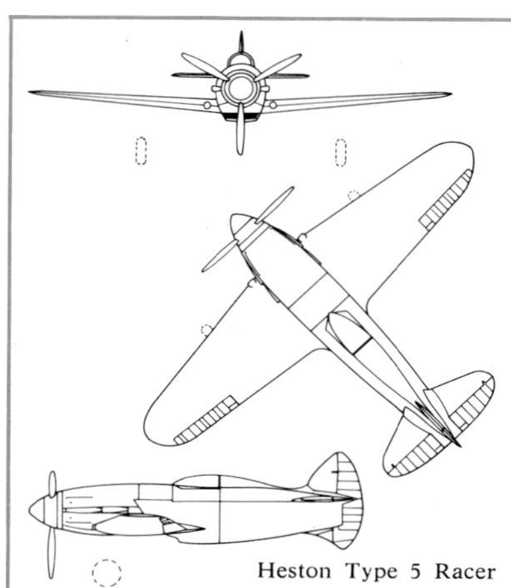
Heston Type 5 Racer

Hughes H-1, which had had its wingspan increased, won the U.S. transcontinental speed record. The flight from Los Angeles to Newark took 7 hours 28 minutes, covering 2,489 miles (4,006 km) at an average speed of 327 mph (526.24 km/h).

Plate 72
Three unforgettable record-breaking aircraft: 1928–1934

In the late twenties and early thirties some exceptional record-breaking airplanes were built, simply to set new world records in a race against time, designed and built by some of the best talent available during the golden age of competition aircraft. Enormous sums were spent on these aircraft and the only visible return was usually that of national prestige, when another world record was broken. Between 1928 and 1930 an Italian airplane was expressly designed to attempt new world endurance records and made a name for itself in international aviation circles. The Savoia Marchetti S.M.64 was the result of a meeting between two dedicated aviation enthusiasts, Alessandro Marchetti and Arturo Ferrarin, and the project was successfully completed thanks to the collaboration between Savoia Marchetti and Fiat and the support of the Italian Air Ministry. Fiat, in fact, built a special version of its A.22 engine, while the Air Force constructed a special cement runway on a slanting gradient at Montecelio near Guidonia to facilitate the S.M.64's takeoff when fully loaded with extra fuel.

After test flights at Cameri (April 1928), the S.M.64 was readied for the attempt at the record. On the night of 31 May the S.M.64 took off on its long flight with Arturo Ferrarin, Carlo Del Prete and flight engineer Capannini. The circuit was flown fifty-one times and at 3.30 on the afternoon of 2 June the airplane landed, having established several records: 58 hours 53 minutes and 15 seconds in the air, having covered 4,763.7 miles (7,663.617 km); this meant that this crew of the S.M.64 had set new world closed-circuit records for endurance and distance and the speed record over 5,000 kilometers (3,100 miles) at 86 mph (139 km/h). A month later Ferrarin and Del Prete took off on a nonstop long-distance flight from Montecelio to Natal (Brazil). They reached their destination or very near it, crashing near Natal on 5 July, but they had beaten the world long-distance flight record, having flown 4,466 miles (7,188 km). The airplane's career was not yet over, however: it was repaired and taken back to Italy where it was modified and called the S.M.64bis. On 31 May 1930, flown by Fausto Cecconi and Umberto Maddalena, the aircraft set a new closed-circuit endurance record at 67 hour 13 minutes in the air, covering a distance of 5,088 miles (8,186 km).

These feats were emulated during the next three years by a French aircraft which, like the Savoia Marchetti S.M.64 had also been specifically designed and constructed to be a record-breaker: the Blériot 110. Filippo Zappata's design was begun in early 1929 and construction was completed by 9 May the following year. A few weeks later it started to win success after success, the first being the national closed-circuit distance record (4,785 miles–7,701 km). In February 1931, with Lucien Bossoutrot and Maurice Rossi at the controls, the Blériot 110 beat the previous record set by the S.M.64, flying 5,468 miles (8,799 km) in 75 hours 23 minutes. A year later on 26 March 1932, they broke their own record by flying 6,587 miles (10,601.480 km) in 76 hours 34 minutes. And then on 5–7 August 1933, Maurice Rossi and Paul Codos established a new long-distance straight-line world record. They flew 5,656 miles (9,104 km) from New York to Rayak, Syria, in 55 hours 30 minutes in the Blériot 110.

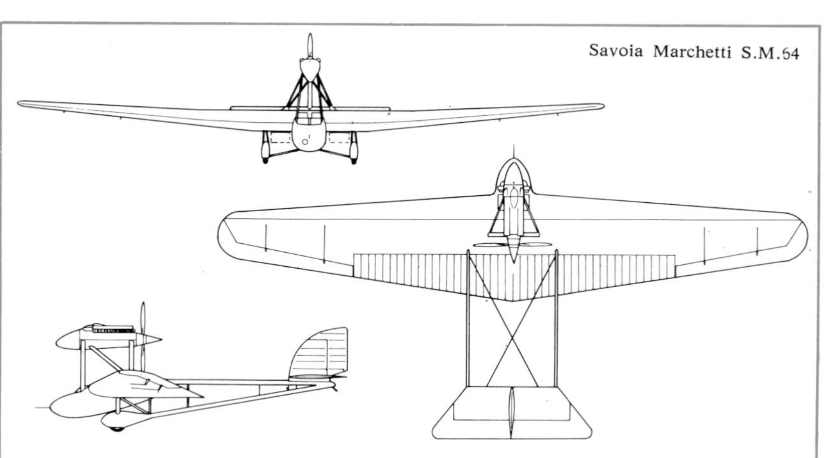
Savoia Marchetti S.M.64

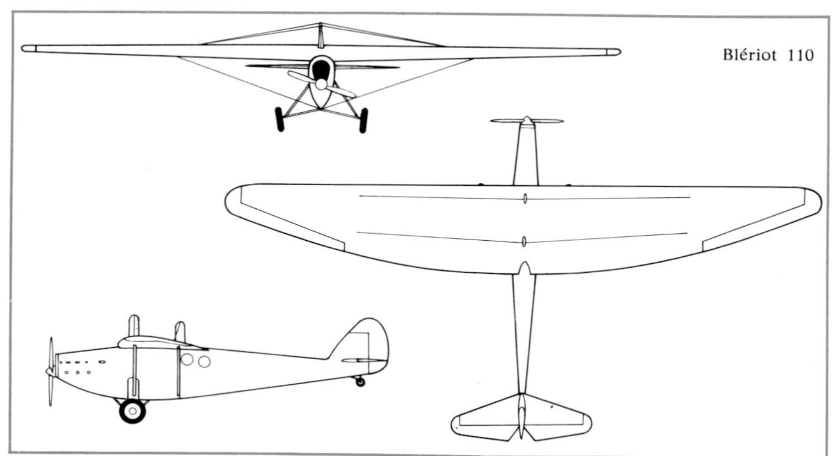
Blériot 110

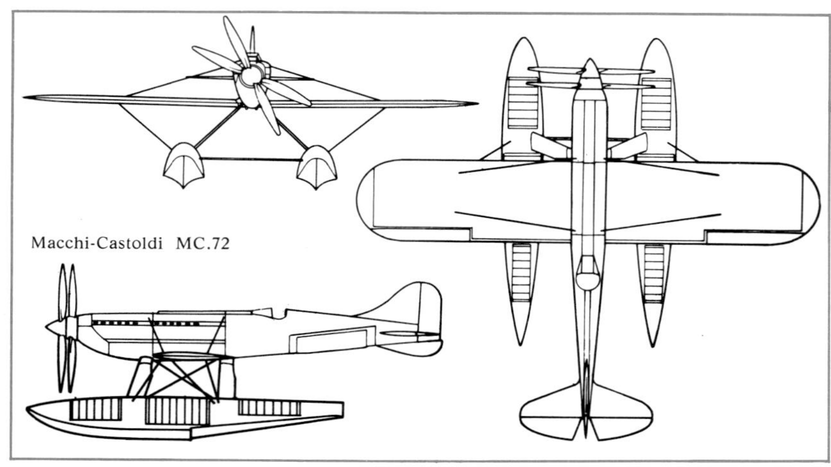
Macchi-Castoldi MC.72

Italy was to produce another quite exceptional racing aircraft built with all the emphasis on speed. The Macchi-Castoldi MC.72 seaplane was to be unique in aviation history, the last and best of an internationally acclaimed series whose *raison d'être* was to compete in the Schneider Trophy contest. The MC.72 had been designed and built to take part in the 1931 Schneider race, but was not ready in time, due to persistent problems with its very large and powerful engine. This was the Fiat A.S.6 which had been built by joining two A.S.5 12-cylinder V engines end to end, forming a single element, a power unit which could develop over 3,000 hp at 3,300 rpm. Considerable modifications were subsequently made to eliminate the engine faults and on 10 April 1933, Francesco Agello broke the world speed record for seaplanes for the first time with the MC.72, reaching a speed of 423.822 mph (682.078 km/h). On 8 October, at Ancona, Casinelli broke the world speed record over 100 kilometers with a speed of 391.071 mph (629.37 km/h). On 23 October 1934, once more at Lake Garda, Francesco Agello flew the last of the five MC.72s built, to its most outstanding achievement when he again set a new world speed record; in four runs the seaplane reached a top speed of 442.081 mph (711.463 km/h), achieving a final average speed of 440.681 mph (709.209 km/h). The MC.72 had reached the limit which could be achieved by a seaplane powered by a piston engine and this record was not to be beaten in the years to come.

The James Gordon Bennett Cup: 1909-1920

Date, Venue, Distance	Place	Pilot	Aircraft	Engine	Race No.	Speed km/h	mph
1909 28 August	1	Glenn Curtiss (USA)	Curtiss Golden Flyer	Curtiss V-8 50 HP	8	75,492	46.918
Reims, (F) 20 km (12.43 miles)	2	Louis Blériot (F)	Blériot XI	E.N.V. V-8 60 HP	22	75,349	46.829
	3	H. Hubert Latham (F)	Antoinette	Antoinette V-8 50 HP	13	68,382	42.499
1910 29 October	1	C. Grahame-White (GB)	Blériot XI bis	Gnôme Rotary 14c. 100 HP	—	98,552	61.250
Belmont, N.Y. (USA) 100 km	2	Moisant (USA)	Blériot XI	Gnôme Rotary 7c. 50 HP	—	50,694	31.506
(62.137 miles)	3	Alec Ogilvie (GB)	Wright C	Wright 4c. 35 HP	—	47,314	29.405
1911 1 July	1	Charles T. Weymann (USA)	Nieuport monoplane	Gnôme Rotary 7c. 100 HP	—	125,633	78.080
Eastchurch, (GB) 150 km (94 miles)	2	A. Leblanc (F)	Blériot	Gnôme Rotary 7c. 100 HP	—	122,037	75.846
	3	M. Nieuport (F)	Nieuport	Gnôme Rotary 7c. 70 HP	—	120,814	75.086
1912 9 September	1	Jules Védrines (F)	Deperdussin	Gnôme Rotary 160 HP	—	169,700	105.469
Chicago, Ill. (USA) 201 km (124,8 miles)	2	Maurice Prévost (F)	Deperdussin	Gnôme Rotary 14c. 100 HP	—	167,050	103.822
	3	* André Frey (F)	Hanriot		—		
1913 29 September	1	Maurice Prévost (F)	Deperdussin	Gnôme Rotary 160 HP	1	200,836	124.820
Reims, (F) 200 km (124.3 miles)	2	Emile Védrines (F)	Ponnier		5	197,907	123.000
	3	Gilbert (F)	Deperdussin	Gnôme Rotary 14c. 160 HP	2	192,275	119.499
1920 28 September	1	Sadi Lecointe (F)	Nieuport 29V	Hispano Suiza V-8 320 HP	10	271,548	168.731
Etampes, (F) 300 km (186.451 miles)	2	Bernard de Romanet (F)	Spad S.20 bis	Hispano Suiza V-8 320 HP	8	181,616	112.875
	3	** Georges Kirsch (F)	Nieuport 29V	Hispano Suiza V-8 320 HP	11		

After French entrants won the Cup for the third successive year it mas awarded outright to the Aéro Club de France
* Withdrew after the 24th lap ** Withdrew after the 3rd lap

The Henry Deutsch de la Meurthe Grand Prix d'Aviation: 1912-1920

Date, Venue, Distance	Place	Pilot	Aircraft	Engine	Race No.	Fastest Lap km/h	mph
1912 1 May Paris (F) 200 km (124.3 miles)	1	Emmanuel Helen (F)	Nieuport	Gnôme 70 HP	—	125,370	77.917
1913 27 October Paris (F) 200 km (124.3 miles)	1	Eugène Gilbert (F)	Deperdussin	Gnôme Rotary 160 HP	—	163,451	101.585
1919 2 September - 24 January Paris (F) 190,399 km (118.333 miles)	1	Sadi Lecointe (F)	Nieuport 29V	Hispano-Suiza 42 275 HP	6	266,314	165.515

The Deutsch de la Meurthe Cup: 1921-1922

Date, Venue, Distance	Place	Pilot	Aircraft	Engine	Race No.	Fastest Lap km/h	mph
1921 1 October	1	Georges Kirsch (F)	Nieuport-Delage	Hispano-Suiza 42 300 HP	7	282,752	175.731
Paris (F) 300 km (186.451 miles)	2	Fernand Lasne (F)	Nieuport-Delage 29V	Hispano-Suiza 42 300 HP	5	259,030	160.988
1922 30 September Paris (F) 300 km (186.451 miles)	1	Fernand Lasne (F)	Nieuport-Delage 29V	Hispano-Suiza 42 300 HP	4	289,902	180.175

London Aerial Derby: 1912-1923

Date, Venue, Distance	Place	Pilot	Aircraft	Engine	Race No.	Fastest Lap km/h	mph
1912 8 June Hendon, (GB) 130,329 km (81 miles)	1	T.O.M. Sopwith (GB)	Blériot XI	Gnôme 70 HP	—	94,062	58.460
1913 20 September Hendon (GB) 152,855 km (95 miles)	1	Gustav Hamel (GB)	Morane-Saulnier	Gnôme 80 HP	—	120,964	75.180
1914 23 May Hendon, (GB) 152,050 km (94.5 miles)	1	William L. Brock (USA)	Morane-Saulnier	Gnôme 80 HP	—	115,622	71.860
1919 21 June	1	Gerald Gathergood (GB)	Airco D.H.4R	Napier Lion II 450 HP	7	212,939	132.343
Hendon, (GB) 304,101 km (189 miles)	2	R.H. Nisbet (GB)	Martinsyde F.4 Buzzard	Rolls-Royce Falcon III 220 HP	10	200,976	124.908
	3	Marcus D. Manton (GB)	Airco D.H.4	Rolls-Royce Eagle VIII 360 HP	8	191,057	118.743
1920 24 July	1	Francis T. Courtney (GB)	Martinsyde Semiquaver	Hispano-Suiza 42 290 HP	15	248,899	154.692
Hendon, (GB) 321,80 km (200 miles)	2	James H. James (GB)	Nieuport & General L.C.1	A.B.C. Dragonfly 295 HP	10	233,734	145.267
	3	Cyril F. Uwins (GB)	Bristol 32 Bullet	Bristol Jupiter I 400 HP	14	219,076	136.157
1921 16 July	1	James H. James (GB)	Gloucestershire Mars I	Napier Lion II 425 HP	21	263,076	163.503
Hendon, (GB) 321,80 km (200 miles)	2	Cyril F. Uwins (GB)	Bristol 32 Bullet	Bristol Jupiter I 400 HP	17	229,948	142.914
	3	Walter H. Longton (GB)	S.E.5a	Hisp.-Suiza Wolseley Viper 210 HP	28	192,643	119.729
1922 7 August	1	James H. James (GB)	Gloucestershire Mars I	Napier Lion II 425 HP	9	287,528	178.700
Croydon, (GB) 318,582 km	2	Rollo A. de Haga Haig (GB)	Bristol 32 Bullet	Bristol Jupiter II 380 HP	8	241,757	150.253
(198 miles)	3	Frederick P. Raynham (GB)	Martinsyde F.6	Hisp.-Suiza Wolseley Viper 210 HP	3	179,482	111.549
1923 6 August	1	Larry L. Carter (GB)	Gloucestershire Gloster I	Napier Lion III 460 HP	—	314,804	195.652
Croydon, (GB) 321,8 km (200 miles)	2	Walter H. Longton (GB)	Sopwith 107 Hawker	Bristol Jupiter III 420 HP	—	267,917	166.512
	3	C.D. Barnard (GB)	de Havilland D.H.9A	Napier Lion Ia 450 HP	—	240,128	149.241

The above results are placings based on speed. Another, handicap, placing was also made.

Louis D. Beaumont Cup: 1923-1925

Date, Venue, Distance	Place	Pilot	Aircraft	Engine	Race No.	Fastest Lap km/h	Fastest Lap mph
1923 14 October Istres, Marseille (F) 300 km (186,451 miles)	*				—	—	—
1924 23 June Istres, Marseille (F) 300 km (186,451 miles)	1	Sadi Lecointe (F)	Nieuport-Delage 42	Hispano-Suiza 51 570 HP	3	317,460	197.46
1925 18 October Istres, Marseille (F) 300 km (186,451 miles)	1	Sadi Lecointe (F)	Nieuport-Delage 42	Hispano-Suiza 51 570 HP	—	312,464	194.155

* Race cancelled due to contestants having scratched

Schneider Trophy: 1913-1931

Date, Venue, Distance	Place	Pilot	Aircraft	Engine	Race No.	Speed km/h	Speed mph
1913 16 April Monaco 280 km (174 miles)	1	Maurice Prévost (F)	Deperdussin	Gnôme Rotary 160 HP	19	73,56	45.7
1914 20 April Monaco 280 km (174 miles)	1	C. Howard Pixton (GB)	Sopwith Tabloid	Gnôme Rotary 100 HP	3	139,73	83.735
	2	Burri (CH)	F.B.A.	Gnôme Rotary 100 HP	7	139,656	86.78
1919 10 September Bournemouth (GB) 370,40 km (230.205 miles)	1	Guido Jannello (I) *	Savoia S.13 bis	Isotta-Fraschini V6 250 HP	7	—	—
1920 21 September Venice (I) 371,17 km (230.683 miles)	1	Luigi Bologna (I)	Savoia S.12 bis	Ansaldo V-12 500 HP	7	170,541	105.971
1921 7 August Venice (I) 394,10 km (244.938 miles)	1	Giovanni De Briganti (I)	Macchi M.7 bis	Isotta-Fraschini V6A 280 HP	1	189,677	117.859
1922 12 August Naples (I) 370,689 km (230.385 miles)	1	Henri C. Biard (GB)	Supermarine Sea Lion II	Napier Lion II 450 HP	14	234,516	145.721
	2	Alessandro Passaleva (I)	Savoia S.M.51	Itala 300 HP	8	229,571	142.679
	3	Arturo Zanetti (I)	Macchi M.17 bis	Isotta-Fraschini V6A 240 HP	9	213,653	132.786
1923 28 September Cowes, Isle of Wight (GB) 344,472 km (214.090 miles)	1	David Rittenhouse (USA)	Curtiss CR-3	Curtiss D-12 450 HP	4	285,303	177.278
	2	Rutledge Irvine (USA)	Curtiss CR-3	Curtiss D-12 450 HP	3	278,975	173.384
	3	Henri C. Biard (GB)	Supermarine Sea Lion III	Napier Lion III 460 HP	7	252,772	157.065
1925 26 October Bay Shore Park, Balt. (USA) 350 km (217.48 miles)	1	James H. Doolittle (USA)	Curtiss R3C-2	Curtiss V-1400 610 HP	3	374,284	232.573
	2	Hubert S. Broad (GB)	Gloster III-A	Napier Lion III 530 HP	5	320,464	199.170
	3	Giovanni De Briganti (I)	Macchi M.33	Curtiss D-12A 507 HP	7	271,026	168.444
1926 13 November Hampton Roads, Norfolk (USA) 350 km (217.48 miles)	1	Mario De Bernardi (I)	Macchi M.39	Fiat A.S.2 V-12 800 HP	5	396,698	246.496
	2	Christian Frank Schilt (USA)	Curtiss R3C-2	Curtiss V-1400 500 HP	6	372,263	231.363
	3	Adriano Bacula (I)	Macchi M.39	Fiat A.S.2 V-12 800 HP	1	350,847	218.052
1927 26 September Venice (I) 350 km (217.48 miles)	1	S.N. Webster (GB)	Supermarine S.5	Napier Lion VIIG 875 HP	6	453,273	281.655
	2	O.F. Worseley (GB)	Supermarine S.5	Napier Lion VIID 875 HP	4	439,369	273.070
1929 7 September Cowes, Isle of Wight (GB) 350 km (217.48 miles)	1	H.R.D. Waghorn (GB)	Supermarine S.6	Rolls-Royce R V-12 1920 HP	2	528,869	328.629
	2	T. Dal Molin (I)	Macchi M.52R	Fiat A.S.3 V-12 1030 HP	—	457,277	284,200
	3	d'Arcy Greig (GB)	Supermarine S.5	Napier Lion VIIG 875 HP	—	453,914	282.110
1931 13 September Lee on Solent (GB) 350 km (217.48 miles)	1	John H. Boothman (GB)	Supermarine S.6B	Rolls-Royce R V-12 2350 HP	—	547,297	340.108

* Victory not ratified

Pulitzer Trophy: 1919-1925

Date, Venue, Distance	Place	Pilot	Aircraft	Engine	Race No.	Speed km/h	Speed mph
1919 28 May Atlantic C., N.J. - Boston, Mass. (USA) 547 km (340 miles)	1	Mansell R. James (USA)	Sopwith Camel				
1920 25 November Long Island, N.Y. (USA) 186,772 km (116.080 miles)	1	Corliss C. Moseley (USA)	Verville VCP-R	Packard 1A 638 HP	63	251,921	156.539
	2	Harold E. Hartney (USA)	Thomas-Morse M.B.3	Wright H-2 326 HP	41	238,432	148.187
	3	Bert Acosta (USA)	Ansaldo A.1 Balilla	SPA 6A 210 HP	56	216,410	134.500
1921 3 November Omaha, Nebr. (USA) 247,134 km (153.595 miles)	1	Bert Acosta (USA)	Curtiss CR-1	Curtiss CD-12 405 HP	4	284,44	176.750
	2	Clarence B. Coombs (USA)	Curtiss-Cox Cactus Kitten	Curtiss C-12 435 HP	3	274,070	170.336
	3	John A. Macready (USA)	Thomas-Morse MB-6	Wright H-2 326 HP	2	258,600	160.721
1922 14 October Mt. Clemens, Mich. (USA) 250 km (155.376 miles)	1	Russel L. Maughan (USA)	Curtiss R-6	Curtiss D-12 468 HP	43	331,288	205.856
	2	Lester J. Maitland (USA)	Curtiss R-6	Curtiss D-12 468 HP	44	319,949	198.850
	3	Harold J. Brow (USA)	Curtiss CR-2	Curtiss D-12 435 HP	40	311,655	193.695
1923 6 October St. Louis, Mo. (USA) 200 km (124.28 miles)	1	Alford J. Williams (USA)	Curtiss R2C-1	Curtiss D-12A 507 HP	9	392,147	243.673
	2	Harold J. Brow (USA)	Curtiss R2C-1	Curtiss D-12A 507 HP	10	389,022	241.779
	3	Lawson H. Sanderson (USA)	Wright F2W-1	Wright T-3 600 HP	8	370,177	230.067
1924 4 October Dayton, Ohio (USA) 200 km (124.28 miles)	1	Henry H. Mills (USA)	Verville-Sperry R-3	Curtiss D-12A 507 HP	70	348,504	216.554
	2	Wendell H. Brookley (USA)	Curtiss R-6	Curtiss D-12A 507 HP	69	344,992	214.414
	3	Rex K. Stoner (USA)	Curtiss PW8A	Curtiss D-12 470 HP	71	270,196	167.928
1925 12 October Long Island, N.Y. (USA) 200 km (124.28 miles)	1	Cyrus Bettis (USA)	Curtiss R3C-1	Curtiss V-1400 500 HP	43	400,680	248.975
	2	Alford J. Williams (USA)	Curtiss R3C-1	Curtiss V-1400 500 HP	40	388,887	241.695
	3	Leo H. Dawson (USA)	Curtiss P-1	Curtiss D-12 470 HP	—	273,369	169.900

The Thompson Trophy: 1930-1939

Date, Venue, Distance	Place	Pilot	Aircraft	Engine	Race No.	Speed km/h	Speed mph
1930 1 September Chicago, Ill. (USA) 160,394 km (100 miles)	1	Charles Holman	Laird LC-DW-300 Solution	P. & W. Wasp Jr. 470 HP	77	324,873	201.910
	2	James Haizlip	Travel Air R *Mystery Ship*	Wright R-975 400 HP	—	321,478	199.800
	3	Ben Howard	Howard *Pete*	Wright Gipsy 90 HP	37	261,945	162.800
1931 7 September Cleveland, Ohio (USA) 160,934 km (100 miles)	1	Lowell Bayles	Gee Bee Z	P. & W. Wasp Jr. 535 HP	4	380,84	236.239
	2	James Wedell	Wedell-Williams 44	P. & W. Wasp Jr. 535 HP	44	366,839	227.992
	3	Dale Jackson	Laird Solution	Wright J-6-9 525 HP	77	339,793	211.183
1932 5 September Cleveland, Ohio (USA) 160,934 km (100 miles)	1	James Doolittle	Gee Bee R-1	P. & W. Wasp Jr. 800 HP	11	406,571	252.686
	2	James Wedell	Wedell-Williams	P. & W. Wasp Jr. 550 HP	44	390,176	242.496
	3	Roscoe Turner	Wedell-Williams	P. & W. Wasp Jr. 550 HP	121	374,964	233.042
1933 4 July Los Angeles, Calif. (USA) 96,560 km (60 miles)	1	James Wedell	Wedell-Williams	P. & W. Wasp Jr. 550 HP	44	382,864	237.952
	2	Leo Gehlbach	Wedell-Williams	P. & W. Wasp Jr. 550 HP	92	361.939	224.947
	3	Roy Minor	Howard *Mike*	Menasco 6 225 HP	38	321,590	199.870
1934 3 September Cleveland, Ohio (USA) 160,934 km (100 miles)	1	Roscoe Turner	Wedell-Williams	P. & W. Hornet 1000 HP	57	399,239	248.129
	2	Roy Minor	Brown *Miss Los Angeles*	Menasco C-6S 300 HP	33	345,820	214.929
	3	J.A. Worthen	Wedell-Williams	P. & W. Wasp Jr. 550 HP	92	335,276	208.376
1935 2 September Cleveland, Ohio (USA) 241,402 km (150 miles)	1	Harold Neumann	Howard DGA-6 *Mr Mulligan*	P. & W. Wasp 830 HP	40	354,292	220.194
	2	Steve Wittman	Wittman *Bonzo*	Curtiss D-12 435 HP	4	351,865	218.686
	3	Roger Don Rae	Rider R-1	Menasco C-65 250 HP	131	344,232	213.942
1936 4-7 September Los Angeles, Calif. (USA) 241,402 km (150 miles)	1	Michel Detroyat	Caudron C-460	Renault Bengali 340 HP	100	425,195	264.261
	2	Earl Ortman	Rider R-3	P. & W. Wasp Jr. 750 HP	54	399,099	248.042
	3	Roger Don Rae	Rider R-4	Menasco B-6S 250 HP	70	380,623	236.559
1937 6 September Cleveland, Ohio (USA) 321,869 km (200 miles)	1	Rudy Kling	Folkerts SK-3 Jupiter	Menasco C-6S4 400 HP	301	413,368	256.910
	2	Earl Ortman	Marcoux-Bromberg	P. & W. Twin Wasp Jr. 800 HP	4	413,284	256.858
	3	Roscoe Turner	Laird-Turner L-RT Meteor	P. & W. Twin Wasp Sr. 1000 HP	29	408,367	253.802
1938 3-5 September Cleveland, Ohio (USA) 482,804 km (300 miles)	1	Roscoe Turner	Laird-Turner L-RT Meteor	P. & W. Twin Wasp Sr. 1100 HP	29	456,021	283.419
	2	Earl Ortman	Marcoux-Bromberg	P. & W. Twin Wasp Jr. 900 HP	3	433,976	269.718
	3	Steve Wittman	Wittman *Bonzo*	Curtiss D-12 485 HP	2	417,031	259.187
1939 2-5 September Cleveland, Ohio (USA) 482,804 km (300 miles)	1	Roscoe Turner	Laird-Turner L-RT Meteor	P. & W. Twin Wasp Sr. 1000 HP	29	454,600	282.536
	2	Tony Le Vier	Schoenfeldt *Firecracker*	Menasco C-6S4 350 HP	70	438,513	272.538
	3	Earl Ortman	Marcoux-Bromberg	P. & W. Twin Wasp Jr. 850 HP	3	409,385	254.435

National Air Races: 1926-1929

Date, Venue, Distance	Place	Pilot	Aircraft	Engine	Race No.	Speed km/h	Speed mph
1926 10 October Philadelphia, Pa. (USA) 193,121 km (120 miles)	1	George Cuddihy	Boeing FB-3	Packard 2A-1500 V-12 600 HP	—	290,416	180.495
	2	Elliott	Curtiss Hawk P-2	Curtiss V-1400 V-12 500 HP	—	287,381	178.609
	3	Ross Hoyt	Curtiss Hawk P-2	Curtiss V-1400 V-12 500 HP	—	274,992	170.909
1927 10 October Spokane, Wash. (USA) 193,121 km (120 miles)	1	Batten	Curtiss Hawk XP-6A	Curtiss V-1570-1 V-12 700 HP	3	323,793	201.239
	2	Lyon	Curtiss Hawk XP-6	Curtiss V-1570-1 V-12 700 HP	14	305,079	189.608
	3	Thomas Jeter	Boeing FB-5	Packard 2A-1500 V-12 600 HP	23	284,696	176.940
1928 10 October Los Angeles, Calif. (USA) 96,560 km (60 miles)	1	Thomas Jeter	Boeing XF4B-1	P. & W. Wasp R-1340-7 450 HP	—	277,166	172.260
	2	Edgar Cruise	Boeing F2B-1	P. & W. Wasp R-1340-3 450 HP	—	257,214	159.860
	3	Harrigan	Boeing F2B-1	P. & W. Wasp R-1340-3 450 HP	—	243,924	151.600
1929 10 October Cleveland, Ohio (USA) 80,467 km (50 miles)	1	Douglas Davis	Travel Air R *Mystery Ship*	Wright R-975 400 HP	31	313,594	194.900
	2	Breene	Curtiss Hawk P-3A	P. & W. Wasp R-1340-3 450 HP	80	300,625	186.840
	3	Roscoe Turner	Lockheed Vega	P. & W. Wasp R-1344 450 HP	—	263,618	163.840

The Bendix Trophy: 1931-1939

Date, Venue, Distance	Place	Pilot	Aircraft	Engine	Race No.	Speed km/h	Speed mph
1931 4 September From Burbank, Calif., to Cleveland, Ohio (USA) 3288 km (2043 miles)	1	James Doolittle	Laird LC-DW-500	P. & W. Wasp Jr. 535 HP	400	374,958	233.038
	2	Harold S. Johnson	Lockheed Orion	P. & W. Wasp 450 HP	—	319,894	198.816
	3	Beeler Blevins	Lockheed Orion	P. & W. Wasp 450 HP	—	304,088	188.992
1932 29 August From Burbank, Calif., to Cleveland, Ohio (USA) 3288 km (2043 miles)	1	James Haizlip	Wedell-Williams	P. & W. Wasp Jr. 550 HP	92	394,205	245.000
	2	James Wedell	Wedell-Williams	P. & W. Wasp Jr. 550 HP	44	373,288	232.000
	3	Roscoe Turner	Wedell-Williams	P. & W. Wasp Jr. 550 HP	121	363.634	226.000
1933 1 July From New York City to Los Angeles, Calif. (USA) 3299 km (2050 miles)	1	Roscoe Turner	Wedell-Williams	P. & W. Wasp Sr. 900 HP	2	345,581	214.780
	2	James Wedell	Wedell-Williams	P. & W. Wasp Jr. 550 HP	44	336.651	209.230
1934 31 August From Burbank, Calif., to Cleveland, Ohio (USA) 3288 km (2043 miles)	1	Douglas Davis	Wedell-Williams	P. & W. Wasp Jr. 550 HP	44	347,925	216.237
	2	John Worthen	Wedell-Williams	P. & W. Wasp Jr. 550 HP	92	326,969	203.213
1935 31 August From Burbank, Calif., to Cleveland, Ohio (USA) 3288 km (2043 miles)	1	Ben Howard	Howard DGA-6 *Mr. Mulligan*	P. & W. Wasp 830 HP	40	384,074	238.704
	2	Roscoe Turner	Wedell-Williams	P. & W. Hornet 1000 HP	57	383,781	238.522
	3	Russel Thaw	Northrop Gamma	Wright Cyclone 775 HP	—	324.902	201.928
1936 4 September From New York City to Los Angeles, Calif. (USA) 3942 km (2450 miles)	1	Louise Thaden	Beech C-17R	Wright R-975 420 HP	62	266,041	165.346
	2	Laura Ingalls	Lockheed Orion 9D	P. & W. Wasp 550 HP	—	253,362	157.466
	3	William Bulick	Vultee VI A	Wright Cyclone 735 HP	—	251,795	156.492
1937 3 September From Burbank, Calif., to Cleveland, Ohio (USA) 3288 km (2043 miles)	1	Frank Fuller Jr.	Seversky Sev-S2	P. & W. Twin Wasp 1000 HP	23	415,511	258.242
	2	Earl Ortman	Marcoux-Bromberg	P. & W. Twin Wasp 700 HP	4	361,756	224.833
	3	Jacqueline Cochran	Beechcraft D-17W	P. & W. Wasp Jr. 450 HP	13	313,336	194.740
1938 3 September From Burbank, Calif., to Cleveland, Ohio (USA) 3288 km (2043 miles)	1	Jacqueline Cochran	Seversky Sev-S2	P. & W. Twin Wasp 1200 HP	13	401,838	249.744
	2	Frank Fuller Jr.	Seversky Sev-S2	P. & W. Twin Wasp 1200 HP	77	383,913	238.604
	3	Paul Mantz	Lockheed Orion	Wright Cyclone 750 HP	23	332,385	206.579
1939 10 October From Burbank, Calif., to Cleveland, Ohio (USA) 3288 km (2043 miles)	1	Frank Fuller Jr.	Seversky Sev-S2	P. & W. Twin Wasp 1000 HP	77	453,895	282.098
	2	Arthur Bussy	Bellanca 28-92	Ranger Menasco 870 HP	99	393,376	244.486
	3	Paul Mantz	Lockheed Orion	Wright Cyclone 750 HP	23	377,913	234.875

Landplane speed records: 1919-1939 (FAI-Class C)

Date	Place	Pilot	Aircraft	km/h	mph
1919 26 June	Mirafiori (I)	Francesco Brak-Papa	Fiat BR	261,629	162.603
1919 25 September	Paris (F)	Sadi Lecointe	Spad-Herbemont S.20bis	265,000	164.698
1919 20 October	Paris (F)	Bernard de Romanet	Nieuport 29V	268,631	166.955
1919 20 November	Montecelio (I)	Elia Liut	—	274,000	170.292
1920 7 February	Villacoublay (F)	Sadi Lecointe	Nieuport 29V	*275,264	171.049
1920 28 February	Villacoublay (F)	Jean Casale	Spad-Herbemont S.20bis	*283,464	176.174
1920 9 October	Buc (F)	Bernard de Romanet	Spad-Herbemont S.20bis	*292,682	181.905
1920 10 October	Buc (F)	Sadi Lecointe	Nieuport 29V	*296,694	184.396
1920 20 October	Villacoublay (F)	Sadi Lecointe	Nieuport 29V	*302,529	188.022
1920 4 November	Buc (F)	Bernard de Romanet	Spad-Herbemont S.20bis	*309,012	192.052
1920 12 December	Villacoublay (F)	Sadi Lecointe	Nieuport 29V bis	*313,043	194.557
1921 26 September	Villesauvage (F)	Sadi Lecointe	Nieuport-Delage sesquiplane	*330,275	205.267
1922 30 April	Mineola (USA)	Bert Acosta	Curtiss Cactus-Kitten	335,000	208.203
1922 26 August	Mirafiori (I)	Francesco Brak-Papa	Fiat R-700	336,132	208.907
1922 21 September	Villesauvage (F)	Sadi Lecointe	Nieuport-Delage sesquiplane	*341,023	211.912
1922 2 October	Mineola (USA)	Russell Maughan	Curtiss R-6	*353,1	219.453
1922 8 October	Mineola (USA)	Russell Maughan	Curtiss R-6	354,774	220.493
1922 13 October	Selfridge Field (USA)	William Mitchell	Curtiss R-6	*358,836	223.018
1923 15 February	Istres (F)	Sadi Lecointe	Nieuport-Delage sesquiplane	*375,000	233.064
1923 29 March	Fairfield (USA)	Russell Maughan	Curtiss R-6	*380,751	236.638
1923 29 March	Fairfield (USA)	Lester Maitland	Curtiss R-6	386,174	240.008
1923 16 September	New York (USA)	Lawson H. Sanderson	Wright F2W-1	398,640	247.756

km/h/mph 200/124 300/186 400/248 500/310 600/372 700/434 800/496

(cont)

Date	Place	Pilot	Aircraft	km/h	mph
1923 16 September	New York (USA)	Alford Williams	Curtiss R2C-1	410,000	254.816
1923 2 November	Mineola (USA)	Harold J. Brow	Curtiss R2C-1	*417,059	259.127
1923 4 November	Mineola (USA)	Alford Williams	Curtiss R2C-1	*429,025	266.640
1924 11 December	Istres (F)	Florentin Bonnet	Bernard V.2	*448,171	278.548
1932 3 September	Cleveland (USA)	James H. Doolittle	Gee Bee	*473,82	294.432
1933 4 September	Chicago (USA)	James R. Wedell	Wedell Williams	*490,08	304.8
1934 25 December	Istres (F)	Ralph Delmotte	Caudron C-460	*505,335	314
1935 13 September	Santa Anna (USA)	Howard Hughes	Hughes Special H-1	*566,490	351.99
1937 11 November	Augsburg (D)	Herman Wurster	Messerschmitt Bf.113R	610,950	380.000
1939 26 April	Augsburg (D)	Fritz Wendel	Messerschmitt Bf.109R	*755,138	468.94

km/h/mph 200/124 300/186 400/248 500/310 600/372 700/434 800/496

* ratified by the Fédération Aéronautique Internationale.

Great Britain
Germany
Italy
France
United States

Seaplane speed records: 1920-1926 (FAI-Class C)

Date	Place	Pilot	Aircraft	km/h	mph
1920 25 April	Monaco-Cannes (F)	Bernard de Romanet	Spad S.26	*211,395	131.382
1922 12 August	Naples (I)	Henri C. Biard	Supermarine Sea Lion II	208,818	129.781
1922 28 December	Sesto Calende (I)	Alessandro Passaleva	Savoia Marchetti S.M.51	*280,155	174.117
1923 30 July	Long Island (USA)	Rutledge Irvine	Curtiss CR-3	282,1	175.326
1924 3 August	Sesto Calende (I)	Alessandro Passaleva	Savoia Marchetti S.M.51	303,37	188.545
1924 4 September	Philadelphia (USA)	George T. Cuddihy	Curtiss CR-3	318, —	197.638
1924 25 October	Bay Shore (USA)	George T. Cuddihy	Curtiss CR-3	*302,684	188.088
1925 13 September	Southampton (GB)	Henri C. Biard	Supermarine S.4	*364,924	226.801
1925 27 October	Bay Shore (USA)	James Doolittle	Curtiss R3C-2	*395,439	245.713
1926 17 November	Hampton Roads-Norfolk (USA)	Mario De Bernardi	Macchi M.39	*416,618	258.929

km/h/mph 200/124 300/186 400/248 500/310 600/372 700/434 800/496

* ratified by the Fédération Aéronautique Internationale.

Closed-circuit distance records: 1920-1939

Date	Place	Pilot	Aircraft	km	miles
1920 3-4 May	Villesauvage (F)	Lucien Bossoutrot - Jean Bernard	Farman Goliath	1.915,2	1,190.105
1923 16-17 April	Dayton (USA)	Oakley C. Kelly - John A. Macready	Fokker T-2	4.050	2,516.67
1925 7-9 August	Etampes-Chartres (F)	Maurice Droulin - Jules Laudry	Farman	4.400	2,734.16
1927 3-5 August	Dessau (D)	Cornelius Edzard - Johann Risztics	Junkers-W 33	4.660,62	2,895.114
1928 31 May/1-2 June	Casale del Prati (I)	Arturo Ferrarin - Carlo Del Prete	Savoia Marchetti S.M.64	7.666,6	4,764.062
1929 15-17 December	Istres (F)	Dieudonné Costes - Paul Codos	Breguet XIX	8.029	4,989.221
1930 31 May/1-2 June	Montecelio (I)	Umberto Maddalena - Fausto Cecconi	Savoia Marchetti S.M.64	8.188,8	5,088 52
1931 30 March/2 April	Oran (DZ)	Anthoine Paillard - Jean Mermoz	—	8.960	5,567.744
1931 7-10 June	Istres (F)	Joseph Le Brix - Marcel Doret	Dewoitine *The Hyphen*	10.371	6,444.571
1932 23-26 March	Oran (DZ)	Lucien Bossoutrot - Maurice Rossi	Blériot 110	10.601,48	6,586.932
1938 13-15 May	Kisarazu (J)	Yuzo Fujita - Fukujiro Takahashi - Chikakichi Sekine	Koken	11.651,01	7,239.938
1939 30 July/1 August	Rome (I)	Angelo Tondı - Roberto Dagasso - Ferruccio Vignoli - Aldo Stagliano	Savoia Marchetti S.M.79	12.935,77	8,038.287

km/miles 2000/1240 4000/2480 6000/3720 8000/4960 10.000/6200 12.000/7440 14.000/8680

Distance records: 1919-1938

Date	From	To	Pilot	Aircraft	km	miles
1919 14-15 June	Saint John's (VO)	Clifden (IRL)	John Alcock-A.W. Brown (GB)	Vickers Vimy	3.115	1,936
1925 3-4 February	Etampes (F)	Villa Cisneros (E)	L. Arrachart-Henri Le Maitre (F)	Breguet XIX	3.166,3	1,967.539
1926 26-27 June	Paris (F)	Shaibah (KWT)	Ludovic Arrachart-Paul Arrachart (F)	Breguet XIX	4.305	2,675.127
1926 14-15 July	Paris (F)	Omsk (USSR)	André Girier-Francis Dordilly (F)	Breguet XIX	4.715,9	2,930.460
1926 31 August/1 September	Paris (F)	Bandar-Abbas (IR)	Léon Challe-René Weiser (F)	Breguet XIX	5.174	3,215.124
1926 28-29 October	Paris (F)	Jäsk (IR)	Dieudonné Costes-Georges Rignot (F)	Breguet XIX	5.396	3,353.074
1927 20-21 May	New York (USA)	Paris (F)	Charles A. Lindbergh (USA)	Ryan NYP *Spirit of St. Louis*	5.809	3,609.713

km/miles 2000/1240 4000/2480 6000/3720 8000/4960 10.000/6200 12.000/7440 14.000/8680

(cont)

Date	From	To	Pilot	Aircraft	km	miles
1927 4-5 June	New York (USA)	Eisleben (D)	Clarence Chamberlin-Charles A. Levine (USA)	Bellanca	6.294	3,911.092
1928 3-5 July	Montecelio (I)	Natal (BR)	Arturo Ferrarin-Carlo Del Prete (I)	Savoia Marchetti S.M.64	7.188,26	4,466.785
1929 27-29 September	Paris (F)	Tsi tsi har (TJ)	Dieudonné Costes-Maurice Bellonte (F)	Breguet XIX	7.905,14	4,912.254
1931 28-30 July	New York (USA)	Istanbul (TR)	Russell N. Boardman-J. Polando (USA)	Bellanca monoplane	8.065	5,011.591
1933 6-8 February	Cranwell (GB)	Walvis Bay (ZA)	O.R. Graiford-C.E. Micholetts (GB)	Fairey	8.544	5,309.242
1933 5-7 August	New York (USA)	Riyaq (SYR)	Maurice Rossi-Paul Codos (F)	Blériot 110	9.104,7	5,655.654
1937 12-14 July	Moscow (USSR)	San Jacinto (USA)	Mikhail Gromov-Andrei Yumashev-Sergei Daniline (USSR)	Tupolev ANT-25	10.148	6,305.967
1938 5-7 November	Ismailia (ET)	Darwin (AUS)	R. Kellett, B.K.Burnett and crews	Vickers Wellesley	11.520,4	7,158.79

km/miles 2000/1240 4000/2480 6000/3720 8000/4960 10.000/6200 12.000/7440 14.000/8680

Great Britain — United States — Germany — Japan — Italy — USSR — France

Altitude records: 1918-1938

Date	Place	Pilot	Aircraft	Altitude m	ft
1918 18 September	Dayton (USA)	Rudolph W. Schroeder	Bristol	8.807	28,897
1919 26 May	Issy-les-Moulineaux (F)	Jean Casale	Nieuport	9.124	29,937
1919 18 September	Garden City (USA)	Roland Rohlfs	Curtiss K-12	9.576	31,420
1919 4 October	Dayton (USA)	Rudolph W. Schroeder	Le Père	9.699	31,821
1921 18 September	Dayton (USA)	John A. Macready	Le Père	10.518	34,508
1923 5 September	Villacoublay (F)	Sadi Lecointe	Nieuport Delage	10.742	35,244.502
1927 25 July	Anacostia (USA)	C.C. Champion	Wright	11.710	38,420.51
1929 25 May	Dessau (D)	Willi Neuenhofen	Junkers	12.739	41,796.659
1930 4 June	Anacostia (USA)	Apollo Soucek	Wright Apache	13.157	43,168.117
1932 16 September	Filton (GB)	Cyril F. Uwins	Vickers	13.404	43,978.524
1933 28 September	Villacoublay (F)	G. Lemoine	Potez	13.661	44,821.741
1934 11 April	Montecelio (I)	Renato Donati	Caproni Ca.113 A.Q.	14.443	47,387.483
1936 14 August	Villacoublay (F)	Georges Datre	—	14.843	48,699.883
1936 28 September	Farnborough (GB)	S.R.D. Swain	Bristol Special	15.223	48,946.663
1937 8 May	Montecelio (I)	Mario Pezzi	Caproni Ca.161bis	15.655	51,364.055
1937 30 June	Farnborough (GB)	M.J. Adam	Bristol	16.440	53,937.24
1938 22 October	Montecelio (I)	Mario Pezzi	Caproni Ca.161bis	17.083	56,049.323

m/ft 8000/26240 9000/29520 10000/32800 11000/36080 12000/39360 13000/42640 14000/45920 15000/49200 16000/52480 17000/55760 18000/59040

Photographic Appendix

Gloucestershire Mars I (Bamel) - 1921, GB (62)

Gloucestershire Gloster I - 1923, GB (62)

Supermarine S.5 - 1927, GB (64)

Supermarine S.6 - 1929, GB (64)

de Havilland D.H.88 Comet - 1934, GB (70)

Heston Type 5 Racer - 1940, GB (71)

Messerschmitt Bf 108B Taifun - 1935, D (71)

Breguet XIX Grand Raid - 1929, F (70)

Blériot 110 - 1930, F (72)

Caudron C.460 - 1934, F (68)

Savoia S.13bis - 1919, I (63)

Macchi M.7bis - 1921, I (63)

Fiat R.700 - 1921, I (61)

Macchi M.39 - 1926, I (64)

Savoia Marchetti S.M.64 - 1928, I (72)

Photographic Appendix

Macchi-Castoldi MC.72 - 1930-31, I (72)

Verville VCP-R - 1920, USA (65)

Curtiss R2C-1 - 1923, USA (66)

Curtiss R3C-2 - 1925, USA (63)

Nardi F.N.305D - 1935, I (71)

Curtiss R-6 - 1922, USA (66)

Curtiss CR-3 - 1923 (63)

Wedell-Williams - 1931, USA (67)

Travel Air R Mystery Ship - 1929, USA (67)

Laird LC-DW-500 Super Solution - 1931, USA (69)

Gee Bee R-1 - 1932, USA (67)

Hughes H-1 - 1935, USA (71)

Howard DGA-6 "Mr. Mulligan" - 1935, USA (68)

Beech C-17R - 1936, USA (69)

Folkerts SK-3 Jupiter - 1937, USA (68)

5.

THE GLAMOROUS YEARS OF CIVIL AVIATION 1928-1940

During the 1930s, while the sporting events and long-distance flights were arousing such widespread interest in aviation, commercial transport was booming. There is a general consensus that the ten years leading up to World War II saw air transport finally come of age; an exciting and rewarding period when the organizational infrastructure and operational network of civil aviation as we know it today took shape. The steady growth of international airways led to an increasingly comprehensive world coverage (due mainly to transoceanic routes being developed) and this momentum gathered pace right up to the eve of World War II, by which time regular services crossed the North Atlantic.

Europe and the United States were at this stage competing on equal terms; the former had the advantage of longer experience, and although America had for some years lagged behind in the development of commercial aviation, this gap could soon be closed by drawing on her vast industrial and technological resources. World War II was to shift the balance of power and the United States was to dominate the world market, remaining the leading nation in Western aviation.

In the late 1920s and early 1930s France fostered the consolidation of her civil aviation industry. Her network of air routes spread from Europe to Africa, Asia and South America. In 1931–32 alone, French airlines handled an impressive amount of business: they flew 11,450,000 miles (18,425,000 km); carried 2,767 tonnes of freight and 360 tonnes of airmail. Air Union was one of the busiest companies, and had taken over Aéronavale's southern routes to Corsica and North Africa and increased its services to London. The Farman Company, which had been renamed Société Générale de Transport Aérien (SGTA) ran services to Germany and Scandinavia; the Compagnie Franco-Roumaine de Navigation Aérienne (which on 1 January 1925, changed its name to the Compagnie Internationale de Navigation Aérienne, CIDNA) had services through Eastern Europe as far as Constantinople (Istanbul).

In 1933 these companies were all affected by far-reaching changes in French air transport policy. In an effort to improve France's position with regard to foreign competitors and in order to control civil aviation more efficiently, the government promoted the consolidation of the major airlines into a single national company. Thus Air France was born and was to become one of the most successful international airlines, still renowned for its efficiency and innovative flair. The company was founded on 30 August 1933, by the merger of Air Orient, Air Union, CIDNA and SGTA. Air France was confronted with a formidable task: it had a route network of over 23,000 miles (38,000 km) and a mixed fleet of 259 aircraft of 35 types, many of which were obsolescent.

A program of aircraft standardization and rationalization of routes was carried out with great efficiency and decisiveness and soon yielded results, at the same time giving great stimulus to the French aircraft industry as a result of orders for new airplanes. Air France's network was considerably expanded, especially on international and intercontinental lines. In 1934 the first mail services between France and South America were inaugurated (the first ocean crossing of the service was on 28 May, with the Couzinet *Arc-en-Ciel*). Two years later a regular passenger service to Dakar was begun, and in 1937 route proving flights over the North Atlantic were initiated. A year later Air France extended its Eastern route from Indo-China to Hong Kong. A few figures suffice to illustrate the growth in France's share of passenger traffic: in 1930 the four chief French airlines (Air Union, Farman, CIDNA and Aéropostale) carried some 55,000 passengers. In 1939, on the eve of World War II, Air France had nearly doubled this total. By this date it was no longer the leading European airline, but was still expanding and came sixth in order of mileage and business after Lufthansa, Aeroflot, Imperial Airways, KLM and Ala Littoria.

A similar process of consolidation took place in Great Britain during the 1930s. While Imperial Airways was extending its services, several new private companies were established. Hillman's Airways was founded in 1932; Spartan Air Lines made its debut in 1933 and United Airways and British Continental Airways were both formed in 1935. These companies mostly operated routes that Imperial Airways did not cover and in 1935, in order to achieve maximum efficiency and profitability, they joined forces to form British Airways.

Founded on 30 September 1935 as Allied British Airways, this new company proved a very dynamic and thoroughly competitive airline which successfully held its own with other European airlines. In 1933 Jersey Airways began operating regular services to Jersey in the Channel Islands, landing on the beach because there was no airdrome; and in 1934 a major British domestic airline, Railway Air Services, was founded by the four main railroad companies and Imperial Airways. Another British operator was Scottish Airways, formed in 1937 after the merger of Highland Airways and Northern and Scottish Airways. British Airways and Imperial Airways had the difficult task of flying the flag in a highly competitive international market which was dominated by the enterprising Dutch airline, KLM, and the formidable German company, Lufthansa, as the airline was styled from 1 January 1934. Intercontinental routes benefited most from British air transport policy of the time and the years just before World War II saw the completion of much of Imperial Airways' ambitious program of expansion. The national airline's network linked the United Kingdom with South Africa, India, Hong Kong, Singapore, and Australia.

Imperial Airways' main task had been to develop air links with British overseas territories and this resulted in a failure fully to exploit European services. Also, Imperial Airways, with a State subsidy, was not allowed to purchase non-British aircraft. British Airways, as a private company, was able to purchase high-speed American aircraft, which it used on European services.

The comparison between the performance of the two airlines, plus certain other considerations, led to a government inquiry in 1937–38 which in turn brought about the decision to merge Imperial Airways and British Airways to form the British Overseas Airways Corporation (BOAC), which formally came into existence on 1 April 1940. However, because of the war, the two airlines worked very closely from September 1939.

Throughout the 1930s the airline which set the pace was Deutsche Lufthansa: meticulously organized to make the most of its operational and commercial potential and benefiting from a steady supply of modern and competitive aircraft which were being clandestinely developed for military as well as civil use and which were to play a fundamental role in the rebirth of German air power. Lufthansa reached the peak of its expansion in the years leading up to the war and in 1938 the German company carried over 254,000 passengers and close on 7,000 tonnes of freight, baggage and mail; its aircraft had flown more than 9,000,000 miles (15,000,000 km). In the following year the number of passengers had risen to almost 280,000. This was a phenomenal achievement when one reflects that in 1930, when Lufthansa was already the European market leader, it had carried just over 58,000 passengers.

Italy was also well-placed among the "Big Four" of commercial aviation in the early 1930s, having made up for lost time very quickly. By 1930, Italy was in third place in terms of passengers carried, with a total of some 40,000, and was to consolidate her progress in the second half of the 1930s when Italian civil aviation continued to expand.

Like France, Germany and Great Britain, Italy felt the need to concentrate available resources and to improve its commercial services; on 28 August 1934, a national airline was founded, Società Ala Littoria, which absorbed SISA, Aero Espresso, SANA and SAM, (SAM had taken over Transadriatica in 1931). The only remaining independent company was Avio Linee Italiane.

Ala Littoria embarked on an ambitious expansion program, aided by the government. The company increased its colonial flights and extended its European routes; on 29 July 1935, a service to Paris via Marseilles was inaugurated. On 7 December 1936, Cadiz and Spanish Morocco were added and, in 1937, routes were extended to Central Europe: to Prague in May and to Bucharest in October. Finally, in 1938 more flights were added, on the Madrid route in particular, and also to other destinations in Spain.

Special attention was paid to developing intercontinental routes. In the years just before World War II, after Ala Littoria established strategic routes to Eritrea, Somaliland and Abyssinia, attention was focused on opening up routes to South America. A new company was founded in 1939 for this purpose, the Linee Aeree Transcontinentali Italiane (LATI) which inaugurated regular flights between Rome and Rio de Janeiro in December 1939, using Savoia Marchetti S.M.83s. Weekly flights were kept up on this route until the end of 1941 and had to avoid French and British territories. In September 1941, LATI had managed to extend its routes to Buenos Aires but, with the war becoming a global conflict, LATI had to suspend all its services.

Throughout the period of expansion of European commercial aviation during the 1930s, the great Dutch national airline, KLM, managed to keep its place among the leading European airlines. It was a well-managed, dynamic company and adopted an aggressive and far-sighted policy, constantly updating and strengthening its fleet. In line with this policy, KLM took the then venturesome step of ending its long collaboration with Fokker, switching to Douglas aircraft. This Dutch company was, in fact, the first in Europe to order the outstanding and modern American DC-2 and not only to put it into service on the busy European routes but also to use it on its Far East flights, where it made considerable savings in flying time. Having ordered 14 DC 2s in 1934, KLM subsequently bought 11 of the larger and more powerful DC-3s; three years later KLM had a total fleet of 26 Douglas aircraft. Operating its modern fleet, KLM had several extremely successful years until World War II virtually destroyed the operations and its fleet, although the airline managed to continue limited operations. During 1939 KLM had carried nearly 170,000 passengers, compared with Ala Littoria's total of some 120,000, and was fourth in order of importance among European airlines.

Perhaps the greatest surprise was the boom in air transport in the Soviet Union. After the small-scale venture of 1921, when Deruluft was formed in collaboration with the Germans, an all-Soviet state airline was established in 1923 and was called Dobrolet. It was this company which laid the basis of a network which would eventually cover the whole of the vast Union of Soviet Socialist Republics. In 1929 Dobroflot, a new state company, was formed by the merger of Dobrolet and Ukrvozdukhput. The entire network was reviewed and routes extended under the first Five Year Plan of 1928. During the period 1928–32 Soviet air transport carried about 67,000 passengers and 6,000 tonnes of mail and cargo over a network of 31,935 kilometers (19,845 miles). A major development took place in 1932 when a new state organization, Grazhdanskii vozdushnii flot, was created, which soon became well known under the name of Aeroflot.

This new organization proved surprisingly effective. In 1932 it had managed to transport only 27,000 passengers and slightly less than 900 tonnes of cargo and mail—not a particularly impressive total. In 1935 the number of passengers carried had risen to 111,000 and the amount of cargo to over 11,000 tonnes. In addition the network of routes extended across the vast Soviet territory, from Leningrad and Moscow in the west to the Pacific coast. In 1939 Aeroflot had reached second place among the major European airlines, surpassed only by Lufthansa, which was then in its heyday. In the following year, the year before the German invasion, the network of services covered 90,910 miles (146,300 km) with the number of passengers totaling 395,000 and the amount of cargo and mail 45,000 tonnes.

On the eve of war, the European airline system included

many minor companies who operated from points all over the Continent and, between them all, they carried nearly as many passengers as Lufthansa alone. Some of the better-known smaller airlines were ČSA (Československé Státní Aerolinie) formed in Czechoslovakia in 1923; ABA (AB Aerotransport), the Swedish company founded in 1924; Swissair, created in 1931; Sabena, the Belgian airline, founded in 1923; the Polish company LOT (Polskjie Linjie Lotnicze) formed in 1929; the Danish airline DDL (Det Danske Luftfartselskab) which began operation in 1920; and Aero O/Y of Finland, which dated from 1923. In Spain LAPE (Lineas Aéreas Postales Españolas) continued to operate until 1936, having, in 1932, replaced CLASSA (Concessionaria Lineas Aéreas Subvencionales) formed in March 1929, by the merger of three airlines—Iberia (established in 1927), UAE (1925) and CETA (1921). This last company had been responsible for launching commercial aviation in Spain on 15 October 1921, when it used D.H.9 biplanes for an airmail service linking Seville and Larache in Spanish Morocco.

While all this activity was going on in Europe, on the other side of the Atlantic the United States had already become the world leader in civil aviation, especially as an innovator in design and technology. As yet there was little direct competition with European airlines and there was still a great deal of room for growth in the world market at the beginning of the 1930s, and the American aircraft industry and airlines tended to concentrate on satisfying the particular demands of its own internal network. Soon, however, an American airline was to challenge European companies on intercontinental routes: this was the giant Pan American Airways which had been founded during the aviation boom of the twenties and had become an extremely well-organized airline with a fleet of very up-to-date aircraft which was to enable it to capture a large proportion of international business. In the mid-1930s the U.S. domestic network was mainly shared by the "Big Four" of American commercial aviation—American Airways (later American Airlines), which had been formed by the merger of four other airlines: United Air Lines, which had absorbed six companies: Eastern Air Lines, resulting from a merger of two smaller airlines; and Transcontinental & Western Air (TWA) which was formed by the consolidation of Transcontinental Air Transport and Western Air Express. Pan American was another major operator. Apart from these colossal companies there was a host of small airlines; by 1930 there were over forty of them, owning a total of 500 aircraft between them and with a network of nearly 31,000 miles (50,000 km) in total. Civil aviation expanded very rapidly and soon the United States was the world leader; as early as 1929 the number of passengers carried in the U.S.A. was over 160,000; 100,000 more than the preceding year and 50,000 more than the total carried by German airlines, which held first place in Europe.

Apart from the specific demands of the home market, the United States had achieved this exceptionally fast growth because of the flexibility and strength of her aeronautical industry, which had progressed from a second-rank position in the year immediately after World War I, gradually making up lost ground and forging ahead to dominate the world market. Such companies as Boeing, Douglas, Lockheed and Sikorsky became famous throughout the world and their names were synonymous with advanced aircraft design. The U.S. aircraft manufacturing industry's contribution to the expansion of commercial aviation cannot be overemphasized since aircraft of American manufacture gradually won an increasingly large share of the international market and promoted another, less direct, form of competition.

Few aircraft have proved so significant as the Boeing 247 of 1933, which was the first really modern commercial airliner, influencing a whole epoch of civil aviation. The appearance of the 247 had far-reaching repercussions and threatened the very survival of several other companies, demonstrating perhaps for the first time, that effective aircraft were of prime importance in capturing business in a highly competitive market. United Air Lines took delivery of the entire initial production of the 247 and by doing so became a danger to its competitor, TWA, since it could now offer a much more efficient and comfortable service and shorter flying time. TWA had no option but to approach the U.S. aircraft industry and ask them to produce an even more competitive aircraft. Thus, in response to the demands and pressures of the market, the precursor of the most famous of all civil aircraft was created, the Douglas DC-1 which led to the DC-2 and the incomparable DC-3. Within a few years these aircraft had formed eighty per cent of American airlines' fleets and for a European company to succeed in buying DC-3s meant that it had an immediate advantage over its rivals.

Pan American's expansion on international routes paralleled the expansion of the domestic market. From 1929 onward, Pan American had built up a complex network of lines throughout the Caribbean; the following year services were extended to the farthest points of South America and in 1935 Pan Am had inaugurated routes over the Pacific and, in 1938, to Alaska. In 1939 transatlantic flights were commenced and the following year New Zealand was added to destinations on its network, completing its vast route coverage, on which first-class aircraft were used. Its position as undisputed world-leader reinforced the conception of the United States' role as aeronautical trail-blazer once and for all.

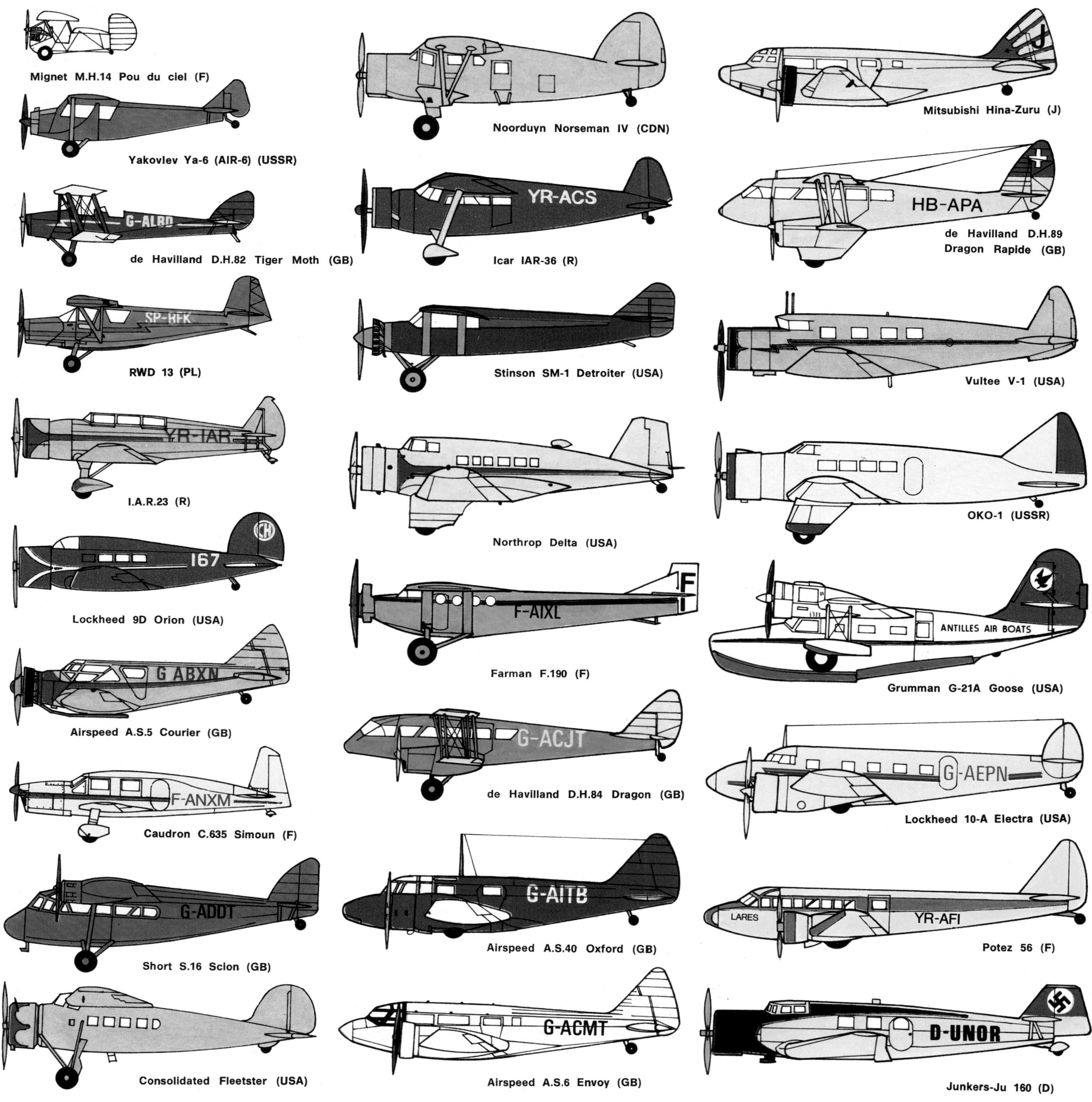

Mignet M.H.14 Pou du ciel (F)

Yakovlev Ya-6 (AIR-6) (USSR)

de Havilland D.H.82 Tiger Moth (GB)

RWD 13 (PL)

I.A.R.23 (R)

Lockheed 9D Orion (USA)

Airspeed A.S.5 Courier (GB)

Caudron C.635 Simoun (F)

Short S.16 Scion (GB)

Consolidated Fleetster (USA)

Noorduyn Norseman IV (CDN)

Icar IAR-36 (R)

Stinson SM-1 Detroiter (USA)

Northrop Delta (USA)

Farman F.190 (F)

de Havilland D.H.84 Dragon (GB)

Airspeed A.S.40 Oxford (GB)

Airspeed A.S.6 Envoy (GB)

Mitsubishi Hina-Zuru (J)

de Havilland D.H.89 Dragon Rapide (GB)

Vultee V-1 (USA)

OKO-1 (USSR)

Grumman G-21A Goose (USA)

Lockheed 10-A Electra (USA)

Potez 56 (F)

Junkers-Ju 160 (D)

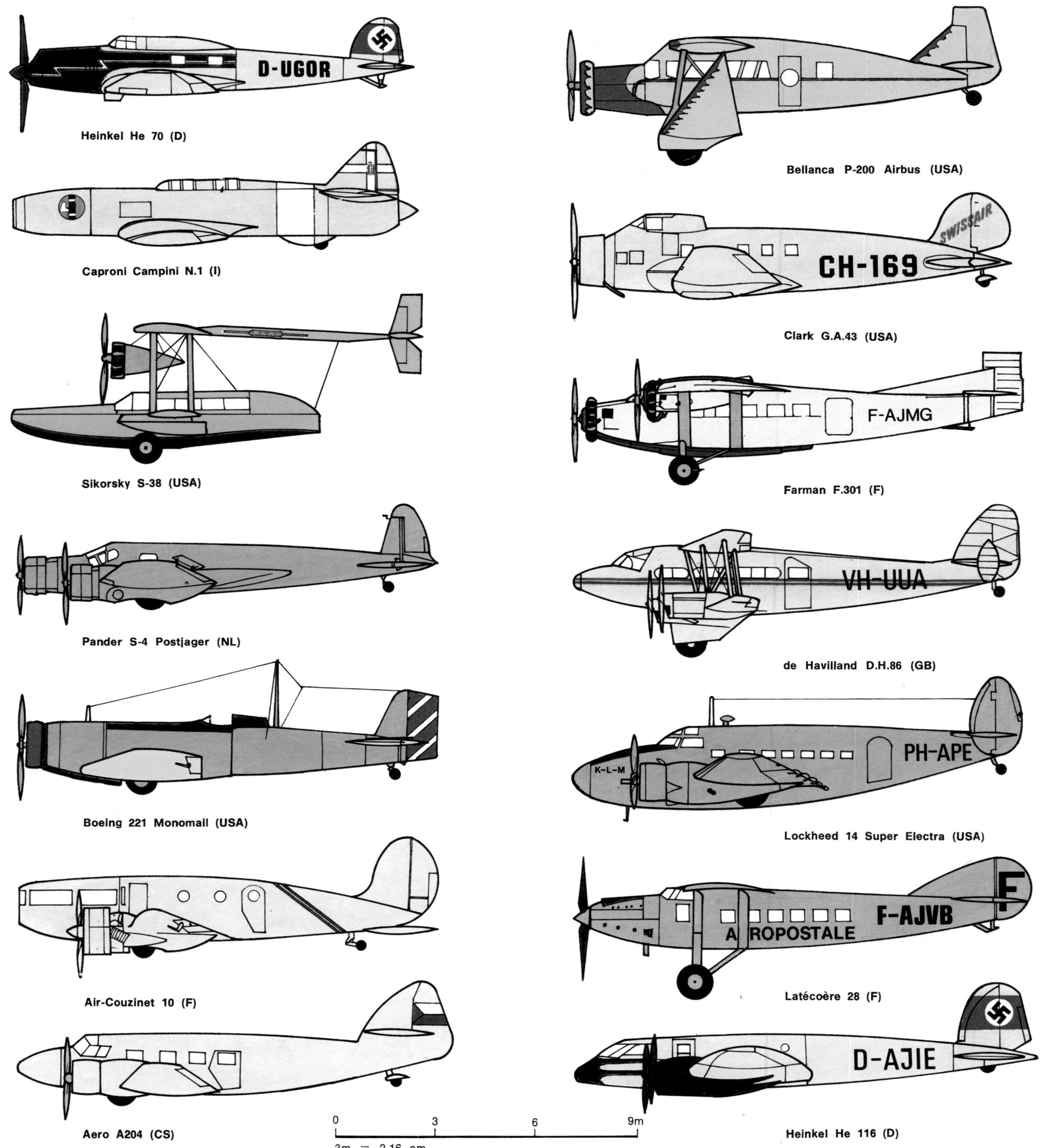

Heinkel He 70 (D)

Caproni Campini N.1 (I)

Sikorsky S-38 (USA)

Pander S-4 Postjager (NL)

Boeing 221 Monomail (USA)

Air-Couzinet 10 (F)

Aero A204 (CS)

Bellanca P-200 Airbus (USA)

Clark G.A.43 (USA)

Farman F.301 (F)

de Havilland D.H.86 (GB)

Lockheed 14 Super Electra (USA)

Latécoère 28 (F)

Heinkel He 116 (D)

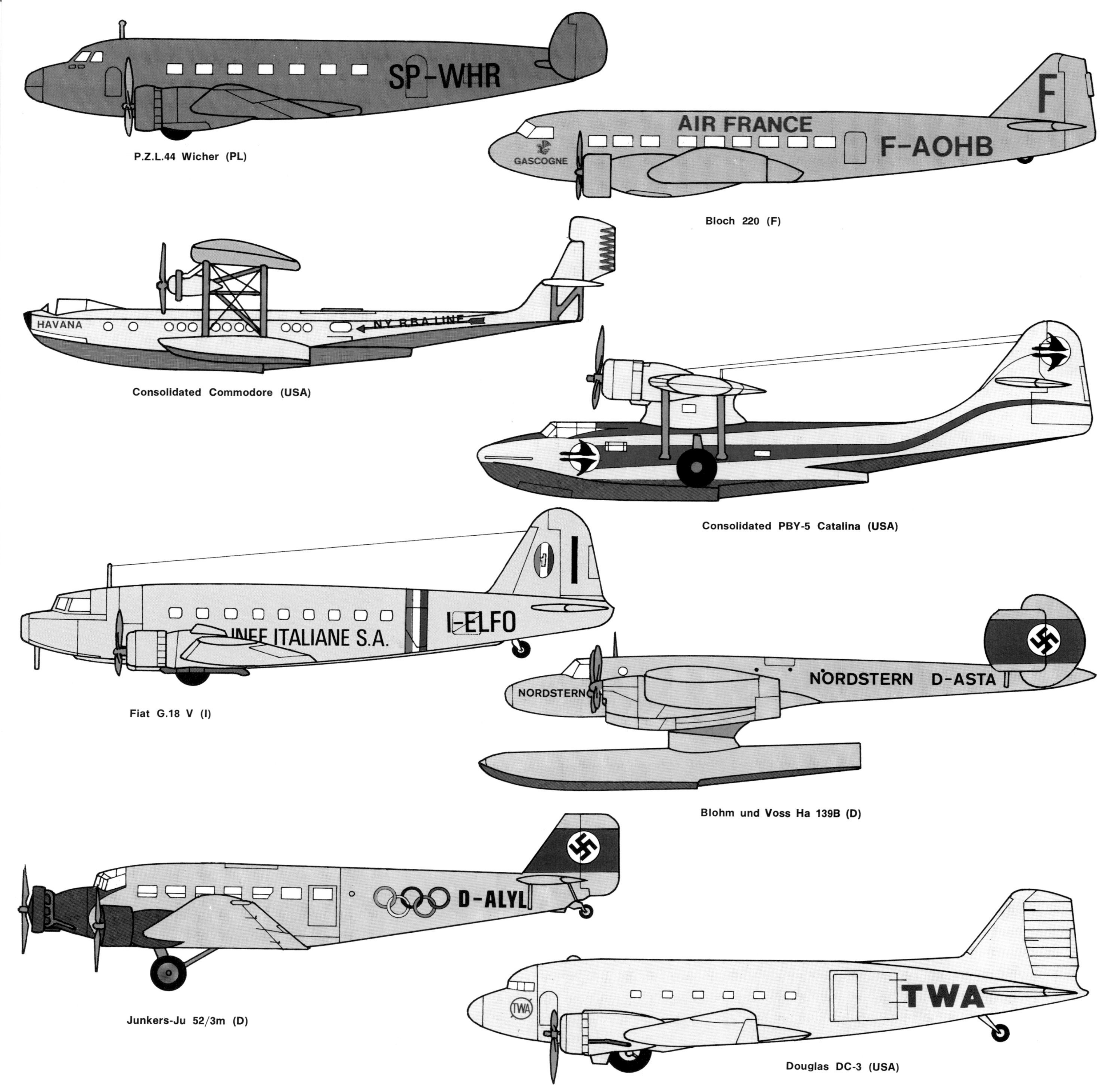

P.Z.L.44 Wicher (PL)

Bloch 220 (F)

Consolidated Commodore (USA)

Consolidated PBY-5 Catalina (USA)

Fiat G.18 V (I)

Blohm und Voss Ha 139B (D)

Junkers-Ju 52/3m (D)

Douglas DC-3 (USA)

Entry into service of the most important aircraft: 1928–1934

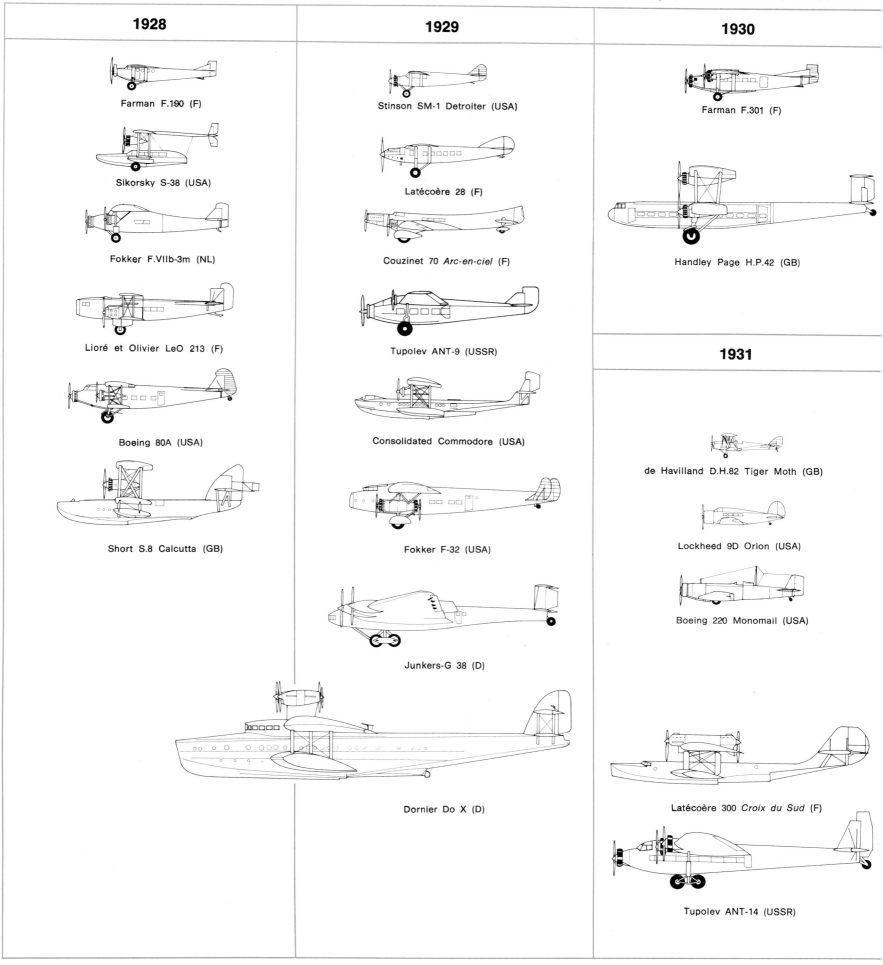

1928	1929	1930
Farman F.190 (F)	Stinson SM-1 Detroiter (USA)	Farman F.301 (F)
Sikorsky S-38 (USA)	Latécoère 28 (F)	Handley Page H.P.42 (GB)
Fokker F.VIIb-3m (NL)	Couzinet 70 *Arc-en-ciel* (F)	
Lioré et Olivier LeO 213 (F)	Tupolev ANT-9 (USSR)	
Boeing 80A (USA)	Consolidated Commodore (USA)	
Short S.8 Calcutta (GB)	Fokker F-32 (USA)	
	Junkers-G 38 (D)	
	Dornier Do X (D)	

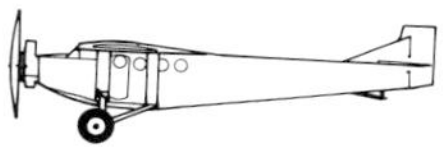

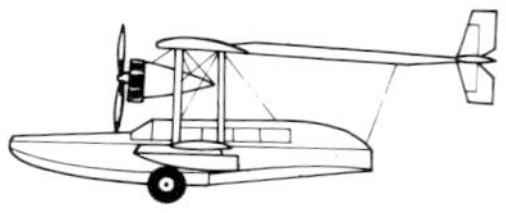

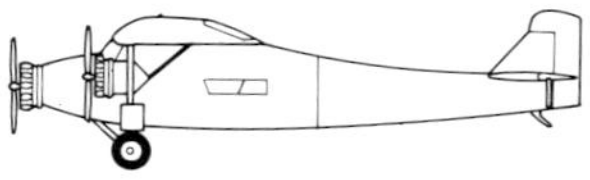

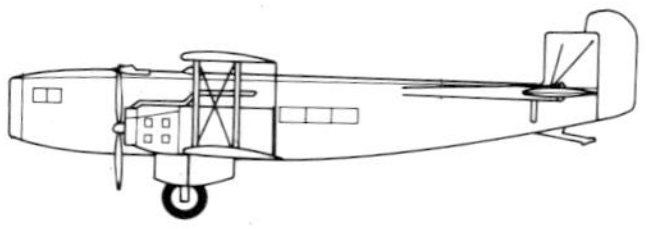

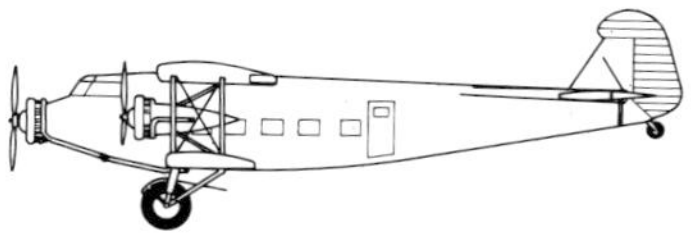

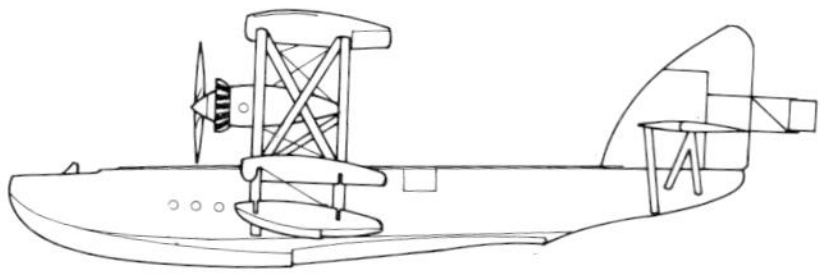

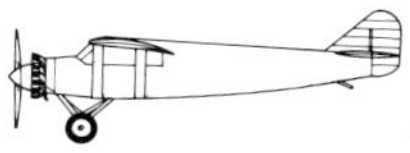

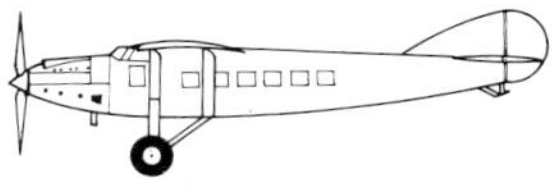

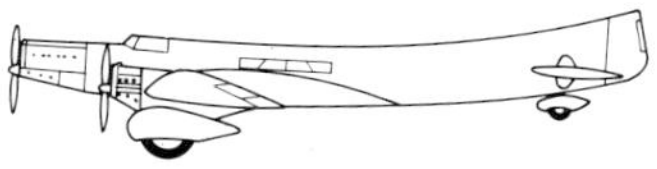

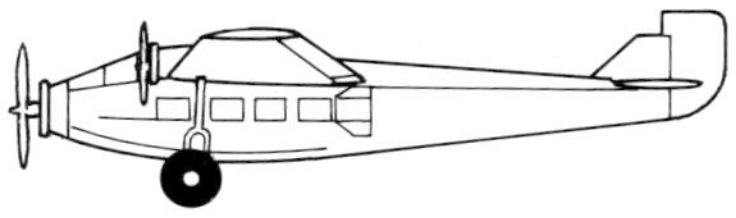

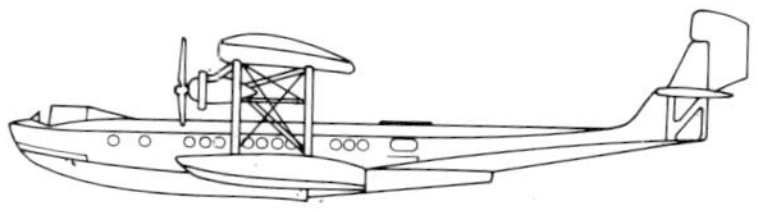

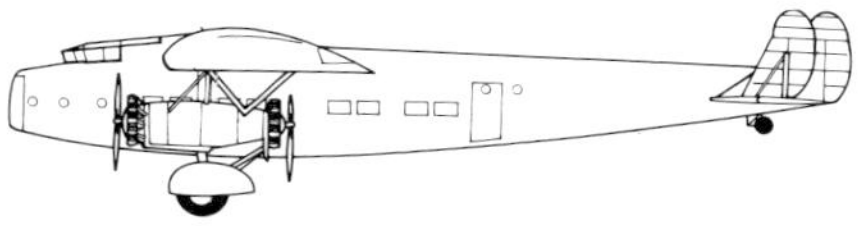

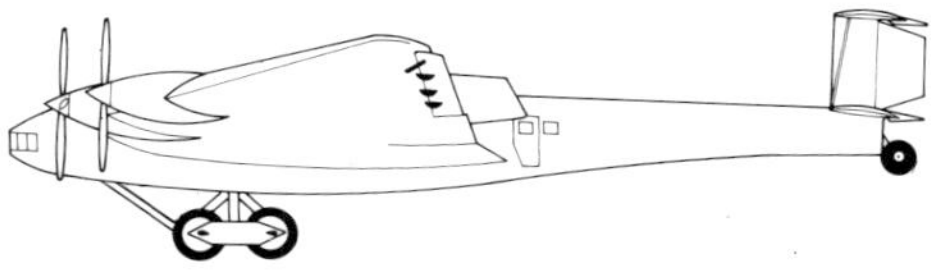

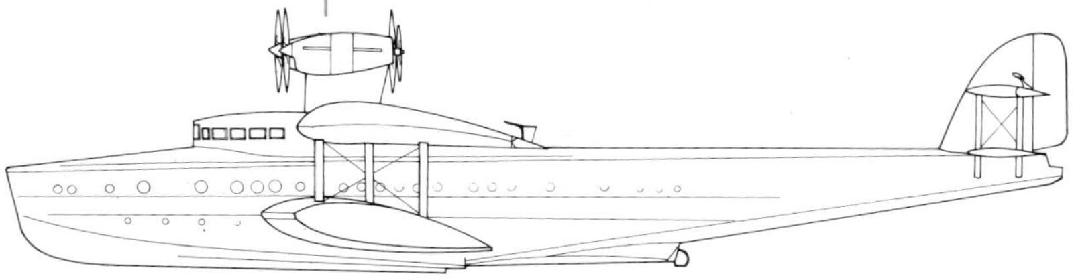

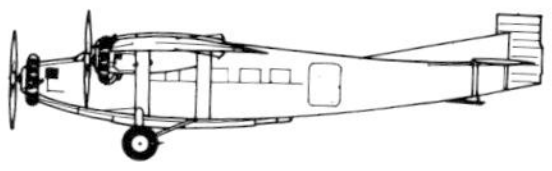

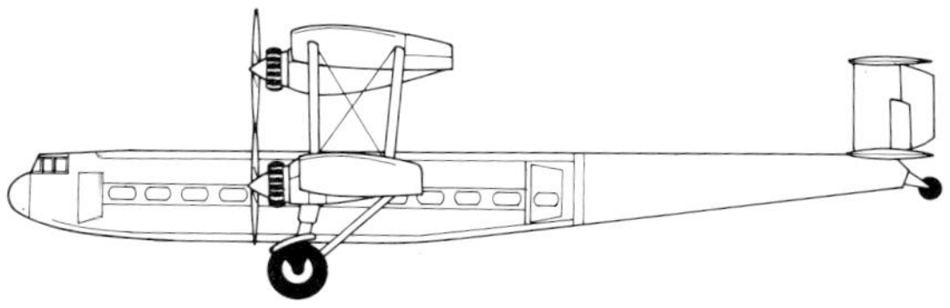

1931
de Havilland D.H.82 Tiger Moth (GB)
Lockheed 9D Orion (USA)
Boeing 220 Monomail (USA)
Latécoère 300 *Croix du Sud* (F)
Tupolev ANT-14 (USSR)

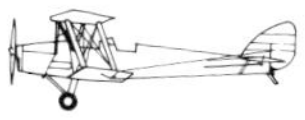

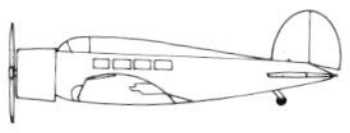

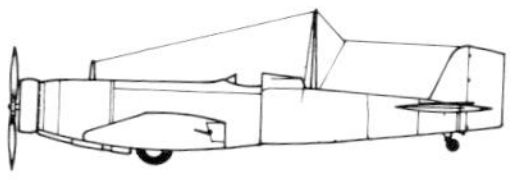

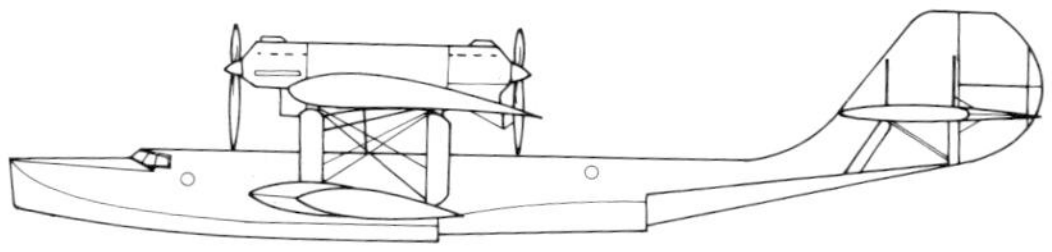

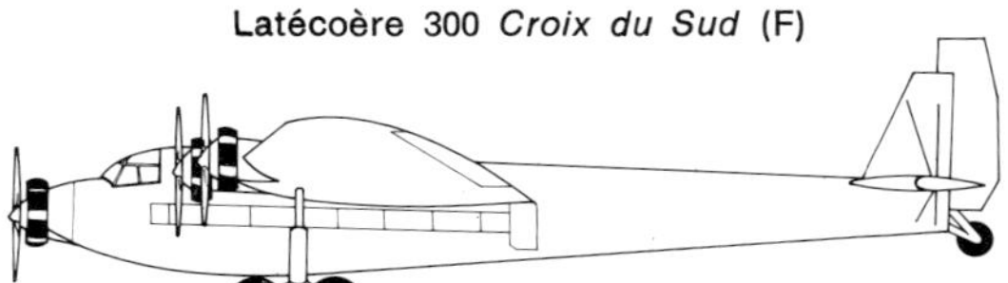

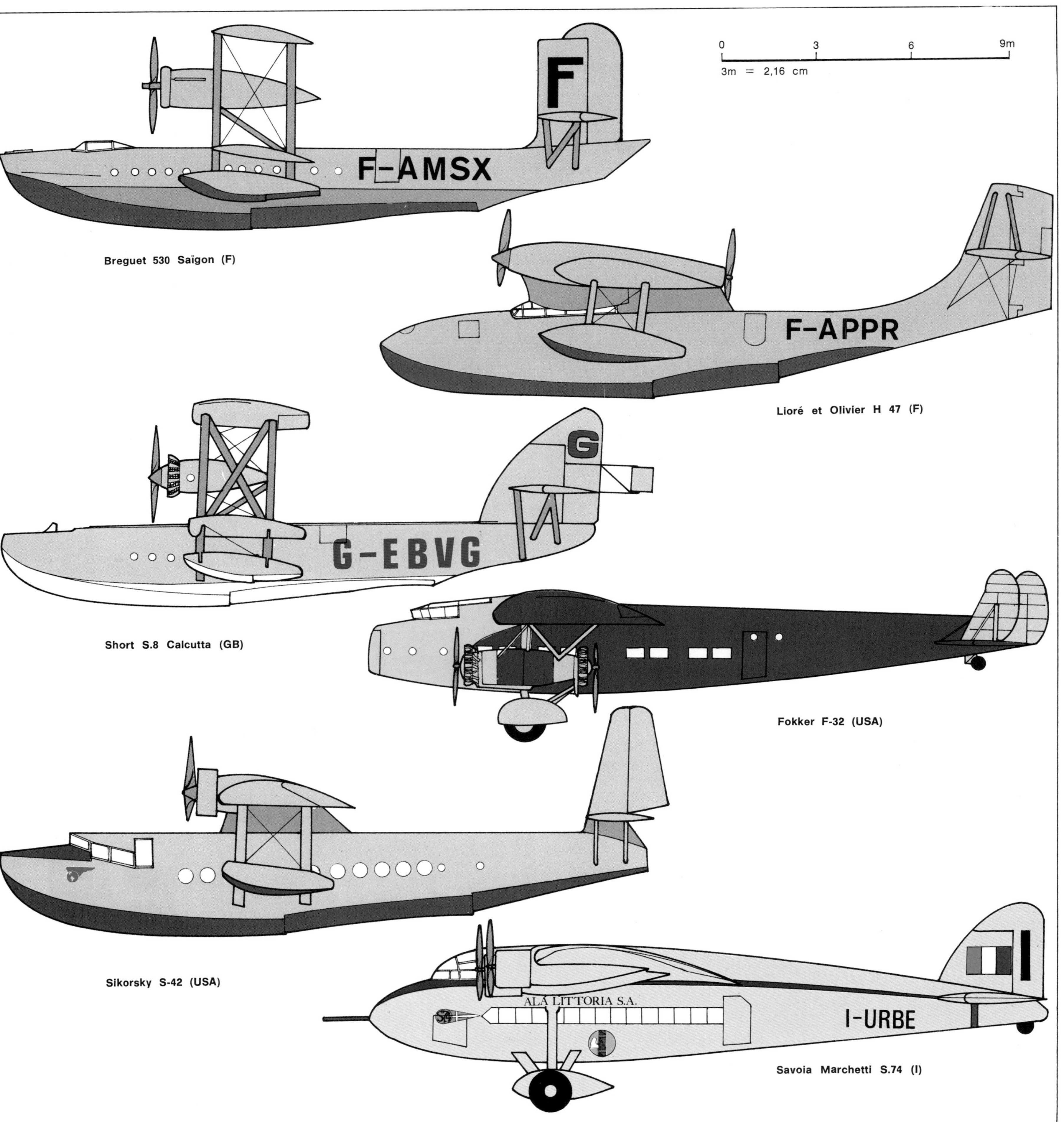

Breguet 530 Saïgon (F)

Lioré et Olivier H 47 (F)

Short S.8 Calcutta (GB)

Fokker F-32 (USA)

Sikorsky S-42 (USA)

Savoia Marchetti S.74 (I)

1932

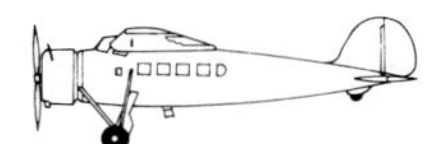

Consolidated 17A Fleetster (USA)

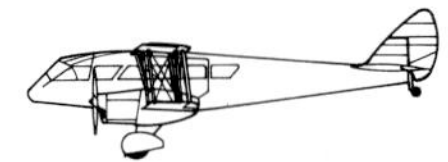

de Havilland D.H.84 Dragon Mk. I (GB)

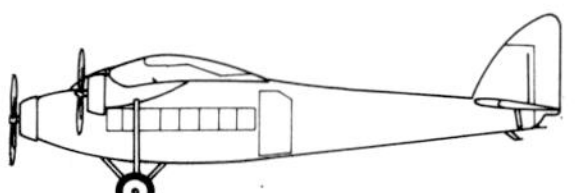

Savoia Marchetti S.71 (I)

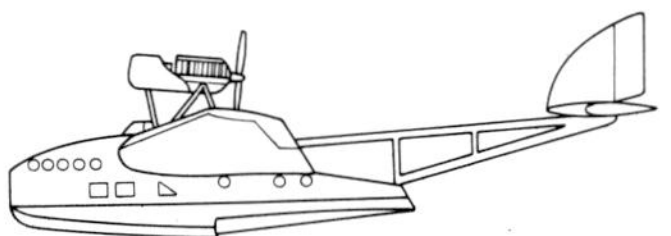

Savoia Marchetti S.66 (I)

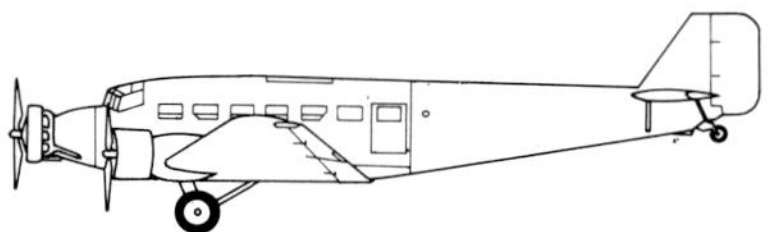

Junkers-Ju 52/3m (D)

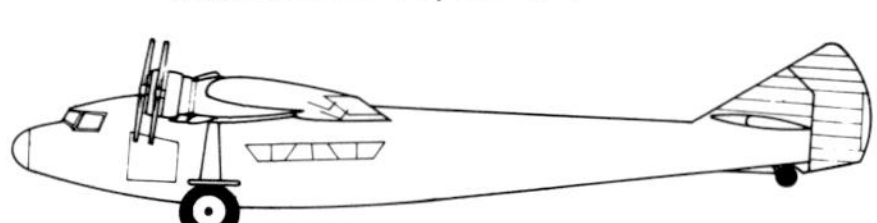

Armstrong Whitworth A.W. XV Atalanta (GB)

1933

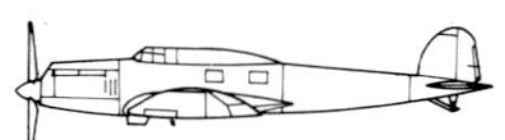

Heinkel He 70 (D)

Curtiss T-32 Condor (USA)

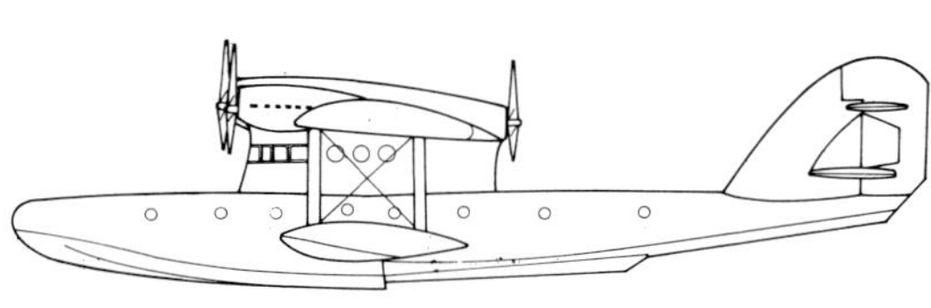

Blériot 5190 *Santos-Dumont* (F)

1934

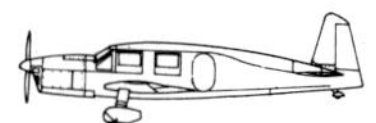

Caudron C.635 Simoun (F)

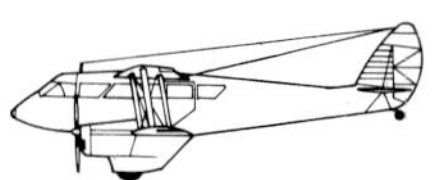

de Havilland D.H.89 Dragon Rapide (GB)

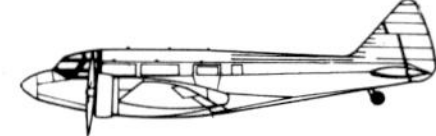

Airspeed A.S.6 Envoy (GB)

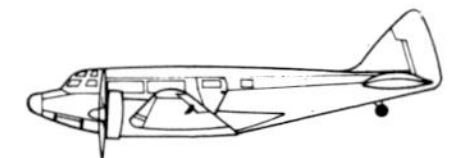

Mitsubishi Hina-Zuru (J)

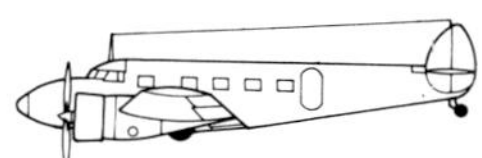

Lockheed 10-A Electra (USA)

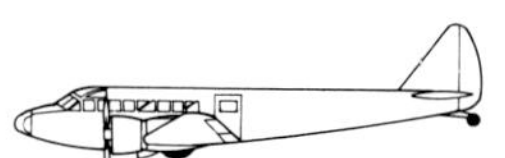

Potez 56 (F)

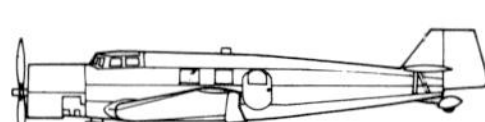

Junkers-Ju 160 (D)

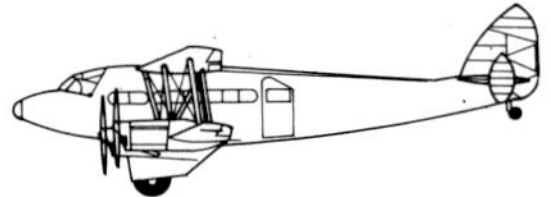

de Havilland D.H.86 (GB)

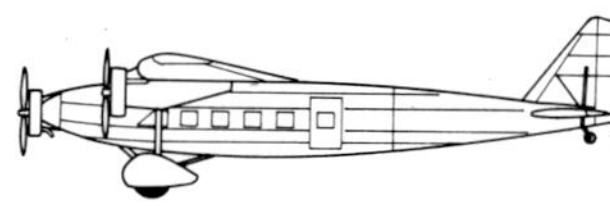

Bloch 120 (F)

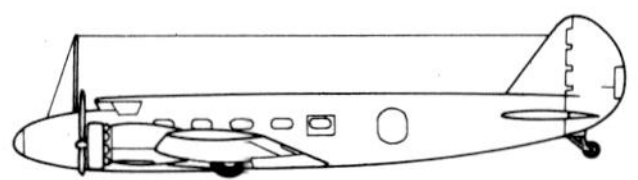

Boeing 247 (USA)

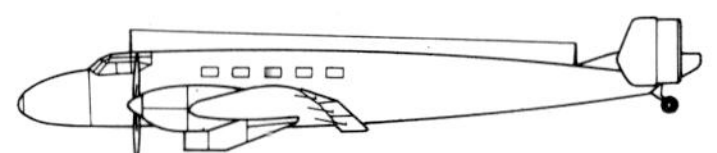

Junkers-Ju 86 (D)

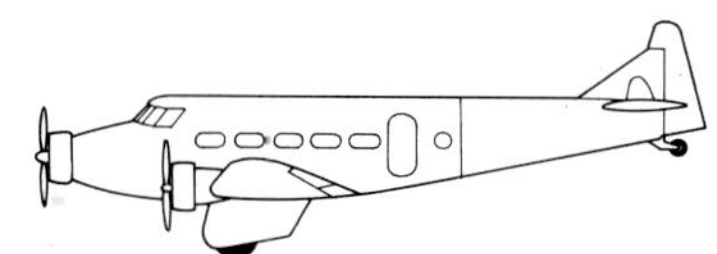

Wibault 283.T12 (F)

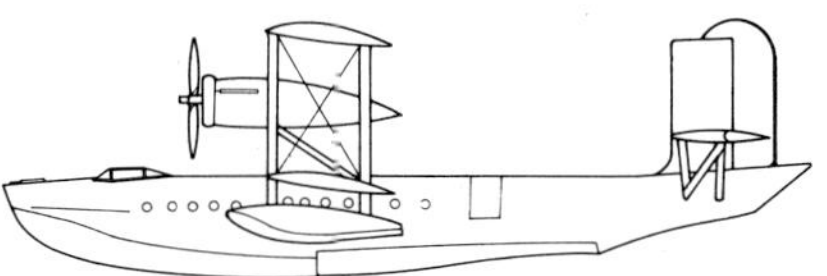

Breguet 530 Saïgon (F)

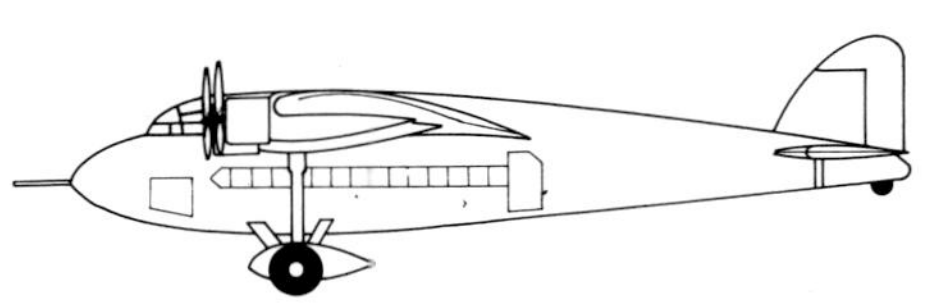

Savoia Marchetti S.74 (I)

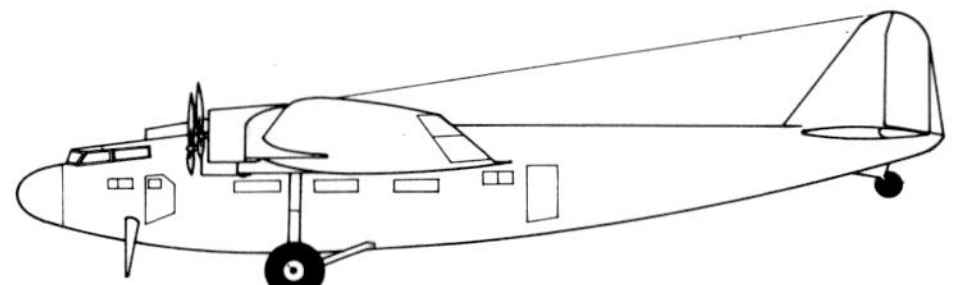

Fokker F.XXXVI (NL)

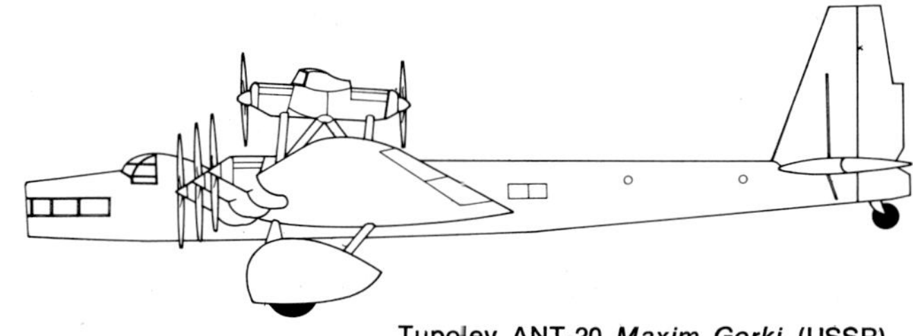

Tupolev ANT-20 *Maxim Gorki* (USSR)

These aircraft are all drawn to the same scale, which is also used for Plates 81, 118, 119, 120, 121

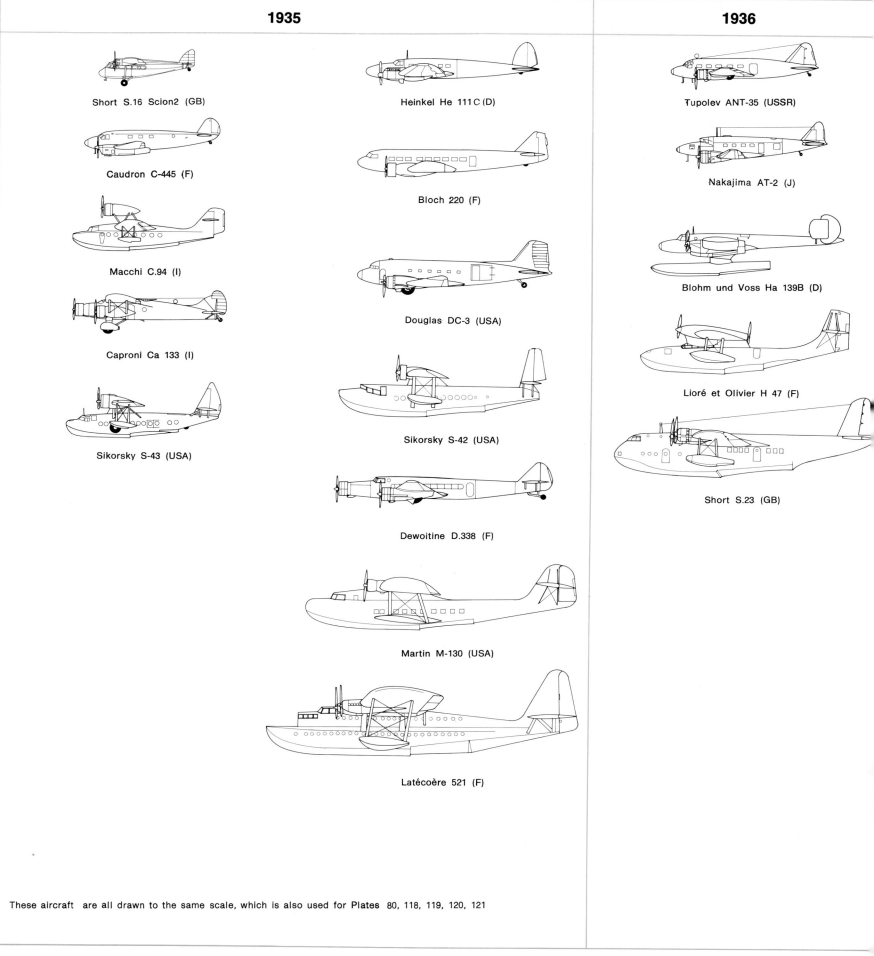

1935

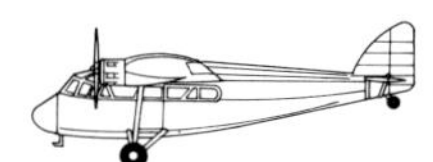
Short S.16 Scion2 (GB)

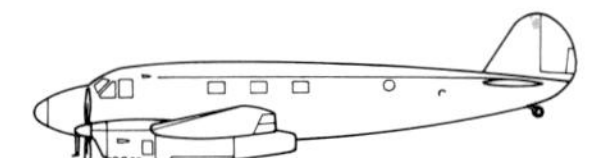
Caudron C-445 (F)

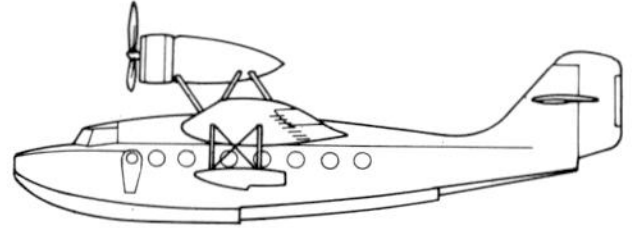
Macchi C.94 (I)

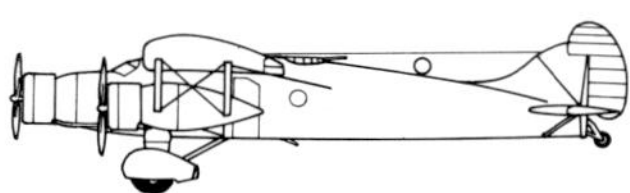
Caproni Ca 133 (I)

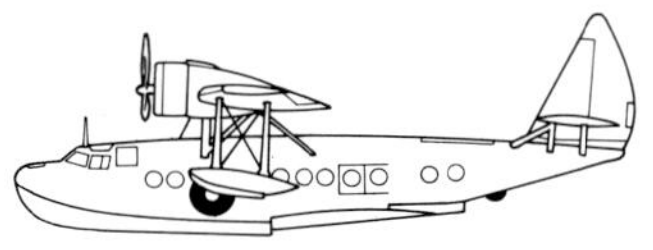
Sikorsky S-43 (USA)

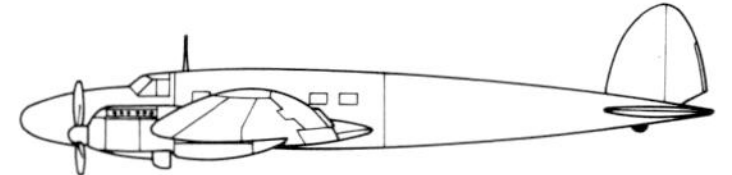
Heinkel He 111C (D)

Bloch 220 (F)

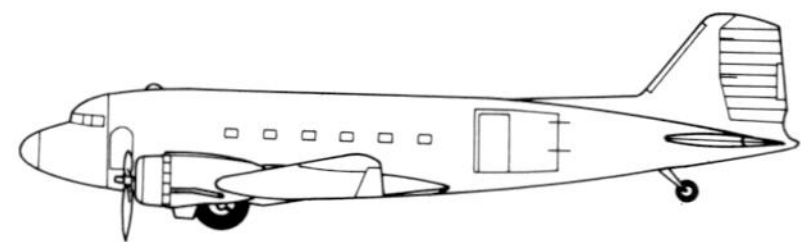
Douglas DC-3 (USA)

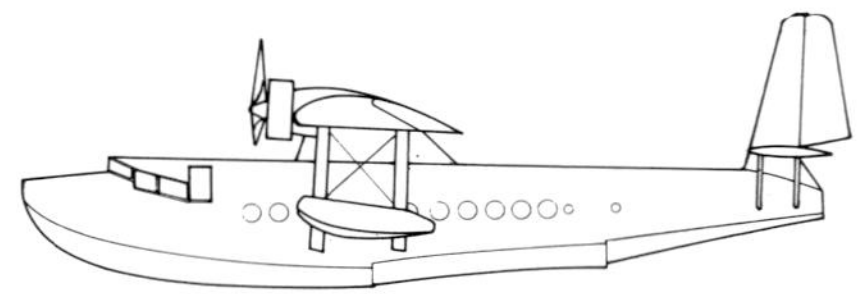
Sikorsky S-42 (USA)

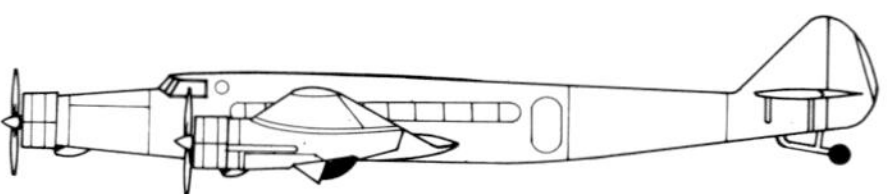
Dewoitine D.338 (F)

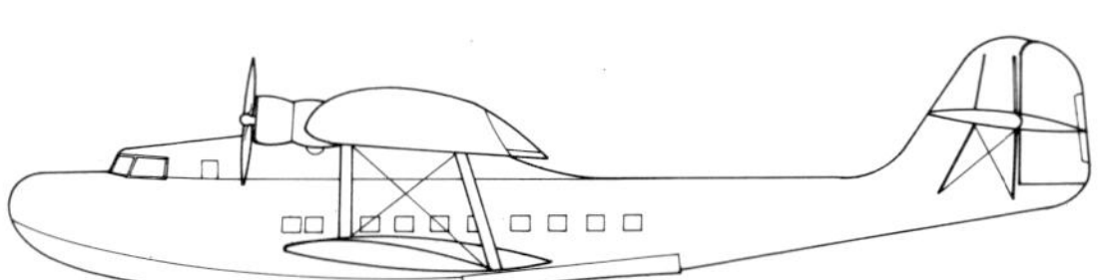
Martin M-130 (USA)

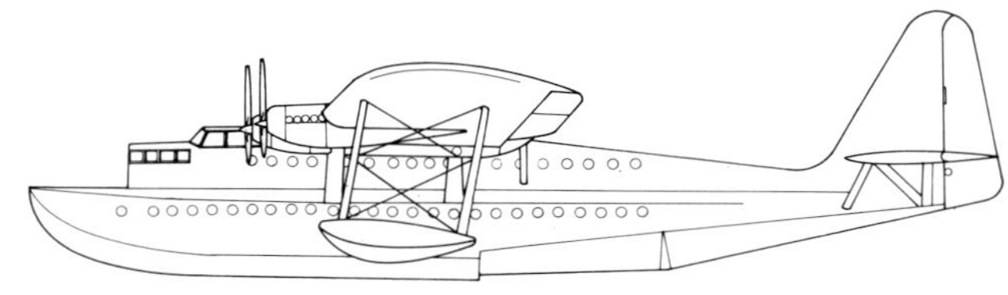
Latécoère 521 (F)

These aircraft are all drawn to the same scale, which is also used for Plates 80, 118, 119, 120, 121

1936

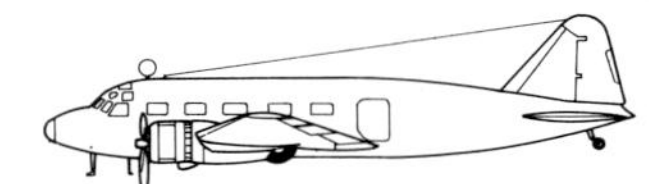
Tupolev ANT-35 (USSR)

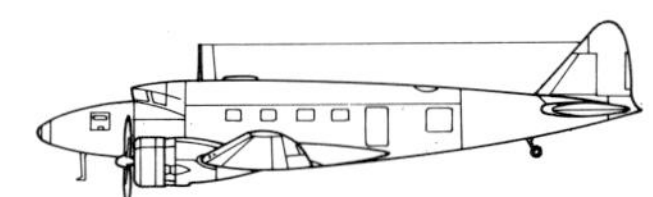
Nakajima AT-2 (J)

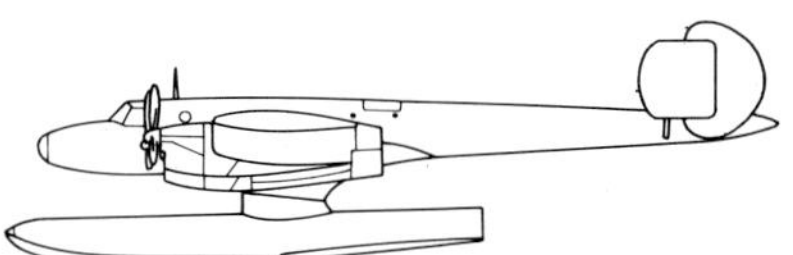
Blohm und Voss Ha 139B (D)

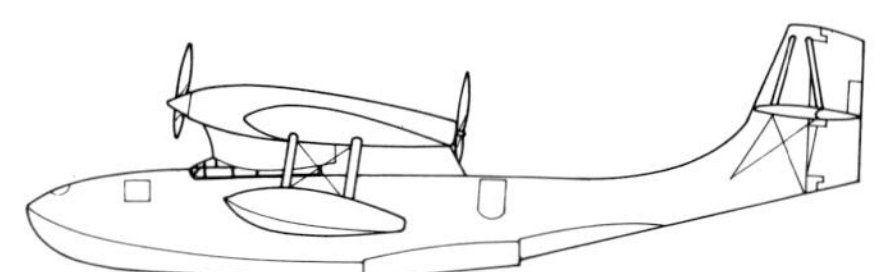
Lioré et Olivier H 47 (F)

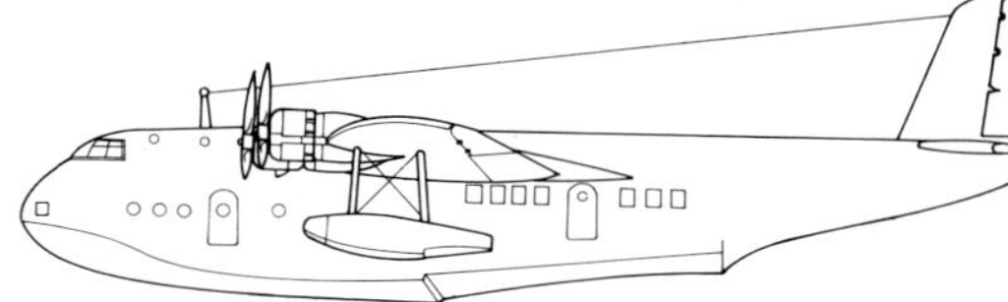
Short S.23 (GB)

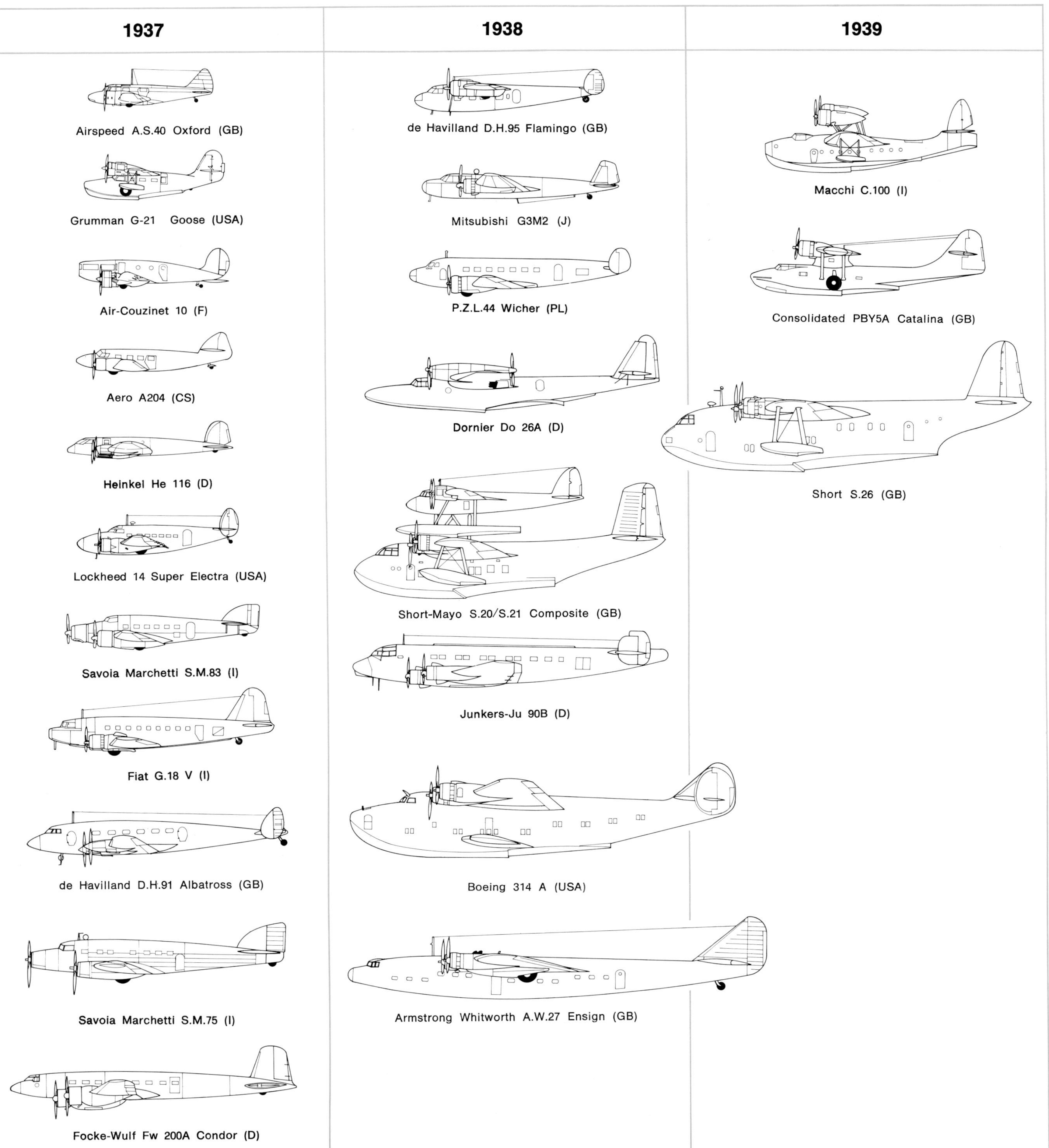
1937
Airspeed A.S.40 Oxford (GB)
Grumman G-21 Goose (USA)
Air-Couzinet 10 (F)
Aero A204 (CS)
Heinkel He 116 (D)
Lockheed 14 Super Electra (USA)
Savoia Marchetti S.M.83 (I)
Fiat G.18 V (I)
de Havilland D.H.91 Albatross (GB)
Savoia Marchetti S.M.75 (I)
Focke-Wulf Fw 200A Condor (D)
1938
de Havilland D.H.95 Flamingo (GB)
Mitsubishi G3M2 (J)
P.Z.L.44 Wicher (PL)
Dornier Do 26A (D)
Short-Mayo S.20/S.21 Composite (GB)
Junkers-Ju 90B (D)
Boeing 314 A (USA)
Armstrong Whitworth A.W.27 Ensign (GB)
1939
Macchi C.100 (I)
Consolidated PBY5A Catalina (GB)
Short S.26 (GB)

Cutaway drawing of the Short S.23 Empire Class flying boat

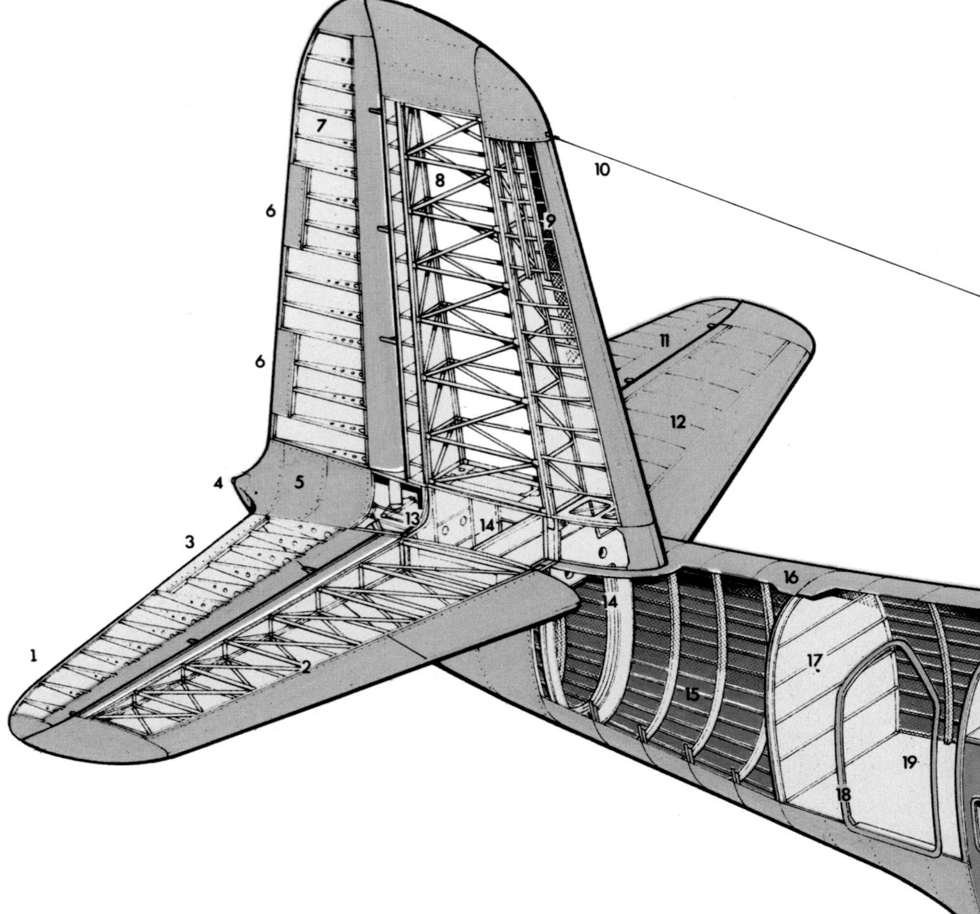

1 starboard elevator
2 tailplane construction
3 elevator tab
4 tail navigation light
5 tailcone
6 rudder tabs
7 fabric covered rudder
8 fin girder construction
9 leading edge construction
10 aerial wire
11 port fabric covered elevator
12 port tailplane
13 rudder and elevator control levers
14 tailplane attachment double frames
15 fuselage frame and stringer construction
16 fuselage skin plating
17 rear bulkhead
18 baggage door
19 aft main baggage bay
20 cabin rear bulkhead
21 window panels
22 bilge keel construction
23 aft cabin, seating six passengers
24 cabin trim panels
25 overhead luggage racks
26 rear entry door
27 bulkhead doorway
28 wing root trailing edge fillet
29 cabin roof bedding stowage
30 window curtains
31 wing root rib
32 starboard dipole aerial mast
33 promenade cabin, eight passengers
34 starboard flap shroud
35 starboard gouge type flap
36 girder construction rear spar
37 trailing edge ribs
38 starboard aileron
39 fixed tab
40 aileron control horns
41 wing tip fairing
42 starboard navigation light
43 wire braced wing rib construction
44 front girder spar
45 leading edge nose ribs
46 float mounting struts
47 diagonal wire bracing
48 starboard wing tip float construction
49 landing/taxi-ing lamp
50 wing stringers
51 overwing exhaust outlet
52 carburetor air intake
53 starboard outer engine nacelle construction
54 engine mounting ring
55 exhaust collector ring
56 detachable engine cowlings
57 oil cooler radiators
58 hull planing bottom forward step
59 midships cabin, three passengers
60 midships window panel
61 starboard inner engine nacelle
62 cooling air flaps
63 nacelle tail fairing
64 heater intake duct
65 cabin heater/exhaust heat exchanger
66 wing/fuselage main spar attachments
67 root rib cut-outs
68 wing spar center section carry-through
69 port gouge-type trailing edge flap
70 flap screw jack
71 port dipole aerial mast
72 flap guide rails
73 port aileron
74 aileron control cables
75 fixed tab
76 port wing-tip fairing
77 port navigation light
78 landing/taxi-ing lamp
79 port outer engine nacelle
80 oil tank
81 Bristol Pegasus XC air cooled 9-cylinder radial engine
82 de Havilland three bladed propeller
83 propeller hub pitch change mechanism
84 port wing tip float
85 ram air intakes
86 oil radiators
87 outboard main fuel tanks
88 port inner engine nacelle
89 exhaust collector ring
90 cooling air flaps
91 overwing exhaust outlet
92 exhaust pipe heat exchanger
93 inboard main fuel tank, total tankage, 600 Imp gal (2,727 l)
94 engine cowl flaps and fuel cock controls
95 ship's clerk's station
96 upper deck crew entry door
97 access ladder between decks
98 steward's galley
99 port side toilet doors, two toilets
100 upper deck level
101 port mail and freight compartment
102 sliding door
103 forward entry door
104 smoking lounge, seven passengers
105 fuselage chine member
106 forward fuselage portholes
107 radio operator's seat
108 radio racks
109 aerial mast
110 pitot tubes
111 cockpit roof hatch
112 chart table
113 cockpit roof trim control cables
114 pilot's seat
115 sliding cockpit side windows
116 copilot's seat
117 control column
118 rudder pedals
119 instrument panel shroud
120 curved windscreen panels
121 mooring hatch
122 marine equipment compartment
123 mooring ladder
124 anchor winch
125 anchor stowage
126 retractable mooring bollard
127 towing cleat

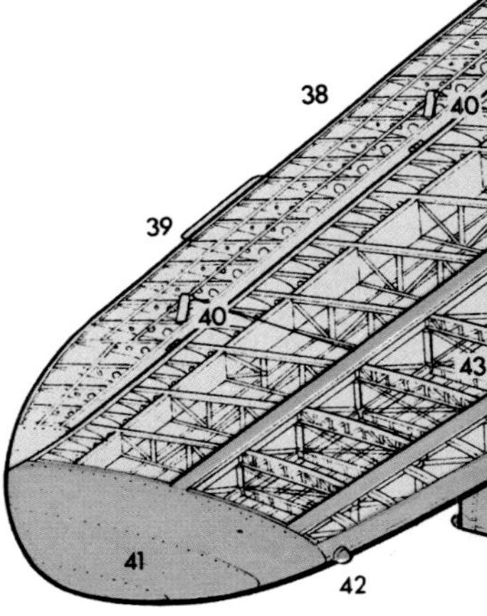

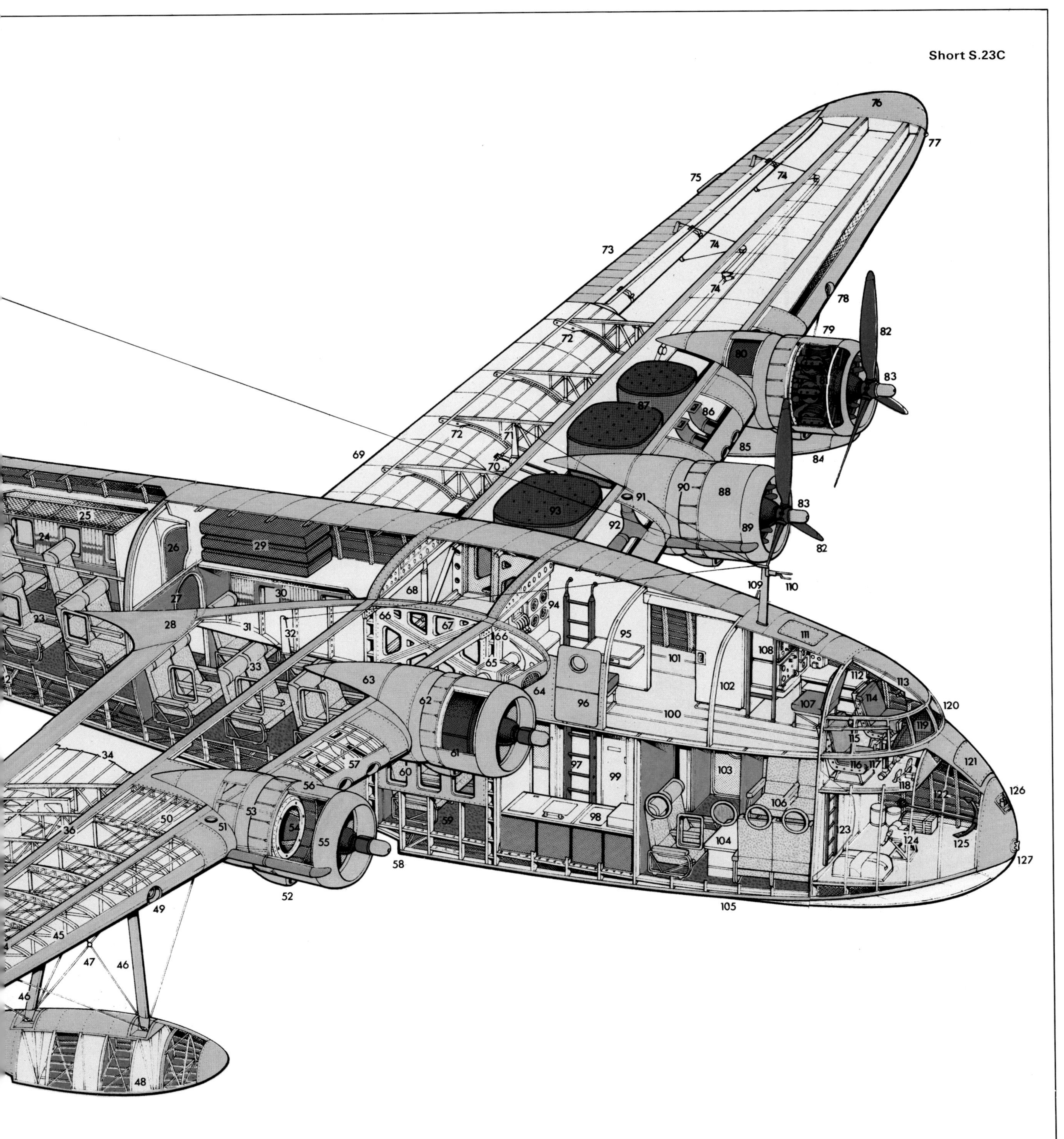
Short S.23C

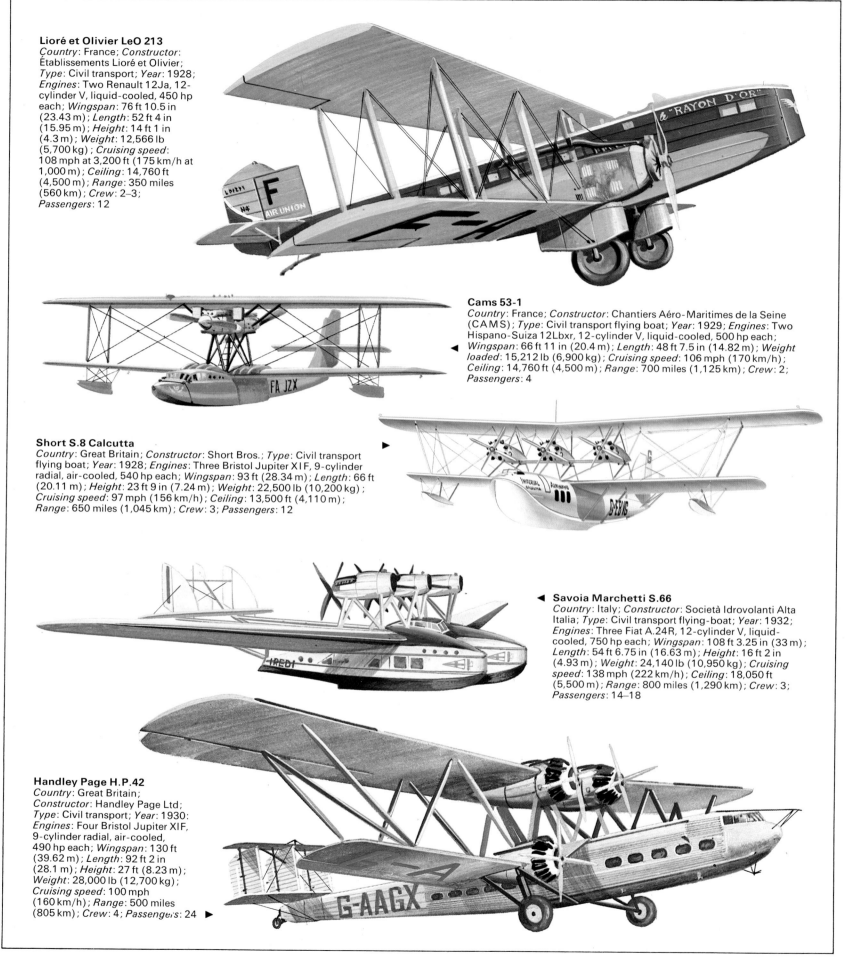

Lioré et Olivier LeO 213
Country: France; *Constructor*: Établissements Lioré et Olivier; *Type*: Civil transport; *Year*: 1928; *Engines*: Two Renault 12Ja, 12-cylinder V, liquid-cooled, 450 hp each; *Wingspan*: 76 ft 10.5 in (23.43 m); *Length*: 52 ft 4 in (15.95 m); *Height*: 14 ft 1 in (4.3 m); *Weight*: 12,566 lb (5,700 kg); *Cruising speed*: 108 mph at 3,200 ft (175 km/h at 1,000 m); *Ceiling*: 14,760 ft (4,500 m); *Range*: 350 miles (560 km); *Crew*: 2–3; *Passengers*: 12

◄ **Cams 53-1**
Country: France; *Constructor*: Chantiers Aéro-Maritimes de la Seine (CAMS); *Type*: Civil transport flying boat; *Year*: 1929; *Engines*: Two Hispano-Suiza 12Lbxr, 12-cylinder V, liquid-cooled, 500 hp each; *Wingspan*: 66 ft 11 in (20.4 m); *Length*: 48 ft 7.5 in (14.82 m); *Weight loaded*: 15,212 lb (6,900 kg); *Cruising speed*: 106 mph (170 km/h); *Ceiling*: 14,760 ft (4,500 m); *Range*: 700 miles (1,125 km); *Crew*: 2; *Passengers*: 4

Short S.8 Calcutta ►
Country: Great Britain; *Constructor*: Short Bros.; *Type*: Civil transport flying boat; *Year*: 1928; *Engines*: Three Bristol Jupiter XIF, 9-cylinder radial, air-cooled, 540 hp each; *Wingspan*: 93 ft (28.34 m); *Length*: 66 ft (20.11 m); *Height*: 23 ft 9 in (7.24 m); *Weight*: 22,500 lb (10,200 kg); *Cruising speed*: 97 mph (156 km/h); *Ceiling*: 13,500 ft (4,110 m); *Range*: 650 miles (1,045 km); *Crew*: 3; *Passengers*: 12

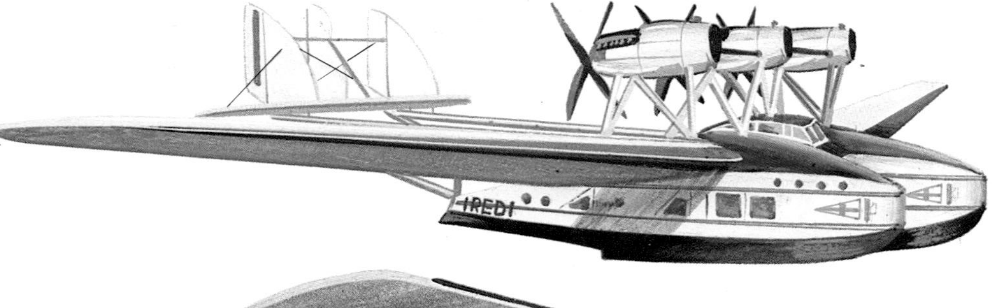

◄ **Savoia Marchetti S.66**
Country: Italy; *Constructor*: Società Idrovolanti Alta Italia; *Type*: Civil transport flying-boat; *Year*: 1932; *Engines*: Three Fiat A.24R, 12-cylinder V, liquid-cooled, 750 hp each; *Wingspan*: 108 ft 3.25 in (33 m); *Length*: 54 ft 6.75 in (16.63 m); *Height*: 16 ft 2 in (4.93 m); *Weight*: 24,140 lb (10,950 kg); *Cruising speed*: 138 mph (222 km/h); *Ceiling*: 18,050 ft (5,500 m); *Range*: 800 miles (1,290 km); *Crew*: 3; *Passengers*: 14–18

Handley Page H.P.42
Country: Great Britain; *Constructor*: Handley Page Ltd; *Type*: Civil transport; *Year*: 1930; *Engines*: Four Bristol Jupiter XIF, 9-cylinder radial, air-cooled, 490 hp each; *Wingspan*: 130 ft (39.62 m); *Length*: 92 ft 2 in (28.1 m); *Height*: 27 ft (8.23 m); *Weight*: 28,000 lb (12,700 kg); *Cruising speed*: 100 mph (160 km/h); *Range*: 500 miles (805 km); *Crew*: 4; *Passengers*: 24 ►

Farman F.180 Oiseau Bleu
Country: France; *Constructor*: Avions H. & M. Farman; *Type*: Civil transport; *Year*:1927; *Engines*: Two Farman 12We, 12-cylinder V, liquid-cooled, 500 hp each; *Wingspan*: 85 ft 3.75 in (26 m); *Length*: 59 ft (18 m); *Weight*: 17,637 lb (8,000 kg); *Cruising speed*: 106 mph (170 km/h); *Ceiling*: 13,000 ft (4,000 m); *Range*: 620 miles (1,000 km); *Crew*: 2; *Passengers*: 24

Farman F.190
Country: France; *Constructor*: Avions H. & M. Farman; *Type*: Civil transport; *Year*: 1928; *Engine*: Gnome-Rhône Titan 5Ba, 5-cylinder radial, air-cooled, 230 hp; *Wingspan*: 47 ft 3 in (14.4 m); *Length*: 34 ft 3.5 in (10.45 m); *Weight*: 3,968 lb (1,800 kg); *Cruising speed*: 100 mph (160 km/h); *Ceiling*: 16,900 ft (5,150 m); *Range*: 530 miles (850 km); *Crew*: 1; *Passengers*: 4

▲
Farman F.220
Country: France; *Constructor*: Avions H. & M. Farman; *Type*: South Atlantic transport version of 1930 bomber; *Year*: 1935; *Engines*: Four Hispano-Suiza 12 Lbr, 12-cylinder V, liquid-cooled, 600 hp each; *Wingspan*: 118 ft 1.25 in (36 m); *Length*: 69 ft (21.03 m); *Weight*: 35,274 lb (16,000 kg); *Cruising speed*: 136 mph at 11,480 ft (219 km/h at 3,500 m); *Ceiling*: 19,680 ft (6,000 m); *Range*: 2,796 miles (4,500 km); *Crew*: 2 or more

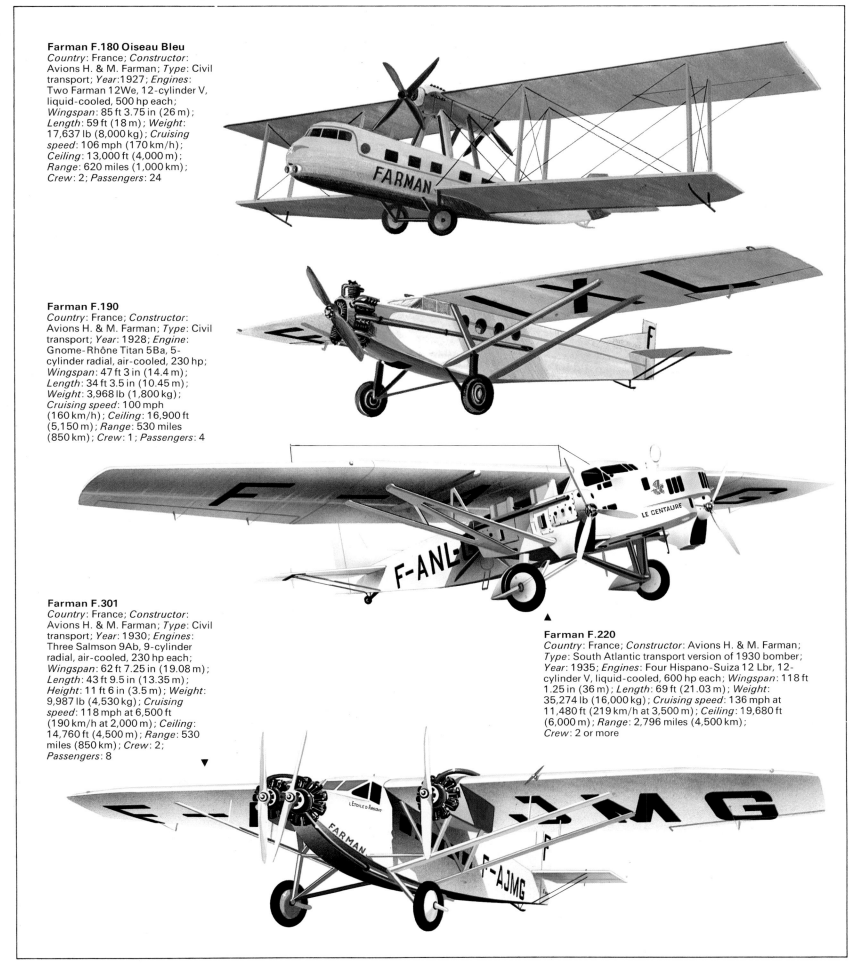

Farman F.301
Country: France; *Constructor*: Avions H. & M. Farman; *Type*: Civil transport; *Year*: 1930; *Engines*: Three Salmson 9Ab, 9-cylinder radial, air-cooled, 230 hp each; *Wingspan*: 62 ft 7.25 in (19.08 m); *Length*: 43 ft 9.5 in (13.35 m); *Height*: 11 ft 6 in (3.5 m); *Weight*: 9,987 lb (4,530 kg); *Cruising speed*: 118 mph at 6,500 ft (190 km/h at 2,000 m); *Ceiling*: 14,760 ft (4,500 m); *Range*: 530 miles (850 km); *Crew*: 2; *Passengers*: 8
▼

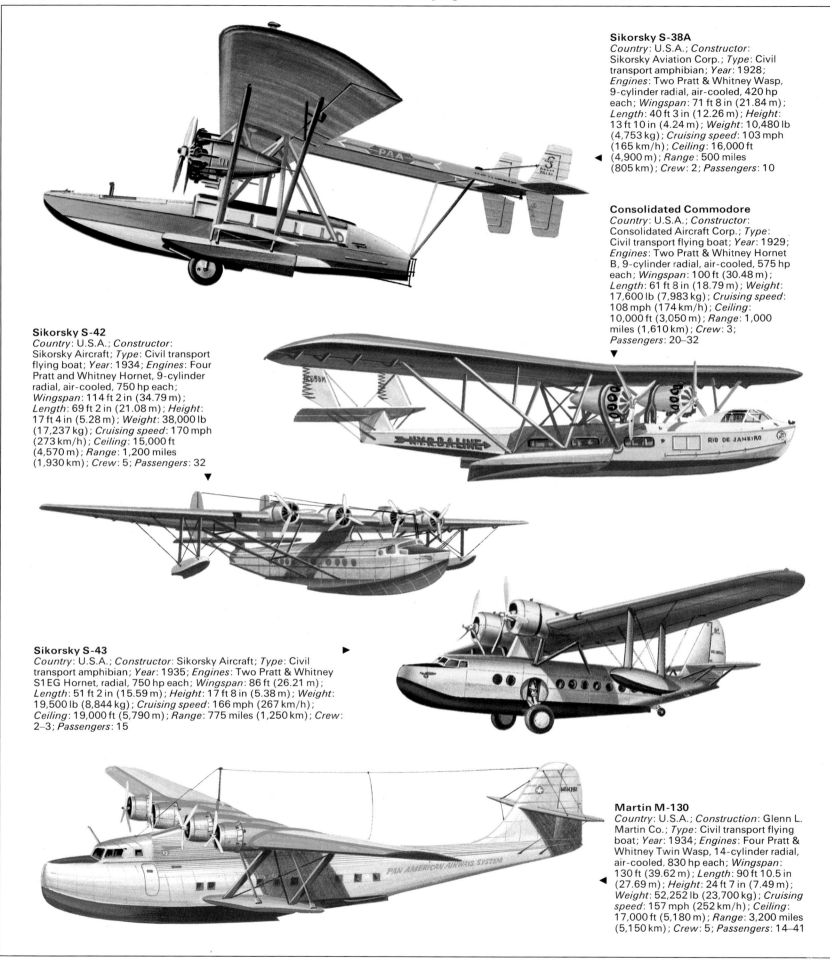

Sikorsky S-38A
Country: U.S.A.; *Constructor*: Sikorsky Aviation Corp.; *Type*: Civil transport amphibian; *Year*: 1928; *Engines*: Two Pratt & Whitney Wasp, 9-cylinder radial, air-cooled, 420 hp each; *Wingspan*: 71 ft 8 in (21.84 m); *Length*: 40 ft 3 in (12.26 m); *Height*: 13 ft 10 in (4.24 m); *Weight*: 10,480 lb (4,753 kg); *Cruising speed*: 103 mph (165 km/h); *Ceiling*: 16,000 ft (4,900 m); *Range*: 500 miles (805 km); *Crew*: 2; *Passengers*: 10

Consolidated Commodore
Country: U.S.A.; *Constructor*: Consolidated Aircraft Corp.; *Type*: Civil transport flying boat; *Year*: 1929; *Engines*: Two Pratt & Whitney Hornet B, 9-cylinder radial, air-cooled, 575 hp each; *Wingspan*: 100 ft (30.48 m); *Length*: 61 ft 8 in (18.79 m); *Weight*: 17,600 lb (7,983 kg); *Cruising speed*: 108 mph (174 km/h); *Ceiling*: 10,000 ft (3,050 m); *Range*: 1,000 miles (1,610 km); *Crew*: 3; *Passengers*: 20–32

Sikorsky S-42
Country: U.S.A.; *Constructor*: Sikorsky Aircraft; *Type*: Civil transport flying boat; *Year*: 1934; *Engines*: Four Pratt and Whitney Hornet, 9-cylinder radial, air-cooled, 750 hp each; *Wingspan*: 114 ft 2 in (34.79 m); *Length*: 69 ft 2 in (21.08 m); *Height*: 17 ft 4 in (5.28 m); *Weight*: 38,000 lb (17,237 kg); *Cruising speed*: 170 mph (273 km/h); *Ceiling*: 15,000 ft (4,570 m); *Range*: 1,200 miles (1,930 km); *Crew*: 5; *Passengers*: 32

Sikorsky S-43
Country: U.S.A.; *Constructor*: Sikorsky Aircraft; *Type*: Civil transport amphibian; *Year*: 1935; *Engines*: Two Pratt & Whitney S1EG Hornet, radial, 750 hp each; *Wingspan*: 86 ft (26.21 m); *Length*: 51 ft 2 in (15.59 m); *Height*: 17 ft 8 in (5.38 m); *Weight*: 19,500 lb (8,844 kg); *Cruising speed*: 166 mph (267 km/h); *Ceiling*: 19,000 ft (5,790 m); *Range*: 775 miles (1,250 km); *Crew*: 2–3; *Passengers*: 15

Martin M-130
Country: U.S.A.; *Construction*: Glenn L. Martin Co.; *Type*: Civil transport flying boat; *Year*: 1934; *Engines*: Four Pratt & Whitney Twin Wasp, 14-cylinder radial, air-cooled, 830 hp each; *Wingspan*: 130 ft (39.62 m); *Length*: 90 ft 10.5 in (27.69 m); *Height*: 24 ft 7 in (7.49 m); *Weight*: 52,252 lb (23,700 kg); *Cruising speed*: 157 mph (252 km/h); *Ceiling*: 17,000 ft (5,180 m); *Range*: 3,200 miles (5,150 km); *Crew*: 5; *Passengers*: 14–41

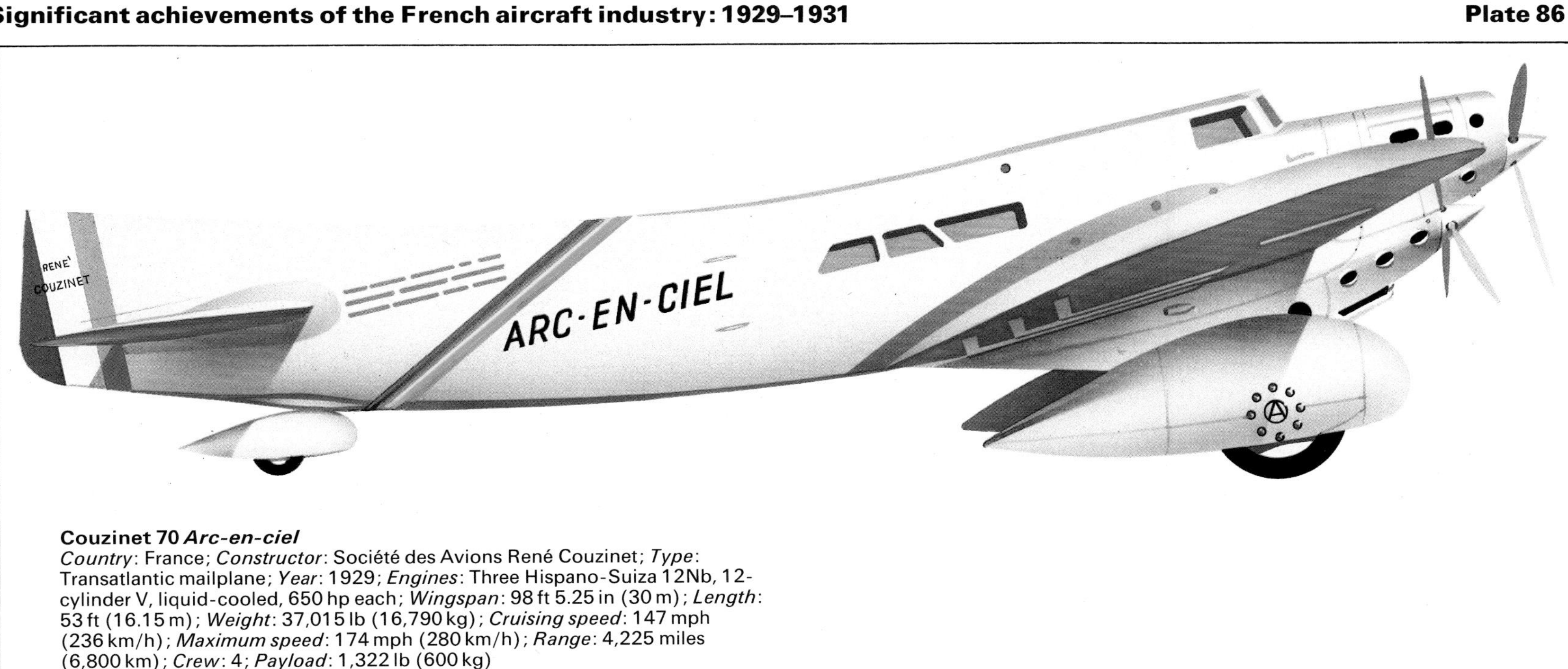

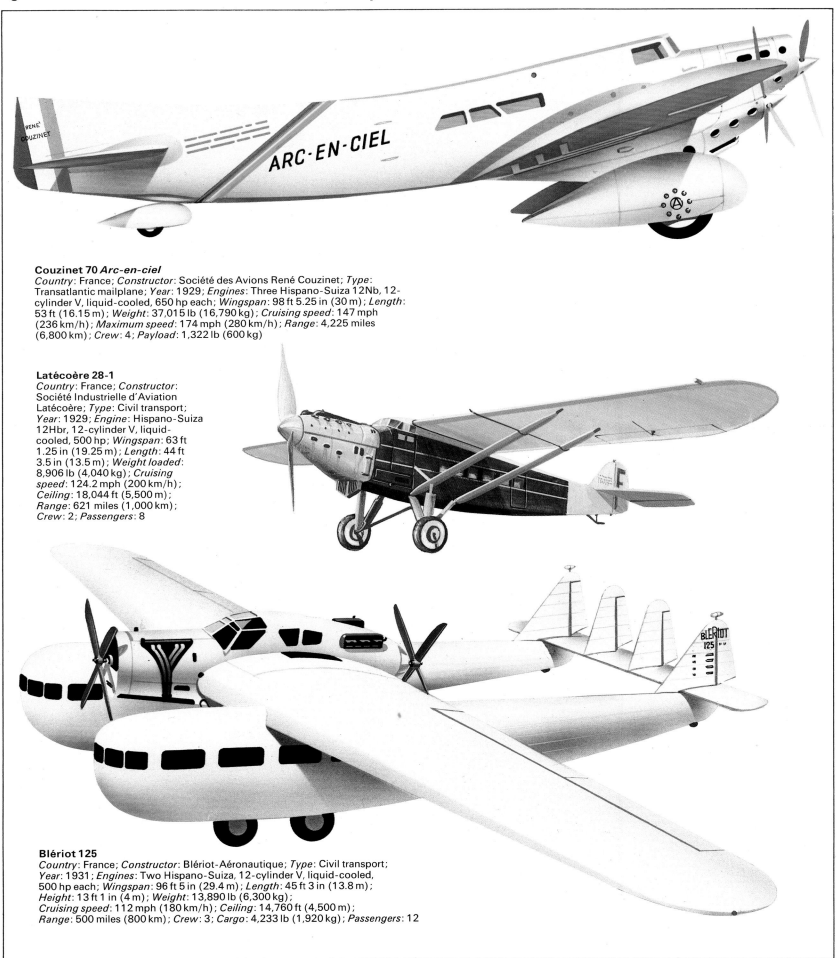

Couzinet 70 *Arc-en-ciel*
Country: France; *Constructor*: Société des Avions René Couzinet; *Type*: Transatlantic mailplane; *Year*: 1929; *Engines*: Three Hispano-Suiza 12Nb, 12-cylinder V, liquid-cooled, 650 hp each; *Wingspan*: 98 ft 5.25 in (30 m); *Length*: 53 ft (16.15 m); *Weight*: 37,015 lb (16,790 kg); *Cruising speed*: 147 mph (236 km/h); *Maximum speed*: 174 mph (280 km/h); *Range*: 4,225 miles (6,800 km); *Crew*: 4; *Payload*: 1,322 lb (600 kg)

Latécoère 28-1
Country: France; *Constructor*: Société Industrielle d'Aviation Latécoère; *Type*: Civil transport; *Year*: 1929; *Engine*: Hispano-Suiza 12Hbr, 12-cylinder V, liquid-cooled, 500 hp; *Wingspan*: 63 ft 1.25 in (19.25 m); *Length*: 44 ft 3.5 in (13.5 m); *Weight loaded*: 8,906 lb (4,040 kg); *Cruising speed*: 124.2 mph (200 km/h); *Ceiling*: 18,044 ft (5,500 m); *Range*: 621 miles (1,000 km); *Crew*: 2; *Passengers*: 8

Blériot 125
Country: France; *Constructor*: Blériot-Aéronautique; *Type*: Civil transport; *Year*: 1931; *Engines*: Two Hispano-Suiza, 12-cylinder V, liquid-cooled, 500 hp each; *Wingspan*: 96 ft 5 in (29.4 m); *Length*: 45 ft 3 in (13.8 m); *Height*: 13 ft 1 in (4 m); *Weight*: 13,890 lb (6,300 kg); *Cruising speed*: 112 mph (180 km/h); *Ceiling*: 14,760 ft (4,500 m); *Range*: 500 miles (800 km); *Crew*: 3; *Cargo*: 4,233 lb (1,920 kg); *Passengers*: 12

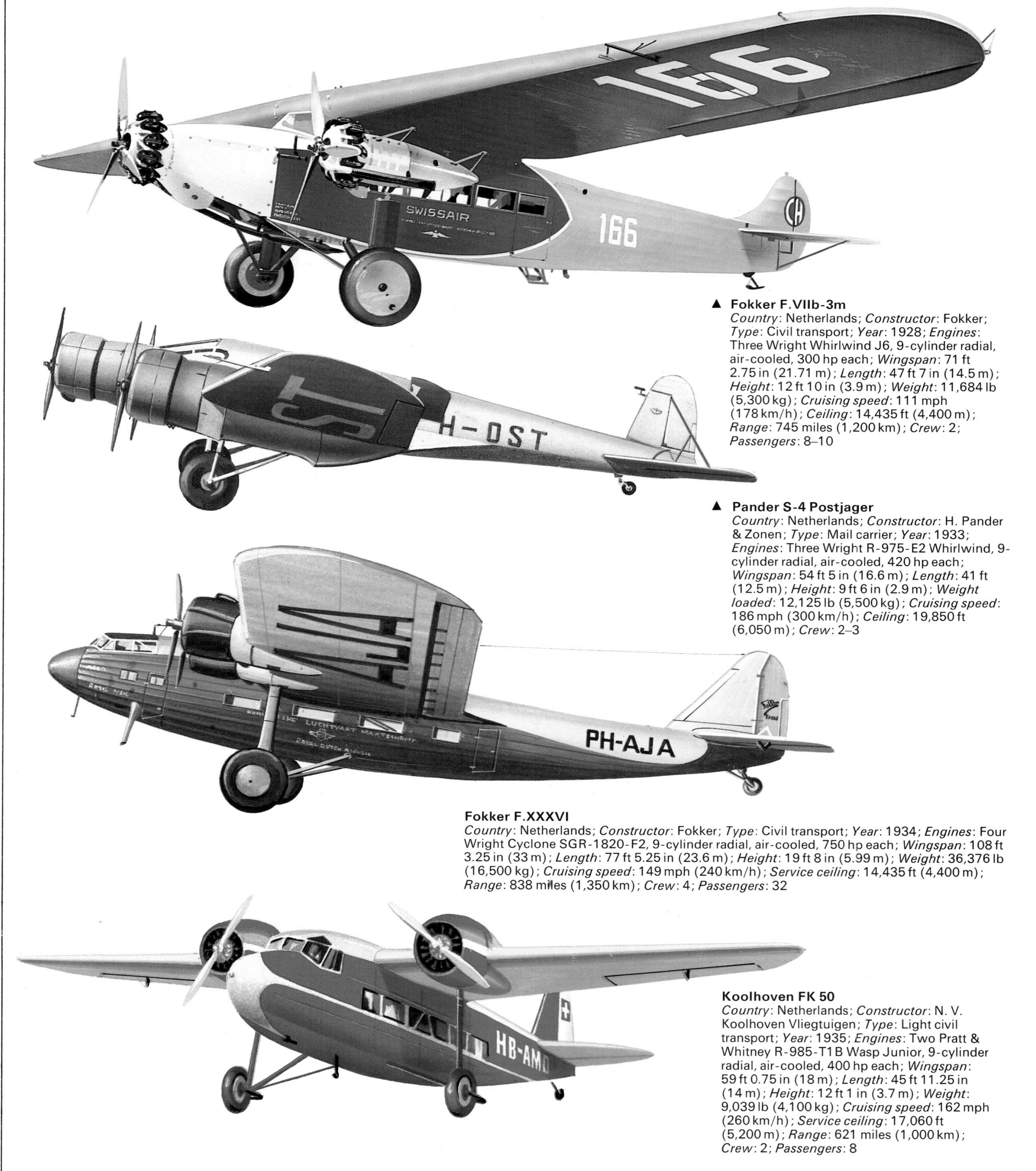

▲ **Fokker F.VIIb-3m**
Country: Netherlands; *Constructor*: Fokker; *Type*: Civil transport; *Year*: 1928; *Engines*: Three Wright Whirlwind J6, 9-cylinder radial, air-cooled, 300 hp each; *Wingspan*: 71 ft 2.75 in (21.71 m); *Length*: 47 ft 7 in (14.5 m); *Height*: 12 ft 10 in (3.9 m); *Weight*: 11,684 lb (5,300 kg); *Cruising speed*: 111 mph (178 km/h); *Ceiling*: 14,435 ft (4,400 m); *Range*: 745 miles (1,200 km); *Crew*: 2; *Passengers*: 8–10

▲ **Pander S-4 Postjager**
Country: Netherlands; *Constructor*: H. Pander & Zonen; *Type*: Mail carrier; *Year*: 1933; *Engines*: Three Wright R-975-E2 Whirlwind, 9-cylinder radial, air-cooled, 420 hp each; *Wingspan*: 54 ft 5 in (16.6 m); *Length*: 41 ft (12.5 m); *Height*: 9 ft 6 in (2.9 m); *Weight loaded*: 12,125 lb (5,500 kg); *Cruising speed*: 186 mph (300 km/h); *Ceiling*: 19,850 ft (6,050 m); *Crew*: 2–3

Fokker F.XXXVI
Country: Netherlands; *Constructor*: Fokker; *Type*: Civil transport; *Year*: 1934; *Engines*: Four Wright Cyclone SGR-1820-F2, 9-cylinder radial, air-cooled, 750 hp each; *Wingspan*: 108 ft 3.25 in (33 m); *Length*: 77 ft 5.25 in (23.6 m); *Height*: 19 ft 8 in (5.99 m); *Weight*: 36,376 lb (16,500 kg); *Cruising speed*: 149 mph (240 km/h); *Service ceiling*: 14,435 ft (4,400 m); *Range*: 838 miles (1,350 km); *Crew*: 4; *Passengers*: 32

Koolhoven FK 50
Country: Netherlands; *Constructor*: N. V. Koolhoven Vliegtuigen; *Type*: Light civil transport; *Year*: 1935; *Engines*: Two Pratt & Whitney R-985-T1B Wasp Junior, 9-cylinder radial, air-cooled, 400 hp each; *Wingspan*: 59 ft 0.75 in (18 m); *Length*: 45 ft 11.25 in (14 m); *Height*: 12 ft 1 in (3.7 m); *Weight*: 9,039 lb (4,100 kg); *Cruising speed*: 162 mph (260 km/h); *Service ceiling*: 17,060 ft (5,200 m); *Range*: 621 miles (1,000 km); *Crew*: 2; *Passengers*: 8

Boeing 80A ►
Country: U.S.A.; *Constructor*: Boeing Airplane Co.; *Type*: Civil transport; *Year*: 1928; *Engines*: Three Pratt & Whitney Hornet, 9-cylinder radial, air-cooled, 525 hp each; *Wingspan*: 80 ft (24.38 m); *Length*: 56 ft 6 in (17.22 m); *Height*: 15 ft 3 in (4.65 m); *Weight*: 17,500 lb (7,938 kg); *Cruising speed*: 125 mph (201 km/h); *Ceiling*: 14,000 ft (4,270 m); *Range*: 460 miles (740 km); *Crew*: 2–3; *Passengers*: 18

Fokker F-32
Country: U.S.A.; *Constructor*: Fokker Aircraft Corp. (USA); *Type*: Civil transport; *Year*: 1929; *Engines*: Four Pratt & Whitney Hornet, 9-cylinder radial, air-cooled, 525 hp each; *Wingspan*: 99 ft (30.18 m); *Length*: 70 ft 2 in (21.38 m); *Height*: 16 ft 6 in (5.03 m); *Weight*: 22,500 lb (10,205 kg); *Cruising speed*: 123 mph (198 km/h); *Ceiling*: 18,000 ft (5,485 m); *Range*: 530 miles (853 km); *Crew*: 2; *Passengers*: 32

Stinson Trimotor SM-6000 ▲
Country: U.S.A.; *Constructor*: The Stinson Aircraft Corp.; *Type*: Civil transport; *Year*: 1930; *Engines*: Three Lycoming R-680, 9-cylinder radial, air-cooled, 215 hp each; *Wingspan*: 60 ft (18.29 m); *Length*: 42 ft 10 in (13.05 m); *Height*: 12 ft (3.65 m); *Weight*: 8,500 lb (3,855 kg); *Cruising speed*: 115 mph (185 km/h); *Ceiling*: 15,000 ft (4,570 m); *Range*: 345 miles (555 km); *Crew*: 1; *Passengers*: 10

Curtiss T-32 Condor ▲
Country: U.S.A.; *Constructor*: Curtiss Aeroplane and Motor Co.; *Type*: Civil Transport; *Year*: 1933; *Engines*: Two Wright Cyclone, 9-cylinder radial, air-cooled, 720 hp each; *Wingspan*: 82 ft (24.99 m); *Length*: 48 ft 7 in (14.81 m); *Height*: 16 ft 4 in (4.98 m); *Weight*: 17,500 lb (7,938 kg); *Cruising speed*: 167 mph (268 km/h); *Service ceiling*: 23,000 ft (7,010 m); *Range*: 716 miles (1,152 km); *Crew*: 2; *Passengers*: 12

Boeing 247D
Country: U.S.A.; *Constructor*: Boeing Airplane Co.; *Type*: Civil transport; *Year*: 1933; *Engines*: Two Pratt & Whitney Wasp S1H1G, 9-cylinder radial, air-cooled, 550 hp each; *Wingspan*: 74 ft (22.56 m); *Length*: 51 ft 7 in (15.72 m); *Height*: 12 ft 1.75 in (3.7 m); *Weight*: 13,650 lb (6,192 kg); *Cruising speed*: 189 mph (304 km/h); *Service ceiling*: 25,400 ft (7,740 m); *Range*: 745 miles (1,200 km); *Crew*: 2–3; *Passengers*: 10 ▼

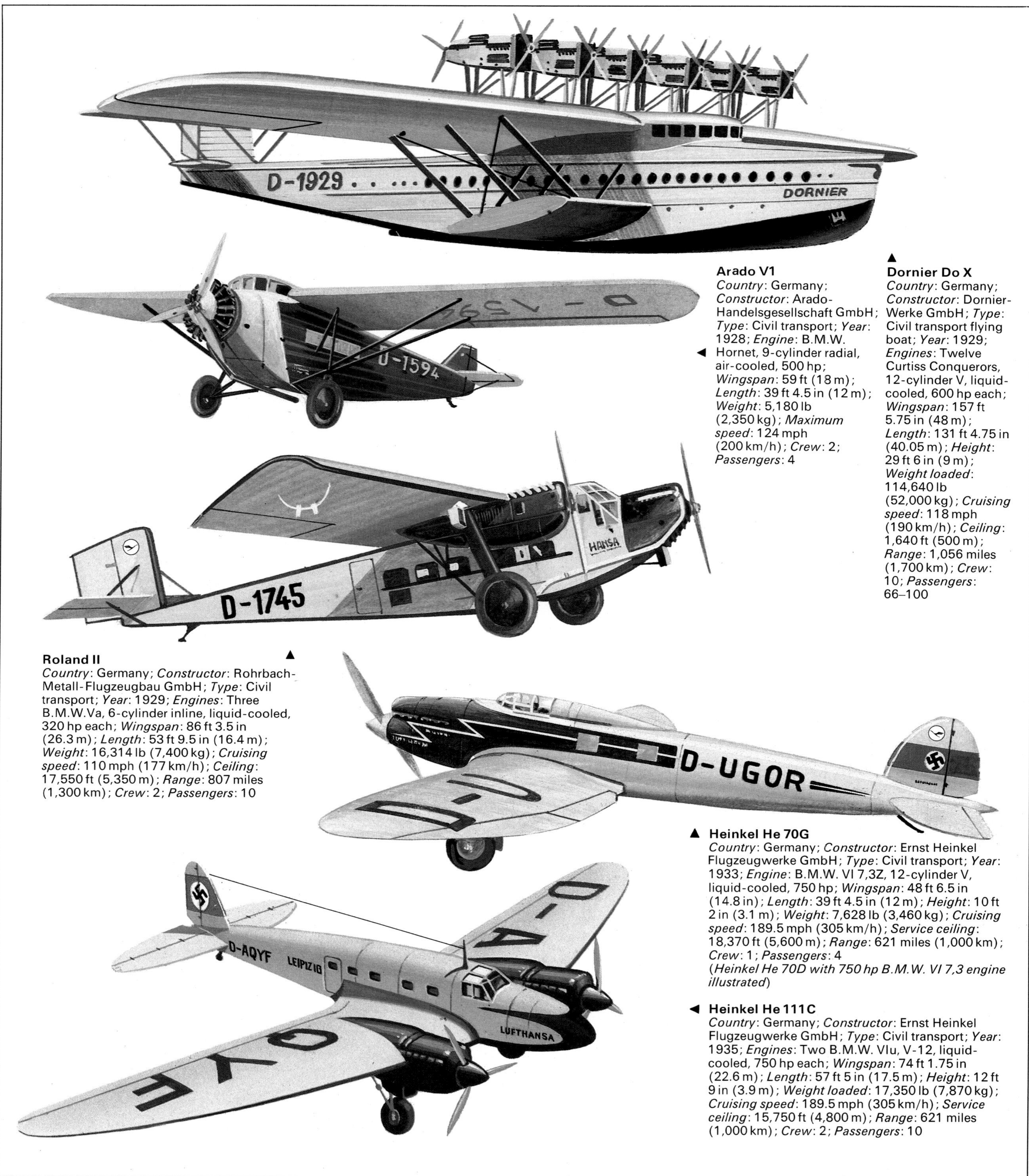

▲ **Dornier Do X**
Country: Germany; *Constructor*: Dornier-Werke GmbH; *Type*: Civil transport flying boat; *Year*: 1929; *Engines*: Twelve Curtiss Conquerors, 12-cylinder V, liquid-cooled, 600 hp each; *Wingspan*: 157 ft 5.75 in (48 m); *Length*: 131 ft 4.75 in (40.05 m); *Height*: 29 ft 6 in (9 m); *Weight loaded*: 114,640 lb (52,000 kg); *Cruising speed*: 118 mph (190 km/h); *Ceiling*: 1,640 ft (500 m); *Range*: 1,056 miles (1,700 km); *Crew*: 10; *Passengers*: 66–100

◄ **Arado V1**
Country: Germany; *Constructor*: Arado-Handelsgesellschaft GmbH; *Type*: Civil transport; *Year*: 1928; *Engine*: B.M.W. Hornet, 9-cylinder radial, air-cooled, 500 hp; *Wingspan*: 59 ft (18 m); *Length*: 39 ft 4.5 in (12 m); *Weight*: 5,180 lb (2,350 kg); *Maximum speed*: 124 mph (200 km/h); *Crew*: 2; *Passengers*: 4

▲ **Roland II**
Country: Germany; *Constructor*: Rohrbach-Metall-Flugzeugbau GmbH; *Type*: Civil transport; *Year*: 1929; *Engines*: Three B.M.W.Va, 6-cylinder inline, liquid-cooled, 320 hp each; *Wingspan*: 86 ft 3.5 in (26.3 m); *Length*: 53 ft 9.5 in (16.4 m); *Weight*: 16,314 lb (7,400 kg); *Cruising speed*: 110 mph (177 km/h); *Ceiling*: 17,550 ft (5,350 m); *Range*: 807 miles (1,300 km); *Crew*: 2; *Passengers*: 10

▲ **Heinkel He 70G**
Country: Germany; *Constructor*: Ernst Heinkel Flugzeugwerke GmbH; *Type*: Civil transport; *Year*: 1933; *Engine*: B.M.W. VI 7,3Z, 12-cylinder V, liquid-cooled, 750 hp; *Wingspan*: 48 ft 6.5 in (14.8 in); *Length*: 39 ft 4.5 in (12 m); *Height*: 10 ft 2 in (3.1 m); *Weight*: 7,628 lb (3,460 kg); *Cruising speed*: 189.5 mph (305 km/h); *Service ceiling*: 18,370 ft (5,600 m); *Range*: 621 miles (1,000 km); *Crew*: 1; *Passengers*: 4
(Heinkel He 70D with 750 hp B.M.W. VI 7,3 engine illustrated)

◄ **Heinkel He 111C**
Country: Germany; *Constructor*: Ernst Heinkel Flugzeugwerke GmbH; *Type*: Civil transport; *Year*: 1935; *Engines*: Two B.M.W. VIu, V-12, liquid-cooled, 750 hp each; *Wingspan*: 74 ft 1.75 in (22.6 m); *Length*: 57 ft 5 in (17.5 m); *Height*: 12 ft 9 in (3.9 m); *Weight loaded*: 17,350 lb (7,870 kg); *Cruising speed*: 189.5 mph (305 km/h); *Service ceiling*: 15,750 ft (4,800 m); *Range*: 621 miles (1,000 km); *Crew*: 2; *Passengers*: 10

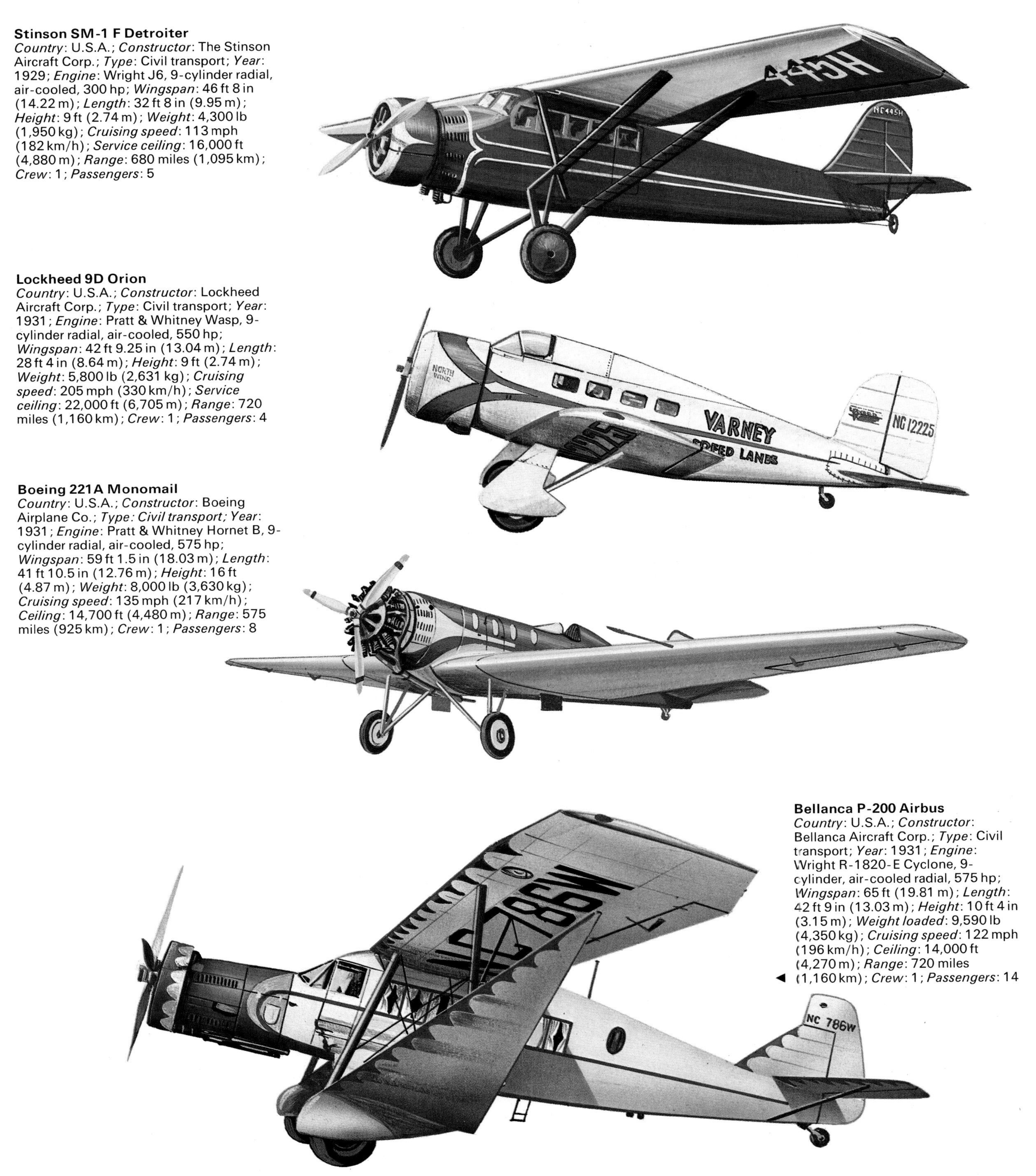

Stinson SM-1 F Detroiter
Country: U.S.A.; *Constructor*: The Stinson Aircraft Corp.; *Type*: Civil transport; *Year*: 1929; *Engine*: Wright J6, 9-cylinder radial, air-cooled, 300 hp; *Wingspan*: 46 ft 8 in (14.22 m); *Length*: 32 ft 8 in (9.95 m); *Height*: 9 ft (2.74 m); *Weight*: 4,300 lb (1,950 kg); *Cruising speed*: 113 mph (182 km/h); *Service ceiling*: 16,000 ft (4,880 m); *Range*: 680 miles (1,095 km); *Crew*: 1; *Passengers*: 5

Lockheed 9D Orion
Country: U.S.A.; *Constructor*: Lockheed Aircraft Corp.; *Type*: Civil transport; *Year*: 1931; *Engine*: Pratt & Whitney Wasp, 9-cylinder radial, air-cooled, 550 hp; *Wingspan*: 42 ft 9.25 in (13.04 m); *Length*: 28 ft 4 in (8.64 m); *Height*: 9 ft (2.74 m); *Weight*: 5,800 lb (2,631 kg); *Cruising speed*: 205 mph (330 km/h); *Service ceiling*: 22,000 ft (6,705 m); *Range*: 720 miles (1,160 km); *Crew*: 1; *Passengers*: 4

Boeing 221A Monomail
Country: U.S.A.; *Constructor*: Boeing Airplane Co.; *Type: Civil transport; Year*: 1931; *Engine*: Pratt & Whitney Hornet B, 9-cylinder radial, air-cooled, 575 hp; *Wingspan*: 59 ft 1.5 in (18.03 m); *Length*: 41 ft 10.5 in (12.76 m); *Height*: 16 ft (4.87 m); *Weight*: 8,000 lb (3,630 kg); *Cruising speed*: 135 mph (217 km/h); *Ceiling*: 14,700 ft (4,480 m); *Range*: 575 miles (925 km); *Crew*: 1; *Passengers*: 8

Bellanca P-200 Airbus
Country: U.S.A.; *Constructor*: Bellanca Aircraft Corp.; *Type*: Civil transport; *Year*: 1931; *Engine*: Wright R-1820-E Cyclone, 9-cylinder, air-cooled radial, 575 hp; *Wingspan*: 65 ft (19.81 m); *Length*: 42 ft 9 in (13.03 m); *Height*: 10 ft 4 in (3.15 m); *Weight loaded*: 9,590 lb (4,350 kg); *Cruising speed*: 122 mph (196 km/h); *Ceiling*: 14,000 ft (4,270 m); *Range*: 720 miles ◄ (1,160 km); *Crew*: 1; *Passengers*: 14

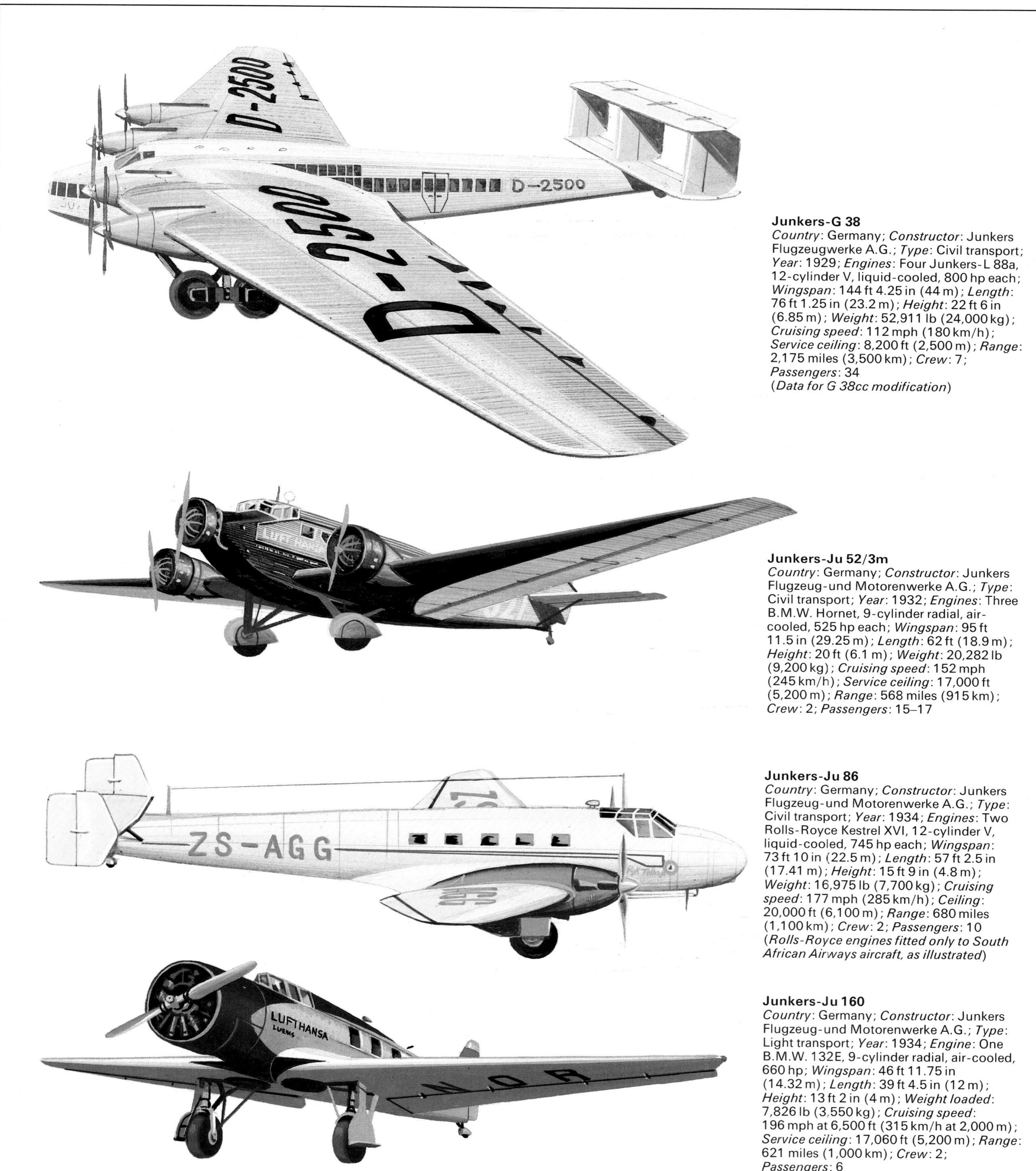

Junkers-G 38
Country: Germany; *Constructor*: Junkers Flugzeugwerke A.G.; *Type*: Civil transport; *Year*: 1929; *Engines*: Four Junkers-L 88a, 12-cylinder V, liquid-cooled, 800 hp each; *Wingspan*: 144 ft 4.25 in (44 m); *Length*: 76 ft 1.25 in (23.2 m); *Height*: 22 ft 6 in (6.85 m); *Weight*: 52,911 lb (24,000 kg); *Cruising speed*: 112 mph (180 km/h); *Service ceiling*: 8,200 ft (2,500 m); *Range*: 2,175 miles (3,500 km); *Crew*: 7; *Passengers*: 34
(*Data for G 38cc modification*)

Junkers-Ju 52/3m
Country: Germany; *Constructor*: Junkers Flugzeug-und Motorenwerke A.G.; *Type*: Civil transport; *Year*: 1932; *Engines*: Three B.M.W. Hornet, 9-cylinder radial, air-cooled, 525 hp each; *Wingspan*: 95 ft 11.5 in (29.25 m); *Length*: 62 ft (18.9 m); *Height*: 20 ft (6.1 m); *Weight*: 20,282 lb (9,200 kg); *Cruising speed*: 152 mph (245 km/h); *Service ceiling*: 17,000 ft (5,200 m); *Range*: 568 miles (915 km); *Crew*: 2; *Passengers*: 15–17

Junkers-Ju 86
Country: Germany; *Constructor*: Junkers Flugzeug-und Motorenwerke A.G.; *Type*: Civil transport; *Year*: 1934; *Engines*: Two Rolls-Royce Kestrel XVI, 12-cylinder V, liquid-cooled, 745 hp each; *Wingspan*: 73 ft 10 in (22.5 m); *Length*: 57 ft 2.5 in (17.41 m); *Height*: 15 ft 9 in (4.8 m); *Weight*: 16,975 lb (7,700 kg); *Cruising speed*: 177 mph (285 km/h); *Ceiling*: 20,000 ft (6,100 m); *Range*: 680 miles (1,100 km); *Crew*: 2; *Passengers*: 10
(*Rolls-Royce engines fitted only to South African Airways aircraft, as illustrated*)

Junkers-Ju 160
Country: Germany; *Constructor*: Junkers Flugzeug-und Motorenwerke A.G.; *Type*: Light transport; *Year*: 1934; *Engine*: One B.M.W. 132E, 9-cylinder radial, air-cooled, 660 hp; *Wingspan*: 46 ft 11.75 in (14.32 m); *Length*: 39 ft 4.5 in (12 m); *Height*: 13 ft 2 in (4 m); *Weight loaded*: 7,826 lb (3,550 kg); *Cruising speed*: 196 mph at 6,500 ft (315 km/h at 2,000 m); *Service ceiling*: 17,060 ft (5,200 m); *Range*: 621 miles (1,000 km); *Crew*: 2; *Passengers*: 6

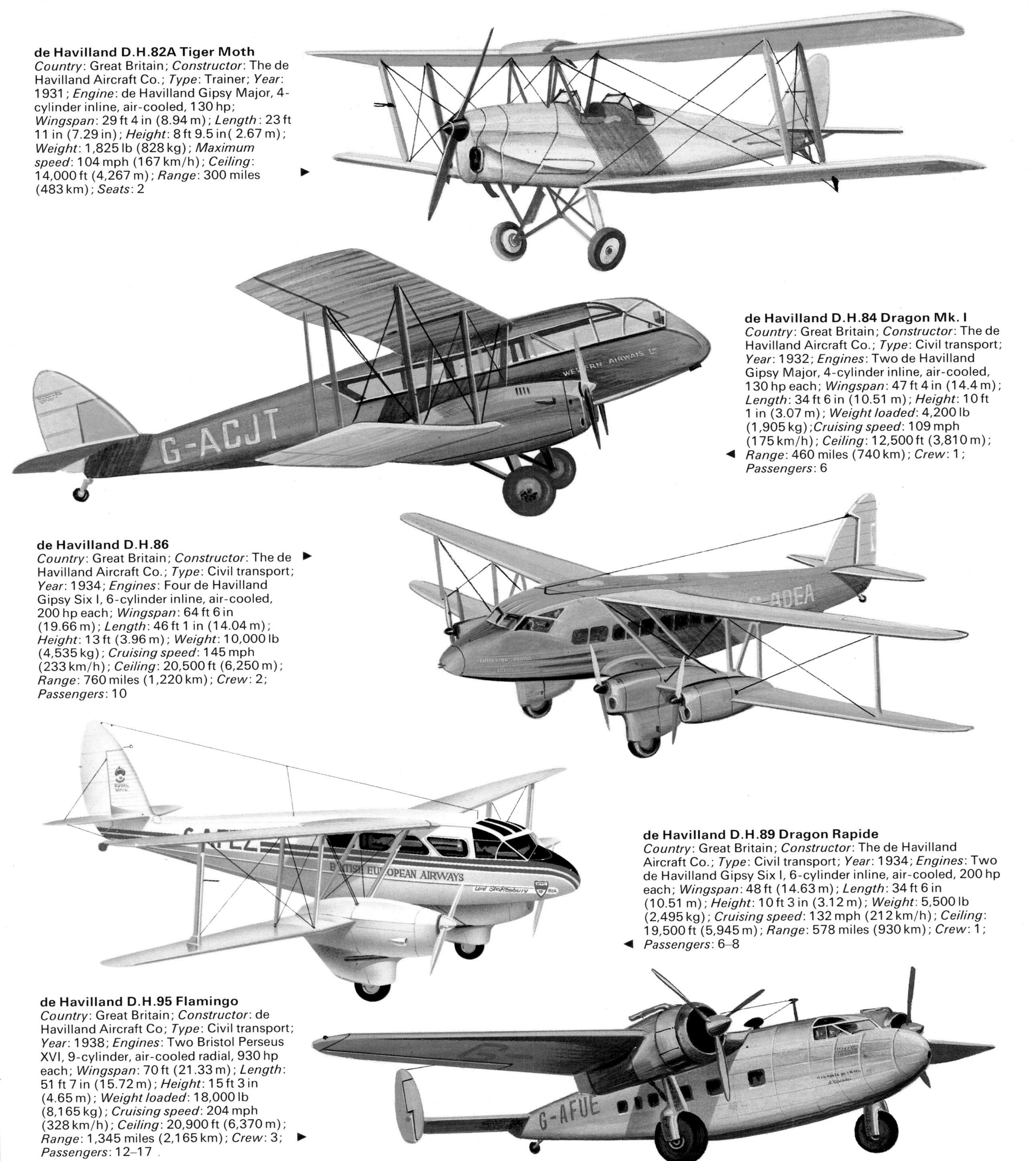

de Havilland D.H.82A Tiger Moth
Country: Great Britain; *Constructor*: The de Havilland Aircraft Co.; *Type*: Trainer; *Year*: 1931; *Engine*: de Havilland Gipsy Major, 4-cylinder inline, air-cooled, 130 hp; *Wingspan*: 29 ft 4 in (8.94 m); *Length*: 23 ft 11 in (7.29 in); *Height*: 8 ft 9.5 in (2.67 m); *Weight*: 1,825 lb (828 kg); *Maximum speed*: 104 mph (167 km/h); *Ceiling*: 14,000 ft (4,267 m); *Range*: 300 miles (483 km); *Seats*: 2 ▸

de Havilland D.H.84 Dragon Mk. I
Country: Great Britain; *Constructor*: The de Havilland Aircraft Co.; *Type*: Civil transport; *Year*: 1932; *Engines*: Two de Havilland Gipsy Major, 4-cylinder inline, air-cooled, 130 hp each; *Wingspan*: 47 ft 4 in (14.4 m); *Length*: 34 ft 6 in (10.51 m); *Height*: 10 ft 1 in (3.07 m); *Weight loaded*: 4,200 lb (1,905 kg); *Cruising speed*: 109 mph (175 km/h); *Ceiling*: 12,500 ft (3,810 m); ◂ *Range*: 460 miles (740 km); *Crew*: 1; *Passengers*: 6

de Havilland D.H.86
Country: Great Britain; *Constructor*: The de ▸ Havilland Aircraft Co.; *Type*: Civil transport; *Year*: 1934; *Engines*: Four de Havilland Gipsy Six I, 6-cylinder inline, air-cooled, 200 hp each; *Wingspan*: 64 ft 6 in (19.66 m); *Length*: 46 ft 1 in (14.04 m); *Height*: 13 ft (3.96 m); *Weight*: 10,000 lb (4,535 kg); *Cruising speed*: 145 mph (233 km/h); *Ceiling*: 20,500 ft (6,250 m); *Range*: 760 miles (1,220 km); *Crew*: 2; *Passengers*: 10

de Havilland D.H.89 Dragon Rapide
Country: Great Britain; *Constructor*: The de Havilland Aircraft Co.; *Type*: Civil transport; *Year*: 1934; *Engines*: Two de Havilland Gipsy Six I, 6-cylinder inline, air-cooled, 200 hp each; *Wingspan*: 48 ft (14.63 m); *Length*: 34 ft 6 in (10.51 m); *Height*: 10 ft 3 in (3.12 m); *Weight*: 5,500 lb (2,495 kg); *Cruising speed*: 132 mph (212 km/h); *Ceiling*: 19,500 ft (5,945 m); *Range*: 578 miles (930 km); *Crew*: 1; ◂ *Passengers*: 6–8

de Havilland D.H.95 Flamingo
Country: Great Britain; *Constructor*: de Havilland Aircraft Co; *Type*: Civil transport; *Year*: 1938; *Engines*: Two Bristol Perseus XVI, 9-cylinder, air-cooled radial, 930 hp each; *Wingspan*: 70 ft (21.33 m); *Length*: 51 ft 7 in (15.72 m); *Height*: 15 ft 3 in (4.65 m); *Weight loaded*: 18,000 lb (8,165 kg); *Cruising speed*: 204 mph (328 km/h); *Ceiling*: 20,900 ft (6,370 m); *Range*: 1,345 miles (2,165 km); *Crew*: 3; ▸ *Passengers*: 12–17

Savoia Marchetti produce a succession of excellent aircraft: 1930–1939

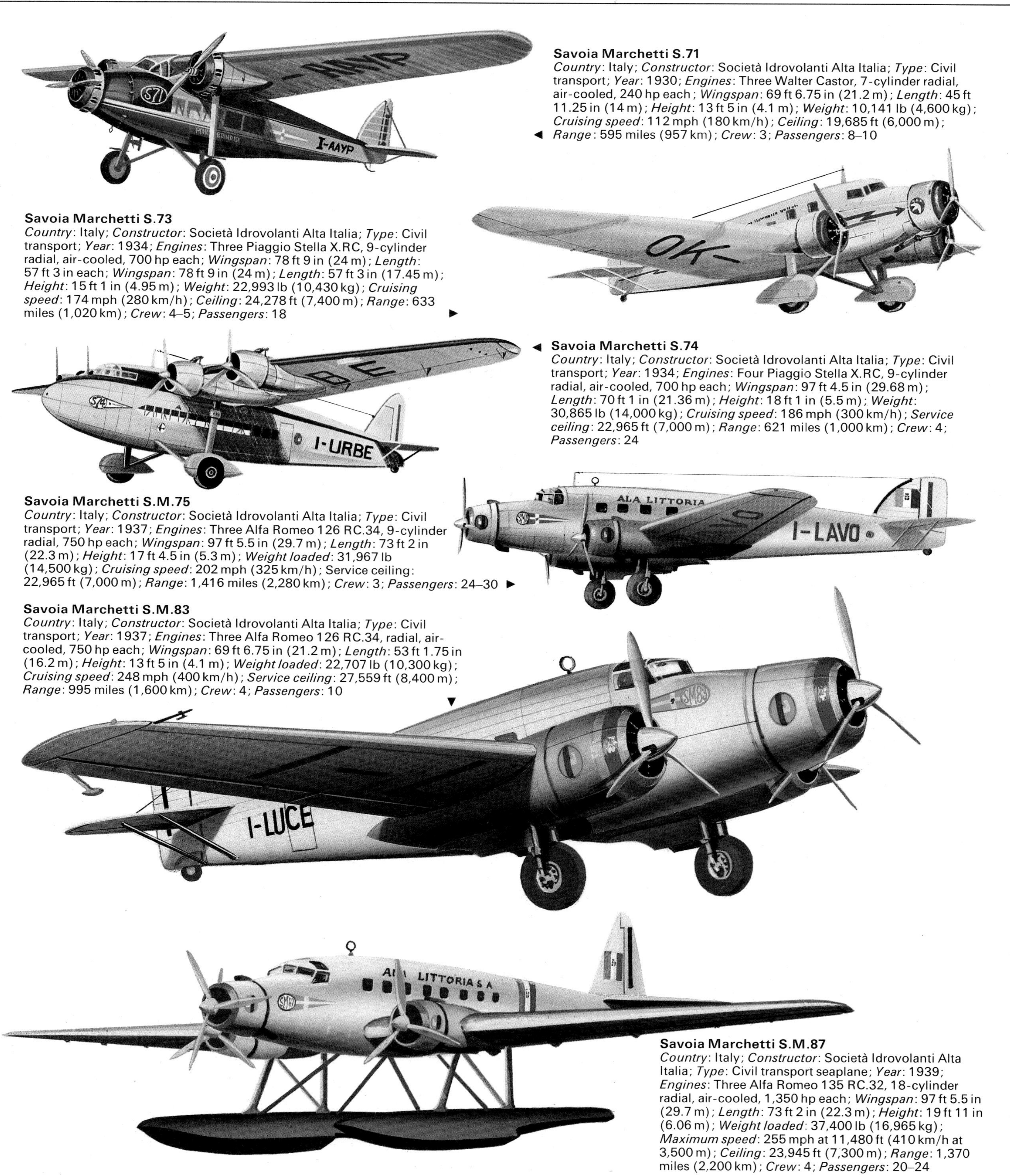

Savoia Marchetti S.71
Country: Italy; *Constructor*: Società Idrovolanti Alta Italia; *Type*: Civil transport; *Year*: 1930; *Engines*: Three Walter Castor, 7-cylinder radial, air-cooled, 240 hp each; *Wingspan*: 69 ft 6.75 in (21.2 m); *Length*: 45 ft 11.25 in (14 m); *Height*: 13 ft 5 in (4.1 m); *Weight*: 10,141 lb (4,600 kg); *Cruising speed*: 112 mph (180 km/h); *Ceiling*: 19,685 ft (6,000 m); *Range*: 595 miles (957 km); *Crew*: 3; *Passengers*: 8–10

Savoia Marchetti S.73
Country: Italy; *Constructor*: Società Idrovolanti Alta Italia; *Type*: Civil transport; *Year*: 1934; *Engines*: Three Piaggio Stella X.RC, 9-cylinder radial, air-cooled, 700 hp each; *Wingspan*: 78 ft 9 in (24 m); *Length*: 57 ft 3 in each; *Wingspan*: 78 ft 9 in (24 m); *Length*: 57 ft 3 in (17.45 m); *Height*: 15 ft 1 in (4.95 m); *Weight*: 22,993 lb (10,430 kg); *Cruising speed*: 174 mph (280 km/h); *Ceiling*: 24,278 ft (7,400 m); *Range*: 633 miles (1,020 km); *Crew*: 4–5; *Passengers*: 18

Savoia Marchetti S.74
Country: Italy; *Constructor*: Società Idrovolanti Alta Italia; *Type*: Civil transport; *Year*: 1934; *Engines*: Four Piaggio Stella X.RC, 9-cylinder radial, air-cooled, 700 hp each; *Wingspan*: 97 ft 4.5 in (29.68 m); *Length*: 70 ft 1 in (21.36 m); *Height*: 18 ft 1 in (5.5 m); *Weight*: 30,865 lb (14,000 kg); *Cruising speed*: 186 mph (300 km/h); *Service ceiling*: 22,965 ft (7,000 m); *Range*: 621 miles (1,000 km); *Crew*: 4; *Passengers*: 24

Savoia Marchetti S.M.75
Country: Italy; *Constructor*: Società Idrovolanti Alta Italia; *Type*: Civil transport; *Year*: 1937; *Engines*: Three Alfa Romeo 126 RC.34, 9-cylinder radial, 750 hp each; *Wingspan*: 97 ft 5.5 in (29.7 m); *Length*: 73 ft 2 in (22.3 m); *Height*: 17 ft 4.5 in (5.3 m); *Weight loaded*: 31,967 lb (14,500 kg); *Cruising speed*: 202 mph (325 km/h); Service ceiling: 22,965 ft (7,000 m); *Range*: 1,416 miles (2,280 km); *Crew*: 3; *Passengers*: 24–30

Savoia Marchetti S.M.83
Country: Italy; *Constructor*: Società Idrovolanti Alta Italia; *Type*: Civil transport; *Year*: 1937; *Engines*: Three Alfa Romeo 126 RC.34, radial, air-cooled, 750 hp each; *Wingspan*: 69 ft 6.75 in (21.2 m); *Length*: 53 ft 1.75 in (16.2 m); *Height*: 13 ft 5 in (4.1 m); *Weight loaded*: 22,707 lb (10,300 kg); *Cruising speed*: 248 mph (400 km/h); *Service ceiling*: 27,559 ft (8,400 m); *Range*: 995 miles (1,600 km); *Crew*: 4; *Passengers*: 10

Savoia Marchetti S.M.87
Country: Italy; *Constructor*: Società Idrovolanti Alta Italia; *Type*: Civil transport seaplane; *Year*: 1939; *Engines*: Three Alfa Romeo 135 RC.32, 18-cylinder radial, air-cooled, 1,350 hp each; *Wingspan*: 97 ft 5.5 in (29.7 m); *Length*: 73 ft 2 in (22.3 m); *Height*: 19 ft 11 in (6.06 m); *Weight loaded*: 37,400 lb (16,965 kg); *Maximum speed*: 255 mph at 11,480 ft (410 km/h at 3,500 m); *Ceiling*: 23,945 ft (7,300 m); *Range*: 1,370 miles (2,200 km); *Crew*: 4; *Passengers*: 20–24

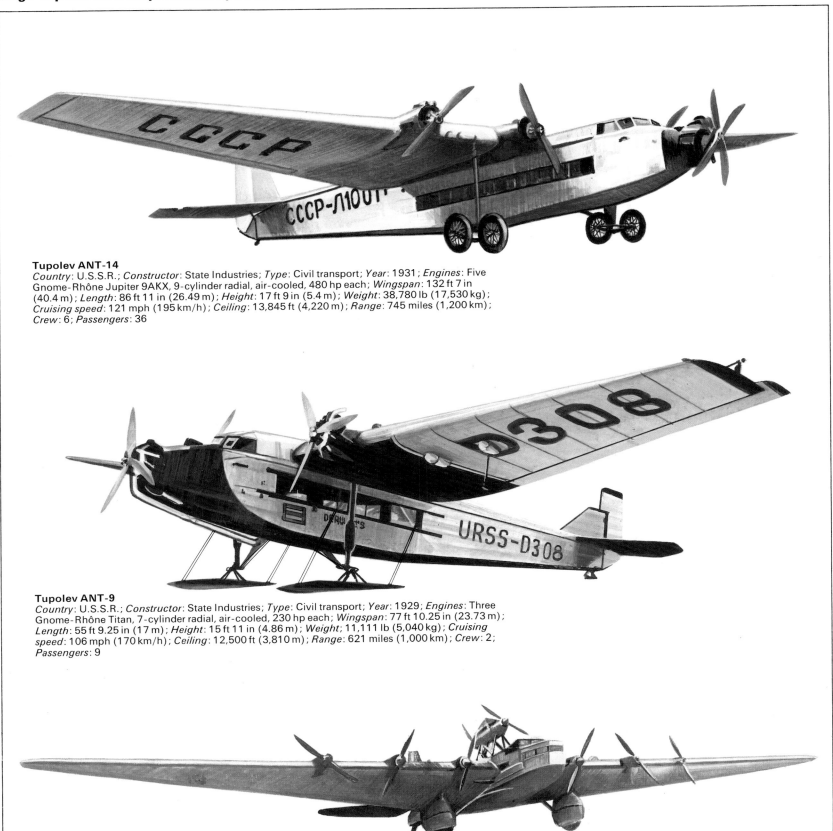

Tupolev ANT-14
Country: U.S.S.R.; *Constructor*: State Industries; *Type*: Civil transport; *Year*: 1931; *Engines*: Five Gnome-Rhône Jupiter 9AKX, 9-cylinder radial, air-cooled, 480 hp each; *Wingspan*: 132 ft 7 in (40.4 m); *Length*: 86 ft 11 in (26.49 m); *Height*: 17 ft 9 in (5.4 m); *Weight*: 38,780 lb (17,530 kg); *Cruising speed*: 121 mph (195 km/h); *Ceiling*: 13,845 ft (4,220 m); *Range*: 745 miles (1,200 km); *Crew*: 6; *Passengers*: 36

Tupolev ANT-9
Country: U.S.S.R.; *Constructor*: State Industries; *Type*: Civil transport; *Year*: 1929; *Engines*: Three Gnome-Rhône Titan, 7-cylinder radial, air-cooled, 230 hp each; *Wingspan*: 77 ft 10.25 in (23.73 m); *Length*: 55 ft 9.25 in (17 m); *Height*: 15 ft 11 in (4.86 m); *Weight*: 11,111 lb (5,040 kg); *Cruising speed*: 106 mph (170 km/h); *Ceiling*: 12,500 ft (3,810 m); *Range*: 621 miles (1,000 km); *Crew*: 2; *Passengers*: 9

Tupolev ANT-20 *Maxim Gorki*
Country: U.S.S.R.; *Constructor*: State Industries; *Type*: Civil transport; *Year*: 1934: *Engines*: Eight AM-34FRN, 12-cylinder V, liquid-cooled, 900 hp each; *Wingspan*: 206 ft 8.25 in (63 m); *Length*: 106 ft 6 in (32.47 m); *Height*: 36 ft 11 in (11.25 m); *Weight*: 92,595 lb (42,000 kg); *Cruising speed*: 137 mph (220 km/h); *Service ceiling*: 14,760 ft (4,500 m); *Range*: 1,200 miles (2,000 km); *Crew*: 8; *Passengers*: 72

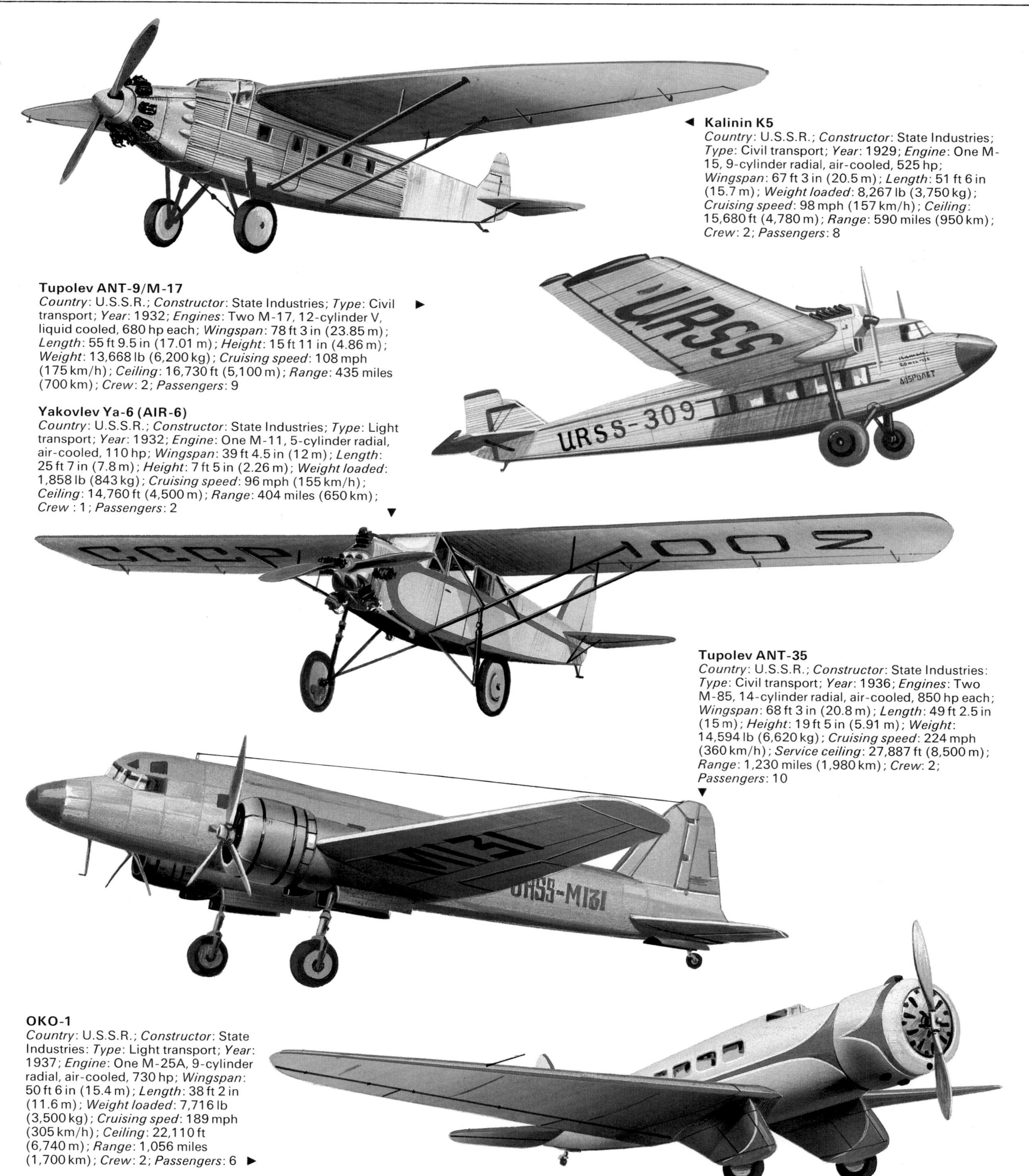

◄ **Kalinin K5**
Country: U.S.S.R.; *Constructor*: State Industries; *Type*: Civil transport; *Year*: 1929; *Engine*: One M-15, 9-cylinder radial, air-cooled, 525 hp; *Wingspan*: 67 ft 3 in (20.5 m); *Length*: 51 ft 6 in (15.7 m); *Weight loaded*: 8,267 lb (3,750 kg); *Cruising speed*: 98 mph (157 km/h); *Ceiling*: 15,680 ft (4,780 m); *Range*: 590 miles (950 km); *Crew*: 2; *Passengers*: 8

Tupolev ANT-9/M-17 ►
Country: U.S.S.R.; *Constructor*: State Industries; *Type*: Civil transport; *Year*: 1932; *Engines*: Two M-17, 12-cylinder V, liquid cooled, 680 hp each; *Wingspan*: 78 ft 3 in (23.85 m); *Length*: 55 ft 9.5 in (17.01 m); *Height*: 15 ft 11 in (4.86 m); *Weight*: 13,668 lb (6,200 kg); *Cruising speed*: 108 mph (175 km/h); *Ceiling*: 16,730 ft (5,100 m); *Range*: 435 miles (700 km); *Crew*: 2; *Passengers*: 9

Yakovlev Ya-6 (AIR-6)
Country: U.S.S.R.; *Constructor*: State Industries; *Type*: Light transport; *Year*: 1932; *Engine*: One M-11, 5-cylinder radial, air-cooled, 110 hp; *Wingspan*: 39 ft 4.5 in (12 m); *Length*: 25 ft 7 in (7.8 m); *Height*: 7 ft 5 in (2.26 m); *Weight loaded*: 1,858 lb (843 kg); *Cruising speed*: 96 mph (155 km/h); *Ceiling*: 14,760 ft (4,500 m); *Range*: 404 miles (650 km); *Crew* : 1; *Passengers*: 2 ▼

Tupolev ANT-35
Country: U.S.S.R.; *Constructor*: State Industries: *Type*: Civil transport; *Year*: 1936; *Engines*: Two M-85, 14-cylinder radial, air-cooled, 850 hp each; *Wingspan*: 68 ft 3 in (20.8 m); *Length*: 49 ft 2.5 in (15 m); *Height*: 19 ft 5 in (5.91 m); *Weight*: 14,594 lb (6,620 kg); *Cruising speed*: 224 mph (360 km/h); *Service ceiling*: 27,887 ft (8,500 m); *Range*: 1,230 miles (1,980 km); *Crew*: 2; *Passengers*: 10 ▼

OKO-1
Country: U.S.S.R.; *Constructor*: State Industries: *Type*: Light transport; *Year*: 1937; *Engine*: One M-25A, 9-cylinder radial, air-cooled, 730 hp; *Wingspan*: 50 ft 6 in (15.4 m); *Length*: 38 ft 2 in (11.6 m); *Weight loaded*: 7,716 lb (3,500 kg); *Cruising sped*: 189 mph (305 km/h); *Ceiling*: 22,110 ft (6,740 m); *Range*: 1,056 miles (1,700 km); *Crew*: 2; *Passengers*: 6 ►

Airspeed A.S.5A Courier
Country: Great Britain; *Constructor*: Airspeed Ltd.; *Type*: Light transport; *Year*: 1933; *Engine*: Armstrong Siddeley Lynx IVC, 7-cylinder radial, air-cooled, 240 hp; *Wingspan*: 47 ft (14.33 m); *Length*: 28 ft 6 in (8.68 m); *Height*: 8 ft 9 in (2.66 m); *Weight loaded*: 3,900 lb (1,771 kg); *Cruising speed*: 132 mph (212 km/h); *Service ceiling*: 13,500 ft (4,120 m); *Range*: 600 miles (965 km); *Crew*: 1; *Passengers*: 5

Airspeed A.S.6 Envoy II
Country: Great Britain; *Constructor*: Airspeed Ltd.; *Type*: Light transport; *Year*: 1934; *Engines*: Two Armstrong Siddeley Lynx IVC, 7-cylinder radial, air-cooled, 240 hp each; *Wingspan*: 52 ft 4 in (15.94 m); *Length*: 34 ft 6 in (10.53 m); *Height*: 9 ft 6 in (2.99 m); *Weight loaded*: 5,850 lb (2,650 kg); *Cruising speed*: 153 mph (246 km/h); *Service ceiling*: 16,500 ft (5,020 m); *Range*: 650 miles (1,045 km); *Crew*: 1; *Passengers*: 6–8

Short S.16 Scion 2
Country: Great Britain; *Constructor*: Short Brothers Ltd.; *Type*: Light transport; *Year*: 1935; *Engines*: Two Pobjoy Niagara III, 7-cylinder radial, air-cooled, 90 hp each; *Wingspan*: 42 ft (12.8 m); *Length*: 31 ft 6 in (9.6 m); *Height*: 10 ft 4.5 in (3.16 m); *Weight loaded*: 3,200 lb (1.452 kg); *Cruising speed*: 116 mph (186 km/h); *Ceiling*: 13,000 ft (3,960 m); *Range*: 390 miles (624 km); *Crew*: 1; *Passengers*: 6

Airspeed A.S.40 Oxford
Country: Great Britain; *Constructor*: Airspeed Ltd.; *Type*: Military trainer converted to light transport; *Year*: 1937; *Engines*: Two Armstrong Siddeley Cheetah X, 7-cylinder radial, air-cooled, 375 hp each; *Wingspan*: 53 ft 4 in (16.25 m); *Length*: 34 ft 6 in (10.51 m); *Height*: 11 ft 1 in (3.38 m); *Weight loaded*: 7,600 lb (3,447 kg); *Cruising speed*: 166 mph at 5,000 ft (267 km/h at 1,525 m); *Ceiling*: 19,500 ft (5,945 m); *Range*: 900 miles (1,450 km); *Crew*: 1–2; *Passengers*: 5–6

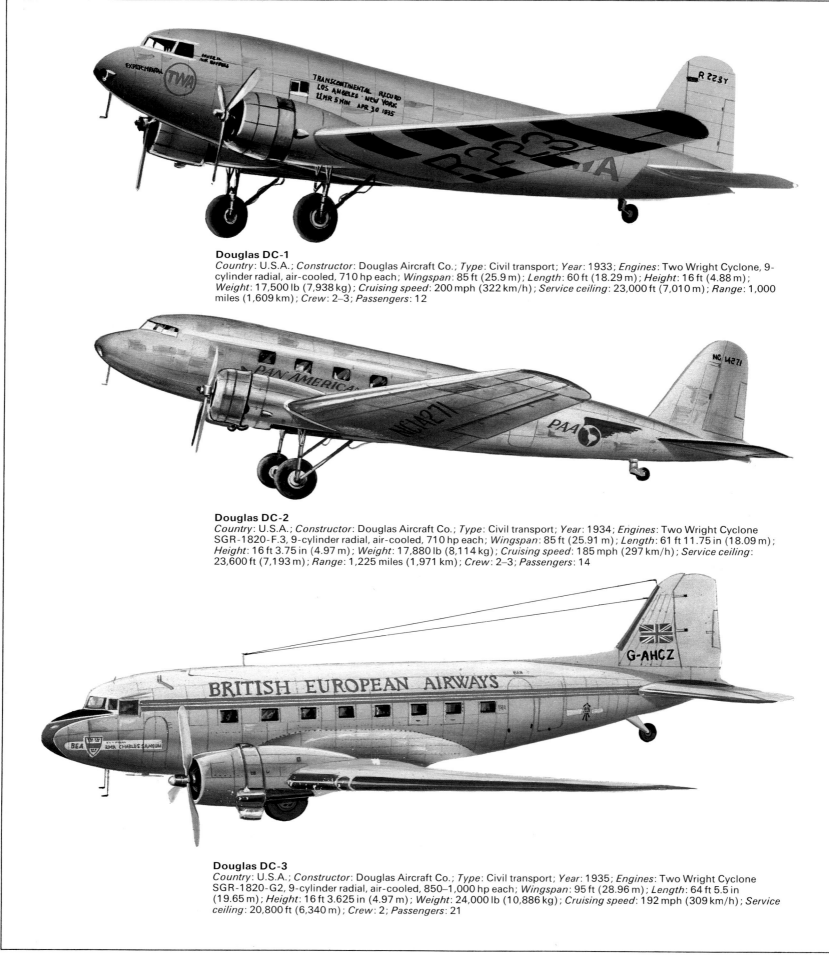

Douglas DC-1
Country: U.S.A.; *Constructor*: Douglas Aircraft Co.; *Type*: Civil transport; *Year*: 1933; *Engines*: Two Wright Cyclone, 9-cylinder radial, air-cooled, 710 hp each; *Wingspan*: 85 ft (25.9 m); *Length*: 60 ft (18.29 m); *Height*: 16 ft (4.88 m); *Weight*: 17,500 lb (7,938 kg); *Cruising speed*: 200 mph (322 km/h); *Service ceiling*: 23,000 ft (7,010 m); *Range*: 1,000 miles (1,609 km); *Crew*: 2–3; *Passengers*: 12

Douglas DC-2
Country: U.S.A.; *Constructor*: Douglas Aircraft Co.; *Type*: Civil transport; *Year*: 1934; *Engines*: Two Wright Cyclone SGR-1820-F.3, 9-cylinder radial, air-cooled, 710 hp each; *Wingspan*: 85 ft (25.91 m); *Length*: 61 ft 11.75 in (18.09 m); *Height*: 16 ft 3.75 in (4.97 m); *Weight*: 17,880 lb (8,114 kg); *Cruising speed*: 185 mph (297 km/h); *Service ceiling*: 23,600 ft (7,193 m); *Range*: 1,225 miles (1,971 km); *Crew*: 2–3; *Passengers*: 14

Douglas DC-3
Country: U.S.A.; *Constructor*: Douglas Aircraft Co.; *Type*: Civil transport; *Year*: 1935; *Engines*: Two Wright Cyclone SGR-1820-G2, 9-cylinder radial, air-cooled, 850–1,000 hp each; *Wingspan*: 95 ft (28.96 m); *Length*: 64 ft 5.5 in (19.65 m); *Height*: 16 ft 3.625 in (4.97 m); *Weight*: 24,000 lb (10,886 kg); *Cruising speed*: 192 mph (309 km/h); *Service ceiling*: 20,800 ft (6,340 m); *Crew*: 2; *Passengers*: 21

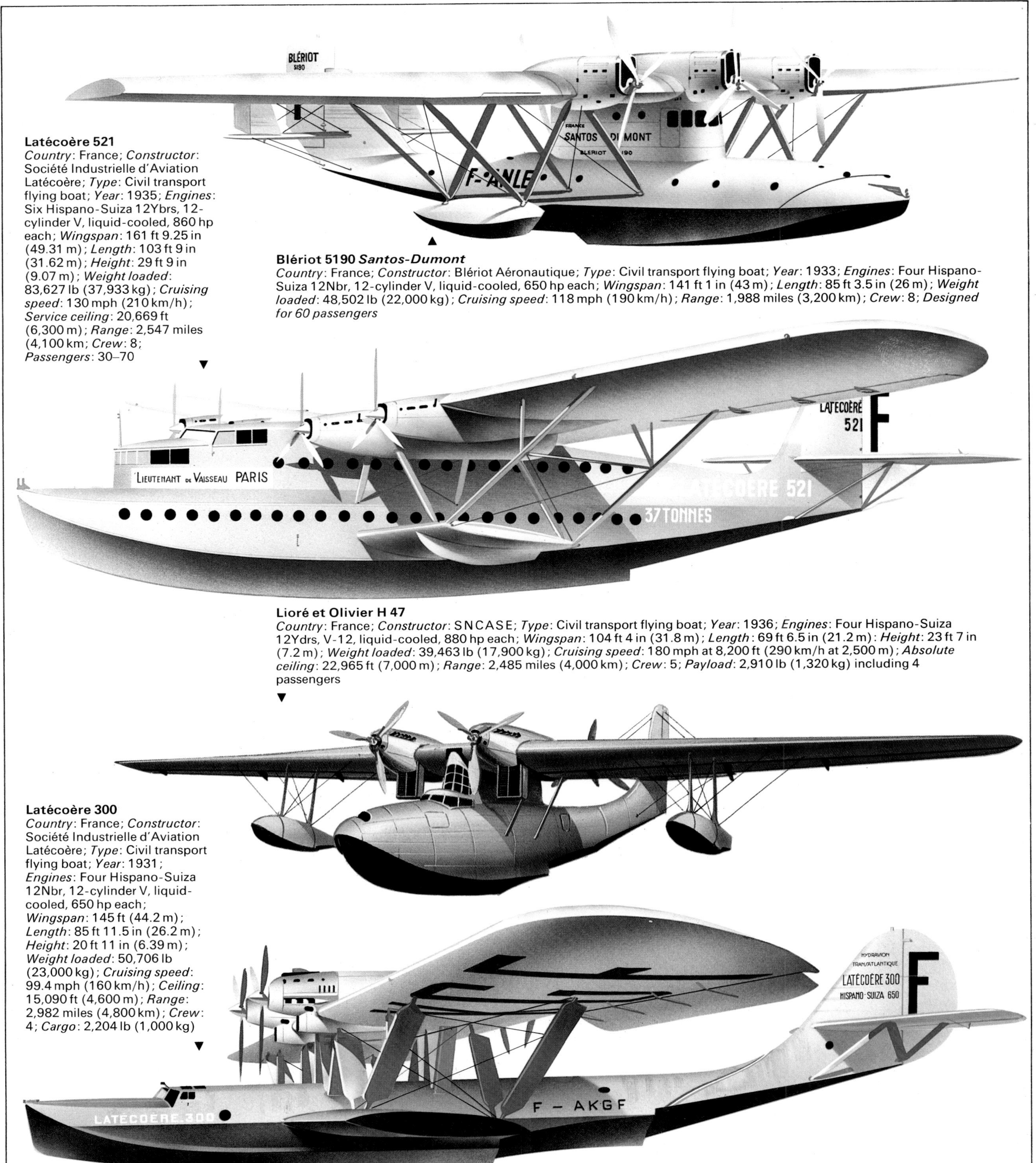

Latécoère 521
Country: France; *Constructor*: Société Industrielle d'Aviation Latécoère; *Type*: Civil transport flying boat; *Year*: 1935; *Engines*: Six Hispano-Suiza 12Ybrs, 12-cylinder V, liquid-cooled, 860 hp each; *Wingspan*: 161 ft 9.25 in (49.31 m); *Length*: 103 ft 9 in (31.62 m); *Height*: 29 ft 9 in (9.07 m); *Weight loaded*: 83,627 lb (37,933 kg); *Cruising speed*: 130 mph (210 km/h); *Service ceiling*: 20,669 ft (6,300 m); *Range*: 2,547 miles (4,100 km; *Crew*: 8; *Passengers*: 30–70

Blériot 5190 *Santos-Dumont*
Country: France; *Constructor*: Blériot Aéronautique; *Type*: Civil transport flying boat; *Year*: 1933; *Engines*: Four Hispano-Suiza 12Nbr, 12-cylinder V, liquid-cooled, 650 hp each; *Wingspan*: 141 ft 1 in (43 m); *Length*: 85 ft 3.5 in (26 m); *Weight loaded*: 48,502 lb (22,000 kg); *Cruising speed*: 118 mph (190 km/h); *Range*: 1,988 miles (3,200 km); *Crew*: 8; *Designed for 60 passengers*

Lioré et Olivier H 47
Country: France; *Constructor*: SNCASE; *Type*: Civil transport flying boat; *Year*: 1936; *Engines*: Four Hispano-Suiza 12Ydrs, V-12, liquid-cooled, 880 hp each; *Wingspan*: 104 ft 4 in (31.8 m); *Length*: 69 ft 6.5 in (21.2 m): *Height*: 23 ft 7 in (7.2 m); *Weight loaded*: 39,463 lb (17,900 kg); *Cruising speed*: 180 mph at 8,200 ft (290 km/h at 2,500 m); *Absolute ceiling*: 22,965 ft (7,000 m); *Range*: 2,485 miles (4,000 km); *Crew*: 5; *Payload*: 2,910 lb (1,320 kg) including 4 passengers

Latécoère 300
Country: France; *Constructor*: Société Industrielle d'Aviation Latécoère; *Type*: Civil transport flying boat; *Year*: 1931; *Engines*: Four Hispano-Suiza 12Nbr, 12-cylinder V, liquid-cooled, 650 hp each; *Wingspan*: 145 ft (44.2 m); *Length*: 85 ft 11.5 in (26.2 m); *Height*: 20 ft 11 in (6.39 m); *Weight loaded*: 50,706 lb (23,000 kg); *Cruising speed*: 99.4 mph (160 km/h); *Ceiling*: 15,090 ft (4,600 m); *Range*: 2,982 miles (4,800 km); *Crew*: 4; *Cargo*: 2,204 lb (1,000 kg)

Armstrong Whitworth A.W.XV Atalanta
Country: Great Britain; *Constructor*: Sir W. G. Armstrong Whitworth Aircraft Ltd.; *Type*: Civil transport; *Year*: 1932; *Engines*: Four Armstrong Siddeley Serval III, 10-cylinder radial, air-cooled, 340 hp each; *Wingspan*: 90 ft (27.43 m); *Length*: 71 ft 6 in (21.79 m); *Height*: 14 ft (4.27 m); *Weight loaded*: 21,000 lb (9,525 kg); *Cruising speed*: 118 mph (190 km/h); *Service ceiling*: 14,200 ft (4,328 m); *Range*: 640 miles (1,030 km); *Crew*: 3; *Passengers*: 9–17

Short S.23 C-Class Empire Flying Boat
Country: Great Britain; *Constructor*: Short Brothers Ltd.; *Type*: Civil transport flying boat; *Year*: 1936; *Engines*: Four Bristol Pegasus XC, 9-cylinder radial, air-cooled, 920 hp each; *Wingspan*: 114 ft (34.74 m); *Length*: 88 ft (26.82 m); *Height*: 31 ft 9.75 in (9.69 m); *Weight loaded*: 40,500 lb (18,370 kg); *Cruising speed*: 164 mph (264 km/h); *Ceiling*: 20,000 ft (6,100 m); *Range*: 760 miles (1,223 km); *Crew*: 5; *Passengers*: 24

de Havilland D.H.91 Albatross
Country: Great Britain; *Constructor*: The de Havilland Aircraft Co. Ltd.; *Type*: Civil transport; *Year*: 1937; *Engines*: Four de Havilland Gipsy Twelve I, 12-cylinder inverted V, air-cooled, 525 hp each; *Wingspan*: 104 ft 8 in (31.9 m); *Length*: 70 ft (21.34 m); *Height*: 20 ft 2 in (6.15 m); *Weight loaded*: 29,500 lb (13,380 kg); *Cruising speed*: 210 mph at 11,000 ft (338 km/h at 3,355 m); *Ceiling*: 17,900 ft (5,455 m); *Range*: 1,040 miles (1,675 km); *Crew*: 4; *Passengers*: 21

Armstrong Whitworth A.W.27 Ensign
Country: Great Britain; *Constructor*: Sir W. G. Armstrong Whitworth Aircraft Ltd.; *Type*: Civil transport; *Year*: 1938; *Engines*: Four Armstrong Siddeley Tiger IXC, 14-cylinder radial, air cooled, 850 hp each; *Wingspan*: 123 ft (37.49 m); *Length*: 111 ft (33.83 m); *Height*: 23 ft (7.01 m); *Weight loaded*: 48,500 lb (22,000 kg); *Cruising speed*: 170 mph at 7,000 ft (274 km/h at 2,135 m); *Service ceiling*: 22,000 ft (6,106 m); *Range*: 860 miles (1,384 km); *Crew*: 5; *Passengers*: 27–40

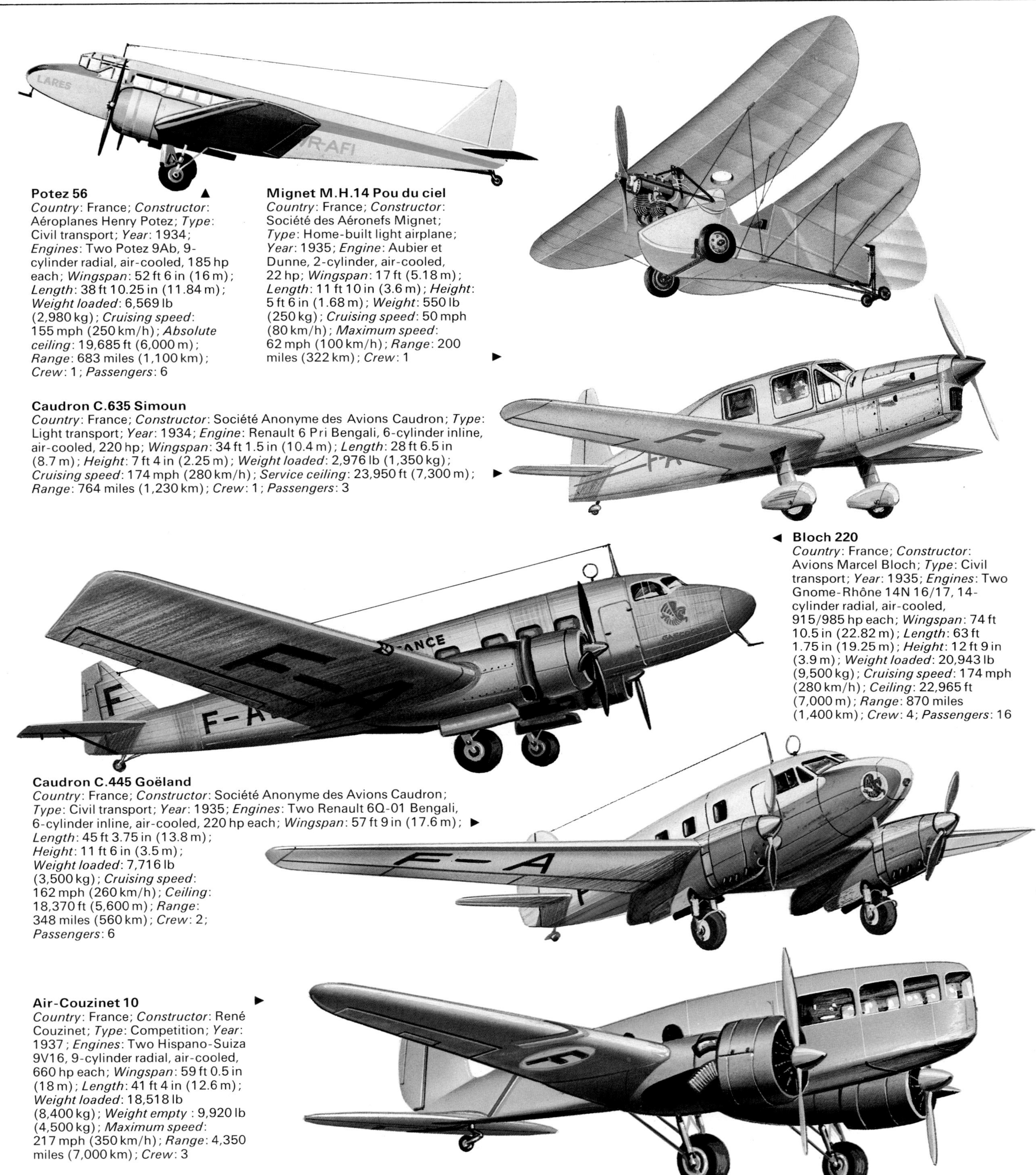

Potez 56 ▲
Country: France; *Constructor*: Aéroplanes Henry Potez; *Type*: Civil transport; *Year*: 1934; *Engines*: Two Potez 9Ab, 9-cylinder radial, air-cooled, 185 hp each; *Wingspan*: 52 ft 6 in (16 m); *Length*: 38 ft 10.25 in (11.84 m); *Weight loaded*: 6,569 lb (2,980 kg); *Cruising speed*: 155 mph (250 km/h); *Absolute ceiling*: 19,685 ft (6,000 m); *Range*: 683 miles (1,100 km); *Crew*: 1; *Passengers*: 6

Mignet M.H.14 Pou du ciel
Country: France; *Constructor*: Société des Aéronefs Mignet; *Type*: Home-built light airplane; *Year*: 1935; *Engine*: Aubier et Dunne, 2-cylinder, air-cooled, 22 hp; *Wingspan*: 17 ft (5.18 m); *Length*: 11 ft 10 in (3.6 m); *Height*: 5 ft 6 in (1.68 m); *Weight*: 550 lb (250 kg); *Cruising speed*: 50 mph (80 km/h); *Maximum speed*: 62 mph (100 km/h); *Range*: 200 miles (322 km); *Crew*: 1 ►

Caudron C.635 Simoun
Country: France; *Constructor*: Société Anonyme des Avions Caudron; *Type*: Light transport; *Year*: 1934; *Engine*: Renault 6 Pri Bengali, 6-cylinder inline, air-cooled, 220 hp; *Wingspan*: 34 ft 1.5 in (10.4 m); *Length*: 28 ft 6.5 in (8.7 m); *Height*: 7 ft 4 in (2.25 m); *Weight loaded*: 2,976 lb (1,350 kg); *Cruising speed*: 174 mph (280 km/h); *Service ceiling*: 23,950 ft (7,300 m); *Range*: 764 miles (1,230 km); *Crew*: 1; *Passengers*: 3 ►

◄ **Bloch 220**
Country: France; *Constructor*: Avions Marcel Bloch; *Type*: Civil transport; *Year*: 1935; *Engines*: Two Gnome-Rhône 14N 16/17, 14-cylinder radial, air-cooled, 915/985 hp each; *Wingspan*: 74 ft 10.5 in (22.82 m); *Length*: 63 ft 1.75 in (19.25 m); *Height*: 12 ft 9 in (3.9 m); *Weight loaded*: 20,943 lb (9,500 kg); *Cruising speed*: 174 mph (280 km/h); *Ceiling*: 22,965 ft (7,000 m); *Range*: 870 miles (1,400 km); *Crew*: 4; *Passengers*: 16

Caudron C.445 Goëland
Country: France; *Constructor*: Société Anonyme des Avions Caudron; *Type*: Civil transport; *Year*: 1935; *Engines*: Two Renault 6Q-01 Bengali, 6-cylinder inline, air-cooled, 220 hp each; *Wingspan*: 57 ft 9 in (17.6 m); ► *Length*: 45 ft 3.75 in (13.8 m); *Height*: 11 ft 6 in (3.5 m); *Weight loaded*: 7,716 lb (3,500 kg); *Cruising speed*: 162 mph (260 km/h); *Ceiling*: 18,370 ft (5,600 m); *Range*: 348 miles (560 km); *Crew*: 2; *Passengers*: 6

Air-Couzinet 10 ►
Country: France; *Constructor*: René Couzinet; *Type*: Competition; *Year*: 1937; *Engines*: Two Hispano-Suiza 9V16, 9-cylinder radial, air-cooled, 660 hp each; *Wingspan*: 59 ft 0.5 in (18 m); *Length*: 41 ft 4 in (12.6 m); *Weight loaded*: 18,518 lb (8,400 kg); *Weight empty* : 9,920 lb (4,500 kg); *Maximum speed*: 217 mph (350 km/h); *Range*: 4,350 miles (7,000 km); *Crew*: 3

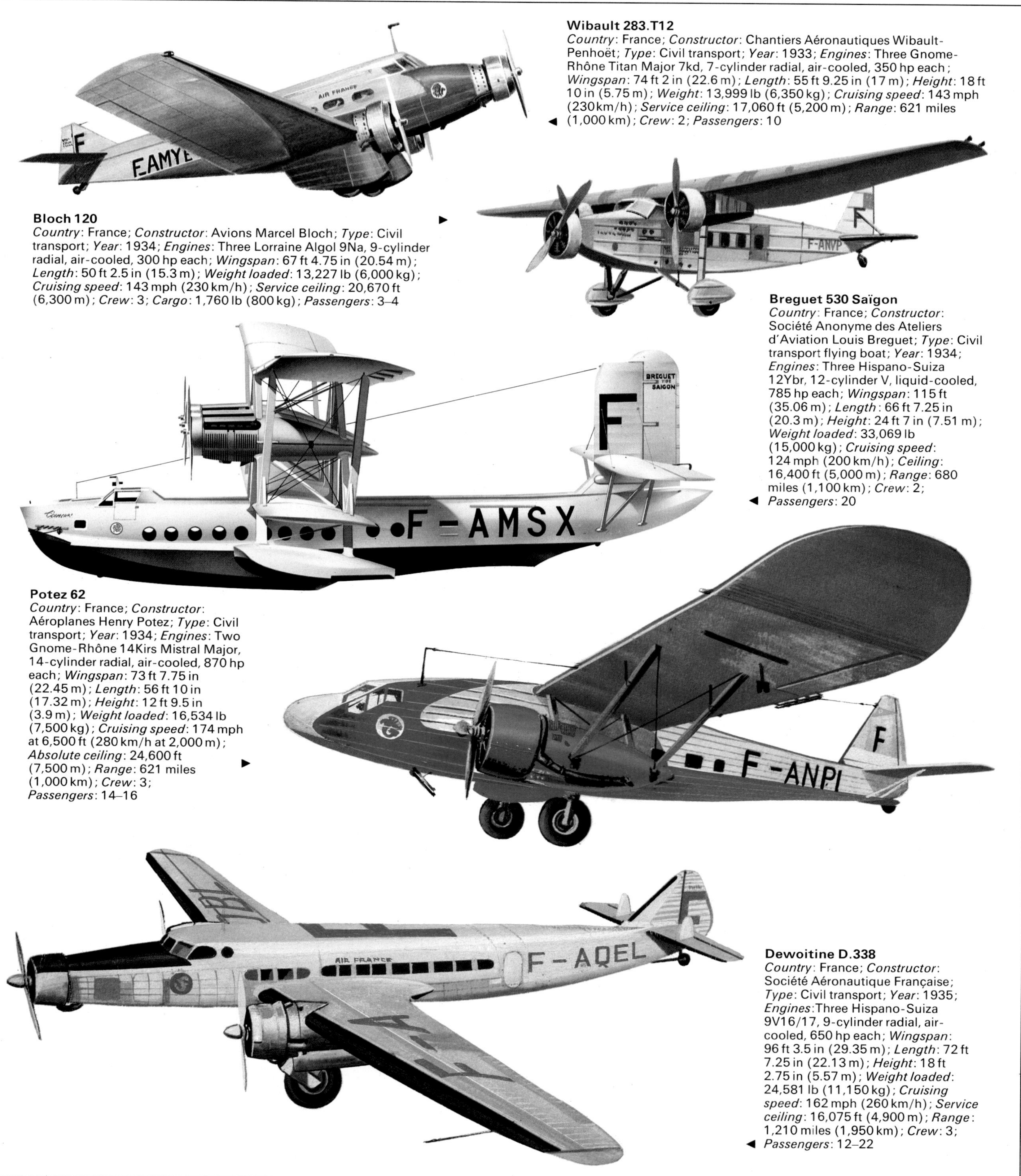

Wibault 283.T12
Country: France; *Constructor*: Chantiers Aéronautiques Wibault-Penhoët; *Type*: Civil transport; *Year*: 1933; *Engines*: Three Gnome-Rhône Titan Major 7kd, 7-cylinder radial, air-cooled, 350 hp each; *Wingspan*: 74 ft 2 in (22.6 m); *Length*: 55 ft 9.25 in (17 m); *Height*: 18 ft 10 in (5.75 m); *Weight*: 13,999 lb (6,350 kg); *Cruising speed*: 143 mph (230 km/h); *Service ceiling*: 17,060 ft (5,200 m); *Range*: 621 miles (1,000 km); *Crew*: 2; *Passengers*: 10

Bloch 120
Country: France; *Constructor*: Avions Marcel Bloch; *Type*: Civil transport; *Year*: 1934; *Engines*: Three Lorraine Algol 9Na, 9-cylinder radial, air-cooled, 300 hp each; *Wingspan*: 67 ft 4.75 in (20.54 m); *Length*: 50 ft 2.5 in (15.3 m); *Weight loaded*: 13,227 lb (6,000 kg); *Cruising speed*: 143 mph (230 km/h); *Service ceiling*: 20,670 ft (6,300 m); *Crew*: 3; *Cargo*: 1,760 lb (800 kg); *Passengers*: 3–4

Breguet 530 Saïgon
Country: France; *Constructor*: Société Anonyme des Ateliers d'Aviation Louis Breguet; *Type*: Civil transport flying boat; *Year*: 1934; *Engines*: Three Hispano-Suiza 12Ybr, 12-cylinder V, liquid-cooled, 785 hp each; *Wingspan*: 115 ft (35.06 m); *Length*: 66 ft 7.25 in (20.3 m); *Height*: 24 ft 7 in (7.51 m); *Weight loaded*: 33,069 lb (15,000 kg); *Cruising speed*: 124 mph (200 km/h); *Ceiling*: 16,400 ft (5,000 m); *Range*: 680 miles (1,100 km); *Crew*: 2; *Passengers*: 20

Potez 62
Country: France; *Constructor*: Aéroplanes Henry Potez; *Type*: Civil transport; *Year*: 1934; *Engines*: Two Gnome-Rhône 14Kirs Mistral Major, 14-cylinder radial, air-cooled, 870 hp each; *Wingspan*: 73 ft 7.75 in (22.45 m); *Length*: 56 ft 10 in (17.32 m); *Height*: 12 ft 9.5 in (3.9 m); *Weight loaded*: 16,534 lb (7,500 kg); *Cruising speed*: 174 mph at 6,500 ft (280 km/h at 2,000 m); *Absolute ceiling*: 24,600 ft (7,500 m); *Range*: 621 miles (1,000 km); *Crew*: 3; *Passengers*: 14–16

Dewoitine D.338
Country: France; *Constructor*: Société Aéronautique Française; *Type*: Civil transport; *Year*: 1935; *Engines*: Three Hispano-Suiza 9V16/17, 9-cylinder radial, air-cooled, 650 hp each; *Wingspan*: 96 ft 3.5 in (29.35 m); *Length*: 72 ft 7.25 in (22.13 m); *Height*: 18 ft 2.75 in (5.57 m); *Weight loaded*: 24,581 lb (11,150 kg); *Cruising speed*: 162 mph (260 km/h); *Service ceiling*: 16,075 ft (4,900 m); *Range*: 1,210 miles (1,950 km); *Crew*: 3; *Passengers*: 12–22

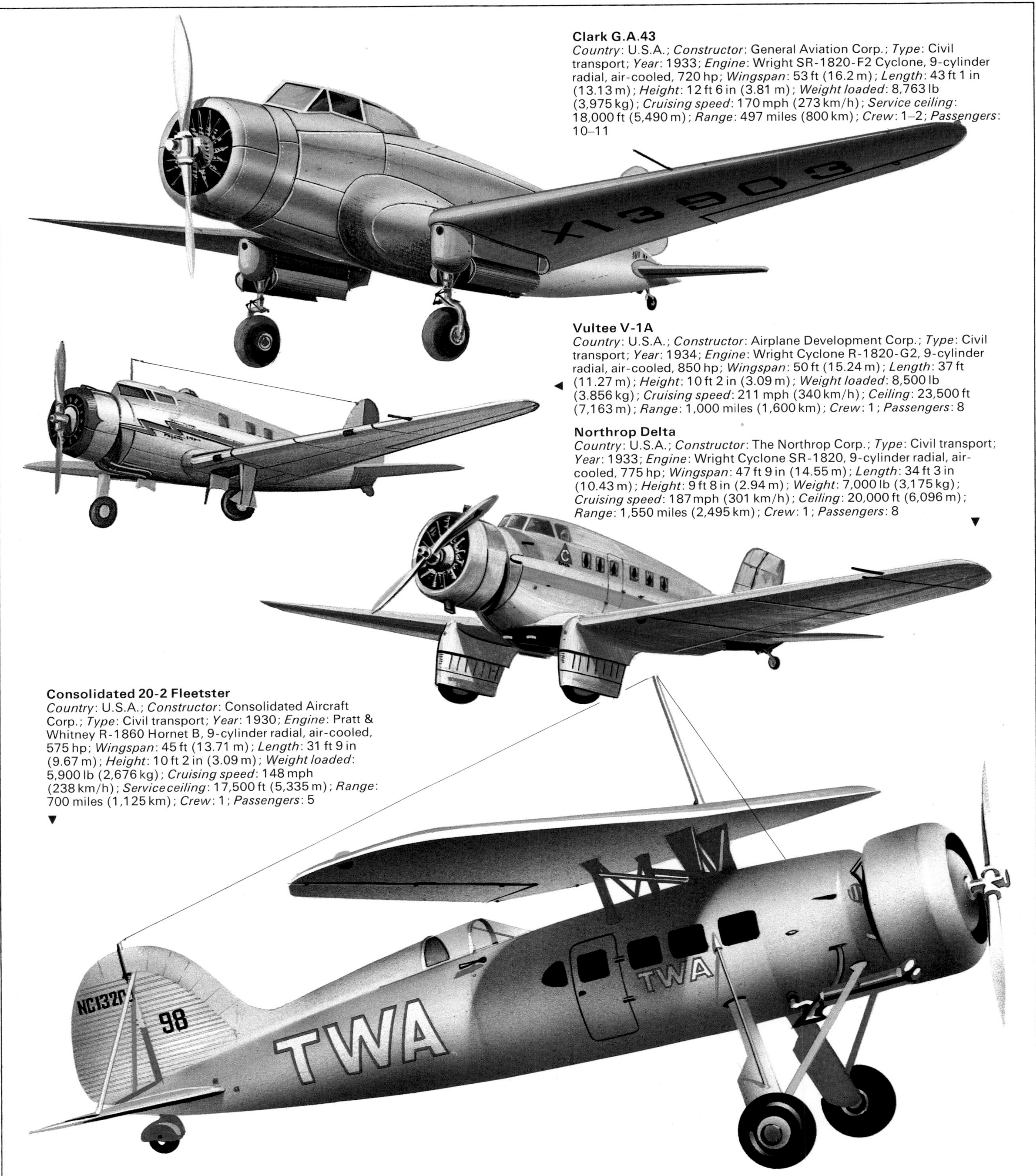

Clark G.A.43
Country: U.S.A.; *Constructor*: General Aviation Corp.; *Type*: Civil transport; *Year*: 1933; *Engine*: Wright SR-1820-F2 Cyclone, 9-cylinder radial, air-cooled, 720 hp; *Wingspan*: 53 ft (16.2 m); *Length*: 43 ft 1 in (13.13 m); *Height*: 12 ft 6 in (3.81 m); *Weight loaded*: 8,763 lb (3,975 kg); *Cruising speed*: 170 mph (273 km/h); *Service ceiling*: 18,000 ft (5,490 m); *Range*: 497 miles (800 km); *Crew*: 1–2; *Passengers*: 10–11

Vultee V-1A
Country: U.S.A.; *Constructor*: Airplane Development Corp.; *Type*: Civil transport; *Year*: 1934; *Engine*: Wright Cyclone R-1820-G2, 9-cylinder radial, air-cooled, 850 hp; *Wingspan*: 50 ft (15.24 m); *Length*: 37 ft (11.27 m); *Height*: 10 ft 2 in (3.09 m); *Weight loaded*: 8,500 lb (3.856 kg); *Cruising speed*: 211 mph (340 km/h); *Ceiling*: 23,500 ft (7,163 m); *Range*: 1,000 miles (1,600 km); *Crew*: 1; *Passengers*: 8

Northrop Delta
Country: U.S.A.; *Constructor*: The Northrop Corp.; *Type*: Civil transport; *Year*: 1933; *Engine*: Wright Cyclone SR-1820, 9-cylinder radial, air-cooled, 775 hp; *Wingspan*: 47 ft 9 in (14.55 m); *Length*: 34 ft 3 in (10.43 m); *Height*: 9 ft 8 in (2.94 m); *Weight*: 7,000 lb (3,175 kg); *Cruising speed*: 187 mph (301 km/h); *Ceiling*: 20,000 ft (6,096 m); *Range*: 1,550 miles (2,495 km); *Crew*: 1; *Passengers*: 8

Consolidated 20-2 Fleetster
Country: U.S.A.; *Constructor*: Consolidated Aircraft Corp.; *Type*: Civil transport; *Year*: 1930; *Engine*: Pratt & Whitney R-1860 Hornet B, 9-cylinder radial, air-cooled, 575 hp; *Wingspan*: 45 ft (13.71 m); *Length*: 31 ft 9 in (9.67 m); *Height*: 10 ft 2 in (3.09 m); *Weight loaded*: 5,900 lb (2,676 kg); *Cruising speed*: 148 mph (238 km/h); *Service ceiling*: 17,500 ft (5,335 m); *Range*: 700 miles (1,125 km); *Crew*: 1; *Passengers*: 5

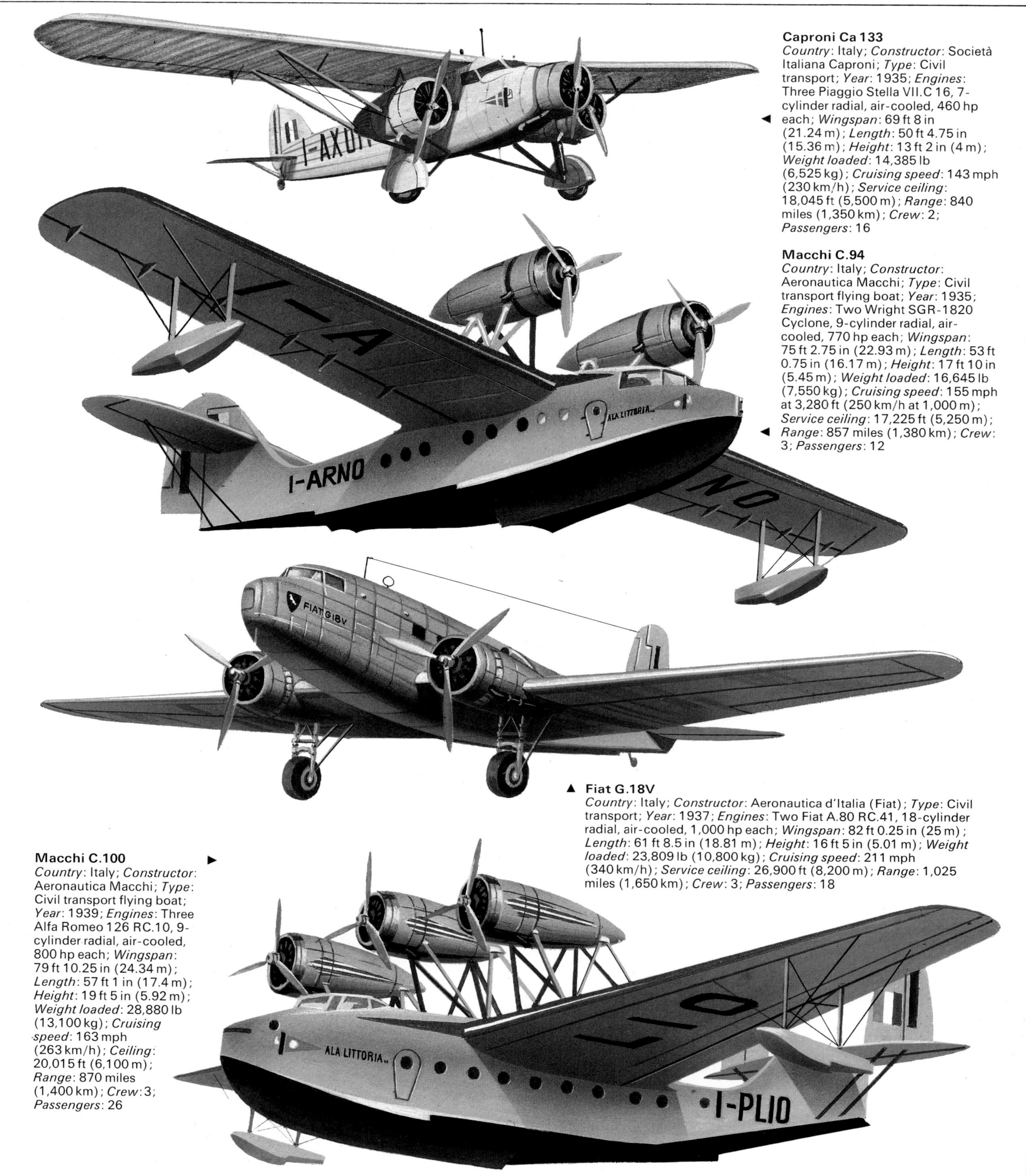

Caproni Ca 133
Country: Italy; *Constructor*: Società Italiana Caproni; *Type*: Civil transport; *Year*: 1935; *Engines*: Three Piaggio Stella VII.C 16, 7-cylinder radial, air-cooled, 460 hp each; *Wingspan*: 69 ft 8 in (21.24 m); *Length*: 50 ft 4.75 in (15.36 m); *Height*: 13 ft 2 in (4 m); *Weight loaded*: 14,385 lb (6,525 kg); *Cruising speed*: 143 mph (230 km/h); *Service ceiling*: 18,045 ft (5,500 m); *Range*: 840 miles (1,350 km); *Crew*: 2; *Passengers*: 16

Macchi C.94
Country: Italy; *Constructor*: Aeronautica Macchi; *Type*: Civil transport flying boat; *Year*: 1935; *Engines*: Two Wright SGR-1820 Cyclone, 9-cylinder radial, air-cooled, 770 hp each; *Wingspan*: 75 ft 2.75 in (22.93 m); *Length*: 53 ft 0.75 in (16.17 m); *Height*: 17 ft 10 in (5.45 m); *Weight loaded*: 16,645 lb (7,550 kg); *Cruising speed*: 155 mph at 3,280 ft (250 km/h at 1,000 m); *Service ceiling*: 17,225 ft (5,250 m); *Range*: 857 miles (1,380 km); *Crew*: 3; *Passengers*: 12

Fiat G.18V
Country: Italy; *Constructor*: Aeronautica d'Italia (Fiat); *Type*: Civil transport; *Year*: 1937; *Engines*: Two Fiat A.80 RC.41, 18-cylinder radial, air-cooled, 1,000 hp each; *Wingspan*: 82 ft 0.25 in (25 m); *Length*: 61 ft 8.5 in (18.81 m); *Height*: 16 ft 5 in (5.01 m); *Weight loaded*: 23,809 lb (10,800 kg); *Cruising speed*: 211 mph (340 km/h); *Service ceiling*: 26,900 ft (8,200 m); *Range*: 1,025 miles (1,650 km); *Crew*: 3; *Passengers*: 18

Macchi C.100
Country: Italy; *Constructor*: Aeronautica Macchi; *Type*: Civil transport flying boat; *Year*: 1939; *Engines*: Three Alfa Romeo 126 RC.10, 9-cylinder radial, air-cooled, 800 hp each; *Wingspan*: 79 ft 10.25 in (24.34 m); *Length*: 57 ft 1 in (17.4 m); *Height*: 19 ft 5 in (5.92 m); *Weight loaded*: 28,880 lb (13,100 kg); *Cruising speed*: 163 mph (263 km/h); *Ceiling*: 20,015 ft (6,100 m); *Range*: 870 miles (1,400 km); *Crew*: 3; *Passengers*: 26

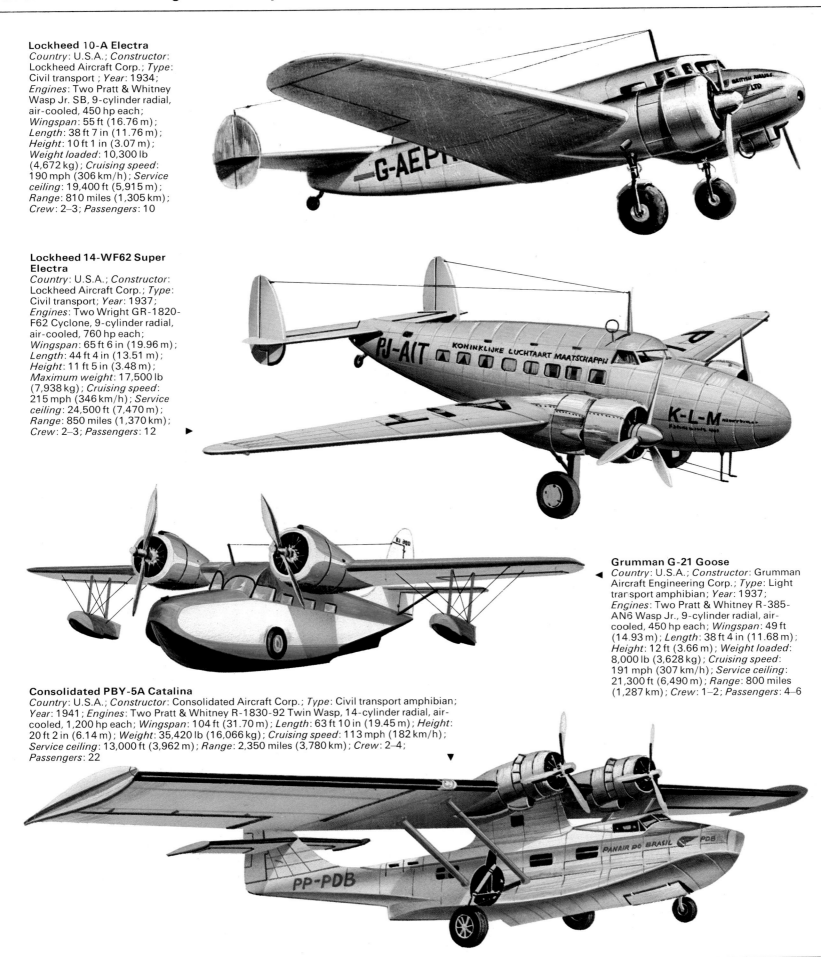

Lockheed 10-A Electra
Country: U.S.A.; *Constructor*: Lockheed Aircraft Corp.; *Type*: Civil transport; *Year*: 1934; *Engines*: Two Pratt & Whitney Wasp Jr. SB, 9-cylinder radial, air-cooled, 450 hp each; *Wingspan*: 55 ft (16.76 m); *Length*: 38 ft 7 in (11.76 m); *Height*: 10 ft 1 in (3.07 m); *Weight loaded*: 10,300 lb (4,672 kg); *Cruising speed*: 190 mph (306 km/h); *Service ceiling*: 19,400 ft (5,915 m); *Range*: 810 miles (1,305 km); *Crew*: 2–3; *Passengers*: 10

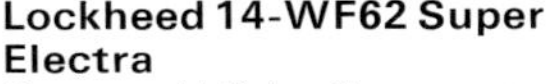

Lockheed 14-WF62 Super Electra
Country: U.S.A.; *Constructor*: Lockheed Aircraft Corp.; *Type*: Civil transport; *Year*: 1937; *Engines*: Two Wright GR-1820-F62 Cyclone, 9-cylinder radial, air-cooled, 760 hp each; *Wingspan*: 65 ft 6 in (19.96 m); *Length*: 44 ft 4 in (13.51 m); *Height*: 11 ft 5 in (3.48 m); *Maximum weight*: 17,500 lb (7,938 kg); *Cruising speed*: 215 mph (346 km/h); *Service ceiling*: 24,500 ft (7,470 m); *Range*: 850 miles (1,370 km); *Crew*: 2–3; *Passengers*: 12 ►

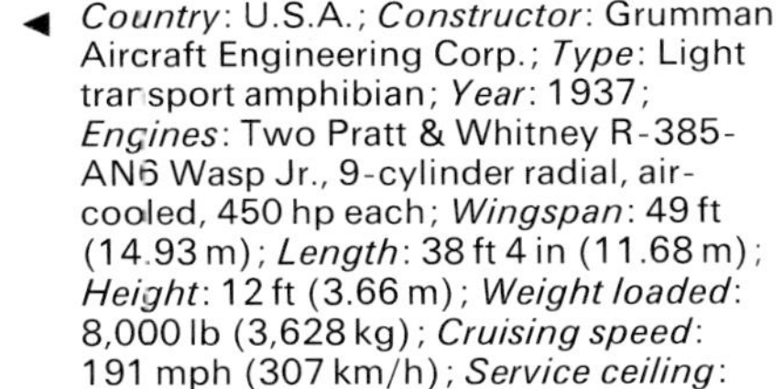

Grumman G-21 Goose
◄ *Country*: U.S.A.; *Constructor*: Grumman Aircraft Engineering Corp.; *Type*: Light transport amphibian; *Year*: 1937; *Engines*: Two Pratt & Whitney R-385-AN6 Wasp Jr., 9-cylinder radial, air-cooled, 450 hp each; *Wingspan*: 49 ft (14.93 m); *Length*: 38 ft 4 in (11.68 m); *Height*: 12 ft (3.66 m); *Weight loaded*: 8,000 lb (3,628 kg); *Cruising speed*: 191 mph (307 km/h); *Service ceiling*: 21,300 ft (6,490 m); *Range*: 800 miles (1,287 km); *Crew*: 1–2; *Passengers*: 4–6

Consolidated PBY-5A Catalina
Country: U.S.A.; *Constructor*: Consolidated Aircraft Corp.; *Type*: Civil transport amphibian; *Year*: 1941; *Engines*: Two Pratt & Whitney R-1830-92 Twin Wasp, 14-cylinder radial, air-cooled, 1,200 hp each; *Wingspan*: 104 ft (31.70 m); *Length*: 63 ft 10 in (19.45 m); *Height*: 20 ft 2 in (6.14 m); *Weight*: 35,420 lb (16,066 kg); *Cruising speed*: 113 mph (182 km/h); *Service ceiling*: 13,000 ft (3,962 m); *Range*: 2,350 miles (3,780 km); *Crew*: 2–4; *Passengers*: 22 ▼

ICAR IAR-36
Country: Romania; *Constructor*: ICAR; *Type*: Civil transport; *Year*: 1934; *Engine*: Armstrong Siddeley Serval, 10-cylinder radial, air-cooled, 360–380 hp; *Wingspan*: 50 ft 6.25 in (15.4 m); *Length*: 32 ft 2.5 in (9.82 m); *Height*: 9 ft 2 in (2.8 m); *Weight loaded*: 4,960 lb (2,250 kg); *Cruising speed*: 133 mph (215 km/h); *Ceiling*: 16,075 ft (4,900 m); *Range*: 435 miles (700 km); *Crew*: 2; *Passengers*: 6

I.A.R. 23
Country: Romania; *Constructor*: Societate Anonima Industria Aeronautica Romana; *Type*: Light monoplane; *Year*: 1934; *Engine*: Hispano-Suiza9 Qa, 9-cylinder radial, air-cooled, 340 hp; *Wingspan*: 39 ft 4 in (12 m); *Length*: 27 ft 5 in (8.35 m); *Height*: 8 ft 10 in (2.7 m); *Weight loaded*: 4,233 lb (1,920 kg); *Maximum speed*: 165 mph (265 km/h); *Absolute ceiling*: 13,500 ft (4,100 m); *Range*: 965 miles (1,550 km); *Seats*: 2

Aero A204
Country: Czechoslovakia; *Constructor*: Aero Tovarna Letadel; *Type*: Light transport; *Year*: 1937; *Engines*: Two Walter Pollux IIR, 9-cylinder radial, air-cooled, 360 hp each; *Wingspan* : 62 ft 4 in (19 m); *Length* : 42 ft 8 in (13 m); *Height*: 11 ft 2 in (3.4 m); *Weight loaded*: 9,480 lb (4,300 kg); *Cruising speed*: 178 mph (286 km/h); *Ceiling*: 19,030 ft (5,800 m); *Range*: 560 miles (900 km); *Crew*: 2, *Passengers*: 8

RWD 13
Country: Poland; *Constructor*: Doświadczałne Warsztaty Lotnicze; *Type*: Light monoplane; *Year*: 1935; *Engine*: Walter Major, 4-cylinder inline, air-cooled, 130 hp; *Wingspan*: 37 ft 9 in (11.5 m); *Length*: 25 ft 9 in (7.85 m); *Height*: 6 ft 9 in (2.05 m); *Maximum weight*: 2,050 lb (930 kg); *Cruising speed*: 112 mph (180 km/h); *Service ceiling*: 13,800 ft (4,200 m); *Range*: 560 miles (900 km); *Crew*: 1; *Passengers*: 2

RWD 11
Country: Poland; *Constructor*: Doświadczałne Warsztaty Lotnicze; *Type*: Civil transport; *Year*: 1936; *Engines*: Two Walter Major-6, 6-cylinder inline, air-cooled, 205 hp; *Wingspan*: 49 ft 10.5 in (15.2 m); *Length*: 34 ft 11.5 in (10.65 m); *Height*: 10 ft 10.75 in (3.3 m); *Weight loaded*: 5,842 lb (2,650 kg); *Cruising speed*: 158 mph (255 km/h); *Service ceiling*: 13,450 ft (4,100 m); *Range*: 500 miles (800 km); *Crew*: 1; *Passengers*: 6

P.Z.L.44
Country: Poland; *Constructor*: Państwowe Zakłady Lotnicze; *Type*: Civil transport; *Year*: 1938; *Engines*: Two Wright GR-1820-G2 Cyclone, 9-cylinder radial, air-cooled, 850–1,000 hp each; *Wingspan*: 78 ft 1.5 in (23.8 m); *Length*: 60 ft 6.75 in (18.45 m); *Height*: 15 ft 9 in (4.8 m); *Maximum weight*: 20,943 lb (9,500 kg); *Cruising speed*: 174 mph (280 km/h); *Service ceiling*: 22,475 ft (6,850 m); *Range*: 1,144 miles (1,840 km); *Crew*: 3–4; *Passengers*: 14

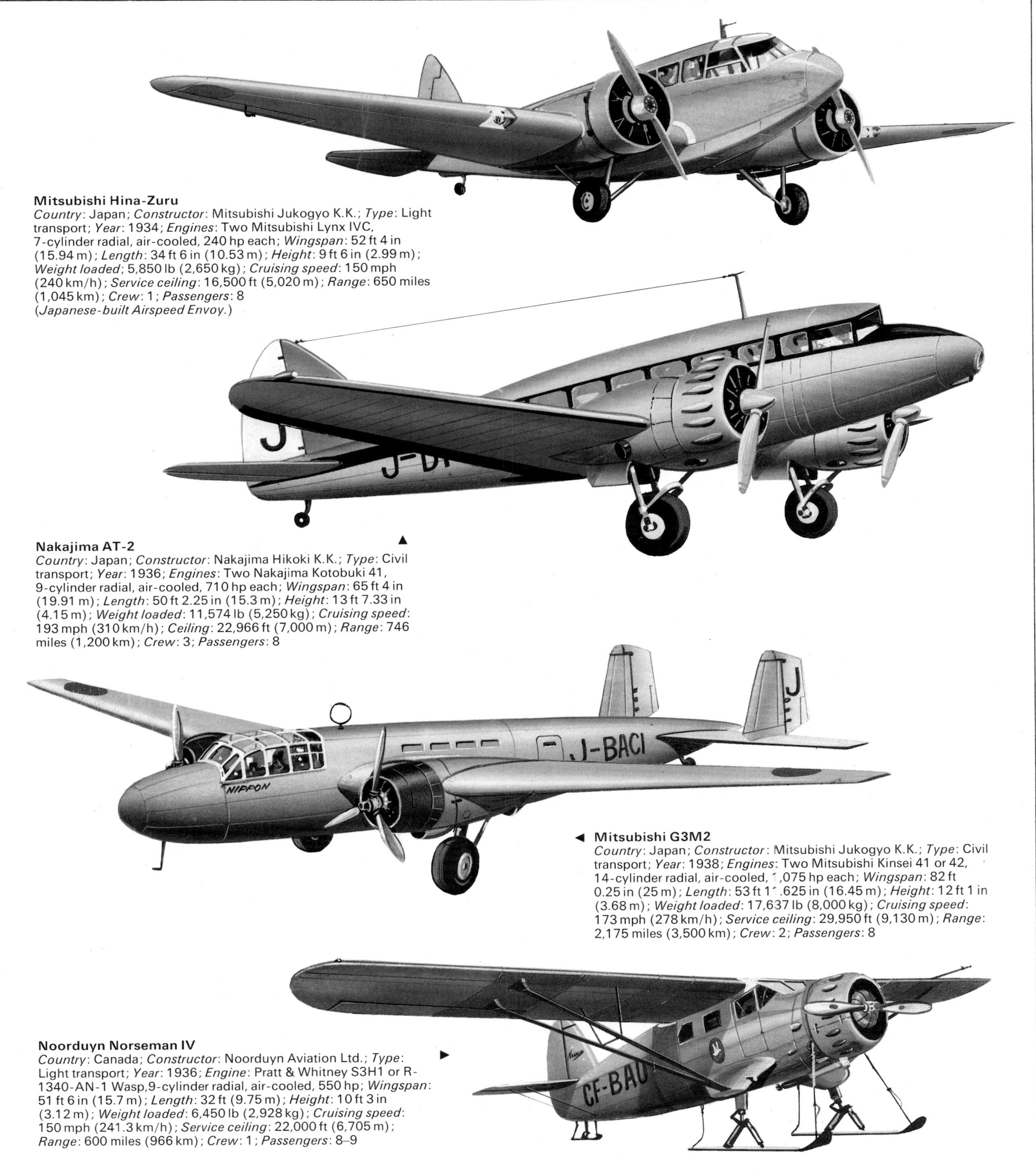

Mitsubishi Hina-Zuru
Country: Japan; *Constructor*: Mitsubishi Jukogyo K.K.; *Type*: Light transport; *Year*: 1934; *Engines*: Two Mitsubishi Lynx IVC, 7-cylinder radial, air-cooled, 240 hp each; *Wingspan*: 52 ft 4 in (15.94 m); *Length*: 34 ft 6 in (10.53 m); *Height*: 9 ft 6 in (2.99 m); *Weight loaded*; 5,850 lb (2,650 kg); *Cruising speed*: 150 mph (240 km/h); *Service ceiling*: 16,500 ft (5,020 m); *Range*: 650 miles (1,045 km); *Crew*: 1; *Passengers*: 8
(*Japanese-built Airspeed Envoy.*)

Nakajima AT-2 ▲
Country: Japan; *Constructor*: Nakajima Hikoki K.K.; *Type*: Civil transport; *Year*: 1936; *Engines*: Two Nakajima Kotobuki 41, 9-cylinder radial, air-cooled, 710 hp each; *Wingspan*: 65 ft 4 in (19.91 m); *Length*: 50 ft 2.25 in (15.3 m); *Height*: 13 ft 7.33 in (4.15 m); *Weight loaded*: 11,574 lb (5,250 kg); *Cruising speed*: 193 mph (310 km/h); *Ceiling*: 22,966 ft (7,000 m); *Range*: 746 miles (1,200 km); *Crew*: 3; *Passengers*: 8

◄ **Mitsubishi G3M2**
Country: Japan; *Constructor*: Mitsubishi Jukogyo K.K.; *Type*: Civil transport; *Year*: 1938; *Engines*: Two Mitsubishi Kinsei 41 or 42, 14-cylinder radial, air-cooled, 1,075 hp each; *Wingspan*: 82 ft 0.25 in (25 m); *Length*: 53 ft 11.625 in (16.45 m); *Height*: 12 ft 1 in (3.68 m); *Weight loaded*: 17,637 lb (8,000 kg); *Cruising speed*: 173 mph (278 km/h); *Service ceiling*: 29,950 ft (9,130 m); *Range*: 2,175 miles (3,500 km); *Crew*: 2; *Passengers*: 8

Noorduyn Norseman IV ►
Country: Canada; *Constructor*: Noorduyn Aviation Ltd.; *Type*: Light transport; *Year*: 1936; *Engine*: Pratt & Whitney S3H1 or R-1340-AN-1 Wasp, 9-cylinder radial, air-cooled, 550 hp; *Wingspan*: 51 ft 6 in (15.7 m); *Length*: 32 ft (9.75 m); *Height*: 10 ft 3 in (3.12 m); *Weight loaded*: 6,450 lb (2,928 kg); *Cruising speed*: 150 mph (241.3 km/h); *Service ceiling*: 22,000 ft (6,705 m); *Range*: 600 miles (966 km); *Crew*: 1; *Passengers*: 8–9

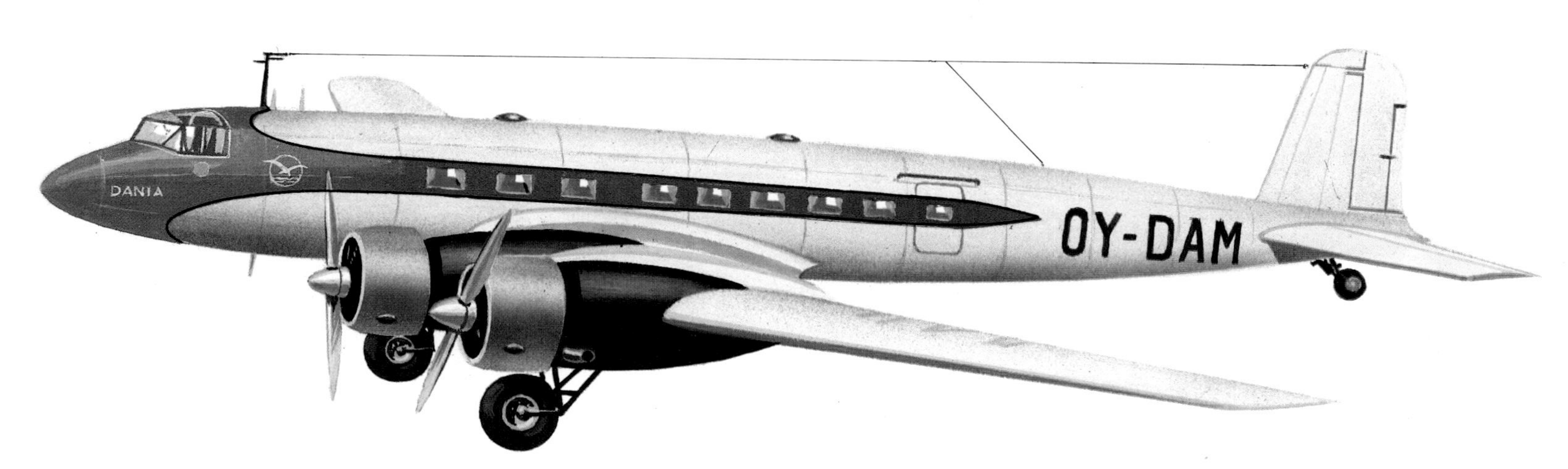

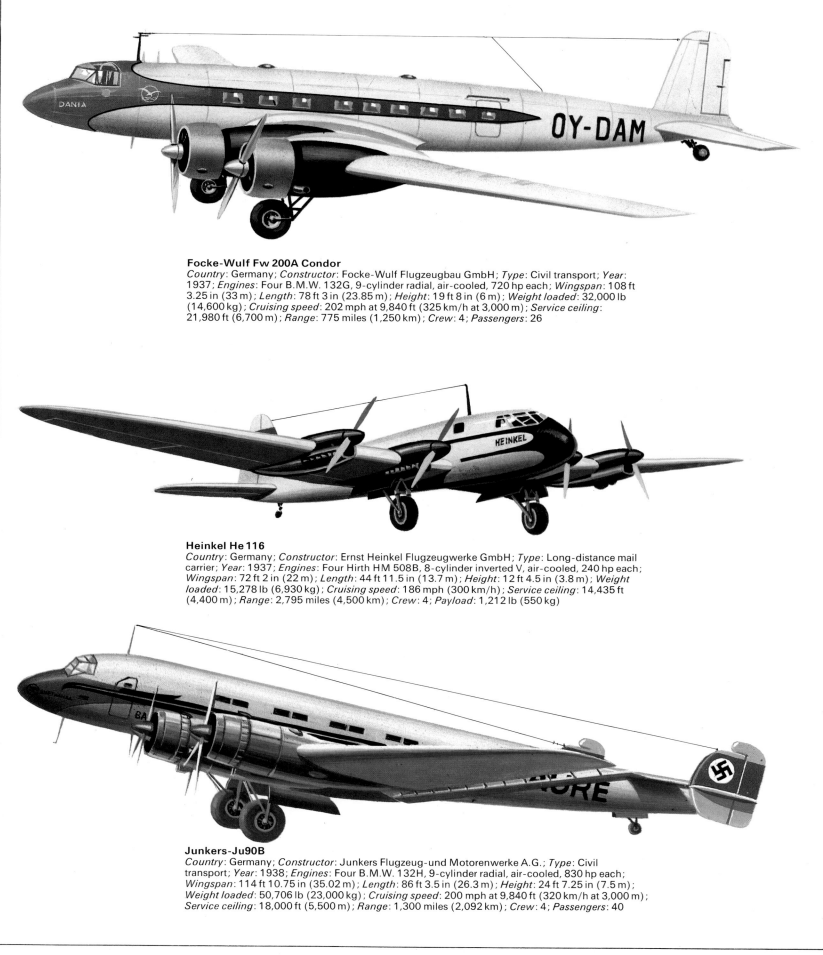

Focke-Wulf Fw 200A Condor
Country: Germany; *Constructor*: Focke-Wulf Flugzeugbau GmbH; *Type*: Civil transport; *Year*: 1937; *Engines*: Four B.M.W. 132G, 9-cylinder radial, air-cooled, 720 hp each; *Wingspan*: 108 ft 3.25 in (33 m); *Length*: 78 ft 3 in (23.85 m); *Height*: 19 ft 8 in (6 m); *Weight loaded*: 32,000 lb (14,600 kg); *Cruising speed*: 202 mph at 9,840 ft (325 km/h at 3,000 m); *Service ceiling*: 21,980 ft (6,700 m); *Range*: 775 miles (1,250 km); *Crew*: 4; *Passengers*: 26

Heinkel He 116
Country: Germany; *Constructor*: Ernst Heinkel Flugzeugwerke GmbH; *Type*: Long-distance mail carrier; *Year*: 1937; *Engines*: Four Hirth HM 508B, 8-cylinder inverted V, air-cooled, 240 hp each; *Wingspan*: 72 ft 2 in (22 m); *Length*: 44 ft 11.5 in (13.7 m); *Height*: 12 ft 4.5 in (3.8 m); *Weight loaded*: 15,278 lb (6,930 kg); *Cruising speed*: 186 mph (300 km/h); *Service ceiling*: 14,435 ft (4,400 m); *Range*: 2,795 miles (4,500 km); *Crew*: 4; *Payload*: 1,212 lb (550 kg)

Junkers-Ju90B
Country: Germany; *Constructor*: Junkers Flugzeug-und Motorenwerke A.G.; *Type*: Civil transport; *Year*: 1938; *Engines*: Four B.M.W. 132H, 9-cylinder radial, air-cooled, 830 hp each; *Wingspan*: 114 ft 10.75 in (35.02 m); *Length*: 86 ft 3.5 in (26.3 m); *Height*: 24 ft 7.25 in (7.5 m); *Weight loaded*: 50,706 lb (23,000 kg); *Cruising speed*: 200 mph at 9,840 ft (320 km/h at 3,000 m); *Service ceiling*: 18,000 ft (5,500 m); *Range*: 1,300 miles (2,092 km); *Crew*: 4; *Passengers*: 40

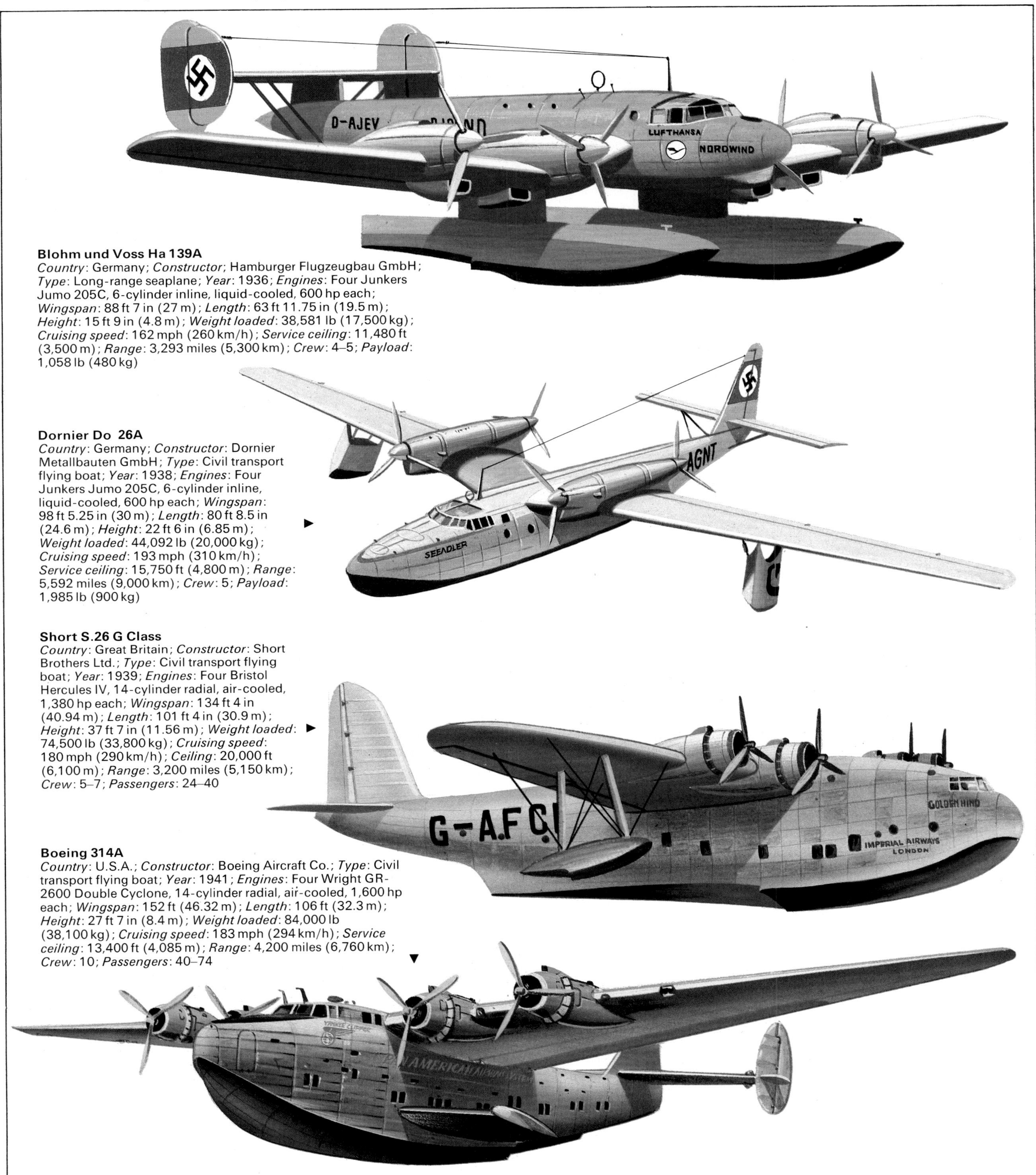

Blohm und Voss Ha 139A
Country: Germany; *Constructor*; Hamburger Flugzeugbau GmbH; *Type*: Long-range seaplane; *Year*: 1936; *Engines*: Four Junkers Jumo 205C, 6-cylinder inline, liquid-cooled, 600 hp each; *Wingspan*: 88 ft 7 in (27 m); *Length*: 63 ft 11.75 in (19.5 m); *Height*: 15 ft 9 in (4.8 m); *Weight loaded*: 38,581 lb (17,500 kg); *Cruising speed*: 162 mph (260 km/h); *Service ceiling*: 11,480 ft (3,500 m); *Range*: 3,293 miles (5,300 km); *Crew*: 4–5; *Payload*: 1,058 lb (480 kg)

Dornier Do 26A
Country: Germany; *Constructor*: Dornier Metallbauten GmbH; *Type*: Civil transport flying boat; *Year*: 1938; *Engines*: Four Junkers Jumo 205C, 6-cylinder inline, liquid-cooled, 600 hp each; *Wingspan*: 98 ft 5.25 in (30 m); *Length*: 80 ft 8.5 in (24.6 m); *Height*: 22 ft 6 in (6.85 m); *Weight loaded*: 44,092 lb (20,000 kg); *Cruising speed*: 193 mph (310 km/h); *Service ceiling*: 15,750 ft (4,800 m); *Range*: 5,592 miles (9,000 km); *Crew*: 5; *Payload*: 1,985 lb (900 kg) ▶

Short S.26 G Class
Country: Great Britain; *Constructor*: Short Brothers Ltd.; *Type*: Civil transport flying boat; *Year*: 1939; *Engines*: Four Bristol Hercules IV, 14-cylinder radial, air-cooled, 1,380 hp each; *Wingspan*: 134 ft 4 in (40.94 m); *Length*: 101 ft 4 in (30.9 m); *Height*: 37 ft 7 in (11.56 m); *Weight loaded*: 74,500 lb (33,800 kg); *Cruising speed*: 180 mph (290 km/h); *Ceiling*: 20,000 ft (6,100 m); *Range*: 3,200 miles (5,150 km); *Crew*: 5–7; *Passengers*: 24–40 ▶

Boeing 314A
Country: U.S.A.; *Constructor*: Boeing Aircraft Co.; *Type*: Civil transport flying boat; *Year*: 1941; *Engines*: Four Wright GR-2600 Double Cyclone, 14-cylinder radial, air-cooled, 1,600 hp each; *Wingspan*: 152 ft (46.32 m); *Length*: 106 ft (32.3 m); *Height*: 27 ft 7 in (8.4 m); *Weight loaded*: 84,000 lb (38,100 kg); *Cruising speed*: 183 mph (294 km/h); *Service ceiling*: 13,400 ft (4,085 m); *Range*: 4,200 miles (6,760 km); *Crew*: 10; *Passengers*: 40–74 ▼

Short-Mayo Composite Aircraft
In an attempt to achieve nonstop North Atlantic range while carrying a payload, Great Britain took an unusual step. Because an aircraft can carry a heavier weight than it can take off with, it was decided to mount a small seaplane on a flying boat. The composite aircraft took off using the power and lift of both aircraft, after which the two aircraft separated, the seaplane crossing the ocean, and the flying boat returning to base.

Short S.21 Maia
Country: Great Britain; *Constructor*: Short Brothers Ltd.; *Type*: Civil transport flying boat; *Year*: 1937; *Engines*: Four Bristol Pegasus XC, 9-cylinder radial, air-cooled, 920 hp each; *Wingspan*: 114 ft (34.74 m); *Length*: 84 ft 11 in (25.87 m); *Height*: 32 ft 7.5 in (9.95 m); *Normal weight loaded*: 38,000 lb (17,237 kg); *Weight for composite air launching*: 27,700 lb (12,564 kg); *Cruising speed*: 165 mph at 5,000 ft (265 km/h at 1,524 m); *Service ceiling*: 20,000 ft (6,100 m); *Range*: 850 miles (1,368 km); *Crew*: 5

Short S.20 Mercury
Country: Great Britain; *Constructor*: Short Brothers Ltd.; *Type*: Civil transport seaplane; *Year*: 1937; *Engines*: Four Napier Rapier V, 16-cylinder inline, air-cooled, 340 hp, each; *Wingspan*: 73 ft (22.25 m); *Length*: 51 ft (15.54 m); *Height*: 20 ft 3 in (6.17 m); *Normal weight loaded*: 12,500 lb (5,670 kg); *Weight for composite air launching*: 20,500 lb (9,298 kg); *Cruising speed*: 180 mph at 10,000 ft (290 km/h at 3,050 m); *Air-launched range*: 3,900 miles (6,275 km); *Crew*: 2; *Payload*: 1,000 lb (450 kg)

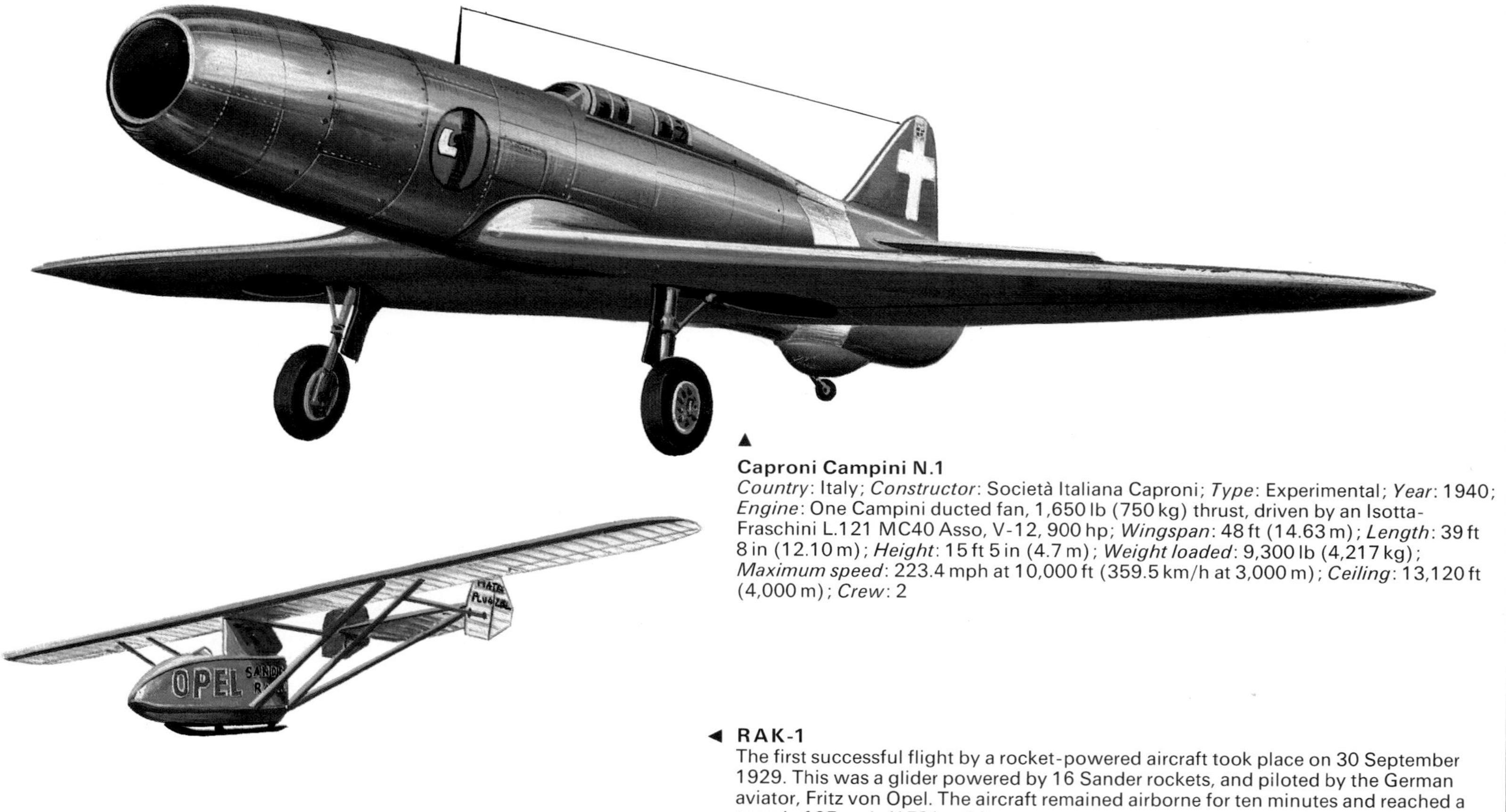

▲ **Caproni Campini N.1**
Country: Italy; *Constructor*: Società Italiana Caproni; *Type*: Experimental; *Year*: 1940; *Engine*: One Campini ducted fan, 1,650 lb (750 kg) thrust, driven by an Isotta-Fraschini L.121 MC40 Asso, V-12, 900 hp; *Wingspan*: 48 ft (14.63 m); *Length*: 39 ft 8 in (12.10 m); *Height*: 15 ft 5 in (4.7 m); *Weight loaded*: 9,300 lb (4,217 kg); *Maximum speed*: 223.4 mph at 10,000 ft (359.5 km/h at 3,000 m); *Ceiling*: 13,120 ft (4,000 m); *Crew*: 2

◄ **RAK-1**
The first successful flight by a rocket-powered aircraft took place on 30 September 1929. This was a glider powered by 16 Sander rockets, and piloted by the German aviator, Fritz von Opel. The aircraft remained airborne for ten minutes and reached a speed of 95 mph (153 km/h).

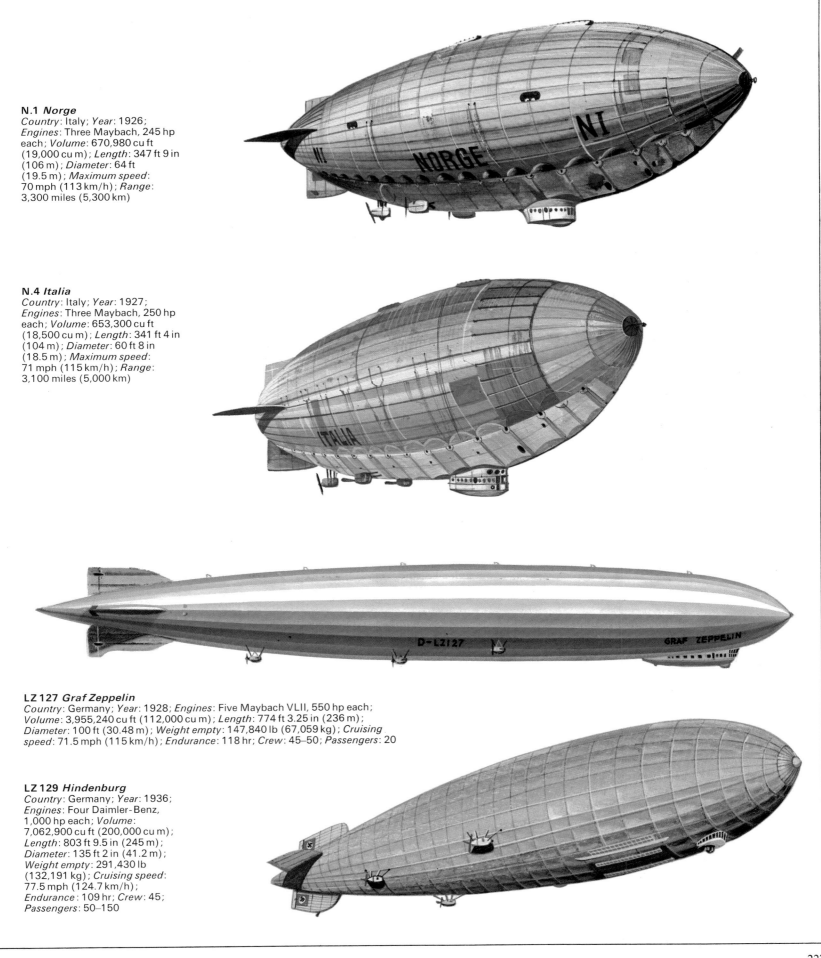

N.1 *Norge*
Country: Italy; *Year*: 1926; *Engines*: Three Maybach, 245 hp each; *Volume*: 670,980 cu ft (19,000 cu m); *Length*: 347 ft 9 in (106 m); *Diameter*: 64 ft (19.5 m); *Maximum speed*: 70 mph (113 km/h); *Range*: 3,300 miles (5,300 km)

N.4 *Italia*
Country: Italy; *Year*: 1927; *Engines*: Three Maybach, 250 hp each; *Volume*: 653,300 cu ft (18,500 cu m); *Length*: 341 ft 4 in (104 m); *Diameter*: 60 ft 8 in (18.5 m); *Maximum speed*: 71 mph (115 km/h); *Range*: 3,100 miles (5,000 km)

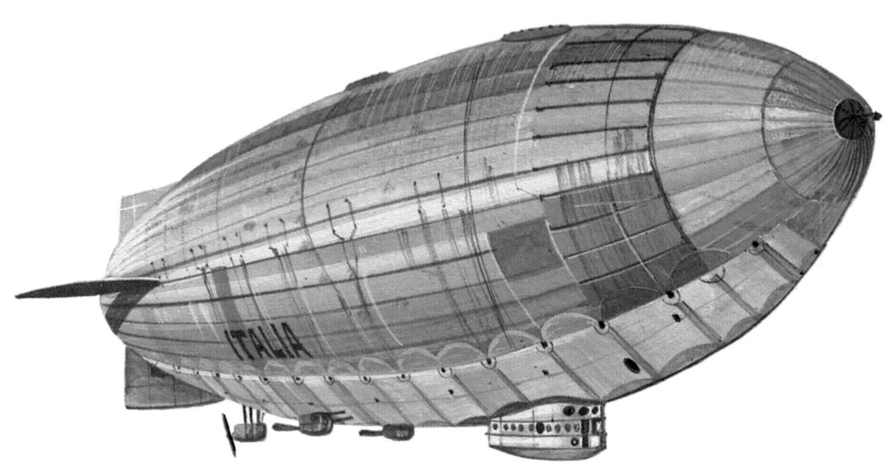

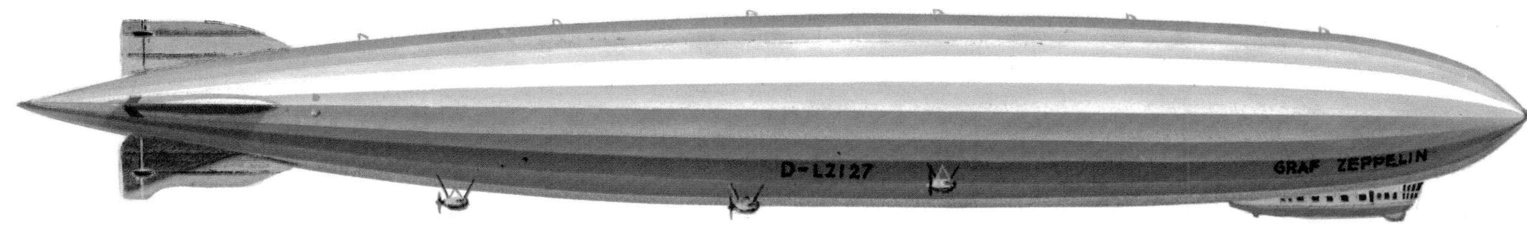

LZ 127 *Graf Zeppelin*
Country: Germany; *Year*: 1928; *Engines*: Five Maybach VLII, 550 hp each; *Volume*: 3,955,240 cu ft (112,000 cu m); *Length*: 774 ft 3.25 in (236 m); *Diameter*: 100 ft (30.48 m); *Weight empty*: 147,840 lb (67,059 kg); *Cruising speed*: 71.5 mph (115 km/h); *Endurance*: 118 hr; *Crew*: 45–50; *Passengers*: 20

LZ 129 *Hindenburg*
Country: Germany; *Year*: 1936; *Engines*: Four Daimler-Benz, 1,000 hp each; *Volume*: 7,062,900 cu ft (200,000 cu m); *Length*: 803 ft 9.5 in (245 m); *Diameter*: 135 ft 2 in (41.2 m); *Weight empty*: 291,430 lb (132,191 kg); *Cruising speed*: 77.5 mph (124.7 km/h); *Endurance*: 109 hr; *Crew*: 45; *Passengers*: 50–150

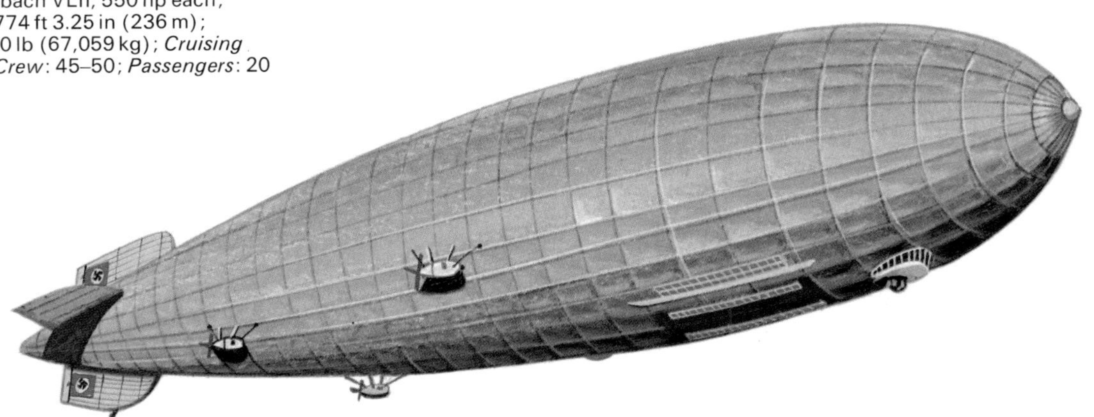

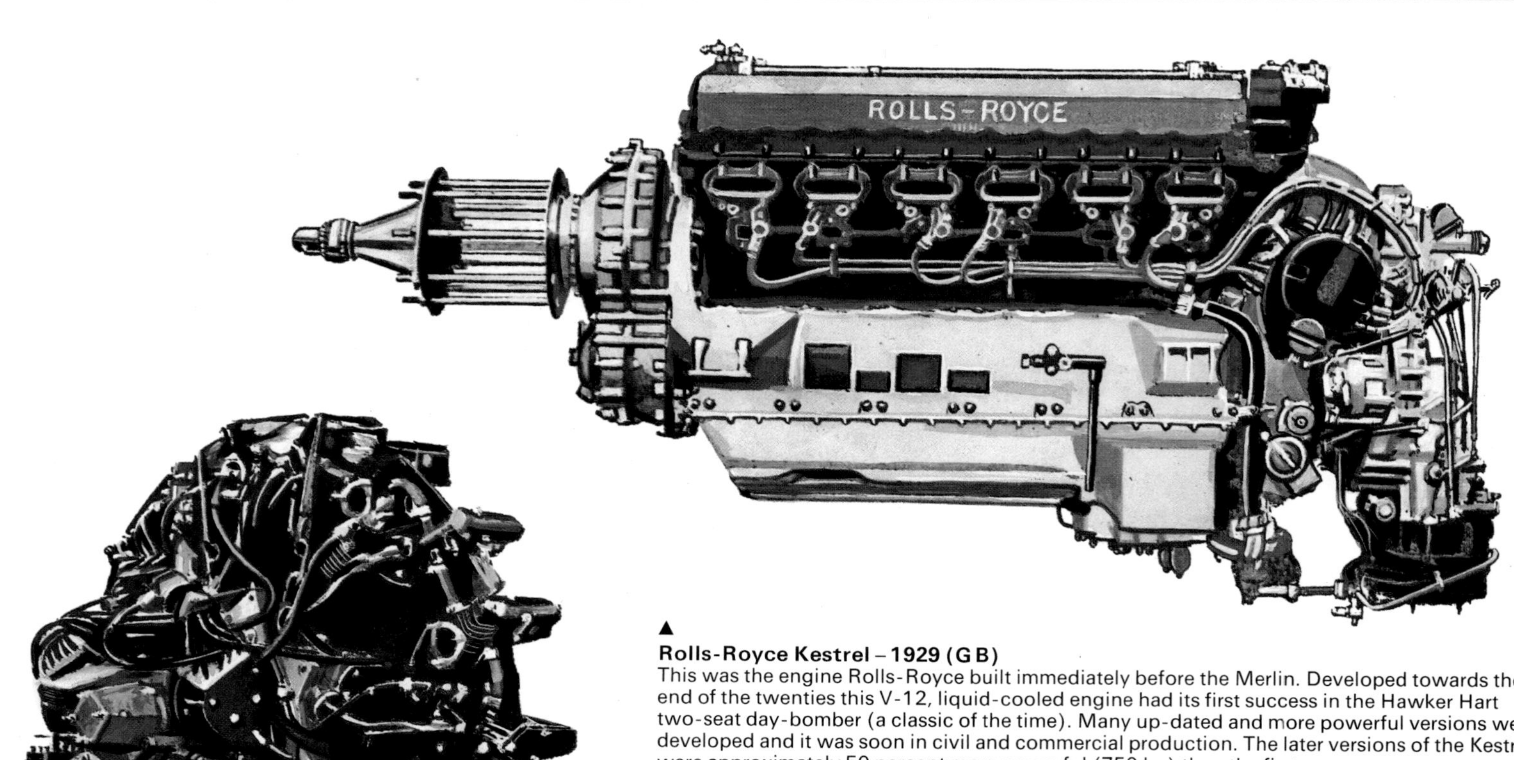

▲
Rolls-Royce Kestrel – 1929 (GB)
This was the engine Rolls-Royce built immediately before the Merlin. Developed towards the end of the twenties this V-12, liquid-cooled engine had its first success in the Hawker Hart two-seat day-bomber (a classic of the time). Many up-dated and more powerful versions were developed and it was soon in civil and commercial production. The later versions of the Kestrel were approximately 50 percent more powerful (750 hp) than the first.

◄ **Lycoming R-680 – 1928 (USA)**
Lycoming, known throughout the world for its light aircraft engines, started its career in 1928 with an engine that was a classic of that period: the R-680, a 9-cylinder radial engine in the 200 hp class. Even after ten years of development, the later versions of the R-680 made ready on the eve of World War II were in much the same class with a maximum of 285 hp. This accounted for the popularity of these engines for use in private and commercial aircraft of the time.

Fiat A.24R – 1930 (I)
This 750 hp 12-cylinder V liquid-cooled engine was one of a series of outstanding engines produced by Fiat during the 1920s and early 1930s. The A.22T had powered Ferrarin's and Del Prete's S.M.64 and the A.S.2 and A.S.3 respectively powered the Macchi M.39 and M.52 racing seaplanes. The A.24R was used to power the S.66 twin-hulled flying boats.
▼

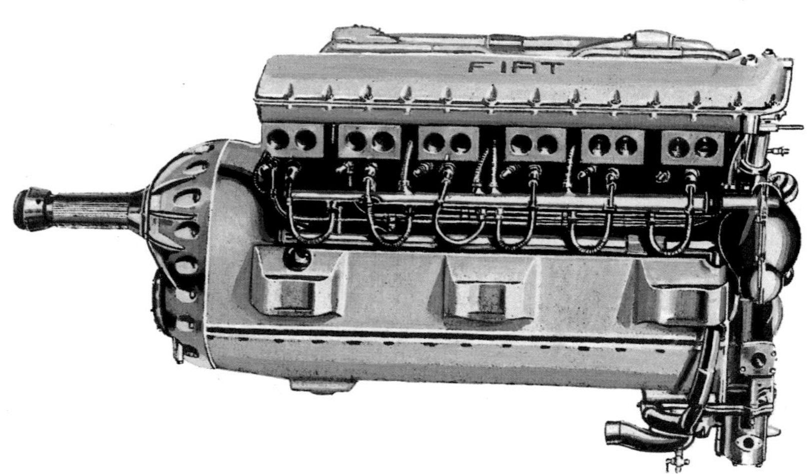

◄ **Gnome-Rhône Mistral – 1930 (F)**
This long-established French aero-engine company, famous for its rotary engines since the pioneering days, entered the field of radial engines by producing, under license, the British Bristol Jupiter. In 1929, the company started to build engines from original designs which were the series K. The 9-cylinder Mistral joined the 7-cylinder Titan Major and the 14-cylinder Titan Major. The distinctive feature of these engines was that all their main parts were interchangeable. The Mistral engines developed 550–740 hp according to the version and the Mistral Major was in the 870–1,100 hp category.

Plate 83
Outstanding aircraft used for cross-Channel and Mediterranean flights: 1928–1932

The late twenties and early thirties saw a tremendous expansion in civil aviation. European companies spared no efforts to capture the largest market share on the most sought-after routes in Europe. Their three main selling-points which were continually stressed were safety, speed and comfort. The French airliner which met these claims was the Lioré et Olivier LeO 21, a twin-engine type, derived from the LeO 20 heavy bomber, which made its name in the history of airline travel as one of the most luxurious airliners of its day. The prototype of the LeO 21 series appeared in 1926 and up to 1931 a total of thirteen aircraft (eleven of them LeO 213s) were built and went into service with Air Union on its two most important routes, on which it was determined to be most competitive, Paris–London and Paris–Lyons–Marseilles. The original LeO 21 and the second one were converted to LeO 212s in 1927 and one was converted into a flying restaurant, offering traditional French excellence in cuisine and service. The original aircraft and ten of the LeO 213s were subsequently taken over by Air France and a great deal of use was made of them until they were taken out of service in 1934.

Much the biggest and most luxurious airliners of the early 1930s were the Handley Page Hannibal and Heracles class four-engine biplanes built for Imperial Airways. Eight H.P.42s were completed in 1930–31 and were built in two versions: the E model for Indian services and African routes which could carry twenty-four passengers, and the W for European routes which could accommodate thirty-eight. During their existence these aircraft were known as H.P.42s, with the suffix E (Eastern) and W (Western). Later it was discovered that the Western type—the Heracles class—was the H.P.45. The H.P.42 prototype flew for the first time on 14 November 1930, and began operating on the London—Paris route on 11 June the following year. The aircraft were all given names of historical or mythological heroes and heroines, such as *Hannibal*, *Horsa*, *Hanno* and *Hadrian* for the H.P.42E models, and *Heracles*, *Hengist*, *Horatius* and *Helena* for the H.P.42Ws. These aircraft clocked up a very high mileage, in aggregate exceeding ten million miles (16,093,400 km), and earned Imperial Airways an unrivaled reputation for reliability and safety.

Another British airplane which helped Imperial Airways to extend its routes was the Short S.8 Calcutta, a three-engine flying boat used on the Mediterranean sector of the London—Karachi route when it opened in 1929. The first of their five Calcuttas took to the air on 20 February 1928, and was put into temporary service between Liverpool and Belfast in September 1928. Together with the four-engine and more comfortable S.17 Kents, the S.8s remained in service until the mid-thirties.

From the early 1930s until the outbreak of World War II, Italian airlines used the equally outstanding Savoia Marchetti S.66 flying boat for Mediterranean flights. This was a three-engine aircraft which had been derived from the successful twin-engine S.55 and could carry up to eighteen passengers. The first airlines to take delivery of the new flying boats were Aero Espresso, buying three, SANA (four) and SAM (seven). Ala Littoria absorbed these fleets, ordered additional examples and eventually had no fewer than twenty-three S.66s in its fleet, which were first put into service on its Rome–Tripoli–Tunis route in April 1934 and from April 1937 worked the Brindisi–Athens–Rhodes–Haifa services.

A small French Flying boat which played an important role in the 1930s was the CAMS 53, derived from a line of military aircraft, the initial variant of which went into service on Mediterranean flights in 1928. The most widely-used model was the 53-1, of 1929, which had a strengthened hull and more powerful, Hispano-Suiza, engines. In 1933 Air France took over twenty-one CAMS 53s and kept most of them in service for two years. One, registered F-AIZB, remained with the airline until 1938.

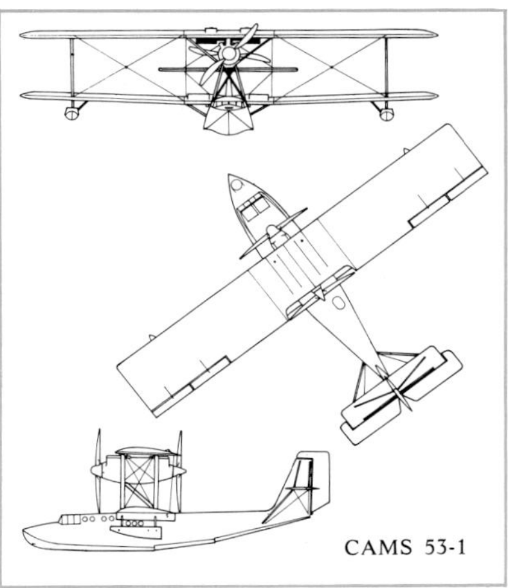
CAMS 53-1

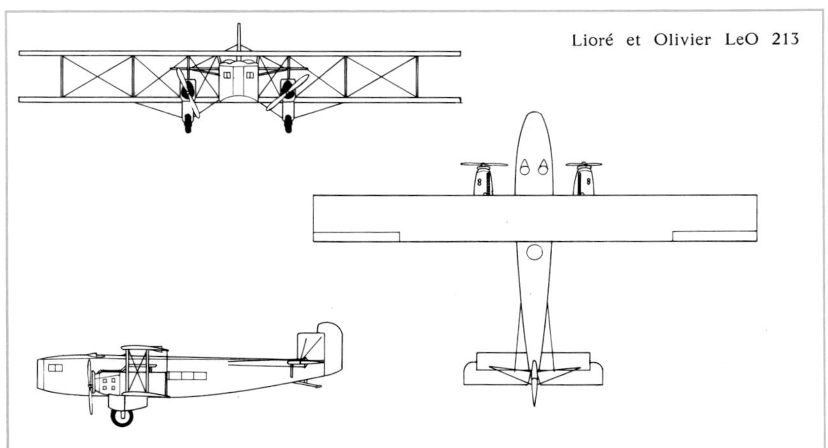
Lioré et Olivier LeO 213

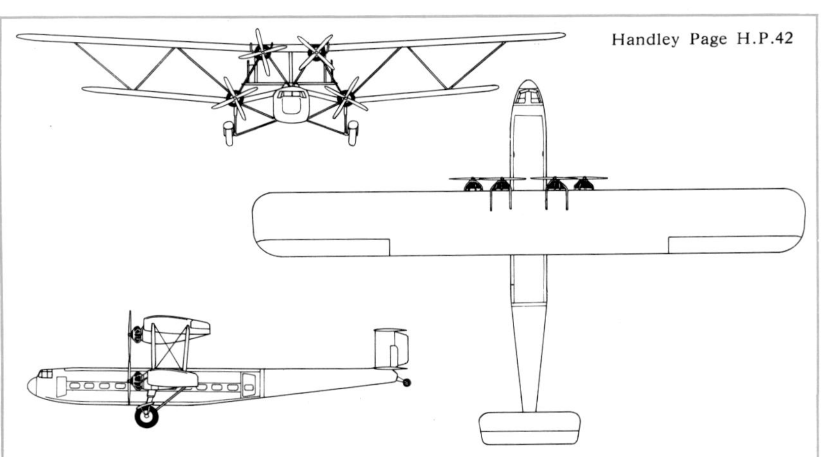
Handley Page H.P.42

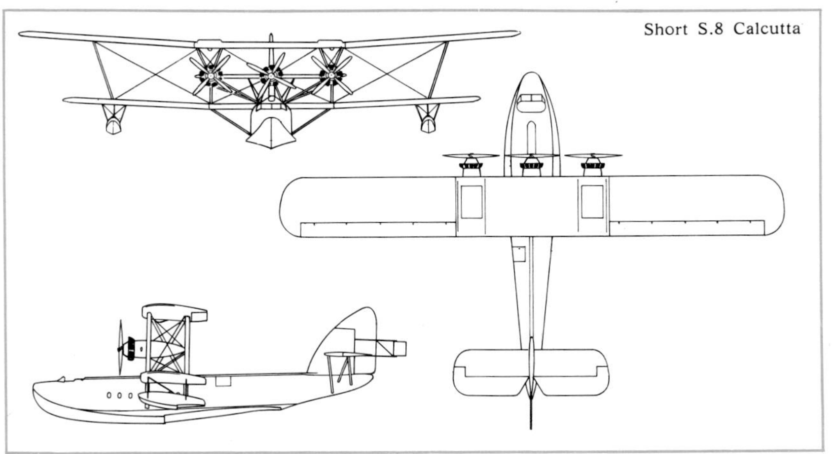
Short S.8 Calcutta

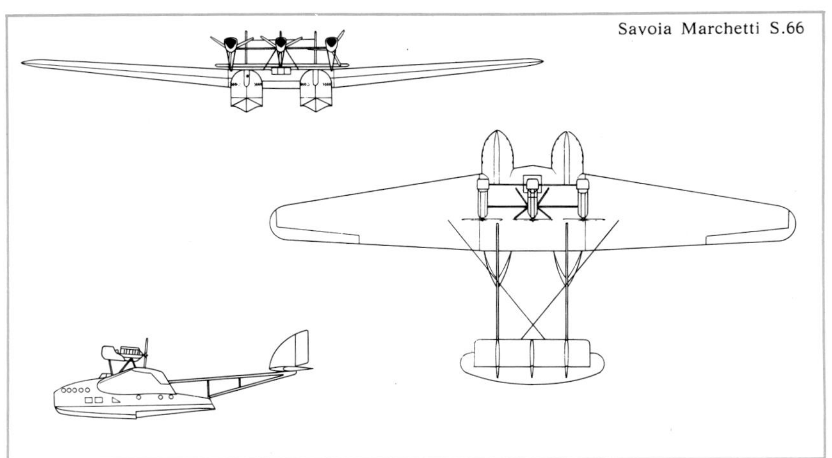
Savoia Marchetti S.66

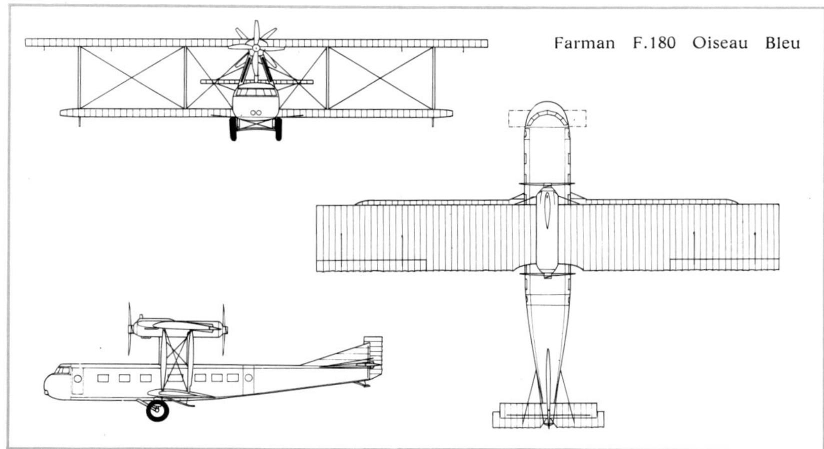
Farman F.180 Oiseau Bleu

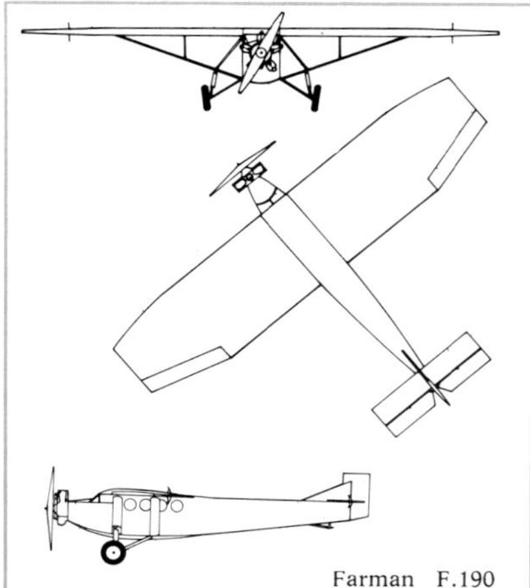
Farman F.190

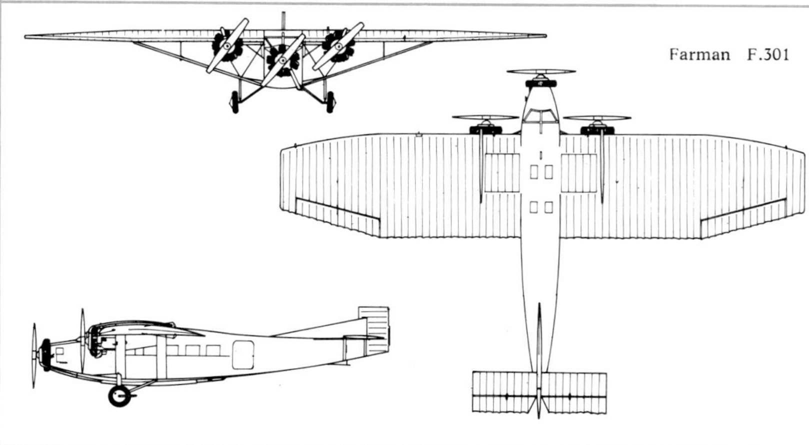
Farman F.301

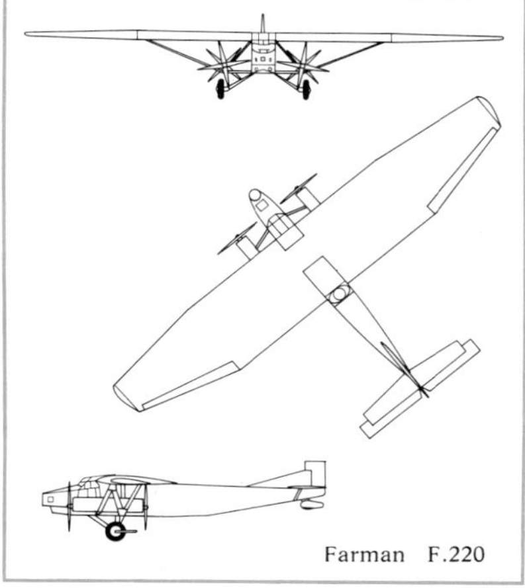
Farman F.220

Plate 84
A selection of Farman aircraft: 1927–1930

In France, Farman can probably be considered to have made the most significant contribution to providing French civil aviation with reliable aircraft during these years of expansion. After the success of the F.60 Goliath in the immediate postwar years, the most unusual Farman airliner, both in design and technical innovations was the F.180 Oiseau Bleu. The prototype of this large unequal-span biplane appeared in 1927. Its two engines were mounted in tandem beneath the center of the upper wing and it had a very streamlined fuselage. The F.180 had originally been designed for an attempt on the North Atlantic crossing, but this project had been dropped and the aircraft was taken over by Farman Lignes in February 1928. Three were built, but there is little evidence that they saw much service.

Another popular contemporary Farman of a different type, the F.190, was the forerunner of a large family of monoplanes which reached the end of its development line with the larger F.300 series in the 1930s. The F.190 project got under way in 1928, with the aim of building a relatively small aircraft which had to be reliable and versatile.

The F.190 found favor with the market and production continued until 1931, in several models, reaching a total of over one hundred. The various models differed mainly in the type of engine used. The F.190 had a 230 hp Gnome-Rhône Titan; the F.192 had a 230 hp Salmson 9Ab; the F.193 was powered by a 230 hp Farman 9Ea; the F.194 by a 250 hp Hispano-Suiza 6Mb; the F. 197 had a 240 hp Lorraine 7Me; a 250 hp Renault 9A was installed in the F.198, and the most powerful variant, the F.199, had a 325 hp Lorraine 9Na. Lignes Farman was the largest operator of this aircraft, having at least fourteen, while Air Union used seven. Air France acquired fifteen in 1933 and kept them in service for several years. Other airlines which flew Farman F.190s were CIDNA, Air Orient in Saigon, LARES in Romania and two companies operating in Africa.

After the success of the F.190 series, the Farman company decided to develop another generation of aircraft which would continue the lines and structure of the earlier model, albeit on a larger scale, with increased range, power and capacity. The new series was the F.300 and the prototype had its maiden flight early in 1930. The major difference compared with the F.190 was the greater size and the installation of three Salmson engines, one in the nose and two in wing nacelles. F.300 production also ran through several variants (six of which went into service) with different power units. Six of the first series, the F.301, were built, powered by three 230 hp Salmson 9Ab radials; then the second model, the F.302, of which only one was built, had a single liquid-cooled 650 hp Hispano-Suiza 12Nb engine. The F.303 of 1931 (six built) reverted to the three-engine formula and was powered by 240 hp Gnome-Rhône Titan radials; the F.305 (two built) had a 380 hp Gnome-Rhône Jupiter 9Aa as its central engine plus a Titan on each wing; the F.306 (four manufactured) had three 240 hp Lorraine 7Me engines, and the series was completed with a private order, the F.304, (powered by three 300 hp Lorraine 9Na's), and the Salmson-powered F.310 twin-float seaplane. These aircraft were given a great deal of use and once again Lignes Farman was the main operator on the principal European routes, giving them the evocative name of "Etoile d'Argent" (Silver Star). Air Orient, Compagnie Transafricaine d'Aviation and the Yugoslav company, Aeroput, also used F.300s. In 1933 Air France took over fifteen of them and kept them in service for some time.

Another significant contribution to the development of commercial aviation was made by the civil types derived from Farman heavy bombers. In addition to the five F.220 series which flew the South Atlantic route from 1935, one of the best known was the only example of the F.220 series to have been a direct conversion of the F.220 bomber. This airplane made its first South Atlantic crossing on 3 June 1935, and three months later it broke the record for a South Atlantic crossing, flying from Dakar to Natal (Brazil) in 13 hours 37 minutes.

Plate 85
American flying boats for South American and Pacific routes: 1928–1935

From the late twenties the development of intercontinental flights from the United States was closely linked to the expansion of a particular airline, Pan American Airways, and during the next decade Pan American was to develop the most extensive commercial network in the world. The aircraft which played a crucial role in this very rapid growth was the flying boat, considered to be the safest type for long flights over water.

The first successful aircraft of this category, built specially for Pan American, was the twin-engine Sikorsky S-38 amphibian, produced in 1928 for use on flights to Central America. This aircraft was derived from another amphibian, the S-36, one of which was used by Pan American, but it was faster and had increased range and capacity compared with its predecessor. There were two main variants, the S-38A and the S-38B, the latter being an improved version. Eleven S-38As were manufactured, the first of which entered service in June 1928. Pan American operated three, as did the Curtiss Flying Service;

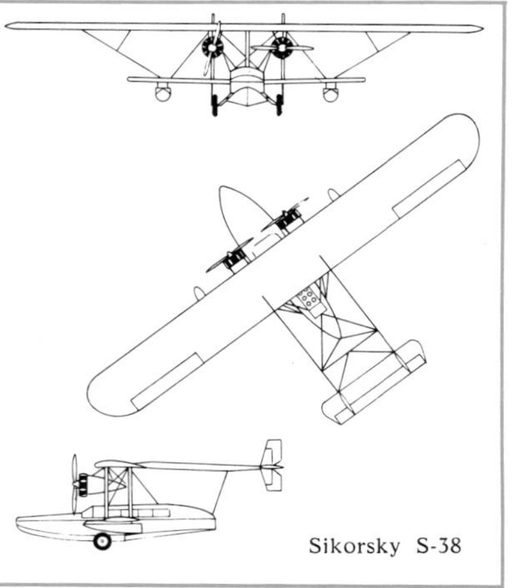
Sikorsky S-38

N.Y.R.B.A. Line used one (this was a very short-lived company, formed in 1929 to fly to South America and was taken over only a year later by Pan American); Western Air Express also used one S-38A.

N.Y.R.B.A. Line inaugurated its Miami–Buenos Aires service in February 1930, with another important flying boat, the Consolidated Commodore, a large airplane which initially could carry twenty passengers over distances of 1,000 miles (1,610 km) at a cruising speed of over 100 mph (160 km/h). This company had taken delivery of ten Commodores and when N.Y.R.B.A. was taken over by Pan American in 1930, Pan Am took the Commodores and the four which had not been delivered. Pan Am flew Commodores on their longest nonstop oversea route of the time: from Jamaica to Panama.

The mid-thirties onward saw Pan American's meteoric rise when the airline ordered the first large four-engine flying boats, the famous "Clippers" from United States aircraft manufacturers. These came to symbolize one of the most fascinating periods in the history of aviation. Pan American's first choice was once more for a Sikorsky design. The first airplane of this type was the S-40, of which three were ordered in 1930. It was the largest aircraft yet built in the United States, capable of carrying thirty-two passengers in some luxury over distances up to 900 miles (1,450 km). Some time after putting the S-40 into service on Caribbean routes, Pan American announced that it was seeking something even more ambitious: a four-engine flying boat to carry at least 300 lb (136 kg) of mail, with a range of 2,500 miles (4,025 km) against a 30 mph (48 km/h) headwind. Two manufacturers submitted designs, Martin and Sikorsky, and Pan American decided to order both.

Sikorsky's proposed aircraft was derived from its previous design, the S-40, and was a four-engine flying boat, the S-42. The airplane did not satisfy Pan American's range specification but it was accepted in spite of this because of the prototype's outstanding performance during test flights (the S-42 had made its maiden flight on 30 March 1934); it set ten altitude records with varying loads. Altogether, Pan American ordered ten S-42s, three of which were B variants which had extra fuel tanks. One of these new S-42 Clippers began making Pacific survey flights in April 1935, but they were mostly used on Latin American routes although later they worked the Manila–Hong Kong route and between New York and Bermuda and Seattle and Alaska.

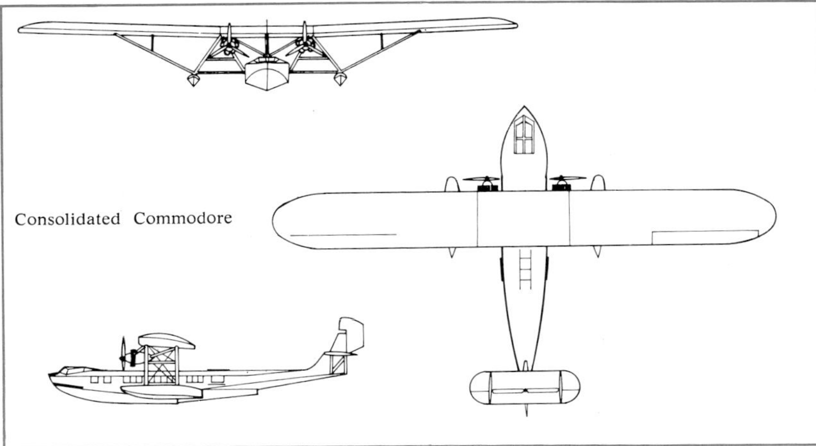
Consolidated Commodore

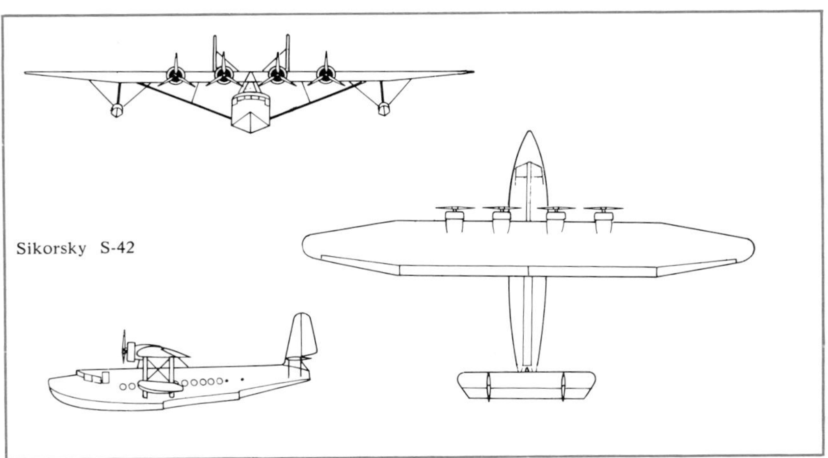
Sikorsky S-42

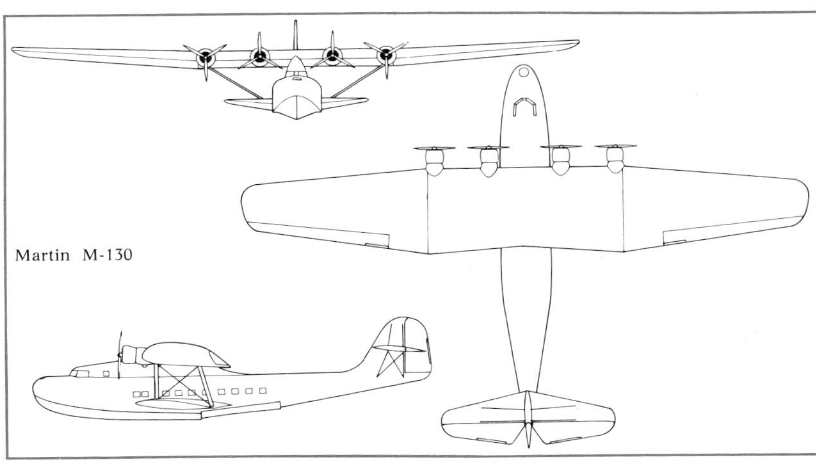
Martin M-130

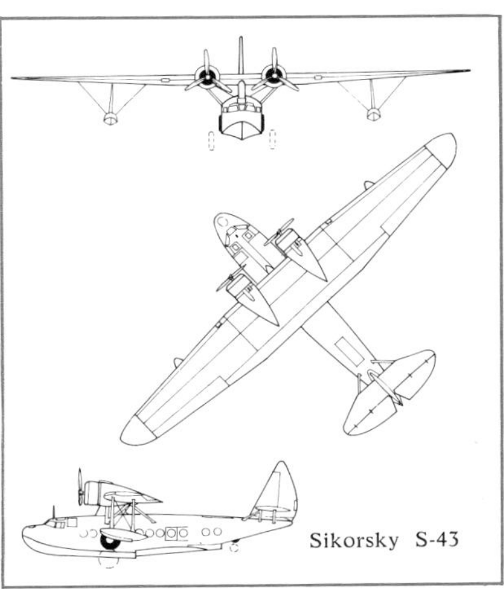
Sikorsky S-43

The first Martin M-130 flew for the first time on 30 December 1934, and all three were delivered late in 1935. In contrast to the Sikorsky S-42's rather disappointing range, these large M-130 flying boats could fly well in excess of the 2,500 miles (4,025 km) required by Pan American. Pan American planned to introduce a direct route across the Pacific from San Francisco to Manila, to be completed in five stages: San Francisco–Honolulu (2,394 miles–3,853 km); Honolulu–Midway Island (1,360 miles–2,200 km); Midway–Wake Island (1,260 miles–2,030 km; Wake Island–Guam (1,450 miles–2,335 km); and Guam–Manila (2,000 miles–3,220 km). Scheduled mail flights began on 22 November 1935, and paying passengers were carried from 21 October 1936; the San Francisco–Manila journey took five days in all: sixty flying hours. Three M-130s were built and flown on this run, being called *China Clipper*, *Philippine Clipper* and *Hawaii Clipper*, but all three soon came to be known collectively as the "China Clippers."

From April 1937 the route was extended to Hong Kong. The M-130 could carry from fourteen passengers on the longest runs to a maximum of forty-one on shorter flights. On night flights eighteen people could be accommodated in sleeping berths in the three main cabins. The M-130s' busy career was to last well into World War II; in 1942 the two surviving Clippers were turned over to the U.S. Navy and used as military transports. By this time the *China Clipper* and the *Philippine Clipper* had each flown a total of over 10,000 hours (the *Hawaii Clipper*, renamed *Hawaiian Clipper*, had been lost at sea in 1938.

Another Sikorsky amphibian which echoed its predecessor's success was the smaller, twin-engine S-43, and for many years this aircraft complemented the larger S-42, proving extremely popular on shorter routes. The S-43 first appeared in 1935 and two versions were built. Pan American was the largest operator of this B series, taking delivery of fourteen and flying them on Latin-American routes.

Plate 86
Significant achievements of the French aircraft industry: 1929–1931

The establishement of regular air services across the South Atlantic was a prime French objective, and considerable effort was put into the design and construction of aircraft capable of crossing the ocean with a commercial payload. The first reliable multi-engine aircraft designed for the ocean crossing was the Couzinet 70 *Arc-en-ciel* (Rainbow), an elegant three-engine monoplane, and although only one was ever built, it made itself quite a reputation with a number of crossings of the South Atlantic in the hands of Aéropostale and Air France.

The event which greatly impressed aviation experts was its inaugural flight from St. Louis, in Senegal, to Natal in Brazil, on 16 January 1933, with the famous Jean Mermoz at the controls, an exceptionally fast crossing of only 14 hours 27 minutes. The *Arc-en-ciel* had originated in 1928 when the young designer, René Couzinet, in collaboration with Marcel Maurice Drouhin, another aviation enthusiast, decided to

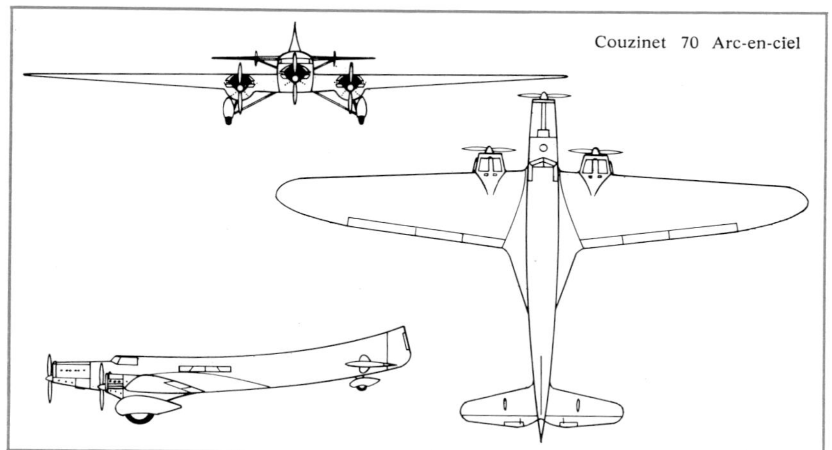
Couzinet 70 Arc-en-ciel

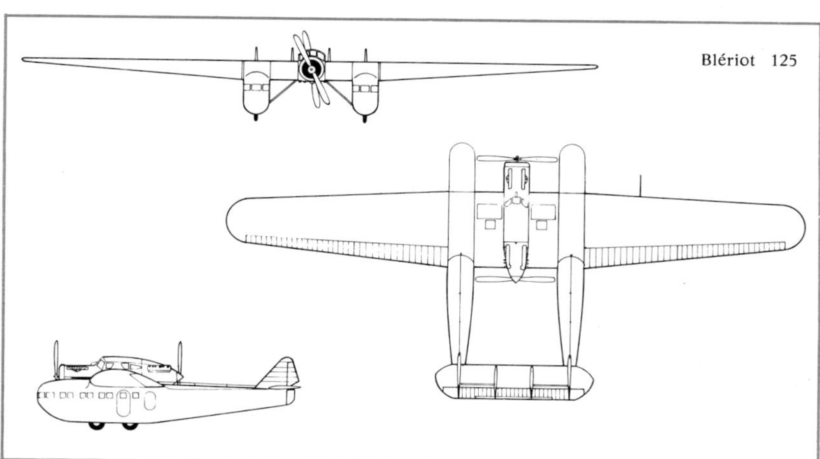
Blériot 125

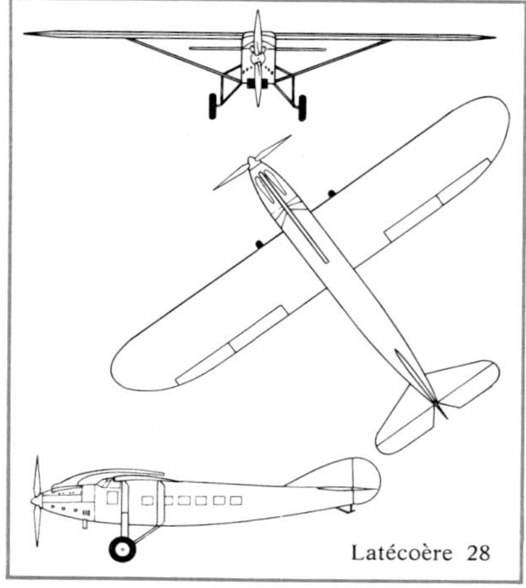
Latécoère 28

build a long-distance aircraft for record-breaking. They had so much faith in their project that they launched a public appeal for funds to construct the airplane. Two million francs were collected and the first *Arc-en-ciel*, the Couzinet 10-01, was completed. This first *Arc-en-ciel* crashed at Orly in August 1928, during a test flight and Drouhin was killed. A second model was destroyed by fire. Although saddened by his friend's death, Couzinet went on with his work and designed further aircraft derived from the prototype. One of these was the Couzinet 70, also called *Arc-en-ciel* which had considerable range, could carry 1,320 lb (600 kg) of mail or freight and subsequently acquitted itself well on Jean Mermoz's historic flight.

Immediately after the January 1933 crossing the Couzinet 70 was extensively modified; the fuselage was lengthened, the tail was altered and different propellers were fitted. Thus remodeled, the *Arc-en-ciel*, as the Couzinet 71, began its regular postal run to South America on 28 May 1934. From 24 July that year there was a monthly crossing, shared with the Latécoère 300 flying boat, eight crossings being safely completed during this period by the *Arc-en-ciel*. Early in 1935 the aircraft was altered once more, to make it more streamlined, but its final operations and fate have not been traced.

The Latécoère 28 had crossed the South Atlantic before the *Arc-en-ciel* but was not suitable for regular crossings, being a single-engine, high-wing monoplane. But it was used on flights between France and West Africa and in South America from about 1930. The Latécoère 28 proved its worth by establishing several world records: in 1930 a Naval seaplane model set nine world records for speed, endurance and distance with loads of 1,100 lb (500 kg); 2,200 lb (1,000 kg) and 4,400 lb (2,000 kg). Another Laté 28 seaplane called the *Comte de la Vaulx*, piloted by Jean Mermoz, flew across the South Atlantic (from St. Louis to Natal) in twenty-one hours on 12–13 May 1930. This was the ocean sector of the first experimental mail flight from Toulouse to Rio de Janeiro.

The prototype Latécoère 28 made its appearance in 1929 and, to meet Aéropostale's requirements, production included several different models, fifty aircraft in all being manufactured. The initial versions, the Laté 28-0 and 28-1 were both landplanes and were powered by the 500 hp Renault 12JG and 500 hp Hispano-Suiza 12Hbr engine respectively. The later 28-3 and 28-5 models were mail carrying seaplanes which had 600 hp and 650 hp engines. These had significantly increased range and capacity compared with earlier models and were used for transatlantic mail services. The Laté 28's career continued without interruption after the formation of Air France in 1933: the new company took over twenty-nine of the landplane models and two seaplanes. A further four Laté 28s went to Aeroposta Argentina and several went to the Venezuelan airline LAV (Linea Aeropostal Venezolana).

During the thirties in France a number of interesting designs and prototypes were projected and although innovative and possibly practical propositions, many never went into production, unlike their more successful contemporaries. the Blériot 125 was one of these which is worthy of mention. The prototype was an unusual twin-engine monoplane with two fuselages, designed to offer its passengers the utmost comfort. Up to twelve people could be accommodated. The two fuselages were completely separate and the three-man crew was housed in a small central cabin above the wing between the two engines, one of which drove a tractor, the other a pusher propeller. There were no less than four fins and rudders.

Plate 87
The Netherlands–Fokker's lead is unchallenged: 1928–1935

The Netherlands continued to play an influential role in European aviation. Following the successful F.VIIa-3m series, Fokker's family of trimotors was extended, introducing an aircraft which was probably the most outstanding of them all: the F.VIIb-3m. The aircraft was built in 1928 and echoed the general lines and design formula of its predecessor but had a bigger wing. The F.VIIb-3m met with almost instant commercial success and about 150 were manufactured: about half being

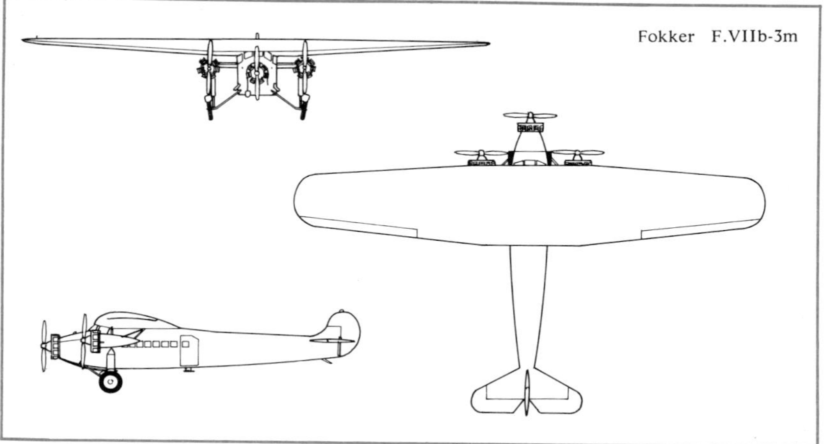
Fokker F.VIIb-3m

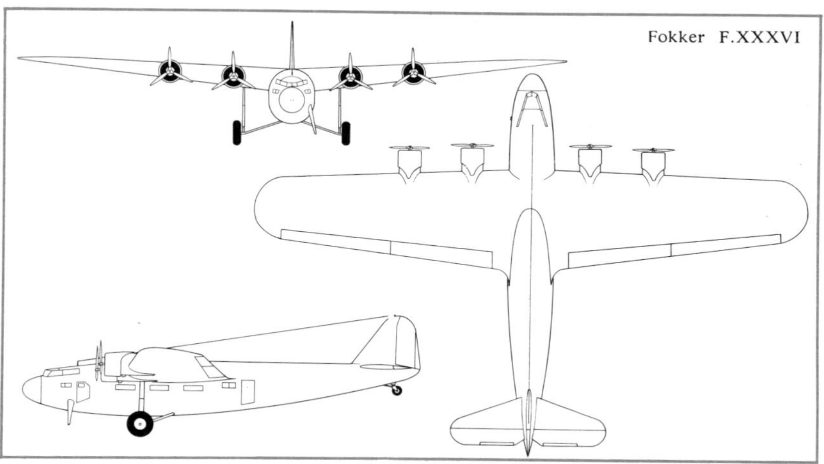
Fokker F.XXXVI

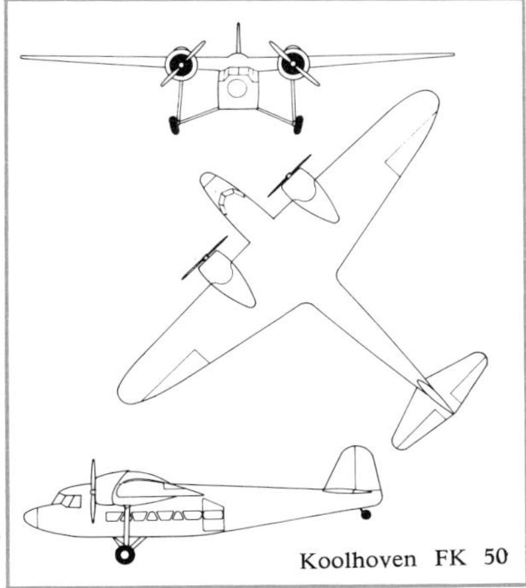
Koolhoven FK 50

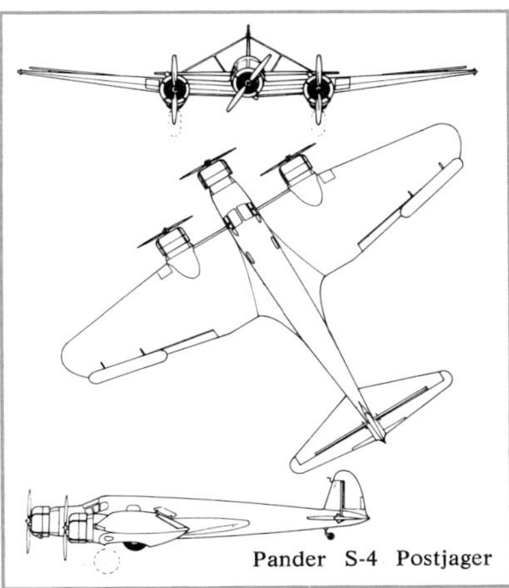
Pander S-4 Postjager

built in the Netherlands by Fokker itself and the rest were constructed under license in several countries, among them Belgium, Czechoslovakia, Poland, Italy and Great Britain. In the United States the very similar F.X and F.Xa were produced. Many major airlines operated Fokker F.VIIb-3ms but they mainly earned a name for themselves through their record-breaking flights and long journeys of exploration.

The most famous of these was Charles Kingsford Smith's first air crossing of the Pacific with a crew of three. His F.VIIb-3m, called the *Southern Cross*, set out from Oakland, California, on 31 May 1928, and landed at Brisbane on 9 June, having been more than 83 hours in the air and landed *en route* at Honolulu and Suva. The *Southern Cross* is still to be seen at Brisbane Airport.

One of Fokker's last commercial designs of the 1930s was for a large four-engine aircraft, the F.XXXVI, designed especially for KLM's long-distance route to the Far East. Six aircraft had been ordered in 1932 but the F.XXXVI had the bad luck of having the more modern and much more efficient American Douglas DC-2 as competition and KLM understandably chose the latter, having done so well in the 1934 London–Melbourne race with its first DC-2. Fokker completed the first F.XXXVI, which had its maiden flight on 22 June 1934, and this example was bought by KLM and generally used on the London–Amsterdam–Berlin route. It was finally sold as a navigational trainer.

Fokker overshadowed other, smaller Dutch aircraft manufacturers although some managed to produce worthwhile aircraft. The Koolhoven FK 50 was one example, a twin-engine airliner which could seat eight passengers. Three FK 50s were built between 1935 and 1938 for the Swiss company, Alpar Luftverkehrs of Berne who kept two of them in service until after the war. Another minor manufacturer had less success with its Pander S-4 Postjager in 1933. The only prototype of this fast and streamlined trimotor monoplane which had been built for use on mail runs to the Netherlands East Indies, made several outstanding flights but failed to find a market.

Plate 88
Multi-engine aircraft developed in the United States: 1928–1933

Fokker's designs had a particularly strong influence on U.S. aircraft manufacturers since he had established an affiliate company in America in 1920, which produced independently for the U.S. market. The Fokker Aircraft Corporation of America traded for nine years, until it was taken over by General Motors in 1929. The great "flying Dutchman's" last design for the U.S. commercial aviation market was his F-32, a large, four-engine high-wing monoplane which could seat 32 passengers. The prototype was designed in 1929 and first flew in September of that same year. Two companies expressed interest in it. The first, Universal Air Lines, canceled its order for the outstanding four F-32s after its first one crashed, but the other customer, Western Air Express, eventually took delivery of two which were flown on the San Francisco–Los Angeles route, but they were not a great success.

Quite apart from this direct influence on the North American market, Fokker's aircraft also had a considerable indirect effect on the types produced by U.S. aircraft manufacturers. His favorite trimotor formula, for instance, was enthusiastically adopted by several American constructors.

Among the constructors to adopt this commercially successful three-engine formula was Boeing, and from 1928 until 1933 Boeing Air Transport operated their Model 80s. The prototype had its first flight in August 1928, and four of the initial production series were built and entered service on the

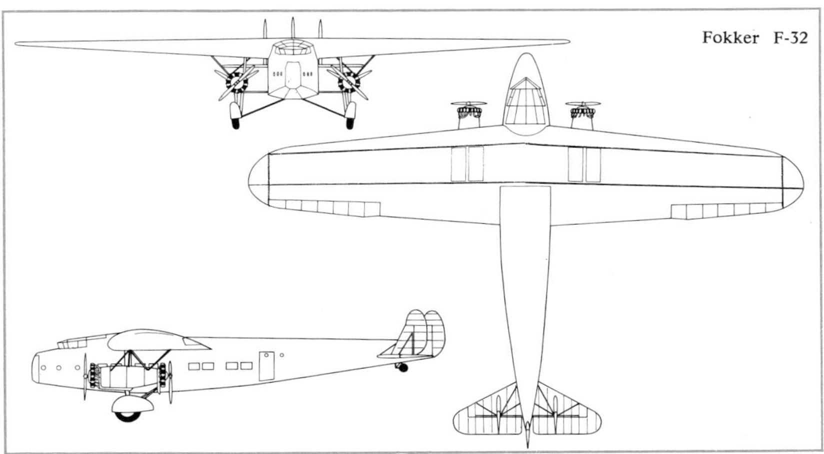
Fokker F-32

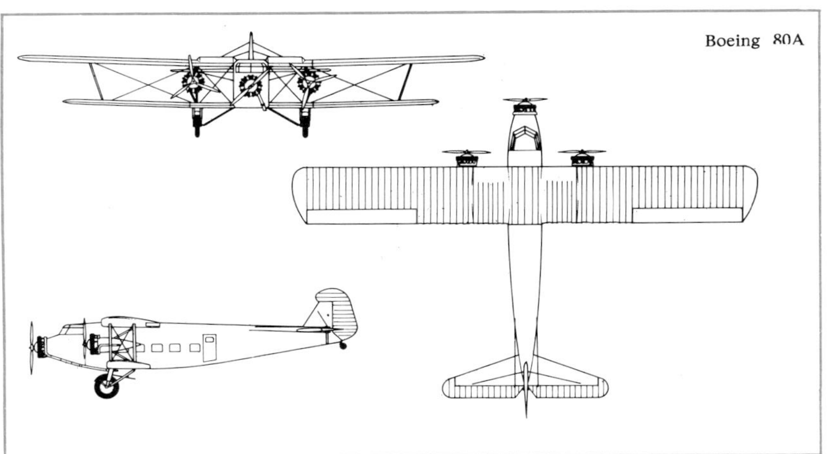
Boeing 80A

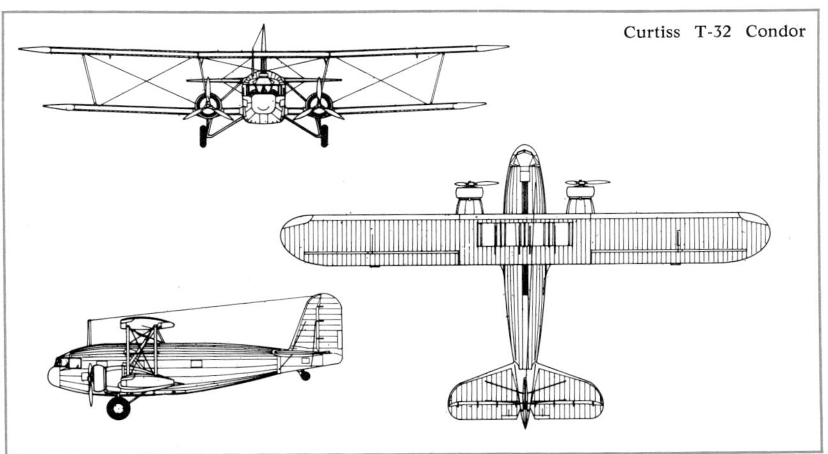
Curtiss T-32 Condor

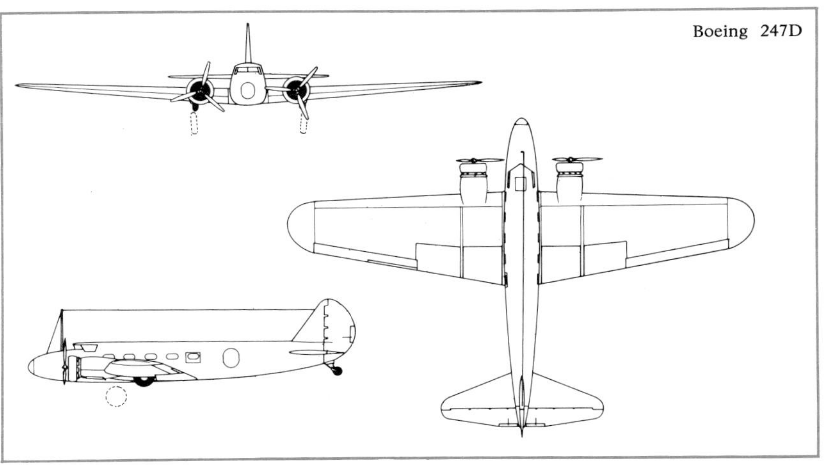
Boeing 247D

San Francisco–Chicago route in October 1928. Production continued with ten of the 80A improved model, which had minor structural modifications and more powerful engines. One of these 80A models had the forward fuselage altered to accommodate an open cockpit and was known as the 80B.

Another trimotor which was very popular with the smaller airlines was the Stinson Trimotor SM-6000, developed in 1930. This was a tough and versatile aircraft which could seat ten passengers over short distances and many companies soon took delivery of their SM-6000s, attracted not only by the aircraft's good qualities but also by its extremely competitive price. The largest operator of the SM-6000 was the Ludington Line which put ten into service on its busy New York–Washington run, flying as many as eleven services daily between the two cities.

The Curtiss T.32 Condor was a very different type of aircraft; it was the last civil transport biplane to be built by the American aircraft industry. A total of forty-five T-32s was manufactured and a number saw service with Eastern Air Transport and American Airways from 1933. In spite of the T.32s being very safe and comfortable (the Condor was one of the first airliners to have sleeping berths for night flights), they were casualties of the appearance of the more advanced Boeing 247, which marked the beginning of a new era in commercial transport. The Boeing 247 prototype made its maiden flight on 8 February 1933, and immediately made the entire world fleet of commercial aircraft seem obsolete. This new aircraft had an all-metal structure and was a low-wing monoplane with retractable undercarriage. It was very streamlined, had good all-round performance and low operating costs. Other interesting technological innovations included a wing and tail de-icing system. The 247 originated in a military specification to Boeing in 1931 for a medium bomber. This aircraft, the B-9, was built in small numbers and Boeing followed it with work on a civil development. United Air Lines, one of the most go-ahead and enterprising airlines of the day, had a complete monopoly of the 247 production aircraft and Boeing Air Transport, part of the United group, introduced the first 247s into service on 30 March 1933. United eventually operated 60 Boeing 247s and had a decided advantage over all its competitors.

The results of putting this new type into service were dramatic; flying times were slashed and at the same time safety was improved. Other airlines began clamoring for new aircraft in their turn. By the time Boeing had managed to manufacture seventy-five 247s another, even more modern and competitive aircraft had appeared: the twin-engine Douglas DC-1/DC-2, the forerunner of the famous DC-3 (widely known as the Dakota) which was to be the greatest airliner of all and which had been developed by Douglas in response to TWA's request for a new commercial transport.

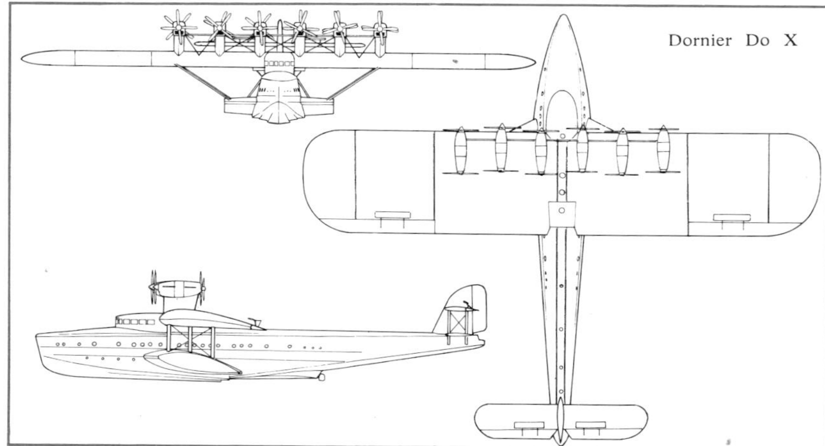
Dornier Do X

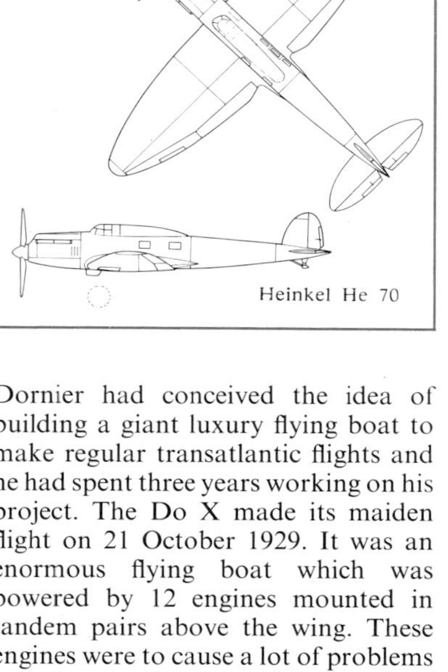
Heinkel He 70

Plate 89
Aircraft for Germany's growing civil aviation fleet: 1928–1935

During the 1920s and 1930s German commercial aviation expanded at a phenomenal rate. Deutsche Luft Hansa forged ahead relentlessly, determined to make up for lost time. It was during this period that some important aircraft were introduced, designed and built by companies which would later become world-famous, laying the bases of future German air power. One of them was Arado Handelsgesellschaft, which in 1928 made one of its few serious attempts at developing a civil transport. This company had ceased trading immediately after World War I, but in 1924 it had started up again, producing small trainers, most of which were biplanes. Deutsche Luft Hansa provided the stimulus which made Arado switch to the production of more modern types, when a mail-plane for the longer postal routes was ordered. Arado's designers wasted no time in producing the V 1, a single-engine high-wing monoplane which met Deutsche Luft Hansa's requirements very satisfactorily.

The Arado V 1 went on display at the Berlin air exhibition in October 1928, and Luft Hansa then took delivery of it and carried out proving flights to Marseilles, Seville, the Canary Islands and Istanbul. The aircraft crashed on 19 December 1929, but its achievements included Berlin–Seville, a distance of 1,610 miles (2,591 km) in 15 hours and Berlin–Istanbul in 11 hours.

In 1926 a larger and more powerful transport, the Rohrbach Roland, was built for Luft Hansa who operated six of them. It was followed in 1929 by the Roland II. These were high-wing trimotor monoplanes designed by Adolf Rohrbach who had also designed the impressive but ill-fated Zeppelin-Staaken E.4/20 in 1919, destroyed by order of the Allied Control Commission.

Nine Roland IIs were built. Luft Hansa employed these aircraft on some of its main European routes including services to Great Britain and Italy and some were still flying in 1936.

The same year, 1929, saw the appearance of the Dornier Do X, one of the most ambitious projects undertaken by the German aircraft industry in the inter-war years. This was the biggest aircraft of its day, weighing 52 tonnes on takeoff and seating up to one hundred passengers. In 1926 Claude Dornier had conceived the idea of building a giant luxury flying boat to make regular transatlantic flights and he had spent three years working on his project. The Do X made its maiden flight on 21 October 1929. It was an enormous flying boat which was powered by 12 engines mounted in tandem pairs above the wing. These engines were to cause a lot of problems and destroy the Do X's chances of success, since it was difficult to cool the rear engines. A great deal of time was devoted to correcting this and other problems and even an extended round-the-Atlantic publicity flight lasting ten months in 1930–1931 was beset by numerous problems. Only two Do X aircraft were ordered by Italy in 1931, intended for SANA to use on its Trieste – Venice – Genoa – Marseilles – Barcelona – Gibraltar – Cadiz service. These two aircraft were named after two famous Italian aviators, *Umberto Maddalena* and *Alessandro Guidoni*, but were never put into service. Instead they were handed over to the Regia Aeronautica for experimental flights and then dismantled.

In the early thirties Germany adopted a policy of rapid expansion for her civil aviation industry, partly as a cloak for her determination to rebuild a strong air force. A prerequisite for this objective was that Lufthansa should equip itself with a totally new generation of airplanes. One of these was the Heinkel He 70, an all-metal elegantly streamlined low-wing monoplane which had a four-passenger cabin. The prototype first flew on 1 December 1932, and the second aircraft broke eight world speed records over various distances with payloads of 500 and 1,000 kilograms. The He 70 was hailed as the fastest airliner in the world and twenty-eight civil and 296 military He 70s and He 170s were manufactured. Lufthansa operated these aircraft on European express services until 1938.

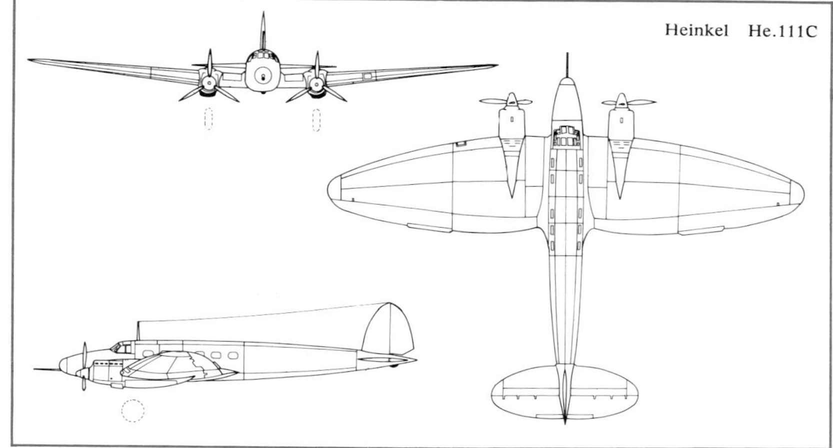
Heinkel He.111C

The revolutionary Heinkel He 70's success was repeated three years later when Heinkel again produced another winner, the He 111. This modern twin-engine type was to be one of the Luftwaffe's most widely-used bombers. The Prototype first flew on 24 February 1935, and only twelve civil examples were built. Six of these were He 111C variants; four were G and L models and Lufthansa also took delivery of the two prototypes. These airplanes saw service from the summer of 1936 and, although they entailed high operating costs, they were given a lot of exposure as a prestige exercise. In spite of being designed for commercial use, these He 111s were not, strictly speaking, true airliners, since their cramped fuselage limited capacity to a maximum of ten passengers.

Plate 90
American single-engine aircraft for mail and passengers: 1929–1931

One of the most interesting aspects of North American civil aviation in the late 1920s and early 1930s was the tremendous growth in the activity of developing airlines which operated a network of routes throughout the United States.

A great many different aircraft were used on these short- and medium-distance routes. One of them was the Stinson Detroiter, of which many variants were developed from 1926, culminating in the SM-1F Detroiter of 1929. These Detroiters made it possible for many small companies to operate profitably; one of them was later to grow into a very large airline: Braniff Airways, founded on 20 June 1928, which began by operating a Stinson SM-1 on the Tulsa—Oklahoma City route.

The Lockheed Orion made just as significant a contribution to the expansion of U.S. airways; this was the last and best of a series of models which had stemmed from J. K. Northrop's original Vega design of 1927. It was the first commercial aircraft to fly at speeds over 200 mph (321 km/h) and the Orion first went into service with Bowen Airlines in 1931, shortly afterwards being adopted by a number of users. Thirty-five Orions were built and five converted from earlier models. Two were operated in Europe by Swissair.

The Bellanca P-200 Airbus, which also came on the market in 1931 did not enjoy the success that it deserved, due to the economic depression. Its able designer and builder, Mario Bellanca, had produced an interesting single-engine type which could comfortably carry fourteen passengers (comparable with many contemporary three-engine commercial transports). Born in Italy, Bellanca had emigrated to the United States and had managed to build up a first-class aircraft manufacturing company. The Airbus prototype first flew in 1931, but only four civil versions were ever built and put on the market.

The Boeing Monomail had an indirect effect on design development and represented an advance in construction techniques; the two Monomails built foreshadowed many technological innovations which Boeing was later to apply to the revolutionary twin-engine 247. They were used to begin with as mailplanes only, and later to carry passengers as well. The original model was the 200 Monomail of 1930; this was followed shortly afterwards by the six-passenger Model 221; both models were subsequently modified and redesignated Model 221A, which could carry eight passengers as well as mail.

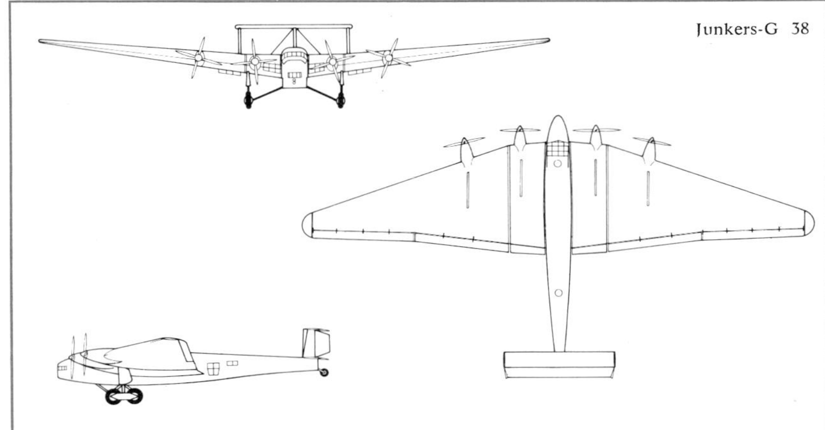

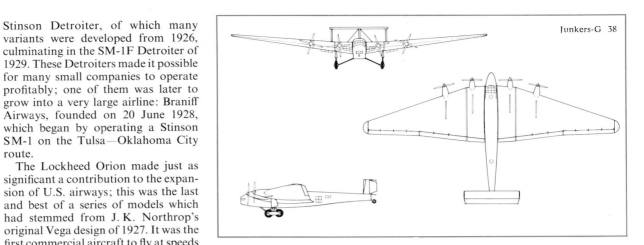

Junkers-G 38

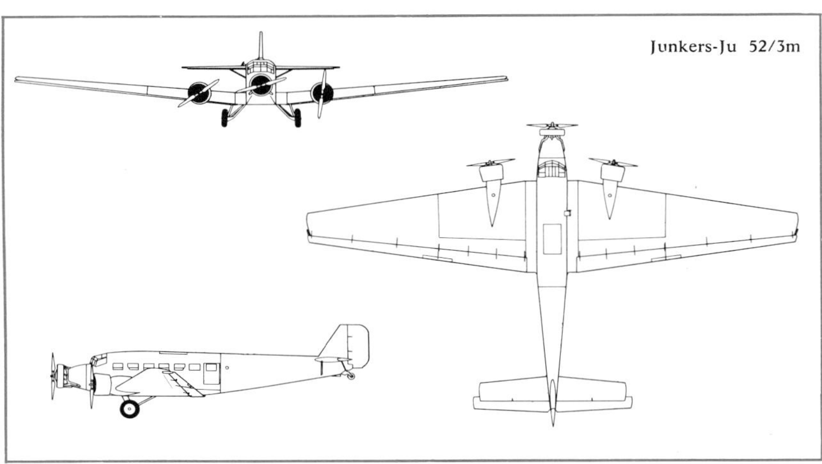

Junkers-Ju 52/3m

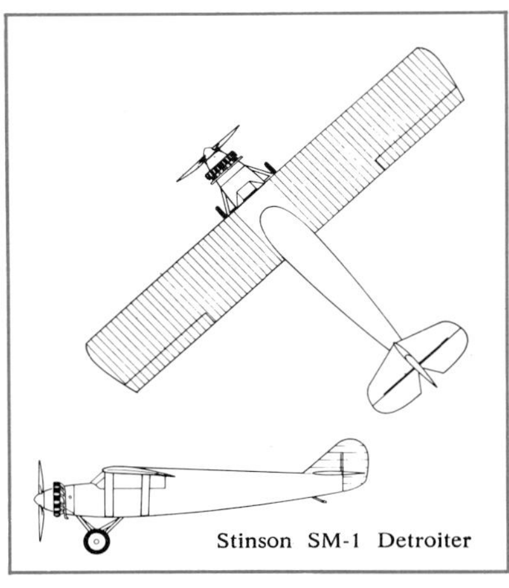

Stinson SM-1 Detroiter

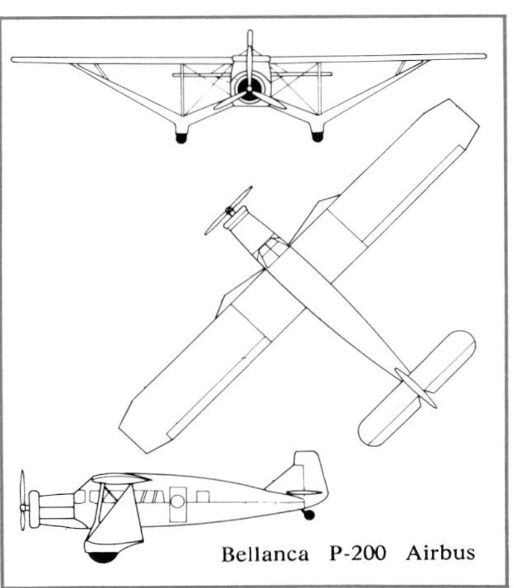

Bellanca P-200 Airbus

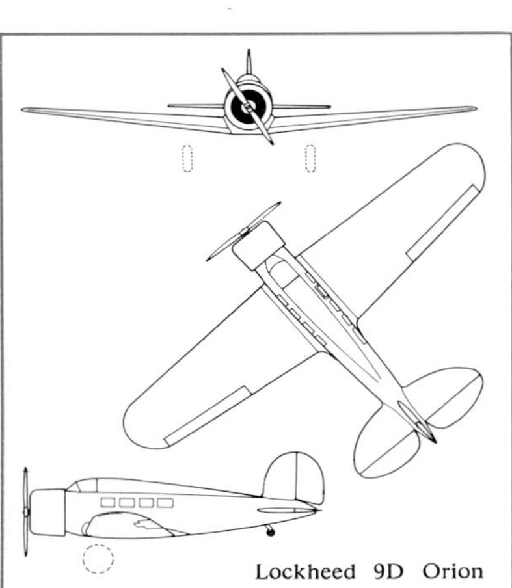

Lockheed 9D Orion

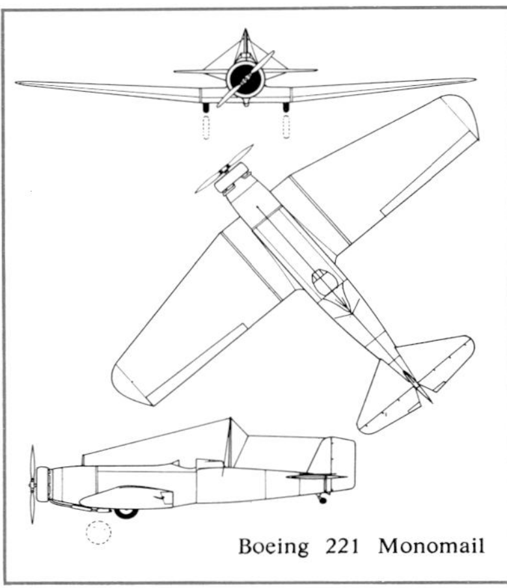

Boeing 221 Monomail

Plate 91
Junkers—a great name in civil aviation: 1929–1934

One of the greatest contributors towards the resurgence of German air power was Professor Hugo Junkers, a designer who had been very successful immediately after World War I. His four-engine G 38 was to be a milestone in civil aviation. This huge transport aircraft was virtually a "flying-wing" which created a sensation in aviation circles because of its originality and daring. Work began on construction in 1928 and the first of two G 38s built flew on 6 November the following year. The aircraft had an enormous wing, spanning 144 ft 4.25 in (44 m) with a root chord of 32 ft 9.5 ins (10 m), and these wings were 5 ft 7 in (1.7 m) thick. Within the multi-spar wings were the engines and fuel-load, part of the passenger accommodation (4 seats) and a large freight storage area. Changes were made in capacity, the accommodation was rearranged and other structural features were introduced in the second model which was delivered on 1 September 1931. Lufthansa put both these aircraft into service on their top international prestige flights and flew them until 1936.

In 1932 Junkers' most famous transport had its maiden flight. The three-engine Ju 52/3m started life as a tough, reliable transport plane and was then used as a warplane—nearly five thousand Ju 52s were manufactured. During the period 1932–39 some 200 Ju 52/3m civil aircraft were built and sold to about thirty airlines around the world and they became an important force in the development of civil aviation. The single-engine Ju 52 pro-

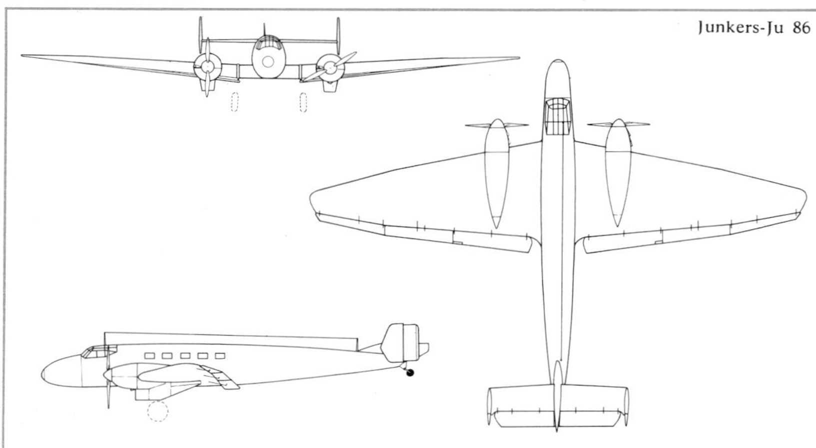
Junkers-Ju 86

totype took to the air on 13 October 1930, but only five of these were built. Instead the seventh or eighth aircraft off the production line was powered by three engines and this was the definitive prototype which first flew in April 1932. Production was soon under way and reached very high levels, in numerous variants, the main difference lying in the engines and equipment installed. Numerous radial as well as a few liquid-cooled engines were used. Lufthansa was the biggest customer for these three-engine aircraft (seventy-eight were still in service with the airline at the end of 1940) and used them on routes in many parts of the world, including Europe and the Far East. These aircraft were still flying well after the end of World War II: Spain and France kept them in service for many years and a few were still airworthy in 1982.

Junkers produced another advanced type in 1934. This was the Ju 86, a twin-engine aircraft which was Junkers' answer to a dual-purpose specification for a transport aircraft which could also be used as a bomber. Some fifty civil Ju 86s were built, but the vast majority of those manufactured (just under a thousand in many variants) went for military use. The prototype flew on 4 November 1934, and Swissair was among the first to take delivery of the new aircraft. Six other airlines

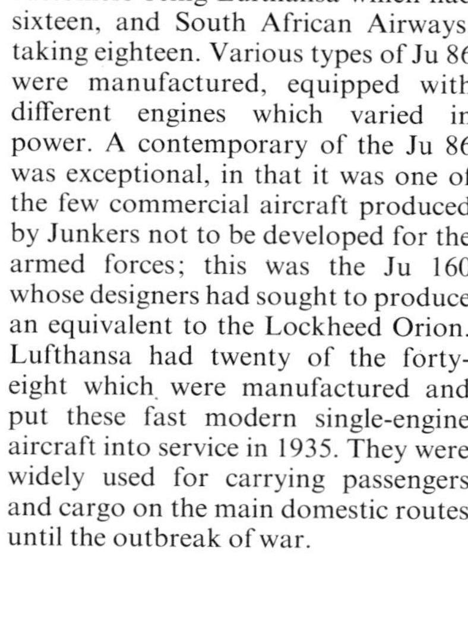

purchased the Ju 86, the two best customers being Lufthansa which had sixteen, and South African Airways, taking eighteen. Various types of Ju 86 were manufactured, equipped with different engines which varied in power. A contemporary of the Ju 86 was exceptional, in that it was one of the few commercial aircraft produced by Junkers not to be developed for the armed forces; this was the Ju 160 whose designers had sought to produce an equivalent to the Lockheed Orion. Lufthansa had twenty of the forty-eight which were manufactured and put these fast modern single-engine aircraft into service in 1935. They were widely used for carrying passengers and cargo on the main domestic routes until the outbreak of war.

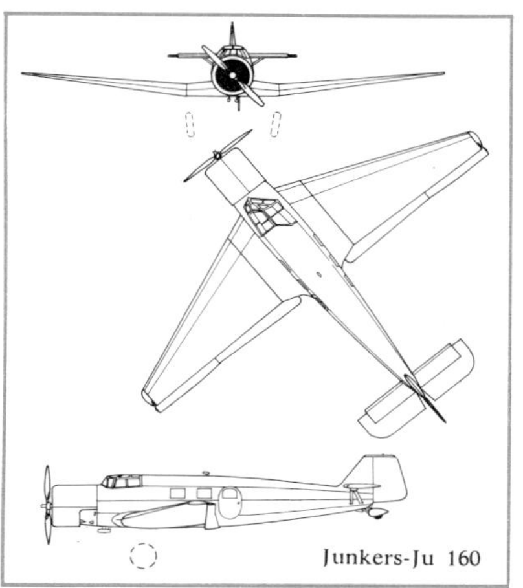
Junkers-Ju 160

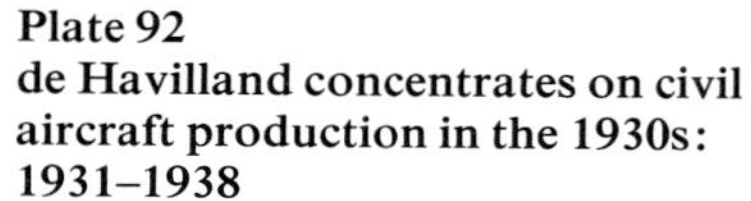

Plate 92
de Havilland concentrates on civil aircraft production in the 1930s: 1931–1938

The de Havilland Aircraft Company was probably more closely associated with the expansion of British civil aviation in the 1930s than any other manufacturer in Britain, and throughout this period de Havilland produced a succession of exceptional light aircraft.

Perhaps the most famous was the D.H.82 Tiger Moth. A total of 8,300 of these small biplane trainers was built and the Royal Air Force used the Tiger Moth as a basic trainer for fifteen years; many are still being flown from small airfields all over the world as they are still a favorite with private owners. The D.H.60 Moth of 1925 was the forerunner of the Tiger Moth. More than 1,700 D.H.60s were built, of which some 1,300 used the Gipsy engine designed and built by the de Havilland company itself. The simplicity, resilience, safety and low cost of this engine were to make it one of the main reasons for the Tiger Moth's success. The Tiger Moth made its maiden flight on 26 October 1931, and large-scale production began almost immediately, mostly for the Royal Air Force. In 1947 the R.A.F. declared the

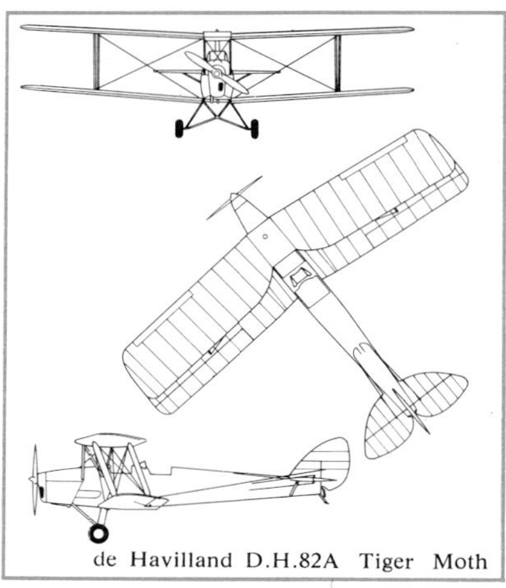
de Havilland D.H.82A Tiger Moth

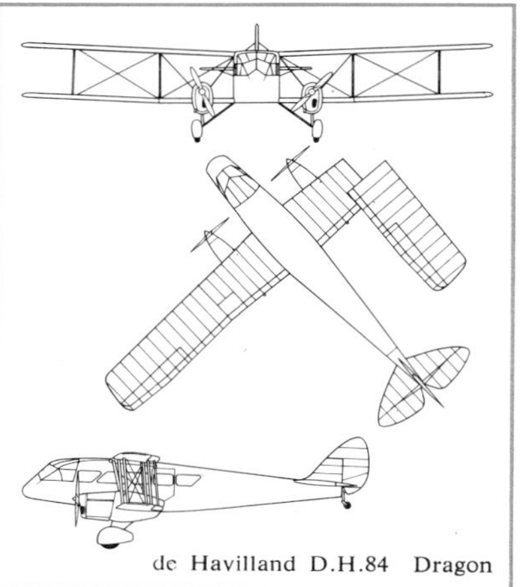
de Havilland D.H.84 Dragon

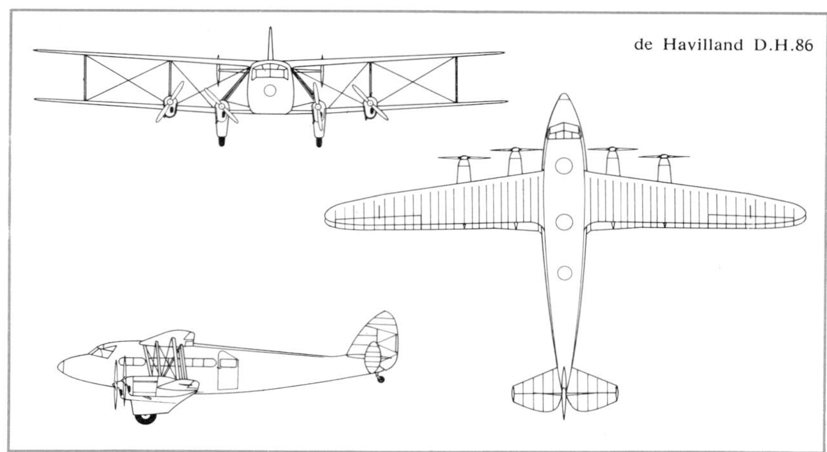
de Havilland D.H.86

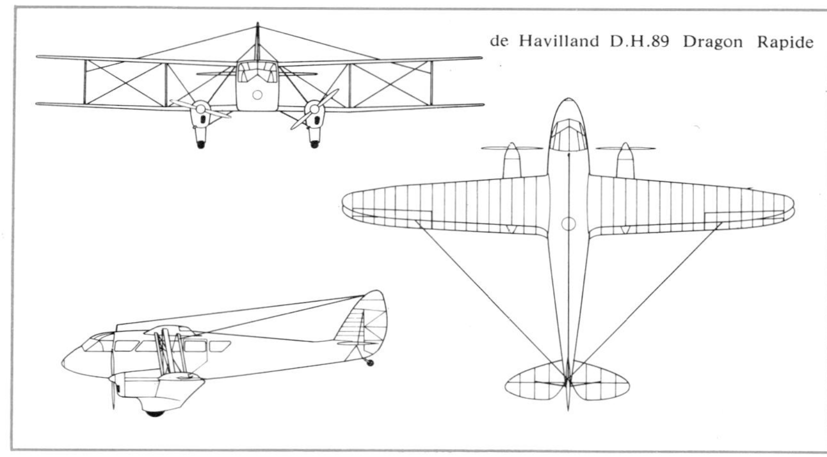
de Havilland D.H.89 Dragon Rapide

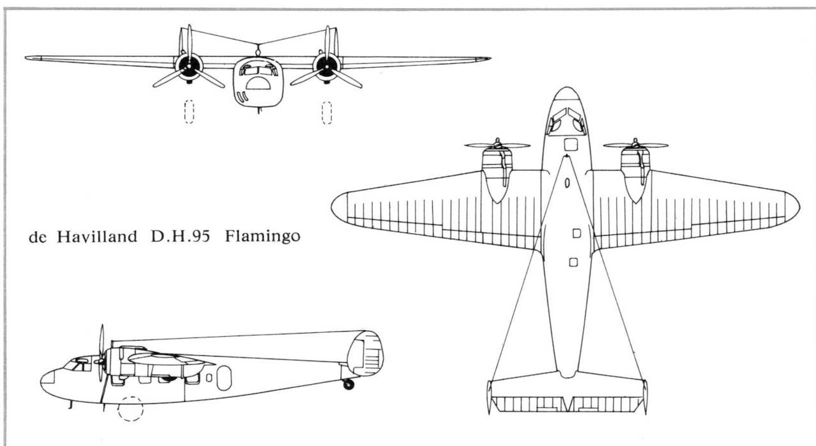
de Havilland D.H.95 Flamingo

Tiger Moth obsolete and thousands of these small biplanes suddenly came on to the civil market, where they were bought by private pilots and flying clubs and were given a second lease of life.

After the success of several de Havilland single-engine types, the company turned once more to the construction of a larger aircraft. The D.H.84 Dragon prototype first flew in 1932 and was the first of a series of famous multi-engine aircraft. The D.H.84 was a twin-engine, six-passenger biplane which had been specially ordered from de Havilland for use as a commercial transport on the Paris route. The Dragon was an instant success and de Havilland manufactured a total of 115 which were bought by numerous small airlines. Much larger than the Dragon, the D.H.86 took to the air on 14 January 1934. The aircraft had been developed for the Australian sector of the England–Australia route and was to be operated by Qantas between Singapore and Brisbane. It was a four-engine development of the D.H.84, which proved very reliable, considerably faster and had increased capacity. The production run totalled 62 and included 20 D.H.86As and 10 D.H.86Bs built in 1936–37 which had modified fuselages and strengthened tail surfaces. The D.H.86 started its career on 20 August 1934, with Railway Air Services and was used for many years in Europe, Africa, the Middle and Far East, New Zealand and, of course, Australia, in the livery of various airlines.

The last of this series was the D.H.89 Dragon Rapide, the prototype of which first flew on 17 April 1934. This aircraft was, in essence, an updating of the twin-engine D.H.84 with more powerful engines and improved performance. More than 700 were built during the course of over ten years and they were even more successful immediately after World War II, when many aircraft of the military variant, the Dominie, built for the R.A.F., came on to the civil market. A few Dragon Rapides are still flying in various parts of the world.

De Havilland's last civil transport aircraft before the outbreak of war was the D.H.95 Flamingo, a modern all-metal twin-engine monoplane, the prototype of which first flew on 28 December 1938. The fact that it was of all-metal construction represented a new departure from de Havilland's well-known tradition of specializing in wooden construction. Sixteen Flamingoes were manufactured, the prototype was operated by Jersey Airways in 1939, and others saw service during the war with BOAC in Africa and the Middle East, and with the Royal Navy.

Plate 93
Savoia Marchetti produces a succession of excellent aircraft: 1930–1939

After the success of its flying boats, especially the S.55 and the S.66, the Italian manufacturer, Società Idrovolanti Alta Italia, known as Savoia-Marchetti, turned to the production of landplanes to serve the civil transport market. The S.71 was the first in a long series of popular trimotors. This was a clean-lined cantilever monoplane of mixed steel, wood and fabric construction and Savoia Marchetti developed this formula which was a general favorite at the time and remained faithful to it for nearly all its subsequent production. The project got under way in 1930 and the S.71 first entered service with SAM two years later. Production was small, and there were two principal variants, one of which was powered by 240 hp Walter Castor engines, the other by 370 hp Piaggio Stella VIIs. SAM operated four aircraft belonging to the first series and two of the second, originally flying them on the Rome–Brindisi route and later on the Rome–Salonika run. The S.71s were to remain operational until 1937, as part of Ala Littoria's fleet.

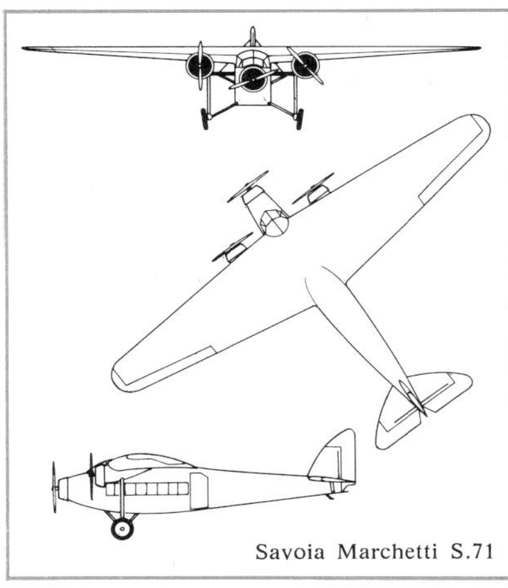
Savoia Marchetti S.71

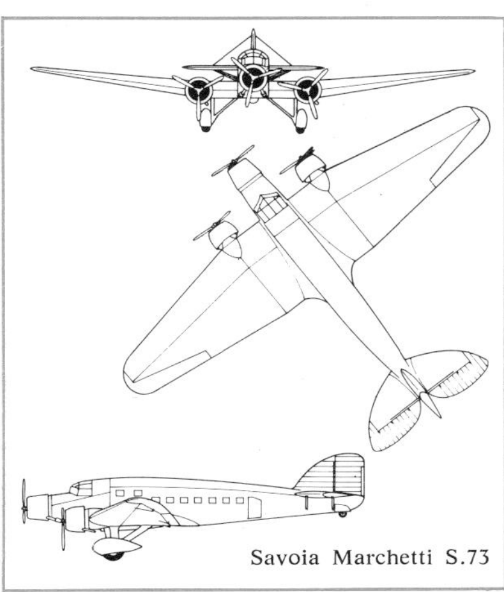
Savoia Marchetti S.73

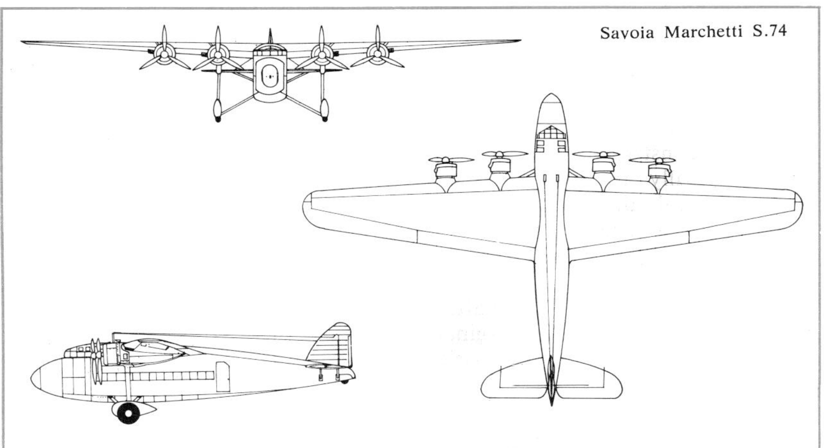
Savoia Marchetti S.74

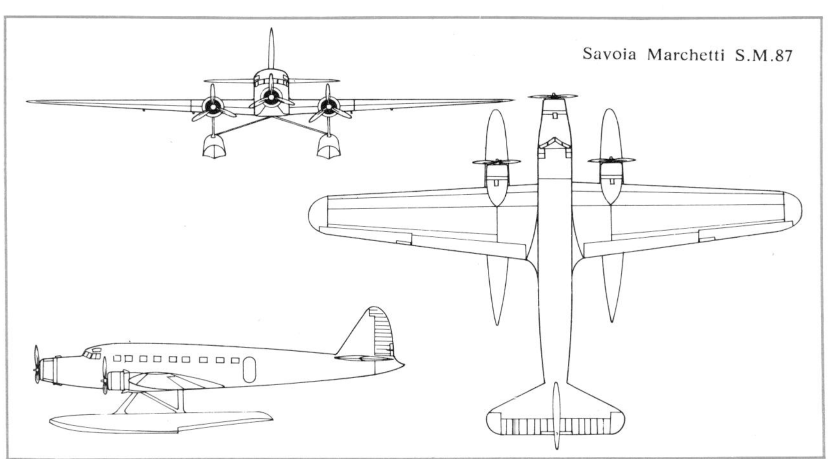
Savoia Marchetti S.M.87

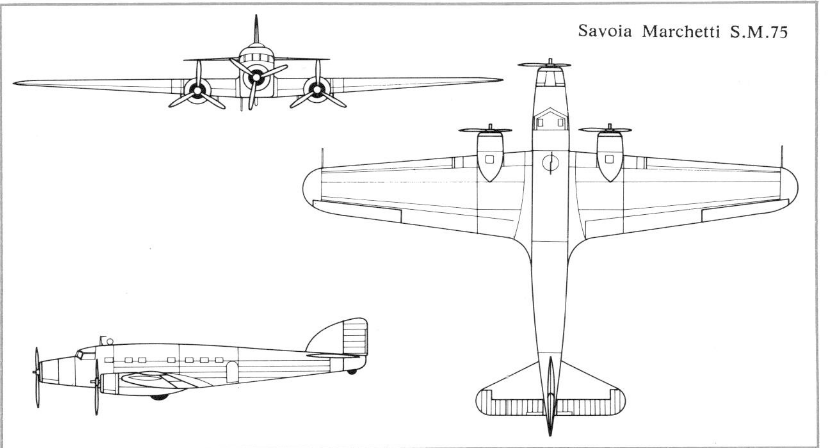
Savoia Marchetti S.M.75

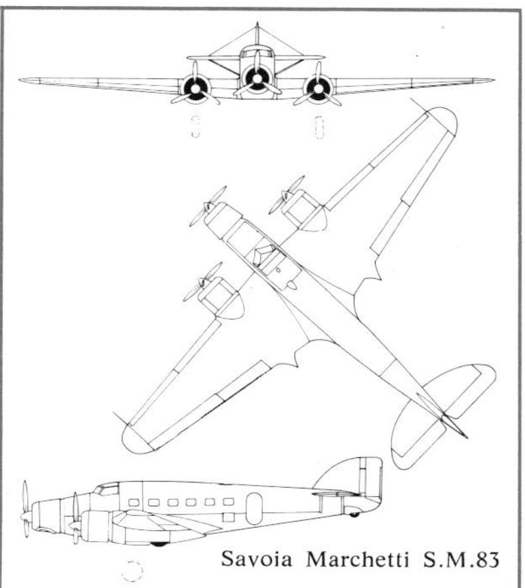
Savoia Marchetti S.M.83

It was the S.73, however, which truly established the Savoia family, resulting in some exceptionally fine aircraft, both civil and military. The prototype appeared in 1934, and had the low-wing, mixed-construction which was to remain virtually unchanged for a decade. Several different types of engine were installed in production series aircraft, including Piaggio Stella, Wright Cyclone, Gnome-Rhône Mistral, Alfa Romeo, and Walter Pegasus, but these made only marginal differences to the S.73's excellent basic performance. Five of the earliest aircraft off the assembly line went to the Belgian airline, Sabena; Ala Littoria bought twenty; Avio Linee Italiane six, and the Czechoslovak company ČSA took delivery of five, commencing in 1937; a further seven aircraft were built under license by SABCA in Belgium for Sabena who used them on European routes and on its demanding and difficult route to the Congo.

The first four-engine aircraft built by Savoia Marchetti was the exception in a long succession of trimotors; the S.74 was a large, high-wing monoplane and only three were built. The prototype first flew on 16 November 1934 and, after protracted proving trials which showed what excellent performance it could deliver, Ala Littoria took on its first S.74, using it to inaugurate their Rome–Marseilles–Lyons–Paris route, on 18 July the following year. From the summer of 1936 the three S.74s plied the Rome–Brindisi run and were later used for flights to Libya. When war started these aircraft were requisitioned by the Regia Aeronautica and used as troop and cargo carriers. All were destroyed during the war.

The first flight of the S.M.75 prototype on 6 November 1937, signaled a return to the three-engine formula. It was intended to be a successor to the S.73 and compared with its predecessor it was larger, decidedly more up-to-date and had improved performance. How much improved was clearly demonstrated when on 10 January 1939, an S.M.73 broke the world speed record over 1,240 miles (2,000 km) with a payload of 22,000 lb (10,000 kg), achieving an average speed of 205.656 mph (330.972 km/h) and also broke the world closed-circuit distance record on 30 July–1 August with 8,037 miles (12,935 km) in 57 hours 35 minutes flying time. Total production was ninety aircraft, many of which went to Ala Littoria which used the aircraft from 1938, on European and African routes. When war started, these aircraft were also handed over to the Regia Aeronautica and some were still flying in 1949. The war did, however, put paid to commercial use of the seaplane version of the S.M.75, the S.M.87, which was to have gone to the Argentine airline, Corporación Sudamericana de Servicios Aéreos, an associate company of the Italian airline, Ala Littoria. Four S.M.87s were completed in 1939 and all were militarized.

The last pre-war Savoia Marchetti civil trimotor was the S.M.83, a derivative of the S.M.79 bomber. The first aircraft appeared in October 1937, and twenty-three were built in three basic variants: the basic model, the S.M.83A, for transatlantic flights, and the S.M.83T mailplane. These were used by LATI (starting in December 1939), the Belgian company, Sabena, and the Romanian airline, LARES.

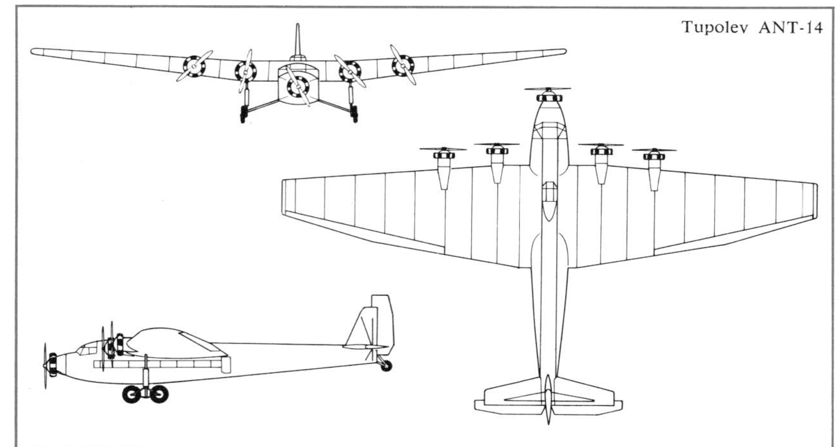
Tupolev ANT-14

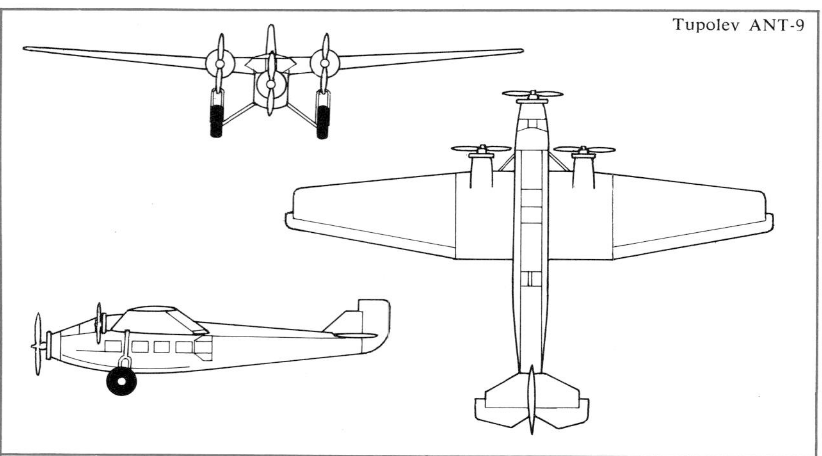
Tupolev ANT-9

Plate 94
Large Tupolev aircraft produced by Soviet state industry: 1929–1934

During the early 1930s very large aircraft were very much in favor in the Soviet Union. Fifteen years after the appearance of the first "giant" aircraft of aviation history, the Sikorsky *Ilya Mourometz*, the Soviet aeronautical industry reverted to the idea of producing an extremely large transport with high load capacity, and the Tupolev ANT-14 was the result. This all-metal monoplane was powered by five engines and could carry thirty-six passengers and six crew over 1,000 kilometers (621 miles). It was designed by Andrei Nikolaevich Tupolev, a young engineer who had started his career in 1920 at the Russian Central Aerodynamic Institute (TsAGI), founded in 1918 to promote aeronautical study, research and development. Tupolev's first project had been a small low-wing monoplane, powered by a 45 hp Anzani engine, but from this modest beginning he had rapidly risen to be one of the foremost aircraft designers of his generation.

In 1923 Tupolev designed the ANT-2, a small, single-engine all-metal transport monoplane; two years later he was responsible for the ANT-3, a two-seat biplane for civil and military use and then for the ANT-4, his first multi-engine aircraft. In 1927 this brilliant design engineer produced his first fighter, the ANT-5 (I-4).

Before designing his large ANT-14, however, Tupolev designed a transport on which work began in 1928. This was the ANT-9 which, with a later version, became one of the most widely-used types in the Soviet Union during the inter-war years. It was a high-wing, three-engine monoplane and was of all-metal construction, as was usual with Tupolev's designs.

The ANT-9 was powered by three 230 hp Gnome-Rhône Titan radials,

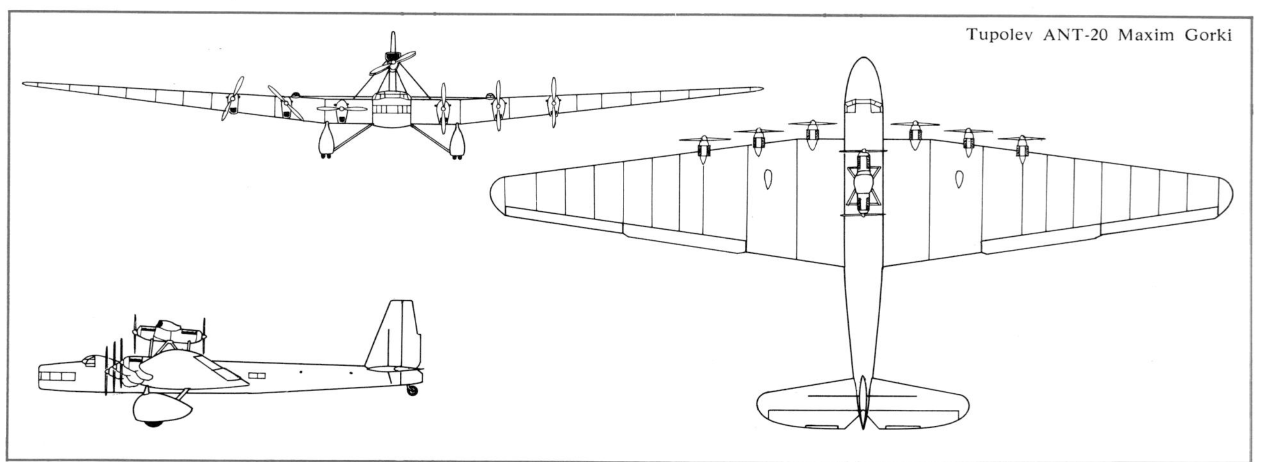
Tupolev ANT-20 Maxim Gorki

could carry nine passengers and, in winter, operate on skis. It had excellent performance and since it could use rough or semi-prepared airstrips it was ideal for communications and transport in the more inaccessible and remote areas of the immense Soviet territory. The prototype was completed on 28 April 1929, and in July and August of that year it made a 5,590 mile (9,000 km) propaganda flight in the livery of Dobrolet, having been named *The Wings of the Soviets*, visiting the main European capitals. One operator of the ANT-9 was the Russo-German company, Deruluft, which in 1932 equipped itself with a fleet of ANT-9s, putting them into service on the Moscow–Königsberg route. These aircraft were, however, also used a great deal for military propaganda flights and a special unit was formed for this purpose and was called the Maxim Gorki Squadron.

The ANT-9's success encouraged Tupolev to design a larger version in 1929. This was the ANT-14 which had almost double the wingspan of its predecessor and four times its capacity. The prototype had its maiden flight on 14 August 1931, but only one is known to have been built. Little is known of how much use was made of this large aircraft, but, called *Pravda* (Truth), it was flown by the Maxim Gorki Squadron on propaganda flights. The ANT-14 was also used for scientific expeditions in the Arctic and Siberia fitted, of course, with skis. It was finally put on view in a Moscow park, where it is reported as having been used as a cinema. Tupolev persisted in designing and building ever larger aircraft. Only one, ANT-20, was ever built and when it first flew on 19 May 1934, it was the largest landplane ever built. It was a vast monoplane with eight engines developing a total of 7,200 hp. Six were wing mounted but two in tandem were carried above the fuselage; the wings were 206 ft 8.25 in (63 m) long and the aircraft weighed 42 tonnes loaded.

The circumstances surrounding the aircraft's design and construction were somewhat unusual. In 1932 the Union of Soviet Writers and Publishers (YURGAZ) is said to have commissioned an aircraft to celebrate the anniversary of Maxim Gorky's first literary success. The ANT-20 was to be named after the famous writer and a squadron, also named after him, was also planned for propaganda purposes. The ANT-20 was not only a gigantic aircraft, it was also a flying laboratory with a small printing plant, a photographic studio, a cinema and a radio transmitting station on board; and as if this was not enough, illuminated signs and slogans could be displayed on the underside of the vast wings. Work got under way on the project in 1933, involving an entire factory and a workforce of 800 people. The aircraft's unusual dimensions made preliminary tests of single structural elements mandatory, so the construction process was very long and laborious. In spite of this the final assembly of the *Maxim Gorki* was completed just over a year later, in March 1934, at Moscow's Central Airport.

After the inaugural flight had taken place and test flights had been concluded the *Maxim Gorki* started to make a concentrated series of propaganda flights. These were not to continue for long, however, for almost exactly a year after the prototype's first flight it was destroyed on 18 May 1935, in a mid-air collision with an I-4 fighter. This disaster took a toll of forty-nine lives and national mourning was declared. Another subscription was launched (the first had raised six million roubles to build the original ANT-20) to pay for the construction of another three aircraft and Tupolev built the ANT-20bis which was just as large but powered by six engines. It is thought that only one of these airplanes was completed, in 1939, which was handed over to Aeroflot in May 1940, and put on the Moscow–Mineral'nyye Vody route as the PS-124.

Plate 95
Varied Soviet aircraft: 1929–1937

A variant of the popular ANT-9 was developed, which first appeared in 1932 designated ANT-9/M-17. The main difference between the two aircraft lay in their power units. Instead of three radials, Tupolev opted for twin 680 hp M-17 V-12s. This change of power unit improved performance and made further streamlining practicable. The operators of this aircraft were Dobrolet, and subsequently, Aeroflot. A total of some seventy of the two ANT-9 variants were reported to have been used by the two airlines.

Tupolev produced his first really up-to-date design when the ANT-35 appeared: a modern, all-metal twin-engine aircraft with a retractable undercarriage which drew its inspiration directly from the American Boeing 247. This project was launched in 1935 and after the prototype had undergone proving trials and test flights it was exhibited at the Paris Air Show the following year. The ANT-35 entered service on 1 July 1937, on the Moscow–Riga–Stockholm route. It is not known how many were built and to this day little is known of this interesting airplane's career. One of the few facts suggests that the ANT-35 was capable of excellent performance: in September 1936 the prototype made an experimental Moscow–Leningrad return flight of 785 miles (1,266 km) in just over three and a half hours, an outstanding achievement for an aircraft of this type.

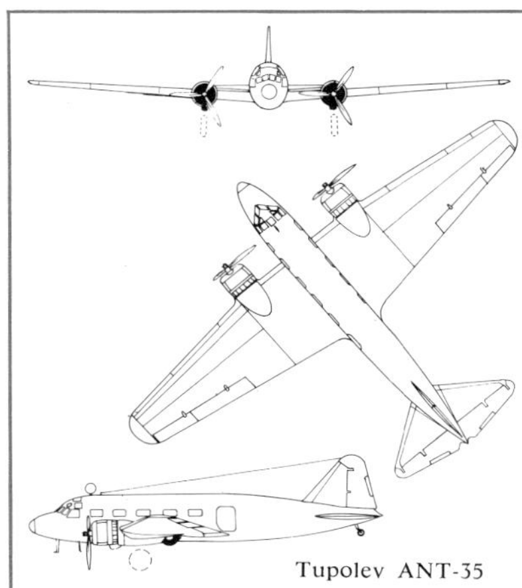
Tupolev ANT-35

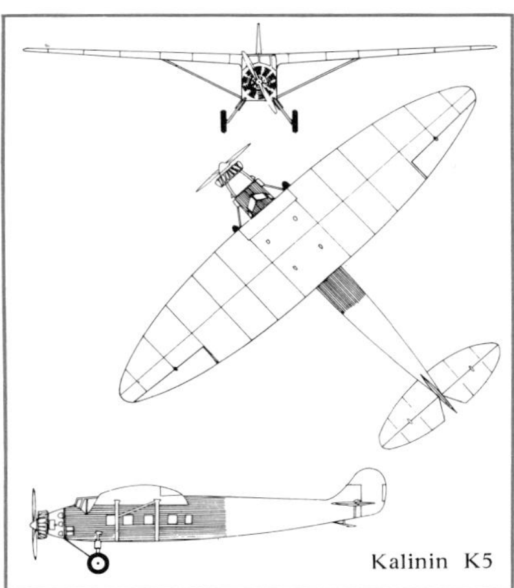
Kalinin K5

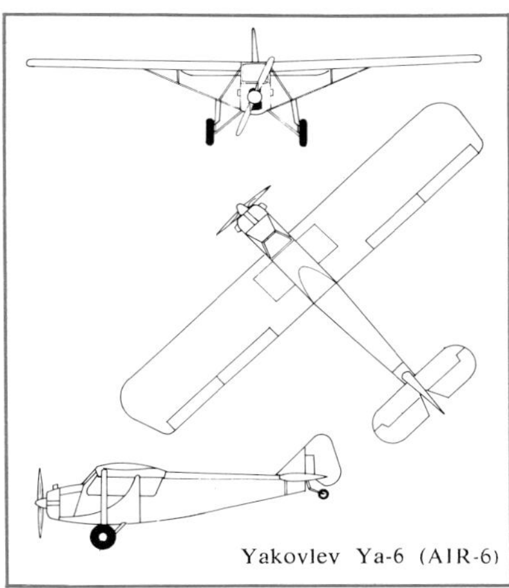
Yakovlev Ya-6 (AIR-6)

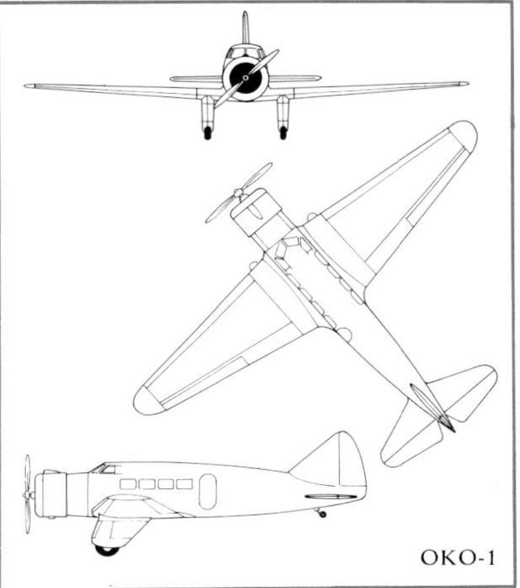
OKO-1

Tupolev, however, was not the only Soviet aircraft designer to produce worthwhile commercial airplanes during the 1930s. The Kalinin K5 was very widely-used on domestic routes in the Soviet Union and about 260 of these reliable and roomy single-engine monoplanes came off the assembly lines. The project had been developed in 1929 by Konstantin Alekseevich Kalinin and was derived from an earlier aircraft, the K4 of 1928, echoing its general lines and elliptical wings. Production centered on two versions, which had different engines and different coverings for the forward fuselage.

A small, multi-purpose monoplane in the light-aircraft category which was extremely widely-used was designed in 1932 by Alexander Sergeievich Yakovlev. The Ya-6, or AIR-6, was intended specifically for use as a short-range mixed transport. It is known that production numbers were very high and there were many variants, although no exact figures are available. Some were operated as seaplanes.

The OKO-1, however, was never to progress beyond the stage of prototype. It was a modern, single-engine experimental aircraft which was developed in 1937 very much along the lines of the Northrop Delta of 1934. The designer was Vsevolod K. Tairov who copied the structure and lines of the U.S. type, but built his model almost entirely of wood. The prototype flew in 1937 and revealed very satisfactory performance.

Plate 96
British light transport aircraft: 1933–1937

In the years leading up to World War II, one of the leading manufacturers of light aircraft in Great Britain was Airspeed. The little A.S.5 Courier was the forerunner of a successful series of aircraft. It was a low-wing monoplane with retractable undercarriage (the first time this feature had been adopted in series production aircraft in Britain), which had been designed in 1932 at the specific request of Sir Alan Cobham, who was planning to make a nonstop flight from Great Britain to India. The prototype was built in 1933 and underwent an exhaustive series of test flights and proving trials which were (in part) aimed at perfecting a practicable system of in-flight refueling. The Courier took off on the long-distance flight on 22 September 1934, but was not successful; Sir Alan had to make a forced landing in Malta and the attempt had to be called off. Meanwhile,

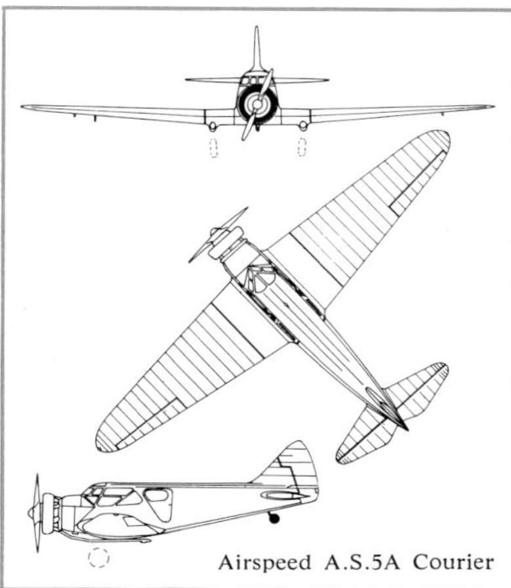
Airspeed A.S.5A Courier

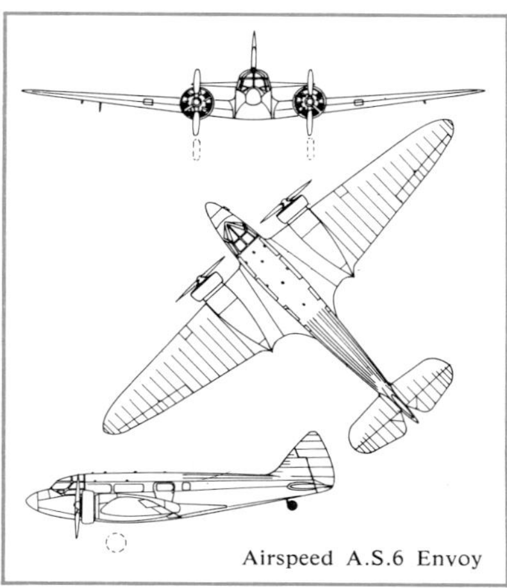
Airspeed A.S.6 Envoy

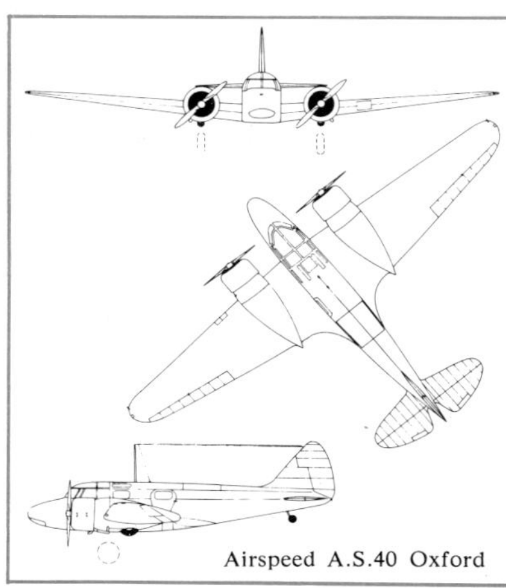
Airspeed A.S.40 Oxford

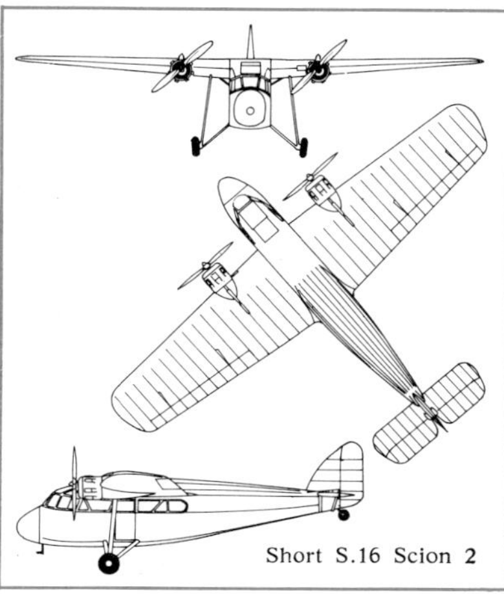
Short S.16 Scion 2

however, Airspeed had laid down a production line of fifteen Couriers, mostly to be designated A.S.5A. Several small companies took delivery of the Couriers and used them on domestic routes and also on flights to Paris. Only one of these Airspeed Couriers survived the war, eventually being scrapped in 1949.

In 1934 Airspeed produced a larger and more powerful successor to the Courier, the twin-engine A.S.6 Envoy. Despite the change to twin-engines and certain other logical alterations, the new aircraft had many features in common with its predecessor; these included the type of airframe and covering, certain sections of the wing and the retractable undercarriage. After the production of a few models belonging to the first series, production was concentrated on the Series II and III with more powerful engines and landing flaps. The Envoy had a brief sporting career, but was used a great deal by small domestic operators, and was particularly successful with such companies as North Eastern Airways and Portsmouth, Southsea and Isle of Wight Aviation which had already used Couriers. Some of these aircraft were also sold to overseas customers in China, India, South Africa and Czechoslovakia. One of the Envoy IIIs (G-AEXX) flew with the King's Flight from 1937 to 1939.

The most interesting development of this series was the A.S.10 Oxford, the prototype of which had its maiden flight on 19 June 1937. An enormous number (more than 8,500 in various models) was built and used in the flying schools of the Royal Air Force and Commonwealth air forces until 1954. A certain number, however, were put to civil use; some of these were used as executive and communications aircraft and assigned to the aircraft industry during the war. Once the war was over some Oxfords, redesignated A.S.40, were used in the civil market, once they had been taken out of service by the R.A.F. Owing to their limited passenger capacity these Oxfords were not very successful as post-war commercial transports and were mainly used as survey and aerial photography airplanes. Apart from armament, these models were identical with the military versions. A more complete civil conversion was the A.S.65 Consul, of which 161 were sold.

One of the Envoy's contemporaries, the Short S.16 Scion, was popular with smaller companies, although only twenty-two were built. The prototype appeared in 1933 and made quite an impression on the market as it marked a completely new departure from Short's usual designs, since this company's name had become synonymous with flying boats. The first four aircraft to be completed underwent a long series of meticulous tests and proving flights and as a result the principal version, the Scion 2, was developed, which appeared in 1935. The Scion was safe, quiet and comfortable and was used on short routes in the United Kingdom, Palestine, West Africa and Australia.

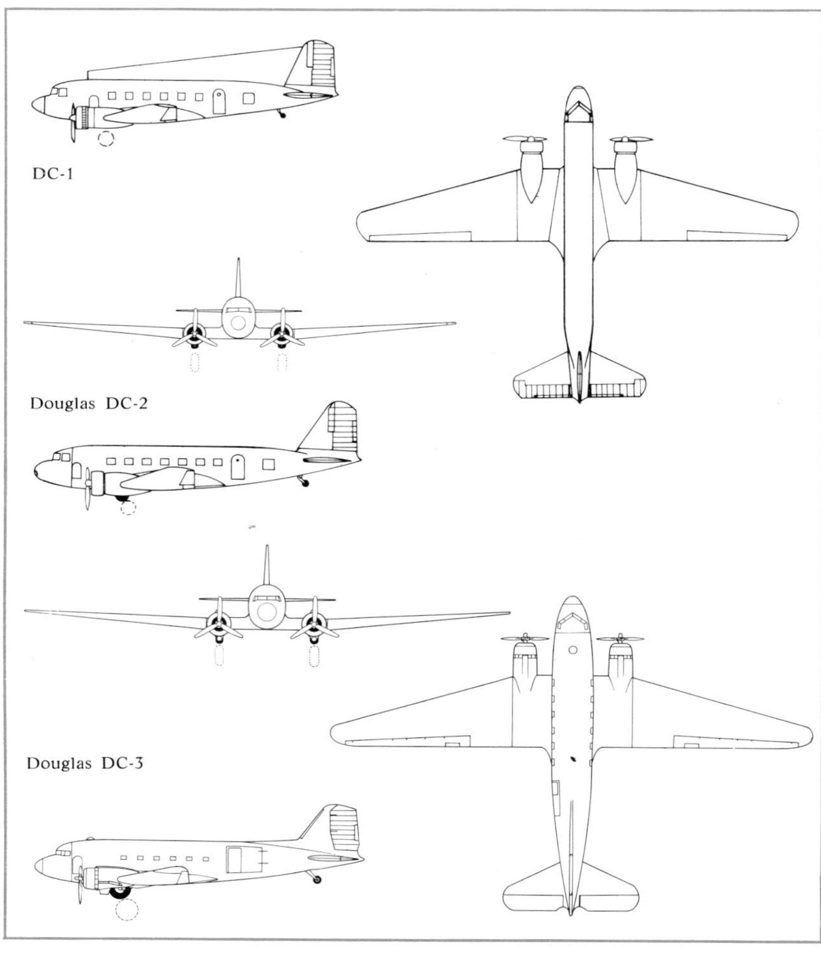

Plate 97
The amazing Douglas DC-3: 1933–1935

The Boeing 247's entry into service acted as a catalyst in the U.S. commercial aviation world. United Air Lines had managed to monopolize this revolutionary new airplane and captured such a large share of the passenger market that, in desperation, the other major airlines had to counter this threat if they were to survive. It was against this background that one of the most outstanding series of commercial aircraft in the history of aviation came into being: the product of a desperate search for an airplane with which to compete. This family was founded by the Douglas DC-1, progressed to the DC-2 and then to the immortal DC-3, the culmination of a great development line. Even today, more than forty-five years after it first appeared, the DC-3 is still flying, having survived not only World War II and other conflicts, but also the radical changes brought about by the evolution of air transport. During the course of its career the DC-3 underwent countless modifications—some authorized, some not, which mainly concerned the type of engines used and the interior layout of the aircraft. None of these affected the aircraft's qualities, except to enhance its performance or payload, and United States production of military and civil versions combined has totaled 10,654.

The project which brought this great family of DC (Douglas Commercial) transports to life originated in 1932 with an order from a vice-president of TWA, Jack Frye, for a new commercial transport to challenge the Boeing 247. The original specification was for a three-engine all-metal aircraft with a cruising speed of 150 mph (241 km/h), a range of 1,080 miles (1,738 km) and a service ceiling of 21,000 ft (6,400 m), which could carry at least twelve passengers in maximum comfort. Five constructors submitted designs, but the Douglas Aircraft Company was the first to respond. Five days after receiving TWA's letter and following the ensuing three weeks' of discussions, the designers James "Dutch" Kindelberger and Arthur Raymond convinced the management of TWA to accept a twin-engine aircraft within the safety

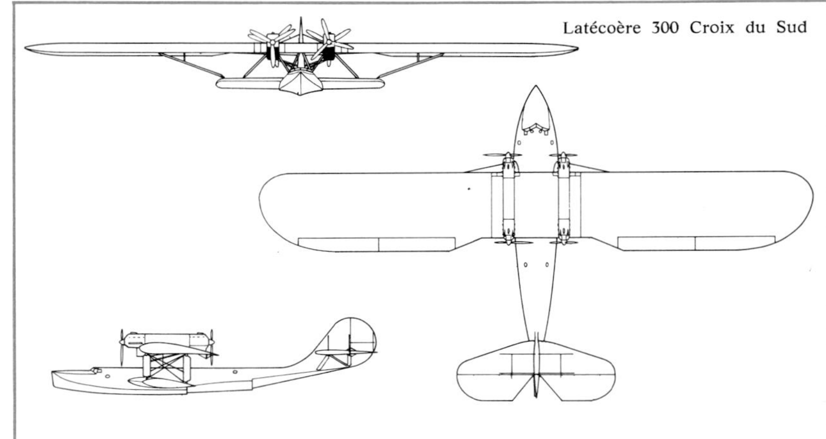
Latécoère 300 Croix du Sud

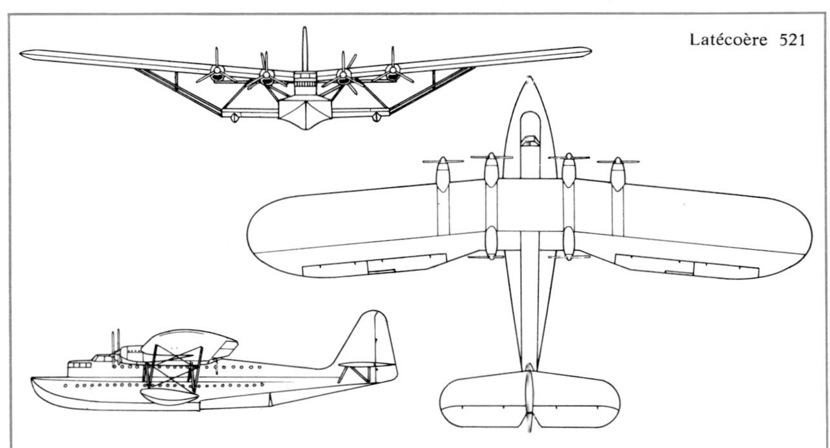
Latécoère 521

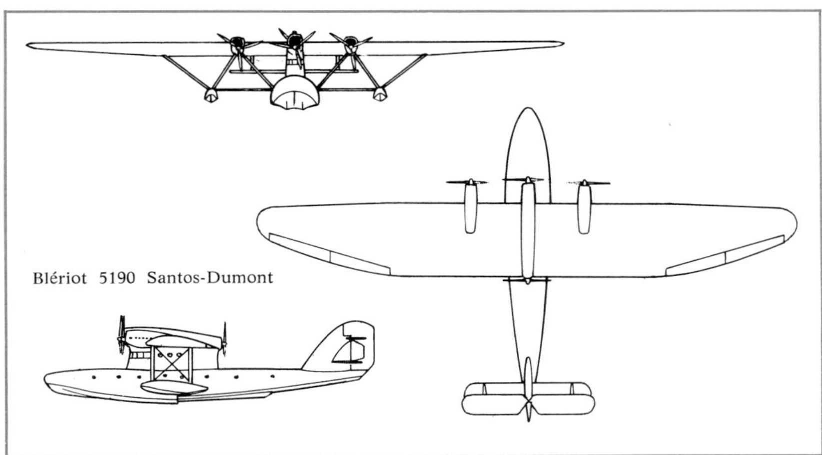
Blériot 5190 Santos-Dumont

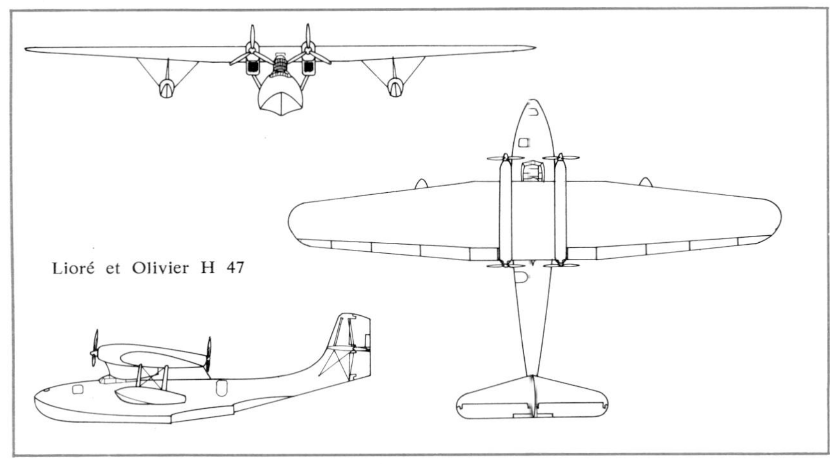
Lioré et Olivier H 47

margins required. On 20 September 1932, the prototype was ordered, with a further option on sixty production aircraft.

Detailed engineering work began immediately and the prototype first flew on 1 July 1933. It was an elegant, low-wing monoplane which not only incorporated the main features of its rival, the 247, but embodied many more advantages. The new aircraft delivered more than TWA had asked for, not only in capacity but also in cruising speed and range. The aircraft was delivered to TWA in December and, on 19 February 1934, it broke the U.S. coast-to-coast speed record, going on to set a whole series of nineteen national and world speed and distance records. When they realized the edge their new aircraft had on the 247, TWA decided to maximize this design's potential and, instead of the DC-1, immediately ordered twenty of the improved 14-passenger model, the DC-2. The DC-2 had increased capacity, more power and even better performance. It flew for the first time on 11 May 1934, and a week later was flying with TWA on the Columbus–Pittsburg–Newark route, bettering all the 247's flying times. On 1 August the DC-2 was put on the longest and most important run, from New York to Los Angeles, a flight lasting 18 hours. This newcomer's devastating success immediately changed the airlines' market shares, with TWA becoming the clear leader.

United Air Lines and all the other companies could only wait their turn in the queue for the Douglas aircraft once TWA's expanded order for thirty-one DC-2s had been completed. This new airplane was also tremendously popular with European airlines. The first European company to take delivery of a DC-2 was KLM and following its splendid performance in the MacRobertson London–Melbourne race in October 1934, the Dutch airline ordered fourteen more DC-2s. Other European companies soon followed suit. In all Douglas built 198 DC-2s and the production line was closed in 1936 when manufacture switched to its successor, the DC-3.

The DC-3 originated in much the same way as the DC-1. This time, however, the request came from American Airlines. In 1934 Douglas was asked to develop a new aircraft to replace the airline's aging Fokker trimotors and Curtiss Condor biplanes on night flights. In a bid to remain competitive, the president of American Airlines, C. R. Smith, sought a stretched version of the DC-2 which could carry as many passengers in sleeping berths as the DC-2 did in daytime seating. The result was a larger, strengthened and more powerful version of the DC-2 which flew for the first time on 17 December 1935, and was originally called the DST (Douglas Sleeper Transport). American Airlines put the first of its new fleet into service on 25 June 1936, on the nonstop New York–Chicago flight. The daytime version, the DC-3 with 21 seats, was even more successful and cost-effective than its predecessor, and Douglas was literally inundated with orders. Up to the time of the Untied States' entry into World War II, a total of 430 DC-3s and DSTs had been built which were used by most American airlines and several major European airlines. In 1939 the DC-3 had achieved the enviable position of accounting for ninety percent of the world's airline trade.

Plate 98
Four French flying boats for transatlantic routes: 1931–1936

The fascination of transatlantic flight continued to stimulate European aircraft manufacturers and nowhere more than in France. Here much effort was put into constructing aircraft for this purpose and some of the best flying boats of the 1930s were produced by French designers. The Latécoère 300 was one of the most famous in its day. It was developed in 1931 in response to a specification from the French Government which was seeking a mailplane which could carry a tonne of mail on the South Atlantic route. This large four-engine flying boat went into service on 31 December 1933, and immediately broke a world record, flying 2,285 miles (3,679 km) from Marseilles to St. Louis, Senegal, in just under twenty-four hours. The prototype was called *Croix du Sud*, (Southern Cross) and completed fifteen crossings from Dakar to Natal but, on 7 December 1936, it was lost at sea with its pilot Jean Mermoz and crew. Six other Laté 300s were built, three for Air France (Laté 301) and three for the French Navy (Laté 302). The civil models were delivered by early 1936.

Another type, the Blériot 5190, designed to meet a 1928 specification, only made its first flight on 11 August 1933. This flying boat had also been ordered as a mailplane for the South American run and the Blériot 5190 made its first Dakar–Natal flight on 27 November 1934. The aircraft was named *Santos-Dumont* and completed twenty-two ocean crossings for Air France, shortening the overall flying times between Toulouse and Buenos Aires considerably.

An extremely ambitious project was

launched by Latécoère when the Model 521, a very large flying boat powered by six engines, was built. This flying boat could carry thirty people across the North Atlantic or seventy passengers over the Mediterranean. Services to the United States never got under way because of the outbreak of war, but the Laté 521 completed an experimental flight to New York during the period 23–31 August 1938, via Lisbon and the Azores, showing that it had great potential. Construction of the big flying boat was begun in 1933 and the prototype, which had been given the name *Lieutenant de Vaisseau Paris*, first flew on 17 January 1935. On its first flight to North America, however, the Laté 521 was sunk in a typhoon on 4 January 1936; it was recovered and had to be almost completely rebuilt. In 1937, after reconstruction, the aircraft broke several speed, distance and load records. Four other Laté 521 series aircraft were built, but these never saw commercial use; one, the Laté 522, was lent to Air France—Transatlantique and the three Laté 523s were bought by the Navy. The war was also to be responsible for circumscribing the development of another interesting flying boat: the Lioré et Oliver H 47, built to a specification issued by the French Government in 1934. The prototype flew on 25 July 1936, but a serious accident hindered progress. Only in 1938 was the first production aircraft completed as part of an Air France order for five H 47s. By this time France faced another war and the H 47s went to the French Navy.

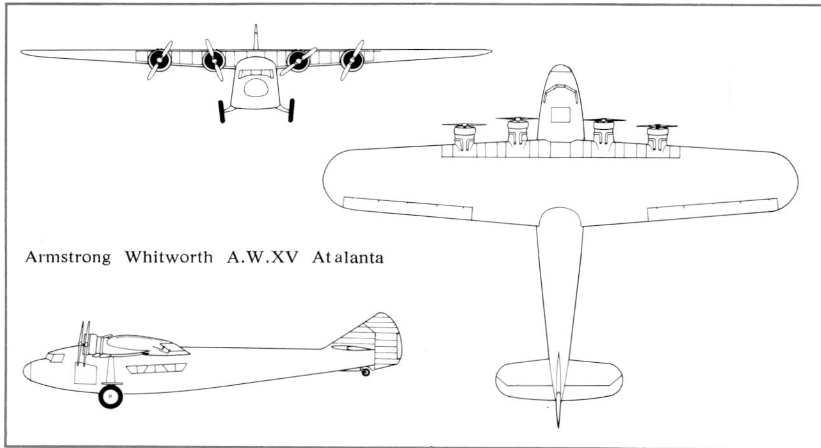
Armstrong Whitworth A.W.XV Atalanta

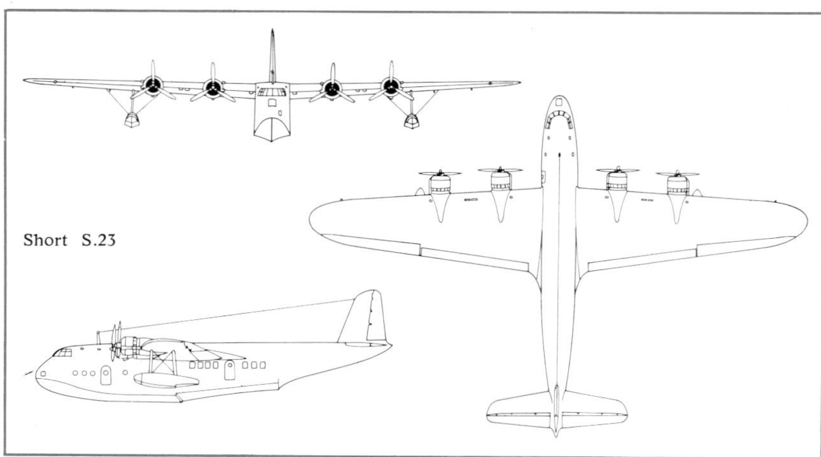
Short S.23

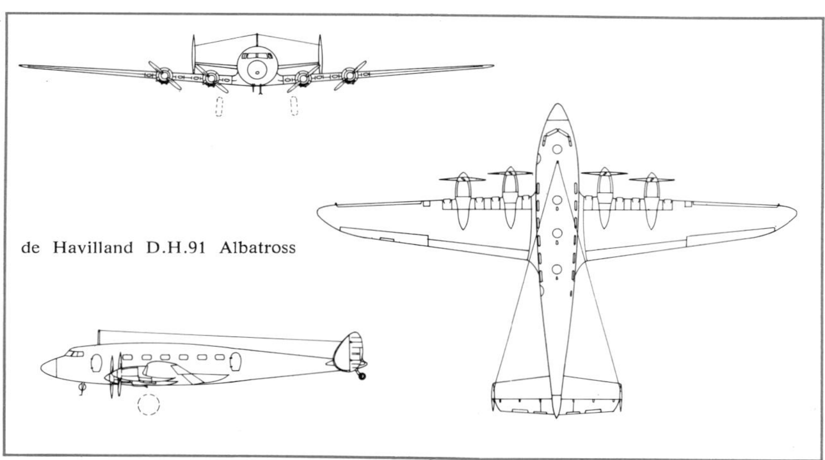
de Havilland D.H.91 Albatross

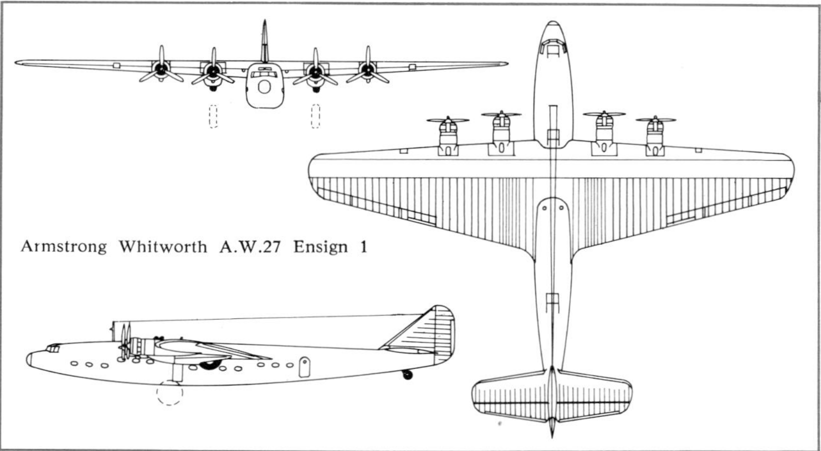
Armstrong Whitworth A.W.27 Ensign 1

Plate 99
British four-engine airliners: 1932–1938

The British aircraft industry was particularly successful in developing four-engine aircraft during the 1930s. Among the first transport of this type was the Armstrong Whitworth A.W.XV Atalanta, an adaptable and safe high-wing monoplane which was evolved to meet the specific needs of Imperial Airways' African and Far Eastern routes. The order was placed in 1931 and the first of eight aircraft manufactured made its first flight on 6 June the following year. A route proving flight from London to Cape Town began on 5 January 1933, and on 29 May the *Astraea* began a survey flight from London to Australia. For several years these aircraft operated the routes between Central and South Africa, and Karachi and Singapore. In 1941 five Atalantas were transferred to the R.A.F. and then to the Indian Air Force.

But the type of aircraft which was the real lynch-pin of Imperial Airways' dependable longhaul services was a long series of flying boats which were built by Shorts and known under the collective name of Empire flying boats. The aircraft which founded this important new family of transports was the S.23, forty-one of which were built in three variants between 1935 and 1939. *Canopus*, the first of these flying boats had its maiden flight on 4 July 1936. The project had been started in 1934 following a decision by the British Government that all first-class mail for British territories should be carried by air without surcharge. Thus it was decided to commission a fleet of new long-range passenger and freight carriers for Empire routes.

Imperial Airways had laid down the technical and operational specifications for the design and placed an order for twenty-eight of these new aircraft. The new fleet was urgently required and the S.23s went straight into series production without waiting for a prototype. Shorts made a brilliant job of solving the quite considerable problems involved by carrying out experiments with two Short S.16 Scions, one of which was a four-engine model. Once proving flights were completed the first S.23 was delivered to Imperial Airways on 20 October 1936, and on the 22nd it left Rochester on its first proving flight to the Mediterranean. The first scheduled C Class service left Alexandria for Athens on 30 October. All the flying boats in this series were given names beginning with the letter C, and they were collectively known as the C Class flying boats. On 8 February 1937, C Class flying boats began regular operation between Southampton and Alexandria; in May they began operating as far as Kisumu on Lake Victoria and on 2 June began working right through to Durban; on 16 June the *Cavalier* opened a Bermuda–New York service; services to Karachi began on 3 October; and on 26 June 1938, the first through flying boat service to Australia left Southampton.

In July 1937 a route proving flight over the North Atlantic was made by one of these S.23s without payload, taking off from Foynes (in Ireland) in the evening of 5 July and reaching New York on 9 July. The commercial success of the S.23 led Imperial Airways to expand their fleet and, late in 1937, the company ordered a further eleven aircraft, eight of which were strengthened and had more powerful engines: these were designated S.30. On 5 August 1939, one of these S.30s inaugurated Imperial Airways' North Atlantic experimental weekly mail service. The other Empire boats ordered that year were designated S.33. The war did not put an end to these flying boats' careers; they maintained essential communications and did outstanding work in the Mediterranean and with Qantas Empire Airways in the southwest Pacific. Thirteen survived the war and continued in commercial operation. The final flight of the last C Class flying boat (*Coriolanus*) took place on 20 December 1947, between Noumea and Sydney, flying in the livery of the Australian airline Qantas.

On European routes in 1938 Imperial Airways began to operate an elegant and fast four-engine landplane, the de Havilland D.H.91 Albatross. Although only five series aircraft were ever built, they proved extremely competitive in service up to the outbreak of war. The project had been initiated, as a transatlantic mail carrier, in 1936, and the first of two prototypes flew for the first time on 20 May the following year, creating something of a sensation when it first appeared; partly because its design seemed to be a completely new departure from de Havilland's previous ideas and partly because of the brilliant performance its excellent aerodynamics made possible. *Frobisher*, the first of the five Albatross passenger aircraft was delivered to Imperial Airways in October 1938. These aircraft were known as the F Class and all bore names beginning with the letter F.

Armstrong Whitworth's last prewar commercial transport was the A.W.27 Ensign, an up-to-date four-engine monoplane which at the time of its entry into service was the largest airliner ever used by Imperial Airways. The first example made its first flight on 24 January 1938, and was followed by eleven of the initial production model and two of the second variant, the Ensign II, which had more powerful engines. It commercial career commenced on 24 October 1938, with *ad hoc* services to Paris. Once World War II had started, these Ensigns (or E Class aircraft, as they were known, again following the first letter of their names) flew with BOAC on routes to Africa and India until January 1946.

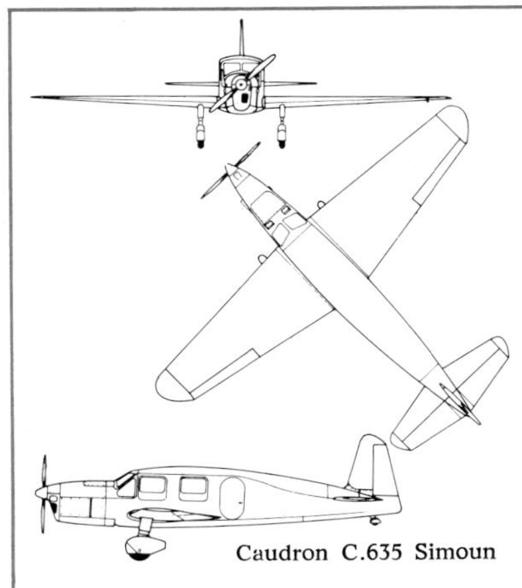
Caudron C.635 Simoun

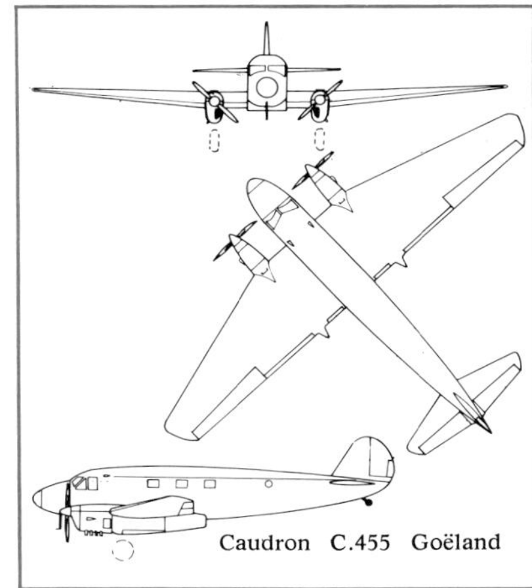
Caudron C.455 Goëland

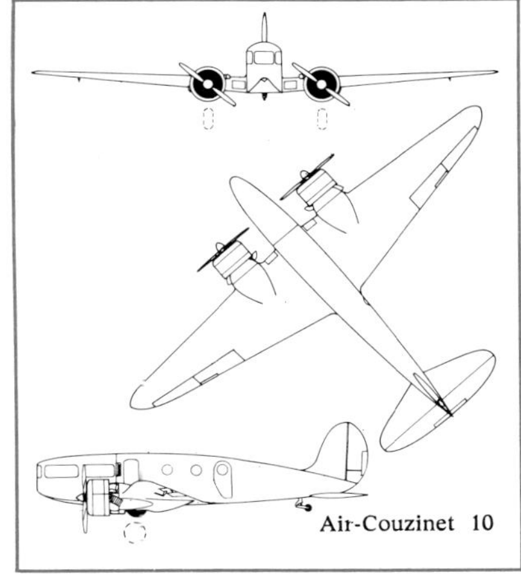
Air-Couzinet 10

Plate 100
Minor French aircraft: 1934–1937

France manufactured airplanes in great numbers during the years leading up to World War II and many of them deserve mention, not only for their contribution to commercial aviation but also for their achievement in record-breaking and, in some cases, simply because of the originality of their design. Among those to be included in this last category was the Mignet Pou du Ciel (The Flying Flea), a tiny, airplane designed for construction by amateurs and the forebear of all today's homemade aircraft. In the years 1933–36 it was popular with British enthusiasts; over 120 were built by enterprising private flyers, whereas in France it was considered dangerous and at that time failed to get a Certificate of Airworthiness. There were several fatal accidents in Britain alone. Its inventor was Henri Mignet, an ingenious enthusiast who decided to built himself his own airplane in which he was going to learn to fly. Having successfully completed his little tandem-winged aircraft, Mignet was so enthusiastic about his idea that he wrote a manual in which he gave details of his design and instructions for building and piloting the aircraft; this sold extremely well.

The Caudron C.630 series Simoun was, in contrast, a thoroughly airworthy light airplane. It became particularly well known through several long-distance flights, its busy competition career and its use on French domestic mail services. This elegant single-engine cabin monoplane was shown for the first time at the 1934 Paris Air Show and scored an instant success. More than seventy Simouns were built for the civil market and there were 140 military models. There were several different versions and the type numbers, such as C.635, identified the particular model. Among its more outstanding achievements was its flight from Le Bourget to Tananarive (Madagascar), covering 5,384 miles (8,664 km) between 18–21 December 1935, in 57 hours 36 minutes flying time. Another commercial light transport, the Potez 56 of 1934, had some success in export sales to Chile and Romania. About 27 civil examples were manufactured, the prototype made its maiden flight on 18 June 1934, and then flew with the Potez Aéro Service between Bordeaux and Bastia from 15 May 1935. Two Potez 56s saw service with the Régie Air Afrique in Algeria and Tunisia and six served LAN-Chile.

The Bloch 220 was a far more impressive twin-engine type, a sound and capacious aircraft which enjoyed a long career on European routes as part of Air France's fleet. The prototype flew in December 1935, and another sixteen 220s were produced. The type was operated from December 1937, on the Paris–Marseilles run. Five Bloch 220s which had survived the war and been equipped with new engines and designated Bloch 221s, were still in Air France service in 1949.

After the war, France's national airline also readopted a small twin-engine monoplane which had first appeared in 1935: the Caudron Goëland, which was one of the most widely-used airplanes of the day. More than 1,700 of these aircraft were manufactured in differing versions which were allocated designations from C.440 to C.449 and production continued well after the end of World War II, during which many of these aircraft were built.

In the prewar years the Goëland was widely employed by small operators in France and in Africa. They operated with Air France and Air Bleu and Régie Air Afrique. Caudron Goëlands also found foreign buyers in Yugoslavia, Bulgaria, Argentina and Spain. Another twin-engine type which appeared in 1937 was built by René Couzinet to compete in the Istres–Damascus–Paris race, to be held in August 1937, but met with bad luck.

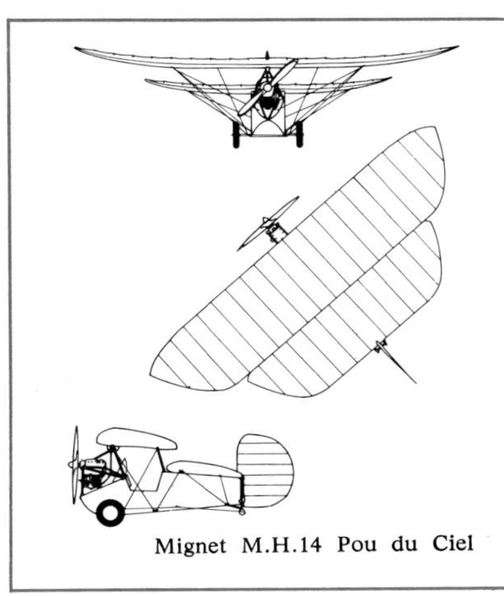
Mignet M.H.14 Pou du Ciel

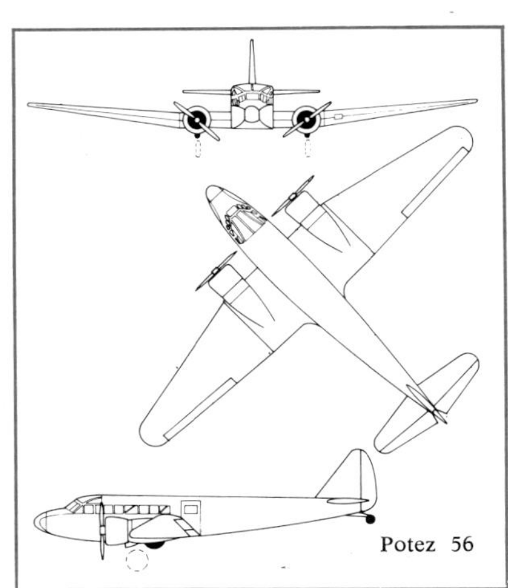
Potez 56

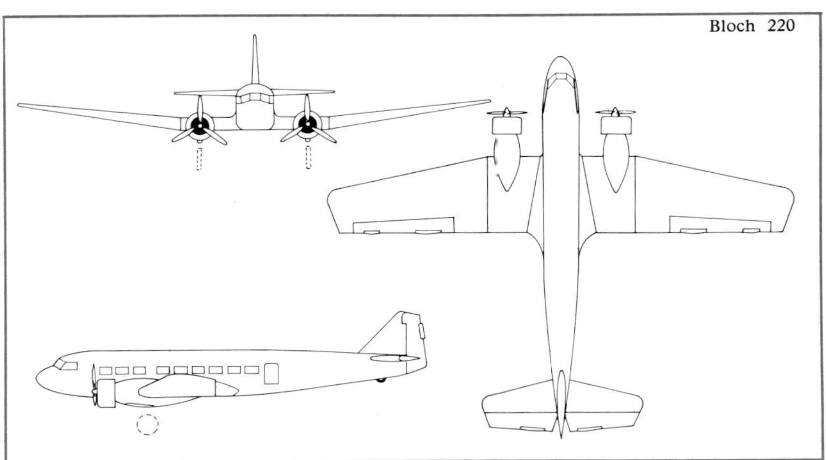
Bloch 220

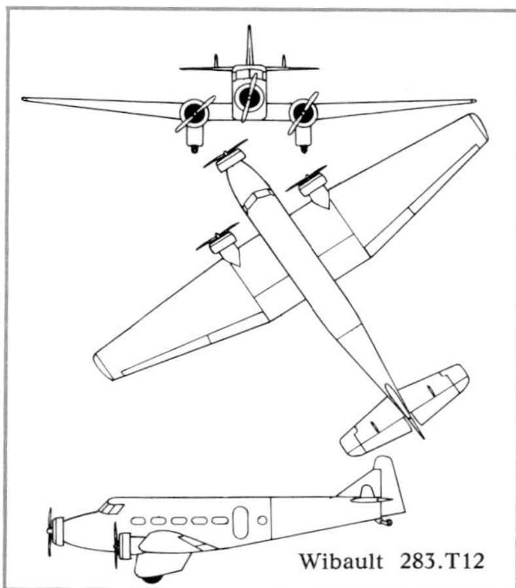
Wibault 283.T12

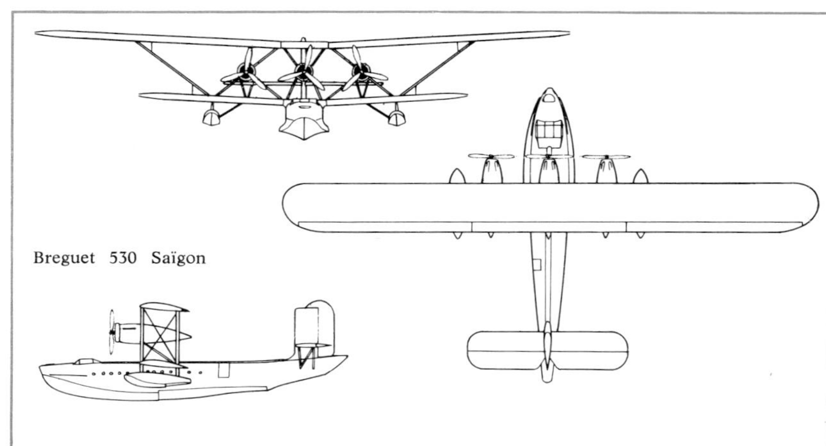
Breguet 530 Saïgon

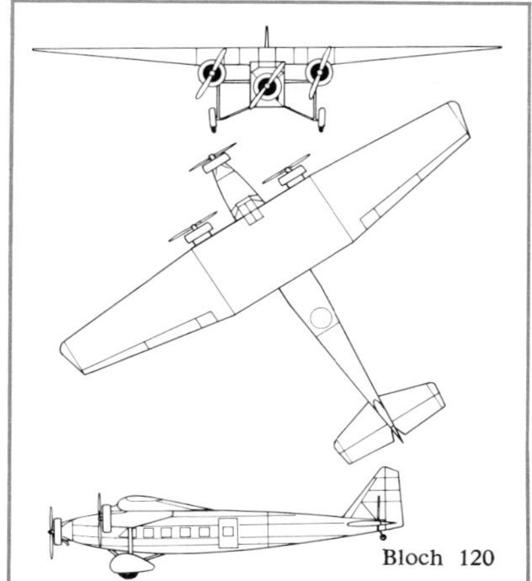
Bloch 120

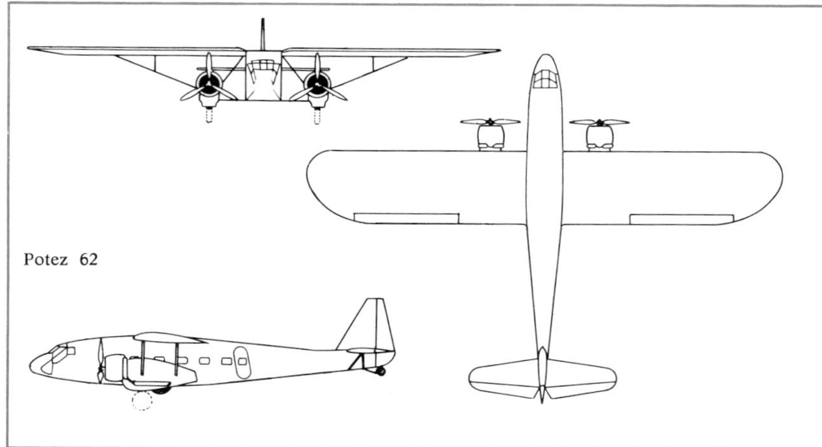
Potez 62

On 16 August, thirteen days after its first flight, the aircraft came to grief during a test flight and could not be repaired in time for the race.

Plate 101
French multi-engine aircraft for European, African and Far Eastern routes: 1933–1935

Some of Air France's most valuable all-purpose short to medium range transports were the aircraft of the Wibault 280.T series which were operated for five years on its main European routes. This was a sound and reliable type which made a very good impression at the Paris Air Show of 1930 when the prototype went on display, so advanced were its lines. It had all-metal structure and skin and was a low-wing monoplane which could comfortably accommodate ten passengers in its roomy fuselage. Two prototypes were built, designated 280.T and 281.T, which had different engines and series production centered mainly on two principal variants, the 282.T12 and the 283.T12 which had more powerful engines and increased fuel capacity. The two prototypes were owned by the French Government and subjected to a long and demanding series of proving trials. CIDNA and Air Union took delivery of the first 282.T12 aircraft completed, for use on their Paris–Istanbul and Paris–London routes. When Air France was formed in 1933, these aircraft were absorbed into the new company's fleet, and a year later the airline took delivery of ten of the second series Wibaults, the 283.T12 which remained in service on main routes until 1938 and were then transferred to secondary routes.

The Bloch 120 was a much more conventional high-wing three-engine aircraft. This airplane was the official choice for services run by a newly-formed company (1934), Régie Air Afrique, and the Bloch 120 inaugurated the Algiers—Niamey (Niger) route on 7 September that same year. Flights were later extended to cover the whole route between Algiers and Madagascar. Only a few Bloch 120s were built but they gave good service and were still in operation in the summer of 1939.

For trans-Mediterranean routes Air France made much use of a large three-engine flying boat, the Breguet 530 Saïgon, for a number of years. This type owed much to the design and construction of the British Short Calcutta, since Breguet had acquired the construction rights to build the Calcutta in 1931. Five Calcuttas had been built in France and Breguet had then developed a larger variant, on which work had commenced in 1932 in response to an order from the French Navy. Thirty of the resulting Type 521 Bizerte were manufactured and at the same time Breguet also constructed two civil examples, the 530 Saïgon, following an order from Air Union. Among the flying boat's most valued qualities were its resilience and its large capacity.

Another invaluable contemporary transport aircraft was the Potez 62, a tough twin-engine aircraft which was a derivative of the Potez 54 bomber. Until the outbreak of World War II, Air France used these airplanes on many of its routes: on European flights including those to Scandinavia; on services to the Far East and in South America. The prototype Potez 62 was completed at the end of 1934 and on 28 January the following year made its first flight. After proving trials had been satisfactorily completed the aircraft went into production and Air France had twelve of the initial radial engine 62-0 series. They began flying the Paris–Marseilles–Rome route in April 1935. In the same year the second production series prototype appeared, which had more powerful liquid-cooled engines and was designated Potez 62-1. Air France ordered ten of these and converted three 62-0s to 62-1 standard, and from 1936 some were put on to South American routes, mainly between Buenos Aires and Santiago, Chile.

The last and best French prewar transport was the Dewoitine D.338, a modern and clean-lined graceful tri-motor. The first, of a total of thirty-one built, made its maiden flight in 1935. This design stemmed from two earlier aircraft, the D.332 of 1933 and the D.333 of 1934 (three of the latter had been bought by Air France) and compared with these it was larger, heavier and more powerful, with more than double the capacity of its predecessors, and with improved performance which was in part due to a retractable undercarriage having been installed, as well as to improved streamlining. Air France put the first D.338 into service in 1936 and later used the D.338s on its most important routes in Europe, the Far East and over the African section of the South America route. Nine aircraft were still serviceable after the war, eight being still in service in 1946 when some were used for a while on the Paris–Nice services.

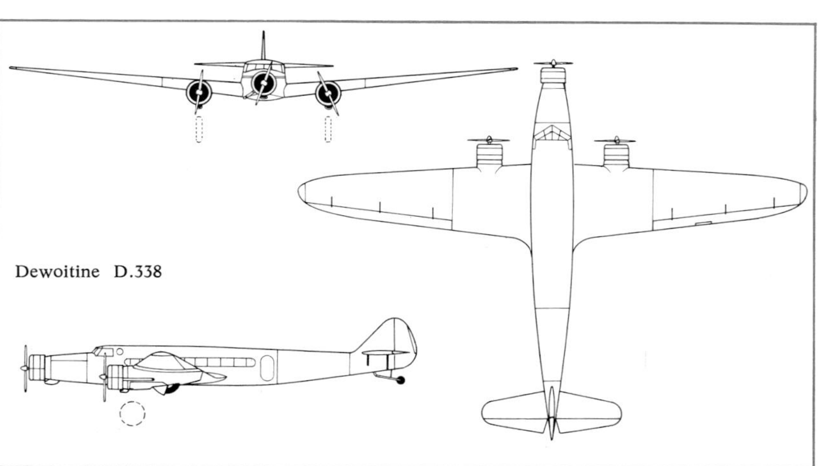
Dewoitine D.338

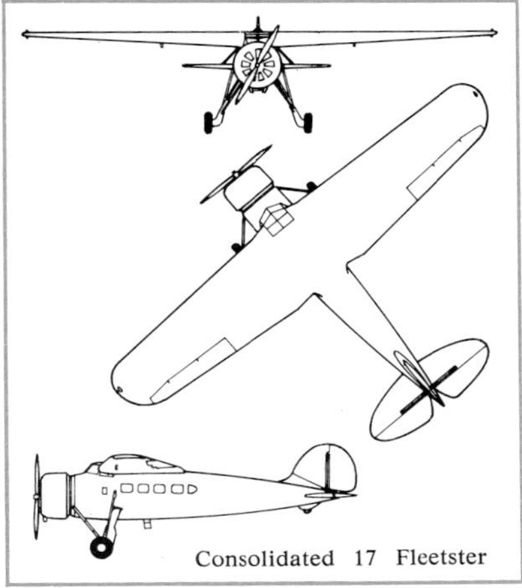
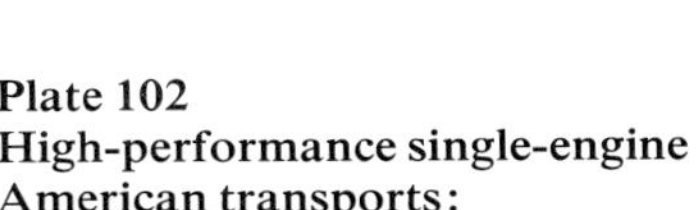
Consolidated 17 Fleetster

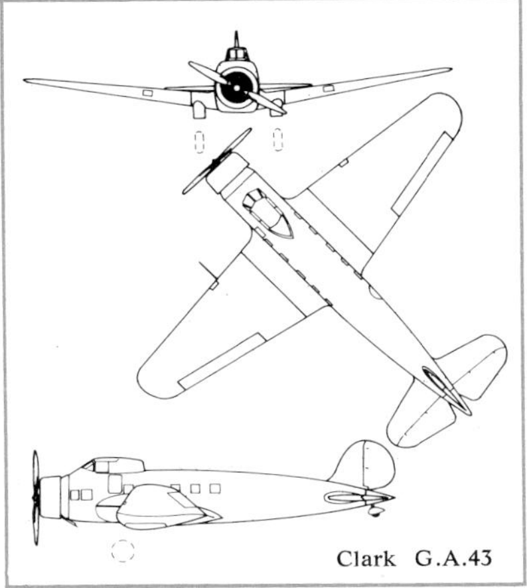
Clark G.A.43

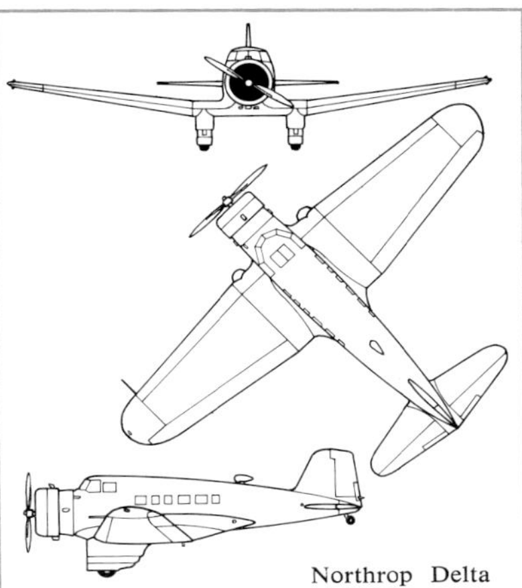
Northrop Delta

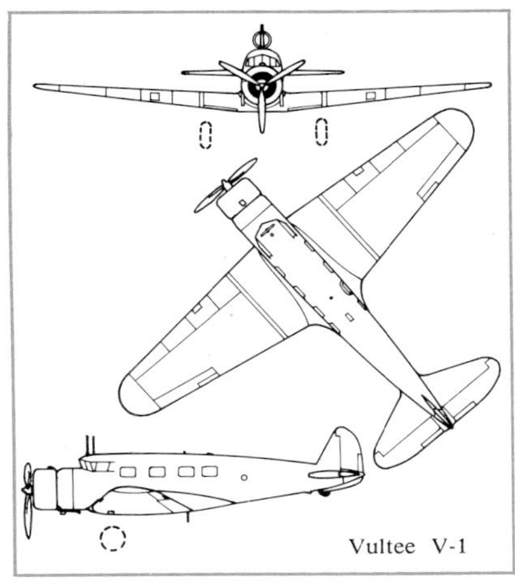
Vultee V-1

Plate 102
High-performance single-engine American transports: 1930–1934

On the eve of the revolution in commercial aviation which the appearance of the Boeing 247 and the Douglas DC-2 triggered off, America's light single-engine aircraft, which had done so much to develop U.S. networks, reached the climax of their development. They belonged, however, to a generation of airplanes which was soon to be relegated to the background of the civil aviation scene.

One of the Lockheed Vega's contemporaries was the Consolidated Fleetster, a small, resilient high-wing monoplane and, although only a limited number was built, this type met with a certain degree of success. The project originated in 1929 with an order from the N.Y.R.B.A (New York, Rio & Buenos Aires Line). One of the founders of the company, Reuben H. Fleet, had also been president of Consolidated Aircraft Corporation, and what he felt was needed was a small, fast airplane which could fly on feeder routes backing up the Commodore flying boats. The prototype, designated Model 17, made its first flight in October 1929 and once proving trials were over, three production aircraft were constructed. These were put into service in early 1930 and two remained in service until 1934 as part of Pan American's fleet, after it had taken over N.Y.R.B.A. Two other variants of the Model 17 were produced. The first was an order for a private owner in 1930, designated 17-2C and had a different engine; three years later this model was sold to Pacific International Airways who used it in Alaska. Three of the second variant, designated 17-AF, were built in 1932 for Ludington Airlines, who put them into service on the busy New York–Washington run. These Fleetster 17-AFs not only had up-rated engines, but were slightly larger and of greater capacity. In 1933 these three aircraft were sold to Pan American.

Series production, however, was based on a new main variant, the Model 20, which had also been developed for N.Y.R.B.A in 1930. The four Model 20s built had a parasol-wing layout in order to make better use of the available fuselage space, and the cockpit, which was open, was repositioned aft of the wings enabling a cargo hold to be accommodated in the deep forward fuselage between the passenger cabin and the engine bay. Three of these aircraft were also subsequently acquired by Pan American. The final Fleetster, the Model 20-2, was essentially an alliance of the parasol-wing Model 20 with the longer wings, modified undercarriage and other improvements of the Model 17-AF. In 1932 seven were built for Transcontinental and Western Air (TWA) in order to operate a Detroit–Indianapolis service. These Fleetsters entered service in October that same year and operated until February 1935. Three were later sold privately and another three found their way to Spain where they were used by the Republican forces in the Civil War.

Another contemporary single-engine aircraft, the Clark G.A.43 met with limited market success in spite of its very advanced design. This low-wing, all-metal monoplane had a retractable undercarriage and useful performance, with capacity for 10–11 passengers. After a very protracted development phase, the Clark G.A.43 made its maiden flight in 1933 and only four production aircraft were built. One of these was purchased by Western Air Express which used it on the Cheyenne–Albuquerque route; another was operated by SCADTA in Colombia, and Swissair took delivery of two. From March 1934, one of Swissair's G.A.43s operated the night mail flight between Zürich and Frankfurt and the passenger routes between Zürich and Vienna and Geneva. It was joined by the second aircraft in 1935. In 1936 one of them crashed and the remaining G.A.43 was then sold.

The all-metal Northrop Delta single-engine transport monoplane was developed in parallel with the Gamma as the last of Northrop's high-performance civil aircraft, and the first example flew in May 1933. However, its commercial success was marred by the U.S. Government's decision in October 1934 that only multi-engine aircraft could be used for carrying passengers at night or over terrain where it was difficult or impossible to make an emergency landing. Thirteen Deltas were built in the United States and a further nineteen military aircraft were built by Canadian Vickers for the Royal Canadian Air Force. The Delta was built in a number of versions including the deep fuselage type with accommodation for six or eight passengers and a more slender-fuselage model with aft-positioned cockpit for two crew. TWA had one passenger aircraft (Delta 1A), Pan American bought a passenger Delta 1B for Mexico, and Swedish Air Lines had one passenger (Delta 1C) and one night mail aircraft (Delta 1E).

The Vultee V-1A marked the end of the era of the single-engine airliner and was one of the most eminent examples of the type which had proved so useful up to this time. American Airlines ordered twenty and introduced the type in September 1934. Bowen Airlines in the U.S.A. also used the V-1A and at least one is reported to have gone to Canadian Colonial Airways. Apart from its commercial career, the Vultee also made a name for itself through several record-breaking flights, one of which earned it a great deal of publicity when, in September 1936, it was piloted by Dick Merrill and Harry Richman on a transatlantic return flight from New York to London. A record time of 18 hours 38 minutes was set, at an average speed of 210 mph (338 km/h). Jimmy Doolittle had previously flown the Vultee coast-to-coast on a record-breaking flight across the United States of 11 hours 59 minutes.

Plate 103
Italian airliners: 1935–1939

There were several very interesting airliners produced in Italy in the years leading up to World War II, although they may not have achieved the same success as the popular Savoia Marchetti series. The Caproni Ca 101s and Ca 133s were ideal for use on routes to and within the African colonies, although they were mainly used in a military role by the Regia Aeronautica.

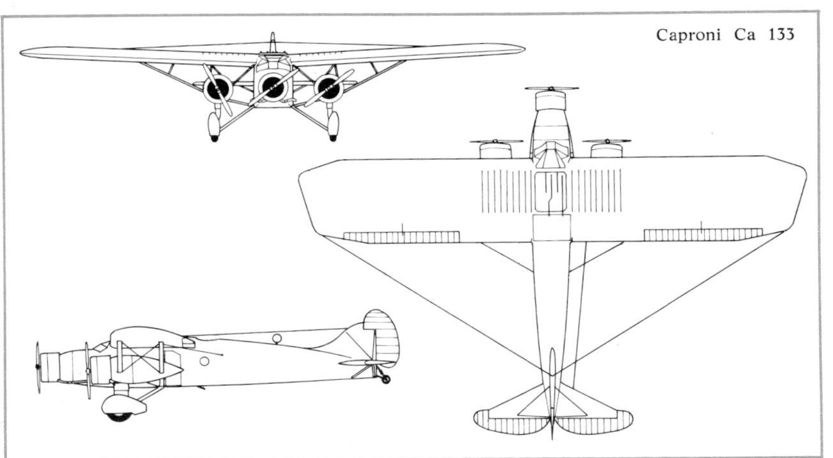
Caproni Ca 133

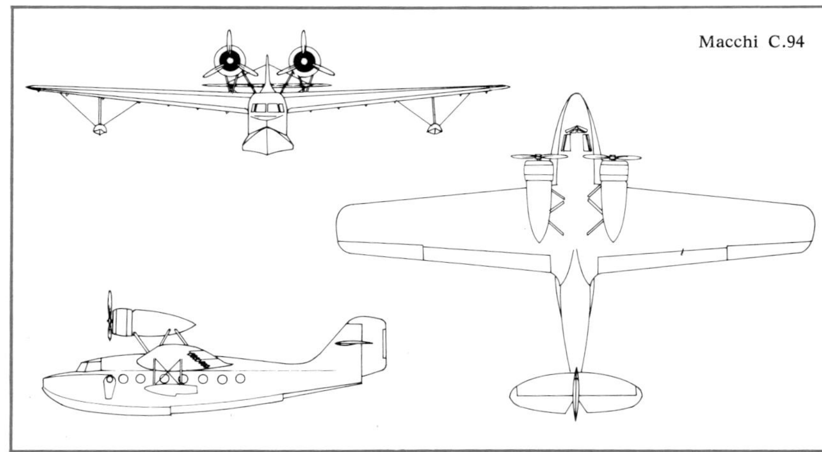
Macchi C.94

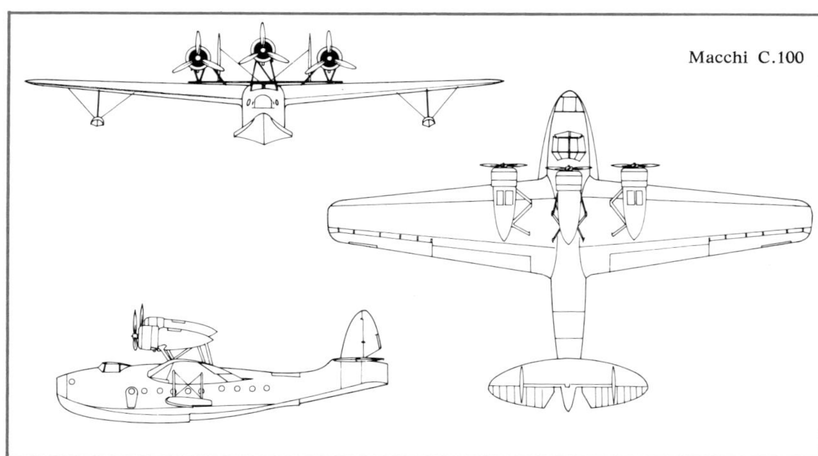
Macchi C.100

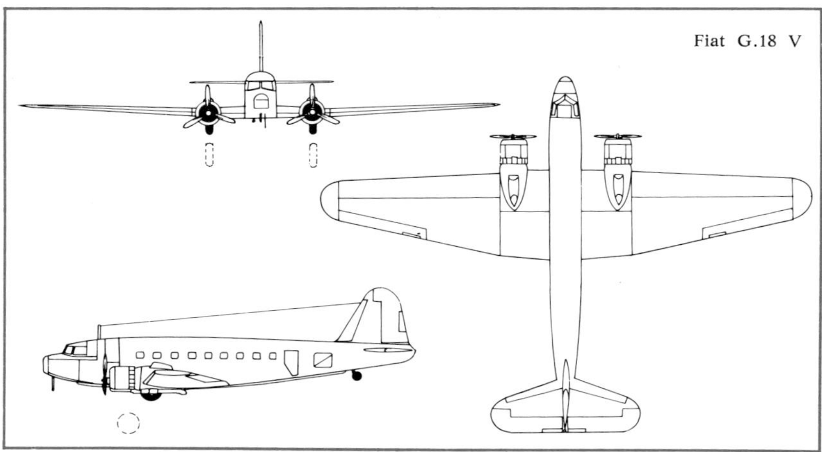
Fiat G.18 V

The Ca 101 was developed in 1930 and several versions were produced, differing in type and number of engines, being mostly three-engine aircraft, although there was a single-engine version and a twin-engine bomber. A few were put to commercial use by the Società Nord-Africa Aviazione in Libya and some of these passed to Ala Littoria. In 1935 the improved model, the Ca 133, appeared. The two aircraft were structurally virtually identical and with the same strut-braced high-wing layout, but the Ca 133 was a better aircraft than its predecessor, being generally cleaned up and with more powerful engines. As a result its overall performance was an improvement over the Ca 101 and it could also carry a greater payload. Production totaled some 275 in all: almost all of these were military aircraft, but twelve were built for civil use and delivered to Ala Littoria. The Regia Aeronautica's Capronis (which were soon nicknamed "Caprone"—or Billy-goat) saw service on all fronts throughout World War II.

The Italian manufacturer, Macchi, concentrated on developing two interesting flying boats during the latter half of the thirties; these were the C.94 and the C.100. The designer of both these aircraft was Mario Castoldi who in 1935 had submitted his initial design for the C.94 to Ala Littoria. This twin-engine, twelve-seat aircraft was also available in an amphibian version, and was intended to be a replacement for the aging Cant 10 on the Northern Adriatic and Mediterranean routes.

The prototype, an amphibian, was exhibited at the International Air Show which was held in Milan in October 1935, and was later put through proving trials. These showed that the retractable undercarriage created too much drag and, when test flights were concluded, it was decided that only the flying boat version would go into production. Ala Littoria placed an initial order for six aircraft, then followed this with an order for another six, powered by different engines (changing from the original 770 hp Wright Cyclones to 800 hp Alfa Romeo 126s). These flying boats went into commercial service in 1936 and, in 1939, three C.94s were sold to Ala Littoria's South American affiliate, Corporación Sudamericana de Servicios Aéreos who flew them between Buenos Aires, Rosario and Montevideo. In Italy, the remaining Macchi flying boats were kept in service throughout the war, having been impressed by Ala Littoria's Communications Unit (Nucleo Comunicazioni). Among the highlights of the C.94's career were the record-breaking flights of the prototype (I-NEPI) on 15 April and 6 May 1937, when it set a new altitude record for an amphibian with a payload of 1,000 kilograms at 21,102 ft (6,432 m); a new 1,240 miles (2,000 km) closed-circuit speed record at 154.67 mph (248.967 km/h); and a new closed-circuit speed record over 621 miles (1,000 km) with a 1,000 kilogram payload, reaching 159.78 mph (257.138 km/h).

In 1938 Mario Castoldi started to formulate designs for a much bigger flying boat than C.94 and the C.100 prototype made its maiden flight on 7 January 1939. This was a considerably larger aircraft, which had three engines and could seat twenty-six passengers. It fell short of its designer's hopes, however, since the design of the hull proved to have shortcomings and the flying boat was unstable in the water, a fault which was never to be satisfactorily rectified. By June 1940, only three had been completed and after very brief commercial use they were militarized and saw service in the war. From August 1940, the C.100s flew missions from Italy to Libya as part of the Communications Unit, ferrying war materials and troops on the outward flight and bringing the wounded back on the return journey. Only one survived until the Armistice in 1943.

In 1935 the airplane which can be considered the most advanced Italian aircraft of its day appeared; a type which could measure up to the most modern contemporary international competition. This was the Fiat G.18, a twin-engine monoplane which was in the same category as the revolutionary American Douglas DC-1 and DC-2. It was designed by Giuseppe Gabrielli who had clearly been influenced by the U.S. designs—the DC-1 had flown in July 1933 followed by the DC-2 in May 1934—and the G.18 prototype first flew on 18 March 1935. Its performance and general lines were very reminiscent of the Douglas aircraft and in some respects on a par with them. Production commenced with two aircraft of the initial series and then came another six of the G.18 V series which had more powerful engines and some structural changes and which made its first flight on 11 March 1937. These Fiat twin-engine airplanes were all bought by Avio Linee Italiane who put them into service on domestic and international routes based on Milan. The G.18s also proved a major contributory factor in the success of the airline's Venice–Milan–Turin–Paris service. From June 1938 services to London and other European capitals were opened. Once war started the Fiat G.18 aircraft were converted into military transports and were employed as troop-carriers.

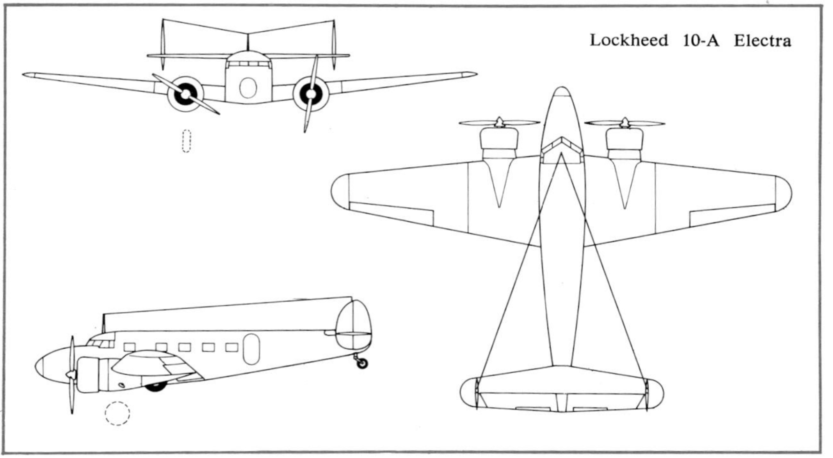
Lockheed 10-A Electra

Plate 104
Famous American twin-engine civil transports: 1934–1941

In the United States the upheaval caused by Boeing and Douglas's new models meant that other aircraft manufacturers had to go all out to improve the quality of their products. The third major protagonist in this battle was Lockheed and this company spared no efforts to rise to the challenge of cutthroat competition, producing their own outstanding new generation of aircraft. The first of their designs for the changed market of the 1930s was the Model 10 Electra, which immediately met with just as much success as the company's previous single-engine series, from the Vega of 1927 to the Orion of 1931. The Electra project was developed in 1933 as Lockheed's answer to the Boeing 247 and Lockheed pushed ahead with the program for nearly a year. Their engineers had to contend with a series of problems which they were bound to encounter since it was the company's first all-metal aircraft. These difficulties were overcome and the twin-engine prototype made its first flight on 23 February 1934, and favorably impressed potential customers with its good overall performance and capabilities. Carrying the same number of passengers as the 247, the Electra was not only faster but had better range and ceiling and was also much cheaper. The Electra's selling price was actually the lowest for any aircraft of its category on the market. Its commercial success was instantaneous.

The first to introduce the new aircraft was Northwest Airlines in August 1934. Total production in several variants, differing in minor details from one another, reached 149. Besides being bought by some of the main U.S. airlines, the Electra found plenty of foreign customers, including Great Britain, Australia and New Zealand. The Lockheed Electra also broke several records and it was during an attempt at a new round-the-world record flight in an Electra that Amelia Earhart was lost in the Pacific.

On 29 July 1937, the prototype of the new, scaled-up model, the Lockheed 14, which was called the Super Electra, first flew. This was a direct development of its immediate predecessor and, although it echoed the lines of the Model 10, it was a much more versatile and capacious airliner. Apart from its commercial function the Super Electra had a distinguished military career which almost made its commercial achievements pale into insignificance. Lockheed built 112 Super Electras and a further 119 were built in Japan but there were 2,941 of the similar Hudsons which were used by Allied air forces during the war.

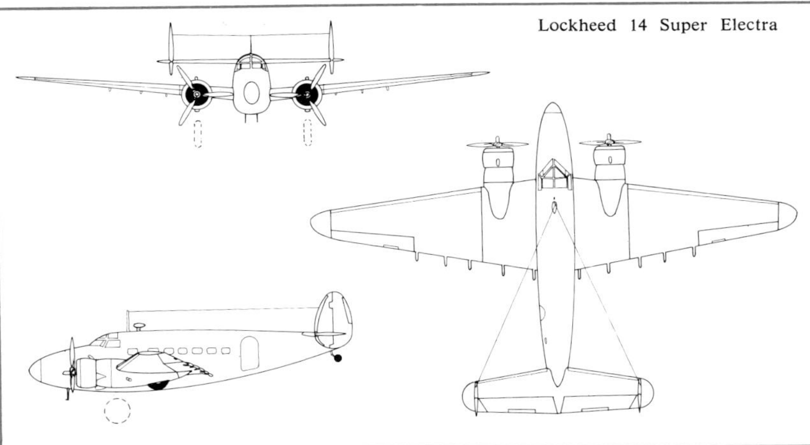

Lockheed 14 Super Electra

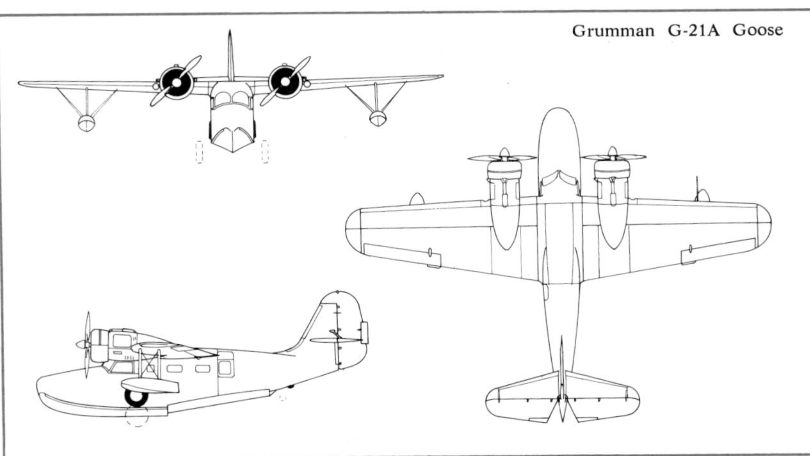

Grumman G-21A Goose

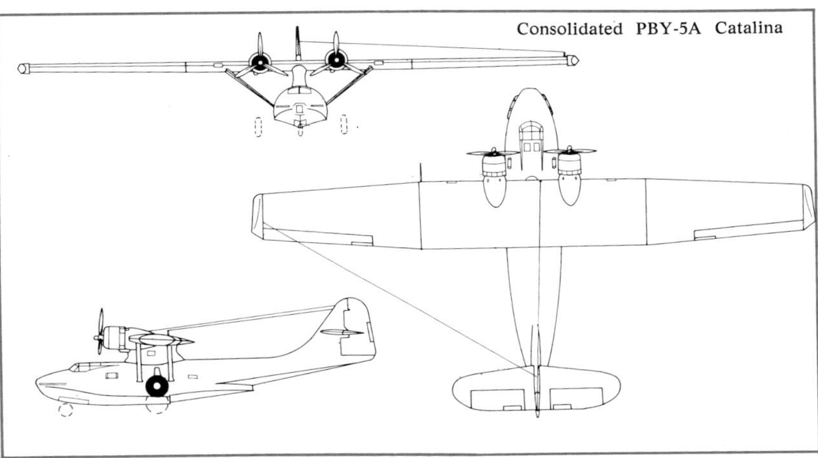

Consolidated PBY-5A Catalina

Commercial success was never in question for the Super Electra; once the prototype had appeared approval came not only from U.S. airlines but also from many foreign customers, with European airlines conspicuous among them. As with the Electra, Northwest Airlines was the first to put the Super Electra into service, in October 1937. The Dutch company, KLM, was the first non-U.S. airline to put the new Lockheed twin-engine aircraft into service and was followed by British Airways, Sabena, LOT Polish Airlines and Aer Lingus. On top of this, orders came in from such buyers as Guinea Airways, Trans-Canada Air Lines and Dai Nippon Koku K.K. of Japan. One of the highlights of the Lockheed Super Electra's long and varied service occurred in July 1938, when the millionaire Howard Hughes completed a round-the-world flight in one of these twin-engine Lockheeds. A total distance of 14,672 miles (23,612 km) was covered in 91.25 hours with a flying time of just over 71 hours.

U.S. aircraft manufacturers were no less successful with their flying boats during this period. The Grumman G-21 Goose is one example; originally flown in June 1937 as a commercial amphibian aircraft, more than 250 were built for civil and military customers before production ended in September 1945. Two other derivant Grumman amphibians were the G-44 Widgeon, which first flew in 1940, and the G-73 Mallard of 1946. A much bigger flying boat was to be the Consolidated PBY Catalina, the unforgettable "Cat" which proved absolutely indispensable to the Allies during the war, when thousands of them were built (3,290 in the U.S.A. and Canada and an unknown number in the U.S.S.R.). The Catalina's career was mainly spent as a military flying boat but after the war numbers of them came on to the international civil aviation markets. After the prototype's first flight on 21 March 1935, the main production models were the PBY-1, 2, 3 and 4 (the first series); the PBY-5 of 1940 was one of those produced in the greatest numbers; then followed the PBY-5A amphibian of 1941 and the final variant, the PBY-6A. The PBY-5A was the most successful model in commercial use: Panair do Brasil used six Catalinas, which had been modified in order to accommodate twenty-two passengers, until 1965. Many sub-series were modified and had different power units installed.

In airline operation the Catalina's greatest achievement was the wartime operation of Qantas services between Western Australia and Ceylon. The distance of more than 3,500 miles (5,600 km) had to be flown in radio silence and the longest crossing took 31 hours 35 minutes. A total of 271 ocean crossings was made between July 1943 and July 1945.

Plate 105
Commercial aviation in Romania, Czechoslovakia and Poland: 1934–1938

While civil aviation was advancing at an accelerating rate in the industrialized nations, the commercial transport scene in less highly industrialized

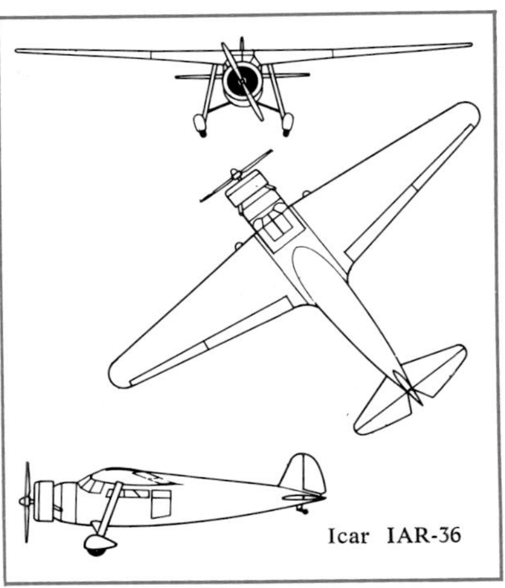

Icar IAR-36

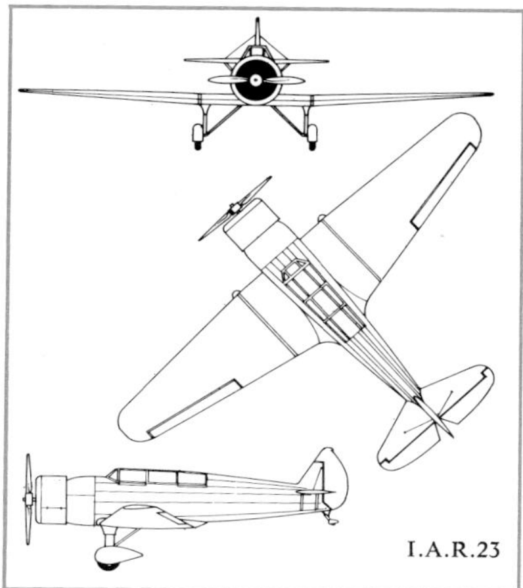
I.A.R.23

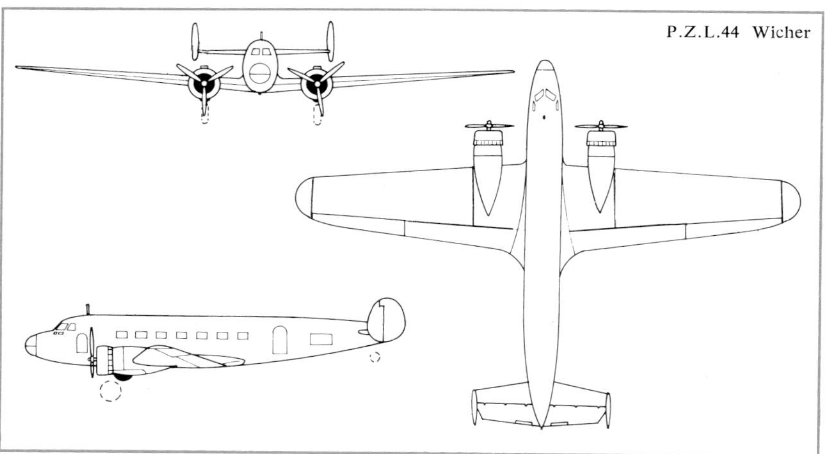
P.Z.L.44 Wicher

countries inevitably felt some of the repercussions of these changes and progress. In many cases this happened slowly but steadily, but some nations, such as Japan, launched themselves wholeheartedly into a program of rapid expansion in this field, starting off a momentum which reached its climax during World War II.

Romania had a well-established and long-standing aeronautical tradition, but limited manufacturing capacity when compared with that of the great air powers. The first Romanian commercial aircraft was built in 1934 by ICAR but had been designed by Messerschmitt. It was the Icar IAR-36. ICAR (Intreprindere Constructii Aeronautice Romane), a company which had been founded in 1925 and had specialized in the construction of light aircraft, such as tourers, trainers and aerobatic types. The IAR-36 had very acceptable performance for its type, particularly as regards speed and range when fully loaded (six passengers). The prototype entered service with LARES on domestic routes, but it is not known whether more than one was built.

In spite of importing large numbers of contemporary Italian and German light aircraft, the Romanian aircraft industry succeeded in producing worthwhile aircraft of its own. One of these was the I.A.R. 23, a low-wing, two-seat monoplane with fixed undercarriage. Immediately after it first appeared it made a name for itself in endurance competitions. In September 1934, piloted by George Banciulescu, an I.A.R. 23 actually took part in three international meetings within the space of five days. On 15 September, Banciulescu flew to Bucharest from Warsaw and back; on the 18th he flew from Pipera to Prague and Bucharest and, the next day, went on to participate in the Bucharest–Vienna–Paris race. This was indeed an exceedingly demanding test of its capabilities, but the little airplane came through with flying colors, demonstrating what a fine design it was.

The influence of the manufacturers of international status was easily discernible all over the world, in such countries as Czechoslovakia, for example, where the Aero A204 twin-engine transport was built. The Aero A204 was developed in the mid-thirties and was somewhat out of place in the context of a national aviation industry which was almost entirely devoted to meeting national military needs. The prototype made its debut in 1937 and it was obvious that much thought had been given to the comfort of the passengers: the cabin was planned in such a way as to make it as spacious and as comfortable as possible for eight people. Each passenger had his own adjustable window seat which was individually lit, heated and ventilated. The Aero A204 was a low-wing, twin-engine monoplane with retractable undercarriage, of mixed construction and with ply-covered wing and fabric-covered fuselage. Its general performance was good, especially its cruising speed. In the event, however, it failed to prove competitive with aircraft produced by other European and American manufacturers and its development lost momentum and then came to a halt when the war started.

Poland was another European country which was very advanced in the aeronautical field during the 1930s. The RWD 13 was a worthwhile light aircraft; a small high-wing monoplane developed in 1934 as the RWD 6bis/II, the prototype first flew in February of the following year. Its main virtue lay in its versatility and slow-flying qualities. The RWD 13 functioned equally with a range of engines, but most had the 120–130 hp P.Z. Inż Major, the 120–130 hp Walter Major or the 130 hp de Havilland Gipsy Major. The RWD 13 was produced in several versions including the RWD 13S ambulance, and numbers were exported, although it was regarded as too expensive for the Polish market. More than 100 had been produced by September 1939.

The RWD 11 twin-engine six-passenger feederliner was designed as a competitor for the government-sponsored P.Z.L.27. Of low-wing layout with retractable undercarriage, the RWD 11 was claimed to be the first passenger transport with fully-slotted wings. The wing was of wooden construction, but the fuselage was a tubular metal structure with ply and fabric covering. The RWD 11 made its first flight in February 1936 and demonstrated its ability to operate from restricted airdromes, but LOT, the Polish national airline, had no interest in the aircraft and it was eventually seized by the Germans.

Another interesting and up-to-date commercial twin-engine monoplane also got no further than the prototype stage: the P.Z.L.44 Wicher (Gale) which had been developed with a view to providing LOT with a dependable nationally-manufactured airliner. This program was launched in 1936 in response to an official specification which laid down that the new airplane had to be comparable with the American Douglas DC-2. The prototype made its first flight in March 1938, but LOT discovered some shortcomings and numerous modifications were made. Although in general appearance the Wicher resembled the DC-2, it had twin fins and rudders. The Wicher took longer to develop than had been foreseen and it was just at this crucial stage that an acrimonious dispute broke out between the airline and the Polish Department of Aeronautics concerning production costs. The argument dragged on and no compromise was reached. Eventually the war put an end to the project for good and all. The prototype was later seized by the invading Russians.

Plate 106
Japan's and Canada's nascent aircraft industries: 1934–1938

Japan's rapid transformation into an aeronautical power of some consequence during the 1920s and 1930s was a particularly interesting phenomenon. Spurred on by her wish to achieve military domination and by her expansionist policies, Japan progressed through a transitional phase of building foreign designs under license to producing Japanese-designed aircraft. This was particularly obvious with military aircraft production, but it also had some effect in the commercial field, since some of the best prewar airliners were early versions of what were to be the most famous and widely-used Japanese bombers of World War II.

The Mitsubishi Hina-Zuru (Crane) was a twin-engine light transport which was built under license from Britain and therefore was typical of the era when Japan was still importing technological experience and design from abroad. This aircraft was, in fact,

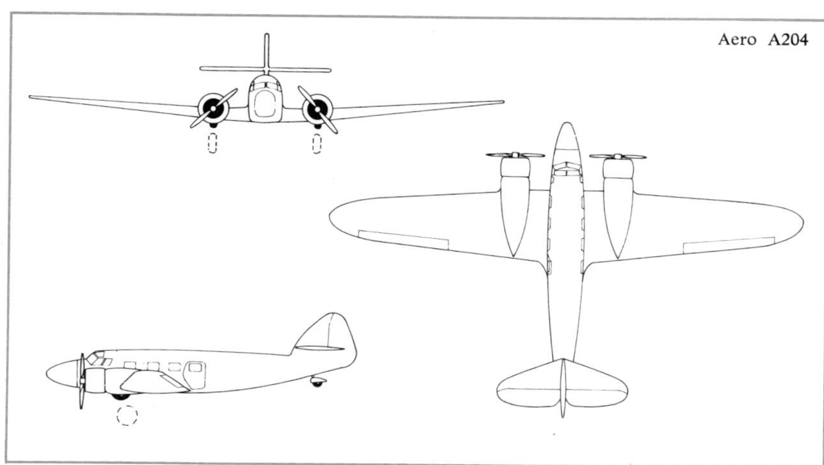
Aero A204

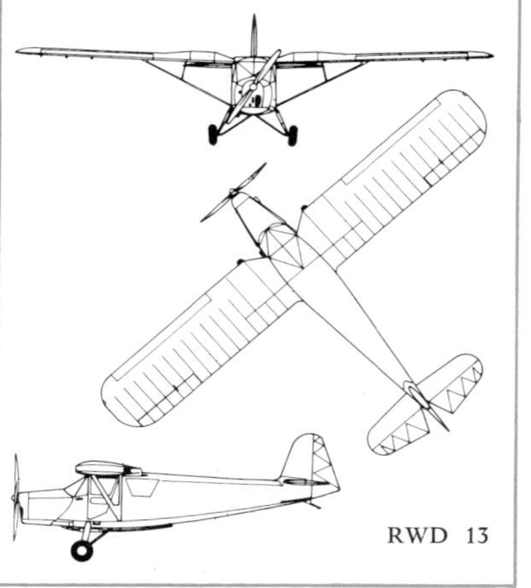
RWD 13

none other than the successful Airspeed A.S.6 Envoy which the British company had managed to sell to Japan during an intensive sales campaign to capture foreign markets for the airplane. This Hina-Zuru only differed from the original Envoy in details: even the engines were manufactured under license by Mitsubishi. It is believed that eleven of these aircraft were built and they were used on domestic services by Japan Air Transport.

On 12 September 1936, the Nakajima AT-2 prototype, the first all-Japanese twin-engine commercial transport, had its maiden flight. The aircraft clearly showed traces of the indirect influence of contemporary foreign designs. Preliminary designs had been drawn up in 1935, immediately after Nakajima had acquired the construction rights of the American Douglas DC-2. Only after they had minutely studied the U.S. construction techniques and methods used to build the DC-2, did the Japanese design engineers get down to designing a smaller version, for short-range flights. After overcoming some minor shortcomings, production got under way and Nakajima built thirty-two AT-2s for operation by Dai Nippon Koku K.K. (Greater Japan Air Lines) and Manchurian Air Transport. A far greater number was built for military use; two military variants (the Army Ki-34 and the Navy L1N1) were manufactured and over 300 left the assembly lines. They saw a great deal of service during the war.

The career of the Mitsubishi G3M was somewhat similar but on a far larger scale. This was an aircraft which was important to the Japanese Imperial Navy. The original G3M1 went into production in 1936 and in 1938 it was decided to convert twenty of the later G3M2s for civil use. Most of these G3M2s were used by Nippon Koku K.K. and subsequently with Dai Nippon Koku K.K., the two main Japanese airlines. The aircraft's brief commercial employment was publicized by a series of spectacular intercontinental flights by several of the civil variants. Among the most sensational of these was the round-the-world flight (26 August–20 October 1939) by the G3M2 J-BAC1 *Nippon* which flew over 32,850 miles (52,860 km) in 194 flying hours.

While Japan was busy during the years leading up to World War II, successfully building up and continually up-dating a first-class aeronautical industry with immense potential for future growth, another great nation, Canada, was continuing to develop her own aviation industry. Although many U.S. and British designed aircraft were manufactured in Canada there was always a need for aircraft specially designed for Canadian conditions. One of the best-known of these in prewar years was the Noorduyn Norseman, a tough, safe and versatile single-engine monoplane, which first flew on 14 November 1935. The main series model of prewar production was the Norseman IV of 1936, with the more powerful 550 hp Pratt & Whitney Wasp engine instead of the 420 hp Wright Whirlwind. Apart from being flown by commercial operators and private owners, the Norseman was also used by the RCAF and the USAAF, and 904 were built. After the war a final model was brought out, the Norseman V, a heavier version, manufactured by the Canadian Car & Foundry Company which had taken over Norseman rights in the spring of 1946.

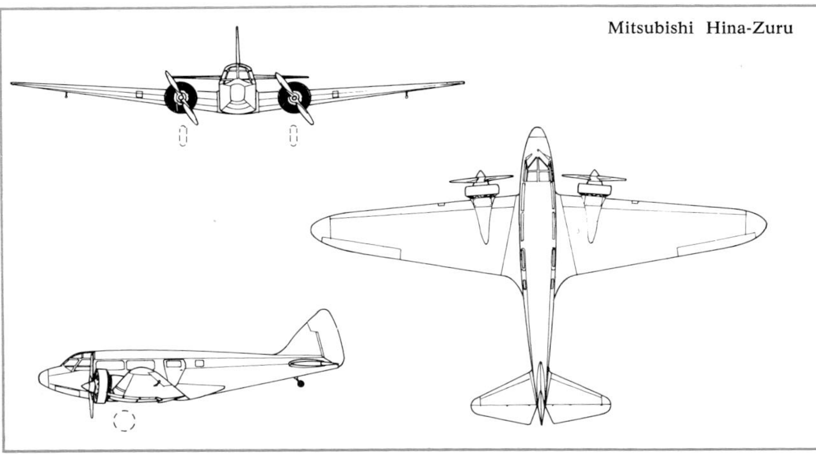
Mitsubishi Hina-Zuru

Nakajima AT-2

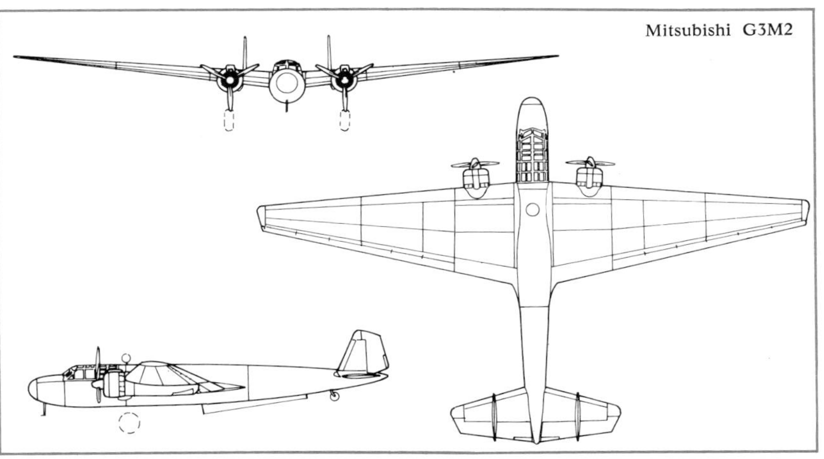
Mitsubishi G3M2

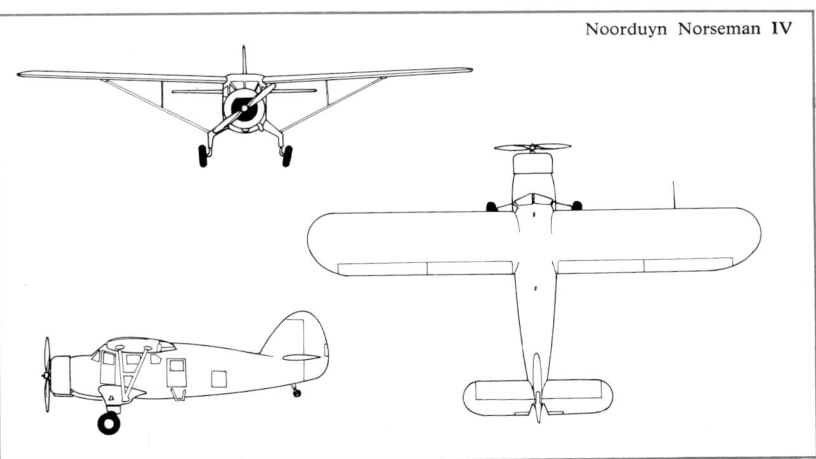
Noorduyn Norseman IV

Plate 107
German four-engine aircraft: 1937–1938

While Japan was unobtrusively pushing ahead with the development of her aircraft industry in the immediately prewar years, Germany's startling buildup of air power and technical advances impressed the whole world. As a side effect of Germany's military aspirations, commercial aviation expanded as never before. Deutsche Lufthansa, which already had a large fleet and excellent organization, added some extremely advanced aircraft to its stock.

The Focke-Wulf Fw 200 Condor is a good example; this was a large, modern four-engine monoplane which had been designed in early 1936 in response to a specification from the national airline which sought a four-engine aircraft for its main routes, with better performance and greater capacity than its Junkers-Ju 52 trimotors. Kurt Tank was in charge of the project and designed an elegant, low-wing, all-metal aircraft with retractable undercarriage. While two prototypes were being readied, an assembly line was laid down for a batch of preproduction aircraft. The first Fw 200 flew on 27 July 1937, and within a short time had completed test flights. Soon afterwards it was joined by the other prototype and the pre-production aircraft, designated Fw 200A-0. The Condor's commercial use started the following year. The first Condor to be put into service may not have been one of Lufthansa's, but possibly one of the two Fw 200s which had been bought by the Danish airline DDL (Det Danske Luftfartselskab) and was introduced in July 1938.

Deutsche Lufthansa operated a total of twelve Condors: the two prototypes, and ten Fw 200As and Fw 200Bs, these last being the improved, more powerful variant. Before the assembly lines were

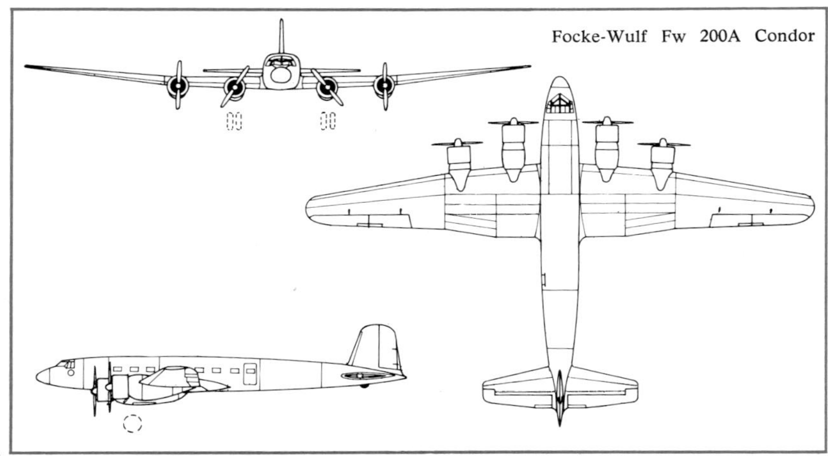
Focke-Wulf Fw 200A Condor

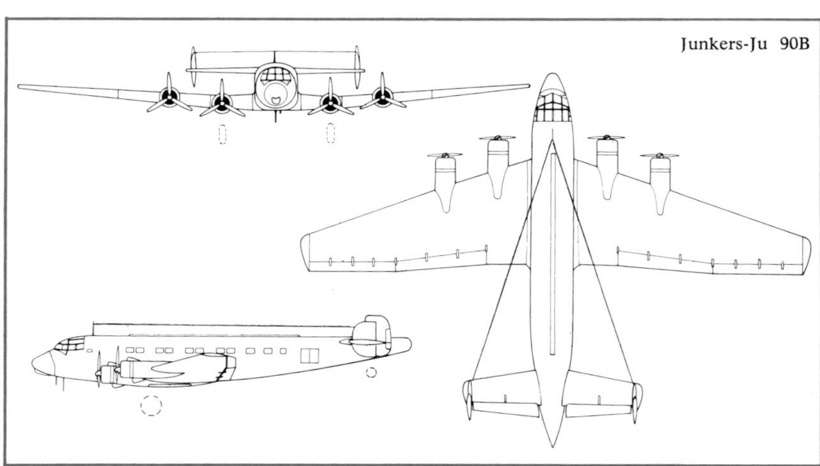
Junkers-Ju 90B

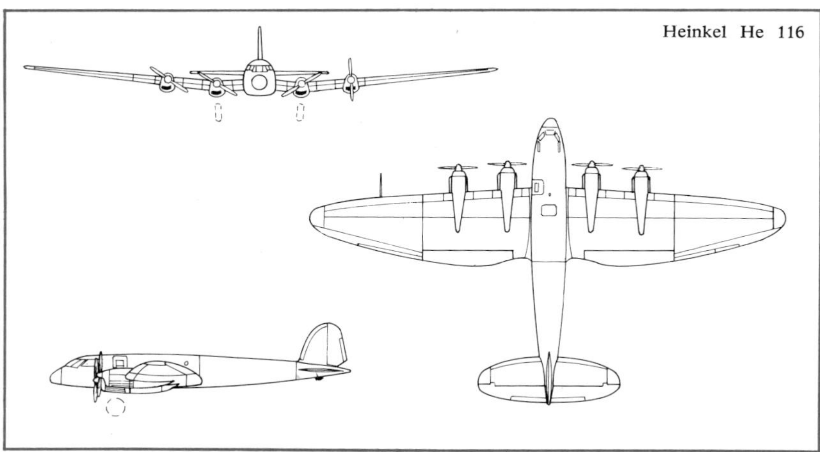
Heinkel He 116

switched wholly to the military versions of the four-engine Focke-Wulf, two Condors were delivered to Syndacata Condor Limitada in Brazil. Another was used by Hitler, but two ordered by Aero O/Y in Finland were not delivered. During the war all but two of Lufthansa's Condors were militarized. The type's last flight with Lufthansa before the airline ceased operation took plane on 14 April 1945, from Barcelona to Berlin. One of the more impressive experimental flights made by the Condor in its early days was the nonstop flight from Berlin to New York of 10–11 August 1938: the journey of over 4,070 miles (6,550 km) was completed in 24 hours 56 minutes on the outward journey and in 19 hours 55 minutes on the return trip, at an average speed of 164 mph (264 km/h) and 205 mph (330 km/h) respectively.

In 1938 another four-engine type joined the Fw 200: the Junkers-Ju 90, of which four prototypes were constructed and ten of the B series model for the civil market, before production was wholly devoted to military orders. The first prototype, with liquid-cooled engines, flew on 28 August 1937, and operational trials were accompanied by a very high-powered publicity campaign. The prototype was not used commercially, but some of the air-cooled-engine Ju 90Bs went to Lufthansa and began operation on the Berlin–Vienna route in 1938. The war prevented full use of the Ju 90s but they were occasionally seen at Croydon and some other Lufthansa stations. In 1940 Ju 90s were operating Berlin–Belgrade services but then these airplanes were requisitioned by the Luftwaffe. The Ju 90 was a very comfortable and capacious aircraft, offering imaginative and practical alternative layouts for passenger accommodation.

Yet another contemporary four-engine aircraft, the Heinkel He 116 was not to find particular favor in the market for which it was intended—as a long-range mailplane. Lufthansa had placed an order in 1936 for its development. The main cause of its failure was the lack of suitable engines which could develop sufficient power at high altitudes—one of the company's particular requirements—since they intended to operate mail routes which would entail flying over the 25,000 ft (8,000 m) high Pamirs on the Afghanistan/Tadzhikistan border on its Far Eastern routes. Before the program was dropped, however, a modified He 116 managed to demonstrate its great potential when, in 1939, it flew 6,213 miles (10,000 km) nonstop in 46 hours 18 minutes, at an average speed of 140 mph (215.6 km/h). Two He 116s were bought by the Japanese.

Plate 108
Transatlantic seaplanes and flying boats: 1936–1941

Britain, France, Germany and the United States all saw the necessity for and advantages of operating air services between Europe and North America, but there were great difficulties in bringing about such operations. The distances were great and strong westerly winds made the westbound crossing extremely difficult. By the second half of the 1930s technical progress was beginning to conquer the problems of achieving adequate range and, eventually, with a commercial load. The Blohm und Voss Ha 139 seaplane was designed in 1935–36 as a transatlantic mailplane. Two were used from 1937, with a third from 1938, in a series of interesting experimental flights across the North Atlantic (the fastest Azores–New York flight was accomplished in 13 hours 40 minutes and the fastest eastward journey in 11 hours 53 minutes); but in the event these aircraft were flown commercially between Africa and South America for a limited period. Using these flights as proving trials and encouraged by the aircraft's initial performance, Lufthansa ordered a flying boat from Dornier which had to have sufficient range to provide a nonstop service between Lisbon and New York. This resulted in the Dornier Do 26, an elegant four-engine flying boat which first flew on 21 May 1938. Proving flights and tests revealed that the Do 26 was fully capable of coping with the required range, but the onset of war terminated any further development. Two Do 26 flying boats were used for mail runs across the South Atlantic, but the third had not been completed when the war began.

The war also put a stop to the commercial introduction of an even better flying boat, the British Short S.26. Three were ordered and the first, *Golden Hind*, flew on 21 July 1939. The stimulus for the development of this enormous flying boat was provided by the great success which Short had enjoyed with its S.23 model, consolidated by all the experience and specialized knowledge the company had acquired during the construction of the military Short S.25 Sunderland, produced in very large numbers. The S.26 program was initiated in 1936 when Imperial Airways sought an aircraft which could fly nonstop mail services across the Atlantic. The *Golden Hind* was delivered to Imperial Airways on 24 September 1939, and together with the other two aircraft was to form the G Class of flying boats. Transatlantic services were interrupted

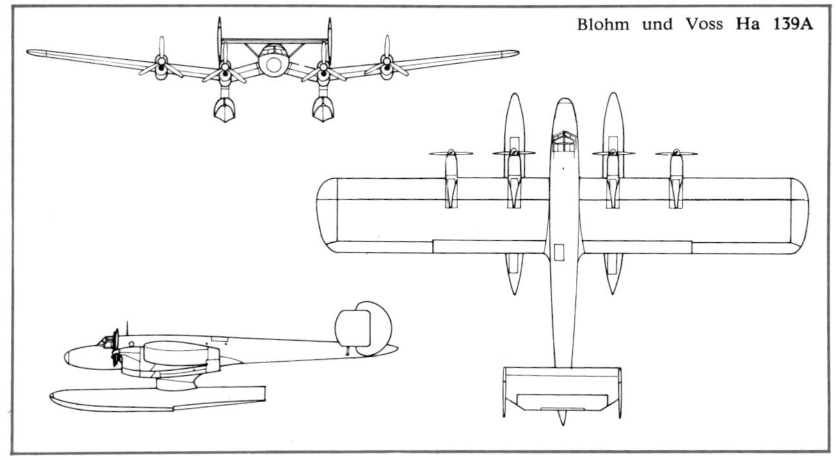
Blohm und Voss Ha 139A

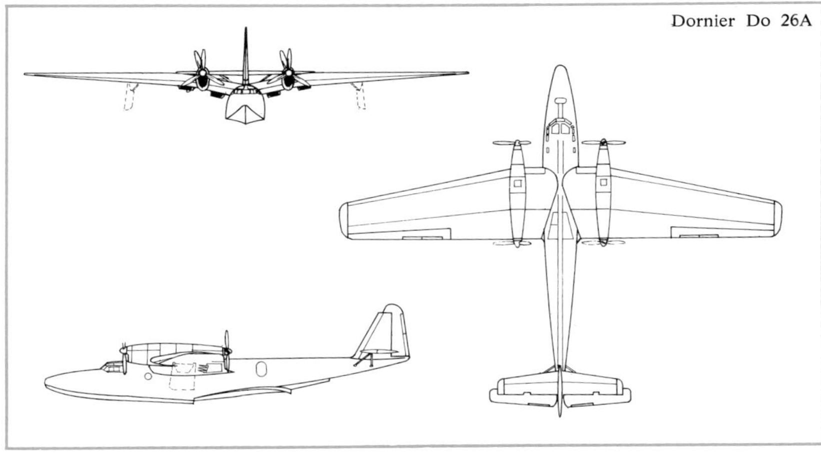

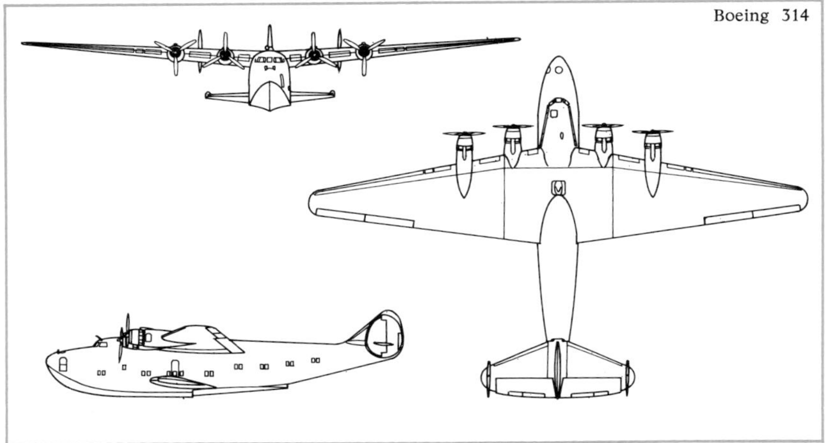

by the war, and the S.26s were militarized, and one was lost with the RAF. The other two of them flew with BOAC from July 1942. After being refurbished as a 24-seater the sole survivor, the *Golden Hind*, began flying a U.K.–Egypt service on 30 September 1946. Eighteen months later it was sold to a private owner but never flew again.

An American flying boat, the Boeing 314 carried out regular flights across the North Atlantic. Pan American Airways ordered six of these large four-engine aircraft and on 20 May 1939, used one (the *Yankee Clipper*) to inaugurate its New York–Marseilles mail service; on 28 June the *Dixie Clipper* was used to launch Pan Am's first regular New York–Lisbon–Marseilles passenger service, and on 8 July *Yankee Clipper* opened the passenger service between New York and Southampton. The advent of World War II meant that these services were canceled, but the twelve Boeings which had been built (three had been handed over to BOAC) were kept busy throughout the war on airline work and with the U.S. Navy. Work had begun on this project in 1935 and the first of the six initial aircraft had flown on 7 June 1938. They were delivered during the first half of 1939 and were later followed by another six of the improved and more powerful variant, the 314A. Only three of these went to Pan American, the other three were bought by the British Government and handed over to BOAC for use on essential services: they survived the war and were returned to the United States in 1948. The American-owned Boeing 314s also saw long service; apart from three which were destroyed, Pan American still had six in service in April 1946. They were sold to charter companies and two of them were lost, one in the Atlantic and the other in the Pacific, but there were no casualties.

Plate 109
Differing approaches to power: 1929–1940

Just how strong was the momentum in aviation during the 1930s and how imperative the achievement of ever longer and more ambitious routes was considered, can be gauged from one of the most ingenious projects to be initiated during this most stimulating period in the history of aviation: the Short-Mayo Composite design, launched in 1937.

The achievement of long range was dependent on efficient engines with modest fuel consumption, adequate tank capacity and the power to lift the aircraft into the air. To lift increasingly heavy aircraft off land or water, demanded ever greater engine power and wing area. But this increased the weight, thus demanding still more power and bigger loads of fuel. An aircraft can fly at a much greater weight than that at which it can take off and therefore Britain experimented with two ways of securing adequate range to cross the North Atlantic against the prevailing westerly winds and with a commercial payload.

One way of achieving increased range was for the aircraft to take off with only a modest fuel load and then refuel in the air. This method was successfully tried using C Class flying boats. The other British solution was to mount a fairly small heavily loaded seaplane onto the back of a large flying boat, achieve takeoff using the lift of both aircraft's wings and the combined power of their eight engines, and then separate them in the air. This last solution resulted in the Short-Mayo Composite Aircraft.

R. H. Mayo, General Manager (Technical) of Imperial Airways, was responsible for the inception of this design with the aim of achieving North Atlantic commercial operation. The idea found favor with the British Government who approved the program and agreed to its development. In 1935 a special company was formed, the Mayo Composite Aircraft Co. Ltd., which was to be responsible for supervising the program, while construction was entrusted to Short Brothers at Rochester, the British company with the greatest expertise in building flying boats, the most suitable craft for this concept. The composite soon took shape, comprising two totally different four-engine aircraft, which were designated the S.20 and S.21. The former was relatively small and was the upper component; it was a high-wing monoplane with twin floats and of good aerodynamic form. The latter was a large flying boat, which was really a modified S.23 C Class aircraft.

Both aircraft were built and tested separately, their maiden flights taking place on 27 July (S.21) and 5 September 1937 (S.20). The lower component was named *Maia* and the upper component *Mercury*. On 20 January the following year, *Maia* and *Mercury* flew as a unit and on 6 February the first inflight separation took place. On 20 July *Mercury* separated from *Maia* near Foynes (Ireland) and set off on a direct flight to Canada, piloted by Captain D. C. T. Bennett. *Mercury* carried a 600 lb (272 kg) payload and touched down at Boucherville (Montreal) after flying for 20 hours 20 minutes, having covered 2,930 miles (4,715 km). This was the first commercial crossing of the North Atlantic by a heavier-than-air aircraft. On 6 October, a second, considerably more ambitious, experimental flight was begun, setting off from Dundee for Cape Town. *Mercury* covered 6,045 miles (9,728 km) in 42 hours and 5 minutes although it did not quite reach its intended destination, but had to alight in the estuary of the Orange River. Nevertheless it had set a record. These proving flights would have continued but for the imminence of war. The Short S.21 was converted into an airliner and handed over to BOAC to be used as a wartime transport. *Mercury* was taken over by the RAF. *Maia* met its end on 11 May 1941, being destroyed by bombing, and *Mercury* was broken up during that year. Before being impressed into the Royal Air Force, the S.20 had helped with Christmas mailloads between Southampton and Alexandria.

Another original experiment was that carried out with the Caproni Campini N.1 (often inaccurately referred to as the CC.2), the first Italian aircraft not to be driven by a propeller and one of the first reaction-powered aircraft. The Germans, at this time, had unquestionably taken the lead in this new field; the first successful flight to be made by a rocket-propelled aircraft had been achieved on 30 September 1929, by the RAK-1, a glider powered by 16 rockets which had been developed by Friedrich Wilhelm

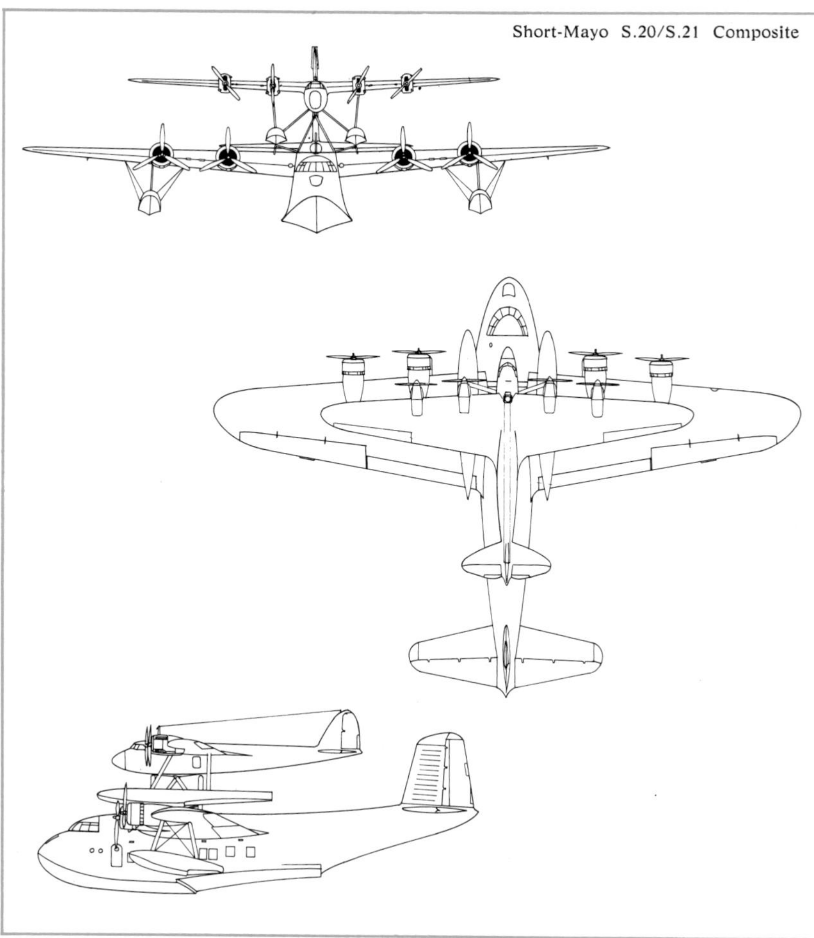

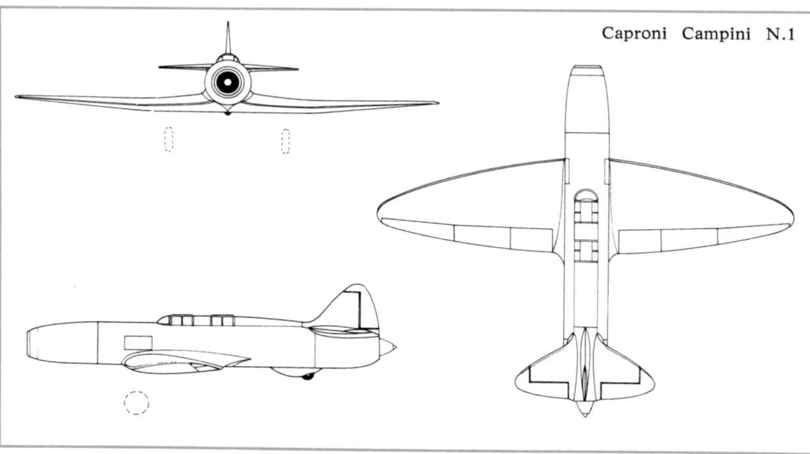

Sander, and piloted by Fritz von Opel. The glider remained airborne for about ten minutes reaching a maximum speed of 95 mph (153 km/h). On 27 August 1939, the first jet aircraft in history made its maiden flight—the Heinkel He 178. In this context the Italian experiment can be seen as an isolated project without any real relevance to contemporary German research, since it made no serious attempt to develop the technology needed to build a jet engine. In point of fact the power-unit which the engineer, Secondo Campini, designed was halfway between a piston engine and a turbine.

The N.1 was a two-seat, all-metal monoplane with a 900 hp Isotta-Fraschini engine mounted within the fuselage, driving a variable-pitch, ducted-fan compressor. A ring of fuel injectors heated the compressed air, to develop thrust of 750 kg.

The Caproni Campini was given its first test flight on 28 August 1940, with Mario De Bernardi at the controls. On 30 November 1941, De Bernardi flew the N.1 from Milan to Rome with a consignment of mailbags as payload; the airplane was then handed over to the Regia Aeronautica at the test center at Guidonia and was evaluated until September 1942.

Plate 110
Four famous dirigibles: 1926–1936

Ironically enough, it was only in the late 1930s that the airplane fully caught up with the achievements which airships had made ten years earlier, in spite of all the concentrated research and effort which had gone into developing heavier-than-air flight. The most famous passenger airship was named *Graf Zeppelin* on 8 July 1928, three months before it made its inaugural flight from Germany to the United States. This dirigible had been designed for training and research into transocean navigation, but it was destined to become the first aircraft to carry passengers on transocean services. Only 20 passengers could be accommodated on board but they were provided with every comfort and facility that luxurious air travel of the day could offer. The *Graf Zeppelin* could cruise at 71.5 mph (115 km/h) and fly about 8,000 miles (12,875 km) non-stop. On 11 October 1928, the airship left Friedrichshafen bound for the United States carrying 10 paying passengers and 10 guests, some freight and a considerable number of sacks of mail containing sixty thousand letters which had been specially franked to commemorate the journey. This was the first in a long series of flights across the Atlantic. In the years which followed, the *Graf Zeppelin* made many journeys, including some hundred over the South Atlantic between Friedrichshafen and Pernambuco (Brasil). In 1935 the airship completed its 100th ocean crossing, its 500th flight, its 50th return flight over the South Atlantic and its 1,000,000th kilometer (621,370 miles).

In addition to scheduled transocean flights the *Graf Zeppelin* made a round-the-world flight in 12 days 14 hours 20 minutes in August 1929, and in 1931 an Arctic cruise as far north as Franz Josef Land. The airship was withdrawn from service after the loss of the *Hindenburg* in 1937, by which time it had flown 1,053,395 miles (1,695,272 km), made 590 flights and carried 13,100 passengers. It was dismantled in 1940.

The airship *Norge* flew over the North Pole on 12 May 1926, three days after the Fokker F.VIIa-3m trimotor *Josephine Ford*, piloted by Richard Byrd and Floyd Bennett. On board the *Norge* (which had been built in Italy to Umberto Nobile's design and was originally designated N.1) was Nobile himself, with the Norwegian explorer, Roald Amundsen and the American Lincoln Ellsworth, who had financed the project. They set off on this great adventure on 10 April, when the *Norge* left Italy. On 7 May the dirigible moored in King's Bay (Spitzbergen) to make its final preparations and, four days later at 10 a.m., the airship took off. The first part of the flight went well, but the later stages were another matter. Bedeviled by fog and bad weather, the *Norge* only managed to land on 14 May, in Alaska.

Nobile was keen to continue such flights, but considerable disagreements had arisen between him and the Norwegians; he therefore decided to go it alone, and the next expedition and the new airship were financed by public subscription. The project was launched in 1927 and the new dirigible was designated N.4 and was called the *Italia*. She was built by the Stabilimento Costruzioni Aeronautiche who had gained considerable experience when constructing the N.1. The *Italia* differed only slightly from the *Norge* in size and structural details. Once the airship was completed it made the voyage to King's Bay, arriving on 6 May 1928, after crossing Central Europe and the Barents Sea in three stages. After one attempt to take off was frustrated by bad weather, the departure was set for the morning of 23 May. *Italia* took off at 4.28 a.m. and the outward journey went well. The return journey was a nightmare: delayed by bad weather and ice forming on the envelope and weighing the dirigible down, the airship crashed at 10.33 a.m. on 25 May. The search for the survivors of the crash, who had managed to pitch a bright red tent, began, lasting forty-eight days and still causes controversy after fifty years. The immediate consequence was that the Italian armed forces took all dirigibles out of service under pressure of public opinion.

The final episode which helped to bring the age of the big rigid airship to an end occurred nine years later; this was the *Hindenburg* tragedy. The LZ 129 *Hindenburg* was the most luxurious passenger airship ever built, the last to enter service in a long line of dirigibles built by Ferdinand von Zeppelin. The LZ 129 was put into service by Deutsche Zeppelin-Reederei on 6 May 1936, on the Frankfurt–New York service. The German airship burst into flames exactly a year later, when coming up to its mooring mast at Lakehurst on the first crossing of the 1937 season.

Thirty-five of the ninety-seven people on board died in or as the result of this disaster and it was decided that no lives must be risked in this way ever again in transatlantic airship flights. The public outcry which ensued effectively put an end to the era of the commercial airship.

Increasing passenger capacity of aircraft: 1928–1940

Plate 112

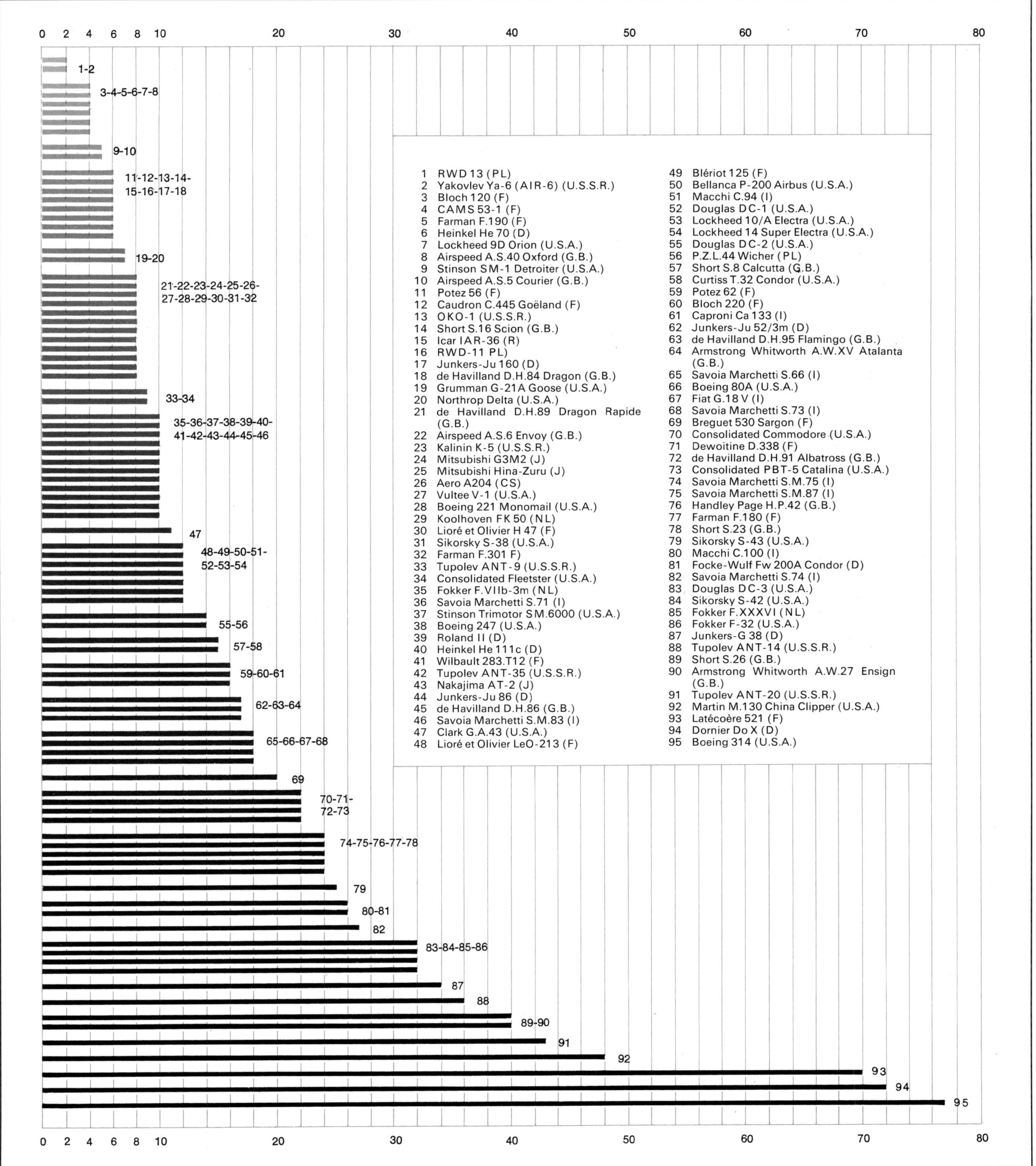
0 2 4 6 8 10 20 30 40 50 60 70 80
1-2
3-4-5-6-7-8
9-10
11-12-13-14-
15-16-17-18
19-20
21-22-23-24-25-26-
27-28-29-30-31-32
33-34
35-36-37-38-39-40-
41-42-43-44-45-46
47
48-49-50-51-
52-53-54
55-56
57-58
59-60-61
62-63-64
65-66-67-68
69
70-71-
72-73
74-75-76-77-78
79
80-81
82
83-84-85-86
87
88
89-90
91
92
93
94
95
1 RWD 13 (PL)
2 Yakovlev Ya-6 (AIR-6) (U.S.S.R.)
3 Bloch 120 (F)
4 CAMS 53-1 (F)
5 Farman F.190 (F)
6 Heinkel He 70 (D)
7 Lockheed 9D Orion (U.S.A.)
8 Airspeed A.S.40 Oxford (G.B.)
9 Stinson SM-1 Detroiter (U.S.A.)
10 Airspeed A.S.5 Courier (G.B.)
11 Potez 56 (F)
12 Caudron C.445 Goëland (F)
13 OKO-1 (U.S.S.R.)
14 Short S.16 Scion (G.B.)
15 Icar IAR-36 (R)
16 RWD-11 PL)
17 Junkers-Ju 160 (D)
18 de Havilland D.H.84 Dragon (G.B.)
19 Grumman G-21A Goose (U.S.A.)
20 Northrop Delta (U.S.A.)
21 de Havilland D.H.89 Dragon Rapide (G.B.)
22 Airspeed A.S.6 Envoy (G.B.)
23 Kalinin K-5 (U.S.S.R.)
24 Mitsubishi G3M2 (J)
25 Mitsubishi Hina-Zuru (J)
26 Aero A204 (CS)
27 Vultee V-1 (U.S.A.)
28 Boeing 221 Monomail (U.S.A.)
29 Koolhoven FK 50 (NL)
30 Lioré et Olivier H 47 (F)
31 Sikorsky S-38 (U.S.A.)
32 Farman F.301 F)
33 Tupolev ANT-9 (U.S.S.R.)
34 Consolidated Fleetster (U.S.A.)
35 Fokker F.VIIb-3m (NL)
36 Savoia Marchetti S.71 (I)
37 Stinson Trimotor SM.6000 (U.S.A.)
38 Boeing 247 (U.S.A.)
39 Roland II (D)
40 Heinkel He 111c (D)
41 Wilbault 283.T12 (F)
42 Tupolev ANT-35 (U.S.S.R.)
43 Nakajima AT-2 (J)
44 Junkers-Ju 86 (D)
45 de Havilland D.H.86 (G.B.)
46 Savoia Marchetti S.M.83 (I)
47 Clark G.A.43 (U.S.A.)
48 Lioré et Olivier LeO-213 (F)
49 Blériot 125 (F)
50 Bellanca P-200 Airbus (U.S.A.)
51 Macchi C.94 (I)
52 Douglas DC-1 (U.S.A.)
53 Lockheed 10/A Electra (U.S.A.)
54 Lockheed 14 Super Electra (U.S.A.)
55 Douglas DC-2 (U.S.A.)
56 P.Z.L.44 Wicher (PL)
57 Short S.8 Calcutta (G.B.)
58 Curtiss T.32 Condor (U.S.A.)
59 Potez 62 (F)
60 Bloch 220 (F)
61 Caproni Ca 133 (I)
62 Junkers-Ju 52/3m (D)
63 de Havilland D.H.95 Flamingo (G.B.)
64 Armstrong Whitworth A.W.XV Atalanta (G.B.)
65 Savoia Marchetti S.66 (I)
66 Boeing 80A (U.S.A.)
67 Fiat G.18 V (I)
68 Savoia Marchetti S.73 (I)
69 Breguet 530 Sargon (F)
70 Consolidated Commodore (U.S.A.)
71 Dewoitine D.338 (F)
72 de Havilland D.H.91 Albatross (G.B.)
73 Consolidated PBT-5 Catalina (U.S.A.)
74 Savoia Marchetti S.M.75 (I)
75 Savoia Marchetti S.M.87 (I)
76 Handley Page H.P.42 (G.B.)
77 Farman F.180 (F)
78 Short S.23 (G.B.)
79 Sikorsky S-43 (U.S.A.)
80 Macchi C.100 (I)
81 Focke-Wulf Fw 200A Condor (D)
82 Savoia Marchetti S.74 (I)
83 Douglas DC-3 (U.S.A.)
84 Sikorsky S-42 (U.S.A.)
85 Fokker F.XXXVI (NL)
86 Fokker F-32 (U.S.A.)
87 Junkers-G 38 (D)
88 Tupolev ANT-14 (U.S.S.R.)
89 Short S.26 (G.B.)
90 Armstrong Whitworth A.W.27 Ensign (G.B.)
91 Tupolev ANT-20 (U.S.S.R.)
92 Martin M.130 China Clipper (U.S.A.)
93 Latécoère 521 (F)
94 Dornier Do X (D)
95 Boeing 314 (U.S.A.)
0 2 4 6 8 10 20 30 40 50 60 70 80

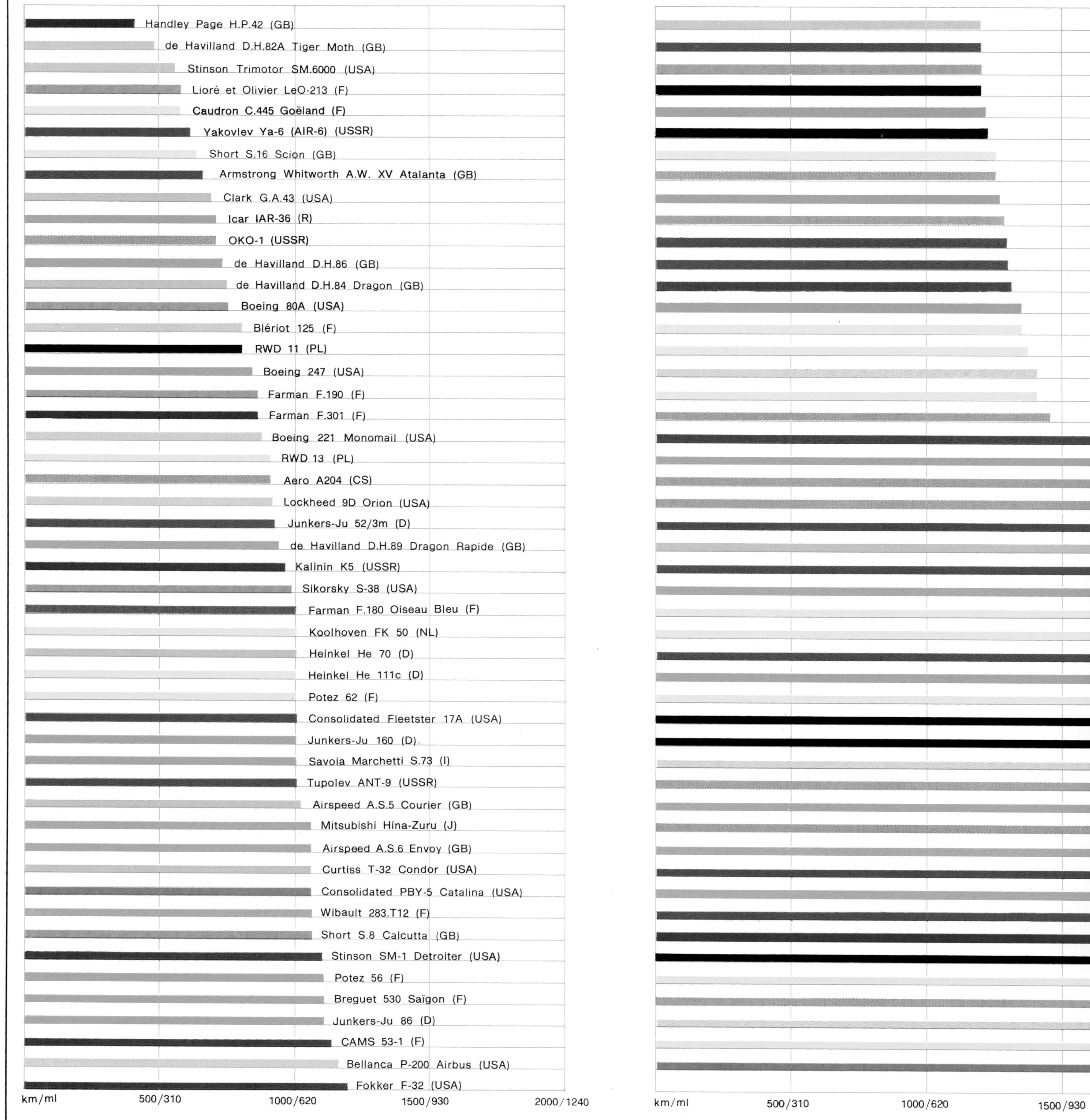
Handley Page H.P.42 (GB)
de Havilland D.H.82A Tiger Moth (GB)
Stinson Trimotor SM.6000 (USA)
Lioré et Olivier LeO-213 (F)
Caudron C.445 Goëland (F)
Yakovlev Ya-6 (AIR-6) (USSR)
Short S.16 Scion (GB)
Armstrong Whitworth A.W. XV Atalanta (GB)
Clark G.A.43 (USA)
Icar IAR-36 (R)
OKO-1 (USSR)
de Havilland D.H.86 (GB)
de Havilland D.H.84 Dragon (GB)
Boeing 80A (USA)
Blériot 125 (F)
RWD 11 (PL)
Boeing 247 (USA)
Farman F.190 (F)
Farman F.301 (F)
Boeing 221 Monomail (USA)
RWD 13 (PL)
Aero A204 (CS)
Lockheed 9D Orion (USA)
Junkers-Ju 52/3m (D)
de Havilland D.H.89 Dragon Rapide (GB)
Kalinin K5 (USSR)
Sikorsky S-38 (USA)
Farman F.180 Oiseau Bleu (F)
Koolhoven FK 50 (NL)
Heinkel He 70 (D)
Heinkel He 111c (D)
Potez 62 (F)
Consolidated Fleetster 17A (USA)
Junkers-Ju 160 (D)
Savoia Marchetti S.73 (I)
Tupolev ANT-9 (USSR)
Airspeed A.S.5 Courier (GB)
Mitsubishi Hina-Zuru (J)
Airspeed A.S.6 Envoy (GB)
Curtiss T-32 Condor (USA)
Consolidated PBY-5 Catalina (USA)
Wibault 283.T12 (F)
Short S.8 Calcutta (GB)
Stinson SM-1 Detroiter (USA)
Potez 56 (F)
Breguet 530 Saïgon (F)
Junkers-Ju 86 (D)
CAMS 53-1 (F)
Bellanca P-200 Airbus (USA)
Fokker F-32 (USA)
km/ml
500/310
1000/620
1500/930
2000/1240
km/ml
500/310
1000/620
1500/930

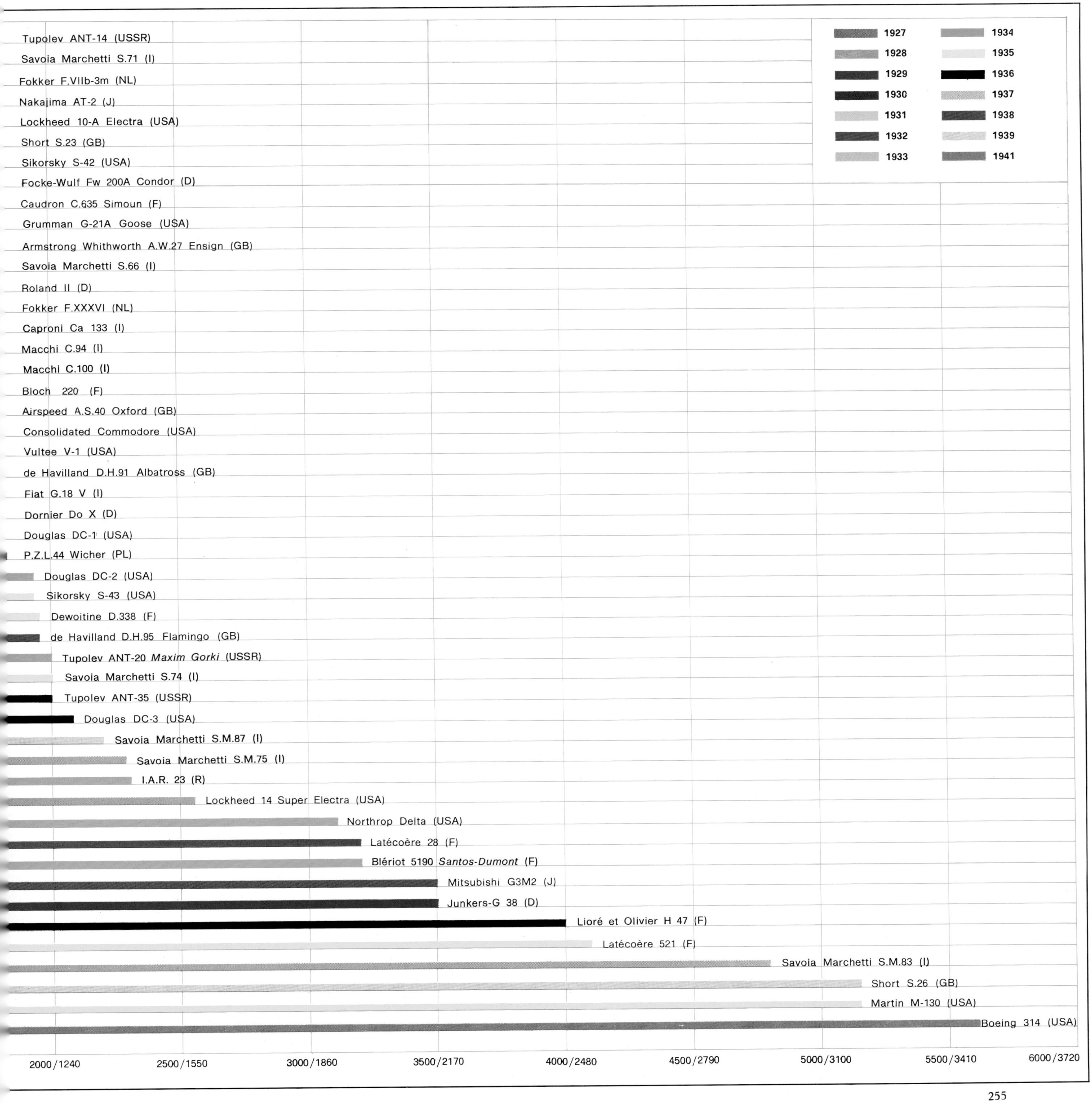

1927	1934
1928	1935
1929	1936
1930	1937
1931	1938
1932	1939
1933	1941

Tupolev ANT-14 (USSR)
Savoia Marchetti S.71 (I)
Fokker F.VIIb-3m (NL)
Nakajima AT-2 (J)
Lockheed 10-A Electra (USA)
Short S.23 (GB)
Sikorsky S-42 (USA)
Focke-Wulf Fw 200A Condor (D)
Caudron C.635 Simoun (F)
Grumman G-21A Goose (USA)
Armstrong Whithworth A.W.27 Ensign (GB)
Savoia Marchetti S.66 (I)
Roland II (D)
Fokker F.XXXVI (NL)
Caproni Ca 133 (I)
Macchi C.94 (I)
Macchi C.100 (I)
Bloch 220 (F)
Airspeed A.S.40 Oxford (GB)
Consolidated Commodore (USA)
Vultee V-1 (USA)
de Havilland D.H.91 Albatross (GB)
Fiat G.18 V (I)
Dornier Do X (D)
Douglas DC-1 (USA)
P.Z.L.44 Wicher (PL)
Douglas DC-2 (USA)
Sikorsky S-43 (USA)
Dewoitine D.338 (F)
de Havilland D.H.95 Flamingo (GB)
Tupolev ANT-20 *Maxim Gorki* (USSR)
Savoia Marchetti S.74 (I)
Tupolev ANT-35 (USSR)
Douglas DC-3 (USA)
Savoia Marchetti S.M.87 (I)
Savoia Marchetti S.M.75 (I)
I.A.R. 23 (R)
Lockheed 14 Super Electra (USA)
Northrop Delta (USA)
Latécoère 28 (F)
Blériot 5190 *Santos-Dumont* (F)
Mitsubishi G3M2 (J)
Junkers-G 38 (D)
Lioré et Olivier H 47 (F)
Latécoère 521 (F)
Savoia Marchetti S.M.83 (I)
Short S.26 (GB)
Martin M-130 (USA)
Boeing 314 (USA)

2000/1240 2500/1550 3000/1860 3500/2170 4000/2480 4500/2790 5000/3100 5500/3410 6000/3720

Comparative table of aircraft speeds: 1927–1941

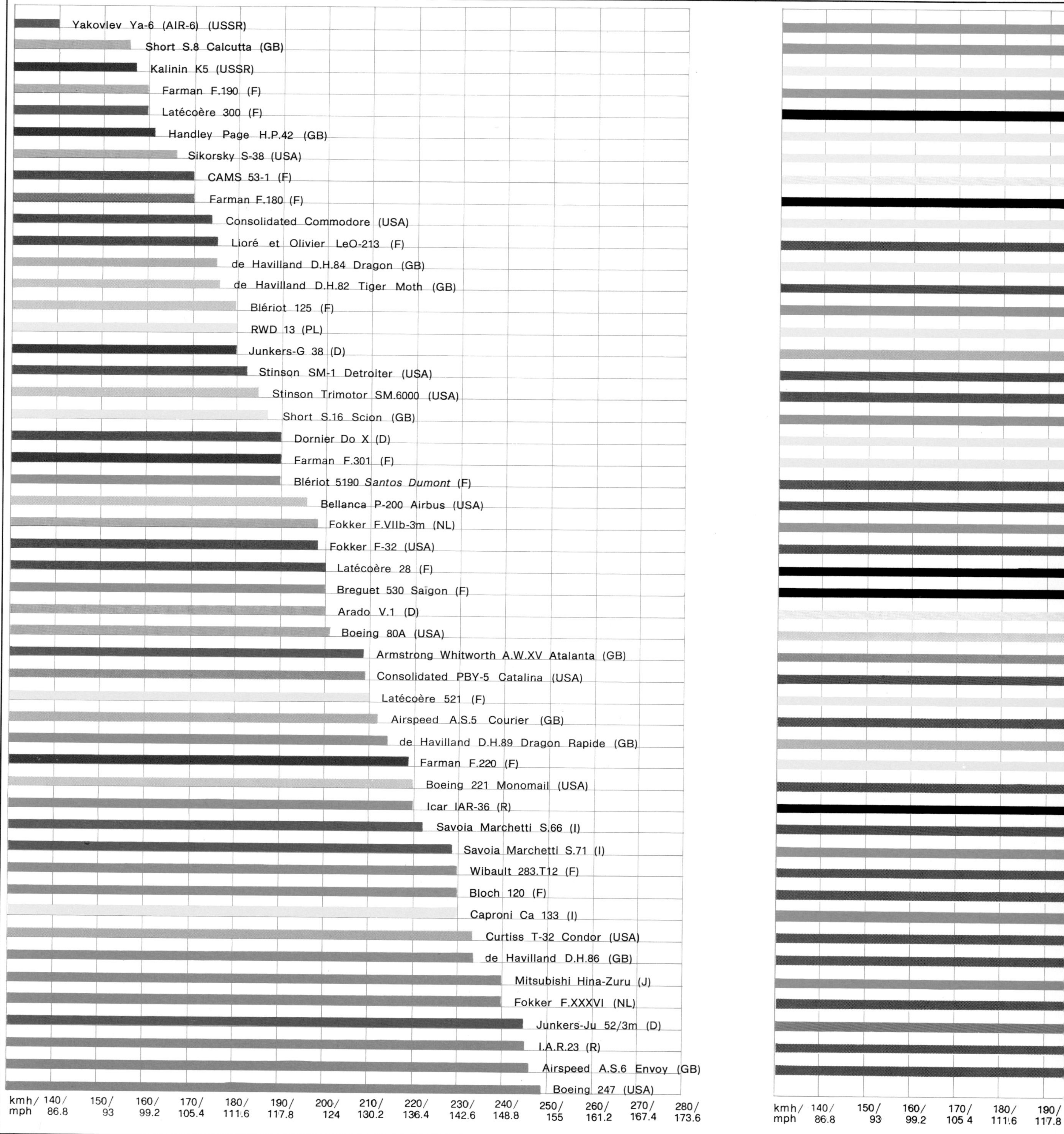
Yakovlev Ya-6 (AIR-6) (USSR)
Short S.8 Calcutta (GB)
Kalinin K5 (USSR)
Farman F.190 (F)
Latécoère 300 (F)
Handley Page H.P.42 (GB)
Sikorsky S-38 (USA)
CAMS 53-1 (F)
Farman F.180 (F)
Consolidated Commodore (USA)
Lioré et Olivier LeO-213 (F)
de Havilland D.H.84 Dragon (GB)
de Havilland D.H.82 Tiger Moth (GB)
Blériot 125 (F)
RWD 13 (PL)
Junkers-G 38 (D)
Stinson SM-1 Detroiter (USA)
Stinson Trimotor SM.6000 (USA)
Short S.16 Scion (GB)
Dornier Do X (D)
Farman F.301 (F)
Blériot 5190 *Santos Dumont* (F)
Bellanca P-200 Airbus (USA)
Fokker F.VIIb-3m (NL)
Fokker F-32 (USA)
Latécoère 28 (F)
Breguet 530 Saïgon (F)
Arado V.1 (D)
Boeing 80A (USA)
Armstrong Whitworth A.W.XV Atalanta (GB)
Consolidated PBY-5 Catalina (USA)
Latécoère 521 (F)
Airspeed A.S.5 Courier (GB)
de Havilland D.H.89 Dragon Rapide (GB)
Farman F.220 (F)
Boeing 221 Monomail (USA)
Icar IAR-36 (R)
Savoia Marchetti S.66 (I)
Savoia Marchetti S.71 (I)
Wibault 283.T12 (F)
Bloch 120 (F)
Caproni Ca 133 (I)
Curtiss T-32 Condor (USA)
de Havilland D.H.86 (GB)
Mitsubishi Hina-Zuru (J)
Fokker F.XXXVI (NL)
Junkers-Ju 52/3m (D)
I.A.R.23 (R)
Airspeed A.S.6 Envoy (GB)
Boeing 247 (USA)
kmh/ mph
140/ 86.8
150/ 93
160/ 99.2
170/ 105.4
180/ 111.6
190/ 117.8
200/ 124
210/ 130.2
220/ 136.4
230/ 142.6
240/ 148.8
250/ 155
260/ 161.2
270/ 167.4
280/ 173.6
kmh/ mph
140/ 86.8
150/ 93
160/ 99.2
170/ 105.4
180/ 111.6
190/ 117.8

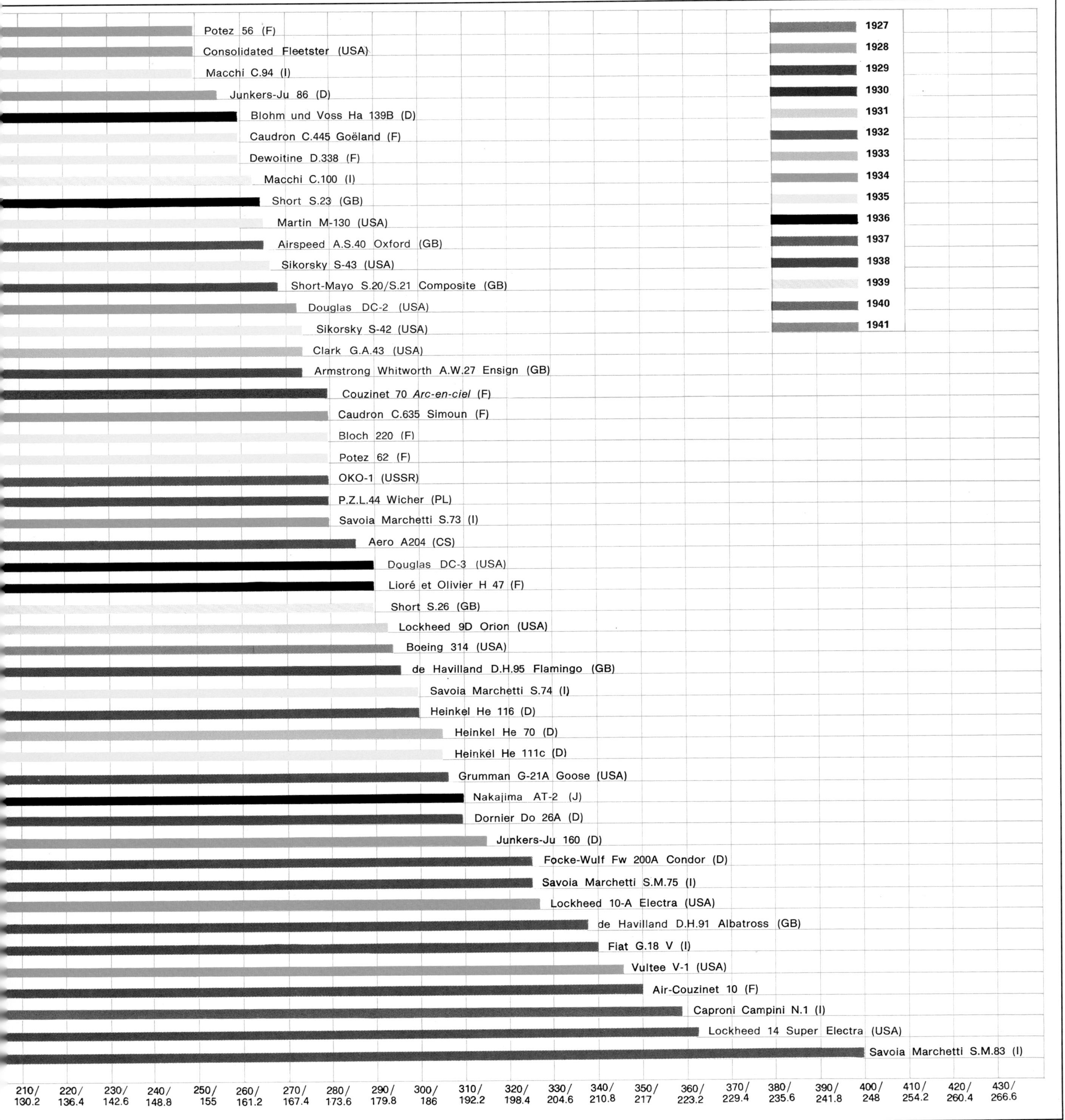

Potez 56 (F)
Consolidated Fleetster (USA)
Macchi C.94 (I)
Junkers-Ju 86 (D)
Blohm und Voss Ha 139B (D)
Caudron C.445 Goëland (F)
Dewoitine D.338 (F)
Macchi C.100 (I)
Short S.23 (GB)
Martin M-130 (USA)
Airspeed A.S.40 Oxford (GB)
Sikorsky S-43 (USA)
Short-Mayo S.20/S.21 Composite (GB)
Douglas DC-2 (USA)
Sikorsky S-42 (USA)
Clark G.A.43 (USA)
Armstrong Whitworth A.W.27 Ensign (GB)
Couzinet 70 Arc-en-ciel (F)
Caudron C.635 Simoun (F)
Bloch 220 (F)
Potez 62 (F)
OKO-1 (USSR)
P.Z.L.44 Wicher (PL)
Savoia Marchetti S.73 (I)
Aero A204 (CS)
Douglas DC-3 (USA)
Lioré et Olivier H 47 (F)
Short S.26 (GB)
Lockheed 9D Orion (USA)
Boeing 314 (USA)
de Havilland D.H.95 Flamingo (GB)
Savoia Marchetti S.74 (I)
Heinkel He 116 (D)
Heinkel He 70 (D)
Heinkel He 111c (D)
Grumman G-21A Goose (USA)
Nakajima AT-2 (J)
Dornier Do 26A (D)
Junkers-Ju 160 (D)
Focke-Wulf Fw 200A Condor (D)
Savoia Marchetti S.M.75 (I)
Lockheed 10-A Electra (USA)
de Havilland D.H.91 Albatross (GB)
Fiat G.18 V (I)
Vultee V-1 (USA)
Air-Couzinet 10 (F)
Caproni Campini N.1 (I)
Lockheed 14 Super Electra (USA)
Savoia Marchetti S.M.83 (I)
1927
1928
1929
1930
1931
1932
1933
1934
1935
1936
1937
1938
1939
1940
1941
210/ 130.2
220/ 136.4
230/ 142.6
240/ 148.8
250/ 155
260/ 161.2
270/ 167.4
280/ 173.6
290/ 179.8
300/ 186
310/ 192.2
320/ 198.4
330/ 204.6
340/ 210.8
350/ 217
360/ 223.2
370/ 229.4
380/ 235.6
390/ 241.8
400/ 248
410/ 254.2
420/ 260.4
430/ 266.6

First regular flights and first airmail services on the Atlantic and Pacific routes: 1933–1939

Date	Route	Crew	Aircraft	Engine	Notes	km	miles
1933 16 January	Paris (F)-Buenos Aires (RA)	Mermoz-Carretier-Mailloux-Couzinet-Bringuier (F)	Couzinet-70 *Arc-en-ciel*	Hispano-Suiza 650 HP	Experimental postal flight	3.200	1,988
1933 15 May	Buenos Aires (RA)-Paris (F)	Mermoz-Carretier-Mailloux-Couzinet-Bringuier (F)	Couzinet-70 *Arc-en-ciel*	Hispano-Suiza 650 HP	Experimental flight with passengers	3.100	1,926
1933 6 May-15 October	Friedrichshafen (D)-Rio de Janeiro (BR)	Lehmann (D)	*Graf Zeppelin*	Maybach	9 return journeys with mail and passengers	10.300	6,401
1934 3 February	Bathurst-Natal Natal-Bathurst	Lufthansa (D)	Dornier-Wal *Monsun* and *Taifun*	BMW 600 HP	Inaugurating regular mail flights	3.100	1,926
1934 26 May-8 September	Friedrichshafen (D)-Rio de Janeiro (BR)	Lehmann (D)	*Graf Zeppelin*	Maybach	11 return flights	10.500	6,525
1935 January - December	Gambia-Brazil Brazil-Gambia	Lufthansa (D)	Dornier Wal	—	Weekly transoceanic service	3.100	1,926
1935 14 February	Senegal-Brazil Brazil-Senegal	Air France (F)	Blériot 5190 *Santos Dumont*	Hispano-Suiza 650 HP	24 return flights	3.100	1,926
1935 17 April	Alameda (USA)-Honolulu (USA)	Musick-Sullivan (Pan American Airways) (USA)	Sikorsky S.42 *Oriental Clipper*	P.&W. Hornet 750 HP	Return flight on 20 April	3.880	2,411
1935 10-15 June	Alameda (USA)-Midway (USA)	Musick-Sullivan (Pan American Airways) (USA)	Sikorsky S.42 *Oriental Clipper*	P.&W. Hornet 750 HP	Returned end June	6.100	3,791
1935 10-17 August	Alameda (USA)-Wake (USA)	Musick-Sullivan (Pan American Airways) (USA)	Sikorsky S.42 *Oriental Clipper*	P.&W. Hornet 750 HP	Returned end August	8.110	5,040
1935 5-14 October	Alameda (USA)-Guam (USA)	Musick-Sullivan (Pan American Airways) (USA)	Sikorsky S.42 *Oriental Clipper*	P.&W. Hornet 750 HP	Returned end October	10.620	6,600
1935 23-28 November	Alameda (USA)-Manila (PI)	Musick (Pan American Airways) (USA)	Glenn Martin M.130 *China Clipper*	P.&W. Hornet 750 HP	Pan American's inaugural flight, returned 6 December	13.160	8,178
1935 6-13 December	Alameda (USA)-Manila (PI)	Sullivan (Pan American Airways) (USA)	Sikorsky S.42 *Philippine Clipper*	P.&W. Hornet 750 HP	Returned end December	13.160	8,178
1936 10-11 September	Azores-New York (USA)	Blankenburg-Von Gablenz (Lufthansa) (D)	Dornier Do 18 *Zephyr*	Junkers Jumo 205 600 HP	Catapult launching from the ship *Schwabenland* returned 25-26 September	4.400	2,734
1936 1-12 September	Azores-New York (USA)	Von Engel (Lufthansa) (D)	Dornier Do 18 *Aeolus*	Junkers Jumo 205 600 HP	Catapult launching from the ship *Schwabenland* returned 22-23 September	4.550	2,827
1936 21-30 October	Alameda (USA)-Kuang-chou (TJ)	Musick (Pan American Airways) (USA)	Glenn Martin M.130 *China Clipper*	P.&W. Hornet 830 HP	First regular passenger and mail flight	14.500	9,011
1937 17-30 March	Alameda (USA)-Auckland (AUS)	Musick (Pan American Airways) (USA)	Sikorsky S.42B *Samoan Clipper*	P.&W. Hornet 750 HP	Experimental flight	11.200	6,920
1937 20-26 March	Italy-Brazil	Kingler-Tonini (Ala Littoria) (I)	Cant Z-506	Alfa Romeo 2250 HP	Returned 2-13 April	4.000	2,480
1937 25 May	USA - Bermuda	Pan American Airways (USA)	Sikorsky S.42	P.&W. Hornet 750 HP	Start of weekly passenger and mail flights	1.250	0,776
1937 25 May	Bermuda - USA	Imperial Airways (USA)	Short S.23 *Cavalier*	Bristol Pegasus 800 HP	on the Hamilton-New York-Hamilton route		
1937 9 June	Bathurst-Natal Natal-Bathurst	Lufthansa (D)	Dornier Do 18	Junkers Jumo 205 600 HP	250 crossing flown on Stuttgart-Santiago de Chile	3.100	1,926
1937 5-6 July	New York (USA)-Southampton (GB)	Gray-De Lima-Masland (Pan American Airways) (USA)	Sikorsky S.42B *Clipper III*	P.&W. Hornet 750 HP	Returned 15 July	3.200	1,988
1937 5-6 July	Southampton (GB) - New York (USA)	Wilcockson-Bowes (Imperial Airways) (USA)	Short S.23 *Caledonia*	Bristol Pegasus 800 HP	Returned 15 July	3.200	1,988
1937 29-30 July	Southampton (GB) - New York (USA)	Powell-Felser (Imperial Airways) (USA)	Short *Cambria*	Bristol Pegasus 800 HP	Returned 7-9 August	3.200	1,988
1937 10-16 August	Germany-Azores-New York (USA)	Blankenburg-Schack (Lufthansa) (D)	Blohm und Voss Ha139 *Normeer*	Junkers Jumo 205 600 HP	Returned 24-26 August	3.970	2,467
1937 15 September	Azores-New York (USA)	Von Engel-Stein (Lufthansa) (D)	Blohm und Voss Ha139 *Norwind*	Junkers Jumo 205 600 HP	Returned 22 September	3.970	2,467
1937 21-22 November	Paris (F)- Santiago (RCH)	Codos-Vauthier (Air France) (F)	Farman 2231 *Chef de Pilote Guerrero*	Hispano-Suiza 900 HP	Commercial record.	3.100	1,926

Date	Route	Crew	Aircraft	Engine	Notes	km	miles
1938 27-29 March	Plymouth (GB)-Brazil	Von Engel (Lufthansa) (D)	Dornier Do 18	Junkers Jumo 205 600 HP		8.500	5,282
1938 25 July 1938 31 July 1938 13 September	Horta-Port Washington/ Port Washington-Horta	Von Engel (Lufthansa) (D) Blankenburg (Lufthansa) (D) Mayr-Blume (Lufthansa) (D)	Blohm und Voss Ha139 *Nordwind* Blohm und Voss Ha139 *Nordmeer* Blohm und Voss Ha139 *Nordstern*	Junkers Jumo 205 600 HP Junkers Jumo 205 600 HP Junkers Jumo 205 600 HP	28 crossings total mileage.......	141.800	88,129
1938 23-31 August	Bordeaux (F)-New York (USA)	Guillaumet-Leclaire (Air France) (F)	Latécoère 521 *Lieut. de Vaisseau Paris*	Hispano-Suiza 860 HP	Returned 6-9 September.	4.600	2,858
1938 26 December	Senegal-Brazil	Air France (F)			Total of 351 crossings flown since inception of bi-weekly mail flights.		
1938 31 December	Gambia-Brazil	Lufthansa (D)			Total of 413 crossings flown since inception of bi-weekly mail flights.		
1939 26-30 March	Baltimore (USA)-Marseille (F)	Gray-Loreer (Pan American Airways) (USA)	Boeing 314A *Yankee Clipper*	Wright Cyclone 1600 HP	First flight on Bermuda-Azores-Lisbon route.	5.500	3,420
1939 3 April	New York (USA)-Bermuda	Pan American Airways (USA)	Boeing 314A *Bermuda Clipper*	Wright Cyclone 1600 HP	First scheduled flight carrying 38 passengers	1.250	0,776
1939 12-16 April	Bermuda-New York (USA)	Gray-Loreer (Pan American Airways) (USA)	Boeing 314A *Yankee Clipper*	Wright Cyclone 1600 HP	First scheduled flight carrying 60 passengers.	1.250	0,776
1939 27-29 May	New York (USA)-Marseille (F)	Culberston (Pan American) Airways) (USA)	Boeing 314A *Atlantic Clipper*	Wright Cyclone 1600 HP	First flight on Azores-Lisbon route. Returned 1-3 June.	9.500	5,904
1939 17-19 June	Biscarrosse (F)-New York (USA)	Guillaumet-Carriou-Comet (Air France) (F)	Latécoère 522 *Ville de St. Pierre*	Hispano-Suiza 860 HP	First flight on Lisbon-Azores-Bermuda route. Returned 22-24 June.	7.600	4,723
1939 27-29 June	Berlin (D)-Rio de Janeiro (BR)	Henke (Lufthansa) (D)	Focke-Wulf Fw 200 Condor *Pommern*	Junkers Jumo 205 720 HP	Returned to Berlin in July.	11.500	7,147
1939 1-3 July	New York (USA)-Biscarrosse (F)	Byrne (American Export Airlines) (USA)	Consolidated *Transatlantic*	Wright Cyclone 800 HP	First flight on Azores-Lisbon route. Returned 5-7 July.	7.500	4,661
1939 14-15 July	New York (USA)-Bordeaux (F)	Guillaumet-Carriou-Comet (Air France) (F)	Latécoère 521 *Lieut. de Vaisseau Paris*	Hispano-Suiza 860 HP	Jamaica Bay-Biscarrosse non-stop.	5.850	3,635
1939 14-15 July	New York (USA)-Bordeaux (F)	Byrne (American Export Airlines) (USA)	Consolidated *Transatlantic*	Wright Cyclone 800 HP	Trepassey Bay-Biscarrosse non-stop. Returned 29-30 July.	4.700	2,921
1939 26-31 July	Berlin (D)-Rio de Janeiro (BR)	Cramer-Von Klausbruck (Lufthansa) (D)	Focke-Wulf Fw 200 Condor *Arumani*	Junkers Jumo 205 720 HP	Returned to Berlin in August.	11.500	7,147
1939 5-6 August	New York (USA)-Southampton (GB)	Pan American Airways (USA)	Boeing 314A *Yankee Clipper*	Wright Cyclone 1600 HP	First flight on the Botwood-Foynes route. Returned 9-10 August.	3.200	1.988
1939 5-7 August	Southampton (GB)-New York (USA)	Imperial Airways (USA)	Short S.23 *Caribou*	Bristol Pegasus 800 HP	First flight on the Foynes-Botwood route. Returned 9-10 August.	3.200	1,988
1939 22-27 August	San Francisco (USA)-New Zealand	Pan American Airways (USA)	Boeing 314A *California Clipper*	Wright Cyclone 1600 HP	Inaugural flight on the Hawaii-Samoa route.	11.200	6,960
1939 2-6 October	Rome-Cape Verde Islands	Tonini-Suster-Rapp (LATI) (I)	Savoia Marchetti S.M.83	Alfa Romeo 2250 HP	Start of experimental/ route proving flights by LATI.	5.300	3,286
1939 18 December	USA-Europe	Pan American Airways (USA)	Boeing 314A *Yankee Clipper*	Wright Cyclone 1600 HP	Total of 100 crossings flown having carried 1,800 passengers on Transatlantic flights.	—	—

Armstrong Whitworth A.W. XV Atalanta - 1932, GB (99)

de Havilland D.H.82A Tiger Moth - 1931, GB (92)

de Havilland D.H.86 - 1934, GB (92)

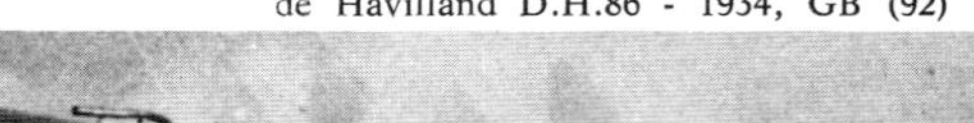

Handley Page H.P.42 - 1930, GB (83)

de Havilland D.H.89 Dragon Rapide - 1934, GB (92)

Short Scion Senior - 1935, GB (96)

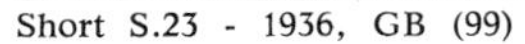
Short S.23 - 1936, GB (99)

Short S.26 - 1939, GB (108)

Dornier Do X - 1929, D (89)

Junkers-Ju 52/3m - 1932, D (91)

Focke-Wulf Fw 200 Condor - 1937, D (107)

Heinkel He 111c - 1935, D (89)

Heinkel He 70 - 1933, D (89)

Rohrbach Roland II - 1929, D (89)

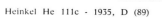

Dornier Do 26 - 1938, D (108)

Blériot 165 between two Lioré et Olivier LeO 213 - 1928, F (83)

Farman F.303 - 1930, F (84)

Wibault 283.T12 - 1934, F (101)

Couzinet 70 Arc-en-ciel - 1929, F (86)

Latécoère 300 - 1931, F (98)

Dewoitine D.338 - 1935, F (101)

Photographic Appendix

Savoia Marchetti S.71 - 1930, I (93)

Macchi C.94 - 1935, I (103)

Caproni Ca 133 - 1935, I (103)

Savoia Marchetti S.M.83 - 1937, I (93)

Fiat G.18 - 1936, I (103)

Savoia Marchetti S.73 - 1934, I (93)

Savoia Marchetti S.66 - 1932, I (83)

Sikorsky S-42 - 1934, USA (85)

Douglas DC-1 - 1933, USA (97)

Douglas DC-2 - 1934, USA (97)

Lockheed 9D Orion - 1931, USA (90)

Consolidated 17 Fleetster - 1930, USA (102)

Douglas DC-3 - 1935, USA (97)

6.

THE GREAT AGE OF EXPANSION IN CIVIL AVIATION

In 1981 the airlines of the 150 member countries of ICAO (International Civil Aviation Organization) carried 728 million passengers on scheduled flights and 11 million tonnes of cargo. These figures were respectively a drop of 2.5 percent and an increase of 3 percent and reflect the impact of the worldwide recession. The peak traffic year was 1979 when the passenger total was 754 million and this figure represented a 3 percent increase on the previous year. In 1979 domestic passenger traffic had increased by 9.8 percent and international passenger traffic by 10.4 percent. Total international traffic, measured in terms of tonne/kilometers had increased by 12.1 percent, as against 10.3 percent for domestic business. Approximately 51 percent of the total traffic had been accounted for by the U.S.A. and the Soviet Union (37 and 14 percent); furthermore, these two countries had between them handled 80 percent of the world's domestic traffic, the shares being: U.S.A. 56 percent and U.S.S.R. 24 percent. On international routes United States airlines handled approximately 17 percent and Great Britain 10 percent of the traffic. The leading nations in commercial aviation were, in order of traffic volume: the U.S.A., the U.S.S.R., Great Britain, followed by Japan, France, Canada, the German Federal Republic and Australia. This was the state of the world market at the end of the 1970s which had proved an extremely prosperous decade, during which passenger traffic had increased at an annual rate of 8.1 percent. These statistics give a useful outline of the state of civil aviation today, the culmination of thirty-five years' postwar progress and changes in world coverage and the infrastructure of the industry, but also encapsulate the phase during which commercial aviation started to undergo profound changes. From the beginning of the 1980s recession hit the developed countries, caused mainly by the energy crisis, and this new situation has already determined future developments. Like many industries, the transport industry has had to undergo yet another period of change.

The history of the last forty years of air transport is first and foremost the story of America's aviation industry, and it is interesting to follow the evolution of this nation's overwhelming supremacy in terms of organization, industrial strength and aircraft.

The outbreak of war in Europe in 1939 and the United States' entry into the conflict at the end of 1941 did not have a traumatic effect on the United States' commercial air transport system. Normal services were able to continue throughout the continent of North America, far removed from any of the theaters of war, and had only the positive effect of giving further stimulus to the process of expansion which had begun in the 1930s, due to the immense war effort demanded of the whole industrial machine. In 1941 the domestic airlines managed to reach their target of carrying 4 million passengers and after a relative lull during the next three years, growth accelerated once more. In 1945 total passenger traffic had risen to 6 million—an increase of 50 percent.

The response to this increase in domestic demand was impressive; in 1951 American Airlines carried 4.9 million passengers; Eastern came second with 3.5 million; United reached a total of 2.8 million; while TWA (which on 17 May 1950, had changed its name to Trans World Airlines) carried some 2.2 million. Close behind the "Big Four" came Capital Airlines, carrying nearly 2 million people while a further seven companies accounted for somewhere between 500,000 and 1,000,000 each.

International air traffic followed a similar pattern. From 1942 onward, the intercontinental giant Pan American was joined by another enterprising company, American Export Airlines, and on 1 June 1945, TWA was authorized to start a transatlantic service, flying to destinations as distant as India, across the Mediterranean and the Middle East. Northwest Airlines was next, and inaugurated services to Japan across the Pacific; Braniff International operated routes to South America, and National Airlines and Chicago & Southern Airlines to the Caribbean. The most sought-after route was still over the North Atlantic, which at that time was shared by Pan American, TWA and American Export (which had changed its name on 10 November 1945 to American Overseas Airlines) and these three enjoyed an absolute monopoly until the spring of 1946. In spite of the European airlines subsequently competing on this route (in 1950 ten companies operated the North Atlantic route; in 1955 this had risen to 14 and by 1960 to 18) the three American airlines managed to keep their dominant position. In 1948, out of a total of 240,000 passengers on the North Atlantic route, 55,000 flew with Pan American; 48,000 with TWA and 45,000 with American Overseas Airlines. After the merger of Pan American and American Overseas in 1950, passengers on this route totaled 311,000; of these, 109,000 flew in aircraft belonging to the new group's fleet and 66,000 with TWA; in 1960 Pan American's passengers totalled 368,000 and TWA's 243,000, out of an overall total of 1,760,000 passengers.

In 1960 the 88 airline companies belonging to IATA (the International Air Transport Association) carried over 106 million passengers. More than 40 percent of this volume of traffic was handled by 12 U.S. member airlines and those known traditionally as the "Big Four" (United, Eastern, American and TWA), together with Pan American, accounted for more than 32 percent. Ten years later, in 1970, total passenger traffic reached 385 million, and U.S. airlines handled 45.8 percent of this; Aeroflot had 19.6 percent; the European airlines accounted for 16.3 percent; Japanese airlines: 3.8 percent; South American companies: 2.8 percent; Canadian airlines: 2.6 percent; Australian: 1.7 percent; and the remaining 7.4 percent by other nations.

Apart from the sheer volume of traffic handled by the United States, another crucial factor in building the prestige of the U.S. aviation industry has been the constant progress and up-dating achieved over the years, which has shaped the entire world of international civil transport. The first revolutionary change was the introduction of the jet engine. Although the U.S.A. was not the first country to put a turbojet-powered airliner into service, it swiftly overtook both Great Britain and the Soviet Union, who had both put jet airliners into service before the U.S., in terms of quality and quantity. Boeing deserves much of the credit for this: the Boeing 707 was not only the first commercial jet manufactured in the United States, it was also the forerunner of a whole family of aircraft whose influence is still felt throughout the Western World's air transport industry. The other two giants of the U.S. aeronautical industry, Douglas and Lockheed, followed their old rival and, between them, these three companies took a large share of the world market, except for the Soviet bloc. Boeing was once more the innovator when it introduced the first wide-bodied jet and put its Model 747 into service, and yet again, in the early 1980s, working on the first examples of a new generation of lower fuel consumption aircraft: the 767 and the 757. The United States did not, however, finally opt for participation in another significant development—that of the supersonic transports in which France and Great Britain have been technically successful with their Concorde. This was not due, however, to lack of technical capability but to a decision that such an aircraft would not be economic.

The other three Western powers which have managed to maintain a significant role since the war are, in fact, Great Britain, France and the Netherlands.

At the end of World War II British civil aviation was beset by serious organizational and technical problems. There was a shortage of modern aircraft, such as those being produced by United States industry, which were at that time the only ones capable of being competitive. A dual approach was therefore needed: on one hand, to start from scratch designing new commercial airplanes and thus close the gap which had widened during the war years; on the other hand Great Britain had to survive the transitional phase and all the risks it entailed whilst trying to recover as quickly as possible. On the organizational level it was decided to make a distinction between European and intercontinental routes. During the war BOAC had carried some 280,000 passengers, using a fleet of 160 aircraft of differing types and origins, covering more than 56,500,000 miles (91,000,000 km). In 1946 BOAC's European operations were hived off into the new corporation, British European Airways (BEA), formed on 1 August 1946. This new company soon proved itself to be both enterprising and responsive to market trends and won a good share of the business available.

In January 1944 a group of shipping companies founded British Latin-American Air Lines and in October 1945 the name was changed to British South American Airways Ltd. This airline began proving flights to South America in January 1946 and, that August, it was nationalized as British South American Airways Corporation (BSAAC). After the failure of the Avro Tudors, the airline was merged with BOAC in July 1949.

Recovery was soon in sight, partly because Britain now had the means to buy American aircraft and also because the British aircraft industry, working flat out, was on the point of launching a new generation of commercial aircraft. British designers and engineers made the most of the advances they had achieved in aero-engines during the war, and Great Britain's clear lead in this field meant that she was the first nation to produce effective turbine engines. There were two major steps forward: the first flight of the prototype Vickers-Armstrongs Viscount (the V.630) on 16 July 1948, and the maiden flight of the de Havilland Comet on 27 July 1949, the former being the first propeller-turbine passenger airliner and the latter the first commercial turbojet aircraft to be put into service.

BOAC began the world's first jet-operated regular passenger services on 2 May 1952, when the Comet G-ALYP left Heathrow for Johannesburg, which was reached in 23 hours 34 minutes. As more Comets were delivered these advanced aircraft were introduced on the routes to India and Ceylon (11 August), Singapore (14 October), and in 1953 to Tokyo (3 April). On all these routes the Comets halved the flight times, but on the first anniversary of their introduction a Comet broke up in a storm near Calcutta and, on 10 January and 8 April 1954, two Comets suffered structural failure off the Italian coast. All Comets were withdrawn from service until the much changed Comet 4 began the first North Atlantic jet services in October 1958.

On 29 July 1950, BEA had operated the first scheduled passenger service anywhere in the world to be flown by a turbine-powered aircraft, when for two weeks the 32-passenger prototype Viscount V.630 was used on the London–Paris route. Then from 15 to 23 August the Viscount flew on the London–Edinburgh route. But the V.630 was considered uneconomic and BEA ordered a fleet of more powerful 47-passenger Viscount V.701s, with regular operation beginning on 18 April 1953, over the London–Rome–Athens–Nicosia route. The Vickers Viscount launched the British airline on a period of remarkable expansion: by 1955 BEA was the leading European airline, carrying just over 1 million passengers on international flights and more than 860,000 on internal routes; by 1961 these two totals had risen to 2.2 million and 1,780,000. In the same years BOAC's share of passenger traffic was 291,000 and 852,000 on intercontinental routes. In 1970 Great Britain ranked third in the world: British airlines carried 2,293 million tonne/kilometers of passengers, cargo and mail; in 1979 it held the same position (still third after the United States and the Soviet Union), with a total of 6,290 million tonne/kilometers. In 1979, British Airways alone (the new airline was formed on 1 April 1972, by the merger of BOAC and BEA) carried a total of 16,906,000 passengers on scheduled flights and was the leading European airline.

The mid-seventies saw the entry into service of what was perhaps the most exciting commercial aircraft ever built: Concorde, which heralded the era of the supersonic transport. British Airways put this aircraft into service on 21 January 1976, on the London–Bahrain route; on the same date Air France inaugurated its "Mach 2" route between Paris and Rio de Janeiro via Dakar. On 24 May flights to North America were commenced, firstly to Washington and then, on 22 November 1977, to New York. These were certainly milestones in the history of aviation, but the driving force behind this achievement was national prestige rather than purely financial considerations.

National prestige was France's main reason for pushing ahead with the great enterprise of supersonic civil transport and also accounted for her efforts to consolidate her position in the forefront of European aeronautical development which she had won for herself since the end of World War II. When peace came, France had to undertake a complete reconstruction of her commercial aviation industry. The French airlines which had survived the German occupation were nationalized and, on 1 January 1946, Société Nationale Air France was re-formed. Recovery was swift: the French adopted a diversified policy in procurement of new aircraft. On the one hand, they encouraged their own manufacturing industry, and at the same time bought the best types available on the international market. As a result the French national airline always had a fleet of first-class, highly competitive aircraft and soon captured a good share of European air traffic. The most successful outcome of this policy was the production of the Caravelle in the mid-1950s, a twin-jet which immediately brought the French aviation industry up to the same quality level as the U.S. manufacturers.

Air France's success in the 1950s and 1960s was largely attributable to this aircraft: the company achieved first place among European companies in 1955 on intercontinental routes, with over 450,000 passengers, and in 1960 it was second with nearly 700,000. In the European sector and on internal flights Air France came a respectable second to BEA, with 650,000 passengers on European international flights and 450,000 on internal flights in 1955, and these figures rose to over 1,250,000 and 950,000 respectively in 1960. France held on to this position throughout the 1970s. In 1979 France was in fifth overall position worldwide, with a total of 5,140 million tonne/kilometers, after Japan, Great Britain, the U.S.S.R. and the U.S.A. On scheduled flights alone Air France had carried 10,767,000 passengers.

Apart from Concorde, one of the most interesting trends in air transport was the European introduction in the 1970s of a new kind of wide-body airliner, called the Airbus A300. This is a high-capacity twin-jet (built by a consortium including France, Great Britain, Germany and the Netherlands) which had a hard struggle even to gain acceptance partly because of the monopoly held by the American industrial giants, in spite of being much superior to any of its rivals. But this very fine airplane has gradually won worldwide sales, and is on its way to becoming one of the best-selling transports of all time. At the beginning of the 1980s the different versions of the Airbus have captured 50 percent of the Western market for wide-bodied medium-range jets and more than 500 had been ordered or optioned by early 1981.

From the postwar years the Soviet state company, Aeroflot, the world's largest airline, has remained unchallenged in terms of mileage covered and passengers carried. A few figures suffice to give an idea of the volume of traffic handled by this giant: in 1970 total tonne/kilometers flown were 8,917 million as against the U.S. companies' total of 26,537 million tonne/kilometers; in 1979 these figures had risen to 17,000 million as against 47,150 million; in the years 1975–80, Aeroflot carried 500 million passengers on 4,400 routes.

Having become the second largest company in Europe just before World War II, Aeroflot's growth has been almost continuous. In 1946, as part of a massive recovery program initiated immediately the war was over, Aeroflot re-equipped with new and up-to-date aircraft and operated a network of 108,000 miles (175,000 km). In 1950 this state airline carried 1.6 million passengers and over 181,000 tonnes of cargo and mail over a network covering 186,000 miles (300,500 km); five years later these figures had risen to 2.5 million passengers, nearly 259,000 tonnes of cargo and mail, over a 200,000-mile (321,500 km) network. In 1959 passenger traffic totalled 12.3 million, the network covered 220,000 miles (355,000 km); 1965's totals were: 42 million passengers; cargo and mail: 1.22 million tonnes; network: 270,000 miles (435,000 km). This development was backed up by very highly sophisticated production: for nearly two years (while the Comet was out of service) Aeroflot was the only airline to have a jet airliner in regular service. This significant period started on 15 September 1956, with the introduction of the Tupolev Tu-104 and ended on 4 October 1958, when the British de Havilland Comet 4 went into service. Other very advanced aircraft were to follow: propeller-turbine types such as the Antonov An-10, Ilyushin Il-18 and the enormous Tupolev Tu-114; then came the Tupolev Tu-124, Tu-134 and the Tu-154 jets, and the most recent jet to go into service, the first Soviet wide body—the Ilyushin Il-86. For a time Aeroflot also operated a supersonic transport similar to the Anglo-French Concorde—the Tupolev Tu-144.

While the leaders of the aeronautical world, those at the forefront of progress, continue to compete with one another, hundreds of airlines all over the world contribute to the everyday operations of commercial aviation. It is, however, virtually impossible to discern or describe any particular pattern or geographical tendency, as could still be done to demonstrate areas of operation in commercial aviation's golden years, before World War II. That war was to alter the balance of power and national wealth, and even in the world of aviation the difference between the stronger and weaker nations widened and had other, surprising sequels. Perhaps the most remarkable example is Japan which, having had more of her industrial structure destroyed than any other nation during the war is, however, today fourth in order of importance in the scale of civil aviation in terms of traffic handled.

Boeing 707-320C

1 nose cone
2 weather radar scanner
3 glide-slope aerial
4 forward pressure bulkhead
5 pitot head
6 nose frames
7 windscreen panels
8 eyebrow windows
9 overhead console
10 First Officer's seat
11 Captain's seat
12 forward frame
13 twin nosewheels
14 nosewheel doors
15 nosewheel box
16 drag struts
17 Navigator's table
18 Observer's seat
19 Navigator's seat
20 Navigator's overhead panel
21 Flight Engineer's seat
22 Flight Engineer's instrument panels
23 flight deck entry door
24 crew coat closet
25 crew toilet
26 crew galley/buffet
27 spare life vest stowage
28 radio (emergency) transmitter
29 life raft stowage (2)
30 VHF aerial
31 smoke and fume-proof curtain
32 forward entry door (24 × 72 ins)
33 escape slide stowage
34 forward underfloor freight hold
35 cabin floor level
36 six cargo pallets (total 4,424 cu ft)
37 ball transfer mat (five segments)
38 door actuator rams
39 main cargo door (raised)
40 engine intakes
41 secondary inlet doors
42 turbocompressor intakes
43 turbocompressor outlets
44 nacelle pylons
45 leading-edge wing flaps
46 main tank no. 3 (4,069 US gals)
47 fuel system dry bay
48 vortex generators
49 main tank no. 4 (2,323 US gals)
50 reserve tank (439 US gals)
51 vent surge tank
52 starboard wingtip
53 starboard outboard aileron
54 aileron balance tab
55 starboard outboard spoiler (extended)
56 starboard outboard flap
57 flap tracks
58 aileron/spoiler actuator linkage
59 starboard inboard aileron
60 control tab
61 starboard inboard flap
62 starboard inboard spoiler (extended)
63 life raft stowage (4)
64 escape straps
65 escape hatches/emergency exits (20 × 38 ins) (4)
66 life raft attachment clips
67 inter-cabin movable bulkhead
68 access door (port walkway)
69 fuselage frames
70 87-passenger Tourist Class cabin configuration (34 ins seat pitch)
71 4-abreast seating row (emergency exit stations)
72 ceiling air-conditioning
73 passenger amenities
74 rear cabin single-row seating
75 cabin windows
76 coat closet
77 life raft stowage (2)
78 spare life vests (and machete)
79 first aid kit
80 aft service door (starboard) (24 × 48 ins)
81 fin fillet
82 starboard tailplane
83 VOR antenna
84 removable fin leading edge
85 rudder control linkage
86 tail fin construction
87 rudder "Q" bellows
88 HF probe antenna
89 LORAN antenna
90 rudder
91 rudder control tab
92 rudder anti-balance tab
93 internal balance panel
94 rudder flutter damper
95 elevator torque tube
96 rudder trim tab
97 tail cone
98 tailplane actuator tab
99 elevator control tab
100 port elevator
101 port tailplane
102 internal balance panel
103 elevator linkage
104 crank assembly
105 elevator quadrant
106 autopilot elevator servo
107 tail fin spar/fuselage joints
108 rear pressure bulkhead
109 aft toilets (2)
110 coat closet
111 aft entry door
112 escape slide stowage
113 vestibule
114 fuselage skinning
115 aft underfloor freight hold
116 wingroot fairing
117 fillet flap
118 landing gear trunnion
119 undercarriage shock strut
120 main undercarriage well
121 side strut
122 torsion links
123 fuel tank end rib
124 wing rear spar/fuselage pick-up point
125 inboard wing stringers
126 wing front spar/fuselage pick-up point
127 fuselage center tank forward face
128 landing lights
129 front spar
130 four-wheel main landing gear
131 port inboard spoilers
132 port inboard flap
133 vortex generators
134 nacelle pylon
135 turbocompressor
136 engine intake
137 Pratt & Whitney JT3D turbofan
138 fan thrust reverser doors
139 engine fuel pump
140 starter
141 primary thrust reverser cascade vanes
142 wing anti-ice check valve
143 wing anti-ice shut-off valve
144 duct temperature sensor
145 leading-edge wing flap
146 dimpled inner skin
147 rear spar
148 leading-edge thermal anti-icing duct
149 integral wing fuel tanks
150 port inboard aileron
151 control tab
152 port outboard spoilers
153 port outboard flap
154 engine access doors (port and starboard)
155 nacelle nose cowl
156 nacelle structure
157 strut/pylon attachment
158 exhaust
159 pylon/wing joint
160 tab
161 leading-edge anti-ice supply manifold
162 port outboard aileron
163 wing skinning
164 port wingtip

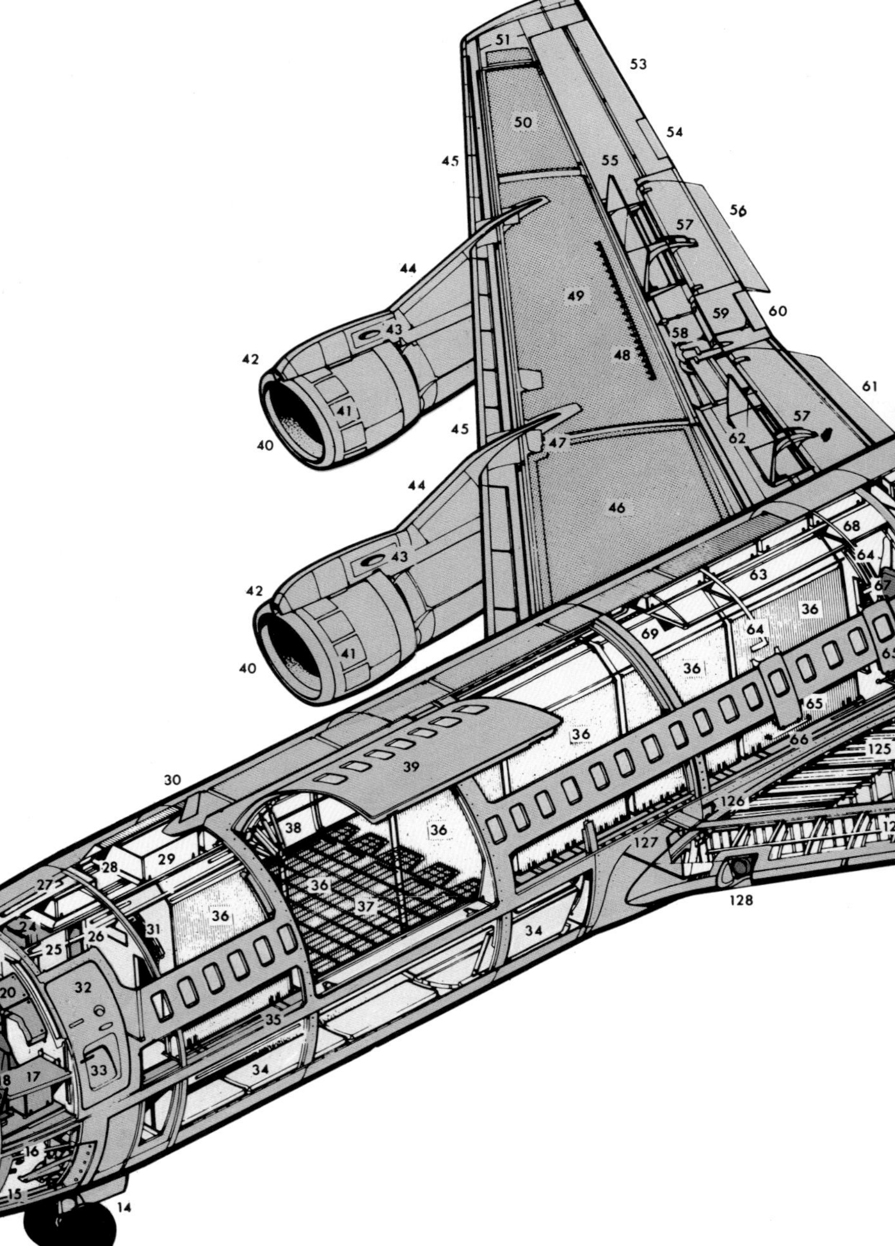

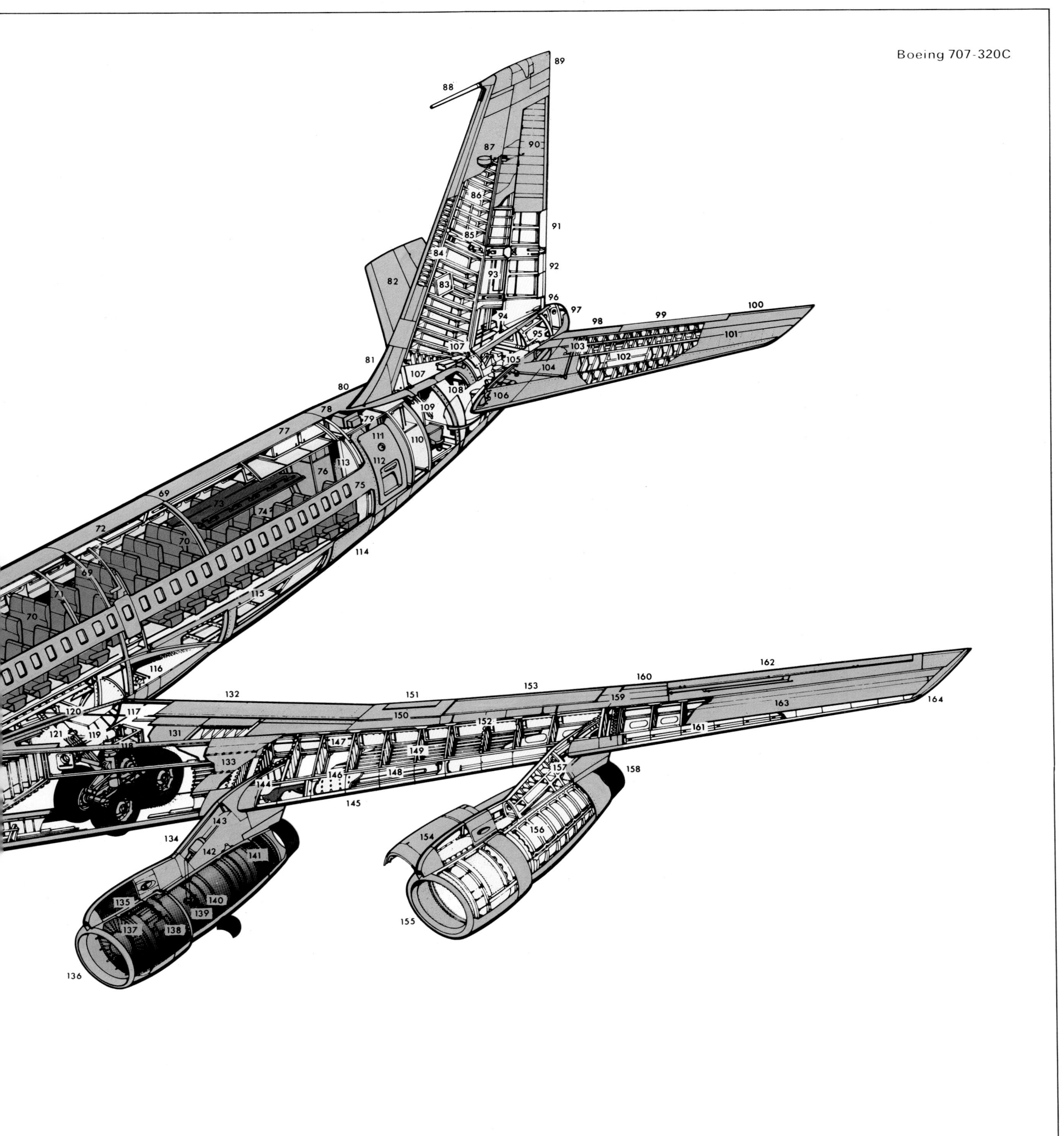
Boeing 707-320C
69
70
71
72
73
74
75
76
77
78
79
80
81
82
83
84
85
86
87
88
89
90
91
92
93
94
95
96
97
98
99
100
101
102
103
104
105
106
107
108
109
110
111
112
113
114
115
116
117
118
119
120
121
131
132
133
134
135
136
137
138
139
140
141
142
143
144
145
146
147
148
149
150
151
152
153
157
154
155
156
158
159
160
161
162
163
164

Aero 145 (CS)
L-200 Morava (CS)
Macchi M.B.320 (I)
I.A. 45 Querandi (RA)
Dornier Do 28 (D)
Dornier Do 27 (D)
de Havilland Canada DHC-2 Beaver I (CDN)
Pilatus PC-6 Porter (CH)
Aero Commander 560 (USA)
Scottish Aviation Prestwick Pioneer (GB)
Airspeed A.S.65 Consul (GB)

Piaggio P.136 (I)
Pilatus Britten-Norman BN-2A Islander (GB)
MR-2 (R)
Miles M.57 Aerovan (GB)
de Havilland DHA-3 Drover (AUS)
Antonov An-14 Pchelka (USSR)
Piaggio P.166 Portofino (I)
de Havilland D.H.104 Dove (GB)
Short Skyliner (GB)

SNCASO SO.95 Corse (F)
de Havilland Canada DHC-3 Otter (CDN)
Short S.A.6 Sealand (GB)
Antonov An-2 (USSR)
Peking (TJ)
Percival Prince (GB)
Cessna Citation (USA)
Scottish Aviation Twin Pioneer (GB)

CASA-201 Alcotan (E)
Aérospatiale SN.601 Corvette (F)
I.A. 35-X-III (RA)
Learjet Model 24 (USA
Yakovlev Yak-16 (USSR
de Havilland D.H.114 Heron (GB)
Britten-Norman BN-2 Trislander (GB)
Lockheed 18-56 Lodestar (USA)
Hawker Siddeley 125 (GB)

de Havilland Canada DHC-6 Twin Otter 300 (CDN)

Grumman G-159 Gulfstream I (USA)

PZL MD-12 (PL)

Vickers-Armstrongs Viking (GB)

Handley Page H.P.R.1 Marathon (GB)

Avro 748 (GB)

MBB HFB 320 Hansa (D)

VFW-Fokker 614 (D)

Dassault Mystère-Falcon 20 (F)

Nord 260 (F)

Bristol 170 Freighter (GB)

Swearingen Metro II (USA)

Avro 683 Lancaster (GB)

SNCASO SO.30 Bretagne (F)

Saab 90 Scandia (S)

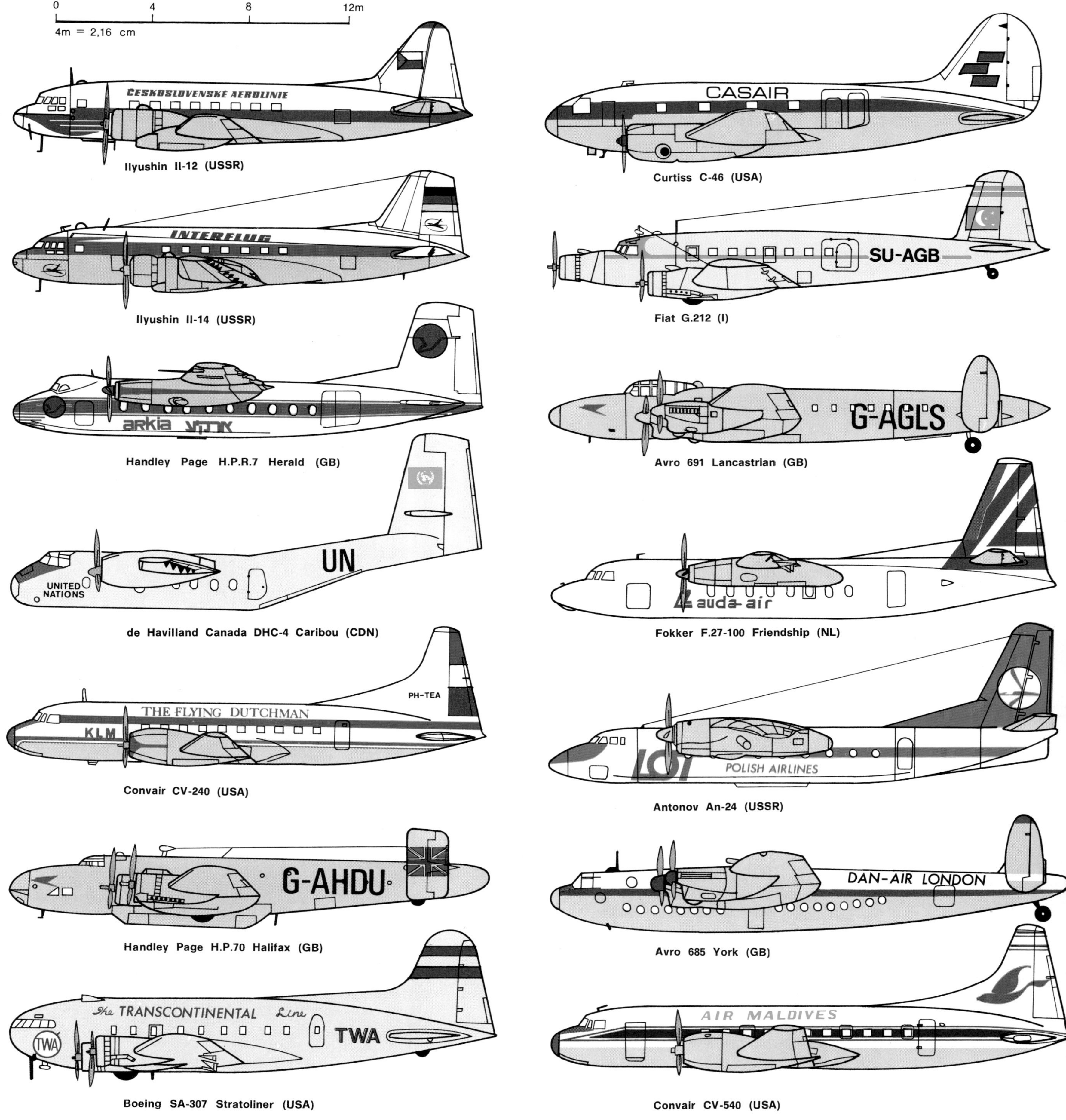

Ilyushin Il-12 (USSR)

Curtiss C-46 (USA)

Ilyushin Il-14 (USSR)

Fiat G.212 (I)

Handley Page H.P.R.7 Herald (GB)

Avro 691 Lancastrian (GB)

de Havilland Canada DHC-4 Caribou (CDN)

Fokker F.27-100 Friendship (NL)

Convair CV-240 (USA)

Antonov An-24 (USSR)

Handley Page H.P.70 Halifax (GB)

Avro 685 York (GB)

Boeing SA-307 Stratoliner (USA)

Convair CV-540 (USA)

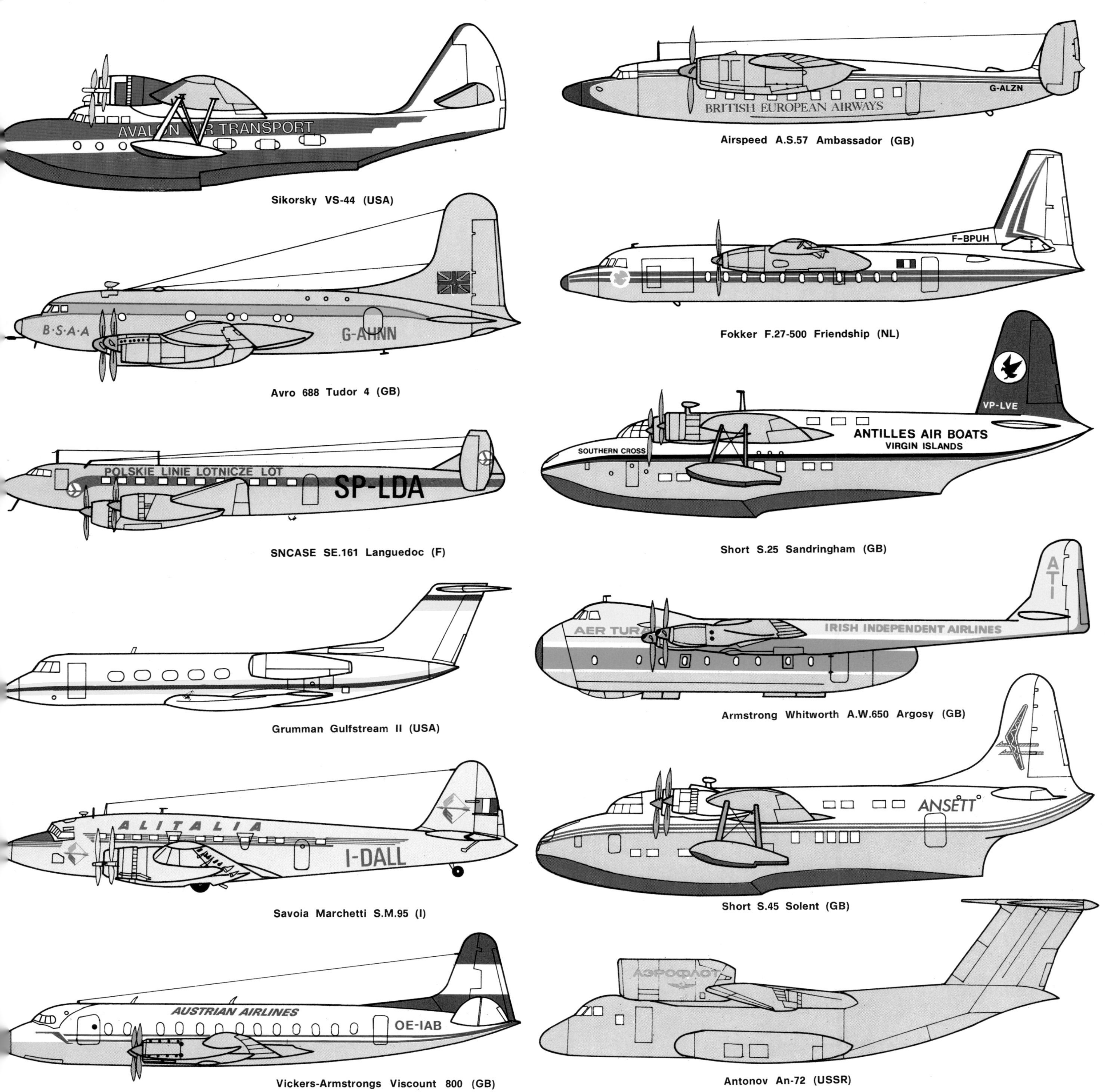

Sikorsky VS-44 (USA)

Avro 688 Tudor 4 (GB)

SNCASE SE.161 Languedoc (F)

Grumman Gulfstream II (USA)

Savoia Marchetti S.M.95 (I)

Vickers-Armstrongs Viscount 800 (GB)

Airspeed A.S.57 Ambassador (GB)

Fokker F.27-500 Friendship (NL)

Short S.25 Sandringham (GB)

Armstrong Whitworth A.W.650 Argosy (GB)

Short S.45 Solent (GB)

Antonov An-72 (USSR)

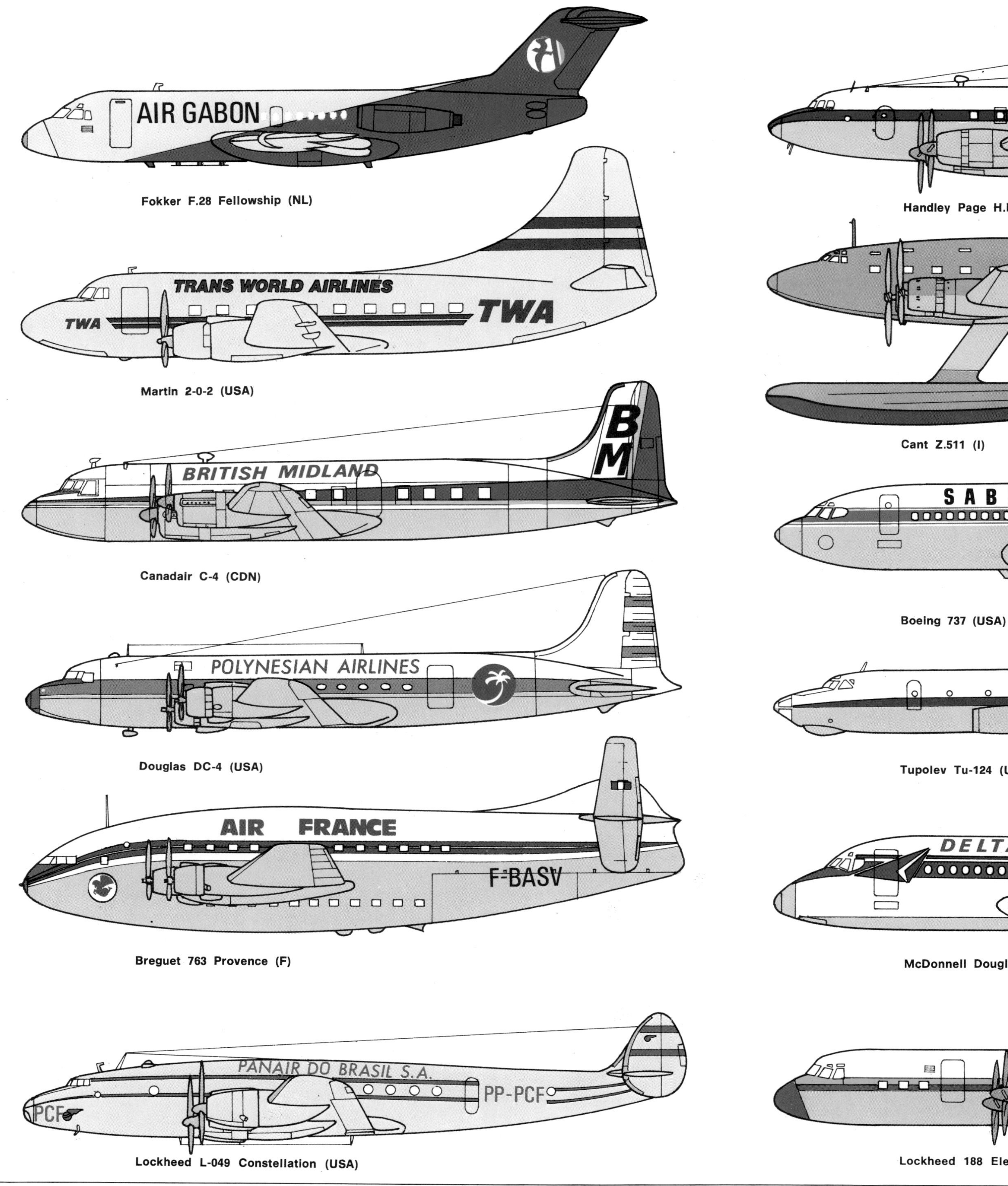

Fokker F.28 Fellowship (NL)

Martin 2-0-2 (USA)

Canadair C-4 (CDN)

Douglas DC-4 (USA)

Breguet 763 Provence (F)

Lockheed L-049 Constellation (USA)

Handley Page H.P.81 Hermes (GB)

Cant Z.511 (I)

Boeing 737 (USA)

Tupolev Tu-124 (USSR)

McDonnell Douglas DC-9-10 (USA)

Lockheed 188 Electra (USA)

Sud-Aviation SE.210 Caravelle (F)

Avro 689 Tudor 2 (GB)

Douglas DC-6 (USA)

BAC One-Eleven 500 (GB)

Sud-Aviation SE.210 Caravelle Super B (F)

Antonov An-12 (USSR)

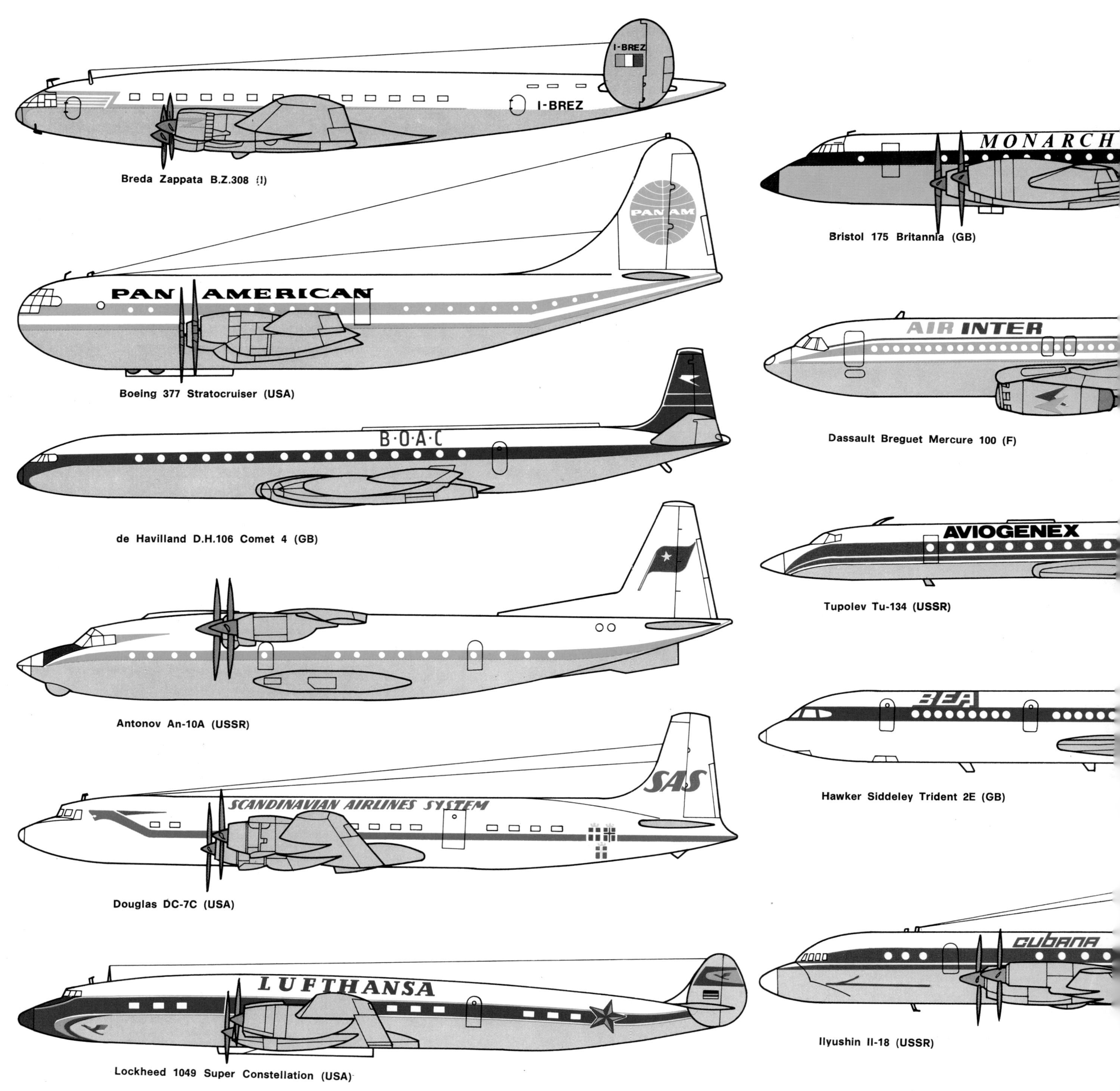

Breda Zappata B.Z.308 (I)

Boeing 377 Stratocruiser (USA)

de Havilland D.H.106 Comet 4 (GB)

Antonov An-10A (USSR)

Douglas DC-7C (USA)

Lockheed 1049 Super Constellation (USA)

Bristol 175 Britannia (GB)

Dassault Breguet Mercure 100 (F)

Tupolev Tu-134 (USSR)

Hawker Siddeley Trident 2E (GB)

Ilyushin Il-18 (USSR)

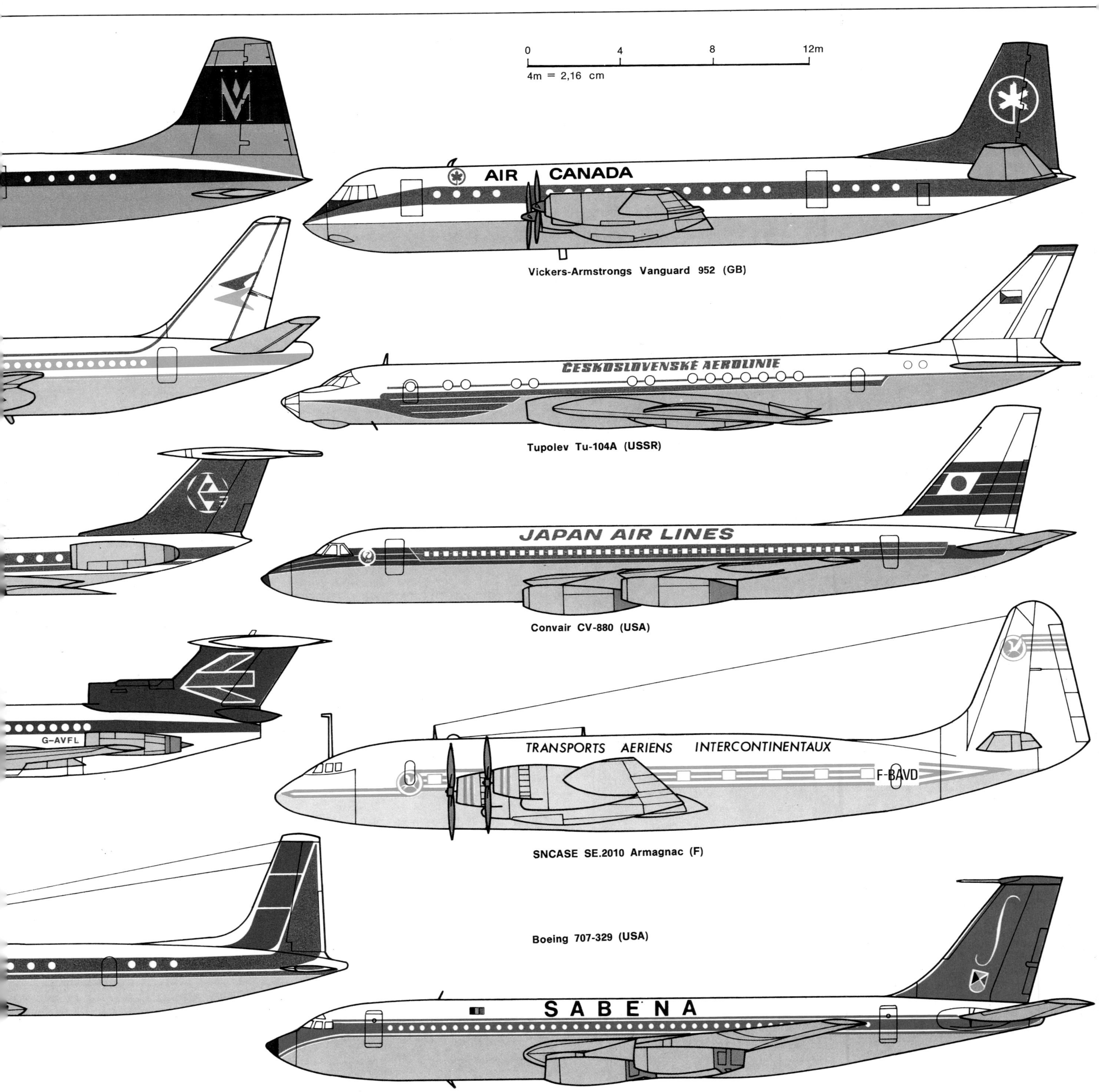

Vickers-Armstrongs Vanguard 952 (GB)

Tupolev Tu-104A (USSR)

Convair CV-880 (USA)

SNCASE SE.2010 Armagnac (F)

Boeing 707-329 (USA)

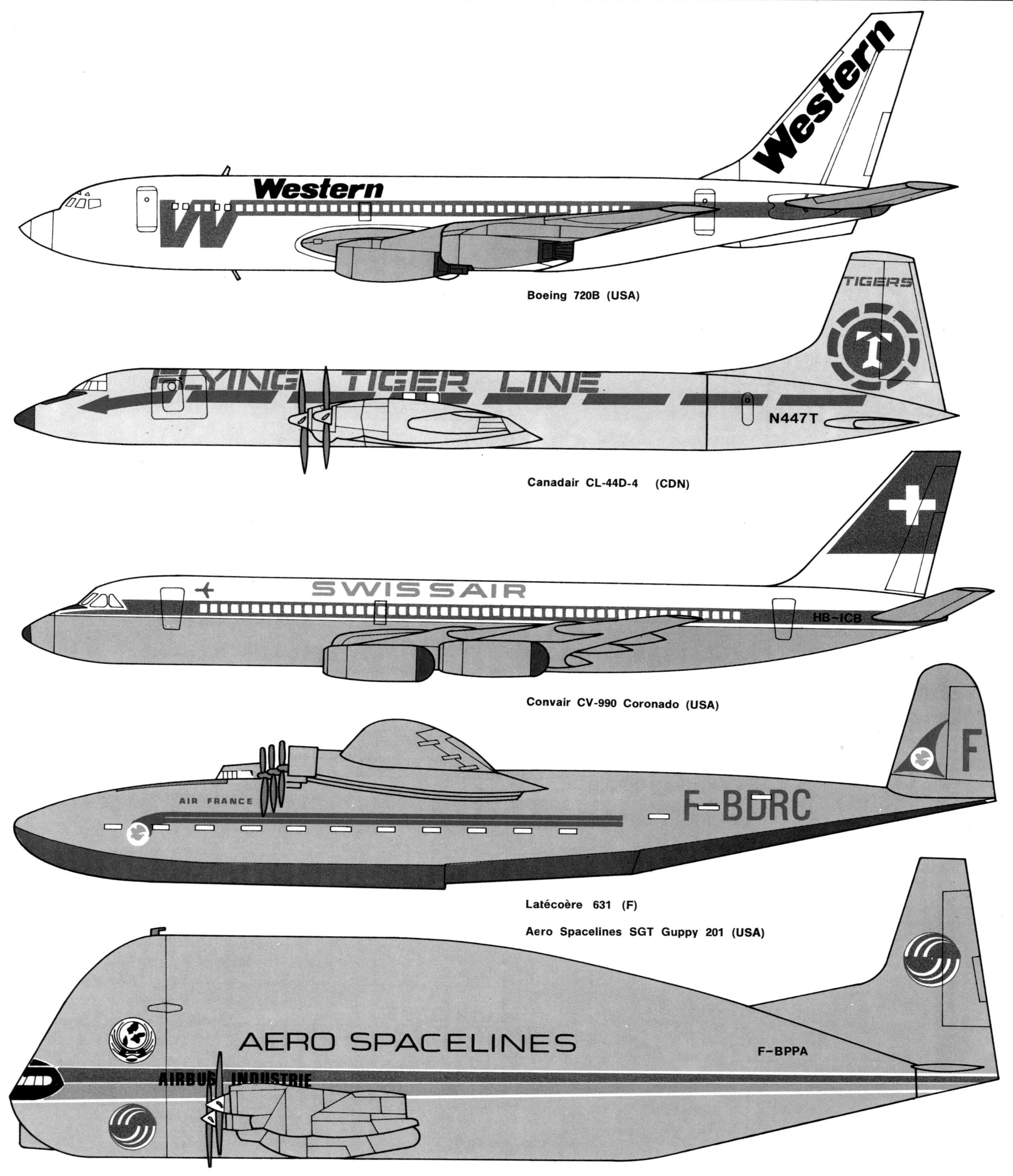

Boeing 720B (USA)

Canadair CL-44D-4 (CDN)

Convair CV-990 Coronado (USA)

Latécoère 631 (F)

Aero Spacelines SGT Guppy 201 (USA)

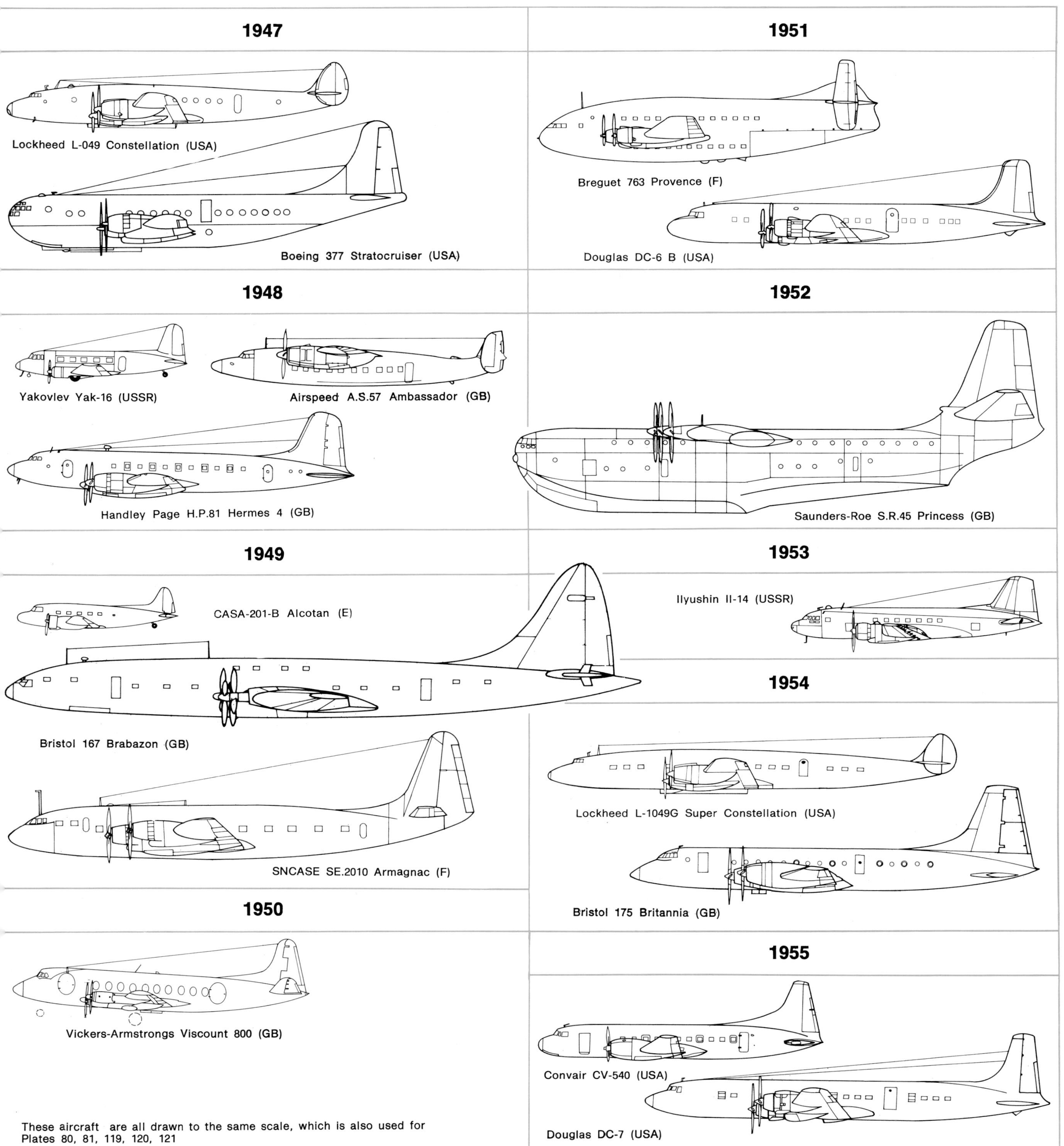

These aircraft are all drawn to the same scale, which is also used for Plates 80, 81, 119, 120, 121

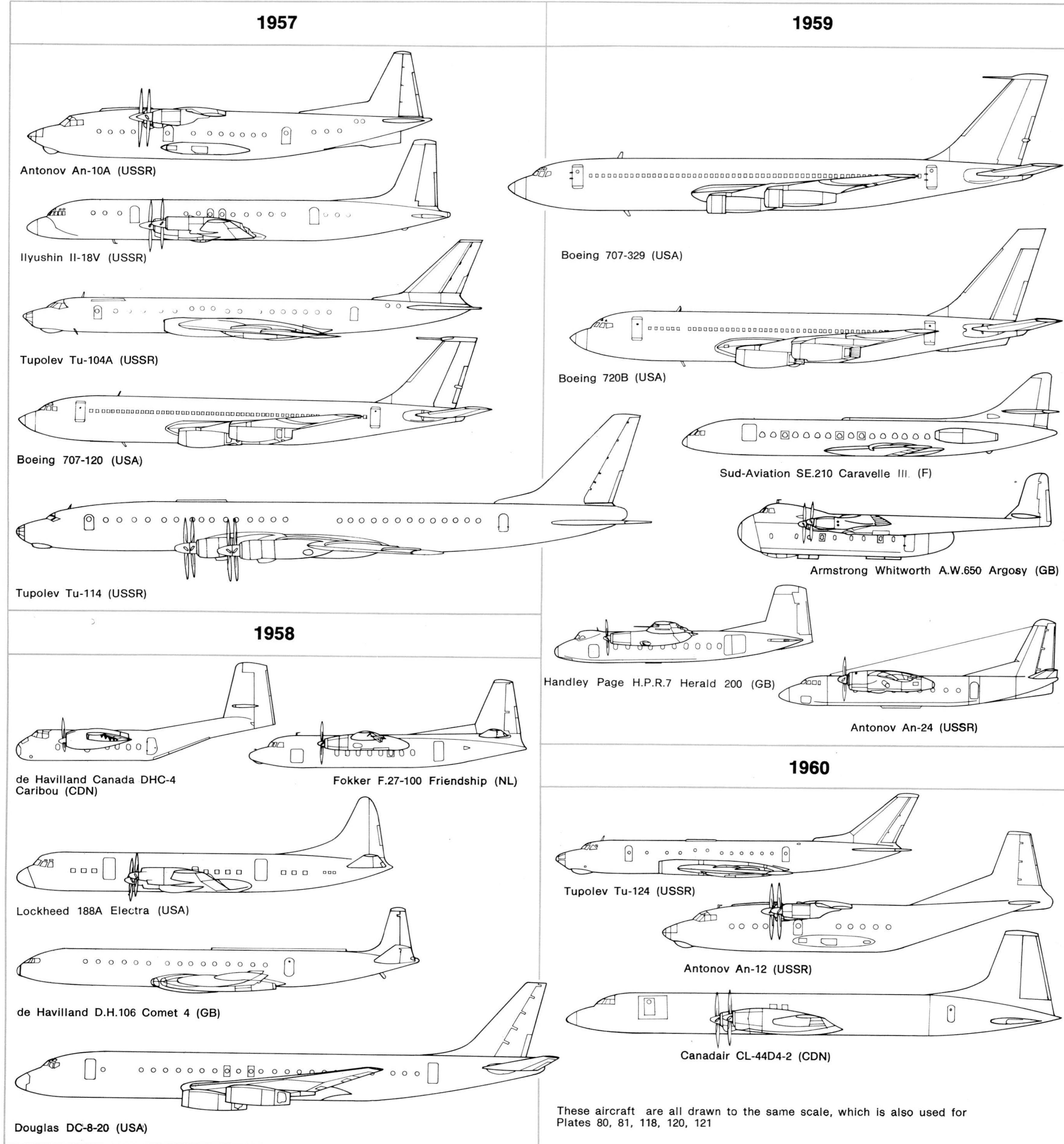

These aircraft are all drawn to the same scale, which is also used for Plates 80, 81, 118, 120, 121

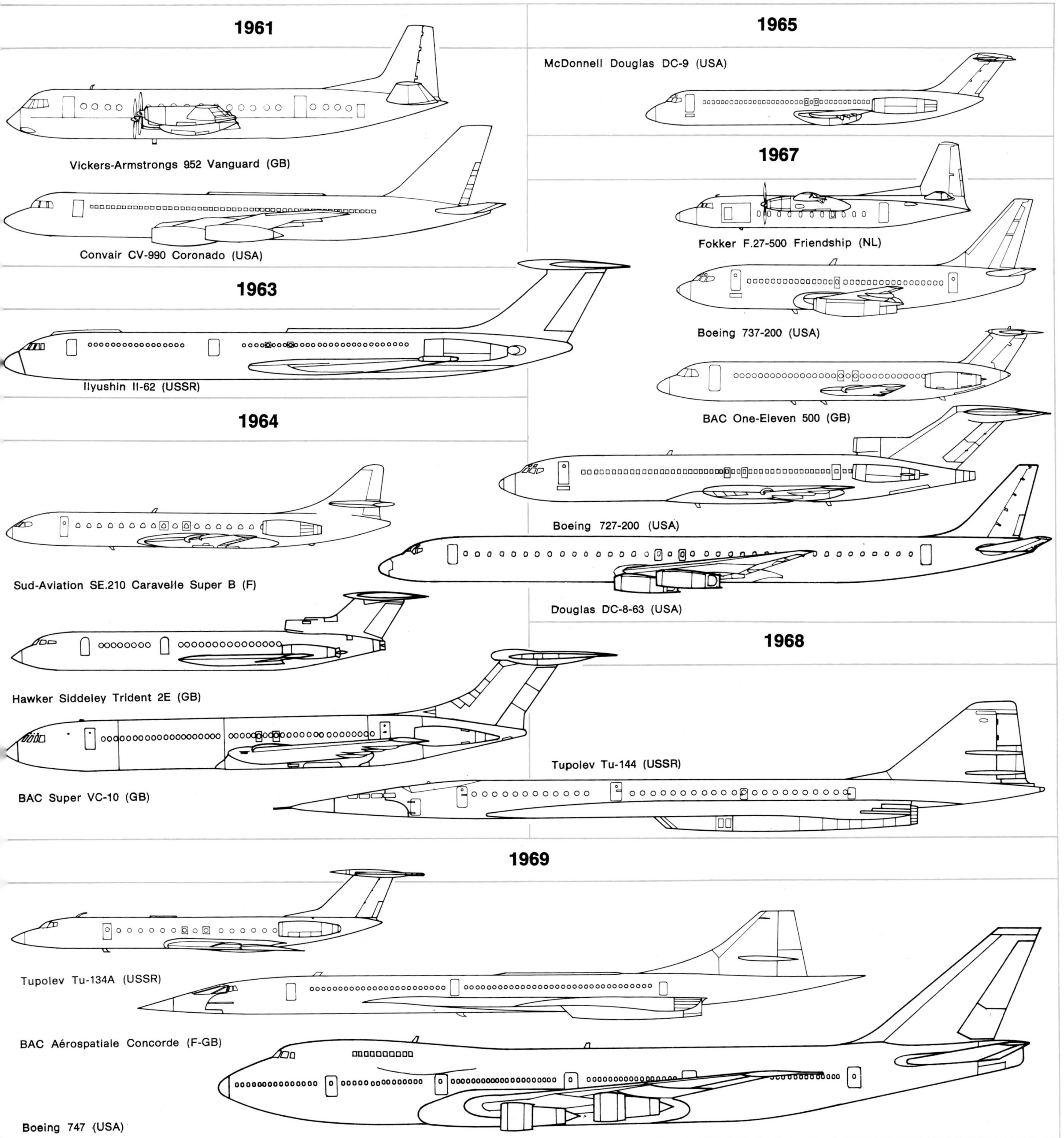
1961
Vickers-Armstrongs 952 Vanguard (GB)
Convair CV-990 Coronado (USA)
1963
Ilyushin Il-62 (USSR)
1964
Sud-Aviation SE.210 Caravelle Super B (F)
Hawker Siddeley Trident 2E (GB)
BAC Super VC-10 (GB)
1965
McDonnell Douglas DC-9 (USA)
1967
Fokker F.27-500 Friendship (NL)
Boeing 737-200 (USA)
BAC One-Eleven 500 (GB)
Boeing 727-200 (USA)
Douglas DC-8-63 (USA)
1968
Tupolev Tu-144 (USSR)
1969
Tupolev Tu-134A (USSR)
BAC Aérospatiale Concorde (F-GB)
Boeing 747 (USA)

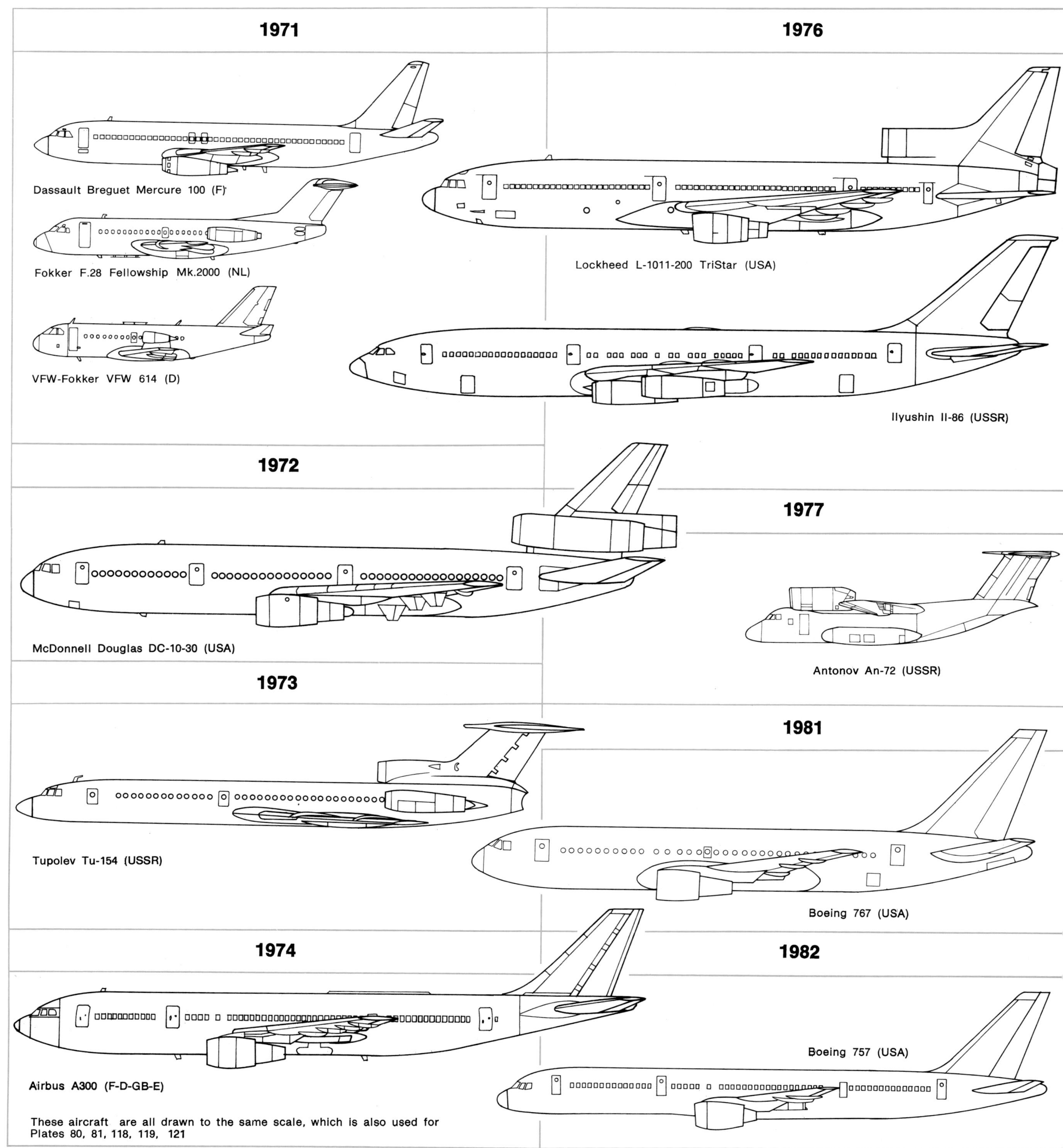

These aircraft are all drawn to the same scale, which is also used for Plates 80, 81, 118, 119, 121

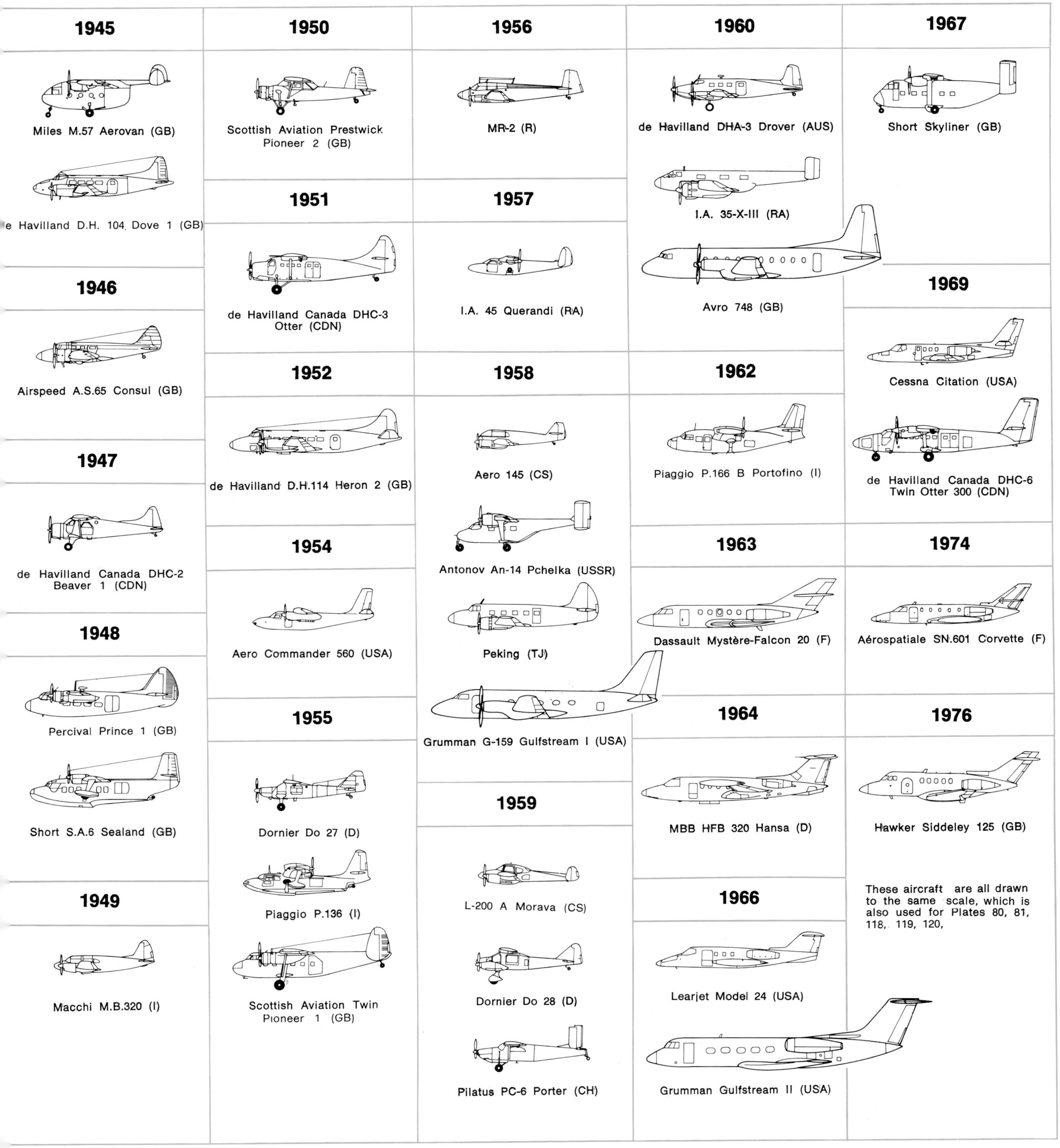

Entry into service of the most important executive and light transport aircraft: 1945–1976

1945

Miles M.57 Aerovan (GB)

de Havilland D.H. 104 Dove 1 (GB)

1946

Airspeed A.S.65 Consul (GB)

1947

de Havilland Canada DHC-2 Beaver 1 (CDN)

1948

Percival Prince 1 (GB)

Short S.A.6 Sealand (GB)

1949

Macchi M.B.320 (I)

1950

Scottish Aviation Prestwick Pioneer 2 (GB)

1951

de Havilland Canada DHC-3 Otter (CDN)

1952

de Havilland D.H.114 Heron 2 (GB)

1954

Aero Commander 560 (USA)

1955

Dornier Do 27 (D)

Piaggio P.136 (I)

Scottish Aviation Twin Pioneer 1 (GB)

1956

MR-2 (R)

1957

I.A. 45 Querandi (RA)

1958

Aero 145 (CS)

Antonov An-14 Pchelka (USSR)

Peking (TJ)

Grumman G-159 Gulfstream I (USA)

1959

L-200 A Morava (CS)

Dornier Do 28 (D)

Pilatus PC-6 Porter (CH)

1960

de Havilland DHA-3 Drover (AUS)

I.A. 35-X-III (RA)

Avro 748 (GB)

1962

Piaggio P.166 B Portofino (I)

1963

Dassault Mystère-Falcon 20 (F)

1964

MBB HFB 320 Hansa (D)

1966

Learjet Model 24 (USA)

Grumman Gulfstream II (USA)

1967

Short Skyliner (GB)

1969

Cessna Citation (USA)

de Havilland Canada DHC-6 Twin Otter 300 (CDN)

1974

Aérospatiale SN.601 Corvette (F)

1976

Hawker Siddeley 125 (GB)

These aircraft are all drawn to the same scale, which is also used for Plates 80, 81, 118, 119, 120.

Icelandair

Scandinavian Airlines System

Scanair

Transair Sweden

Finnair O/Y

Aeroflot

Air France

Air Littoral

Air Inter

Air Alpes

Touraine Air Transport

Union de Transports Aériens

Sabena-
Belgian World Airlines

Condor
Flugdienst

Luftransport-Unternehmen

Bavaria Germanair

Interflug

LOT - Polskie Linie
Lotnicze

Ceskoslovenske Aerolinie

Swissair

Aviaco-
Aviacion Y Comercio

Alitalia - Linee Aeree Italiane

Aero Trasporti Italiani

Air Malta

Jugoslovenski Aerotransport

Inex Adria Airways

Egyptair

Air Mali

Air Niger

Sudan Airways

Ethiopian Airlines

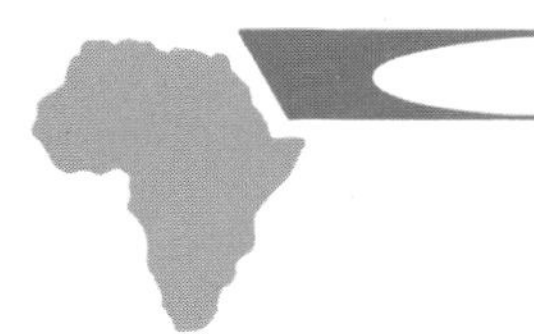

Air-Guinnée

Air Zaire

Air Tanzania

Air Kenya

TAAG - Linhas Aéreas de Angola

Zambia Airways

Air Malawi

LAM
Lineas Aereas de Mocambique

MEA - Middle East
Airlines Air Liban

Trans Mediterranean Airways

Syrian Arab Airlines

Iraqi Airways

El Al Israel Airlines

Arkia
Israel Inland Airways

Air-India

Indian Airways

Airlanka

MIAT
Air Mongol

CAAC - Civil Aviation Administration of China

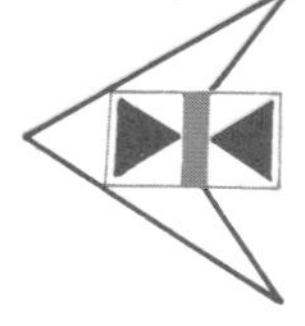

Cathay Pacific Airways

Aer Lingus
Irish Airlines

British Airways

Air UK

Britannia Airways

British Caledonian Airways

Laker Airways

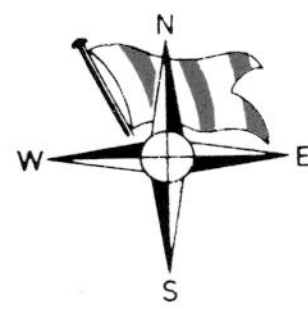

Dan-Air Services

Monarch Airlines

Sterling Airways A/S

Sobelair - Société Belge de Transports Par Air

Trans European Airways

Luxair

Koninklijke Luchtvaart Maatschapij NV

Martinair Holland

Transavia Holland

Lufthansa

Balair

Crossair

Austrian Airlines

TAROM - Transporturile Aeriene Romane

TAP - Air Portugal (Transportes Aéreos Portugueses)

Iberia

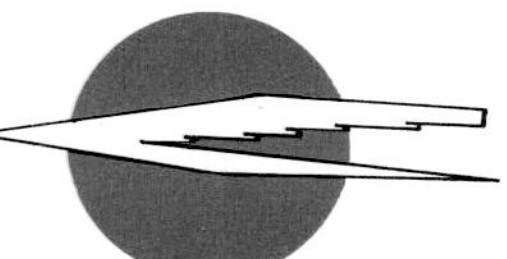

Spantax Trasportes Aereos

Aviogenex

Olympic Airways

Balkan Bulgarian Airlines

Royal Air Maroc

Air Algerie

Tunis Air

Libyan Arab Airlines

Air Afrique

Air Ivoire

Ghana Airways

Nigeria Airways

Cameroon Airlines

Air Gabon

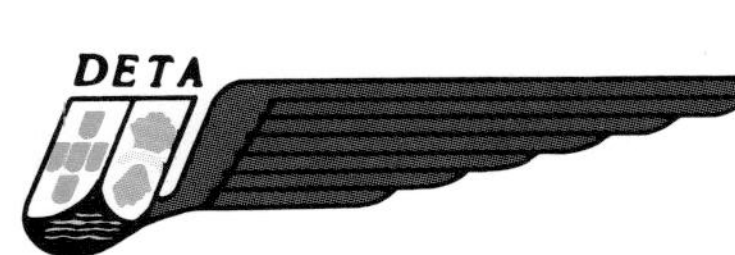

Direccao de Exploracao dos Transportes Aéreos

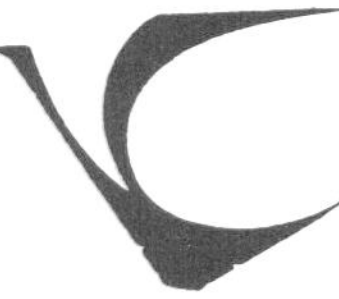

Air Madagascar

South African Airways

Safair Freighters

Cyprus Airways

Turk Hava Yollari

Alia-Royal Jordanian Airlines

Saudia

Kuwait Airways

Gulf Air

Yemenia

Iran Air

PIA
Pakistan International Airlines

China Airlines

Korean Air Lines

Japan Air Lines

All Nippon Airways

Japan Asia Airways

TDA - Domestic Airlines

Southwest Air Lines

Royal Nepal Airlines

Bangladesh Biman

Burma Airways

Thai Airways International

Thai Airways

MAS Malaysian Airlines System

PAL Philippine Airlines

Wardair International

Nordair

Okanagan Helicopters

Trans World Airlines

Pan American World Airways

American Airlines

United Airlines

Pacific Southwest Airlines

Northwest Orient

National Airlines

Alaska International Air

Air California

Aeroamerica

Seaboard World Airlines

SMB Stage Line

World Airways

Wien Air Alaska

Western Airlines

Texas International Airlines

Piedmont Airlines

Ozark Air Lines

Transamerica Airlines

Aeromech Airlines

Golden West Airlines

Alaska Airlines

Frontier Airlines

Federal Express

Belize Airlines

Lineas Aereas Costaricenses

Air Panama Internacional

Empresa Consolidada Cubana de Aviacion

Bahamasair

Air Jamaica

Ecuatoriana

Antilles Air Boats

British West Indian Airways

AeroPeru

Cruzeiro do Sul

VOTEC Servicos Aéreos Regionais

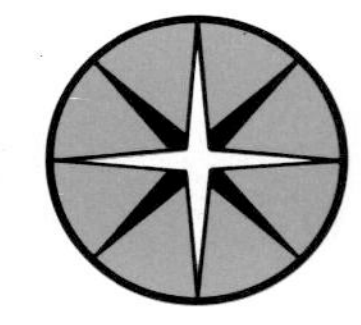
VARIG - Viacao Aérea Rio Gradense

PLUNA Primeras Lineas Uruguayas de Navegacion Aérea

Air Calédonie

Air Niugini

Talair TPY

Surinam Airways

Qantas Airways

Sterling Philippine Airways

SIA
Singapore Airlines

Royal Brunei Airlines

Garuda
Indonesian Airways

Air Canada

CP Air
Canadian Pacific Airlines

Quebecair

Braniff International

Flying Tiger Line

Continental Airlines

USAIR

Capitol International Airways

Eastern Air Lines

Delta Air Lines

Air Florida

Republic Airlines

Cochise Airlines

Evergreen International Airlines

Rio Airways

Sierra Pacific Airlines

Hughes Airwest

Hawaiian Airlines

Aloha Airlines

Sea Airmotive

Zantop International Airlines

Trans Continental Airlines

Aspen Airways

Southern Airways

Aeromexico

Mexicana

SAHSA
Servicio Aereo de Honduras SA

Aviateca
Aerolineas de Guatemala

Dominicana

Caribbean Airways

Aerovias Nacionales de Colombia

Aerocondor
Aerovias Condor de Colombia

Venezolana International
de Aviacion SA

Lloyd Aereo Boliviano

Viacao Aérea Sao Paulo

Transbrasil S/A
Linhas Aereas

Rio-Sul

LADECO
Linea Aerea del Cobre

Lan Chile

Aerolineas Argentinas

Austral Lineas Aereas

East-West Airlines

Ansett Airlines of Australia

Trans-Australia Airlines

Polynesian Airlines

Air New Zealand

IATA - International Air
Transport Association

Airline	Prefix
American Airlines	AA
Air Cortez	AB
Air Canada	AC
Airborne Express	AE
Air France	AF
Air Algerie	AH
Air-India	AI
Altair Airlines	AK
Allegheny Commuter	ALC
Aeromexico	AM
Ansett (AUS)	AN
AVIACO	AO
Aspen Airways	AP
Aloha Airlines	AQ
Aerolinas Argentinas	AR
Alaska Airlines	AS
Royal Air Maroc	AT
Austral	AU
AVIANCA	AV
Air Niger	AW
Aero Transit	AW
Finnair	AY
Alitalia	AZ
British Airways	BA
Air Great Lakes	BB
Brymon Airways	BC
British Midland Airways	BD
Centennial Airlines	BE
Alaska International Air	BF
Bangladesh Biman	BG
Air U.S.	BH
Royal Brunei Airlines	BI
Devoe Airlines	BJ
Chalk's Int'l Airlines	BK
Bradley Air Services	BL
ATI	BM
Bouraq Indonesia Airlines	BO
Air Botswana	BP
Aer Mediterranea	BQ
British Caledonian Airways	BR
Lance Aviation	BS
Air Lines of Northern Australia	BT
Braathens S.A.F.E.	BU
North West Airlines	BV
BWIA Int'l Trinidad and Tobago Airways	BW
CAAC — Civil Aviation Administration of China	CA
Commuter Airlines	CB
Inland Empire Airways	CC
Trans-Provincial Airlines	CD
Air Virginia	CE
Faucett	CF
Clubair	CG
Safair Freighters	CG
Bemidji Airlines	CH
China Airlines	CI
Colgan Airways	CJ
Capitol Air	CL
COPA	CM
James Air	CN
Continental Airlines	CO
CP Air	CP
Aero Chaco	CQ
Colorado Airlines	CS
A.A.A. Air Enterprises	CT
Command Airways, (Magnum Helicopters)	CT
Cubana	CU
Cargolux	CV
Cathay Pacific Airways	CX
Cyprus Airways	CY
Cascade Airways	CZ
Dan-Air Services	DA
Air Niagara (cargo)	DB
Brittany Air Int'l	DB
Trans Catalina Airlines	DC
Command Airways	DD
Aerovias Darienietas	DG
Air Charter Services (cargo)	DH
Tonga Air Service (passenger)	DH
Delta Air	DI
Air Djibouti	DJ
Delta Air Lines	DL
Maersk	DM
Freedom Airlines	DN
Dominicana de Aviacion	DO
Cochise Airlines	DP
Great Western Airlines	DQ
Air Limousin	DQ
Aydev Airlines of Australia	DR
Air Senegal	DS
TAAG — Angola Airlines	DT
Summit Airlines (cargo)	DU
Roland Air (passenger)	DU
DLT German Domestic Airlines	DW
Danair	DX
Alyemda — Democratic Yemen Airlines	DY
Douglas Airways	DZ
Eastern Airlines	EA
T Thomas Air Transport	EB
Air Ecosse (passenger)	EC
Miller Air Transporters (cargo)	EC
Andes (cargo)	ED
Sunbird Airlines (passenger)	ED
Eagle Commuter Airlines	EE
Far Eastern Air Transport	EF
Japan Asia Airways	EG
Roederer Aviation	EH
Aer Lingus	EI
New England Airlines	EJ
Masling Commuter Services	EK
Nihon Kinkyori Airways	EL
Hammonds Air Service	EM
Eastern Airways	EN
Euroflite	EO
Pelita Air Service	EP
Tropic Air Services	EP
TAME	EQ
DHL Airlines	ER
Airways of New Mexico	ES
Ethiopian Airlines	ET
Ecuatoriana	EU
Atlantic Southeast Airlines	EV
East-West Airlines	EW
Eagle Airways	EX
Europe Aero Service	EY
Evergreen Int'l Airlines	EZ
Finnaviation	FA
Chaparral Airlines	FC
Texas Star Airlines	FD
Air Link	FF
Ariana Afghan Airlines	FG
Mall Airways	FH
Icelandair	FI
Air Pacific (Fiji)	FJ
Frontier Airlines	FL
New South Wales Airlines	FO
Compagnie Aerienne du Languedoc	FQ
Susquehanna Airlines	FR
Flying Tiger Line (cargo)	FT
Metro Int'l Airways (passenger)	FT
Air Littoral	FU
Erie Airways	FV
Wright Airlines	FW
Metroflight Airlines	FY
Air Chico	FZ
Garuda	GA
Air Inter Gabon	GB
Lina Congo	GC
Bahamas Caribbean Airlines	GD
Guernsey Airlines	GE
Gulf Air	GF
North American Airlines	GG
Ghana Airways	GH
Air Guinee	GI
Airlines of South Australia	GJ
Laker Airways	GK
Global Int'l Airways	GL
Gronlandsfly	GL
Scheduled Skyways	GM
Air Gabon	GN
Hadag General Air	GP
Big Sky Airlines	GQ
Aurigny Air Services	GR
BAS Airlines	GS
GB Airways	GT
Aviateca	GU
Talair	GV
Golden West Airlines	GW
Air Ontario	GX
Guyana Airways Corpn.	GY
Copper State Airlines	GZ
Hawaiian Air	HA
Air Express Int'l (cargo)	HB
Air Melanésie (passenger)	HB
New York Helicopter	HD
First Air	HF
Harbor Airlines	HG
Somali Airlines	HH
Pinehurst Airlines	HI
South Pacific Island Airways	HK
Air Seychelles	HM
NLM Dutch Airlines	HN
Mid Pacific Airlines	HO
Air Hawaii	HP
Gold Coast Airlines	HR
Air Tchad	HT
Guy America Airways	HX
Metro Airlines	HY
Henebery Aviation (passenger)	HZ
Island Airlines Hawaii (cargo)	HZ
Iraqi Airways	IA
Iberia	IB
Indian Airlines	IC
Apollo Airways	ID
Solomon Islands Airways	IE
Interflug	IF
Alisarda	IG
Imperial Airlines	II
TAT — Touraine Air Transport	IJ
Air Central	IK
Island Air	IL
Jamaire	IM
Ipec Aviation	IN

Airline	Code
T.A.T. Export	IO
H C Sleigh Airlines	IP
Caribbean Airways	IQ
Iran Air	IR
Eagle Air	IS
Air Inter	IT
Midstate Airlines	IU
Air Traffic Executive Jet Service	IX
Yemen Airways	IY
Arkia-Israel Airlines	IZ
Bankair	JA
Pioneer Airways	JB
Rocky Mountain Airways	JC
Toa Domestic Airlines	JD
Swedair	JG
Gull Air	JI
Astec Air East	JJ
JAL-Japan Air Lines	JL
Air Jamaica	JM
Holiday Airlines	JO
Trans-Jamaica Airlines	JQ
Mid Continental Airlines	JR
Chosonminhang (CAA of DPR of Korea)	JS
Air Oregon	JT
JAT — Jugoslavenski Aerotransport	JU
Bearskin Lake Air Service	JV
Bougair-Bougainville Air Services	JX
Jersey European Airways	JY
Golden Air AB	JZ
C & M Airlines	KA
Burnthills Aviation	KB
Aeromech	KC
Kendell Airlines	KD
Korean Air Lines	KE
Catskill Airways	KF
Cook Island Airways	KH
Time Air	KI
Iscargo	KJ
Transportes Aereos Regionais	KK
KLM — Royal Dutch Airlines	KL
Air Malta	KM
Tyee Airlines	KN
Kodiak Western Alaska Airlines	KO
Air Alma	KP
Kenya Airways	KQ
Kar-Air	KR
Caribbean Air Services (cargo)	KT
Turtle Airways (passenger)	KT
Kuwait Airways	KU
Transkei Airways	KV
Crown Air	KW
Cayman Airways	KX
LAN-Chile	LA
LAB-Lloyd Aero Boliviano	LB
LAC	LC
LADE — Lineas Aereas del Estado	LD
Magnum Airlines	LE
Linjeflyg	LF
Luxair	LG
Lufthansa — German Airlines	LH
Liat (1974)	LI
Sierra Leone Airways	LJ
Letaba Airways	LK
Bell-Air	LL
ALM — Antillean Airlines	LM
Jamahiriya Libyan Arab Airlines	LN
LOT — Polskie Linie Lotnicze	LO
Air Alpes	LP
LACSA — Lineas Aereas Costarricenses	LR
Express Air Services (cargo)	LS
Marco Island Airways (passenger)	LS
Shasta Air Inc.	LU
Lav-Linea Aeropostal Venezolana	LV
Air Nevada	LW
Crossair	LX
EL AL — Israel Airlines	LY
Balkan — Bulgarian Airlines	LZ
MALEV — Hungarian Airlines	MA
Muse Air	MC
Air Madagascar	MD
MEA — Middle East Airlines Air Liban	ME
Aerosun Int'l	MF
Pompano Airway	MG
MAS — Malaysian Airline System	MH
S.M.B. Stage Lines	MJ
Air Mauritius	MK
Midway Airlines	ML
S.A.M.	MM
Commercial Airways	MN
Calm Air Int'l	MO
Air Mauritanie	MR
Egyptair	MS
Macknight Airlines	MT
Misrair	MU
Airlines of Western Australia	MV
Maya Airways	MW
Mexicana	MX
Air Mali	MY
Merpati Nusantara	MZ
A/S Nordsjoefly	NA
Newair	NC
Nordair	ND
Air Vanuatu	NF
Green Hills Aviation	NG
All Nippon Airways	NH
Namakwaland Lugdiens	NJ
Norcanair	NK
Air Liberia	NL
Mount Cook Airlines	NM
Air Martinique	NN
Air North	NO
Cumberland Airlines	NQ
Norontair	NR
Neurenberger Flugdienst	NS
Southwest Airlines (Okinawa)	NU
Northwest Orient Airlines	NW
New Zealand Air Charter	NX
New York Air	NY
Air New Zealand — Domestic	NZ
Olympic Airways	OA
Opal Air	OB
Air Cal	OC
Noosa Air	OF
Air Guadeloupe	OG
Comair	OH
CSA — Ceskoslovenske Aerolinie	OK
OLT — Ostfriesische Lufttransport	OL
Air Mongol — MIAT	OM
Air Nauru	ON
Sun Aire Lines	OO
Air Panama Internacional	OP
Royale Airlines	OQ
Air Comores	OR
Austrian Airlines	OS
Butler Airlines	OT
Air Atonabee	OU
Air Olympia	OW
Ozark Air Lines	OZ
Pan American World Airways	PA
Air Burundi	PB
Fiji Air	PC
Pem Air	PD
People Air Express	PE
Providence Airlines	PF
Polynesian Airlines	PH
Piedmont Aviation	PI
Air St. Pierre	PJ
PIA — Pakistan Int'l Airlines	PK
AeroPeru	PL
Pilgrim Airlines	PM
Princeton Aviation	PN
Aeropelican (passenger)	PO
Profit Airlines (cargo)	PO
Prinair	PQ
Philippine Air Lines	PR
Pacific Southwest Airlines	PS
Provincetown — Boston Airline & Naples Airline	PT
Pluna	PU
Eastern Provincial Airways	PV
Pacific Western Airlines	PW
Air Niugini	PX
Suriname Airways	PY
LAP — Lineas Aereas Paraguayas	PZ
Quebecair	QB
Air Zaire	QC
Transbrasil	QD
Air Tahiti	QE
Qantas	QF
Sky West Aviation	QG
Air Florida	QH
Cimber Air	QI
Arizona Pacific Airlines	QJ
Lesotho Airways	QL
Air Malawi	QM
Bush Pilots Airways	QN
Bar Harbor Airlines	QO
Sunbird Aviation	QP
Inter City Airlines (passenger)	QT
Tampa Airlines (cargo)	QT
Uganda Airlines	QU
Lao Aviation	QV
Turks and Caicos Nat'l Airline	QW
Horizon Airlines	QX
Aero Virgin Islands	QY
Zambia Airways	QZ
Royal Nepal Airlines	RA
Syrian Arab Airlines	RB
Republic Airlines	RC
Alderney Air Ferries	RD
Aer Arann	RE
Rossair	RF
VARIG	RG

(cont)

Airline	Code
Air Zimbabwe	RH
Eastern Airlines (AUS)	RI
Alia - Royal Jordanian Airlines	RJ
Air Afrique	RK
Aeronica	RL
Wings West	RM
Royal Air Inter	RN
TAROM — Romanian Air Transport	RO
Precision Airlines	RP
Maldives Int'l Airlines	RQ
A/S Norving	RT
Britt Airways	RU
Reeve Aleutian Airways	RV
Capitol Air Service	RX
Sun International Airways	RY
South African Airways	SA
Cruzeiro do Sul	SC
Sudan Airways	SD
Scruse-Air	SF
Atlantis Airlines	SG
SAHSA — Servicio Aereo de Honduras	SH
Southern Air	SJ
SAS — Scandinavian Airlines System	SK
Superior Airways	SM
Sabena Belgian World Airlines	SN
Austria Air Services	SO
SATA (Azores)	SP
Singapore Airlines	SQ
Swissair	SR
Clinton Aero	SS
Singleton Air Service	ST
Aeroflot	SU
Saudia	SV
Namib Air	SW
Christman Air System	SX
Air Alsace	SY
Pro Air Service	SZ
TACA Int'l Airlines	TA
Air Tanzania Corpn.	TC
Transavia	TD
Air New Zealand International	TE
Vee Neal Airlines	TF
Thai International	TG
Thai Airways	TH
Texas Int'l Airlines	TI
Ocean Air	TJ
Turk Hava Yollari	TK
Trans-Mediterranean Airways	TL
LAM - Linhas Aereas de Mozambique	TM
TAA — Trans-Australia Airlines	TN
Trans-North Turbo Air	TO
TAP — Transportes Aereos Portugueses	TP
Las Vegas Airlines	TQ
Air Benin	TS
Tunis Air	TU
Transamerica Airlines	TV
TWA — Trans World Airlines	TW
TAN — Transportes Aereos Nacionales	TX
Air Caledonie	TY
Sansa	TZ
United Air Lines	UA
Burma Airways Corpn.	UB
Ladeco — Lineas Aerea del Cobre	UC
United Air Services	UD
Sydaero	UF
Norfolk Island Airlines	UG
Austin Airways	UH
Flugfelag Nordurlands	UI
Cen-Tex Airlines	UJ
Air UK	UK
Air Lanka	UL
East Coast Airlines	UN
Direct Air Inc.	UO
Bahamasair	UP
Mission Air Lines	UQ
Empire Airlines	UR
U.T.A. — Union de Transports Aériens	UT
Reunion Air Service	UU
Perimeter Airlines	UW
Air Illinois	UX
Cameroon Airlines	UY
Nefertiti Aviation	UZ
VIASA	VA
Westair Commuter Airlines	VB
Avensa — Aerovias Venezolanas	VE
Golden Airways	VF
City Flug	VG
Air Volta	VH
Vieques Air Link	VI
Trans Colorado Airlines	VJ
Air Tungaru	VK
Mid South Commuter Airlines	VL
Tyrolean Airways	VO
VASP — Viacao Aerea Sao Paulo	VP
Oxley Airlines	VQ
Transportes Aereos de Cabo Verde	VR
Air Polynesie	VT
Air Ivoire	VU
Semo Aviation	VV
Ama-Flyg	VW
Aces	VX
Coral Air	VY
Aquatic Airways	VZ
Western Airlines	WA
SAN — Servicios Aereos Nacionales	WB
Wien Air Alaska	WC
VOTEC — Servicios Aereos Regionalis	WE
Wideroe's Flyveselskap	WF
Alag	WG
Torontair	WJ
Westkustenflug	WK
Aeroperias	WL
Windward Island Airways Int'l	WM
World Airways	WO
Princeville Airways	WP
Wings Airways	WQ
Wheeler Flying Service	WR
Regionair	WS
Nigeria Airways	WT
Rhine Air	WU
Trans-West	WW
Air New South Wales	WX
Trans Western Airlines of Utah	WZ
Spacegrand Aviation	XF
Air North	XG
Mesaba Aviation	XJ
Aerotal — Aerolineas Territoriales de Colombia	XK
Rio Airways	XO
Avior	XP
Trans Mo Airlines	XU
Mississippi Valley Airways	XV
Walker's Cay Airlines	XW
Munz Northern Airlines	XY
Air Tasmania	XZ
All Seasons Air Pacific	YB
Alaska Aeronautical Industries	YC
Ama Air Express	YD
Commodore Airlines	YJ
Cyprus/Turkish Airways	YK
Montauk Caribbean Airways Ocean Reef Airways	YL
Arkansas Traveler Airline	YM
Heli-Air Monaco	YO
Pagas Airlines	YP
Lakeland Aviation	YQ
Scenic Airlines	YR
San Juan Airlines	YS
Skywest Airlines	YT
William Air	YX
Linhas Aereas da Guine-Bissau	YZ
Genair	ZA
Air Vectors Airways	ZB
Royal Swazi National Airways	ZC
Air Berlin USA	ZF
Silver State Airlines	ZG
Royal Hawaiian Air Service	ZH
Lucas Air Transport	ZI
Hazelton Air Services	ZL
Trans Central Aviation	ZM
Tennessee Airways	ZN
Virgin Air	ZP
Lawrence Aviation	ZQ
Cassair Aviation Services	ZR
Air Midwest	ZV
Air Wisconsin	ZW
Air BC	ZX
Air Pennsylvania	ZY
DHL Cargo	2D
Executive Helicopters	2E
Sunflower Airlines	2S
Wairarapa Airlines	2W
Euroair Transport	3E
Air-Lift Commuter	3L
Air New Orleans	3N
Pioneer Airlines	3P
Upali Airlines	3U
Trans Island Airways	4T

Country	Letters
Afghanistan	YA
Albania	ZA
Algeria	7T
Angola	D2
Antigua	VP-LAA/VP-LJZ
Argentina	LQ, LV
Australia	VH
Austria	OE
Bahamas	C6
Bahrain	A9C
Bangladesh	S2
Barbados	8P
Belgium	OO
Belize (British Honduras)	VP-H
Benin	TY
Bermuda	VR-B
Bolivia	CP
Boputhatswana	ZS
Botswana	A2
Brazil	PP, PT
Brunei	VR-U
Bulgaria	LZ
Burma	XY, XZ
Burundi	9U
Cameroun	TJ
Canada	C
Cayman Islands	VR-C
Central African Republic	TL
Chad	TT
Chile	CC
China (Nationalist)	B
China (People's Republic)	B
Colombia	HK
Comoro	D6
Congo (People's Republic)	TN
Costa Rica	TI
Cuba	CU
Cyprus	5B
Czechoslovakia	OK
Denmark	OY
Dominican Republic	HI
Ecuador	HC
Egypt	SU
El Salvador	YS
Equatorial Guinea	3C
Ethiopia	ET
Falkland Islands	VP-F
Fiji	DQ
Finland	OH
France	F
Gabon	TR
Gambia	C5
Germany (Democratic Republic)	DDR
Germany (Federal Republic)	D
Ghana	9G
Gibraltar	VR-G
Greece	SX
Grenada	VQ-G
Guatemala	TG
Guiné-Bissau	J5
Guinea (Republic of)	3X
Guyana	8R
Haiti	HH
Honduras	HR
Hong-Kong	VR-H
Hungary	HA
Iceland	TF
India	VT
Indonesia	PK
Iran	EP
Iraq	YI
Ireland	EI, EJ
Israel	4X
Italy	I
Ivory Coast	TU
Jamaica	6Y
Japan	JA
Jordan	JY
Kampuchea	XU
Kenya	5Y
Korea (Democratic Republic)	P
Korea (Republic of)	HL
Kuwait	9K
Lao	RDPL
Lebanon	OD
Lesotho	7P, VQ-Z
Liberia	EL
Libya	5A
Liechtenstein	HB
Luxembourg	LX
Malagasy (Madagascar)	5R
Malawi	7Q-Y
Malaysia	9M
Maldives	8Q
Mali	TZ
Malta	9H
Mauritania	5T
Mauritius	3B
Mexico	XA, XB, XC
Monaco	3A
Mongolia	HMAY
Montserrat	VP-L
Morocco	CN
Mozambique	C9
Nauru	C2
Nepal	9N
Netherlands	PH
Netherlands Antilles	PJ
New Hebrides	F/H4
New Zealand	ZK, ZL, ZM
Nicaragua	AN
Niger	5U
Nigeria	5N
Norway	LN
Oman	A40
Pakistan	AP
Panama	HP
Papua New Guinea	P2
Paraguay	ZP
Peru	OB
Philippines	RP
Poland	SP
Portugal	CR, CS
Qatar	A7
Romania	YR
Ruanda	9XR
St. Helena	VQ-H
St. Kitts/Nevis/Anguilla	VP-LKA/VP-LLZ
St. Lucia	VQ-L
St. Vincent	VP-V
São Tomé and Principé	S9
Saudi Arabia	HZ
Sénégal	6V, 6W
Seychelles	S7
Sierra Leone	9L
Singapore	9V
Solomon Islands	H4
Somalia	6O
South Africa	ZS, ZT, ZU
Spain	EC
Sri Lanka	4R
Sudan	ST
Surinam	PZ
Swaziland	3D
Sweden	SE
Switzerland	HB
Syria	YK
Tanzania	5H
Thailand	HS
Togo	5V
Trinidad and Tobago	9Y
Tunisia	TS
Turkey	TC
Uganda	5X
United Arab Emirates	A6
United Kingdom	G
United Kingdom Colonies and Protectorates	VP, VQ, VR
United States of America	N
Upper Volta	XT
Uruguay	CX
U.S.S.R.	CCCP (SSSR)
Venezuela	YV
Vietnam	XV
Virgin Islands (British)	VP-LVA/VP-LZZ
West Irian	PK
Western Samoa	5W
Yemen, Arab Republic	4W
Yemen, Democratic Republic	7O
Yugoslavia	YU
Zaïre	9Q
Zambia	9J
Zimbabwe	VP-W, VP-Y

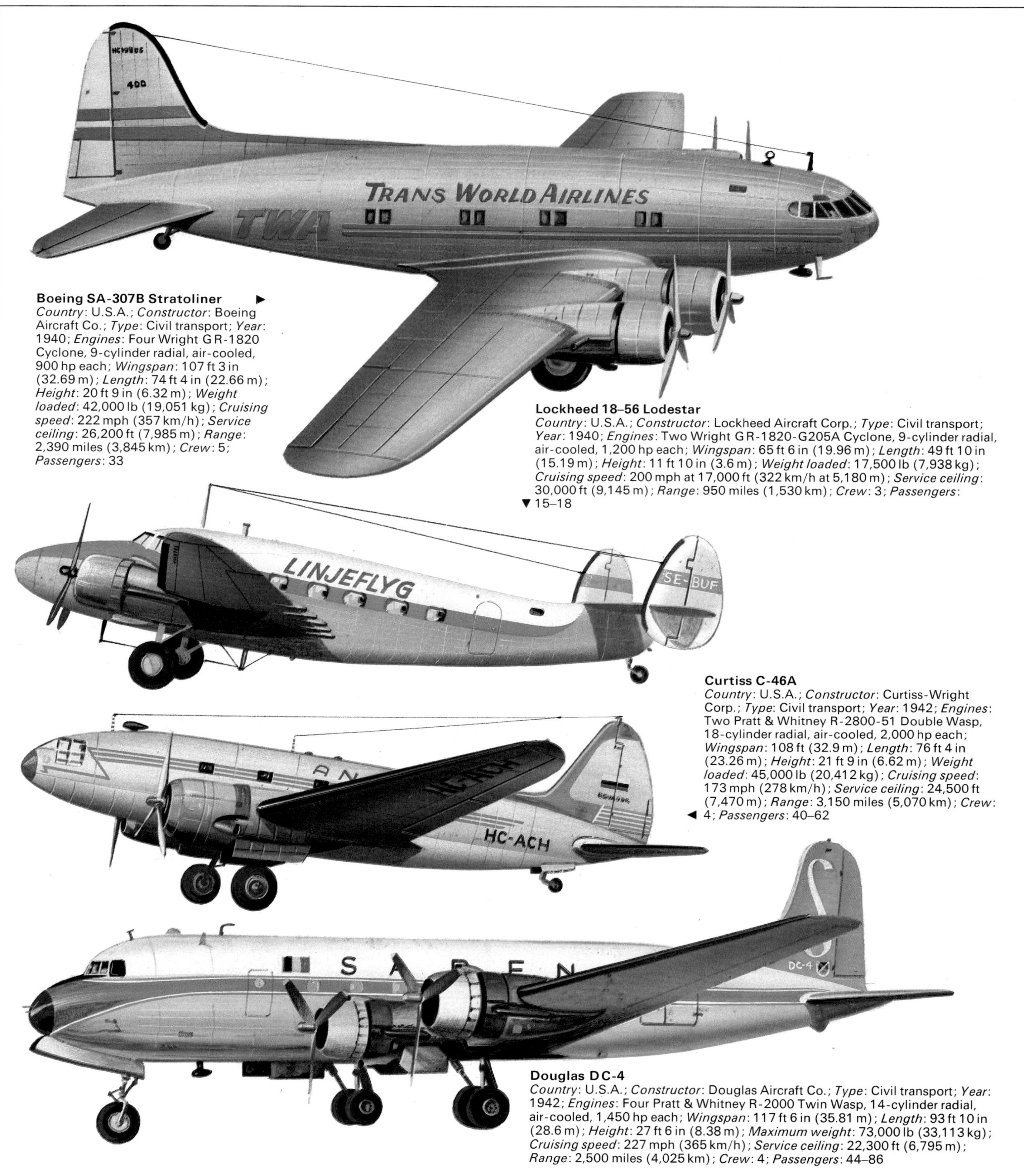

Boeing SA-307B Stratoliner ▶
Country: U.S.A.; *Constructor*: Boeing Aircraft Co.; *Type*: Civil transport; *Year*: 1940; *Engines*: Four Wright GR-1820 Cyclone, 9-cylinder radial, air-cooled, 900 hp each; *Wingspan*: 107 ft 3 in (32.69 m); *Length*: 74 ft 4 in (22.66 m); *Height*: 20 ft 9 in (6.32 m); *Weight loaded*: 42,000 lb (19,051 kg); *Cruising speed*: 222 mph (357 km/h); *Service ceiling*: 26,200 ft (7,985 m); *Range*: 2,390 miles (3,845 km); *Crew*: 5; *Passengers*: 33

Lockheed 18–56 Lodestar
Country: U.S.A.; *Constructor*: Lockheed Aircraft Corp.; *Type*: Civil transport; *Year*: 1940; *Engines*: Two Wright GR-1820-G205A Cyclone, 9-cylinder radial, air-cooled, 1,200 hp each; *Wingspan*: 65 ft 6 in (19.96 m); *Length*: 49 ft 10 in (15.19 m); *Height*: 11 ft 10 in (3.6 m); *Weight loaded*: 17,500 lb (7,938 kg); *Cruising speed*: 200 mph at 17,000 ft (322 km/h at 5,180 m); *Service ceiling*: 30,000 ft (9,145 m); *Range*: 950 miles (1,530 km); *Crew*: 3; *Passengers*: ▼ 15–18

Curtiss C-46A
Country: U.S.A.; *Constructor*: Curtiss-Wright Corp.; *Type*: Civil transport; *Year*: 1942; *Engines*: Two Pratt & Whitney R-2800-51 Double Wasp, 18-cylinder radial, air-cooled, 2,000 hp each; *Wingspan*: 108 ft (32.9 m); *Length*: 76 ft 4 in (23.26 m); *Height*: 21 ft 9 in (6.62 m); *Weight loaded*: 45,000 lb (20,412 kg); *Cruising speed*: 173 mph (278 km/h); *Service ceiling*: 24,500 ft (7,470 m); *Range*: 3,150 miles (5,070 km); *Crew*: ◀ 4; *Passengers*: 40–62

Douglas DC-4
Country: U.S.A.; *Constructor*: Douglas Aircraft Co.; *Type*: Civil transport; *Year*: 1942; *Engines*: Four Pratt & Whitney R-2000 Twin Wasp, 14-cylinder radial, air-cooled, 1,450 hp each; *Wingspan*: 117 ft 6 in (35.81 m); *Length*: 93 ft 10 in (28.6 m); *Height*: 27 ft 6 in (8.38 m); *Maximum weight*: 73,000 lb (33,113 kg); *Cruising speed*: 227 mph (365 km/h); *Service ceiling*: 22,300 ft (6,795 m); *Range*: 2,500 miles (4,025 km); *Crew*: 4; *Passengers*: 44–86

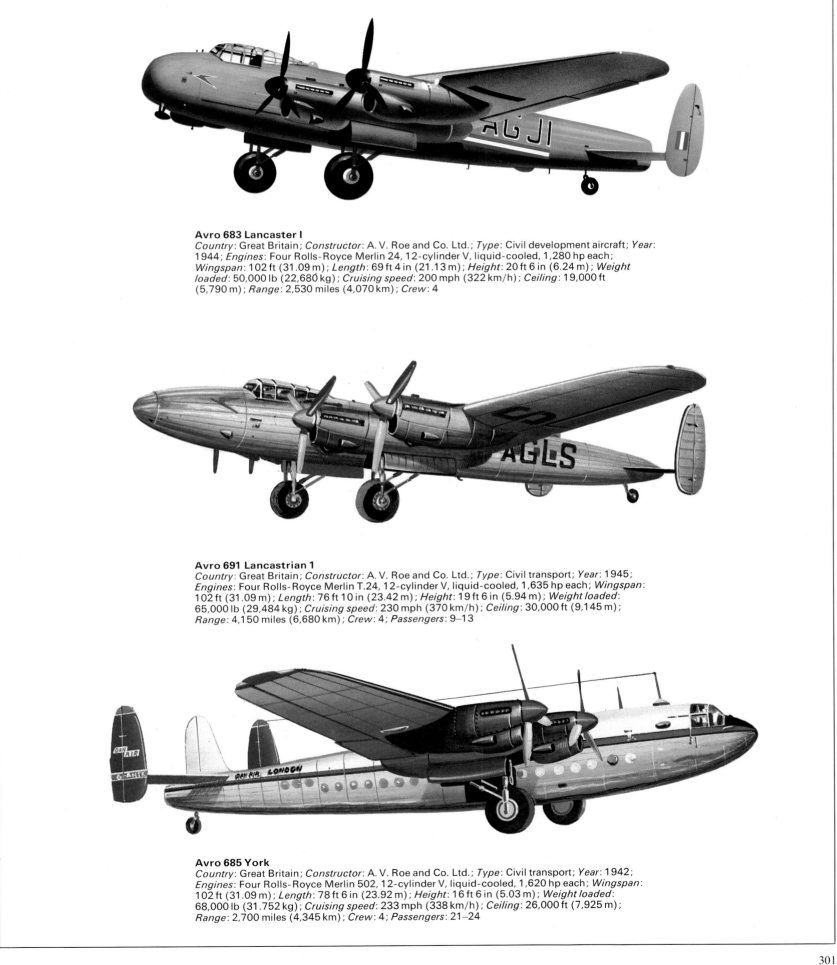

Avro 683 Lancaster I
Country: Great Britain; *Constructor*: A. V. Roe and Co. Ltd.; *Type*: Civil development aircraft; *Year*: 1944; *Engines*: Four Rolls-Royce Merlin 24, 12-cylinder V, liquid-cooled, 1,280 hp each; *Wingspan*: 102 ft (31.09 m); *Length*: 69 ft 4 in (21.13 m); *Height*: 20 ft 6 in (6.24 m); *Weight loaded*: 50,000 lb (22,680 kg); *Cruising speed*: 200 mph (322 km/h); *Ceiling*: 19,000 ft (5,790 m); *Range*: 2,530 miles (4,070 km); *Crew*: 4

Avro 691 Lancastrian 1
Country: Great Britain; *Constructor*: A. V. Roe and Co. Ltd.; *Type*: Civil transport; *Year*: 1945; *Engines*: Four Rolls-Royce Merlin T.24, 12-cylinder V, liquid-cooled, 1,635 hp each; *Wingspan*: 102 ft (31.09 m); *Length*: 76 ft 10 in (23.42 m); *Height*: 19 ft 6 in (5.94 m); *Weight loaded*: 65,000 lb (29,484 kg); *Cruising speed*: 230 mph (370 km/h); *Ceiling*: 30,000 ft (9,145 m); *Range*: 4,150 miles (6,680 km); *Crew*: 4; *Passengers*: 9–13

Avro 685 York
Country: Great Britain; *Constructor*: A. V. Roe and Co. Ltd.; *Type*: Civil transport; *Year*: 1942; *Engines*: Four Rolls-Royce Merlin 502, 12-cylinder V, liquid-cooled, 1,620 hp each; *Wingspan*: 102 ft (31.09 m); *Length*: 78 ft 6 in (23.92 m); *Height*: 16 ft 6 in (5.03 m); *Weight loaded*: 68,000 lb (31.752 kg); *Cruising speed*: 233 mph (338 km/h); *Ceiling*: 26,000 ft (7,925 m); *Range*: 2,700 miles (4,345 km); *Crew*: 4; *Passengers*: 21–24

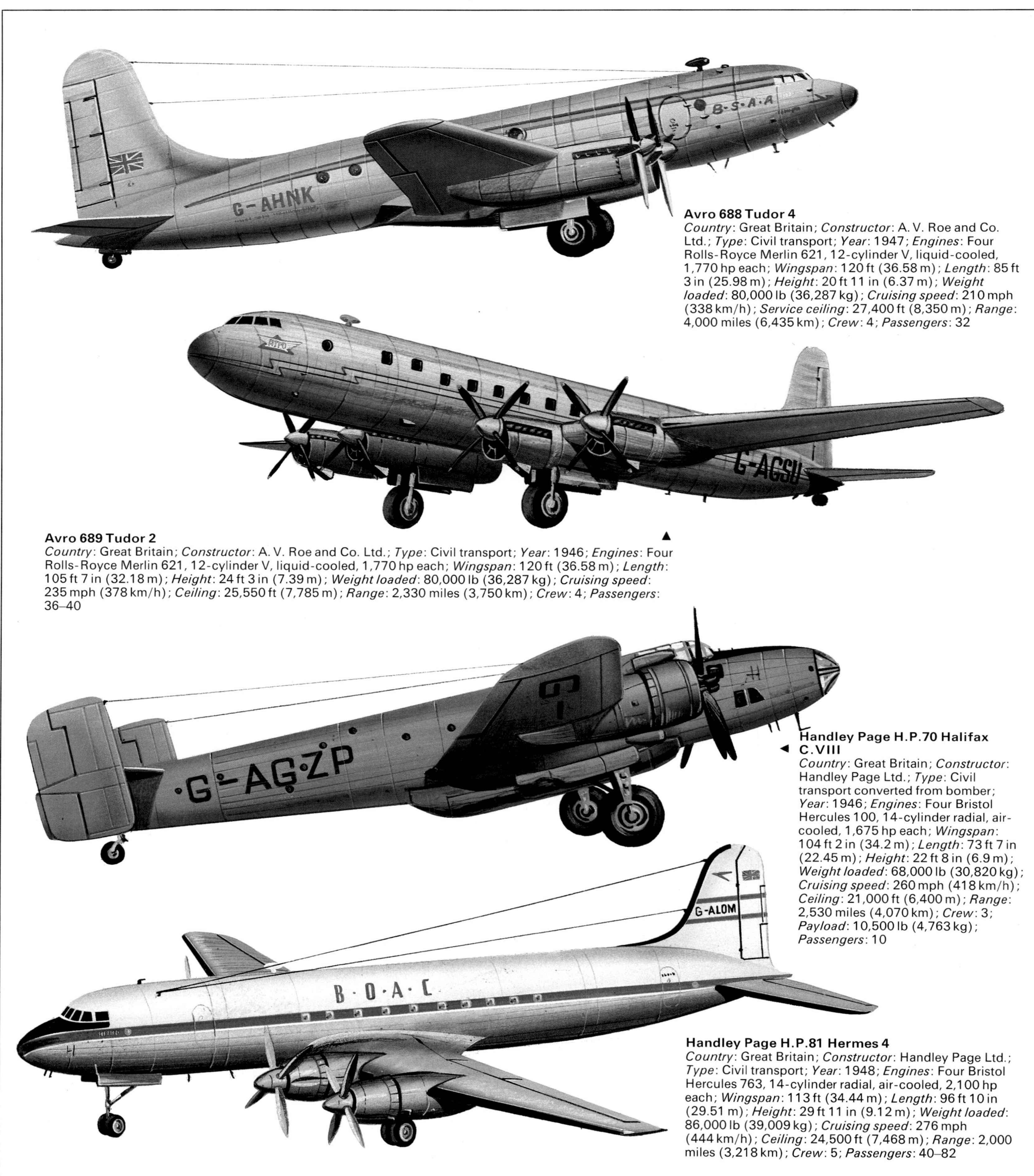

Avro 688 Tudor 4
Country: Great Britain; *Constructor*: A. V. Roe and Co. Ltd.; *Type*: Civil transport; *Year*: 1947; *Engines*: Four Rolls-Royce Merlin 621, 12-cylinder V, liquid-cooled, 1,770 hp each; *Wingspan*: 120 ft (36.58 m); *Length*: 85 ft 3 in (25.98 m); *Height*: 20 ft 11 in (6.37 m); *Weight loaded*: 80,000 lb (36,287 kg); *Cruising speed*: 210 mph (338 km/h); *Service ceiling*: 27,400 ft (8,350 m); *Range*: 4,000 miles (6,435 km); *Crew*: 4; *Passengers*: 32

Avro 689 Tudor 2 ▲
Country: Great Britain; *Constructor*: A. V. Roe and Co. Ltd.; *Type*: Civil transport; *Year*: 1946; *Engines*: Four Rolls-Royce Merlin 621, 12-cylinder V, liquid-cooled, 1,770 hp each; *Wingspan*: 120 ft (36.58 m); *Length*: 105 ft 7 in (32.18 m); *Height*: 24 ft 3 in (7.39 m); *Weight loaded*: 80,000 lb (36,287 kg); *Cruising speed*: 235 mph (378 km/h); *Ceiling*: 25,550 ft (7,785 m); *Range*: 2,330 miles (3,750 km); *Crew*: 4; *Passengers*: 36–40

◄ **Handley Page H.P.70 Halifax C.VIII**
Country: Great Britain; *Constructor*: Handley Page Ltd.; *Type*: Civil transport converted from bomber; *Year*: 1946; *Engines*: Four Bristol Hercules 100, 14-cylinder radial, air-cooled, 1,675 hp each; *Wingspan*: 104 ft 2 in (34.2 m); *Length*: 73 ft 7 in (22.45 m); *Height*: 22 ft 8 in (6.9 m); *Weight loaded*: 68,000 lb (30,820 kg); *Cruising speed*: 260 mph (418 km/h); *Ceiling*: 21,000 ft (6,400 m); *Range*: 2,530 miles (4,070 km); *Crew*: 3; *Payload*: 10,500 lb (4,763 kg); *Passengers*: 10

Handley Page H.P.81 Hermes 4
Country: Great Britain; *Constructor*: Handley Page Ltd.; *Type*: Civil transport; *Year*: 1948; *Engines*: Four Bristol Hercules 763, 14-cylinder radial, air-cooled, 2,100 hp each; *Wingspan*: 113 ft (34.44 m); *Length*: 96 ft 10 in (29.51 m); *Height*: 29 ft 11 in (9.12 m); *Weight loaded*: 86,000 lb (39,009 kg); *Cruising speed*: 276 mph (444 km/h); *Ceiling*: 24,500 ft (7,468 m); *Range*: 2,000 miles (3,218 km); *Crew*: 5; *Passengers*: 40–82

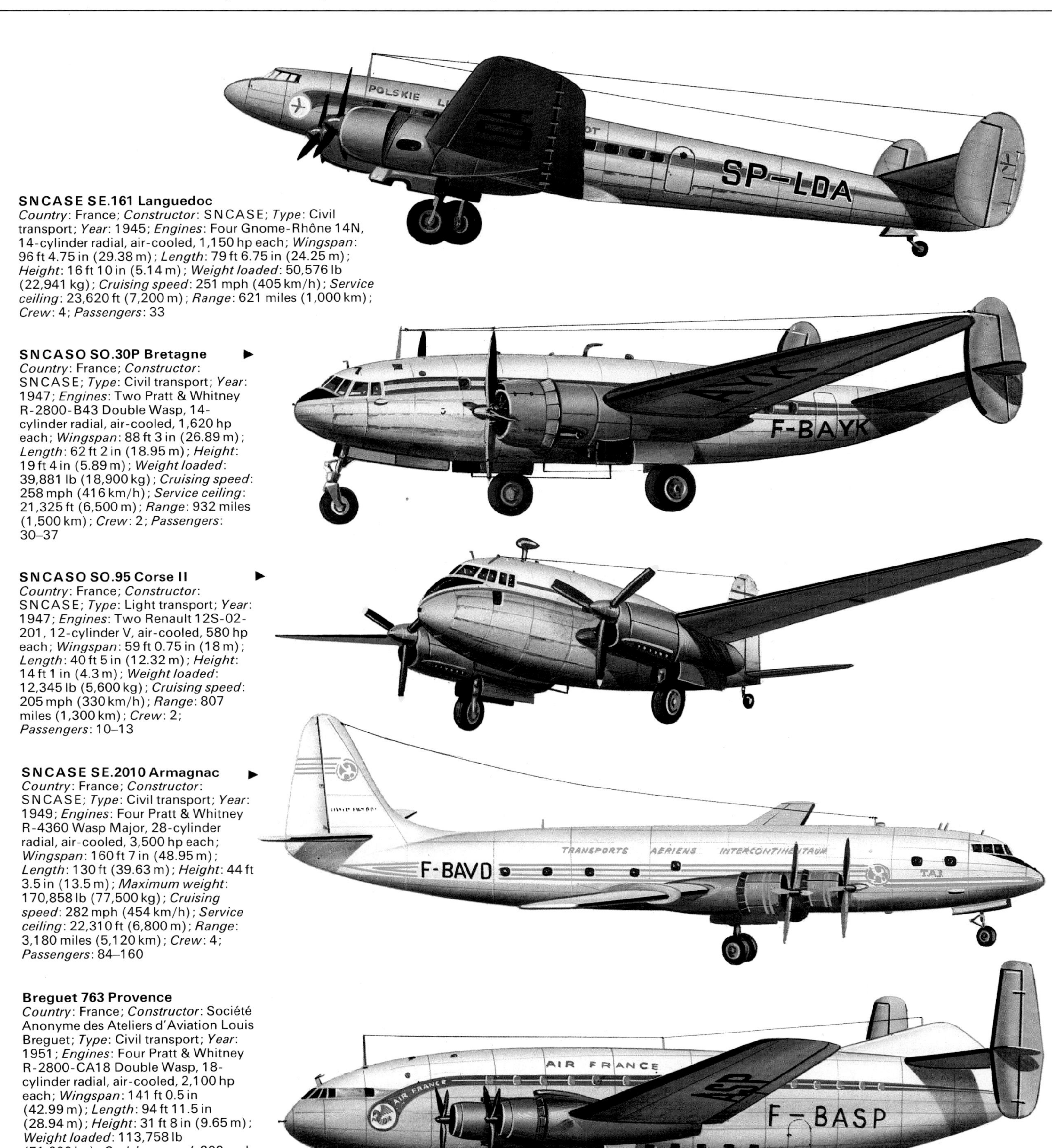

SNCASE SE.161 Languedoc
Country: France; *Constructor*: SNCASE; *Type*: Civil transport; *Year*: 1945; *Engines*: Four Gnome-Rhône 14N, 14-cylinder radial, air-cooled, 1,150 hp each; *Wingspan*: 96 ft 4.75 in (29.38 m); *Length*: 79 ft 6.75 in (24.25 m); *Height*: 16 ft 10 in (5.14 m); *Weight loaded*: 50,576 lb (22,941 kg); *Cruising speed*: 251 mph (405 km/h); *Service ceiling*: 23,620 ft (7,200 m); *Range*: 621 miles (1,000 km); *Crew*: 4; *Passengers*: 33

SNCASO SO.30P Bretagne ►
Country: France; *Constructor*: SNCASE; *Type*: Civil transport; *Year*: 1947; *Engines*: Two Pratt & Whitney R-2800-B43 Double Wasp, 14-cylinder radial, air-cooled, 1,620 hp each; *Wingspan*: 88 ft 3 in (26.89 m); *Length*: 62 ft 2 in (18.95 m); *Height*: 19 ft 4 in (5.89 m); *Weight loaded*: 39,881 lb (18,900 kg); *Cruising speed*: 258 mph (416 km/h); *Service ceiling*: 21,325 ft (6,500 m); *Range*: 932 miles (1,500 km); *Crew*: 2; *Passengers*: 30–37

SNCASO SO.95 Corse II ►
Country: France; *Constructor*: SNCASE; *Type*: Light transport; *Year*: 1947; *Engines*: Two Renault 12S-02-201, 12-cylinder V, air-cooled, 580 hp each; *Wingspan*: 59 ft 0.75 in (18 m); *Length*: 40 ft 5 in (12.32 m); *Height*: 14 ft 1 in (4.3 m); *Weight loaded*: 12,345 lb (5,600 kg); *Cruising speed*: 205 mph (330 km/h); *Range*: 807 miles (1,300 km); *Crew*: 2; *Passengers*: 10–13

SNCASE SE.2010 Armagnac ►
Country: France; *Constructor*: SNCASE; *Type*: Civil transport; *Year*: 1949; *Engines*: Four Pratt & Whitney R-4360 Wasp Major, 28-cylinder radial, air-cooled, 3,500 hp each; *Wingspan*: 160 ft 7 in (48.95 m); *Length*: 130 ft (39.63 m); *Height*: 44 ft 3.5 in (13.5 m); *Maximum weight*: 170,858 lb (77,500 kg); *Cruising speed*: 282 mph (454 km/h); *Service ceiling*: 22,310 ft (6,800 m); *Range*: 3,180 miles (5,120 km); *Crew*: 4; *Passengers*: 84–160

Breguet 763 Provence
Country: France; *Constructor*: Société Anonyme des Ateliers d'Aviation Louis Breguet; *Type*: Civil transport; *Year*: 1951; *Engines*: Four Pratt & Whitney R-2800-CA18 Double Wasp, 18-cylinder radial, air-cooled, 2,100 hp each; *Wingspan*: 141 ft 0.5 in (42.99 m); *Length*: 94 ft 11.5 in (28.94 m); *Height*: 31 ft 8 in (9.65 m); *Weight loaded*: 113,758 lb (51,600 kg); *Cruising speed*: 209 mph (336 km/h); *Ceiling*: 22,310 ft (6,800 m); *Range*: 1,423 miles (2,290 km); *Crew*: 4; *Passengers*: 107

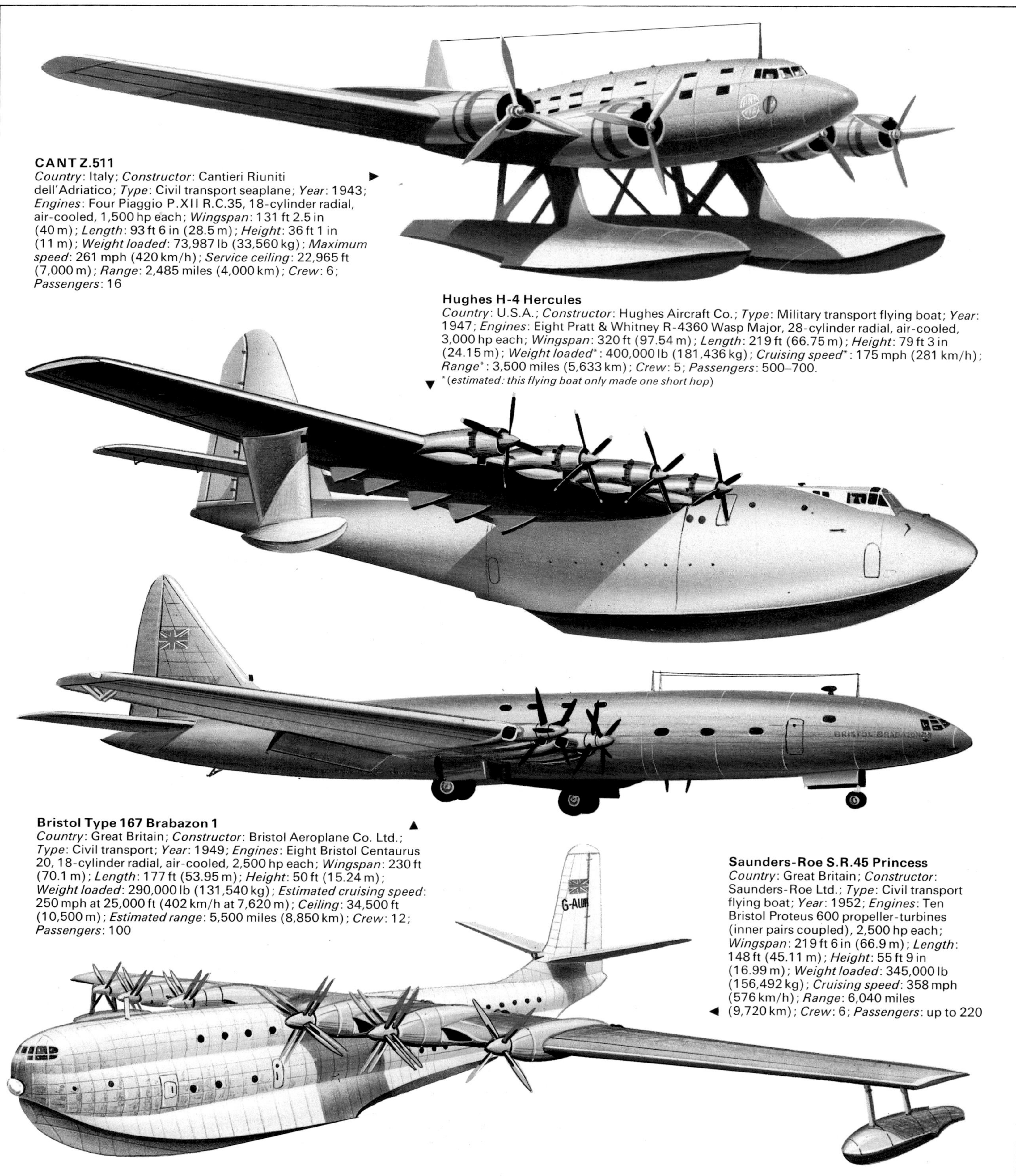

CANT Z.511
Country: Italy; *Constructor*: Cantieri Riuniti dell'Adriatico; *Type*: Civil transport seaplane; *Year*: 1943; *Engines*: Four Piaggio P.XII R.C.35, 18-cylinder radial, air-cooled, 1,500 hp each; *Wingspan*: 131 ft 2.5 in (40 m); *Length*: 93 ft 6 in (28.5 m); *Height*: 36 ft 1 in (11 m); *Weight loaded*: 73,987 lb (33,560 kg); *Maximum speed*: 261 mph (420 km/h); *Service ceiling*: 22,965 ft (7,000 m); *Range*: 2,485 miles (4,000 km); *Crew*: 6; *Passengers*: 16

Hughes H-4 Hercules
Country: U.S.A.; *Constructor*: Hughes Aircraft Co.; *Type*: Military transport flying boat; *Year*: 1947; *Engines*: Eight Pratt & Whitney R-4360 Wasp Major, 28-cylinder radial, air-cooled, 3,000 hp each; *Wingspan*: 320 ft (97.54 m); *Length*: 219 ft (66.75 m); *Height*: 79 ft 3 in (24.15 m); *Weight loaded**: 400,000 lb (181,436 kg); *Cruising speed**: 175 mph (281 km/h); *Range**: 3,500 miles (5,633 km); *Crew*: 5; *Passengers*: 500–700.
* *(estimated: this flying boat only made one short hop)*

Bristol Type 167 Brabazon 1
Country: Great Britain; *Constructor*: Bristol Aeroplane Co. Ltd.; *Type*: Civil transport; *Year*: 1949; *Engines*: Eight Bristol Centaurus 20, 18-cylinder radial, air-cooled, 2,500 hp each; *Wingspan*: 230 ft (70.1 m); *Length*: 177 ft (53.95 m); *Height*: 50 ft (15.24 m); *Weight loaded*: 290,000 lb (131,540 kg); *Estimated cruising speed*: 250 mph at 25,000 ft (402 km/h at 7,620 m); *Ceiling*: 34,500 ft (10,500 m); *Estimated range*: 5,500 miles (8,850 km); *Crew*: 12; *Passengers*: 100

Saunders-Roe S.R.45 Princess
Country: Great Britain; *Constructor*: Saunders-Roe Ltd.; *Type*: Civil transport flying boat; *Year*: 1952; *Engines*: Ten Bristol Proteus 600 propeller-turbines (inner pairs coupled), 2,500 hp each; *Wingspan*: 219 ft 6 in (66.9 m); *Length*: 148 ft (45.11 m); *Height*: 55 ft 9 in (16.99 m); *Weight loaded*: 345,000 lb (156,492 kg); *Cruising speed*: 358 mph (576 km/h); *Range*: 6,040 miles (9,720 km); *Crew*: 6; *Passengers*: up to 220

Latécoère 631
Country: France; *Constructor*: Société Industrielle d'Aviation Latécoère; *Type*: Civil transport flying boat; *Year*: 1942; *Engines*: Six Wright GR-2600-A5B Cyclone, 14-cylinder radial, air-cooled, 1,600 hp each; *Wingspan*: 188 ft 5 in (57.43 m); *Length*: 142 ft 7 in (43.46 m); *Height*: 33 ft 2 in (10.1 m); *Weight loaded*: 157,300 lb (71,350 kg); *Cruising speed*: 185 mph (297 km/h); *Range*: 3,750 miles (6,035 km); *Crew*: 5; *Passengers*: 46

Sikorsky VS-44A
Country: U.S.A.; *Constructor*: Vought Sikorsky Aircraft; *Type*: Civil transport flying boat; *Year*: 1942; *Engines*: Four Pratt & Whitney R-1830-S1C3G Twin Wasp, 14-cylinder radial, air-cooled, 1,200 hp each; *Wingspan*: 124 ft (37.79 m); *Length*: 79 ft 3 in (24.15 m); *Height*: 27 ft 7.25 in (8.41 m); *Weight loaded*: 57,500 lb (26,082 kg); *Cruising speed*: 160 mph at 10,000 ft (257 km/h at 3,050 m); *Service ceiling*: 19,000 ft (5,790 m); *Range*: 3,600 miles (5,795 km); *Crew*: 9; *Passengers*: 16–47

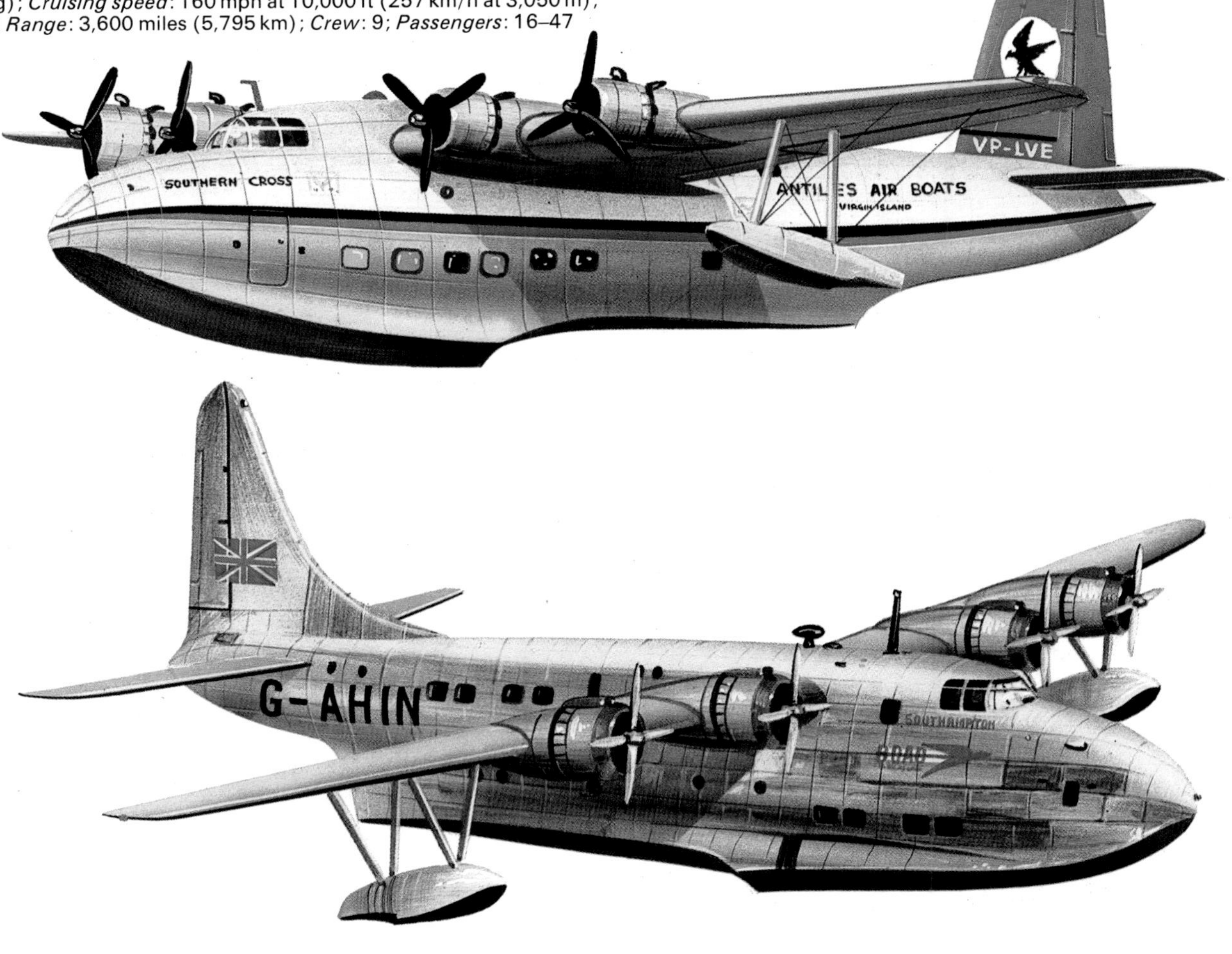

Short S.25/V Sandringham 4
Country: Great Britain; *Constructor*: Short Brothers Ltd.; *Type*: Civil transport flying boat; *Year*: 1946; *Engines*: Four Pratt & Whitney R-1830-92C Twin Wasp, 14-cylinder radial, air-cooled, 1,200 hp each; *Wingspan*: 112 ft 9.5 in (34.38 m); *Length*: 86 ft 3 in (26.29 m); *Height*: 22 ft 10.5 in (6.97 m); *Weight loaded*: 56,000 lb (25,400 kg); *Cruising speed*: 221 mph (356 km/h); *Ceiling*: 21,300 ft (6,490 m); *Range*: 2,410 miles (3,880 km); *Crew*: 5; *Passengers*: 30

Short S.45A Solent 2
Country: Great Britain; *Constructor*: Short Brothers Ltd.; *Type*: Civil transport flying boat; *Year*: 1946; *Engines*: Four Bristol Hercules 637, 14-cylinder radial, air-cooled, 1,690 hp each; *Wingspan*: 112 ft 9 in (34.37 m); *Length*: 87 ft 8 in (26.7 m); *Height*: 34 ft 3.25 in (10.44 m); *Weight loaded*: 78,000 lb (35,400 kg); *Cruising speed*: 244 mph (392 km/h); *Service ceiling*: 17,500 ft (5,335 m); *Range*: 1,800 miles (2,896 km); *Crew*: 4; *Passengers*: 34–44

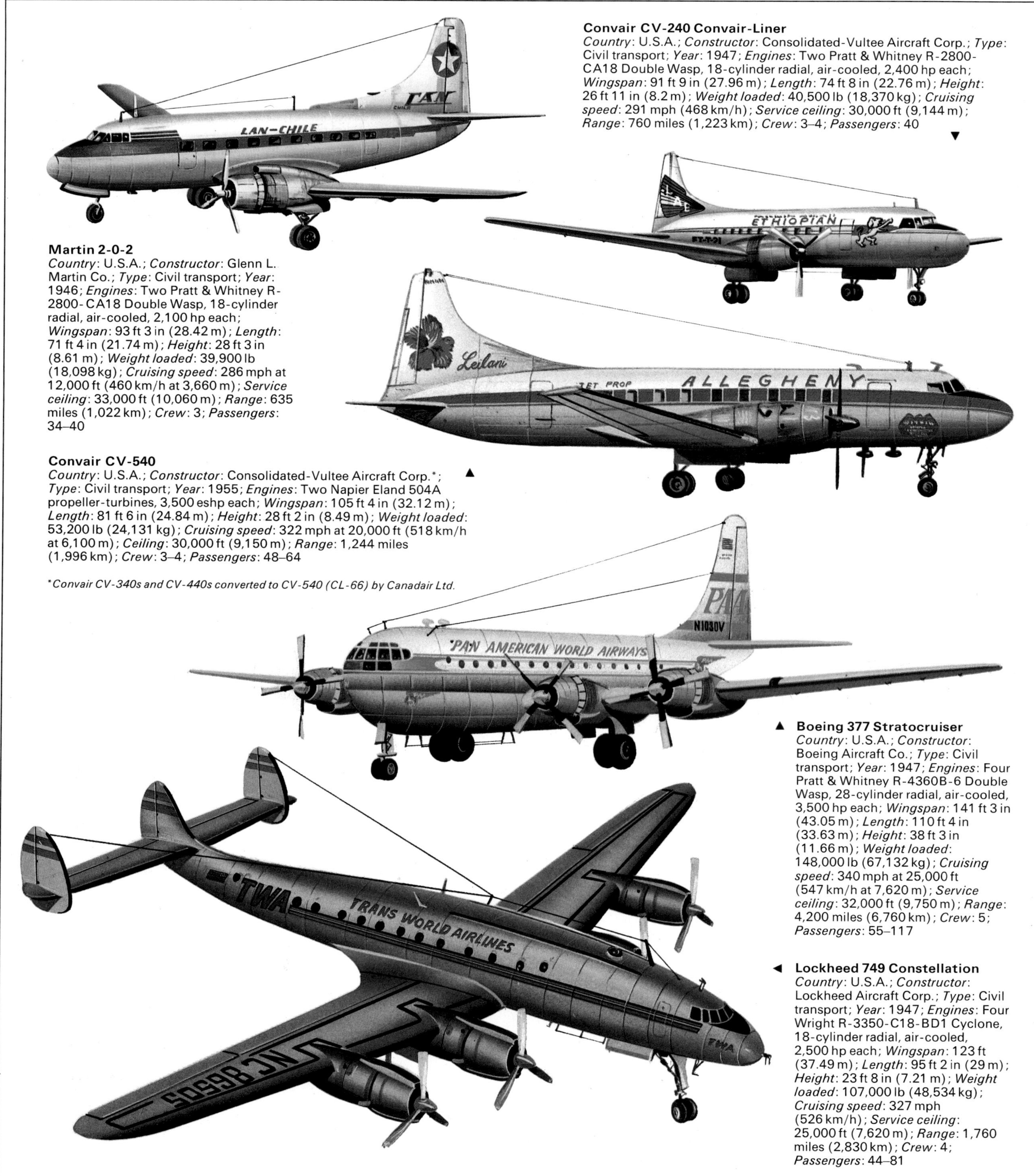

Convair CV-240 Convair-Liner
Country: U.S.A.; *Constructor*: Consolidated-Vultee Aircraft Corp.; *Type*: Civil transport; *Year*: 1947; *Engines*: Two Pratt & Whitney R-2800-CA18 Double Wasp, 18-cylinder radial, air-cooled, 2,400 hp each; *Wingspan*: 91 ft 9 in (27.96 m); *Length*: 74 ft 8 in (22.76 m); *Height*: 26 ft 11 in (8.2 m); *Weight loaded*: 40,500 lb (18,370 kg); *Cruising speed*: 291 mph (468 km/h); *Service ceiling*: 30,000 ft (9,144 m); *Range*: 760 miles (1,223 km); *Crew*: 3–4; *Passengers*: 40 ▼

Martin 2-0-2
Country: U.S.A.; *Constructor*: Glenn L. Martin Co.; *Type*: Civil transport; *Year*: 1946; *Engines*: Two Pratt & Whitney R-2800-CA18 Double Wasp, 18-cylinder radial, air-cooled, 2,100 hp each; *Wingspan*: 93 ft 3 in (28.42 m); *Length*: 71 ft 4 in (21.74 m); *Height*: 28 ft 3 in (8.61 m); *Weight loaded*: 39,900 lb (18,098 kg); *Cruising speed*: 286 mph at 12,000 ft (460 km/h at 3,660 m); *Service ceiling*: 33,000 ft (10,060 m); *Range*: 635 miles (1,022 km); *Crew*: 3; *Passengers*: 34–40

Convair CV-540 ▲
Country: U.S.A.; *Constructor*: Consolidated-Vultee Aircraft Corp.*; *Type*: Civil transport; *Year*: 1955; *Engines*: Two Napier Eland 504A propeller-turbines, 3,500 eshp each; *Wingspan*: 105 ft 4 in (32.12 m); *Length*: 81 ft 6 in (24.84 m); *Height*: 28 ft 2 in (8.49 m); *Weight loaded*: 53,200 lb (24,131 kg); *Cruising speed*: 322 mph at 20,000 ft (518 km/h at 6,100 m); *Ceiling*: 30,000 ft (9,150 m); *Range*: 1,244 miles (1,996 km); *Crew*: 3–4; *Passengers*: 48–64

**Convair CV-340s and CV-440s converted to CV-540 (CL-66) by Canadair Ltd.*

▲ **Boeing 377 Stratocruiser**
Country: U.S.A.; *Constructor*: Boeing Aircraft Co.; *Type*: Civil transport; *Year*: 1947; *Engines*: Four Pratt & Whitney R-4360B-6 Double Wasp, 28-cylinder radial, air-cooled, 3,500 hp each; *Wingspan*: 141 ft 3 in (43.05 m); *Length*: 110 ft 4 in (33.63 m); *Height*: 38 ft 3 in (11.66 m); *Weight loaded*: 148,000 lb (67,132 kg); *Cruising speed*: 340 mph at 25,000 ft (547 km/h at 7,620 m); *Service ceiling*: 32,000 ft (9,750 m); *Range*: 4,200 miles (6,760 km); *Crew*: 5; *Passengers*: 55–117

◄ **Lockheed 749 Constellation**
Country: U.S.A.; *Constructor*: Lockheed Aircraft Corp.; *Type*: Civil transport; *Year*: 1947; *Engines*: Four Wright R-3350-C18-BD1 Cyclone, 18-cylinder radial, air-cooled, 2,500 hp each; *Wingspan*: 123 ft (37.49 m); *Length*: 95 ft 2 in (29 m); *Height*: 23 ft 8 in (7.21 m); *Weight loaded*: 107,000 lb (48,534 kg); *Cruising speed*: 327 mph (526 km/h); *Service ceiling*: 25,000 ft (7,620 m); *Range*: 1,760 miles (2,830 km); *Crew*: 4; *Passengers*: 44–81

The Americans build the last successful four-engine piston-engine transports: 1951–1955

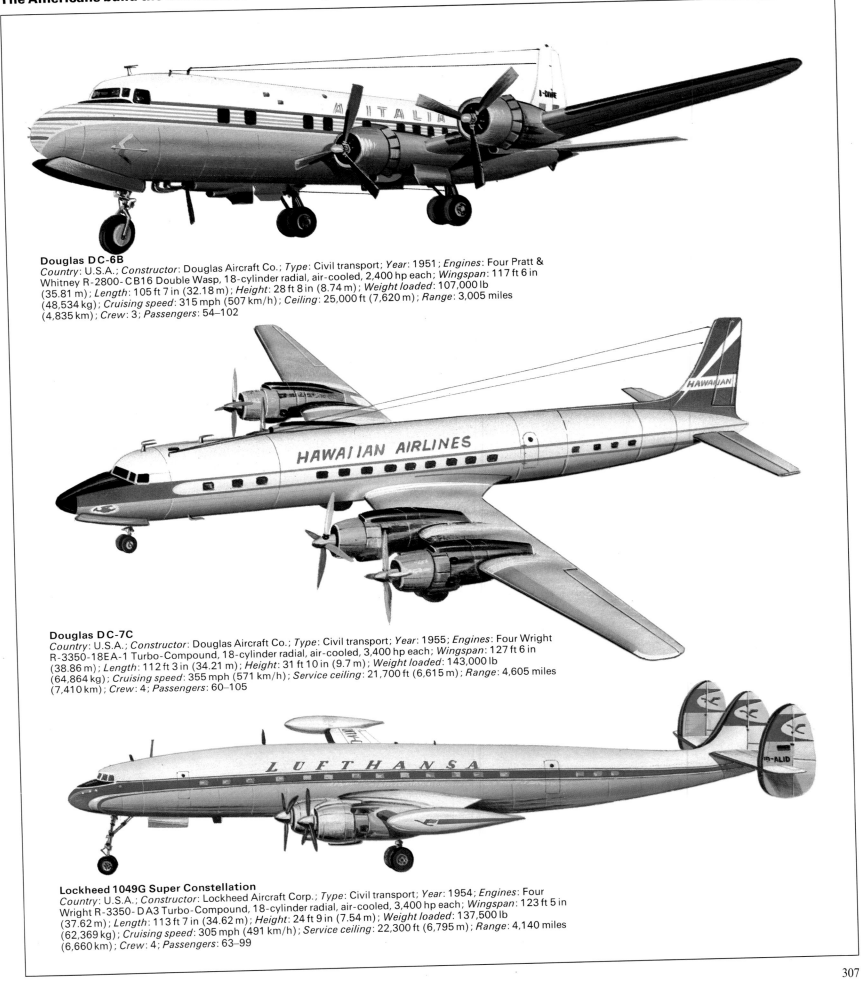

Douglas DC-6B
Country: U.S.A.; *Constructor*: Douglas Aircraft Co.; *Type*: Civil transport; *Year*: 1951; *Engines*: Four Pratt & Whitney R-2800-CB16 Double Wasp, 18-cylinder radial, air-cooled, 2,400 hp each; *Wingspan*: 117 ft 6 in (35.81 m); *Length*: 105 ft 7 in (32.18 m); *Height*: 28 ft 8 in (8.74 m); *Weight loaded*: 107,000 lb (48,534 kg); *Cruising speed*: 315 mph (507 km/h); *Ceiling*: 25,000 ft (7,620 m); *Range*: 3,005 miles (4,835 km); *Crew*: 3; *Passengers*: 54–102

Douglas DC-7C
Country: U.S.A.; *Constructor*: Douglas Aircraft Co.; *Type*: Civil transport; *Year*: 1955; *Engines*: Four Wright R-3350-18EA-1 Turbo-Compound, 18-cylinder radial, air-cooled, 3,400 hp each; *Wingspan*: 127 ft 6 in (38.86 m); *Length*: 112 ft 3 in (34.21 m); *Height*: 31 ft 10 in (9.7 m); *Weight loaded*: 143,000 lb (64,864 kg); *Cruising speed*: 355 mph (571 km/h); *Service ceiling*: 21,700 ft (6,615 m); *Range*: 4,605 miles (7,410 km); *Crew*: 4; *Passengers*: 60–105

Lockheed 1049G Super Constellation
Country: U.S.A.; *Constructor*: Lockheed Aircraft Corp.; *Type*: Civil transport; *Year*: 1954; *Engines*: Four Wright R-3350-DA3 Turbo-Compound, 18-cylinder radial, air-cooled, 3,400 hp each; *Wingspan*: 123 ft 5 in (37.62 m); *Length*: 113 ft 7 in (34.62 m); *Height*: 24 ft 9 in (7.54 m); *Weight loaded*: 137,500 lb (62,369 kg); *Cruising speed*: 305 mph (491 km/h); *Service ceiling*: 22,300 ft (6,795 m); *Range*: 4,140 miles (6,660 km); *Crew*: 4; *Passengers*: 63–99

Bristol Type 175 Britannia 102

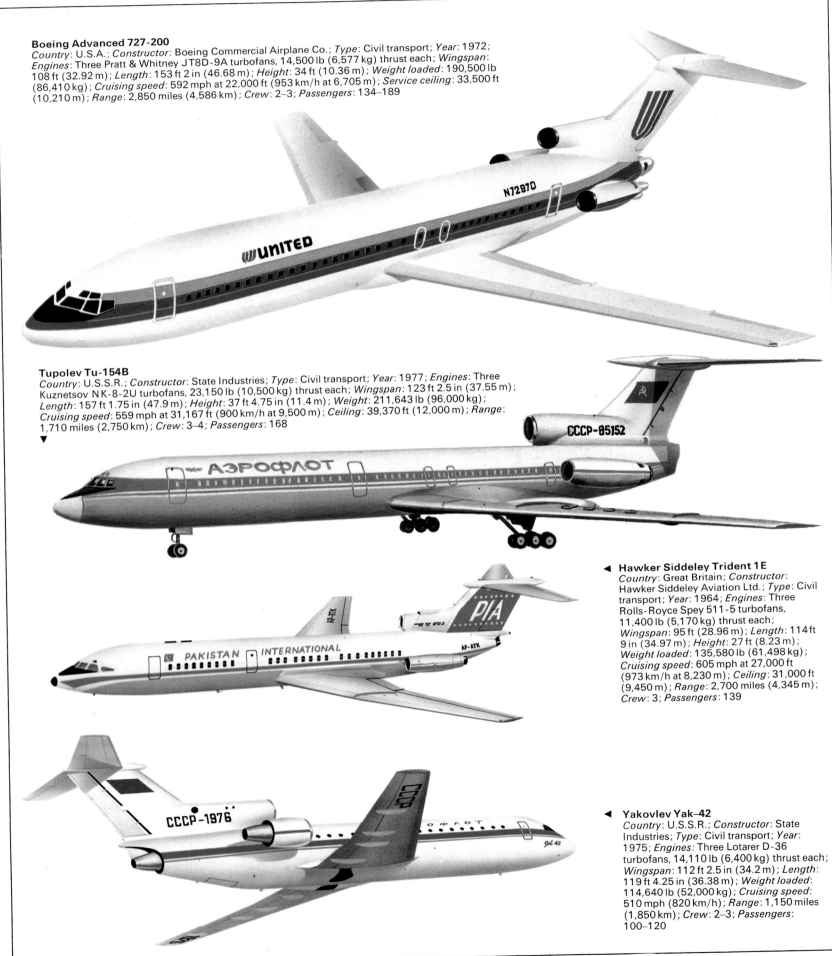

Boeing Advanced 727-200
Country: U.S.A.; *Constructor*: Boeing Commercial Airplane Co.; *Type*: Civil transport; *Year*: 1972; *Engines*: Three Pratt & Whitney JT8D-9A turbofans, 14,500 lb (6,577 kg) thrust each; *Wingspan*: 108 ft (32.92 m); *Length*: 153 ft 2 in (46.68 m); *Height*: 34 ft (10.36 m); *Weight loaded*: 190,500 lb (86,410 kg); *Cruising speed*: 592 mph at 22,000 ft (953 km/h at 6,705 m); *Service ceiling*: 33,500 ft (10,210 m); *Range*: 2,850 miles (4,586 km); *Crew*: 2–3; *Passengers*: 134–189

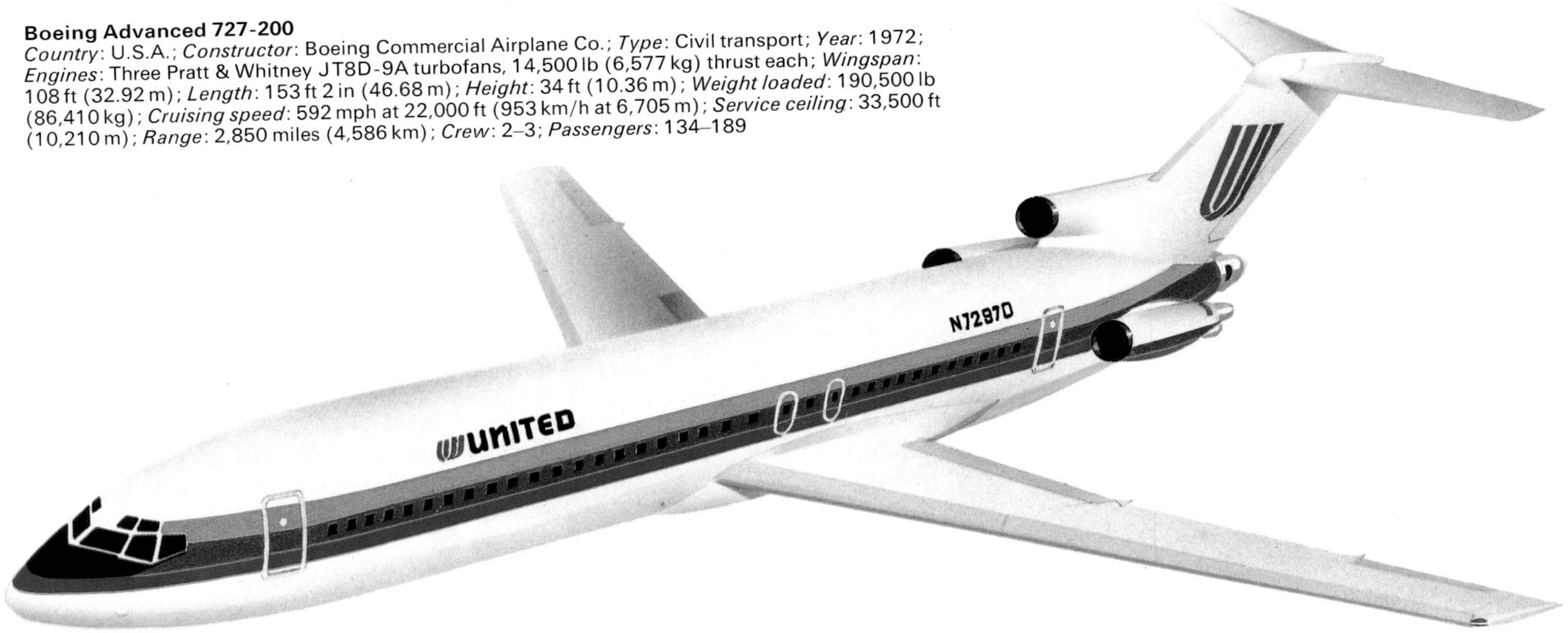

Tupolev Tu-154B
Country: U.S.S.R.; *Constructor*: State Industries; *Type*: Civil transport; *Year*: 1977; *Engines*: Three Kuznetsov NK-8-2U turbofans, 23,150 lb (10,500 kg) thrust each; *Wingspan*: 123 ft 2.5 in (37.55 m); *Length*: 157 ft 1.75 in (47.9 m); *Height*: 37 ft 4.75 in (11.4 m); *Weight*: 211,643 lb (96,000 kg); *Cruising speed*: 559 mph at 31,167 ft (900 km/h at 9,500 m); *Ceiling*: 39,370 ft (12,000 m); *Range*: 1,710 miles (2,750 km); *Crew*: 3–4; *Passengers*: 168
▼

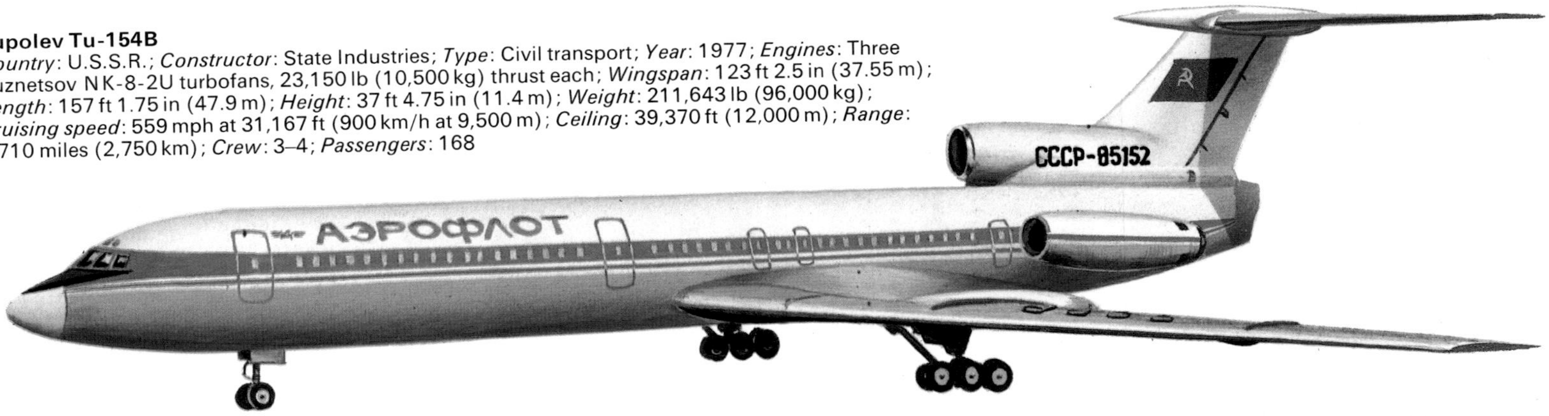

◄ **Hawker Siddeley Trident 1E**
Country: Great Britain; *Constructor*: Hawker Siddeley Aviation Ltd.; *Type*: Civil transport; *Year*: 1964; *Engines*: Three Rolls-Royce Spey 511-5 turbofans, 11,400 lb (5,170 kg) thrust each; *Wingspan*: 95 ft (28.96 m); *Length*: 114 ft 9 in (34.97 m); *Height*: 27 ft (8.23 m); *Weight loaded*: 135,580 lb (61,498 kg); *Cruising speed*: 605 mph at 27,000 ft (973 km/h at 8,230 m); *Ceiling*: 31,000 ft (9,450 m); *Range*: 2,700 miles (4,345 m); *Crew*: 3; *Passengers*: 139

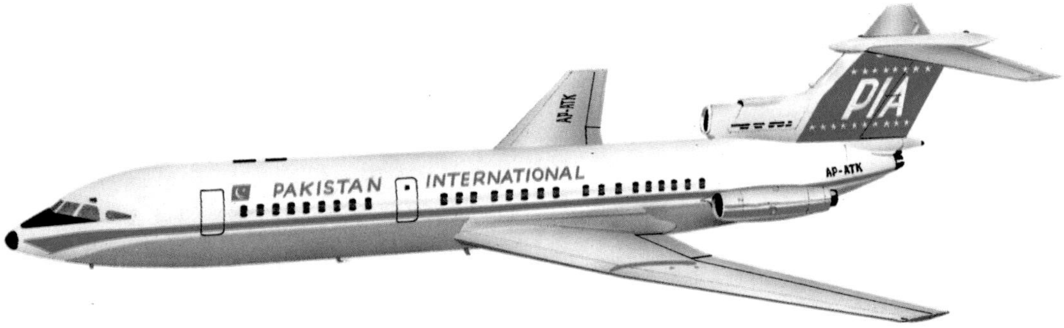

◄ **Yakovlev Yak–42**
Country: U.S.S.R.; *Constructor*: State Industries; *Type*: Civil transport; *Year*: 1975; *Engines*: Three Lotarer D-36 turbofans, 14,110 lb (6,400 kg) thrust each; *Wingspan*: 112 ft 2.5 in (34.2 m); *Length*: 119 ft 4.25 in (36.38 m); *Weight loaded*: 114,640 lb (52,000 kg); *Cruising speed*: 510 mph (820 km/h); *Range*: 1,150 miles (1,850 km); *Crew*: 2–3; *Passengers*: 100–120

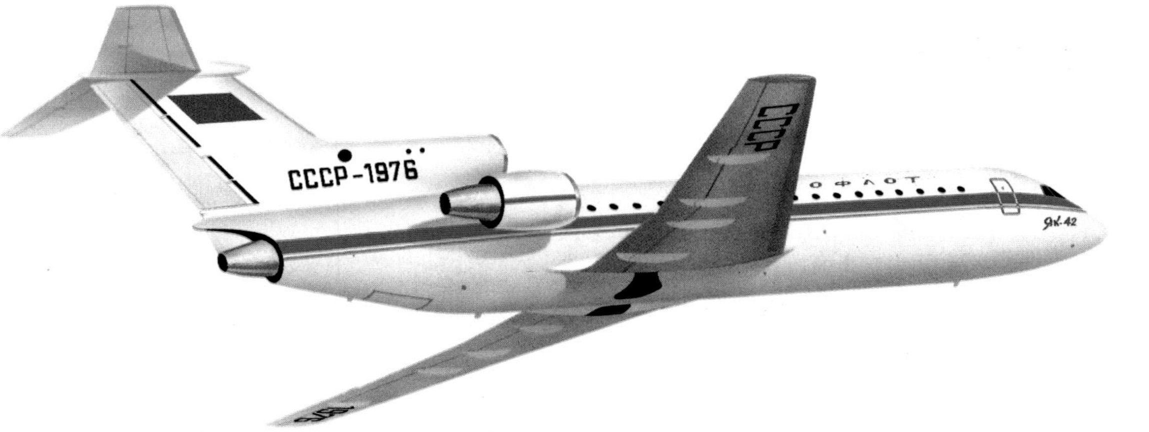

Airbus A300B4
Countries: France, Germany, Great Britain, The Netherlands, Italy and Spain; *Constructor*: Airbus Industries; *Type*: Civil transport; *Year*: 1974; *Engines*: Two General Electric CF6-50C turbofans, 51,000 lb (23,133 kg) thrust each; *Wingspan*: 147 ft 1 in (44.84 m); *Length*: 176 ft 4 in (53.75 m); *Height*: 54 ft 3 in (16.53 m); *Weight loaded*: 346,125 lb (157,000 kg); *Cruising speed*: 569 mph at 30,000 ft (917 km/h at 9,145 m); *Service ceiling*: 35,020 ft (10,675 m); *Range*: 2,993 miles (4,818 km); *Crew*: 3; *Passengers*: 336 maximum

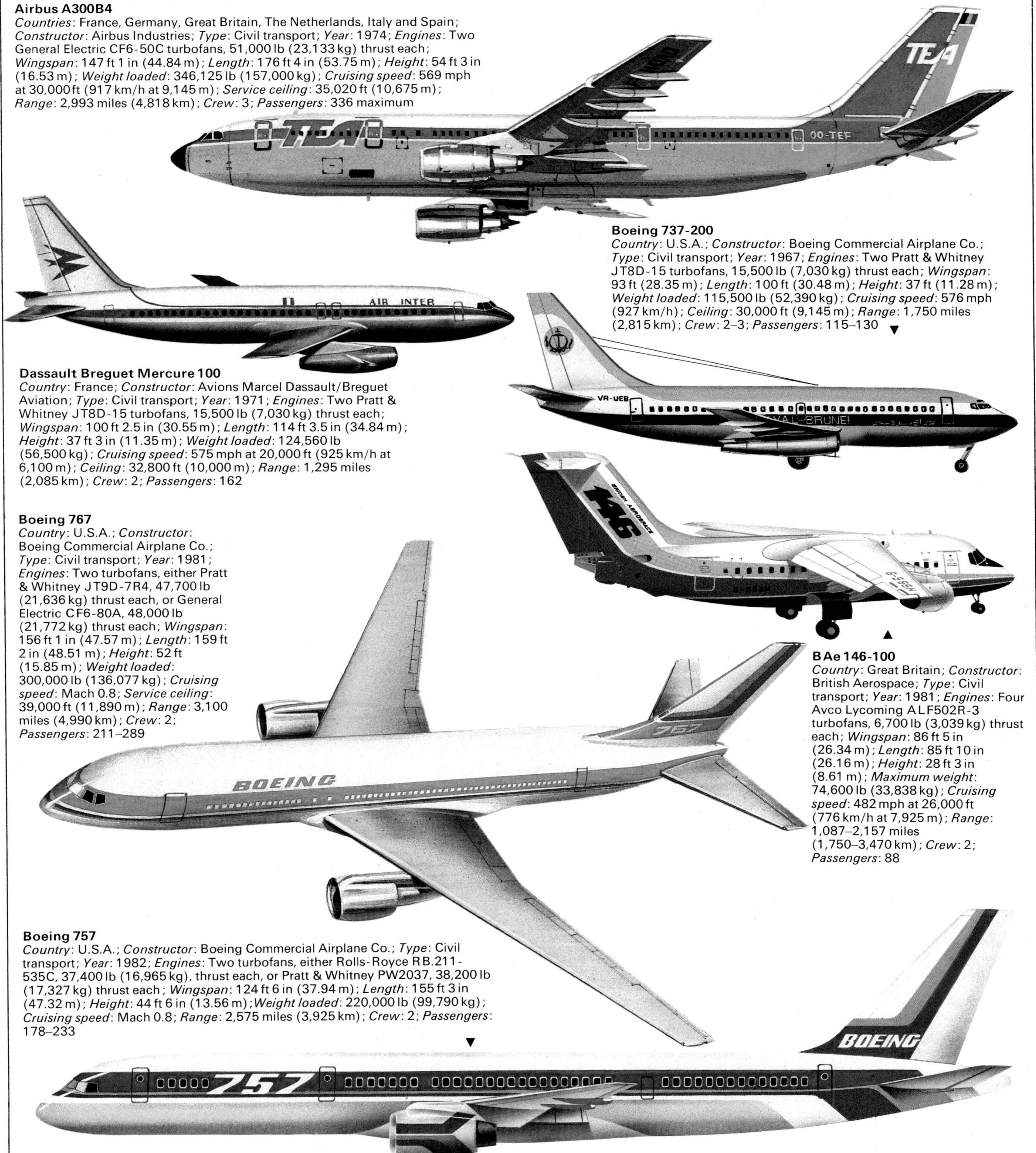

Boeing 737-200
Country: U.S.A.; *Constructor*: Boeing Commercial Airplane Co.; *Type*: Civil transport; *Year*: 1967; *Engines*: Two Pratt & Whitney JT8D-15 turbofans, 15,500 lb (7,030 kg) thrust each; *Wingspan*: 93 ft (28.35 m); *Length*: 100 ft (30.48 m); *Height*: 37 ft (11.28 m); *Weight loaded*: 115,500 lb (52,390 kg); *Cruising speed*: 576 mph (927 km/h); *Ceiling*: 30,000 ft (9,145 m); *Range*: 1,750 miles (2,815 km); *Crew*: 2–3; *Passengers*: 115–130 ▼

Dassault Breguet Mercure 100
Country: France; *Constructor*: Avions Marcel Dassault/Breguet Aviation; *Type*: Civil transport; *Year*: 1971; *Engines*: Two Pratt & Whitney JT8D-15 turbofans, 15,500 lb (7,030 kg) thrust each; *Wingspan*: 100 ft 2.5 in (30.55 m); *Length*: 114 ft 3.5 in (34.84 m); *Height*: 37 ft 3 in (11.35 m); *Weight loaded*: 124,560 lb (56,500 kg); *Cruising speed*: 575 mph at 20,000 ft (925 km/h at 6,100 m); *Ceiling*: 32,800 ft (10,000 m); *Range*: 1,295 miles (2,085 km); *Crew*: 2; *Passengers*: 162

Boeing 767
Country: U.S.A.; *Constructor*: Boeing Commercial Airplane Co.; *Type*: Civil transport; *Year*: 1981; *Engines*: Two turbofans, either Pratt & Whitney JT9D-7R4, 47,700 lb (21,636 kg) thrust each, or General Electric CF6-80A, 48,000 lb (21,772 kg) thrust each; *Wingspan*: 156 ft 1 in (47.57 m); *Length*: 159 ft 2 in (48.51 m); *Height*: 52 ft (15.85 m); *Weight loaded*: 300,000 lb (136,077 kg); *Cruising speed*: Mach 0.8; *Service ceiling*: 39,000 ft (11,890 m); *Range*: 3,100 miles (4,990 km); *Crew*: 2; *Passengers*: 211–289

▲
BAe 146-100
Country: Great Britain; *Constructor*: British Aerospace; *Type*: Civil transport; *Year*: 1981; *Engines*: Four Avco Lycoming ALF502R-3 turbofans, 6,700 lb (3,039 kg) thrust each; *Wingspan*: 86 ft 5 in (26.34 m); *Length*: 85 ft 10 in (26.16 m); *Height*: 28 ft 3 in (8.61 m); *Maximum weight*: 74,600 lb (33,838 kg); *Cruising speed*: 482 mph at 26,000 ft (776 km/h at 7,925 m); *Range*: 1,087–2,157 miles (1,750–3,470 km); *Crew*: 2; *Passengers*: 88

Boeing 757
Country: U.S.A.; *Constructor*: Boeing Commercial Airplane Co.; *Type*: Civil transport; *Year*: 1982; *Engines*: Two turbofans, either Rolls-Royce RB.211-535C, 37,400 lb (16,965 kg), thrust each, or Pratt & Whitney PW2037, 38,200 lb (17,327 kg) thrust each; *Wingspan*: 124 ft 6 in (37.94 m); *Length*: 155 ft 3 in (47.32 m); *Height*: 44 ft 6 in (13.56 m); *Weight loaded*: 220,000 lb (99,790 kg); *Cruising speed*: Mach 0.8; *Range*: 2,575 miles (3,925 km); *Crew*: 2; *Passengers*: 178–233
▼

Boeing 747-200B
Country: U.S.A.; *Constructor*: Boeing Commercial Airplane Co.; *Type*: Civil transport; *Year*: 1970; *Engines*: Four Pratt & Whitney JT9D-7AW turbofans, 47,670 lb (21,620 kg) thrust each; *Wingspan*: 195 ft 8 in (59.64 m); *Length*: 231 ft 4 in (70.51 m); *Height*: 63 ft 5 in (19.33 m); *Weight loaded*: 775,000 lb (351,534 kg); *Cruising speed*: 601 mph at 30,000 ft (967 km/h at 9,145 m); *Ceiling*: 45,000 ft (13,715 m); *Range*: 6,447 miles (10,375 km); *Crew*: 4; *Passengers*: 385 (typical)

▲ **Ilyushin Il-86**
Country: U.S.S.R.; *Constructor*: State Industries; *Type*: Civil transport; *Year*: 1976; *Engines*: Four Kuznetsov NK-86 turbofans, 28,660 lb (13,000 kg) thrust each; *Wingspan*: 157 ft 8 in (48.06 m); *Length*: 195 ft 4 in (59.54 m); *Height*: 51 ft 7 in (15.81 m); *Weight loaded*: 454,150 lb (206,000 kg); *Cruising speed*: 590 mph at 36,000 ft (950 km/h at 11,000 m); *Service ceiling*: 36,000 ft (11,000 m); *Range*: 2,235 miles (3,600 km); *Crew*: 3–4; *Passengers*: 350

◄ **Lockheed L-1011-100 TriStar**
Country: U.S.A.; *Constructor*: Lockheed Aircraft Corp.; *Type*: Civil transport; *Year*: 1970; *Engines*: Three Rolls-Royce RB.211-22F turbofans, 43,500 lb (19,730 kg) thrust each; *Wingspan*: 155 ft 4 in (47.35 m); *Length*: 177 ft 8 in (54,46 m); *Height*: 55 ft 4 in (16.87 m); *Weight loaded*: 466,000 lb (211,374 kg); *Cruising speed*: 495 mph (796 km/h); *Service ceiling*: 42,000 ft (12,800 m); *Range*: 4,465 miles (7,185 km); *Crew*: 3; *Passengers*: 256–400

◄ **McDonnell Douglas DC-10-30**
Country: U.S.A.; *Constructor*: McDonnell Douglas Corp.; *Type*: Civil transport; *Year*: 1972; *Engines*: Three General Electric CF6-50A turbofans, 49,000 lb (22,226 kg) thrust each; *Wingspan*: 165 ft 4 in (50.39 m); *Length*: 182 ft 7 in (55.35 m); *Height*: 58 ft 1 in (17.7 m); *Weight loaded*: 555,000 lb (251,744 kg); *Cruising speed*: 574 mph at 30,000 ft (924 km/h at 9,145 m); *Service ceiling*: 33,400 ft (10,180 m); *Range*: 4,690 miles (7,550 km); *Crew*: 3–4; *Passengers*: 255–380

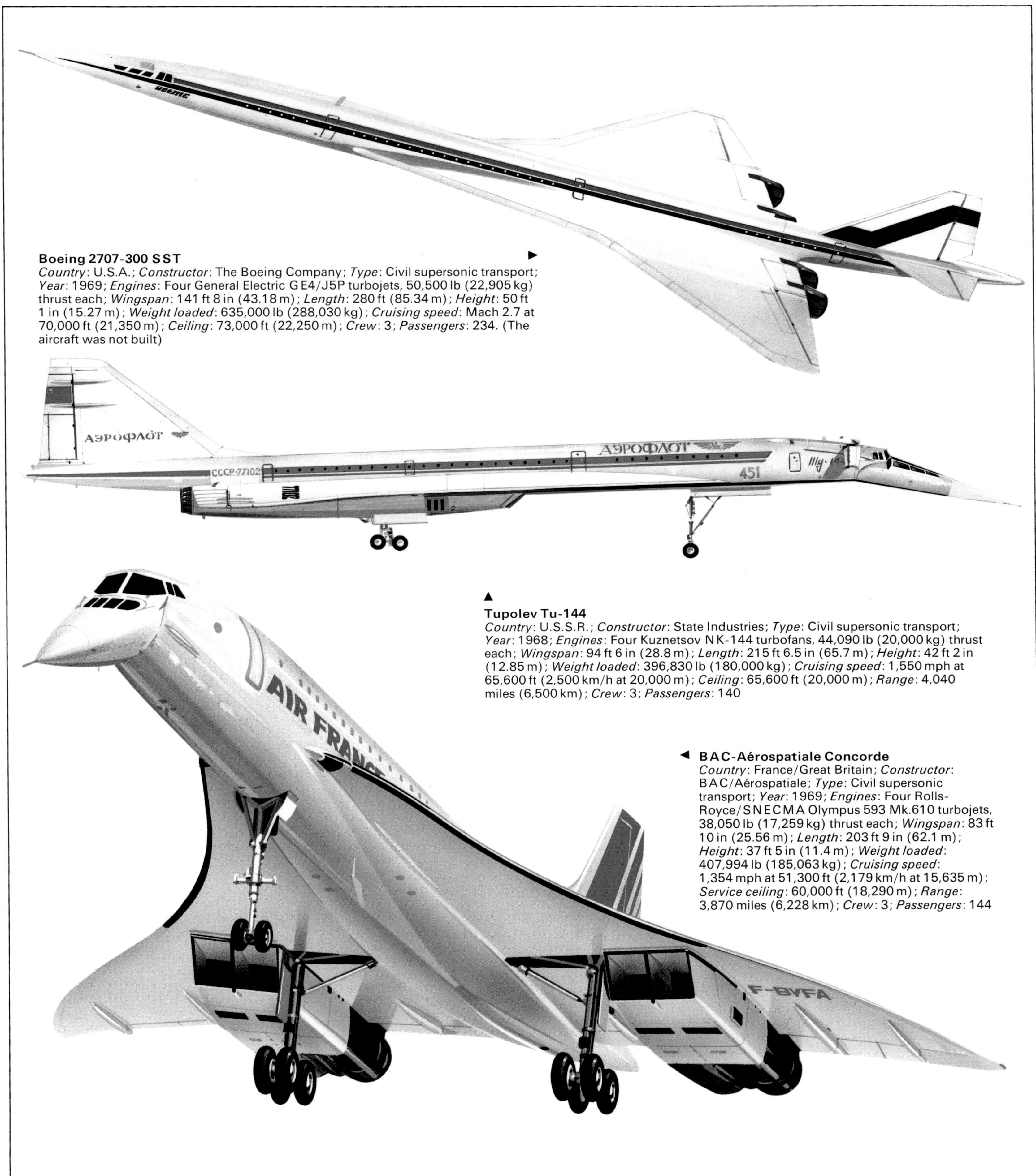

Boeing 2707-300 SST ►
Country: U.S.A.; *Constructor*: The Boeing Company; *Type*: Civil supersonic transport; *Year*: 1969; *Engines*: Four General Electric GE4/J5P turbojets, 50,500 lb (22,905 kg) thrust each; *Wingspan*: 141 ft 8 in (43.18 m); *Length*: 280 ft (85.34 m); *Height*: 50 ft 1 in (15.27 m); *Weight loaded*: 635,000 lb (288,030 kg); *Cruising speed*: Mach 2.7 at 70,000 ft (21,350 m); *Ceiling*: 73,000 ft (22,250 m); *Crew*: 3; *Passengers*: 234. (The aircraft was not built)

▲
Tupolev Tu-144
Country: U.S.S.R.; *Constructor*: State Industries; *Type*: Civil supersonic transport; *Year*: 1968; *Engines*: Four Kuznetsov NK-144 turbofans, 44,090 lb (20,000 kg) thrust each; *Wingspan*: 94 ft 6 in (28.8 m); *Length*: 215 ft 6.5 in (65.7 m); *Height*: 42 ft 2 in (12.85 m); *Weight loaded*: 396,830 lb (180,000 kg); *Cruising speed*: 1,550 mph at 65,600 ft (2,500 km/h at 20,000 m); *Ceiling*: 65,600 ft (20,000 m); *Range*: 4,040 miles (6,500 km); *Crew*: 3; *Passengers*: 140

◄ **BAC-Aérospatiale Concorde**
Country: France/Great Britain; *Constructor*: BAC/Aérospatiale; *Type*: Civil supersonic transport; *Year*: 1969; *Engines*: Four Rolls-Royce/SNECMA Olympus 593 Mk.610 turbojets, 38,050 lb (17,259 kg) thrust each; *Wingspan*: 83 ft 10 in (25.56 m); *Length*: 203 ft 9 in (62.1 m); *Height*: 37 ft 5 in (11.4 m); *Weight loaded*: 407,994 lb (185,063 kg); *Cruising speed*: 1,354 mph at 51,300 ft (2,179 km/h at 15,635 m); *Service ceiling*: 60,000 ft (18,290 m); *Range*: 3,870 miles (6,228 km); *Crew*: 3; *Passengers*: 144

▲ **Savoia Marchetti S.M.95**
Country: Italy; *Constructor*: Società Idrovolanti Alta Italia; *Type*: Civil transport; *Year*: 1947; *Engines*: Four Bristol Pegasus 48, 9-cylinder radial, air-cooled, 740 hp each; *Wingspan*: 112 ft 5.75 in (34.28 m); *Length*: 81 ft 3 in (24.77 m); *Height*: 17 ft 2.5 in (5.25 m); *Weight loaded*: 48,502 lb (22,000 kg); *Cruising speed*: 184 mph at 11,480 ft (296 km/h at 3,500 m); *Service ceiling*: 22,300 ft (6,800 m); *Range*: 1,250 miles (2,000 km); *Crew*: 5; *Passengers*: 20–38

Fiat G.212 CP Monterosa
Country: Italy; *Constructor*: Fiat S.A.; *Type*: Civil transport; *Year*: 1948; *Engines*: Three Pratt & Whitney R-1830-S1C3-G Twin Wasp, 14-cylinder radial, air-cooled, 1,065 hp each; *Wingspan*: 96 ft 3 in (29.34 m); *Length*: 75 ft 7.5 in (23.05 m); *Height*: 21 ft 4 in (6.5 m); *Weight loaded*: 38,360 lb (17,400 kg); *Cruising speed*: 186 mph (300 km/h); *Service ceiling*: 24,600 ft (7,500 m); *Range*: 1,550 miles (2,495 km); *Crew*: 3; *Passengers*: 24–30

Breda-Zappata B.Z.308
Country: Italy; *Constructor*: Società Italiana Ernesto Breda; *Type*: Civil transport; *Year*: 1948; *Engines*: Four Bristol Centaurus 568, 18-cylinder radial, air-cooled, 1,750 hp each; *Wingspan*: 138 ft 1 in (42.1 m); *Length*: 109 ft 11 in (33.52 m); *Height*: 23 ft 5 in (7.15 m); *Maximum weight*: 88,185 lb (40,000 kg); *Cruising speed*: 261 mph at 14,100 ft (420 km/h at 4,300 m); *Ceiling*: 24,100 ft (7,350 m); *Range*: 3,105 miles (5,000 km); *Crew*: 3–4; *Passengers*: 55 ◄

◄ **Macchi M.B.320**
Country: Italy; *Constructor*: Aeronautica Macchi; *Type*: Light transport; *Year*: 1949; *Engines*: Two Continental E.185, 6-cylinder horizontally opposed, air-cooled, 185 hp each; *Wingspan*: 42 ft 7.75 in (13 m); *Length*: 28 ft 5 in (8.66 m); *Height*: 10 ft 6 in (3.19 m); *Weight loaded*: 5,511 lb (2,500 kg); *Cruising speed*: 157 mph at 6,560 ft (252 km/h at 2,000 m); *Service ceiling*: 14,763 ft (4,500 m); *Range*: 994 miles (1,600 km); *Crew*: 2; *Passengers*: 4

Piaggio P.136-L1
Country: Italy; *Constructor*: Industrie Aeronautiche e Meccaniche Rinaldo Piaggio S.p.A.; *Type*: Light transport amphibian; *Year*: 1955; *Engines*: Two Lycoming GO-480-B1A6, 6-cylinder horizontally-opposed, air-cooled, 270 hp each; *Wingspan*: 44 ft 4.75 in (13.53 m); *Length*: 35 ft 5.25 in (10.8 m); *Height*: 12 ft 7 in (3.83 m); *Weight loaded*: 5,996 lb (2,720 kg); *Cruising speed*: 170 mph (273 km/h); *Service ceiling*: 18,370 ft (5,600 m); *Range*: 715 miles (1,150 km); *Crew*: 1; *Passengers*: 4

Piaggio P.166B Portofino
Country: Italy; *Constructor*: Industrie Aeronautiche e Meccaniche Rinaldo Piaggio S.p.A.; *Type*: Light transport; *Year*: 1962; *Engines*: Two Lycoming IGSO-540-A1C, 6-cylinder horizontally-opposed, air-cooled, 360 hp each; *Wingspan*: 46 ft 9 in (14.25 m); *Length*: 39 ft (11.89 m); *Height*: 16 ft 5 in (5 m); *Weight*: 8,377 lb (3,800 kg); *Cruising speed*: 176 mph (283 km/h); *Service ceiling*: 29,100 ft (8,870 m); *Range*: 1,500 miles (2,410 km); *Crew*: 1–2; *Passengers*: 6–9

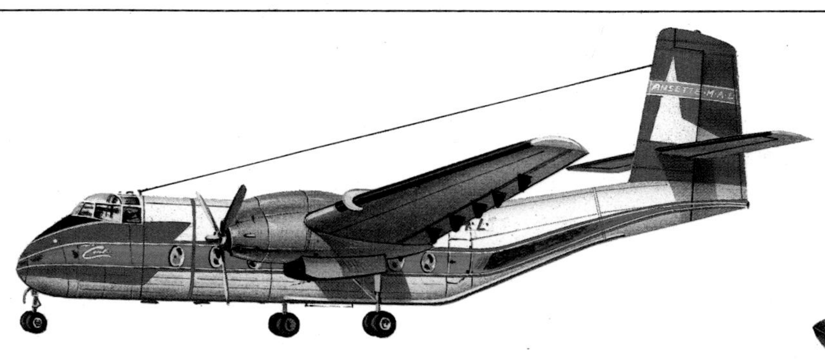

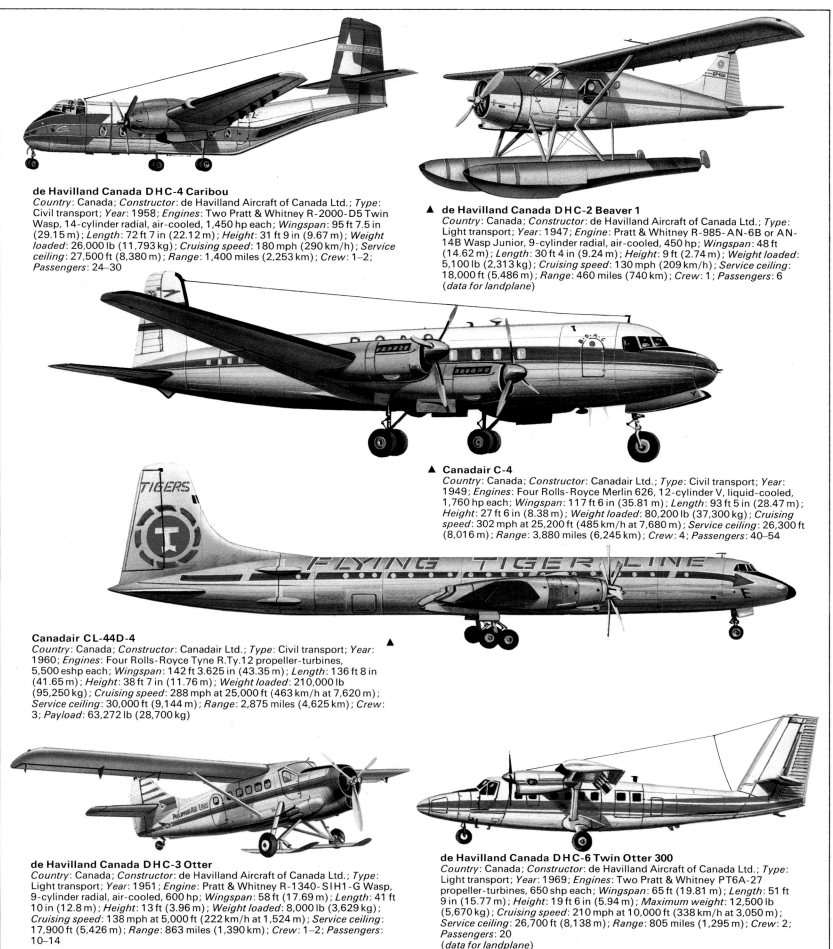

de Havilland Canada DHC-4 Caribou
Country: Canada; *Constructor*: de Havilland Aircraft of Canada Ltd.; *Type*: Civil transport; *Year*: 1958; *Engines*: Two Pratt & Whitney R-2000-D5 Twin Wasp, 14-cylinder radial, air-cooled, 1,450 hp each; *Wingspan*: 95 ft 7.5 in (29.15 m); *Length*: 72 ft 7 in (22.12 m); *Height*: 31 ft 9 in (9.67 m); *Weight loaded*: 26,000 lb (11,793 kg); *Cruising speed*: 180 mph (290 km/h); *Service ceiling*: 27,500 ft (8,380 m); *Range*: 1,400 miles (2,253 km); *Crew*: 1–2; *Passengers*: 24–30

▲ **de Havilland Canada DHC-2 Beaver 1**
Country: Canada; *Constructor*: de Havilland Aircraft of Canada Ltd.; *Type*: Light transport; *Year*: 1947; *Engine*: Pratt & Whitney R-985-AN-6B or AN-14B Wasp Junior, 9-cylinder radial, air-cooled, 450 hp; *Wingspan*: 48 ft (14.62 m); *Length*: 30 ft 4 in (9.24 m); *Height*: 9 ft (2.74 m); *Weight loaded*: 5,100 lb (2,313 kg); *Cruising speed*: 130 mph (209 km/h); *Service ceiling*: 18,000 ft (5,486 m); *Range*: 460 miles (740 km); *Crew*: 1; *Passengers*: 6 (*data for landplane*)

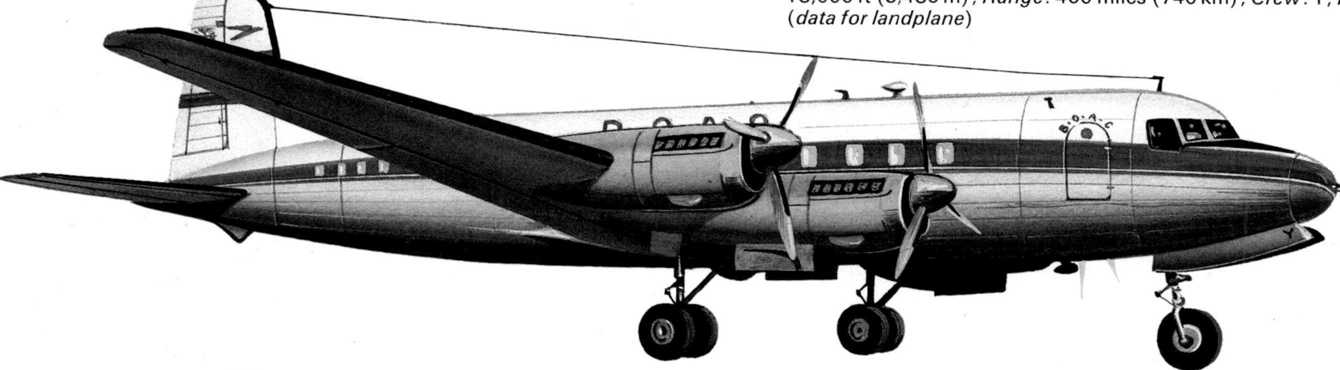

▲ **Canadair C-4**
Country: Canada; *Constructor*: Canadair Ltd.; *Type*: Civil transport; *Year*: 1949; *Engines*: Four Rolls-Royce Merlin 626, 12-cylinder V, liquid-cooled, 1,760 hp each; *Wingspan*: 117 ft 6 in (35.81 m); *Length*: 93 ft 5 in (28.47 m); *Height*: 27 ft 6 in (8.38 m); *Weight loaded*: 80,200 lb (37,300 kg); *Cruising speed*: 302 mph at 25,200 ft (485 km/h at 7,680 m); *Service ceiling*: 26,300 ft (8,016 m); *Range*: 3,880 miles (6,245 km); *Crew*: 4; *Passengers*: 40–54

Canadair CL-44D-4 ▲
Country: Canada; *Constructor*: Canadair Ltd.; *Type*: Civil transport; *Year*: 1960; *Engines*: Four Rolls-Royce Tyne R.Ty.12 propeller-turbines, 5,500 eshp each; *Wingspan*: 142 ft 3.625 in (43.35 m); *Length*: 136 ft 8 in (41.65 m); *Height*: 38 ft 7 in (11.76 m); *Weight loaded*: 210,000 lb (95,250 kg); *Cruising speed*: 288 mph at 25,000 ft (463 km/h at 7,620 m); *Service ceiling*: 30,000 ft (9,144 m); *Range*: 2,875 miles (4,625 km); *Crew*: 3; *Payload*: 63,272 lb (28,700 kg)

de Havilland Canada DHC-3 Otter
Country: Canada; *Constructor*: de Havilland Aircraft of Canada Ltd.; *Type*: Light transport; *Year*: 1951; *Engine*: Pratt & Whitney R-1340-SIH1-G Wasp, 9-cylinder radial, air-cooled, 600 hp; *Wingspan*: 58 ft (17.69 m); *Length*: 41 ft 10 in (12.8 m); *Height*: 13 ft (3.96 m); *Weight loaded*: 8,000 lb (3,629 kg); *Cruising speed*: 138 mph at 5,000 ft (222 km/h at 1,524 m); *Service ceiling*: 17,900 ft (5,426 m); *Range*: 863 miles (1,390 km); *Crew*: 1–2; *Passengers*: 10–14

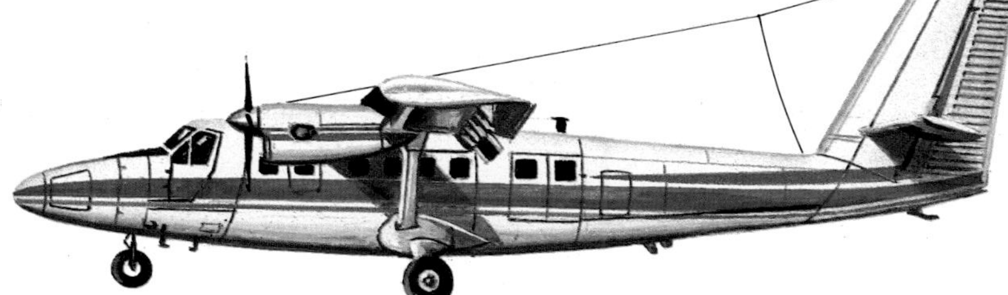

de Havilland Canada DHC-6 Twin Otter 300
Country: Canada; *Constructor*: de Havilland Aircraft of Canada Ltd.; *Type*: Light transport; *Year*: 1969; *Engines*: Two Pratt & Whitney PT6A-27 propeller-turbines, 650 shp each; *Wingspan*: 65 ft (19.81 m); *Length*: 51 ft 9 in (15.77 m); *Height*: 19 ft 6 in (5.94 m); *Maximum weight*: 12,500 lb (5,670 kg); *Cruising speed*: 210 mph at 10,000 ft (338 km/h at 3,050 m); *Service ceiling*: 26,700 ft (8,138 m); *Range*: 805 miles (1,295 m); *Crew*: 2; *Passengers*: 20
(*data for landplane*)

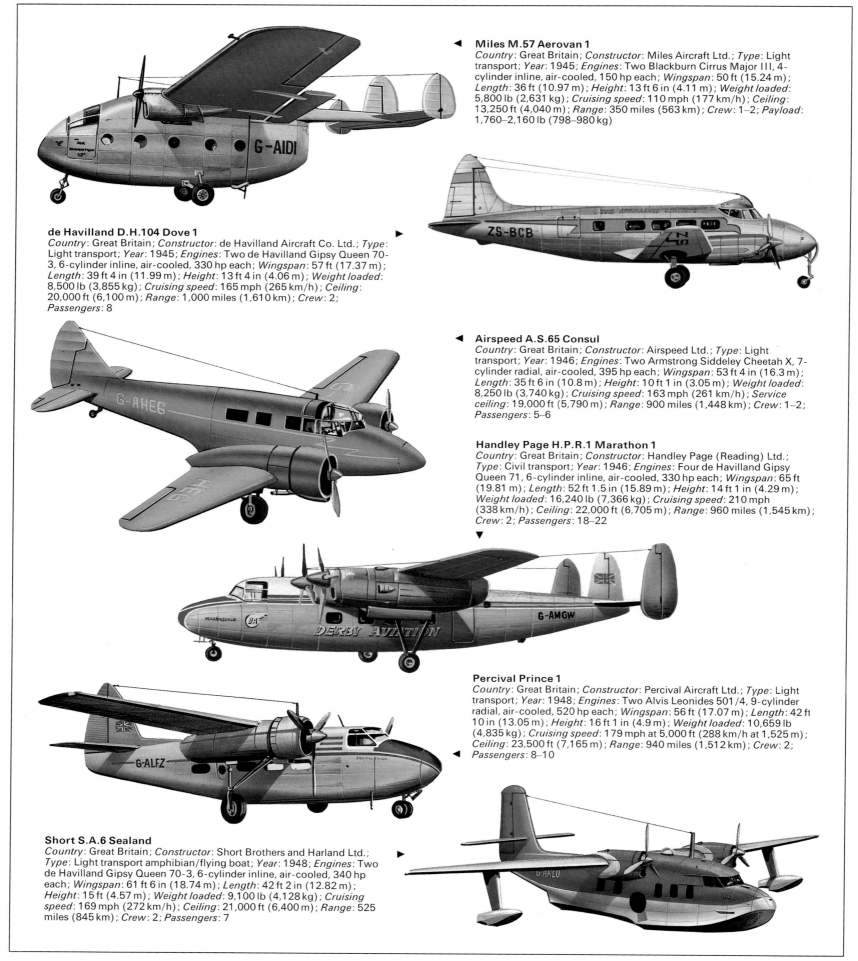

◄ **Miles M.57 Aerovan 1**
Country: Great Britain; *Constructor*: Miles Aircraft Ltd.; *Type*: Light transport; *Year*: 1945; *Engines*: Two Blackburn Cirrus Major III, 4-cylinder inline, air-cooled, 150 hp each; *Wingspan*: 50 ft (15.24 m); *Length*: 36 ft (10.97 m); *Height*: 13 ft 6 in (4.11 m); *Weight loaded*: 5,800 lb (2,631 kg); *Cruising speed*: 110 mph (177 km/h); *Ceiling*: 13,250 ft (4,040 m); *Range*: 350 miles (563 km); *Crew*: 1–2; *Payload*: 1,760–2,160 lb (798–980 kg)

de Havilland D.H.104 Dove 1 ►
Country: Great Britain; *Constructor*: de Havilland Aircraft Co. Ltd.; *Type*: Light transport; *Year*: 1945; *Engines*: Two de Havilland Gipsy Queen 70-3, 6-cylinder inline, air-cooled, 330 hp each; *Wingspan*: 57 ft (17.37 m); *Length*: 39 ft 4 in (11.99 m); *Height*: 13 ft 4 in (4.06 m); *Weight loaded*: 8,500 lb (3,855 kg); *Cruising speed*: 165 mph (265 km/h); *Ceiling*: 20,000 ft (6,100 m); *Range*: 1,000 miles (1,610 km); *Crew*: 2; *Passengers*: 8

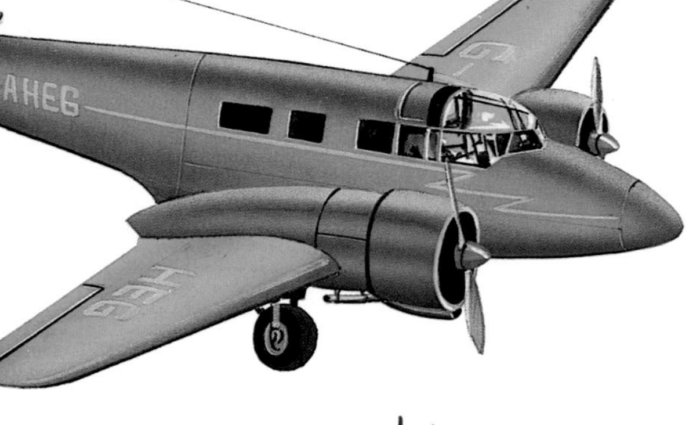

◄ **Airspeed A.S.65 Consul**
Country: Great Britain; *Constructor*: Airspeed Ltd.; *Type*: Light transport; *Year*: 1946; *Engines*: Two Armstrong Siddeley Cheetah X, 7-cylinder radial, air-cooled, 395 hp each; *Wingspan*: 53 ft 4 in (16.3 m); *Length*: 35 ft 6 in (10.8 m); *Height*: 10 ft 1 in (3.05 m); *Weight loaded*: 8,250 lb (3,740 kg); *Cruising speed*: 163 mph (261 km/h); *Service ceiling*: 19,000 ft (5,790 m); *Range*: 900 miles (1,448 km); *Crew*: 1–2; *Passengers*: 5–6

Handley Page H.P.R.1 Marathon 1
Country: Great Britain; *Constructor*: Handley Page (Reading) Ltd.; *Type*: Civil transport; *Year*: 1946; *Engines*: Four de Havilland Gipsy Queen 71, 6-cylinder inline, air-cooled, 330 hp each; *Wingspan*: 65 ft (19.81 m); *Length*: 52 ft 1.5 in (15.89 m); *Height*: 14 ft 1 in (4.29 m); *Weight loaded*: 16,240 lb (7,366 kg); *Cruising speed*: 210 mph (338 km/h); *Ceiling*: 22,000 ft (6,705 m); *Range*: 960 miles (1,545 km); *Crew*: 2; *Passengers*: 18–22
▼

Percival Prince 1
Country: Great Britain; *Constructor*: Percival Aircraft Ltd.; *Type*: Light transport; *Year*: 1948; *Engines*: Two Alvis Leonides 501/4, 9-cylinder radial, air-cooled, 520 hp each; *Wingspan*: 56 ft (17.07 m); *Length*: 42 ft 10 in (13.05 m); *Height*: 16 ft 1 in (4.9 m); *Weight loaded*: 10,659 lb (4,835 kg); *Cruising speed*: 179 mph at 5,000 ft (288 km/h at 1,525 m); *Ceiling*: 23,500 ft (7,165 m); *Range*: 940 miles (1,512 km); *Crew*: 2;
◄ *Passengers*: 8–10

Short S.A.6 Sealand ►
Country: Great Britain; *Constructor*: Short Brothers and Harland Ltd.; *Type*: Light transport amphibian/flying boat; *Year*: 1948; *Engines*: Two de Havilland Gipsy Queen 70-3, 6-cylinder inline, air-cooled, 340 hp each; *Wingspan*: 61 ft 6 in (18.74 m); *Length*: 42 ft 2 in (12.82 m); *Height*: 15 ft (4.57 m); *Weight loaded*: 9,100 lb (4,128 kg); *Cruising speed*: 169 mph (272 km/h); *Ceiling*: 21,000 ft (6,400 m); *Range*: 525 miles (845 km); *Crew*: 2; *Passengers*: 7

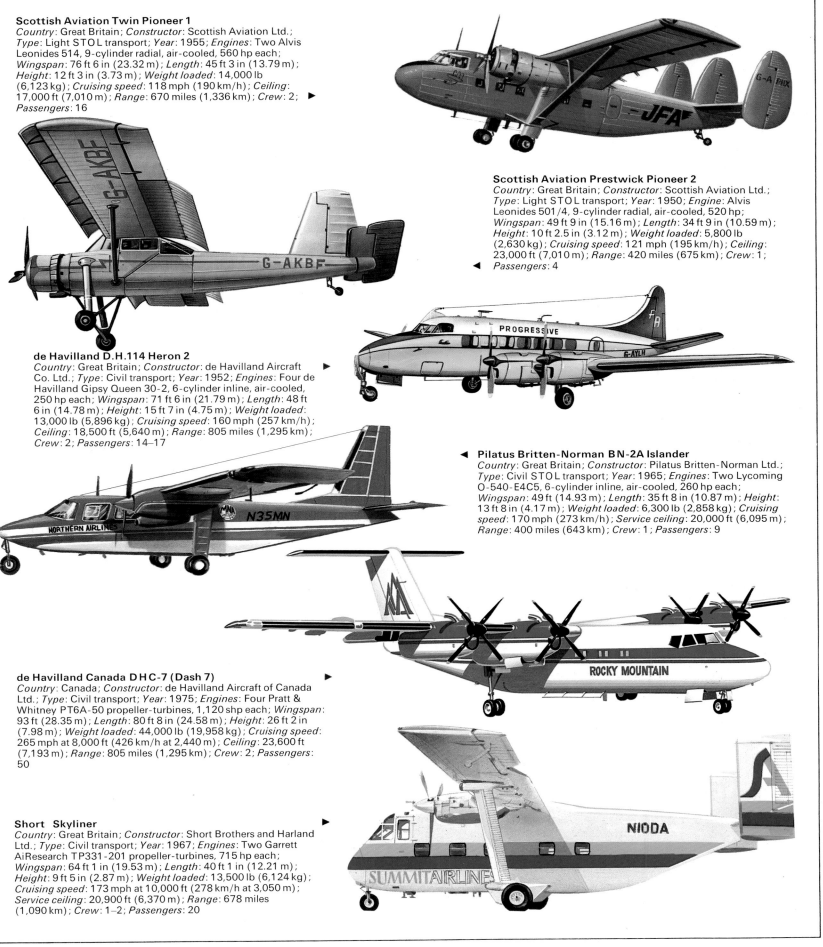

Scottish Aviation Twin Pioneer 1
Country: Great Britain; *Constructor*: Scottish Aviation Ltd.; *Type*: Light STOL transport; *Year*: 1955; *Engines*: Two Alvis Leonides 514, 9-cylinder radial, air-cooled, 560 hp each; *Wingspan*: 76 ft 6 in (23.32 m); *Length*: 45 ft 3 in (13.79 m); *Height*: 12 ft 3 in (3.73 m); *Weight loaded*: 14,000 lb (6,123 kg); *Cruising speed*: 118 mph (190 km/h); *Ceiling*: 17,000 ft (7,010 m); *Range*: 670 miles (1,336 km); *Crew*: 2; *Passengers*: 16

Scottish Aviation Prestwick Pioneer 2
Country: Great Britain; *Constructor*: Scottish Aviation Ltd.; *Type*: Light STOL transport; *Year*: 1950; *Engine*: Alvis Leonides 501/4, 9-cylinder radial, air-cooled, 520 hp; *Wingspan*: 49 ft 9 in (15.16 m); *Length*: 34 ft 9 in (10.59 m); *Height*: 10 ft 2.5 in (3.12 m); *Weight loaded*: 5,800 lb (2,630 kg); *Cruising speed*: 121 mph (195 km/h); *Ceiling*: 23,000 ft (7,010 m); *Range*: 420 miles (675 km); *Crew*: 1; *Passengers*: 4

de Havilland D.H.114 Heron 2
Country: Great Britain; *Constructor*: de Havilland Aircraft Co. Ltd.; *Type*: Civil transport; *Year*: 1952; *Engines*: Four de Havilland Gipsy Queen 30-2, 6-cylinder inline, air-cooled, 250 hp each; *Wingspan*: 71 ft 6 in (21.79 m); *Length*: 48 ft 6 in (14.78 m); *Height*: 15 ft 7 in (4.75 m); *Weight loaded*: 13,000 lb (5,896 kg); *Cruising speed*: 160 mph (257 km/h); *Ceiling*: 18,500 ft (5,640 m); *Range*: 805 miles (1,295 km); *Crew*: 2; *Passengers*: 14–17

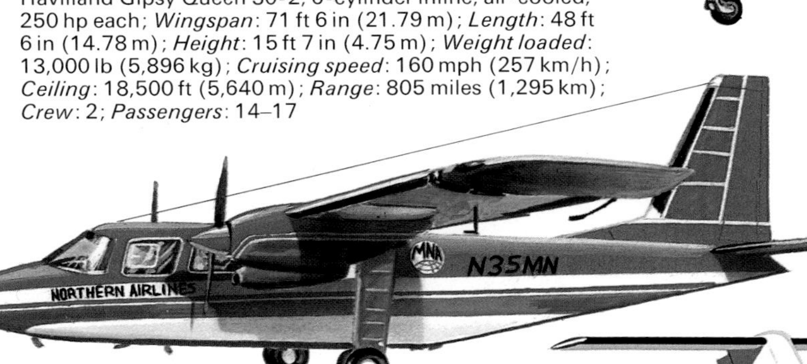

Pilatus Britten-Norman BN-2A Islander
Country: Great Britain; *Constructor*: Pilatus Britten-Norman Ltd.; *Type*: Civil STOL transport; *Year*: 1965; *Engines*: Two Lycoming O-540-E4C5, 6-cylinder inline, air-cooled, 260 hp each; *Wingspan*: 49 ft (14.93 m); *Length*: 35 ft 8 in (10.87 m); *Height*: 13 ft 8 in (4.17 m); *Weight loaded*: 6,300 lb (2,858 kg); *Cruising speed*: 170 mph (273 km/h); *Service ceiling*: 20,000 ft (6,095 m); *Range*: 400 miles (643 km); *Crew*: 1; *Passengers*: 9

de Havilland Canada DHC-7 (Dash 7)
Country: Canada; *Constructor*: de Havilland Aircraft of Canada Ltd.; *Type*: Civil transport; *Year*: 1975; *Engines*: Four Pratt & Whitney PT6A-50 propeller-turbines, 1,120 shp each; *Wingspan*: 93 ft (28.35 m); *Length*: 80 ft 8 in (24.58 m); *Height*: 26 ft 2 in (7.98 m); *Weight loaded*: 44,000 lb (19,958 kg); *Cruising speed*: 265 mph at 8,000 ft (426 km/h at 2,440 m); *Ceiling*: 23,600 ft (7,193 m); *Range*: 805 miles (1,295 km); *Crew*: 2; *Passengers*: 50

Short Skyliner
Country: Great Britain; *Constructor*: Short Brothers and Harland Ltd.; *Type*: Civil transport; *Year*: 1967; *Engines*: Two Garrett AiResearch TP331-201 propeller-turbines, 715 hp each; *Wingspan*: 64 ft 1 in (19.53 m); *Length*: 40 ft 1 in (12.21 m); *Height*: 9 ft 5 in (2.87 m); *Weight loaded*: 13,500 lb (6,124 kg); *Cruising speed*: 173 mph at 10,000 ft (278 km/h at 3,050 m); *Service ceiling*: 20,900 ft (6,370 m); *Range*: 678 miles (1,090 km); *Crew*: 1–2; *Passengers*: 20

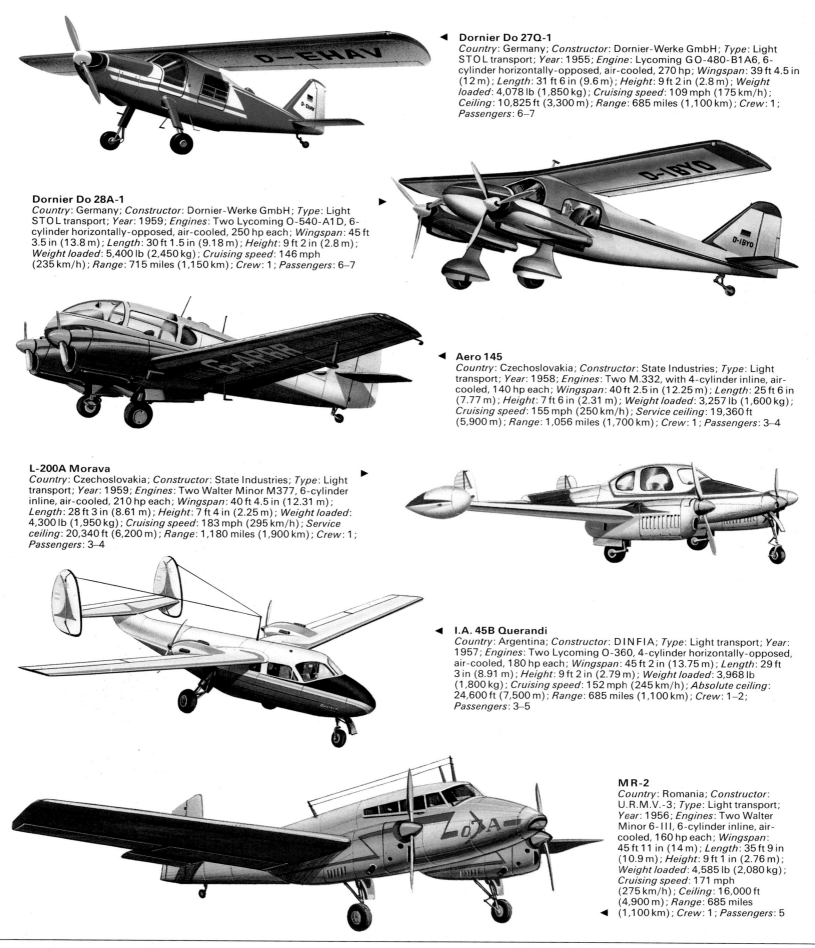

◄ **Dornier Do 27Q-1**
Country: Germany; *Constructor*: Dornier-Werke GmbH; *Type*: Light STOL transport; *Year*: 1955; *Engine*: Lycoming GO-480-B1A6, 6-cylinder horizontally-opposed, air-cooled, 270 hp; *Wingspan*: 39 ft 4.5 in (12 m); *Length*: 31 ft 6 in (9.6 m); *Height*: 9 ft 2 in (2.8 m); *Weight loaded*: 4,078 lb (1,850 kg); *Cruising speed*: 109 mph (175 km/h); *Ceiling*: 10,825 ft (3,300 m); *Range*: 685 miles (1,100 km); *Crew*: 1; *Passengers*: 6–7

Dornier Do 28A-1 ►
Country: Germany; *Constructor*: Dornier-Werke GmbH; *Type*: Light STOL transport; *Year*: 1959; *Engines*: Two Lycoming O-540-A1D, 6-cylinder horizontally-opposed, air-cooled, 250 hp each; *Wingspan*: 45 ft 3.5 in (13.8 m); *Length*: 30 ft 1.5 in (9.18 m); *Height*: 9 ft 2 in (2.8 m); *Weight loaded*: 5,400 lb (2,450 kg); *Cruising speed*: 146 mph (235 km/h); *Range*: 715 miles (1,150 km); *Crew*: 1; *Passengers*: 6–7

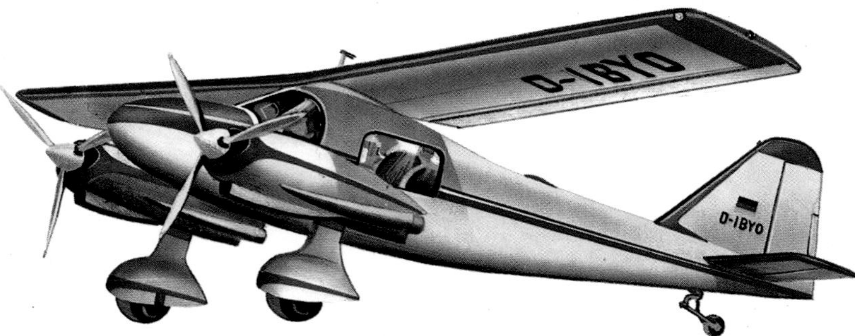

◄ **Aero 145**
Country: Czechoslovakia; *Constructor*: State Industries; *Type*: Light transport; *Year*: 1958; *Engines*: Two M.332, with 4-cylinder inline, air-cooled, 140 hp each; *Wingspan*: 40 ft 2.5 in (12.25 m); *Length*: 25 ft 6 in (7.77 m); *Height*: 7 ft 6 in (2.31 m); *Weight loaded*: 3,257 lb (1,600 kg); *Cruising speed*: 155 mph (250 km/h); *Service ceiling*: 19,360 ft (5,900 m); *Range*: 1,056 miles (1,700 km); *Crew*: 1; *Passengers*: 3–4

L-200A Morava ►
Country: Czechoslovakia; *Constructor*: State Industries; *Type*: Light transport; *Year*: 1959; *Engines*: Two Walter Minor M377, 6-cylinder inline, air-cooled, 210 hp each; *Wingspan*: 40 ft 4.5 in (12.31 m); *Length*: 28 ft 3 in (8.61 m); *Height*: 7 ft 4 in (2.25 m); *Weight loaded*: 4,300 lb (1,950 kg); *Cruising speed*: 183 mph (295 km/h); *Service ceiling*: 20,340 ft (6,200 m); *Range*: 1,180 miles (1,900 km); *Crew*: 1; *Passengers*: 3–4

◄ **I.A. 45B Querandi**
Country: Argentina; *Constructor*: DINFIA; *Type*: Light transport; *Year*: 1957; *Engines*: Two Lycoming O-360, 4-cylinder horizontally-opposed, air-cooled, 180 hp each; *Wingspan*: 45 ft 2 in (13.75 m); *Length*: 29 ft 3 in (8.91 m); *Height*: 9 ft 2 in (2.79 m); *Weight loaded*: 3,968 lb (1,800 kg); *Cruising speed*: 152 mph (245 km/h); *Absolute ceiling*: 24,600 ft (7,500 m); *Range*: 685 miles (1,100 km); *Crew*: 1–2; *Passengers*: 3–5

MR-2
Country: Romania; *Constructor*: U.R.M.V.-3; *Type*: Light transport; *Year*: 1956; *Engines*: Two Walter Minor 6-III, 6-cylinder inline, air-cooled, 160 hp each; *Wingspan*: 45 ft 11 in (14 m); *Length*: 35 ft 9 in (10.9 m); *Height*: 9 ft 1 in (2.76 m); *Weight loaded*: 4,585 lb (2,080 kg); *Cruising speed*: 171 mph (275 km/h); *Ceiling*: 16,000 ft (4,900 m); *Range*: 685 miles ◄ (1,100 km); *Crew*: 1; *Passengers*: 5

CASA-201-B Alcotan
Country: Spain; *Constructor*: Construcciones Aeronauticas S.A.; *Type*: Civil transport; *Year*: 1949; *Engines*: Two ENMA Sirio S-VII-A, 7-cylinder radial, air-cooled, 475 hp each; *Wingspan*: 60 ft 4 in (18.4 m); *Length*: 45 ft 3 in (13.8 m); *Height*: 12 ft 8 in (3.85 m); *Weight loaded*: 12,125 lb (5,500 kg); *Cruising speed*: 193 mph (310 km/h); *Service ceiling*: 20,000 ft (6,100 m); *Range*: 621 miles (1,000 km); *Crew*: 2; *Passengers*: 8–10 ▶

◀ **Swearingen SA226 TC Metro II**
Country: U.S.A., *Constructor*: Swearingen Aviation Corp. (*now* Fairchild Swearingen); *Type*: Light transport; *Year*: 1970; *Engines*: Two Garrett-AiResearch TPE331-3UW-303G propeller-turbines, 940 shp each; *Wingspan*: 46 ft 3 in (14.1 m); *Length*: 59 ft 4.75 in (18.1 m); *Height*: 16 ft 8 in (5.08 m); *Maximum weight*: 12,500 lb (5,670 kg); *Cruising speed*: 294 mph at 10,000 ft (473 km/h at 3,050 m); *Service Ceiling*: 27,000 ft (8,230 m); *Range*: 685 miles (1,102 km); *Crew*: 2; *Passengers*: 20

I.A.35 Pandora ▶
Country: Argentina; *Constructor*: DINFIA; *Type*: Light transport; *Year*: 1957; *Engines*: Two I.A.-R-19-SR.1 El Indio, 9-cylinder radial, air-cooled, 750 hp each; *Wingspan*: 64 ft 3 in (19.6 m); *Length*: 46 ft 6 in (14.17 m); *Height*: 15 ft 5 in (4.7 m); *Weight loaded*: 13,670 lb (6,200 kg); *Cruising speed*: 191 mph at 9,840 ft (308 km/h at 3,000 m); *Service ceiling*: 20,835 ft (6,350 m); *Range*: 930 miles (1,500 km); *Crew*: 3; *Passengers*: 10

◀ **Peking No. 1**
Country: People's Republic of China; *Constructor*: Institute of Aeronautical Engineering of Peking; *Type*: Light transport; *Year*: 1958; *Engines*: Two Ivchenko AI-14R, 9-cylinder radial, air-cooled, 260 hp each; *Wingspan*: 57 ft 5 in (17.5 m); *Length*: 42 ft 7.75 in (13 m); *Cruising speed*: 162 mph (261 km/h); *Service ceiling*: 15,750 ft (4,800 m); *Range*: 668 miles (1,075 km); *Crew*: 2; *Passengers*: 8

Pilatus PC-6 Porter ▶
Country: Switzerland; *Constructor*: Pilatus Flugzeugwerke A.G.; *Type*: Light STOL transport; *Year*: 1959; *Engine*: Lycoming GSO-480-B1A6, 6-cylinder horizontally-opposed, air-cooled, 340 hp; *Wingspan*: 49 ft 10 in (15.2 m); *Length*: 33 ft 5.5 in (10.2 m); *Height*: 10 ft 6 in (3.2 m); *Weight loaded*: 4,320 lb (1,960 kg); *Cruising speed*: 135 mph (217 km/h); *Service ceiling*: 23,950 ft (7,300 m); *Range*: 750 miles (1,200 km); *Crew*: 1; *Passengers*: 7–11

◀ **de Havilland DHA-3 Drover 3**
Country: Australia; *Constructor*: de Havilland Aircraft Pty Ltd. (Hawker Siddeley Group); *Type*: Light transport; *Year*: 1959; *Engines*: Three Lycoming O-360-A1A, 4-cylinder horizontally-opposed, air-cooled, 180 hp each; *Wingspan*: 57 ft (17.37 m); *Length*: 36 ft 2 in (11.02 m); *Height*: 9 ft 9 in (2.97 m); *Weight loaded*: 6,500 lb (2,950 kg); *Cruising speed*: 144 mph (232 km/h); *Range*: 540 miles (870 km); *Crew*: 2; *Passengers*: 8

P.Z.L. MD-12
Country: Poland; *Constructor*: Osrodek Konstrukcji Lotniczych; *Type*: Civil transport; *Year*: 1959; *Engines*: Four Narkiewicz WN-3, 7-cylinder radial, air-cooled, 330 hp each; *Wingspan*: 69 ft 11 in (21.31 m); *Length*: 51 ft 10 in (15.8 m); *Height*: 19 ft 1 in (5.82 m); *Weight loaded*: 16,534 lb (7,500 kg); *Cruising speed*: 177 mph at 8,200 ft (285 km/h at 2,500 m); *Ceiling*: 17,060 ft (5,200 m); *Range*: 590 miles (950 km); *Crew*: 2; *Passengers*: 20 ▶

Aero Commander 560
Country: U.S.A.; *Constructor*: Aero Design and Engineering Corp.; *Type*: Light transport; *Year*: 1954; *Engines*: Two Lycoming GO-480-B, 6-cylinder horizontally-opposed, air-cooled, 270 hp each; *Wingspan*: 44 ft (13.42 m); *Length*: 34 ft 2.5 in (10.44 m); *Height*: 14 ft 9 in (4.49 m); *Weight loaded*: 5,500 lb (2,495 kg); *Cruising speed*: 200 mph at 10,000 ft (320 km/h at 3,050 m); *Service ceiling*: 22,000 ft (6,706 m); *Range*: 1,100 miles (1,770 km); *Crew*: 1; *Passengers*: 5–6

Grumman G-159 Gulfstream I
Country: U.S.A.; *Constructor*: Grumman Aircraft Engineering Corp.; *Type*: Light transport; *Year*: 1958; *Engines*: Two Rolls-Royce Dart Mk. 529 propeller-turbines, 2,210 ehp each; *Wingspan*: 78 ft 6 in (23.93 m); *Length*: 63 ft 8 in (19.4 m); *Height*: 22 ft 9 in (6.93 m); *Weight loaded*: 35,100 lb (15,920 kg); *Cruising speed*: 348 mph at 25,000 ft (560 km/h at 7,620 m); *Service ceiling*: 33,600 ft (10,240 m); *Range*: 2,540 miles (4,088 km); *Crew*: 2; *Passengers*: 24

Beech G18S
Country: U.S.A.; *Constructor*: Beech Aircraft Corp.; *Type*: Light transport; *Year*: 1959; *Engines*: Two Pratt & Whitney R-985-AN 14B Wasp Junior, 9-cylinder radial, air-cooled, 450 hp each; *Wingspan*: 49 ft 8 in (15.14 m); *Length*: 35 ft 2.5 in (10.7 m); *Height*: 9 ft 8 in (2.94 m); *Weight loaded*: 9,700 lb (4,400 kg); *Cruising speed*: 204 mph at 5,000 ft (328 km/h at 1,525 m); *Service ceiling*: 21,600 ft (6,580 m); *Range*: 1,585 miles (2,550 km); *Crew*: 2; *Passengers*: 5–9

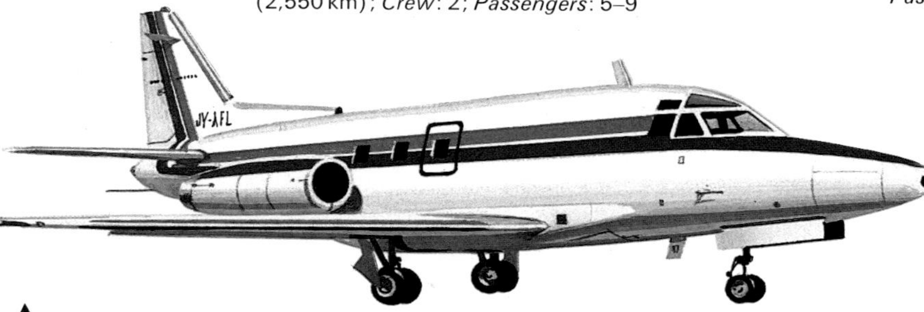

Rockwell Sabreliner 75A
Country: U.S.A.; *Constructor*: Rockwell International; *Type*: Executive transport; *Year*: 1974; *Engines*: Two General Electric CF700-2D-2 turbofans, 4,315 lb (1,960 kg) thrust each; *Wingspan*: 50 ft 5 in (15.37 m); *Length*: 46 ft 11 in (14.3 m); *Height*: 17 ft 3 in (5.26 m); *Weight loaded*: 23,000 lb (10,432 kg); *Cruising speed*: 560 mph (901 km/h); *Ceiling*: 45,000 ft (13,715 m); *Range*: 1,970 miles (3,170 km); *Crew*: 2; *Passengers*: 10

Lockheed 1329 JetStar 6
Country: U.S.A.; *Constructor*: Lockheed Aircraft Corp.; *Type*: Civil transport; *Year*: 1960; *Engines*: Four Pratt & Whitney JT12A-6 turbojets, 3,000 lb (1,360 kg) thrust each; *Wingspan*: 53 ft 8 in (16.36 m); *Length*: 60 ft 5 in (18.41 m); *Height*: 20 ft 6 in (6.25 m); *Maximum weight*: 42,000 lb (19,051 kg); *Cruising speed*: 507 mph (816 km/h); *Service ceiling*: 38,000 ft (11,580 m); *Range*: 2,345 miles (3,775 km); *Crew*: 2; *Passengers*: 10

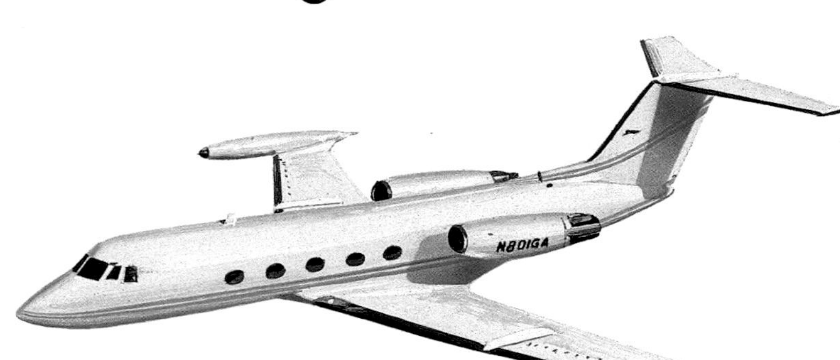

Grumman Gulfstream II
Country: U.S.A.; *Constructor*: Grumman American Aviation Corp.; *Type*: Civil transport; *Year*: 1966; Engines: Two Rolls-Royce Spey Mk.511-8 turbofans, 11,400 lb (5,170 kg) thrust each; *Wingspan*: 71 ft 9 in (21.87 m); *Length*: 79 ft 11 in (24.36 m); *Height*: 24 ft 6 in (7.47 m); *Weight loaded*: 65,500 lb (29,710 kg); *Cruising speed*: 581 mph at 25,000 ft (935 km/h at 7,620 m); *Service ceiling*: 43,000 ft (13,105 m); *Range*: 4,120 miles (6,630 km); *Crew*: 2–3; *Passengers*: 19

Cessna Citation 500
Country: U.S.A.; *Constructor*: Cessna Aircraft Co.; *Type*: Executive transport; *Year*: 1969; *Engines*: Two Pratt & Whitney of Canada JT15D-1 turbofans, 2,200 lb (998 kg) thrust each; *Wingspan*: 47 ft 1 in (14.35 m); *Length*: 43 ft 6 in (13.26 m); *Height*: 14 ft 3 in (4.36 m); *Weight loaded*: 11,850 lb (5,375 kg); *Cruising speed*: 400 mph (644 km/h); *Ceiling*: 38,400 ft (11,704 m); *Range*: 1,535 miles (2,470 km); *Crew*: 2; *Passengers*: 6

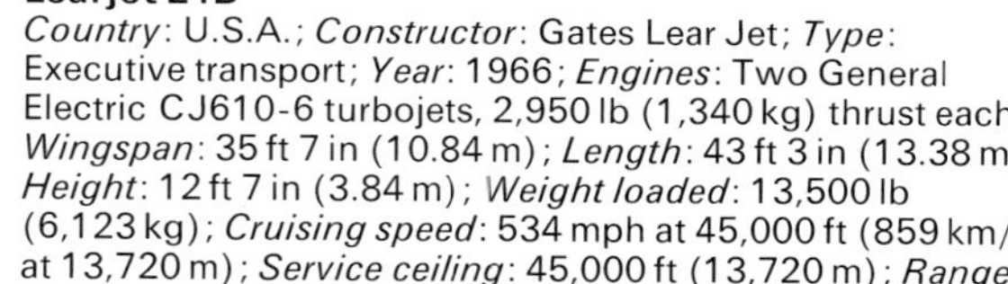

Learjet 24B
Country: U.S.A.; *Constructor*: Gates Lear Jet; *Type*: Executive transport; *Year*: 1966; *Engines*: Two General Electric CJ610-6 turbojets, 2,950 lb (1,340 kg) thrust each; *Wingspan*: 35 ft 7 in (10.84 m); *Length*: 43 ft 3 in (13.38 m); *Height*: 12 ft 7 in (3.84 m); *Weight loaded*: 13,500 lb (6,123 kg); *Cruising speed*: 534 mph at 45,000 ft (859 km/h at 13,720 m); *Service ceiling*: 45,000 ft (13,720 m); *Range*: 1,746 miles (2,810 km); *Crew*: 2; *Passengers*: 6

Hawker Siddeley 125 Series 700
Country: Great Britain; *Constructor*: British Aerospace; *Type*: Executive transport; *Year*: 1976; *Engines*: Two Garrett AiResearch TFE 731-3-H turbofans, 3,700 lb (1,678 kg) thrust each; *Wingspan*: 47 ft (14.33 m); *Length*: 50 ft 8.5 in (15.46 m); *Height*: 17 ft 7 in (5.37 m); *Weight loaded*: 25,500 lb (11,567 kg); *Cruising speed*: 502 mph at 27,500 ft (808 km/h at 8,380 m); *Ceiling*: 41,000 ft (12,500 m); *Range*: 2,900 miles (4,670 km); *Crew*: 2; *Passengers*: 8–10

Dassault Mystère-Falcon 20
Country: France; *Constructor*: Avions Marcel Dassault; *Type*: Civil transport; *Year*: 1963; *Engines*: Two General Electric CF700-2D-2 turbofans, 4,500 lb (1,900 kg) thrust each; *Wingspan*: 53 ft 6 in (16.30 m); *Length*: 56 ft 3 in (17.15 m); *Height*: 17 ft 5 in (5.32 m); *Weight loaded*: 28,660 lb (12,000 kg); *Cruising speed*: 536 mph at 25,000 ft (860 km/h at 7,620 m); *Absolute ceiling*: 42,000 ft (12,800 m); *Range*: 2,080 miles (3,050 km); *Crew*: 2; *Passengers*: 14

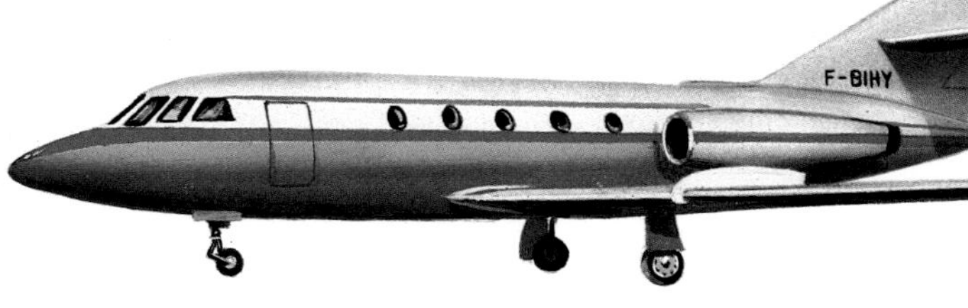

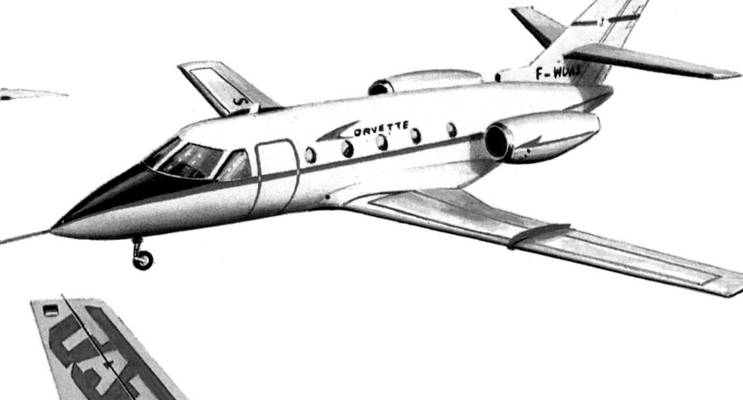

Aérospatiale SN.601 Corvette
Country: France; *Constructor*: Aérospatiale; *Type*: Civil transport; *Year*: 1972; *Engines*: Two Pratt & Whitney Aircraft of Canada JT15D-4 turbofans, 2,500 lb (1,134 kg) thrust each; *Wingspan*: 42 ft 2.5 in (12.87 m); *Length*: 45 ft 4.5 in (13.83 m); *Height*: 13 ft 10 in (4.23 m); *Weight loaded*: 14,550 lb (6,600 kg); *Cruising speed*: 472 mph at 29,525 ft (760 km/h at 9,000 m); *Service ceiling*: 41,000 ft (12,500 m); *Range*: 967 miles (1,555 km); *Crew*: 1–2; *Passengers*: 6–14

VFW-Fokker VFW 614
Country: Germany; *Constructor*: VFW-Fokker; *Type*: Civil transport; *Year*: 1971; *Engines*: Two Rolls-Royce M45H Mk.501 turbofans, 7,280 lb (3,302 kg) thrust each; *Wingspan*: 70 ft 6 in (21.5 m); *Length*: 67 ft 7 in (20.6 m); *Height*: 25 ft 8 in (7.84 m); *Weight loaded*: 43,982 lb (19,950 kg); *Cruising speed*: 438 mph at 25,000 ft (705 km/h at 7,620 m); *Range*: 748 miles (1,204 km); *Crew*: 2; *Passengers*: 44

MBB HFB 320 Hansa
Country: Germany; *Constructor*: Messerschmitt-Bölkow-Blohm GmbH; *Type*: Executive transport; *Year*: 1964; *Engines*: Two General Electric CJ610-5 turbojets, 2,950 lb (1,335 kg) thrust each; *Wingspan*: 47 ft 6 in (14.48 m); *Length*: 54 ft 6 in (16.61 m); *Height*: 16 ft 2 in (4.94 m); *Weight loaded*: 20,280 lb (9,200 kg); *Cruising speed*: 513 mph at 25,000 ft (825 km/h at 7,620 m); *Service ceiling*: 37,500 ft (11,430 m); *Range*: 1,500 miles (2,415 km); *Crew*: 2–3; *Passengers*: 7–12

Antonov An-72
Country: U.S.S.R.; *Constructor*: State Industries; *Type*: STOL transport; *Year*: 1977; *Engines*: Two Lotarev D-36 turbofans, 14,330 lb (6,500 kg) thrust each; *Wingspan*: 84 ft 9 in (25.83 m); *Length*: 87 ft 2.5 in (26.58 m); *Height*: 27 ft (8.23 in); *Weight loaded*: 76,203 lb (34,565 kg); *Cruising speed*: 447 mph (720 km/h); *Ceiling*: 36,100 ft (11,000 m); *Range*: 621 miles (1,000 km); *Crew*: 3; *Cargo*: 16,535 lb (7,500 kg), or 52 passengers

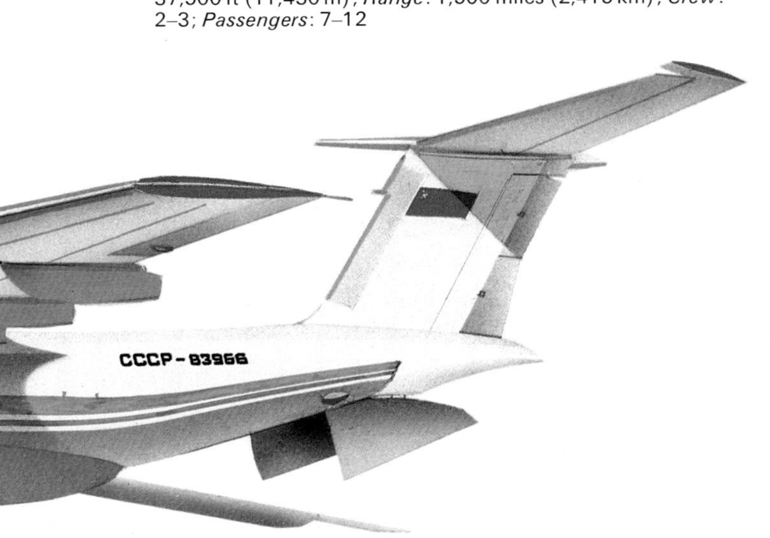

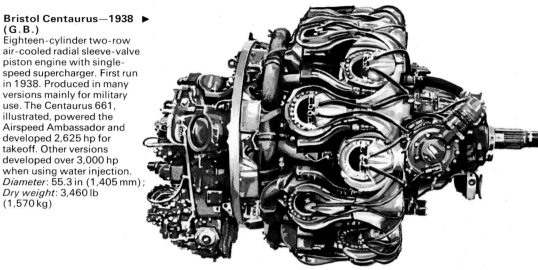

Bristol Centaurus—1938 ▶ (G.B.)
Eighteen-cylinder two-row air-cooled radial sleeve-valve piston engine with single-speed supercharger. First run in 1938. Produced in many versions mainly for military use. The Centaurus 661, illustrated, powered the Airspeed Ambassador and developed 2,625 hp for takeoff. Other versions developed over 3,000 hp when using water injection. *Diameter*: 55.3 in (1,405 mm); *Dry weight*: 3,460 lb (1,570 kg)

Pratt & Whitney R-4360 Wasp Major—1943 (U.S.A.)
Twenty-eight cylinder four-row geared and turbo-supercharged air-cooled radial piston engine. The ultimate development of the long series of Wasp engines. Used to power the Boeing B-50 bomber and some versions of the C-97 military transport, the R-4360 was the power plant used in the Boeing Stratocruiser. Takeoff power was 3,500 hp and some versions developed 3,800 hp when using water injection. *Diameter*: 55 in (1,397 mm); *Dry weight*: 3,670 lb (1,665 kg)

▲
Rolls-Royce Dart—1946 (G.B.)
Propeller-turbine with two-stage centrifugal compressor and two-stage turbine. First run in 1946 and first flown in October 1947. It was the first propeller-turbine to go into service. The original engine in the Viscount V.630 developed 1,130 ehp, the Dart 505, illustrated, produced 1,400 shp for takeoff plus 365 lb (165 kg) of jet thrust and the Dart 542 in the Japanese YS-11A produces 3,060 ehp. Darts power the Viscount, F.27 Friendship, Herald, Argosy, H.S.748 and Gulfstream I. More than 7,000 Darts have been built. *Diameter*: 37.9 in (963 mm); *Length*: 95.125 in (2,416 mm); *Dry weight*: 1,030 lb (467 kg)

Bristol Proteus—1947 (G.B.)
Propeller-turbine with twelve axial-flow and one centrifugal-flow compressors. First run February 1947. The Proteus Series 700 powered the Bristol Britannias; the 705 (illustrated) in the Britannia 100, the 755 the Britannia 250, 300 and 310. The Proteus 705 developed 3,446 shp plus 1,090 lb (495 kg) of jet thrust for takeoff, the Proteus 755 gave 3,650 shp plus 1,220 lb (553 kg) of jet thrust. Later Proteus power increased to 4,400 shp. The Coupled-Proteus was developed for the Saunders-Roe Princess flying boat and the Bristol Brabazon Mk.II.

Proteus 705—*Diameter*: 40.1 in (1,019 m); *Length*: 100.6 in (2,555 mm); *Dry weight*: 2,945 lb (1,336 kg)

Pratt & Whitney JT3C—1949 (U.S.A.)
Twin-spool axial-flow turbojet. Original engine was military J57 for which the design was accepted in 1949 and production began in February 1953. The civil JT3C-6 powered the Boeing 707-120 and DC-8-10. It had a takeoff thrust of 13,500 lb (6,125 kg) when using water injection. By mid-1961 about 18,000 J57s and 1,000 JT3Cs had been delivered. The more efficient JT3D was a turbofan development. *Diameter*: 38.88 in (988 mm); *Length*: 167.53 in (4,255 mm); *Dry weight*: 4,234 lb (1,920 kg) ►

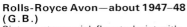

Rolls-Royce Avon—about 1947–48 (G.B.)
Sixteen-stage axial-flow turbojet with three-stage turbine (Avon RA.29). The Avon was originally a twelve-stage engine developed after World War II as a replacement for the Nene. It was shown for the first time in 1948. The RA.1 developed 6,500 lb (2,948 kg) of thrust. The RA.29 was developed as a civil engine and several versions were used to power the Comet 4 series and the Caravelle I, III and VI. The RA.29/6 produced 12,600 lb (5,715 kg) of thrust. *Diameter*: 39 in (990 mm); *Length*: 134 in (3,403 mm); *Dry weight*: 3,491 lb ◄ (1,583 kg)

Wright R-3350 Turbo-Compound—1949 (U.S.A.) ►
Eighteen-cylinder air-cooled radial combining the earlier R-3350 with three exhaust-driven blow-down turbines which increased the power and reduced fuel consumption by 20 per cent for a given rating. Completed first 50-hour test October 1949. It was the last major U.S. high power piston engine. Used in Douglas DC-7 series, Lockheed Super Constellation and 1649A Starliner. TC18DA1 model takeoff power 3,250 hp, TC18EA1 3,400 hp. *Diameter*: 56.6 in (1,438 mm); *Dry weight*: 3,645 lb (1,653 kg) EA1

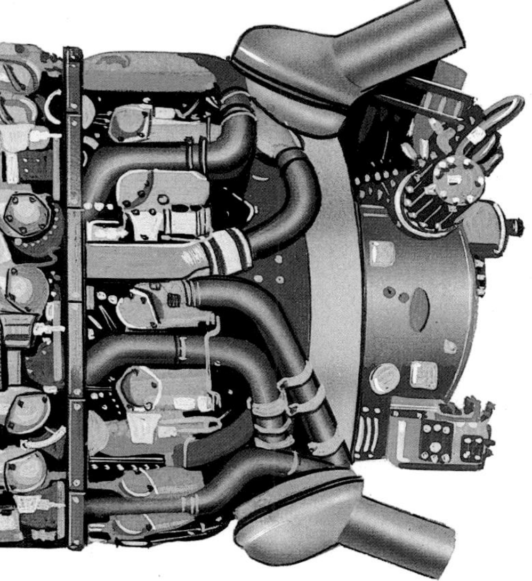

Pratt & Whitney JT4—1957 (U.S.A.)
Axial-flow turbojet with two-spool fifteen-stage compressor. Civil version of military J75 developed between 1951 and 1954 for supersonic fighters. Commercial certification March 1957. Numerous versions including 15,800 lb (7,167 kg) thrust -3 and -5, 16,800 lb (7,620 kg) thrust -9 and -10 and 17,500 lb (7,938 kg) thrust -11 and -12. Used in Boeing 707-303 and DC-8-20 and -30. *Diameter*: 43 in (1,092 mm); *Length*: 144.1 in (3,660 mm)

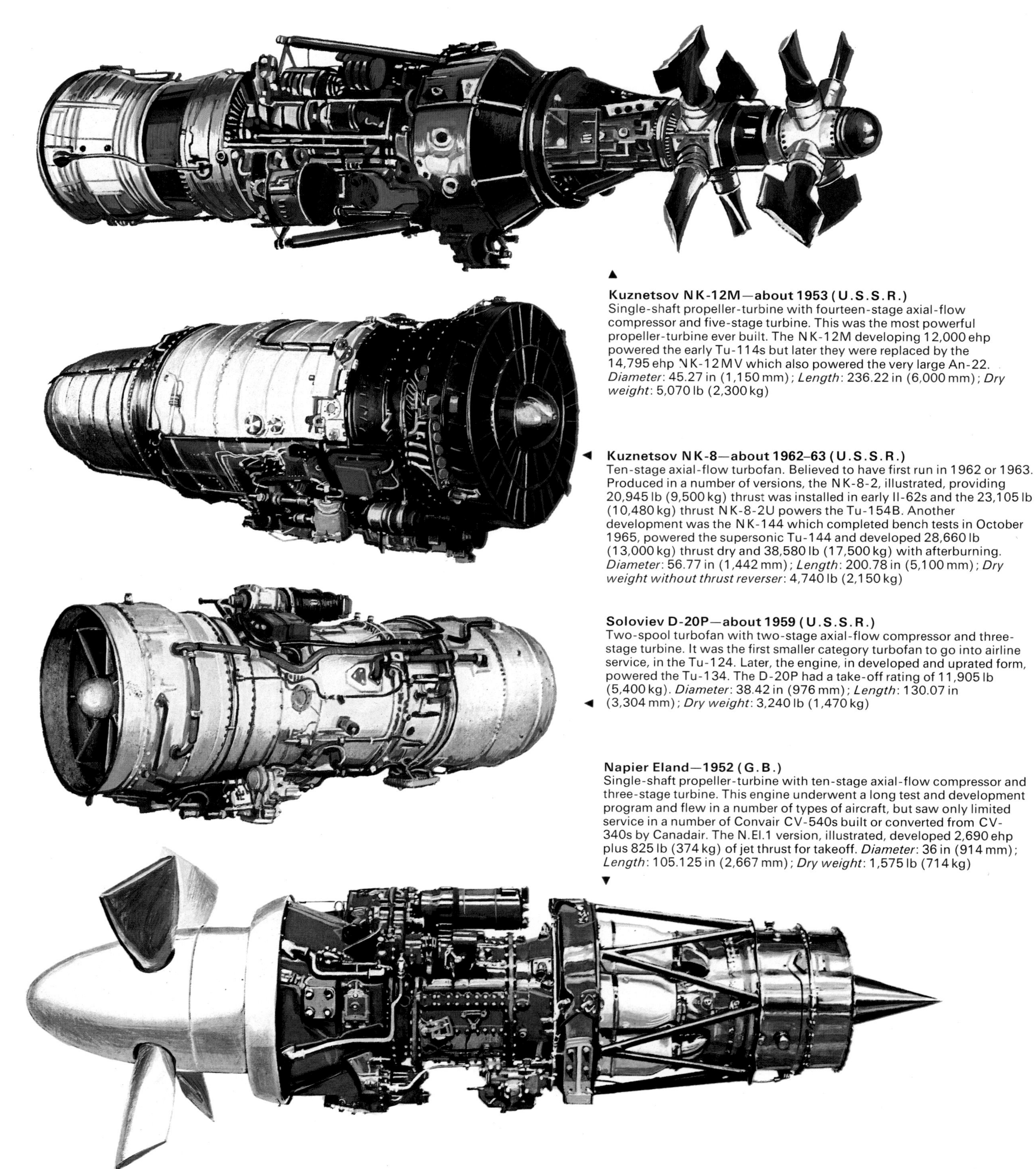

▲

Kuznetsov NK-12M—about 1953 (U.S.S.R.)
Single-shaft propeller-turbine with fourteen-stage axial-flow compressor and five-stage turbine. This was the most powerful propeller-turbine ever built. The NK-12M developing 12,000 ehp powered the early Tu-114s but later they were replaced by the 14,795 ehp NK-12MV which also powered the very large An-22. *Diameter*: 45.27 in (1,150 mm); *Length*: 236.22 in (6,000 mm); *Dry weight*: 5,070 lb (2,300 kg)

◀ **Kuznetsov NK-8—about 1962–63 (U.S.S.R.)**
Ten-stage axial-flow turbofan. Believed to have first run in 1962 or 1963. Produced in a number of versions, the NK-8-2, illustrated, providing 20,945 lb (9,500 kg) thrust was installed in early Il-62s and the 23,105 lb (10,480 kg) thrust NK-8-2U powers the Tu-154B. Another development was the NK-144 which completed bench tests in October 1965, powered the supersonic Tu-144 and developed 28,660 lb (13,000 kg) thrust dry and 38,580 lb (17,500 kg) with afterburning. *Diameter*: 56.77 in (1,442 mm); *Length*: 200.78 in (5,100 mm); *Dry weight without thrust reverser*: 4,740 lb (2,150 kg)

Soloviev D-20P—about 1959 (U.S.S.R.)
Two-spool turbofan with two-stage axial-flow compressor and three-stage turbine. It was the first smaller category turbofan to go into airline service, in the Tu-124. Later, the engine, in developed and uprated form, powered the Tu-134. The D-20P had a take-off rating of 11,905 lb (5,400 kg). *Diameter*: 38.42 in (976 mm); *Length*: 130.07 in ◀ (3,304 mm); *Dry weight*: 3,240 lb (1,470 kg)

Napier Eland—1952 (G.B.)
Single-shaft propeller-turbine with ten-stage axial-flow compressor and three-stage turbine. This engine underwent a long test and development program and flew in a number of types of aircraft, but saw only limited service in a number of Convair CV-540s built or converted from CV-340s by Canadair. The N.El.1 version, illustrated, developed 2,690 ehp plus 825 lb (374 kg) of jet thrust for takeoff. *Diameter*: 36 in (914 mm); *Length*: 105.125 in (2,667 mm); *Dry weight*: 1,575 lb (714 kg)
▼

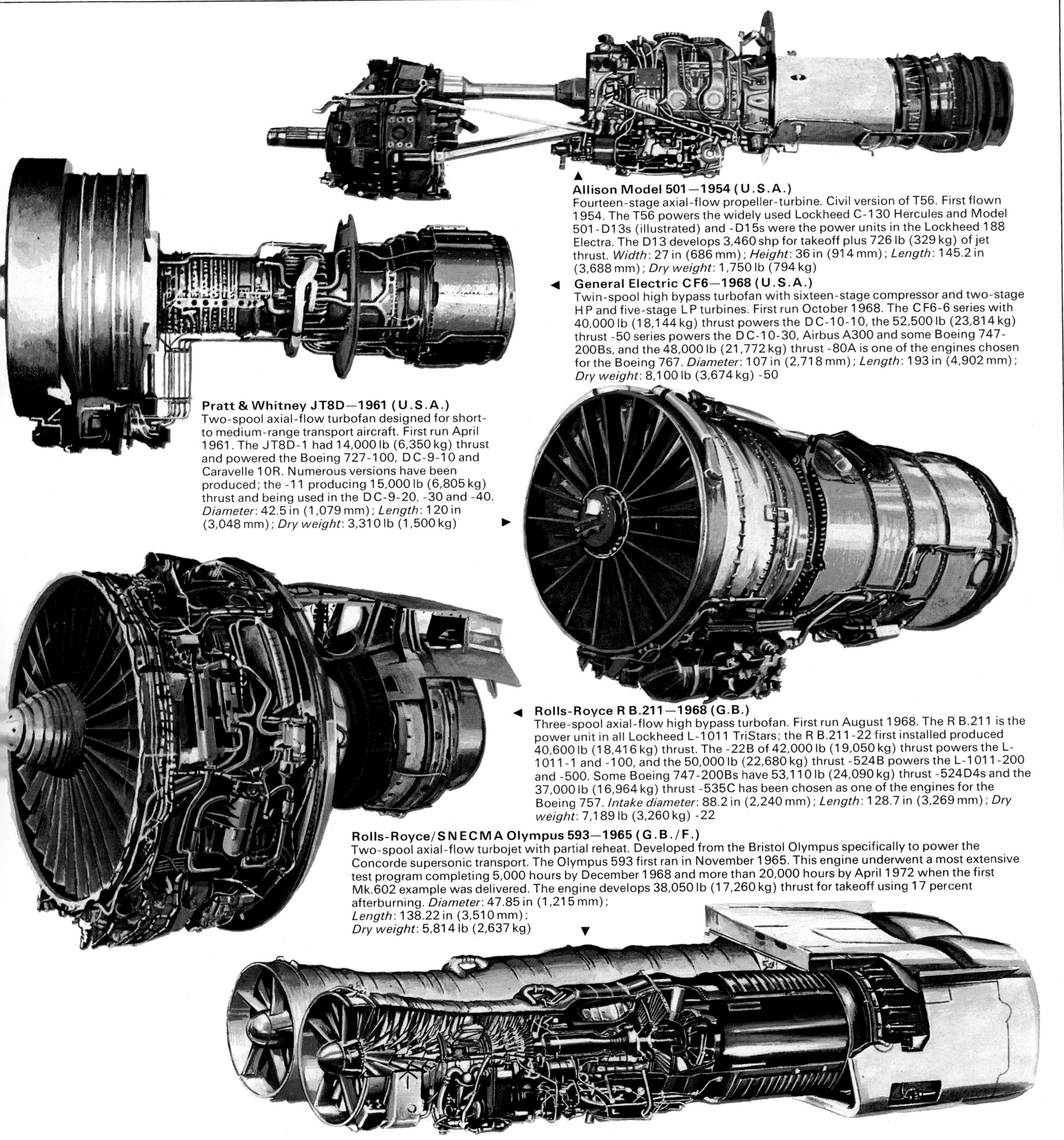

▲ **Allison Model 501—1954 (U.S.A.)**
Fourteen-stage axial-flow propeller-turbine. Civil version of T56. First flown 1954. The T56 powers the widely used Lockheed C-130 Hercules and Model 501-D13s (illustrated) and -D15s were the power units in the Lockheed 188 Electra. The D13 develops 3,460 shp for takeoff plus 726 lb (329 kg) of jet thrust. *Width*: 27 in (686 mm); *Height*: 36 in (914 mm); *Length*: 145.2 in (3,688 mm); *Dry weight*: 1,750 lb (794 kg)

◄ **General Electric CF6—1968 (U.S.A.)**
Twin-spool high bypass turbofan with sixteen-stage compressor and two-stage HP and five-stage LP turbines. First run October 1968. The CF6-6 series with 40,000 lb (18,144 kg) thrust powers the DC-10-10, the 52,500 lb (23,814 kg) thrust -50 series powers the DC-10-30, Airbus A300 and some Boeing 747-200Bs, and the 48,000 lb (21,772 kg) thrust -80A is one of the engines chosen for the Boeing 767. *Diameter*: 107 in (2,718 mm); *Length*: 193 in (4,902 mm); *Dry weight*: 8,100 lb (3,674 kg) -50

Pratt & Whitney JT8D—1961 (U.S.A.)
Two-spool axial-flow turbofan designed for short-to medium-range transport aircraft. First run April 1961. The JT8D-1 had 14,000 lb (6,350 kg) thrust and powered the Boeing 727-100, DC-9-10 and Caravelle 10R. Numerous versions have been produced; the -11 producing 15,000 lb (6,805 kg) thrust and being used in the DC-9-20, -30 and -40. *Diameter*: 42.5 in (1,079 mm); *Length*: 120 in (3,048 mm); *Dry weight*: 3,310 lb (1,500 kg) ►

◄ **Rolls-Royce RB.211—1968 (G.B.)**
Three-spool axial-flow high bypass turbofan. First run August 1968. The RB.211 is the power unit in all Lockheed L-1011 TriStars; the RB.211-22 first installed produced 40,600 lb (18,416 kg) thrust. The -22B of 42,000 lb (19,050 kg) thrust powers the L-1011-1 and -100, and the 50,000 lb (22,680 kg) thrust -524B powers the L-1011-200 and -500. Some Boeing 747-200Bs have 53,110 lb (24,090 kg) thrust -524D4s and the 37,000 lb (16,964 kg) thrust -535C has been chosen as one of the engines for the Boeing 757. *Intake diameter*: 88.2 in (2,240 mm); *Length*: 128.7 in (3,269 mm); *Dry weight*: 7,189 lb (3,260 kg) -22

Rolls-Royce/SNECMA Olympus 593—1965 (G.B./F.)
Two-spool axial-flow turbojet with partial reheat. Developed from the Bristol Olympus specifically to power the Concorde supersonic transport. The Olympus 593 first ran in November 1965. This engine underwent a most extensive test program completing 5,000 hours by December 1968 and more than 20,000 hours by April 1972 when the first Mk.602 example was delivered. The engine develops 38,050 lb (17,260 kg) thrust for takeoff using 17 percent afterburning. *Diameter*: 47.85 in (1,215 mm); *Length*: 138.22 in (3,510 mm); *Dry weight*: 5,814 lb (2,637 kg) ▼

Plate 126
Some U.S. airliners: 1940–1942

The threat of another world war had little effect on the rate of expansion of U.S. airlines and, in fact, it was at the very beginning of the 1940s that a new generation of airliners came on to the market; aircraft which were to be converted to military use and after a great deal of service in the war were to form the basis of postwar recovery. One of the most significant, technologically speaking, was the Boeing 307 Stratoliner, the first four-engine commercial aircraft to have a pressurized passenger cabin.

Although only ten were built (production had to be concentrated on the B-17 bomber), the Stratoliner was visible proof that a new milestone in civil aviation development had been passed; airliners could now fly at high altitudes, above many of the cloud layers, avoiding weather disturbances and providing even faster and more comfortable travel. The Stratoliner project was initiated towards the end of 1935, soon after the appearance of the B-17 bomber, of which the airliner used the wing, tailplane and power installation. The fuselage differed considerably, however, since it had to be redesigned to allow for pressurization, and to accommodate thirty-three passengers comfortably. Boeing was well aware that this design was very advanced and judged it prudent to wait until some orders were forthcoming from airlines before building a prototype. They did not have to wait long: Pan American ordered four and TWA's management, who fully appreciated the advantages of pressurization since they had conducted research in this field starting in the early 1930s, initially ordered six 307s but then reduced this to five. The first Stratoliner flew on 31 December 1938, and was followed in 1940 by the other series models (designated S-307) ordered by Pan American. The five Stratoliners for TWA were also completed in 1940 and were designated SA-307B, with detail changes. The last series aircraft, the SB-307B, was bought by the millionaire, Howard Hughes, to attempt a new distance record but was eventually turned into a luxurious "executive" aircraft. Pan American and TWA took their Stratoliners out of service in 1948 and 1951 respectively, the TWA aircraft having been rebuilt and re-engined after the war. Some continued to fly for more than a decade under French ownership.

On 2 February 1940, the first production model of an important twin-engine light transport made its first flight: the Lockheed 18 Lodestar, the third in the family of twin-engine transports originating with the Electra of 1934. The Lodestar was to echo the Electra and the Super Electra's success, both as a military aircraft and on the civil market. It was more up to date, powerful and capacious than its direct predecessor; the airlines took to it immediately and, from 1940 onward, it was used in the U.S.A., South America, South Africa and Europe. Immediately after the war many of the military models were taken out of service and came on to the civil market; these were also very popular, especially with the smaller airlines.

The Curtiss C-46's development was somewhat similar. This large, twin-engine aircraft had been designed in 1935–36 as the CW-20 to succeed and replace the Douglas DC-3, but the program was interrupted by World War II and production was entirely given over to producing the developed C-46 military versions, known as the Commando. A total of 3,182 were built and all saw service during the war. The CW-20's exceptional performance and obvious potential led to its being chosen as a military transport after the prototype made its first flight on 26 March 1940; military observers were so impressed by the new airplane that they decided that production should commence immediately, and this reached a very high volume. The three main variants were the C-46A (1,491 built); the C-46D (1,410) and the C-46F (234). The only example to be put to civil use during the war was the prototype which was handed over to Great Britain in November 1941, and commenced service with BOAC at the beginning of the following year. The commercial career of the C-46 was, however, really to start once the war was over, when hundreds were taken out of military use and were sold on the open market. They were widely used, particularly in Latin America and the U.S.A., flew in all parts and some are still in operation.

The armed forces also had first call on another popular commercial airliner, the DC-4, which Douglas hoped would repeat the success of the DC-3; when the prototype had made its maiden flight on 14 February 1942, and Douglas already had 61 firm orders from the main U.S. airlines, the assembly lines were directed exclusively to the manufacture of aircraft for the U.S.A.A.F. More than 1,300 DC-4s were built and most saw wartime service with the U.S.A.A.F. as C-54s and with the U.S. Navy as R5Ds. After the war, Douglas resumed its original civil program and built another 79 aircraft which joined the large numbers of demilitarized DC-4s in commercial use.

The DC-4 was first put into service as a civil airliner at the end of October 1945, by American Overseas Airlines when they inaugurated their New York–Hurn transatlantic service which took 23 hours 48 minutes, including

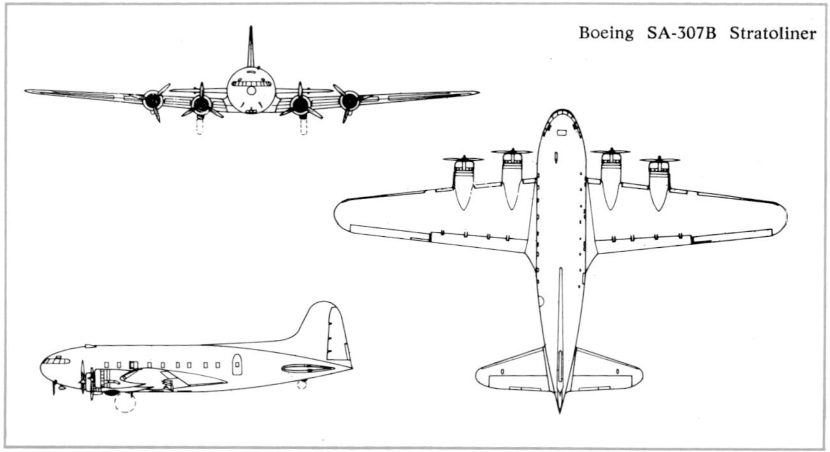
Boeing SA-307B Stratoliner

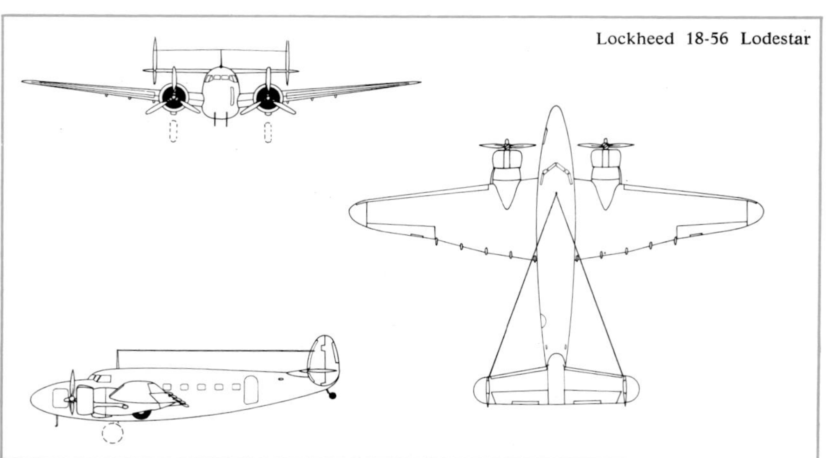
Lockheed 18-56 Lodestar

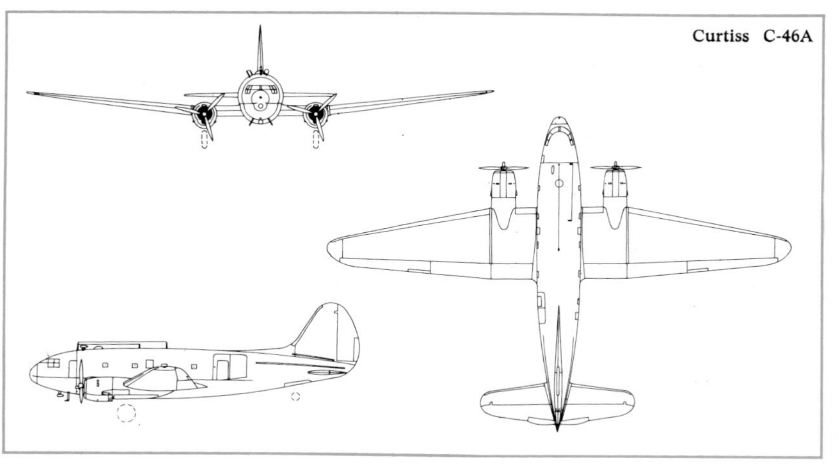
Curtiss C-46A

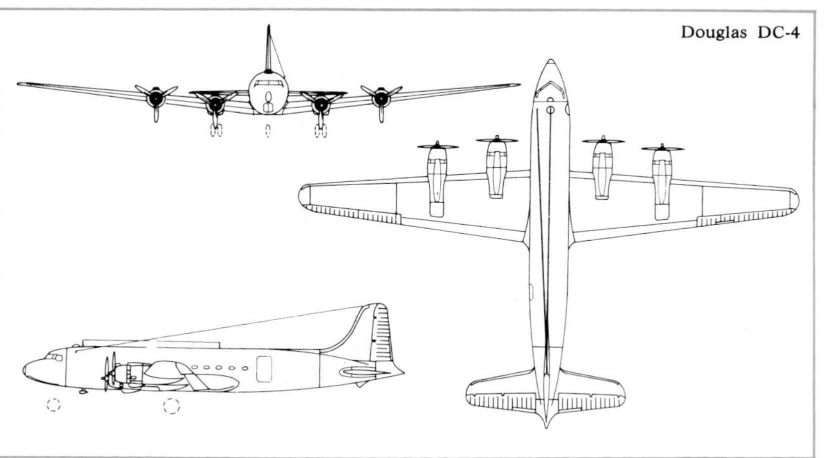
Douglas DC-4

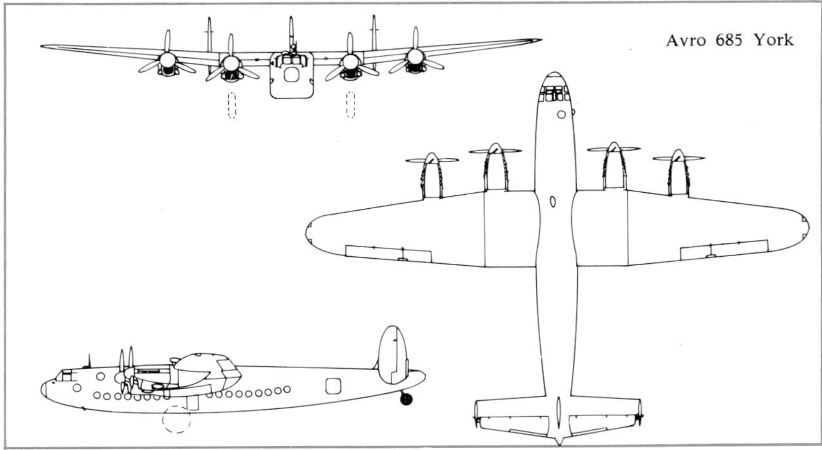

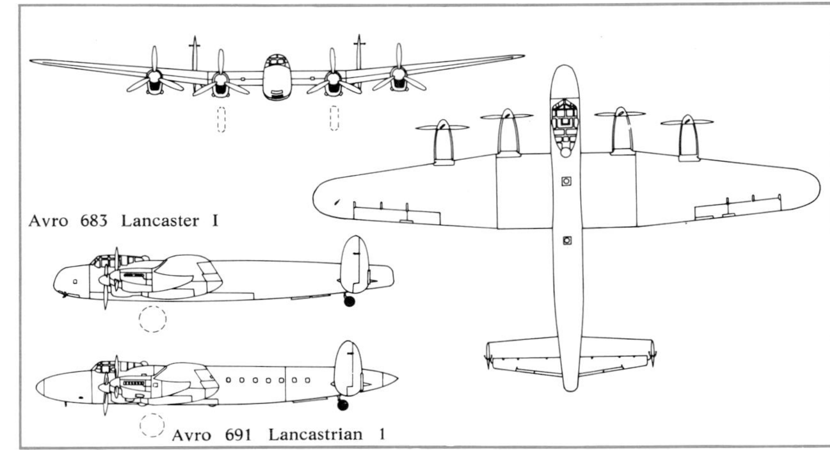

two refueling stops. On 7 March 1946, American Airlines used the DC-4 for the first time on U.S. internal routes, putting them on the New York–Los Angeles service. This reliable Douglas four-engine airliner was subsequently widely used by many European airlines and in Africa, Asia, Australia, the Far East and Latin America.

Plate 127
British bombers modified and used for civil aviation: 1942–1945

British commercial aviation also benefited greatly from military aircraft production, but followed a different pattern from that of the United States. The first British postwar generation of commercial aircraft were all derived from bombers and the best example concerns the famous Avro Lancaster.

The Avro 685 York had been the first of this famous series. R.A.F. Transport Command had issued a specification which led to the project; the prototype first flew on 5 July 1942, and a total of 257 were built. This useful four-engine monoplane started its airline career in 1944 when BOAC put five Yorks from an R.A.F. order into regular service on the Cairo route. At the end of 1945 the British airline acquired another twenty-five Yorks and modified them, equipping them with more powerful engines and giving them the designation "M Class," operating them on its main international routes and keeping them in service until 7 October 1950. These were joined by a further nine Yorks which from 1946 onward were built for British South American Airways which took twelve; Skyways purchased three and the Argentine company, FAMA, bought five.

The York had been derived from the Lancaster, but it had, of course, been necessary to design a completely new fuselage for carrying passengers. Two other commercial derivatives of the Lancaster involved minor modifications: the Avro 683 and the Avro 691 Lancastrian. The former even retained the name which the Lancaster bomber had made so famous, and the civil Avro 683 Lancaster was delivered on 20 January 1944, and was used by BOAC's experimental unit for the best part of three years, as an equipment test bed for future commercial aircraft.

The Lancastrian made a significant contribution to the revival of commercial aviation after the war. Trans-Canada Air Lines was the first company to adapt the bomber in 1943, when on 22 July it used the first of nine modified bombers to launch a Canadian Government transatlantic mail service to Great Britain. BOAC was next, placing an order at the beginning of 1945 for thirty-two (only twenty were completed) of the final Lancaster production series aircraft to be converted. These were known as the Lancastrian 1, and were put through a lengthy series of proving flights on the long-distance routes to Australia and New Zealand, being finally put into regular service by BOAC on 31 May 1945. The Lancastrian's more austere accommodation did not compare with that of the luxurious pre-war flying boats which had served the Imperial routes, but they were fast, efficient, dependable and played a vital part in the postwar reorganization of BOAC, helping to restore considerable prestige. It was the Lancastrian which equipped British South American Airways when it began operations in 1946, opening the first British air service to South America (London–Buenos Aires) on 15 March. Other Lancastrians were used by Qantas and some operated by Flight Refuelling Ltd. played a part in North Atlantic refueling trials before making a major contribution to the Berlin Airlift. In 1946 another twelve Lancastrians were put to commercial use; three were bought by Silver City Airways; four by Skyways; and five received by the newly established airline, Alitalia. The Lancastrians were mostly sold off to smaller operators.

Plate 128
Avro and Handley Page's transitional aircraft for postwar British civil aviation: 1946–1948

Avro's military production led to another commercial project which was to be one of the most ambitious undertaken by the British aeronautical industry to meet the demands of postwar civil aviation; it was also to be one of the most ill-fated. The Tudor was a large, four-engine pressurized aircraft intended for use on transatlantic flights. It was to serve a dual purpose as the vehicle for the regeneration of British airlines and also as the means to fight American dominance of the civil aviation market. It failed on both counts.

In 1943 the original design was drawn up for a commercial derivative of the Avro Lincoln bomber, the last development of the Lancaster design. The Tudor had a very similar wing and engine installation to the Lincoln, but the fuselage and tail unit had been completely redesigned. Two prototypes of the long-range model, the Avro 688 Tudor 1, were ordered in September 1944, and then a third aircraft, the Avro 689 Tudor 2, which was to lead to a second variant with reduced range but much increased capacity. Orders for production aircraft were placed by the three airlines who hoped to operate the new aircraft: BOAC, Qantas and South African Airways. By April 1945, a steady flow of orders had been received for a total of twenty Tudor 1 aircraft and seventy-nine Tudor 2s. But this promising start was soon to wither away. The Tudor 1 prototype flew on 14 June 1945, and put up a disappointing performance, being difficult to handle. The modifications which had to be made meant that long delays ensued and further time was taken up by a seemingly

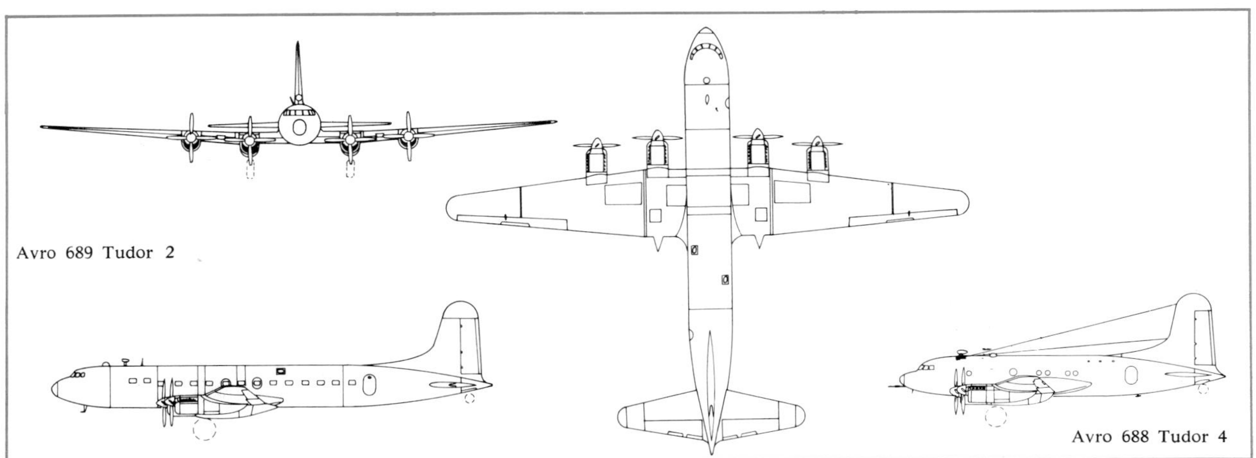

endless succession of changing customer requirements (more than three hundred from BOAC alone). On 11 April 1947, BOAC canceled its order, having decided that the Tudor was not suited to its needs. Ten production Tudor 1s were built: two were completed as Tudor 3s for the Ministry of Supply and twelve as thirty-two-seat Tudor 4s and 4Bs, which were offered to British South American Airways who used them in Latin America until early 1949. The Tudor 2 was just as unfortunate: the prototype had its maiden flight on 10 March 1946, and showed much the same drawbacks as the earlier model; BOAC began to lose interest and orders fell away to only eighteen. In the event six were built with reduced seating capacity as the Tudor 5 and in 1948 five of these were sold to BSAA but they were soon converted to an all-freight configuration. The Tudor did, however, serve a useful purpose when it was used during the Berlin Airlift.

This historic rescue operation coincided with the culmination of another transitional transport aircraft's career; a type which had also been derived from a bomber in the same way as the Lancaster-Lancastrian. This was the Handley Page Halifax, the transformation consisting of minor changes to the fuselage, and on some the installation of an under-fuselage freight container. Work had begun in 1946 with the last two production models, Mk.VI and Mk.VIII, to meet R.A.F. Transport Command's requirements. The resulting airplane was practical and, having no direct competition, found favor on the civil market and many Halifaxes were bought by specialist freight operators. Twelve Halifax C.VIIIs were also used as passenger airliners for more than a year from summer 1946, in the livery of BOAC, mainly on the London–West Africa routes. These Halifaxes were renamed Halton 1. Another contemporary four-engine Handley Page, the Hermes, was a more important civil aircraft; although it was mainly destined for R.A.F. use (under the name Hastings) it met BOAC's needs on their African routes from 1950. The project was put in train toward the end of the war, and before the armed forces monopolized production, the intention had been to prepare an airliner for postwar use. Its development phase was, however, protracted. The first commercial prototype (H.P.68 Hermes 1) first flew on 2 December 1945 (but crashed and was destroyed on that flight), followed by a second (H.P.74 Hermes 2) on 2 September 1947; and finally, on 5 September 1948, by the prototype of twenty-five production H.P.81 Hermes 4 aircraft for BOAC, although not all were taken by the airline.

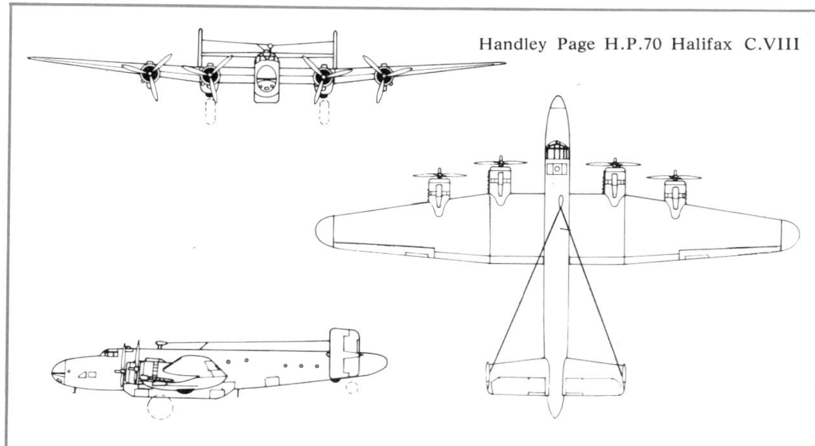

Handley Page H.P.70 Halifax C.VIII

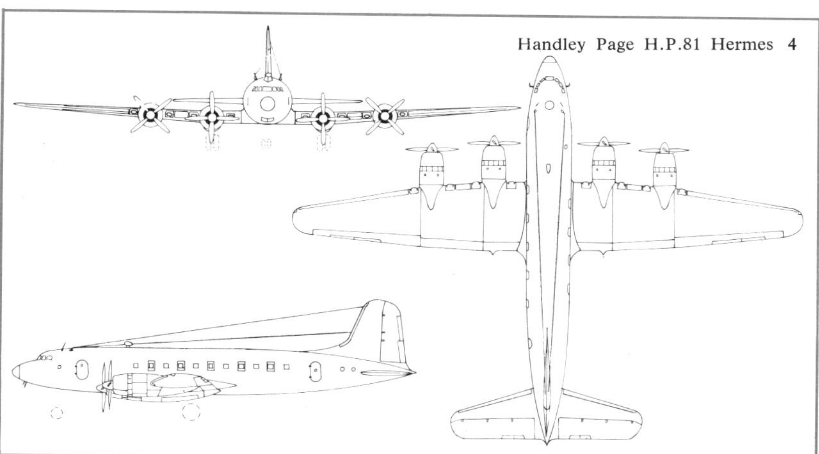

Handley Page H.P.81 Hermes 4

Plate 129
The French aircraft industry's first steps toward recovery: 1945–1951

France, too, was very anxious to revive her moribund commercial aviation industry. Before the war France had enjoyed considerable prestige in this field and was therefore absolutely determined to build up her famous airline, Air France, again, and the French aeronautical industry was exhorted to give of its best. One of the most widely-operated French civil transports during the first years of peace was the SNCASE SE.161 Languedoc, a four-engine aircraft which had first been designed in the 1930s as the Bloch 161, but was still a viable proposition after the war. Production totaled 100 aircraft, made up of assorted civil and military variants and their commercial career continued well into the 1950s. The original project (the Bloch 161) gave rise to a prototype which first flew in September 1939, but the war had halted series production. Once the stimulus had been given for recovery, the first series aircraft was built, which incorporated considerable modifications and was redesignated SE.161. On 17 September 1945, this aircraft had its maiden flight and Air France, duly impressed, placed an order for forty. Thirteen were built by early 1946 and, after completing a series of experimental flights, these aircraft went into regular airline service on 28 May. During the same year, Languedocs were introduced on African routes and the main European routes. At the end of 1946 these aircraft were temporarily grounded because of a number of problems including lack of de-icing equipment. The defects were cured and it was decided that the original Gnome-Rhône power units should be replaced by American Pratt & Whitney engines. These changes led to the Languedoc designation being changed yet again, to SE.161/P7, and they were returned to regular flying duties in March 1947. In the same year LOT, the Polish airline, bought five Languedocs powered by French engines, but later re-engined. Air France began to phase out its Languedocs gradually from the end of 1949.

Two interesting twin-engine aircraft in the medium-range category were both designed in the early years of World War II and built once peace was restored. The SNCASO SO.30 and the SO.95 Corse were not only used as military aircraft, but also flown by smaller civil operators and in French overseas possessions. The SO.30 first took to the air in its definitive form, as the SO.30P Bretagne, on 11 December 1947, and production totaled 45; four

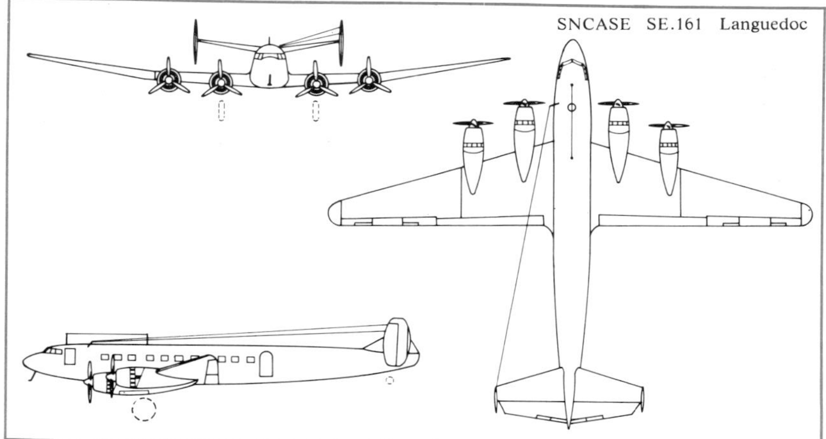

SNCASE SE.161 Languedoc

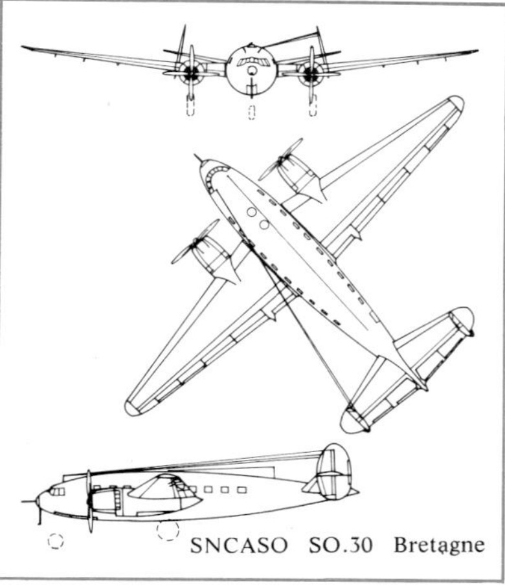

SNCASO SO.30 Bretagne

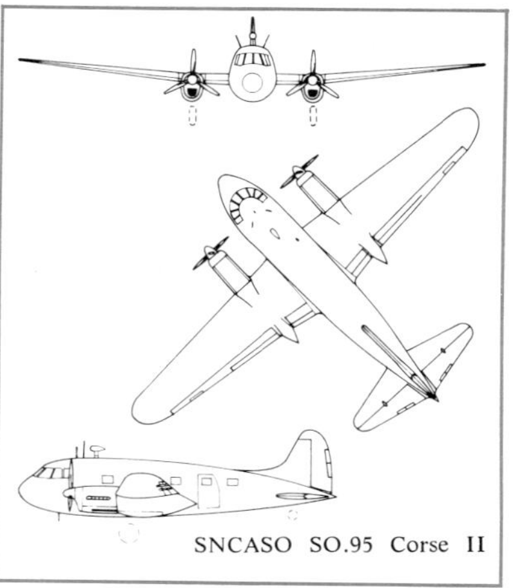

SNCASO SO.95 Corse II

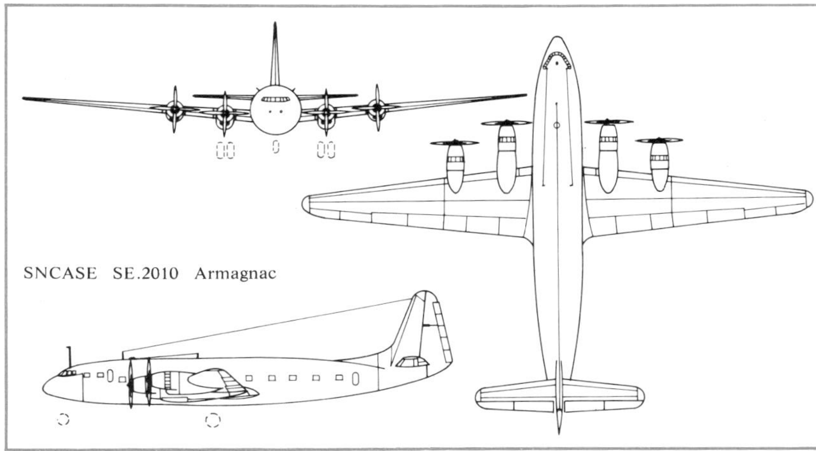

SNCASE SE.2010 Armagnac

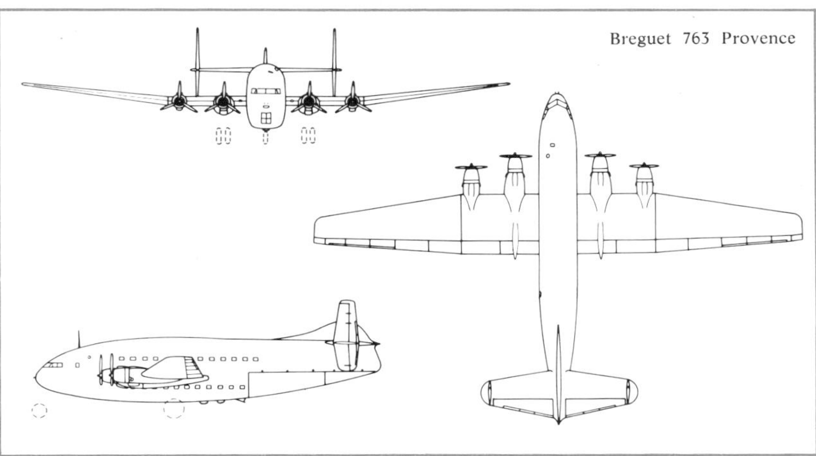

Breguet 763 Provence

of which were flown for a while by Air France; eight served with Air Algérie and twelve with Air Maroc. Some of the remainder were bought by minor companies and some flew with units of Transport Command. The SO.95 Corse II production totaled 60 (the prototype having flown on 17 July 1947) and most of these were used by the Aéronavale's light transport units. Only two SO.95s saw regular passenger service, with Air Services of India, flying between Bombay, Bangalore and Delhi, and these aircraft were taken out of service in October 1950.

Just as had been the case in Britain, many ambitious French designs were put forward at this juncture only to prove impracticable. The SE.2010 Armagnac was a case in point; this was a large four-engine airplane designed mainly for transatlantic routes. In common with many aircraft of its time, the Armagnac had been formulated during the war and the project had been taken up again in 1945. The prototype first flew on 2 April 1949. A production line was laid down on the strength of an order for fifteen aircraft of which eight were intended for Air France.

This program was, however, never to be completed. Air France decided that the Armagnac was not, after all, a competitive proposition when compared with contemporary American output (mainly because of its high operating costs). The order was canceled and only eight SE.2010s were completed with four being taken by Transports Aériens Intercontinentaux (TAI). These were put into service in late 1952, but withdrawn only eight months later because of their poor economics. The Armagnacs ended up as military transports with SAGETA in the war in Indochina from late 1953 onward.

The Breguet 763 Provence was altogether more successful. It was given the nickname "Deux Ponts" (Two Decks) because of the two decks in the very deep fuselage. The first prototype, the Breguet 761, flew on 15 February 1949, and was followed by three pre-series aircraft (Breguet 761S) which were used for proving trials. On 20 July 1951, the first of twelve production aircraft ordered by Air France made its first flight, in what was to be its definitive configuration; this aircraft, the Breguet 763, had a number of modifications and more powerful engines and commenced regular flights to North Africa on 16 March 1953. The Provence, as it was named by Air France, was exceptionally useful because of its great capacity; it could carry 107 passengers on medium-range flights. As more modern aircraft came on to the market, Air France sold six of their Breguets to the French Air Force (which already flew military versions of this four-engine transport, designated Breguet 765 Sahara) and converted the other six into both all-cargo and mixed configurations; this latter variant, the name of which was changed to the Universal, could carry a maximum of twenty-nine passengers. The Universal could be used for a wide variety of tasks because of its extremely capacious fuselage (over 93 cubic meters) and the resulting high tonnage—it could carry over 13 tonnes. In 1966 these aircraft were still being profitably put to use on short hauls between France and Great Britain, and they were finally withdrawn in 1971 after eighteen years' service.

Plate 130
Very large aircraft meet with small success: 1943–1952

Once the war was over the most advanced aeronautical powers started to envision particularly ambitious designs for enormous airplanes which, on paper at any rate, were to be the means of revolutionizing civil aviation, and of expanding its operations at an even faster rate. These projects went no further than the experimental stage and, although they represented technological advances, they were doomed by the over-grandiose thinking which lay behind them and by their total lack of economic and commercial viability. Seaplanes and flying boats were included in these experiments; the mere fact that this type of aircraft did not have to use an airport with all its limitations such as length of runways and other restrictions meant that it was easier for designers to give free reign to their more ambitious plans regarding weight and size. The Italian Cant Z.511 falls into this category; it was designed before the war as a transatlantic passenger carrier and was the largest seaplane ever built. Work started on the design in 1937 at the request of Ala Littoria, but was not to meet with success; the specification was changed considerably which led to delays, and the Cant Z.511 never progressed beyond the prototype stage. It first flew in September 1943.

A similar lack of success was in store for the gigantic Hughes H-4 Hercules, a monster flying boat powered by eight engines which delivered a total of 24,000 hp; and having a wingspan of 320 ft (97.54 m), which Howard Hughes, the "flying millionaire," had designed to show off his prowess as an aeronautical engineer. On 2 November 1947, the Hercules managed to climb about 33 ft (10 m) above the water in the Los Angeles roadstead in front of a crowd of fifty thousand excited spectators, and flew for about a mile before being moored for good back in the immense hangar which had been specially built to house it, there to remain. Hughes had conceived the project in 1942 and it was meant to be a classic flying boat which could be used to ferry troops and supplies to the various war zones, thus avoiding the enemy submarine menace which threatened merchantmen. As time went by, however, this plan no longer had any strategic relevance and in 1945 it was abandoned by the armed forces.

The end of the big commercial flying boat was signaled in 1954 with the cancelation of Britain's Princess flying boat program, under which three very large Saunders-Roe S.R.45 Princess boats had been built, although only the first one was ever flown. Saunders-Roe had received a specification for a flying boat which could accommodate some 100 passengers on transcontinental flights, and in May 1946 an order was placed for three prototypes. The construction program ran into difficulties and fell behind schedule and, in 1951, BOAC announced that it no longer intended to adopt the new flying boat, having opted to use only landplanes in its fleet. The three Princesses were eventually scrapped without ever going into service.

A promising landplane, the Bristol 167 Brabazon, was one of the biggest and most ambitious projects ever attempted by the British aircraft indus-

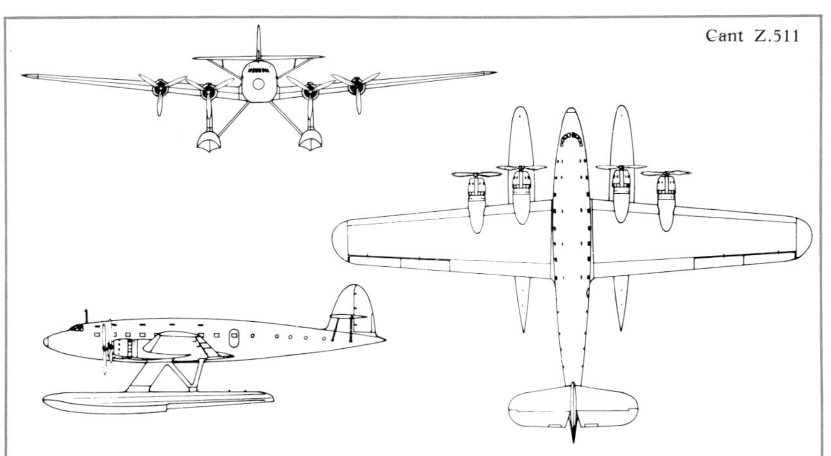

Cant Z.511

Plate 131
The last large passenger flying boats: 1942–1946

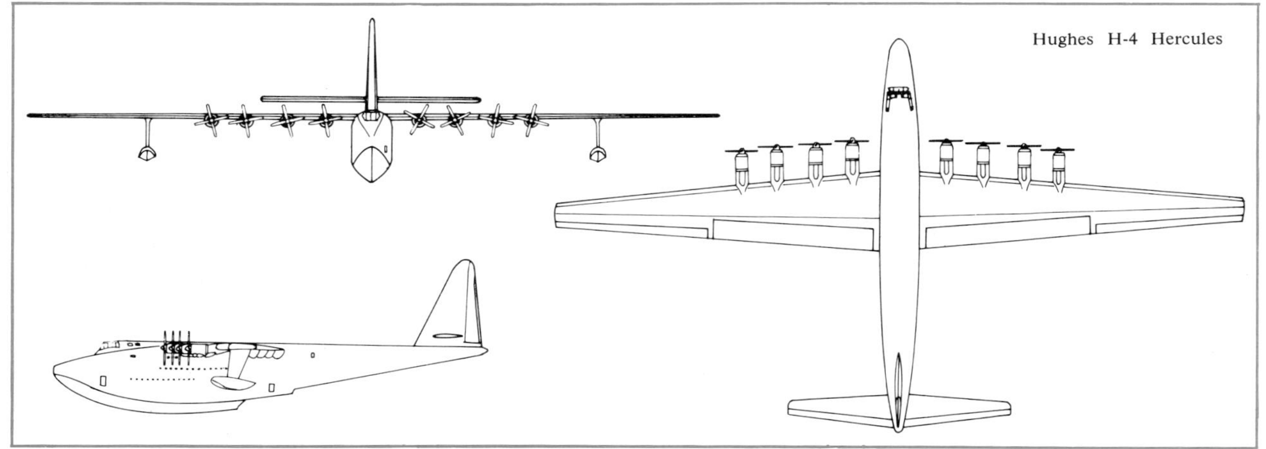

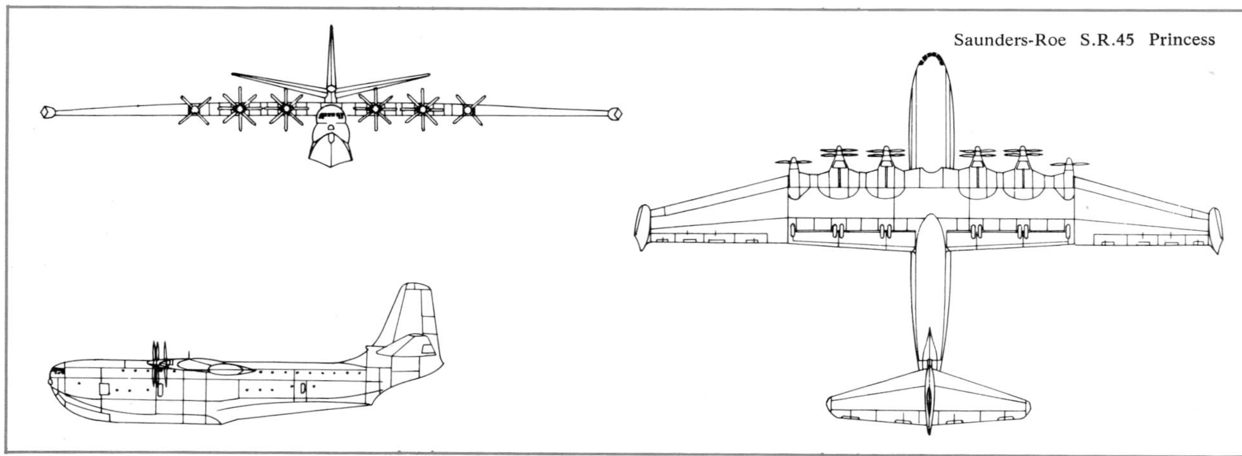

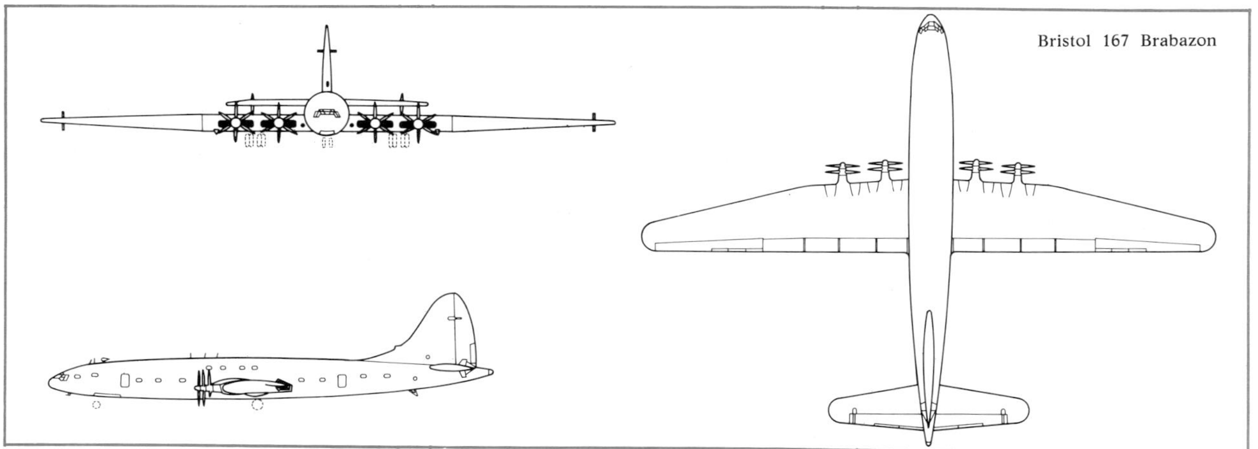

The flying boat which had been such a popular means of transport in the 1930s had another short lease of life immediately after the war, before the new generation of landplanes ousted it from the scene.

Spurred on by the need to restructure and expand France's civil aviation, Air France was eager to put the first of eight Latécoère 631s into service and did so on 26 July 1947. These large six-engine flying boats had been designed as long before as 1938, the maiden flight had taken place on 4 November 1942, and the program had been revived once the war was over. Air France only used three of these aircraft for a short time. One crashed in August 1948, and the other two were withdrawn from service. Eight had been built and one of these was converted and used as a freighter by a private company. The rest were scrapped. British flying boats were to play an important role in the rebuilding of BOAC during the first years of peace. Until November 1950, when landplanes took over from the Solents on the United Kingdom–South Africa route, BOAC had operated a fleet of flying boats on the old Empire routes to Africa, India and Australia. These were the last of a long series of Short flying boats: the final types were the Sandringham and the Solent.

The former was a direct conversion of the famous Sunderland. In November 1945 the first Sandringham 1 was launched and it could accommodate twenty-two passengers in daytime layout and sixteen when used as a sleeper transport. Conversions went ahead smoothly and comprised several variants which differed mainly in capacity and cabin layout.

BOAC took delivery of nine Sandringham 5s (Plymouth Class with 22 seats) and three Sandringham 7s (Bermuda Class with 30 seats) from 1947. These flying boats remained in service until 1949 on Far Eastern and Australian services. They were then sold to smaller companies such as Aquila Airways and the Australian company, Ansett Airways. Five 37-seat Sandringham 6s were used by DNL and SAS on services between Oslo and Tromsø.

The Short Solent was used for a much shorter time. Like the Sandringham it was derived from a military flying boat, the Short Seaford of 1945, and twelve Solents were ordered for BOAC in 1946. These were designated Solent 2. The first of these took to the air on 1 December 1946, the last was launched on 8 April 1948, and the Solents entered regular service in May 1948, on the United

try. It was technologically far ahead of its time and originated in the middle of the war (1943), following the Brabazon Committee's recommendations as to the types of aircraft which should be ready for Britain's postwar civil aviation. There was considerable prestige attached to producing an aircraft which could carry 100 passengers nonstop from London to New York and this was the main attraction, but practical, economic and, above all, political, factors all militated against the Brabazon going into series production. The Brabazon 1 prototype flew for the first time on 4 September 1949, two years behind schedule; designs for the Brabazon Mk. 2 were drawn up which was to have had four 7,000-ehp Coupled-Proteus 710 propeller-turbines (instead of the original eight Bristol Centaurus radials of the Mk. 1) but this version was shelved in 1952 before the second prototype was fully completed. In February 1952, the government decided to suspend work, partly due to embarrassingly high costs. On 9 July 1953, the program was finally abandoned and the only Brabazon completed went to the breakers.

Latécoère 631

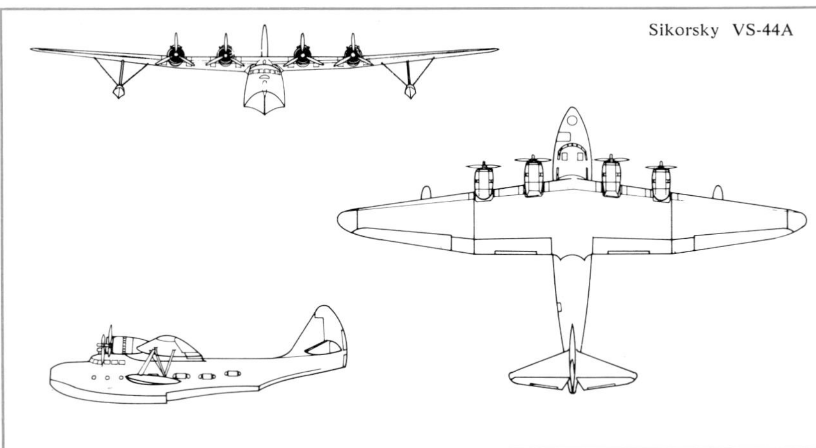
Sikorsky VS-44A

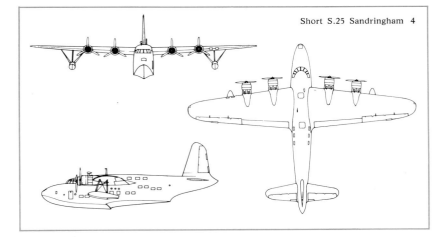

Short S.25 Sandringham 4

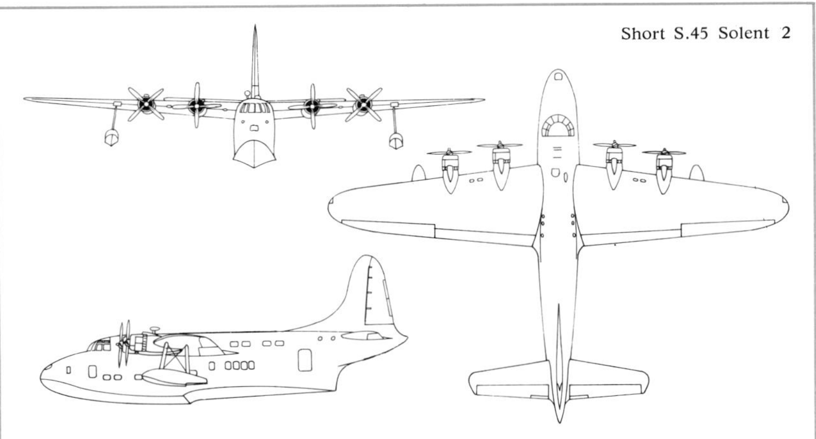
Short S.45 Solent 2

Kingdom–South Africa route, replacing the obsolescent Avro Yorks. These early Solents were joined, in May 1949, by the first of three improved Solent 3s. Once the decision had been taken to phase out all flying boats these aircraft were mostly sold off to minor operators. Aquila Airways was the company which made the most use of them, flying to Madeira until 30 September 1958.

In the United States the last large commercial flying boat was the Sikorsky VS-44A. Only three of these four-engine flying boats were built—the first making its maiden flight on 18 January 1942—and they were used throughout the war as transatlantic military transports, but operated by American Export Airlines. These three VS-44As were called *Excalibur*, *Excambia* and *Exeter*, and only *Excambia* was used commercially to any extent after the war, flying until 1971, first with Avalon Air Transport and then with Antilles Air Boats. At the height of their wartime career, these three VS-44As broke several speed and distance records, including the transatlantic record between Europe and the United States, the fastest nonstop flight from the Old World to New York.

Plate 132
Some outstanding American post-war airliners: 1946–1955

Some of the most dramatic technological advances and growth in production expertise seen in the post-war period were achieved in the United States. A new generation of excellent airplanes was soon coming off the production lines. The various Convair and Martin models were aircraft which deserved to capture a good market share in the short- to medium-range category. The Martin 2-0-2 was the first civil twin-engine aircraft of this type to be designed and go into service in the U.S.A. in the immediately postwar years. Northwest Airlines took delivery of 25 Martin 2-0-2s and introduced the type in November 1947; four went to the Chilean company, LAN, and two to the Venezuelan company, LAV. Unfortunately one of Northwest's 2-0-2s suffered an inflight wing failure, the type was withdrawn and a number of orders for the aircraft were canceled. Only 33 were built. A modified version, the 2-0-2A, appeared in 1950 and twelve were built for TWA. Some of the older 2-0-2s were brought to the improved standard and served with U.S. local service airlines, as did ten of the TWA aircraft. The final version, the 4-0-4, entered service with TWA in October 1951. This had a pressurized cabin, seats for 48 passengers and more powerful engines. Apart from the prototype there were 41 for TWA, 60 for Eastern Air Lines and two for the U.S. Coast Guard. Most, eventually, went to U.S. local service airlines. A few are still in service.

The large family of twin-engine Convairs achieved far greater success than the contemporary aircraft produced by its direct competitor, Martin. In fact the CV-240 Convair-Liner was so versatile that it was a worthy successor to the immortal DC-3. The first prototype, Convair CV-110, made its maiden flight in July 1946, and although it was not really competitive, due to low carrying capacity for its range, it was used as a basic design for the development of later variants. The first successful version was the Convair CV-240 which first flew on 16 March 1947. Although it was only slightly larger and had more powerful engines, this aircraft showed an appreciable increase in carrying capacity and range over the CV-110 and met with instant approval from various companies. The largest operator of the CV-240 was American Airlines which ordered a fleet of more than 70 out of a civil production total of 176. To this figure there were added a further 395 completed as military transports (C-131) and trainers (T-29). Production of the

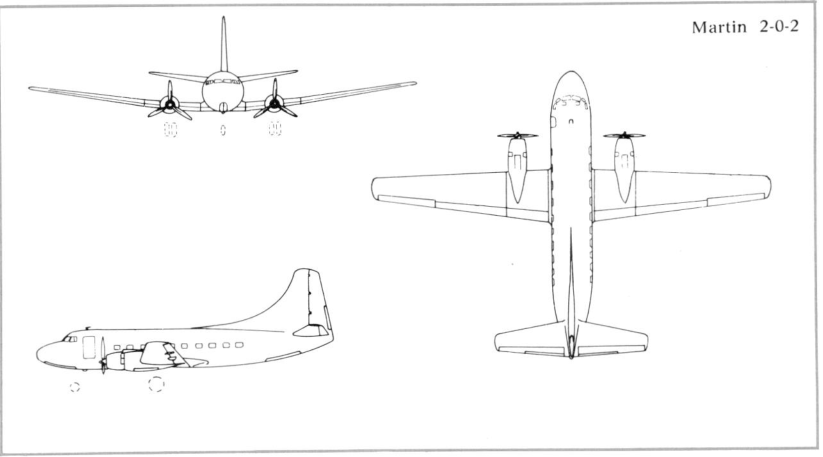
Martin 2-0-2

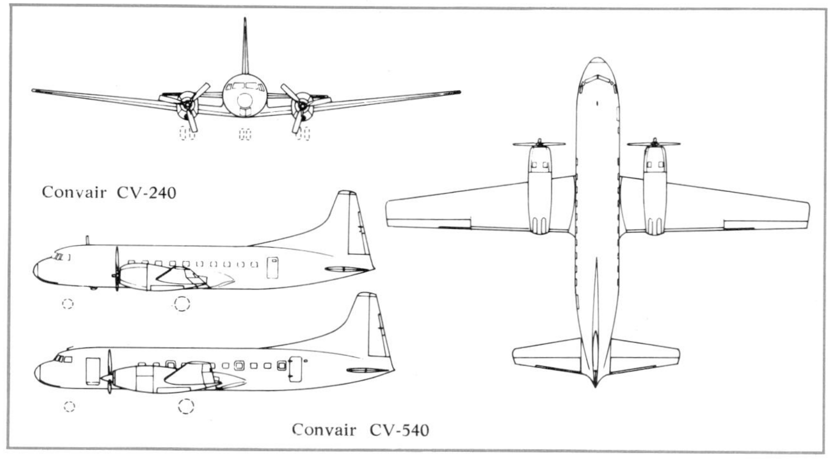

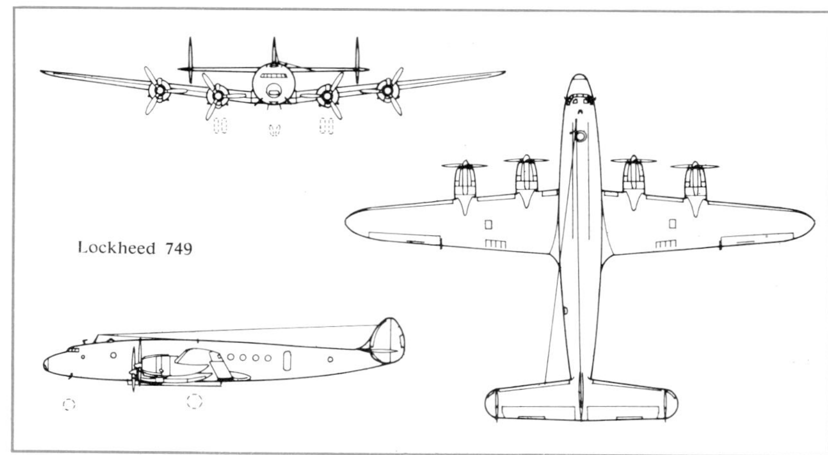

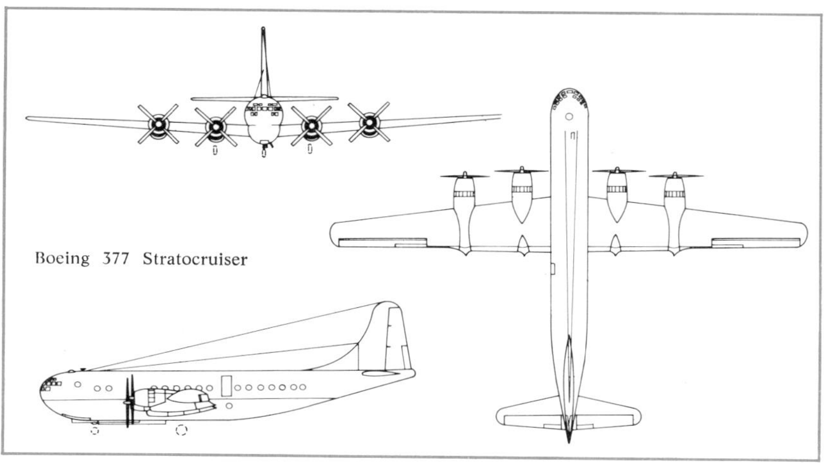

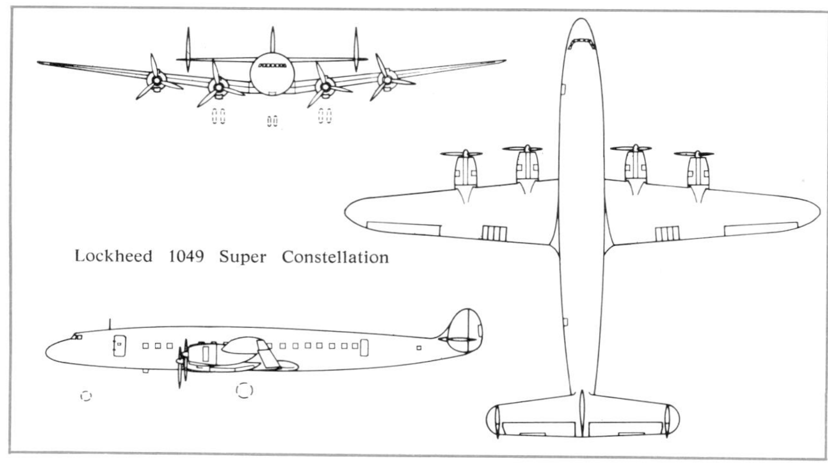

CV-240 ended in 1958. The second model was the CV-340 (first flight 5 October 1951) which had more powerful engines, an increased wingspan, lengthened fuselage and could carry more passengers. 209 civil CV-340s were taken by various American, European, Asian and South American operators and a further 107 were manufactured for military use. The next Convair model, the CV-440, which was to be called the Metropolitan was a further improved version with 56 seats and much reduced cabin noise level; 181 CV-440s were built and in total there were more than 1,000 Convair-Liners. A new chapter in the career of this versatile twin-engine airplane opened in 1955 when a CV-340 was successfully converted to propeller-turbine power which brought this already very successful airframe right up to date. The first of the new variants was designated Convair CV-540 and the prototype flew for the first time in June 1955, powered by Napier Elands. The second major conversion resulted in the CV-580 (which went into service in 1964) using two Allison 501s. Then came the CV-600/640 variants powered by Rolls-Royce Darts. More than 250 CV-240s and CV-340s were converted to turbine power and many of these aircraft are still in service.

The four-engine Boeing 377 Stratocruiser, derived, albeit indirectly, from the B-29 Superfortress, made a considerable impact on the long-range, large-capacity commercial sector. Production of this impressive aircraft originated with a military specification of 1942, and the XC-97 prototype flew on 15 November 1944. 888 C-97s and KC-97s were manufactured and saw service as transports and flying tankers. Boeing decided to develop an exclusively civil version of this successful type, fitted out so that it could carry a maximum of 100 passengers on long-distance flights, and this made its first flight on 8 July 1947. The fifty-five Stratocruisers manufactured were bought by several airlines: Pan American which took twenty; American Overseas Airlines (8); Northwest (10); United Air Lines (7); and in Europe BOAC took delivery of ten. BOAC kept the Stratocruiser in service for the longest time: from 6 December 1949 until May 1959.

The Lockheed O49 Constellation was the first of a series of four-engine aircraft which managed to achieve a large share of the civil market until the arrival of the first jets. Designed to meet a 1939 requirement of TWA and ordered by that airline and Pan American, the first Constellation flew in January 1943 and was put into military service as the C-69. When the war ended, military orders were curtailed and the 51 aircraft left over from the military order were available to the commercial sector. The first company to put the Constellation into service was Pan American which, on 3 February 1946, inaugurated the New York–Bermuda route. Three days later TWA started its service between Washington and Paris, and from 15 February the Constellation was used on domestic routes. The first version to be specifically designed for postwar civil use was the Model 649 which went into service in May 1947, and had improved engines and carrying capacity. This was followed a year later by the Model 749 with increased weight and appropriate modifications to the positioning and capacity of the fuel tanks for overseas operation. This model was joined by a sub-series version, the strengthened Model 749A, which could carry an extra payload of 4,850 lb (2,200 kg). These variants of the Constellation won many orders from the large American airlines (TWA and Pan American took delivery of the largest numbers) and they were used successfully on both international and internal routes. Total production reached 233 aircraft.

Plate 133
The Americans build the last successful four-engine piston-engine transports: 1951–1955

Lockheed's four-engine aircraft were to become even more widely used when the Super Constellation came on the market. The first prototype, Model 1049, flew on 13 October 1950: the fuselage had been lengthened by more than 18 ft (5.5 m), the airframe had been reinforced and more powerful engines installed. The new Super Constellation immediately won orders from the airlines: Eastern Airlines took delivery of 14 followed by TWA, which took 10, and the aircraft first went into service with Eastern on 7 December 1951. The next civil version was the Model 1049C (derived from the Model 1049B which had been developed for the U.S. Navy) and was given more powerful engines with the adoption of the Wright Turbo-Compound. The first Model 1049C flew on 17 February 1953, and in all 48 aircraft were built. The main airlines to order it were Air France, Eastern Air Lines, KLM, TCA and TWA. Two passenger airliners followed: the Model 1049E (28 built) and the Model 1049G (102 built); these were the most widely used of all the Super Constellations. When production of the Super

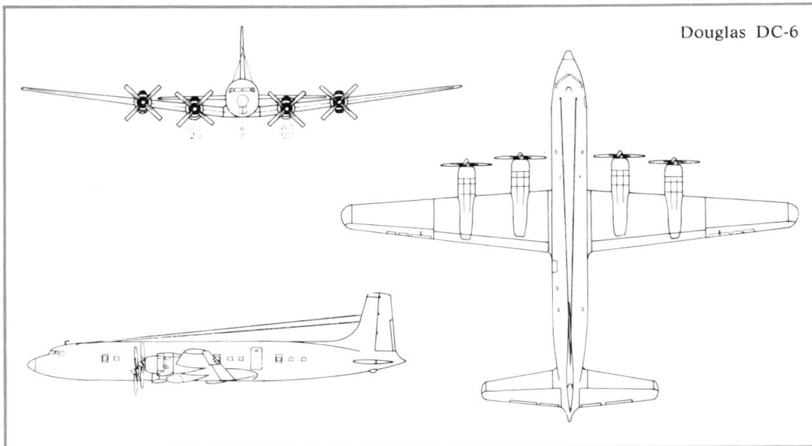
Douglas DC-6

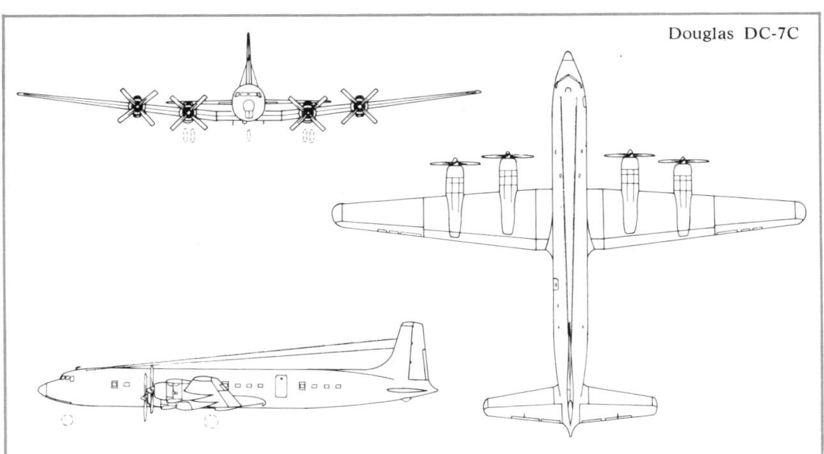
Douglas DC-7C

Constellation came to an end, after a total of 579 civil and military aircraft had been built, Lockheed went ahead with another development of this basic design formula. This was the Model 1649A Starliner which had an even longer fuselage and an entirely new wing. The prototype flew on 10 October 1956, but the aircraft had a short service life; the total production of 43 Starliners soon had to make way for the first jets.

Meanwhile another aircraft constructor was designing and producing a series of equally famous aircraft which were to typify the last piston-engine commercial transports. These were Douglas's DC-6 and DC-7, the culmination of a long line of aircraft which stretched back to the DC-1 of the 1930s. The DC-6 was a more powerful and enlarged version of the DC-4 and managed to make its mark on the civil market. The military prototype had flown on 15 February 1946, but Douglas subsequently decided to focus production on the civil model and the airline companies gave it an enthusiastic reception. United was the first to put the DC-6 into service in April 1947 and the total number of aircraft built reached 175. Two years later the second major production version, the DC-6A, appeared of which 74 were built. These were more powerful and longer with greater carrying capacity. Then, in 1951, came the DC-6B, the final variant, which reached a production total of 288. These airliners were used by nearly all the major operators and by many smaller companies and more than 100 remained in service into the 1980s.

The Douglas DC-7 was not only the direct successor to the DC-6 series, but actually retained many features of the DC-6B's airframe, and the prototype flew for the first time on 18 May 1953. It was built in response to a request from American Airlines who wanted an aircraft which could compete with the Super Constellations ordered by their direct rival, TWA. 110 of the first variant of the DC-7s were completed which had more powerful Wright Turbo-Compound engines, a longer fuselage and reinforced airframe. These were followed by 112 DC-7Bs (the prototype made its maiden flight in October 1954) and was intended to compete for use on transatlantic routes. The prototype of the last version, the DC-7C, first flew on 20 December 1955, and showed that the Douglas designers had managed to identify and eradicate all the shortcomings of the previous production series (which included noise inside the passenger cabin and inadequate North Atlantic fuel capacity), largely by restructuring the wing and lengthening the fuselage.

Plate 134
British and Swedish medium-range transports: 1946–1947

In the immediate postwar years the British aircraft industry spared no efforts to launch a new generation of civil aircraft in the short- to medium-range, large-capacity sector. There were many difficulties and setbacks, but some commercially successful medium-range aircraft were produced. Several types made a significant contribution to the recovery of the smaller operators, as well as forming the main fleet of the newly-created BEA, which was formed on 1 August 1946, to handle European and British Isles routes.

The Bristol 170 was a large and unglamorous twin-engine dual-purpose freighter/passenger carrier which gave sterling service as a general work-horse. The service which made it most popular was its use as a cross-Channel car ferry. The Type 170 was designed during the last years of the war and was originally to be used by the R.A.F., but the end of the war meant that it was no longer needed for military purposes and it was therefore converted to commercial use. There were two prototypes: the 170 Freighter (first flight 2 December 1945) which could carry either passengers or freight with double nose doors for easy loading of heavy freight; next came the prototype 170 Wayfarer (on 30 April 1946), an all-passenger version. The Freighter was the more successful of the two and only 16 Wayfarers were built, most of which went for export and many of these were subsequently converted to cargo use. In 1948, the first of the Mk.21 freighters appeared—a total of 92 was built and these had a modified and stronger wing and more powerful engines than the prototype. These aircraft inaugurated Silver City Airways' car ferry service across the Channel, starting on 14 July 1948. This proved to be an extremely shrewed business initiative and was very popular. Production continued with the Mk.31, which had more power and increased weight, and in 1953 progressed to the Mk.32 which had a redesigned tail unit and a lengthened nose making it possible to carry three vehicles instead of two. The total number of Bristol 170s reached 214.

BEA was fortunate in having a thoroughly reliable twin-engine airliner, the Vickers-Armstrongs Viking, when it took over responsibility for the European routes. BEA kept its Vikings in service from 1946 to 1954. The first of the three prototypes made its maiden flight on 22 June 1945, and there followed an exhaustive cycle of operational trials. The Ministry of

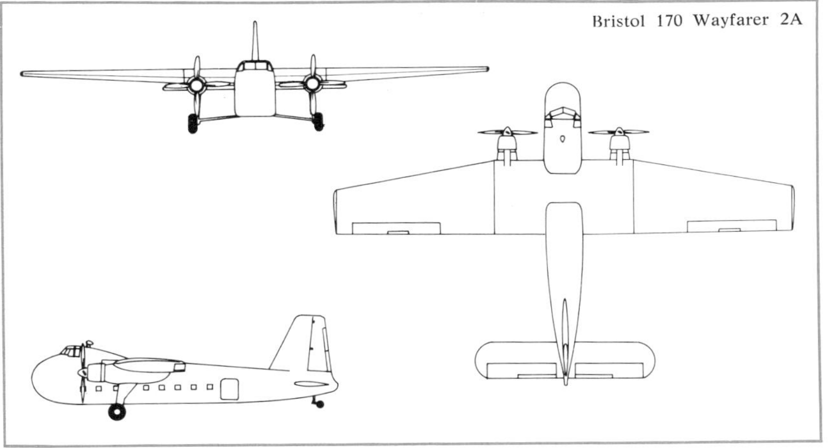
Bristol 170 Wayfarer 2A

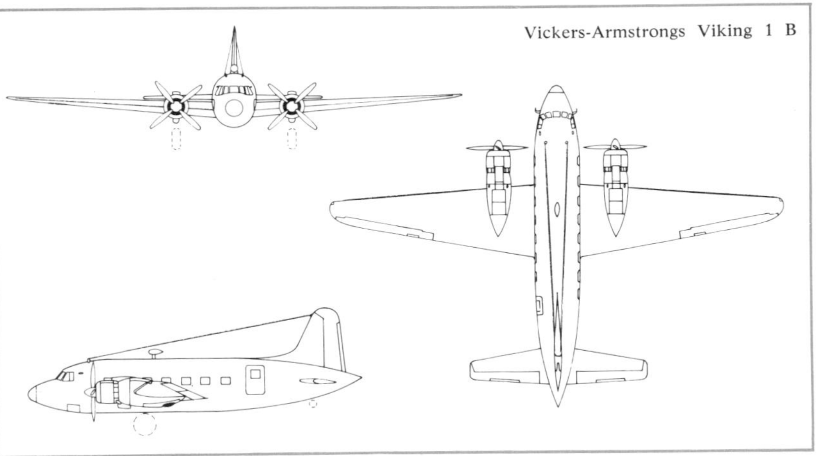
Vickers-Armstrongs Viking 1 B

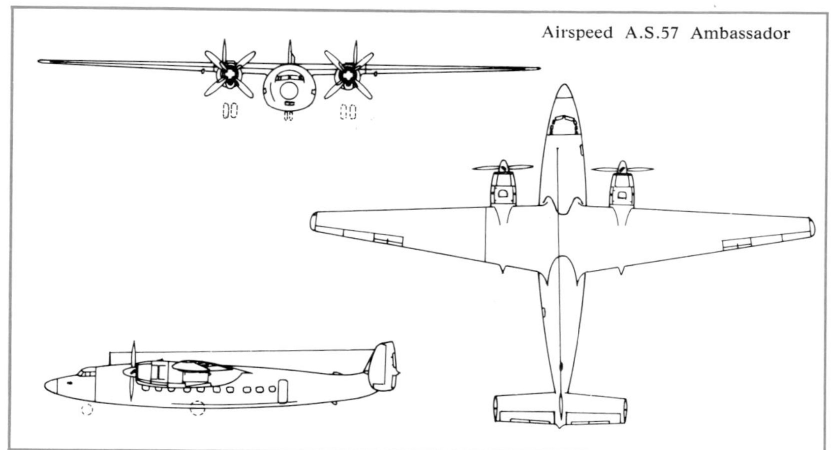

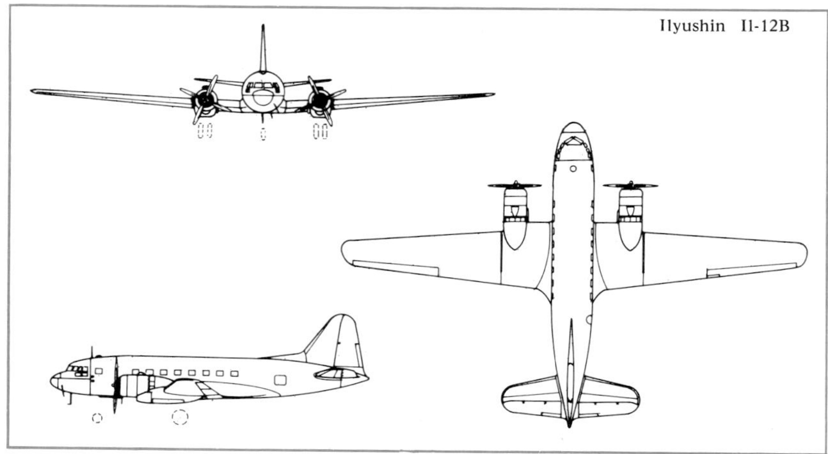

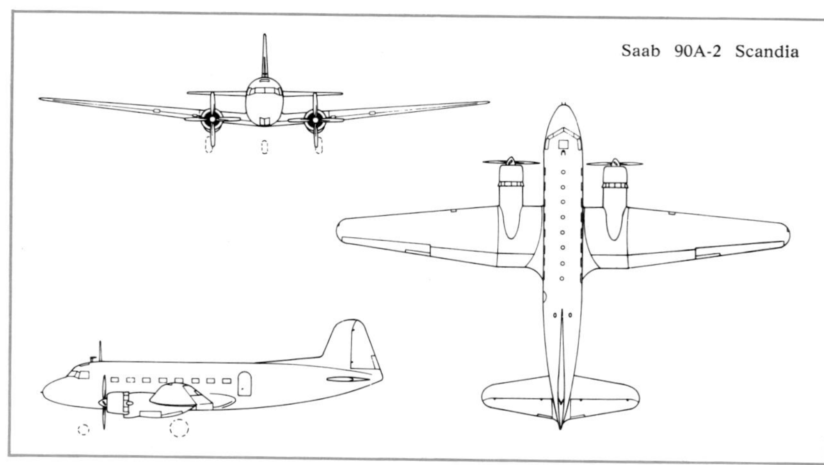

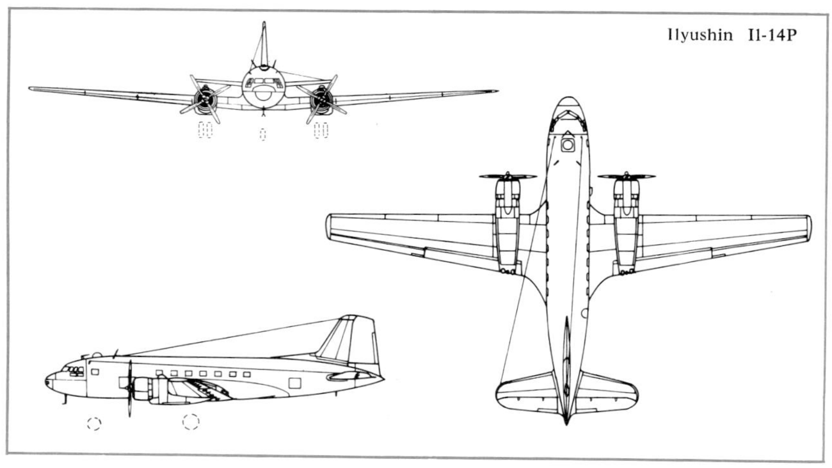

Aircraft Production placed an order for 50 in April 1946 and production began of what was to become the Viking 1A, with fabric-covered wings. Nineteen were built, of which eleven went into regular service. These were followed by the lengthened Viking 1B which had metal-skinned wings and became the standard production version. Apart from the large BEA fleet, many Vikings were exported and total production came to 163 with a further 263 examples of the Valetta military transport version.

On 27 March 1952, BEA's Vikings were joined in regular service by another medium-range twin-engine aircraft, the Airspeed A.S.57 Ambassador, which gave a very good account of itself as part of BEA's fleet until 30 July 1958. The prototype took to the air for the first time on 10 July 1947, and was followed, on 26 August 1948, by the second prototype. On 22 August 1951, BEA took delivery of the first aircraft of its order for twenty A.S.57s and after nearly seven months spent testing the aircraft and training air crews it inaugurated the service to Paris.

The market potential for short- to medium-range, medium-capacity transport category aircraft was so great that the Swedish aircraft industry committed itself to producing an aircraft which could replace the DC-3. This gave rise to the Saab 90 Scandia, an efficient twin-engine type which might have succeeded in capturing its share of this market had it been given sufficient backing. As a result only 17 production aircraft (designated A-2) were built, including six made by Fokker. The Saab Scandia made its maiden flight on 16 November 1946, but the first order was not placed until 1948. Eight Scandias were put into service by SAS (starting in November 1950) and ten by the Brazilian airlines Aerovias Brasil and VASP, the latter buying SAS's Scandias in 1957 and keeping them in its fleet until the mid-sixties.

Plate 135
Aeroflot's aircraft of the early post-war era: 1946–1958

The Soviet Union was also faced with the prospect of finding a worthy successor to the ubiquitous DC-3 in the immediate postwar years. Over 2,000 twin-engine DC-3s had been constructed under license as the Lisunov Li-2, but although quite outstanding, they could not fulfil the particular requirements of Aeroflot's expansion program. It was therefore necessary to design an aircraft which approached the caliber of the Dakota, but which would be more up to date. The prototype of the Ilyushin Il-12 appeared in early 1946 and was to be the first of a succession of effective medium-range twin-engine aircraft which were produced in very large numbers. The final variant, the Il-14, is still in service in China and the U.S.S.R.

Aeroflot put its new Il-12s into service on 22 August 1947, and within a few months was using large numbers of them on its main domestic and international routes. Throughout the 1950s the Ilyushins were used widely and intensively and were only withdrawn in spring 1965. The Ilyushin was also exported and used in countries beyond the Iron Curtain, where it was popular for civil and military use. As many as 3,000 aircraft, both passenger and cargo variants, are believed to have left the assembly lines. Apart from Aeroflot, the main operators of this aircraft were the Czechoslovak airline ČSA and the Polish LOT. The Il-12's success was to be repeated and bettered by the second main production model, the Il-14 of 1953, which had structural improvements and more powerful engines. After the appearance of the prototype, the initial production was for the Soviet Air Force. The first commercial variant was called the Il-

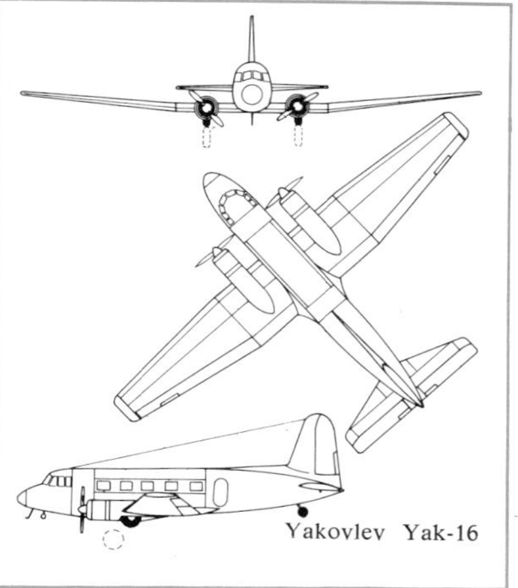

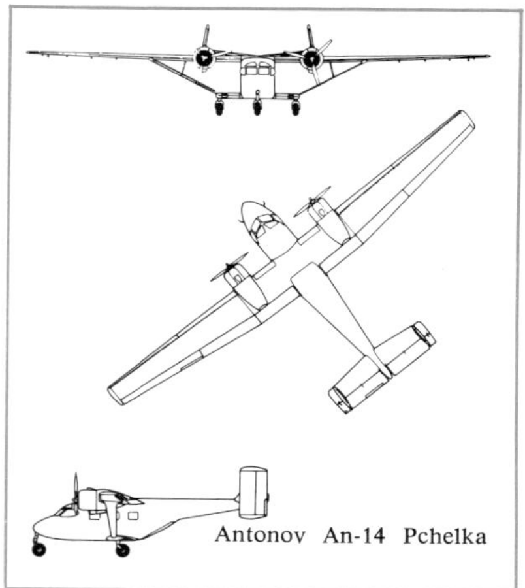

14P and put into service by Aeroflot on 30 November 1954. In 1956 this was followed by the Il-14M with a slightly lengthened fuselage and increased capacity. The next version was the Il-14G which was only used for freight. The Il-14 was exported to Eastern bloc countries and also to Africa and Asia besides being constructed under licence in East Germany and Czechoslovakia; in the latter country they were manufactured by Avia which also developed an executive version (the Avia-14 Salon) and one with a pressurized cabin called the Avia-14 Super in which the passenger capacity was increased to 42.

The Il-12/14 were so successful that they overshadowed other contemporary designs, and one of these was the twin-engine Yak-16, which stood very little chance of being a really competitive aircraft because of its limited passenger capacity and unexciting performance. Although it was an up-to-date design, Aeroflot turned it down on seeing the prototype in 1947 and, in spite of a very energetic sales campaign, it also failed to win any orders from the satellite countries. Only a few Yak-16s were built: some were used on commercial routes, others saw service with the Air Force.

The state airline, Aeroflot, went through a period of such rapid expansion after the war that it needed other types of aircraft apart from freighters and modern passenger aircraft. Thousands of light aircraft were used for countless different purposes and the most outstanding of these was the Antonov An-2, a tough and versatile biplane which first appeared in 1947 and is still in production (at Mielec in Poland, under license) and being flown in many parts of the world. The An-2 has been an absolutely invaluable work-horse, reflected by the number of variants produced, the main versions being the An-2P general transport; the An-2S, M and R for agricultural use; the An-2V seaplane; the An-2L fire-fighting variant and the An-2ZA for meteorological research. Total production has exceeded 12,000 aircraft; 7,500 had been built in Poland alone by the beginning of 1978, quite apart from the many thousands produced by the Soviet aircraft industry and those constructed under license in East Germany and China.

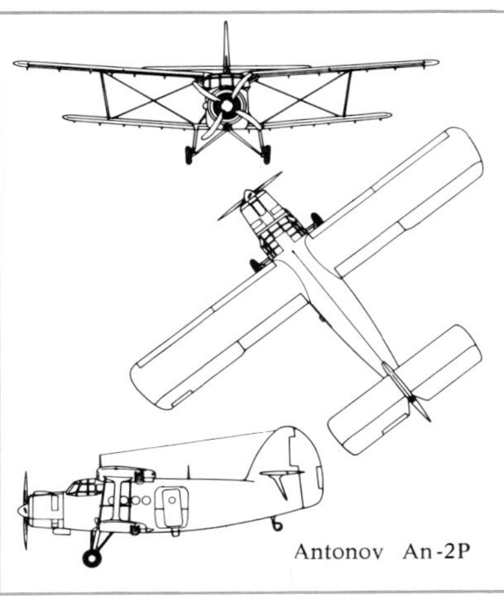
Antonov An-2P

Another versatile aircraft was designed by Antonov in 1957 and named Pchelka (Bee): this was the An-14. The prototype of this little twin-engine monoplane made its first flight on 15 March 1958, but was only put into service in 1965 after protracted development and major modifications to almost every component. The An-14 was built in three basic civil variants: for passenger transport, as an ambulance and for agricultural work.

Plate 136
British and Russian propeller-turbine airliners: 1950–1962

The position of the main competitors in worldwide commercial aviation was to be dramatically altered in 1950 when, after the crisis of the immediately postwar period, the British aircraft industry successfully challenged American dominance. Britain was able to bring off such a coup chiefly because she had led the world in postwar development of new engine technology.

The propeller-turbine represented the transition between the piston-engine and the pure-jet and on 29 July 1950, BEA started a month's trial service on the London–Paris and London–Edinburgh routes using the Vickers-Armstrongs Viscount 630 prototype, the world's first propeller-turbine airliner. A new age had been ushered in by the British aircraft industry and the aeronautical world was soon to follow its lead. The production Viscount went into regular service from 18 April 1953, and from then the European and American airlines sought early delivery of their share of the 445 Viscounts built up till 1959. The V.630 prototype first flew on 16 July 1948, and the prototype V.700 series aircraft on 28 August 1950. The second principal production series, the Viscount 800 of 1956 was a larger version with more powerful engines. A great many variants were manufactured, each specially tailored for customers, and were allotted different design numbers for each operator. At the end of 1981, there were still a hundred Viscounts in service.

During the 1950s other British aircraft manufacturers put some useful propeller-turbine aircraft on the market; one of the best medium-range transports was the Handley Page H.P.R.7 Herald, which was derived from the H.P.R.3 piston-engine prototypes, the first of which made its initial flight on 25 August 1955. The prototype H.P.R.7, better known as the Dart Herald, flew on 11 March 1958. After a batch of four Series 100 aircraft, production switched to the lengthened Series 200 and military Series 400. Only 48 production aircraft were completed and 29 of these were still in service at the end of 1981.

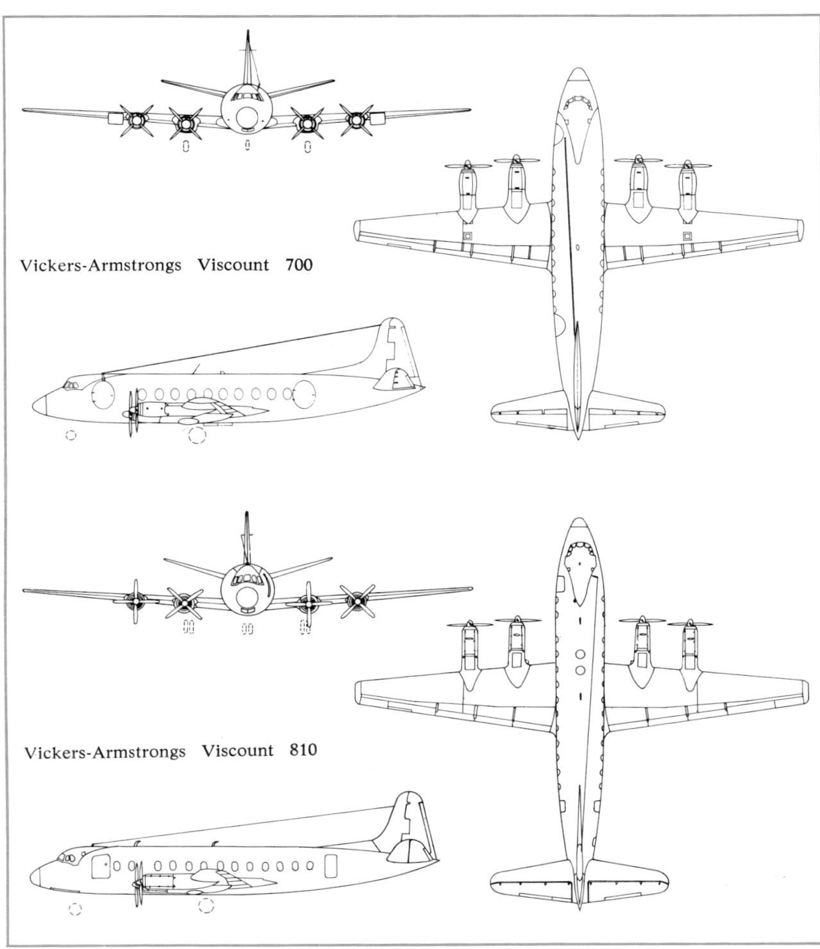
Vickers-Armstrongs Viscount 700

Vickers-Armstrongs Viscount 810

Another propeller-turbine, powered type which was similar, but much more popular, was the Avro 748 which first flew on 24 June 1960, and was the last type to bear the illustrious name of Avro before the company was taken over by Hawker Siddeley. Avro's designers were aiming to produce an aircraft which would enable airlines to keep operating and maintenance costs down and to achieve maximum utilization. The extent to which they succeeded is shown by the aircraft's popularity. Toward the end of 1959, six months before the prototype's first flight, the Indian Government applied for the construction licence, having chosen the 748 as a military transport. This was the first indication of the favorable reception which awaited the 748. Production continued uninterruptedly from 1960. The most important models were the 748 Series 1 (the first version) and the 748 Series 2 of 1961, which was generally improved

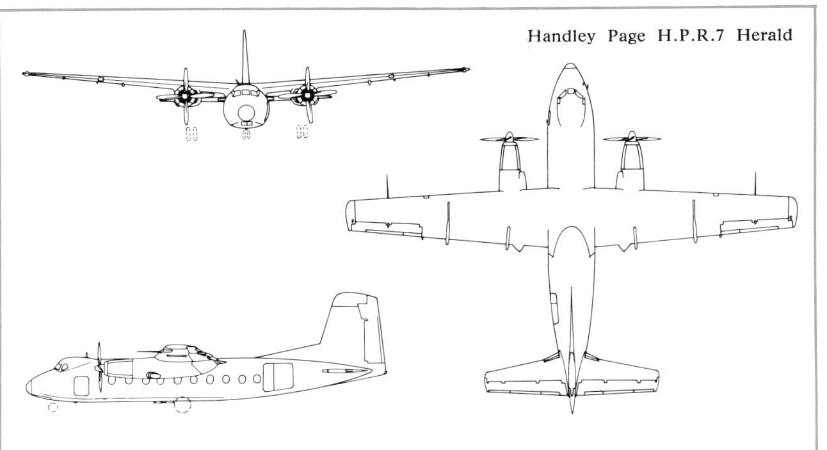
Handley Page H.P.R.7 Herald

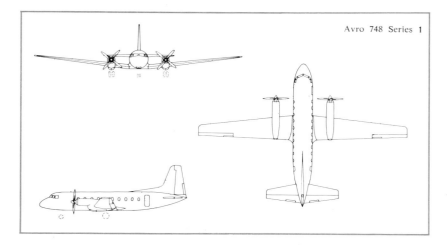

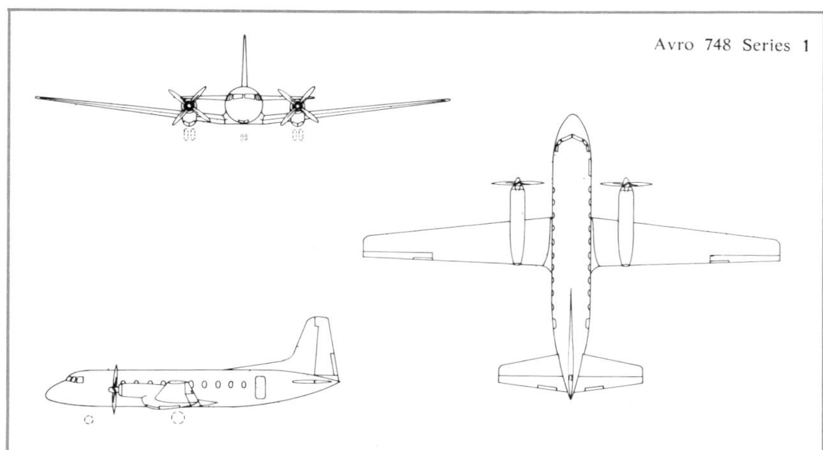
Avro 748 Series 1

and had more powerful engines. By the end of 1981 a total of 360 Avro 748s had been ordered by a variety of airlines and air forces.

The Soviet Union also produced a useful propeller-turbine aircraft in the same category as the Herald and the 748; this was the Antonov An-24, a resilient and versatile twin-engine type, the prototype of which first flew on 20 December 1959, having been designed as a replacement for the aging Ilyushin Il-12 and Ilyushin Il-14. The most important production variants were the An-24V and the An-24TV (the latter being a freighter). Counting militarized variants, more than 1,100 of these twin-engine Antonovs are thought to have been manufactured and well over 800 are still flying in the U.S.S.R., Eastern bloc countries, Cuba, Africa and Asia. The Soviet Union also extended the use of propeller-turbine power to its heavy transport aircraft, and the first belonging to this category, the Antonov An-10, went into service on 22 July 1959. The subsequent, improved An-10A version could carry 100 passengers. Some 300 aircraft are thought to have been built in both versions.

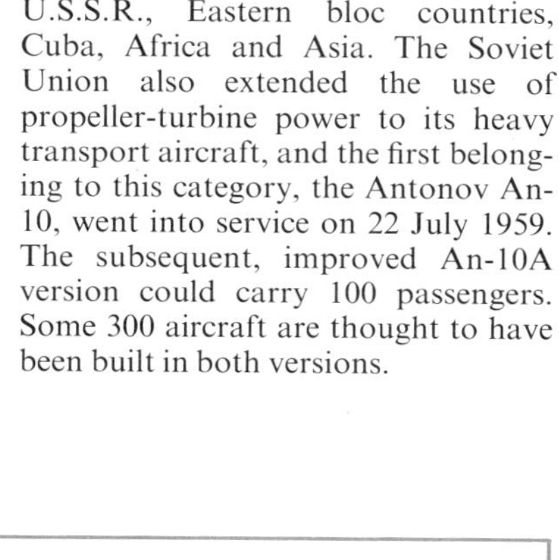

Plate 137
European airlines are first to put jet aircraft into commercial service: 1952–1964

Although jet aircraft form the backbone of the world's airline fleets, it was Great Britain that produced the world's first turbojet airliner, the de Havilland Comet, although the Avro Canada Jetliner flew only two weeks after the first Comet. The Jetliner never entered service but the Comet 1 enjoyed a brilliant success before its promising career ended in disaster.

The story starts in 1942, when the Brabazon Committee recommended its Type IV North Atlantic turbojet mailplane. Numerous designs were produced and rejected and eventually the Comet was designed as a passenger aircraft. The first prototype of the de Havilland D.H.106 Comet flew on 27 July 1949, and was immediately subjected to an exhaustive series of proving trials and then joined by a second prototype on 27 July 1950. In the meantime production of the fourteen aircraft ordered by BOAC (later reduced to nine) and called Comet 1s, went ahead, and the first of these flew in January 1951, and the last in September of the following year. On 2 May 1952, the milestone of the first all-jet commercial flight was passed when BOAC inaugurated its regular Comet passenger service between London and Johannesburg. BOAC and de Havilland appeared to have achieved an outstanding success. Further orders were soon being fulfilled: the Comet 1A (heavier and with greater power) and the Comets 2 and 3 which were still more powerful and had lengthened fuselages. Enthusiasm for the new aircraft was dampened suddenly by a series of seemingly inexplicable accidents which took place on 2 May 1953, 10 January and 8 April 1954, in which three of BOAC's Comets were destroyed. After the second and third accidents the entire fleet of Comets was grounded and an immediate investigation as to the cause of these disconcertingly similar accidents was ordered. In the fall of 1954 the verdict was given: a structural failure due to metal fatigue which led to the disintegration of the fuselage.

De Havilland had to redesign the aircraft before they could resume their production program: the first of the new Comet 4s made its first flight on 27 April 1958, but by this time U.S. jet aircraft, the Boeing 707 and Douglas DC-8, were in production. In spite of this, production of Comet 4s, 4Bs and 4Cs went ahead. The main customers for these Comets, apart from BOAC and BEA, were Greek, Middle East, South American and African airlines.

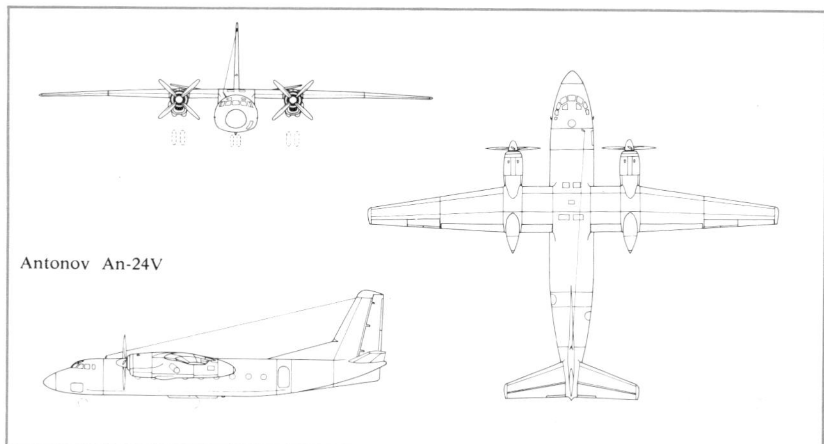
Antonov An-24V

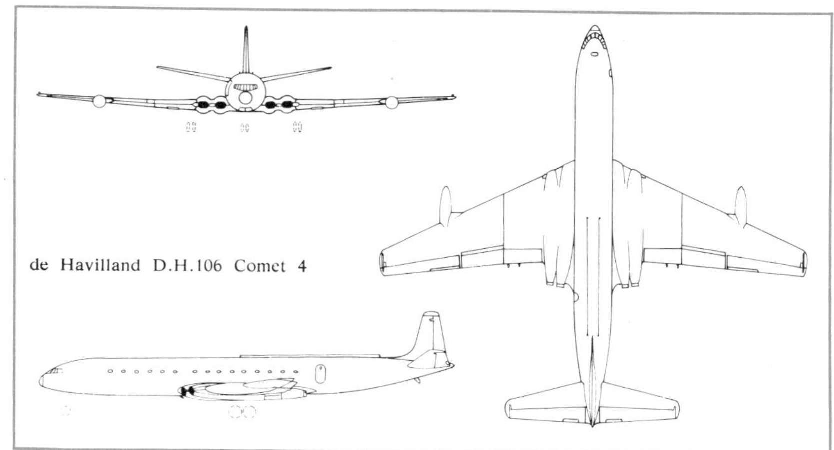
de Havilland D.H.106 Comet 4

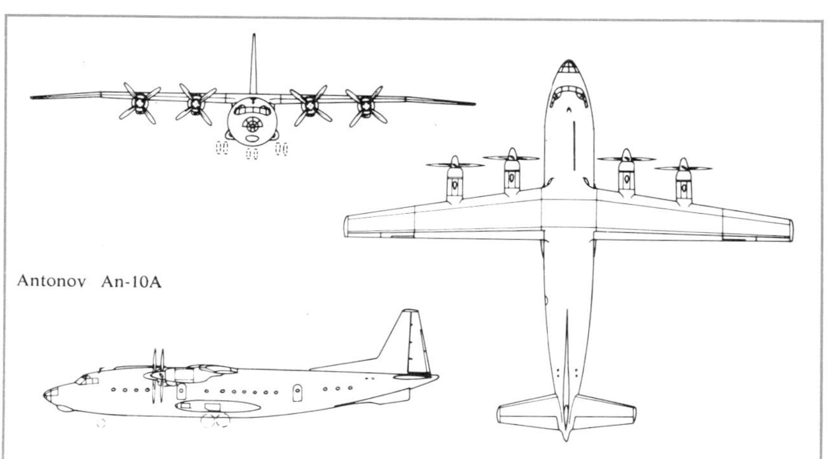
Antonov An-10A

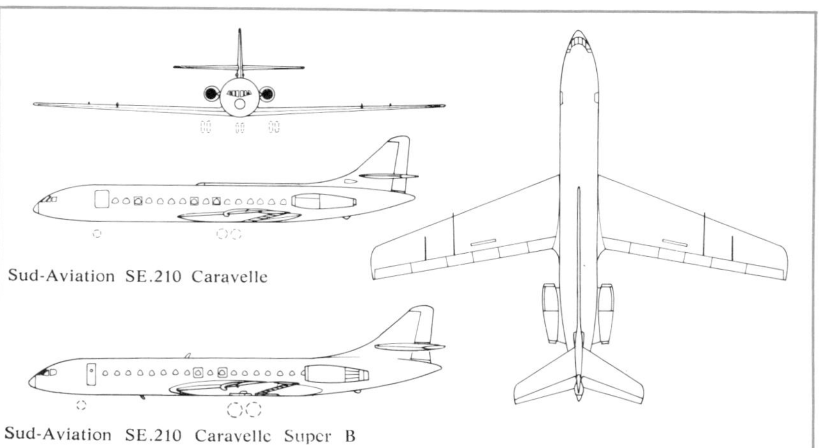
Sud-Aviation SE.210 Caravelle

Sud-Aviation SE.210 Caravelle Super B

The last Comet was only withdrawn from service in November 1980.

The European aeronautical industry was to challenge American dominance again, however, when the French company, Sud-Aviation, produced the SE.210 Caravelle, a versatile and successful twin-jet which was the first to have rear-mounted engines; this became a classic formula for short- to medium-range commercial transport aircraft. The maiden flight of the Caravelle prototype took place on 27 May 1955, only two years after the program had received the go-ahead. Its commercial success was promoted by support from the French Government. The first Series I aircraft were ordered by Air France and put into service on the Paris–Rome–Istanbul route. Other airlines started queuing up to buy the airplane and production was soon in full swing. The next version was the Caravelle IA, which first flew on 11 February 1960, and had modified engines; followed by the Caravelle III (first flight 30 December 1959) which had more powerful engines, increased payload and better performance, entering service with Alitalia on 23 May 1960. The Caravelle VI appeared in 1961 in two versions: the VIN and the VIR; the latter was bought by the American company, United Air Lines. A year later the first production type Caravelle to be powered by American engines (Pratt & Whitney) appeared: this was the Caravelle 10B later known as the 10R. Then came the lengthened Super B, which flew on 3 March 1964. The final stretch of the original design was reached with the Series 11R Freighter and 12B which had longer fuselages and aerodynamic and technical improvements. The prototype of the Caravelle 11 first flew on 21 April 1970, and that of the Caravelle 12 on 29 October 1970. Production ended when 280 Caravelles of all versions had been built.

Plate 138
The Boeing 707 and the Douglas DC-8 win instant popularity: 1957–1967

The United States aircraft industry was to regain the lead in commercial aviation with devastating efficiency. This was achieved by Boeing and Douglas who must both take credit for having put the first economically viable and reliable jet aircraft on to the Western market. These two airplanes, the 707 and the DC-8, dominated the world of air transport for several years. The first of the two to go into regular airline service was the Boeing production model 707-120 on 26 October 1958, in the livery of Pan American. Boeing had started work on the design in the early 1950s, when they were already well ahead with production of the B-47 bomber. The experience and technological knowledge which had been acquired through the military production program contributed a great deal to the development of the commercial model, although a damper was put on progress for a while by the civil market's slowness in realizing the potential of this revolutionary aircraft when it was still in the early stage of its development. Boeing decided to make a logical, though financially extremely risky decision and in April 1952 authorized the expenditure of $16,000,000 to go ahead with the project. It was a carefully calculated risk and the prototype (designated Model 367-80 but known as "Dash Eighty") was built in great secrecy, flew for the first time on 15 July 1954, and went on to complete a long and demanding series of operational tests. The first positive reaction came from the U.S.A.A.F., which in September 1954 ordered 29 aircraft for use as flying tankers (KC-135). This was the first of a long succession of military orders and also the beginning of the aircraft's successful commercial career.

Boeing was inundated with orders. The first was from Pan American which ordered twenty Boeing 707s on 13 October 1955; three years later orders totaled 184. By April 1967, 568 Boeing 707s in the various production models had been delivered and a further 150 were on order. All in all—if one includes the aircraft's "younger brother," the 720—production reached a total of 962 airplanes. The principal series models were the 707-120 (first flight 20 December 1957) and the 707-320 (11 January 1959), the latter being larger with increased range and capacity for intercontinental flights. There were many sub-series, which were designated according to the engines used and whether the aircraft had main deck cargo-carrying capacity. At the end of 1981 over 500 Boeing 707s and 720s were still in regular airline service.

The Boeing 707's direct rival was the Douglas DC-8, the second commercial jet aircraft produced by the United States, which proved to be just as competitive and effective, posing a certain threat to the Boeing jet. The decision to go ahead was announced on 7 June 1955, and Douglas profited from strong demand for this type of aircraft, focusing its efforts on one basic design, which was only altered in the mid-1960s when Douglas produced the three variants of the Series 60. Two of these had a fuselage lengthened by more than 36 ft (11 m) which almost doubled the aircraft's capacity. The DC-8-10 prototype was followed by the first models of four other basic production series: the DC-8-20 which had more powerful engines; the DC-8-

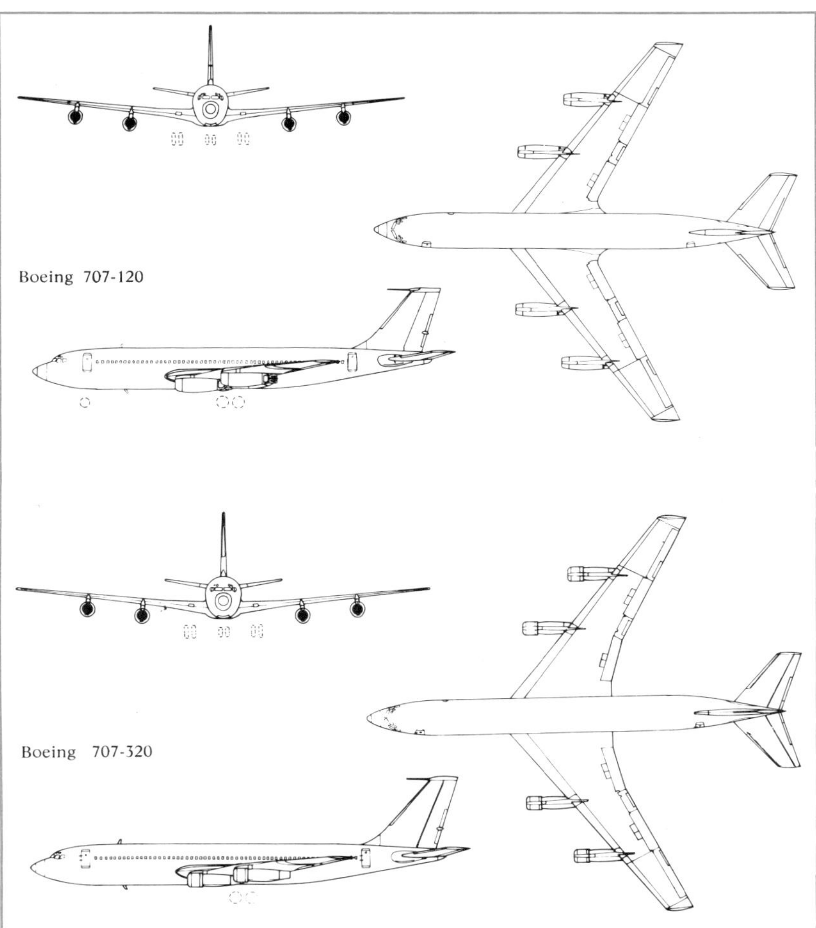

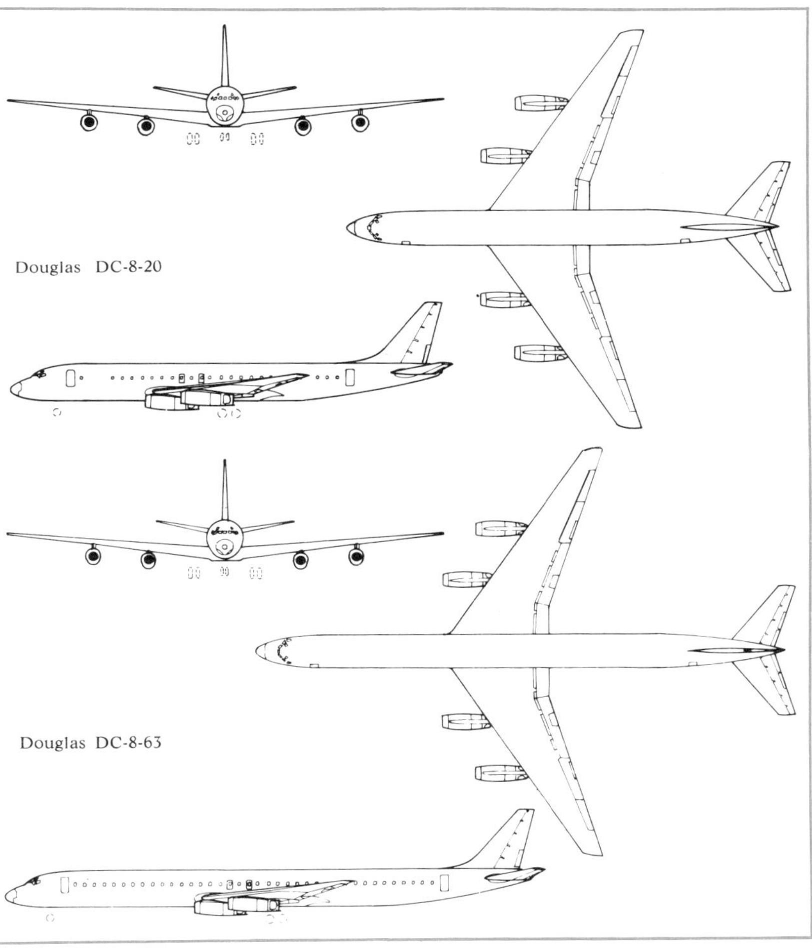

30 for intercontinental routes (first flight 20 February 1959); the DC-8-40, powered by Rolls-Royce Conway engines (23 July 1959); and the DC-8-50 which had Pratt & Whitney turbofans: the first of the -50s first took to the air on 20 December 1960. Once again Pan American was the first airline to ask for the DC-8, ordering 25 in October 1955, and its commercial success was such that by the time the prototype first flew, orders for a total of 130 airplanes had already been placed. In all, 294 DC-8s, comprising aircraft from Series 10 to 50, were built. A new momentum was given to DC-8 production when, in April 1965, Douglas announced three new, lengthened fuselage versions: the DC-8-61 which first flew on 14 March 1966; the DC-8-62 (first flight 29 August) which had a different wing; and the DC-8-63 which adopted the modifications of the two earlier models. 262 of these versions of the DC-8 were manufactured, including all cargo variants. They were even more successful than the early production series, mainly because of their outstanding ratio of payload to range. When the last DC-8 was delivered in 1972 a total of 556 had been built. More than 300 were still in service at the beginning of 1982.

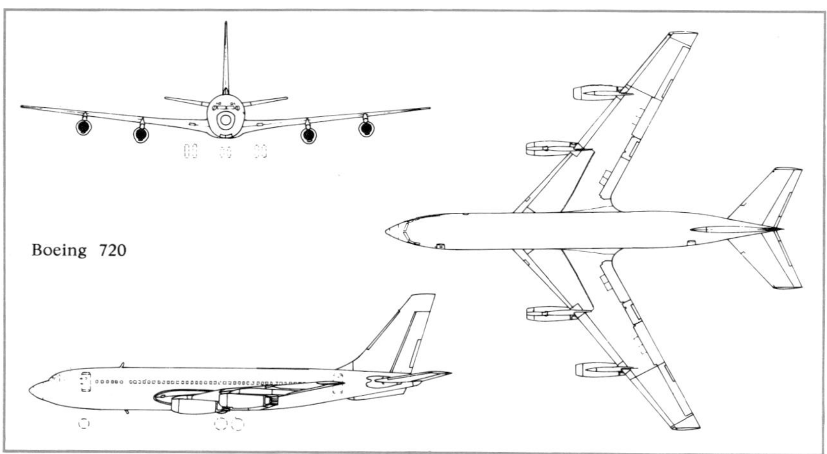
Boeing 720

Plate 139
American and Russian medium-range jetliners: 1957–1960

The Boeing 720 was the third successful model based on the four-engine 707 and was designed as a short- to medium-haul aircraft capable of using shorter runways. The announcement of the plans for an addition to the Boeing "family" was made in July 1957, and the prototype first flew on 23 November 1959. It was an immediate commercial success and United was the first airline to put 720s into service, on 5 July 1960, eventually taking delivery of a total of 29 aircraft. The other main U.S. airlines soon followed suit and used the 720 for domestic flights. The aircraft was further developed and the 720B version (October 1960) had JT3D-1 turbofans, which reduced fuel consumption and consequently increased the airplane's range. The 720B was first used on 12 March 1961, on American Airline's services, but it was particularly popular with foreign buyers. A total of 154 Boeing 720s and 720Bs was built and about half of these were still in airline service at the start of 1982.

Another major American company decided to compete for the medium-range market. Convair chose their four-engine CV-880 to challenge Boeing's and Douglas's hold on the market. This type was very similar in appearance to the Boeing 707. The maiden flight of the prototype took place on 27 January 1959, and although the aircraft showed that it had extremely good overall performance, particularly where speed was concerned, the Convair CV-880 never managed to capture a worthwhile share of sales. Sixty-five 880s were built (20 of which were the intercontinental M variant) and these were eventually operated by the smaller airline companies. It was followed by the Convair CV-990, a more powerful version, which first flew on 24 January 1961, only 37 of which were built, 11 of which remained in service in 1981.

The U.S.S.R. took second place in the race to put the first commercial jet into service and gained tremendous prestige through this achievement. Although the Comet was the first jet airliner to enter regular service, the Tupolev Tu-104 (which went into service on 15 September 1956) was to benefit from the difficulties encountered by the de Havilland aircraft and until the Comet was put back into regular service on 4 October 1958, the Tu-104 was the only jet airliner in service. The design began in 1953 and progress was speeded up by using

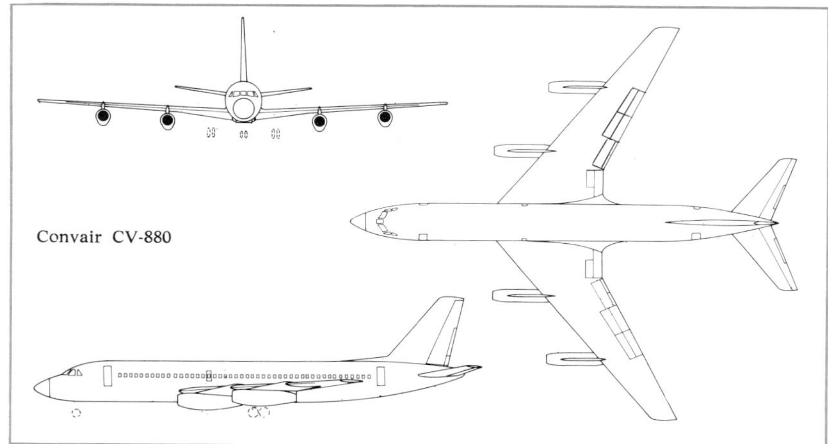
Convair CV-880

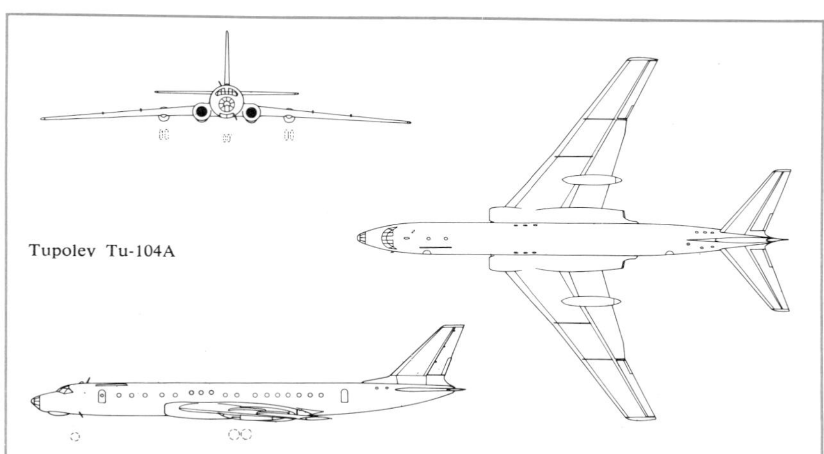
Tupolev Tu-104A

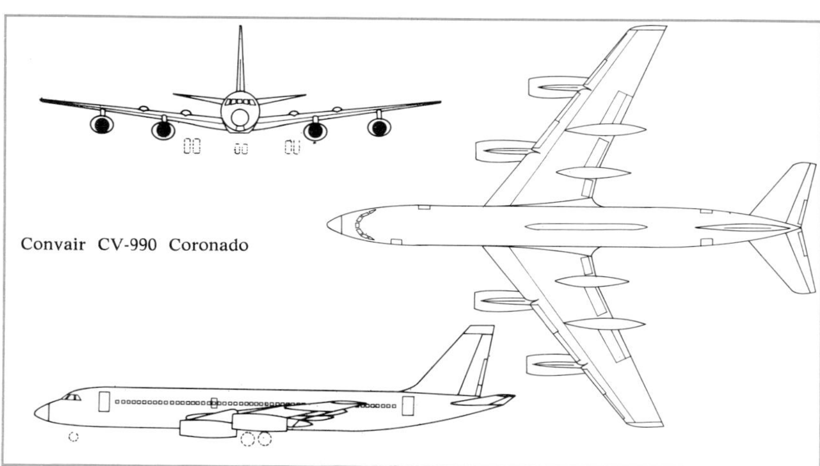
Convair CV-990 Coronado

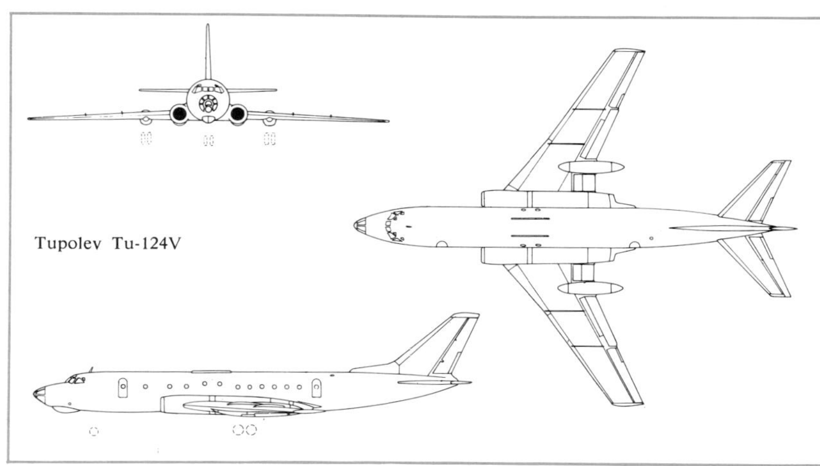
Tupolev Tu-124V

structural experience gained during production of the Tu-16 bomber and by the use of Tu-16 components married to a new fuselage. The Tu-104 prototype made its maiden flight on 17 June 1955, and on 3 July was put on display at Tushino airport. Eight months later the prototype was flown to London and duly impressed Western observers. The regular service on the Moscow–Omsk–Irkutsk route with this aircraft was inaugurated on 15 September 1956. Only twenty of the first Tu-104 were built; they were soon followed on the production lines by the second version, the Tu-104A, with increased capacity and more powerful engines. The prototype of this new production series was displayed in June 1957, and showed its mettle by setting a number of records for its category. On 6 September it set a new payload to altitude record: 44,209 lb (20,053 kg) to 6,561 ft (2,000 m) and an altitude record: 36,814 ft (11,221 m). On 11 September there followed the 1,242-mile (2,000-km) circuit speed record with loads of 2,200 lb and 4,400 lb (1,000 kg and 2,000 kg) at 557.67 mph (897.498 km/h). The following year the final production variant, the Tu-104B, made its appearance. It had almost double the capacity of the original model and even more powerful engines than the Tu-104A. These Tupolevs went into service on the Moscow–Leningrad route on 15 April 1959, and joined the two previous versions of the airplane on the most important routes handled by Aeroflot. It is thought that production of all three models exceeded 200.

Armed with two years' experience in operating a jet airliner, Aeroflot proceeded to order a smaller capacity short- to medium-range jet aircraft. Once again, Tupolev produced a design, which, although it was effectively just a scaled-down version of the Tu-104, was more impressive since it was powered by the new turbofans. The Tu-124 prototype took to the air in June 1960 and started its career in Aeroflot's fleet on 2 October 1962, flying between Moscow and Tallinn. Aeroflot took delivery of almost all the approximately 100 built. Use of the Tu-124 soon became widespread and in 1964 the network of routes covered by these aircraft totaled 22,725 miles (36,570 km). Two years later the Tu-124s were being used on more than 70 routes and in 1966 alone they carried two million passengers. The Czechoslovak airline CSA operated three 124s, as did Interflug and the Indian Air Force. Iraqi Airways is reported to have had two.

Plate 140
Propeller-turbine freighters: 1959–1970

Passenger transport was not the only sector of commercial aviation to feel the benefits of propeller-turbine power. At the same time aircraft were being built specifically for cargo transport—although many were mixed configuration types which could be used for freight, or passengers or both. A new generation of airplanes took their place in commercial aviation and propeller-turbine power proved particularly suitable for this type of aircraft. The first propeller-turbine powered freighter was British, the Armstrong Whitworth A.W.650 Argosy. The project had been launched in 1956 and the prototype made its first flight two years later, on 8 January 1958. Armstrong Whitworth were confident of the commercial potential of their new four-engine aircraft and went straight ahead with preparing a production line for ten aircraft. This policy was amply justified when an order was placed for four (later increased to seven) of the first Argosy production model aircraft (the Series 100) by the American company, Riddle Airlines, who put them into service on 15 January 1961. At the end of 1960 BEA decided to take a greater part in the air freight market and in April 1961 ordered the remaining three Argosy Series 100 aircraft. BEA's aircraft took the designation 102. Later BEA traded in its Series 100 aircraft and took six of the heavier and more powerful Series 200. The biggest order was the R.A.F.'s, for 56 A.W.660 Argosy C Mk.1s.

The Soviet Union placed very heavy demands on designers and manufacturers to provide the great numbers of large freighters and mixed traffic aircraft which she needed so badly. Oleg Antonov specialized in this type of aircraft and his An-12 was for bulky cargo, and was developed shortly after the previous model, the capacious An-10. Most of the An-12s were for military use, but a certain number were used by Aeroflot. The specialized civil variant was designated An-12B and started regular cargo flights between Moscow and Paris on 3 February 1966. A year later the aircraft was put into service on the longest and most important domestic flights in the Soviet Union. The An-12s also saw more international service when they were later flown on the Moscow–Djakarta route.

Among the many cargo transports built were the quite remarkable Guppy aircraft produced by Aero Spacelines from 1962 onward. These aircraft were conversions of the old four piston-engine Boeing 377 Stratocruiser and were invaluable for transporting outsize loads, such as ballistic missiles and

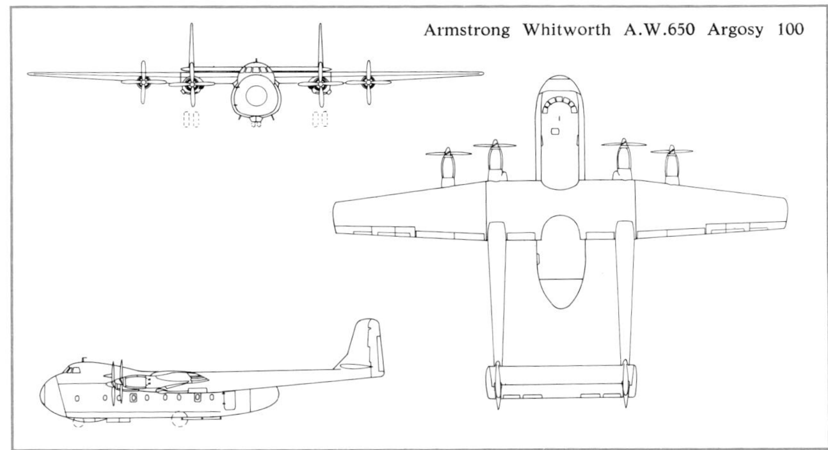
Armstrong Whitworth A.W.650 Argosy 100

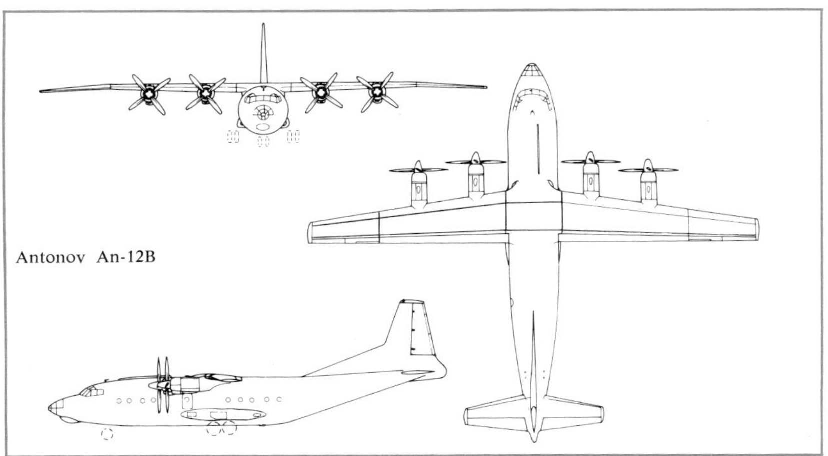
Antonov An-12B

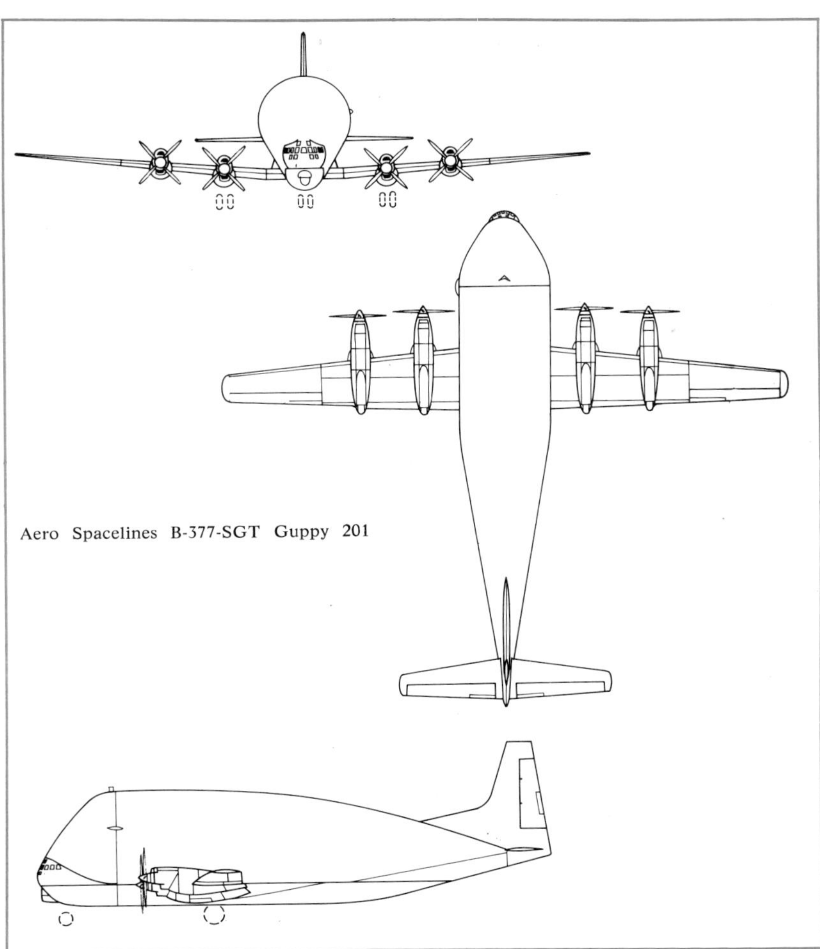
Aero Spacelines B-377-SGT Guppy 201

aircraft fuselages which could be stowed comfortably in the enormous fuselage. Only a small number was built.

It was the particular function of transporting the various stage rockets used in the N.A.S.A. space program which led to Aero Spacelines launching the Guppy project. The first two Guppies built were the B-377PG Pregnant Guppy (first flight 19 September 1962) and the B-377SG Super Guppy (first flight 31 August 1965). These two aircraft had differing fuselages, engines and loading bays; the former, the B377PG, had a removable rear fuselage; the B-377SG had a hinged nose. The Super Guppy was powered by four 7,000-eshp Pratt & Whitney T34 propeller-turbines and could carry both the third stage of the Saturn V rocket and the lunar module at the same time. N.A.S.A. and the Defense Department used these outsize transports a great deal and this encouraged Aero Spacelines to put three other models into production, varying mainly in size, weight, power-plant and capacity. These were the B-377MG Mini Guppy (which first flew on 24 May 1967), powered by piston engines like the original 377, and with a hinged rear fuselage for loading; then came the B-377SGT Guppy-201 (first flight 24 August 1970), powered by four 4,912-eshp Allison 501 propeller-turbines, and which had a hinged forward fuselage for easy loading. The next model was the B-377MG-101 which was in fact a Mini Guppy powered by propeller-turbines and which appeared on 13 March 1970. Among the Guppy's more noteworthy uses was for transporting the fuselage and components of Concorde and the A300 Airbus between factories and assembly lines.

Plate 141
Short- to medium-range twin-engine propeller-turbine transports: 1958–1967

Turning to passenger transport, in this category the propeller-turbine powered aircraft not only fared well in competition with the turbojet aircraft, but was actually preferred for the medium-capacity short- to medium-range routes. At the beginning of the 1980s the Fokker F.27 Friendship is still regarded as the most successful example of this type of aircraft and is still in production and very widely used, more than twenty-five years after the flight of the first prototype. By the end of 1981, sales had reached more than 730 (including 206 built under licence by Fairchild in the United States) and Fokker still have no plans to terminate the program.

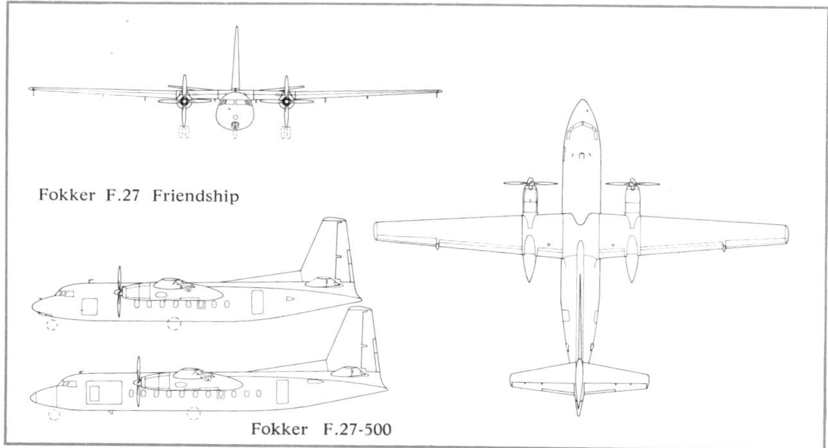
Fokker F.27 Friendship
Fokker F.27-500

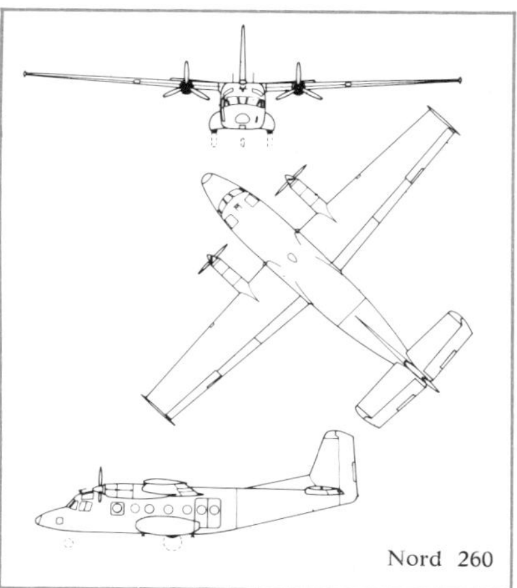
Nord 260

The project was launched at the beginning of the 1950s and progressed rapidly. Starting in May 1951, a long series of wind-tunnel tests was carried out and in 1952 a mock-up fuselage was built. The need to meet deadlines meant that in 1953 the decision was taken to build four prototypes (two flying aircraft and two test structures). The first of these made a satisfactory maiden flight on 24 November 1955.

By this time its commercial success was already assured and, by the spring of 1956, thirty F.27s had already been ordered. In April of that same year Fokker entered into a license agreement with Fairchild in the U.S.A. Series production of the F.27 was started almost simultaneously in the Netherlands and the U.S.A. The first Dutch production F.27-100 flew on 23 March 1958, followed in April by the first Fairchild aircraft. The most important later Series were the F.27-200 (the F.27A in the United States) which had up-rated power units; the F.27-300 and the F.27-400 (F.27B and C respectively in U.S. designations). These models were more versatile, having a large freight loading door in the forward fuselage to permit mixed passenger and freight operations. The next version was the F.27-500 which appeared in November 1967 and had a stretched fuselage, but apart from this resembled the Series 200; this was followed by the F.27-600 (first flight 28 November 1968) which was a development of the F.27-200 and had a large freight door. The military versions were the 500M and the 600M and the Maritime, which was designed for marine patrol and reconnaissance. The prototype of the Maritime model appeared on 25 March 1976. By the middle of 1980 orders had been received from Spain, the Philippines and the Netherlands.

Aérospatiale's N.262 was in the same class as the Fokker Friendship, but not nearly so successful. The original M.H.250 project had been started in 1957 by Avions Max Holste and was a high-wing, twin piston-engine aircraft seating up to twenty-two passengers. After the prototype's maiden flight on 20 May 1959, it was decided that a propeller-turbine variant (the M.H.260) should be developed and this first flew on 29 July 1960. Due to lack of orders, production came to an end when ten had been built and in the spring of 1961 Nord-Aviation, which had taken over the project, developed a new version which was more powerful, generally improved and pressurized. The Nord 262 prototype flew on 24 December 1962, and the production line was soon busy with a series of orders, one of which was for twelve aircraft from Lake Central Airlines in the U.S.A. There were 100 production Nord 262s including A, B, C and D models. Numbers of Nord 262Cs and Ds were modified, given up-rated engines and named Frégate. Finally some of the A series aircraft were re-engined for Allegheny Airlines and redesignated Mohawk 298.

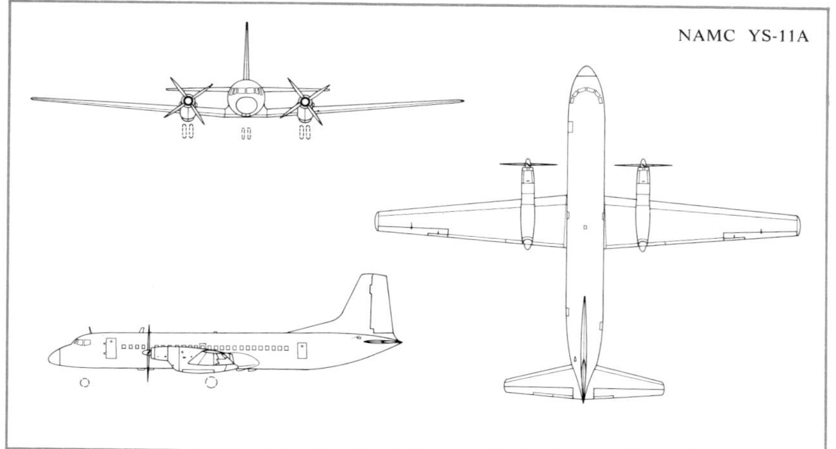
NAMC YS-11A

Japan also wanted to develop a short- to medium-range civil airliner and at the beginning of the 1960s decided to try to produce an effective commercial transport powered by two propeller-turbines. This resulted in the NAMC YS-11, the prototype of which flew on 30 August 1962. A financial consortium was formed by six major companies in which the Japanese Government had a majority shareholding, while the six companies shared manufacturing activities in proportion to their shareholdings.

Production was halted after 182 YS-11s had been built and these were quite well received in the market. The main series models were the YS-11-100 (first flight 23 October 1964) which could seat 60 passengers and of which production continued until October 1967, forty-seven production aircraft and two prototypes being built, of which six were completed as troop carriers; and the YS-11A-200 (first flight 22 November 1967). This version had more powerful engines, and seventy-five of them were built, four being A.S.W. versions for the naval wing of the Self-Defense Force. From these a small number of the YS-11A-300 mixed-traffic version (first flight in the summer of 1968) were derived, which could accommodate forty-six passengers; this was followed by the YS-11A-400 (which first took to the air on 17 September 1969) in all-cargo configuration, and the YS-1A-500 and 600, both of which had greatly increased payloads. Deliveries of YS-11s to operators started in March 1965, and apart from the Japanese airlines, these included Olympic Airways of Athens which took six and the American line, Piedmont, which bought twenty-one.

Plate 142
Large propeller-turbine transports: 1952–1961

Long-range, high-density commercial aviation did not offer a great deal of scope for propeller-turbine powered aircraft. Although they were reliable, the pure-jet had such an advantage over them in terms of speed that inevitably this new power unit would be used for long-distance and intercontinental flights. The golden age of the propeller-turbine can therefore be said to have lasted for about ten years from the mid-fifties to the mid-sixties. The best Western-produced propeller-turbine powered aircraft were without doubt of British design and manufacture. The first four-engine aircraft in this category to fly a regular service was the Bristol 175 Britannia.

In 1947 BOAC issued a specification for a Medium Range Empire (MRE) transport and Bristol designed a piston-engine aircraft to meet this requirement. The design was steadily developed and, in July 1949, a contract was signed for 25, initially having Centaurus sleeve-valve engines, but later Proteus propeller-turbines. In the following year BOAC asked that the aircraft, the Bristol 175, should be delivered with Proteus engines and the prototype Britannia 101 first flew on 16 August 1952. BOAC received its first two production Britannia 102s on 30 December 1955, and after icing problems were cured, the type entered service on the London–Johannesburg route on 1 February 1957. Meanwhile BOAC had ordered a fleet of the longer and heavier Britannia 312s for North Atlantic services. The prototype Britannia 310 flew on 31 December 1956 and, on 19 December 1957, BOAC began nonstop London–New York services with the Britannia. Britannias were also delivered to several other airlines including El Al, Canadian Pacific, Cubana and Ghana Airways, and the Royal Air Force employed a fleet of twenty-three Britannia 253s. Although the Britannia was a superb airplane it appeared too late and only 85 were built. Ten remained in airline service at the end of 1981.

The Vickers-Armstrongs Vanguard was even less successful commercially, mainly due to increasing competition from pure-jets and because it was regarded as too big for its time. The Vanguard was first envisaged in 1951 as a successor to the Viscount. Only forty-four of these four-engine aircraft were completed and these were bought by just two major airlines, BEA and the Canadian airline, TCA, although later most passed to smaller operators. The program was assured on 20 July 1956, when BEA placed an order for twenty of the initial Vanguard 951 series. While the factory was fulfilling this order, Vickers proposed a variant with increased capacity, the 952, which appealed to TCA and, in January 1957, this airline ordered twenty of this model (another three were ordered later). In July 1958 Vickers announced the Type 953 with reduced range but increased payload, and BEA revised its order to six Type 951 and fourteen Type 953. The Vanguard prototype first flew on 20 January 1959, and the initial series aircraft began *ad hoc* service with BEA on 17 December 1960. On 1 May 1961, the Vanguard 953 made its first flight and BEA received its last aircraft, completing its order, on 30 March of the following year. TCA had taken delivery of its first Vanguard 952 at the end of 1960 and had put it into service on 1 February 1961. As the jet aircraft made its presence increasingly widely felt, many of these Vanguards were relegated to use as freighters.

In the United States commercial propeller-turbine powered aircraft were never really highly regarded. The first U.S. transport aircraft of this type was the Lockheed 188 Electra, designed in 1955, and 170 were built in two variants: the Models 188A and the 188C, which differed in range and weight. The prototype's first flight took place on 6 December 1957. Commercial success seemed assured: by the end of 1957 there were 144 aircraft on order, but a few months after the Lockheed Electra went into service with Eastern Air Lines (12 January 1959) and American Airlines (23 January 1959) two serious accidents revealed structural weaknesses in the Electra's wing and production was halted. Only in January 1961 was Lockheed able to go ahead with a program of recalling and strengthening those aircraft already in service and modifying the Electras which were still in production. Following the accidents a speed restriction had been put on the Electra and from then no further orders were placed, although the highly successful Orion military variant is still in production. More than half the Electras built were still in airline service at the beginning of 1982.

The Soviet Union managed to produce satisfactory propeller-turbine powered aircraft of this type. The Ilyushin Il-18 was very similar to the Electra and 565 were manufactured, nearly four hundred of which went to Aeroflot during the expansion of its route network and the remainder went for export. The project was launched in late 1954 and the first prototype flew on 4 July 1957. Series production soon reached high levels and Aeroflot put its new airplanes into service on 20 April 1959. After small numbers of the original model, the principal variants were the 18V of 1962, with greater capacity; the D of 1965 and the E, both

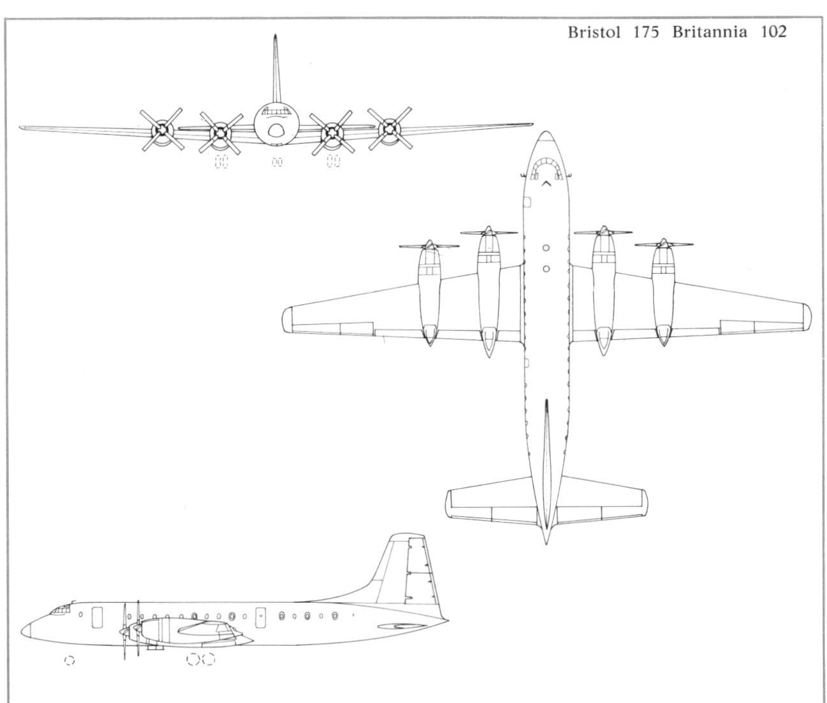
Bristol 175 Britannia 102

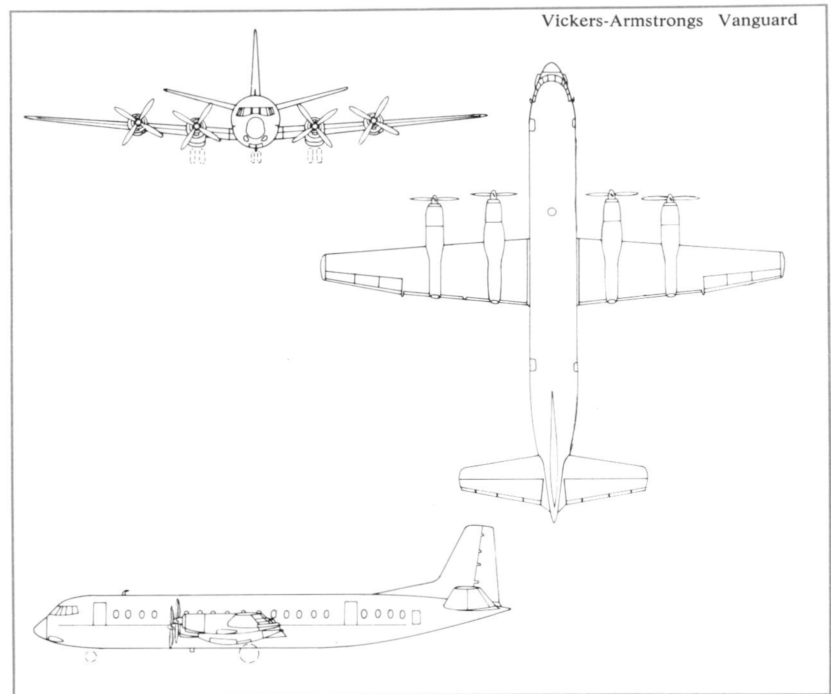
Vickers-Armstrongs Vanguard

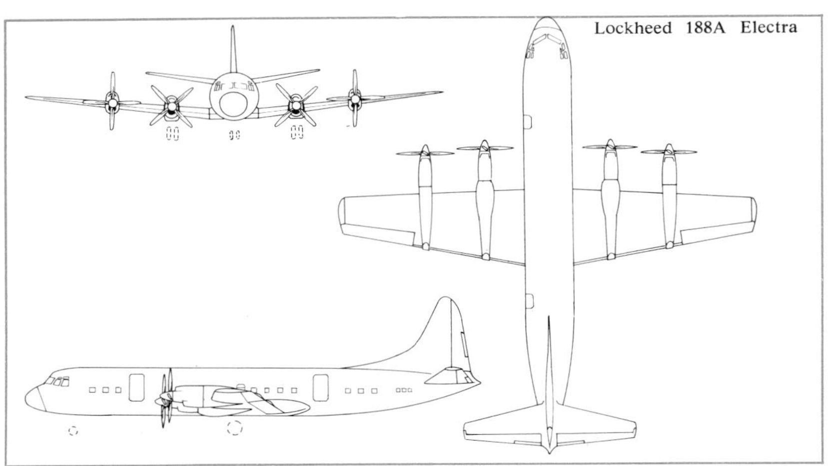
Lockheed 188A Electra

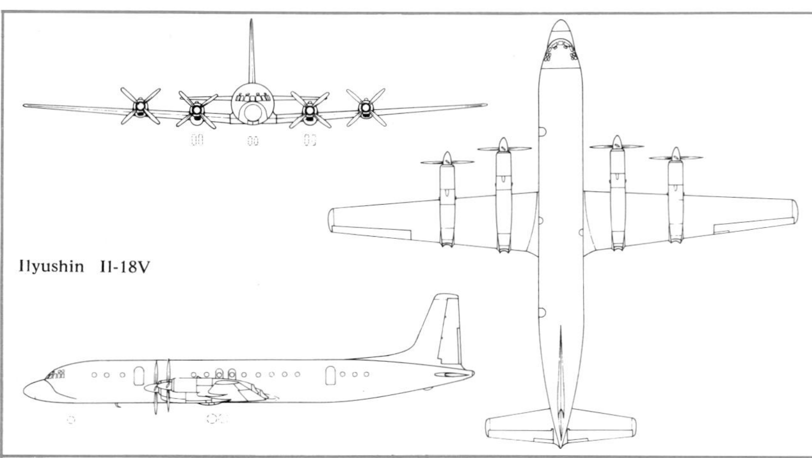
Ilyushin Il-18V

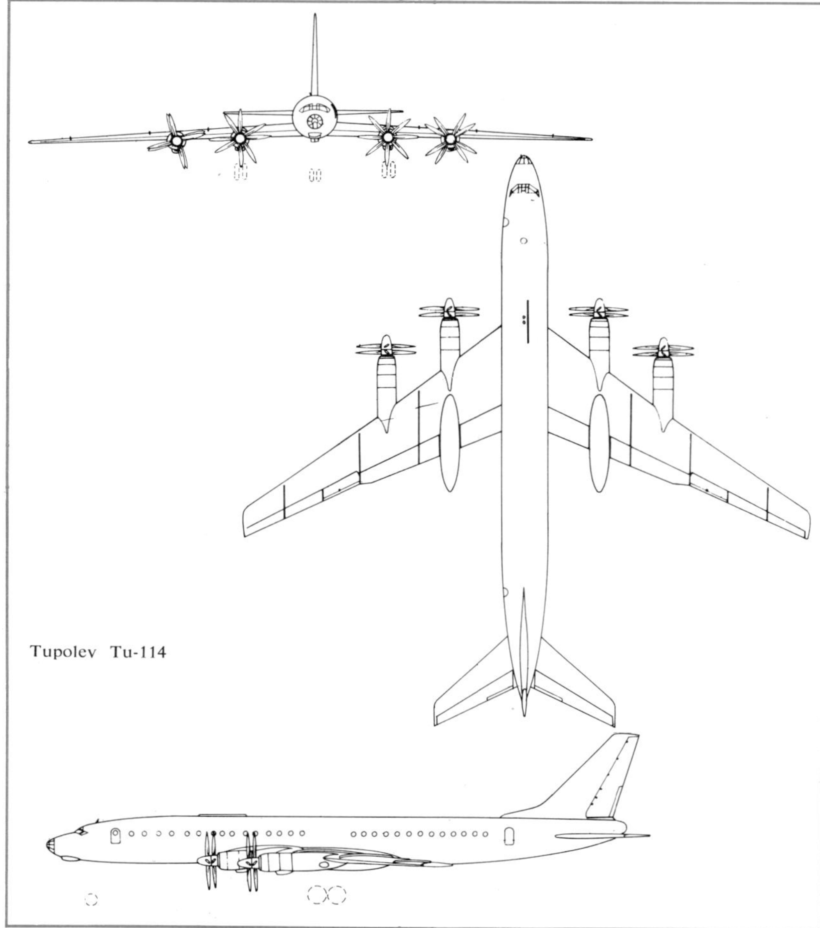
Tupolev Tu-114

of which had up-dated equipment and differing layouts. The Il-18D series had engines with improved fuel consumption and had much longer range.

The largest of all was the Tupolev Tu-114, very large four-engine airplane derived from the Tu-94 bomber, which when it first flew on 3 October 1957, was the heaviest commercial aircraft in the world. Aeroflot put the Tu-114 into regular airline service on 24 April 1961, between Moscow and Khabarovsk, near the Chinese border, and it covered the 4,287 miles (6,900 km) in 8 hours 15 minutes. Over the next few years the Tu-114 was introduced on a number of international routes: from Moscow to Havana and to Delhi in 1963; Moscow to Accra in 1965 and to Montreal in 1966; and in 1967 from Moscow to Tokyo. From the fall of 1967 onward, these Tu-114s (about thirty of which were manufactured) were gradually replaced by the four-jet Ilyushin Il-62. A mixed mail and freight variant of the Tu-114 was produced: the Tu-114D, three of which were built and which had very long range: 6,200 miles (10,000 km).

Plate 143
Rear-engine T-tail airliners: 1963–1971

The construction formula which had been introduced at the beginning of the 1950s in the French Caravelle with its rear-mounted twin jets was widely copied. The Caravelle's keenest competitor was the American Douglas DC-9, an extremely successful aircraft, over one thousand of which had been built by the end of 1980, with plans for production to continue in the years to come.

Douglas announced its intention to produce the DC-9 in 1963 and the first prototype flew on 25 February 1965. At the time of that first flight, Douglas had orders for only 58 DC-9s from six airlines, less than half the number of orders for the DC-8 when it first flew. There was no indication then of the enormous success this aircraft was destined to achieve. Since its inception the DC-9 has undergone continuous development and the sales success was mainly due to the introduction of the higher capacity versions. The basic variants were: the DC-9-10 (first flight 1965), 90 seats; the DC-9-20 (18 September 1968) which was specially designed to operate from short runways and of the same capacity; the DC-9-30 (1 August 1966) with a longer fuselage and increased wingspan, seating 115 passengers—this was the variant built in the greatest numbers, nearly 600 were manufactured. Then came the DC-9-40 (28 November 1967) seating 125; the DC-9-50 (17 December 1974) with an even longer fuselage and 139 seats. In October, 1977 a major up-dating program was undertaken with the construction of the Super 80; the fuselage in this variant was lengthened by just over fourteen feet (more than four meters) compared with the DC-9-50, which increased seating capacity to a maximum of 172; the wing was redesigned and made more aerodynamically efficient; Pratt & Whitney JT8D-209 low-consumption, low-decibel engines were installed. The first DC-9 Super 80 was delivered on 12 September 1980, to Swissair.

The British BAC One-Eleven twin-jet was designed in 1961 and more than two hundred have been completed in five basic variants. The first version, the Series 200, made its first flight in prototype form on 20 August 1963, and the type entered service with British United Airways in 1965. The Series 200 was followed by a small batch of Series 300s which had more powerful engines and increased fuel capacity. On 13 July 1965, the One-Eleven Series 400 prototype was flown—this was for the American market. The Series 500 (which made its maiden flight on 30 June 1967) had a considerably lengthened fuselage, a redesigned wing, increased capacity and more powerful engines. The One-Eleven Series 475 prototype flew on 27 August 1970, combining the wing and engines of the Series 500 with the fuselage of the Series 400, making the aircraft more versatile since it could be used on Class 2 airfields.

The Russians also followed the fashion set by the Caravelle when they built the Tupolev Tu-134 in 1964. After a series of experimental flights on internal Aeroflot routes, the Tu-134 was put on to international services starting in September 1967. Three years later a second version (the Tu-134A) entered service, with a lengthened fuselage, increased seating, more powerful engines and better overall performance.

The most recent twin-jet of this type is the Dutch Fokker F.28 Fellowship, a short-range aircraft which Fokker built in 1962 in the hopes of repeating their success with the F.27. By the end of 1981, 189 of these aircraft had been ordered by more than fifty operators from a wide variety of nations and the manufacturer's production projections envisage a total of 230 by 1985. The F.28 prototype flew for the first time on 9 May 1967, and production allowed for continual up-dating such as had been the case with the DC-9, in order to increase the aircraft's capacity and versatility; this gave rise to varying fuselage lengths, differing wings and up-rated engines. The main series models were the initial version, the F.28-1000, seating 65 passengers; the F.28-2000 (maiden flight 28 April 1971) which had a longer fuselage and could seat 79 passengers; the F.28-4000 (20 October 1976), which was even longer, had more powerful engines and wings of improved aerodynamic efficiency. This model could seat 85 passengers. It was from this series that the F.28-3000 was derived, which returned to the standard fuselage of the initial series; the final variants are the Series 5000 and the Series 6000 (the prototype first flew on 27 September 1973) which were still further improved and more powerful.

The British Vickers-Armstrongs VC10 and the Soviet Ilyushin Il-62 both had four rear-mounted engines and had many other features in common. The VC10 was the earlier type, built at the beginning of the 1960s. The program had been launched in May 1957, and work was started on construction of the prototype in January 1959. After its first flight (29 June 1962) production got under way on twelve aircraft ordered by BOAC, two for Ghana Airways and three for BUA; these aircraft differed in structural details and were classified as the Series 1100. In order to satisfy the demand for increased capacity, particularly on North Atlantic routes, a

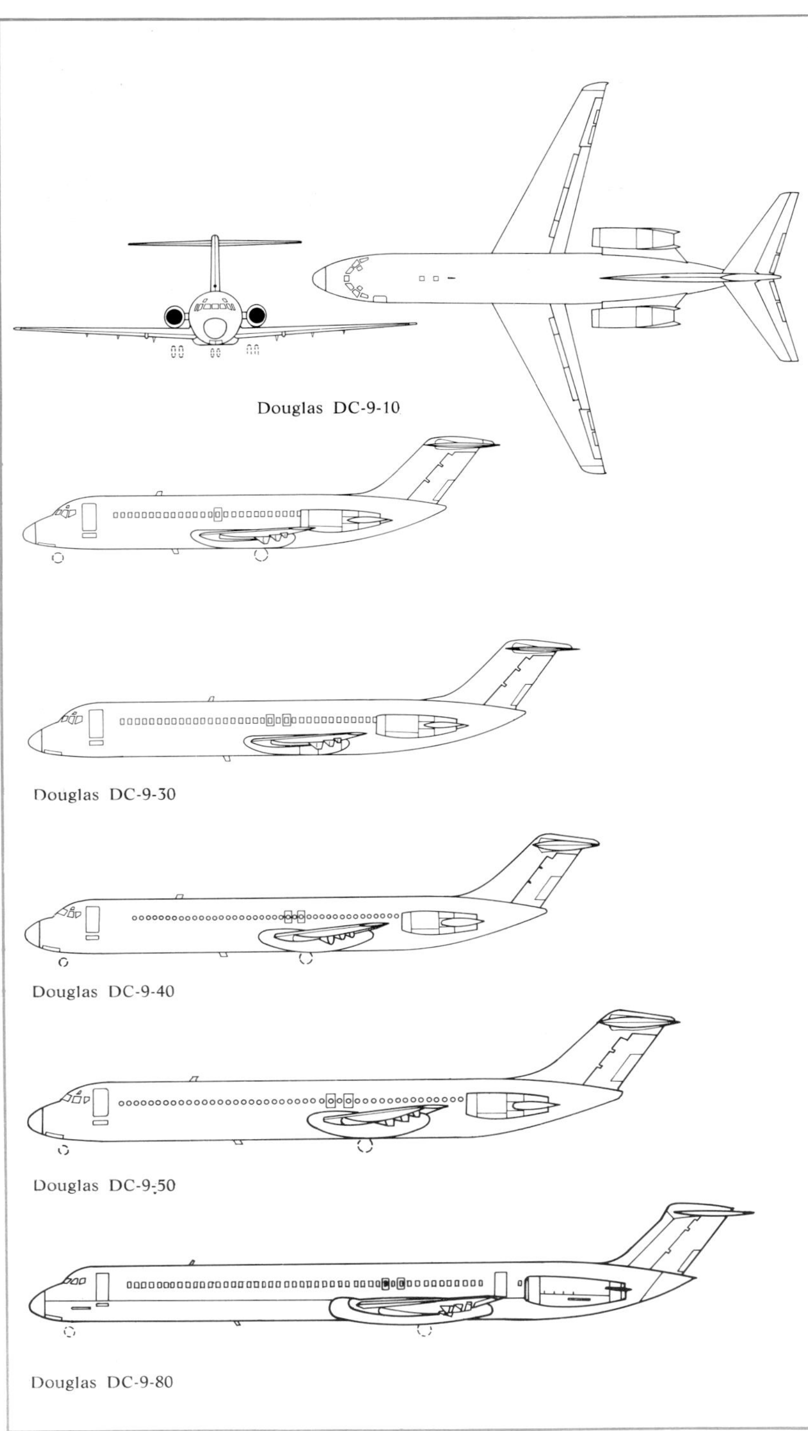

Douglas DC-9-10

Douglas DC-9-30

Douglas DC-9-40

Douglas DC-9-50

Douglas DC-9-80

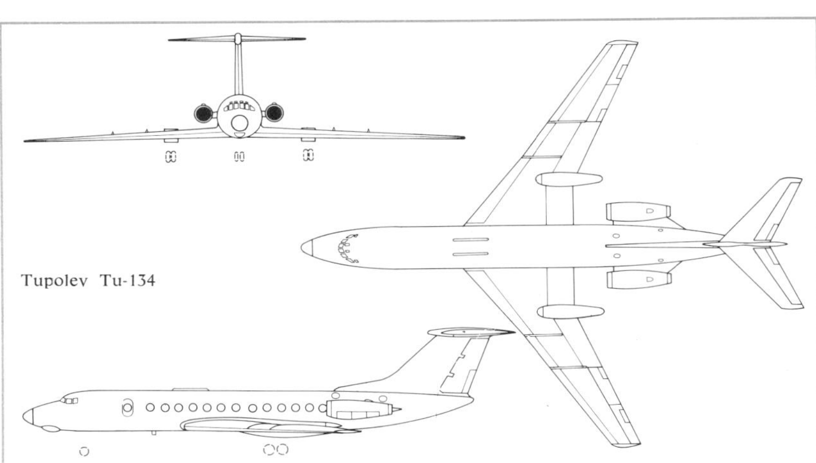

Tupolev Tu-134

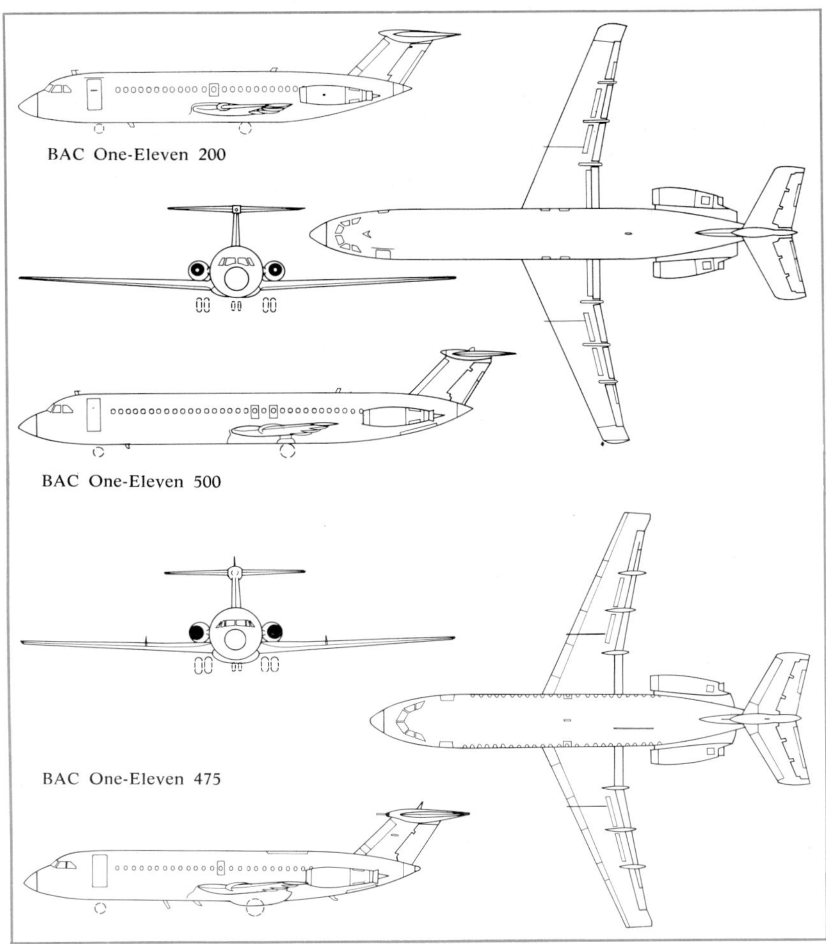

BAC One-Eleven 200

BAC One-Eleven 500

BAC One-Eleven 475

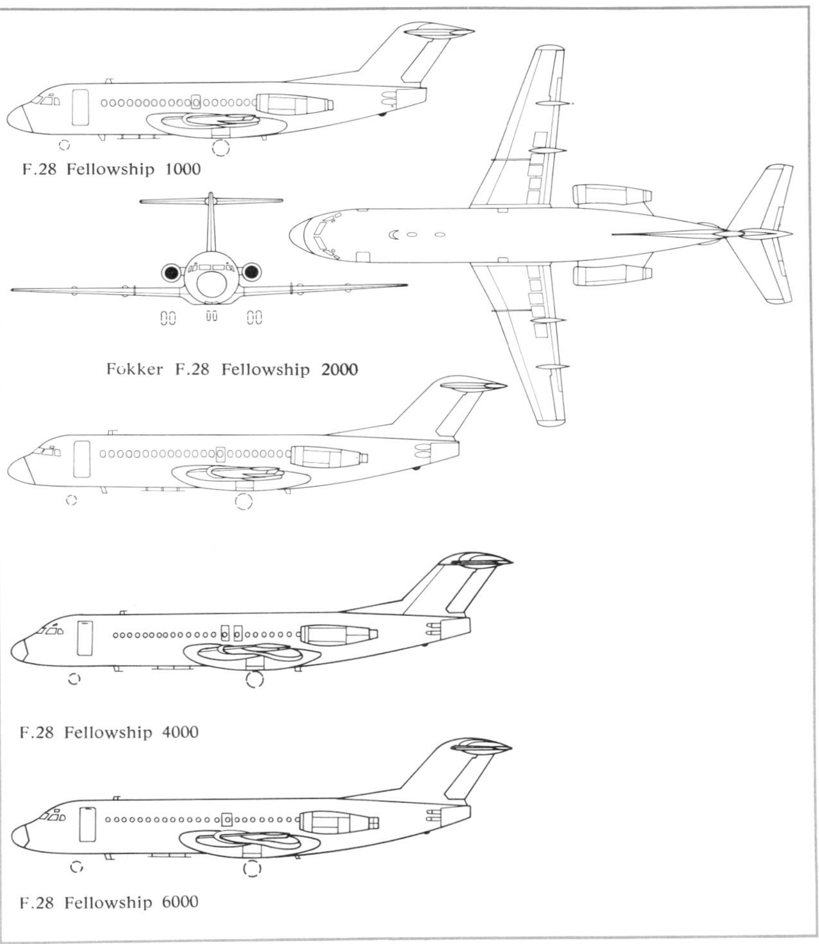

F.28 Fellowship 1000

Fokker F.28 Fellowship 2000

F.28 Fellowship 4000

F.28 Fellowship 6000

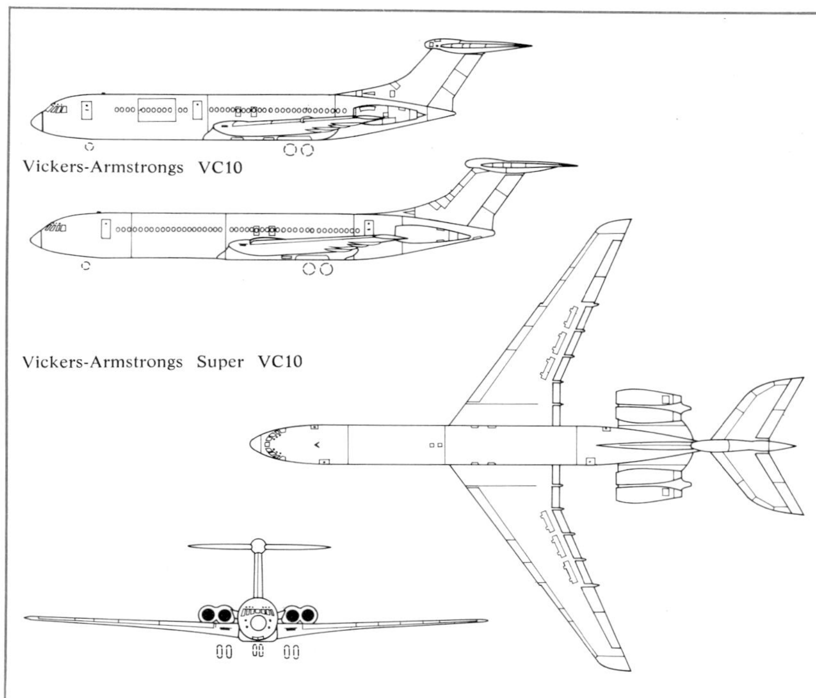
Vickers-Armstrongs VC10

Vickers-Armstrongs Super VC10

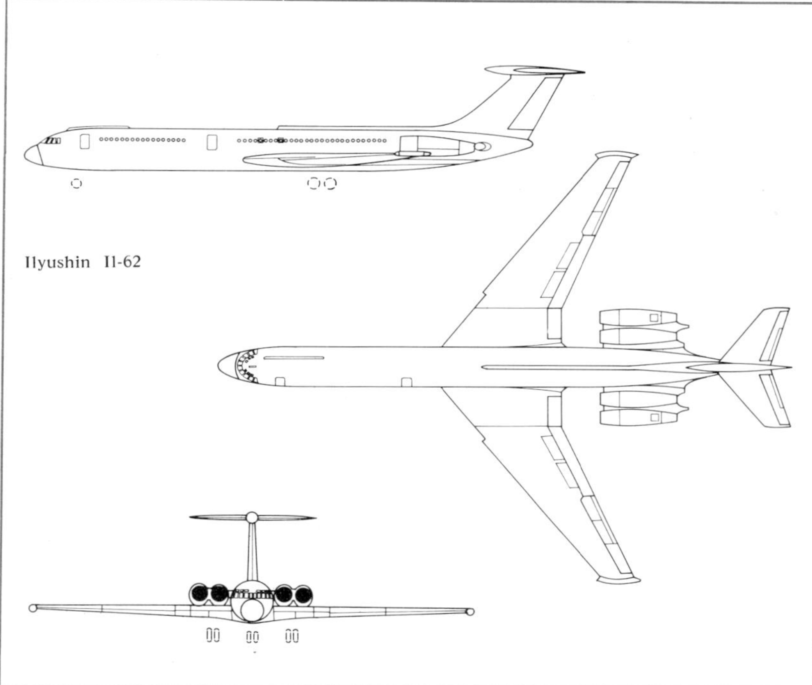
Ilyushin Il-62

lengthened and strengthened version was built, which was called the Super VC10. The first example flew on 7 May 1964, and BOAC took delivery of 17 of the new aircraft which it put into service between London and New York on 1 April 1965. Production terminated with the completion of East African Airways' order for five aircraft early in 1970.

The Ilyushin Il-62 (the first long-range four-jet aircraft built in the U.S.S.R.) first flew in January 1963, and was followed by a second prototype and three pre-production examples which were used for operational proving flights. The Il-62's service with Aeroflot was inaugurated on 10 March 1967 on the Moscow–Khabarovsk and Moscow–Novosibersk routes. Il-62s took over from Tu-114s on the Moscow–Monteal route on 15 September 1967, and continued on to New York from 15 July 1968. Il-62s are used on many of Aeroflot's major intercontinental routes. Production is thought to have totaled over 200 aircraft, and a small number was exported to satellite states and to China and to Cuba. In 1971 a new variant was put on display at the Paris Air Show: the Il-62M, which had more powerful engines and considerably longer range.

Plate 144
Three important trijet transports: 1964–1977

In the great race to capture world markets, Boeing managed to reach the enviable position of manufacturing the best-selling transport aircraft in the Western world: the 727 trijet, orders for which came to 1,825 at the end of 1981, with 1,786 delivered. This successful project began in 1956, when Boeing began studies for a new short-to medium-range civil transport which in the initial versions would seat a maximum of 119 passengers. The 727 has been gradually changed through continual and shrewd up-dating of the various production series, increasing its fully-laden weight by thirty per cent, and maximum seating by nearly sixty percent in the most recent version, the Advanced 200. The 727 prototype first flew on 9 February 1963, and initial series production was far advanced. The first airline to take delivery of the 727 was United Air Lines, in October 1963, and the type was put into regular service in February 1964 by both United and Eastern. The following series was the 727-200, lengthened and more powerful, the prototype of which flew on 27 July 1967. The Advanced 200 series aircraft (delivered from 1973) were subject to a variety of modifications: internal rearrangement, structural changes and quieter engines. The 727 can be used for a very wide variety of duties and the all-cargo and convertible passenger/cargo versions have been mainly adaptations of the first production series aircraft. In early 1977 a more up-to-date convertible version was derived from the Series 200, the 727-200C, which could seat a minimum of 137 passengers in variable configuration. In the all-cargo version, however, the aircraft can take as many as eleven standard containers, making a total payload of over 20 tonnes, and still have a range of 1,950 miles (3,150 km). These improvements in range and capacity have been made possible by the adoption of a more powerful version of the Pratt & Whitney JT8D engine.

The British equivalent of the Boeing 727 was the Hawker Siddeley Trident, 117 of which were sold in five variants and at the end of 1981, 82 Tridents were flying. The project was begun in 1957 in response to a specification from BEA which called for a new short-range commercial jet to be put into service in 1964. The prototype flew on 9 January 1962, and the first batch of 24 Trident 1s were for BEA, commencing regular service on 1 April 1964. Fifteen Trident 1Es followed (first flight 2 November 1964) which had up-rated power units, increased wingspan and longer range. Nearly all these were exported. In 1965 BEA ordered fifteen aircraft of a third version for use on its longer routes to the Middle East, and the first of these aircraft (the Trident 2E) flew on 27 July 1967. Regular Trident 2E service commenced on 18 April the following year. It was BEA again which took delivery of most of the production run of another, high-density route version, the Trident 3B, which could seat 180 passengers. The prototype of this version appeared on 11 December 1969; it had a stretched fuselage (16 ft 5 in—5 m) longer, an improved wing and a fourth, booster, engine was added. These Trident 3Bs entered service on 1 April 1971. The second major operator of the Trident was CAAC, the airline of the People's Republic of China, which bought three Series 1E aircraft; thirty-three 2Es and two of the last variant, the Super 3B, the prototype of which had its maiden flight on 9 July 1975.

The Soviets' answer to the Boeing 727 and the Trident is the Tupolev Tú-154 on which design work was started in the mid-sixties. The program aimed to replace the Tupolev Tu-104, the Ilyushin Il-18 and the Antonov An-10 in the medium- to long-range category (with a maximum range of 3,725 miles—6,000 km) which could also serve feeder routes. The first of six prototypes took to the air on 4 October 1968 and, after completing a series of proving trials, the seventh aircraft to be built was handed over to Aeroflot in the fall of 1970. The aircraft commenced mail and freight flights in May, and in the early summer of 1971 the first route-proving passenger flights got under way on the Moscow–Tiflis route. The Tu-154 entered regular service on 15 November 1971, between Moscow and Simferopol and Moscow and Mineral'nye Vody. About sixty of the initial series aircraft were delivered to the Soviet state airline, before the next model, the Tu-154A of 1973, appeared, which incorporated a number of general improvements. The next variant was the Tu-154B of 1977, with more sophisticated instrumentation and control systems and modifications to the interior allowing greater flexibility of loading. Tu-154s have been exported to many Eastern bloc countries and to Egypt, although the Egyptian aircraft were returned. It was reported from the Soviet Union that Aeroflot was to have 600 Tu-154s. An aircraft destined to play an important role on Soviet domestic services is the Yak-42 which made its first flight on 7 March 1975, and entered service with Aeroflot in December 1980. The Yak-42 has been designed to operate in temperatures ranging from minus 50 deg. C to plus 50 deg. C. The first production batch numbers 200 and it has been reported that a total of 2,000 may be required.

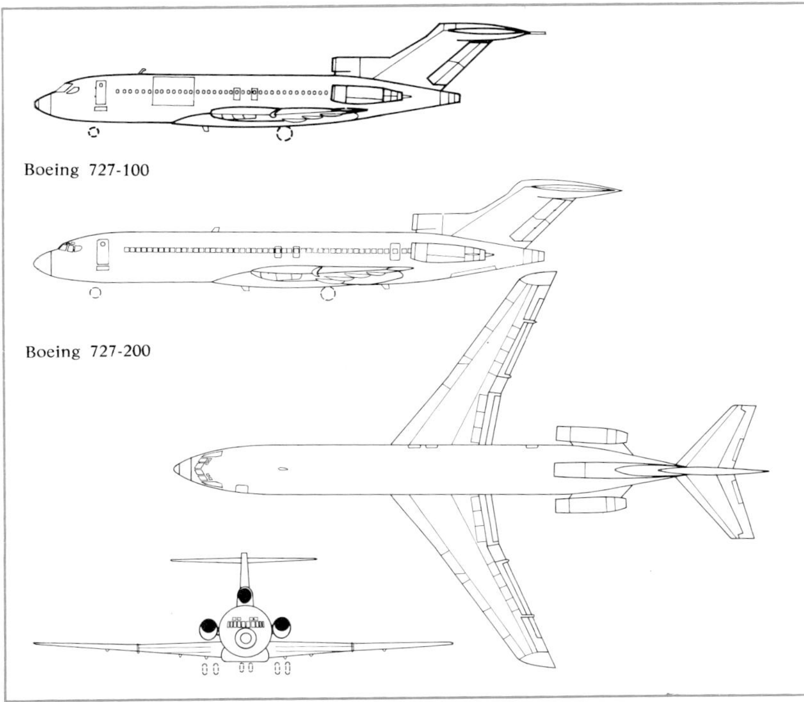
Boeing 727-100

Boeing 727-200

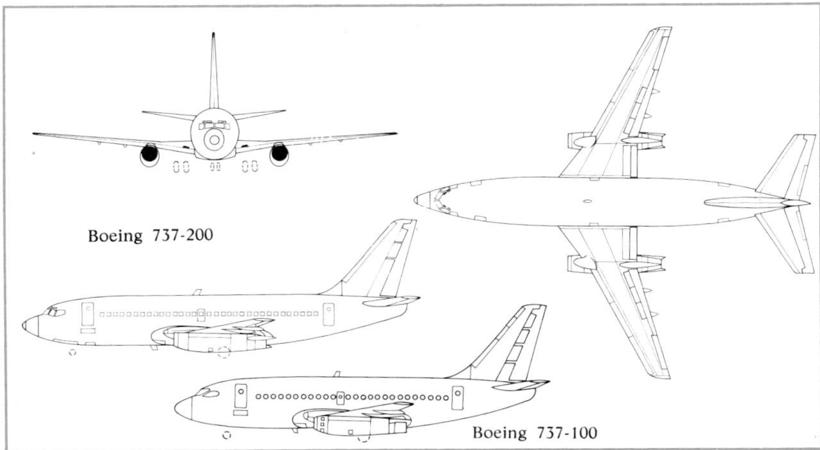
Boeing 737-200

Boeing 737-100

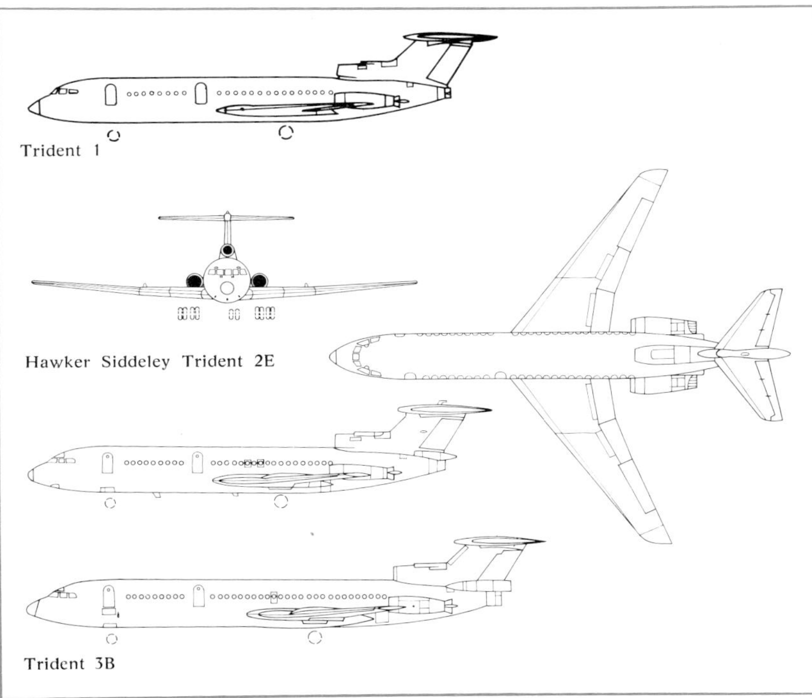
Trident 1

Hawker Siddeley Trident 2E

Trident 3B

Plate 145
Short- to medium-range large capacity jetliners: 1967–1982

The smallest of the most recent generation of short-haul jets is the 737, a twin-engine high-density aircraft. This program got under way in May 1964 and, by the time Boeing announced their plans on 19 February the following year, Lufthansa had already placed a firm order for twenty-one aircraft. Production was started up immediately, achieving considerable economies in time and money by utilizing the same fuselage cross-section as the larger 727 and 707. The prototype flew on 9 April 1967, and deliveries started toward the end of the year. There were two basic versions which were still in full production at the beginning of the 1980s; the 737-200 and the 737-200C/QC cargo and passenger/cargo convertible.

By the end of 1981 a total of 990 737s had been ordered and of these 823 had been delivered. In March 1981 Boeing announced that it was going ahead with the considerably modified 737-300 which is to be available in 1984. The most recent British competitor for this market is the four-engine BAe 146, a low-noise, fuel-efficient, short-haul jet transport. The first Series 100 made its maiden flight on 3 September 1981, and deliveries were scheduled for the fall of 1982. The longer 106-passenger BAe 146-200 is to be ready for delivery early in 1983.

In the late 1960s France made a courageous attempt to challenge the American monopoly in high-capacity, short-range civil transports. The construction of the Dassault Breguet (formerly just Dassault) Mercure was begun in 1968, a large twin-turbofan transport which could seat up to 162 passengers. The development program was prolonged, the early aircraft was deficient in performance, and there was only one customer. Two prototypes were built, the first of which flew on 28 May 1971, and ten production aircraft (Mercure 100) were built for the French domestic airline, Air Inter. In 1976–77 Dassault-Breguet attempted to launch a new, stretched version as the Mercure 200 after design changes which included more powerful engines and an improved, modified wing, in order to give the aircraft increased capacity and better its general performance.

European civil aviation made its come-back in the second half of the 1970s when the Airbus A300 was built. This was the first European "wide-body" airliner, a high-density, medium-range, twin-jet which was the result of a joint venture launched by an international consortium which included the French company, Aérospat-

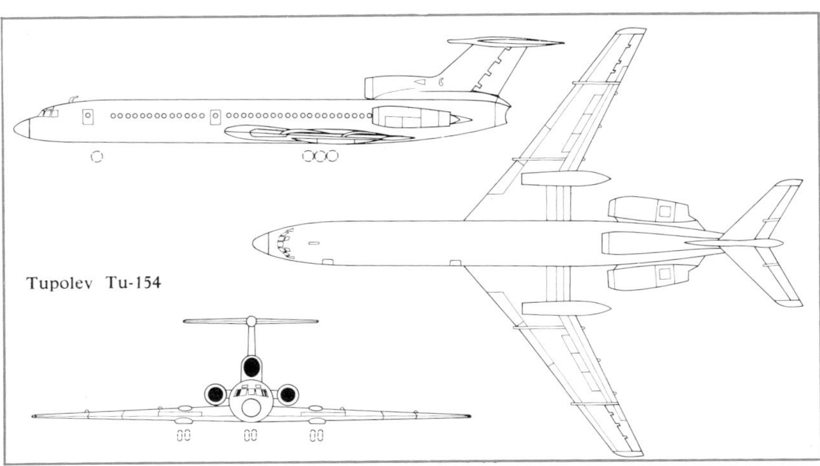
Tupolev Tu-154

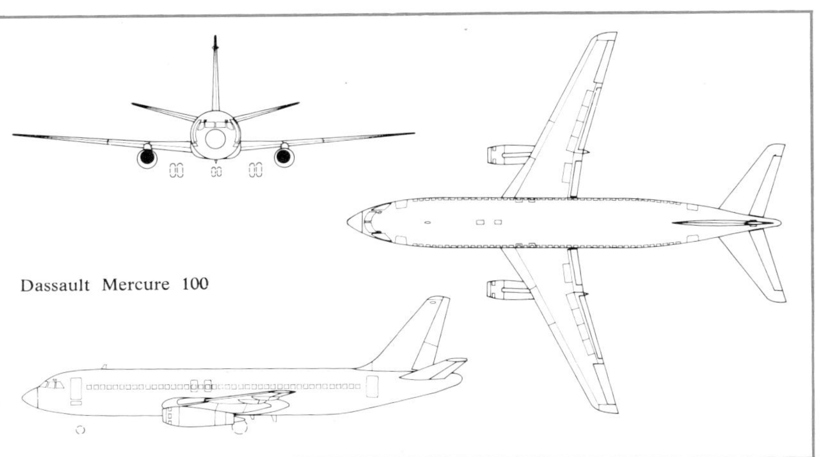
Dassault Mercure 100

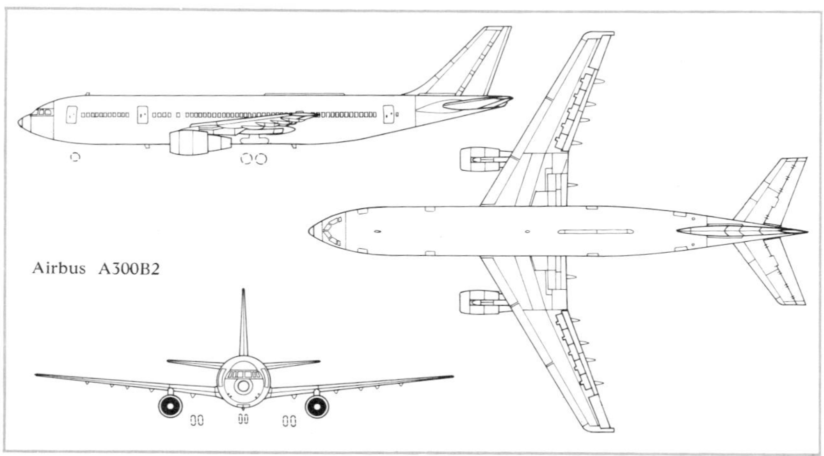
Airbus A300B2

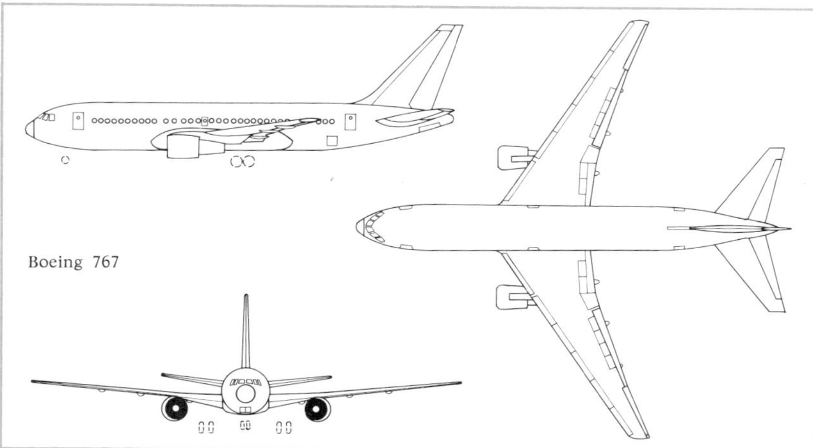
Boeing 767

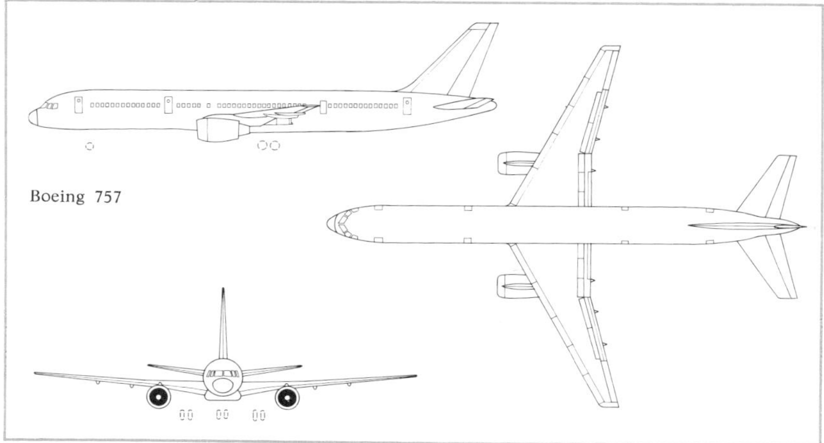
Boeing 757

iale, the German companies, MBB and VFW-Fokker, Britain's Hawker-Siddeley Aviation, Fokker-VFW (Netherlands) and CASA (Spain). The first prototype flew on 28 October 1972, and production gradually got under way. The first basic variant was the A300B2, first flown on 28 June 1973, which went into service with Air France on 23 May the following year. The next Airbus variant was the longer-range A300B4 which had its maiden flight on 26 December 1974. This variant entered service with Germanair on 1 June 1975. The latest basic version is the A310, with a shortened fuselage, which can seat 220 passengers and has a completely new wing. The A310 made its first flight early in 1982. At 31 January 1982, 43 customers had ordered 346 A300s and A310s and taken options on another 159 to give a total of 505. At that date 160 A300s were in service with 28 airlines.

The United States should have considerable success with two new jetliners, the Boeing 767 and the Boeing 757, launched at the beginning of the 1980s. Both these types are powered by much quieter, low fuel consumption engines and achieve lower overall operating costs. The Boeing 767 prototype made its maiden flight on 26 October 1981, and the first production aircraft delivery, for United Airlines, was scheduled for August 1982. By early 1982 a total of 173 firm orders and 138 options had been placed by seventeen airlines.

The next aircraft, the Boeing 757, made its maiden flight on 20 February 1982. British Airways and Eastern placed major orders in March 1979, and these were followed by further orders from Delta, American Airlines, TransBrasil and Monarch. Boeing claims that the 757 can achieve a fuel saving of roughly twenty percent compared with the consumption of the early models of the 727.

Plate 146
The wide-bodied airliners: 1970–1976

At the end of the 1960s Boeing ushered in a new and revolutionary era in civil aviation and in doing so achieved the distinction of designing and manufacturing the largest aircraft put into commercial service to date. The age of the wide-bodied jet transports began on 9 February 1969, when the Boeing 747 first took to the air. A very large aircraft initially capable of seating over 400 passengers, it was approximately double the weight of the previous generation of big jets and had twice the capacity. The impact which the 747 has made on the civil aviation scene is illustrated by a few statistics: in 1966, three years before the 747 prototype's maiden flight, Boeing had already received orders worth 1,800 million U.S. dollars. During the first six months in service, the 747s carried over a million passengers; by the end of 1981 they had carried 368 million passengers; by 31 December 1981, the assembly lines had completed 540 747s and still had to meet orders for forty-six more. The 500th Boeing 747 came off the production line on 17 December 1980.

Boeing have developed numerous variants, giving the aircraft increased power, range and payload. The first production model, the 747-100, entered service between London and New York with Pan American on 22 January 1970. The first variant to have different dimensions from the original 747 was the 747SP, which has a shortened fuselage and consequently reduced accommodation, but longer range and reduced specific fuel consumption. The 747SR is a high-density, short-haul variant capable of carrying 550 passengers. Another option offered by Boeing is the 747-100 Combi convertible/freighter, and the 747F pure freighter with hinged nose for freight loading can transport 111 tonnes payload over a range of 5,125 miles (8,250 km).

Boeing's challenge was taken up by other United States aircraft manufacturers. McDonnell Douglas designed the second wide-bodied type, the DC-10. McDonnell Douglas was spurred on to launch this program by an outline specification from American Airlines, which called for a wide-bodied 250-passenger aircraft capable of flying with full payload on such routes as Chicago to the U.S. West Coast and between New York and Chicago when operating from LaGuardia's limited runways. The first DC-10-10 trijet flew on 29 August 1970, and production aircraft entered service on 5 August the following year on the Los Angeles–Chicago route, with American Airlines. On 21 June 1972, the DC-10-30 first flew, an extended-range variant for intercontinental routes which had more powerful engines, a third main undercarriage unit and increased-span wing. Deliveries to airlines began in November, beginning with KLM and Swissair. The even more powerful version was the Series 40 which first flew under its original designation of DC-10-20 on 28 February 1972. Douglas also built convertible freighter versions, the DC-10-10CF and the DC-10-30CF; the prototype of the latter had its maiden flight on 28 February 1973. By the end of 1981

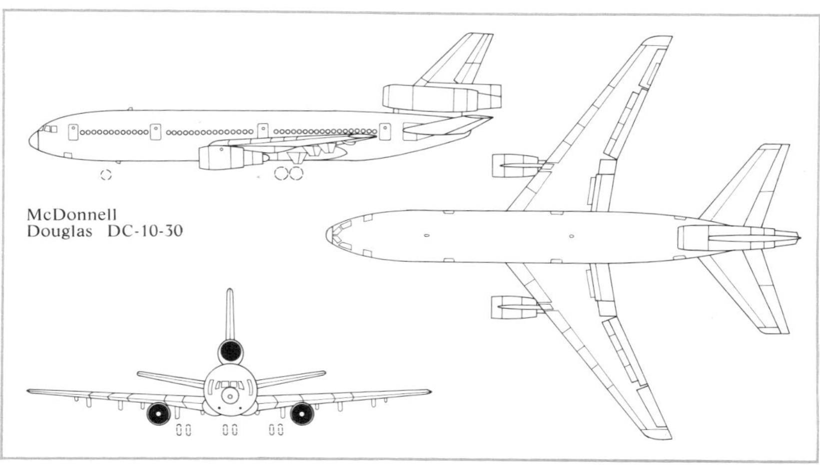
McDonnell Douglas DC-10-30

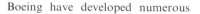

total orders had reached 367.

The same market requirements which had led to the development of the DC-10 in 1966 also triggered off the TriStar program for the production of another high-density trijet which Lockheed developed to appeal to American airlines' needs for U.S. domestic routes. The project, designated L-1011, was launched in March 1968, with 144 orders and options, and the first aircraft flew on 16 November 1970. Production allowed for several developed models, of increased power and gross weights. The initial version was the L-1011-1, which entered regular airline service with Eastern Air Lines on 26 April 1972. The Series 100 TriStars followed, with increased range and an optimal increase in power. Lockheed then proposed several developments of the TriStar and the L-1011-200 was built, first taking to the air on 10 April 1976, powered by an even more powerful version of the Rolls-Royce RB211 engine, which improved this plane's performance on takeoff and landing. In 1977 Lockheed planned the L-1011-250 which has increased range and payload but it was not built. In order to widen the TriStar's operational potential, a new extended-range version, the L-1011-500, was built with a shortened fuselage and this model first flew on 16 October 1978. By the end of 1981, 250 TriStars had been ordered and more than 200 were in airline service, but Lockheed announced its intention of terminating production in 1984.

The Soviet Union was slow off the mark in building its own wide-bodied airliner. The Ilyushin Il-86 project got under way in the early 1970s and the first public appearance of a model of the aircraft was in the spring of 1972. The configuration which was eventually adopted was very different from this early design, however, and appeared some months later. As first projected, the aircraft's configuration resembled that of the Il-62 very closely, but by the end of the year the design had been changed to a more "classic" layout for this type of airplane. The prototype had the appearance of a compromise between a Boeing 747 and a 707, having four engines in underwing pods and low-set tailplane. Unusual design features were the main undercarriage, consisting of three six-wheel bogies, one under the center of the fuselage, and the entrance vestibules and airstairs, obviating the need for complex handling equipment at every airport. The Il-86 can seat some 350 passengers. The prototype had its maiden flight on 22 December 1976. On 24 October 1977, the first production aircraft made its first flight, and regular airline service with Aeroflot is reported to have begun on 26 December 1980.

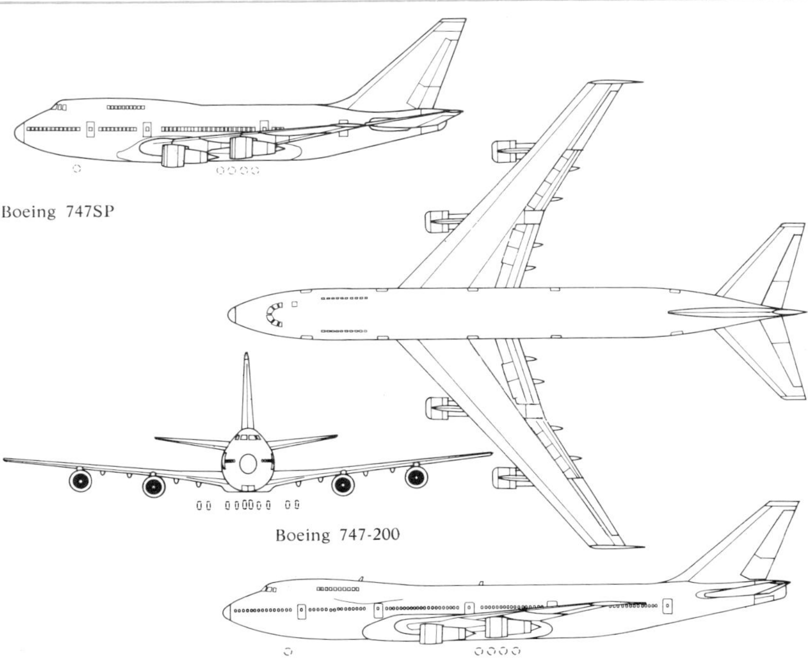

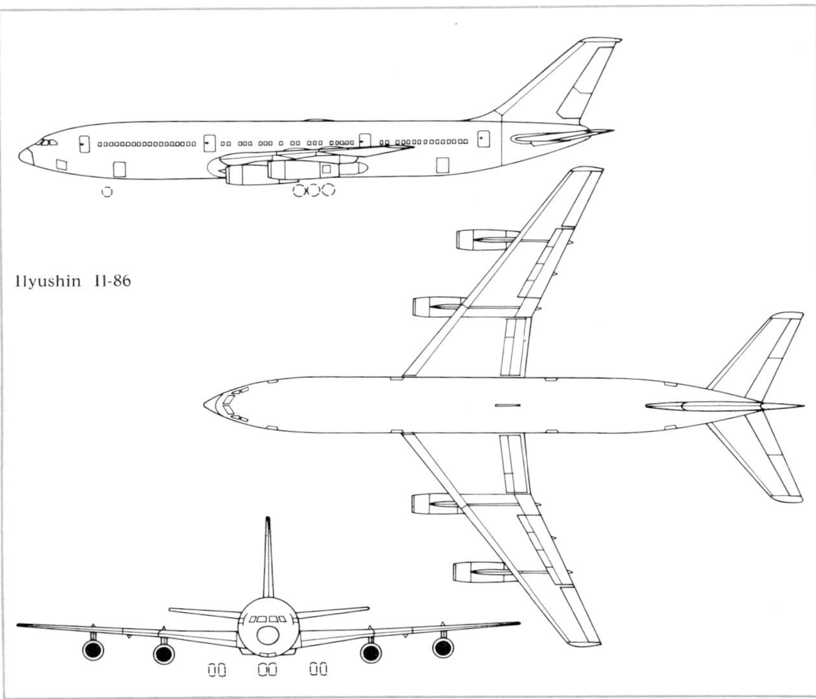

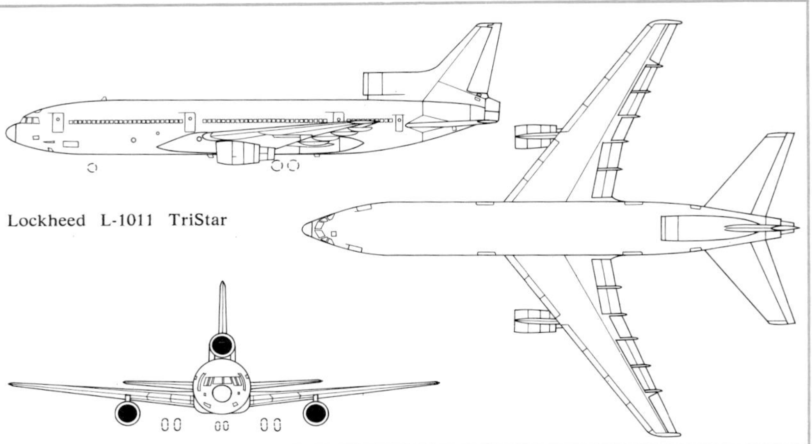

Plate 147
Concorde and the Tu-144 usher in the era of the supersonic transport: 1968–1969

The most breathtaking project undertaken in international civil aviation in the 1960s developed into a keenly-fought competition between the world airpowers: the United States, France, Great Britain and the U.S.S.R. The aim was to put the first supersonic civil transport into the air. A tremendous amount of prestige was involved and new areas of aircraft technology had to be explored and mastered. All this involved vast budgets. In a sense, there were two winners and one loser. The Soviet Tupolev Tu-144 was the first to fly (on 31 December 1968), but remained at a virtually experimental and development stage for nearly ten years. The Anglo-French program for the construction of Concorde, which went through a protracted preliminary design phase to study the feasibility of an SST, was to be the only aircraft of its type to remain in regular commercial service, from 21 January 1976, although its only operators are Air France and British Airways. The American company, Boeing, saw its supersonic transport program killed off on 24 March 1971, when the U.S. Senate refused to approve the enormous budget necessary to see the project through.

A model of the Tupolev Tu-144 was first exhibited at the Paris Air Show in 1965. The first of three prototypes flew on 31 December 1968, and was airborne for thirty-eight minutes. Supersonic speed was achieved for the first time by the Tu-144 on 5 June 1969, followed by the first excursion beyond Mach 2 on 26 May 1970, when the Tu-144 flew at 1,336 mph (2,150 km/h). The Tu-144 required a very long period of development: in 1973 the production configuration, a major redesign of the Soviet SST, was put on display in Paris; this example had a new wing, relocated engine nacelles, a new undercarriage and retractable foreplanes for improved slow-speed handling. This particular Tu-144, the second production aircraft, broke-up in flight during the 1973 Paris Show, but no acknowledgement of any difficulties with the airplane was ever made by the Russians. As production continued (at least ten Tu-144s are known to have been built) other structural modifications and changes in equipment were introduced. The Tu-144 began flying a twice weekly cargo service between Moscow and Alma Ata on 26 December 1975, and began carrying passengers over that route on 1 November 1977. However, the Tu-144 continued to have its problems and in June 1978 the aircraft was withdrawn from service. Since that time a

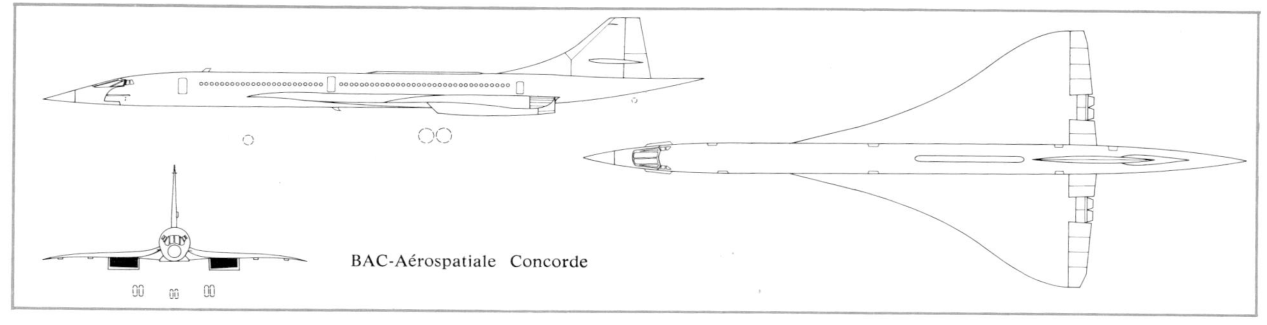

BAC-Aérospatiale Concorde

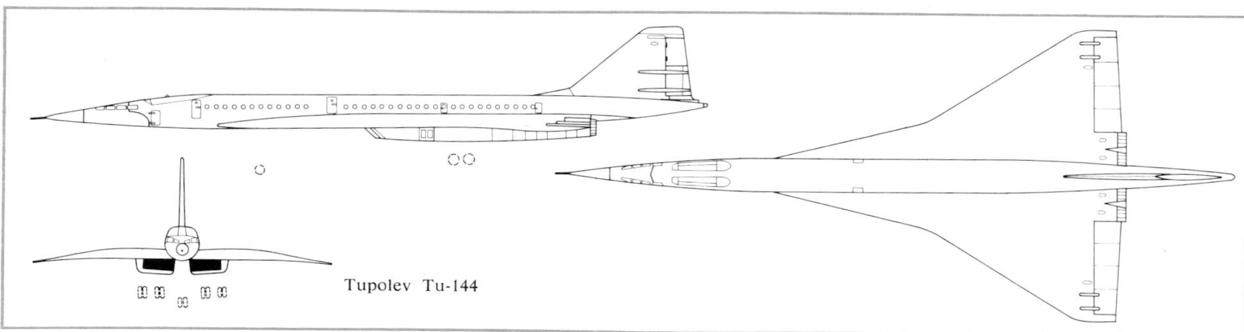

Tupolev Tu-144

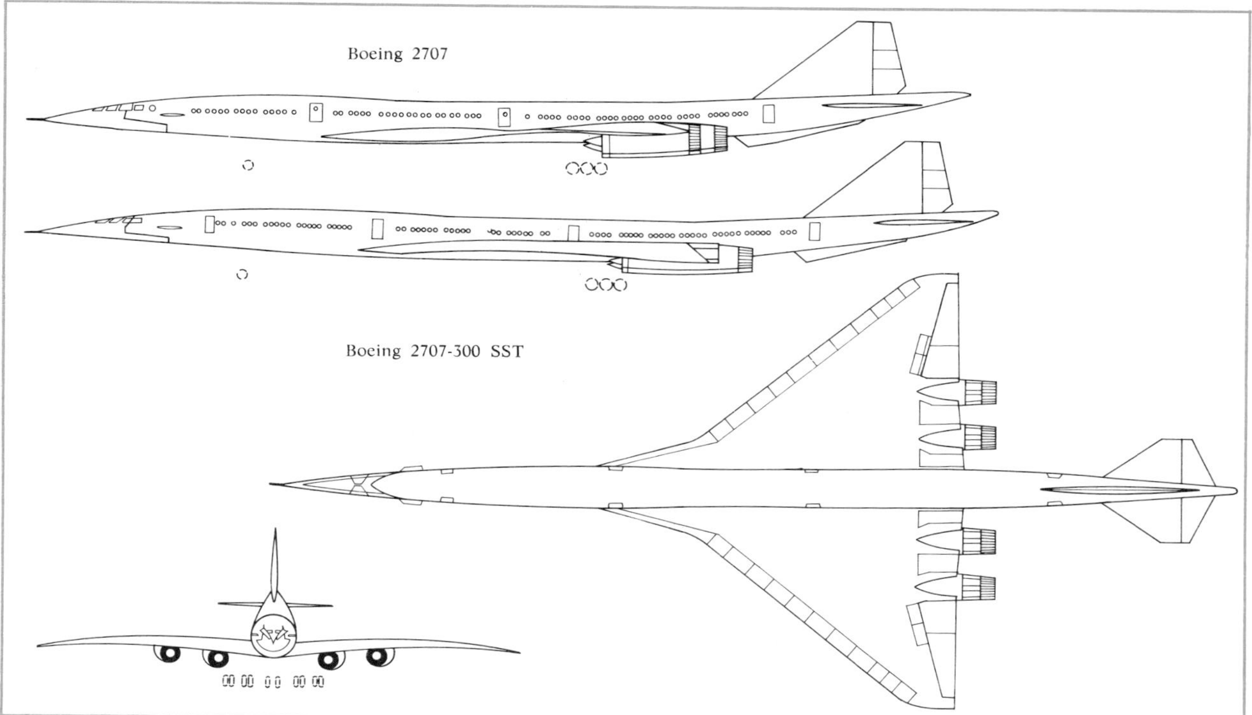

Boeing 2707

Boeing 2707-300 SST

modified version, Tu-144D, has made trial flights between Moscow and Khabarovsk, but it has not gone into service.

The Concorde program was launched on 29 November 1962, with the signing of a protocol of agreement between France and Great Britain and between the companies involved in the joint project in both countries. The principal airframe companies involved were the British Aircraft Corporation and Aérospatiale, and the engine companies were Rolls-Royce and SNECMA. The Concorde program initially allowed for the construction of two prototypes, two pre-production aircraft and two static test aircraft. The first prototype flew on 2 March 1969, later than planned, and two months after the Soviet supersonic transport's debut. The two aircraft had many features in common, however, especially as regards aerodynamics, although the production Tupolev Tu-144 appeared to be larger, with more powerful engines. The second Concorde flew on 9 April the same year, followed on 17 December 1971 and 10 January 1973 by the two pre-series aircraft. By that time the two partners' national airlines, BOAC and Air France, had both placed orders, the former for five Concordes, the latter for four. The first of these production aircraft flew on 6 December 1973. Extensive development flying and an exhaustive series of route proving flights were made, spread over nearly two years, the aim being to try out various international routes and also to promote the airplane and to arouse the interest of the international airline market. Regular service began on 21 January 1976, when the fifth production aircraft, F-BVFA, inaugurated Air France's supersonic service from Paris to Dakar and Rio de Janeiro and the G-BOAA launched British Airways' London–Bahrein supersonic service. On 24 May 1976, operations from Paris and London on the important route across the North Atlantic to Washington were commenced simultaneously. Although Concorde's use was further extended, this European commercial supersonic transport has not been a commercial success. Only sixteen production Concordes were built and at the beginning of 1982 British Airways and Air France each had seven. In 1982, against a background of an extremely serious general crisis in civil aviation, caused by world recession and the large increase in fuel costs, suggestions were widely voiced that since the two airlines were making such heavy losses, Concorde should be grounded.

Boeing's ill-fated project, which was given the company designation of Model 2707-300, was formally announced in October 1968, two years after the program had been initiated and after a previous design study for a variable-geometry aircraft had been canceled. On 23 September 1969, the U.S. Congress approved the construction of two prototypes, voting a budget of 1,300 million U.S. dollars—90 percent of the project costs. By the time the Senate blocked any further development of the supersonic transport eighteen months later, Boeing had almost completed final design work and had built 15 percent of the first airframe.

Plate 148
The Italian aviation industry's post-war recovery: 1946–1962

There can be no question that since the end of World War II, aircraft development has been dominated by the technological pre-eminence of the victorious nations, with the United States well to the fore. In Europe, only Great Britain and France have managed to retain their leading roles in the world of aviation, although until the success of the Airbus they never seriously threatened the dominance of the American manufacturing giants. Among the nations which had to adopt a secondary role after the war, Italy has managed to make a slow, unspectacular recovery by producing some worthwhile commercial airplanes, although she cannot hope to regain her former position as an aviation world leader during the 1930s.

Savoia Marchetti's last four-engine civil transport was the S.M.95, which began life in the early war years as a military transport, only three being completed before the end of the war in Europe. In 1946 only one S.M.95 was left in Italy and, from 10 April 1946, it was used on a service flown by the Italian air force from Rome to Milan. In late 1946 the first of six S.M.95 civil

Savoia Marchetti S.M.95

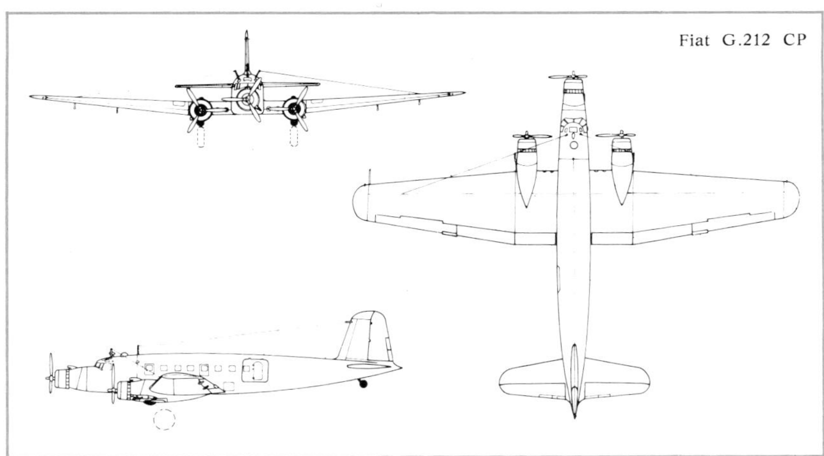
Fiat G.212 CP

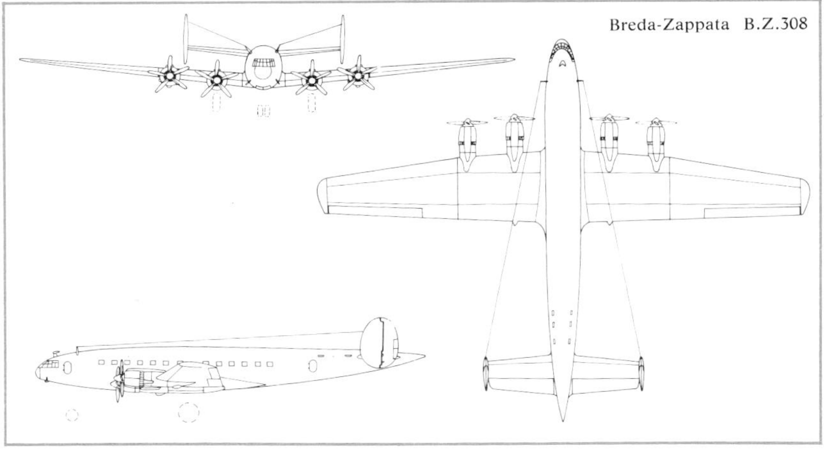
Breda-Zappata B.Z.308

aircraft appeared, entering service in 1947 with the recently-formed airline, Alitalia. On 6 August, the S.M.95 *Marco Polo*, registration I-DALL, inaugurated Alitalia's first international route from Rome to Oslo. On 3 April 1948, the first regular flights to Great Britain (Rome to London, Northolt) commenced and, four days later, the Rome – Milan – London – Manchester service was launched. A further three S.M.95s went to LATI and, in July 1949, they began weekly flights to Caracas. This was a fairly testing route: the last leg involved more than 2,485 miles (4,000 km) nonstop. The LATI aircraft were taken over by Alitalia but withdrawn from service in 1951. The only other operator of S.M.95s was the Egyptian airline SAIDE which had three.

The last trimotor to be produced by the Italian aircraft industry was the Fiat G.212 which was developed from the smaller G.12. The prototype first flew on 19 January 1947. Nine aircraft of the commercial variant, the G.212 CP Monterosa, were built; six were flown by ALI from 1948 until March 1952, and three were operated by the Egyptian airline SAIDE until the early 1950s. A project which might have led to a really internationally important commercial aircraft had it not been for the war was the Breda-Zappata B.Z.308, a large, efficient four-engine airplane which had been designed in 1942 but only appeared in prototype form in August 1948. Construction of this aircraft was first interrupted by the intervention of the Allied Control Commission and then further delayed by late-delivery of the British Bristol Centaurus engines. When the B.Z.308 finally commenced flight tests and proving trials, it was already too late and would have been uneconomical to set up a production line, especially in view of the fierce competition from the American aircraft industry. The only B.Z.308 ever built was bought by the Italian Air Force in 1949.

On the whole, Italian light aircraft was rather more up to standard, although there were some ventures which were unsuccessful, commercially speaking. One example was the M.B.320, which was developed by Macchi after the war, the prototype appearing in 1949. Although the aircraft had no specific faults, it suffered from being operated in precisely those climatic conditions least suited to its construction, having been bought by East African Airways, and the adverse effects on the aircraft's performance hardly enhanced its reputation. Six M.B.320s were built before production was shut down.

In contrast the Piaggio P.136-166 series of twin-engine light aircraft sold extremely well. The prototype P.136 first flew on 29 August 1948. This was a gull-wing amphibian aircraft with a pusher propeller and was both versatile and cheap to operate. The first order was placed in 1950 by the military authorities for eighteen aircraft. A further order followed for fifteen of the second version, the P.136-L. Commercial sales began with the more powerful variants, the L1 of 1955 and the L2 of 1957, and more than twenty were exported to the United States, under the names of Royal Gull and Royal Gull Super 200. The most important development of the design was the P.166, a larger, landplane version with greater capacity. Production commenced in 1958 and included several variants: the initial model A executive and light transport aircraft, thirty-two of which were built; followed by the Piaggio P.166B Portofino of 1962 (six built) which had up-rated engines, and the C of 1964 (three built) with increased capacity. The military versions were the M for the Italian Navy (fifty-one built) and the S model, twenty of which were exported to South Africa in 1968. The last variants were the DL2 (2 May 1975) which had a redesigned wing and increased fuel capacity, and the DL3 (3 july 1976).

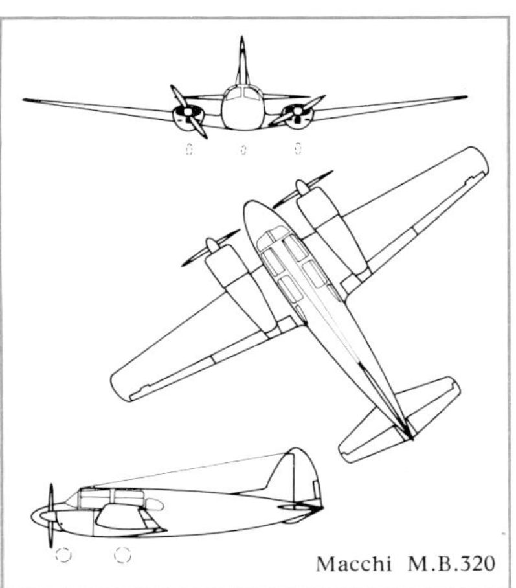
Macchi M.B.320

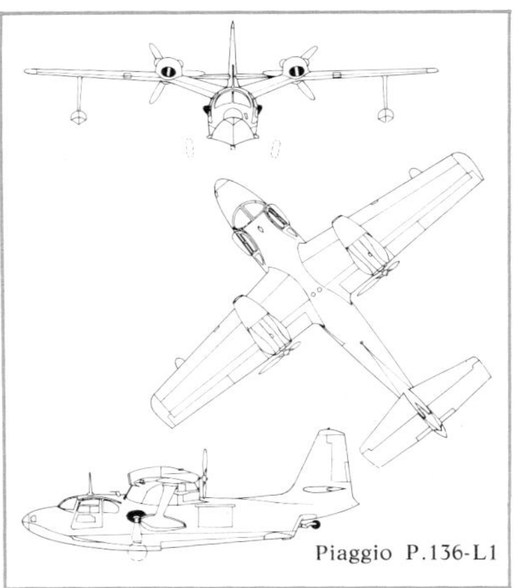
Piaggio P.136-L1

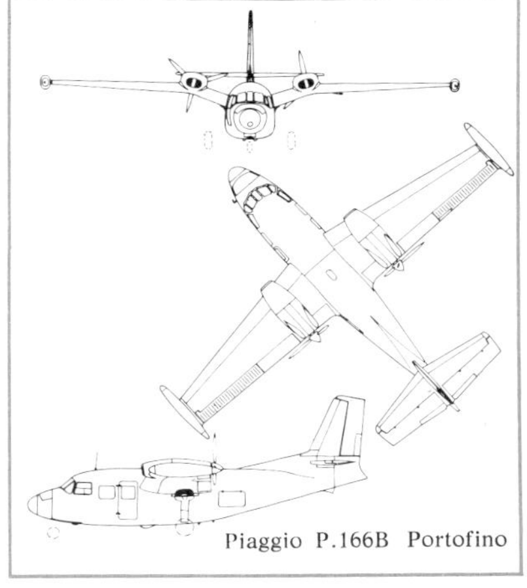
Piaggio P.166B Portofino

Plate 149
Canadian civil aircraft: 1947–1969

The Canadian aircraft industry expanded considerably after the war, having previously been very dependent on the United States and Great Britain for its aircraft. Once the war was over, more civil aircraft were manufactured in Canada itself, mainly by de Havilland Aircraft of Canada, which had originally been founded in 1928 as a subsidiary of the British parent company. The DHC-2 Beaver prototype first flew on 16 August 1947, and was the forerunner of an important series of

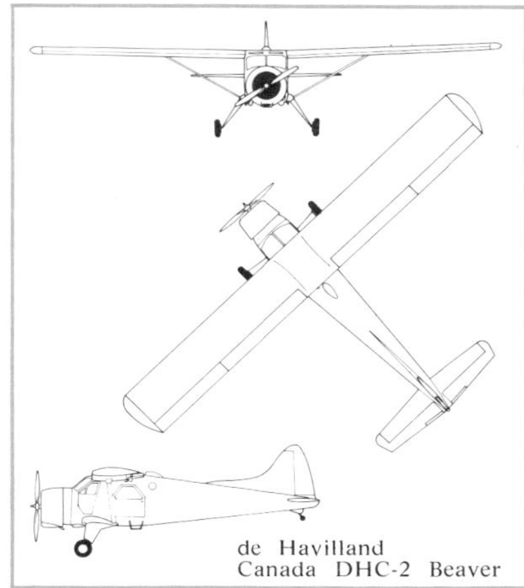
de Havilland Canada DHC-2 Beaver

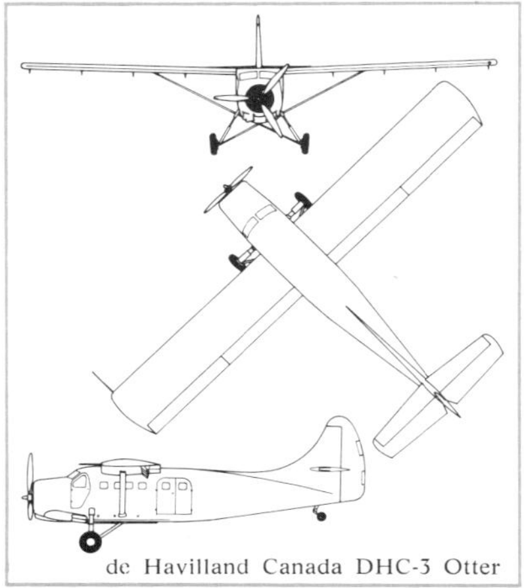
de Havilland Canada DHC-3 Otter

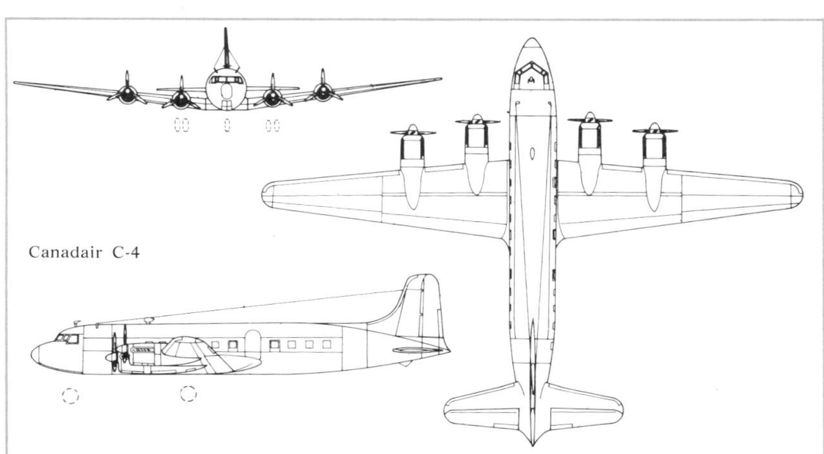
Canadair C-4

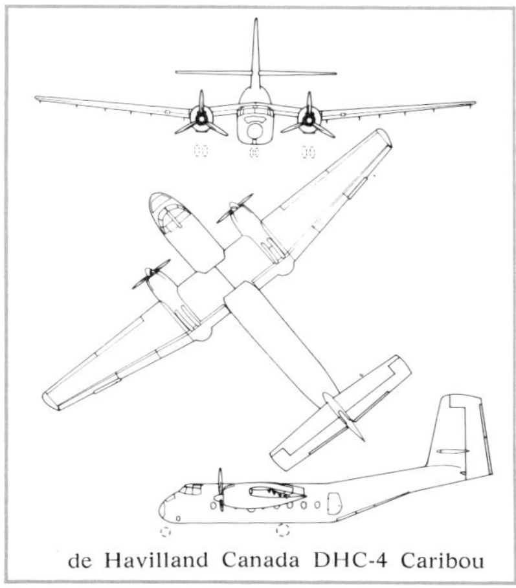
de Havilland Canada DHC-4 Caribou

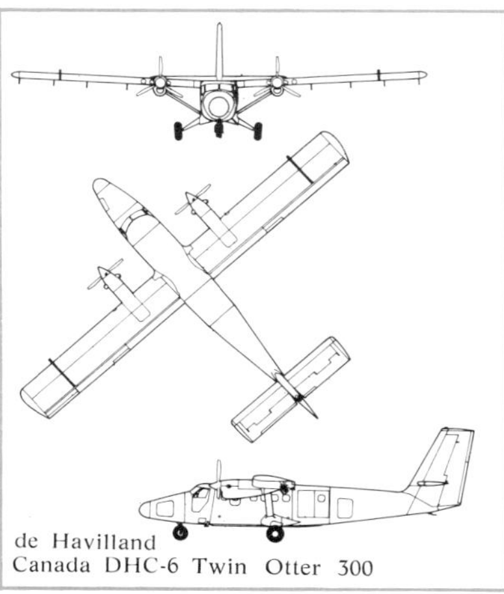
de Havilland Canada DHC-6 Twin Otter 300

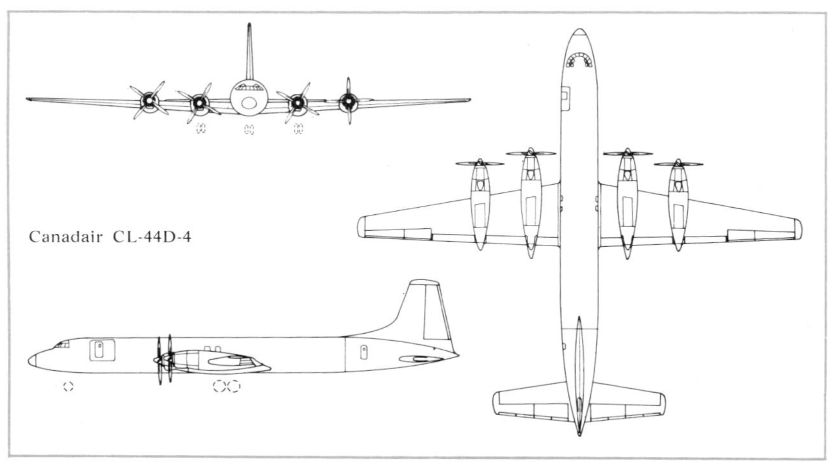
Canadair CL-44D-4

STOL (short takeoff and landing) aircraft, which sold well in world markets. The DHC-2 basic design evolved through the DHC-3 Otter, the twin-engine DHC-4 Caribou and the DHC-5 Buffalo, to developments such as the twin propeller-turbine DHC-6 Twin Otter light transport and the four-engine DHC-7 (Dash 7).

The DHC-2 program was begun immediately after the war and led to a tough and versatile high-wing monoplane with such good performance that it was an immediate commercial success. Production proceeded uninterruptedly, fed by large military orders from the United States and a few from Great Britain, which led to orders being received from fifteen other air forces. 1,692 Beavers were manufactured, many of which were sold on the civil market, and after more than 1,600 aircraft had been completed, the aircraft was modified considerably, a 550 hp Pratt & Whitney PT6A-6 propeller-turbine being installed. This version was designated the Turbo Beaver III, had its maiden flight on 31 December 1963, and sixty were built.

The Beaver's success was to a lesser extent repeated by the DHC-3 Otter (first flight 12 December 1951) which in essence was a larger, more powerful version of the Beaver. More than half the production, totaling 466 aircraft, were sold to the U.S.A.F. and the R.C.A.F. and the other Otters were bought by a very wide range of small commercial operators and individuals in thirty-six countries. The larger DHC-4 Caribou and DHC-5 Buffalo nearly all went for military use, and of these two variants, the DHC-4 had more success on the civil market since it had excellent load capacity (although only a limited number were sold). The prototype flew for the first time on 30 July 1958, and production totaled 307.

Plans for constructing the DHC-6 Twin Otter were announced in 1964 and the first flight took place on 20 May 1965. This light transport aircraft has made its mark as one of the most outstanding in its category and was equally well received by civil and military buyers. It is a powerful and very versatile twin-engine propeller-turbine powered type with a non-retractable undercarriage, and by the end of 1979 over 700 had been constructed, 344 of which had been purchased by commercial operators. The initial production model, the Series 100 (115 built), was followed by the Series 200 and then by the Series 300 which was certificated on 25 April 1968.

In the heavy transport category, two Canadian products, the C-4 and the CL-44, sold well. Both were constructed by Canadair. They were not original designs, since both these four-engine transports were developments of aircraft already in production in the U.S.A. and Great Britain. The former had evolved from the Douglas DC-4, having had Rolls-Royce Merlin engines installed to become the C-54GM, DC-4M and the Canadair C-4; the CL-44 stemmed from the Bristol Britannia which had undergone considerable modifications, leading to the first all-cargo aircraft to have a hinged rear fuselage to facilitate freight-loading operations. The first Canadair Four to fly took to the air on 15 July 1946 under its original designation of DC-4M-1, and was followed in August 1947 by the definitive prototype which had a pressurized cabin (the DC-4 M-2). Apart from its military career, the unpressurized version entered regular commercial service with Trans-Canada Air Lines in April 1947, this airline taking twenty-three aircraft as North Stars, and four commenced flying with Canadian Pacific Airlines in July 1949; from August 1949 twenty-two were flown as Argonauts by BOAC which operated the type until April 1960. The CL-44 prototype appeared on 15 November 1959, and was initially meant for the Royal Canadian Air Force in the CC-106 Yukon version; two production series aircraft were subsequently marketed, a total of twenty-seven being built for the civil market, and these reverted to the original loading system. These variants were designated CL-44D-4 (first flown on 16 November 1960) and the CL-44J (8 November 1965) which had a stretched fuselage. The main operators were Flying Tiger Line, Seabord World, Slick Airways and Icelandic Airlines. The Icelandic company was the first to use these large propeller-turbine powered aircraft as passenger transports, starting in 1964 on the transatlantic route via Iceland. This low-cost, high density service proved so popular that Icelandic Airways changed the aircraft they had on order for a CL-44J and subsequently had the three aircraft (CL-44D-4) which they had already received modified to stretched versions. Fourteen CL-44s were still in airline service at the end of 1981.

Plate 150
British light transports: 1945–1948

Light transports often have to satisfy the demands of private operators, charter lines and executive use and this category has developed along similar lines to the large airliners. In Great Britain, when industry was recovering after the war, the aircraft manufacturers produced many aircraft of this type. On 26 January 1945, the

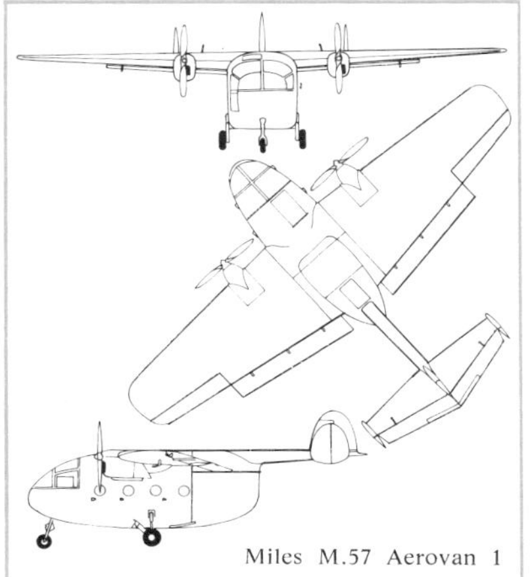

Miles M.57 Aerovan 1

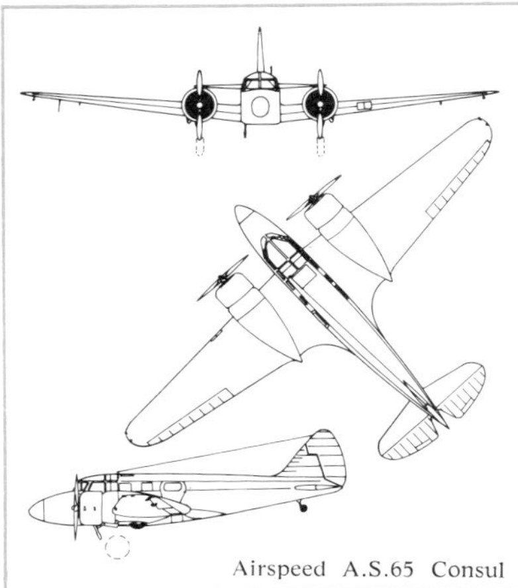

Airspeed A.S.65 Consul

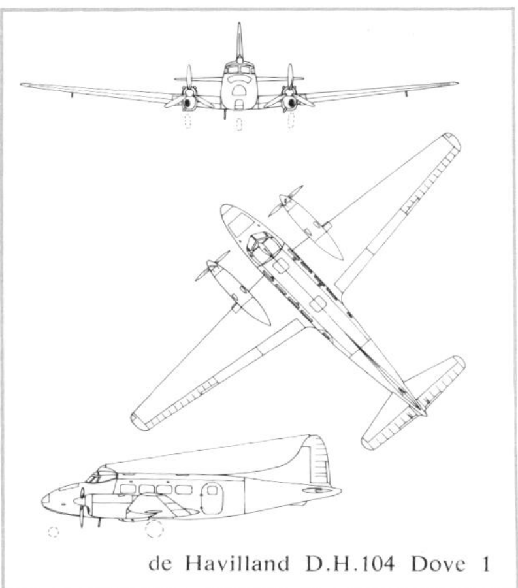

de Havilland D.H.104 Dove 1

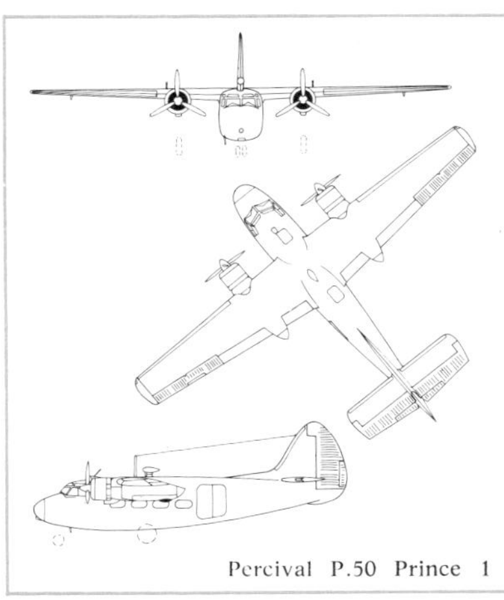

Percival P.50 Prince 1

prototype of one of the most useful all-purpose transports of that period made its maiden flight. The Miles M.57 Aerovan was a small twin-engine monoplane especially designed to meet expected demand for short-range mixed transports which could cope with bulky loads. Production centered on the Aerovan 4 which accounted for forty-three out of the total production of fifty-four. These were followed by single examples of the Aerovan 5 and 6, which had different engines. The aircraft's sales surpassed all expectations and orders came in from many small specialist operators who continued to use the Aerovan through the 1950s.

The de Havilland D.H.104 Dove was a bestseller. The famous British manufacturer planned this little twin-engine airplane as a successor to its famous family of light transports of the 1930s. There were two prototypes and 526 production aircraft, and they were sold to customers throughout the world. The first prototype made its maiden flight on 25 September 1945, and production was launched with the initial series aircraft, the Dove 1. In 1948 this was joined by an executive variant, the Dove 2, especially aimed at the export market, with seating reduced from eight to six. Developed versions of these two aircraft were produced simultaneously; improvements included up-rated engines. These up-dated versions were the 1B and the 2B of 1952 (powered by 340 hp Gipsy Queen engines) and the Dove 5 and Dove 6 of 1953, with 380 hp engines. The last two main variants were the Dove 7 of 1960 which was still more powerful and the Dove 8 executive transport, seating six passengers.

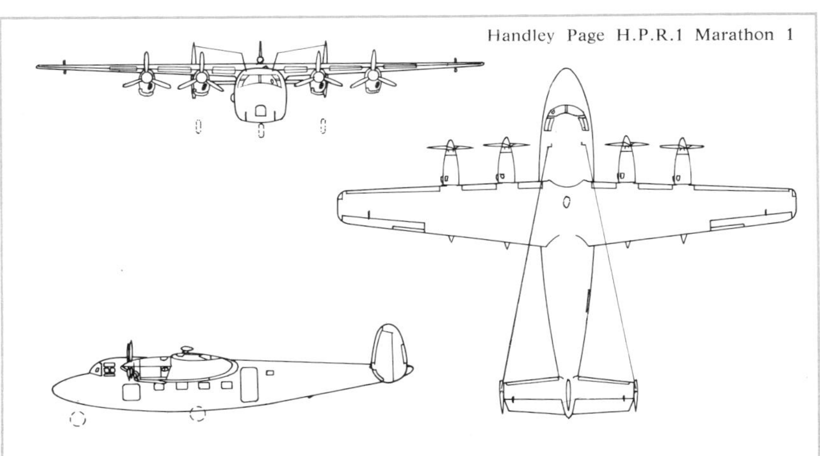

Handley Page H.P.R.1 Marathon 1

Another aircraft in the same category as the Dove was the Airspeed A.S.65 Consul, derived from the series of twin-engine light transport which went back to the Envoy of 1934, and the best of which had been the Oxford of 1937. The Consuls were civil conversions of Oxfords, the main difference being in the fuselage layout which was redesigned to seat six passengers and accommodate their baggage. The first Consul was certificated in March 1946, and more than 150 conversions were made, with very satisfactory sales.

A contemporary, the Handley Page H.P.R.1 Marathon, was not so successful. It was developed immediately after the war by Miles Aircraft Ltd., with the ambitious aim of offering a worthwhile short-haul light transport. Things started to go wrong in 1948 (the prototype having appeared on 19 May 1946) when Miles went into liquidation, and did not improve, since the new aircraft was rejected by the major airlines after Handley Page had taken it over. This small four-engine aircraft was eventually adopted by the R.A.F. as a navigational trainer and was also used by small, mainly foreign, operators. The Marathon 2 variant, the only example of which flew on 23 July 1949, was interesting since it was modified by the installation of two 1,010 ehp Armstrong Siddeley Mamba propeller-turbines, to become the third British propeller-turbine powered transport to fly.

The Percival Prince was a sturdy high-wing twin-engine monoplane, which was subsequently superseded by an improved President and the Pembroke military variant, which was produced until 1958 for the R.A.F. The Prince won a few domestic and overseas sales. The prototype had its first flight on 13 May 1948 and production got under way with ten aircraft, designated Prince 1. Seven Prince 2s followed. They incorporated modifications found necessary after lengthy proving flights by the first three aircraft of the initial production series, in Africa, the Middle East, India and Asia. Ten improved, more powerful Prince 3s were then constructed in 1952. The final versions were the Prince 4 and 6 which, like the Prince 3, were heavier.

The greater part of production of the only amphibian built in Britain in the immediately postwar years, the Short S.A.6 Sealand, went for export. The

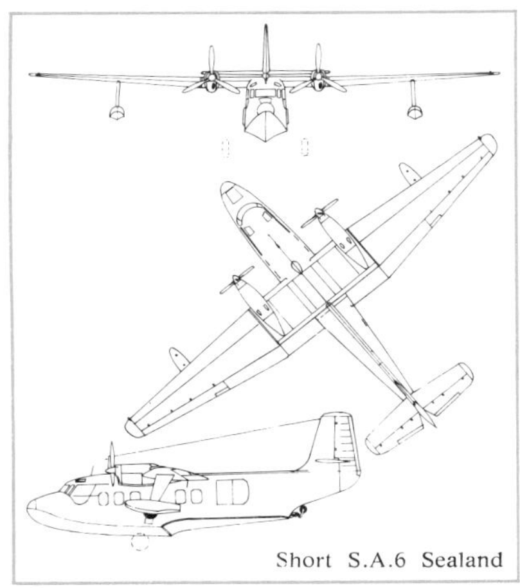

Short S.A.6 Sealand

prototype first flew on 22 January 1948, and production totaled twenty-four aircraft which were manufactured until 1952. After a very hard-selling series of promotional flights in Europe, the U.S.A. and South America, several smaller operators showed interest in the Sealand and certain airlines, such as the Norwegian Vestlandske Luftfartselkap and British West Indian Airways, also bought this aircraft, although the BWIA order was canceled. The biggest fleet was operated by the Indian Navy.

Plate 151
British and Canadian light transports: 1950–1975

Scottish Aviation's first original project was to lead to the first STOL transport to be built in Great Britain: the Pioneer, a small high-wing monoplane with excellent handling qualities. The Pioneer was not widely sold, however, partly because the military authorities were lukewarm about it and partly because it was soon replaced by the larger Twin Pioneer. The prototype was first flown in 1947, powered by a 240 hp Gipsy Queen engine. It was extensively modified and as the Pioneer 2 powered by a 520 hp Alvis Leonides radial engine it flew in June 1950. This variant was adopted by the R.A.F. which bought forty in 1953 and the total built was 59 including some for the air forces of Ceylon and Malaya. From 1955 onward, however, the Pioneer was joined by its improved and more versatile "big brother," the Twin Pioneer, which flew in prototype on 25 June of that year. This twin-engine light transport had such outstanding takeoff and landing performance that Scottish Aviation planned to build 200 in expectation of large-scale sales, but only 87 were built including 39 for the R.A.F. There were three main production series; the first variant was powered by 560 hp Alvis Leonides engines; the Twin Pioneer 2 of 1958

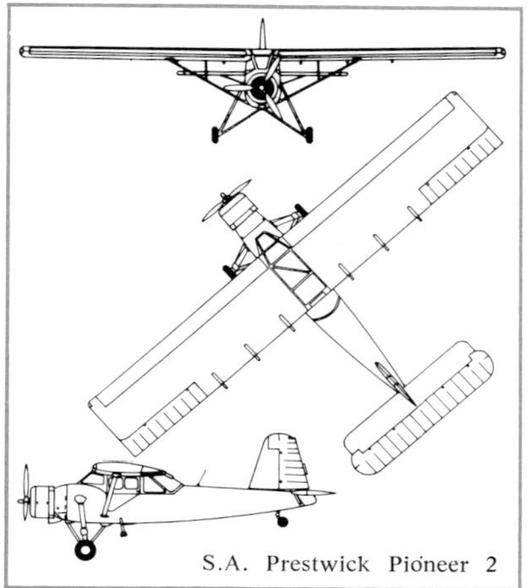
S.A. Prestwick Pioneer 2

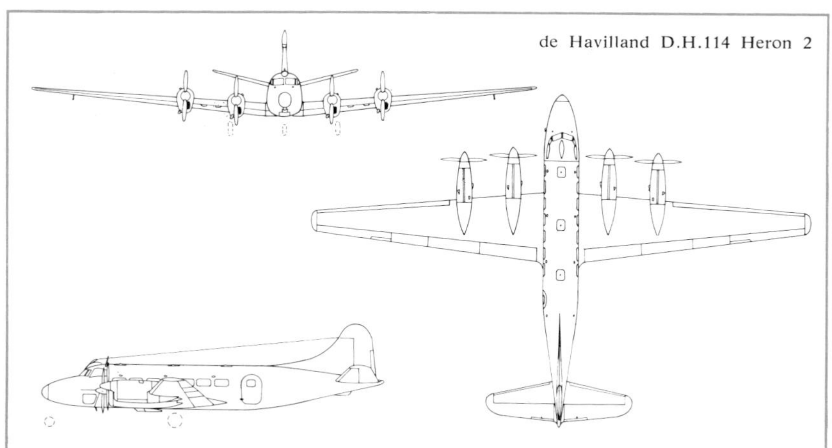
de Havilland D.H.114 Heron 2

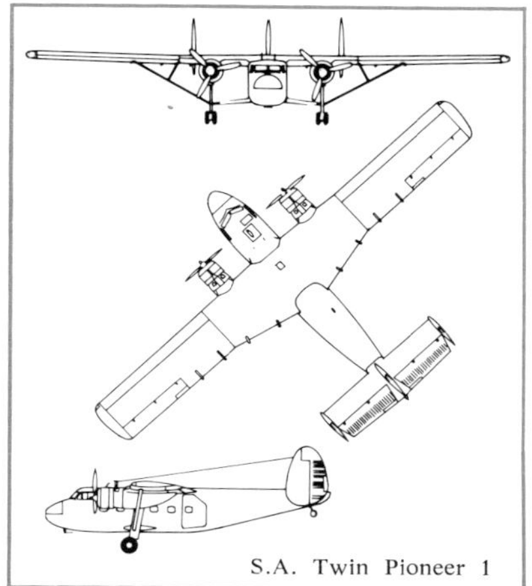
S.A. Twin Pioneer 1

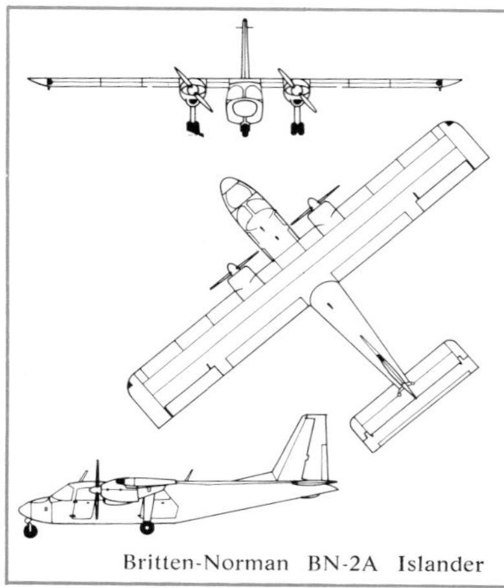
Britten-Norman BN-2A Islander

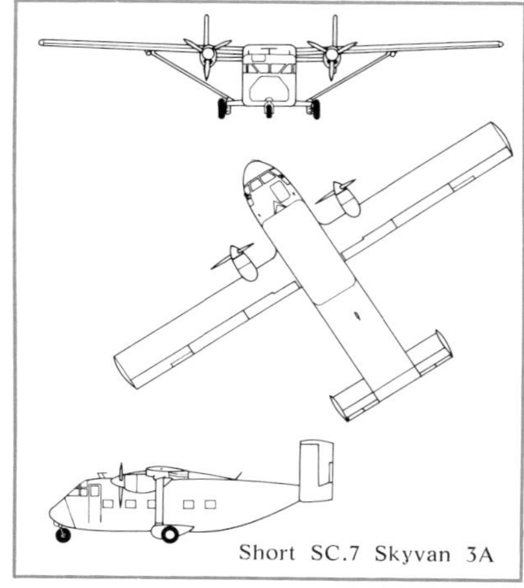
Short SC.7 Skyvan 3A

had two 600 hp Pratt & Whitney Wasps; and the Twin Pioneer 3, also of 1959, had 640 hp Alvis Leonides engines.

Remaining faithful to the policy which had determined their production in the 1930s, de Havilland developed a larger, improved version of their successful D.H.104 Dove in 1949. This was the D.H.114 Heron, a small, four-engine light transport which made its mark in the medium-range category. The Heron prototype made its maiden flight on 10 May 1950, and after completion of proving trials, the assembly lines were set up for the initial series production. The seventh production aircraft became the prototype for the second main variant: the basic difference consisted in the installation of a retractable undercarriage in place of the previous non-retractable undercarriage, which had originally been chosen for simplicity. When tested on 14 December 1952, the D.H.114 Heron 2 showed an improvement in performance and fuel consumption. It won immediate popularity, particularly with the smaller operators. Even the larger airlines were, however, taken with the Heron, among them being Garuda Indonesian Airways, Japan Air Lines, New Zealand National, DHY in Turkey, Indian Airlines, Aviaco in Spain and BEA. The first company to put the little four-engine aircraft into service was BEA, on 4 August 1951, on the London (Northolt)–Jersey run. As with the Dove, there were a number of improved variants and later many Herons were extensively modified and powered by American engines. A total of 149 Herons of all variants were produced including the prototype.

During the 1960s and 1970s other small transports managed to capture a worthwhile market, the Britten-Norman BN-2A Islander and the Short S.C.7 Skyvan, both of which were very versatile and ideally suited for the small operator. The Islander prototype flew for the first time on 20 August 1966, and deliveries started a year later. This twin-engine aircraft has been very successful. In 1977 over 750 had been delivered to customers in 117 countries with orders for some hundred more for completion. In 1979 orders had totalled 900. There have also been several popular military variants, and a three-engine version, the Trislander, of 11 September 1970, for which over a hundred orders have been placed. The company has now been taken over by the Swiss Pilatus company.

The Short S.C.7 Skyvan was designed in 1959 as a general transport, a small "flying boxcar" which was originally powered by Continental piston engines (in the Series 1 and 1A) but was soon converted to propeller-turbine power. The prototype flew on 17 January 1963, and the first turbine-powered Skyvan was tested on 2 October 1963. The first pre-production Skyvan 2 flew on 29 October 1965, with Turbomeca Astazou engines, and the Garrett AiResearch powered Skyvan 3, flew on 15 December 1967. By the end of 1979 approximately 130 Skyvans had been completed, mainly in the final series model, the Skyvan 3, which was built as the Skyvan 3A passenger transport, the Skyvan 3M military transport, and as the all-passenger Skyliner. Larger developments are the 30-passenger 330 and 36-passenger 360.

De Havilland of Canada extended its range in 1972 with the DHC-7 (Dash 7), a 50-passenger STOL transport powered by four propeller-turbines. The prototype flew on 27 March 1975, and the first production aircraft made its maiden flight on 2 April 1977. Apart from the military variant, the Ranger, 110 civil aircraft had been ordered from de Havilland by the end of 1981 and 46 were in airline service.

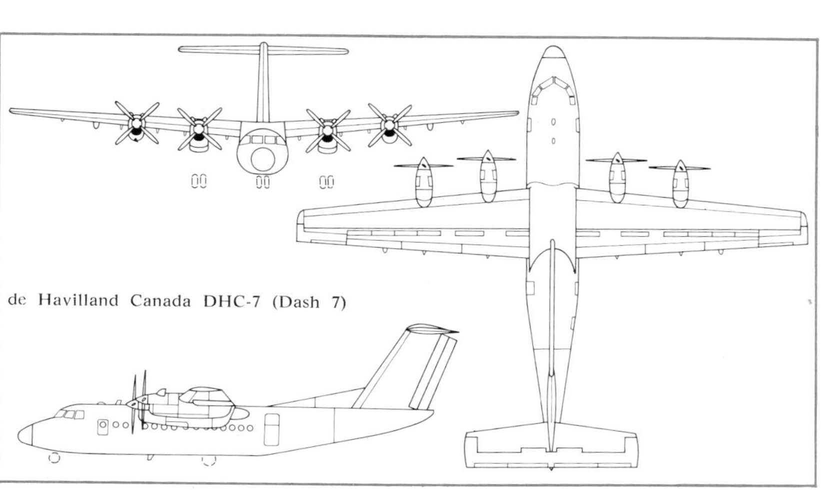
de Havilland Canada DHC-7 (Dash 7)

Plate 152
General purpose aircraft of the 1950s: 1955–1959

The light-transport sector underwent considerable expansion in the immediate postwar period and not only in the more aeronautically advanced countries. In fact it was precisely in those countries which no longer held a significant place in aviation that some very interesting aircraft were produced. This production served a dual purpose of supporting that particular sector of industry without running the risk of becoming involved in the more fiercely competitive markets. A case in point is Germany, relegated after the war to a marginal role; this was the only activity permitted by the victorious Allies.

During the 1950s, among the more typical examples of aircraft designed in Germany were two light transports produced by Dornier, the Do 27 and the Do 28. The former was a small high-wing single-engine type which had excellent performance and was reminiscent of the Fieseler Fi 156 Storch of wartime production. The Do 27 had been developed almost clandestinely in Spain during the first half of the 1950s. The prototype flew on 27 June 1955, and was so impressive that large orders were placed to equip the new Luftwaffe and to meet the German Army's requirement for light aircraft. Production included several variants, and totaled well over 600

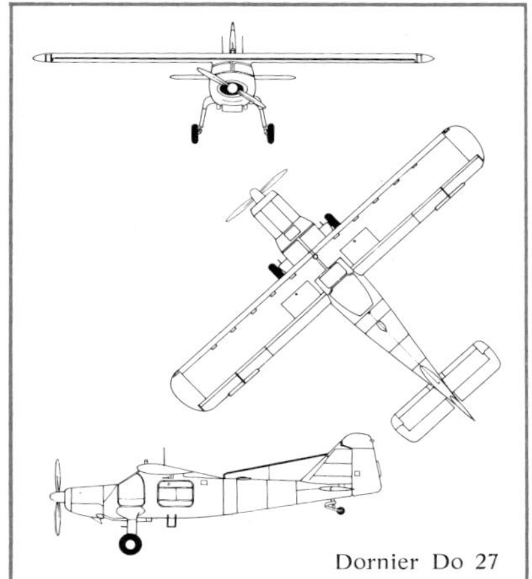
Dornier Do 27

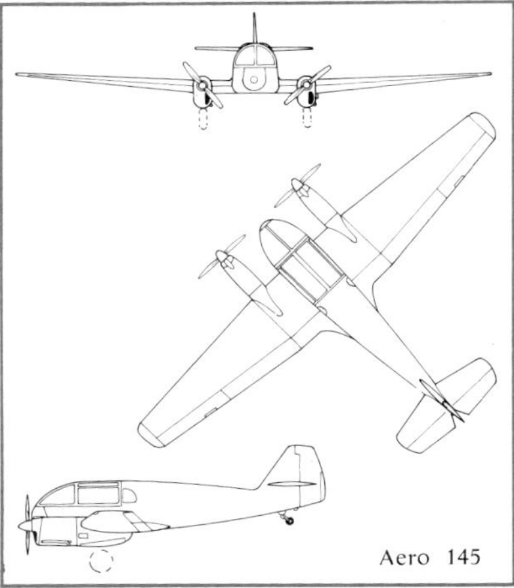
Aero 145

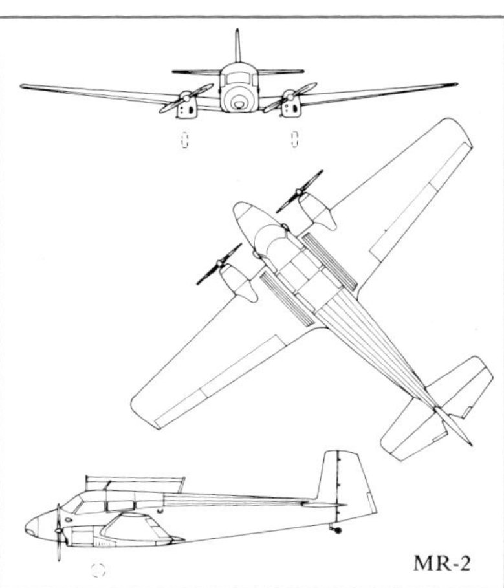
MR-2

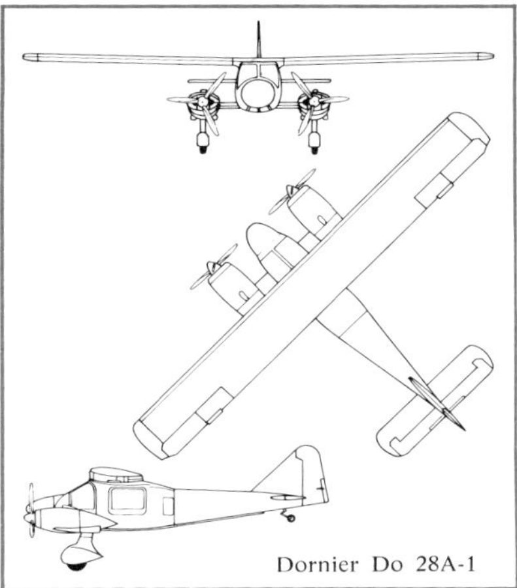
Dornier Do 28A-1

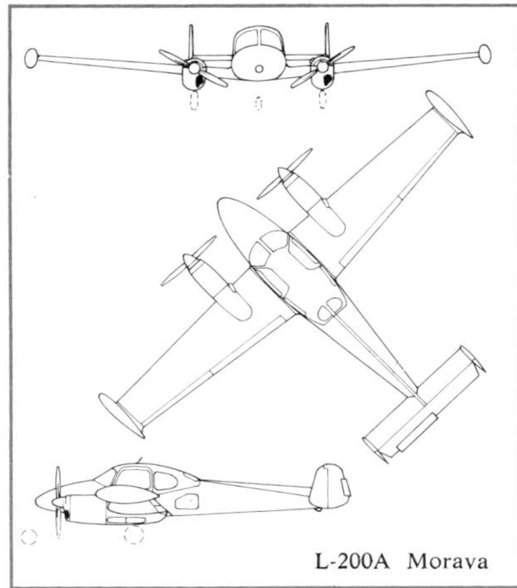
L-200A Morava

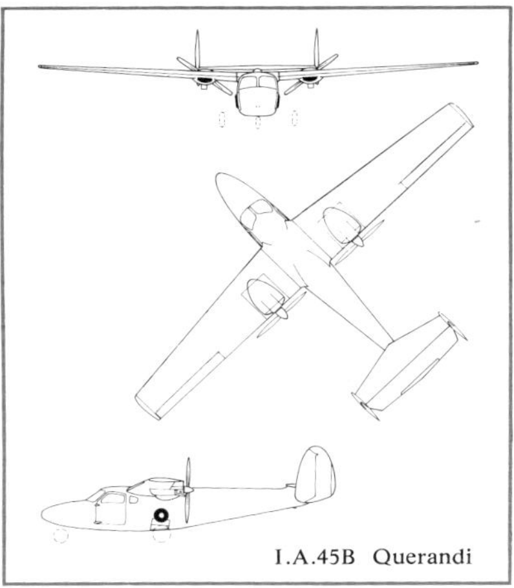
I.A.45B Querandi

aircraft, 420 of which were for military use. Four years later Dornier developed a twin-engine version of this successful model, the Do 28, and the prototype made its maiden flight on 29 April 1959. The assembly lines started work immediately on the first A-1 series aircraft, which sold well to small air transport companies, and in 1963 production was switched to the second main variant, the Do 28B, which had more powerful engines. Manufacture of this twin-engine light transport aircraft totaled 120 by 1966, when the prototype of the Do 28D Skyservant appeared, a complete redesign which was much larger with greater capacity and improved performance and which replaced the Do 28B. By the end of 1979 over 200 Skyservants had been sold to twenty-three countries.

Among Eastern bloc countries, the Czechoslovak aviation industry produced some good light transports. The Aero 145 was popular and was a development of the Model 45 of 1947. Several versions were produced and the type remained in production until 1961, about 700 being built, most of which were exported. The Aero 145 prototype flew in 1958 and only differed from its predecessor in having more powerful engines. The L-200 Morava was another reliable type, designed by Ladislav Smrček as a successor to the Aero design. It was more up to date with improved general performance and the prototype of this elegant twin-engine airplane, built by the National Aircraft Works, first flew on 8 April 1957. Three main variants were manufactured and total production reached over 500 aircraft. The first variant was powered by two 160 hp Walter Minor 6-III engines, the second (the L-200A) by 210 hp Walter Minor M337 engine and the third (the L-200D of 1962) had a strengthened undercarriage, improved hydraulics and three-blade propellers.

Romania produced the MR-2 at about this time—it was a type similar to the L-200 Morava—designed in 1953 and the prototype had first flown three years later. This small twin-engine aircraft was built as a light transport, in particular for air-ambulance work and could accommodate two stretchers. An all-freight version was also built which could carry a payload of half a tonne.

Turning to Latin-America, one of the most interesting light transport aircraft designs of the 1950s was the twin-engine Argentine I.A.45 Querandi, the prototype of which appeared on 23 September 1957. In addition to the first model, which was an executive aircraft, an air-rescue version was built and in 1960 a third variant appeared, designated I.A.45B, which was more powerful.

Plate 153
Light transports of seven nations: 1949–1970

Of contemporary Spanish aircraft, mention should be made of the CASA-201 Alcotan, even though it was eventually put to military use, since it was the first twin-engine transport of all-Spanish design and manufacture. The prototype flew on 11 February 1949, and a total of 112 were built, in three main variants: the 201-B passenger transport; the 201-F for radio and navigational training; and the 201-G for training in bombing and photographic reconnaissance. The transport version could seat up to ten passengers and could also be used as a freighter and as an air-ambulance.

In the same general class as the Spanish twin-engine Alcotan, the Argentine I.A.35 prototype first flew on 21 September 1953, and was the forerunner of a prolific series of military aircraft which were developed throughout the 1960s. There were five models: the Type 1A advanced trainer; the Type 1U for training bombardiers and air-gunners; the Type II light transport; the Type III air-ambulance; and the Type IV photographic-reconnaissance version. Apart from these models a decision was made to develop a civil transport. This was the Pandora which first flew on 28 May 1960, but it never went into series production.

Returning to European civil aviation, it is interesting to note that in the late 1950s the Polish aircraft industry tried to develop a commercial light transport of its own in order to replace the obsolete Soviet aircraft still in use. This project led to the P.Z.L. MD-12 which first flew on 21 July 1959. It was a small, four-engine low-wing monoplane, with a retractable nosewheel undercarriage, which was particularly suited to short-haul operations. Three prototypes were built and handed over to the state airline, LOT, which put them through lengthy proving trials which lasted for three years; however, the airline rejected the MD-12.

From 1928, Flugzeugbau A. Comte in Switzerland designed and built several types of light transport aircraft, but Switzerland's greatest success in this field came with the Pilatus PC-6 Porter STOL transport monoplane which first flew on 4 May 1959. Its box-like fuselage and large loading door made it a useful freighter as well as a passenger aircraft, while its rugged construction and good airfield performance made it particularly suitable for operation in remote areas. The Porter was built in a number of piston-engine versions, and on 2 May 1961, the propeller-turbine powered Turbo-

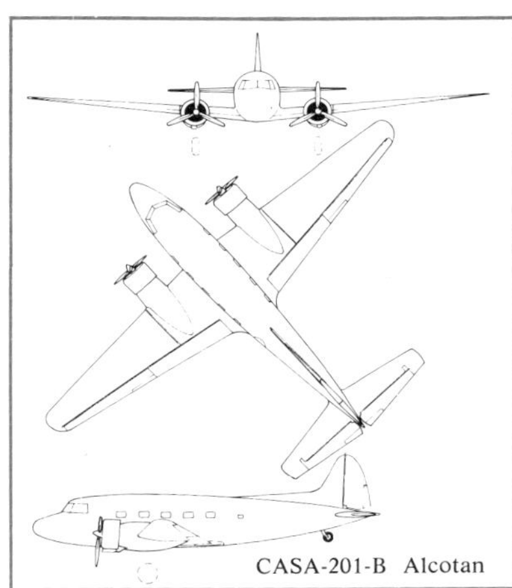
CASA-201-B Alcotan

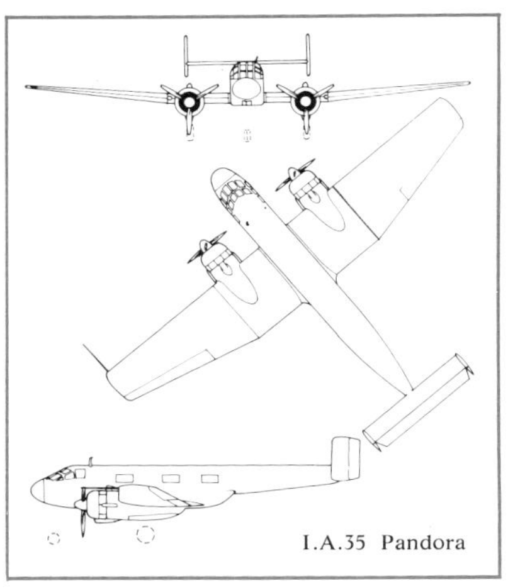
I.A.35 Pandora

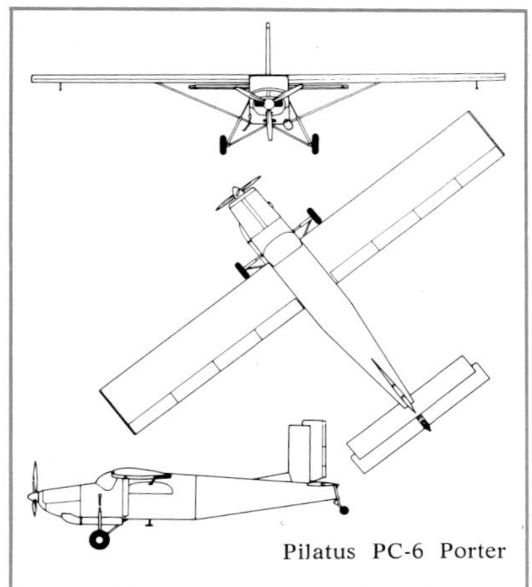
Pilatus PC-6 Porter

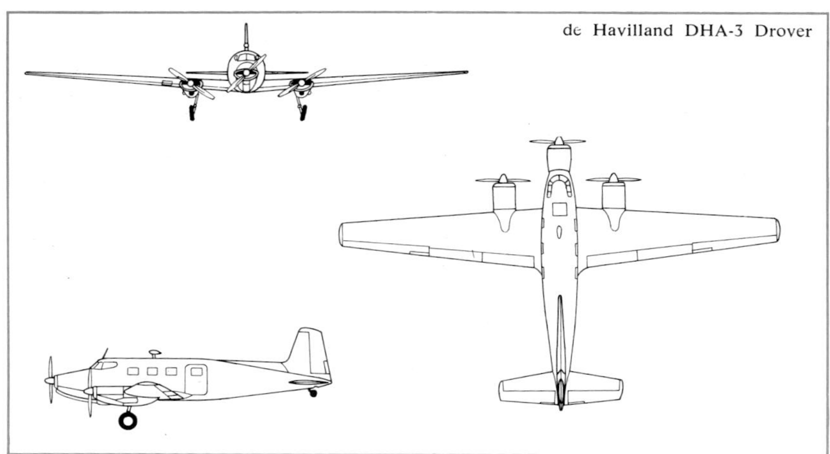
de Havilland DHA-3 Drover

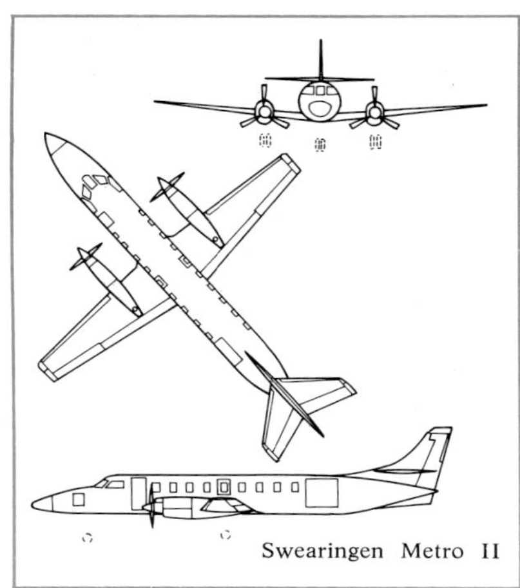
Swearingen Metro II

Porter made its first flight. Turbo-Porters operated one of the most unusual air services when Air-Alpes introduced them on flights to ski resorts, operating from altiports at elevations of up to 2,000 meters. The Turbo-Porter was produced in a number of versions and more than 400 had been built by the late 1970s.

Australia also decided to produce her own aircraft, after having been traditionally dependent on British and U.S. products, and built a light transport, the de Havilland DHA-3 Drover, a small three-engine low-wing monoplane, which was simple to operate and extremely sturdy; many of the D.H.104 Dove parts were utilized for its construction. The Australian subsidiary of de Havilland initiated this program in the late 1940s; the prototype made its maiden flight on 23 January 1948, and production got under way in 1949. By 1953, a total of twenty aircraft had been constructed in two basic variants, the Drover 1 initial variant and the Drover 2, which had double-slotted flaps. In 1959 the Royal Flying Doctor Service decided to modernize its seven Drovers and have 180 hp Lycoming engines in place of the original Gipsy Majors. Other improvements were made, including the fitting of constant-speed feathering propellers. When re-engined this ambulance version was known as the Drover 3 and the first re-engined example made its first flight on 10 November 1959. It could carry pilot, two stretcher cases, doctor and nurse, or pilot and eight passengers.

One of the first transport aircraft projects to be undertaken by The People's Republic of China was the Peking No. 1; this was a small twin-engine light transport built within the space of three months in 1958, flown for the first time on 24 September 1958, and delivered to the Chinese civil aviation authorities on 1 October for testing. Little is actually known of the development of this aircraft; it is probable, however, that some production aircraft have since been built. The Peking No. 1 had a retractable nosewheel undercarriage and was powered by two Ivchenko radial engines. It could seat eight passengers.

The aircraft produced by some of the lesser known aircraft manufacturers also benefited from the introduction of the propeller-turbine. In the United States, the Swearingen company produced an outstandingly original family of light transport aircraft, which originated in 1965 with the Merlin-Metro series of high-performance, reliable twin-propeller-turbine commuter transports. The Metro, in particular, represents the culmination of this development line and can be classified as a sophisticated "mini" airliner for third-level airlines. The Metro I prototype flew in 1969 and was later joined by the improved Metro II. The main feature of this aircraft is its versatility which led to its adoption by many companies. By 1980 over two hundred were in service.

Plate 154
The United States' world leadership in executive aircraft production: 1954–1974

A field in which the United States has taken the lead and still retains its advantage is that of light transport and executive aircraft.

The very large number of aircraft to have been produced in the last thirty years can only be covered somewhat cursorily here, by concentrating on the more widely-used and important models. Among the best piston-engine light-aircraft were the Aero Commander variants, developed from 1944 and continually up-dated until the mid-sixties, giving rise to total production of over 1,200, before changing to propeller-turbine versions. The first of this succession of Aero Commanders first flew on 23 April 1948, and the first series model was the Aero Commander 520 of 1951 (150 built); three years later the series 560 was introduced (80 built), followed by twelve variants which differed in structural details and were powered by various types of engines. Production moved on to the Grand Commander in 1962 and to the Turbo Commander in 1964.

The Beech 18 was even more successful. This was a small twin-engine monoplane which had originated in 1937 as a civil transport; thousands had been built for military use during the war and the aircraft had been modernized and put back on the commercial market after the war, being continually up-dated and remaining extremely competitive. These commercial models were joined on the civilian market by the U.S.A.F. and U.S. Navy's surplus models (the C-45 and the JRB). The new production model was the D18. In 1953 a new variant appeared with a considerably improved wing and more powerful engines (this was the Super 18; first flight 10 December 1953); six years later the G18S model made its debut. This, too, had structural modifications and was more powerful, and in 1962 it was joined by the H18S, which was offered both as a nine-seat executive and as a transport for feeder airlines. A total of 6,326 Beech 18s had been built when production ceased in 1957 and Super 18s numbered 762 when final production ended in 1969—a run of more

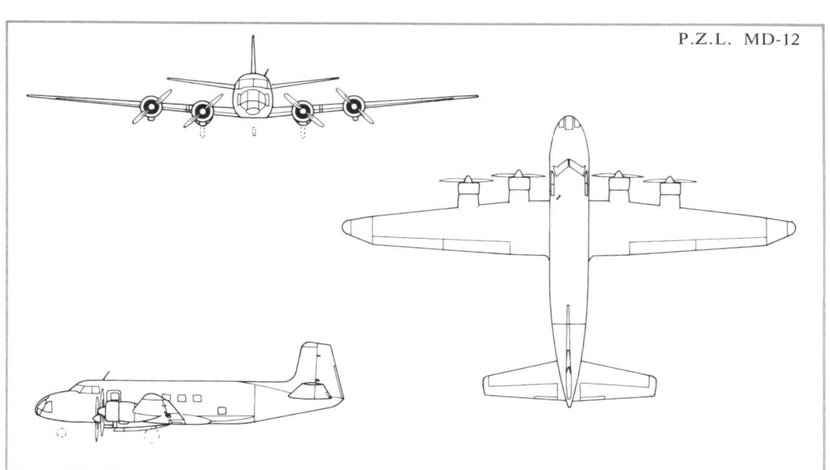
P.Z.L. MD-12

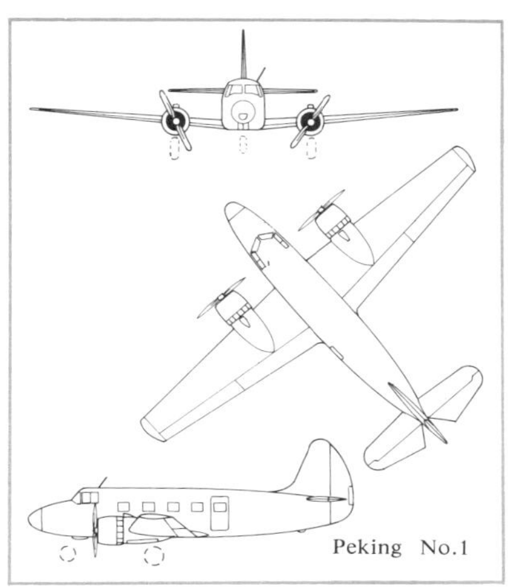
Peking No.1

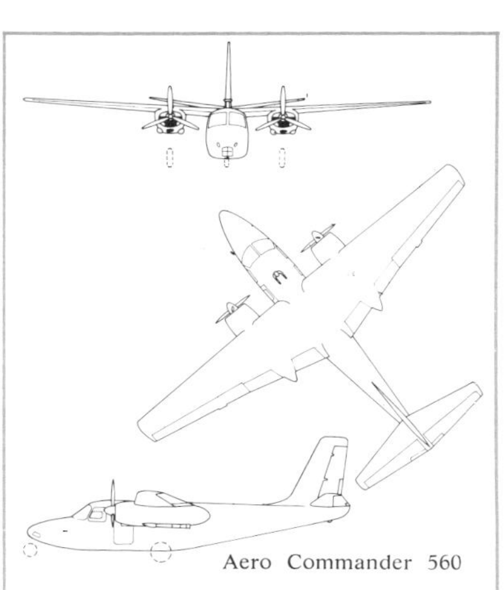
Aero Commander 560

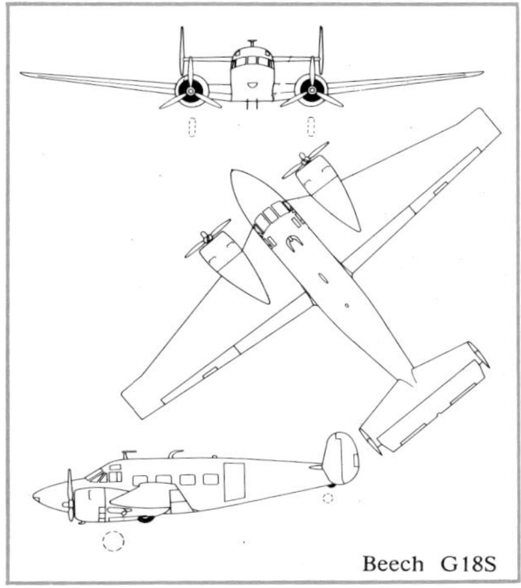
Beech G18S

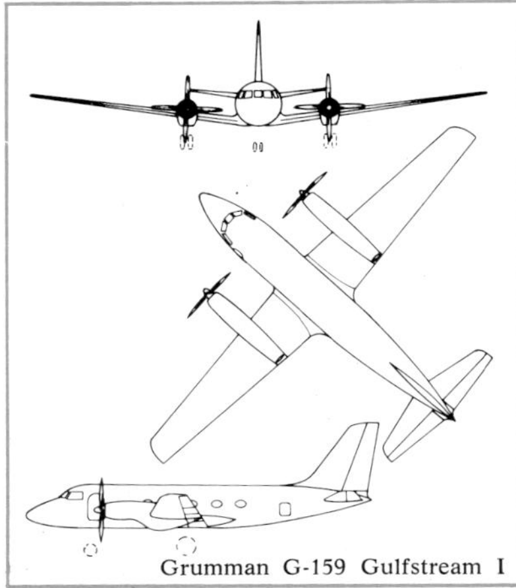
Grumman G-159 Gulfstream I

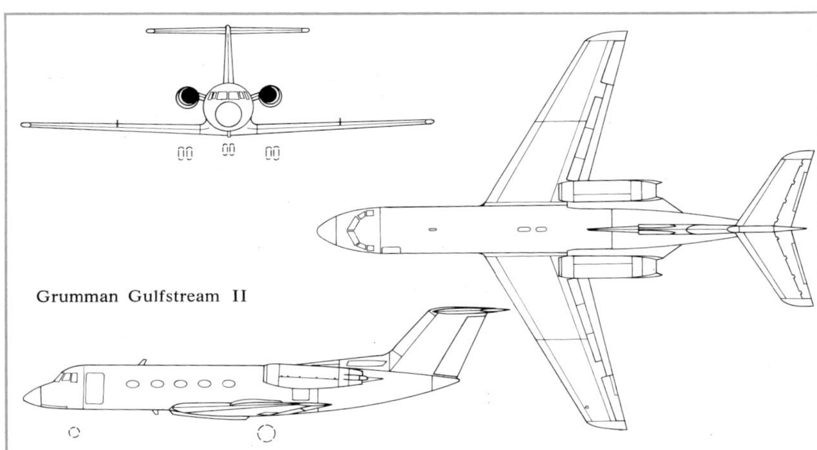
Grumman Gulfstream II

than thirty years. Many Beech 18s are still flown today, by clubs and private owners. These aircraft have undergone a great many unofficial modifications to extend their uses, from interior rearrangement to substitution or change of some of the main components: the original undercarriage, for example, has been replaced by a nosewheel type in some instances, and propeller-turbines have been installed in place of the original power units.

The first turbine-engine executive aircraft was the Grumman G-159 Gulfstream I, design work for which began in 1956, the prototype making its first flight on 14 August 1958. This is a modern, extremely efficient and reliable twin-propeller-turbine corporate transport; 200 had been built when production ended in 1969. Its successor, the Gulfstream II, was announced in May 1965, providing facilities and standards of comfort and performance comparable with international airline standards. The Gulfstream II was powered by two rear-mounted turbofans and could comfortably seat nineteen passengers. Test flights started on 2 October 1966, and deliveries commenced on 6 December 1967.

Although the Gulfstream II was aimed at a somewhat limited market, it sold very well. By 1 January 1979, deliveries totaled more than 240 and the Gulfstream II had been made even more competitive by the option of supplementary wing-tip tanks which increased range by fourteen per cent. The latest version, the Gulfstream III, has a redesigned wing with tip winglets. It first flew in November 1979.

The Gates Learjet series had outstanding performance and was to prove extraordinarily successful. The Learjet 23 prototype had its maiden flight on 7 October 1963, and deliveries started a year later. When 104 Learjets had been built, production was switched to the improved model, the Learjet 24 of 1966, the world's bestselling business jet, of which an initial production run of 80 aircraft was completed. Numerous sub-series were developed, the 24B and the 24D being the main variants; the 24E and the 24F of 1976 were the final variants. The Model 25, which also appeared in 1966, was longer and had increased capacity, as did the Models 35 and 36 of 1973. By the end of 1977 production had reached a total of nearly 800 aircraft. Cessna also adopted the twin-jet formula, drawing on its very long experience in this field. The Citation 500 was announced on 7 October 1968, and the prototype had its first test flight on 15 September of the following year. Deliveries commenced in 1971 and production soon reached high levels: 52 aircraft in 1972, 80 in 1973 and 120 in 1974; overall production totaled 350 by the end of 1976. In September of that year a new, more powerful variant (the Citation I) replaced the preceding model on the assembly lines. Later variants were the Citation II (first flown on 31 January 1977) and the Citation III, which was still larger with a completely redesigned wing.

The Lockheed 1329 JetStar was powered by four engines in rear-mounted pairs, and the first prototype flew on 4 September 1957. This powerful and sophisticated ten-seat executive was a steady seller, and 146 JetStar 6s and 8s were delivered before a new variant, with more powerful engines, was introduced: the JetStar II, the first example of which flew on 18 August 1976.

An important series of twin-jet executive aircraft was developed in the late 1950s by North American (later North American Rockwell and Rockwell International) for military needs. The main civil variants, the Series 40 and the Series 60, were derived from the early T-39 and CT-39 military models and differed in fuselage length and capacity; about one hundred and fifty were sold by March 1969. In 1977 the Series 75 made its debut, being an improved and more powerful version, and then followed the first Sabreliner 75A, with more powerful engines, and a larger tailplane.

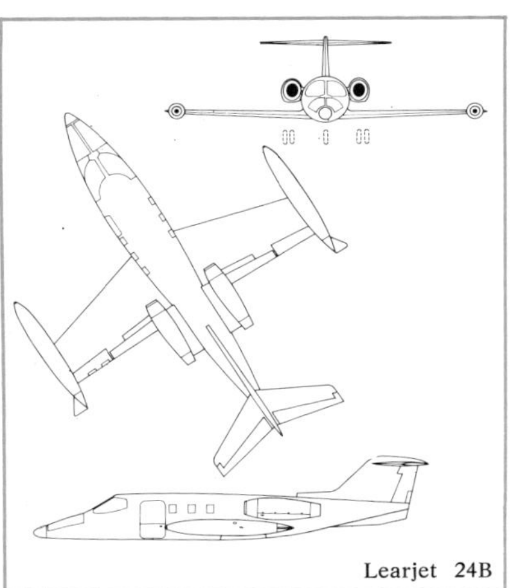
Learjet 24B

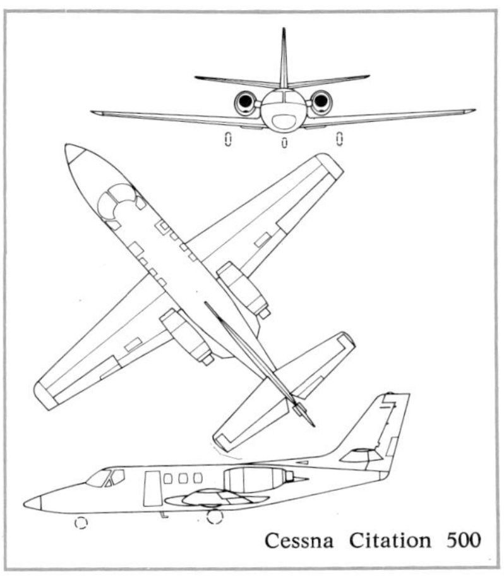
Cessna Citation 500

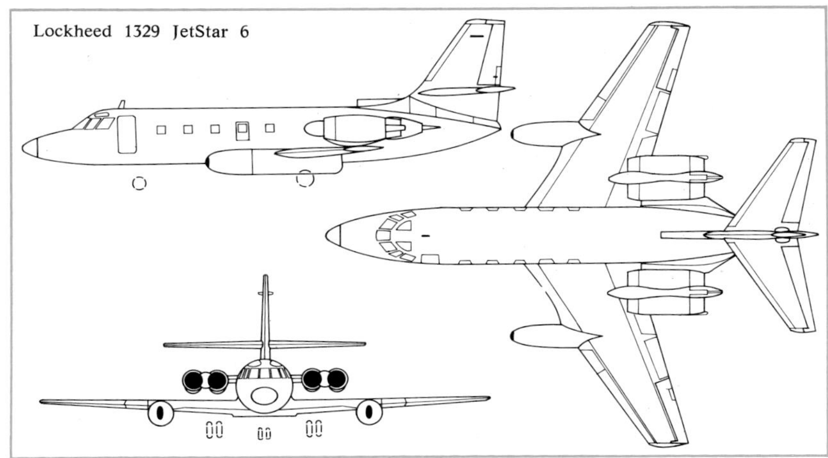
Lockheed 1329 JetStar 6

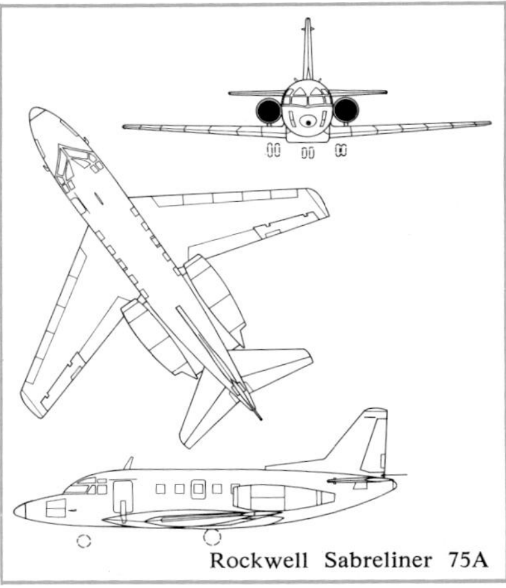
Rockwell Sabreliner 75A

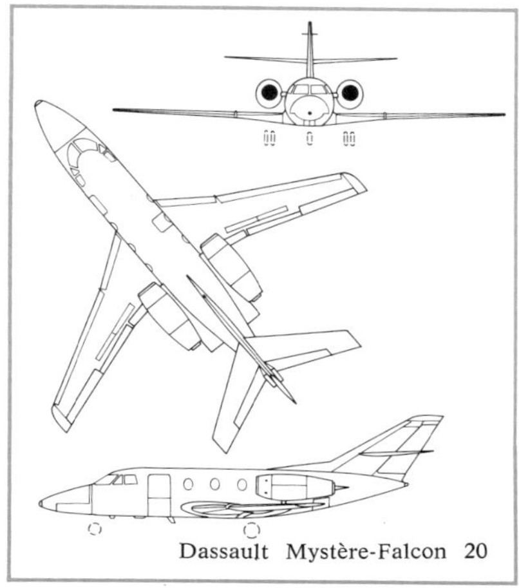
Dassault Mystère-Falcon 20

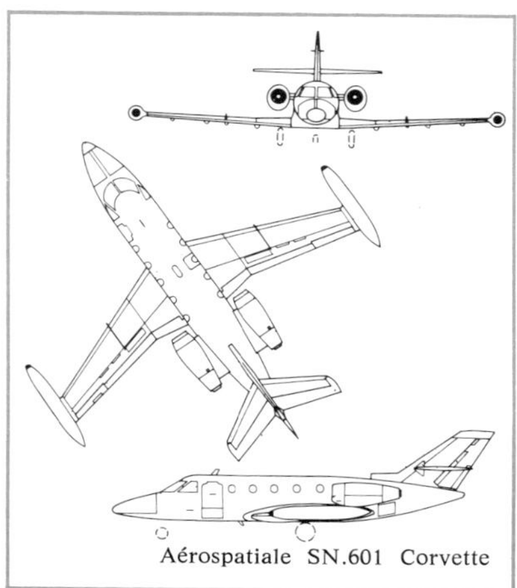
Aérospatiale SN.601 Corvette

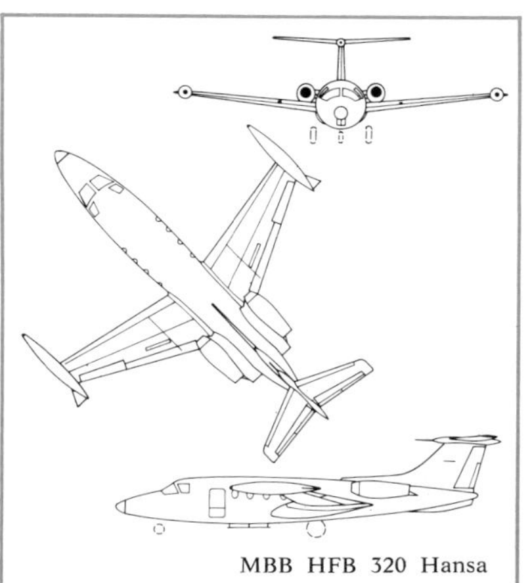
MBB HFB 320 Hansa

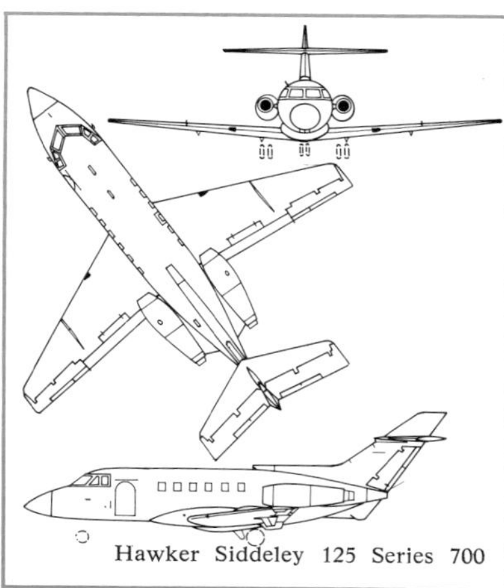
Hawker Siddeley 125 Series 700

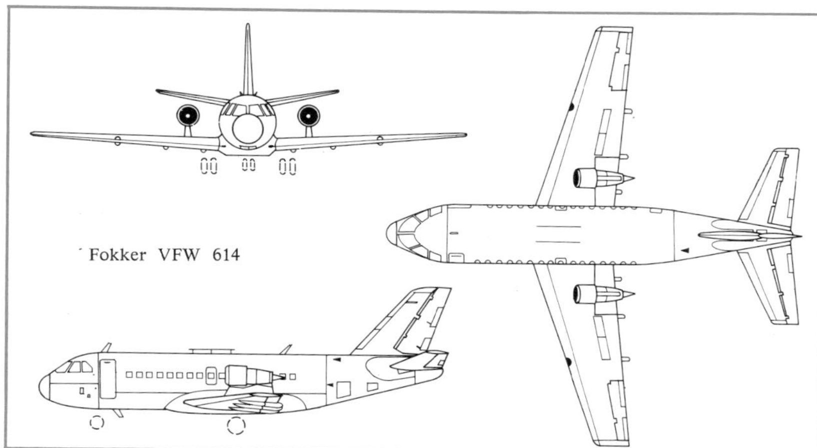
Fokker VFW 614

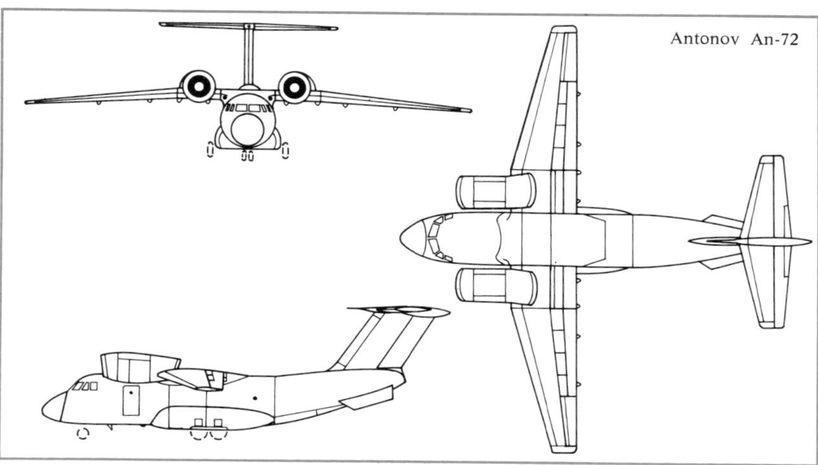
Antonov An-72

Plate 155
European executive and light transport aircraft of the 1960s and 1970s: 1973–1977

The European aviation industry strove to develop worthwhile alternatives to American executive production, often with very satisfactory results. One of the most interesting and prolific executive jets was the Mystère series, built by Dassault in the early sixties and still being up-dated after twenty years in production; hundreds of these aircraft have been sold all over the world. The project was a joint venture with Sud-Aviation, later Aérospatiale, and construction of the prototype began in January 1962. This flew for the first time on 4 May 1963, a small, elegant twin-jet which could seat ten passengers, powered by rear-mounted turbojets. The aircraft caught Pan American's interest and this airline's Business Jets Division ordered 54 production aircraft in August 1963, with an option on a further 106 for distribution on the U.S. market. This marked the beginning of the Mystère's commercial success; in the U.S.A. it was known by the name Fan Jet Falcon. Production continued at very high levels in successive production batches, the main variants being the F of 1969 (more fuel capacity, up-rated engines and new leading and trailing edge flaps), and the G of 1976, powered by more powerful Garrett turbofans. A year later, total sales had reached nearly 400, of which 225 were to the American market. Dassault developed two other variants from the Mystère 20, one smaller model (the Mystère 10 of 1970, over a hundred of which were built), and a larger three-engine derivative, the Mystère 50, which appeared in November 1976. Deliveries started in 1979: this latter variant has a supercritical wing.

Another aircraft of this type was manufactured by Aérospatiale in 1972, the SN.601 Corvette, an attractive twin-jet which closely resembles the Mystère. The first prototype, designated SN.600, flew on 16 July 1970, but was short-lived, crashing eight months later. Drawing on information gathered while testing the prototype which was destroyed, Aérospatiale developed the initial production series, redesignated SN.601, which commenced proving trials on 20 December 1972. The aircraft received its certification in September 1974, and deliveries started immediately afterwards. By mid-1978, thirty-six had been sold.

The British Hawker Siddeley 125 was a more popular aircraft of this type, over 500 of which had been sold by the end of 1981 to customers throughout the world. This was started as a private venture in 1960 as the D.H.125 and the first of the two prototypes flew on 13 August 1962. Production progressed through many variants, some of which were adapted for military use. Eighty-five of the Series 1, 1A and 1B aircraft were built and the R.A.F. took delivery of the whole of the Series 2 production (a total of 20 Dominie T.Mk.1s); 65 Series 3 aircraft were produced, followed by the Series 400 (116) and the Series 600 (72). The latest variant is the Series 700 which first flew on 28 June 1976, and is powered by turbofans. More than 100 Series 700 aircraft have been delivered.

The German Federal Republic has also ventured into the manufacture of these similar transport types. An original design, the HFB 320 Hansa was initiated in the early 1960s by Messerschmitt-Bölkow-Blohm and was extremely distinctive in having a forward-swept wing. The first prototype started flight tests on 21 April 1964, and when certificated, became the first German executive jet to receive formal international aeronautical approval. Production got under way in 1965 and deliveries started in February of the following year. A total of fifty Hansas was built, eight of which were taken by the German Air Force. In the executive version, this twin-jet can seat 7–9 passengers, and up to 12 in higher-density layout. Another salient characteristic is the ease with which the fuselage can be converted for freight transport.

Another, much more ambitious project, since it concerned a much larger, higher-capacity aircraft, was undertaken by VFW (later VFW-Fokker), backed by the Federal Government: the VFW 614 twin-jet. The prototype of this short-range aircraft made its maiden flight on 14 July 1971. This unusual airplane, with its turbofans mounted above the wing, went into service with the Danish airliner Cimber Air in November 1975 and a few saw service with French airlines, but the type was not popular; only sixteen or seventeen were built and production ended in December 1977.

A much larger but equally unusual transport airplane is the Soviet Antonov An-72 with its two turbofans mounted forward of the high-mounted wing and close beside the forward fuselage. Designed to carry 52 passengers in production form, and having STOL performance, the An-72 prototype first flew in 1977.

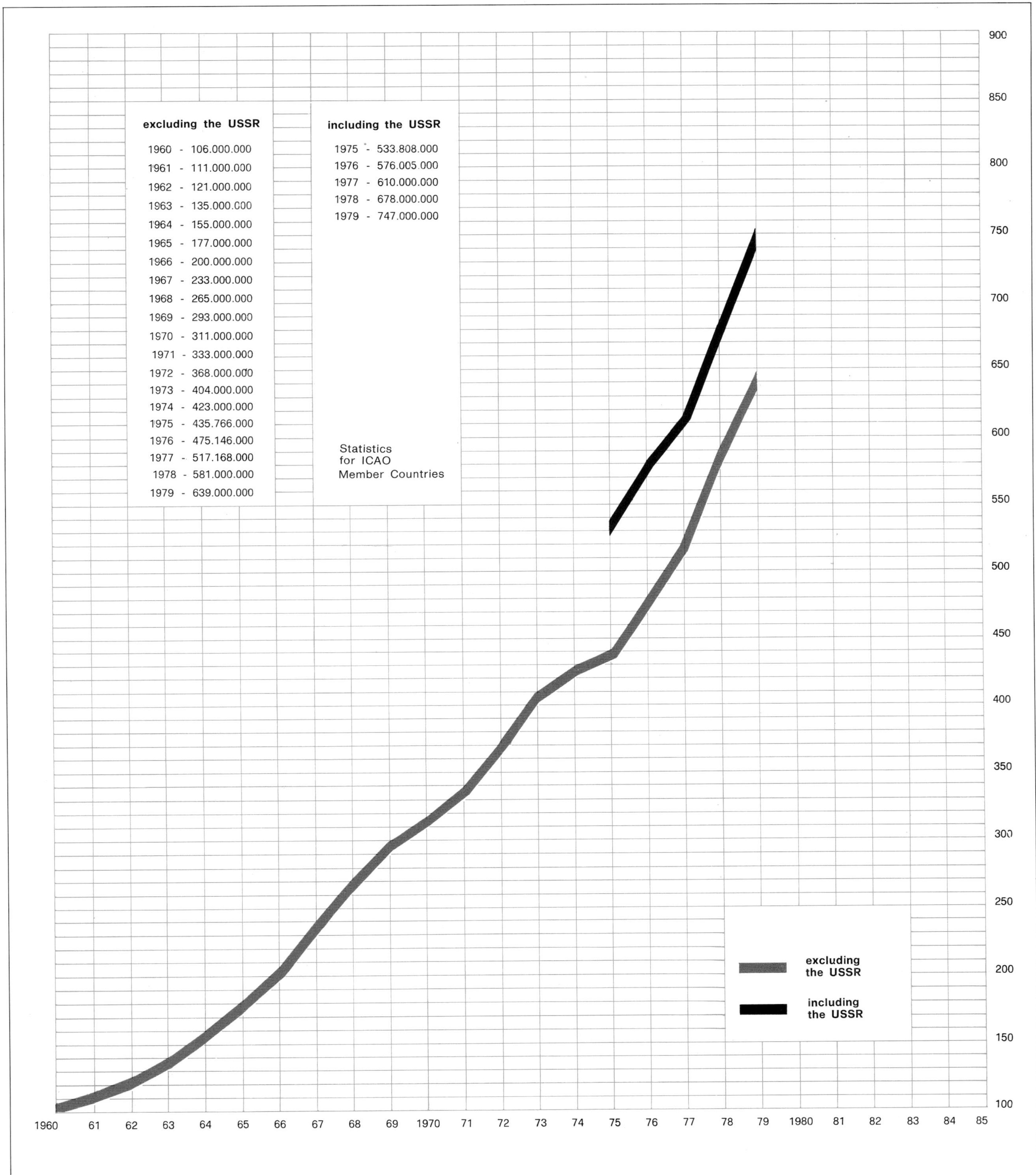
excluding the USSR
1960 - 106.000.000
1961 - 111.000.000
1962 - 121.000.000
1963 - 135.000.000
1964 - 155.000.000
1965 - 177.000.000
1966 - 200.000.000
1967 - 233.000.000
1968 - 265.000.000
1969 - 293.000.000
1970 - 311.000.000
1971 - 333.000.000
1972 - 368.000.000
1973 - 404.000.000
1974 - 423.000.000
1975 - 435.766.000
1976 - 475.146.000
1977 - 517.168.000
1978 - 581.000.000
1979 - 639.000.000
including the USSR
1975 - 533.808.000
1976 - 576.005.000
1977 - 610.000.000
1978 - 678.000.000
1979 - 747.000.000
Statistics for ICAO Member Countries
excluding the USSR
including the USSR
900
850
800
750
700
650
600
550
500
450
400
350
300
250
200
150
100
1960
61
62
63
64
65
66
67
68
69
1970
71
72
73
74
75
76
77
78
79
1980
81
82
83
84
85

Passenger capacity of transport aircraft from 1940 to the present day

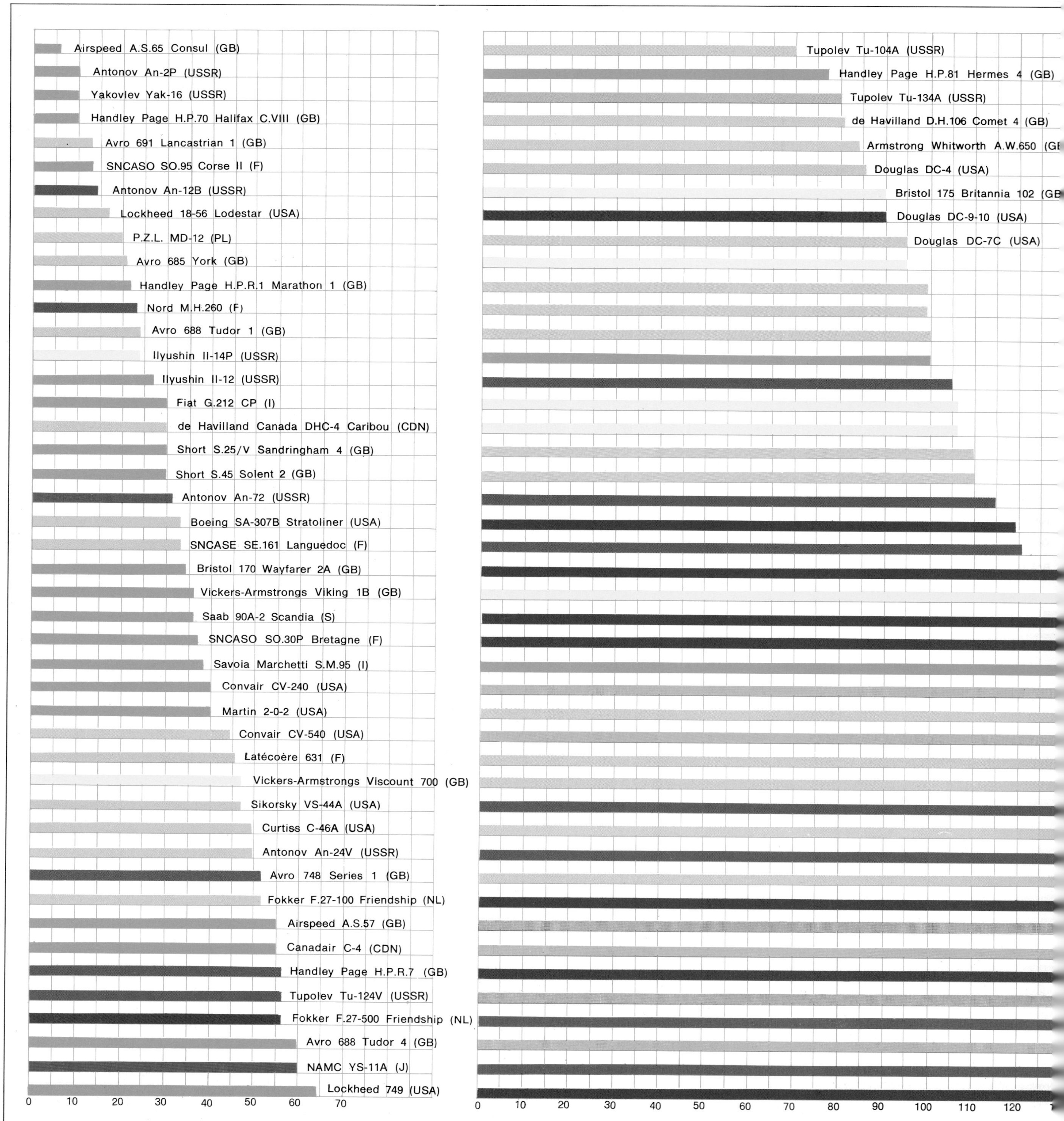
Airspeed A.S.65 Consul (GB)
Antonov An-2P (USSR)
Yakovlev Yak-16 (USSR)
Handley Page H.P.70 Halifax C.VIII (GB)
Avro 691 Lancastrian 1 (GB)
SNCASO SO.95 Corse II (F)
Antonov An-12B (USSR)
Lockheed 18-56 Lodestar (USA)
P.Z.L. MD-12 (PL)
Avro 685 York (GB)
Handley Page H.P.R.1 Marathon 1 (GB)
Nord M.H.260 (F)
Avro 688 Tudor 1 (GB)
Ilyushin Il-14P (USSR)
Ilyushin Il-12 (USSR)
Fiat G.212 CP (I)
de Havilland Canada DHC-4 Caribou (CDN)
Short S.25/V Sandringham 4 (GB)
Short S.45 Solent 2 (GB)
Antonov An-72 (USSR)
Boeing SA-307B Stratoliner (USA)
SNCASE SE.161 Languedoc (F)
Bristol 170 Wayfarer 2A (GB)
Vickers-Armstrongs Viking 1B (GB)
Saab 90A-2 Scandia (S)
SNCASO SO.30P Bretagne (F)
Savoia Marchetti S.M.95 (I)
Convair CV-240 (USA)
Martin 2-0-2 (USA)
Convair CV-540 (USA)
Latécoère 631 (F)
Vickers-Armstrongs Viscount 700 (GB)
Sikorsky VS-44A (USA)
Curtiss C-46A (USA)
Antonov An-24V (USSR)
Avro 748 Series 1 (GB)
Fokker F.27-100 Friendship (NL)
Airspeed A.S.57 (GB)
Canadair C-4 (CDN)
Handley Page H.P.R.7 (GB)
Tupolev Tu-124V (USSR)
Fokker F.27-500 Friendship (NL)
Avro 688 Tudor 4 (GB)
NAMC YS-11A (J)
Lockheed 749 (USA)
0 10 20 30 40 50 60 70
Tupolev Tu-104A (USSR)
Handley Page H.P.81 Hermes 4 (GB)
Tupolev Tu-134A (USSR)
de Havilland D.H.106 Comet 4 (GB)
Armstrong Whitworth A.W.650
Douglas DC-4 (USA)
Bristol 175 Britannia 102
Douglas DC-9-10 (USA)
Douglas DC-7C (USA)
0 10 20 30 40 50 60 70 80 90 100 110 120

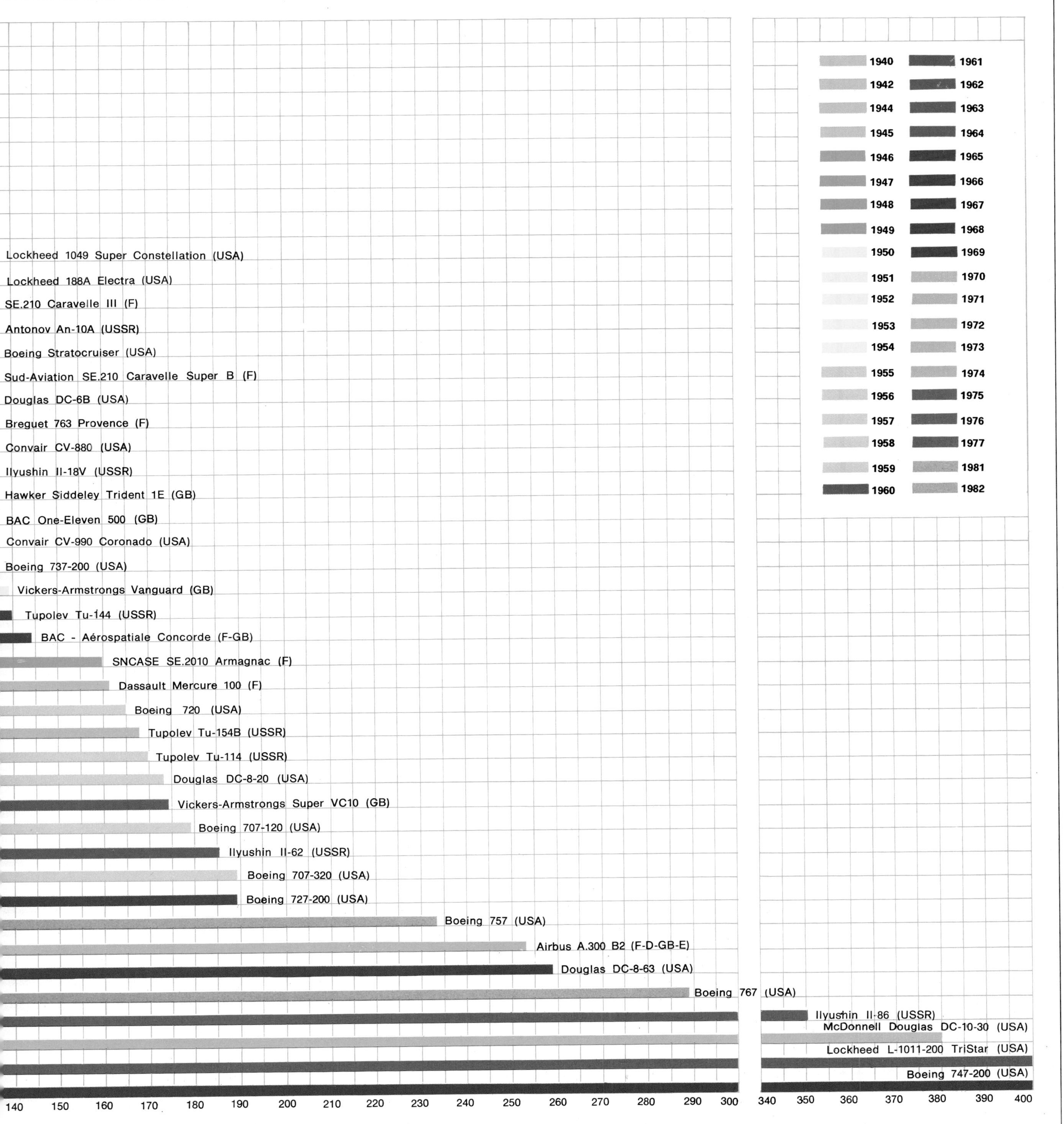
1940
1942
1944
1945
1946
1947
1948
1949
1950
1951
1952
1953
1954
1955
1956
1957
1958
1959
1960
1961
1962
1963
1964
1965
1966
1967
1968
1969
1970
1971
1972
1973
1974
1975
1976
1977
1981
1982
Lockheed 1049 Super Constellation (USA)
Lockheed 188A Electra (USA)
SE.210 Caravelle III (F)
Antonov An-10A (USSR)
Boeing Stratocruiser (USA)
Sud-Aviation SE.210 Caravelle Super B (F)
Douglas DC-6B (USA)
Breguet 763 Provence (F)
Convair CV-880 (USA)
Ilyushin Il-18V (USSR)
Hawker Siddeley Trident 1E (GB)
BAC One-Eleven 500 (GB)
Convair CV-990 Coronado (USA)
Boeing 737-200 (USA)
Vickers-Armstrongs Vanguard (GB)
Tupolev Tu-144 (USSR)
BAC - Aérospatiale Concorde (F-GB)
SNCASE SE.2010 Armagnac (F)
Dassault Mercure 100 (F)
Boeing 720 (USA)
Tupolev Tu-154B (USSR)
Tupolev Tu-114 (USSR)
Douglas DC-8-20 (USA)
Vickers-Armstrongs Super VC10 (GB)
Boeing 707-120 (USA)
Ilyushin Il-62 (USSR)
Boeing 707-320 (USA)
Boeing 727-200 (USA)
Boeing 757 (USA)
Airbus A.300 B2 (F-D-GB-E)
Douglas DC-8-63 (USA)
Boeing 767 (USA)
Ilyushin Il-86 (USSR)
McDonnell Douglas DC-10-30 (USA)
Lockheed L-1011-200 TriStar (USA)
Boeing 747-200 (USA)
140
150
160
170
180
190
200
210
220
230
240
250
260
270
280
290
300
340
350
360
370
380
390
400

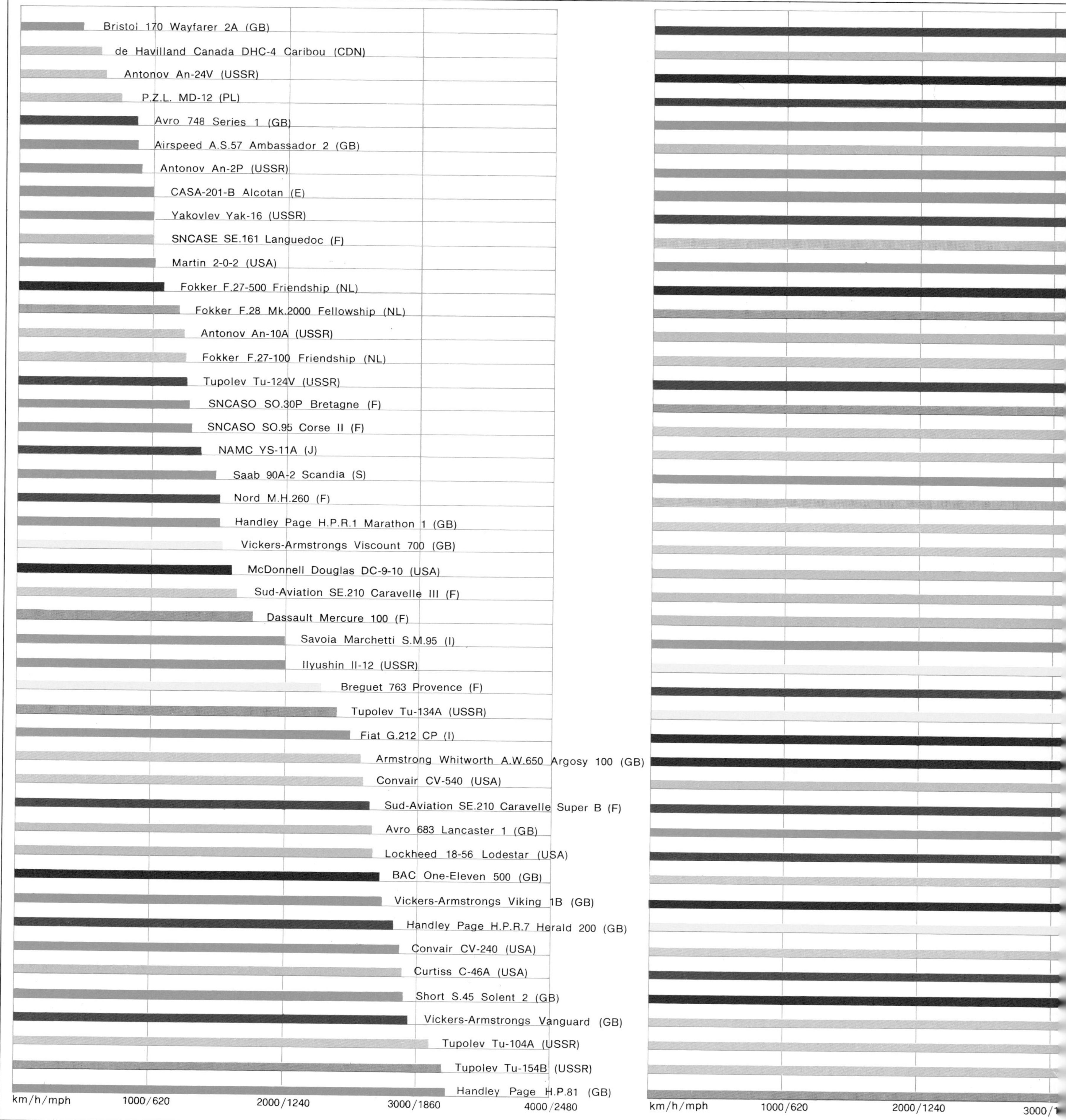
Bristol 170 Wayfarer 2A (GB)
de Havilland Canada DHC-4 Caribou (CDN)
Antonov An-24V (USSR)
P.Z.L. MD-12 (PL)
Avro 748 Series 1 (GB)
Airspeed A.S.57 Ambassador 2 (GB)
Antonov An-2P (USSR)
CASA-201-B Alcotan (E)
Yakovlev Yak-16 (USSR)
SNCASE SE.161 Languedoc (F)
Martin 2-0-2 (USA)
Fokker F.27-500 Friendship (NL)
Fokker F.28 Mk.2000 Fellowship (NL)
Antonov An-10A (USSR)
Fokker F.27-100 Friendship (NL)
Tupolev Tu-124V (USSR)
SNCASO SO.30P Bretagne (F)
SNCASO SO.95 Corse II (F)
NAMC YS-11A (J)
Saab 90A-2 Scandia (S)
Nord M.H.260 (F)
Handley Page H.P.R.1 Marathon 1 (GB)
Vickers-Armstrongs Viscount 700 (GB)
McDonnell Douglas DC-9-10 (USA)
Sud-Aviation SE.210 Caravelle III (F)
Dassault Mercure 100 (F)
Savoia Marchetti S.M.95 (I)
Ilyushin Il-12 (USSR)
Breguet 763 Provence (F)
Tupolev Tu-134A (USSR)
Fiat G.212 CP (I)
Armstrong Whitworth A.W.650 Argosy 100 (GB)
Convair CV-540 (USA)
Sud-Aviation SE.210 Caravelle Super B (F)
Avro 683 Lancaster 1 (GB)
Lockheed 18-56 Lodestar (USA)
BAC One-Eleven 500 (GB)
Vickers-Armstrongs Viking 1B (GB)
Handley Page H.P.R.7 Herald 200 (GB)
Convair CV-240 (USA)
Curtiss C-46A (USA)
Short S.45 Solent 2 (GB)
Vickers-Armstrongs Vanguard (GB)
Tupolev Tu-104A (USSR)
Tupolev Tu-154B (USSR)
Handley Page H.P.81 (GB)
km/h/mph
1000/620
2000/1240
3000/1860
4000/2480
km/h/mph
1000/620
2000/1240

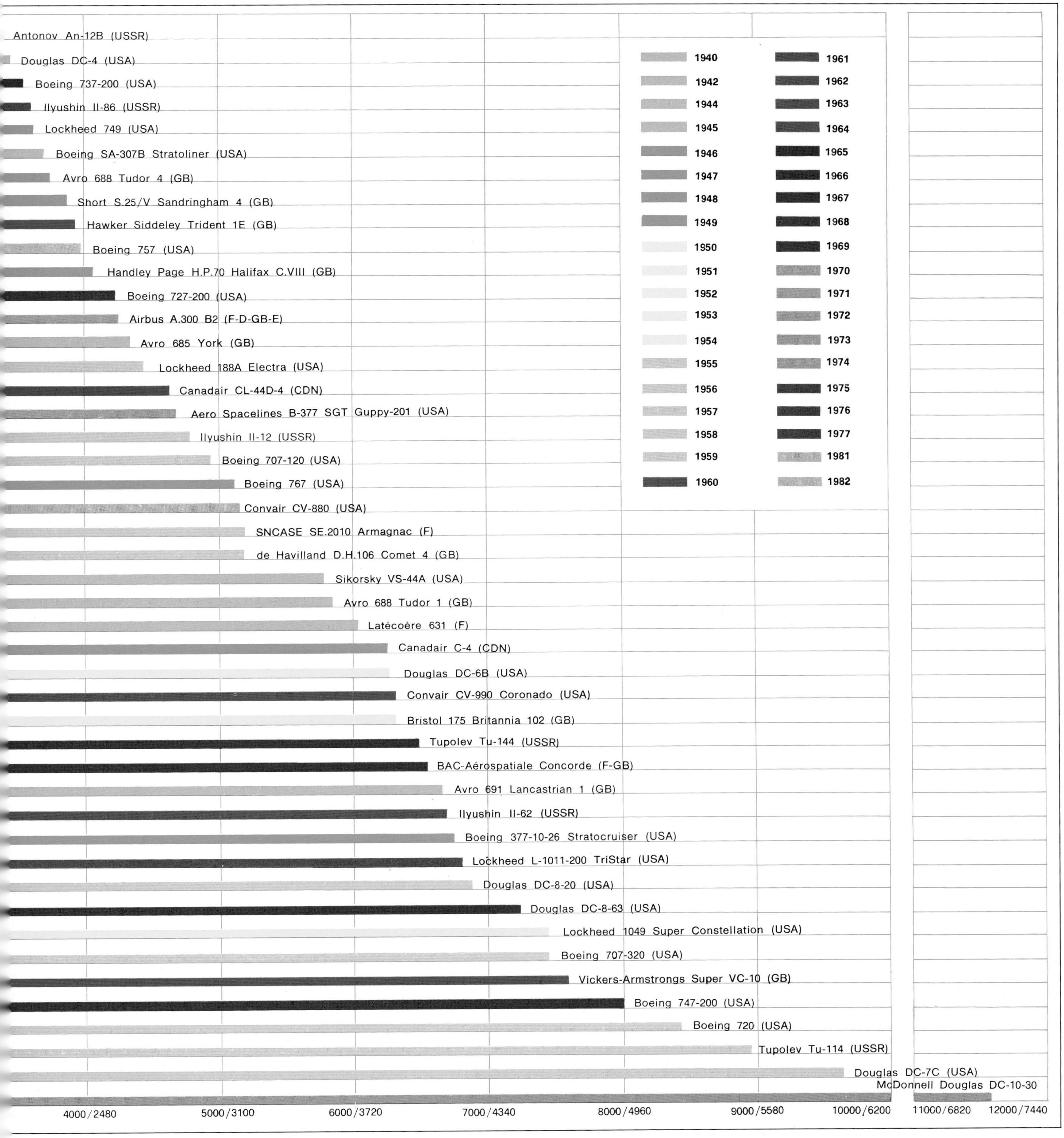

Antonov An-12B (USSR)
Douglas DC-4 (USA)
Boeing 737-200 (USA)
Ilyushin Il-86 (USSR)
Lockheed 749 (USA)
Boeing SA-307B Stratoliner (USA)
Avro 688 Tudor 4 (GB)
Short S.25/V Sandringham 4 (GB)
Hawker Siddeley Trident 1E (GB)
Boeing 757 (USA)
Handley Page H.P.70 Halifax C.VIII (GB)
Boeing 727-200 (USA)
Airbus A.300 B2 (F-D-GB-E)
Avro 685 York (GB)
Lockheed 188A Electra (USA)
Canadair CL-44D-4 (CDN)
Aero Spacelines B-377 SGT Guppy-201 (USA)
Ilyushin Il-12 (USSR)
Boeing 707-120 (USA)
Boeing 767 (USA)
Convair CV-880 (USA)
SNCASE SE.2010 Armagnac (F)
de Havilland D.H.106 Comet 4 (GB)
Sikorsky VS-44A (USA)
Avro 688 Tudor 1 (GB)
Latécoère 631 (F)
Canadair C-4 (CDN)
Douglas DC-6B (USA)
Convair CV-990 Coronado (USA)
Bristol 175 Britannia 102 (GB)
Tupolev Tu-144 (USSR)
BAC-Aérospatiale Concorde (F-GB)
Avro 691 Lancastrian 1 (GB)
Ilyushin Il-62 (USSR)
Boeing 377-10-26 Stratocruiser (USA)
Lockheed L-1011-200 TriStar (USA)
Douglas DC-8-20 (USA)
Douglas DC-8-63 (USA)
Lockheed 1049 Super Constellation (USA)
Boeing 707-320 (USA)
Vickers-Armstrongs Super VC-10 (GB)
Boeing 747-200 (USA)
Boeing 720 (USA)
Tupolev Tu-114 (USSR)
Douglas DC-7C (USA)
McDonnell Douglas DC-10-30

4000/2480 5000/3100 6000/3720 7000/4340 8000/4960 9000/5580 10000/6200 11000/6820 12000/7440

1940 1942 1944 1945 1946 1947 1948 1949 1950 1951 1952 1953 1954 1955 1956 1957 1958 1959 1960
1961 1962 1963 1964 1965 1966 1967 1968 1969 1970 1971 1972 1973 1974 1975 1976 1977 1981 1982

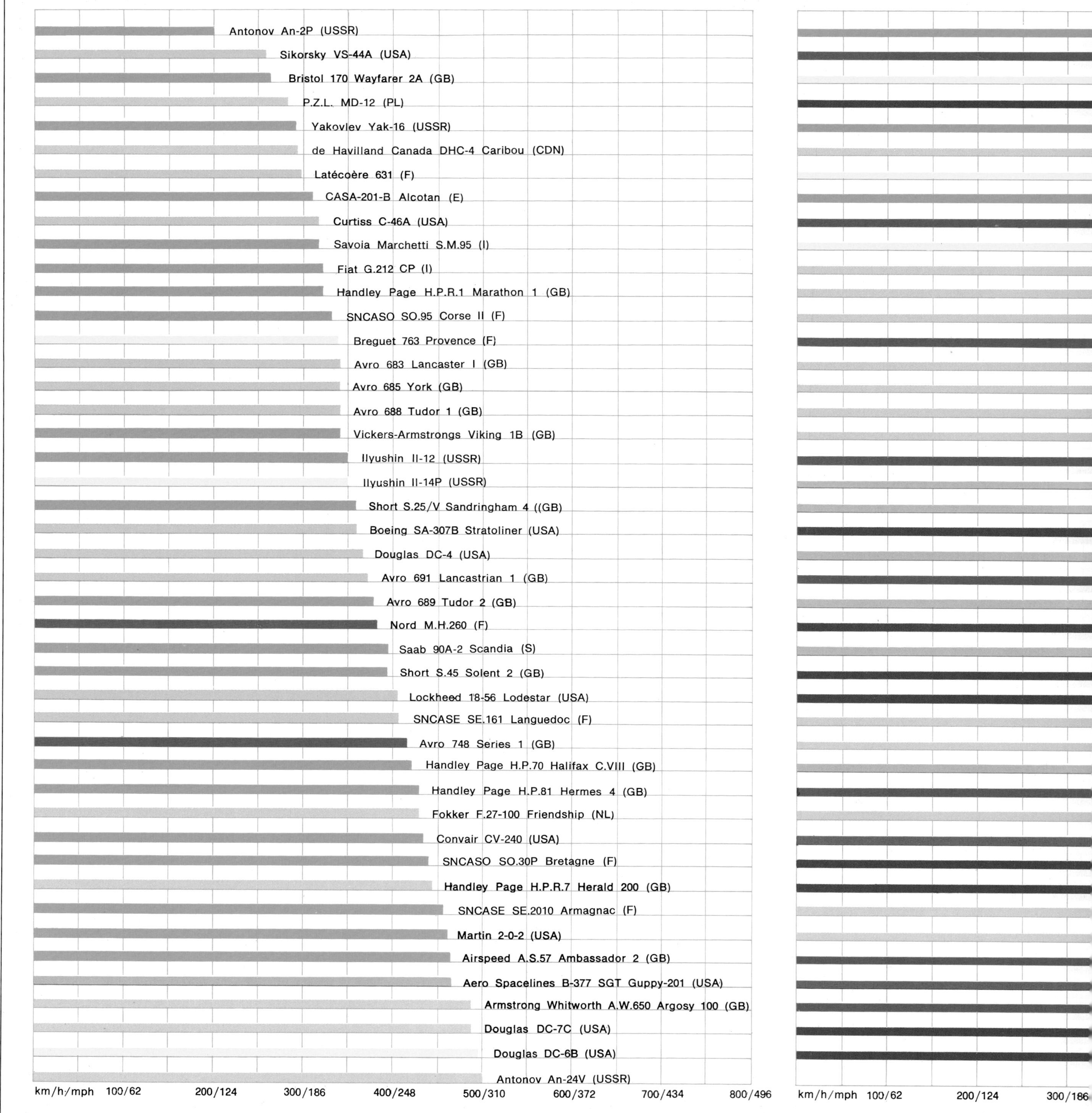

Antonov An-2P (USSR)
Sikorsky VS-44A (USA)
Bristol 170 Wayfarer 2A (GB)
P.Z.L. MD-12 (PL)
Yakovlev Yak-16 (USSR)
de Havilland Canada DHC-4 Caribou (CDN)
Latécoère 631 (F)
CASA-201-B Alcotan (E)
Curtiss C-46A (USA)
Savoia Marchetti S.M.95 (I)
Fiat G.212 CP (I)
Handley Page H.P.R.1 Marathon 1 (GB)
SNCASO SO.95 Corse II (F)
Breguet 763 Provence (F)
Avro 683 Lancaster I (GB)
Avro 685 York (GB)
Avro 688 Tudor 1 (GB)
Vickers-Armstrongs Viking 1B (GB)
Ilyushin Il-12 (USSR)
Ilyushin Il-14P (USSR)
Short S.25/V Sandringham 4 ((GB)
Boeing SA-307B Stratoliner (USA)
Douglas DC-4 (USA)
Avro 691 Lancastrian 1 (GB)
Avro 689 Tudor 2 (GB)
Nord M.H.260 (F)
Saab 90A-2 Scandia (S)
Short S.45 Solent 2 (GB)
Lockheed 18-56 Lodestar (USA)
SNCASE SE.161 Languedoc (F)
Avro 748 Series 1 (GB)
Handley Page H.P.70 Halifax C.VIII (GB)
Handley Page H.P.81 Hermes 4 (GB)
Fokker F.27-100 Friendship (NL)
Convair CV-240 (USA)
SNCASO SO.30P Bretagne (F)
Handley Page H.P.R.7 Herald 200 (GB)
SNCASE SE.2010 Armagnac (F)
Martin 2-0-2 (USA)
Airspeed A.S.57 Ambassador 2 (GB)
Aero Spacelines B-377 SGT Guppy-201 (USA)
Armstrong Whitworth A.W.650 Argosy 100 (GB)
Douglas DC-7C (USA)
Douglas DC-6B (USA)
Antonov An-24V (USSR)
km/h/mph 100/62 200/124 300/186 400/248 500/310 600/372 700/434 800/496
km/h/mph 100/62 200/124 300/186

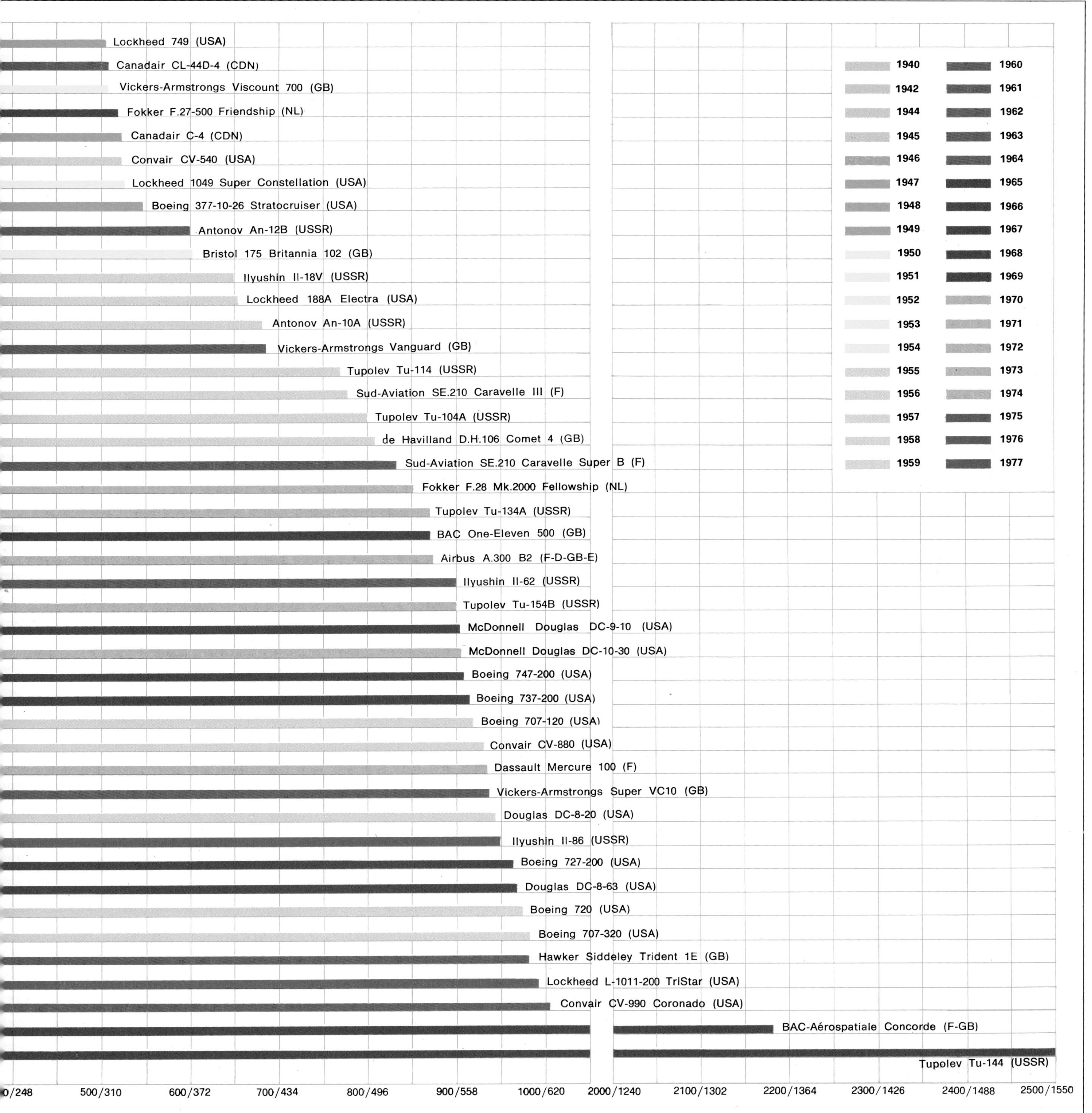

Lockheed 749 (USA)
Canadair CL-44D-4 (CDN)
Vickers-Armstrongs Viscount 700 (GB)
Fokker F.27-500 Friendship (NL)
Canadair C-4 (CDN)
Convair CV-540 (USA)
Lockheed 1049 Super Constellation (USA)
Boeing 377-10-26 Stratocruiser (USA)
Antonov An-12B (USSR)
Bristol 175 Britannia 102 (GB)
Ilyushin Il-18V (USSR)
Lockheed 188A Electra (USA)
Antonov An-10A (USSR)
Vickers-Armstrongs Vanguard (GB)
Tupolev Tu-114 (USSR)
Sud-Aviation SE.210 Caravelle III (F)
Tupolev Tu-104A (USSR)
de Havilland D.H.106 Comet 4 (GB)
Sud-Aviation SE.210 Caravelle Super B (F)
Fokker F.28 Mk.2000 Fellowship (NL)
Tupolev Tu-134A (USSR)
BAC One-Eleven 500 (GB)
Airbus A.300 B2 (F-D-GB-E)
Ilyushin Il-62 (USSR)
Tupolev Tu-154B (USSR)
McDonnell Douglas DC-9-10 (USA)
McDonnell Douglas DC-10-30 (USA)
Boeing 747-200 (USA)
Boeing 737-200 (USA)
Boeing 707-120 (USA)
Convair CV-880 (USA)
Dassault Mercure 100 (F)
Vickers-Armstrongs Super VC10 (GB)
Douglas DC-8-20 (USA)
Ilyushin Il-86 (USSR)
Boeing 727-200 (USA)
Douglas DC-8-63 (USA)
Boeing 720 (USA)
Boeing 707-320 (USA)
Hawker Siddeley Trident 1E (GB)
Lockheed L-1011-200 TriStar (USA)
Convair CV-990 Coronado (USA)
BAC-Aérospatiale Concorde (F-GB)
Tupolev Tu-144 (USSR)
1940
1942
1944
1945
1946
1947
1948
1949
1950
1951
1952
1953
1954
1955
1956
1957
1958
1959
1960
1961
1962
1963
1964
1965
1966
1967
1968
1969
1970
1971
1972
1973
1974
1975
1976
1977
0/248
500/310
600/372
700/434
800/496
900/558
1000/620
2000/1240
2100/1302
2200/1364
2300/1426
2400/1488
2500/1550

Avro 685 York - 1942, GB (127)

de Havilland D.H.104 Dove - 1945, GB (150)

Avro 691 Lancastrian - 1945, GB (127)

Short S.25 Sandringham - 1946, GB (131)

Vickers-Armstrongs Viking 1B - 1948, GB (134)

Short S.A.6 Sealand - 1948, GB (150)

Vickers-Armstrongs Viscount 700 - 1950, GB (136)

de Havilland D.H.114 Heron 1 - 1950,GB (151)

Bristol 175 Britannia 300 - 1957, GB (142)

Vickers-Armstrongs Viscount 802 - 1956, GB (136)

de Havilland D.H.106 Comet 4B - 1959, GB (137)

Armstrong Whitworth A.W.650 Argosy - 1959, GB (140)

Avro (Hawker Siddeley) 748 Series 2 - 1961, GB (136)

Vickers-Armstrongs Vanguard 951 - 1959, GB (142)

Vickers-Armstrongs VC10 - 1962, GB (143)

Hawker Siddeley Trident - 1962, GB (144)

Pilatus Britten-Norman BN-2A Islander - 1965, GB (151)

Short Skyvan - 1963, GB (151)

BAC One-Eleven 500 - 1967, GB (143)

Hawker Siddeley 125 Series 700 - 1976, GB (155)

Saab 90A-2 Scandia - 1946, S (134)

SNCASE SE.2010 Armagnac, seen as an engine testbed - 1949, F (129)

Breguet 763 Provence - 1951, F (129)

Sud-Aviation SE.210 Caravelle - 1955, F (137)

Dassault Mystère-Falcon 20 - 1963, F (155)

BAC-Aérospatiale Concorde - 1969, F-GB (147)

Dassault Mercure 100 - 1971, F (145)

Aérospatiale SN.601 Corvette - 1972, F (155)

Airbus A300 - 1974, F-GB-D-NL-E (145)

Dornier Do 27 - 1955, D (152)

Dornier Do 28A-1 - 1959, D (152)

VFW-Fokker VFW 614 - 1971, D (155)

Fokker F.28 Mk.1000 Fellowship - 1967, NL (143)

Fokker F.27-100 Friendship - 1958, NL (141)

Savoia Marchetti S.M.95 - 1947, I (148)

MBB HFB 320 Hansa - 1964, D (155)

Fokker F.27-400 Friendship - 1961, NL (141)

Cant Z.511 - 1943, I (130)

Fiat G.212 - 1947, I (148)

Breda-Zappata B.Z.308 - 1948, I (148)

Macchi M.B.320 - 1949, I (148)

Piaggio P.136-L - 1955, I (148)

Piaggio P.166B Portofino - 1962, I (148)

Pilatus PC-6 Turbo-Porter - 1961, CH (152)

CASA-201 Alcotan - 1949, E (153)

Ilyushin Il-14 - 1953, USSR (135)

Tupolev Tu-104A - 1957, USSR (139)

Tupolev Tu-114 - 1957, USSR (142)

Ilyushin Il-18 - 1957, USSR (142)

Antonov An-12 - 1960, USSR (140)

Ilyushin Il-62 - 1963, USSR (143)

Tupolev Tu-124 - 1960, USSR (139)

Tupolev Tu-134 - 1963, USSR (143)

Tupolev Tu-144 - 1968, USSR (147)

Tupolev Tu-154 - 1973, USSR (144)

Ilyushin Il-86 - 1976, USSR (146)

de Havilland Canada DHC-3 Otter - 1951, CDN (149)

Canadair Four - 1947, CDN (149)

de Havilland Canada DHC-2 Beaver - 1947, CDN (149)

de Havilland Canada DHC-4 Caribou - 1958, CDN (149)

Canadair CL-44D-4 - 1960, CDN (149)

de Havilland Canada DHC-6 Twin Otter 300 - 1969, CDN (149)

de Havilland Canada DHC-7 (Dash 7) - 1975, CDN (151)

Curtiss C-46 - 1942, USA (126)

Lockheed 18-56 Lodestar - 1940, USA (126)

Douglas DC-4 - 1942, USA (126)

Boeing 377 Stratocruiser - 1947, USA (132)

Lockheed 149 Constellation - 1947, USA (132)

Convair CV-240 Convair-Liner - 1947, USA (132)

Douglas DC-6A - 1949, USA (133)

Aero Commander 560 - 1954, USA (154)

Lockheed 1049G Super Constellation - 1954, USA (133)

Boeing 707-121 - 1957, USA (138)

Lockheed 188 Electra (cargo conversion) - 1957, USA (142)

Grumman G-159 Gulfstream I - 1958, USA (154)

Boeing 720 - 1959, USA (139)

Convair CV-880 - 1959, USA (139)

Douglas DC-9 - 1965, USA (143)

Learjet 24B - 1966, USA (154)

Boeing 707-320 - 1959, USA (138)

Convair CV-990 Coronado - 1960, USA (139)

Douglas DC-10 - 1970, USA (146)

Douglas DC-8-20 - 1959, USA (138)

Boeing 737 - 1967, USA (145)

Boeing 727-200 - 1972, USA (144)

Boeing 747 - 1969, USA (146)

Lockheed L-1011 TriStar - 1970, USA (146)

NAMC YS-11A-300 - 1968, J (141)

I.A.45 Querandi - 1957, RA (152)

I.A.35 - 1957, RA (153)

7. SUPERSONIC AND SPACE FLIGHT

By means of television hundreds of millions of people were able to watch the first space shuttle, *Columbia*, come back to earth on 14 April 1981. The landing was not only a profoundly thrilling moment, it was also the most recent milestone in the history of aviation as well as in space travel. Almost exactly twenty years after man's first journey into space and twelve years after the first moon landing, scientists and engineers have managed to harmonize two methods of travel—the airplane and the spacecraft. The conquest of space has tended to be appreciated on the level of an exciting science-fiction story and has appealed to the public's emotions, since it has been difficult to keep track of any connecting thread or readily understood explanation which can be related to everyday life. So far progress has taken on the appearance of isolated feats of technological virtuosity, an end in themselves. The *Columbia* flight changed all this. For a start, the philosophy which led to its construction was completely different: an aircraft was to be built which could operate a shuttle service between earth and space, in the same way as our familiar airliners fly regularly from one airport to another around the world. The space shuttle was, of course, launched in the same way as a spacecraft and orbited the earth 36 times, but the most critical stage of its journey was its re-entry, and this was not accomplished in the same way as with earlier spacecraft but as an airplane. It was an incredibly sophisticated airplane at that, with its advanced control and computer systems, but it also relied on the most elementary form of flight which had fascinated hundreds of pioneers a century before—gliding.

Columbia landed as a glider, albeit a very heavy one, after having withstood the tremendous pressures and extremely high temperatures generated by re-entry into the earth's atmosphere, decelerating from high orbital speeds. It made a perfect landing, descending gently on to the landing strip on the dry bed of Lake Rogers at Edwards Air Force Base, in the Californian Mojave Desert.

The space shuttle is the very latest evidence of what has been achieved after years of research and experimentation during which the airplane and aeronautical technology has evolved continuously. War has always speeded up progress and given great impetus to innovation. But since World War II aerospace research has become as important a reason for research as military requirements. It is somewhat difficult to separate the two facets today since experimental work, and research and development, some of it successful and some not, have been almost uninterrupted during the past forty years. The history of experimental aircraft parallels mainstream aviation, with its own important dates, events, places and names, all caught up in the struggle towards increasingly ambitious goals. The benefits of this research have not been confined to producing increasingly sophisticated weapons, but have had an even greater effect on commercial aviation which has led to ever more progress and growth.

Speed still mesmerizes those involved in the development of aviation. The first step was to build more powerful engines. By the end of World War II it was obvious that the piston-engine had almost reached the end of its development line, although speeds of piston-engine aircraft had been greatly increased.

Once the first jet aircraft had established themselves the next step was to fly faster than the speed of sound. This was no easy achievement, since it not only involved problems in engine technology, but opened up a whole new unexplored area of aerodynamics. Research concentrated on structural and aerodynamic problems and especially those of the wing. The delta wing was designed as a development of the swept-back wing and was in turn followed by the variable-geometry wing which could combine the advantages of the straight wing for low speeds with a wing sweep necessary for high speeds. Advances continued to be made: the sound barrier was broken, and flying faster than the speed of sound became normal with second generation jet fighters, but efforts were already being made to double and even triple this speed.

This in turn brought new problems and obstacles to be overcome. Speeds of this order posed apparently insuperable high temperature problems. Experiments then also had to include work on new materials, the discovery of new metals and complex new alloys which could withstand such high temperatures. Mach 2 and Mach 3 were reached by aircraft in service and not just by experimental aircraft. New break-throughs were being made after long and painstaking work, pushing back the frontiers of stratospheric and space flight. Two countries have obviously been the main architects of this continual and spectacular progress, the opposing super-powers of the United States and the Soviet Union. The space race has been particularly hotly contested between the two nations, with first one and then the other drawing ahead. Continuous experiments undertaken in the United States during the last forty years, first by NACA, the National Advisory Committee for Aeronautics, then by its successor, NASA, have led to the accumulation of a vast fund of knowledge and expertise across the entire field of aviation and must inevitably be the strongest influence on the future evolution of aviation.

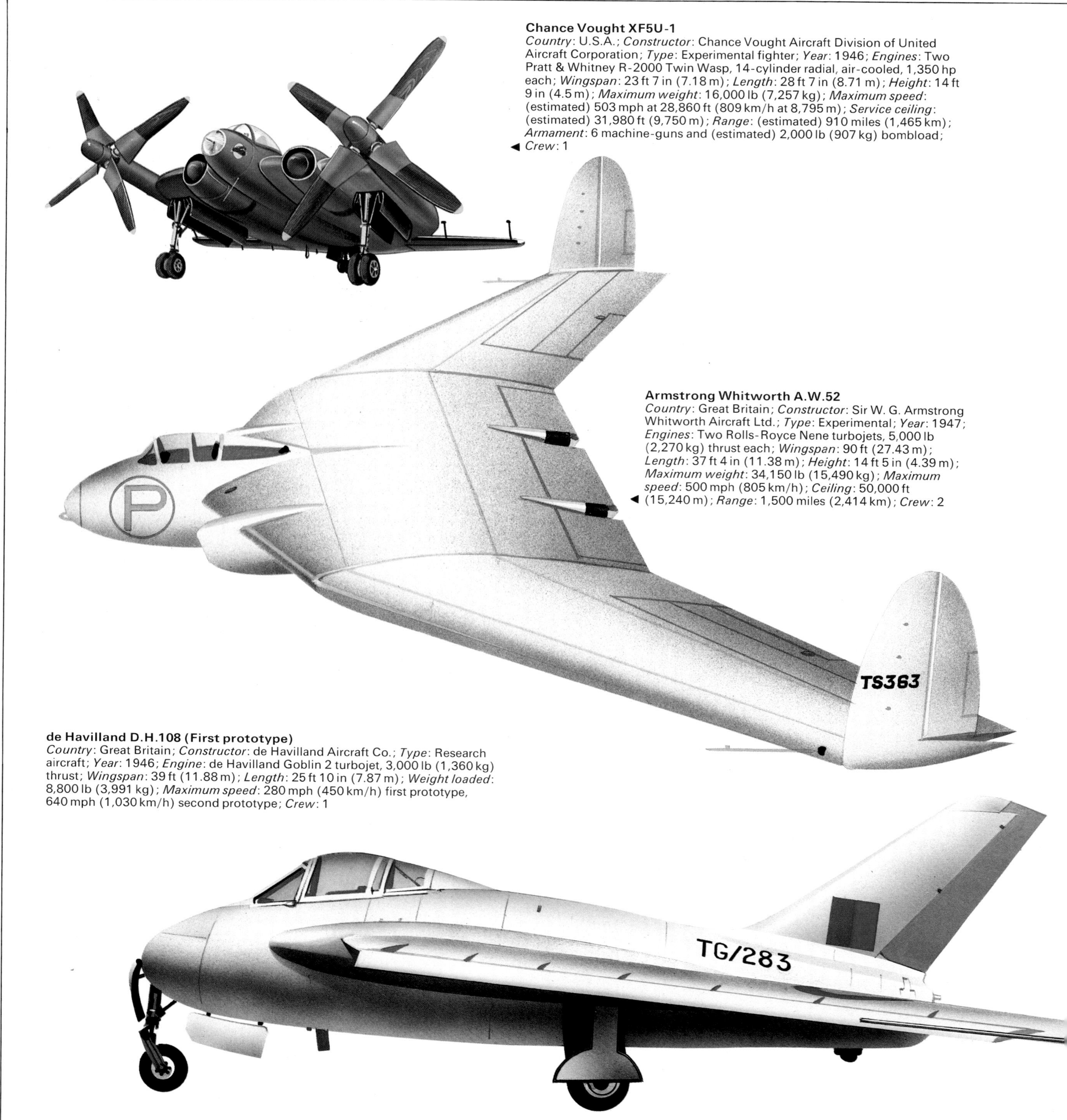

Chance Vought XF5U-1
Country: U.S.A.; *Constructor*: Chance Vought Aircraft Division of United Aircraft Corporation; *Type*: Experimental fighter; *Year*: 1946; *Engines*: Two Pratt & Whitney R-2000 Twin Wasp, 14-cylinder radial, air-cooled, 1,350 hp each; *Wingspan*: 23 ft 7 in (7.18 m); *Length*: 28 ft 7 in (8.71 m); *Height*: 14 ft 9 in (4.5 m); *Maximum weight*: 16,000 lb (7,257 kg); *Maximum speed*: (estimated) 503 mph at 28,860 ft (809 km/h at 8,795 m); *Service ceiling*: (estimated) 31,980 ft (9,750 m); *Range*: (estimated) 910 miles (1,465 km); *Armament*: 6 machine-guns and (estimated) 2,000 lb (907 kg) bombload; *Crew*: 1

Armstrong Whitworth A.W.52
Country: Great Britain; *Constructor*: Sir W. G. Armstrong Whitworth Aircraft Ltd.; *Type*: Experimental; *Year*: 1947; *Engines*: Two Rolls-Royce Nene turbojets, 5,000 lb (2,270 kg) thrust each; *Wingspan*: 90 ft (27.43 m); *Length*: 37 ft 4 in (11.38 m); *Height*: 14 ft 5 in (4.39 m); *Maximum weight*: 34,150 lb (15,490 kg); *Maximum speed*: 500 mph (805 km/h); *Ceiling*: 50,000 ft (15,240 m); *Range*: 1,500 miles (2,414 km); *Crew*: 2

de Havilland D.H.108 (First prototype)
Country: Great Britain; *Constructor*: de Havilland Aircraft Co.; *Type*: Research aircraft; *Year*: 1946; *Engine*: de Havilland Goblin 2 turbojet, 3,000 lb (1,360 kg) thrust; *Wingspan*: 39 ft (11.88 m); *Length*: 25 ft 10 in (7.87 m); *Weight loaded*: 8,800 lb (3,991 kg); *Maximum speed*: 280 mph (450 km/h) first prototype, 640 mph (1,030 km/h) second prototype; *Crew*: 1

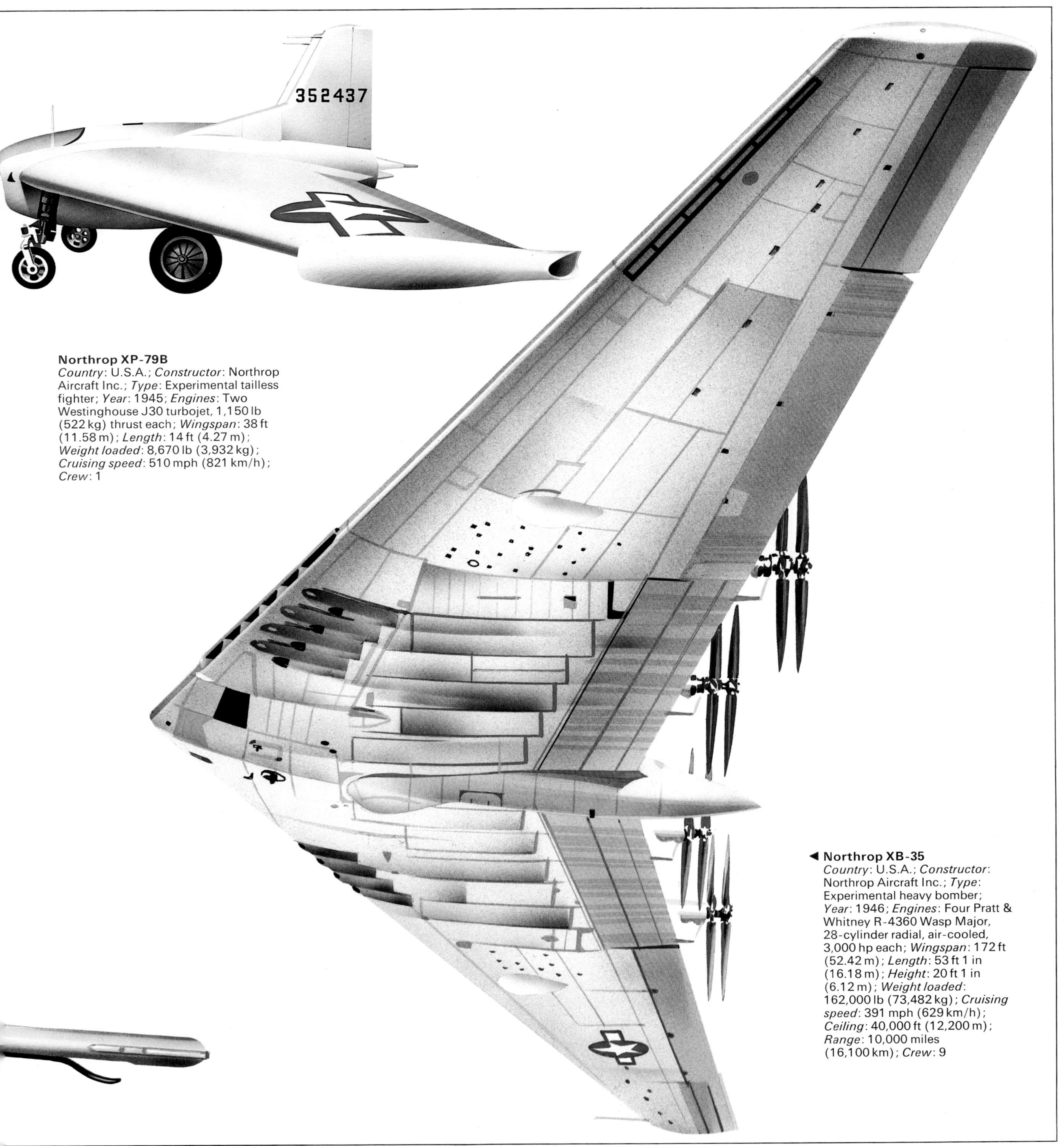

Northrop XP-79B
Country: U.S.A.; *Constructor*: Northrop Aircraft Inc.; *Type*: Experimental tailless fighter; *Year*: 1945; *Engines*: Two Westinghouse J30 turbojet, 1,150 lb (522 kg) thrust each; *Wingspan*: 38 ft (11.58 m); *Length*: 14 ft (4.27 m); *Weight loaded*: 8,670 lb (3,932 kg); *Cruising speed*: 510 mph (821 km/h); *Crew*: 1

◀ **Northrop XB-35**
Country: U.S.A.; *Constructor*: Northrop Aircraft Inc.; *Type*: Experimental heavy bomber; *Year*: 1946; *Engines*: Four Pratt & Whitney R-4360 Wasp Major, 28-cylinder radial, air-cooled, 3,000 hp each; *Wingspan*: 172 ft (52.42 m); *Length*: 53 ft 1 in (16.18 m); *Height*: 20 ft 1 in (6.12 m); *Weight loaded*: 162,000 lb (73,482 kg); *Cruising speed*: 391 mph (629 km/h); *Ceiling*: 40,000 ft (12,200 m); *Range*: 10,000 miles (16,100 km); *Crew*: 9

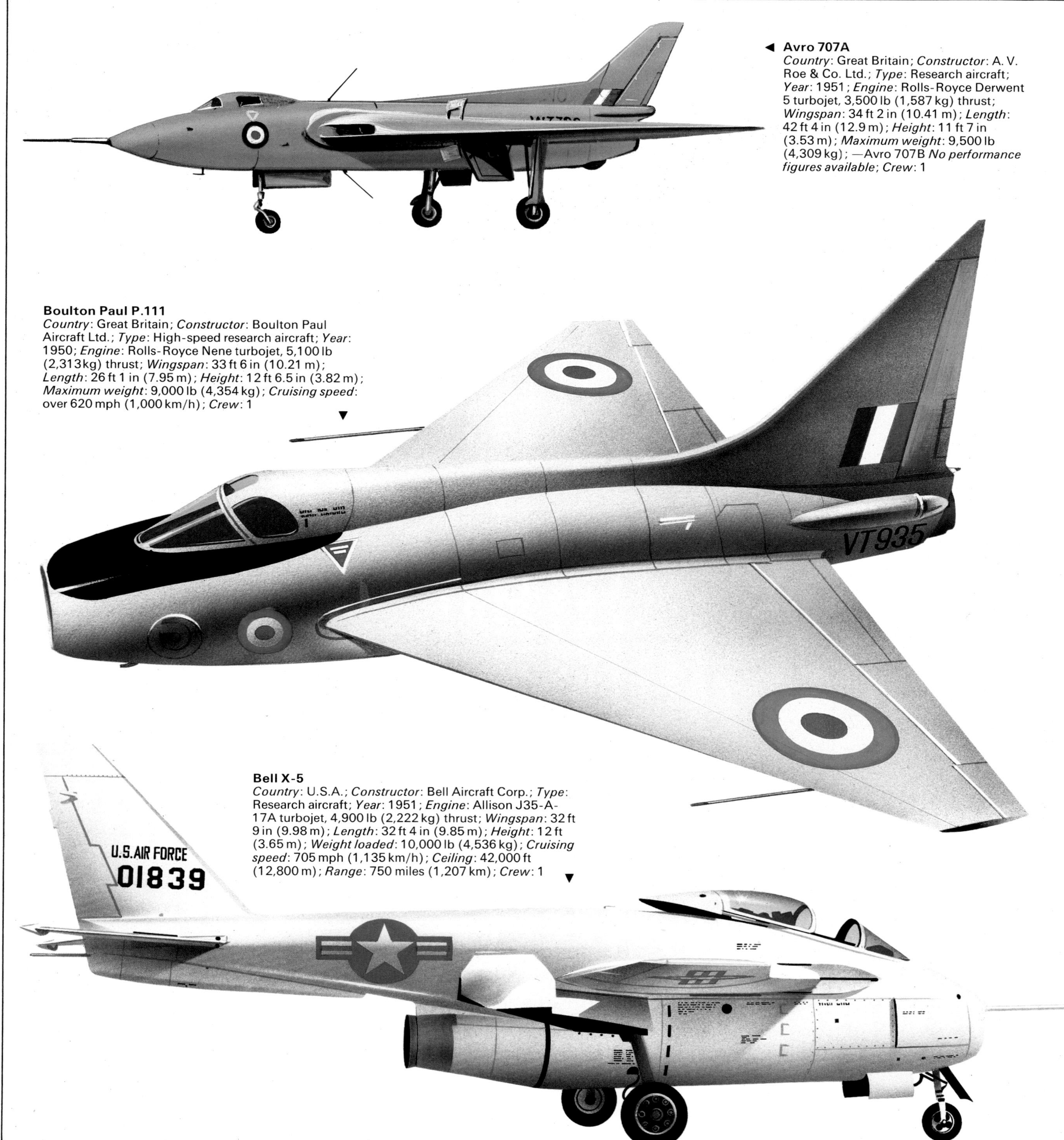

◄ **Avro 707A**
Country: Great Britain; *Constructor*: A. V. Roe & Co. Ltd.; *Type*: Research aircraft; *Year*: 1951; *Engine*: Rolls-Royce Derwent 5 turbojet, 3,500 lb (1,587 kg) thrust; *Wingspan*: 34 ft 2 in (10.41 m); *Length*: 42 ft 4 in (12.9 m); *Height*: 11 ft 7 in (3.53 m); *Maximum weight*: 9,500 lb (4,309 kg); —Avro 707B *No performance figures available*; *Crew*: 1

Boulton Paul P.111
Country: Great Britain; *Constructor*: Boulton Paul Aircraft Ltd.; *Type*: High-speed research aircraft; *Year*: 1950; *Engine*: Rolls-Royce Nene turbojet, 5,100 lb (2,313 kg) thrust; *Wingspan*: 33 ft 6 in (10.21 m); *Length*: 26 ft 1 in (7.95 m); *Height*: 12 ft 6.5 in (3.82 m); *Maximum weight*: 9,000 lb (4,354 kg); *Cruising speed*: over 620 mph (1,000 km/h); *Crew*: 1 ▼

Bell X-5
Country: U.S.A.; *Constructor*: Bell Aircraft Corp.; *Type*: Research aircraft; *Year*: 1951; *Engine*: Allison J35-A-17A turbojet, 4,900 lb (2,222 kg) thrust; *Wingspan*: 32 ft 9 in (9.98 m); *Length*: 32 ft 4 in (9.85 m); *Height*: 12 ft (3.65 m); *Weight loaded*: 10,000 lb (4,536 kg); *Cruising speed*: 705 mph (1,135 km/h); *Ceiling*: 42,000 ft (12,800 m); *Range*: 750 miles (1,207 km); *Crew*: 1 ▼

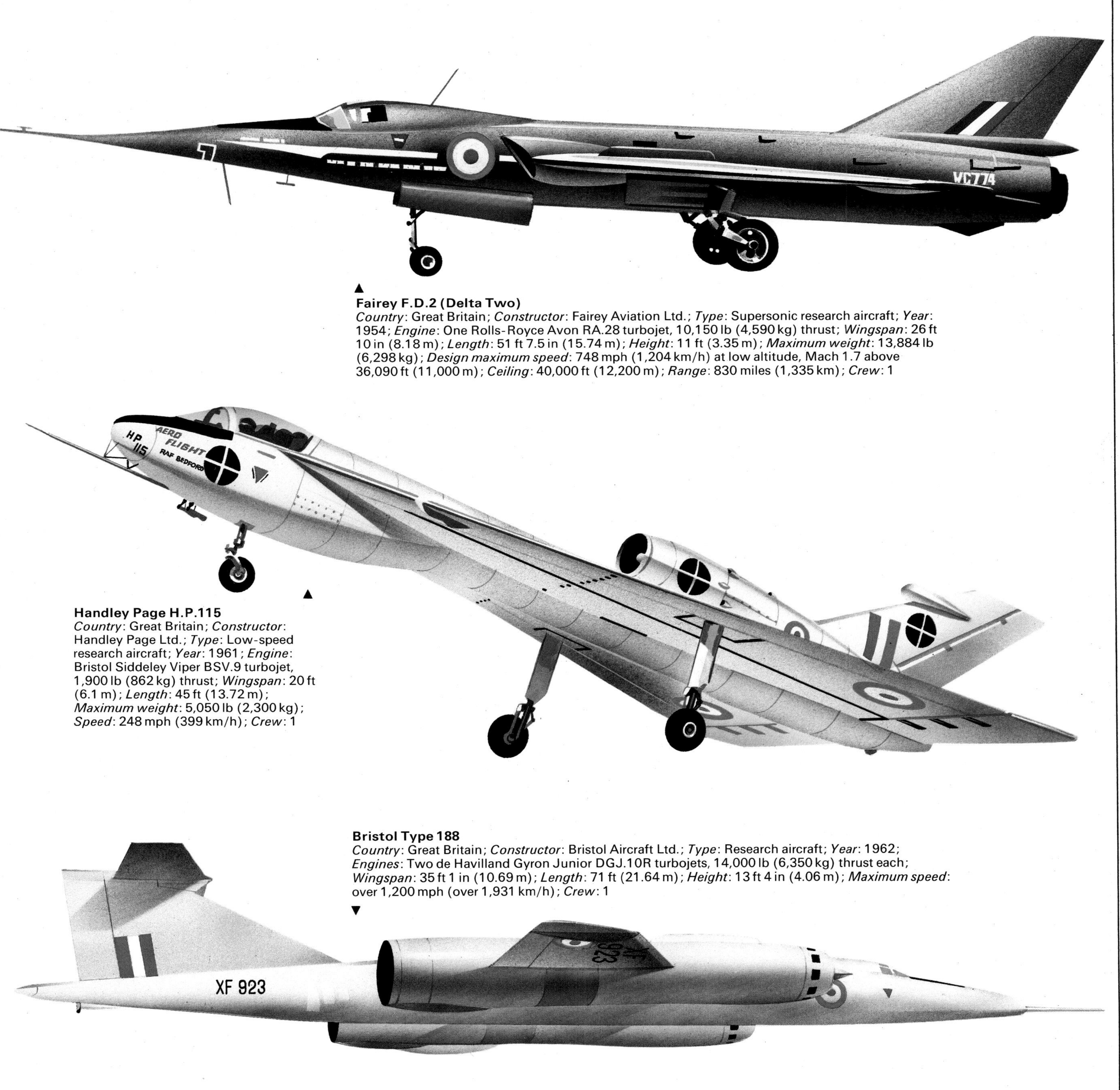

▲
Fairey F.D.2 (Delta Two)
Country: Great Britain; *Constructor*: Fairey Aviation Ltd.; *Type*: Supersonic research aircraft; *Year*: 1954; *Engine*: One Rolls-Royce Avon RA.28 turbojet, 10,150 lb (4,590 kg) thrust; *Wingspan*: 26 ft 10 in (8.18 m); *Length*: 51 ft 7.5 in (15.74 m); *Height*: 11 ft (3.35 m); *Maximum weight*: 13,884 lb (6,298 kg); *Design maximum speed*: 748 mph (1,204 km/h) at low altitude, Mach 1.7 above 36,090 ft (11,000 m); *Ceiling*: 40,000 ft (12,200 m); *Range*: 830 miles (1,335 km); *Crew*: 1

▲
Handley Page H.P.115
Country: Great Britain; *Constructor*: Handley Page Ltd.; *Type*: Low-speed research aircraft; *Year*: 1961; *Engine*: Bristol Siddeley Viper BSV.9 turbojet, 1,900 lb (862 kg) thrust; *Wingspan*: 20 ft (6.1 m); *Length*: 45 ft (13.72 m); *Maximum weight*: 5,050 lb (2,300 kg); *Speed*: 248 mph (399 km/h); *Crew*: 1

Bristol Type 188
Country: Great Britain; *Constructor*: Bristol Aircraft Ltd.; *Type*: Research aircraft; *Year*: 1962; *Engines*: Two de Havilland Gyron Junior DGJ.10R turbojets, 14,000 lb (6,350 kg) thrust each; *Wingspan*: 35 ft 1 in (10.69 m); *Length*: 71 ft (21.64 m); *Height*: 13 ft 4 in (4.06 m); *Maximum speed*: over 1,200 mph (over 1,931 km/h); *Crew*: 1
▼

Bell X-1 ▲
Country: U.S.A.; *Constructor*: Bell Aircraft Corp.; *Type*: Supersonic research aircraft; *Year*: 1946; *Engine*: Reaction Motors Model 6000 C4, 6,000 lb (2,721 kg) thrust; *Wingspan*: 28 ft (8.53 m); *Length*: 31 ft (9.45 m); *Height*: 10 ft 10 in (3.3 m); *Weight loaded*: 13,400 lb (6,078 kg); *Maximum speed*: 1,000 mph (1,609 km/h); *Crew*: 1

Douglas X-3 Stiletto ▶
Country: U.S.A.; *Constructor*: Douglas Aircraft Co.; *Type*: Research aircraft; *Year*: 1952; *Engines*: Two Westinghouse XJ34-WE-17 turbojets, 4,200 lb (1,905 kg) thrust (with afterburning) each; *Wingspan*: 22 ft 8.25 in (6.91 m); *Length*: 66 ft 9 in (20.35 m); *Height*: 12 ft 6.31 in (3.82 m); *Maximum weight*: 22,400 lb (10,160 kg); *Maximum speed*: 706 mph (1,136 km/h); *Absolute ceiling*: 38,000 ft (11,580 m); *Crew*: 1

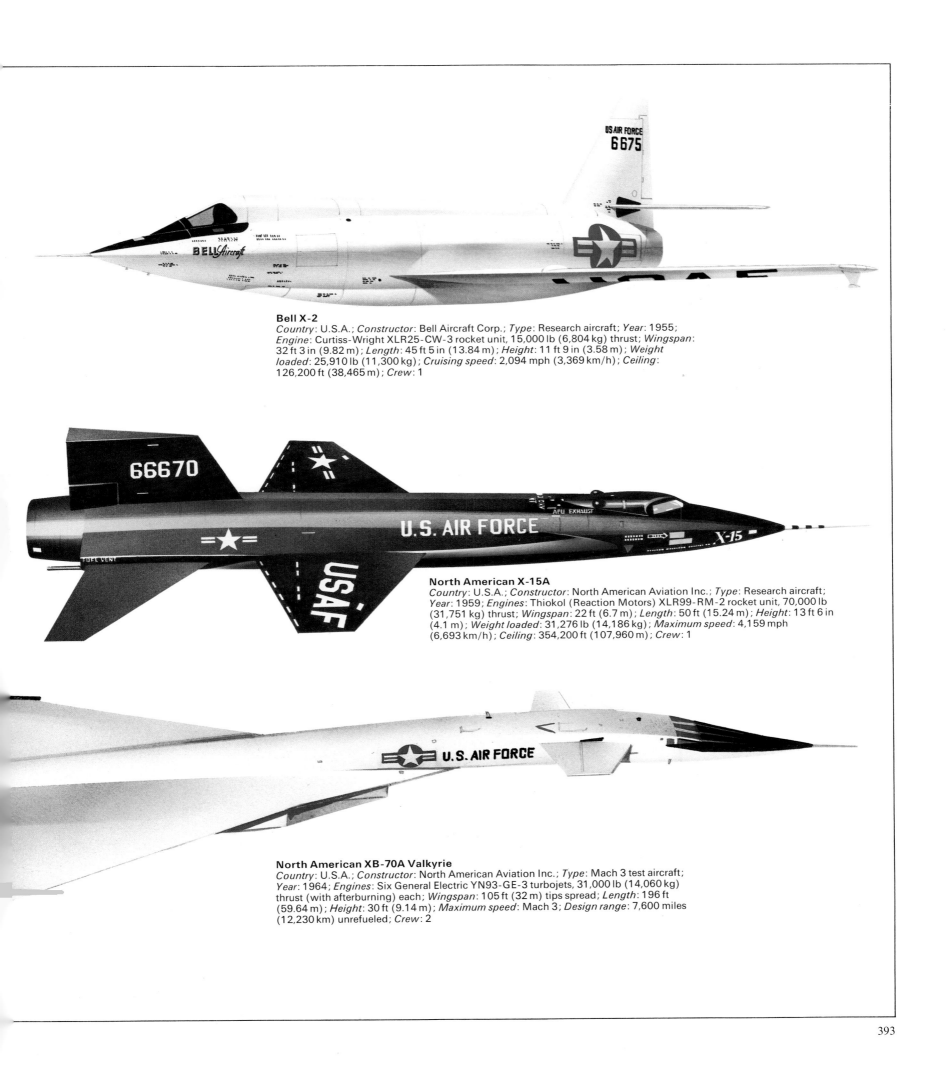

Bell X-2
Country: U.S.A.; *Constructor*: Bell Aircraft Corp.; *Type*: Research aircraft; *Year*: 1955; *Engine*: Curtiss-Wright XLR25-CW-3 rocket unit, 15,000 lb (6,804 kg) thrust; *Wingspan*: 32 ft 3 in (9.82 m); *Length*: 45 ft 5 in (13.84 m); *Height*: 11 ft 9 in (3.58 m); *Weight loaded*: 25,910 lb (11,300 kg); *Cruising speed*: 2,094 mph (3,369 km/h); *Ceiling*: 126,200 ft (38,465 m); *Crew*: 1

North American X-15A
Country: U.S.A.; *Constructor*: North American Aviation Inc.; *Type*: Research aircraft; *Year*: 1959; *Engines*: Thiokol (Reaction Motors) XLR99-RM-2 rocket unit, 70,000 lb (31,751 kg) thrust; *Wingspan*: 22 ft (6.7 m); *Length*: 50 ft (15.24 m); *Height*: 13 ft 6 in (4.1 m); *Weight loaded*: 31,276 lb (14,186 kg); *Maximum speed*: 4,159 mph (6,693 km/h); *Ceiling*: 354,200 ft (107,960 m); *Crew*: 1

North American XB-70A Valkyrie
Country: U.S.A.; *Constructor*: North American Aviation Inc.; *Type*: Mach 3 test aircraft; *Year*: 1964; *Engines*: Six General Electric YN93-GE-3 turbojets, 31,000 lb (14,060 kg) thrust (with afterburning) each; *Wingspan*: 105 ft (32 m) tips spread; *Length*: 196 ft (59.64 m); *Height*: 30 ft (9.14 m); *Maximum speed*: Mach 3; *Design range*: 7,600 miles (12,230 km) unrefueled; *Crew*: 2

Martin Marietta X-24A
Country: U.S.A.; *Constructor*: Martin Marietta Corp.; *Type*: Lifting-body research aircraft; *Year*: 1967; *Engines*: Thiokol (Reaction Motors) XLR11-RM-13 rocket unit, 8,000 lb (3,630 kg) thrust; *Width*: 13 ft 8 in (4.16 m); *Length*: 24 ft 6 in (7.47 m); *Height*: 10 ft 4 in (3.15 m); *Maximum launching weight*: 11,000 lb (4,990 kg); *Speed*: Mach 2; *Ceiling*: 100,000 ft (30,480 m); *Endurance*: ◀ 15 min; *Crew*: 1

Northrop/NASA M2-F2
Country: U.S.A.; *Constructor*: Northrop Corp.; *Type*: Lifting-body research vehicle; *Year*: 1965; *Engines*: Thiokol (Reaction Motors) XLR11 rocket unit, 8,000 lb (3,630 kg) thrust; *Width*: 9 ft 7 in (2.92 m); *Length*: 22 ft 2 in (6.76 m); *Height*: 8 ft 10 in (2.69 m); *Maximum launching weight*: 9,400 lb (4,265 kg); *Crew*: 1 ▶

◀ **Northrop/NASA HL-10**
Country: U.S.A.; *Constructor*: Northrop Corp.; *Type*: Lifting-body research vehicle; *Year*: 1966; *Engine*: One rocket Thiokol (Reaction Motors) XLR11 rocket unit, 8,000 lb (3,630 kg) thrust; *Width*: 15 ft 1 in (4.6 m); *Length*: 22 ft 2 in (6.76 m); *Height*: 11 ft 5 in (3.48 m); *Maximum launching weight*: 9,400 lb (4,625 kg); *Crew*: 1

NASA/Rockwell International Space Shuttle Orbiter
Country: U.S.A.; *Constructor*: Rockwell International; *Type*: Space shuttle; *Year*: 1976; *Engines*: Three Rocketdyne SSME (Space Shuttle Main Engines), 470,000 lb (213,188 kg) thrust each; *Wingspan*: 78 ft 0.5 in (23.79 m); *Length*: 122 ft 2.5 in (37.24 m); *Height*: 56 ft 8 in (17.27 m); *Approximate landing weight*: 187,000 lb (84,778 kg) ▶

The space shuttle orbiter *Columbia* with the astronauts Commander John Young and Captain Robert Crippen on board, on the launching pad shortly before the beginning of its first historic flight. The shuttle completed 36 earth orbits before re-entry and powerless ◀ descent and landing

Columbia landing on the specially prepared strip on the dry bed of Lake Rogers at Edwards Air Force Base in the Californian Mojave Desert at a speed of 214 mph (345 km/h): 14 April 1981

Plate 162
Circular-wing and tailless aircraft: 1945–1947

During World War II, apart from producing tremendous numbers of military aircraft, the most aeronautically advanced nations devoted a great deal of their resources to research and experimentation. It would be a mistake to assume that all this work was carried out for military ends. Although many experiments were directed towards this sector, a considerable number were channeled towards the development of new-technology airliners, the achievement of greater safety in the air and the general evolution of aircraft for the future. One of the most significant results of this technical effort was certainly the jet engine, but apart from perfecting this revolutionary means of propulsion (in which field both the Germans and the British were world leaders), a large proportion of experiments tended to concentrate on the development of new and more efficient wing shapes which became necessary to achieve greater speeds. The achievement of ever-higher speeds was made feasible by the development of the jet engine, but these speeds could only be reached if the wing underwent a dramatic change. A great many prototype aircraft were built, especially in Great Britain, the United States and Germany. (In the closing stages of the war the vast mass of documents relating to German research and development studies, many of which were far in advance of those conducted by any other nation, fell into the hands of the invading forces and made a major contribution to their subsequent experimental work.

The Chance Vought XF5U-1 (nicknamed the "Flying Pancake") was the culmination of a great deal of research into the potential of a wing of roughly circular planform which constituted the main structure. These studies had been embarked upon as far back as 1933, by Charles H. Zimmerman, and during the war the U.S. Navy had become interested in the design's potential, which led to a program being undertaken by Chance Vought. Work centered on two aspects: the production and testing of a full-scale flying model, known as the V-173, and the construction of the experimental fighter itself. The V-173 flew successfully in 1942 but the XF5U-1 suffered from a series of technical faults, mainly connected with the propellers and transmission system, which meant that this prototype never flew. The aircraft was completed on 25 June 1945, and test flights were scheduled to begin the following year but never took place, since by then the Navy had lost all interest in the project and it was therefore canceled.

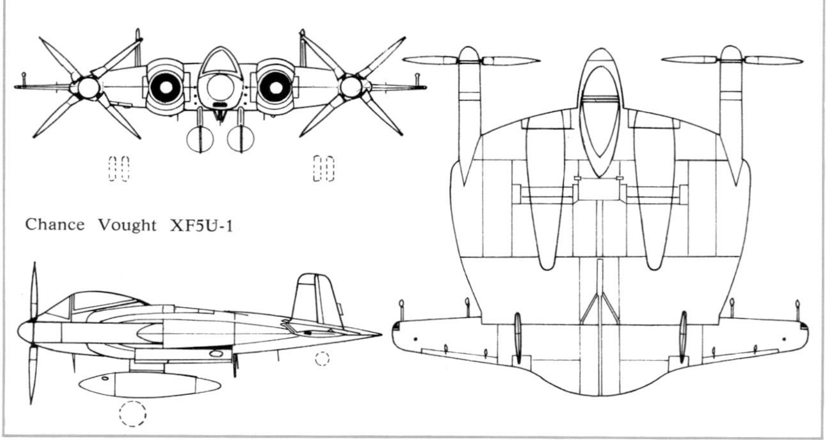
Chance Vought XF5U-1

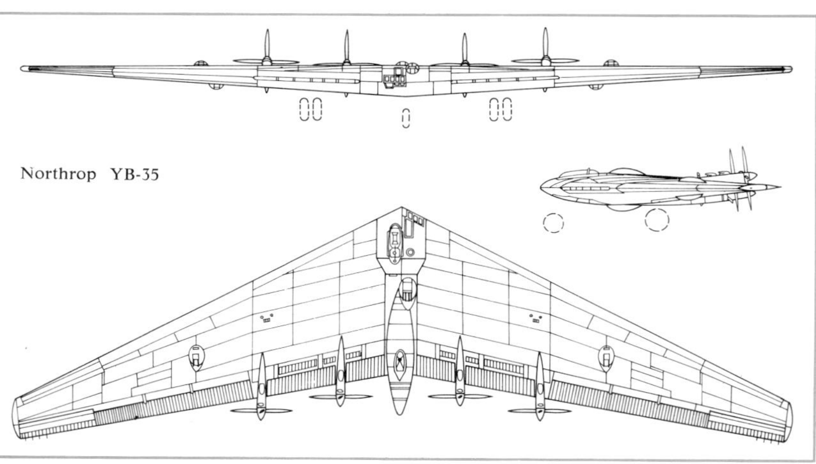
Northrop YB-35

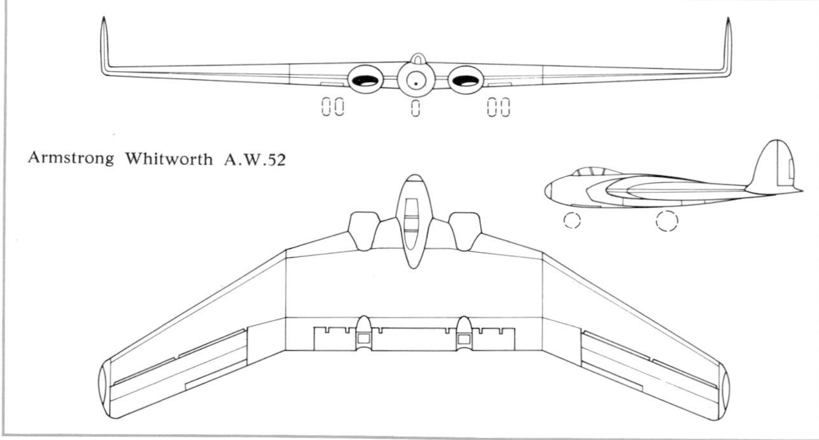
Armstrong Whitworth A.W.52

Northrop's long series of research programs proved more fruitful. This company had undertaken research into flying wing aircraft (with no identifiable fuselage, merely a fuselage nacelle built around the centerline of the wing for the crew). The earliest prototype for this type of design had appeared in 1928 and successive experimental projects had been undertaken by this great American aircraft manufacturer during the twenty years which had elapsed since then. One of the most original was the XP-79 of 1944. This was a fighter, powered by two jet engines and its function was to be very unorthodox—to bring down enemy aircraft by ramming their tails. The wing had, therefore, to be exceptionally strong, the leading edge being constructed of thick magnesium, strong enough in theory to withstand the shock of impact; the pilot lay prone in the central cockpit. This unusual aircraft was to be rocket-powered but since no suitable power units of this type were available the XP-79B prototype was equipped with twin Westinghouse J30 turbojets. The aircraft had its maiden flight on 12 September 1945, and this ended in disaster, due to the failure of its directional control system.

This set-back did not jeopardize an even more ambitious program which was already under development, for a flying wing bomber (the B-35) powered by four piston-engines and capable of very high performance in terms of speed and range. The project had been supported from 1941 by the military authorities and, spurred on by the prospect of an order for 200 aircraft, Northrop had built a special factory and entered into co-operation agreements with other aeronautical manufacturers. Work started on the first of two prototypes ordered (the XB-35) in January 1943; the original contract provided for the construction of thirteen pre-series aircraft (YB-35) two of which were to be suitable for the installation of eight jet engines (the YB-49). The first XB-35 was flown on 25 June 1946. The results of the series of proving flights were, however, disappointing; serious problems occurred with the reversible-pitch pusher propellers and simpler propellers had to be installed. These changes only concerned the pre-series aircraft (the first YB-35 flew on 13 May 1948), for meanwhile the U.S.A.F.'s interest had centered on the jet-powered variant. The YB-49 flew for the first time on 21 October 1947. A contract for 200 B-35As was placed but this was canceled, as was an order for 30 reconnaissance RB-49s. Conversion of nine YB-35s to jet power was also ordered but only one conversion was completed by November 1949, when the program was abandoned, in favor of Convair's more promising, and conventional, B-36.

The British aeronautical industry also conducted research into tailless aircraft, although on a more limited scale. The most interesting program of experiments was carried out by Armstrong Whitworth immediately after the war, with the A.W.52 prototypes, a flying wing powered by two Rolls-Royce turbojets. The construction of two prototypes followed research carried out with the A.W.52G glider. The first, Nene-powered, A.W.52 flew successfully on 13

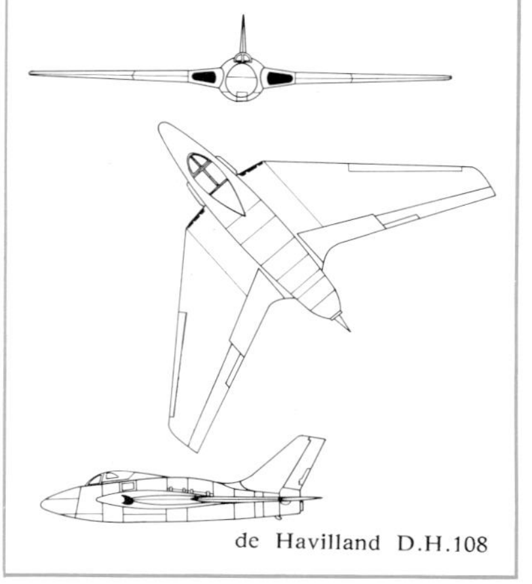
de Havilland D.H.108

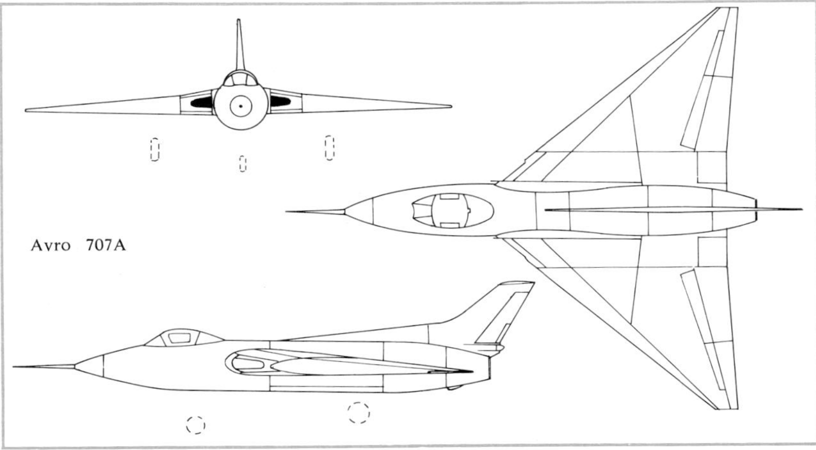

Avro 707A

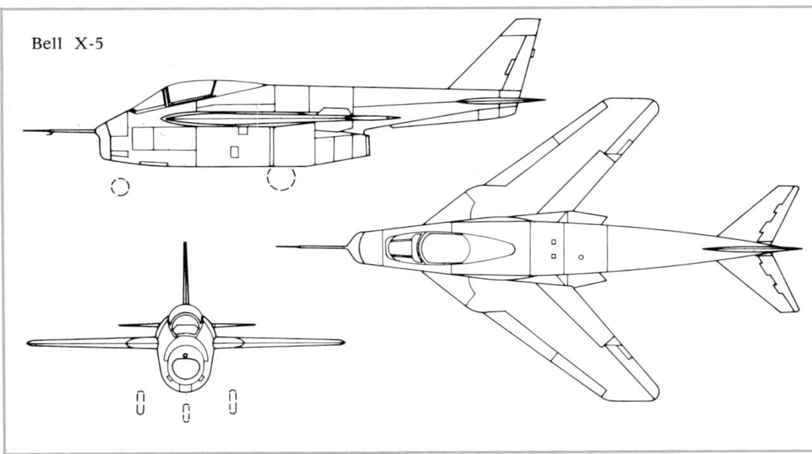

Bell X-5

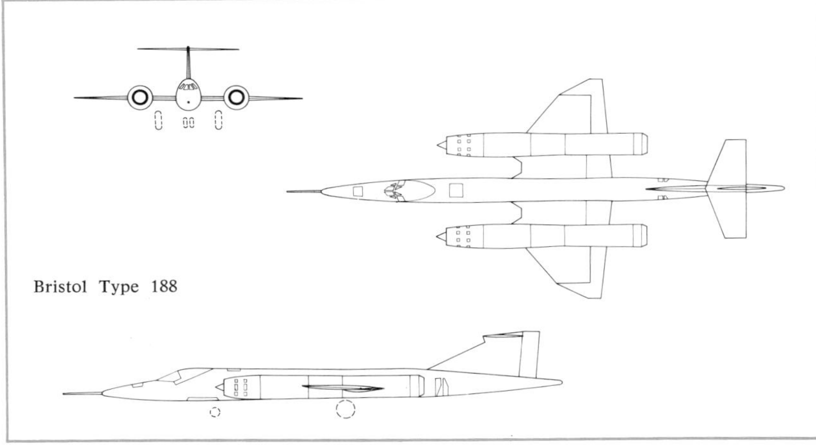

Bristol Type 188

November 1947, and it was followed on 1 September 1948, by the second aircraft which had Derwent turbojets. On 30 May 1949, flutter developed in one wingtip and quickly spread across the entire wing. The pilot ejected from the aircraft which landed in open country with little damage. This incident, combined with disappointing test results, led to Armstrong Whitworth abandoning further work on flying wing aircraft.

During the design studies for the Comet jet airliner consideration was given to a tailless aircraft with sweptback wings. In order to study the behaviour and control problems of sweptback wings, de Havilland, in 1945, began the design of a tailless research aircraft using the Vampire fighter fuselage combined with a wing having 43 degrees sweep. Three different examples were built and the first flew on 15 May 1946. This aircraft was destroyed in a fatal accident. The second prototype was potentially supersonic, had an up-rated engine and 45 degrees wing sweep. It first flew on 23 August 1946. The third prototype had yet more power and made its first flight on 24 July 1947. On 27 September 1946, during a high-speed flight the second prototype broke up, killing its pilot Geoffrey de Havilland. It appears to have achieved a speed of about Mach 0.9. The third aircraft, flown by John Derry, set a new 100 km closed-circuit record on 12 April, 1948, with a speed of 605.23 mph (974 km/h) and, on 9 September that year, Derry exceeded Mach 1 with the D.H.108 during a dive from 40,000 ft (12,190 m) to 30,000 ft (9,145 m). This was the first time the speed of sound had been exceeded in Britain.

Plate 163
Progress toward supersonic flight—from the delta to the variable-geometry wing: 1950–1962

The delta wing aircraft was tested in the early 1950s in Great Britain as part of an ambitious military aircraft project: the construction of the Avro Vulcan strategic bomber, the first jet bomber to have a delta wing. Avro designed and built five approximately one-third scale aircraft with which to carry out all the basic research and to provide information which would be used in the final design of the Vulcan. The Type 707 was, therefore, the first British aircraft designed for delta wing research. The first prototype flew on 4 September 1949, but was destroyed in an accident a little over three weeks later. It was followed by a second prototype, the Type 707B, on 6 September 1950, built for low-speed research. The third prototype, the 707A, flew for the first time on 14 June 1951: it was built for high-speed research, and to hasten the research program a second 707A was constructed (first flown on 20 February 1953). The final example was the two-seat 707C which flew on 1 July 1953.

Another interesting experimental delta wing aircraft built in Great Britain was the Boulton Paul P.111 prototype, constructed to investigate the delta wing at transonic speeds. The project was initiated in 1946 and the prototype made its first flight on 10 October 1950. A landing accident held up the program for a while, but the aircraft was repaired and modified internally and externally to a certain extent and was redesignated P.111A. The test program was resumed on 2 July 1953. Five years later the aircraft made its last flight with the Royal Aircraft Establishment.

The 1950s also saw the first experiments with a new type of wing, which was only to be applied to the construction of military aircraft in the 1960s: the variable-geometry wing, which is, today, in the 1980s, used for the Tornado. This research was aimed at achieving the practical advantage of improving the otherwise poor handling qualities of heavily-swept aircraft at low speeds by reducing the angle of sweep and so giving them the handling characteristics of aircraft with unswept or moderately swept wings, while still retaining the performance that a heavily swept wing can offer. The first prototype ever built with a variable-sweep wing was the American Bell X-5, design work for which started in 1948, heavily influenced by the Messerschmitt P.1101 wartime concept. An original innovation was the operating mechanism varying the sweepback angle of the wings from a minimum of twenty degrees to a maximum of sixty degrees. Two aircraft were built and the first one flew on 20 June 1951. On 27 July, the mechanism altering the

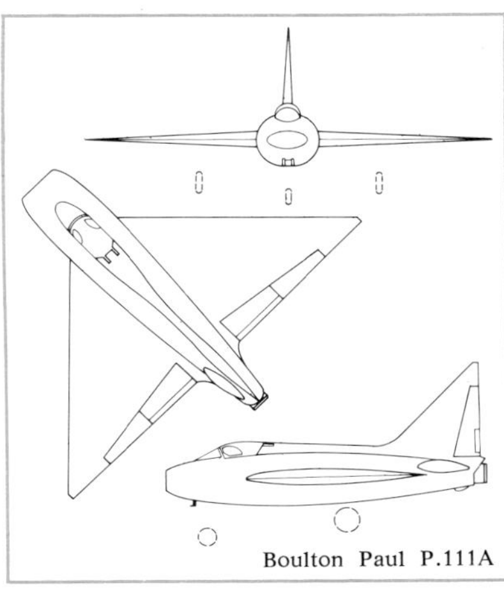

Boulton Paul P.111A

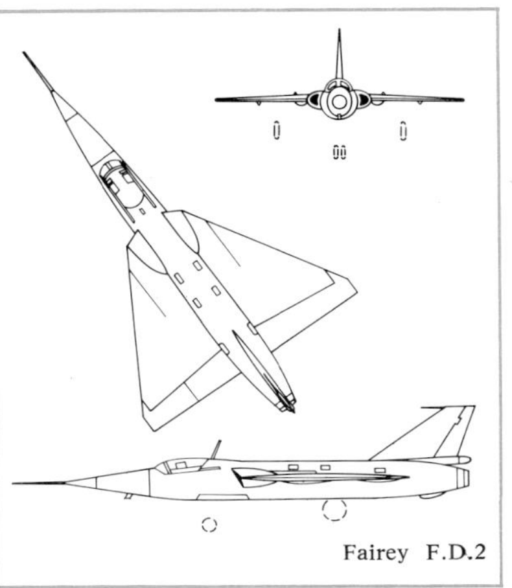

Fairey F.D.2

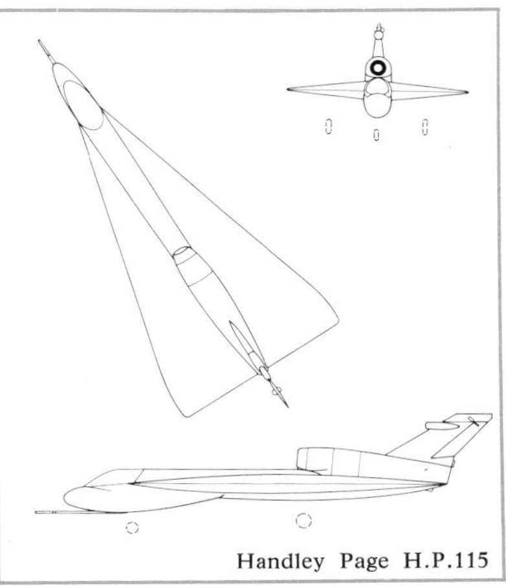

Handley Page H.P.115

sweepback was given limited testing. Some days later the whole operation was successfully tried out during the prototype's ninth flight. A demanding series of proving flights continued until 1955. Only one aircraft, the first prototype, completed the series of tests and is now in the Wright-Patterson Air Force Museum in Ohio; the other crashed on 4 October 1953.

The variable-geometry wing was an extremely complex structure and some years were to pass while it remained at the experimental stage and it took time to replace the delta wing with its proven advantages. Just how real these advantages were where speed was concerned was demonstrated in Great Britain in 1956 by an interesting research aircraft, the Fairey Delta Two (F.D.2) which on 10 March of that year became the first aircraft to set a world speed record of over 1,000 mph; an average of 1,132 mph (1,821 km/h) when flown by the test pilot Peter Twiss. This airplane had been designed in the early fifties for the purpose of investigating the characteristics of flight and control at transonic and supersonic speeds and two examples were built; the first began test flights on 6 October 1954, the second on 15 February 1956. The first F.D.2 research aircraft had a significant influence on the design of the Anglo-French Supersonic Civil Transport, Concorde. The aircraft was redesigned by British Aircraft Corporation, given a lengthened fuselage and slim ogee wing to obtain experience of high-speed handling of the Concorde wing design. Redesignated Bristol 221 it made its first flight on 1 May 1964.

The little Handley Page H.P.115, on the other hand, was especially built for the Concorde program, and was in essence, a flying test-bed for research into the behavior of slender delta wings at low speeds. Among the more interesting facets of the design was the detachable leading-edge which permitted flight testing of a wide variety of shapes, if required.

In its attempt to accumulate further knowledge of high-speed flight the British aircraft industry built an interesting prototype in the late 1950s, the Bristol Type 188, designed to investigate prolonged flight at speeds of up to Mach 2. Two aircraft were built, the first flew on 14 April 1962, and the second on 29 April 1963. Apart from its extreme aerodynamic sophistication, the most notable feature of the Bristol 188 was its fabrication of special stainless steel, to meet the problems of kinetic heating. No results of flight tests have been published although it is known that the aircraft's research program was cut short because the high fuel consumption restricted its flight time too severely at high speed.

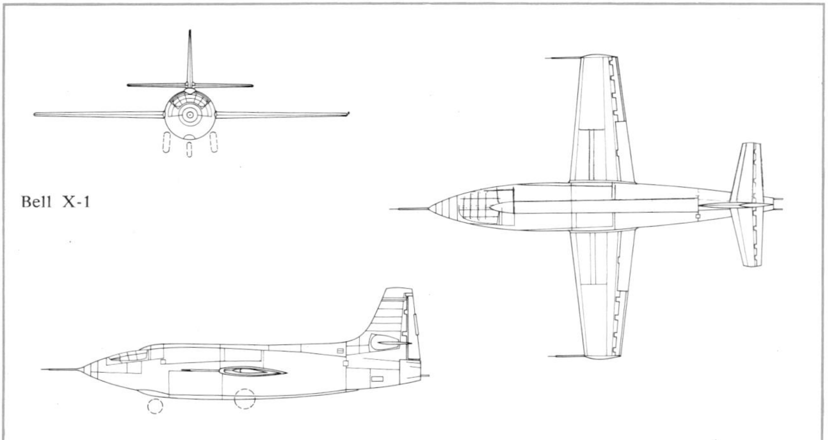
Bell X-1

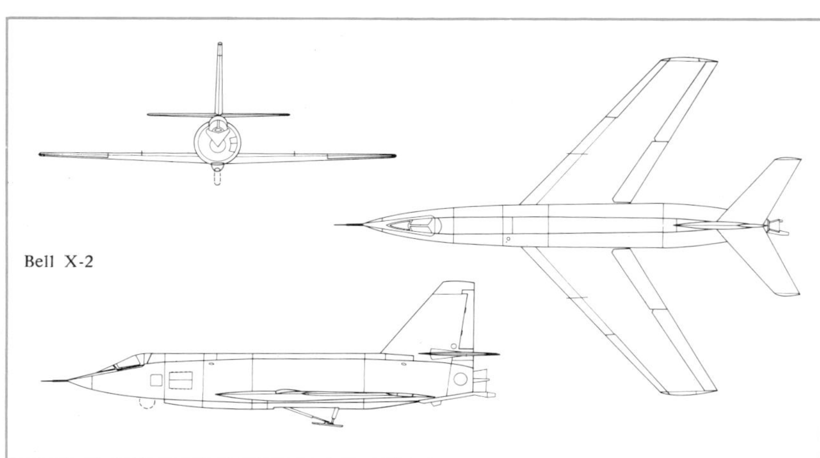
Bell X-2

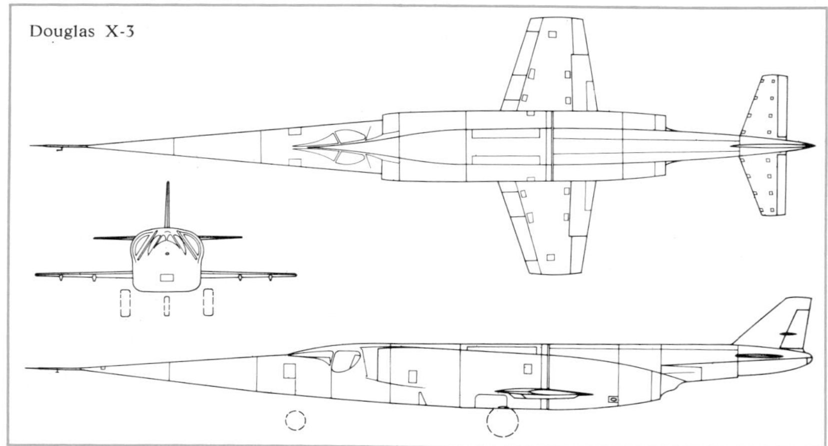
Douglas X-3

Plate 164
From the X-1 to the Valkyrie: 1946–1964

A sustained research program which has probably contributed more than any other to the development of the airplane was launched by the United States in 1942, under the name of the Experimental Research Aircraft Program. The major U.S. aircraft manufacturers, funded by the United States Air Force and the Navy under the supervision of NACA (later NASA), produced the famous X-series of aircraft—X standing, of course, for experimental. These were experimental aircraft in the truest sense, developed for pure research and in order to identify and overcome hitherto unknown dangers and supersonic flight problems. The X aircraft enabled many further stages in the development of modern aviation to be reached and mastered. The initial X-1 was the first manned airplane to exceed the speed of sound in level flight; variable-geometry wings were first tried out in one of these X aircraft. Other achievements of this series included: the first aircraft to fly at an altitude of over 328,000 feet (100,000 m); and the first to reach a speed of Mach 6.

The first of this amazing series was the Bell X-1, the first American aircraft to be rocket powered, built for the investigation of supersonic flight problems. Supersonic flight was acheived by the first of the three X-1 prototypes on 14 October 1947, ten months after its maiden flight under its own power. The pilot on this historic occasion was Charles Yeager, who was air-launched from a B-29 at an altitude of about 29,500 feet (9,000 m) and reached a speed of 670 mph; 1,078 km/h or Mach 1.015 in level flight. On 8 August 1949, another achievement was recorded, when Frank Everest flew the aircraft to an altitude of 71,881 feet (21,925 m). Another three improved aircraft were built in the late 1950s, with even more ambitious goals (the X-1A, the X-1B and the X-1D). In the first of these Charles Yeager flew at 1,650 mph (2,655 km/h) or Mach 2.435 on 12 December 1953, and Arthur Murray reached an unconfirmed altitude of over 90,000 feet (27,435 m) on 4 June 1954. The last of this series was the X-1E, converted from the second X-1, having its maiden flight on 12 December 1955, intended for research leading to the development of a new wing. The X-1 program continued until 1958; the X-1s made a total of 156 flights; the X-1A made 21; the X-1B, (27), the X-1D made one flight and the X-1E, 26.

The next Bell experimental aircraft was the X-2: two prototypes were ordered in 1946 to operate at still higher speeds and altitudes than those reached by the X-1 and to test the swept wing. These aircraft had stainless steel wings and tails. The first, unpowered example, was lost in May 1954 when it was jettisoned from its B-50 carrier. The second X-2 made its first powered flight on 18 November 1955, and was destroyed in an accident on 27 September 1956. The main achievements of the X-2 were the altitude record established on 7 September 1956, when, piloted by Iven Kinchloe, it reached 126,200 feet (38,405 m); and the speed record: 2,094 mph (3,370 km/h) or Mach 3.2, when piloted by Captain Milburn Apt, who was killed when the aircraft went out of control and crashed just after the record had been set.

Douglas built the X-3 Stiletto as a research vehicle for the development of high-speed military aircraft. It was to be capable of sustained speeds in excess of Mach 1 and have a top speed in excess of Mach 2. However, the engines available never produced sufficient power and the X-3 was only capable of exceeding Mach 1 in a dive. The X-3 was of unusual appearance having a long slender fuselage and short straight tapered wing. The aircraft first flew on 20 September 1952; it did a limited amount of flying until May 1956 and, in spite of its restricted performance, contributed considerably to the development of high-speed flight.

The most famous of all these X-series aircraft was the X-15 which flew far faster and higher than the X-1 and the X-2, reaching the limits of stratospheric flight, up to the threshold of space. NACA issued a specification for the X-15 on 24 June 1952, when the U.S.A.F. was still working on the X-1 program and getting the X-2 program commissioned. The specification called for a rocket-powered aircraft which could reach an altitude of not less than 264,000 feet (80,465 m)—50 miles (80 km)—and capable of speeds up to Mach 7. The task envisaged for the X-15s was the collection of data on high-speed control, stability, heating and atmosphere re-entry. The program was put out to tender towards the end of 1954 and North American was awarded the contract, for three aircraft, in December 1955. Design and construction presented problems of unprecedented complexity involving the use of then new materials such as titanium which had to withstand extreme temperatures (minus 300°F and plus 1,200°F), and the difficulties connected with perfecting efficient rocket motors. The X-15 left the factory on 15 October 1958, and flew for the first time under the wing of its specially-modified B-52 carrier on 10 March 1959. On 8 June 1959, the first unpowered free flight was made and the second prototype made the first powered flight on 17 September the same year. Maximum performance could not be achieved before the definitive XLR99 rocket motor was installed, in place of the original two LR11-RM-5 rocket motors which only developed 8,000 lb (3,630 kg) of thrust, but which North American had had to use as the XLR99 was not delivered until May, 1960. After a series of ground tests, during which an engine exploded, the X-15 was ready for further test flights. The second aircraft started these on 15 November 1960; by August 1961 the first X-15 was also ready, the last to receive the new engine. With the new engines the X-15s achieved outstanding performance. On 9 November 1961, Robert White reached 4,093 mph (6,587 km/h); on 30 April 1962, Joseph Walker reached an altitude of 246,700 feet (75,194 m); on 22 August 1963, this same pilot reached an even higher altitude of 354,200 feet (or 67.08 miles)—107,796 m. Accidents did happen, however: on 9 November 1962, the No.2 aircraft was involved in an accident on landing and was returned to North American and rebuilt with its fuselage lengthened by 73 cm and with additional propellants in large external tanks, giving it extra fuel capacity. The entire airframe was coated with Emerson Electric T-500 ablative material so that it could tolerate far higher temperatures. The aircraft was redesignated X-15A-2 and flew faster than any other: on 3 October 1967, piloted by William Knight, it reached 4,534 mph (7,296 km/h). After this record-breaking flight, however, the aircraft made another forced landing and suffered irreparable damage and, its flying days over, the X-15A-2 was donated to the Wright-Patterson Air Force Museum. From then on it was only a question of time before the X-15 program was wound up. Another reason for termination was the loss of X-15A-3 on 15 November 1967, in a crash. The last surviving prototype made eight more flights, the last of which was on 24 October 1968.

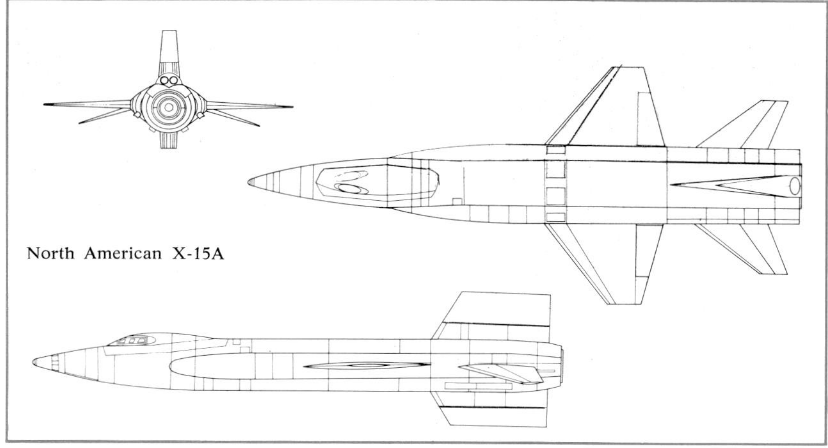
North American X-15A

In addition to producing the fastest experimental aircraft in the world, North American were also responsible for the largest and most sophisticated experimental aircraft: the XB-70 Valkyrie. This very advanced aircraft was planned originally as a strategic bomber, but was relegated to the role of aerodynamic research in 1961, having been superseded by the advent of intercontinental ballistic missiles. The aircraft had a design range of 7,600 miles (12,230 km) unrefueled and was designed to travel the entire distance to the target and back at Mach 3 carrying nuclear and conventional weapons. Two XB-70As were built and the first flew for the first time on 21 September 1964. They made a succession of proving trials. The objective of this program was to carry out aerodynamic tests and assess control and stability at very high altitudes and at speeds exceeding Mach 3. The XB-70A was a very interesting airplane of unusual configuration. It had a very long slim fuselage and a wide-chord delta wing of thin section. There was full-span anhedral and, seen in front elevation, the wing had a slight twist. There were twelve elevons along the trailing edge and the outer sections of the wing folded down 25 degrees for low-level supersonic flight and 65 degrees for high-altitude Mach 3 cruise. The leading edge was swept back 65 degrees 34 minutes. Just aft of the flight deck was a foreplane with trailing-edge flaps. The engines were grouped side by side at the rear of a massive underwing power duct. The forward fuselage was built mainly of titanium and the rear fuselage over the wing was a stainless steel honeycomb sandwich. The entire wing was covered by brazed stainless steel honeycomb sandwich panels which had welded joints. The crew seats formed selfcontained emergency ejection capsules, and a retractable visor was used to smooth the nose contours at high speed. After the first flight, the program was continued almost exclusively with the first XB-70A; the second prototype was lost on 8 June 1966, when an F-104 Starfighter involved in a photographic sortie collided with it. The top speed of Mach 3.08 was reached in January 1966; the highest altitude, 73,980 feet (22,550 m) in March. The last flight was made on 4 February, 1969.

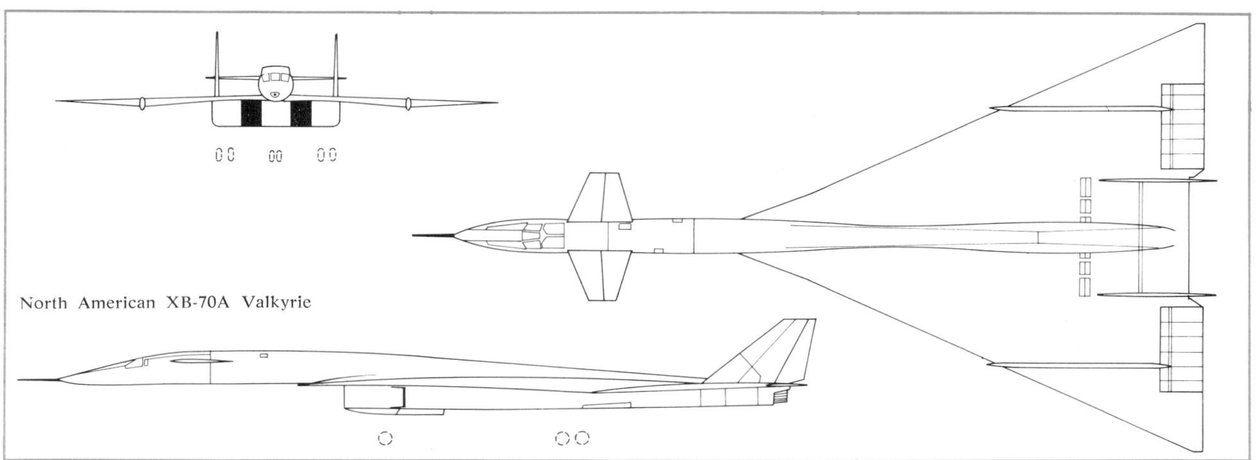
North American XB-70A Valkyrie

Plate 165
Landing after space flight: 1965–1981

In terms of aeronautical progress all the research undertaken with experimental aircraft throughout the world, not only in the U.S.A., and the vast sums invested in these projects, to say nothing of the lives lost, seems to have been worthwhile. The advanced experimental aircraft prepared the way for space flight by exploring the limits of stratospheric flight. Proof of this can be seen today, in the most recent experimental aircraft which prepare the way for NASA's task in the years to come: the establishment of a manned space station and the perfecting of a transport system between this station and the earth by means of the Space Shuttle. A major problem which had to be overcome was developing a vehicle which could withstand re-entry from space into the earth's atmosphere and to make a controled descent and land at a predetermined point. In the early sixties, NASA developed two projects (built by Northrop) which led to the first "lifting-bodies": wingless re-entry research vehicles which achieved lift through the design of their fuselages. Such were the M2-F2 and the HL-10. These two craft were, in a sense, structurally complementary. The M2-F2 had a basic delta planform and its fuselage was D-shaped in cross-section, the flat side of the D forming the top. In the case of the HL-10 the flat surface was on the underside. Apart from this the two vehicles' performance was similar. These "lifting-bodies" were taken to the required altitude by a specially-modified B-52,

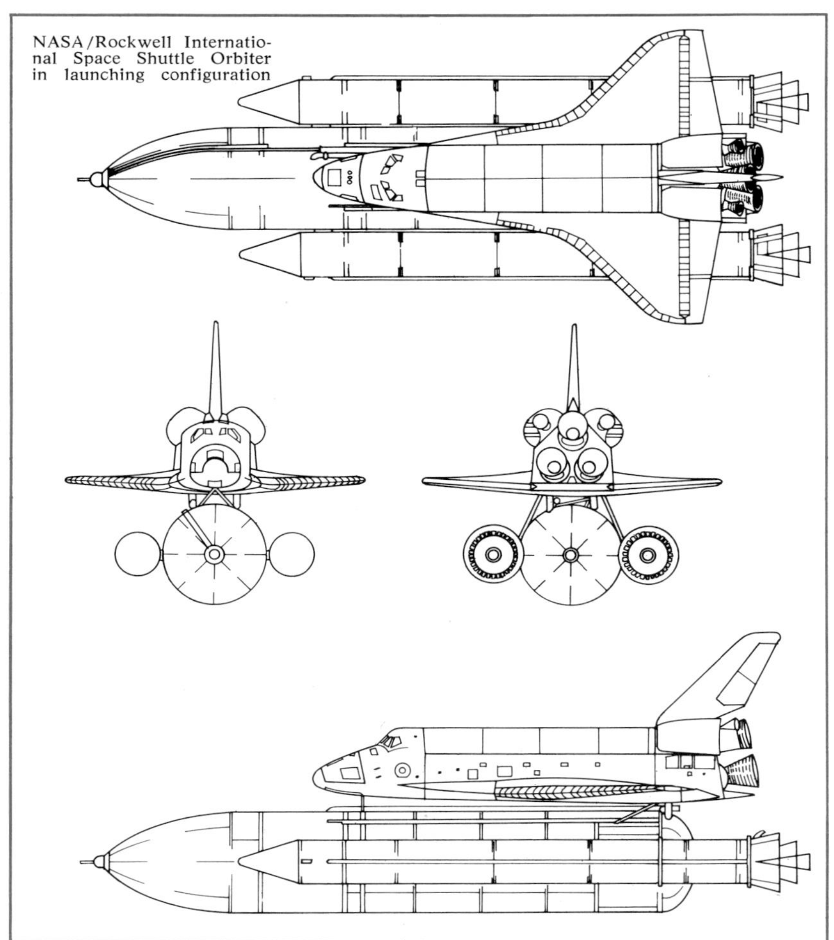
NASA/Rockwell International Space Shuttle Orbiter in launching configuration

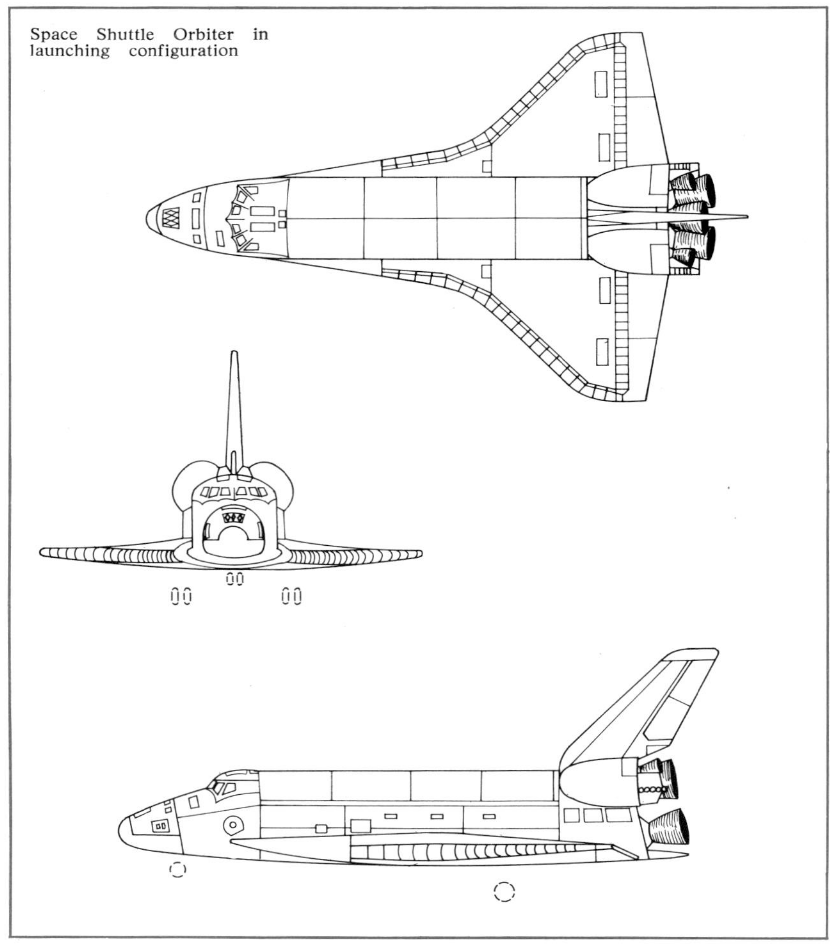
Space Shuttle Orbiter in launching configuration

were dropped, and then, under their own rocket power, they gained altitude and speed and then made controled gliding descents back to earth. The M2-F2 was delivered to NASA on 15 June 1965, made its first unpowered flight on 12 July of the following year and by the end of the year was ready for powered test flights. After a landing accident, however, on 10 May 1967, the M2-F2 was completely rebuilt and some modifications were made. It was redesignated M2-F3 and commenced testing on 25 November 1970, completing the program of proving flights on 20 December 1972. The HL-10 was delivered to NASA on 19 January 1966, and on 22 December made its first unpowered flight and by the end of 1971 had made 37 flights, 25 of which under its own power. During the program the HL-10 reached a maximum altitude of 90,200 feet (27,500 m) and a speed of Mach 1.861.

Considerable work on lifting-body aircraft was also undertaken by the Martin Marietta Corporation. It began with six years' work and millions of hours of investigation and wind-tunnel testing of models. Then in 1964 the U.S.A.F. ordered four small-scale vehicles known as SV-5D PRIME (Precision Recovery Including Maneuvering Entry) and X-23A to the Air Force. Then in 1966 the U.S.A.F. ordered the manned SV-5P (X-24A) to explore the lower speed behavior. The X-24A was delivered on 11 July 1967. The scheduled flight profile was to release the X-24A from its B-52 carrier at about 45,000 feet (13,715 m) after which it would use rocket power to achieve Mach 2 and climb to 100,000 feet (30,480 m). From that height it would make a powerless descent and land after a total of 15 minutes from launching. Landing speeds were very high, with a design maximum of over 350 mph (more than 560 km/h). The X-24A made its first powered flight on 19 March 1970; in 1972 it was rebuilt as the X-24B (flying on 1 August 1973); and it made its final flight on 23 September 1975.

Meanwhile the Space Shuttle project, which had been launched on 26 July 1972, had already begun to take shape. Rockwell International was awarded the contract for two (later five) orbiters and the first of five was rolled out in September 1976; on 18 February 1977 the first unmanned flight was made mounted on top of a specially modified Boeing 747. On 18 June the first manned flight took place. In November 1980 the vehicle which was to be used for the first space flight was transferred to the factory where the final work was carried out. The maiden flight of the first Space Shuttle, *Columbia*, was successfully completed on 14 April 1981. The Space Shuttle consists of an Orbiter which can glide like an airplane and has a very large storage hold. At least 100 missions are envisaged. Launching is by conventional means, with two solid fuel booster rockets which are recoverable and can be re-used, and with three Orbiter vehicle engines, fueled from an external fuel tank. The booster rockets fall away at an altitude of approximately 27 miles and once the external fuel tank has been jettisoned, the Orbiter was designed to undertake various missions. Being launched from the Kennedy Space Center in Florida with orbital insertion at 100 nautical miles (185 km), it can carry a payload of 29,484 kilograms or, with a 270 nautical mile orbital insertion, 11,340 kilograms. Launched from Vandenberg Air Force Base in California with orbital insertion at 100 nautical miles the payload is 14,515 kilograms. Length of mission may vary between seven and thirty days. Re-entry into the earth's atmosphere starts at an altitude of 76 miles (122 km) at a speed of about 17,450 mph (28,000 km/h); in gliding flight the Orbiter can reach a base 1,242 miles (2,000 km) away and reduce its speed on landing to 212–226 mph (341–364 km/h).

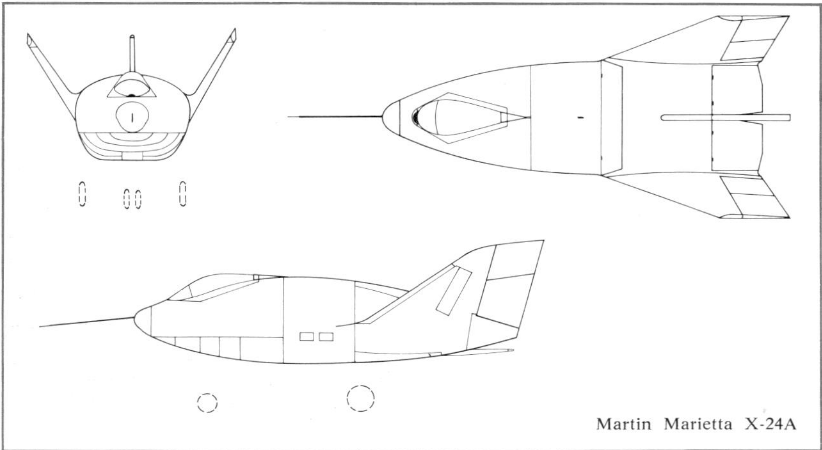
Martin Marietta X-24A

Armstrong Whitworth A.W.52G glider - 1945, GB (162)

Bell X-1 - 1946, USA (164)

Bell X-2 - 1955, USA (164)

North American X-15 - 1959, USA (164)

Bell X-5 - 1951, USA (163)

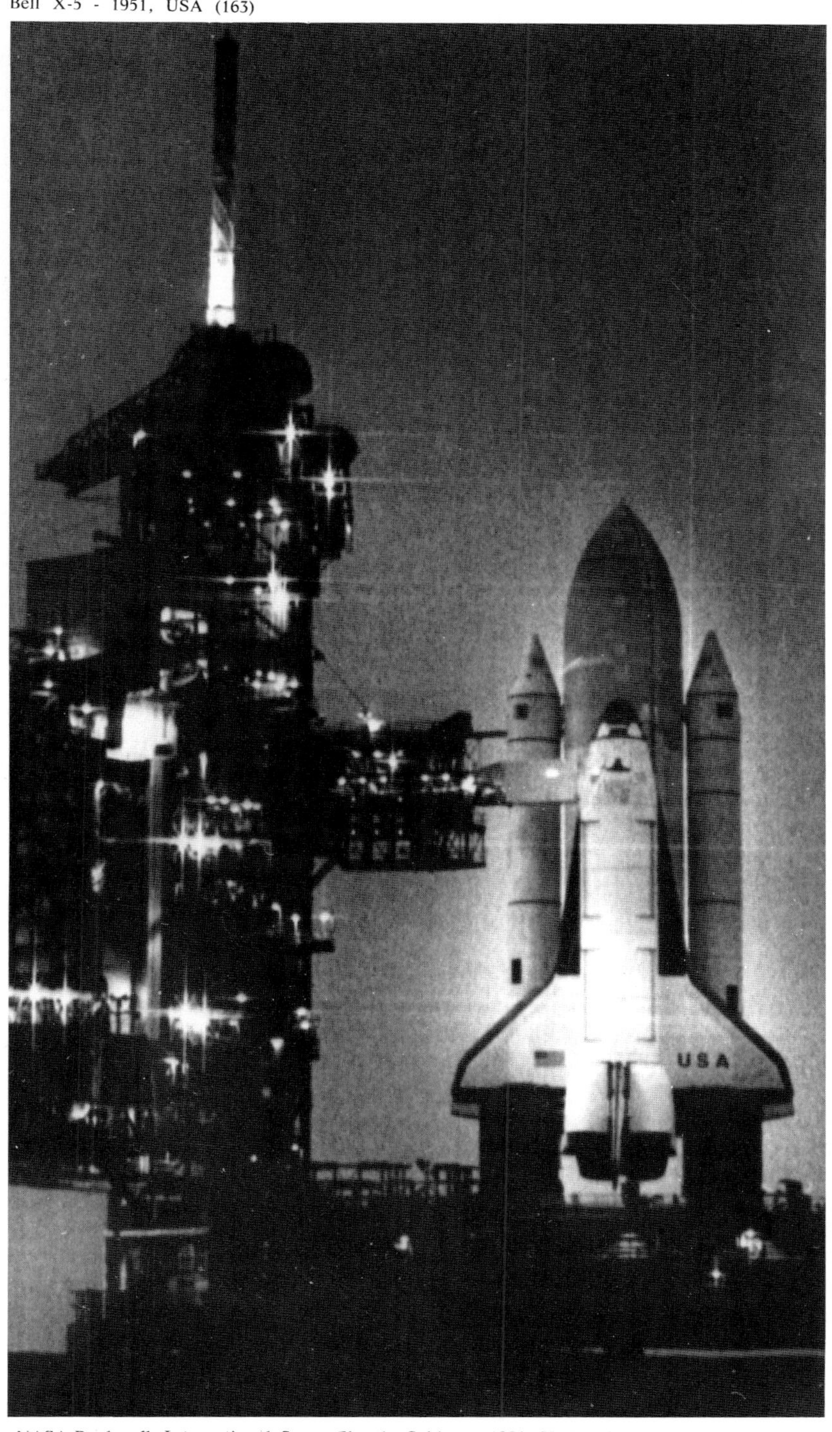

NASA-Rockwell International Space Shuttle Orbiter - 1981, USA (165)

Picture Sources

The abbreviations next to the page numbers below indicate the position of the illustration on the page:
a = above; b = below; c = center; l = left; r = right

Aeronews, 372a, 378b, 379, 380c, 381cr, 382br, 383br, 384ca
Air France, 135al, 263al, 376a
Bruno Benvenuti Archives, 380a, 380cl
Giorgio Apostolo Archives, 176, 178, 179, 264ar, 264c
Ervin Archives, 42, 43, 44, 45, 82, 83, 84, 85, 133, 134, 135, 260, 261, 262, 263, 264, 265, 372, 373, 374, 375, 376, 377, 378, 380, 381, 382, 383, 384, 385, 401
British Airways, 372a, 380b
Iberia, 385ar
Lufthansa, 134a, 134c, 135bl, 26bl, 262, 385al
Luxair, 377c
Valerio D'Orio, picture research

BIBLIOGRAPHY

INDEX BY COUNTRY

GENERAL INDEX

BIBLIOGRAPHY

Abate Rosario - Lazzati Giulio, *I velivoli Macchi dal 1912 al 1963*, Milan, Ali nel Tempo, 1963.

Abate Rosario, *Storia dell'Aeronautica Italiana*, Milan, Bietti, 1974.

Achard André - Tribot - Laspierre Jack, *Répertoire des Aéronefs de Construction Française pour la période 1890-1967*, Paris, Doc. Air Espace, Centre de Documentation de l'Armement, 1968.

Aircraft Year Book, Aero Chambers of Commerce of America.

Allard Noel, *Speed: The Biography of Charles W. Holman*, Noel E. Allard, 1976.

Allen C. B. - Lyman Lauren D., *The Wonder Book of the Air*, Chicago, The John C. Winston Company, 1936.

Allen C. B. - Sanders R., *Revolution in The Sky: The Fabulous Lockheed. The Pilots Who Flew Them*, Vermont, The Stephens Greene Press, 1964.

Allen C. B. - Sanders R., *The American Heritage History of Flight*, American Heritage Publishing Co. Inc. 1962.

Allen Roy, *Pictorial History of KLM*, London, Ian Allen Ltd., 1978.

American Heritage, *History of Flight*, New York, Simon & Schuster, 1962.

Amundsen R., *Il mio volo polare*, Milan, Arnoldo Mondadori Editore, 1925.

Andrews Allen, *The Flying Machine*, New York, G. P. Putnam's Sons, 1977.

Andrews C. F., *Vickers Aircraft since 1908*, London, Putnam & Co. Ltd., 1969.

Angelucci Enzo, *Gli Aeroplani*, Verona, Arnoldo Mondadori Editore, 1972.

Angelucci Enzo - Matricardi Paolo, *Guida agli Aeroplani di tutto il mondo "dalle origini alla prima guerra mondiale", "dal 1918 al 1935", "modelli civili dal 1935 al 1960"*, Verona, Arnoldo Mondadori Editore, 1975-1978.

Apostolo, G. et al - *Storia dell'aviazione*, Milan, Fratelli Fabbri, 1973.

Apostolo, G. et al - *Aviazione oggi*, Milan, Fratelli Fabbri, 1975.

Arena Nino, *Dai Wright all'avvento del Jet 50 anni di aviazione commerciale nel mondo*, Rome, Edizioni Bizzarri, 1976.

Barker Ralph, *The Schneider Trophy Races*, London, Chatto & Windus, 1972.

Barnes C. H., *Bristol Aircraft since 1910*, London, Putnam & Co. Ltd., 1970.

Barnes C. H., *Handley Page Aircraft since 1907*, London, Putnam & Co. Ltd., 1976.

Barnes C. H., *Short Aircraft since 1900*, London, Putnam & Co. Ltd., 1967.

Beckford L., *An ABC of Aeronautics*, London, Cassell, 1957.

Bellinger - Vice Admiral Patrick N. L., *Sailors in The Sky*, Washington, National Geographic Society.

Bergman J., *Ninety Seconds to Space: The X-15 Story*, New York, Doubleday, 1960.

Bignozzi G. - Catalanotto B., *Storia degli aerei d'Italia*, Rome, Editrice Cielo, 1962.

Black Archibald, *The Story of Flying*, Whittlesey House, McGraw-Hill Book Company Inc., 1943.

Blake John, *Early Airplanes*, New York, Golden Press, 1974.

Bonifacio S., *Il velivolo moderno*, Milan, Hoepli, 1929.

Boni P. - Fellini, *Uomini dell'aria*, Rome, Centro Editoriale dell'Osservatore, 1956.

Bowers P. M., *Boeing Aircraft since 1916*, London, Putnam & Co. Ltd., 1966.

Briand Paul L. Jr., *Daughter of The Sky: The Story of Amelia Earhart*, New York, Duell, Sloan & Pearce, 1960.

Brooks P. W., *The Modern Airliner: its Origin and Development*, London, Putnam & Co. Ltd., 1961.

Broomfield G. A., *Pioneer of The Air*, Aldershot, Gale and Polden, 1953.

Bruce J. M., *British Aeroplanes 1914-1918*, London, Putnam & Co. Ltd., 1957.

Bruno Harry, *Wings over America*, New York, Halcyon House, 1942.

Cameron J., *Wings of the Morning*, London, Hodder & Stoughton, 1962.

Chambre R., *Histoire de l'Aviation*, Paris, Flammarion, 1972.

Chapman Ted, *Cornwall Aviation Company*, Falmouth, Glasney Press, 1979.

Claidin Martin, *Barnstorming*, New York, Duell, Sloan & Pearce, 1965.

Clarke D. H., *What Were They Like to Fly?*, London, Ian Allan Ltd., 1964.

Clayton Donald C., *Handley Page: an Aircraft Album*, London, Ian Allan Ltd., 1970.

Cleveland Carl M., *"Upside-Down" Pangbom: King of the Barnstormers*, Aviation Book Company, 1978.

Cobham Sir Alan, *A Time to Fly*, London, Shepheard-Walwyn, 1978.

Cobianchi M., *Pionieri dell'aviazione in Italia*, Rome, 1938.

Colliers Encyclopedia, vols. 9, 15, New York, P. F. Collier & Son Corp., 1958.

Conradis H., *Design for Flight*, London, MacDonald Ltd., 1960.

Cook David C., *The Story of Aviation*, New York, Archer House, 1958.

Crosby Maynard, *Flight Plan for Tomorrow. The Douglas Story: a condensed History*, Santa Monica, Douglas Aircraft Co., 1962.

Cunningham Frank, *Sky Master, The Story of Donald Douglas*, Philadelphia, Dorrance & Co., 1943.

Davies R. E. G., *A History of the World's Airlines*, London, Oxford University Press, 1964.

Davies R. E. G., *Airlines of The United States since 1914*, London, Putnam & Co. Ltd., 1972.

Davy M. J. B., *Henson and Stringfellow*, London, Science Museum, Her Majesty's Stationery Office, 1931.

Davy M. J. B., *Interpretive History of Flight*, London, Her Majesty's Stationery Office, 1948.

De Beires S., *Asas que Naufragam*, Lisbon, Teixeira & C., 1927.

de Havilland Sir G., *Sky Fever*, Ontario, London & Don Mills, 1961.

de la Cierva, J., *Wings of Tomorrow: the Story of Autogiro*, New York, Brewer, Warren and Putnam, 1931.

Demand C. - Emde H., *Les Conquérants de l'Air*, Lausanne, Edita S. A., 1968.

Dempster D., *The Tale of the Comet*, London, Allan Wingate, 1959.

Desoutter D. M., *All about Aircraft*, London, Faber & Faber Ltd., 1955.

D. L. H., *Deutschen Luftverkehr Lufthansa*, 1930.

D. L. H., *History of Lufthansa German Airlines*, 1968.

Dollfus C. - Beaubois H. - Rougeron C., *L'Homme, l'Air et l'Espace: Aéronautique, Astronautique*, Paris, 1965.

Dollfus C. - Bouche H., *Histoire de l'aéronautique*, Paris, L'Illustration, 1932.

Dornier C., *Das Flugschiff Do. X*, Munich, F. Bruckmann, 1929.

Dornier C., *Metallflugzeuge*, Munich, F. Bruckmann, 1921.

Dornier C., *Ueber eine Familie Ähnlicher Flugboote*, Munich, F. Bruckmann, 1928.

Dornier C., *Vortrage und Abhandlugen aus dem Gebiete des Flugzeugbaues and*

Luftschiffbaues 1914-1930.
Dumont Villaves Henriques, *Foto- Historia de Santos Dumont 1898-1910*, São Paulo, Comp. Melhoramentos de São Paulo, 1956.
Dumont Villaves Henriques, *Santos Dumont, il padre dell'aviazione*, São Paulo Comp. Melhoramentos de São Paulo, 1956.
Duncan, Richard M. C., *Stunt Flying*, The Goodheart-Wilcox Co., 1930.
Duval G. R., *British Flying Boats and Amphibians 1909-1952*, London, Putnam & Co. Ltd., 1966.
Dwiggins Don, *The Air Devils*, New York, Grosset & Dunlop, 1966.
Dwiggins Don, *The Barnstormers: Flying Daredevils of the Roaring Twenties*, New York, Grosset & Dunlop, 1968.
Dwiggins Don, *They Flew the Bendix Race: the History of the Competition for the Bendix Trophy*, Philadelphia, J. B. Lippincott, 1965.
Emde Heimer - Demand Carlo, *Conquerors of the Air*, Lausanne, Edita S. A., 1968.
Emme, E. M., *A History of Space Flight*, Washington, Holt, Rinehart and Winston, 1965.
Endres Gunther G., *World Airlines Fleets*, Hounslow, Airline Publications Sales Ltd., 1976–1980.
Fokker-The Man and the Aircraft, Letchworth, Herts, Harleyford Publications Ltd., 1961.
Foxworth Thomas G., *The Speed Seekers*, London, MacDonald & Jane's, 1975.
Freeman, R. A., *The Mighty Eighth*, London, McDonald, 1970.
Gablehouse Charles, *Helicopters and Autogyros*, London, Frederick Muller Ltd., 1968.
Galland A., *The first and the last*, London, Methuen & Co. Ltd., 1955.
Garber Paul E., *The National Aeronautical Collections*, Washington, D.C. Smithsonian Institution, National Air Museum, 1965.
Giacomelli R., *Gli scritti di Leonardo da Vinci sul volo*, Rome, 1936.
Gianvanni Paolo, *I trasporti aerei in Italia dalla guerra all'era del getto*, Florence, Edizioni Aeronautiche Italiane.
Gibbs-Smith Charles H., *A Brief History*, London, Science Museum, Her Majesty's Stationery Office, 1967.
Gibbs-Smith Charles H., *A Directory and Nomenclature of the First Aeroplanes 1809 to 1909*, London, Science Museum, Her Majesty's Stationery Office, 1966.
Gibbs-Smith Charles H., *Aeronautics 1: Early flying up to Reims Meeting*, London, Science Museum, Her Majesty's Stationery Office, 1966.
Gibbs-Smith Charles H., *Leonardo Da Vinci's Aeronautics*, London, Science Museum, Her Majesty's Stationery Office, 1967.
Gibbs-Smith Charles H., *Sir George Cayley 1773-1857*, London, Science Museum, Her Majesty's Stationery Office, 1968.
Gibbs-Smith Charles H., *The Aeroplane: An Historical Survey of its Origins and Development*, London, Science Museum, Her Majesty's Stationery Office, 1960.
Gibbs-Smith Charles H., *The Invention of the Aeroplane 1799-1909*, London, Faber & Faber Ltd., 1966.
Gibbs-Smith Charles H., *The World's First Aeroplane Flights*, London, Science Museum, Her Majesty's Stationery Office, 1965.
Gibbs-Smith Charles H., *The Wright Brothers*, London, Science Museum, Her Majesty's Stationery Office, 1963.
Glines Carroll V., *Jimmy Doolittle: Daredevil Aviator and Scientist*, New York, Macmillan, 1972.
Godfrey Arthur, *Above the Pacific*, Fallbrook Calif., Aero Publisher Inc., 1966.
Goldstrom J., *A Narrative History of Aviation*, New York, Macmillan, 1930.
Goma José, *Historia de la aeronautica española*, Madrid, Graficas Huerfanos Ejercito del Aire, 1950.
Grace Dick, *I Am Still Alive*, New York, Rand McNally, 1931.
Grace Dick, *Visibility Unlimited*, New York, Longmans Green & Co., 1950.
Grahame - White, C. - Harper, H., *The Aeroplane, Past, Present and Future*, London, T. Werner - Laurie, 1911.
Green William - Pollinger Gerald, *The Aircraft of the World*, London, Macdonald & Co. Ltd., 1965.
Green William, *The Observer's Basic Book of Aircraft—Civil*, New York, Frederick Warne & Co. Ltd., 1967.
Gregory H. F., *The Helicopter*, London, Allen & Unwin, 1949.
Gunston Bill, *The World's Greatest Airplanes*, Birmingham, Basinghalls Books Limited, 1980.
Gunston Bill, *The Illustrated Encyclopedia of Commercial Aircraft*, London, Phoebus Publishing, 1980.
Gunston Bill, *The Illustrated Encyclopedia of Propeller Airlines*; London, Phoebus Publishing, 1980.
Haddow G. W. - Grosz P. M., *The German Giants*, London, Putnam & Co. Ltd.
Halle G., *Otto Lilienthal*, Düsseldorf, 1956.
Hardy Michael, *World Civil Aircraft since 1945*, London, Ian Allan Ltd., 1979.
Harris Sherwood, *The First to Fly: Aviation's Pioneer Days*, New York, Simon & Schuster, 1970.
Hart I. B., *The Mechanical Investigations of Leonardo da Vinci*, London, Chapman & Hall, 1925.
Hatfield D. D., *Aeroplane Scrapbook No. 1*, Northrop University Press, 1976.
Hatfield D. D., *Los Angeles Aeronautics 1920-1929*, Northrop University Press, 1976.
Hawks Ellison, *British Seaplanes Triumph in The International Schneider Trophy Contest 1913-1931*, Southport, Real Photographs.
Hébrard J., *L'aviation des origines à nos jours*, Paris, Robert Laffont, 1954.
Heinkel E., *A l'assault du Ciel*, Paris, Plon, 1955.
Historical Aviation Album, vols. I-VIII, Temple City, Calif., Paul R. Matt, 1965-1970.
Hodgson J. E., *The History of Aeronautics in Great Britain*, London, Milford, 1924.
Hooftman H., *Alles over de Fokker Friendship*, Amsterdam, L.J. Veens Uitgevermij N. V.
Hooftman, H., *Russian Aircraft*, Fallbrook Calif., Aero Publisher Inc., 1965.
Howard F. - Gunston B., *La conquista dell'aria*, Milan, Silvana Ed., 1962.
Hudson K., *Air Travel*, Bath, Adams & Dart, 1972.
Hummelchen G., *Die Deutschen Seeflieger*, Munich, Lehmanns Verlag, 1973.
Hunsaker J. C., *Aeronautics at the Mid-Century*, New Haven, Connecticut, 1952.
Ingells Douglas J., *The Plane that Changed the World*, Fallbrook Calif., Aero Publishers Inc., 1966.
Ingells Douglas J., *Tin Goose, The Fabulous Ford Trimotor*, Fallbrook Calif., Aero Publishers Inc., 1968.
Inoguchi R. - Nakajima T. - Pinean R., *The Divine Wind*, Annapolis, United States Institute, 1958.
International Academy of Astronautics, *Astronautical Multilingual Dictionary*, Amsterdam, Praha Academia, Elsevier P. C., 1970.
Jackson A. J., *Avro Aircraft since 1908*, London, Putnam & Co. Ltd., 1965.
Jackson A. J., *Blackburn Aircraft since 1909*, London, Putnam & Co. Ltd., 1968.
Jackson A. J., *British Civil Aircraft 1919-59*, vols. I, II, London, Putnam & Co. Ltd., 1959-60.
Jackson A. J., *De Havilland Aircraft*, London, Putnam & Co. Ltd., 1962.
James Derek N., *Gloster Aircraft since 1917*, London, Putnam & Co. Ltd., 1971.
Juptner Joseph P., *U.S. Civil Aircraft*, vols. I-VIII, Fallbrook Calif., Aero Publishers Inc., 1962-1967.
Keller Ulrich, *Propellerflugzeuge im Dienste des Schweizerischen Fluglinienverkehrs 1919-1968*, Basle and Stuttgart, Birkhäuser Verlag, 1969.
Kelly F. C., *Miracle at Kitty Hawk: the Letters of Wilbur and Orville Wright*, New York, 1951.
Kelly F. C., *The Wright Brothers*, New York and London, 1944.
Kens K. - Nowarra H. J., *Die Deutschen Flugzeuge 1933-1945*, Munich, Lehmanns Verlag, 1974.
Killian Gary L., *The Convair Twins 240 to 640*, London, Macdonald & Jane's Airline Publications, 1979.
Kinert Reed, *Racing Planes and Air Races*, vols. I-IV, Fallbrook Calif., Aero Publishers Inc., 1967-1968.
King H. F. - Taylor J. W. R., *Jane's 100 Significant Aircraft 1909-1969*, London, Jane's Yearbook, 1969.
King H. F., *Aeromarine Origins*, London & Fallbrook Calif., Aero Publishers Inc., 1966.
King H. F., *The World's Fighters*, London, The Bodley Head Ltd., 1971.
Komons Nick A., Bonfires to Beacons: *Federal Civil Aviation Policy under the Air Commerce Act 1926-1938*, U.S. Department of Transportation 1978.
Lacey G. W. B., *Aeronautics, 2: Flying since 1913*, London, Science Museum, Her Majesty's Stationery Office, 1966.
Lewis F. Allen, *Only Yesterday*, New York, Bantam Books, 1946.
Lewis Peter, *British Aircraft 1909-14*, London, Putnam & Co. Ltd., 1962.
Lewis Peter, *British Racing and Record-Breaking Aircraft*, London, Putnam & Co. Ltd., 1971.
Lindbergh Charles, *The Spirit of St. Louis*, New York, Scribner, 1953.
Liptrot R. N. - Woods J. D., *Rotorcraft*. London, Butterworth, 1955.
Lockheed's Family Tree: A History of the Company's Early Aircraft, Lockheed Aircraft Corporation, 1978.
Lynn S. R., Boeing Production, Hounslow, Airline Publications & Sales Ltd.
Mackintosh Ian, *Encyclopedia of Airline Colour Schemes*, vol. I, Hounslow, Airline Publications & Sales Ltd., 1979.
Mancini Luigi, *Grande Enciclopedia Aeronautica*, Milan, Edizioni Aeronautica, 1936.
Mandrake Charles, *National Air Races 1932*, Speed Publishing, 1976.
Mandrake Charles, *The Gee Bee Story*, Robert R. Longo, 1956.
Mason Francis K. - Windrow Martin C., *Air Facts and Feats*, London, Guinness Superlatives Ltd., 1970.
Mason Francis K., *Hawker Aircraft since 1920*, London, Putnam & Co. Ltd., 1961.
McFarland Marvin W., *The Papers of Wilbur and Orville Wright*, vols. I-II, New York, Arno Press, Inc., 1953.
Mermoz Jean, *Mes Vols*, Paris, Flammarion, 1937.
Miller Ronald - Sawers Davis, *The Technical Development of Modern Aviation*, London, Routledge & Kegan Paul, 1968.
Mondini A., *La gloriosa parabola del dirigibile*, Rome, 1969.
Morgan Leu, *The Douglas DC-3*, New York, Arco Publishing Co. Inc., 1964.
Morgan Leu - Shannon R. P., *The Planes the Aces Flew*, New York, Arco Publishing Co. Inc., 1964.
Morgan Terry, *The Lockheed Constellation*, New York, Arco Publishing Co. Inc., 1967.
Morris Lloyd - Smith Kendall, *Ceiling Unlimited: The Story of American Aviation from Kitty Hawk to Supersonics*, New York, Macmillan Co., 1953.
Munson Kenneth, *Aircraft the World Over*, London, Ian Allan Ltd., 1963.
Munson Kenneth, *Civil Aircraft of Yesteryear*, London, Ian Allan Ltd., 1967.
Munson Kenneth, *Civil Airlines since 1946*, London, Blandford Press Ltd., 1967.
Munson Kenneth, *Flying Boats and Seaplanes Since 1910*. London, Blandford Press Ltd., 1971.
Munson Kenneth, *Helicopters and other Rotorcraft since 1907*, London, Blandford Press Ltd., 1968.
Munson Kenneth, *Pioneer Aircraft 1903-1914*, London, Blandford Press Ltd., 1969.
Munson Kenneth, *Private Aircraft since 1946*, London, Blandford Press Ltd., 1967.
Munson Kenneth - Swanborough Gordon, *Boeing: an Aircraft Album*, London, Ian Allan Ltd., 1971.
Nayler J. L. - Ower E., *Aviation: its Technical Development*, London, Chester Springs, 1965.
Nevin David, *The Pathfinders*, Virginia, Time-Life Books, 1980.
Nowarra Heinz J., *Die Sowjetischen Flugzeuge 1941-1966*, Munich, J. F. Lehmanns Verlag, 1967.
Nowarra Heinz J., *Eisernes Kreuz und Balkenkreuz*, Mainz, Verlag Dieter Hoffmann, 1968.
Nozawa Tadashi, *Encyclopedia of Japanese Aircraft 1900-1945*, Tokyo, Shuppan-Kyodo, 1958-1966.
O'Dea W. T., *Aeronautica*, London, Science Museum, Her Majesty's Stationery Office, 1966.
O'Neil Paul, *Barnstormers & Speed Kings*, Virginia, Time-Life Books, 1981.
Oriebar A. H., *Schneider Trophy: A Personal Account of High-Speed Flying & the Winning of the Schneider Trophy*, London, Seeley Service & Co. Ltd., 1929.
Oughton James D., *Bristol an Aircraft Album*, London, Ian Allan, 1973.
Palmer Henry R. Jr., *This was Air Travel*, Seattle, Superior Publishing Company, 1960.
Penrose Harald, *British Aviation: The Pioneer Years*, London, Putnam & Co. Ltd., 1967.
Peterson Houston, *See Them Flying*, New York, Richard W. Baron Publishing Co. Inc., 1969.
Petit Edmond, *Histoire mondiale de l'aviation*, Paris, Librairie Hachette, 1967.

Piaggio & C., *75 anni di attività*, Genoa, Piaggio & C., 1960.

Rae John B., *Climb to Greatness. The American Aircraft Industry, 1920-1960*, Cambridge, USA, Massachusetts Institute of Technology Press, 1968.

Reynolds Quentin, *The Amazing Mr. Doolittle: A Biography of Lieutenant General James H. Doolittle*, New York, Appleton-Century-Crofts, 1953.

Rhode Bill, *Baling Wire, Chewing Gum, and Guts: The Story of the Gates Flying Circus*. New York, Simon & Schuster, 1970.

Robertson Bruce, *Aircraft Camouflage and Markings 1907-1954*, Letchworth, Herts, Harleyford Publications Ltd., 1956.

Robertson Bruce, *Aircraft Markings of the World 1912-1967*, Letchworth, Herts, Harleyford Publications Ltd., 1967.

Robinson Douglas H., *LZ 129 Hindenburg*, Dallas, Morgan Aviation Books, 1964.

Rocchi Renato, *La Meravigliosa Avventura*, Rome, Stato Maggiore Aeronautica, 1976.

Rolfe D. - Dawydoff A., *Airplanes of the World, from Pusher to Jet, 1904 to 1954*, New York, 1954.

Rolt L. T. C., *The Aeronauts*, London and New York, 1966.

Ronnie Art, *Locklear: The Man Who Walked on Wings*, San Diego, A. S. Barnes, 1973.

Roseberry C. R., *Glenn Curtiss: Pioneer of Flight*, New York. Doubleday & Co. Inc., 1972.

Roseberry C. R., *The Challenging Skies: The Colorful Story of Aviation's Most Exciting Years, 1919-1939*, New York, Doubleday, & Co. Inc., 1966.

Rust Kenn C., ed., *Historical Aviation Album: All American Series*, vols. 10-14, Historical Aviation Album, 1971.

Saladin Raymond, *Les Temps Héroiques de l'Aviation*, Paris, Editions Arcadiennes, 1949.

Schamburger Page, *Classic Monoplanes*, New York, Sports Car Press Ltd., 1966.

Schamburger Page - Christy Joe, *Command The Horizon*, New York, A. S. Barnes and Co., 1968.

Scharff Robert - Taylor Walter S., *Over Land and Sea: Glenn A. Curtiss*, New York, David McKay Co. Inc., 1968.

Schiff Barry J., *The Boeing 707*, New York, Arco Publishing Co. Inc., 1967.

Schmidt Heinz A. F., *Historische Flugzeuge*, Vols I-II, Stuttgart, Motorbuch-Verlag, 1968-1970.

Schmidt S. H. - Weaver Truman C., *Golden Age of Air Racing*, 1940, EAA Air Museum, Foundation Inc., 1963.

Shrader W. A., *Fifty Years of Flight: a Chronicle of the Aviation Industry in America*, Cleveland Ohio, 1953.

Sikorsky Igor I., *The Story of the Winged-S*, London, Robert Hale Ltd., 1939.

Silvestri A., *A cinquant'anni dalla trasvolata delle Alpi*, Milan, 1960.

Simonson, G. R., *The History of the American Aircraft Industry (Anthology)*, Cambridge, USA, Massachusetts Institute of Technology Press, 1968.

Smith G. G., *Gas Turbines and Jet Propulsion*, London and New York, 1955.

Smith Robert T., *Classic Biplanes*, New York, Sports Car Press Ltd., 1963.

Staddon T. G., *History of Cambrian Airways, The Welsh Airline from 1935-1976*, Hounslow, Airline Publications & Sales Ltd.

Stehling Kurt R. - Beller Williams, *Skyhooks*, New York, Doubleday & Co. Inc., 1962.

Stewart Oliver, *Aviation: the Creative Ideas*, London and New York, 1966.

Stinton D., *The Anatomy of the Aeroplane*, London and New York, 1966.

Storia dell'Aviazione, Istituto Geografico De Agostini, Novara, 1978.

Stroud John, *Annals of British and Commonwealth Air Transport*, London, Putnam & Co. Ltd., 1962.

Stroud John, *European Transport Aircraft since 1910*. London and Fallbrook, California, 1966.

Stroud John, *The World's Airlines*, London, The Bodley Head Ltd., 1971.

Sunderman James F., *Early Air Pioneers*, New York, Franklin Watts Inc., 1961.

Swanborough F. G., *Turbine-Engined Airliners of the World*, London, Temple Press Book Ltd., 1962.

Swanborough F. G., *Vertical Flight Aircraft of the World*, Fallbrook, California, Aero Publishers Inc., 1964.

Taylor John W. R., *Aircraft, Aircraft*, London, The Hamlyn Publishing Group Ltd., 1967.

Taylor, John W. R., *Aircraft Annual*, London, Ian Allan Ltd., 1962.

Taylor John W. R., *Aircraft Identification Guide*, London, C. Tinling & Co. Ltd.

Taylor John W. R., *Aircraft Sixty Nine*, London, Ian Allan Ltd., 1968.

Taylor John W. R., *Civil Aircraft of the World*, London, Ian Allan Ltd., 1968.

Taylor John W. R., *Civil Aircraft Recognition*, London, Ian Allan Ltd., 1955.

Taylor John W. R., *Flight*, London, Edward Hilton, 1959.

Taylor John W. R., *Helicopters and Vtol Aircraft*, Garden City, N.Y., Doubleday & Co., 1968.

Taylor Patrick Gordon, *Pacific Flight: the Story of the Lady Southern Cross*, Sydney, Angus and Robertson Ltd., 1935.

Taylor Patrick Gordon, *The Sky Beyond*, Boston, Houghton Mifflin Co., 1963.

The American Heritage History of Flight, New York, American Heritage Publ. Co. Inc., 1962.

The Flyer's Handbook, London, Marshall Editions Ltd., 1978.

The Lore of Flight, Gothenburg, Tre Tryckare Cagner & Co., 1970.

Thetford Owen, *Aircraft of the Royal Air Force since 1918*, London, Putnam & Co. Ltd., 3rd edition, 1962.

Thetford Owen, *British Naval Aircraft Since 1912*, London, Putnam & Co. Ltd., 1962.

Thomas Lowell - Thomas Lowell Jr., *Famous First Flights that changed History*, Garden City, N.Y., Doubleday & Co., 1968.

Thompson Jonathan, *Italian Civil and Military Aircraft 1930-45*, Fallbrook, California, Aero Publishers Inc., 1963.

Tuck W. J., *Power to Fly*, London, Science Museum, Her Majesty's Stationery Office, 1966.

Turner P. St. John - Nowarra Heinz J., *Junkers an Aircraft Album*, London, Ian Allan Ltd., 1971.

Über den Wolken, Munich, Südwest-Verlag, 1962.

Underwood John W., *Acrobats in the Sky*, Glendale, Calif., Aviation Book Co., 1972.

Underwood John W., *The World's Famous Racing Aircraft*, Los Angeles, Floyd Clymer, 1955.

Van Ronau W., *Un idrovolante intorno al mondo*, Milan, Arnoldo Mondadori Editore, 1933.

Various authors, *Airplanes of the World*, New York, Simon & Schuster, 1962.

Various authors, *Scienziati e tecnologi*, Milan, Mondadori, 1974/1975.

Viemeister Peter, *Flight in the Ocean of Air*, New York, Doubleday & Co. Inc., 1959.

Voisin Gabriel, *Men, Women and 10,000 Kites*, London and Toronto, 1963.

Vorderman Don, *The Great Air Races*, New York, Doubleday & Co. Inc., 1969.

Weaver Truman C., *62 Rare Racing Planes*, New York, Arenar Publications.

Weeks E. O., *Lincoln Beachy's Last Ride*, American Aviation, Historical Society Journal, 1961.

Weyl A. R., *Fokker: The Creative Years*, London, Putnam & Co. Ltd., 1965.

Whitehouse Arch, *The Years of the Sky Kings*, New York, Doubleday & Co. Inc., 1959.

Whittle Sir F., *Jet*, London, Frederick Muller, 1953.

Wigton Don C., *From Jenny to Jet*, New York, Bonanza Books, 1963.

Wilson Charles - Reader William, *Men and Machines - A History of D. Napier & Son, Engineers Ltd., 1908-1958*, London, Weidenfeld and Nicolson, 1958.

Wright Orville, *How we invented the Aeroplane*, New York, F. C. Kelly, 1953.

Wykeham Peter, *Santos-Dumont: A Study in Obsession*, London and Toronto, 1962.

Wynn Hymphrey, *World Airline Insignia*, London, Hamlyn Publishing Group Ltd., 1973.

Periodicals

Aircam "Specials" Series, vols. I-VII, Canterbury, Osprey Publications Ltd., 1969-71.

Aircam Aviation Series, vols. I-XVIII, Canterbury, Osprey Publications Ltd., 1969-71.

"Air Classic", Canoga Park, Challenge Publications, Inc.

"Aircraft Illustrated", Ian Allan Ltd.

"Air Pictorial", London, Air League.

"Air Progress", New York, The Condé Nast Publications, Inc.

"Ala Rotante", Rome, Costruzioni Aeronautiche Giovanni Agusta S.p.A.

"Année Aeronautique" 1931-1932, Hirschauer & Dollfuss.

"Aviation Magazine International", Paris, Union de Presse Européenne.

"Aviation Week & Space Technology", New York, McGraw-Hill.

"Aviazione di Linea Aeronautica e Spazio", Rome.

"Camouflage & Markings", London, Ducimus Books Ltd.

"Cross & Cockade", Leicester, Society of World War I Aero Historians.

"Der Flieger", Postfach, Luftfahrt-Verlag, Walter Zuerl.

"Esso Air World", New York, Esso International Inc.

"Flight International", London, IPC Business Press Ltd.

"Flug Revue - Flugwelt", Stuttgart, Vereinigte Motor-Verlage GmbH.

"Flying Review International", London, Haymarket Press Ltd.

"Icare, Revue de l'Aviation Française", Orly.

"Interavia", Geneva, Interavia S.A.

"Interconair Aviazione Marina", Genoa, Interconair S.A.

"Koku-Fan", Tokyo, Bunrin-do Co. Ltd.

"I primi cinquant'anni dell'aviazione italiana", Rome, Rivista Aeronautica.

"L'Album du Fanatique de l'Aviation", Paris, Editions Larivière.

"Profile", Windsor, Profile Publications Ltd.

"The Aeroplane", London.

Yearbooks

Aerospace Facts and Figures, Aerospace Industries Association of America Inc. - Aviation Week & Space Technology, New York, McGraw-Hill.

Jane's All The World's Aircraft, London, Sampson Low, Merston & Co. Ltd., from 1909.

The Aerospace Year Book, Washington, D.C., Book Inc., from 1922.

INDEX BY COUNTRY

Listed below are only those aircraft for which specifications are given.

GENERAL INDEX

Numbers in bold type refer to illustrations, those in roman type to the text.

A

O

P

Q

R

S

T

U

V

W

Y

Z